COMPREHENSIVE HANDBOOK
OF
PSYCHOLOGICAL ASSESSMENT

COMPREHENSIVE HANDBOOK
OF
PSYCHOLOGICAL ASSESSMENT

VOLUME 3
BEHAVIORAL ASSESSMENT

Stephen N. Haynes

Elaine M. Heiby

Volume Editors

Michel Hersen

Editor-in-Chief

WILEY

John Wiley & Sons, Inc.

We would like to acknowledge Vicky Keogh, who provided valuable assistance at every phase of the development and preparation of this book.

Library of Congress Cataloging-in-Publication Data:

Comprehensive handbook of psychological assessment / editor-in-chief, Michel Hersen.
    p. cm.
    Includes bibliographical references and index.
    Contents: v. 1 Intellectual and neuropsychological assessment / editors, Gerald Goldstein
and Sue R. Beers — v. 2. Personality assessment / editors, Mark J. Hilsenroth and Daniel L.
Segal — v. 3. Behavioral assessment / editors, Stephen N. Haynes and Elaine M. Heiby — v. 4.
Industrial and organizational assessment / editor, Jay C. Thomas.
    ISBN 0-471-41610-X (set : hardcover : alk. paper) — ISBN 0-471-41611-8 (v. 1 :
hardcover : alk. paper) — ISBN 0-471-41612-6 (v. 2 : hardcover : alk. paper) — ISBN
0-471-41613-4 (v. 3 : hardcover : alk. paper) — ISBN 0-471-41614-2 (v. 4 : hardcover :
alk. paper)
    1. Psychological tests. I. Hersen, Michel.
BF176 .C654 2003
150′.28′7—dc21

                                      2002193381

Contents

v

Handbook Preface

Over the last century the scope of activity of clinical psychologists has increased exponentially. In earlier times psychologists had a much more restricted range of responsibilities. Today psychologists not only provide assessments but treat a wide variety of disorders in an equally wide variety of settings, consult, teach, conduct research, help to establish ethical policies, deal with human engineering factors, have a strong media presence, work with law enforcement in profiling criminals, and have had increasing influence in the business world and in the realm of advertising, to identify just a few of the major activities in which they are engaged. Nonetheless, the hallmark of psychologists has always been assessment and it continues to be a mainstay of their practices in the twenty-first century. Indeed, in each of the activities just described, psychologists and their assistants are performing assessments of some sort.

In the nineteenth century our predecessors in Germany began to study individual differences and abilities in what then was the most scientific way. In the more than 120 years that have elapsed since these early efforts were carried out, the field of psychological assessment has seen many developments and permutations, ranging from educational needs to identify individuals with subnormal intelligence to attempts to measure unconscious dynamics with unstructured stimuli, wide-range governmental efforts to measure intelligence and other capabilities to screen out undesirable military recruits during wartime, development of evaluative tools to ensure successful personnel selection, the advent of behavioral and physiological assessments, the increased reliance on computerized assessments, and, most recently, the spectacular innovation of virtual reality assessments using the latest electronic technologies.

Thousands of specific assessment strategies and tests that are carried out on both an individual and group basis have been devised for almost every conceivable type of human endeavor. Many of these strategies have been carefully developed, tested, and refined, with norms available for many populations and excellent reliability and validity data reported. To keep abreast of all new developments in the field of assessment is a near impossibility, although scores of journals, books, and yearly publications are available that catalog such developments.

In considering how the field of psychological assessment has evolved over the last century with the resulting explosion of new technologies and new assessment devices, it seemed to us imperative to create a resource (*Comprehensive Handbook of Psychological Assessment:* CHOPA) that distilled this vast reservoir of data in a more manageable format for researchers, clinicians, educators, and students alike. Therefore, Tracey Belmont, our editor at John Wiley & Sons, the volume editors (Gerald Goldstein, Sue R. Beers, Mark J. Hilsenroth, Daniel L. Segal, Stephen N. Haynes, Elaine M. Heiby, and Jay C. Thomas), and I as editor-in-chief developed this four-volume format. This decision was both conceptual, in order to best capture the scope of the field, and pragmatic, so that individuals wishing to purchase a single volume (as a consequence of their unique interest) would be able to do so.

CHOPA includes four volumes with a total of 121 chapters written by renowned experts in their respective areas of expertise. In order the volumes are: 1, Intellectual and Neuropsychological Assessment; 2, Personality Assessment; 3, Behavioral Assessment; and 4, Industrial and Organizational Assessment. Each volume has an introductory chapter by the editor. In the case of Volume 2, there is an introductory chapter for objective tests and an introductory chapter for projective tests. In general, introductory chapters are concerned with a historical review, range of tests, theoretical considerations, psychometric concerns, range of populations for which the tests are appropriate, cross-cultural factors, accommodation for persons with disabilities, legal and ethical issues, computerization, and future perspectives. Chapters on individual tests or approaches cover many of the same areas but in much more specific detail, in addition, of course, to the test description and development. Other chapters are more conceptual and theoretical in nature and articulate an approach to evaluation, such as the chapters on clinical interviewing and program evaluation in Volume 3.

In developing the CHOPA concept and selecting chapters and contributors, our objective has been to be comprehensive in a global sense but not encyclopedic (i.e., detailing every conceivable and extant assessment strategy or test). However, we believe that we are sufficiently comprehensive so that the interested reader can move to greater specificity, if needed, on the basis of the very current list of references for each chapter.

An endeavor as complicated as CHOPA has required the efforts of many people, and here we would like to acknowledge their various contributions. First, I personally would like to thank Tracey Belmont and her superb staff at John Wiley & Sons for recognizing the value of this project and for helping to bring the pieces together. Second, I thank the volume editors for their Herculean efforts in monitoring, reviewing, and reworking the contributions of their colleagues. Next, we owe a debt of gratitude to our eminent contributors, who so graciously have shared their high levels of expertise with us. And finally, I would like to thank all of our staff here at Pacific University who contributed technical assistance to bringing this four-volume set to publication: Carole Londeree, Kay Waldron, Angelina Marchand, and Alex Duncan.

Michel Hersen
Forest Grove, Oregon

Contributors

Heather K. Alvarez, BA
Virginia Polytechnic Institute & State University
Blacksburg, VA

Krista A. Barbour, MA
University of Southern California
Los Angeles, CA

Billy A. Barrios, PhD
University of Mississippi
Oxford, MS

Bruce F. Chorpita, PhD
University of Hawaii at Manoa
Honolulu, HI

Gerald C. Davison, PhD
University of Southern California
Los Angeles, CA

Thomas J. Dishion, PhD
University of Oregon
Eugene, OR

Georg H. Eifert, PhD
Chapman University
Orange, CA

Matthew T. Feldner, PhD
University of Vermont
Burlington, VT

Kyle E. Ferguson, BA
University of Nevada
Reno, NV

Rocío Fernández-Ballesteros, PhD
Autonoma University of Madrid
Spain

Sarah E. Francis, MA
University of Hawaii at Manoa
Honolulu, HI

Michael D. Franzen, PhD
Allegheny General Hospital
Pittsburgh, PA

Howard N. Garb, PhD
Pittsburgh V.A. Healthcare System
University of Pittsburgh
Pittsburgh, PA

Candace P. Girdwood, BA
MCP Hahnemann University
Philadelphia, PA

Brett R. Goldberg, MA
Hofstra University
Hempstead, NY

Isabela Granic, PhD
University of Oregon
Eugene, OR

Ross W. Greene, BA
Massachusetts General Hospital & Harvard Medical School
Boston, MA

Donald P. Hartmann, PhD
University of Utah
Salt Lake City, UT

Stephen N. Haynes, PhD
University of Hawaii at Manoa
Honolulu, HI

Elaine M. Heiby, PhD
University of Hawaii at Manoa
Honolulu, HI

Richard E. Heyman, PhD
State University of New York at Stony Brook
Stony Brook, NY

John Hunsley, PhD
University of Ottawa
Ottawa, Canada

Mary E. Kaplar, BA
Bowling Green State University
Bowling Green, OH

Thomas R. Kratochwill, PhD
University of Wisconsin-Madison
Madison, WI

Dean Lauterbach, BA
Eastern Michigan University
Ypsilanti, MI

Scott O. Lilienfeld, PhD
Emory University
Atlanta, GA

Eric J. Mash, PhD
University of Calgary
Calgary, Alberta
Canada

Jennifer J. McGrath, MA
Bowling Green State University
Bowling Green, OH

Katherine M. McKnight, PhD
University of Arizona
Tucson, AZ

Kevin R. Murphy, PhD
Pennsylvania State University
University Park, PA

Rosemery O. Nelson-Gray, PhD
University of North Carolina at Greensboro
Greensboro, NC

Arthur M. Nezu, PhD
MCP Hahnemann University
Philadelphia, PA

Christine Maguth Nezu, PhD
MCP Hahnemann University
Philadelphia, PA

William H. O'Brien, PhD
Bowling Green State University
Bowling Green, OH

William T. O'Donohue, PhD
University of Nevada
Reno, NV

Thomas H. Ollendick, PhD
Virginia Polytechnic Institute & State University
Blacksburg, VA

James F. Paulson, BA
University of North Carolina at Greensboro
Greensboro, NC

Michelle A. Peacock, BA
MCP Hahnemann University
Philadelphia, PA

David C.S. Richard, PhD
Eastern Michigan University
Ypsilanti, MI

Patricia J. Robinson, PhD
Mountainview Consulting Group, Inc.
Moxee, WA

Sarah E. Rzasa, BA
Pennsylvania State University
University Park, PA

Kurt Salzinger, PhD
American Psychological Association
Washington, DC

Lee Sechrest, PhD
University of Arizona
Tucson, AZ

Mark R. Serper, PhD
Hofstra University
Hempstead, NY

Elisa Steele Shernoff, BA
University of Wisconsin-Madison
Madison, WI

Amy M. Smith Slep, BA
State University of New York at Stony Brook
Stony Brook, NY

Joshua P. Smith, BA
University of Cincinnati
Cincinnati, OH

Kirk D. Strosahl, PhD
Mountainview Consulting Group, Inc.
Moxee, WA

Hoi K. Suen, PhD
Pennsylvania State University
University Park, PA

Junko Tanaka-Matsumi, PhD
Kwansei Gakuin University
Nishinomiya-City
Japan

Giao Q. Tran, PhD
University of Cincinnati
Cincinnati, OH

David D. Wood, PhD
Private Practice
Visalia, CA

James M. Wood, PhD
University of Texas at El Paso
El Paso, TX

INTRODUCTION TO BEHAVIORAL ASSESSMENT

CHAPTER 1

Introduction to Behavioral Assessment

ELAINE M. HEIBY AND STEPHEN N. HAYNES

OVERVIEW OF THE BEHAVIORAL ASSESSMENT VOLUME

Behavioral Assessment, one of four volumes in the *Comprehensive Handbook of Psychological Assessment,* presents the history, conceptual foundations, methods, applications, and future directions of behavioral assessment. In this first chapter of Section One, we present an overview of behavioral assessment and discuss the definition and distinguishing features of behavioral assessment, emphasizing its scientific and empirical bases. In Chapter 2, Ollendick, Alvarez, and Greene review the history of behavioral assessment. They trace the development of the science of psychological assessment and the impact of disease-oriented and scientifically based behavioral approaches to understanding, measuring, and treating behavior disorders.

Section Two includes chapters on the conceptual foundations of behavioral assessment. Suen and Rzasa (Chapter 3) discuss the psychometric foundations of behavioral assessment. They present an overview of the sign versus sample assumptions underlying measurement, the precision of measures, approaches to reliability and interobserver agreement, generalizability models for estimating sources of variance in obtained measures, measurement errors, and concepts of approaches to validity. O'Donohue and Ferguson (Chapter 4)

introduce the basic learning principles that, when applied to complex human behavior, dictate the precision of the methods used in both behavioral assessment and inextricably behavior and cognitive-behavior therapy. They describe learning mechanisms, such as classical, operant, and cognitive conditioning processes, that must be considered when identifying situational and behavioral targets to be measured in a particular case. They point out how an understanding of learning principles facilitates hypothesizing causal variables of problem behaviors and the acquisition and generalization of new behaviors. In Chapter 5, O'Brien, Kaplar, and McGrath, present models of causality that underlie behavioral assessment strategies. They discuss the role of behavior-environment interactions, complex functional relations, chains of causal variables, and multiple modes of causal factors. Eifert and Feldner (Chapter 6) discuss additional aspects of the conceptual foundations of behavioral assessment. They examine the epistemology associated with behavioral theory and how that epistemology affects the goals of behavioral assessment, its focus on functional relations, the contexts of behavior, the use of multiple sources of information and multiple targets, measurement specificity, and time-series measurement. The authors also discuss trends and challenges in behavioral assessment as the paradigm encounters a widening range of measured phenomena. The assessment method most strongly associated with behavioral assessment is systematic observation. Hartmann, Barrios, and Wood (Chapter 7) review the background, underlying rationale, applications, and methods of behavioral observation, with a focus on strategies for developing a behavioral observation coding system. They provide guidance for the development of behavioral categories, operational definitions, observation settings, temporal considerations in observation, recording methods, and the use of technological aids. Hartmann et al. also discuss validity, sources of error, and the application of generalizability theory to examine the dependability of observation measures. In Chapter 8, Tanaka-Matsumi addresses the role of individual difference variables in behavioral assessment, particularly within the client's cultural context. She points out how the basic principles of behavioral assessment involve identifying causal behavioral and situational variables that inevitably include ones related to ethnocultural factors in order to be ecologically sound.

Section Three includes chapters on the methods of behavioral assessment. Each chapter describes the method and its variations, its conceptual foundations, and its clinical and research applicability and utility. Sources of variance in obtained measures and potential errors are considered, and psychometric foundations are reviewed. Each chapter also considers future developments and offers recommendations for strengthening the precision, validity, applicability, and utility of the method. Chapter 9 by Dishion and Granic focuses on behavioral observation in the natural environment. They note that the use of trained observers assessing behavior across time and in context provides data that minimize error found in devices that rely upon self-report or contrived settings and yields information amenable to a functional analysis. They also point out that the use of naturalistic observation has become more cost-efficient with the use of videotaping and digital recording technology. They provide concrete examples of how such observations can involve some structure in order to elicit situation-specific behaviors that can be coded and that are relevant to a case conceptualization and evaluation of treatment outcome. Chapter 10 by Heyman and Smith Slep reviews behavioral observation in analogue environments where the situation is designed and manipulated in order to code clinically relevant behaviors. They underscore how analogue observations, like naturalistic observations, yield data conducive to hypothesis testing of functional relations among situational and behavioral causal factors and the target behavior. However, they also point out that analogue observations may be more cost-efficient than naturalistic observation in some individuals because there is more opportunity to control the situation to elicit the behaviors of interest. They provide a case study of a married couple, which

describes how the use of self-report information can guide hypothesis testing and the design of analogue observational situations. Chapter 11 by Barbour and Davison reviews the characteristics of behavioral interviewing, noting that the clinical interview is one of the most common and useful assessment devices used by clinicians. Behavioral interviews are distinguished by their structure in terms of how the interviewer behaves in order to obtain information about current environmental conditions under which the problem and causal behaviors are exhibited. They review structured interviews that have been developed to identify problem behaviors as classified by the *Diagnostic and Statistical Manual of Mental Disorders* (*DSM-IV*) as well as those designed to also assess some potential causal variables. They also review semistructured interviews that permit the behavioral assessor to obtain information critically relevant to developing a functional analysis so that the information yielded is directly relevant to treatment planning and evaluation. They provide an example of a semistructured behavioral interview that nicely illustrates how the interviewer elicits information relevant to cognitive-behavior therapy planning. Chapter 12 by Fernández-Ballesteros addresses the role of self-report questionnaires in behavioral assessment, another of the more common methods used in both clinical and research settings but one that was eschewed in the early behavioral assessment literature. She provides a history of the role of self-report questionnaires within behavioral assessment and how the development of narrow-band, low-inference questionnaires facilitated the acceptance of behavioral assessment methods within psychological assessment at large. She also indicates that behavioral self-report questionnaires are distinctive in that they are more likely than broadband personality questionnaires to be conducive to repeated measurement and causal model testing. She provides examples of how the information from behavioral self-report questionnaires can complement data obtained by other behavioral assessment methods, such as direct observation and psychophysiological indices, to guide treatment planning and outcome evaluation. Chapter 13 by Richard and Lauterbach reviews how various methods of behavioral assessment can be computerized, rendering them more cost-effective and facilitating data management and analysis needed for evaluation of hypothesis-testing. Their literature review documents a trend toward greater use of computerized behavioral assessment (both hardware and software) that has been facilitated by the availability of handheld computers. Computerized methods and tools, including the Internet, that they describe include simulation training of both clinical assessors to enhance accuracy of assessment and clients so that situational and behavioral problems can be identified and treatment outcome evaluated when doing so in vivo is not practical (e.g., skills needed for the use of a wheelchair and parent-child interactions). They also describe computerized methods that have been developed for the use of behavioral observation, physiological indices, self-monitoring, self-report questionnaires, interviews, and rating scales. Chapter 14 on program evaluation by McKnight and Sechrest underscores how behavioral assessment principles provide guidelines for the development, ongoing evaluation, and determination of programs. The authors underscore the need for highly specific and operationalized components of programs' low-inference variables for the evaluation of the program. They indicate how evaluations need to include multiple methods (referred to as multiplism) when assessing both causal and outcome variables over time. They also point out that determining cost-effectiveness is inherent in a behavioral approach to program evaluation.

Applications of behavioral assessment in particular settings and with particular populations are presented in Section Four. Tran and Smith (Chapter 15) discuss behavioral assessment of treatment outcome. The authors review effectiveness and efficacy evaluations, methods of evaluating treatment-related change, clinical significance, reliability, validity, clinical utility, efficiency, and sensitivity of treatment outcome measures. The authors emphasize these dimensions in the measurement of treatment outcome with social anxiety disorders. Francis and Chorpita present an overview of behavioral assessment of children in outpatient settings (Chapter 16). They point out developmental considerations in the selection and application of specific behavioral assessment devices, such as situational factors related to the family, school, and peers as well as age-specific behavioral competencies. They provide a session-by-session case example of assessment and treatment of a 9-year-old girl who presented a number of behavioral problems (e.g., anxiety, peer relations, tantrums, vomiting) and indicate how target behaviors were selected and treatment outcome evaluated. In Chapter 17, Serper, Goldberg, and Salzinger examine behavioral assessment in restricted environments, with a focus on inpatient psychiatric units. They discuss the origins of severely maladaptive behavior, including the role of stimulus control, competing behaviors, and reinforcing contingencies. They review methods of measurement in restricted environments, such as Gordon Paul's observational systems, event sampling, duration measures, interviews, self-report questionnaires, rating scales, and self-monitoring. They also discuss cognitive and other assessment approaches to behavior problems such as delusions and hallucinations, depression, suicidal behaviors, aggression, and adaptive functioning. Murphy (Chapter 18) provides an overview of the conceptual bases and methods

of behavioral assessment for personnel selection and job performance in work settings. The role of biodata, structured interviews, standardized tests, cognitive ability tests, and personality tests are covered. Murphy also reviews work samples and simulations and the multimethod strategies associated with assessment centers. These methods and concepts are integrated in a case study of the development and validation of a selection test battery. Behavioral assessment in educational settings is reviewed in Chapter 19 by Shernoff and Kratochwill. The authors review the conceptual foundations and methodological underpinnings of behavioral assessment as applied to the design, outcome measurement, and modification of interventions in the classroom. Assessment and intervention with a girl experiencing selective mutism is used to illustrate behavioral assessment strategies. In Chapter 20, Franzen presents a behavioral approach to neuropsychological assessment, demonstrating how this traditionally nonbehavioral area of assessment can be conducive to the tenets of behavioral assessment. He finds an overlap between the methods used in traditional neuropsychological assessment and behavioral assessment, such as behavioral checklists, physiological indices, and use of the observation both in vivo and by informants. He also points out conceptual overlaps, such as the relation between assessment information and treatment planning. In its early stages, neuropsychological assessment was primarily concerned with inferring the locus of brain damage, but contemporary approaches involve a greater focus on specific behavioral strengths, deficits, and targets for rehabilitation. Chapter 21 by Nezu, Nezu, Peacock, and Girdwood provides an overview of the behavioral assessment implications of cognitive-behavior therapy, one of the most broadly applied empirically supported treatments. They underscore the need to generate and evaluate theory and data-driven hypotheses regarding causal variables of an individual's presenting problems. They note the fallibility of clinical decision making that is not empirically guided and self-correcting. They also provide four models of case formulation, including a problem-solving paradigm, an integration of cognitive therapy and functional analysis, a framework derived from dialectical behavior therapy, and quantitative functional analytic causal modeling. Common themes across these models include the need for causal modeling and an ongoing evaluation of treatment outcome. The role of behavioral assessment in the era of managed care is addressed in Chapter 22 by Strosahl and Robinson. They provide a contextual argument that the ethics, standards, and scientific soundness of behavioral assessment are consistent with the health care industry's reimbursement criteria of cost-effectiveness and accountability. They underscore the practical implications for applied psychologists' economic survival at a time when all health care providers are facing declining incomes. They note that behavioral health care involves evaluation at the clinical, individual, and system level and that such evaluation is best served by methods used by behavioral assessors. Therefore, the authors predict that use of behavioral assessment in the future must expand if applied psychologists wish to sell their services to third-party payers.

Section Five concerns how the tenets of behavioral assessment interface with certain aspects of the common culture of nonbehavioral assessment. Chapter 23 by Garb, Lilienfeld, and Wood discusses the role of projective techniques in assessment given the popularity of these highly inferential instruments among applied psychologists, the empirical support for these instruments, and their use in the context of the ethics and standards of behavioral assessment. They review the three most popular projective techniques: the Rorschach, thematic apperception test, and human figure drawings. They address the controversy over the use of these instruments in the field, focusing on difficulties of interpretation of test data owing to situational effects on responses, a high rate of false negatives in identifying problem behavior, and lack of incremental validity in identifying both causal variables and problem behaviors. They provide a detailed review of the inadequacy of projectives in the identification of child sexual abuse to illustrate the need for extreme caution in the use of projectives. Although they do note some validity evidence for these projective techniques in the identification of a few problem behaviors, their review yields no clear rationale for including projectives in an assessment battery when the goal is case formulation and ongoing evaluation of treatment outcome. In Chapter 24, Nelson-Gray and Paulson present the interaction and integration of behavioral assessment with the hegemony of psychiatry's diagnostic system within both research and applied psychology. They point out that, although early behavioral psychologists eschewed psychiatric diagnoses for sound reasons, much recent work on behavioral assessment and treatments has accepted the utility of classifying target problems according to the American Psychiatric Association's *DSM* system despite limitations of its reliability and validity. While the authors note weaknesses in the manual, they also argue that a clinical science requires some taxonomy in order to organize findings in a systematic fashion, and a more precise taxonomy more congruent with the principles of behavioral assessment has not been fully developed or widely accepted. Until such a system is developed, the authors point out that a diagnosis from the *DSM* can be a starting point in providing more specification of the problem behaviors and their causal factors necessary for a case conceptualization.

Section Six consists of the final chapter by Mash and Hunsley that integrates the volume and its implications for the future of behavioral assessment. It should be noted that the authors did not have the benefit of studying all of the volume's final chapters owing to publication deadlines. They end this volume on a very positive note, stating that behavioral assessment is becoming so integrated with psychological assessment that its principles, methods, and applications are often not recognized as "behavioral." They conclude that the era for wide applications of behavioral assessment has arrived.

We should point out that there are topics relevant to behavioral assessment that are not covered in depth in this volume. Section One on the overview of principles, strategies, and methods would have benefited by a chapter on the ethics of behavioral assessment (see Hayes, Follette, Dawes, & Grady, 1995). Section Two on conceptual foundations could have included an additional chapter on the learning principles upon which behavioral assessment is grounded (see Haynes & O'Brien, 2000). Section Three on methods of behavioral assessment fails to include chapters on self-monitoring (see Cole & Bambara, 2000), psychophysiological methods (see Sturgis & Gramling, 1998), and informant reports (see Haynes & O'Brien, 2000). Section Four on the applications of behavioral assessment could have a chapter on assessment of adults in outpatient settings (see Haynes, Nelson, Thacher, & Kaholokula, 2002). Section Five on the interaction/integration between behavioral and nonbehavioral methods would be more useful if it also included a chapter on behavioral approaches to the writing of psychological evaluations, although the case examples in several chapters of Sections Three and Four provide guidelines.

OVERVIEW AND DEFINITION OF BEHAVIORAL ASSESSMENT

The first challenge to describing a psychological assessment paradigm is to construct a definition. Behavioral assessment is particularly difficult to define for several reasons. Most important, behavioral assessment is primarily defined by an epistemology of behavioral science, rather than by a circumscribed set of assessment methods or a model of behavior disorders. That is, it is defined by assumptions about the best approach to developing a science of psychological assessment. It is presumed that a scientific approach to psychological assessment will lead to an effective set of assessment methods and valid and useful models of behavior disorders. We address the scientific roots of behavioral assessment further below.

Partially as a function of its scientific basis, behavioral assessment is a dynamic paradigm. The methods, underlying models of behavior, and applicability of behavioral assessment evolve as we learn more about measurement and the phenomena that are measured. While behavioral assessment was originally associated with behavioral observation and manipulation of hypothesized controlling variables in analogue and naturalistic settings, behavioral assessment methods now include self-report interviews and questionnaires, psychophysiological assessment, computerized assessment, rating scales, self-monitoring, and product-of-behavior measures (e.g., school grades, blood-sugar levels). The targets of behavioral assessment now include not only observable behaviors, but physiological events, thoughts, expectancies, environmental settings and events, behavior chains, change in behavior and events over time, and interactions between persons and between persons and their environments.

The applicability of behavioral assessment also has expanded. As the following chapters illustrate, behavioral assessment is being used to develop clinical case formulations, measure treatment outcome and process, investigate the causes and correlates of behavior problems, enhance educational programs, provide data for psychiatric diagnoses, and aid in workplace and community-based decisions and interventions.

The supraordinate, guiding principle of behavioral assessment is that psychological assessment should be based on principles of scientific *inquiry and inference.* That is, measures and inferences derived from them should be precise, minimally inferential, based on a strong foundation of validation research, with well-documented sources of variance and error. A focus on sources of error in assessment encourages the use of multiple sources of information (e.g., parents, teachers) and methods of assessment (e.g., observation, self-report), in order to reduce errors that would occur if inferences were based on only one source or method.

The scientific epistemology of behavioral assessment is discussed in greater detail later in this chapter. At this point, we emphasize that it is the primary force underlying the paradigm's evolution and that it leads to the defining characteristics and methods discussed in the next sections.

An emphasis on the science of psychological assessment applies to three of the major foci of behavioral assessment—the measurement of *change,* the measurement of *functional relations,* and measurement of these phenomena for *individuals.* Many applications of behavioral assessment involve time-series measurement—the frequent measurement of behavior and environmental events in order to capture their dynamic aspects. The focus on functional relations is central to the use of behavioral assessment for clinical case formulation because it facilitates the identification of events

that control clients' behavior problems or the acquisition of their goals. Inferences are derived for individual clients because change in behavior and environmental events, and functional relations, can differ in important ways across persons.

To summarize: *Behavioral assessment is a scientific approach to psychological assessment that emphasizes the use of minimally inferential measures, the use of measures that have been validated in ways appropriate for the assessment context, the assessment of functional relations, and the derivation of judgments based on measurement in multiple situations, from multiple methods and sources, and across multiple times.*

APPLICABILITY, UTILITY, AND GOALS OF BEHAVIORAL ASSESSMENT

As documented in the chapters that follow, behavioral assessment has been used in most applied assessment settings and for most applied assessment purposes (see overviews in Sections Three and Four: Bellack & Hersen, 1998; Haynes & O'Brien, 2000). Perhaps more important, the applicability and utility of behavioral assessment is increasing, sometimes in the context of decreasing use of alternative assessment strategies (e.g., the decreasing use of projective and personality assessment methods in managed care; Chapter 22).

Behavioral assessment is used in the measurement of treatment process and outcome (Chapter 15), in program evaluation (Royse & Thyer, 1996), for case formulation and treatment planning (Chapter 21), to enhance the validity of psychiatric diagnostic decisions (Chapter 24), to facilitate decisions in the workplace (Chapter 18), as a screen for behavior problems in primary care settings (Chapter 13), for basic research across a range of psychology subdisciplines (e.g., developmental psychology, learning, psychobiology), and to identify the causes and correlates of behavior problems (e.g., Cicchetti & Rogosch, 1999).

As we reviewed earlier, behavioral assessment is also applicable across a range of assessment settings. It has been used in classrooms and schools (Chapter 19), the home (Chapter 7), outpatient psychiatric settings (Chapter 16), inpatient psychiatric settings (O'Brien & Haynes, 1993; Chapter 17), the workplace (Chapter 18), community settings (Tolan, 1999), and medical settings (see overview in George, 1991; Simeonsson & Rosenthal, 2001).

Behavioral assessment has been used with persons across many dimensions of individual differences. It has been used with infants (Singer & Zeskind, 2001), children and adolescents (Greene & Ollendick, 2000), adults and older adults

(Haynes, 2000; Rybarczyk & Lopez, 1999), persons from diverse cultures and ethnicities (Chapter 8), and across a range of developmental and cognitive abilities (Simeonsson & Rosenthal, 2001). Behavioral assessment also has been used in the assessment of couples (Floyd, Haynes, & Kelly, 1997) and families, and persons with physical disabilities (Malec & Lemsky, 1995) and acute or chronic medical illnesses (Simeonsson & Rosenthal, 2001; Tait, 1999).

The broad applicability and utility of behavioral assessment is a consequence of its emphasis on a science of assessment rather than on a set of methods or fixed models of behavior disorders. Foremost, behavioral assessment presumes that scientific principles of psychological assessment are applicable across most assessment settings, dimensions of individual differences, client behavior problems and goals, and assessment purposes. Regardless of the application, assessment strategies can entail carefully constructed measurement of carefully defined and precisely measured targets (Haynes & O'Brien, 2000; Mash & Terdal, 1997; Shapiro & Kratochwill, 2000). However, it is noteworthy that there are some contexts for which some behavioral scientists question the current applicability of a science of assessment. For example, judgments about whether a person was legally "insane" at the time a crime was committed cannot currently be subjected to the same degree of validation as many other clinical judgments.

A scientific approach to assessment permits a diverse set of methods (e.g., Bellack & Hersen, 1998; Shapiro & Kratochwill, 2000). Most personality assessment methods, for example, require that respondents have at least a moderate level of verbal comprehension and communicative abilities. These methods often require the respondent to provide retrospective and integrative judgments (e.g., about beliefs, past events, emotions, and perceptions) to written, pictorial, or verbally presented queries. The requirement of a moderate level of cognitive and communicative functioning reduces the applicability of these instruments for the assessment of infants and young children, persons with developmental and other cognitive disabilities, family and social systems, and of functional relations among multiple events.

In contrast, the behavioral assessment paradigm includes a broad and flexible collection of methods. Some behavioral self-report and cognitive assessment methods also require a minimal level of comprehension and communicative abilities (e.g., parent reports of their child's behaviors). When clients lack cognitive or communicative abilities, other methods, such as naturalistic and analogue observation, experimental functional analyses, psychophysiological assessment, and informant reports often can be substituted.

OVERLAP OF BEHAVIORAL WITH NONBEHAVIORAL ASSESSMENT PARADIGMS

Many authors (e.g., Bellack & Hersen, 1998; Haynes & O'Brien, 2000; see overviews in Mash & Terdal, 1997; Shapiro & Kratochwill, 2000) have outlined facets of behavioral assessment that differentiate it from other psychological assessment paradigms (see also Chapter 6). Before we present these discriminative facets, we note that behavioral assessment and some other psychological assessment paradigms overlap in several ways. For example, neuropsychological and psychophysiological assessment (often included in books on behavioral assessment; e.g., see Chapter 20) and empirically based personality assessment paradigms stress the use of validated measures to draw carefully constrained inferences. These psychological assessment paradigms address, as does behavioral assessment, sources of error (e.g., malingering and faking good, effects of test administration variables), reliability and validity, the precision of measured constructs, and clinical utility.

Differences between these paradigms and behavioral assessment are more apparent when the specifics of psychometric evaluations are considered. For example, because of the types of measures derived and assumptions about the stability of measures, content validity assumes a greater role and temporal stability assumes a lesser role in the validation of behavioral observation systems (see Chapter 3). Similarly, many behavioral assessment instruments are assumed to sample events from a domain of interest (e.g., to sample some oppositional behaviors of a child in a classroom) rather than to derive indirect indices (i.e., signs) of latent constructs (e.g., to measure multiple markers of narcissism; see Chapter 6).

Other facets of behavioral and nonbehavioral assessment paradigms also overlap. For example, psychophysiological and neuropsychological assessment also focus on dynamic aspects of behavior—the measurement of behavior change over time and as a function of environmental events and states. Psychophysiological assessment (Tomarken, 1999), as with behavioral assessment, often entails extensive time-series assessment—many samples of events in order to track their time course and effects of interventions. The time-series measurement strategy of behavioral assessment differs from these paradigms in that it often involves the measurement of multiple behaviors and events in order to estimate their functional relations (e.g., estimating the degree to which daily mood changes of arthritis patients are affected by their pain and social interactions; Thacher & Haynes, 2001).

The overlap of behavioral with other psychological assessment paradigms is further discussed in several chapters in this book. Garb and colleagues (Chapter 23) discuss the relation between behavioral and projective methods. Nelson-Gray and Paulson (Chapter 24), discuss behavioral assessment and psychiatric diagnosis. Barbour and Davison (Chapter 11) discuss behavioral assessment and structured interviews. Strosahl and Robinson (Chapter 22) discuss behavioral and nonbehavioral approaches to assessment in managed care.

ETHICS AND PRACTICE STANDARDS OF BEHAVIORAL ASSESSMENT

The ethical principles underlying behavioral assessment techniques include an emphasis not only on science in general, but specifically on cost-efficiency and incremental validity (Haynes & O'Brien, 2000)—principles that are congruent with the industrialization of health care (see Chapter 22) and, of course, consumer protection. These ethical principles represent more strict standards than those of the American Psychological Association (APA, 1990), which govern practice in most states in the United States. Dawes (1994) pointed out that the APA's ethical standards simply require a psychologist to be aware of the scientific knowledge related to services rendered. The ethics do not require psychologists to use the most valid and cost-efficient techniques. This is in sharp contrast to the ethical code of the American Medical Association (AMA, 1989), which explicitly requires physicians to use the most valid techniques and explicitly prohibits the use of ineffective or outdated ones. The APA permits psychologists to use invalid and ineffective techniques as long as they are aware that they are doing so. Adherents to the use of behavioral assessment follow ethical principles that are more similar to those followed by the AMA than the APA. The need for higher ethical standards for psychologists has been underscored by McFall (1991), who proposed a manifesto involving the cardinal principle that a scientific psychology is the only legitimate and acceptable psychology. He provided a corollary that reiterates the ethical principles underlying behavioral assessment, particularly that the assessment must be validated and have benefits that outweigh the costs.

In 1995, the American Association of Applied and Preventive Psychology (AAAPP) held a conference and published the proceedings on practice standards (Hayes, Follette, Dawes, & Grady, 1995). The speakers at the conference agreed on the following conclusions, among others, that are congruent with behavioral assessment: (1) applied psychologists should use empirically valid repeated measures of problems being treated; (2) applied psychologists should only use interventions that are protective of the consumer, effective, and empirically validated; (3) the entire discipline of psychology should develop and follow hortatory and mina-

tory standards of scientific practice; (4) consumers of applied psychology should be informed of the scientific status of services offered; and (5) if scientifically supported treatments are not effective and no scientifically supported alternative treatments exist, the applied psychologist should emphasize to the consumer points (1) and (4).

Therefore, it may require not only market factors but also a change in ethics for behavioral assessment to be common in clinical psychology training programs and to be the primary method of assessment in research and practice. Hayes et al. (1995) called upon the AAAPP to develop standards of practice and be open to psychologists who believe in developing procedures that meet the above-delineated standards.

BEHAVIORAL ASSESSMENT, PSYCHOLOGICAL ASSESSMENT, AND PRINCIPLES OF SCIENCE

As indicated above, the principles of behavioral assessment are congruent with the basic tenets of science. These tenets include posing constructs and hypotheses that are testable (refutable) and parsimonious (minimizing inference and unnecessary explanatory mechanisms). The history of modern science since the Renaissance shows that advancements occur when more direct measurement devices are developed. As examples, the invention of the telescope, microscope, and thermometer as well as socially permissible dissection of the human body resulted in replacing dogma and speculation with mechanical and direct observations. More direct measurement led to great developments in the natural and life sciences and provided a model for a science of psychology. Psychological physiologists in the early nineteenth century measured gross human motor behavior by direct observation (e.g., reaction time), sensorimotor behavior by psychophysiological methods (e.g., electrical stimulation of the brain), and covert behavior such as perception by self-report (verbalizing the color seen when exposed to a visual stimulus). In the late nineteenth century German scientists applied these approaches to more complex human behavior by adopting broader human phenomenology as a legitimate focus of study, and thereby ushered in the birth of psychological science and eventually applied psychology (Boring, 1950). Therefore, the origins of assessment in psychology involved methods that curiously are now viewed as a fairly modern behavioral approach (see Chapter 2).

A curiosity concerns whether it would be necessary to classify assessment of human behavior into the types represented in this *Comprehensive Handbook of Psychological Assessment* if psychologists had maintained the same approach to measurement that established the discipline. Perhaps there would not be a need for this volume entitled *Behavioral Assessment,* as all assessment in psychology would be what we now call behavioral. Instead, the *Handbook* might be organized around a taxonomy of clinically relevant behaviors, their causal and maintenance variables, and methods of assessment that are conducive to particular individuals and contexts. In this volume's final chapter, Mash and Hunsley conclude that behavioral assessment is rapidly becoming integrated with psychological assessment, suggesting the possibility that future handbooks may be organized differently than this one.

It is beyond the scope of this chapter to summarize the history of psychology's twists and turns regarding its adherence to the basic tenets of science and the development of various approaches to assessment. However, it is instructive to consider briefly how behavioral assessment evolved from psychological physiology, psychological physics, and psychological philosophy that emerged in the late nineteenth and early twentieth centuries. The predecessors to psychologists became interested in complex individual differences that had applied implications, such as success in educational or work settings and identification of psychopathology. The term *mental tests* was coined by Cattell in his 1890 paper "Mental Tests and Measurement," in which he proposed 50 assessment devices. These tests focused on direct observation of multiple measures over time (i.e., reaction time and self-report of perceptions). Binet, around the same time, sampled behaviors of children through observation and self-report that were directly relevant to skills needed in school settings. Binet's low-inference measures became reified decades later into the higher-level construct of intelligence. Other highly inferential psychological tests, such as the projectives, were developed to measure personality constructs and abnormal behavior. However, what we now call behavioral assessment techniques invented by the predecessors to psychology (observational, psychophysiological, and self-report) were never abandoned. These techniques came to be labeled *behavioral* when a school of thought that evolved out of objective psychology was founded by Watson's 1913 paper "Psychology as the Behaviorist Views It" (see Chapter 2). Watson assessed behavior using both observational and self-report measures while contemporaries such as Lashley focused on psychophysiological measures (Boring, 1950). Modern behaviorists have expanded upon these techniques, developing low-inference self-report measures that include interviewing, self-monitoring, and questionnaires. At the same time, the field of psychological assessment reflects the influence of philosophy and authoritarianism that has permitted untestable psychological theories, highly inferential approaches to measurement, and treatments that have little or no empirical support.

Recently, McFall (2002) observed that modern applied psychologists can be divided into two basic types: those who adhere to a science of psychology (clinical scientists and scientist-practitioners) and those who are guided by a more intuitive approach. Therefore, behavioral assessment, which adheres to the tenets and ethics of science, has not dominated the history of psychological assessment nor its current practice. The differences between scientists and philosophers remain evident in the different epistemologies of today's approaches to applied psychology.

The modern rediscovery of behavioral assessment is evident in the chapters of this volume. Other promising indices suggest the influence of behavioral assessment will continue to grow and return applied psychology to its scientific roots. Most empirically supported treatments are products of behavioral theories and research. For example, Fisher, Hayes, and O'Donohue (in press) describe 69 empirically supported therapies, which have evolved primarily from behavioral research that inherently is conducted with behavioral assessment techniques. Their book provides clinicians with a guide for using assessment and treatment approaches that can be justified for third-party reimbursement. Insurance companies have begun to demand evidence that procedures used by clinicians are scientifically sound. This era of accountability has led more clinicians to appreciate the contributions of behavioral approaches to assessment and treatment that they formerly eschewed. In 1993, Piotrowski and Zalewski found that training in behavioral assessment was provided in only a little over half of clinical psychology doctoral programs, but the teaching and use of behavioral assessment was predicted to increase. Consistent with this prediction, the number of paid subscriptions to behavioral journals has, on average, increased 23% between 1992 and 1997 (Haynes & O'Brien, 2000). Indeed, Strosahl and Robinson's Chapter 22 in this volume notes that managed care companies are becoming unwilling to pay for most traditional assessment techniques and are demanding the type of data gathered by behavioral assessment techniques to justify reimbursement for clinical services. Therefore, applied psychologists seem to be returning to the basic scientific approaches of experimental psychology, and, oddly enough, it may be market factors rather than an adherence to science that is promoting this trend.

TENETS OF THE BEHAVIORAL ASSESSMENT PARADIGM

The emphasis on a scientific approach to psychological assessment mandates that behavioral assessment strategies reflect empirical findings on the characteristics and causes of behavior disorders, treatment process and outcome, and principles of measurement. Therefore, the foci and methods of behavioral assessment reflect the importance of behavior-environment functional relations, dynamic aspects of behavior, and the idiographic nature of behavior disorders and their causes.

Functional Relations Between Behavior and the Environment

A central and well-supported tenet of behavioral paradigms is that variance in behavior and behavior problems often can be understood through an examination of behavior-environment functional relations (Pierce & Epling, 1999; Plaud & Eifert, 1998).[1] These functional relations most often involve differences in the rates or other dimensions of behavior across different contexts and settings and as a function of different response contingencies. Functional relations also can involve extended social systems.

A Focus on Settings, Contexts, and Consequences

An examination of the *settings and contexts* associated with different rates (or other dimensions, such as duration or intensity) of behavior can provide information about factors that affect the behavior (e.g., Bandura & Goldman, 1995; Boutin & Nelson, 1998). For example, it can be helpful for the design of intervention programs to know how often or to what extent a client expresses delusions of persecution. But it is even more helpful to identify the environmental settings in which the client's delusions are most likely to occur or in which they are most strongly believed, the degree to which the client's delusions are affected by specific environmental stressors or medication adherence, and the degree to which their rate or intensity varies in the presence of different persons.

The probability of a behavior problem often differs across contexts. That is, it can exhibit differential conditional probabilities (see overview in Bellack & Hersen, 1998)—it is more likely to occur in some settings or following some events. For example, for some persons, domestic violence is more likely when a spouse is intoxicated.

Often, particular settings are associated with a higher likelihood of a behavior problem because the setting has been associated with an elevated probability of reinforcement for the behavior—the setting has acquired *discriminative stimulus properties*. These properties elicit affect, direct behavior, and function as reinforcers (Staats, 1968). Thus, a child may be more likely to exhibit tantrums with one parent than with another if tantrum-like demands for attention, toys, or escape from an aversive situation have been reinforced more often by one parent.

Context refers to stimuli and conditions that accompany specific antecedent-response-consequence associations. Contexts can involve environmental settings, complex behavior and behavior-environment chains, interaction effects involving multiple stimuli, and physiological states (see overview in Morris, 1988). In following with the above example, the probability of violent domestic interactions can be significantly affected by the intoxication state of a partner as well as the recent history of couple conflict and occupational and financial difficulties of one partner (see overview of domestic violence in Holtzworth-Munroe, Smutzler, Bates, & Sandin, 1997).

Specific *antecedent stimuli* also may acquire discriminative properties. A behavior problem can be elicited by particular persons, words, noises, thoughts, internal physiological stimuli, objects, animals, smells, and locations. These events often function as conditional stimuli because of past associations with unconditional or other conditional stimuli. For example, a bedroom previously associated with sexual assault and hyperventilation previously associated with a panic episode can elicit anxious thoughts and physiological responses.

An important aspect of functional relations is the sequelae to responses—the events following a response. Since the writings of Thorndike, Watson, and Skinner, the behavioral paradigm has emphasized the importance of *response contingencies* for understanding why behavior is more or less likely to occur (see Chapter 2 on history of behavioral assessment). For many clients, the factors that account for the occurrence of a behavior problem, or for the nonoccurrence of a positive alternative to a behavior problem, can be ascribed to the effect of those behaviors on the environment, the consequences of the behavior. The environment can be said to *select* behaviors, because only some behaviors are strengthened by reinforcing consequences in particular contexts (Pierce & Epling, 1999). As noted, the degree to which a response is selected can vary across contexts.

Response contingencies are only one of many potential causal factors for behavior problems (see Chapter 5 on causal models in behavioral assessment). However, an extensive empirical literature documents that many behavior problems—such as self-injurious behaviors, aggression, pain expressions, oppositional behaviors, obsessive and compulsive behaviors, ingestive behaviors, substance use, social avoidance, and medication intake—are affected by their immediate consequences.

A Focus on Contemporaneous Functional Relations

Many important functional relations for behavior problems are historical. That is, the initial causes of behavior problems are often historical events and learning experiences. The onset of eating, anxiety, mood, self-injurious, aggressive, anti-social, and other behavior problems often can be partially attributed to early learning experiences, developmental events, and parent-child interactions (e.g., Turner, 1994, with personality disorders). Historical causal factors are often the focus of traditional psychotherapies.

While acknowledging the importance of historical events (and other causal factors such as intrauterine conditions, early diet and stimulation, and genetic factors) in the development of behavior problems, a behavioral assessment paradigm pays special attention to contemporaneous behavioral, cognitive, and social environmental factors that may be maintaining the behavior problem. These contiguous factors are often the most useful for designing intervention programs. Thus, although a client's depressed mood and social anxiety can be a partial function of early learning and difficult childhood family environments, behavioral assessors are more likely than assessors from other paradigms to emphasize the causal role of contemporaneous self-statements and expectations, conditional responses to environmental stimuli, social interactions, and stress coping strategies.

A contemporaneous focus often leads to greater attention to *moderator variables,* variables that affect the strength of relations between two other variables. For example, we would be interested in the variables (e.g., social supports, cognitive variables) that affect depressed mood responses to early trauma, loss of a job, or physical injury.

Given a focus on contemporaneous behavior and causal variables, a scientific approach to assessment is also important when the focus is on historical events. For example, several studies have noted that the validity and precision of clients' self-reports about the history of such events as substance use, health problems, major life stressors, and episodes of panic and depressed mood can be strengthened with the use of timeline follow-back methods (Sobell & Sobell, 1994). Additionally, there is a growing empirical literature on variables that affect, and ways to enhance, the validity of self-report (Chapter 12; Stone et al., 2000).

A Focus on Extended Social Systems

Although the preceding sections emphasize the importance of immediate contextual factors, antecedent stimuli, and response contingencies, many factors that affect behavior problems are less contiguous and immediate and often involve events that affect persons in the client's social environment (Mash & Terdal, 1997). For example, the ability of a parent to respond appropriately to an oppositional child might be affected by financial worries, the need to spend large amounts of time at work, conflicts between the parent and other chil-

dren in the family, marital conflict and distress, and health problems. Also, how staff members on a psychiatric inpatient unit interact with patients might be affected by hospital administration policies, conflicts among staff members on the unit, patient-staff ratios, and factors affecting the staff member outside of work.

The principle here is that any factor that affects the functional relations relevant for a client's behavior problem can serve as an important causal factor for that behavior problem. Anything that affects a parent's response to his or her child, a teacher's response to children in the classroom, a spouse's response to his or her partner, and a staff member's response to patients can be important causal variables in a chain ending in the behavior problem of the child, spouse, and patient. The obvious implication is that assessment strategies must broadly focus on extended social systems. For example, it may be a mistake to implement a parent-training program for a parent who is facing severe life stressors or who shows signs of major affective disorder without first addressing these treatment outcome moderators. These factors are likely to be part of a complex causal matrix, and it may be difficult for the parent to follow treatment program requirements.

The Dynamic Nature of Behavior Problems, Causal Variables, and Functional Relations

A substantive literature documents the dynamic nature of many behavior problems and many events that affect them (see overviews in Collins & Horn, 1991; Haynes, 1992). Mood, oppositional behaviors, delusions, substance use, weight, blood pressure, autistic behaviors, infant feeding problems, and marital distress are just a few of the behavior problems that change, sometimes rapidly, over time. Also, many factors that affect clients' behaviors can change—for example, the behavior of clients' partners, parents, and children; the frequency or intensity of daily hassles; the behavior of staff members, supervisors, and teachers; the frequency or duration of exposure to life stressors and conditioned aversive stimuli; demands to perform feared behaviors; injuries and illnesses; and medication effects. Further, therapeutic interventions can produce change, both in behavior problems and in causal variables.

Complicating the task of measuring dynamic variables is dyssynchrony across dimensions and modes (e.g., cognitive, behavioral, physiological) of behavior problems and causal variables. The dimensions of behavior and causal events can change differentially across time. For example, the frequency, intensity, and duration of panic episodes can change differentially over time and as a function of treatment (see overview of panic in Baillie & Rapee, 2002; Baker, Patterson, &

Barlow, 2002). Additional cognitive, behavioral, and emotional facets of behavior problems can change in dyssynchronous fashion. Also, the life stressors encountered by a client can change in intensity, frequency, and/or duration (see discussion in Bandura, 1982).

Idiographic Nature of Behavior Problems and Causal Variables

The behavioral assessment paradigm emphasizes the idiographic nature of behavior problems and causal factors (Cone, 1986; Haynes & O'Brien, 2000; Nelson-Gray, 1996; Pervin, 1984). Not only can the form, dimensions, and time course of behavior problems and their causal variables differ across time and contexts, they can differ across persons. We know that the specific symptoms associated with depression, oppositional, and other behavior problems often differ across persons with the same diagnosis (Hersen & Porzelius, 2002). Further, the factors that affect a behavior problem can also differ across persons (Goldberger & Breznitz, 1993). The causal importance of automatic negative thoughts and social skills deficits can differ across persons with the same affective disorder. As discussed in the next sections (also see Chapter 24), behavioral assessment often includes both nomothetic and idiographic strategies, and clinical inferences are often based on a combination of nomothetic and idiographic information and measures.

Behavioral Assessment and Psychological Paradigms

We have outlined the close association between behavioral assessment and elements of behavior therapy and the behavioral paradigm. However, as suggested earlier, a scientific approach to psychological assessment is not tied to a particular theoretical paradigm. An approach to assessment that emphasizes the derivation of precise and minimally inferential measures, measures that are sensitive to changes across time and contexts, measures subjected to validation appropriate for their application, inferences based on multiple sources of information, and measures that address potential causal factors for behavior problems and treatment outcome is relevant whatever the assessors' ideas about the nature of behavior and its causes.

One reason behavioral assessment is not tied to a particular theoretical paradigm is that there exists no generally accepted paradigm in psychology. The theoretical nature of the discipline of psychology has changed little since Staat's 1983 book *Psychology's Crisis of Disunity: Philosophy and Methods for a Unified Science*. Staats pointed out that psychology is a relatively young science that is riddled with competing and often redundant and simplistic theories of a particular complex behavior. Integrative theories are difficult to publish in a preparadigmatic science. He also pointed out that research guided by one particular theory is often ignored rather than integrated with research guided by concurrent or subsequent theories. The field of psychology lacks integration also in the sense that theories often introduce new terms that are constructs that have already been defined but labeled differently in prior theories. For example, the behavioral competencies of self-monitoring, self-evaluation, and self-reinforcement have been referred to in the literature as self-control, self-regulation, and self-management, among other terms.

Thus the behavioral assessor is faced with a myriad of theoretically proposed and sometimes redundant empirically supported causal factors for any particular problem behavior. For example, a recent book in a series published under the auspices of the Association for the Advancement of Behavior Therapy (AABT), *Practitioner's Guide to Empirically Based Measures of Depression* (Nezu, Ronan, Meadows, & McClure, 2000) reviews the psychometric status of 52 assessment devices for depression and 42 assessment devices for potential causal variables of depression. The measures in this *Guide* are amenable to behavioral assessment and include observational, self-report, and psychophysiological techniques that can be applied repeatedly at little cost. Yet the clinician and researcher are faced with selecting which measures are relevant to assess depression and potential causal factors under a particular context with a particular individual. The selection of measures would most likely be guided by the degree to which the assessor is influenced by the empirical support of particular theories of depression, such as cognitive (Beck, 1967), radical behavioral (Ferster, 1973), social skills (Lewinsohn, 1974), learned helplessness (Abramson, Seligman, & Teasdale, 1978), self-control (Rehm, 1977), or paradigmatic behavioral (Heiby & Staats, 1990). Therefore, one challenge for all behavioral assessors is to be familiar with the empirical status of potential causal variables for a disorder. While the *Guides* being developed by the AABT are a great step forward in helping to identify available behavioral assessment tools, the discipline has yet to develop a zeitgeist that encourages integrative, empirically supported theories of problem behaviors to assist in the selection of targeted causal and outcome variables.

FUTURE DIRECTIONS OF BEHAVIORAL ASSESSMENT

As indicated earlier, approaches to assessment typically not classified as behavioral are often referred to as nonbehavioral, and there is an overlap between these approaches to assessment. Nonbehavioral approaches are also referred to as traditional, even though, as pointed out earlier, assessment devices used by the predecessors of psychology and the early psychologists are what we now call behavioral. A more philosophical than scientific epistemology often characterizes what is generally referred to as traditional assessment. Some of these traditional methods evolved from theories that posit untestable hypotheses (e.g., psychodynamic). Other traditional methods evolved from trait theories that posit stability in behavior across situations and time. Many traditional methods of assessment (e.g., projective techniques, personality inventories, and intelligence tests) lead to highly inferential information. Interpretation of the results to address practical questions, such as what situational and behavioral deficiencies should be the targets of treatment, requires theoretical inferences that may or may not be empirically supported.

Traditional assessment also often occurs only for diagnostic, prognostic, and treatment outcome purposes. Interpretation of the results generally is based largely on instruments designed to identify whether behavioral disorders are present. The episodic nature of the assessment precludes feedback about the effect of intervention techniques on different targets of treatment (e.g., modification of self-control skills and attributional style to alleviate depression). When dealing with behaviors that have been shown to be somewhat stable (e.g., performance on intelligence tests), infrequent assessment can be justified in terms of cost-efficiency and incremental validity. When dealing with unstable dysfunctional behaviors with varying causal factors over time, however, infrequent and diagnosis-oriented assessment fails to provide feedback for correction of the targets of the intervention and the type of intervention. Strosahl and Robinson's Chapter 22 in this volume notes that managed care companies have come to require assessment throughout treatment in order to justify continuation of reimbursement for services. Repeatedly administering most traditional assessment techniques, such as an inkblot test, would not provide the type of information required by managed care companies (e.g., behavioral changes directly related to adaptive functioning).

Traditional assessment techniques not only provide little feedback on the ongoing effectiveness of an intervention, most are very time-consuming and expensive. Their cost-efficiency and utility in establishing quality assurance are being questioned by both scientist-practitioners and the health care industry (Hayes, Barlow, and Nelson-Gray, 1999). These authors argue that behavioral assessment techniques are more justifiable than most traditional ones in both applied research and program evaluation/treatment outcome settings. Their

analysis of the culture of accountability and guidelines for the use of psychological assessment reflect the values of behavioral assessment, including the accompanying ethical standards. They point out the need to justify the use of any expensive assessment device, be it traditional (e.g., intelligence test) or modern behavioral (e.g., naturalistic outpatient observations). If Hayes and colleagues are correct, the context for a broader acceptance of behavioral assessment may be evolving as Mash and Hunsley conclude in the final chapter of this volume.

The evolution of behavioral assessment, as mentioned earlier, is a rediscovery of the precise measurement emphasized when psychology was a subspecialty of physiology and physics (Boring, 1950). For example, responding to color in an inkblot at the beginning of the science of psychology was viewed as a measure of color perception. With the influence of theories focusing on hypothetical constructs in the early and mid-twentieth century, responding to color in an inkblot came to be viewed by some psychologists as a measure of emotional expression and mood disorders. Even if responding to the color in an inkblot were to correspond with emotional expression, one would still not be informed as to the nature of the expression, such as type (e.g., anger, anxiety, sadness, euphoria), duration (e.g., episodic or chronic), intensity (e.g., happy or manic), or situational specificity. One also would not be informed regarding the causal and maintenance factors for the emotional expression.

Within behavioral assessment, if one wants to measure an emotion, such as anxiety, the approach would be much more direct and situation specific—such as asking the person to rate the degree to which he or she feels tense, observing approach and avoidance behavior, and measuring heart rate. Variables associated with anxiety that are targets for intervention also would be assessed, such as assertiveness in confronting others or the basic instrumental skills needed to carry out a necessary task that is being avoided. In addition, because anxiety, like many behaviors, may be exhibited differently over time and across situations, the assessment would be conducted to consider these dynamic aspects. Causal, maintenance, and outcome indices would be collected throughout any intervention so adjustments can be made based on objective feedback and the outcome can be documented.

The emphasis of behavioral assessment on the collection of precise idiographic time-series data for unstable behavior is in keeping with current advancements in the natural and life sciences, namely chaos theory or nonlinear dynamic modeling (Haynes, 1995; Haynes, Blaine, & Meyer, 1995; Heiby, 1995a, 1995b). Nonlinear dynamical modeling of time-series data can identify a deterministic temporal structure of a behavior that is not captured by statistics based on the general linear model and that is difficult to ascertain by visual inspection of time-series graphics. Simulated data suggest chaotic affective disorders perseverate in such a way that they may respond best to interventions applied before clinical levels are exhibited (Huber, Braun, & Krieg, 1999, 2000, 2001). Some research has shown that the prediction of episodes of bipolar disorder can be improved by considering the nonlinear deterministic structure of the time-series assessment of the symptoms (e.g., Gottschalk, Bauer, & Whybrow, 1995). Only a behavioral assessment can provide the type of time-sensitive data required for chaos theory testing.

It is common practice in the natural and life sciences to collect precise time-series data, and these sciences have benefited from the application of nonlinear dynamical modeling (e.g., Glass and Mackey, 1988). In contrast, psychology has been slow to develop chaos theory testing (Barton, 1994; Heath, 2000), perhaps partly because behavioral assessment does not yet dominate the discipline. Advances in computer software have made it more likely that future behavioral assessment research and applications will consider both linear and nonlinear temporal characteristics of problem behaviors and maintenance factors.

Haynes and O'Brien (2000) provided some survey data regarding the use of behavioral versus projective assessment devices in treatment outcome studies published in the *Journal of Consulting and Clinical Psychology* between 1968 and 1996. They found projective techniques were not used in articles published since 1980. The most common device was narrow-band behavioral self-report questionnaires. Other common outcome measures were behavioral observation, self-monitoring, and psychophysiological indexes. This survey suggests that in research settings there is evidence that clinical scientists are less likely to use traditional assessment devices and are more likely to use behavioral ones.

Although it is unknown how often traditional and behavioral assessment devices are used in direct service settings, the findings of Piotrowski and Zalewski (1993)—indicating that clinicians are commonly trained in traditional methods—suggests that they most likely use those methods in practice. At least one survey of clinical psychologists indicated that the most frequently used tests are broadband personality questionnaires and projectives (Watkins, Campbell, Niebering, & Hallmark, 1995). One of the more popular psychological assessment graduate textbooks dedicates one chapter to behavioral assessment and eight chapters to traditional, non-behavioral assessment approaches, although the author does acknowledge that the future of psychological assessment will more likely reflect the tenets of behavioral assessment owing to the requirements of managed care to demonstrate the cost-effectiveness of psychological evaluations and relate the eval-

uations to treatment strategies and outcome (Groth-Marnat, 1997). Given that behavioral devices and approaches to assessment seem to have greater scientific support and veridicality with the health care industry and research granting agencies, it seems critical to offer continuing education opportunities to clinicians trained primarily in traditional approaches to assessment.

Retooling clinicians should facilitate their survival in practice settings (Hayes et al., 1999; Chapter 22). But this retooling must also consider the realities of applied work. Perhaps another reason behavioral assessment is not equivalent to psychological assessment is that the tenets and techniques can involve more effort on the part of the clinician. It is far easier to sit a client in a room with a projective test, broadband personality inventory, and intelligence test kept in a file drawer than it is to conduct a case conceptualization, select and obtain multiple methods of assessing a variety of causal and outcome variables, and apply the assessment on an ongoing basis. Development of a case conceptualization may be facilitated in the future when a scientific approach to psychological assessment is legitimately tied to a particular theoretical paradigm.

Discovering available behavioral assessment techniques also has not been easy for clinicians or researchers. Obtaining references to these techniques has been facilitated by Hersen and Bellack's (2002) *Dictionary of Behavioral Assessment Techniques.* This dictionary provides a brief summary of the purposes and psychometric status of 285 behavioral assessment techniques. The techniques include observational, psychophysiological, and self-report measures of situational factors, potential causal variables, and behavioral problems. Obtaining the actual measurement devices has been facilitated by two volumes of *Measures for Clinical Practice* by Fischer and Corcoran (1994a, 1994b). The first volume reproduces instruments designed for couples, families, and children, while the second volume reproduces instruments designed for adults. While Fischer and Corcoran do not explicitly espouse a behavioral approach to assessment, most of the instruments they elected to reproduce are designed to assess highly specific behavioral problems and maintenance variables and are conducive to ongoing assessment. As indicated earlier, obtaining behavioral assessment devices also has been facilitated by a series of practitioner's guides to empirically supported measures published under the auspices of the Association for the Advancement of Behavior Therapy (Antony, Orsillo, & Roemer, 2001; Nezu et al., 2000). Hopefully, this volume on *Behavioral Assessment* will provide further continuing education for clinicians who are not familiar with the assets of behavioral assessment, inspire their application, and promote their further development.

NOTE

1. A functional relation is any relation between events that can be described as an equation. It often takes the form of significant correlations, *F* statistics, conditional probabilities, chi-squares, or graphical displays of differential means and trends. Some functional relations also are presumed to be causal, in that changes in one variable will lead to changes in the other.

REFERENCES

Abramson, L., Seligman, M.E.P., & Teasdale, J.D. (1978). Learned helplessness in humans: Critique and reformulation. *Journal of Abnormal Psychology, 87,* 49–74.

American Medical Association (1989). *Current opinions: The council on ethical and judicial affairs of the American Medical Association.* Chicago: American Medical Association.

American Psychological Association (1990). Ethical principles of psychologists (amended June 2, 1989), *American Psychologist, 45,* 390–395.

Antony, M.M., Orsillo, S.M., & Roemer, L. (Eds.). (2001). *Practitioner's guide to empirically based measures of anxiety.* New York: Kluwer Academic/Plenum.

Baillie, A.J., & Rapee, R.M. (2002). Panic and agoraphobia. In M. Hersen & L.K. Porzelius (Eds.), *Diagnosis, conceptualization, and treatment planning for adults—A step-by-step guide* (pp. 113–132). Mahwah, NJ: Erlbaum.

Baker, S.L., Patterson, M.D., & Barlow, D.H. (2002). Panic disorder and agoraphobia. In M.M. Antony & D.H. Barlow (Eds.), *Handbook of assessment and treatment planning for psychological disorders* (pp. 67–112). New York: Guilford Press.

Bandura, A. (1982). The psychology of chance encounters and life paths. *American Psychologist, 37,* 747–755.

Bandura, M.M., & Goldman, C. (1995). Expanding the contextual analysis of clinical problems. *Cognitive and Behavioral Practice, 2,* 119–141.

Barton, S. (1994). Chaos, self-organization, and psychology. *American Psychologist, 49,* 5–14.

Beck, A.T. (1967). *Depression: Clinical, experimental, and theoretical aspects.* New York: Harper & Row.

Bellack, A.S., & Hersen, M. (Eds.). (1988). *Behavioral assessment: A practical handbook* (4th ed.). Needham Heights, MA: Allyn & Bacon.

Boring, E.G. (1950). *A history of experimental psychology.* New York: Appleton-Century-Crofts.

Boutin, M.E., & Nelson, J.V. (1998). The role of context in classical conditioning: Some implications for cognitive behavior therapy. In W. O'Donohue (Ed.), *Learning and behavior therapy* (pp. 59–84). Needham Heights, MA: Allyn & Bacon.

Cicchetti, D., & Rogosch, F.A. (1999). Conceptual and methodological issues in developmental psychopathology research. In P.C. Kendall, J.N. Butcher, & G.N. Holmbeck (Eds.), *Handbook of research methods in clinical psychology* (2nd ed., pp. 433–465). New York: Wiley.

Cole, C.L., & Bambara, L.M. (2000). Self-monitoring: Theory and practice. In E.S. Shapiro & T.R. Kratochwill (Eds.), *Behavioral assessment in schools: Theory, research, and clinical foundations* (2nd ed., pp. 202–232). New York: Guilford Press.

Collins, L.M., & Horn, J.L. (Eds.). (1991). *Best methods for the analysis of change. Recent advances, unanswered questions, future directions.* Washington, DC: American Psychological Association.

Cone, J.D. (1986). Idiographic, nomothetic, and related perspectives in behavioral assessment. In R.O. Nelson & S.C. Hayes (Eds.), *Conceptual foundations of behavioral assessment* (pp. 111–128). New York: Guilford Press.

Dawes, R.M. (1994). *House of cards: Psychology and psychotherapy built on myth.* New York: Free Press.

Ferster, C.B. (1973). A functional analysis of depression. *American Psychologist, 28,* 857–870.

Fischer, J., & Corcoran, K. (1994a). *Measures for clinical practice: Volume 1.* New York: Free Press.

Fischer, J., & Corcoran, K. (1994b). *Measures for clinical practice: Volume 2.* New York: Free Press.

Fisher, J., Hayes, S.C., & O'Donohue, W.O. (Eds.) (in press). *Empirically supported techniques of cognitive behavioral therapy: A step-by-step guide for clinicians.* New York: Wiley.

Floyd, F.J., Haynes, S.N., & Kelly, S. (1997). Marital assessment: A dynamic functional-analytic approach. In W.K. Halford & H.J. Markman (Eds.), *Clinical handbook of marriage and couples interventions* (pp. 349–377). New York: Wiley.

George, A. (1991). Medical assessment. In M. Hersen, A.E. Kazdin, & A.S. Bellack (Eds.), *The clinical psychology handbook* (2nd ed., pp. 491–505). Elmsford, NY: Pergamon Press.

Glass, L., & Mackey, M.C. (1988). *From clocks to chaos.* Princeton, NJ: Princeton University Press.

Goldberger, L., & Breznitz, S. (Eds.). (1993), *Handbook of stress: Theoretical and clinical aspects.* New York: Free Press.

Gottschalk, A., Bauer, M.S., & Whybrow, P.C. (1995). Evidence of chaotic mood variation in bipolar disorder. *Archives of General Psychiatry, 52,* 947–959.

Greene, R.W., & Ollendick, T.H. (2000). Behavioral assessment of children. In G. Goldstein & M. Hersen (Eds.), *Handbook of psychological assessment* (3rd ed., pp. 453–470). New York: Pergamon-Elsevier Science.

Groth-Marnat, G. (1997). *Handbook of psychological assessment.* New York: Wiley.

Hayes, S.C., Barlow, D.H., & Nelson-Gray, R.O. (1999). *The scientist practitioner: Research and accountability in the age of managed care* (2nd ed.). Needham Heights, MA: Allyn & Bacon.

Hayes, S.C., Follette, V.M., Dawes, R.M., & Grady, K.E. (Eds.). (1995). *Scientific standards of psychological practice: Issues and recommendations.* Reno, NV: Context Press.

Haynes, S.N. (1992). *Models of causality in psychopathology: Toward synthetic, dynamic and nonlinear models of causality in psychopathology.* Des Moines, IA: Allyn & Bacon.

Haynes, S.N. (1995). Introduction to the special section on chaos theory and psychological assessment. *Psychological Assessment, 7,* 3–4.

Haynes, S.N. (2000). Behavioral assessment of adults. In G. Goldstein & M. Hersen (Eds.), *Handbook of psychological assessment* (3rd ed., pp. 471–502). New York: Pergamon-Elsevier Science.

Haynes, S.N., Blaine, D., & Meyer, K. (1995). Dynamical models for psychological assessment: Phase space functions. *Psychological Assessment, 7,* 17–24.

Haynes, S.N., Nelson, K.G., Thacher, I., & Kaholokula, J.K. (2002). Outpatient behavioral assessment and treatment target selection. In M. Hersen & L.K. Porzelius (Eds.), *Diagnosis, conceptualization, and treatment planning for adults—A step-by-step guide* (pp. 35–70). Mahwah, NJ: Erlbaum.

Haynes, S.N., & O'Brien, W.H. (2000). *Principles and practice of behavioral assessment.* New York: Kluwer Academic/Plenum.

Heath, R.A. (2000). *Nonlinear dynamics: Techniques and applications in psychology.* Mahwah, NJ: Erlbaum.

Heiby, E.M. (1995a). Chaos theory, nonlinear dynamical models, and psychological assessment. *Psychological Assessment, 7,* 5–9.

Heiby, E.M. (1995b). Assessment of behavioral chaos with a focus on transitions in depression. *Psychological Assessment, 7,* 10–16.

Heiby, E.M., & Staats, A.W. (1990). Depression: Classification, explanation, and treatment. In G.H. Eifert & I.M. Evans (Eds.), *Unifying behavior therapy: Contributions of paradigmatic behaviorism.* New York: Springer.

Hersen, M., & Bellack, A.S. (2002) *Dictionary of behavioral assessment techniques.* Clinton Corners, NY: Percheron Press.

Hersen, M., & Porzelius, L.K. (Eds.). (2002). *Diagnosis, conceptualization, and treatment planning for adults: A step-by-step guide.* Mahwah, NJ: Erlbaum.

Holtzworth-Munroe, A., Smutzler, N., Bates, L., & Sandin, E. (1997). Husband violence: Basic facts and clinical implications. In W.K. Halford & H.J. Markman (Eds.), *Clinical handbook of marriage and couples interventions* (pp. 129–156). New York: Wiley.

Huber, M.T., Braun, H.A., & Krieg, J.C. (1999). Consequences of deterministic and random dynamics for the course of affective disorders. *Biological Psychiatry, 46,* 256–262.

Huber, M.T., Braun, H.A., & Krieg, J.C. (2000). Effects of noise on different disease states of recurrent affective disorders. *Biological Psychiatry, 47,* 634–643.

Huber, M.T., Braun, H.A., & Krieg, J.C. (2001). On the impact of episodic sensitization of the course of recurrent depression. *Journal of Psychiatric Research, 35,* 49–57.

Lewinsohn, P.M. (1974). A behavioral approach to depression. In R. Friedman & M. Katz (Eds.), *The psychology of depression: Contemporary theory and research.* New York: Wiley.

Malec, J.F., & Lemsky, C. (1995). Behavioral assessment in medical rehabilitation: Traditional and consensual approaches. In L.A. Cushman & M.J. Scherer (Eds.), *Medical rehabilitation* (pp. 199–236). Washington, DC: American Psychological Association.

Mash, E.J., & Terdal, L.G. (Eds.). (1997). *Assessment of childhood disorders* (3rd ed., pp. 130–193). New York: Guilford Press.

McFall, R.M. (1991). Manifesto for a science of clinical psychology. *Clinical Psychologist, 44,* 75–88.

McFall, R.M. (2002). Training for prescriptions v. prescriptions for training: Where are we now? Where should we be? How did we get there? *Journal of Clinical Psychology, 58,* 659–676.

Morris, E.K. (1988). Contextualism: The world view of behavior analysis. *Journal of Experimental Child Psychology, 46,* 289–323.

Nelson-Gray, R.O. (1996). Treatment outcome measures: Nomothetic or idiographic? *Clinical Psychology, Science and Practice, 3,*164–167.

Nezu, A.M., Ronan, G.F., Meadows, E.A., & McClure, K.S. (2000). *Practitioner's guide to empirically based measures of depression.* New York: Kluwer Academic/Plenum.

O'Brien, W.H., & Haynes, S.N. (1993). Behavioral assessment in the psychiatric setting. In A.S. Bellack & M. Hersen (Eds.). *Handbook of behavior therapy in the psychiatric setting* (pp. 39–71). New York: Plenum Press.

Pervin, L.A. (1984). Idiographic approaches to personality. In N.S. Endler & J.M. Hunt (Eds.), *Personality and the behavior disorders* (pp. 261–282). New York: Wiley.

Pierce, W.D., & Epling, W.F. (1999). *Behavior analysis and learning* (2nd ed.). Upper Saddle River, NJ: Prentice-Hall.

Piotrowski, C., & Zalewski, C. (1993). Training in psychodiagnostic testing in APA-approved PsyD and PhD clinical psychology programs. *Journal of Personality Assessment, 61,* 394–405.

Plaud, J.J., & Fifert, G.H. (Eds.) (1998). *From behavior theory to behavior therapy.* Boston: Allyn & Bacon.

Rehm, L.P. (1977). A self-control model of depression. *Behavior Therapy, 8,* 787–804.

Royse, D., & Thyer, B.A. (1996). *Program evaluation: An introduction* (2nd ed.). Chicago: Nelson-Hall.

Rybarczyk, B., & Lopez, M. (1999). Focus chapter: Research methods with older adults. In P.C. Kendall, J.N. Butcher, & G.N. Holmbeck (Eds.), *Handbook of research methods in clinical psychology* (2nd ed., pp. 662–680). New York: Wiley.

Shapiro, E.S., & Kratochwill, T.R. (Eds.). (2000). *Behavioral assessment in schools: Theory, research, and clinical foundations* (2nd ed.). New York: Guilford Press.

Simeonsson, R.J., & Rosenthal, S.L. (Eds.) (2001). *Psychological and developmental assessment—Children with disabilities and chronic conditions.* New York: Guilford Press.

Singer, L.T., & Zeskind, P.S. (Eds.) (2001). *Biobehavioral assessment of the infant.* New York: Guilford Press.

Sobell, L.C., & Sobell, M.B. (1994). *Timeline followback.* Toronto, Ontario, Canada: Addiction Research Foundation (also instructional video at same place).

Staats, A.W. (1968). Social behaviorism and human motivation: Principles of the attitude-reinforcer-discriminative system. In A.R. Gilgen (Ed.), *Contemporary scientific psychology* (pp. 183–239). New York: Plenum Press.

Staats, A.W. (1983). *Psychology's crisis of disunity: Philosophy and methods for a unified science.* New York: Academic Press.

Sturgis, E.T., & Gramling, S.E. (1998). Psychophysiological assessment. In A.S. Bellack & M. Hersen (Eds.), *Behavioral assessment—A practical handbook* (4th ed.), pp. 126–157. Boston: Allyn & Bacon.

Stone, A.A., Turkkan, J.S., Bachrach, C.A., Jobe, J.B., Kurtzman, H.S., & Cain, V.S. (Eds.) (2000). *The science of self-report—Implications for research and practice.* Mahwah, NJ: Erlbaum.

Tait, R.C. (1999). Evaluation of treatment effectiveness in patients with intractable pain: Measures and methods. In R.J. Gatchel & D.C. Turk (Eds.), *Psychosocial factors in pain: Critical perspectives* (pp. 457–480). New York: Guilford Press.

Thacher, I., & Haynes, S.N. (2001). A multivariate time series regression study of pain, depression symptoms, and social interaction in rheumatoid arthritis. *International Journal of Clinical and Health Psychology, 1,* 159–180.

Tolan, P.H. (1999). Focus chapter: Research methods in community-based treatment and prevention. In P.C. Kendall, J.N. Butcher, & G.N. Holmbeck (Eds.), *Handbook of research methods in clinical psychology* (2nd ed., pp. 403–418). New York: Wiley.

Tomarken, A.J. (1999). Focus chapter: Methodological issues in psychophysiological research. In P.C. Kendall, J.N. Butcher, & G.N. Holmbeck (Eds.), *Handbook of research methods in clinical psychology* (2nd ed., pp. 251–275). New York: Wiley.

Turner, R.M. (1994). Borderline, narcissistic, and histrionic personality disorders. In M. Hersen & R.T. Ammerman (Eds), *Handbook of prescriptive treatments for adults* (pp. 393–420). New York: Plenum.

Watkins, C.E., Campbell, V.L., Niebering, R., & Hallmark, R. (1995). Contemporary practice of psychological assessment by clinical psychologists. *Professional Psychology: Research and Practice, 26,* 54–60.

CHAPTER 2

Behavioral Assessment: History of Underlying Concepts and Methods

THOMAS H. OLLENDICK, HEATHER K. ALVAREZ, AND ROSS W. GREENE

INTRODUCTION

Developments in the field of psychology have occurred largely as a function of philosophical leanings and social ideologies present at given points in time, combined with the slow but steady accumulation of scientific and practical knowledge throughout history. As will be outlined in this chapter, the growth of behavioral assessment also follows this overall pattern of development. To appreciate the true developmental course and history of behavioral assessment, including its underlying concepts and methods, one must first understand the changing nature of society, innovations within scientific psychology, and developments in clinical practice.

This chapter will briefly highlight historical developments that have provided a foundation for current trends and ideas related to behavioral assessment. These developments have not only led to notable gains in the science and practice of behavioral assessment *and* behavior therapy, but also have influenced changes in the methods and goals of psychology more generally.

Acknowledgment: The authors would like to acknowledge the assistance of Jennifer C. Goring in the preparation of this chapter.

Before proceeding further in our discourse, it should be noted that the history of behavioral assessment is neither linear nor straightforward. This is largely due to the parallel yet somewhat independent scientific and conceptual contributions to the field of behaviorism from which behavioral assessment practices evolved. In addition, dissatisfaction with the effectiveness of clinical practice, as well as the limited professional status of psychologists within clinical practice, led to the search for viable alternatives. Thus, behavioral assessment can be considered a product of both scientific and clinical developments whose paths joined during the middle of the twentieth century and remain enjoined into the twenty-first century.

HISTORICAL FOUNDATIONS

Early Influences

Although the history of behavioral assessment is often associated with recent influences and discoveries, the use of assessment procedures to understand and predict behavior can be traced to far earlier times. As noted by both Sattler (1988) and Routh (1998), Chinese emperors who set up civil service programs around 2200 B.C. were among the first to devise and use assessment procedures. However, the understanding of psychological problems was constrained by the religious and magical thinking characteristic of the time (Brems, Thevenin, & Routh, 1991). The conception of "mental illness" through a religious lens remained dominant well into the Renaissance. Abnormal behavior was largely considered to be due to supernatural forces and was treated with spiritual methods (e.g., purification rites, magical rituals). Thus, assessment and treatment of persons with psychological problems were considered within the domain of priests, who were assumed to have powers to contact and influence spirits (Kazdin, 1978).

Fortunately, important philosophical influences eventually led to a shift in the perception of mental illness and human behavior. Advances in medical knowledge led to a greater understanding of the human condition and, in turn, served to redirect the focus of assessment and treatment of abnormal behavior. For instance, Hippocrates and others suggested that mental illness, like physical illness, stemmed from biological causes (Brems et al., 1991; Kazdin, 1978; Walker & Shelton, 1985). The communication of these ideas through the great philosophers of the Classical Era led to advancements in both theory and practice. Further, these theoretical viewpoints brought alternative methods of treatment that focused more upon physiological or bodily changes than spiritual ones and brought clinical practice into the realm of medical practitioners rather than priests and shamans.

More sophisticated conceptualizations of human behavior and greater attention to both normal and abnormal human processes continued during the Renaissance. Assessment methodologies likewise evolved from religious speculation to an emphasis on rational exploration and explanations of behavior. The implementation of formal observation and evaluation techniques over time led to greater and more precise description of clinical symptoms and syndromes (Brems et al., 1991).

Nineteenth Century: Psychology as a Budding Science

During the last half of the nineteenth century, it was common to consider psychology as the "science of the mind." Despite use of the term *science,* psychology was studied largely through introspective methods and, as a result, remained largely within the domain of philosophical thought and inquiry. However, a number of critical experimental developments helped move the field from the realm of art into the age of science (Baum, 1994). Specifically, researchers and theoreticians such as William James and Wilhelm Wundt became deeply committed to the advancement of objectivity in psychology and began to apply the objective methods of other sciences to the study of human behavior.

In addition to advances in the United States and Germany, the work of three prominent Russian researchers was instrumental in the advancement of objectivism. First, Pavlov applied scientific methodology and learning theory to the study of the central nervous system and conditioned reflexes through his laboratory work with dogs as experimental subjects. Pavlov was also interested in how his findings pertained to human learning, hypothesizing that humans, like his animal subjects, have a set of innate reactions to the environment as well as learning processes that allow for the acquisition of more complex behavior. Sechenov also introduced objective experimentation in his study of the physiological bases of psychological problems. According to Sechenov, all behavior, whether voluntary or involuntary, reflected environmental stimulation. Finally, Bechterev, like his colleagues, subscribed to objective methods of study. He went further to suggest that these ideas should be viewed as a discipline separate from psychology. According to Bechterev,

> The new science, which we call reflexology, has for its aim the study of personality by means of objective observation and experiment, and the registration of all its external manifestations and their external causes, present or past, which arise from the social environment and even from the framework of inherited character. In other words, the aim of reflexology is the strictly objective study, in their entirety, of the correlations of the human being with the environment through the mediation of man's facial features, his gestures, the content and form of his speech, his behaviour, and, in general, everything by which he manifests himself in the environment (Bechterev, 1933, p. 81).

While he envisioned a separate field of study to specifically consider behavior-environment relationships, others were more optimistic about changes that could be made in psychology to incorporate this line of inquiry (Kazdin, 1978). Furthermore, although later applications of behavioral theory recognized a more complex etiology and course of human behavior, the importance of these early developments cannot be underestimated.

Movement to Clinical Psychology

As the experimental domain of psychology accentuated the establishment of objective scientific methodologies and sound theoretical advancements, the clinical or applied side of the field attempted to make similar strides in the description, explanation, and prediction of human behavior. The preponderance of clinical work during this time period revolved around investigation of the individual as the sole source of psychopathology. This work took the form of biological disease models, following in the earlier medical tradition, as well as intrapsychic models, where underlying personality structures were deemed to be of greatest importance (Routh, 1998).

Disease Models

Inasmuch as the study of human behavior remained largely in the domain of medical practitioners, definitions and models for understanding behavior remained within the framework of medicine. Given earlier success in formulating diagnosis and treatment of physical illnesses within a disease model, it seemed probable that similar benefits would derive from this conceptualization of mental illness. Specifically, using the disease model, physicians tried to devise a method to identify underlying disorders, expressed through specific patterns of symptoms (i.e., behaviors) that could be treated. Although specific organic bases for some abnormal behaviors were indeed found, this model was also extended to illnesses with no known organic pathology. Attempts to categorize and distinguish patterns of abnormal behavior led to the development of diagnostic systems, including that of Kraepelin in 1883, and other explanatory structures focusing on the individual as the sole source of pathology. The disease model of abnormal behavior remained dominant through the early twentieth century (and, in some circles, even into the present). Its impact led to further investigations of the individual as the source of psychopathology and supported the model's application to assessment and treatment practices.

Their impact notwithstanding, the classification systems applied in the medical model of psychopathology were severely criticized. For instance, researchers and clinicians alike found traditional classification systems to be of little prognostic value (Redd, Porterfield, & Andersen, 1979). Additionally, diagnostic assessment practices found little consensus among clinicians, such that patients often were provided different and sometimes multiple diagnoses. Finally, even with one or more diagnoses, diagnostic assessment was often not connected with treatment. Specifically, while early investigators found certain biochemical explanations for such problem behaviors as psychosis, these results did not lead to a consistent body of treatment strategies (Nay, 1976).

Personality Theory

Although the twentieth century was a time of change and progress in the understanding of human behavior, this period also was fraught with continued repressive attitudes and Victorian withholding of knowledge about human functioning, including human sexuality (Brems et al., 1991). Psychoanalysis, as formulated by Freud, marked the beginning of a clini-

cal method in psychology that combined the ideology of the early twentieth century with the theoretical developments of early philosophers, psychologists, and scientists. Psychoanalytic theory largely followed the notions of psychic determinism, such that the contents of the unconscious served as the underlying force driving the individual's actions. Freud was less interested in the process and study of behavior than he was in the motives associated with it.

The ramifications of this theory on the goals and methodology of clinical assessment have been profound. According to Freud, the appropriate way to predict behavior was through an assessment of the inferred characteristics underlying that behavior. Given the perspective that behavior depended on the personality characteristics of the individual, it was assumed that consistencies in behavior would exist independent of situational variances (Goldfried & Kent, 1972). Thus, behavior was important only to the degree to which it informed the hypothesized personality constructs and the theory underlying them (Cone, 1977).

Although this perspective became highly popular within psychological practice, it also led to much controversy due to its practical and theoretical limitations. First, as recognized by Goldfried and Kent (1972), according to psychoanalytic theory, it could be assumed that consistencies in behavior exist independent of situational variances. However, such classic work as Hartshorne and May's (1928) study of honesty and studies of aggressive and cooperative behavior reviewed by Mischel (1968) failed to support this assertion. Second, as noted by Hersen (1976), indirect assessment practices (i.e., projective techniques) are neither impartial nor objective. Hersen asserted that an individual's responses to ambiguous stimuli are highly dependent on overt and covert manipulations within the assessment environment. Third, such methods of assessment place little emphasis on the selection of appropriate therapeutic procedures, such that minimal interplay exists between assessment and treatment (Hersen, 1976; Hersen & Bellack, 1977; Ollendick & Hersen, 1984).

Psychology as a Science of Behavior

Early Behaviorism

Continued dissatisfaction with the methods of psychological study, combined with the influences of early research in learning theory, led to the introduction of a new domain of psychology called behaviorism (Calhoun & Turner, 1981). Although Watson attempted to disseminate his ideas years earlier, it was not until the 1913 publication of *Psychology as the Behaviorist Views It* that behaviorism gained popularity. A complete discussion of this theory and its implications is beyond the scope of this chapter, but those factors leading to the practical application of Watson's ideas will be highlighted. In line with the current growth of objectivism in research, Watson advocated for the empirical study of observable behavior and rejected subjective modes of inquiry that dominated the field of clinical practice. According to Watson, psychology should no longer consider consciousness as its domain of study. Rather, a focus on overt behavior and, specifically, the relations between environmental stimuli and the responses they evoke was recommended. Thus, Watson argued, the study of behavior would best be accomplished by the methods established by early animal researchers. In particular, Watson suggested the use of conditioned reflexes much like the work of Pavlov and Bechterev. Further, within the behavioral framework, personality was viewed primarily as an abstraction that one would make after observing a person behaving across a comprehensive sampling of situations (Cone & Hawkins, 1977). This conception of personality had important implications for the assessment and treatment of human behavior.

Empirical Tests of Behaviorism: Clinical Research

Initial examination of the tenets of behaviorism primarily focused on clinical research, specifically behavior modification and the treatment of diverse forms of psychopathology. The first published accounts of the use of behavioral strategies included the 1924 work of Mary Cover Jones, who under the supervision of Watson successfully treated a 3-year-old boy with severe anxiety for furry objects (Ollendick & Cerny, 1981; Redd et al., 1979). Later, Mowrer and Mowrer (1938) established a treatment for enuresis with a specially designed pad that buzzed when it came into contact with moisture. Additional research contributions included the evaluation of conditioning principles to treat both alcohol and morphine addiction by Kantorovich in 1929 and Rubenstein in 1931, respectively (Kazdin, 1978).

Increased attention to advancing clinical research in the academic domain resulted in alternative theoretical explanations to describe and predict abnormal behavior. During this time, other researchers independently initiated additional examination of these issues, serving as a foundation for the clinical application of behaviorism. First, Wolpe, Lazarus, and colleagues, in their search for clinical techniques that could be empirically validated, introduced conditioning principles for the treatment of phobias and other anxiety disorders (Hersen, 1976).

Eysenck and others furthered this scientific movement by voicing criticisms of projective techniques and traditional psychoanalysis. Eysenck spearheaded critical investigations of the validity and reliability of psychoanalytic methodology

and suggested, in its place, empirically based analysis and modification of behavior. Additionally, a 1943 report by Sears, who evaluated 166 articles that attempted to empirically evaluate some of Freud's propositions, failed to find support for psychodynamic theory. Soon, a close relationship between clinical research and practice developed (Hersen, 1976), such that assessment and treatment techniques were largely scientifically based and more closely entwined.

Clinical Applications of Behaviorism

Behavioral Assessment Is Born

By the late 1950s, clinical psychologists had become increasingly dissatisfied with the limited effectiveness of traditional assessment and diagnostic approaches. Some began to challenge their restricted role as assessment agents. While this development was taking place among practitioners, another advancement in the field was also occurring: the advent of behavior therapy.

According to Cone and Hawkins (1977), behavioral assessment was an obvious by-product of the emergence of behavior therapy. In particular, behavioral assessment techniques developed in the 1960s from a need to determine treatment effectiveness and appropriateness within this new clinical discipline (Nelson, 1983; Nelson & Hayes, 1976). Although still quite popular among many clinicians, traditional assessment techniques such as projective tests and personality inventories did not adequately serve those who were adopting the behavioral ideology. Behavioral assessment also represented a backlash against the stigmas associated with diagnostic labels and the traditional view that mental illness was a function of "personality" (Redd et al., 1979).

Decade of Development

The growth of behaviorism in the late 1960s and early 1970s is reflected in many advances that occurred during these decades. The Association for the Advancement of Behavior Therapy was established in 1966, followed by the European Association of Behavior Therapy in 1971. Also, with the success of behavioral therapeutic techniques came a proliferation of assessments to measure diverse behaviors of both children and adults. In 1978, the first journal devoted exclusively to behavioral assessment—*Behavioral Assessment*—was founded and its first issue was published under the editorship of Rosemery Nelson in 1979. At that time, Nelson and Hayes (1976) indicated that behavioral assessment could be "distinguished from other types of assessment in its emphasis on both meaningful response units and their controlling variables. Behavior is defined functionally, in relation to its present controlling variables (both environmental and organismic) and to its responsiveness to intervention strategies." They went on to indicate that behavioral assessment "is seen to produce situation-specific samples of behavior in one or more response categories: motor, verbal-cognitive, and physiological-emotional" and that behavioral assessment "excludes trait assumptions and sign-oriented approaches to measurement." Although Nelson and Hayes did not specify the *methods* of assessment, it was clear that traditional approaches to assessment that were in vogue at the time (e.g., projective instruments, personality tests) were to be abandoned.

In its earliest stages, behavioral assessment relied almost exclusively on the identification and specification of discrete and highly observable target behaviors (cf. Ullmann & Krasner, 1965). As such, assessment was limited to gathering information solely from the motoric (i.e., overt behavioral) response modality. This early assessment approach followed logically from theoretical assumptions of the operant school of thought. Early on, behaviorally oriented clinicians posited that the only appropriate behavioral domain for empirical study was that which was directly observable (Skinner, 1953). Contending that objective demonstration of behavior change following intervention was of utmost importance, behaviorists relied upon data that could be measured objectively and reliably. Subjectivity and the inferential process associated with subjectivity were eschewed. Hence, the frequency, intensity, and duration (i.e., "hard core" measures) of problematic behaviors were pursued. Although the existence of cognitions and affective states was not denied, they were simply not deemed appropriate subject matter for experimental analysis.

As behavioral treatment approaches were broadened to include cognitive and self-control techniques in the 1970s (c.g., Bandura, 1977; Kanfer & Phillips, 1970; Meichenbaum, 1977), it became apparent that assessment strategies would have to expand their reach into the cognitive and affective domains as well. Furthermore, even though operant techniques were shown to be efficacious in producing behavior change under controlled conditions, the clinical significance and social validity of these changes were less evident. This state of affairs prompted behaviorists to expand their assessment net and to obtain information from a variety of sources (including self- and other-report measures), even though these sources provided only "indirect" measures of behavior (Cone, 1978). Hence, other-report and self-report measures became important sources of information.

The scope of behavioral assessment has also been expanded to include the impact of large-scale social systems (e.g., work settings, schools, neighborhoods) on behavior

(see, for example, Patterson, 1976, and Wahler, 1976). Although inclusion of these additional factors serves to complicate the assessment process, they are an indispensable part of contemporary behavioral assessment (Ollendick & Greene, 1997). The ideologies and expectations of seemingly distal social systems often have immediate and profound effects on individual behavior (see Winett, Riley, King, & Altman, 1989, for discussion of these issues).

In sum, behavioral assessment has progressed from sole reliance on measurement of target behaviors to a broader approach that takes into account cognitive and affective processes of the individual that serve to mediate behavior change and the social contexts (i.e., families, schools, work settings, communities) in which the problematic behaviors occur. The assessment techniques that have accompanied this broader approach include indirect behavioral measures such as behavioral interviews and self- and other-report instruments. These measures are utilized in addition to direct behavioral observations that remain the cornerstone of behavioral assessment (Cone, 1992; Mash & Terdal, 1981, 1989; Ollendick & Hersen, 1984, 1993).

THEORETICAL UNDERPINNINGS

As noted above, the behavioral approach flourished, at least in part, due to dissatisfaction with the psychodynamic approach. This dissatisfaction can be found in early discussions of behavioral assessment that compared and contrasted this approach with traditional assessment approaches (e.g., Bornstein, Bornstein, & Dawson, 1984; Cone & Hawkins, 1977; Goldfried & Kent, 1972; Hayes, Nelson, & Jarrett, 1986; Haynes, 1978; Hersen & Bellack, 1976; Mash & Terdal, 1981, 1989; Mischel, 1968; Ollendick & Hersen, 1984). Although such comparisons often resulted in oversimplification of both approaches, they served to elucidate the theoretical underpinnings of the behavioral approach and its unique contributions. In this section, we will contrast the theoretical assumptions that guide behavioral assessment and traditional assessment and discuss the practical implications of these assumptions for behavioral assessment.

Concept of Personality and Behavior

The most fundamental difference between traditional and behavioral assessment lies in the conception of "personality" and behavior (we place the construct *personality* in quotation marks because early behaviorists would have objected to use of this term, given its subjectivity and imprecise meaning). In the traditional assessment approach, personality is viewed as a reflection of underlying and enduring traits, and behavior is assumed to be a function of these internal personality characteristics (*personolgism*). Aggressive behavior, for example, is assumed to reside *in* the person and to be caused by an underlying dynamic process attributed perhaps to hostility or anger and resulting from deep-seated intrapsychic conflict. In contrast, behavioral approaches avoid references to underlying personality constructs, focusing instead on what the person does under specific conditions. From the behavioral perspective, "personality" refers to situational patterns rather than causes of behavior (Staats, 1975, 1986). Indeed, behavior is viewed as a result of current environmental factors (*situationalism*) and of these current environmental factors interacting with organismic variables (*interactionism*). Thus, the role of the current environment is stressed more in behavioral assessment than it is in traditional assessment. The focus of assessment is on what the person does in that situation rather than on what he or she *has* or *is* (Mischel, 1968). As a result, behavioral assessment requires a lower level of inference than does traditional assessment.

It is important not to oversimplify the behavioral view of the causes of behavior, however. It often has been erroneously asserted that the behavioral approach focuses on external determinants of behavior at the exclusion of organismic states or internal cognitions and affects. To be sure, behavioral views of psychological disorders have emphasized the significant role of environmental factors in the manifestation and maintenance of behavior. However, organismic variables that influence behavior are not ignored or discounted, as indicated early on by Nelson and Hayes (1976) and reaffirmed by others in recent years (Haynes, 1990; Ollendick & Greene, 1990; Ollendick & Hersen, 1993). Among the organismic variables—referred to as cognitive social learning person variables (CSLPVs) by Mischel (1973)—found to be important are variables such as competencies (skills that the individual possesses such as social skills, problem-solving skills), encoding strategies (the manner in which a person perceives or encodes information about his or her environment), expectancies (expectancies about performance, including self-efficacy and outcome expectancies), subjective values (a person's likes or dislikes, preferences or aversions), and self-regulatory systems and plans (the individual's capacity for and manner of self-imposing goals and standards and self-administering consequences for his or her behavior). A thorough behavioral assessment should attempt to identify controlling variables, whether environmental or organismic in nature. Recently, we have reviewed a wide array of self-report instruments tapping CSLPVs and related cognitive and affective modalities for use in behavioral assessment (Greene & Ollendick, 2000). As Mash and Terdal (1981) point out, "the

relative importance of organismic and environmental variables and their interaction . . . should follow from a careful analysis of the problem" (p. 23).

The traditional conception of personality as made up of stable and enduring traits implies that behavior will be relatively persistent over time and consistent across situations. The behavioral emphasis on situational specificity, by contrast, posits that, because behavior is in large part a function of situational determinants and CSPLVs that are engaged under certain specified conditions, a person's behavior will change as these situational factors are altered or the person variables are enacted. Similarly, consistency of behavior across the temporal dimension is not necessarily expected. The expanded scope of behavioral assessment—focusing on the combination of person and situational variables that contribute to variations in an individual's behavior—are consistent with current models of development emphasizing the transactional/reciprocal processes that contribute to an individual's outcome. Such models (see Belsky, 1980; Cicchetti & Lynch, 1993, 1995; Sameroff, 1975) posit that an individual's outcome is a function of the degree of "fit" or "compatibility" between characteristics of the person and characteristics of his or her environment. A high level of person-environment compatibility is thought to produce optimal outcomes, whereas a high level of incompatibility is thought to produce less optimal outcomes.

Hence, as noted above, an aggressive act such as a child hitting another child might be seen from the traditional viewpoint as a reflection of underlying hostility that, in turn, might be related to early life experiences or intrapsychic conflict. Little or no attention would be given to specific situational factors or the environmental context in which the aggressive acts occur. From the behavioral perspective, an attempt would be made to identify those variables that elicit and maintain the aggressive act in that particular situation (i.e., in what situations does incompatibility between characteristics of a child and his or her environment contribute to the manifestation of aggressive behavior in the child?). That the child may aggress in a variety of situations is explained in terms of his or her learning history and not in terms of an underlying personality trait such as hostility. For example, aggressive acts may have been reinforced previously, thereby making it more likely that the child would respond to similar situational factors with aggression. However, it is also possible that situational factors evoke in the child a state of arousal that makes it difficult to access and perform previously learned adaptive responses (Greene & Doyle, 1999). From this analysis, it is clear that actual behavior is of primary importance to behaviorists, because it represents a sample of the individual's behavioral repertoire (or the lack thereof) in a specific situation. From the traditional viewpoint, in contrast, the behavior assumes importance only insofar as it is a sign of some underlying trait.

These differing assumptions have direct implications for the assessment process. In behavioral assessment, the emphasis on situational specificity necessitates an approach that samples behavior across time, interaction partners, and settings. Hence, assessment of the individual's behavior at home, at work, or in school is of equal importance. Furthermore, the information obtained from these various settings likely would not, and in fact need not, be consistent. The child who is aggressive, for example, may behave aggressively in school and on the playground with peers but not at home with siblings or parents. This lack of consistency in behavior would be problematic for the traditional approach, but not for the behavioral approach. From a behavioral perspective, situational inconsistency provides crucial information about the interplay between environmental and organismic factors that give rise to adaptive and maladaptive behavior.

At one point, it was relatively easy to differentiate behavioral from traditional assessment on the basis of the methods employed. Direct behavioral observation was the defining characteristic and often the sole assessment technique of the behavioral approach, whereas clinical diagnostic interviews, self-report measures, and possibly projective techniques characterized traditional assessment. However, as behavioral assessment broadened to include a wider repertoire of assessment methods, it has become more difficult to differentiate behavioral and traditional assessments simply on the basis of methodology. It is not uncommon for behaviorists to utilize information from clinical interviews and self-report instruments and to pursue perceptions and expectancies of significant others in the person's environment. Thus, there is considerable overlap in actual assessment practices, although projective techniques would rarely be found in the armamentarium of the behavioral assessor. The difference between traditional and behavioral assessment is then not so much in the methods employed, but rather in the approach to assessment and the manner in which data from assessment sources are subsequently used (Cone, 1992; Nelson-Gray, Gaynor, & Korotitsch, 1997; Ollendick & Greene, 1997). Traditional approaches interpret assessment data as signs of underlying personality functioning. These data are used to diagnose and classify the person and to make prognostic statements. From the behavioral perspective, assessment data are used to identify target behaviors and their controlling conditions (again, be they overt or covert). Information obtained from assessment serves as a sample of the individual's behavior under specific circumstances. This information guides the selection of appropriate treatment procedures. Because behavioral assessment is ongoing, such information serves as an index by which to continually evaluate the effects of treatment and to make appropriate revisions in treatment.

Nomothetic and Idiographic Distinction

In addition to these differences, Cone (1986) has highlighted the nomothetic and idiographic distinction between traditional and behavioral assessment. Stated briefly, the nomothetic approach is concerned with the discovery of general laws as they are applied to large numbers of individuals. Usually, these laws provide heuristic guidelines as to how certain variables are related to one another. Such an approach can be said to be variable-centered because it deals with particular characteristics (traits) such as intelligence, achievement, assertion, aggression, and so on. In contrast, the idiographic approach is concerned more with the uniqueness of a given person and is said to be person-centered rather than variable-centered. Unlike the nomothetic approach, the idiographic perspective emphasizes the discovery of relationships among variables that are uniquely patterned in each individual. The idiographic approach is most akin to the behavioral perspective, whereas the nomothetic approach is closely related to the traditional approach. As Mischel (1968) observed, "Behavioral assessment involves an exploration of the unique or idiosyncratic aspects of the single case, perhaps to a greater extent than any other approach" (p. 190). Cone (1986) illustrates how the idiographic/nomothetic distinction relates to the general activities of behavioral assessors by exploring five basic questions: What is the purpose of assessment? What is its specific subject matter? What general scientific approach guides this effort? How are differences accounted for? And, to what extent are currently operative environmental variables considered? Although further discussion of these important issues is beyond the scope of the present chapter, Cone's schema helps us recognize the pluralistic nature of behavioral assessment and calls our attention to meaningful differences in the diverse practices contained therein. As Cone (1986) concludes, "There is not one behavioral assessment, there are many" (p. 126).

In sum, traditional and behavioral assessment approaches operate under different assumptions regarding the individual and his or her behavior. These assumptions, in turn, have implications for the assessment process. Of paramount importance for behavioral assessment is the need to tailor the assessment approach to the specific difficulties of the individual in order to identify the problem accurately, specify treatment, and evaluate treatment outcome. Such tailoring requires ongoing assessment from a number of sources under appropriately diverse stimulus situations.

DESCRIPTION OF ASSESSMENT METHODS AND PROCEDURES

Multimethod behavioral assessment entails the use of a wide variety of specific procedures. As behavioral approaches evolved from sole reliance on operant procedures to those involving cognitive and self-control procedures, the methods of assessment changed accordingly. As noted earlier, the identification of discrete target behaviors has been expanded to include assessment of cognitions and affect as well as large-scale social systems that influence the individual (e.g., families, communities, work settings, schools).

Information regarding these additional areas can be obtained most efficiently through behavioral interviews, self-reports, and other reports. Cone (1978) describes these assessment methods as indirect ones; that is, although they may be used to measure behaviors of clinical relevance, they are obtained at a time and place different from when and where the behaviors occur. In both behavioral interviews and self-report questionnaires, a verbal representation of the behaviors of interest is obtained. Other reports or ratings by others such as parents, teachers, partners, and coworkers also are included in the indirect category because they too involve retrospective descriptions of behavior.

As noted by Cone (1978), ratings such as these should not be confused with direct observation methods, which assess behaviors of interest at the time and place of their occurrence. Of course, information regarding cognition and affect, as well as the situations or settings in which they occur, also can be obtained through direct behavioral observations, either by trained observers or via self-monitoring. In the sections that follow, both indirect and direct methods are reviewed briefly. More extended discussions are included in subsequent chapters.

Behavioral Interviews

The first method of indirect assessment to be considered is the behavioral interview. Of the many procedures employed by behavioral clinicians, the interview is the most widely used (Swann & MacDonald, 1978), and it is generally considered an indispensable part of assessment (Gross, 1984; Linehan, 1977). Behavioral interviews are frequently structured to obtain information about the target behaviors and their controlling variables and to begin the formulation of specific treatment plans. Although the primary purpose of the behavioral interview is to obtain information, one cannot underestimate the importance of traditional "helping" skills—including reflections, clarifications, and summary statements—that help put the individual at ease and greatly

facilitate collection of relevant information (Ollendick & Cerny, 1981). As with traditional therapies, it is important to establish rapport with the person or the child and his or her family and to begin to develop a therapeutic relationship and alliance (i.e., agreement on the goals and procedures of therapy) in this first assessment session.

Undoubtedly, the popularity of the behavioral interview is derived, at least in part, from a number of practical considerations associated with its use. While direct observation of target behaviors remains the hallmark of behavioral assessment, such observations are not always practical or feasible. At times, especially in outpatient clinical settings, the clinician might have to rely on the person's self-report to obtain critical details about problem behaviors and their controlling variables. Further, the interview affords the clinician the opportunity to obtain information regarding overall functioning in a number of settings (e.g., home, school, work, church, neighborhood) in addition to specific information about the target behaviors. The flexibility inherent in the interview also allows the clinician to build a relationship with the individual and his or her family and to obtain information that otherwise might not be revealed. As noted early on by Linehan (1977), some family members may be more likely to divulge information verbally in the context of a professional relationship than to write it down on a form to be entered into a permanent file. That is, certain family members report little or no difficulties on intake reports or on self-report measures, yet they divulge a number of problem areas during the behavioral clinical interview.

Ratings and Checklists

Significant others in the person's environment also may be requested to complete rating forms or checklists. Such a practice is especially useful in the assessment of children. In general, responses on these forms provide an overall description of the child's behavior, help specify dimensions or response clusters that characterize the child's behavior, and can serve as measures for the evaluation of treatment outcome. Many of these forms contain items related to broad areas of functioning such as school achievement, peer relationships, activity level, and self-control. As such, they provide a cost-effective picture of the child and his or her level of functioning. Further, the forms are useful in eliciting information that may have been missed in the behavioral interview (Novick, Rosenfeld, Bloch, & Dawson, 1966). Finally, the forms can be useful in the search for the best match between various treatments (e.g., systematic desensitization, cognitive restructuring, and self-control) and subtypes of children as revealed on these forms (Ciminero & Drabman, 1977; Ollendick & Cerny, 1981).

Self-Report Instruments

Concurrent with the collection of ratings and reports from significant others, self-reports of attitudes, moods, and behaviors also may be obtained. As noted earlier, behaviorists initially eschewed such data, maintaining that the only acceptable datum was observable behavior. To a large extent, this negative bias against self-report was an outgrowth of early findings indicating that reports of subjective states did not always coincide with observable behaviors (Finch & Rogers, 1984). While congruence is not always observed, researchers have cogently argued that the person's perceptions of his or her own behavior and its consequences may be as important for behavior change as the behavior itself (Finch, Nelson, & Moss, 1983; Ollendick & Hersen, 1984, 1993). Furthermore, as we noted earlier, although different assessment procedures may yield slightly different information, data from these sources can be compared and contrasted in order to arrive at the best snapshot of the individual and to derive treatment goals and procedures. Although self-report instruments have specific limitations, they can provide valuable information about the person and his or her presenting problem; furthermore, they can be used as an index of change following treatment.

Self-Monitoring

Self-monitoring differs from self-report in that it constitutes an observation of clinically relevant target behaviors (e.g., thoughts, feelings, actions) at the time of their occurrence (Cone, 1978). As such, it is a direct method of assessment. Self-monitoring requires the person to observe his or her own behavior and then to record its occurrence systematically. Typically, the individual is asked to record the behavior as it occurs or shortly thereafter in a diary or on a rating form. Although self-monitoring procedures have been used widely (see Cone, 1999, and Korotitsch & Nelson-Gray, 1999, for recent reviews), at least three considerations must be attended to for their effective use: behaviors should be clearly defined, prompts to use the procedures should be readily available, and rewards for their use should be provided. Younger children, in particular, may be less aware of when the target behavior is occurring and will require coaching and assistance prior to establishing a monitoring system. Other young children may have difficulty remembering exactly what behaviors to monitor and how those behaviors are defined. For these reasons, it is generally considered advisable to provide the child a brief description of the target behavior or, better yet, a picture of it, and to have the child record only one or two behaviors at a time. Finally, both adults and children should be reinforced adequately following successful self-monitoring; in the absence of such reinforcement, self-monitoring behavior frequently desists.

In general, the exact methods of self-monitoring are highly variable and depend on the specific behavior being monitored and its place of occurrence. For example, Shapiro, McGonigle, and Ollendick (1980) had children with mental retardation and emotional disturbance self-monitor on-task behavior in a school setting by placing gummed stars on assignment sheets, Ollendick (1981) had children with tics place tally marks upon the occurrence of tics on a colored index card carried in their pocket, and Ollendick (1995) had adolescents diagnosed with panic disorder and agoraphobia indicate the extent of their agoraphobic avoidance on a 1–5 point scale each time they encountered the feared situation. He also asked the adolescents to indicate their confidence (i.e., self-efficacy) in coping with their fear on a similar 1–5 point scale. Wrist counters with children and adults whose targeted behaviors occur while they are on the move also have been used. Such devices are not only easy to use but serve as visual prompts to self-record. The key to successful self-monitoring is the use of uncomplicated recording procedures. They must be highly portable, simple, time-efficient, and relatively unobtrusive (Greene & Ollendick, 2000).

Behavioral Observation

Direct observation of the person's behavior in the natural environment remains the hallmark of behavioral assessment. As described early on by Johnson and Bolstad (1973), the development of naturalistic observation procedures represents one of the major, if not the major, contribution of the behavioral approach to assessment and treatment. Such procedures involve obtaining a direct sample of the person's behavior at the time and place of its occurrence. As such, it is the least inferential of the assessment methods described heretofore. However, behavioral observations in the naturalistic environment should not be viewed as necessarily better than other methods of assessment. Rather, direct observations should be viewed as complementary to the other methods, with each method providing different and potentially valuable information.

In behavioral observation systems, a single behavior or set of behaviors identified as problematic (generally through the aforementioned procedures) are operationally defined, observed, and recorded in a systematic fashion. In addition, events that precede and follow behaviors of interest are recorded and subsequently used in the development of specific treatment programs. Although Jones, Reid, and Patterson (1975) have recommended use of "trained impartial observer-coders" for collection of these data, this is rarely possible in the practice of behavioral assessment in the clinical setting. Frequently, time constraints, lack of trained personnel, and insufficient resources preclude use of highly trained and impartial observers. In some cases, significant others in the child's environment (e.g., parents, teachers, siblings) have been observers of the targeted behavior. Although not impartial, these observers can be trained adequately to record behaviors in the natural environment. In other cases, behavioral clinicians have resorted to laboratory or analogue settings that are similar but not identical to the natural environment. In these simulated settings, the child or adult may be asked to behave as if he or she is angry with his or her parents or partner, to role play assertive responding, or to approach a highly feared object. Behaviors can be directly observed or videotaped and reviewed retrospectively. The distinguishing characteristic of behavioral observations, whether made in the naturalistic environment or in simulated settings, is that a direct sample of the person's behavior is obtained.

Current Status of Behavioral Assessment Methods

As noted by Haynes (1998), Cone (1998), Ollendick and Greene (1997) and others, the nature of behavioral assessment has changed over the years, both in terms of the scope of assessment and the methods employed in the assessment process. First, it should be noted that *Behavioral Assessment,* the first journal devoted exclusively to issues and practices of behavioral assessment, desisted as an independent journal in 1992. At that time, it merged with the journal *Behaviour Research and Therapy,* becoming a special subsection of that journal. As noted by Cone (1992), editor of *Behavioral Assessment* at the time, this decision was a difficult one and one that was due to myriad forces. On the positive side, this merger allowed for publication of behavioral intervention and assessment articles in the same outlet—an outcome consonant with the original purposes of behavioral assessment (i.e., to serve treatment) and one that potentially could bridge the assessment-treatment gap that is often noted in the science and practice of clinical psychology and related disciplines. On the negative side, however, it was also noted by Cone that the number of submissions to the journal had declined greatly over the years and that apparent interest in behavioral assessment had diminished.

This trend was also evidenced by a sister journal, also begun in 1979, the *Journal of Behavioral Assessment.* This journal was expanded in 1985 and was renamed the *Journal*

of Psychopathology and Behavioral Assessment, at least partially in response to decreased submissions in the area of behavioral assessment. On the positive ledger, however, its new name was adopted because the journal, under the editorship of Henry Adams and Samuel Turner, desired to integrate current developments in experimental and clinical psychopathology with behavioral assessment. That is, a merger between behavioral assessment and psychopathology was enacted. Thus, both of these developments with the two major behavioral assessment journals were pursued in an attempt to integrate—or more precisely reintegrate—behavioral assessment back into the broader fields of basic clinical psychopathology and clinical treatment. Of course, as others have noted (see Taylor, 1999), two other assessment journals have been spawned in recent years: *Psychological Assessment* (a spin-off of the *Journal of Consulting and Clinical Psychology*) in 1989 and in 1994 the journal simply named *Assessment.* These latter two journals continue to publish a fair number of articles on behavioral assessment issues and practices. Thus, the dearth of submissions to "behavioral" journals may be due to the greater number of outlets for such work, not necessarily a reduction in interest in behavioral assessment per se.

However, as noted by Cone in his closing editorial comment for *Behavioral Assessment* in 1992, entitled "That Was Then, This Is Now," there had not only been a decline in articles submitted to the journal, there was also a decline in the number of articles submitted and published on direct observational methods and, simultaneously, an increase in articles on self-report methods of assessment (the proportion of articles on other methods of assessment such as interview measures, reports of others, and psychophysiological methods remained constant—about 20% of submitted and published articles). Steven Taylor, editor of the special section on behavioral assessment in *Behaviour Research and Therapy,* offered a similar conclusion in 1999. Taylor (1999) noted that the trend identified by Cone continued under his editorship. As can be seen in Figure 2.1, the trends are self-evident. Taylor (1999) also noted that this trend "raises the question of whether assessment researchers (and consumers of assessment research) are tending to over-rely on self-report instruments" (p. 477).

Although these trends may be disconcerting, a national survey of members of the Association for the Advancement of Behavior Therapy conducted by Elliott, Miltenberger, Kaster-Bundgaard, and Lumley (1996) revealed that a majority of both practitioners and academics aligned with behavior therapy continue to use, at least "sometimes," behavioral observation and self-monitoring assessment procedures (see Table 2.1). They also tend to use indirect methods of assessment,

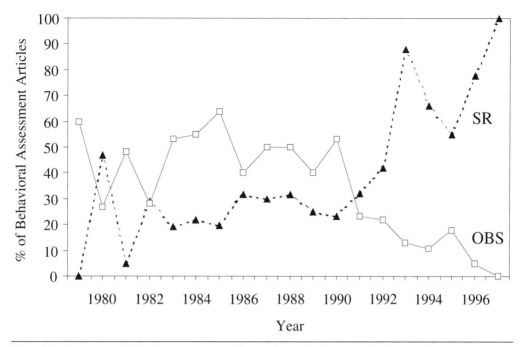

Figure 2.1   Percentage of behavioral assessment articles on observational methods (OBS) and self-report (SR) methods of assessment. S. Taylor (1999). Behavioral assessment: Review and prospect. *Behaviour Research and Therapy, 37,* 475–482. Figure 1, p. 477. Reproduced with permission.

TABLE 2.1   Assessment Procedures

	Practitioners		Academics	
Procedure	% Therapists Sometimes Use	% Clients Receive	% Therapists Sometimes Use	% Clients Receive
Interview with identified client	99.1	94.1	95.7	93.3
Interview with significant others	94.1	42.0	89.5	45.7
Information from other professionals	88.7	38.0	92.6	41.7
Self-monitoring	83.6	44.1	74.7	47.5
Behavioral rating scales/questionnaires	80.5^	43.7**	89.5^	67.3**
Direct observation	76.5	52.3	82.1	51.9
Mental status exam	65.8	36.1	58.9	26.6
Role play	62.9	19.4	64.9	25.3
Personality inventories	61.1	15.9	57.9	19.6
Intellectual assessment	58.2	14.2	61.0	14.1
Structured diagnostic interview	50.4	22.6	57.9	28.6
Neuropsychological assessment	37.1	5.8	38.9	7.1
Projective tests	27.6	4.7	17.9	2.5
Analogue functional assessment	23.5	10.0*	31.6	16.3*
Other	5.1	3.0	4.3	4.2

Note. The categories were provided in the survey. The column "% clients receive" represents the mean percentage of clients with whom therapists reported using the technique. The column "% therapists sometimes use" indicates the percentage of therapists who endorsed the item (suggesting they use the technique with at least some clients). Chi-square tests were conducted comparing the percentage of practitioners and academics who used the various assessment techniques (^), and two-tailed *t* tests were conducted comparing the percentage of clients with whom practitioners and academics used these procedures (*). Due to multiple comparisons, only findings with p < .003 should be viewed as significant according to a Bonferroni correction.
**p < .003. *p < .05. ^p < .05.
Source: A.G. Elliott, R.G. Miltenberger, J. Kaster-Bundgaard, & V. Lumley (1996). A national survey of assessment and therapy techniques used by behavior therapists. *Cognitive and Behavioral Practice, 3,* 107–125. Reprinted with permission.

including interviews, rating scales, and self-report instruments. Moreover, practitioners and academicians alike report that assessment practices are very important to them, ranking their importance 1.8 on a 7-point rating scale ranging from 1 = extremely important to 7 = extremely unimportant. These survey results mirrored those obtained from earlier surveys conducted by Swann and MacDonald (1978) and Wade, Baker, and Hartmann (1979). Thus, although the number and type of submitted and published articles are on the decline, it appears that behavioral assessment remains a stable ingredient of many behaviorally oriented practitioners and researchers.

FUTURE DIRECTIONS

A number of directions for future research and development in behavioral assessment may be evident to the reader. What follows is our attempt to highlight those areas that appear most promising and in need of greater articulation. Some of these areas are undoubtedly more important in the assessment of children than adults, but all of them deserve our careful consideration.

First, it seems to us that greater attention must be given to developmental factors as they affect the selection of behavioral assessment procedures for individuals of varying ages and development. Although behavioral assessment procedures should be developmentally sensitive, behavioral assessors have frequently ignored this admonition. One of the most distinguishing characteristics of children is developmental change. Such change encompasses basic biological growth and maturity as well as affective, behavioral, and cognitive fluctuations that may characterize them at different age levels. Although the importance of accounting for developmental level when assessing behavior may be obvious, ways of integrating developmental concepts and principles into behavioral assessment are less evident. Edelbrock (1984) has noted three areas for the synthesis of developmental and behavioral principles: (1) use of developmental fluctuations in behavior to establish normative baselines of behavior, (2) determination of age and gender differences in the expression and covariation of behavioral patterns, and (3) study of stability and change in behavior over time. Clearly, these areas of synthesis and integration are in their infancy and in need of greater articulation (e.g., Harris & Ferrari, 1983; Ollendick & Hersen, 1983; Rutter & Garmezy, 1983; Sroufe & Rutter, 1984). Moreover, the implications of development need to be extended to adults as well. Just as an 8-year-old differs from a 16-year-old, we maintain that a 21-year-old differs from a 42-year-old and a 63-year-old and that developmental processes remain important in adulthood. Development continues

across the lifespan and does not cease when one becomes 21 years of age. As Ollendick and Vasey (1999) and Ollendick, Grills, and King (2001) note, the promise of a developmental-behavioral synthesis remains unfulfilled at this time.

Second, greater attention must be focused on the incremental validity of the multimethod approach, especially when used for individuals of varying ages. In this chapter, the importance of a multimethod approach consisting of interviews, self- and other-reports, self-monitoring, and behavioral observations was highlighted. Some of these procedures may be more appropriate at some age levels than others. Further, the psychometric properties of these procedures may vary with age. For example, self-monitoring requires the ability to compare one's own behavior against a standard and to accurately judge occurrence or nonoccurrence of targeted events and behaviors. Most children below 8 years of age lack the requisite ability to self-monitor and may not profit from such procedures. In fact, the limited research available suggests that self-monitoring may be counterproductive when used with young children (e.g., Higa, Thorp, & Calkins, 1978). These findings suggest that self-monitoring procedures are better suited for individuals who possess sufficient cognitive abilities to benefit from their use (Shapiro, 1984). Similarly, age-related variables place constraints on use of certain self-report measures with young children. Ollendick and Hersen (1993) review additional age-related findings for other procedures and suggest caution in using these procedures without due regard for their developmental appropriateness and related psychometric properties. To our knowledge, no one has addressed this important issue with adults. What are the effects, for example, of being observed or being asked to self-monitor behavior at varying ages? Do these procedures work equally well across age? Moreover, what are the effects of undertaking such practices at one's workplace? At one's home or church? And, in one's intimate relationships? Might there be important differences in the utility (and reliability) of various assessment practices, not only in different settings, but also due to accumulated experiences and learning across time?

If certain procedures were found to be less reliable or valid at different age levels, their indiscriminate use, of course, would not be valid, let alone recommended. Inasmuch as these strategies are found to be inadequate, their combination in a multimethod approach would serve only to compound their inherent limitations (Mash & Terdal, 1981). In addition, the different procedures might vary in terms of their treatment utility across ages. The sine qua non of behavioral assessment is that the procedures to be employed must be empirically validated (Ollendick & Hersen, 1984).

A related issue is that of treatment utility, which refers to the degree to which assessment strategies are shown to contribute to beneficial treatment outcomes (Hayes et al., 1987). More specifically, treatment utility addresses issues related to the selection of specific target behaviors and to the choice of specific assessment strategies. For example, we might wish to examine the treatment utility of using self-report questionnaires to guide treatment planning, above and beyond that provided by direct behavioral observation of persons who are phobic of social encounters (i.e., those diagnosed with social phobia). All persons could complete a fear schedule and be observed in a social situation, but the self-report data for only half of the individuals would be made available for treatment planning. If the individuals for whom self-reports were made available improved more than those whose treatment plans were based solely on behavioral observations, then the treatment utility of using self-report data would be established. In a similar fashion, the treatment utility of interviews, role-plays, behavioral avoidance tests, and other devices could be evaluated (Hayes et al., 1987). Of course, it would be important to examine treatment utility from a developmental perspective as well. Certain procedures might be shown to possess incremental validity at one age (whether adult or child) but not another. Although the concept of treatment utility is relatively unexplored at this time, it shows considerable promise as a strategy to evaluate the incremental validity of the multimethod assessment approach. We should not necessarily assume that more assessment is better assessment.

Third, considerable energy must be directed to the development of behavioral assessment methods that are culturally sensitive. In recent years, numerous individuals have called attention to the internationalization of the world and, for example, the "browning of America" (e.g., Malgady, Rogler, & Constatino, 1987; Vasquez, DeLeon, & Del Valle, 1990). The very same behavioral assessment practices are being used with non-Caucasian children and adults for whom Standard English may not be the primary language, and many procedures developed in the United States and other Western countries are being applied, oftentimes indiscriminately, in other countries. Development of assessment procedures that are culture-fair, language-fair, and culture-specific is of utmost importance. Of course, many cultural issues must be considered in the assessment process. Cultural differences may be expressed in child-rearing practices, family values, parental expectations, communication styles, nonverbal communication patterns, and family structure and dynamics. As but one example, certain behaviors characteristic of ethnic minority children may be seen as emotionally or behaviorally maladaptive by persons who have little or no appreciation for cultural variations (e.g., Prewitt-Diaz, 1989). Thus, cultural differences are likely to occur early in the assessment process. In a particularly informative and sensitive commentary,

Vasquez and colleagues (1996) have suggested several steps that can be taken to minimize cultural biases in the assessment process: (1) include extended family members in the information-gathering process; (2) use interpreters, if necessary, in the interview process; (3) familiarize oneself with the culture of specific groups; and (4) use instruments that have been translated into the native language of reporters and for which norms are available for specific ethnic groups. In sum, a clear challenge before us in the years ahead is to attend to important cultural factors that impinge on our assessment armamentarium and to develop and promulgate culturally sensitive methods that are also developmentally appropriate and empirically validated.

In short, the future directions of behavioral assessment are numerous and varied. Even though a technology for behavioral assessment has evolved and is in force, we need to begin to explore the issues raised before we can conclude that the procedures are maximally productive and in the best interests of individuals throughout the world.

SUMMARY

Behavioral assessment, as with other movements in psychology, has mirrored important philosophical, scientific, and practical developments. Certain theoretical assumptions guide behavioral assessment that set it apart from traditional assessment. Foremost among these is the premise that behavior is a function of situational determinants and not a sign of underlying personality traits. To assess adequately the situational determinants and to obtain as complete a picture of the person as possible, a multimethod assessment approach is recommended that utilizes both direct and indirect methods of assessment. Even though direct behavioral observation remains the hallmark of behavioral assessment, information from these other sources is considered not only valuable but also integral in the understanding and subsequent treatment of diverse behavior problems. Hence, although the identification and specification of discrete target behaviors was once considered sufficient, current behavioral assessment involves serious consideration and systematic assessment of cognitive and affective aspects of the person's behavior and of developmental, social, and cultural factors that influence the individual, as well as direct observation of the problematic behavior in situ. Current trends support the utility and importance of a wide array of behavioral assessment methods.

Several areas of future research remain, however. These include clearer specification of developmental variables, a closer examination of the utility of the multimethod approach at different age levels and in different contexts, and the influence of culture and the need for models of assessment that take cultural forces into consideration. Although the basis for a technology of behavioral assessment exists, considerable fine-tuning remains to be done. Behavioral assessment is at a critical juncture in its own development. Based on chapters in this volume, however, behavioral assessment appears to be in good hands and remains an indispensable aspect of our efforts to better understand people and their behavior.

REFERENCES

Bandura, A. (1977). Self-efficacy: Toward a unifying theory of behavioral change. *Psychological Review, 84,* 191–215.

Baum, W.M. (1994). *Understanding behaviorism: Science, behavior, and culture.* New York: HarperCollins College Publishers.

Bechterev, V.M. (1933). *General principles of human reflexology: An introduction to the objective study of personality.* London: Jarrolds.

Belsky, J. (1980). Child maltreatment: An ecological integration. *American Psychologist, 35,* 320–335.

Bornstein, P.H., Bornstein, M.T., & Dawson, B. (1984). Integrated assessment and treatment. In T.H. Ollendick, & M. Hersen (Eds.), *Child behavioral assessment: Principles and procedures* (pp. 223–243). New York: Pergamon Press.

Brems, C., Thevenin, D.M., & Routh, D.K. (1991). The history of clinical psychology. In C.E. Walker (Ed.), *Clinical psychology: Historical and research foundations* (pp. 3–36). New York: Plenum Press.

Calhoun, K.S., & Turner, S.M. (1981). Historical perspectives and current issues in behavior therapy. In S.M. Turner, K.S. Calhoun, & H.E. Adams (Eds.), *Handbook of clinical behavior therapy* (pp. 1–11). New York: Wiley.

Cicchetti, D., & Lynch, M. (1993). Toward an ecological/transactional model of community violence and child maltreatment. *Psychiatry, 56,* 96–118.

Cicchetti, D., & Lynch, M. (1995). Failures in the expectable environment and their impact on individual development: The case of child maltreatment. In D. Cicchetti & D.J. Cohen (Eds.), *Developmental psychopathology: Vol. 2. Risk, disorder, and adaptation* (pp. 32–71). New York: Wiley.

Ciminero, A.R., & Drabman, R.S. (1977). Current developments in the behavioral assessment of children. In B.B. Lahey & A.E. Kazdin (Eds.), *Advances in clinical child psychology* (Vol. 1, pp. 47–82). New York: Plenum.

Cone, J.D. (1977). The relevance of reliability and validity for behavioral assessment. *Behavior Therapy, 8,* 411–426.

Cone, J.D. (1978). The behavioral assessment grid (BAG): A conceptual framework and a taxonomy. *Behavior Therapy, 9,* 882–888.

Cone, J.D. (1986). Ideographic, nomothetic, and related perspectives in behavioral assessment. In R.O. Nelson & S.C. Hayes (Eds.),

Conceptual foundations of behavioral assessment (pp. 111–128). New York: Guilford Press.

Cone, J.D. (1992). That was then! This is now! *Behavioral Assessment, 14,* 219–228.

Cone, J.D. (1998). Psychometric considerations: Concepts, contents, and methods. In A.S. Bellack & M. Hersen (Eds.), *Behavioral assessment: A practical handbook* (pp. 22–46.) Needham Heights, MA: Allyn & Bacon.

Cone, J.D. (1999). Introduction to the special section on self-monitoring: A major assessment method in clinical psychology. *Psychological Assessment, 11,* 411–414.

Cone, J.D., & Hawkins, R.P. (1977). Current status and future directions in behavioral assessment. In J.D. Cone & R.P. Hawkins (Eds.), *Behavioral assessment: New directions in clinical psychology* (pp. 381–392). New York: Brunner/Mazel.

Edelbrock, C.S. (1984). Developmental considerations. In T.H. Ollendick & M. Hersen (Eds.), *Child behavioral assessment: Principles and procedures* (pp. 20–37). Elmsford, NY: Pergamon Press.

Elliott, A.J., Miltenberger, R.G., Kaster-Bundgaard, J., & Lumley, V. (1996). A national survey of assessment and therapy techniques used by behavior therapists. *Cognitive and Behavioral Practice, 3,* 107–125.

Finch, A.J., Nelson, W.M. III, & Moss, J.H. (1983). Stress inoculation for anger control in aggressive children. In A.J. Finch, W.M. Nelson, & E.S. Ott (Eds.), *Cognitive-behavioral procedures with children: A practical guide* (pp. 148–205). Newton, MA: Allyn & Bacon.

Finch, A.J., & Rogers, T.R. (1984). Self-report instruments. In T.H. Ollendick & M. Hersen (Eds.), *Child behavioral assessment: Principles and procedures* (pp. 106–123). Elmsford, NY: Pergamon Press.

Goldfried, M.R., & Kent, R.N. (1972). Traditional versus behavioral personality assessment: A comparison of methodological and theoretical assumptions. *Psychological Bulletin, 77,* 409–420.

Greene, R.W., & Doyle, A.E. (1999). Toward a transactional conceptualization of oppositional defiant disorder: Implications for assessment and treatment. *Clinical and Family Psychology Review, 2,* 129–147.

Greene, R.W., & Ollendick, T.H. (2000). Behavioral assessment of children. In G. Goldstein & M. Hersen (Eds.), *Handbook of psychological assessment* (3rd ed., pp. 453–470). Oxford, England: Elsevier Science/Pergamon Press.

Gross, A.M. (1984). Behavioral interviewing. In T.H. Ollendick & M. Hersen (Eds.), *Child behavioral assessment: Principles and procedures* (pp. 61–79). Elmsford, NY: Pergamon Press.

Harris, S.L., & Ferrari, M. (1983). Developmental factors in child behavior therapy. *Behavior Therapy, 14,* 54–72.

Hartshorne, H., & May, M.A. (1928). *Studies in the nature of character. Vol I. Studies in deceit.* New York: Macmillan.

Hayes, S.C., Nelson, R.O., & Jarrett, R.B. (1986). Evaluating the quality of behavioral assessment. In R.O. Nelson & S.C. Hayes

(Eds.), *Conceptual foundations of behavioral assessment* (pp. 463–503). New York: Guilford Press.

Hayes, S.C., Nelson, R.O., & Jarrett, R.B. (1987). The treatment utility of assessment: A functional approach to evaluating assessment quality. *American Psychologist, 42,* 963–974.

Haynes, S.N. (1978). *Principles of behavioral assessment.* New York: Gardner Press.

Haynes, S.N. (1990). Behavioral assessment of adults. In G. Goldstein & M. Hersen (Eds.), *Handbook of psychological assessment* (2nd ed., pp. 423–463). New York: Pergamon Press.

Haynes, S.N. (1998). The changing nature of behavioral assessment. In A.S. Bellack & M. Hersen (Eds.), *Behavioral assessment: A practical handbook* (4th ed., pp. 1–21). Boston: Allyn & Bacon.

Hersen, M. (1976). Historical perspectives in behavioral assessment. In M. Hersen & A.S. Bellack (Eds.), *Behavioral assessment: A practical handbook* (pp. 3–22). New York: Pergamon Press.

Hersen, M., & Bellack A.S. (Eds.) (1976). *Behavioral assessment: A practical handbook.* New York: Pergamon Press.

Hersen, M., & Bellack, A.S. (1977). Assessment of social skills. In A.R. Ciminero, K.S. Calhoun, & H.E. Adams (Eds.), *Handbook of behavioral assessment* (pp. 509–554). New York: Wiley.

Higa, W.R., Tharp, R.G., & Calkins, R.P. (1978). Developmental verbal control of behavior: Implications for self-instructional testing. *Journal of Experimental Child Psychology, 26,* 489–497.

Johnson, S.M., & Bolstad, O.D. (1973). Methodological issues in naturalistic observations: Some problems and solutions for field research. In L.A. Hammerlynck, L.C. Handyx, & E.J. Mash (Eds.), *Behavior change: Methodology, concepts, and practice* (pp. 7–67). Champaign, IL: Research Press.

Jones, R.R., Reid, J.B., & Patterson, G.R. (1975). Naturalistic observation in clinical assessment. In P. McReynolds (Ed.), *Advances in psychological assessment* (Vol. 3, pp. 42–95). San Francisco: Jossey-Bass.

Kanfer, F.H., & Phillips, J.S. (1970). *Learning foundations of behavior therapy.* New York: Wiley.

Kazdin, A.E. (1978). *History of behavior modification.* Baltimore: University Park Press.

Korotitsch, W.J., & Nelson-Gray, R.O. (1999). An overview of self-monitoring research in assessment and treatment. *Psychological Assessment, 11,* 415–425.

Linehan, M. (1977). Issues in behavioral interviewing. In J.D. Cone & R.P. Hawkins (Eds.), *Behavioral assessment: New directions in clinical psychology* (pp. 30–51). New York: Brunner/Mazel.

Malgady, R., Rogler, L., & Constatino, G. (1987). Ethnocultural and linguistic bias in mental health evaluation of Hispanics. *American Psychologist, 42,* 228–234.

Mash, E.J., & Terdal, L.G. (1981). Behavioral assessment of childhood disturbance. In E.J. Mash & L.G. Terdal (Eds.), *Behavioral assessment of childhood disorders* (pp. 3–76). New York: Guilford Press.

Mash, E.J., & Terdal, L.G. (1989). Behavioral assessment of childhood disturbance. In E.J. Mash & L.G. Terdal (Eds.), *Behavioral assessment of childhood disorders* (2nd ed., pp. 3–65). New York: Guilford Press.

Meichenbaum, D.H. (1977). *Cognitive behavior modification.* New York: Plenum Press.

Mischel, W. (1968). *Personality and assessment.* New York: Wiley.

Mischel, W. (1973). Toward a cognitive social learning reconceptualization of personality. *Psychological Review, 80,* 252–283.

Mowrer, O.H., & Mowrer, W.A. (1938). Enuresis: A method for its study and treatment. *American Journal of Orthopsychiatry, 8,* 436–447.

Nay, R.W. (1976). *Behavioral intervention: Contemporary strategies.* New York: Gardner Press.

Nelson, R.O. (1983). Behavioral assessment: Past, present, and future. *Behavioral Assessment, 5,* 195–206.

Nelson, R.O., & Hayes, S.C. (1976). Nature of behavioral assessment. In M. Hersen & A.S. Bellack (Eds.), *Behavioral assessment: A practical handbook* (2nd ed., pp. 3–37). New York: Plenum Press.

Nelson-Gray, R., Gaynor, S.T., & Korotitsch, W.J. (1997). Behavior therapy: Distinct but acculturated. *Behavior Therapy, 28,* 563–572.

Novick, J., Rosenfeld, E., Bloch, D.A., & Dawson, D. (1966). Ascertaining deviant behavior in children. *Journal of Consulting and Clinical Psychology, 30,* 230–238.

Ollendick, T.H. (1981). Self-monitoring and self-administered overcorrection: The modification of nervous tics in children. *Behavior Modification, 5,* 75–84.

Ollendick, T.H. (1995). Cognitive-behavioral treatment of panic disorder with agoraphobia in adolescents: A multiple baseline design analysis. *Behavior Therapy, 26,* 517–531.

Ollendick, T.H., & Cerny, J.A. (1981). *Clinical behavior therapy with children.* New York: Plenum Press.

Ollendick, T.H., & Greene, R.W. (1990). Behavioral assessment of children. In G. Goldstein & M. Hersen (Eds.), *Handbook of psychological assessment* (2nd ed., 403–422). Elmsford, NY: Pergamon Press.

Ollendick, T.H., & Greene, R.W. (1997). Principles and practices of behavioral assessment with children. In A.S. Bellack & M. Hersen (Eds.), *Comprehensive clinical psychology* (Vol. 4, pp. 131–156). New York: Elsevier Science.

Ollendick, T.H., Grills, A.E., & King, N.J. (2001). Applying developmental theory to the assessment and treatment of childhood disorders: Does it make a difference? *Clinical Psychology and Psychotherapy, 8,* 304–314.

Ollendick, T.H., & Hersen, M. (1983). *Handbook of child psychopathology.* New York: Plenum Press.

Ollendick, T.H., & Hersen, M. (1984). *Child behavioral assessment: Principles and procedures.* New York: Pergamon Press.

Ollendick, T.H., & Hersen, M. (1993). Child and adolescent behavioral assessment. In T.H. Ollendick & M. Hersen (Eds.), *Hand-*

book of child and adolescent behavioral assessment (pp. 3–14). New York: Pergamon Press.

Ollendick, T.H., & Vasey, M.W. (1999). Developmental theory and the practice of clinical child psychology. *Journal of Clinical Child Psychology, 28,* 457–466.

Patterson, G.R. (1976). The aggressive child: Victim and architect of a coercive system. In E.J. Mash, L.A. Hammerlynck, & L.C. Hardy (Eds.), *Behavioral modification and families* (pp. 267–316). New York: Brunner/Mazel.

Prewitt-Diaz, J. (1989). *The process and procedures for identifying exceptional language minority children.* State College: Pennsylvania State University.

Redd, W.H., Porterfield, A.L., & Andersen, B.L. (1979). *Behavior modification: Behavioral approaches to human problems.* New York: Random House.

Routh, D.K. (1998). Hippocrates meets Democritus: A history of psychiatry and clinical psychology. In A.S. Bellack & M. Hersen (Eds.), *Comprehensive clinical psychology* (Vol. 1, pp. 1–48). New York: Elsevier Science.

Rutter, M., & Garmezy, N. (1983). Developmental psychopathology. In E.M. Hetherington (Ed.), *Socialization, personality, and social development: Vol. 14. Mussen's handbook of child psychology* (pp. 775–911). New York: Wiley.

Sameroff, A. (1975). Early influences on development: Fact or fancy? *Merrill-Palmer Quarterly, 21,* 263–294.

Sattler, J.M. (1988). *Assessment of children* (3rd ed.). San Diego: Author.

Shapiro, E.S. (1984). Self-monitoring. In T.H. Ollendick & M. Hersen (Eds.), *Child behavioral assessment: Principles and procedures* (pp. 148–165). Elmsford, NY: Pergamon Press.

Shapiro, E.S., McGonigle, J.J., & Ollendick, T.H. (1980). An analysis of self-assessment and self-reinforcement in a self-managed token economy with mentally retarded children. *Journal of Applied Research in Mental Retardation, 1,* 227–240.

Skinner, B.F. (1953). *Science and human behavior.* New York: Macmillan.

Sroufe, L.A., & Rutter, M. (1984). The domain of developmental psychopathology. *Child Development, 55,* 17–29.

Staats, A.W. (1975). *Social behaviorism.* Homewood, IL: Dorsey Press.

Staats, A.W. (1986). Behaviorism with a personality: The paradigmatic behavioral assessment approach. In R.O. Nelson & S.C. Hayes (Eds.), *Conceptual foundations of behavioral assessment* (pp. 242–296). New York: Guilford Press.

Swann, G.E., & MacDonald, M.L. (1978). Behavior therapy in practice: A rational survey of behavior therapists. *Behavior Therapy, 9,* 799–807.

Taylor, S. (1999). Behavioral assessment: Review and prospect. *Behaviour Research and Therapy, 37,* 475–482.

Ullmann, L.P., & Krasner, L. (Eds.) (1965). *Case studies in behavioral modification.* New York: Holt, Rinehart, & Winston.

Vasquez Nuttall, E., DeLeon, B., & Del Valle, M. (1990). Best practice in considering cultural factors. In A. Thomas & J. Grimes (Eds.), *Best practices in school psychology II* (pp. 219–233). Washington, DC: National Association of School Psychologists.

Vasquez Nuttall, E., Sanchez, W., Borras Osorio, L., Nuttall, R.I., & Varvogil, L. (1996). Assessing the culturally and linguistically different child with emotional and behavioral problems. In M.J. Breen & C.R. Fiedler (Eds.), *Behavioral approach to assessment of youth with emotional/behavioral disorders: A handbook for school-based practitioners* (pp. 451–502). Austin, TX: ProEd.

Wade, T.C., Baker, T.B., & Hartmann, D.P. (1979). Behavior therapists' self-reported views and practices. *The Behavior Therapist, 2,* 3–6.

Wahler, R.G. (1976). Deviant child behavior in the family: Developmental speculations and behavior change strategies. In H. Leitenberg (Ed.), *Handbook of behavior modification and behavior therapy* (pp. 516–543). Englewood Cliffs, NJ: Prentice-Hall.

Walker, C.E., & Shelton, T. (1985). An overview of behavioral medicine. In A. Zeiner, D. Bendell, & C.E. Walker (Eds.), *Health Psychology* (pp. 63–82). New York: Plenum Press.

Winett, R.A., Riley, A.W., King, A.C., & Altman, D.G. (1989). Preventive strategies with children and families. In T.H. Ollendick & M. Hersen (Eds.), *Handbook of child psychopathology* (2nd ed., pp. 499–521). New York: Plenum Press.

SECTION TWO

CONCEPTUAL FOUNDATIONS OF BEHAVIORAL ASSESSMENT

CHAPTER 3

Psychometric Foundations of Behavioral Assessment

HOI K. SUEN AND SARAH E. RZASA

SIGN AND SAMPLE NATURE OF BEHAVIORAL ASSESSMENT DATA

How we view the quality of data from behavioral assessment and what evidence is needed to demonstrate the quality of data depend on how we view the epistemological nature of these data. During the middle of the twentieth century, Skinnerian behaviorism, which is a form of logical positivism expressed in the area of psychology (Phillips, 1992; Phillips & Burbules, 2000), and operant conditioning were dominant perspectives. The epistemological underpinning of this view of human behavior is that we should study what is directly observable through our senses (or extensions through instrumentation). That which is not observable is conjecture and is not a proper focus of assessment. From this perspective, data collected from the observation of behaviors are the direct object of investigation without further inference into unobserved "conjectures." The behaviors being assessed are themselves an end, not a means to an end.

A second view of behavioral assessment is that the scores are reflections of deeper and covert psychological constructs or traits. For a discussion on the nature of behavioral assessment data, we need not get tangled in the debate regarding the nature of constructs and their existence. Suffice to say that constructs are not directly observable. In this case, ob-

servable behaviors are viewed as manifestations of these unobservable latent constructs.

These two perspectives regarding the nature of behavioral assessment data have been described as the sample and sign measures (Messick, 1989; Cone, 1986). When one adopts the stance of behaviorism, the behavior being observed is the target. As such, the observed data represent a sample of all potential incidents of the behavior. For example, we might observe the frequency of an aggressive behavior such as hitting done by a child during an observation session and use the data as a sample of the child's general frequency of hitting behavior. On the other hand, when one views a behavior as a manifestation of a covert construct, the observed data represent a sign of the underlying construct. For example, we might observe that same frequency of hitting behaviors as an indicator of the covert "propensity toward violence" of the child. The two different perspectives lead to different implications for what is necessary to ascertain data quality.

With sample measures, the major issue of data quality is that of score accuracy or precision. Issues of score precision typically are conceptualized under the nomenclature of *reliability*. In addition to issues of score accuracy, sign measures raise questions of meaningful representation. Issues of meaningfulness generally are conceptualized under the nomenclature of *validity*. In both cases, issues of utility or usefulness are important. Utility also falls under the nomenclature of validity. Hence, the mix of reliability and validity evidence necessary to justify a particular use of a given set of behavioral assessment scores will differ according to one's epistemological stance. In the remainder of this chapter, we focus on issues and techniques related to the collection of a proper mix of reliability and validity evidence.

A hybrid of the two perspectives is one in which the object of interest is an unobservable theoretical construct. However, data obtained through the direct observation of behaviors are considered the sine qua non measure of the construct. Data thus obtained are considered the ultimate standard upon which the quality of data obtained through other means such as self-report or assessment are to be judged (Hartmann, 1977, 1982). In terms of mix of evidence, this perspective still treats behavioral assessment results as sign measures, albeit the method that requires the least amount of inferential leap to the construct and thus the least amount of validity evidence.

CONSIDERATIONS RELATED TO
SCORE PRECISION

Evidence of score precision is typically derived by examining the reliability of the scores obtained through the behavioral assessment procedure. Because reliability is concerned with the precision of scores as such, it is fundamentally a statistical concept. A very large body of literature since the early twentieth century has examined techniques to evaluate reliability. Possibly due to this large and diverse body of literature and its many suggestions and approaches, there are numerous pitfalls in the assessment of reliability. Many of these pitfalls have led to some common errors and misconceptions. Before we discuss the methods to estimate reliability and measurement errors, it is important to keep in mind a number of issues that will directly affect how we proceed with deriving evidence of reliability.

First, all existing theories of reliability and measurement errors focus on the statistical properties of the *scores,* not on the reliability of an instrument. Therefore, reliability refers not to the reliability of an observation procedure, a behavioral checklist, a test, a scale, an inventory nor of any other similar entity. Neither is it the reliability of an observer. Rather, reliability refers to the reliability of the results of an observer using such an entity following a certain prescribed procedure under a certain prescribed or natural set of conditions. That is, reliability is of the scores, and thus it is the result of the interaction of all these factors. This conceptual distinction is not mere semantic hairsplitting; it has important consequences in terms of reliability estimation. This is because any given

behavioral assessment may produce many scores, including composite scores, subscale scores, score profiles, and item scores. Further, interpretations and decisions often are based on some mathematical combination of scores such as the difference or ratio between scores on different subscales. For each of these scores, differences, and ratios, the reliability would be different. Although all these scores come from the same instrument, reliability changes as a function of the scores of interest. Hence, reliability is not a property of an instrument, nor of an observer, but is a descriptor of the degree of precision of a particular score.

Related to the concept of reliability of scores is the issue of the unit of analysis for reliability estimation. In behavioral assessment, the behavior of interest is based on a certain level of data and aggregation. For example, we might assess a sample or a sign at the molecular or the molar level. Molar behaviors are aggregates of a class of molecular behaviors. For example, we might study how often a child talks out of turn in class. Alternatively, we might study the frequency with which a child talks out of turn, being off task, being out of seat, and so on under a larger rubric of inappropriate classroom behavior. Within this context, talking out of turn by itself would be a molecular behavior, whereas inappropriate classroom behavior would be a molar behavior. The scores reflecting molar behaviors, being aggregates of molecular behaviors, can be expected to be more reliable than the scores of molecular behaviors. Thus, when examining reliability, it is important to ascertain the proper level of behavior of interest and make sure that the reliability and measurement error estimates correspond to the level of behavior aggregation of interest.

Another aspect of the unit of analysis issue is that of the sampling unit along the time continuum. Behaviors occur in time. Some behavior data are based on behaviors exhibited over a long period of time, while other data are based on a sample of behaviors during a brief period. Data based on long periods can be expected to be more reliable than data based on brief periods. Thus, when assessing reliability, it is important to ascertain that the time unit on which the reliability estimate is derived corresponds to the time unit on which the actual behaviors are used in subsequent research or treatment. For example, in behavioral assessment, a common approach to estimating reliability is to observe a behavior of interest during an observation session that is divided into many observation intervals. Reliability is estimated based on the degree of interval-by-interval agreement between two independent observers and is typically expressed in the form of either a percentage agreement index or a kappa coefficient. This approach provides a measure of observer interchangeability (we will discuss these issues in greater depth later) relative to the *interval* scores. Yet the scores typically used for decisions and/or research are the *session* scores. Session scores are generally more reliable than interval scores. Thus, by estimating the reliability of the interval scores, we usually underrepresent the reliability of the actual scores being used.

Behavioral assessment data may be interpreted in an absolute or a relative manner (Brennan & Kane, 1977). With the absolute approach, behavioral data are interpreted in relation to some absolute standard. In traditional paper-and-pencil assessment, this approach is referred to as a criterion-referenced interpretation. For example, a company might hire an individual only if he or she scores above a certain cutoff score on a job performance rating scale. When we treat the frequency and prevalence of a particular behavior as a sample measure, the sample data can be interpreted relative to an absolute zero (i.e., treat frequency and prevalence as ratio scale data). As such, a frequency of 20, for instance, is 20 times above zero. On the other hand, we may ask a respondent to rate his or her own behavior on a rating scale. For example, students might be asked to rate themselves on a scale of conscientiousness. Because no natural metric exists for a rating scale such as this, there is no natural absolute point of origin such as zero. In this case, we might interpret the scores in either of two approaches. We might determine, through some policy decision, that a certain score on the rating scale is a minimum cutoff between two different decisions or actions. This would suggest an absolute approach. Or we might compare one person's score to scores of that person's norm group and make decisions based on the relative position of the person (e.g., provide treatment if lower than the bottom 5% or if more than 1.5 standard deviations below the mean). In this case, the scores are treated in a relative manner, a method called norm-referenced interpretation.

Whether scores are interpreted in a relative or absolute manner will have important implications on the assessment of score reliability. In an absolute approach, all score inconsistencies are measurement errors. However, in a relative approach, some types of inconsistencies are not necessarily errors (Brennan & Kane, 1977). Hence, reliability of the same scores under a relative interpretation can be expected to be higher than those same scores under an absolute interpretation. To illustrate, two independent raters rate the level of marital accord between spouses based on observation of the interactions between spouses in treatment sessions. Let us say that one rater is systematically more lenient and consistently gives 5 more points to each couple than does the other rater. This inconsistency between the two raters would be of concern when we interpret the scores against some absolute standard, because it would make a difference as to which rater's score is used. On the other hand, this same inconsistency is

of no consequence to the rank order of couples so long as we consistently use the data from either the same rater or the composite (e.g., average) of the two raters. In other words, those couples who score highest in terms of marital accord will consistently be identified by using data from either rater separately or from a combination of the two data sources. Thus, this inconsistency is measurement error under the absolute approach but is irrelevant to reliability under the relative approach. Hence, prior to assessing score reliability, it is necessary to determine how one intends to interpret the scores from the assessment device.

Finally, reliability is relative to the extent of generalization. Measurement error may arise from many different sources. One way to remove measurement errors is through standardization and limiting our generalization. Hence, behavioral data obtained under controlled conditions such as observations in clinical settings or measurement of bio-indicators of behaviors can be expected to contain less measurement error. But this reduction in measurement error may come with a price. The more controlled the conditions under which data are gathered, the less authentic is the behavioral data. In other words, data from a very controlled laboratory situation may not be applicable to real-world settings. For example, observing an ADHD child's play behavior with a researcher in a laboratory setting will undoubtedly yield results that are different from the child's behavior at home or at school when other individuals are present and in which other situations may arise. Similarly, measurement errors can be reduced through standardization, which minimizes potential errors due to observer bias, background, perspectives, item errors, and various interactions among these sources. These standardization steps also have the potential to render the observed behavior different from natural behaviors. This is similar to the classic tradeoff between internal and external validity in conventional experimentation. Hence, reliability is relative to the intended extent of generalization of the data (Kane, 1982).

INDICES OF SCORE RELIABILITY

Statistically, score reliability has been expressed in a number of ways. A most common approach is to express it in the form of a reliability coefficient. An alternative method is to express reliability in another coefficient-like index called the signal-to-noise ratio and another related index called the separation index (Wright, 1996), which is the square root of the signal-to-noise ratio. Finally, reliability can be expressed from the perspective of its absence in the form of measurement error. Under the classical theory (e.g., Gulliksen, 1950) as well as the generalizability theory of measurement (Cronbach, Gleser, Nanda, & Rajaratnam, 1972), the variance of scores obtained from behavioral measures can be decomposed into true variance (σ_T^2) and error variance (σ_E^2). True variance reflects the amount of score variation due to true differences in behaviors among subjects, across time, or across other types of objects of measurement. Error variance reflects the amount of score variation due to factors unrelated to differences in behaviors. The reliability coefficient expresses the relative magnitudes of these two components as a proportion of the observed variance being true variance. Specifically:

$$\text{Reliability coefficient} = \rho_{XT}^2 = \frac{\sigma_T^2}{\sigma_T^2 + \sigma_E^2}. \quad (1)$$

As a proportion, the values of a reliability coefficient range between 0 and 1, with 1 indicating the complete absence of error variance and 0 indicating the complete absence of true variance. The signal-to-noise ratio expresses a similar idea. Instead of a proportion, it compares the magnitude of the true variance against that of the error variance (Brennan & Kane, 1977):

$$\text{Signal-to-noise ratio} = \Psi = \frac{\sigma_T^2}{\sigma_E^2}. \quad (2)$$

The larger the value of the signal-to-noise ratio, the larger is the relative size of the true variance, and, thus, the amount of measurement error is smaller.[1] Finally, score reliability also may be expressed in the form of its absence through the standard error of measurement (SEM). SEM is the square root of the error variance, and it can be estimated either directly under the generalizability theoretical approach or indirectly through the reliability coefficient under classical theory:

$$\text{SEM} = \sqrt{\sigma_E^2} = \sigma_X\sqrt{1 - \rho_{XT}^2}, \quad (3)$$

where σ_X is the standard deviation of the observed scores, and σ_{XT}^2 is the reliability coefficient. The *SEM* is also sometimes described as the margin of error and can be used to build confidence intervals around the scores. For example, the 95% confidence interval for a given score is:

$$95\% \text{ C.I.} = x \pm 1.96 \, (SEM) \quad (4)$$

where x is the observed score, and the 95% C.I. can be interpreted as the range within which there is a 95% chance that the true score falls.

Various measurement theories differ in how these various indices are emphasized and estimated. With classical theory,

the focus is on the estimation of the reliability coefficient. Once an estimate of the reliability coefficient is obtained, other indices such as the standard error of measurement can be estimated based on the reliability coefficient. With generalizability theory, the focus is on the estimation of the magnitudes of the true variance and error variance. From these components, reliability coefficients (called *G*-coefficients) can be built, and SEM can be estimated. In the Item Response theoretical approach, only the SEM is of primary interest. Other indices are generally not estimated.

Classical Approach

The classical approach to estimating score reliability is to focus on the estimation of the reliability coefficient. This is accomplished through the correlation between scores on two "classically parallel" tests, which are essentially two interchangeable instruments whose only differences are random (cf. Lord & Novick, 1968). Algebraically, the simple Pearson's correlation between the scores on two such parallel measures can be demonstrated to be numerically equivalent to the proportion of the observed variance being true variance; that is, equivalent to the reliability coefficient. If such parallel assessment instruments can be found, we can estimate the reliability coefficient of the scores on either of these two interchangeable instruments.

The main task to estimating the reliability coefficient of a particular set of behavioral scores obtained from a particular assessment device or set of procedures or protocol is, thus, to find another assessment device, procedure, or protocol that is parallel or interchangeable with this one. This is conventionally accomplished for paper-and-pencil tests and/ or self-report scales through several common strategies: the test-retest method, the equivalent forms method, and the internal consistency method. With the test-retest method, the same assessment device is given to the same group twice, and the two sets of scores are considered scores from two parallel assessment devices. Because the same instrument is given twice, there is strong rationale to argue that indeed the two instruments are interchangeable and that the only differences between the two sets of scores are random errors. The only drawback with this method is that the sample, and thus true variance, may have changed between the two administrations. To maintain the interchangeability between the two assessment instruments, it is necessary that the true scores and thus true variance does not change between the two measures. Because behavioral assessment data are often quite unstable over time, this strategy is not often useful. However, for behaviors that are quite stable over time, the test-retest strategy can be employed.

A second strategy in the classical approach is the equivalent forms method. With this method, we deliberately construct two parallel (i.e., interchangeable) forms of the same instrument and administer both to the same group of individuals at the same time. The correlation between the scores on the two versions is then used as an estimate of score reliability coefficient. This strategy is readily adaptable to behavioral assessment when the assessment involves an observer or rater (as opposed to biological monitors or self-report). It can be argued that two similarly trained observers using an identical set of behavioral definitions observing the same set of behaviors following an identical protocol may be considered an analogue of two equivalent forms of the same assessment device; that is, the two observers are analogous to two parallel forms. Thus, the correlation between the scores from two similarly trained observers can be considered an estimate of score reliability—provided that the two observers have been trained to the point of interchangeability—and thus considered parallel.

The third strategy of internal consistency methods, parallel tests, are simulated from within a single test by dividing the items in a paper-and-pencil test into subscales and assume that they are interchangeable. The correlations between these parallel subscales are corrected through the Spearman-Brown prophecy formula to estimate the reliability coefficient for the overall scores.[2] A behavioral assessment analogue of this strategy can be obtained when no observer is involved (e.g., biological monitor) and relatively stable data are collected repeatedly over time (e.g., daily record of dietary behaviors). Data over time can be randomly divided into two sets of data and treated as parallel assessment devices, provided that the behavior of interest is not expected to have changed during the time period. The correlation of scores from these parallel assessments would be corrected through the Spearman-Brown prophecy formula to estimate the reliability coefficient of the composite scores over time. The Spearman-Brown formula is:

$$\text{Corrected–reliability coefficient} = \frac{K\rho_{XT}^2}{1-(K-1)\rho_{XT}^2}, \quad (5)$$

where K is the factor by which the length of the instrument is to be changed, and ρ_{XT}^2 is the reliability coefficient estimated based on the part assessment. For the behavioral assessment application in which N observation points over time are divided into two parallel assessments, ρ_{XT}^2 would be the correlation between the scores on the two parallel assessments, and K would be 2.

Because the classical approach only considers random measurement error, results of these approaches are not appropriate for behavioral data intended to be interpreted against some absolute standard or in a criterion-referenced manner. The reliability coefficient would indicate the proportion of true variance if and only if the scores are to be interpreted in a relative or norm-referenced manner. The estimates of reliability coefficients obtained through these strategies can be applied to Equations 3 and 4 to obtain confidence intervals. Additionally, the square roots of these reliability coefficients provide estimates of the correlation between observed and true scores. If the correlation is very high, one can argue that the observed scores approach a linear transformation of the true scores; that is, observed scores are true scores expressed on some metric.

Interobserver "Reliability" and Classical Approach

Because the classical approach relies on the strategy of using parallel assessment instruments to attain an estimate of the score reliability coefficient, it is inherently unable to accommodate such concepts as coefficients of stability, equivalence, internal consistency, and interobserver reliability. That is, in order to estimate the reliability coefficient of the scores, we need to assume that the scores are already stable when we use the test-retest strategy, that the two forms are already equivalent when we use the equivalent forms strategy, and that the items are already internally consistent when we use the internal consistency strategy. These assumptions are necessary conditions for the estimation of score reliability. The same inherent limitation applies to the so-called interobserver reliability approach in behavioral assessment. If we treat two observers as two equivalent forms, the correlation of scores from the two observers would provide an estimate of reliability coefficient. However, we logically cannot use that same piece of information to assess whether the observers are interchangeable (i.e., whether they are consistent with one another) because in order to use the correlation as an estimate of *score* reliability coefficient, we necessarily assume that the observers are indeed interchangeable.

Shouldn't we be concerned about whether observers are interchangeable? Observer interchangeability is indeed important, as its absence would indicate an important source of measurement error. However, observer interchangeability is not score reliability, the latter being a concept related to the precision of scores, not quality of observers. Thus, concepts such as interobserver reliability, stability, equivalence, and internal consistency are best considered important formative characteristics of an assessment procedure. A reliability coefficient is the summative evaluation of the quality of the scores. Measurement errors may come from a lack of observer interchangeability, lack of stability, lack of internal consistency, and so on. If we are willing to assume that two observers are sufficiently trained and that they are already interchangeable, the correlation between their scores would be an estimate of classical score reliability. If we are unwilling to assume that the two observers are interchangeable, the correlation will be a measure of their interchangeability and cannot logically be considered at the same time a reliability coefficient of scores.

For formative purposes, such as observer training, the Pearson's product-moment correlation coefficient of scores between two observers may be used as a measure of observer interchangeability. This correlation is indicative of the consistency of scores between the two observers as long as scores are interpreted in a norm-referenced manner. This is because only random measurement errors are considered in the Pearson's correlation. For criterion-referenced interpretations, we need to consider systematic measurement errors as well as random errors. In this case, correlation-based measures such as Pearson's correlation would not be appropriate. One would use indices that consider both random and systematic errors. The proportion agreement index (p_o) is perhaps the most popular example of an interobserver agreement index:

$$p_o = \frac{\text{Frequency of agreements}}{\text{(Frequency of agreements)} + \text{(Frequency of disagreements)}} \quad (6)$$

The problem with this index is that it is often inflated by chance agreement. For example, imagine that two observers are observing a behavior that in reality occurs in 10 of the intervals in a 100-interval session. The first observer reports that the behavior occurs in 10 of the 100 intervals. The second observer did not record any of the behavior occurrences. The frequency of agreements in this example is found to be equal for 90 of the 100 intervals, and the frequency of disagreements is found to be equal to 10. Thus, using the equation above, the proportion agreement index would be equal to 90%. Although the second observer did not record a single occurrence of behavior, the interobserver agreement using the above equation appears to be rather large at 90% due to chance agreement. In order to correct for chance, the kappa (κ) coefficient, which is the proportion agreement index, p_o, with the proportion of chance agreements (p_c) removed, can be utilized:

$$\kappa = \frac{p_o - p_c}{1 - p_c} \quad (7)$$

Caution also should be taken to ensure that the unit of analysis used in the evaluation of observers formatively will ultimately contribute to the overall summative score reliability. For example, consider a situation in which behavioral data are gathered through observations in a number of observation sessions, and decisions are to be made or analyses are to be done on the session scores. To ensure observer interchangeability, we train observers and gather data by dividing each observation session into many small time intervals. We then calculate the proportion agreement index value based on the scores in these intervals. The result is a measure of observer interchangeability at the interval level, not the session score level. Fortunately, in this case, a high degree of interval interchangeability will enhance session score reliability. However, the reverse is not the case. That is, if observer interchangeability is gauged at the session level and we are to use interval scores for decisions and treatment, a high session level interchangeability may not enhance the reliability of interval scores. Overall, it is important to ensure that, when gauging the degree of observer interchangeability, we use data at the same unit and level as the scores whose reliability we wish to eventually evaluate. It is also important to note that measurement errors come from many potential sources and observers are but one of many. Thus, a high degree of observer interchangeability will enhance, but not guarantee, high score reliability (Reckase, 1995).

Generalizability Approach

Classical methods of estimating score reliability coefficients are inherently summative in nature and cannot accommodate concepts that specify potential origins of errors such as those implied by the concepts of stability, internal consistency, or observer reliability. As such, a low score reliability coefficient only indicates a large proportion of random error variance. It does not provide any information as to the possible sources of these errors despite the exact method used to approximate parallel assessment instruments. Additionally, the reliability coefficient estimated applies only to the specific score under investigation and is only appropriate if the score is interpreted in a norm-referenced, relative manner. Another limitation is that data for the estimation of reliability must be collected in a fully-crossed design. For example, when we use observers as parallel assessments to estimate reliability coefficient through the correlation between the scores from the two observers, both observers must observe and score all subjects in the study. This is not always feasible in behavioral assessment.

Given the multifaceted nature of behavioral assessment, the generalizability approach is particularly appropriate for the assessment of score reliabilities (e.g., Suen, Logan, Neisworth, & Bagnato, 1995; Suen, Lu, Neisworth, & Bagnato, 1993). All the problems related to the classical approach described above are removed or minimized in the generalizability approach (Brennan, 1983; Cronbach, Gleser, Nanda, & Rajaratnam, 1972; Shavelson & Webb, 1989). This is accomplished through a two-step process. In the first step, called the G-study (generalizability-study) stage, sample data are collected as appropriate for the intended extent of score generalization (e.g., only trained observers are used, and they observe only certain well-defined behaviors). Based on these sample data, the magnitudes of all variance components implicit in the defined data collection design are estimated statistically through analyses of variance procedures. Examination of the magnitudes of these estimated variance components helps evaluate possible sources of measurement error, and steps might be taken to revise the assessment method to minimize these errors. In the second step, called the D-study (decision-study) stage, the variance component estimates from the G-study stage are applied to specific expected usage scenarios (e.g., norm-referenced or criterion-referenced, cross or nested design, number of observers used). For each of the scenarios, the final variance components are estimated based on those from the G-study. These final components are then sorted into those considered true variances, those considered error variances, and those considered irrelevant to the particular scenario. Reliability coefficients, called G-coefficients, are then built by dividing true variances by the sum of true and error variances, in the manner of Equation 1, for each scenario. Theoretically, an unlimited number of possible G- and D-studies exist for the same set of data from a particular behavioral assessment, leading to a theoretically infinite number of possible reliability coefficients (G-coefficients), each appropriate for a very specific usage scenario. Below, we focus on several common behavioral assessment scenarios.

Single (Observer) Facet Design

A common behavioral assessment situation is one in which one or more trained observers either record the occurrences or nonoccurrences of a particular behavior or rate the extent or prevalence of a particular behavior on a rating scale under standardized controlled conditions. Given that the conditions for observations are standardized and no attempt is made to generalize the assessment outcomes beyond the controlled conditions, the only sources of measurement error of concern in this case are systematic and random errors due to observers. This forms what is referred to as a single observer facet case.

The most appropriate data collection design for the G-study for this case is a cross design in which a sample of k trained observers (o) are used to record or rate the target behavior of

a sample of n persons (p). Both k and n must be greater than 1, otherwise there is no variance to speak of, and should be as large as feasible. The resulting n by k data matrix is then submitted to a two-way analysis of variance. The results of this analysis are three mean square statistics: mean square due to persons (MS_p), mean square due to observers (MS_o), and mean square due to the interaction between persons and observers (MS_{po}).[3] Based on these MS values, the variance component due to person, observer, and interaction can be estimated as follows, respectively:

$$\hat{\sigma}_p^2 = \frac{MS_p - MS_{po}}{k}, \quad (8)$$

$$\hat{\sigma}_o^2 = \frac{MS_o - MS_{po}}{n}, \quad (9)$$

$$\hat{\sigma}_{po}^2 = MS_{po}, \quad (10)$$

The relative magnitude of each of these components can be compared to determine sources of score variation.

These variance components can be used to assess reliabilities for specific D-study scenarios. One general scenario is to use trained observers like those used in the G-study to generate scores that will be used in a norm-referenced manner. For this D-study scenario, the reliability coefficient can be estimated through:

$$\text{Norm-referenced G-coefficient} = \frac{\hat{\sigma}_p^2}{\hat{\sigma}_p^2 + \frac{\hat{\sigma}_{po}^2}{N_o}}, \quad (11)$$

where N_o is the number of observers intended to be used for each person observed in the scenario. For instance, if in future applications of the observation procedure, only one trained observer will be used for each person, and assessments will be made based on the scores from the single observer, N_o would be set to 1 in Equation 11. If future applications of the assessment instrument will be such that decisions on an individual will be based on the average scores from two observers, N_o would equal 2, and so on. As consistent with the spirit of the Spearman-Brown formula (i.e., Equation 5), scores that are based on the average across many observers would result in higher G-coefficients than those based on few observers.

If scores from future applications of this assessment instrument will be interpreted in an absolute or criterion-referenced manner, the reliability coefficient would instead be estimated through:

Criterion-referenced G-coefficient

$$= \frac{\hat{\sigma}_p^2}{\hat{\sigma}_p^2 + \dfrac{\hat{\sigma}_o^2}{N_o} + \dfrac{\hat{\sigma}_{po}^2}{N_o}}, \quad (12)$$

As expressed through the difference between Equations 11 and 12, criterion-referenced reliabilities can be expected to be less than or equal to their norm-referenced counterparts because systematic error (in this case σ_o^2) is irrelevant in norm-referenced situations but is a source of error in criterion-referenced situations. If future assessments are to be conducted so that different trained observers or sets of observers will be used for different persons, the resulting D-study design is a nested design in which observers are nested in persons. In this scenario, only Equation 12 will apply regardless of norm- or criterion-referenced interpretation.

Single (Item) Facet Design

Another common behavioral assessment situation is to have a person report or rate his or her own behaviors on a standardized checklist or scale following standardized procedures. No external observer is involved. This situation is entirely analogous to the observer facet situation described above, with items replacing observers. Hence, all G-study and D-study procedures described above apply to this situation as well by substituting items for observers (i.e., replace subscript o with subscript i and po with pi in Equations 8 through 12). An interesting aspect of the item facet situation is with the norm-referenced D-study scenario. For this scenario, the G-coefficient analogous to Equation 11 is:

$$\text{Norm-referenced G-coefficient} = \frac{\hat{\sigma}_p^2}{\hat{\sigma}_p^2 + \dfrac{\hat{\sigma}_{pi}^2}{N_i}}, \quad (13)$$

In this particular case, if N_i (i.e., number of items) is set to equal the number of items on the standardized checklist or scale, which implies that decisions will be made only based on the summation or composite score from the entire scale or checklist, the G-coefficient estimated based on Equation 13 is mathematically equivalent to Hoyt's intraclass correlation coefficient (Hoyt, 1941):

$$\text{Hoyt's intraclass correlation} = \frac{MS_p - MS_{po}}{MS_p}, \quad (14)$$

which is also mathematically equivalent to the popular Cronbach's alpha coefficient (Cronbach, 1951). If all the items on the checklist or scale are dichotomously scored, in

addition to being equivalent to Hoyt's intraclass correlation and Cronbach's alpha, this G-coefficient is also equivalent to KR-20 (Kuder & Richardson, 1937), which is another commonly used coefficient in classical paper-and-pencil tests.

Two-Facet Design

A slightly more complex but common behavioral assessment situation is one in which a number of trained observers record or rate the behaviors of a person on a standardized checklist or scale following standardized procedures. The potential sources of measurement errors are those related to observers and those related items on the checklist or scale. The most informative G-study data collection design for this situation is a fully-crossed design in which n_o observers observe or rate all of n_p persons on all n_i items on the scale or checklist. In this case, n_o, n_p, and n_i must all be greater than 1. The n_o by n_p by n_i data matrix is then submitted to a 3-way repeated measures ANOVA, which would yield seven mean squares as follows: MS_p, MS_o, MS_i, MS_{po}, MS_{pi}, MS_{oi}, and MS_{poi}. The seven corresponding variance components can be estimated through:

$$\hat{\sigma}_p^2 = \frac{MS_p - MS_{pi} - MS_{po} + MS_{poi}}{n_i n_o}, \quad (15)$$

$$\hat{\sigma}_i^2 = \frac{MS_i - MS_{pi} - MS_{oi} + MS_{poi}}{n_p n_o}, \quad (16)$$

$$\hat{\sigma}_o^2 = \frac{MS_o - MS_{po} - MS_{oi} + MS_{poi}}{n_i n_p}, \quad (17)$$

$$\hat{\sigma}_{pi}^2 = \frac{MS_{pi} - MS_{poi}}{n_o}, \quad (18)$$

$$\hat{\sigma}_{po}^2 = \frac{MS_{po} - MS_{poi}}{n_i}, \quad (19)$$

$$\hat{\sigma}_{oi}^2 = \frac{MS_{oi} - MS_{poi}}{n_p}, \quad (20)$$

$$\hat{\sigma}_{poi}^2 = MS_{poi}, \quad (21)$$

With these seven variance components, numerous potential D-study scenarios can be investigated. We will focus on only a few common scenarios. For norm-referenced interpretation in which scores and decisions are based on the average of N_o observers on N_i items and all observers score all persons on all items (i.e., cross design):

Norm-referenced G-coefficient

$$= \frac{\hat{\sigma}_p^2}{\hat{\sigma}_p^2 + \dfrac{\hat{\sigma}_{pi}^2}{N_i} + \dfrac{\hat{\sigma}_{po}^2}{N_o} + \dfrac{\hat{\sigma}_{poi}^2}{N_i N_o}}. \quad (22)$$

The criterion-referenced counterpart to Equation 22 is:

Criterion-referenced G-coefficient

$$= \frac{\hat{\sigma}_p^2}{\hat{\sigma}_p^2 + \dfrac{\hat{\sigma}_i^2}{N_i} + \dfrac{\hat{\sigma}_o^2}{N_o} + \dfrac{\hat{\sigma}_{pi}^2}{N_i} + \dfrac{\hat{\sigma}_{po}^2}{N_o} + \dfrac{\hat{\sigma}_{oi}^2}{N_i N_o} + \dfrac{\hat{\sigma}_{poi}^2}{N_i N_o}}. \quad (23)$$

If the observers used are considered fixed—that is, no generalization is made beyond the observers employed and scores are interpreted only relative to the specific observers used (e.g., teachers, therapists)—

Norm-referenced G-coefficient

$$= \frac{\hat{\sigma}_p^2 + \dfrac{\hat{\sigma}_{po}^2}{N_o}}{\hat{\sigma}_p^2 + \dfrac{\hat{\sigma}_{pi}^2}{N_i} + \dfrac{\hat{\sigma}_{po}^2}{N_o} + \dfrac{\hat{\sigma}_{poi}^2}{N_i N_o}}, \text{ and} \quad (24)$$

Criterion-referenced G-coefficient

$$= \frac{\hat{\sigma}_p^2 + \dfrac{\hat{\sigma}_{po}^2}{N_o}}{\hat{\sigma}_p^2 + \dfrac{\hat{\sigma}_i^2}{N_i} + \dfrac{\hat{\sigma}_{pi}^2}{N_i} + \dfrac{\hat{\sigma}_{po}^2}{N_o} + \dfrac{\hat{\sigma}_{oi}^2}{N_i N_o} + \dfrac{\hat{\sigma}_{poi}^2}{N_i N_o}}. \quad (25)$$

If observers are considered random and are nested within subjects, Equation 23 would be applied to both norm-referenced and criterion-referenced interpretations. Similarly, if observers are considered fixed and are nested, Equation 25 would be applied. The potential D-study scenarios are too numerous for this situation to discuss in detail. Suffice to say that the above scenarios are the common ones. Other scenarios might involve considering the items fixed, having observers nested in persons, having observers nested in items, and so on. For detailed treatments of various complex designs, consult specialized texts such as Brennan (1983), Cronbach et al. (1972), and Shavelson and Webb (1981, 1989).

Estimating True Scores Directly

The focus of both the classical and generalizability approaches is to estimate reliability coefficients and variance components. Although it is possible to estimate the true behavioral score (T) from the observed score (X) through:

$$\hat{T} = \hat{\rho}_{XT}^2 (X - \hat{\mu}_X) + \hat{\mu}_X, \quad (26)$$

where $\hat{\rho}_{XT}^2$ is the classical reliability coefficient or the G-coefficient as appropriate and $\hat{\mu}_X$ is the mean observed scores, this is generally not done. This is because the resulting true scores will only be a linear transformation of the observed scores; that is, observed scores expressed on a different metric. Both classical and generalizability theory are interested in describing the precision of the observed score in representing the true score. True scores in these two theories are defined as mean observed scores. As such, no attempt is made to refer to some latent covert construct. Hence, these approaches are relevant to both sample and sign measures of behavior.

Other approaches, however, attempt to estimate the latent construct scores directly. These techniques are generally not concerned about the quality of the observed scores. Instead, observed data are used as the basis to estimate the underlying "true" covert construct scores. These techniques are hence only appropriate for sign measures of behavior.

One such approach is an application of factor analysis. While classical and generalizability approaches attempt to partition observed variance into true variance and error variance, factor analysis further partitions true variance into common factor variance and unique factor variance. The focus is to examine the portion that is due to the common factor. Unique variance and error variance are generally not separated but are considered together as the residual. As such, factor analysis is interested in the relationship between the observed score and the latent construct. The latent construct may or may not be the intended one; this is a question of validity, which will be addressed later in this chapter. Factor analysis is most often used to provide a piece of validity evidence. However, it also can be viewed as a method for estimating the "true" covert construct score directly. This is generally accomplished through the factor scoring method in exploratory factor analysis.

Another approach that attempts to estimate latent construct true scores directly is the item response theoretic (IRT) approach. The general IRT approach can be viewed as a nonlinear version of factor analysis in which items are scored dichotomously (see Kamata, 2001; McDonald, 1999). Through a process somewhat similar to logistic regression, IRT approaches attempt to estimate a person's true latent score based on the observed pattern of his or her behavior scores. There are a number of statistical models in IRT. Of particular relevance to behavioral assessment is the faceted Rasch model developed by Linacre (1989). This model is applicable to situations in which a number of observers record or rate the behaviors of a number of persons on a number of items on a checklist or scale. Through maximum likelihood estimation procedures in the faceted Rasch model, the latent true score of each person, the difficulty of each item, and the leniency/stringency of each observer can be estimated. Errors of estimation are expressed in the forms of a standard error and a fit statistic.

POTENTIAL SOURCES OF MEASUREMENT ERRORS

Although it is possible to identify sources of measurement error in the generalizability approach, these will only inform the researcher as to the possible sources of error. To maximize reliability, steps should be taken from the start in the development of the behavioral assessment protocol. Measurement errors may arise from many different sources. By and large, establishing a standard procedure and adhering to that procedure will maximize reliability. Other commonsense practices such as making sure that behavioral definitions are unambiguous, making sure wording used in checklists and scales are clear and easily understood, minimizing interference and situational variability during assessment, and so on will all help. In behavioral assessment, steps should be taken to minimize two well-known sources of potential measurement errors.

One source of measurement error is the use of observers. Observers bring with them personal perspectives, biases, prejudices, habits, and various random interpretive or careless errors. These errors can be minimized through training. Typically, two or more observers are trained simultaneously by having them practice the application of given behavioral definitions on past behaviors, such as those on videotapes. They are trained until they are essentially interchangeable or their scores are interchangeable with those from a master observer. Such training will minimize random errors and some forms of systematic errors and will hence maximize score reliability. However, caution should be taken to make sure that such training does not compromise the validity of the scores (e.g., Suen, Logan, Neisworth, Bagnato, 1995). Specifically, observers should be trained to be interchangeable only if the specific observers used are expected to be interchangeable. In some observation situations, different observers with different perspectives are used in order to obtain the benefit of different perspectives (e.g., parent and professional rating of children or representatives from different constituent groups in an interview).

Another potential source of measurement error is in the behavior recording method used. Certain methods such as

time sampling are known to contain systematic errors. The use of these methods reduces the reliability of scores, particularly when scores are to be interpreted in an absolute, criterion-referenced manner. Specifically, it is generally known that in the measurement of behavior duration or prevalence, partial-interval sampling, in which the observer notes whether a behavior has or has not occurred during each equally timed interval in an observation session, will tend to produce an overestimate. Whole-interval sampling, in which the observer notes whether the behavior has occurred continuously during the entire interval, will tend to produce an underestimate. Momentary time sampling, in which the behavior of interest is observed only at one instance within an interval, will tend to produce an unbiased estimate. That is, the former two methods contain systematic and random errors, whereas momentary time sampling contains only random errors. These errors can be minimized but not removed by using very short intervals in the observation. Thus, to maximize reliability when duration or prevalence of behavior is of interest, these methods should be avoided in favor of continuous observation. If used, momentary time sampling is preferred. Momentary time sampling with very short intervals leads to the least amount of measurement error among these techniques. It is also known that these methods systematically underrepresent frequencies of behavior regardless of which specific method is used. There are some possible remedies to these methods, but these remedies generally require some degree of continuous observation and complex post hoc correction procedures based on a number of statistical assumptions (see, for example, Quera, 1989).

IMPLICATIONS OF SCORE RELIABILITY

Reliability is concerned with the precision of the scores. As such, it is primarily a quantitative concept with mathematical solutions. Although much work has been done in this area over the past century, the volume of cumulative work in this area is not necessarily indicative of its relative importance. Indeed, the importance and role of reliability in behavioral assessment varies with different situations. One such situational factor is whether the behavioral data are intended to be interpreted as a sign measure or a sample measure. If they are to be interpreted as a sign of some underlying construct, evidence of validity will be by far much more important, and reliability is only of secondary importance and may even be considered one of the many pieces of the validity puzzle. If the behavioral data are to be interpreted as a sample measure, however, reliability becomes quite important. As a sample measure, the most critical issue of quality would be one of sampling adequacy. Several questions address sampling adequacy: Is the sample sufficiently large to minimize sampling errors? Are the contents of the sample representative? Are the contents of the sample relevant? Does the way the sample data are gathered lead to a representative sample? Of these questions, the first is one of reliability. The other three are validity questions falling under the nomenclature of content-based evidence and process-based evidence, which will be discussed in the next section of this chapter.

The importance of reliability is also relative to the intended use of and potential decisions to be made based on the behavioral data. If behavioral data are to be used for research purposes only or if only group statistics are to be used, a very high reliability coefficient may or may not be important. First, the reliability of group statistics such as group mean scores can be expected to be higher than the reliability of the scores for individuals. Therefore, a low reliability coefficient, which indicates the reliability for the individual scores, does not automatically imply a low reliability for the group statistic. In general, the larger the group, the higher is the reliability of the group mean. Second, for the purpose of research, high reliability will enhance statistical power in significance testing. However, statistical power is also enhanced by having larger sample sizes, larger effect sizes, and more homogeneous subjects. Thus, reliability is helpful but not a determining factor in statistical power. If statistical significance is found, whether the reliability coefficient is too high or too low becomes moot for this purpose.

Finally, having a high reliability coefficient is generally important when we use behavioral assessment data to make clinical decisions and/or take actions regarding an individual, especially when the potential consequences of these decisions and/or actions are serious. Even here, we need to keep reliability in perspective. Having a low reliability does not mean that we cannot make individual decisions and/or take actions. It means we have an obligation to take the large margin of potential measurement error into consideration when we make these decisions. With high reliability, we can make fine judgments and comparisons. With low reliability, only coarse judgments and comparisons are possible. A researcher should be cautious in making inferences from data with low reliability. There is really no such thing as a minimum level of reliability coefficient for all situations. Any nonzero reliability coefficient indicates that using the behavioral assessment procedure will produce data that are better than random guessing. The question we need to consider is whether the coarseness of the data is worth the efforts put into gathering the behavioral data. In this regard, the following statement by Thorndike and Hagen (1969, p. 194) is quite illuminating:

> If we must make some decision or take some course of action with respect to an individual, we will do so in terms of the best information we have, however unreliable it may be, provided only that the reliability is better than zero.

Similarly, the problem of overemphasizing the role of reliability was observed by Lindquist as early as 65 years ago:

> Reliability coefficients can usually be easily determined. For this reason, there has been a tendency to give a great deal of prominence to the concept of reliability, not because of its significance, but because it is so easy to measure and describe quantitatively. . . . The reliabilities of a number of assessments intended for the same purpose may, in fact, even be negatively related to their validities. . . . If one assessment can be shown to be more valid than another for a given purpose, then it is to be preferred for that purpose, regardless of the comparative reliabilities of the two assessments (Lindquist, 1936, p. 99).

GATHERING EVIDENCE OF VALIDITY

The concept of validity has undergone numerous changes in the twentieth century (see Geisinger, 1992; Moss, 1992), starting from the relatively simplistic view of validity as a statistic measured through a validity coefficient in the 1930s to various complex models reflecting differing epistemologies today. Perhaps the most commonly cited model among textbooks today is what is sometimes referred to as the Trinitarian model. This is a view advocated by the 1966 Joint Committee Standards of the American Educational Research Association (AERA), American Psychological Association (APA), and the National Council on Measurement in Education (NCME) (Standards, 1966). In this perspective, validity is divided into three types: content validity, criterion-related validity, and construct validity. Content validity refers to the extent to which the content of the test is representative and relevant to the domain of interest. When applied to behavioral assessment, it refers to the extent to which the actual behaviors being observed are representative and relevant to the larger domain or repertoire of potential behaviors that one can observe. Criterion-related validity refers to the extent to which the results of the assessment instrument correlate statistically with an appropriate external criterion measure. In behavioral assessment, an example might be how highly scores on an observation scale correlate with some other accepted measure of the construct of interest. Finally, according to the 1966 standards, construct validity refers to the extent to which an instrument measures what it purports to measure.

Since 1966, three more joint committees have produced new sets of standards in 1974, 1985, and then again in 1999. The 1974 committee attempted to clarify the definitions of content validity and construct validity to make them more measurable and precise (Standards, 1974). Construct validity was further defined to be an accumulation of evidence based on formulating and testing hypotheses. Verifying the construct validity of a measure was considered an ongoing process of collecting evidence for the assessment. An important contribution of this committee was the first recognition of the social consequences of test use, including issues of test bias and adverse impact.

Despite its popularity among textbook writers, the Trinitarian model is generally rejected by measurement specialists today. In fact, for the first time since 1966, the 1985 standards introduced the first new definition of validity (Standards, 1985). Validity was no longer considered to be of varying types. Instead, validity became recognized as a unitary concept that can be supported through various processes in which various types of evidence—content-related evidence, criterion-related evidence, and construct-related evidence—are gathered. Although the 1985 definition was somewhat vague, this unitary definition of validity has continued to be the most widely accepted view of validity today, particularly with the refinements of Messick's theory.

Messick (1989) introduced a faceted model of validity that included both the interpretation and use of the assessment. For the first time, the consequences of participating in a testing situation were considered in measurement theory. Similar to previous definitions, Messick suggested that researchers should accumulate evidence—including content-related evidence, criterion-related evidence, and construct-related evidence—to support the interpretation of a score. Again, as discussed above, Messick theorized that rather than there being several types of validity, construct validity of a measure can be supported through various types of evidence. Regarding the social consequences of assessment, Messick favored collecting evidence regarding the appropriate use or utility of the assessment and value implications or the consequences of a particular interpretation of the assessment.

Although Messick's model dominates the views of many modern validity theorists, other alternative models have emerged. Kane (1992) developed a theory of validation as a process of systematic arguments. According to Kane, test designers provide evidence through these arguments supporting possible interpretations of scores and refuting competing interpretations. Although a given interpretative argument, and thus corresponding validity, cannot be proven, enough evidence should be collected to support that the interpretative argument is plausible given the obtainable evidence. Similarly, Cronbach (1988) also viewed validity as a system of arguments. These models, based on a social rhetoric perspective, are strikingly different than the statistical data used in yesteryear to support the validity of a measurement.

In behavioral assessment, theorists also conceive validity as having a large verbal component. Cone (1998) theorized that validity is a value judgment or "verbal behavior reflecting the believability of empirical and theoretical evidence supporting the characterization of assessment instruments as discriminative for certain behaviors of persons having contact with them" (p. 37). Cone theorized that several types of validation should be performed in order to support the overall validity of the behavioral assessment. Consistent with Messick's theory, Cone emphasizes the importance of consequential validation, which looks at the social consequences of the assessment. Representational validation refers to the extent to which the assessment instrument adequately represents the construct of interest. This category subsumes previously used definitions of content validity, convergent and discriminant validity, and face validity. Elaborative validation analyzes the usefulness of the measure and the meaning behind the data. This type of validation subsumes previously used definitions of construct validity and criterion-related validity.

The most recent standards of the AERA, APA, and NCME (Standards, 1999) combine several theories. Validation is defined as "the degree to which evidence and theory support the interpretations of test scores entailed by proposed uses of tests" (p. 9). Validation once again, is viewed as a unitary concept that can be supported through the collection of different types of evidence. Validation is an ongoing process that can never be proven. Rather, judgment is made after compilation of much evidence to determine whether a given interpretation of an instrument is valid. The standards specifically discuss five sources of validity evidence: evidence based on the content of the assessment, evidence based on response processes, evidence based on internal structure, evidence based on relations to other variables, and evidence based on consequences of the assessment. Table 3.1 concisely summarizes some of the similarities and differences between traditional pencil-and-paper tests and behavioral assessment instruments regarding these five types of validity evidence, which are discussed further below. Note that Table 3.1 is meant to be illustrative but not exhaustive.

TYPES OF VALIDITY EVIDENCE

Evidence Based on Content of the Assessment

Evidence based on assessment content is similar to the previously used terms *content validity* or *content-related evidence.* This source of evidence analyzes the relationship between an intended domain or construct and the content of the assessment, including "themes, wording, and format of

TABLE 3.1   Comparison of Traditional Versus Behavioral Assessments Regarding Validity Evidence

Type of Validity Evidence	Traditional Pencil-and-paper Tests	Behavioral Assessment Instruments
Evidence Based on Content	• Themes, wording, and format of items • Guidelines for administration and scoring	• Themes and wording of individual behavioral codes • Format of coding sheet • Instructions for observers • Method of time sampling
Evidence Based on Response Processes	• Evidence showing the test-taker is responding to items using the appropriate processes	• Evidence showing the observers are rating in the appropriate manner • Observer training to reduce drift, bias, and fatigue
Evidence Based on Internal Structure	• Factor analysis	• Not assessed in molecular signs/samples or molar samples • Same as for traditional tests for molar signs
Evidence Based on Relations to Other Variables	• Convergent and discriminant evidence, multitrait multimethod • Structural equation modeling • Nomological net	• Same as for traditional tests
Evidence Based on Consequences	• Consequences to the test-taker • Hit rate, sensitivity, specificity, predictive power • Unintended consequences to individual/social system	• Consequences to the observed individual • Hit rate, sensitivity, specificity, predictive power • Treatment utility • Unintended consequences to individual/social system

items, tasks, or questions on a test, as well as the guidelines for procedures regarding administration and scoring" (Standards, 1999). In traditional assessments, this type of evidence is dependent upon how representative and relevant the item sample is to the universe of all possible items measuring the given construct. In behavioral assessment, evidence based on content includes the behaviors sampled, the instructions given to the observers, and the method of time sampling. In analogue observation assessments, the settings that are sampled also may be included in evidence based on content. Both the entire coding system and the individual behavioral codes can be evaluated in terms of relevance and representation. In terms of the individual behavioral codes, how evidence related to content is viewed depends on the epistemological view of sign versus sample as well as whether the level being considered is molecular or molar.

In most cases, researchers utilizing an instrument analyzing molecular samples of behavior need to be less concerned with evidence related to the content of the assessment. For example, if a researcher is interested in the number of times a person smokes a cigarette, the molecular sample of "number of cigarettes smoked" is the object of measurement. In this instance, the object of measurement is equivalent to the domain, and therefore it is unnecessary to provide validity evidence related to the assessment content. However, one needs to be aware of all the possible environmental stimuli that may threaten the results of the instrument. For example, if the researcher only watches smoking behavior while the individual is at work in a nonsmoking environment, then smoking behavior at home, which is likely to vary extremely, will be missed. In order to provide evidence related to content, the

researcher needs to explicitly identify the situational factors, such as time and location, to which the results can be generalized. If the researcher is only interested in the individual's at-work smoking behavior, then the above situation shows validity evidence related to content. If the researcher is interested in the individual's smoking behavior as a whole, then the above situation is inadequate and does not provide evidence for validity related to content. One way to ensure that the instrument is valid is to restrict the domain of the object of measurement to list all possible environmental stimuli.

If an instrument measures molecular signs, the researcher must also specify the domain including environmental factors to limit threats to validity. However, there are several additional concerns for this type of measurement. First, the researcher must provide evidence that the molecular sign is indeed an indication of the more complex construct. For example, seeing an individual drink an alcoholic beverage may or may not be indicative of the larger construct of being an alcoholic. A second precaution the researcher must take is ensuring that the molecular sign is a comprehensive sign of the construct. Say, for example, a researcher uses instances of crying to indicate the larger construct of depression. Psychologists may suggest that there are many other indicative signs of depression such as changes in sleep habits, eating habits, or other activities. Instances of crying may not be comprehensive enough to definitively state that an individual is experiencing depression.

A researcher creating an instrument with molar sample behaviors also must be concerned with ensuring the representativeness of the behavior to the domain including all environmental stimuli, as discussed previously. Similar to the concerns for molecular signs, the researcher must also ensure that the molecular samples contributing to the overall molar sample are both comprehensive and representative of the domain. For example, a researcher interested in children's aggressive acts should not only include molecular samples of hitting, kicking, biting, etc., but also verbal acts of aggression such as yelling at others, calling names, etc.

Utilizing an instrument with molar signs also has similar concerns of environmental stimuli such as time and location. Again, care must be taken to ensure that both the overall molar sign is indicative of the larger domain and that each molecular component is indicative of the molar sign. The researcher must ensure that all possible components are included in the rating scale. Each molecular sign should be relevant and representative of the domain.

Most of the evidence related to content is primarily judgmental and often built into the writing process. Experts specializing in the construct of interest can be asked to ensure that the items included in the rating scale are representative and relevant to the domain. For traditional tests, rules and algorithms often associated with test specifications can be utilized to standardize the item-writing process as much as possible. Unfortunately, this often cannot be used in the creation of behavioral assessment. Instead, the Standards recommend that experts be used to judge "the relative importance, criticality, and/or frequency" of the items. The Standards also emphasize that if the assessment instrument is being considered for a use different from what was originally intended, the appropriateness of that instrument should be reevaluated.

Evidence Based on Response Processes

In traditional tests, evidence should be gathered to show that the test taker is responding to the items using the processes the test was designed to measure. In behavioral assessment, many times raters or observers are used instead of test takers. Therefore, this type of evidence attempts to ensure that the observers are responding in the manner for which the instrument was designed. "Assessments often rely on observers or judges to record and/or evaluate examinee's performances or products. In such cases, relevant validity evidence includes the extent to which the processes of observers or judges are consistent with the intended interpretation of scores" (Standards, 1999). Threats against validity often can be reduced through strict observer training and various processes that ensure that raters respond in the manner consistent with the goal of the instrument. Evidence based on response processes includes detailed descriptions of rater training, including the processes used to reduce threats to validity. For example,

systematic errors can occur due to observer drift, observer bias, and fatigue.

Observer bias occurs when the rater responds to an item due to extraneous factors unintended by the instrument. For example, an observer may respond to an item that he or she believes is consistent with the research hypothesis (Rosenthal & Jacobson, 1968). This threat to validity can be reduced by not revealing the research hypothesis to the raters. Also, researchers should not reinforce or reward raters for responding to an item in a manner congruent with the research hypothesis. Observer bias also can result from ambiguous behavioral codes. Clear behavioral codes and intentional overtraining of raters can reduce observer bias in the behavioral assessment.

Observer drift occurs when raters systematically change the criteria by which they respond to each item. This may occur for several reasons, such as rater fatigue or changing definitions in the coding scheme as the study progresses. One way to monitor raters for observer drift is to periodically analyze inter-rater agreements. However, researchers should be aware that this would not find evidence of possible consensual drift, which occurs when more than one rater shifts the criteria simultaneously. To reduce consensual drift, raters should not be allowed to watch one another rating in order to reduce copying or being influenced by others. Periodically drilling and retraining of raters can reduce problems of both observer drift and bias. However, researchers should enforce that all raters attend training sessions so that everyone receives the same information and multiple methods of rating do not result.

Evidence Based on Internal Structure

Another important source of validity evidence comes from analysis of the internal structure of the assessment instrument. Evidence based on internal structure can be used to gain an understanding of the relationship between the structure of the assessment and the structure of the construct of interest. A construct may be composed of a single or several dimensions. Theoretically, the items on an instrument or protocol should have the same structure as the hypothesized structure of the corresponding construct. Whether a behavioral assessment deals with signs or samples will determine whether examination of the internal structure of the instrument is necessary. For molecular or molar samples, examination of internal structure is not assessed because no inference is made beyond the frequency of the behavior. An instrument measuring molecular signs only has one dimension and therefore has no internal structure. The molecular behavior cannot be further broken down into smaller parts. However, an instrument using molar signs does have an internal structure that should be examined to see if the assessment structure corresponds to the theoretical structure.

The most common method of this type of evidence is through factor analysis. Today's software programs make performing a factor analysis a simple task. For further information regarding exploratory and confirmatory factor analysis, see Bollen (1989), Kline (1998), and Loehlin (1998) among many others. It should be emphasized that factor analytic techniques are used to verify whether the assessment instrument has an internal structure similar to that of the theoretical underlying construct. Factor analysis will only find the best mathematical internal structure of an instrument; it will not find the structure of a theoretical construct.

Evidence Based on Relations to Other Variables

Analysis of an assessment's relationship with other variables constitutes yet another important source of validity. The nomological net of a construct refers to the network of other concepts that may or may not be related to the construct of interest. A construct does not exist in a vacuum. Rather, the construct exists in an interconnecting system with other constructs. Some of these constructs are theorized to be similar and some dissimilar to the construct of interest. A researcher can indirectly assess the instrument with other theoretical constructs in the network to provide evidence for validity. If an instrument is shown to agree with those other constructs that were hypothesized to agree, then validity of the instrument is supported. If the assessment disagrees with those other constructs that were hypothesized to agree, two possible scenarios result: (1) the assessment may not be measuring the intended construct, or (2) the theory among the constructs may not be correct. Validity evidence is garnered by performing many different studies and showing that most theories agree with the data.

Evidence related to the nomological net often comes in the form of convergent and discriminant evidence, previously called criterion-related or criterion validity. If two assessment devices that are theoretically measuring similar constructs show a relationship, convergent evidence is obtained. For example, an assessment instrument measuring children's reading comprehension may be hypothesized to be similar to a teacher's ratings of the same children's reading comprehension. Discriminant evidence is provided through relationships between measures of theoretically dissimilar constructs. For example, an assessment instrument measuring spatial ability should not be related to assessment instruments measuring reading comprehension. In most cases, convergent and discriminant evidence is obtained through the use of Pearson's r correlational studies. Multitrait-multimethod has been es-

tablished as a research tool for simultaneously investigating convergent and discriminant evidence for different constructs. Traditionally, multitrait-multimethod has been performed utilizing a correlation matrix that provides an assessment of both reliability and validity. A reliability coefficient is obtained through analysis of the maximally similar measures of the same construct. The correlation between dissimilar measures of the same construct provides convergent evidence of validity. Discriminant evidence is obtained using the difference between the convergent evidence correlation and the correlation between two dissimilar measures of two different constructs (Campbell and Fisk, 1959). More recent theories suggest utilizing generalizability theory (Kane, 1982) and structural equation modeling (e.g., Loehlin, 1998) to arrive at evidence of convergent and discriminant validity.

Utilizing correlational data does have some limitations. The strongest Pearson's r results only when the criterion measure is a duplicate of or a linear transformation of the original measure. Classical theory's reliability coefficients are obtained by the square of the Pearson's r between the original and the true score, and thus the square of the correlation between the observed score and the criterion measure. Thus, the correlation between the original score and the criterion measure can never be greater than the square root of the reliability coefficient. For this reason, high reliability coefficients are desired so that the evidence for validity based on external variables has the potential to be maximized. Researchers also must be cautious of data with restricted range that can influence the Pearson's r. If an assessment instrument contains data from only a small portion of the possible scores, Pearson's r may not reveal relationships that actually exist for the overall range. If collecting data from all possible scores is not feasible, utilizing Lord and Novick's (1968) correction for Pearson's r may reveal a stronger relationship between the original and the criterion measure.

Some of these problems with Pearson's r can lead to variability in validity studies from one situation to the next. Comparison of local validity evidence from one administration to the next can vary considerably. However, research has shown that much of this variability is often due to reliability of the instrument or the criterion, restricted range, and other various sources of sampling error. Statistically removing error due to the above sources often reduces considerably the variability in validity evidence based on relations to other variables. Validity generalization (Schmidt, 1988; Schmidt & Hunter, 1977) is analogous to a meta-analysis of evidence obtained through correlations of the original score with other criterion variables removing the above sources of error. Providing validity generalization summaries of previous validation studies of an instrument can be useful in estimating the relationship between the original assessment instrument and the criterion measure in a new situation. If there exist many validation studies on the instrument in which the assessment situation is similar to the situation of interest, a validity generalization study may provide more meaningful and valuable information than a local validity study. If few studies on the instrument exist that are similar in nature to the current administration, a validity generalization study may not be adequate to provide validity evidence for that current administration. The characteristics of the situations that a researcher should consider include: "(a) differences in the way the predictor construct is measured, (b) the type of job or curriculum involved, (c) the type of criterion measure used, (d) the type of test takers, and (e) the time period in which the study was conducted" (Standards, 1999). In behavioral assessment, researchers also may wish to include aspects such as observer training characteristics, the location and conditions of the observation, and specifics such as frequency and duration of the observation periods.

Another method of obtaining information for a construct's relationships with other variables in the nomological net is through structural equation modeling. This powerful research tool allows for assessment of a hypothesized structure of causal or correlational relationships among multiple variables, thus exceeding the capabilities of Pearson's r correlations tremendously. With the advent of recent software packages, performing an analysis using structural equation modeling has become feasible. Typically, a pictorial representation, or a path diagram, is created to provide a clearer understanding of the structure of the construct. Bollen and Lennox (1991) identify two basic types of structural equation models. Effect indicator models are those in which the construct is theorized to cause the individual's response on the assessment instrument. Due to this expectation, evidence for internal consistency should be shown for these models. Causal indicator models are those in which the responses on the assessment instrument are theorized to cause the construct. Because the construct is seen to determine results of the assessment instrument, evidence for internal consistency of the instrument does not need to be shown. When running the model, using statistical software such as EQS or Amos, various goodness of fit indices are given, providing information on whether the theorized structure is plausible. Validity evidence is obtained for the instrument if the goodness of fit indices are acceptable. Bollen (1989), Bryne (1994), and Kline (1998), among others, provide comprehensive treatments of structural equation modeling.

Evidence based on relationships with other variables is not necessarily gauged through results of correlational analyses. Essentially, a nomological net poses many different theory-based hypotheses of relationships with other variables. The investigation of many of these hypothesized relations may employ correlational techniques. Other hypothesized relations may be best investigated through experimental designs, group comparisons, and so on.

Evidence Based on Consequences

Incorporating Messick's emphasis on social consequence, the final source of validity evidence is based on the consequences regarding the use of the assessment itself. Researchers need to be aware of both the intended and unintended consequences associated with uses of assessment results. Scores from an assessment instrument are generally used to foster some sort of benefit. For example, certain assessment devices are used to identify individuals in need of additional academic help, to identify individuals qualified for a job, to identify children in need of early intervention, or to identify individuals who may have a disorder so they may seek therapy. Researchers need to show that these intended beneficial uses of the instruments indeed occur.

When behavioral assessment scores are used to place individuals into categories or classifications for various purposes of treatment, employment, placement, or other decisions, the question of utility becomes an important aspect of validity. In these situations, one of the most important validity questions is that of use. Utility is often assessed statistically through the correspondence between assessment-based classification/categorization and some external criterion such as subsequent functioning, performance, and placement decisions made independent of the results of the assessment instrument. For example, a behavioral assessment procedure may be used to classify a child with a case of conduct disorder. The criterion measure used to evaluate the utility of this assessment-based classification may be future placement of the child based on information and criteria other than the assessment. For these uses, the relations of interest are those between the assessment-based classification and the subsequent criteria variables. Statistics such as hit rate, sensitivity, specificity, positive predictive power, and negative predictive power are indices used to evaluate the utility of these decisions (see Diamond, 1987; Taylor and Russell, 1939).

Behavioral assessment can be considered a form of functional assessment whose "content, focus, and product is determined by its function" (Haynes & Waialae, 1994). Because the function of behavioral assessment in many cases is to identify a problem and determine a course of action in a clinical setting, researchers using such instruments need to be concerned with treatment utility. In a counseling situation, treatment utility refers to the degree to which an assessment instrument can be shown to foster treatment outcomes that are beneficial to the patient or client. Treatment utility goes beyond the identification of problems, as discussed above, which is often analyzed statistically, to include both selection and evaluation of treatments for the patient or client. Specifically, does the assessment device identify the best possible treatment for the client? Does the assessment device improve treatment outcomes? Recommendations for test users emphasize the importance of providing evidence regarding beneficial outcomes for the test taker. However, the empirical evidence supporting that assessment can lead to improved treatment outcomes in the counseling situation is minimal (Braden & Kratochwill, 1997).

The assessment specialist should still consider the consequences on the individual participating in an assessment. If the purpose of an assessment is to identify individuals who will receive differential treatments, the researcher must show that this differential treatment is beneficial and effective. For example, "tests should not be used to assign children to different educational treatments unless it can be shown that those treatments are differentially effective; that is, children with a given test score must be better off as a result of the special placement than they would have been in the normal or usual placement" (Camilli & Shepard, 1994). Assessment users need to be aware that sometimes unintended consequences can transpire. In particular, if negative social consequences arise due to assessment invalidity sources, such as construct irrelevance, then assessment use for that given interpretation is questioned and may be invalid. If negative social consequences arise even though other types of validity evidence have been shown, assessment usage may be a function of social policy rather than invalidity. "Adverse social consequences associated with valid test interpretation and use may implicate the attributes validly assessed, to be sure, as they function under the existing social conditions of the applied setting, but they are not in themselves indicative of validity" (Messick, 1989). For example, if the use of an employment assessment instrument results in few individuals of minority races accepted for a particular position, yet the instrument validly measures the constructs necessary to perform that position, then that instrument is still valid.

CONSIDERATIONS OF ASSESSMENT BIAS

One important consequence that assessment developers need to be consistently aware of is the possibility of bias in their assessment in content, interpretation, and use. Bias, as defined by Cole and Moss (1989), is "differential validity of a given interpretation of a test score for any definable, relevant subgroup of test takers." Bias is found through investigating rival hypotheses and accumulating evidence that the interpretation of a score is the same for all subgroups of individuals, including those defined by race, gender, or ethnicity. As discussed above, bias does not necessarily include social conditions, such as adverse impact, as group differences in scores are not necessarily evidence of bias.

Bias in content refers to an assessment instrument being composed of items that are somehow unfair to a particular subgroup (Flaugher, 1978). A sensitivity review is a judgmental method in which a panel of experts reviews each item to identify those that may provide sources of irrelevant content. Sensitivity reviews also are designed to eliminate content that may be seen as offensive to any particular subgroup. Unfortunately, often the results of these judgmental methods do not agree with statistical processes of identifying biased items, because some content may not be obviously unfavorable to a particular subgroup (Camilli & Shepard, 1994). Therefore, statistical methods, such as various differential item functioning (DIF) techniques, can be used to identify items that function differently for members of different subgroups. There are several methods of performing DIF, including contingency table and item response theory (IRT) methods. Other methods include the delta plot technique (Angoff, 1972) and the Mantel-Haenszel method (1959). DIF procedures compare item responses of individuals from different subgroups at the same ability level. If individuals at the same ability level score markedly different on a particular item, the item may be functioning differently for the different subgroups. It is important to note that an average difference in overall scores does not necessarily indicate bias, but in fact may be a source of assessment validity in identifying a true difference between the subgroups. A major drawback for most researchers in utilizing DIF procedures to obtain important validity information is the necessary sample size for the minority group of concern. Therefore, most DIF studies are limited to large-scale testing programs.

The types of validity evidence that a researcher gathers on a particular instrument may depend on the specific content and context of the assessment instrument. Although validation is never proven, accumulation of multiple types of evidence will support the case that the instrument is valid. In behavioral assessment, using multiple methods of assessing a phenomenon is often valued. As certain assessment methods may have limitations, using multiple methods for assessing a phenomenon may be optimal to support interpretations or decisions from the instrument. For example, Rychtarik & McGillicuddy (1998) suggest that biological indicators, collateral reports, and self-reports should be used together when diagnosing addictive disorders. Each method has limitations that can be mitigated by using other methods to support the diagnosis. However, if a researcher is utilizing multiple methods, evidence should still be provided for validity and reliability of each method.

CONCLUSION

The psychometric evidence gathered for a particular instrument will vary based on the method and the purpose. Whether a researcher intends to interpret behavioral assessment results as signs of a covert construct or samples of an overt behavior will determine the appropriate evidence needed to support the instrument as psychometrically sound.

Based on the specific characteristics of an assessment device, a researcher may wish to focus more on validity evidence than on showing the assessment is reliable. Traditionally, psychometricians assumed that an assessment instrument could not have validity if reliability was not present. Because of this standpoint, much focus in measurement was placed on maximizing the reliability of the instrument (i.e., Knott & Bartholomew, 1993). However, recently there has been a shift to focus more on the validity of instruments than on reliability. Some theorists suggest that reliability is no longer a necessary condition for an instrument to be valid (i.e., Moss, 1994). Based on certain characteristics of the assessment instrument, such as the emphasis on gathering qualitative information, reliability may no longer be obtainable. In situations such as these, a researcher may wish to focus more on gathering validity evidence than on striving for an elusive reliability coefficient that may not be appropriate for that particular instrument.

Recent advances in computing have changed the nature of some behavioral assessments. Computer software has facilitated performing time-series and other analyses. Hand-held computers can be used for self-monitoring purposes, allowing for an easy way to collect information immediately and to facilitate analyses (Haynes, 1998). For self-report methods, these computers can provide a prompt to remind subjects to enter the appropriate information at a given time, thus reducing error associated with retrospective methods and allowing for collection of data in a more natural setting.

Other technological advances include devices that collect information on biological indicators of behavior without the need for subjective sources of rating. For example, actigraphs, which directly collect information about a person's movement, can be used to study sleep patterns. Some authors (i.e., Tyron, 1997) have argued that utilizing these measures reduces the need for providing evidence of basic psycho-

metric principles. However, reliability and validity of the scores, interpretation, and use must still be demonstrated, because the information collected is still typically indicative of a greater construct. For example, actigraph data correlate only with measures of sleep and wake states and are not a perfect measure of the sleep cycle (Haynes, 1998). Thus, related validity and utility information such as specificity and sensitivity of the biological indicator should be collected prior to use.

Another aspect of behavioral assessment that requires additional exploration are the psychometric considerations in the use of functional relations for behavioral problems in clinical settings. Instead of just focusing on one particular variable in an assessment, the analyst may wish to better understand the relationship among the client's various behaviors. "[B]ehavior analysts are interested in describing a client's behaviors but are especially interested in describing the variables that trigger those behaviors, set the occasions for their occurrence, that maintain them across time and situations, and that may mediate their magnitude and duration" (Haynes and Waialae, 1994). This process involves integration of results on various instruments, each of which should be shown to be psychometrically sound in terms of reliability and validity, in order to create a profile for each client. Bornstein, Bornstein, and Dawson (1984) describe several models for functional analysis. Doubtless the integration of information on multiple instruments would require complex analyses, yet yield a more meaningful and rich understanding of the individual.

This chapter is designed to be an introductory chapter on the psychometric foundations regarding behavioral assessment. For more detailed works on psychometric foundations, see Suen and Ary (1989) and Silva (1994).

NOTES

1. Some (e.g., Wright, 1996) have suggested the use of a separation index, which is the square root of the signal-to-noise ratio, as yet another measure of score reliability. It is suggested that the separation index indicates the number of categories into which the scores can be divided reliably.

2. A special case of the internal consistency approach is the Cronbach-Guttman Alpha method, which is based on a set of somewhat more relaxed assumptions called *essentially tau-equivalent assumptions,* instead of the classical parallel tests assumptions. KR-20 is a special case of Cronbach's alpha, and KR-21 is a special case of KR-20.

3. Because this is a repeated measures design with only one observation per cell, there is no residual mean square in this analysis of variance.

REFERENCES

American Educational Research Association, American Psychological Association, and National Council on Measurement in Education. (1966). *Standards for educational and psychological assessments and manuals.* Washington, DC: Author.

American Educational Research Association, American Psychological Association, and National Council on Measurement in Education. (1974). *Standards for educational and psychological assessments and manuals.* Washington, DC: Author.

American Educational Research Association, American Psychological Association, and National Council on Measurement in Education. (1985). *Standards for educational and psychological assessment.* Washington, DC: American Psychological Association.

American Educational Research Association, American Psychological Association, and National Council on Measurement in Education. (1999). *Standards for educational and psychological assessment.* Washington, DC: Author.

Angoff, W.H. (1972, September). *A technique for the investigation of cultural differences.* Paper presented at the annual meeting of the American Psychological Association, Honolulu, HI. (ERIC Document Reproduction Service No. ED 069 686).

Bollen, K. (1989). *Structural equations with latent variables.* New York: Wiley.

Bollen, K., & Lennox, R. (1991). Conventional wisdom on measurement: A structural equation perspective. *Psychological Bulletin, 110,* 305–314.

Bornstein, P.H., Bornstein, M.T., & Dawson, B. (1984). Integrated assessment and treatment. In T.H. Ollendick & M. Hersen (Eds.), *Child behavioral assessment: Principles and procedures.* New York: Pergamon Press.

Braden, J.P., & Kratochwill, T.R. (1997). Treatment utility of assessment: Myths and realities. *School Psychology Review, 26,* 475–485.

Brennan, R.L. (1983). *Elements of generalizability theory.* Iowa City: IA: ACT.

Brennan, R.L., & Kane, M.T. (1977). An index of dependability for mastery assessments. *Journal of Educational Measurement, 14,* 277–289.

Bryne, B. (1994). *Structural equation modeling with EQS and EQS/Window.* Thousand Oaks, CA: Sage.

Camilli, G., & Shepard, L. (1994). *Methods for identifying biased assessment items.* Thousand Oaks, CA: Sage.

Campbell, D.T. & Fiske, D.W. (1959). Convergent and discriminant validation by the multitrait-multimethod matrix. *Psychological Bulletin, 56,* 81–105.

Cole, N.S., & Moss, P.A. (1989). Bias in assessment use. In R.L. Linn (Ed.), *Educational Measurement* (3rd ed., pp. 201–219). New York: Macmillan.

Cone, J.D. (1986). Ideographic, nomothetic, and related perspectives in behavioral assessment. In R.O. Nelson & S.C. Hayes (Eds.), *Conceptual foundations of behavioral assessment* (pp. 111–128). New York: Guilford Press.

Cone, J.D. (1998). Psychometric considerations: Concepts, contents, and methods. In A. Bellack & M. Hersen (Eds.), *Behavioral assessment: A practical handbook.* Needham Heights, MA: Allyn & Bacon.

Cronbach, L.J. (1951). Coefficient alpha and the internal structure of assessments. *Psychometrika, 16,* 297–334.

Cronbach, L.J. (1988). Five perspectives on the validity argument. In H. Wainer & H.I. Braun (Eds.), *Assessment validity* (pp. 3–18). Hillsdale, NJ: Erlbaum.

Cronbach, L.J., Gleser, G.C., Nanda, H., & Rajaratnam, N. (1972). *The dependability of behavioral measurements: Theory of generalizability for scores and profiles.* New York: Wiley.

Diamond, K.E. (1987). Predicting school problems from preschool developmental screening: A four year follow-up of the Revised Denver Developmental Screening Assessment and the role of parent report. *Journal of the Division of Early Childhood, 11,* 247–253.

Flaugher, R. (1978). The many definitions of assessment bias. *American Psychologist, 33,* 671–679.

Geisinger, K.F. (1992). The metamorphosis of assessment validation. *Educational Psychologist, 27*(2), 197–222.

Gulliksen, H. (1950). *Theory of mental assessments.* New York: Wiley.

Hartmann, D.P. (1977). Considerations in the choice of interobserver reliability estimates. *Journal of Applied Behavioral Analysis, 10,* 103–115.

Hartmann, D.P. (1982). Assessing the dependability of observational data. In D.P. Hartmann (Ed.), *Using observers to study behavior* (pp. 51–66). San Francisco: Jossey-Bass.

Haynes, S. (1998). The changing nature of behavioral assessment. In A. Bellack & M. Hersen (Eds.), *Behavioral assessment: A practical handbook.* Needham Heights, MA: Allyn & Bacon.

Haynes, S., & Waialae, K. (1994). Psychometric foundations of behavioral assessment. In R. Fernandez-Ballestros (Ed.), *Evaluación conducto hoy.* Madrid, Spain: Ediciones Piramide.

Hoyt, C.J. (1941). Assessment reliability estimated by analysis of variance. *Psychometrika, 6,* 153–160.

Kamata, A. (2001). Item analysis by the Hierarchical Generalized Linear Model. *Journal of Educational Measurement, 38*(1), 79–93.

Kane, M.T. (1982). A sampling model for validity. *Applied Psychological Measurement, 6*(2), 125–160.

Kane, M. (1992). An argument-based approach to validity. *Psychological Bulletin, 112,* 527–535.

Kline, R.B. (1998). *Principles and practice of structural equation modeling.* New York: Guilford Press.

Knott, M., & Bartholomew, D.J. (1993). Constructing measures with maximum reliability. *Psychometrika, 58,* 331–338.

Kuder, G.F., & Richardson, M.W. (1937). The theory of the estimation of reliability. *Psychometrika, 2,* 151–160.

Linacre, J.M. (1989). *Many-faceted Rasch measurement.* Chicago: MESA.

Lindquist, E.F. (1936). The theory of assessment construction. In H.E. Hawkes, E.F. Lindquist, & C.R. Mann (Eds.), *The construction and use of achievement examinations* (pp. 17–106). Boston: Houghton Mifflin.

Loehlin, J. (1998). *Latent-variable models.* Mahwah, NJ: Erlbaum.

Lord, F.M., & Novick, M.R. (1968). *Statistical theories of mental assessment scores.* Reading, MA: Addison-Wesley.

Mantel, N., & Haenszel, W. (1959). Statistical aspects on the analysis of data from retrospective studies of disease. *Journal of the National Cancer Institute, 22,* 719–748.

McDonald, R. (1999). *Test theory.* Hillsdale, NJ: Erlbaum.

Messick, S. (1989). Validity. In R. Linn (Ed.), *Educational measurement* (3rd ed., pp. 13–103). Washington, DC: American Council on Education and National Council on Measurement in Education.

Moss, P.A. (1992). Shifting conceptions of validity in educational measurement: Implications for performance assessment. *Review of Educational Research, 62*(3), 229–258.

Moss, P.A. (1994). Can there be validity without reliability? *Educational Researcher (5),* 5–12.

Phillips, D.C. (1992) *The social scientist's bestiary: A guide to fabled threats to, and defences of, naturalistic social science.* Oxford, England: Pergamon Press.

Phillips, D.C., & Burbules, N.C. (2000). *Postpositivism and educational research.* Oxford, England: Rowman & Littlefield.

Quera, V. (1989). Estimación de frecuencia y duración en el muestero temporal de la conducta. *Anuario de Psicologia, 43*(4), 33–62.

Reckase, M.D. (1995). The reliability of ratings versus the reliability of scores. *Educational Measurement: Issues and Practice, 14* (4), 31.

Rosenthal, R., & Jacobson, L. (1968). *Pygmalion in the classroom.* New York: Holt, Rinehart & Winston.

Rychtarik, R., & McGillicuddy, N. (1998). Assessment of appetitive disorders: Status of empirical methods in alcohol, tobacco, and other drug use. In A. Bellack & M. Hersen (Eds.), *Behavioral assessment: A practical handbook.* Needham Heights, MA: Allyn & Bacon.

Schmidt, F.L. (1988). Validity generalization and the future of criterion-related validity. In H. Wainer & H.I. Braun (Eds.), *Assessment validity* (pp. 173–190). Mahwah, NJ: Erlbaum.

Schmidt, F.L., & Hunter, J. (1977). Development of a general solution to the problem of validity generalization. *Journal of Applied Psychology, 62,* 529–540.

Shavelson, R.J., & Webb, N.M. (1981). Generalizability theory: 1973–1980. *British Journal of Mathematical and Statistical Probability, 34,* 133–166.

Shavelson, R.J., & Webb, N.M. (1989). Generalizability theory. *American Psychologist, 44,* 922–932.

Silva, F. (1994). *Psychometric foundations and behavioral assessment.* Newbury Park, CA: Sage.

Suen, H.K., & Ary, D. (1989). *Analyzing quantitative behavioral observation data.* Hillsdale, NJ: Erlbaum.

Suen, H.K., Logan, C., Neiswork, J., & Bagnato, S. (1995). Parent/ professional congruence: Is it necessary? *Journal of Early Intervention, 19,* 257–266.

Suen, H.K., Lu, C.H., Neisworth, J.T., & Bagnato, S. (1993). Measurement of team decision making through generalizability theory. *Journal of Psychoeducational Assessment, 11,* 120–132.

Taylor, H.C., & Russell, J.T. (1939). The relationship of validity coefficient to the practical validity of assessments in selection: Discussion and tables. *Journal of Applied Psychology, 23,* 565–578.

Thorndike, R.L., & Hagen, E. (1969). *Measurement and evaluation in psychology and education.* New York: Wiley.

Tyron, W.W. (1997). Toward unified assessment. *Contemporary Psychology, 42,* 1031–1032.

Wright, B. (1996). Reliability and separation. *Rasch Measurement, 9*(4), 472.

CHAPTER 4

Learning and Applied Behavior Analysis: Foundations of Behavioral Assessment

WILLIAM T. O'DONOHUE AND KYLE E. FERGUSON

Behavioral assessment at its core is concerned with accurately measuring variables of interest to the clinician and researcher. Accurately measuring behavioral phenomena or constructs (i.e., how to minimize the deviance between the obtained score and the true score) is a key issue but not the focus of this chapter. This chapter will focus on another critical issue: how to choose among a myriad of possibilities the most useful constructs and variables that ought to be measured. In brief, the core insight motivating this chapter is that measuring variables involved in behavioral mechanisms can pay off experimentally and clinically, as these are the processes by which behavior is developed, maintained, and modified. It is beyond the scope of this chapter to describe all such mechanisms. The reader is referred to general texts that provide more comprehensive overviews (see Catania, 1992; O'Donohue, 1998; Pierce & Epling, 1999). Rather, this chapter deals with only those learning mechanisms that historically have proven most germane to behavioral assessment strategies.

Although there is some consensus regarding what are the mechanisms of human behavior (ontic commitments), there are two that are controversial. First, the major controversy in behavior therapy has involved the importance or even the existence of cognitive mechanisms. In this chapter we will discuss a subset of cognitive processes: rule-governed behavior. We think much of the traditional antagonism between the Skinnerians and cognivitists has been misplaced (see O'Donohue and Ferguson, 2001, chapter 6, for an exegesis of Skinner's views on cognition). The second controversy

concerns the mechanisms underlying clinical problems. Clients will not present with a note from an indubitable source indicating which process or processes are underlying their clinical problem(s). Rather, the therapist must form interpretative hypotheses and test these. This skill will, of course, vary tremendously across therapists. Information can be gained regarding mechanisms involved in problem development, maintenance, and modification. However, some of these assessment strategies are quite expensive. Later we will discuss the issue of the tradeoff between accuracy of information regarding mechanisms versus the cost of this information.

In this chapter we will discuss four major mechanisms: habituation/sensitization (reflexive processes), classical conditioning processes, operant conditioning, and cognitive processes from a behavior analytic orientation. These processes are in many ways the "classical" mechanisms upon which behavior therapies have been traditionally constructed (O'Donohue, Henderson, Hayes, Fisher, & Hayes, 2001). Thus, a clear knowledge of these is essential to understanding the workings of behavior therapy. Specifically, knowledge of these enables clinicians to better understand what treatments work for what clients, and in what settings (Paul, 1969). In fact, an even stronger statement should be made: Without an understanding of these learning processes, the behavioral clinician cannot understand and may not be able to competently implement a behavioral intervention.

Assessing the relevance of these processes also leads to more useful, treatment-relevant information. If these are the processes by which behavior is developed and maintained, then understanding the relevance of these processes is useful for:

- Understanding the etiology of change-worthy behavior
- Understanding how new behaviors are acquired
- Understanding how already existing behaviors increase or decrease
- Understanding how positive behavior change maintains and generalizes.

O'Donohue (1998) also notes three felicitous commonalities between basic learning research and clinical concerns: (1) Learning researchers are attempting to discover how experience changes behavior. This focus precisely addresses the general question in psychotherapy: How can therapists structure experience so that relatively enduring changes occur in clients' behavior? (2) Much learning research involves the intensive experimental analysis of behavior of individual organisms. The clinician is rarely concerned with group averages but rather is concerned with manipulable variables that are functionally related to enduring changes in an individual organism. (3) Learning researchers, particularly Skinnerian researchers, eschew statistical significance and instead attempt to identify controlling variables that result in highly reliable, high-magnitude changes. This is fortuitous, because clinicians generally want or need their outcome variables to undergo similar large changes.

This is in direct contrast to assessment information that is less treatment relevant. Understanding variables that are static, nonmanipulable, correlational, or proxy may not only be expensive but also irrelevant to clinical outcomes. For example, many diagnostic, psychometrically based systems have little to no empirical support with respect to treatment utility; there are no data where the "assessment is shown to contribute to a beneficial treatment outcomes" (Hayes, Nelson, & Jarrett, 1987, p. 963).

However, learning research by its nature attempts to strip the phenomena of some of its complexity. The laboratory is meant to study more simple preparations. The phenomena that the clinician sees will generally be much more complex. Part of the complexity may be that the phenomena are multiply determined or that different aspects of the clinical picture are determined by different processes. Some learning research has already recognized this. The two-factor fear theory (McAllister & McAllister, 1991), for example, postulates that first classical conditioning processes are involved in the development of a fear response to a conditioned stimulus, but then escape is maintained by operant processes. Thus, it can be difficult to apply laboratory-derived results to more complex natural phenomena. The behavioral assessor

is in a similar position to the engineer. The engineer extrapolates simple physical processes to the more complex natural environment.

REFLEXIVE PROCESSES

Habituation and Sensitization

Repeated presentations of a constant eliciting stimulus can produce five major patterns of responding: (1) response magnitude can remain the same; (2) response magnitude can increase; (3) response magnitude can decrease; (4) response magnitude can vary unsystematically; and (5) response magnitude can fluctuate between these in some complex way. When (3) occurs and is not due to physiological fatigue or sensory adaptation, then habituation is occurring. With (2), sensitization is occurring.

Habituation and sensitization are often considered the simplest and most fundamental kinds of conditioning. These are thought to be simple as these involve a two-term relation between stimulus and response (S-R), rather than a three-term relation involved in operant conditioning (S^D-R-S^+), or four-term relations involved in classical conditioning (CS-US-UR-CR) and operant conditioning (S^E: S^D-R-S^+). Habituation and sensitization are considered to be more fundamental because they occur in phylogenetically simple organisms and because their occurrence can be a precondition for the occurrence of other conditioning processes. For example, emotional responding to the experimental chamber often needs to habituate before operant or classical conditioning takes place.

In general, in Thompson and Spencer's (1966) dual process model, sensitization processes are predominant in early trials of stimulus repetition. However, habituation tends to predominate when the stimulus intensity is low, and sensitization tends to predominate when stimulus intensity is high. These processes can have obvious evolutionary advantages: low intensity, "insignificant" stimuli might need to be attended to initially (orienting response), but when they are constant, they should soon result in less responding so the organism can devote its behavioral resources to potentially more valuable stimuli. On the other hand, high intensity stimuli that are repetitive might be significant, and therefore the organism, at least initially, might need to increase the amount of resources devoted to processing and behaving. Clinically, habituation has been hypothesized to be involved in decreased sexual arousal to a constant partner (O'Donohue & Geer, 1993), drug tolerance (Siegel, 1977), anxiety reduction (e.g., decreased startle response; Barlow, 1988), and orientation problems in dementia (Langley, Overmier, Knopman, & Prod'homme, 1998).

Relevance to Assessment

There are three general levels of information that can guide the assessor.

(1) Hypothesis Generation. In this level the assessor makes an educated guess that a particular mechanism is involved. The mechanism becomes a working hypothesis and is used to generate testable predictions. For example, the assessor might reason: given the clinical picture (i.e., high initial sexual arousal to mate that diminishes over time, fairly constant sexual interactions, and literature support for the habituation of sexual arousal), it is hypothesized that the client's current complaint of low sexual arousal for his mate is due to habituation (at least in part). Thus, if the sexual interaction is varied so it is relatively novel (e.g., partner wears a wig), sexual arousal ought to increase. In order to minimize the habituation problem and relapse, the client needs to be instructed in other dishabitory practices that fit with the literature and general pattern of the purported mechanisms involved. Corroboration or falsification occurs in the evaluation of the intervention. On one hand, this working hypothesis approach is useful because it can cheaply and quickly lead to intervention implementation. However, on the other hand, it can turn out to be costly if the clinician's hypotheses are erroneous, and, as a result, numerous ineffective interventions are tried.

(2) Low-Cost Data Gathering. The second general level of information is to actively gather data that lend support for or against the working hypothesis. Clinically, this can be done through treatment as described above, but it also can be done in a nonintervention mode. Interviews can be conducted to see if the client's verbal behavior is consistent with the supposed mechanism ("When my wife and I are on vacation, I seem to be more interested in sex," lends some support to the hypothesis that low sexual arousal is due to habituation). Questionnaires can be completed to determine stimulus preferences (e.g., turn-ons), etc. This is usually a bit more expensive, and it is unclear to what extent incremental validity is increased. Much of the remainder of this handbook provides information relevant to these possibilities.

(3) Functional Analysis. A functional analysis in which variables are manipulated to see if they respond in the pattern predicted by the mechanism is the best but most expensive manner of gaining information. A hallmark of behavior therapy is that assessment can be treatment and treatment can be assessment. Usually, functional analyses can uncover the maintaining conditions and, in so doing, also point to the intervention needed to improve the problem. Because of the

expense and required expertise and effort, this procedure is rarely used as recommended in the literature (see *Journal of Applied Behavior Analysis*).

Thus, the process of habituation and sensitization has several component aspects. Each must be present in order for habituation or sensitization processes to be present. Thus, a single negative finding can falsify this hypothesis. The behavioral assessor can systematically evaluate whether each component is present to come to a determination about whether habituation or sensitization are occurring.

The general questions that should be addressed to see if habituation and sensitization are involved are:

1. Is there an S-R connection (i.e., does a stimulus regularly give rise to a response?)
2. Were there repeated presentations of the stimulus?
3. Did responding either systematically increase (sensitization) or decrease (habituation)?
4. Can other explanations be ruled out for this change (e.g., response fatigue, sensory adaptation, reinforcement)?

RESPONDENT PROCESSES

Crudely speaking, stimuli occurring with some association with a reflex can alter the organism's behavior. Thus, given a biological reflex (UCS-UCR), a stimulus that is associated with the UCS will soon elicit a response similar to the UCR. This new stimulus is commonly called the conditioned stimulus (CS), and the new response is called the conditioned response (CR). CRs are sometimes identical to the UCR but can differ in key ways such as magnitude and latency (i.e., duration between the presentation of the CS and elicitation of the CR).

Classical conditioning procedures are generally categorized by two major dimensions: *excitatory* (i.e., the CS becomes a signal for the presentation of the UCS) and *inhibitory* (i.e., CS is a signal for the absence of the UCS). There are five major types of excitatory conditioning:

1. *Simultaneous conditioning:* The CS and UCS are presented concurrently.
2. *Short-delayed conditioning:* The onset of the CS precedes the onset of the US by a brief period (usually several seconds).
3. *Trace conditioning:* The US is presented after the CS, and there is a temporal gap between the end of the CS and the start of the US.
4. *Long-delayed conditioning:* The CS remains present about 5–10 minutes before the US is delivered.

5. *Backward conditioning:* The CS is presented after the US is presented.

Like habituation, respondent processes can be involved in fear and anxiety. The famous early research of Watson (Watson & Rayner, 1920) and Mary Cover Jones (Jones, 1924) showed how fears could be learned and extinguished. Since that time classical conditioning mechanisms have been involved in most behavioral theories of fear and other anxiety disorders (e.g., PTSD, Panic Disorder), including two-factor theory (Mowrer, 1960) and more contemporary theories such as Barlow's alarm theory (Barlow, 1988). As a result, extinction (i.e., the presentation of the CS without the UCS) is a major mode of intervention.

In addition to fear and anxiety (Wolpe, 1995), classical conditioning also has been implicated in numerous clinical phenomena, including the placebo effect (Montgomery & Kirsch, 1997), cues for dysfunctional drinking (Marlatt & Gordon, 1985), and anticipatory nausea shown in patients undergoing chemotherapy (Manne et al., 1994).

Classical conditioning can be analyzed using several criteria. Each criterion should be assessed for evaluation of any hypothesis regarding the relevance of classical conditioning. To hypothesize that this process may be involved in the phenomena, the assessor needs to consider the following questions:

1. Can a reflex be identified? (i.e., first there must be a UCS-UCR connection)

2. Was there a neutral stimulus that is now no longer neutral? (i.e., can a possible CS be identified?)

3. Was there a pairing of this neutral stimulus with the reflex? (i.e., are the CS and UCS somehow associated in time or space?)

4. Are other conditioning processes involved, such as generalization and extinction?

5. Can other processes be ruled out that can also account for this behavior change (e.g., pseudo-conditioning)?

OPERANT PROCESSES

Respondent learning processes are unidirectional. To be precise, frequent pairings with the US potentiates an otherwise neutral stimulus into becoming a CS. Responding (i.e., the CR) does not reciprocally cause changes to the environment. Drug paraphernalia (CS) to a heroin addict, for example, elicits a CR (i.e., physiological adaptation) that counteracts the effects of the drugs (UR) (Siegel, Hinson, Krank, & McCully, 1982). The CR does not alter the drug's molecular structure.

Responding that operates on the environment producing certain consequences is called operant behavior (Pierce & Epling, 1995, p. 92; Skinner, 1953, p. 65). Simply, the environment exerts influence on behavior, and behavior in turn acts upon the environment (Skinner, 1957). The outcome of this behavior-environmental interplay increases, decreases, or maintains the rate of operant responding (responding/unit of time).

The ability to be operantly conditioned provided a tremendous selective advantage in the evolution of many species (Skinner, 1984). The behavior of the organism could be sensitive to and track changes in the environment. For example, when food distribution changed so that less food was under rocks and more under leaves, organisms sensitive to the consequences of their foraging behavior would be selected in by the environment. These organisms would have an increased likelihood of living long enough to bear offspring. Organisms not sensitive to the consequences of their foraging behavior would be selected out. That is to say, many would starve to death or become too diseased from malnourishment to bear offspring.

Operant conditioning processes are inherently bidirectional. For example, the intense behavioral displays shown in clients diagnosed with Borderline Personality Disorder (BPD) shapes the interpersonal response patterns of those around them (e.g., they eventually ignore certain suicidal gestures). Likewise, those response patterns in turn shape the behavior of the person with BPD (e.g., the parasuicidal behaviors become more dangerous over time; Linehan, 1993). Patterson's coercion theory describes a similar process in how a child's aggressive behavior evokes parental cessation of demands, which, correspondingly, differentially reinforce the child's aggressive behavior (Patterson, Chamberlain, & Reid, 1982).

With respect to behavioral assessment, if the client is cutting herself,[1] the clinician must first ask: What is(are) the function(s) (i.e., changes in the environment) of the parasuicidal behavior given the client's purported conditioning history? The clinician then gathers information (e.g., via self-monitoring or interviewing others) that either refutes or lends support to the working hypothesis or hypotheses (e.g., cutting as a means of experiential avoidance; Hayes, Strosahl, & Wilson, 1999). Of course, a functional analysis of parasuicidal behavior is contraindicated, because this could result in accidental death.

Three-Term Contingency

The three-term contingency is the simplest conceptual model of operant conditioning (Holland & Skinner, 1961). A more complex model, a four-term contingency that also takes into account overarching contextual stimuli, will be taken up shortly. The three-term contingency consists of a discriminative stimulus (also called an antecedent stimulus, symbolically, S^D), behavior, and the consequences of behavior (Catania, 1992). According to the three-term contingency, discriminative stimuli in the environment occasion or evoke behavior. In their presence, the emission of certain operants is more likely while the emission of other operants is less likely. Operant conditioning thus operates probabilistically.

Discriminative Stimuli and S-deltas

Discriminative stimuli acquire the power to evoke behavior or, technically, achieve stimulus control by way of frequent pairings with the reinforcer. Responding is said to be under stimulus control when discriminative stimuli differentially increase the probability of certain behaviors under certain environmental conditions, while decreasing the probability of other classes of responses (Michael, 1993).[2] In teaching a child with mental retardation stimulus discrimination using a matching-to-sample preparation, for example, after a certain number of pairings with the reinforcer, the sample stimulus (S^D) differentially evokes the "correct" response in the presence of "incorrect" comparison stimuli. Assessing performance would entail presenting the sample stimuli in the absence of feedback. The metric commonly employed in such conditional discrimination tasks is percent correct. Criteria for performance are arbitrary (e.g., conventionally, 90% in the stimulus equivalence literature).

While a discriminative stimulus increases the probability of emission of a particular class of operants, an S-delta (S^Δ) decreases the likelihood of responding (Pierce & Epling, 1999). An S-delta signals that an extinction condition is in effect (i.e., the withholding of reinforcement—see the section entitled "Extinction and Resistance to Extinction"). Planned ignoring, a form of time-out, is frequently used by special education teachers contingent on the emission of problem behavior (Nelson & Rutherford, 1983). In creating an extinction condition for the child, educators make the S^Δ stimuli explicit (e.g., orienting their attention elsewhere), so as to produce a great deal of contrast between time-out and time-in (Friman, in press).

Identifying the conditions under which reinforcement is not forthcoming is important data gathered from the assessment, as S^Δs often prompt unwanted behavior. Because S^Δs are inherently aversive, individuals often emit unwanted behavior (e.g., attention-seeking) as a means of escaping these stimuli. In our above example, a child might throw a pencil at the teacher or slap his or her neighbor as a means of escape.

In determining the extent to which these processes (S^Ds or S^Δs) are affecting target behavior, the assessor needs to consider the following questions:

1. Does the presence of the stimulus in question evoke responding (i.e., is there an increased probability of responding when one alternates between presenting the stimulus and withdrawing it)?
2. If such is the case, what aspects or dimensions of the stimulus seem to be most critical in evoking the response (e.g., volume measured in decibels)?
3. Does the presence of the stimulus in question lower the probability of responding?
4. If so, what about the stimulus seems most crucial in suppressing responding (i.e., valence)?

The behavioral assessor is certainly concerned with such contingencies and chains of contingencies. The assessor is looking for how these events change the probability of other events. In relapse prevention with sex offenders, for example, offense chains are examined to teach the client how to break such links (Laws, Barbaree, & Marshall, 1990). Offenses are often seen to be the last link in chains that start with negative emotion → driving in car → going to park → talking with child → thoughts of touching child → offense. Similarly, in Dialectical Behavior Therapy (DBT), clients are inculcated in conducting a chain analysis of problematic behavior:

> At the first level, when therapy is beginning, the therapist will need to mix more general analyses of the overall pattern of problem behaviors, their antecedents, and their consequences with more detailed analyses of some specific instances.... At the second level, chain analyses will focus on any instances of DBT target behaviors that have occurred since the last session or that are ongoing in the current therapeutic interaction.... At the third level, if no DBT high-priority behaviors are relevant for analysis or a crisis situation has developed demanding attention, the focus of the analysis is determined by the patient (Linehan, 1993, pp. 258–259).

Positive Reinforcement

Four contingent relationships are possible in the three-term contingency: positive reinforcement, negative reinforcement, positive punishment, and negative punishment.

According to Skinner (1953), a positive reinforcer is "any stimulus the presentation of which strengthens the behavior upon which it is made contingent" (p. 195).[3] In other words, a positive reinforcer increases the probability of the emission of the behavior it consistently follows. As a case in point, consider the all-too-common effect of giving in to a child's demands when he or she is having a tantrum. Naturally, parents who do this are positively reinforcing such behavioral displays, as evidenced by increases in the rate (or maintenance, if it's currently problematic) of acting out when in toy stores, supermarkets, and the like.

Invariably, the assessment must bring to light positive reinforcers for two important reasons. First, positive reinforcers often maintain dysfunctional behavior. For example, Wilder, Masuda, O'Connor, & Baham (2001) demonstrated via an experimental (functional) analysis that the maintenance of bizarre vocalizations emitted by an adult diagnosed with schizophrenia was social attention, a powerful reinforcer for most individuals. Second, positive reinforcers are always used in differentially reinforcing appropriate behavior, behavior that is incompatible with that which is problematic. For example, Jones, Swearer, and Friman (1997) used an abbreviated habit reversal procedure for maladaptive self-biting. Treatment involved, among other things, differentially reinforcing two competing responses.

Extinction and Resistance to Extinction

In the absence of reinforcement, responding eventually ceases. When behavior terminates as a result of withholding reinforcement, the operant undergoes extinction, usually after an extinction burst (Catania, 1992). The point to notice here is that extinction occurs only after a response has been maintained by reinforcement. Returning to our child having a tantrum example, if the parent ignores the acting out that has proven effective in the past, the wailing and screaming will eventually cease.

Thus, the most important question to ask that points to the principle of extinction is whether the individual emitted the behavior in the past. If so, the follow-up question, naturally, is what has changed in the person's environment since that time? In the case of a client diagnosed with Major Depression, for example, the question to ask is what has he or she done differently that prevents access to these naturally occurring reinforcers? If the individual seldom or has never emitted the behavior in question, then the principle of extinction is irrelevant.

Two phenomena arise during operant extinction: extinction burst and spontaneous recovery (Sulzer-Azaroff & Mayer, 1991). Extinction burst refers to increased variability in performance arising from the withholding of reinforcement (Galbicka, 1994). Colloquially, when behavior proves ineffective, individuals simply try something else. Along with trying something else, emotional responding is also elicited (colloquially, the person shows frustration).

One can easily produce the extinction burst phenomenon by removing the out-of-order sign on a malfunctioning soda machine. Naïve people first try what usually works (i.e., placing the necessary amount of coins in the slot and making their selection). After this fails (thus producing an extinction

condition), performance varies. Intense emotional behavior becomes increasingly apparent as individuals struggle as new strategies fail. Individuals may try punching the button with greater force, pound the machine hoping to dislodge the jammed apparatus, or begin tipping the machine. More resourceful people may write down the distributor's telephone number and demand compensation. Behavior thus varies along a response generalization gradient, moving farther away from what response produced reinforcement under initial conditions (Pierce & Epling, 1999).

Returning to our example of a person with BPD, the principle is the same. As other people begin ignoring parasuicidal behavior (i.e., producing a condition of extinction), responding varies, becoming more extreme.[4] At some point, the behavior commands attention (e.g., the client is hospitalized). Thus, more extreme behavior is differentially reinforced. Again, individuals try ignoring the new topographical features of parasuicidal behavior when the patient is discharged (e.g., cutting in lieu of scratching). Behavioral intensity correspondingly increases. As new forms command attention, the cycle continues. In extreme cases, parasuicidal gestures result in inadvertent suicide (i.e., help does not arrive in time, the person bleeds to death or overdoses).

After responding extinguishes, initially, if one waits several days or more before presenting the discriminative stimulus, again, the behavior can be evoked. This phenomenon is called spontaneous recovery (Catania, 1992). Over time the "spontaneous recovery" weakens in the absence of reinforcement. Eventually, the discriminative stimulus will lose the power to evoke the target response.

Regarding behavioral deficits, understanding the concept of extinction is fundamentally important because the assessor always needs to determine to what extent is the target a skills deficit versus a contingency deficit (Mager & Pipe, 1984). For example, if there is reason to believe that the client was unable to emit the target behavior in the past, training is necessary. If such were the case, simply increasing reinforcement density, removing punishers, and the like would likely be a waste of time. Conversely, additional training is thus contraindicated and a waste of time if there is a contingency deficit. If such were the case, increasing reinforcement density, removing punishers, and so on would be most appropriate.

Resistance to Extinction

The schedule of reinforcement determines the extent to which responding resists extinction (Ferster & Skinner, 1957). What is meant by "resistance to extinction" is how many responses the individual emits after reinforcement is withdrawn (Miller, 1997). When the reinforcer follows every response and performance reaches a steady state, this generates a condition in which there is little resistance to extinction (Sidman, 1960). Technically speaking, a Continuous Reinforcement schedule (CRF) or Fixed Ratio 1 schedule (FR1) produces a rapid decline in responding by withholding the reinforcer (Ferster & Skinner, 1957). As a side note, such schedules of reinforcement also produce response stereotypy—that is, behavior varies little topographically from one emission to the next (Pierce & Epling, 1999). The range of variability produced by extinction thus narrows.

In contrast with the patterns of behavior associated with CRF schedules, other schedules produce what is called the partial or intermittent reinforcement effect (Pierce & Epling, 1999, p. 156). The partial reinforcement effect is synonymous with the resistance-to-extinction notion mentioned above. It is generated by intermittent schedules of reinforcement (i.e., the reinforcer is not delivered after every response). Intermittent schedules engender greater resistance to extinction relative to continuous reinforcement (Skinner, 1956).

Intermittent schedules of reinforcement can be temporally based—called interval schedules—or response based—called ratio schedules of reinforcement (Ferster & Skinner, 1957). Interval schedules require that some interval of time has elapsed before the reinforcer becomes available. After the interval times out, the next response produces reinforcement. For example, in certain abstinence models of treating addictions, clients cannot attend sessions until they have abstained for a certain period of time from ingesting their drug of choice (Cummings & Cummings, 2000). Ratio schedules require a set number of responses before producing the reinforcer. Masturbation is fundamentally based on this principle (i.e., Variable Ratio schedule of reinforcement).

The schedules, interval and ratio, can be delivered on a fixed or variable basis. For example, an FR3 requires that individuals emit three responses before obtaining the reinforcer. A FI3 sec. schedule entails making the reinforcer available only after 3 seconds has elapsed. After 3 seconds, the next response eventuates in reinforcement. A VR3 on average reinforces every third response (e.g., sometimes one response would produce reinforcement, sometimes four responses, sometimes two, etc.). A VI3 sec. schedule makes the reinforcer available after some average period of time (e.g., after 1 second, 4 seconds, 3 seconds, etc.).

Fixed Ratio and Interval and Variable Ratio and Interval schedules produce predictable patterns of responding. Fixed ratio schedules produce a run of responses followed by a post-reinforcement pause (PRP; Ferster & Skinner, 1957). Longer PRPs are caused by greater ratio requirements, and, in fact, when those requirements are stretched too far, the individual stops responding due to performance strain (Catania, 1992). Orgasmic Disorder (not due to hysterectomy or drugs), a recurrent delay or absence of orgasm, is to some extent caused by ratio strain (American Psychiatric Association, 1994). Following the normal excitement phase of sexual activity, the effort to achieve orgasm at times becomes "more trouble than it's worth." Thus, individuals eventually become less sexually active.

A Fixed Interval schedule of reinforcement produces a characteristic scalloped pattern on a cumulative record (Ferster & Skinner, 1957). As the interval winds down, there is a characteristic acceleration in responding. Regarding variable ratio and interval schedules, both result in steady responding. However, in general, ratio schedules produce a greater number of responses (Pierce & Epling, 1999).

There are exceptions to schedule-induced patterns of responding. Humans capable of emitting verbal behavior often fail to produce such patterns of responding. Verbally able humans are "insensitive" to programmed contingencies (Hayes, 1989). Contingency insensitivity is purportedly due to verbally mediated statements of the contingencies (Lowe, 1979; Poppen, 1982). This will be taken up shortly in the section on language and cognition, but first let us consider how these principles are relevant to behavioral assessment.

Although it is often impossible to determine what exact schedule (or concurrent schedules) is (are) maintaining behavior in naturalistic settings (because there are simply too many variables to account for), clinicians can arrive at some hypothesis by directly observing the behavior of interest (e.g., momentary time sampling procedure) or interviewing those who work closely with the client. For example, the verbal reports of caregivers who care for family members with Alzheimer's disease can speak volumes about what schedules of reinforcement might be maintaining unwanted behavior. Take repetitive questioning as a case in point. Many caregivers report the following: First, they answer specific questions (e.g., when is lunch?); some might even go so far as answer several times in a row. Eventually, however, caregivers begin ignoring the preservative questioning, responding only occasionally. This pattern, of course, settles into a VR schedule. Each emission of the operant (i.e., questioning) does not produce reinforcement (i.e., answering the question). Rather, the operant is reinforced intermittently as the caregiver responds only occasionally. Interval schedules might also apply, because the individual has to wait a certain amount of time before caregivers will answer the question (e.g., "I'll tell you after 5 minutes").

Negative Reinforcement

Behavior that is effective in removing something (or escaping) from the current environment, and there is a corresponding increase in the rate of responding over time, is negatively reinforced (Sulzer-Azaroff & Mayer, 1991). Negative reinforcement invariably involves escape—escape from the actual stimulus and escape from those stimuli signaling its return (i.e., avoidance behavior).

In the interests of assessment, especially regarding higher functioning clients, a comprehensive assessment should not only target overt stimuli but also address covert stimuli (so-called experiential avoidance, Hayes et al., 1999, p. 58). For example, in assessing the ritual behavior of clients diagnosed with Obsessive Compulsive Disorder (OCD; e.g., compulsive hand washing, checking, counting, etc.), one might ask the following: What would happen if you didn't engage in the compulsive behavior? This question, of course, attempts to uncover maladaptive rule-governed behavior (e.g., fear of contamination as in the case of compulsive hand-washing) that sustains the overt target response (see the section titled "Rule-governance").

Positive (Type I) Punishment

Observe too, that in adding something to the current environment or taking something away, there may also be a corresponding *decrease* in behavior. While both types of reinforcement contingencies (positive and negative) increase responding, punishment decreases responding (Skinner, 1953).

Behavior that decreases in frequency in response to something being introduced into the environment, following the contingent emission of behavior, is positively punished (Pierce & Epling, 1999). This principle is also referred to as Type I Punishment (Foxx, 1982). Consider a child who has a history of petting strange dogs. Should a strange dog eventually bite the child's hand drawing blood, and on future occasions the child is less inclined to pet strange dogs, then the child's petting behavior has been positively punished by the bite.

The classic Little Albert study was one of the first experiments illustrating how phobias might develop by way of positive punishment (Watson & Rayner, 1920). Recall that Watson and his assistant produced an earsplitting noise whenever their famous subject approached the rat. Over and above intense anxiety (conditioned responding due to respondent processes), which of course generalized to other white furry objects (e.g., Santa's beard), Albert without fail emitted escape behavior in their presence. By contrast, before the intervention Albert earnestly sought out the rat, and in all likelihood, did not emit escape behavior when in the presence of beards.

Negative (Type II) Punishment or Response Cost

The second form of punishment is negative punishment—also called Type II Punishment and response cost (Sulzer-Azaroff & Mayer, 1991). The principle of negative punishment works

as follows. Upon removing something immediately present in the environment, contingent on responding, if we see a corresponding decrease in responding then negative punishment is said to be operating on behavior.

The stimulus removed is essentially something of value; technically, it functions as a reinforcer. For example, if taking away a child's favorite toy contingent on hitting his or her sister results in a behavioral reduction in hitting behavior, behavior is negatively punished. The reader should note that using aversive techniques that do not produce the anticipated behavioral effect are not considered punishment according to the functional definition of responding. There needs to be a behavioral reduction.

In determining whether these processes (i.e., reinforcement or punishment) might be differentially affecting the behavior of interest, the assessor needs to consider the following questions:

1. Is there an increase or decrease in responding? An increase (or maintenance under some circumstances) suggests reinforcement. A decrease suggests punishment or extinction.
2. Specifically, is there a corresponding increase in response frequency after presenting a certain stimulus? If so, positive reinforcement is likely the process maintaining behavior.
3. If such is the case, is responding being maintained on a continuous or intermittent schedule of reinforcement?
4. Is there a corresponding increase in response frequency contingent on the removal of the stimulus? If so, negative reinforcement is likely the process maintaining behavior.
5. Is the reduction in behavior related to the contingent (1) delivery of a stimulus (pointing to positive reinforcement), (2) removal of a stimulus (pointing to negative punishment), or simply a result of (3) withholding an established reinforcer (pointing to extinction)?

Contextual Stimuli

Although the original models of operant conditioning were comprised of three terms (i.e., S^D-R-S^+), recent models include a fourth variable, a contextual stimulus (Sulzer-Azaroff & Mayer, 1991, p. 254). This chapter will discuss one such variable, establishing operations (EOs).

When an individual is deprived of food for long enough, food becomes reinforcing. Conversely, food is not reinforcing after a big meal. Likewise, when an individual is deprived of sleep for long enough, the opportunity to sleep becomes reinforcing. By contrast, further sleep does not function as a reinforcer when one is well rested. Both examples are called establishing operations (Michael, 1993). EOs are comparable to the behavioral processes of deprivation and satiation (in this case, Unconditioned Establishing Operations; cf. Conditioned Establishing operations, Michael, 1993).

Establishing operations are environmental events that affect behavior in two characteristic ways (Michael, 1993; Vollmer & Iwata, 1991). (1) EOs momentarily alter the reinforcing effectiveness or punishing qualities of events. (2) EOs serve an evocative function (Michael, 1993, p. 58). Let us consider an example illustrating these functions.

When individuals experience severe migraine headaches (EO) their experience of typical events drastically alters. A throbbing headache will intensify aversive properties of other stimuli (first effect). An otherwise comfortable warm room becomes stuffy and uncomfortable (the EO increases the punishing characteristics of ambient temperature). Any noise that could otherwise be easily ignored such as the typical clamor of sports on television sounds like a jackhammer (the EO increases the punishing characteristics of ambient noise). On the contrary, reinforcing events such as socializing with friends and making love become far less reinforcing when this EO is in effect. In short, the interoceptive stimuli entailed in migraine move environmental stimuli along the reinforcing-punishing continuum toward punishment and away from reinforcement.

Regarding the second effect, we will most likely find this hapless individual scrounging for medication while seeking a dark, quiet place to lie down and rest. Medication- and solitude-seeking behaviors are emitted because in the past they produced a reduction in symptom severity during a migraine attack (Michael, 1993). Here the migraine, an Unconditioned EO, serves an evocative function. The presence of the covert migraine stimuli (e.g., throbbing pain, scintillations, nausea), evoke behavior that has been successful in removing such aversive private stimulation.

The questions that should be addressed in assessing the potential influences of EOs are:

1. What aspects of the social context seem to correlate with the target behavior (e.g., peers, members of the opposite sex, family)?
2. What aspects of the physical context seem to correlate with the target behavior (e.g., crowed room, air temperature, room ventilation, noise)?
3. What organismic variables (i.e., biological context) coincide with the emission of the target behavior (e.g., does problem behavior arise after sleep deprivation or while the person is intoxicated)?

COGNITIVE PROCESSES

Rule-Governance

A behavioral view of cognitive phenomena places an emphasis on how language (verbal behavior) interrelates with nonverbal behavior in a bidirectional manner (Hayes & Gifford, 1997). Of particular importance for assessment is a class of verbal behavior called rule-governed behavior (Hayes, 1989; Parrott, 1987; Skinner, 1966).

Rules are special classes of verbal behavior, defined in functional terms, according to their participation as discriminative stimuli (Baum, 1994; Catania, Shimoff, & Matthews, 1989, p. 120). Verbally generated rules, therefore, serve as contingency-specifying stimuli; they specify the antecedents, behavior, and consequences before an individual actually contacts the contingencies to which they refer (Hayes, 1989). Of course, once an individual emits the behavior and thus contacts the contingencies, subsequent responding is not considered rule governed. It becomes contingency-shaped behavior.

Pliance

Zettle and Hayes (1982) maintain that rule-governed behavior is comprised of three principle functional units. The first functional unit of the rule-follower's behavior is termed pliance. The rule itself is called a ply. Pliance is rule-following per se, or "rule-governed behavior primarily under the control of speaker-mediated consequences for a correspondence between the rule and relevant behavior" (Zettle & Hayes, 1982, p. 80). In following the rule, "Turn that !@#$ music down (or else)!" is considered pliance should the person's behavior come under the control of these verbal stimuli. The person does so because of a threat of speaker-mediated consequences that include further yelling, smashing the person's stereo, or a punch to the nose. On the contrary, a person might also choose to defy the speaker by leaving his or her stereo at its present volume. In so doing, the person's behavior is still under speaker-mediated influences, and as such his or her rule-following behavior is considered pliance.[5] In either case, the person establishing the rule mediates the consequences for rule-following.

The notion of pliance is of central importance in assessing for interpersonal violence and abuse. When clients say things comparable to "Because I have to" or "I don't want to upset my husband," clinicians must explore these verbal reports carefully, especially assessing around the consequences of noncompliance. What specifically, for example, does one's spouse do when the client is noncompliant, what does it mean when he or she is "upset"?

Tracking

The second principle unit of rule-governed behavior is termed tracking (Zettle & Hayes, 1982, p. 81; the rule itself is called a track). Tracking is rule-governed behavior influenced by the correspondence of the rule with how the world is arranged. Should tracking lead to auspicious outcomes, or if the person has avoided many pitfalls by following such rules, he or she is more likely to follow tracks. Conversely, if a person has a history of following inaccurate tracks leading to a hefty response cost (e.g., time or money) or positive punishment, then his or her behavior is less likely to come under the control of similar tracks. Examples of tracks include advice (e.g., "the blue dress is more flattering"), admonitions (e.g., "stop smoking"), proverbs (e.g., "a stitch in time saves nine"), and recipes, to name only a few.

Cognitively oriented therapies mostly deal with tracking of various sorts (and augmenting, see below). Cognitive restructuring is the core strategy in cognitive therapy and many cognitive-behavior therapies (Mahoney, 1977). It is a treatment technique aimed at directly modifying such rules that purportedly mediate maladaptive behavioral and emotional responding (Foa & Rothbaum, 1998; Last, 1989).

Panic Disorder is an obvious example of how tracking can lead to maladaptive behavior (Sullivan, Kent, & Coplan, 2000). While most individuals normalize internal events related to panic (e.g., shortness of breath, dizziness, dry mouth, etc.) by taking into account base rates (e.g., "what are the odds of having a heart attack at 20 years of age?"), such individuals on their way to developing Panic Disorder catastrophize attacks as something potentially fatal (Barlow, 1988).

Augmenting

Zettle and Hayes (1982, pp.81–82) also include a third fundamental unit in their formulation of rule-governed behavior called augmenting (the rule per se is called an augmental). Augmenting is rule-governed behavior under the "apparent changes in the capacity of events to function as reinforcers or punishers" (Zettle & Hayes, 1982, p. 81). As Hayes, Zettle, and Rosenfarb (1989, p. 206) observe, an augmental is a verbal stimulus that also serves as an establishing stimulus. That is, it has an evocative effect on related behavior, as well as momentarily increases the reinforcing effectiveness or punishing properties of other events (Michael, 1993). "I hate the way he is treating me," "she should stay out of my business," and "they are all pitted against me," are a few such examples—all of which can potentially change the reinforcing-punishing and evocative properties of other verbal and/or nonverbal stimuli.

Ellis's (1962, 1971, 1994) Rational Emotive Therapy (RET) is implicitly based on the notion of augmental rules. Namely, RET "concentrates on people's current beliefs, attitudes and self-statements as contributing to or 'causing' and maintaining their emotional and behavioral disturbances" (Ellis, McInerney, DiGiuseppe, & Yeager, 1988, pp. 1–2).

In determining whether these processes (i.e., rule-governed behavior) might be differentially affecting the behavior of interest, the assessor needs to consider the following questions:

1. To what extent is verbal behavior related to the client's presenting problem (e.g., are inaccurate rules getting the client into trouble at work or in the home)?
2. Where do these rules come from (e.g., are they self-generated tracks or pliance based)?

CONCLUSION

We have presented a brief overview of some of the major learning processes and discussed their relevance to behavioral assessment. We suggest that the more the behavioral assessor knows the underlying behavioral process the better he or she will understand the development, maintenance, and modification of a client's behavior.

NOTES

1. According to Linehan (1993), clients are almost always women.
2. Difference response forms that achieve similar ends.
3. See Meehl's (1950), transsituational reinforcement law that breaks out of the circularity inherent in this definition.
4. Of course, parasuicidal behavior might also diminish. Hopefully, these more adaptive behaviors will engender social reinforcement.
5. Or technically, we would call this *counterpliance* (Zettle & Hayes, 1982, p. 84).

REFERENCES

American Psychiatric Association. (1994). *Diagnostic and statistical manual of mental disorders* (4th ed.). Washington, DC: Author.

Barlow, D.H. (1988). *Anxiety and its disorders: The nature and treatment of anxiety and panic.* New York: Guilford Press.

Baum, W.M. (1994). *Understanding behaviorism.* New York: Harper Collins College Publishers.

Catania, A.C. (1992). *Learning* (3rd ed.). Englewood Cliffs, NJ: Prentice-Hall.

Catania, A.C., Shimoff, E., & Matthews, B.A. (1989). An experimental analysis of rule-governed behavior. In S.C. Hayes (Ed.), *Rule-governed behavior: Cognition, contingencies, and instructional control* (pp. 119–150). New York: Plenum Press.

Cummings, N.A., & Cummings, J.L. (2000). *The first session with substance abusers: A step-by-step guide.* San Francisco: Jossey-Bass.

Ellis, A. (1962). *Reason and emotion in psychotherapy.* New York: Lyle Stuart.

Ellis, A. (1971). *Growth through reason.* North Hollywood, CA: Wilshire.

Ellis, A. (1994). *Anger: How to live with and without it.* New York: Carol.

Ellis, A., McInerney, J.F., DiGiuseppe, R., & Yeager, R.J. (1988). *Rational-emotive therapy with alcoholics and substance abusers.* Boston: Allyn & Bacon.

Ferster, C.B., & Skinner, B.F. (1957). *Schedules of reinforcement.* New York: Appleton-Century-Crofts.

Foa, E.B., & Rothbaum, B.O. (1998). *Treating the trauma of rape: Cognitive-behavioral therapy for PTSD.* New York: Guilford Press.

Foxx, R.M. (1982). *Increasing behaviors of persons with severe retardation and autism.* Champaign, IL: Research Press.

Friman, P.C., & Finney, J.W. (in press). Teaching patients to use time-out and time-in. In W.T. O'Donohue, J.E. Fisher, & S.C. Hayes (Eds.), *Empirically-supported techniques of cognitive behavioral therapy: A step-by-step guide for clinicians.* New York: Wiley.

Galbicka, G. (1994). Shaping in the 21st century: Moving percentile schedules into applied settings. *Journal of Applied Behavior Analysis, 27,* 739–760.

Hayes, S.C. (Ed.). (1989). *Rule governed behavior: Cognition, contingencies, and instructional control.* New York: Plenum Press.

Hayes, S.C., & Gifford, E.V. (1997). The trouble with language: Experiential avoidance, rules, and the nature of verbal events. *Psychological Science, 8,* 170–173.

Hayes, S.C., Nelson, R.O., & Jarrett, R.B. (1987). The treatment utility of assessment: A functional approach to evaluating assessment quality. *American Psychologist, 42,* 963–974.

Hayes, S.C., Strosahl, K.D., & Wilson, K.G. (1999). *Acceptance and commitment therapy.* New York: Guilford Press.

Hayes, S.C., Zettle, R.D., & Rosenfarb, I. (1989). Rule following. In S.C. Hayes (Ed.), *Rule governed behavior: Cognition, contingencies, and instructional control* (pp. 191–220). New York: Plenum Press.

Holland, J.G., & Skinner, B.F. (1961). *The analysis of behavior: A program for self-instruction.* New York: McGraw-Hill.

Jones, K.M., Swearer, S.M., & Friman, P.C. (1997). Relax and try this instead: Abbreviated habit reversal for maladaptive self-biting. *Journal of Applied Behavior Analysis, 30,* 697–699.

Jones, M.C. (1924). A laboratory study of fear: The case of Peter. *Pedagogical Seminary, 31,* 308–315.

Langley, L.K., Overmier, J.B., Knopman, D.S., & Prod'homme, M.M. (1998). Inhibition and habituation: Preserved mechanisms of attentional selection in aging and Alzheimer's disease. *Neuropsychology, 12,* 353–366.

Last, C.G. (1989). Cognitive restructuring. In A.S. Bellack & M. Hersen (Eds.), *Dictionary of behavior therapy techniques* (pp. 59–60). New York: Pergamon Press.

Laws, D.R., Barbaree, H.E., & Marshall, W.L. (Eds.) (1990). *Handbook of sexual assault: Issues, theories and treatment of the offender.* New York: Plenum Press.

Linehan, M.M. (1993). *Cognitive-behavioral treatment of borderline personality disorder.* New York: Guilford Press.

Lowe, C.F. (1979). Determinants of human operant behavior. In M.D. Zeiler & P. Harzem (Eds.), *Reinforcement and the structure of behavior* (pp. 159–192). New York: Wiley.

Mager, R.F., & Pipe, P. (1984). *Analyzing performance problems or you really oughta wanna* (2nd ed.). Belmont, CA: Pitman.

Mahoney, M.J. (1977). Reflections on the cognitive learning trend in psychotherapy. *American Psychologist, 32,* 5–13.

Manne, S.L., Sabbioni, M., Bovbjerg, D.H., Jacobsen, P.B., Taylor, K.L., & Redd, W.H. (1994). Coping with chemotherapy for breast cancer. *Journal of Behavioral Medicine, 17,* 41–55.

Marlatt, G.A., & Gordon, J.R. (1985). *Relapse prevention: Maintenance strategies in the treatment of addictive behaviors.* New York: Guilford Press.

McAllister, D.E., & McAllister, W.R. (1991). Fear theory and aversively motivated behavior: Some controversial issues. In M.R. Denny (Ed.), *Fear, avoidance, and phobias: A fundamental analysis* (pp. 35–163). Hillsdale, NJ: Erlbaum.

Meehl, P.E. (1950). On the circularity of the law of effect. *Psychological Bulletin, 47,* 52–75.

Michael, J.L. (1993). *Concepts and principles of behavior analysis.* Kalamazoo, MI: Association for Behavior Analysis.

Miller, L.K. (1997). *Principles of everyday behavior analysis* (3rd ed.). Pacific Grove, CA: Brooks/Cole.

Montgomery, G.H., & Kirsch, I. (1997). Classical conditioning and the placebo effect. *Pain, 72,* 107–113.

Mowrer, O.H. (1960). *Learning theory and behavior.* New York: Wiley.

Nelson, C.M., & Rutherford, R.B. (1983). Timeout revisited. Guidelines for its use in special education. *Exceptional Education Quarterly, 3,* 56–67.

O'Donohue, W.T. (Ed.). (1998). *Learning and behavior therapy.* Boston: Allyn & Bacon.

O'Donohue, W.T., & Geer, J.H. (Eds.). (1993). *Handbook of sexual dysfunctions.* Boston: Allyn & Bacon.

O'Donohue, W.T., & Ferguson, K.F. (2001). *The psychology of B. F. Skinner.* Thousand Oaks, CA: Sage.

O'Donohue, W.T., Henderson, D.A., Hayes, S.C., Fisher, J.E., & Hayes, L.J. (Eds.). (2001). *A history of the behavioral therapies: Founders' personal histories.* Reno, NV: Context Press.

Parrott, L.J. (1987). Rule-governed behavior: An implicit analysis of reference. In S. Mogil and C. Mogil (Eds.), *B. F. Skinner: Consensus and controversy.* London: Falmer.

Patterson, G.R., Chamberlain, P., & Reid, J.B. (1982). A comparative evaluation of parent training procedures. *Behavior Therapy, 13,* 638–650.

Paul, G.L. (1969). Behavior modification research: Design and tactics. In C.M. Franks (Ed.), *Behavior therapy: Appraisal and status* (pp. 29–62). New York: McGraw-Hill.

Pierce, W.D., & Epling, W.F. (1999). *Behavior analysis and learning* (2nd ed.). Upper Saddle River, NJ: Prentice-Hall.

Poppen, R. (1982). The fixed-interval scallop in human affairs. *The Behavior Analyst, 5,* 127–136.

Sidman, M. (1960). *Tactics of scientific research.* New York: Basic Books.

Siegel, S. (1977). Morphine tolerance acquisition as an associative process. *Journal of Experimental Psychology: Animal Behavior Processes, 3,* 1–13.

Siegel, S., Hinson, R.E., Krank, M.D., & McCully, J. (1982). Heroin "overdose" death: The contribution of drug-associated environmental cues. *Science, 216,* 436–437.

Skinner, B.F. (1953). *Science and human behavior.* New York: Free Press.

Skinner, B.F. (1956). A case history in scientific method. *American Psychologist, 11,* 221–233.

Skinner, B.F. (1957). *Verbal behavior.* New York: Appleton-Century-Crofts.

Skinner, B.F. (1966). An operant analysis of problem solving. In B. Kleinmuntz (Ed.), *Problem solving: Research, method and theory* (pp. 225–257). New York: Wiley.

Skinner, B.F. (1984). The evolution of behavior. *Journal of the Experimental Analysis of Behavior, 41,* 217–222.

Sullivan, G.M., Kent, J.M., & Coplan, J.D. (2000). The neurobiology of stress and anxiety. In D.I. Mostofsky & D.H. Barlow (Eds.), *The management of stress and anxiety in medical disorders* (pp. 15–35). Boston: Allyn & Bacon.

Sulzer-Azaroff, B., & Mayer, G.R. (1991). *Behavior analysis for lasting change.* New York: Harcourt Brace.

Thompson, R.F., & Spencer, W.A. (1966). Habituation: A model phenomenon for the study of neural substrates of behavior. *Psychological Review, 73,* 16–43.

Vollmer, T.R., & Iwata, B.A. (1991). Establishing operations and reinforcement effects. *Journal of Applied Behavior Analysis, 24,* 279–291.

Watson, J.B., & Rayner, R. (1920). Conditioned emotional reactions. *Journal of Experimental Child Psychology, 3,* 1–14.

Wilder, D.A., Masuda, A., O'Connor, C., & Baham, M. (2001). Brief functional analysis and treatment of bizarre vocalizations in an adult with schizophrenia. *Journal of Applied Behavior Analysis, 34,* 65–68.

Wolpe, J. (1995). Reciprocal inhibition: Major agent of behavior change. In W.T. O'Donohue & L. Krasner (Eds.), *Theories of behavior therapy: Exploring behavior change* (pp. 23–57). Washington, DC: American Psychological Association.

Zettle, R.D., & Hayes, S.C. (1982). Rule-governed behavior: A potential theoretical framework for cognitive-behavior therapy. In P.C. Kendall (Ed.), *Advances in cognitive-behavioral research and therapy* (Vol. 1, pp. 73–118). New York: Academic Press.

CHAPTER 5

Broadly Based Causal Models of Behavior Disorders

WILLIAM H. O'BRIEN, MARY E. KAPLAR, AND JENNIFER J. MCGRATH

"Our inquiry aims at knowledge, and we think we know
    something only when we find the reason why it is so."
                                                —Aristotle

INTRODUCTION

In nearly every clinical and research setting, behavioral
scientist-practitioners engaged in assessment (hereafter referred to simply as assessors for parsimony) must grapple
with the issue of causality. This is particularly true when they
are designing treatments where a primary goal is to determine
the form and function of behaviors that are in need of change.
That is, assessors must construct a causal model that details
information about the many factors believed to be exerting
important influences on behaviors that are to be targeted in
treatment.

Although many of the variables contained in a causal
model may be extremely salient to both the client and the
assessor, some will undoubtedly operate in a much more indirect, obscure fashion and may be several steps removed
from the client's presenting problem. Additionally, clients often present with a complex array of problems, many of which
have overlapping causes and manifestations. Finally, the problems of a given client may be conditional and dynamic, meaning that they may vary across situations and time periods. It
is thus the case that causal models can be quite complicated,
often including dynamic, multivariate, indirect, and nonlinear
causal relationships.

Beyond complexity, it is also important to recognize that
causal models are hypothetical in nature, meaning that one
can never be sure whether a particular causal model adequately captures critical aspects of a client's functioning. Be-

cause the construction of causal models involves a degree of subjectivity and because many of the variables involved are dynamic, one must regard causal models as a constant work in progress. Thus, even after a model has been constructed, one must continually reevaluate it and make adjustments as new information is collected.

Consider, for example, the following transcript of the initial *few moments* of an intake interview that occurred between the first author and "Anna," a female client in her mid-20s who was referred for assessment and treatment for problems that were described by the referring psychologist as "anxiety and panic." (Minor editing of the transcription was conducted to guard client confidentiality and to facilitate a more efficient presentation of information.) As you read, note the richness and complexity of information provided about target behaviors and potential causal events.

Assessor: Please tell me about . . . what's happening, what brought you here today?

Client: [clears throat] It's . . . I've always functioned at a high level of anxiety, I mean, that's just, I tend to be a very tense person. I come from a family that, you know, typically is very tense; it's genetic, I think. But it's just this past year has been . . . it seems like it's been getting out of hand or at least I've been noticing it more. Maybe that's what it is, it's . . . I have difficulty going out, sitting in class. I have stomach problems. I feel like I have to go to the bathroom like, whenever I leave the house, and I'm always conscious of that. I always know where the restrooms are, and, regardless of where I go, I typically don't go anywhere that I know that a facility isn't available for me.

It's . . . it's been . . . interrupting my concentration in class. I've been . . . towards the beginning of the semester I was getting up in class an awful lot and just leaving. And I was, that's initially why I came, because I was worried that I wasn't going to get through the semester. I'm graduating in May and I was worried that this semester was going to screw that up. And, last semester I was having problems, I thought, because I was applying to grad school and I was, you know, taking the GRE and I had tests and a lot of stuff going on. Then this semester it seems more laid back, my schedule's more relaxed, but it's just, it's still of the same intensity as it was.

Assessor: [nods] Mmm hmm.

Client: So, I'm not, I'm not sleeping at night, I'm very paranoid, I like to sleep with my lights on and the door of my room locked, you know, and I, my heart palpi-

tates. I went to a cardiologist for that a couple years ago, because my mom has mitral valve and they thought that I had the same thing. But they didn't find any indication of that at that time. Um, I worry about that a lot, I'm worried that my heart's going to stop beating.

I, lately, like when I eat I have a fear of choking. I don't like to eat unless somebody's there. And when I do, I have the cordless phone in my lap [laughs].

Assessor: [nods] Mmm hmm.

Client: Doesn't make any sense, but . . . um . . . so that's basically what, what's going on. I, um, seems to be a lot of different things. My sister has panic disorder, and, but, it's like what she has and what I'm feeling, I mean, I can talk to her but they don't seem the same because she'd, you know, go into, into like, she couldn't go to school, she couldn't go, you know, and she'd like go into like seizures and stuff.

I . . . I don't do that, but sometimes when I'm out in public, I feel panicky, my heart races and I feel like I just gotta, gotta leave, and I feel shortness of breath and I feel like I just gotta get out of there.

Assessor: Well, that's certainly plenty to be worried about, a lot of things going on all at the same time. Before I ask you more specific questions about these various areas of difficulty, . . . I'm thinking that you have tried a number of things to try to fix these problems. What are the things that you've tried?

Client: My sister tells me to sit there and breathe, deep breathing. I've tried, reminding myself of my options. Like if I need to leave, I can leave you know, and try to remind myself, you know, that my heart's not going to stop beating, you know, that I've had this problem before, and you know, that I'm still living. And, I've gone to medical doctors about my digestive problems, to see if it was medical, and they can't find anything and I've been going to doctors for that since I was in 6th grade. Like I went to the doctor about my heart, to try and ease my mind about that, but it still doesn't. Dr. Smith [the referring psychologist] gave me a relaxation tape to listen to, and that helps me go to sleep at night because I do it right before I go to bed, but it's difficult because sometimes I have to do it three times before I don't get any muscle spasms you know, and that's about . . . I like, just try to remind myself of my options but it's just, rationality doesn't seem to be working.

In terms of causal model construction, this client has described many potential target behaviors (e.g., anxiety, worry, stomach discomfort, fear of going to the bathroom in public, concentration difficulties, fear of having a heart attack, feeling panicky, sleeping difficulties, fear of choking, etc.) and causal variables (genetics, academic stress, exposure to public situations and classrooms, negative self-statements, escape and avoidance behaviors, etc.). She has also provided information about efforts used to manage the target behaviors (reassuring self-statements, deep breathing), as well prior medical assessments that ruled out the presence of an organic condition that could account for her difficulties.

It is important to reiterate that this exchange of information occurred within the first *few moments* of the assessment interview and that only two questions have been posed by the assessor. Much more information will be shared in the remaining moments of the interview and subsequent assessment and intervention sessions. This quantity of information exchange is by no means rare in clinical contexts. A critical question in behavioral assessment and causal model construction thus arises: How can assessors sort through this complex array of target behaviors and potential causal variables in order to develop a causal model that can inform treatment?

Making sense out of these myriad variables is vitally important, because the way a causal model is constructed has many implications. Causal models affect not only the methods and focus of assessment, but also the ultimate case formulation (see Nezu and Nezu in this text) and resultant treatment design. Additionally, construction of a causal model is particularly useful in treatment implementation where efforts are often aimed at direct modification of causal variables.

In this chapter, we present an approach to assessment that is based on cognitive-behavioral theory and is designed to aid in causal model construction for the purposes of intervention design. First, we will review the key requirements for causal inference. Following that, we will summarize the features of causal relationships that are particularly relevant to clinical contexts. Next, we will explain how these causal principles can be used to construct causal models for individual clients that, in turn, can be used for treatment design. Finally, to illustrate the application of these principles, we will return to the interview, assessment, and treatment program designed for Anna.

ARE WE JUSTIFIED IN OUR ATTEMPTS TO INFER CAUSALITY?

One of the central questions that must be considered in causal modeling is whether we are indeed justified in making causal inferences at all. Perhaps most importantly, we must examine the basic assumption that causality exists independently of our perceptions of it. For if causality is merely a fabrication

of the human mind, meaning that there exist no actual causal relationships in the world that have an objective reality of their own, our discussion of causality would, in fact, be moot. Therefore, before discussing the construction of causal models and the complexity of causal relationships, we will first examine whether this basic assumption of causal models is met. That is, is causality *real* in that it exists apart from our perceptions of it?

Selected Historical Ideas About the Nature of Causality

Many philosophers, including David Hume, an eighteenth-century Scottish philosopher, wrote extensively on the topic of causality. Hume focused on three conditions for inferring causality: (a) *contiguity* between the presumed cause and effect, (b) *temporal precedence* (i.e., the cause must precede the effect), and (c) *constant conjunction,* whereby whenever the effect is obtained, the cause must be present, of which the last is the most important (Cook & Campbell, 1979). It should be noted that Hume's requirement of spatial and temporal contiguity does not preclude the existence of remote causes, provided one is able to effectively demonstrate a causal chain between the remote cause and its effect (Beauchamp & Rosenberg, 1981).

Hume argued that, because one must infer causal relationships from one's perceptions, there is no reason to believe that causality exists apart from our perceptions of it. In order to illustrate his point, Hume used the following example in his classic work, *A Treatise of Human Nature:* "Here is a billiard-ball lying on the table, and another ball moving towards it with rapidity. They strike; and the ball, which was formerly at rest, now acquires a motion. . . . There was no interval betwixt the shock and the motion" (Hume, as cited in Beauchamp & Rosenberg, 1981). Upon witnessing this, most individuals would conclude that the action of the first billiard ball had, in fact, caused the second billiard ball to move. Hume, however, claimed that the causal relationship between the first and second billiard ball can only be inferred from our perceptions, which, in turn, are based on observation of coincidence in space and time.

A clinically relevant example can clarify this point. Suppose, for example, that a client's anxiety levels improve shortly after taking an anxiolytic medication. Although it may be tempting to conclude that the medication caused the improvement, Hume would argue that this inference is based solely on the observation of coincidence in space and time. Further, this causal inference would be influenced by presuppositions, beliefs, expectations, prior experience, and myriad other psychological factors that are not rooted in the *real* world, but rather in the mind of the observer.

As an empiricist, Hume denied conceptual status to unobserved phenomena. Thus, he asserted that conclusions about causality must be based exclusively on the observation of past coincidences or correlations among variables. This strategy of moving from a specific fact or set of facts that one has observed to more general statements or relationships (such as the assertion that a causal relationship exists in the collision of the two billiard balls), requires inductive logic. However, Hume's inductive logic proves to be inadequate in that the mere fact that two variables were correlated in the past does not necessitate that they will correlate in the future, nor is it the case that a high degree of correlation in itself adequately demonstrates causation (Cook & Campbell, 1979). For example, social withdrawal is often correlated with sleep disturbances in depressed individuals. However, one cannot conclude from this correlation that social withdrawal causes sleep disturbances or vice versa.

By examining the work of Hume it is apparent that causation cannot be directly observed, and it is thus impossible to empirically demonstrate causation. Instead, causal relationships must be based on a problematic form of inductive logic. That is, an individual concludes that one thing appears to cause another because: (a) the two are temporally and spatially close, (b) one precedes the other, and (c) one expects that this relationship will hold true in the future. It should be noted that throughout the history of philosophy of science many scholars have attempted to develop formal rules for induction equivalent to the more stringent standards of deductive logic; however, no one has succeeded in doing so (Hage & Meeker, 1988). Thus, in scientific and clinical contexts, it is important to acknowledge that the demonstration of a causal relationship is essentially a matter of persuasion using scientific methodology and careful data analysis.

In addition to Hume, John Stuart Mill, a nineteenth-century philosopher, wrote extensively on the problem of demonstrating causal relationships. Mill argued that in order to infer causality three conditions must be met: (a) the cause must precede the effect (i.e., temporal precedence), (b) the cause and effect must be related, and (c) all other explanations of the cause-effect relationship must be eliminated. One of the key contributions of Mill's methodology is that it provides guidance about how one can rule out threats to valid causal inference.

Mill proposed that three methods can be used to help rule out alternative cause-effect relationships. The *method of agreement* states that an effect will be present whenever the presumed cause is present. The *method of difference* states that the effect will not occur when the cause is not present, and the *method of concomitant variation* states that when relationships are observed using both of the above methods, one's causal inference will be stronger since one can rule out other interpretations of the covariation between the two variables (Cook & Campbell, 1979).

Let us return for a moment to Hume's example of the billiard ball. Using the method of agreement, one sees that whenever the second ball moves, the first ball also has moved. In addition, using the method of difference, one sees that if the first ball does not move, the second ball does not move. Finally, the purported causal relationship between the two billiard balls is strengthened by the method of concomitant variation, since both the method of agreement and the method of difference can be successfully used to demonstrate the nature of the relationship (i.e., the second ball will not move unless the first ball has struck it and whenever the first ball strikes the second ball, the second ball moves).

A clinical example also can be used to illustrate these important points. Suppose, for example, that an assessor wishes to evaluate the extent to which stimulant medication reduces impulsive and hyperactive symptoms in a child diagnosed with attention deficit hyperactivity disorder. The method of agreement requires that we observe a reduction in symptoms whenever medication is taken. The method of difference would require that symptom reduction should not occur unless medication is first taken. Finally, the method of concomitant variation states that all increases or decreases in symptoms can be accounted for by variation in the presence or absence of the medication.

In Mill's critique of Hume, he raised the possibility of "plurality of causes." Mill was also particularly emphatic in his position that instances of covariation are often not causal, even when the condition for temporal precedence is met, because a third variable may be responsible for the relationship. For example, an assessor may observe that a client's reports of marital distress and depressed mood are reliably correlated. This correlation, however, may be due to a third causal variable that can affect both marital distress and depressed mood such as substance abuse, work stress, and/or child behavior problems. By studying Mill, one sees that the ability to rule out alternative explanations (such as the presence of a third variable), in addition to temporal precedence and the relation of cause and effect, is crucial to inferring causal relationships (Van Overwalle, 1997).

Contemporary Ideas Regarding the Nature of Causality in Clinical Contexts

Given the aforementioned philosophical perspectives, it is apparent that one can infer causation only on the basis of certain cues, including covariation, temporal order, and the ability to rule out plausible alternative explanations. Although the issue of whether causality exists apart from our perceptions of it may have been a contentious issue in eighteenth- and nineteenth-century philosophy; most behavioral scientists appear to be much more willing to assume that causal relationships exist and are of critical importance in assessment and intervention activities (Haynes, 1992; James, Mulaik, & Brett, 1982). It can be further argued that, for the behavioral scientist-practitioner, what matters most is that certain variables are reliably and strongly associated with certain outcomes and that manipulating these variables often leads to positive, powerful change in clients with various forms of psychopathology (Haynes & O'Brien, 2000). Thus, the contemporary behavioral scientist-practitioner is in a position in which he or she is able to adopt more flexible standards for inferring causality.

Contemporary standards that guide the formation and validation of causal inference in clinical contexts incorporate much of Mill's thought concerning causality. Some of the more commonly accepted of these standards are:

1. *Covariation between variables or increased conditional probabilities:* Two variables must covary, meaning that they must have shared variance. Lack of correlation between variables precludes one from inferring a causal relationship between two variables.

2. *Temporal precedence, wherein cause precedes effect:* A hypothesized causal variable must reliably precede its effect. Without establishing that *X* precedes *Y,* it is difficult to rule out the possibility that *X* is the result of, rather than the cause of, *Y* or, alternatively, that both *X* and *Y* are caused by some common third variable.

3. *Logical basis for inferring causality:* For a variable to be considered causal, it must have a logical connection with the effect. This requires that one identify the causal mechanism, or the particular way that *X* causes *Y.* However, it should be noted that a given logical mechanism is often presumed rather than specifically identified. For example, the exact mechanisms underlying the effects of certain antidepressants and other psychotropic medications are often presumed rather than explicitly identified.

4. *Exclusion of plausible alternative explanations:* It may be that two variables covary not because of a causal relationship between the two, but rather because of the presence of a third variable. Excluding plausible alternative explanations, such as the presence of a third variable, is perhaps the most difficult condition to meet, in part because so many hypothesized causal relationships in the behavioral sciences are open to alternative explanations. Thus, the number of plausible alternative explanations becomes very relevant, because a hypothesized causal relationship that is open to many alternative explanations is of little use to most assessors and researchers.

Summary

The problem of causality has long been debated among philosophers and continues to pose a challenge to modern behavioral scientists. A variety of criteria have been proposed for identifying causal relationships, some of which are still applicable today. Among behavioral scientist-practitioners, a more flexible standard for inferring causality appears to be acceptable. In turn, this more flexible causal inference can help guide the assessment process (see Table 5.1). Contemporary standards required for inferring causality within clinical contexts include covariation between variables or increased conditional probabilities, temporal precedence, a logical basis for inferring causality, and the exclusion of plausible alternative explanations. It thus becomes crucial for assessors to use procedures that will permit them to identify and estimate the magnitude of covariation among target behaviors and causal variables. Additionally, attention to the temporal ordering of variables will be required in an assessment. Finally, through familiarity with both theoretical and empirical research, assessors can educe a logical basis for causal inference and simultaneously consider and/or rule out plausible alternative explanations.

THEORETICAL AND EPISTEMOLOGICAL CHARACTERISTICS OF CLINICAL CAUSAL MODELS

In order to develop an individualized causal model of a clinical disorder, hereafter referred to as a clinical causal model, it is helpful to understand the key theoretical and epistemological characteristics that underlie this approach to assessment. The first, and perhaps most important, characteristic is *functionalism.* This assumption can be thought of as the belief that target behaviors are not randomly emitted, but occur as a function of complex causal influences that arise from intrapersonal events (e.g., internal causal factors such as physiological states, cognitive experiences, etc.), interpersonal events (e.g., social relationships), and environmental events (e.g., changes in the nonsocial environment such as temperature, season, setting, etc.). Behavior is thus construed as a logical outcome of interactions among many specific causal events. Further, it is assumed that learning theories can best guide the process through which relationships among causal events and target behaviors are identified and integrated into a causal model. Thus, our search for potential causal variables will emphasize those events that can be conceptualized as discriminative stimuli, reinforcers, aversive consequences, and conditional stimuli.

TABLE 5.1   Key Requirements for Causal Inference and Implications for Assessment

Causal Principle	Definition	Implications for Assessment
Covariation	Clinically relevant levels of correlation or increased conditional probabilities among target behaviors and one or more causal variables.	Collect assessment information data that will permit unambiguous evaluation of interrelationships between target behaviors and causal variables.
Temporal Precedence	Causal inference is strengthened when one can demonstrate that presumed causal variables precede changes in the target behavior.	Collect assessment information across time so that temporal sequences can be evaluated. Conduct experimental manipulations in which one can systematically manipulate the causal variable and then measure the effect on the target behavior.
Logical Basis for Causal Inference	Causal inference is strengthened when there is a logical basis for this inference.	Be familiar with the evolving theoretical and research literature that investigates the causes, correlates, and interventions for the behavior disorder under investigation.
Exclusion of Plausible Alternative Explanations	Establish that it is improbable to infer that another unmeasured variable may account for the observed relationship between the target behavior and causal variable.	Identify key alternative causal variables and systematically evaluate the extent to which they may be exerting a clinically significant effect on the target behavior.

An *idiographic emphasis* is a second key characteristic of clinical causal modeling. Specifically, because it is believed that behavior arises as a function of interactions among intrapersonal, interpersonal, and environmental causal events, it is also believed that optimal understanding results when assessment and causal model construction occur at the individual level. Thus, clinical causal model construction will tend to rely on methodological and statistical procedures that permit plausible causal inference using data collected from an individual client (e.g., single-subject design, time-series analyses).

A third characteristic associated with clinical causal modeling is *empiricism*. The empiricist position is represented in a preference for assessment procedures that use precise and minimally inferential measures of target behaviors and causal variables. This characteristic is also reflected in a strong preference for the use of empirical data yielded by functional analyses or treatment-outcome studies to guide treatment selection and validation.

In sum, a clinical causal modeling approach carries with it characteristics about why target behaviors occur, the favored level of analysis, and the preferred strategy for detecting and evaluating causal relationships. At the operational level, these assumptions are evidenced in the use of specific assessment procedures designed to yield data from carefully defined and well-validated measures of target behaviors and causal events for an individual client. In turn, these data are best evaluated using statistical and methodological decision aids designed for single-subject analysis.

Returning to Anna's case, functionalism is evidenced in our belief that her many target behaviors were the product of multiple causal factors operating in the external environment (e.g., conditioned responses to situational cues such as the availability for escape), intrapersonal events (e.g., catastrophic beliefs, stomach sensations), and interpersonal events (e.g., only eating when another person is present). We also believed that these relationships among target behaviors and causal events were the result of direct operant and classical conditioning experiences, social learning processes (e.g., learning through observation and modeling), and probable biological predispositions. The idiographic and empirical characteristics are reflected in our belief that the best way to proceed was to carefully define and measure target behaviors and causal variables that were unique to Anna. Finally, we developed ways to evaluate causal relationships using empirically validated methods that were appropriate for single-subject data.

CHARACTERISTICS OF CAUSAL RELATIONSHIPS IN CLINICAL CAUSAL MODELS

Causal relationships encountered in clinical settings have multiple characteristics. These characteristics have been described in a vast research literature that indicates that simple cause-effect relationships involving a single target behavior and a single causal variable do not adequately capture the complexity of most clinical phenomena. In this section, some of the more important characteristics of causal relationships will be presented. For a more detailed description and critical review of these characteristics, see Haynes (1992) and Haynes and O'Brien (2000).

Directionality

Causal relationships can be either unidirectional, whereby a given variable affects a second variable ($A \rightarrow B$), or bidirectional, whereby two variables simultaneously affect each other ($A \leftrightarrow B$). In the behavioral sciences, the direction of a given causal relationship may be unclear because it is often hard to determine whether A causes B or B causes A. For example, one might ask whether marital distress leads to depression or whether depression leads to marital distress. Alternatively, it may be the case that both of these variables simultaneously influence each other bidirectionally.

Complexity

In the simplest form of a causal relationship, known as a univariate causal relationship, only one variable operates on a specific outcome. For example, one might make the case that genetic factors alone are sufficient to cause schizophrenia. In the behavioral sciences, however, many disorders emerge as multivariate in origin, meaning that multiple causal variables contribute to a given disorder. For example, research has shown that schizophrenic symptoms may intensify as a function of exposure to stressful environmental contexts, genetic factors, interpersonal difficulties, financial strain, modification of medications, and a host of other factors (cf. Schneider & Deldin, 2001). Alternatively, multivariate causation also can refer to the phenomenon of different variables affecting the same behavior disorder across individuals.

Direct Versus Indirect/Mediated Causal Relationships

Causal relationships can be either direct or indirect. In a direct causal relationship, two variables are directly related with no intervening variables. For example, one might argue that a spinal cord injury directly leads to paralysis below the level of the injury. The path by which A causes B, or, more generally, a path that connects these two variables in the absence of other intervening variables, is called a direct causal path.

In many cases, causal relationships prove to be complex. Accordingly, one often finds *indirect* paths connecting two variables through other variables. In a *mediated* causal rela-

tionship, A and B are related through the operation of a third variable. To demonstrate mediation, the relationship between A and B is eliminated or minimized when the third variable is introduced into the causal model (James, Mulaik, & Brett, 1982). A causal variable may affect a given disorder through multiple mediators, or, alternatively, multiple causal variables may operate through the same mediator. In a *moderated* causal relationship, the magnitude of the moderator variable (sometimes referred to as a buffering variable) may weaken or augment the causal relationship between two other variables. For instance, social support is a commonly cited moderating variable that can buffer individuals against psychological and physiological reactivity to stress (Anthony & O'Brien, 1999).

Temporal Characteristics

Often, the causal variables and paths associated with a given disorder change over time, thereby necessitating a *dynamic* model that is able to account for these changing relations. For example, separation from a parent may cause extreme anxiety and behavior problems in a young child, which then lessen dramatically as the child matures. Sometimes, a given causal relation may be operational, whereas at other times it may not. Similarly, the magnitude of a given causal relationship may be substantial at one time point and trivial at another. These dynamic changes that occur in causal relations can be explained by many factors, including repeated exposure to a causal variable, the duration of action of a causal variable, changes in moderating or mediating variables, changes in context or situation, and maturation or other developmental changes, as well as the emergence of new causal variables and the disappearance of old causal variables (Haynes & O'Brien, 2000).

Additive Versus Interactive Effects

Also referred to as the summative character of causal effects, *additive* causal relationships occur when two or more causal variables exert unique and separate effects on another variable (Bunge, 1979, p. 166). In other words, in additive causal relationships, the whole is represented by a sum of the parts, such that the individual contributions of each variable account for the overall effect.

Interactive causality, on the other hand, is present when the combined causal effect of two or more causal variables is different from the sum of individual causal effects. This difference in impact may be greater than the individual effects. An example of this would be the synergistic effects of alcohol consumption and barbiturates on arousal (Nishino,

Mignot, & Dement, 1995). Alternatively, when two variables exert antagonistic effects, the interactive effects may be smaller than individual effects.

Nonlinear Causal Relations

Many causal relationships encountered in clinical contexts are *nonlinear*. Two variables share a nonlinear causal relationship when the strength of the relationship between two variables varies across the values of each or across time. For example, the effects of certain drugs are nonlinear in that the effects may not become apparent until blood concentrations reach a certain threshold level. Alternatively, a small dose of a drug may have effects that are opposite to a large dose of the same drug. For instance, in small doses, alcohol is experienced as a mood enhancer, whereas in large doses it acts as a depressant (Haynes, 1992). Other examples of nonlinear relationships include triggering mechanisms, curvilinear relationships, functional plateaus, and chaotic patterns (e.g., McCauley, Hannay, & Swank, 2001; VanLaningham, Johnson, & Amato, 2001).

Levels of Specificity

Causal relations may occur at a variety of levels of specificity, ranging from molar-level causal variables, such as nutrition, genetics, and one's social environment, to variables at a much higher level of specificity, such as inadequate iron consumption, a missing chromosome, or a lack of positive parental reinforcement. Here, the term *specificity* refers to the number of causal variables and relations contained in a given causal relationship (Haynes & O'Brien, 2000).

For instance, one can say that, on one level, depression may be caused by a life stressor, while on another level, it may be due to the reduced availability of serotonin in the presynaptic terminals. One could further explain the causes of depression using more and more microscopic levels of causation, ad infinitum. It is important to note that several different explanations, each at a different level of specificity, may be equally valid. That is, the correctness of a causal explanation at one level of specificity does not rule out the correctness of another causal explanation at a different level of specificity.

Given the potential for several equally valid models of a given disorder, it is a challenge to select the optimal degree of specificity. This decision is particularly important because the degree of specificity can have an important impact on treatment design. For example, molecular explanations are more compatible with pharmacological interventions, and molar-level explanations are more compatible with behavioral or systems interventions.

Summary

Causal relationships, many of which are quite complex, are essential to the study and practice of psychology and manifest themselves in a variety of ways. Causal relationships may be unidirectional or bidirectional, univariate or multivariate, direct or indirect, stable or dynamic, additive or interactive, linear or nonlinear, and may operate at different levels of specificity. Common contemporary standards for inferring causality include covariation between variables or increased conditional probabilities, temporal precedence (wherein cause precedes effect), a logical basis for inferring causality, and the exclusion of plausible alternative explanations. The key characteristics underlying individualized causal models are functionalism (target behaviors are not random, but occur as a result of complex causal influences), an idiographic emphasis (clinical causal model construction relies on procedures that permit causal inference using data from an individual client), and empiricism (utilizing assessment procedures that use precise and minimally inferential measures of target behaviors and causal variables). Although constructing clinical causal models may be a formidable task for assessors, it is nevertheless of great importance because it aids in the prediction of problematic behavior and in the design of intervention programs.

GENERAL PRINCIPLES OF CAUSAL MODELING

Thus far, we have reviewed issues related to the logic (or illogic, according to Hume) of causal inference, the cues or conditions that indicate the potential presence of a causal relationship, theoretical assumptions underlying the types of causal inferences used for clinical causal modeling, and the various forms that a causal relationship or set of causal relationships may take. An understanding of these principles and concerns can help the assessor single out and evaluate individual causal relationships or sets of causal relationships. Several additional principles, however, should be considered when multiple sets of causal relationships are integrated into a broadly based clinical causal model. These additional principles are described in this section.

Determining Domains and Boundary Conditions

Given the assumption that causal relationships are dynamic and context bound, it follows that a clinical causal model will be valid in certain domains but not in others. It is thus essential to establish the domain of a given clinical causal model, where domain refers to the conditions under which it is presumed that the model is valid and operational (Haynes, 1992, 1998). Some examples of boundary conditions that can be considered in establishing the domain include developmental level, environmental contexts, physiological status, and the presence of other key causal variables.

Clinical Causal Models Are Probabilistic

In drawing causal inferences among two or more variables, it is important to remember that such relationships are probabilistic rather than deterministic. That is, a certain degree of ambiguity is inherent in every clinical causal model. The probabilistic nature of causal variables and clinical causal modeling stems from many factors, including, but not limited to: the highly complex nature of many models (including the multiplicity of both identified and unidentified causal variables), the dynamic nature of many of the variables involved, chance occurrences of certain variables, and the fact that one can never be sure that his or her underlying assumptions are indeed correct (Haynes & O'Brien, 2000). Therefore, one must think in terms of probability, or what is most likely to have caused a given effect, recognizing that this may or may not have been the case.

Clinical Causal Models Should Be Amenable to Change

Clinical causal models should not be considered invariant or exclusive of other models. Rather, models should be open to change since many variables are dynamic and can be operationalized at multiple levels of reduction. Furthermore, it should be recognized that there can exist two or more equally good causal models, each from a particular orientation or emphasizing different variables. Thus, a particular clinical causal model cannot preclude the correctness or utility of an alternative clinical causal model. This point is extremely important given the dynamic nature of many variables, as well as the potential wealth of knowledge that may emerge from future research on causal variables.

Comprehensiveness Versus Parsimony

Although clinical causal models seek to illustrate the relations among important variables in substantial detail and to explain the greatest amount of variance as possible, one must be careful not to include so many variables as to render the model too complex to be useful. Instead, one should include only variables that add substantial predictive power or that facili-

tate interventions (Haynes, 1992). In determining what one should include in a given causal model, it may be useful to incorporate the historical principle of parsimony known as Occam's razor.

Named after its proponent, the medieval Franciscan philosopher William of Ockham, this principle is as follows: "what can be explained by the assumption of fewer things is vainly explained by the assumption of more things" (Ockham; appears in Magill, 1990). In other words, one should attempt to construct the simplest theory or model that still adequately accounts for data or explains a given phenomenon. The parameters of simplicity may vary from the number of presupposed axioms to the characteristics of curves drawn between data points (Honderich, 1995).

Ockham's principle supports the position that a causal model should be as parsimonious as possible while still adequately accounting for all the major variables, pathways, and other components in a given disorder. One should seek to avoid superfluous variables and include only those that significantly increase the model's explanatory power or that contribute in some other substantial way to the model's utility (e.g., in designing interventions). At the same time, however, it may be necessary to construct rather complex models, because the causes of behavior disorders are typically multidetermined and multidimensional. Thus, it is important to attempt to achieve a balance between comprehensiveness and parsimony.

Provides Considerable Explanatory Power and Is Useful for Treatment Design

A clinical causal model should be able to explain a substantial amount of the variance in the onset of problem behaviors, as well as the maintenance and termination of such behaviors. Any model lacking significant explanatory power is of little use to the assessor and should be abandoned in favor of a model with greater explanatory power. Additionally, a clinical causal model should help the assessor accurately identify crucial causal variables, thereby allowing for the design of more effective treatment strategies.

Specifies Type, Direction, and Magnitude of Causal Relationships

A clinical causal model should depict the complexity of causal relationships involved, including directionality (univariate, multivariate), magnitude (amount of variance accounted for), and controllability or capacity for change. Furthermore, the model should communicate the dynamic nature of the variables involved and whether certain relationships are additive or interactive.

CLINICAL CAUSAL MODEL CONSTRUCTION

The assumptions and principles outlined in the preceding sections of this chapter are reflected in many contemporary models of behavioral disorders. For example, vulnerability-stress models of panic disorder (Stewart et al., 2001), schizophrenia (Schneider & Deldin, 2001), social anxiety (Crozier & Alden, 2001), suicidal behavior (Weyrauch, Roy-Berne, Katon, & Wilson, 2001), and adolescent depression (Lewinsohn & Joiner, 2001) all posit that multiple causal variables explain the onset and maintenance of target behaviors. Thus, when constructing a clinical causal model, assessors must make important decisions regarding the selection of: (a) assessment methods that can yield data that will reasonably characterize the complex relationships among target behaviors and causal variables; (b) data analytic methods that can be used to evaluate the magnitude of relationships among variables; and (c) data organization methods that can be used to interpret complex patterns of relationships. In the remainder of this chapter, we will present information about these important areas of decision making.

Variables Incorporated Into a Clinical Causal Model

Clinical causal models incorporate two major sets of variables—target behaviors and causal variables. Therefore, one of the initial assessment tasks is to generate *topographical descriptions* of each. Topographical descriptions are precise and quantifiable operational definitions of target behaviors and causal variables. In this section, the major dimensions of target behavior and causal variable topography are reviewed.

Topographical Descriptions of Target Behaviors

Human behavior can be operationalized along an infinite number of dimensions. For assessors constructing clinical causal models, however, the topographical dimensions of greatest relevance typically fall into the following categories: (a) mode of response—which can be partitioned into cognitive-verbal, affective-physiological, and overt-motor response systems; (b) magnitude of response—such as the peak level of responding or degree of change from a baseline or comparison condition; and (c) temporal characteristics of response—such as frequency and duration.

Topographical Descriptions of Causal Variables

Causal variables can be operationalized along topographical dimensions that are similar to target behaviors. Analogous to the concept of mode of responding, causal variables can be classified according to type. Specifically, causal variables can be broadly partitioned into situational and intraindividual dimensions. Further, the situational dimension can be subdivided into domains or behavior settings that have been described by ecological psychologists as fundamental situational units (e.g., a classroom, hospital unit, assessor's office, etc.) where recurrent patterns of behavior are typically observed (e.g., Schoggen, 1989). Behavior settings, in turn, can be subdivided into (a) milieu variables (e.g., a classroom structure, lighting, temperature, humidity) and (b) social variables that can include human-human and human-nonhuman (e.g., pets) interactions (O'Brien & Haynes, 1995). For example, a hospital unit is a behavior setting where one will observe recurrent patterns of behavior such as shift rotations, nursing care schedules, and medication delivery. Additionally, a hospital setting contains many milieu variables (e.g., lighting, noise levels, room arrangement) and interpersonal variables (e.g., other patients, specific medical personnel, etc.) that can exert substantial causal effects on target behaviors and can be measured in terms of magnitude, frequency, and duration.

Intraindividual causal variables can be thought of as the internal contexts associated with target behaviors. Like target behaviors, the intraindividual causal factors can be described according to mode, magnitude, and temporal characteristics. For example, cognitive appraisals of other members in a group therapy experience (a cognitive-verbal causal variable) may exert a significant impact on treatment outcome (Anthony & O'Brien, in press; O'Brien, Korchynsky, Fabrizio, McGrath, & Swank, 1999). Importantly, intraindividual causal factors may account for variance in the topography of the target behavior separate from that accounted for by setting characteristics, milieu variables, and interpersonal variables.

Identifying and Evaluating Causal Relationships and the Role of Presuppositions

After the topographical descriptions of target behaviors and potential causal factors have been generated, the assessor must determine the strength of causal relationships. Given the multiple ways that target behaviors and causal variables can be operationalized, there are also many ways that causal factors and target behaviors can potentially interact, and it is unlikely that an assessor can reasonably assess all possible interactions and incorporate them into a clinical causal model (Garb, 1996; O'Brien, McGrath, & Haynes, in press). Thus, a priori causal presuppositions must be made regarding which of the many potential interactions are most likely to be important, controllable, and causal (Forsyth, Chase, & Hackbert, 1997).

Causal presuppositions used by assessors to reduce the complexity of collected assessment data most likely arise from personal experience, training, and individual differences (Garb, 1996; Hayes & Follette, 1992). For example, an assessor with training and experience in psychophysiological assessment may presuppose that a client's migraine headaches are apt to be caused by maladaptive coping strategies or excessive sympathetic nervous system reactivity in response to stress. His or her topographical description may then emphasize assessment of a limited number of intraindividual causal variables (e.g., frequency and intensity of catastrophic self-statements, negative expectations regarding the probability of headaches, elevated heart rate and excessive vasoconstriction) and situational causal variables (e.g., exposure to interpersonal or situational stressors). Alternatively, an assessor with training and experience in social learning models of pain may presuppose that problematic patterns of reinforcement (e.g., increased social attention for pain expression) and poor self-regulation of activity levels are critical causal variables. His or her topographical description may thus emphasize assessment of patterns of social interaction, social reinforcement, and levels of activity.

The published literature is a second factor that can influence presuppositions to the causal field. For example, Hayes and colleagues (e.g., Hayes, Wilson, Strosahl, Gifford, & Follette, 1996) posit that a functional classification scheme partially based on emotional experience avoidance (i.e., the client organizes his or her behaviors so that exposure to unpleasant emotional experiences and or disturbing thoughts is minimized) can be used to guide treatment design. Thus, assessors familiar with this developing line of research may be apt to reduce their set of potential causal variables to those that would indicate the presence of problematic self-appraisals and self-acceptance.

While presuppositions to the causal field are needed to simplify an extraordinarily complex assessment task, assessors should guard against developing an excessively rigid or narrow set of a priori assumptions. To avoid this, assessors should routinely evaluate their assessment skills and biases (e.g., review audio or videotapes) and keep data on the accuracy or treatment utility of their clinical predictions and decisions (Arkes, 1981; Garb, 1989, 1996). Second, assessors should create opportunities for discussing cases with colleagues and supervisors in order to obtain alternative viewpoints. Third, regular reading of the published assessment and treatment outcome literature is recommended. Finally,

assessors should strive to update their skills and knowledge by conducting research, affiliating with training programs and academic departments, and attending conventions or workshops.

Identifying and Evaluating Causal Functional Relationships: Assessment Strategies

Once a topographical description has been generated and the causal field has been simplified, the assessor must attempt to discern causal relationships out of the many noncausal interactions among causal factors and target behaviors. As noted earlier, reliable covariation between a causal event and some topographical aspect of a target behavior is the sine qua non of a causal functional relationship. However, covariation alone does not imply causality. As noted earlier, differentiating causal functional relationships from noncausal functional relationships requires a demonstration of (a) temporal order—the changes in the causal variable should precede effects on the target behavior, (b) a logical explanation for the relationship (often based on empirical research and theory), and (c) the exclusion of plausible alternative explanations for the observed relationship.

Three primary methods can be used to identify causal functional relationships. Each method also has strengths and limitations in relation to causal inference and suitability for clinical settings. In the following section we will present these methods for identifying causal relationships in clinical contexts.

Marker Variable Strategy

The use of marker variables is, in all likelihood, the most commonly used strategy for identifying causal functional relationships (O'Brien, McGrath, & Haynes, in press). A marker variable is an easily obtained measure that is reliably associated with the strength of a causal relationship. Empirically validated marker variables can be derived from self-report inventories specifically designed to identify functional relationships, as well as structured interviews, psychophysiological assessments, and role-playing exercises. The Motivational Assessment Scale for self-injurious behavior (Durand, 1990) and the School Refusal Assessment Scale (Kearney & Silverman, 1990) are two examples of self-report measures that can be used to identify causal relationships in criterion settings.

Although the marker variable strategy can provide important information about the presence of causal relationships, only a few empirically validated marker variables have, as yet, been identified in the behavioral literature (Haynes & O'Brien, 2000). As a result, to identify causal functional relationships, assessors typically rely on unvalidated marker variables, such as verbal reports of causal relationships obtained during unstructured clinical interviews (e.g., a patient diagnosed with post-traumatic stress disorder may report that increased flashback frequency is caused by increased job stress), administration of traditional self-report inventories and assigning causal inference (e.g., administering the Minnesota Multiphasic Personality Inventory and then inferring that the pattern of scores represents a personality structure, which, in turn, is postulated to be the cause of the presenting problems), and in-session observation of target behavior–causal variable interactions (e.g., a patient with a social phobia shows increased sympathetic activation and topic avoidance when asked to describe feared situations).

The major advantage to the marker variable strategy is convenience. Specifically, an assessor can quickly identify potential causal relationships with a limited investment of time and effort. For example, many markers of potential causal relationships can be collected during a single interview. The most significant problem with using marker variables is lack of validity. Specifically, it is impossible to determine whether the most commonly used marker variables—such as patient reports, self-report inventory responses, in-session observation, and laboratory evaluations—correlate with "real life." For those situations in which empirically validated marker variables are available, the magnitude of correlation between the marker variable and real-life causal relationships can vary substantially for an individual client. Thus, it has been recommended that when marker variables are used, the assessor should collect additional assessment data that will permit empirical validation of the hypothesized causal functional relationship (O'Brien & Haynes, 1995).

Observation and Self-monitoring of Naturally Occurring Target Behavior–Causal Variable Interactions

A second procedure commonly used by assessors to obtain basic information on causal relationships is systematic observation of target behavioral–causal variable interactions. Most commonly, assessors instruct clients to self-monitor these variables (O'Brien, McGrath, & Haynes, in press). Alternatively, direct observation of these interactions can be conducted by trained observers or participant observers in naturalistic (e.g., the client's home, workplace, etc.) and/or analogue (e.g., assessor's office, laboratory, etc.) environments.

Self-monitoring and direct observation methods can yield data that permit strong causal inference (O'Brien, 1995; see also special series on self-monitoring in *Psychological Assessment,* Vol. 11, 1999). However, these techniques have

two practical limitations. First, clients or observers must be carefully trained and be available so that the target behaviors and causal factors are consistently, accurately, and reliably recorded. Second, as the number and/or complexity of the variables to be observed increases, accuracy and reliability often decrease (Hartman & Wood, 1990; Paul, 1986).

Functional Analytic Experimental Manipulation

The third method that can be used to identify causal relationships is experimental manipulation. Experimental manipulations involve systematically modifying setting factors and observing consequent changes in target behavior topography (see Heyman in this text for detailed discussion of analogue observation, which is one type of experimental manipulation; also see the special series on analogue behavioral observation in *Psychological Assessment,* Vol. 13, 2001). These manipulations can be conducted in naturalistic settings (e.g., Sasso et al., 1992), analogue settings (e.g., Iwata, Smith, & Michael, 2000), psychophysiological laboratory settings (e.g., Anthony & O'Brien, 1999), and during assessment/therapy sessions (Kohlenberg & Tsai, 1991).

A number of single-subject experimental designs have been developed that enable the assessor to plausibly infer causality (cf. Kazdin, 1998). Although most were designed to evaluate the causal *effects* of an intervention, they also can be used to evaluate relationships between target behaviors and causal variables during pretreatment assessments. For example, an A-B-A-B design (where A = no treatment or baseline condition, B = treatment condition) can be used to obtain information about the causal effects of a contingency management procedure on school refusal. However, this same design (A = home with television privileges, B = home without television privileges) could also be used to evaluate the extent to which access to a tangible reinforcer (e.g., watching television on skipped days) is causally related to school refusal (Kearney & Silverman, 1990).

Data obtained from well-designed experimental manipulations allow for strong causal inference. Further, manipulations conducted in laboratory and analogue settings often can be accomplished at a minimum of cost to the client and assessor. Despite the potential treatment utility of experimental manipulations, important questions remain. First, the psychometric properties (e.g., reliability, validity) of experimental manipulations are not well developed. Second, most demonstrations of the treatment utility of experimental manipulations have been limited to a very restricted population of clients who were presenting with a restricted number of behavior problems. Thus, utility of this procedure for identifying the target behavior–causal variable relationships may not generalize to other client populations, problem behaviors, and settings.

In sum, marker variables, behavioral observation, and experimental manipulations can be used to gather data on causal functional relationships. As Haynes (1992) noted, however, the strength of causal inference associated with each method varies inversely with clinical applicability. Experimental manipulations, self-monitoring, and behavioral observation can yield data that permit strong causal inference. However, each method requires a significant investment of effort, and only a few target behaviors and causal factors can be reasonably evaluated. In contrast, the marker variable strategy supports only weak causal inference. However, it is easily administered and can provide information on a substantial number of potential target behavior–causal variable relationships.

It is thus logical to employ different methods at different points in the construction of a clinical causal model. In the early stages of model design, the assessor can rely on marker variables so that many potential causal relationships can be identified. Later, after additional information has been collected on target behavior–causal variable interactions, the assessor can select a subset of potentially important and controllable causal relationships and subject them to more intensive scrutiny using self-monitoring, observation, and/or systematic manipulation.

Summary

Contemporary models of disordered behavior are often complex. As a result, assessors must be able to identify and evaluate many relationships among causal factors and target behaviors. Part of the ability to accomplish this task relies on a sound knowledge of (a) the different dimensions of topography that can be quantified, (b) the multiple ways in which causal variables and target behaviors can interact for a particular behavior disorder, and (c) one's own presuppositions and decisional strategies used to narrow causal fields.

In addition to knowledge, specific assessment methods such as the marker variable strategy, self-monitoring, direct observation, and experimental manipulation can be used to empirically identify causal functional relationships. Each method has strengths and limitations related to the strength of causal inference that can be derived from collected data and degree of clinical applicability. In general, methods that support stronger causal inference (self-monitoring, observation, experimental manipulation) are costly and limited in focus. In contrast, methods that are inexpensive and broadly focused (marker variable strategy) tend to permit only weak causal inference. Thus, early in the pretreatment assessment process, the use of broadly focused and inexpensive assess-

ment devices may be most appropriate. Later, after the range of hypothesized causal functional relationships has been narrowed, assessment strategies that permit stronger causal inference are recommended.

CASE ILLUSTRATION

To illustrate interviewing and assessment strategies that can be used to construct a clinical causal model, we will return to Anna's case.[1] In terms of presuppositions, the assessor approached this case with a number of assumptions that narrowed the search for causal variables. Specifically, it was presupposed that anxiety and panic disorders are manifestations of an interaction between biological predispositions, classical conditioning principles, operant conditioning principles, and problematic cognitive schemas. Consequently, the assessor focused on identification of family patterns of anxiety-related problems, instances of pairing of panic states with specific situational and/or intraindividual variables, evidence of contingent reinforcement for target behaviors, and distorted thinking patterns related to anxiety states and their sequelae.

This part of the interview immediately follows the client's initial description of her concerns that were presented earlier. The assessor now asks a series of questions designed to gather information about the topography of target behaviors and potential causal variables. Again, in keeping with the overall thrust of this chapter, which highlights the complexity of causal models, note how a wealth of information is exchanged about target behaviors and causal variables. Additionally, note how the client describes a number of nonlinear, dynamic, bidirectional, multivariate, and mediated causal pathways.

Initial Interview Transcript with Commentary

Assessor: Okay, let me go back and ask you about these different concerns. . . . Let's go with the GI concerns first because that's the first thing you mentioned to me. I'd like to ask you a little bit more about what the nature of this problem is. So, I'm going to ask you about two parts of it. The first part is, what does this experience feel like . . . what are you thinking about, what are the symptoms you experience. Then I will ask you about where, when, and how it occurs. So let me ask you the first part. Tell me about the GI symptoms you are experiencing; what are the thoughts? Let's start with the thoughts that you have when you're at a point where you're feeling like this GI problem is going to occur.

Client: That I have to go to the bathroom?

Assessor: So you're thinking "I have to go to the bathroom."

Client: Yeah, I'm thinking I'm going to embarrass myself. Because, I mean I've gone to the bathroom in my pants once before, and I'm just thinking that I don't want to embarrass myself. I'm thinking that, that it's out of my control . . . I can't . . . and there's nothing I can do about it. That's, that's basically all, that's, it's like I, my sister tells me to try to breathe through that, but I can't, you know, because I can't risk that, I can't risk, you know . . .

Assessor: Going in your pants. Are we talking about having a bowel movement, or . . .

Client: Mmm hmm.

Assessor: Okay, so the thought is something like, oh my god . . .

Client: Yeah.

Assessor: . . . I'm gonna go.

Client: It's like I'm 24 years old.

Assessor: In front of all these people in class. What would happen then, if you got to that point? What do you anticipate would be the consequences?

Client: Yeah, I've thought about that. And I've thought about well, if I get up in class and I don't make it to the bathroom in time, it's like, should I take my books? Should I not take my books? If I don't take my books and then I go to the bathroom and I don't make it in time then I have to go back in and get my books.

Assessor: Mmm hmm.

Client: So, that's probably the toughest thing, you know, is that problem, because wherever I go that's the first thing I think about when I leave the house.

Assessor: That you might have an accident and . . . I can see how this thought could start spinning real fast. Do you find yourself concentrating on those thoughts a great deal?

Client: Yeah. That's all—I mean, my parents went on a house-hunting trip, during the summer because we just moved. I didn't go. I sat in the hotel the entire time because there were some houses that weren't finished and, you know and, I'm like, well I can't go.

Assessor: How often are you having these kinds of thoughts in a typical day?

Client: Whenever I leave the house. It's like never out of my mind.

Assessor: Okay.

Client: It's always there. And sometimes when I go out, I'll go. I mean I try not, I go anyway, I try to leave the house anyway, because I don't want to . . . my sister was agoraphobic and I don't want to be stuck in the house. So, I go out, but if I go out with my friends I'll stand by the door, stand by the bathroom the entire night. So, it's like I do it, but, I kinda modify myself to fit the situation.

Assessor: Okay. So that's the thought part of this fear. Tell me a little bit more about the physical and emotional part of this fear. What are the physical symptoms you might be experiencing as these thoughts are racing through your mind?

Comment. After gathering information about the cognitive mode of responding, the assessor will then ask questions about the affective-physiological and overt-motor modes. Additionally, the assessor will solicit information regarding the magnitude of responding and temporal characteristics (frequency, duration, and rate of symptom onset).

Client: My heart pounds. It races. I can feel it, I feel like my stomach's expanding, and I don't know, like I feel like I get really hot, and I touch my face and try to get it to cool down. Sometimes I'll grab onto things, like my papers or my books or something and squeeze really really hard and try to get myself to think about hurting my hand rather than, you know . . . and uh, I'll do that. It's like, it's a cramp. I mean, some people, they get an upset stomach when they eat something and I can tell the difference. I know the difference. My doctor back in high school, he medicated me for irritable bowels, but the medication didn't help. I stopped taking that about oh, I'd say, last year.

Assessor: So your heart is pounding, you feel your stomach expanding . . . tell me a little bit more about what stomach expanding feels like.

Client: It feels like I'm—blowing up. It's like my pants— my waist tightens, you know, like I'm just all bloated. And I, it starts to gurgle, you know, like I can hear it. And, like, when I was talking to Dr. Smith he wanted me to see what happened first, whether I felt my stomach gurgling or my heart started racing, and sometimes it's one and sometimes it's the other. It's, they're, I haven't noticed a pattern.

Assessor: Okay. And you feel hot, and you mentioned you grab onto things—tell me more about that.

Client: I'll grab onto a book or a pencil or myself or something, typically I'll gather my books up in class and just sit there on the edge of my desk, then I'm worried that everybody's noticing that I'm gathering my stuff up and I don't want to call attention to myself. And I worry about getting up and leaving the room and then I'm gonna call attention to myself, but then if I just sit there, I'm gonna really call attention to myself.

Assessor: Any other sensations? You're aware of some of these symptoms from your sister. To what extent are there changes in your breathing patterns?

Comment. In cases where there is an indication of panic-like states, specific questions about symptoms associated with sympathetic activation can yield helpful information about the target behaviors. In the next several exchanges, specific questions related to these various physiological experiences were asked. The client reported experiencing sweatiness and choking sensations but not dizziness, tingling, or de-realization. She labeled the total emotional experience as fear. The next set of questions focused on learning about the history of the presenting concerns and then developing a set of possible causal variables.

Assessor: Okay. You mentioned that you had a couple of accidents in the past—tell me more about them. When and where did they happen?

Client: One time when I was real little, and I was out with a neighbor, and we were at a playground. And I was really embarrassed.

Assessor: How old were you?

Client: I don't even know, I think that I was somewhere in grade school. Probably in kindergarten or first grade. And then around fifth and sixth grade, I had tests done because I was having chronic diarrhea. They just said that I was just a nervous child. And they didn't find anything so they said that I should just put more fiber in my diet. So I was conscious of that for a while, and then when I got older, I was just like, this is crazy. I'm like, I'm not taking this for the rest of my life. I was only, maybe, 12. And then, then it seemed to subside for a while, and then I had an accident when I was on a walk with my sisters when I was in tenth or eleventh grade. And I had to walk home. . . . So those were the only two times.

Comment. The client has indicated that there is a history of GI problems, but no extensive history of accidents occurring in public situations. In a later session, the client provided more details about the first accident. She noted it was extremely embarrassing because she had a bowel movement while getting a ride in a neighbor's car. The neighbor was

very agitated and reportedly required that she sit on a newspaper for the return trip and subsequent trips. The client recalled she experienced great humiliation and fear that she would have another accident. This experience could have established some of the initial conditioned effects: (a) unconditioned stimuli—being severely reprimanded combined with social rejection; (b) unconditioned responses—fear, sympathetic activation; (c) conditioned stimuli—GI discomfort, riding in a car (a situation where escape and/or access to the bathroom is difficult); (d) conditioned responses—fear, sympathetic activation. Upon re-exposure to riding situations and situations where bathrooms were inaccessible, the client would have experienced anticipatory fear and sympathetic activation (i.e., a conditioned response). If she successfully avoided or escaped from similar situations, then the avoidance and escape behaviors would be negatively reinforced by the reduction in fear and symptoms of sympathetic activation.

Assessor: Okay. So you haven't had any in the recent past. So the fear is not based on accident experiences you're having on a regular basis.

Client: No.

Assessor: Well, that's helpful to know. We've talked about the thoughts that go along with this experience and the physical symptoms. In terms of the physical symptoms, let me ask you this one more thing—all these different symptoms, do you notice whether they come on real suddenly, or if it's a gradual build-up once you're leaving the house?

Comment. This question about rate of onset is primarily designed to aid in generating a *DSM-IV* (American Psychiatric Association, 1994) diagnosis of a panic disorder. Although there have been many articles written about the shortcomings of the *DSM* and its incompatibility with an individualized clinical causal modeling approach to assessment (e.g., Bisset & Hayes, 1999), it is often a necessary component in many managed care systems. Further, much of the assessment and treatment-outcome literature is organized around *DSM* diagnostic categories.

The client reported the onset is rapid and thus provided sufficient details to confirm a *DSM-IV* diagnosis of panic disorder (rapid onset of symptoms that are characterized by panic-like states, sympathetic activation, thoughts related to catastrophic outcomes, and escape/avoidance behaviors). The assessor then gathered information about the topography of overt-motor responses.

Assessor: What are the actions that would be associated with this experience? We have the thoughts, the physical symptoms, if you had a video camera following you, for example, and I was watching you when you're having this experience versus when you're not, how would you look different? What would you be doing differently that would be a strong cue that you are feeling this way?

Client: In class, I pull out a sheet of paper and I try to focus on something else and I'll start a real quick things-to-do list, and I'll write down everything that I have to do when I get home, so then I'm thinking that will make the time go faster. I'll put that away, and then I'll close my books and open my books back up contemplating whether or not to leave, gather my stuff up and look like I'm gonna leave, and then if it subsides, then I'll open my books back up. I grab onto things. I don't . . . I can't tell whether or not I shake, but I worry that I do, because I'm afraid that the person behind me is gonna notice something. I don't want that, so I try to sit there; that's why I grab onto something.

Assessor: Okay. Now, let's say this feeling hits you when you're not in class, when you're in another situation, like . . .

Client: Grocery store?

Assessor: Okay.

Client: [laughs]

Assessor: What would you look like there?

Client: I was in a grocery store with my Mom on Sunday and it happened. She said that I had this look of terror on my face. And I just grabbed onto the cart and I said where's the bathroom? And she said it's over there, and I'm like, I'll be back in a second, and then I walked that way, and then I didn't go that way because my sister says that if you give in every time, you'll become a constant problem. So, I'm like okay, I'm not going to do that. So it was like I looked like I'm torn between having to go do something and not.

Comment. Thus far, overt-motor responses include scanning the environment for restrooms or avenues of escape, asking questions, avoidance, and escape. The assessor then began gathering information about potential causal relationships. Following the requirements for causal inference, the aim is to identify intraindividual and/or situational factors that reliably covary and precede or contingently follow target behaviors.

Assessor: You identified *what* this experience is like. . . . *When* do you have this experience?

Client: They're sometimes worse—no, and I can't really say when that is, it's always on my mind, I'm always conscious of where things are, like I had an internship over the summer, and I wouldn't eat, because then I thought if I don't eat, then I'm not gonna have to go to the bathroom. So, I do that, and then some days I'd go to work and I wouldn't have a problem, and some days I would. And I think it all just depended on what I was concentrating on, if I had a high work load that day, then I couldn't concentrate on my work and think about me, you know, and I think sometimes that's why I'm having more difficulty this semester, because I'm only taking 13 credit hours, and I have a little more time on my hands, so sometimes I think that maybe I'm just trying to find things to worry about that aren't as constructive.

Assessor: So depending on how busy you are, that may be associated with more or less intense symptoms, and if you go to a class—every single class are you having this experience, or just some classes?

Client: Just some classes. There's one class in particular that I'm having the worst problem, and the door's up front, right by the professor, and I don't like that because I feel trapped, so I'll sit right by the door, but since the door's right by him then I'm afraid that if, that he's gonna notice if I leave. I feel like I can't leave. So I feel kinda trapped in there.

Assessor: Is that a general rule, would you say, that in situations where it may be hard to leave or harder to leave, you feel more fear?

Client: Yeah, because I had a class last semester where the door was up front, and there was more of a space between the first seat and the door, and that made me nervous, real nervous, and I had a problem in that class too.

Comment. The client confirms that a critical environmental stimulus for fear is the availability of, or access to, an escape route.

Assessor: And so escape from the room is something that you're using as a cue, or at least you're paying very close attention to. Is that the same for other places, like a restaurant, if the bathroom's far away, or you don't know where it is, would that be a more anxiety-provoking situation?

Client: I typically always find out where it is, or I like to sit so I can face the door, so I can see the door, I don't like to face towards the restaurant, and my parents know that, so they just automatically sit there, like when we go places, I prefer to be by the door or by the bathroom.

Assessor: How about other situations, if you're just going for a walk, let's say. You're just going to go outside, nowhere in particular in mind, or when you're driving?

Client: I don't walk [laughs]. I used to, but when I go to class, I go so that I know the distance between my apartment and the first restroom, and then every restroom in each building along the way to my class. Because Dr. Smith and I talked about that; he said have you ever tried exercise and I said well, I don't like to go to the recreation center because the restroom is in the locker room, on the next floor. I'm up there and I have to go down the stairs to the bathroom so that's not a comfortable place for me.

Assessor: How about driving?

Client: I don't drive [laughs]. This past weekend was the first time I've driven since August. I don't really feel comfortable driving. When I do drive, I usually don't have a problem, I'll go to the bathroom before I leave, and then I know that it's not going to be long before I get somewhere else. Usually I'm pretty okay with that.

Therapist: Okay but lately you haven't been driving?

Client: I haven't.

Assessor: And is it because of this same fear, or is it something else?

Client: I just . . . sometimes . . . I have a fear of driving because I have a fear of losing control.

Assessor: Of the car?

Client: Yeah. So I don't drive much. I haven't ever since I've started driving.

Assessor: Okay. That brings me to another question. I wanted to ask you about certain actions that you might take associated with this problem. You mentioned that sometimes you might avoid eating so that you wouldn't have a BM—how often are you using that as a strategy for coping, would you say?

Client: Every Tuesday and Thursday. [laughs]

Assessor: What's on Tuesday and Thursday?

Client: The class where the door's up front.

Assessor: So what do you do?

Client: I usually wait until I'm home for the night to eat. That's usually what I do. And I've been taking, like if I'm feeling nervous before I leave for classes, I'll take Pepto-Bismol and I've been falling back on that a little more than I'd like to because I'm not a big pill-taker. I'm not a big drug-taker. I don't like any kind of med-

ications in me. So I don't really like that, but I'll do that regardless of whether or not symptoms are actually physical; I feel better that I've taken something.

Comment. Eating avoidance is related to specific days where exposure to a more intense anxiety-provoking situation will occur. In addition, the client has reported another aspect of her target behavior—Pepto-Bismol consumption.

Assessor: What does the Pepto-Bismol do for you?

Client: I don't know. [laugh] It just says that it's for nausea and diarrhea and stomach. So I thought that if I take that then maybe I won't have a problem.

Assessor: So it's a preventive thing.

Client: Yeah.

Assessor: Do you use vomiting sometimes as a way of getting food out of your system?

Client: No.

Assessor: Okay. Normally, I know it's hard to talk about bowel movements, but I might as well get through that. How are your bowel movements?

Client: They're fine. Normal.

Assessor: No diarrhea? How often do you typically go?

Client: I don't know, once a day. They're not, I don't think they're irregular, you know, usually when I get nervous and I feel like I have to go to the bathroom, I don't end up going. There's been a couple of times when I've run to the bathroom and I have gone, and sometimes I think that reinforces the fact that I am going to go.

Assessor: It's also the case that sometimes you feel like you have to go to the bathroom and nothing happens? I know this is a hard question, but what's the ratio? For example, number of times to the bathroom, how many times do you actually end up going, would you say?

Client: I would say 50% of the time.

Assessor: 50%. . . . and so 50% of the time you actually go to the bathroom—there are many times you end up not going and nothing seems to happen?

Comment. The client's sensation of having to go to the bathroom is not a reliable predictor of actually having a bowel movement. This will be important for later cognitive therapy targeting probability overestimation and symptom interpretation.

Client: Yeah.

Assessor: I'm going to ask you a little bit more about some of the other areas that you're worried about as well, so the GI is the number one and it seems like it's related to the other problems too. But you mentioned you also have some worries about your cardiovascular system, or having some problems there. Could you tell me more about them, too, please?

Client: [laughs] That's been going on ever since I was real, real little, probably around 6 years old because I would play tiny tot soccer, and I'd run up and down the field with my hand on my heart because I was afraid if I ran too fast that my heart would stop beating. That's been going on for a long time. I never went to get it checked out until it was right after I graduated high school I was out with my cousin and my heart pumped—it like skipped a beat, and I fell over because, I don't know what it did, it interrupted the blood flow to my brain or something. So I went into the doctor because that happened twice in a matter of a week. They didn't find anything significant, they said that my heart races a lot because they put me on the monitor for 24 hrs and they said that my heart races a lot. And that I should probably keep an eye on that because there's mitral valve prolapse in the family, but that's not anything really life-threatening, anyways. But it's like I hear what the doctor says, but I don't really believe them. It's with my heart, it's with other things. Like one time I had a headache and I went to the eye doctor and he thought that it might be eyestrain, and then he couldn't find eyestrain, and he said that it was on one side of the head, so they said maybe I should go to a neurologist to see if there's anything, and then he said that he'd run a test to see if there was pressure on the back of my eye, and I was crying and I told my mom that he thought that I had a brain tumor. Like my doctor in high school, he knew that I was a little irrational, so one time I had a cyst behind my ear, and he sat me down and said it's not cancer. And then I went home anyways and told my mom that I had cancer because I just don't think that they tell you the truth.

Assessor: And you're going to think, in absence of information, worst-case scenarios?

Client: Yes, so my mom, now even though I'm 23, she still goes to the doctor with me, because she wants to know what's going on, because she knows that I probably won't. . . .

Assessor: So, this really is troubling you more now?

Client: Well, my uncle died of a heart attack two weeks ago, and I guess for a little while I thought that God was sending me a signal that like maybe I'm not being irrational about wondering about my heart.

Assessor: It made it all more real for you.

Client: I sleep with my lights on and the phone right by my head. Usually I don't sleep very well because I'm afraid that I'm not going to wake up.

Assessor: Is this since your Uncle died?

Client: No, this has been going on since—it started in my junior year, two years ago. I started getting real bad. My sophomore year was worse than my freshman year; it seems to have gotten worse, and this semester is just, I mean I used to not always sleep sitting up, I would sometimes if I felt weird, but I do now, sit up all the time.

Assessor: How does that help you?

Client: I don't know, I just feel like that if I'm sitting up, then I'll stay awake, or if I'm sitting up then I'm able to breathe better. I don't know. It just makes me feel better.

Assessor: Do you feel that you're less at risk for having heart trouble?

Client: Yeah. I feel like it usually palpitates more when I'm lying down, or at least I notice it more, so I think that if I sit up, then it won't do it.

Assessor: Okay. So you feel your heart more when you lay down, and when you're sitting up, you don't feel it.

Comment. The client has identified another distinct area of target behavior. Having a catastrophic cardiovascular event (e.g., acute MI). Like the GI problem, it has a long history. Additionally, the client is describing a number of behaviors (e.g., sitting up) that allow her to escape from cardiac sensations, sleep, and fears that help will be unavailable (i.e., having a phone nearby). After interviewing her about the topography of the target behaviors and causal variables, it appeared that the panic and fear associated with having a heart attack was similar to the panic and fear associated with having a BM accident. In both cases, the client was perceiving benign physical symptoms to be indicators of an imminent and catastrophic event. Additionally, the client was using avoidance behaviors (e.g., sitting up, keeping lights on, having a telephone nearby, avoiding medical evaluations) to limit exposure to the physical sensations (intraindividual causal variables) and/or situations (milieu causal variables and interpersonal causal variables) that provoke the target behaviors. Unlike the GI-related panic, this fear of a heart attack was more erratic and episodic. It was also more situationally specific (occurring primarily when she retires for the evening).

The client also reported a number of positive aspects of her life, including supportive family relationships, academic

TABLE 5.2   Topography of Target Behaviors

Cognitive-Verbal	Affective-Physiological	Overt-Motor

Catastrophic Self-statements
  "I'm going to embarrass myself"
  "It's out of control"
  "I can't risk it"
  "I've got to get out of here"
	Sympathetic Activation
	  Heart pounds
	  Heart races
	  Feel hot
	  Feel cramps
	  Stomach bloating
	  Feel sweaty
	  Choking sensation
		Avoidance Behaviors
		  Breathe deep
		  Scan for bathroom
		  Stand near bathroom
		  Avoid places where escape is difficult or
		    bathrooms are unavailable
		  Take Pepto-Bismol
		  Avoid driving
		  Avoid eating

Inaccurate Prediction of Negative Event
  "I'm going to have an accident"
  "I'm going to have a heart attack"
  "I'm going to choke"
	Sleep Difficulties	

Concentration Difficulties		*Escape Behaviors*
		  Scan for exit or bathroom
		  Grab something
		  Get ready to leave
		  Leave

TABLE 5.3   Topography of Causal Variables

Situational-Milieu	Situational-Interpersonal	Intraindividual

*Settings Where Bathroom Access
    and/or Escape Is Limited*
  Classroom
  Grocery store
  Recreation center
  Outdoors
  Driving/riding in car
	Original Panic Attack
	  History of BM accident with
	    severe social sanctions
		Interoceptive Cues
		  GI sensations
		  Cardiac sensations

	Negative Life Events
	  Uncle with recent heart attack
		*Family History: Susceptibility for
		    Excessive Sympathetic
		    Activation*

Settings Where Help Is Unavailable
  Driving alone in car
  In bedroom at night
	Social Reinforcement
	  Family and friends arrange for
	    preferred seating at restaurants,
	    may support other avoidance
	    and escape behaviors
		Catastrophic Self-statements

		Inaccurate Prediction of Negative Event
		Avoidance Behaviors Negative reinforcement
		Escape Behaviors Negative reinforcement

success, plans for graduate school, and a supportive intimate relationship. After collecting information about these more positive aspects of her life, the assessor gathered medical, demographic, occupational, educational, and family history. This information was helpful in constructing the historical components of the causal model. Additionally, the family history questions revealed that she has a sister who received outpatient psychotherapy for panic, agoraphobia, and suicidal tendencies. She also reported that her mother experienced difficulties with agoraphobia. No medical diagnoses were applicable, and the patient had undergone extensive prior medical evaluations as well.

Subsequent to information gathering, the assessor provided a preliminary causal model, developed with the client her goals for therapy (she hoped for a significant reduction in panic frequency, avoidance/escape behaviors, and the chronic anxiety associated with both GI and cardiac symptoms), and oriented the client to the cognitive-behavioral approach to therapy.

Finally, self-monitoring forms were provided, and the client was asked record information about the topography of panic, along with situations in which panic attacks occurred.

Clinical Causal Model for Anna

The topography of Anna's target behaviors and causal behaviors are summarized in Tables 5.2 and 5.3. A clinical causal model of the client's problems is presented in Figure 5.1. This model, based on the assessment information and knowledge of the research literature, illustrates the complex nature of causal relationships for an individual client (for a more detailed discussion of idiographic causal model construction, see Haynes, Leisen, & Blaine, 1997). The causal variables at the top of the figure are referred to as original causal variables. These were postulated to be early learning experiences or genetic susceptibility variables that created the original conditions for extreme fear responses or "panic at-

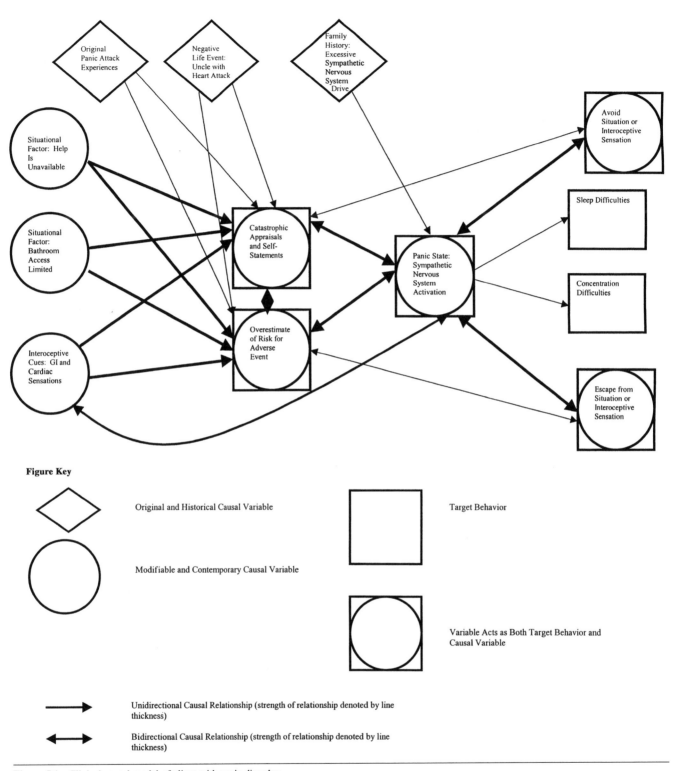

Figure 5.1   Clinical causal model of client with panic disorder.

tacks." More specifically, genetic susceptibility combined with critical childhood experiences (i.e., the initial loss of bowel control and episodes of cardiovascular activation during exercise) may have provoked the initial panic attacks. Through the process of classical conditioning, milieu stimuli (situations where help was unavailable such as her bedroom at night; where bathrooms were inaccessible; or escape was difficult, such as classrooms, driving, walking outdoors) and interoceptive cues (i.e., gastrointestinal sensations, cardiac sensations that were closely associated with these initial panic attacks) became conditioned stimuli for fear responses. Thus, upon re-exposure to these situations or interoceptive cues, the client experienced heightened levels of fear (defined in her case as increased sympathetic activation, which is bidirectionally associated with catastrophic self-statements and overestimation of her levels of risk for an adverse outcome such as a BM accident or a heart attack). In order to reduce the likelihood of experiencing additional conditioned fear responses or intensified fear, she learned to avoid or leave situations where bathrooms may be inaccessible or escape may be difficult. She also learned to avoid activities or positions where cardiovascular activation could be more readily perceived (e.g., lying down or during exercise). These avoidance and escape behaviors were negatively reinforced via anxiety reduction (as evidenced by the bidirectional causal indicators, which suggest that increased sympathetic activation and problematic appraisals both lead to escape and avoidance behaviors and are diminished by escape and avoidance behaviors) and also social support (e.g., family and friends supported Anna's requests for special seating, driving avoidance, etc.).

The hypothesized causal relationships contained in this model were initially identified during the interview provided above using the marker variable strategy. That is, the client's verbal reports of potential causal relationships served as a marker of potential causal relationships. In subsequent sessions, self-monitoring data provided information about the frequency, duration, and situations where panic attacks were most likely to occur. Additionally, in later sessions, experimental manipulations in the form of in vivo interoceptive exposure exercises allowed us to gain enhanced measures of the cognitive, physiological, and behavioral responses associated with panic.

The clinical causal model was used to design a cognitive-behavioral intervention that was partially based on the mastery of anxiety and panic protocol developed by Craske and Barlow (Craske, Barlow, & O'Leary, 1992). This intervention targeted for change the factors that were believed to be exerting the greatest amount of control over the client's behavior problems (as illustrated by the wider vector lines in Figure 5.1). She was thus provided with: (1) training in relaxation and breathing strategies that allowed her to gain improved control of her physiological activation patterns, (2) training in cognition modification skills designed to improve her ability to detect and correct problematic self-statements, and (3) graded exposure to fear-provoking stimuli, which included internal physiological sensations and situations where bathroom access and escape is difficult (i.e., walking outdoors

away from bathroom facilities, attending classrooms and sitting away from the exit, driving alone, etc.).

Goals of the Intervention

The intervention was designed to promote the following outcomes: (a) improved control of sympathetic reactivity via relaxation training, (b) improved control of problematic beliefs about panic—specifically catastrophic appraisals of normal physiological activation patterns and probability overestimation (i.e., a tendency to overpredict that panic would occur in various situations), (c) a reduction in panic attack frequency, (d) reductions in daily anxiety levels and worry about panic, and (e) reductions in avoidance and escape behaviors.

Evaluation of Progress in Therapy

A summary of the essential components of each session are presented in Table 5.4. Daily self-monitored ratings of panic attacks, anxiety, depression, and worry about having a panic

TABLE 5.4   Summary of Intervention and Outcomes

Session Number	Components of Session	No. of Panic Attacks
1	Interview, self-monitoring.	
2	Review of self-monitoring data, education about panic, present behavioral model of panic	8
3	Review of self-monitoring, relaxation training, daily relaxation practice	12
4	Review of self-monitoring, review of relaxation practice, identification of problematic thoughts, identification of alternative thoughts, conducted prediction of panic exercises	6
5	Review self-monitoring, prediction of panic, development of panic symptom hierarchy, identification of catastrophic thoughts and alternative thoughts	2
6	Review self-monitoring, interoceptive exposure; challenged catastrophic interpretations of symptoms and guided client through alternative thoughts and interpretations, daily self-exposure for the upcoming week	0
7	Review self-monitoring, continued interoceptive exposure, added interoceptive exposure in high-risk situations (outdoors in open field far from buildings). Interoceptive exposure in high-risk situations for homework	0
8	Review self-monitoring, continued interoceptive exposure in high-risk situations (library 8th floor—no access to bathroom + elevator ride). Continued self-exposure in high-risk situations	0
9	Review self-monitoring, relapse prevention, discussion of self-guided exposure during summer	0

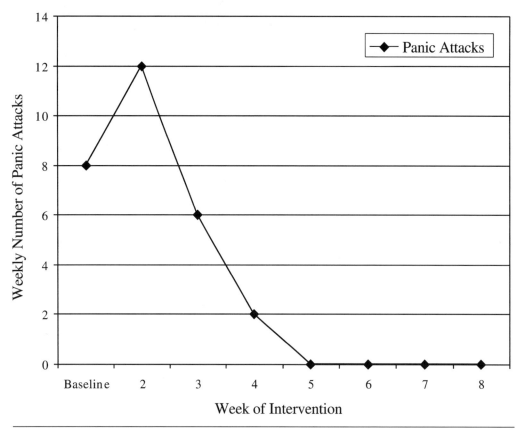

Figure 5.2 Panic attack frequency across the 8 weeks of the intervention.

attack are summarized in Table 5.4 and Figures 5.2 and 5.3. An analysis of these data indicated that daily ratings of panic frequency, anxiety, and worry were significantly associated with the delivery of treatment ($R^2 = .37$ for panic, $R^2 = .42$ for anxiety, and $R^2 = .54$ for worry). Specifically, as treatment progressed, panic frequency, daily anxiety ratings, and daily worry about panic decreased.

Daily depression ratings were evaluated using an alternative statistical model because day-to-day ratings were highly correlated. Results of this analysis indicated depression ratings were not significantly associated with treatment ($F (1, 46) = 1.5, p = .23$). Visual inspection of depression ratings suggests that this lack of significance may be due to an increase in depression ratings that occurred toward the end of the intervention. The client reported that part of this increased level of depression ratings stemmed from the sadness that she felt as she anticipated graduating from college. Because depressed mood was not a major target of the intervention and because the rating was still rather low at the conclusion of treatment, we did not choose to continue treatment in an effort to promote further reductions in this negative mood.

SUMMARY AND CONCLUSIONS

Clinical causal models can be used to better understand the form and function of target behaviors and to aid in the design of interventions. The process of creating clinical causal models requires familiarity with the basic standards by which it is reasonable to form causal inferences. Additionally, as the research literature in psychopathology has expanded, it has become apparent that causal relationships can take on many forms and can vary according to time and context. Thus, clinical causal models, which subsume many target behaviors and causal variables, can become exceedingly complex.

In order to reduce the complexity of causal model construction, the assessor can educe several causal principles and conceptual foundations about the nature of problem behavior and the ways that it should be measured. Additionally, most assessors will simplify the assessment task by applying presuppositions that guide the selection and measurement of causal variables.

In addition to knowledge of causal principles, conceptual foundations, and presuppositions, Assessors should also be

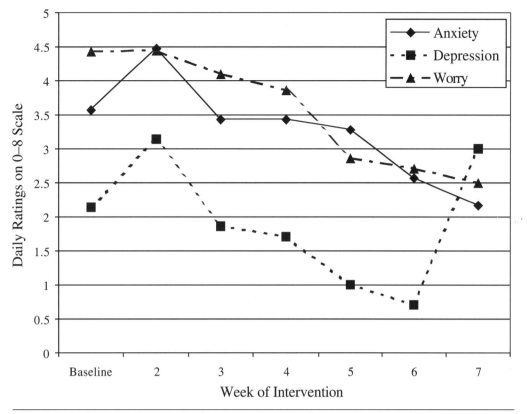

Figure 5.3 Anxiety, depression, and worry levels across the intervention.

familiar with specific strategies that can be used to identify functional relationships. Each method has strengths and limitations related to the strength of causal inference that can be derived from collected data and the degree of clinical applicability. Clinical causal modeling is offered as a method for organizing, interpreting, and communicating complex information about the form and function of target behaviors. A causal illustration demonstrates how the clinical causal model can summarize assessment information into a parsimonious depiction of client functioning and can assist with the design of an intervention. Several important questions about clinical causal modeling merit further investigation. First, to what extent does the use of a clinical causal model lead to more effective interventions? Second, can assessors be trained to reliably identify and evaluate causal relationships? Third, how generalizable are clinical causal models across clients, behaviors, and settings? A final important question for future consideration is the treatment utility of clinical causal models in light of the growing use of treatment protocols. Specifically, what are the relative costs and benefits of individualized treatments compared to nomothetically based treatment protocols?

NOTE

1. There are many other purposes for the initial interview beyond identification of target behavior topography and function. Specifically, the interviewer must provide many nonspecific and process-oriented intervention techniques, such as empathic support, paraphrasing, and reassurance. These are critical for establishing rapport and helping the client begin to examine his or her difficulties in a constructive, approach-oriented manner.

REFERENCES

American Psychiatric Association (1994). *Diagnostic and statistical manual of mental disorders* (4th ed.). Washington, DC: Author.

Anthony, J.L., & O'Brien, W.H. (1999). An evaluation of the impact of social support manipulations on cardiovascular reactivity to laboratory stressors. *Behavioral Medicine, 25,* 78–87.

Anthony, J.L., & O'Brien, W.H. (in press). The impact of a social support intervention on cardiovascular function, stress, depression, anxiety, and physical symptoms. *Small Group Research.*

Arkes, H.R. (1981). Impediments to accurate clinical judgment and possible ways to minimize their impact. *Journal of Consulting and Clinical Psychology, 49,* 323–330.

Beauchamp, T.L., & Rosenberg, A. (1981). *Hume and the problem of causation*. New York: Oxford University Press.

Bissett, R.T., & Hayes, S.C. (1999). The likely success of functional analysis tied to the DSM. *Behaviour Research and Therapy, 37,* 379–383.

Bunge, M. (1979). *Causality and modern science*. New York: Dover.

Cook, T.D., & Campbell, D.T. (1979). *Quasi-experimentation: Design & analysis issues for field settings*. Boston: Houghton Mifflin.

Craske, M.G., Barlow, D.H., & O'Leary, T.A. (1992*). Mastery of your anxiety and worry*. San Antonio, TX: Psychological Corporation.

Crozier, W.R., & Alden, L.E. (2001). *International handbook of social anxiety: Concepts, research, and interventions related to the self and shyness*. New York: Wiley.

Durand, V.M. (1990). *Severe behavior problems: A functional communication training approach*. New York: Guilford Press.

Forsyth, J.P., Chase, P.N., & Hackbert, L. (1997). A behavior analytic interpretation of attributions in the context of behavior therapy. *Journal of Behavior Therapy and Experimental Psychiatry, 28,* 17–29.

Garb, H.N. (1989). Clinical judgment, clinical training, and professional experience. *Psychological Bulletin, 105,* 387–396.

Garb, H.N. (1996). *Studying the clinician: Judgment research and psychological assessment*. Washington, DC: American Psychological Association.

Hage, J., & Meeker, B.F. (1988). *Social causality*. Winchester, MA: Allen & Unwin.

Hartmann, D.P., & Wood, D.D. (1990). Observational methods. In A.S. Bellack, M. Hersen, & A.E. Kazdin (Eds.), *International handbook of behavior modification and therapy* (2nd ed., pp. 107–138). New York: Plenum.

Hayes, S.C., & Follette, W.C. (1992). Can functional analysis provide a substitute for syndromal classification? *Behavioral Assessment, 14,* 345–365.

Hayes, S.C., Wilson, K.G., Strosahl, K., Gifford, E., & Follette, V.M. (1996). Experiential avoidance and behavioral disorders: A functional dimensional approach to diagnosis and treatment. *Journal of Consulting and Clinical Psychology, 64,* 1152–1168.

Haynes, S.N. (1992). *Models of causality in psychopathology: Toward synthetic, dynamic, and nonlinear models of causality in psychopathology*. Boston: Allyn & Bacon.

Haynes, S.N. (1998). The assessment-treatment relationship and functional analysis in behavior therapy. *European Journal of Psychological Assessment, 14,* 26–35.

Haynes, S.N., Leisen, M., & Blaine, D.D. (1997). Design of individualized behavioral treatment programs using functional analytic clinical case models. *Psychological Assessment, 9,* 334–348.

Haynes, S.N. & O'Brien, W.H. (2000). *Principles and practice of behavioral assessment*. New York: Plenum.

Honderich, T. (1995). *The Oxford companion to philosophy*. Oxford, England: Oxford University Press.

Irwin, T. & Fine, G. (Eds.) (1995). *Aristotle: Selections*. Indianapolis, IN: Hackett.

Iwata, B.A., Smith, R.G., & Michael, J. (2000). Current research on the influence of establishing operations on behavior in applied settings. *Journal of Applied Behavior Analysis, 33,* 411–418.

James, L.R., Mulaik, S.A., & Brett, J.M. (1982). *Causal analysis: Assumptions, models, and data*. Beverly Hills, CA: Sage.

Kazdin, A.E. (1998). *Research design in clinical psychology* (3rd ed.). Boston: Allyn & Bacon.

Kearney, C.A., & Silverman, W.K., (1990). A preliminary analysis of a functional model of assessment and treatment for school refusal behavior. *Behavior Modification, 14,* 340–366.

Kohlenberg, R.J., & Tsai, M. (1991). *Functional analytic psychotherapy: Creating intense and curative therapeutic relationships*. New York: Plenum.

Lewinsohn, P.M., & Joiner, T.E. (2001). Evaluation of cognitive diathesis-stress models in predicting major depressive disorder in adolescents. *Journal of Abnormal Psychology, 110,* 203–215.

Magill, F.N. (Ed.). (1990). *Masterpieces of world philosophy*. New York: Harper Collins.

McCauley, S.R., Hannay, H.J., & Swank, P.R. (2001). Use of the disability rating scale recovery curve as a predictor of psychosocial outcome following closed head injury. *Journal of the International Neuropsychological Society, 7,* 457–467.

Nishino, S., Mignot, E., & Dement, W.C. (1995). Sedative-hypnotics. In A. F. Schatzberg & C.B. Nemeroff (Eds.), *Textbook of psychopharmacology* (pp. 405–416). Washington, DC: American Psychiatric Press.

O'Brien, W.H. (1995). Inaccuracies in the estimation of functional relationships using self-monitoring data. *Journal of Behavior Therapy and Experimental Psychiatry, 26,* 351–357.

O'Brien, W.H., & Haynes, S.N. (1995). A functional analytic approach to the assessment and treatment of a child with frequent migraine headaches. *In Session: Psychotherapy in Practice, 1,* 65–80.

O'Brien, W.H., Korchynsky, R., Fabrizio, J., McGrath, J., & Swank, A. (1999). Evaluating group process in a stress management intervention: Relationships between perceived process and cardiovascular reactivity to stress. *Research on Social Work Practice, 9,* 608–630.

O'Brien, W.H., McGrath, J.J., & Haynes, S.N. (in press). Assessment of psychopathology: Behavioral approaches. In J. Graham & J. Naglieri (Eds.) *Handbook of psychological assessment*. New York: Wiley.

Paul, G.L. (1986). *The time sample behavioral checklist: Observational assessment instrumentation for service and research.* Champaign, IL: Research Press.

Sasso, G.M., Reimers, T.M., Cooper, L.J., Wacker, D., Berg, W., Steege, M., Kelly, L., & Allaire, A. (1992). Use of descriptive and experimental analysis to identify the functional properties of aberrant behavior in school settings. *Journal of Applied Behavior Analysis, 25,* 809–821.

Schneider, F., & Deldin, P.J. (2001). *Comprehensive handbook of psychopathology* (3rd ed.). New York: Kluwer Academic.

Stewart, S.H., Taylor, S., Jang, K.L., Cox, B.J., Watt, M.C., Federoff, I.C., & Borger, S.C. (2001). Causal modeling of relations among learning history, anxiety sensitivity, and panic attacks. *Behaviour Research and Therapy, 39,* 443–456.

VanLaningham, J., Johnson, D.R., & Amato, P. (2001). Marital happiness, marital duration, and the U-shaped curve: Evidence from a five-wave panel study. *Social Forces, 79,* 1313–1341.

Van Overwalle, F. (1997). A test of the joint model of causal attribution. *European Journal of Social Psychology, 27,* 221–236.

Weyrauch, K.F., Roy-Berne, P., Katon, W., & Wilson, L. (2001). Stressful life events and impulsiveness in failed suicide. *Suicide and Life Threatening Behavior, 31,* 311–319.

CHAPTER 6

Conceptual Foundations of Behavioral Assessment Strategies: From Theory to Assessment

GEORG H. EIFERT AND MATTHEW T. FELDNER

Behavioral assessment is an integrated set of principles, beliefs, values, hypotheses, and methods primarily advocated by behavior analysts and therapists. In this broad sense, behavioral assessment is not different from other psychological assessment paradigms (Haynes, 1998). It includes hypotheses about the best level of measurement precision such as accuracy and validity (Cone, 1998a), the causal variables most likely to affect behavior, the mechanisms that underlie functional relations, the role of assessment in the design and evaluation of treatment, and the best methods for obtaining assessment data. The major difference between behavioral and other approaches to assessment is that these principles, beliefs, values, hypotheses, and methods are primarily derived from, and influenced by, behavioral theory and its underlying assumptions. Apart from behavioral theory, however, other sources of influence have increasingly grown stronger over the past three decades. This is particularly true in regard to the greater focus on cognitive behavior and processes (Forsyth, Lejuez, Hawkins, & Eifert, 1996).

Behavioral clinicians and researchers develop problem conceptualizations based on behavioral or cognitive-behavioral theories, which result in hypotheses regarding how a particular problem developed, what variables currently maintain it, and what strategies are likely to lead to behavioral changes in a desired direction. For example, a clinician may draw upon theoretical accounts of the anxiety-maintaining function of

avoidant behavior when deciding to implement an exposure-based treatment that targets a patient's avoidance behavior to reduce phobic anxiety. If that individual's anxiety is indeed reduced following such treatment, assessment of behavior before, during, and after treatment will have served to test the utility, or practical validity, of the initial hypotheses regarding the anxiety-maintaining function of avoidance behavior.

The conceptual foundations of behavioral theory and assessment are closely linked because behavioral assessors formulate hypotheses derived from behavioral theory supported by our current knowledge of behavioral models of specific clinical disorders (Eifert, 1992; Eifert, Schulte, Zvolensky, Lejuez, & Lau, 1997). As a result of this close link, many of the controversies and shortcomings in behavioral theory and therapy (Evans & Eifert, 1990) also apply to, and exert an influence on, behavioral assessment. For instance, the unresolved status of cognitive concepts in behavior theory has implications for behavioral assessment. In other words, answers to the question of whether private events cause, set the stage for, follow, or merely coincide with overt behavior have implications for behavioral interventions (e.g., whether such private events should, or even can be, directly changed). At the same time, this issue also affects assessment decisions in terms of whether and how we should attempt to assess private events.

The current chapter will focus on the bridge between the conceptual foundations of behavioral theory and assessment in the context of the various specific strategies and methods used in assessment. Also, we will focus on how developments in behavioral assessment should be closely tied to developments in behavioral theory. Yet the practice of behavioral assessment is not always inspired by behavioral theory. For example, medical researchers often know little about behavioral theory but frequently use behavioral measures to assess the effects of medications in clinical trials. Similar situations occur for assessment in the workplace and in managed care. Many of these researchers know very little about behavioral theory, or about the basic concepts of behavioral assessment, but implement behavioral assessment strategies (particularly as opposed to projective or personality assessment strategies) quite successfully.

Before we turn to a discussion of the relation between theory and assessment strategies, it is important to address specific conceptual foundations of behavioral theory. Specifically, we will consider the epistemological position and associated assumptions adopted by behaviorism in regard to the function and context of behavior as well as the overarching goals of behavioral assessment.

EPISTEMOLOGY

Epistemology is the philosophical study of knowledge and how one arrives at knowledge, which directly influences such aspects of science as methodology and theory development. Behaviorism has adopted an empirical epistemology, which roughly translates to a reliance on sensory perception to arrive at knowledge (Haynes & O'Brien, 2000; Nelson & Hayes, 1986). Therefore, the only route to *true* knowledge within behaviorism is to observe the phenomenon under question. Fundamentally, an empirical approach to science emphasizes the use of observation and systematic experimentation. As an approach that assumes an empirical epistemology, behavioral *theory* development is based on observation via scientific investigations in both naturalistic as well as contrived laboratory environments. In other words, behavioral theory develops as controlled observations are made available by researchers and clinicians. For example, behavioral theories of anxiety reduction developed when Mary Cover Jones reported that phobic anxiety in young children can be reduced if they eat chocolate in the presence of the fear-evoking stimulus, or when Joseph Wolpe published his observation that cats became less fearful of being in a cage where they had been shocked when they were given food to eat in those cages.

Similarly, given the shared adoption of an empirical epistemology, new developments and advances in behavioral *as-*

sessment should be the result of new empirical findings. For instance, the development and use of specific measures should be grounded and supported by empirical data such as reliability and validity data obtained from studying carefully defined groups of individuals that share a particular functional problem (e.g., Eifert et al., 2000a). An example is the assessment of hyperventilation in some individuals with anxiety disorders. As a result of increasing evidence pointing to the role of hyperventilation in the etiology and maintenance of heart-focused anxiety (Eifert, 1992) and panic disorder (Barlow, 2001), researchers developed standardized tests of hyperventilation and other biological challenge procedures (Zvolensky & Eifert, 2000). These tests, grounded in empirical data and studied in conjunction with other theoretically relevant variables, have yielded useful information for improving our understanding of the etiology of anxiety-related disorders. As such, they also have been useful for assessment and treatment purposes in both research and clinical settings.

Assessment strategies also must be designed to test hypotheses derived from behavioral theory. Although the current chapter does not allow for a thorough discussion of the relation between theory and data, a brief discussion is warranted. As an empirical approach, behavioral theory is continually developed based on available and emerging data (Plaud & Eifert, 1998). At the same time, empirical investigations (including research and clinical assessment) are guided by behavioral theory. For example, the behavioral theory of panic disorder (e.g., Barlow, 2001) predicts that individuals with panic disorder are more sensitive to interoceptive arousal. This prediction has been subjected to several empirical tests (e.g., Asmundson, Sandler, Wilson, & Norton, 1993; Rapee, 1994; Schmidt, Lerew, & Trakowski, 1997) and also has implications for treatment. Immanuel Kant proposed the aforementioned reciprocal development of theory and data in his celebrated dictum, "thoughts without content are empty and intuitions without concepts are blind," which has been paraphrased as, "theory without data is groundless and data without theory are uninterpretable" (cited in Reese, 1994). In terms of our discussion, behavioral assessment yields meaningless ("empty") data without the guiding framework provided by behavioral theory. To extend this concept to behavior therapy, theory-less assessment data result in clinical hypotheses constructed on notions or hunches rather than rational or empirical bases (Franks, 1998).

Kant's dictum neither argues for an inductive (data-driven theory) nor deductive (theory-driven data collection) approach. Rather, it suggests that, in order for developments in science to occur, there must be both theory and data, regardless of which comes first. For example, an inductive approach may yield large sets of valid data on parent-child interactions across time. However, the data remain uninterpretable unless a scholar eventually comes up with some general statements regarding the relation between parent and child behaviors across time. If no such general statements are developed, the researcher will only know what happened between the parents and children being studied at the particular time and place when the interaction occurred. On the other hand, if a scholar states that parent-child interactions are influenced by certain environmental variables, but has no data to support the theory, the theory is meaningless.

TRUTH CRITERION

A second assumption involved in psychological theory that warrants consideration is how the value of an approach is evaluated. In other words, what is the theory's truth criterion? Behaviorism, and by extension behavior therapy, often has adopted a pragmatic or functional approach, which suggests that behaviorism as a theory should be evaluated based on how well it guides clinicians, researchers, and assessors toward approaches that achieve assumed goals (Evans & Wilson, 1983; Hayes, Nelson, & Jarrett, 1987). Indeed much of clinical behavioral assessment is conducted to contribute to and document treatment progress and outcome. Of course, behavioral assessment strategies also may be useful in problem screening, making decisions about child placements, and identifying individuals at risk for future problems (e.g., relapse, violence, etc.). Yet the value of the assessment strategy is similarly determined by how well the assessment guides the assessor's decision.

Behavior theory is not primarily aimed at merely describing behavior, but at providing tools for analyzing behavior in functional terms with a goal of being able to change that behavior, if such change is deemed desirable. In other words, behavior theory offers an outline for determining the function(s) maintaining a problem behavior. For instance, reinforcement theory suggests that a behavior is maintained by its relation to a reinforcement contingency. Therefore, an analysis of the relation between a particular behavior and its consequences allows a clinician to manipulate contingencies such that the behavior is changed in a desirable fashion. As an example, if a child's temper tantrum results in increased attention, which then maintains the tantrum behavior, the clinician can instruct the parents to refrain from reinforcing the behavior with attention. In the same way, clinical behavioral assessment strategies are deemed useful if they provide information that helps design and implement behavioral change strategies and examine their effectiveness (Hayes et al., 1987). Thus, the practical impact and utility of using a particular

assessment strategy, or as Cone (1998a) described it, the "consequential validity," is the ultimate criterion for the value of a behavioral assessment strategy.

Although we have adopted this pragmatic truth or utility criterion for the purposes of this chapter, other truth criteria have been adopted within behaviorism (see Hayes, Hayes, Reese, & Sarbin, 1993, for a discussion of other truth criteria). However, in an attempt to preserve continuity (and achieve *our* functional goals for this chapter), we will limit our discussion to the implications of a pragmatic truth and utility criterion. As an additional caveat to the reader, we will use the term *function* in this chapter to refer both to how well an approach achieves its goals and to the relation between a behavior and its consequences. In order to adhere to terminology generally used in discussions of these two issues, and hopefully minimize confusion, we will not introduce new terms to separate these two meanings of function.

GOALS

Within a functional approach, the utility of an assessment strategy or technique is determined by its ability to help achieve the goals of the assessment. Although a comprehensive discussion of the goals of behavioral assessment is beyond the scope of our chapter (see Haynes & O'Brien, 2000, for a discussion), a few points are particularly relevant to the current discussion. One major goal of assessment is to increase the validity of clinical judgments. Subsumed within this broad goal, assessment aims to identify different facets of behavior problems and environmental factors maintaining such problems. Thus, theory guides clinical hypotheses regarding what facets of behavior should be examined and what aspects of an environment may be maintaining behavior. For example, behavioral theory suggests that one of the core functions of compulsive behavior is to avoid or escape from certain anxiety-inducing stimuli. This behavior is maintained because it leads to a reduction of anxiety or tension. These conceptual notions then guide clinical hypotheses and assessment strategies. For instance, a clinician may directly assess the compulsive behavior (e.g., by counting the number of times a patient engages in the act) and evaluate those data in relation to other patient data (e.g., anxiety ratings). In this sense, assessment data are used to test the hypotheses offered by theory. Additionally, clinical behavioral assessment aims to contribute to, and document, treatment progress and outcome. As such, behavioral assessment is inextricably linked to behavioral theory in that it is testing, monitoring, and documenting the effectiveness of treatments developed based upon behavioral theory.

Given these shared foundations of behavioral theory and assessment and our conceptualization of why theory and assessment are closely linked, we now turn our attention to how these foundations relate to specific assessment strategies. Specifically, our discussion will focus on the implications of the epistemological, functional, and goal-related assumptions of behavioral assessment in terms of specific strategies. Our discussion will include an emphasis on functional relations and functional diagnostic dimensions, a focus on context, the importance of using measures with validation data, incorporating multiple sources of information, focusing on multiple targets, and using specific (as opposed to higher-order) assessments. Finally, we will discuss how behavioral assessment strategies are affected by the same changes in the professional zeitgeist that affect behavior theory and how these influences may offer interesting challenges to behavioral assessors.

IMPLICATIONS OF THE CONCEPTUAL FOUNDATIONS OF BEHAVIORAL ASSESSMENT FOR SPECIFIC ASSESSMENT STRATEGIES

Identifying Functional Relations and Incorporating Diagnostic Dimensions

The most basic tenet of behavioral theory is that behavior is controlled by the context (i.e., antecedents and consequences) within which it occurs (e.g., Bouton & Nelson, 1998; Hayes et al., 1993; Skinner, 1953). Identification of the contextual variables that give rise to a particular behavior is therefore a primary concern of behavioral assessment strategies. In addition to providing a richer understanding of the etiology and maintaining factors of a behavior, the identification of a behavior's function(s) is directly relevant for clinical interventions. Assessments that provide insight into the etiology and maintaining functions of behavior also guide clinical decision making toward interventions that most effectively target functions of behavior. Thus, identifying functional relations between a behavior and the environment also will increase the likelihood of making valid clinical judgments. For example, a clinical decision to not use time-out procedures with a child exhibiting problem behavior is likely valid after determining that the child's behavior is reinforced (via time away from parental arguments) when the child is in a time-out room. We also need to recognize, however, that behavior seems to be only partially controlled by context. Although there is strong evidence that some variance is accounted for by context, there are many other sources of variance (e.g., HIV infection, brain injury, fetal alcohol syndromes, early physical abuse), which are not incompatible with behavioral formulations. In-

deed, comprehensive models of abnormal behavior (Eifert, Beach, & Wilson, 1998; Staats, 1996) include these sources of variance in their analyses.

A functional analysis is an assessment strategy that aims to identify and synthesize the situational, cognitive, and behavioral factors that control and/or set the stage for some aspect of a particular behavior's topography, such as its frequency, intensity, or duration (Haynes, Leisen, & Blaine, 1997). Behavior therapists are particularly interested in that subset of functional relations that involves influential, controllable variables, the manipulation of which will result in a clinically significant change in a target behavior of an individual client. For example, based on direct observations of the therapist and a patient's self-reports, a functional analysis may show that the escape behavior of a woman with panic disorder is maintained by reductions of anxiety that occur immediately when she leaves the place (e.g., a department store) where a panic attack occurs. This analysis is useful because it guides the clinician toward a particular treatment. A behavioral analysis of this example suggests that escape behavior is negatively reinforced through anxiety reduction. As a consequence, treatment would be aimed at preventing escape behavior and keeping the woman in the department store until her panic subsides without escaping from the feared environment.

Identifying the idiosyncratic function of individual problem behavior enhances the ability of an assessment strategy to achieve its goals and has long been considered the holy grail of behavioral assessment. Yet functional analyses are plagued by a number of problems because they are highly idiographic and at times difficult to replicate and impractical (Hayes, Wilson, Gifford, Follette, & Strosahl, 1996). Furthermore, contemporaneous foci of behavioral assessment are the social systems affecting behavior problems (i.e., an extended functional analysis). In work with children, for example, we are concerned with the contexts and contingencies that affect the caregivers. For instance, a parent with significant social support problems, depressed mood, medical problems, or financial stressors cannot easily implement behavioral management strategies necessary to deal with an oppositional child. Thus, it is insufficient to base treatment only on traditional functional analyses of the child's behavior. Similarly, treatment programs often cannot be implemented in psychiatric units because contingencies that affect staff behavior (e.g., union rules, supervision practices) are not congruent with needed changes in their behavior. Consequently, it often is insufficient to simply examine immediate antecedent and consequent factors for behavior problems. These problems are largely responsible for the decline in the use of functional analyses over the past 20 years (Haynes & O'Brien, 2000;

Scotti, Morris, McNeil, & Hawkins, 1996). Because they are sometimes vague, functional analyses also may fall prey to the well-documented errors common to clinical judgment.

According to Hayes and associates (1996), one of the most promising solutions to these problems is the development of functional diagnostic dimensions. Functional diagnostic dimensions seek to denote common processes of etiology or maintenance that suggest a similar course of action. These dimensions point to widely accepted pathological processes and may integrate contributions from various theoretical perspectives. How do we arrive at such dimensions? Hayes and colleagues suggest that if one performs many individual functional analyses tied to the same dimension, these analyses might then be arranged into a larger category with related or even common assessment methods and treatment recommendations. As indicated, the guiding principle behind these collections is the identification of a common process of etiology or maintenance that leads to a particular intervention strategy.

Experiential avoidance is an example of a functional diagnostic dimension that illustrates the potential benefits of using such dimensions rather than discrete diagnostic categories. Experiential avoidance is a rigid emotion regulation strategy functionally oriented toward escaping from and preventing experiential contact with aversive internal events (e.g., bodily sensations) and the contexts that occasion them (Hayes et al., 1996). For instance, a person with agoraphobia not only avoids public places, but also avoids experiencing private events, such as thoughts and emotions, associated with panic in those public places (Friman, Hayes, & Wilson, 1998). Avoidance of both overt stimuli and related thoughts and feelings are functionally related to anxiety, because both types of avoidance are likely to be negatively reinforced and maintained in so far as they both prevent or terminate the presentation of an aversive state (Forsyth & Eifert, 1998).

As an individual difference variable, experiential avoidance is a construct that captures a common process involved in the development and maintenance of maladaptive responding to internal stimuli in a variety of clinical problems that are topographically quite dissimilar and traditionally diagnosed using different categories of the *Diagnostic and Statistical Manual of Mental Disorders* (*DSM-IV*, American Psychiatric Association, 1994). Thus, an intriguing feature of experiential avoidance is that it is not just functionally related to one particular traditional diagnostic category, such as anxiety disorders, but that it also captures a core behavioral process in depression, substance abuse, and borderline personality disorder (see Hayes at al., 1996, for a more detailed discussion). In this sense, experiential avoidance refers to a class of behavior and yields information regarding an individual's response tendency across a number of different situations that share functional or contextual similarities.

Information gained from the assessment of experiential avoidance is relevant for treatment planning because it provides information about what motivates and maintains avoidance behavior. This information can then be readily translated into treatment programs that target particular behaviors in specific situations. For instance, a person with agoraphobia is instructed to stay in a store while having a panic attack; a depressed person who recently lost a partner is asked to elicit the memory of the deceased loved one without distraction; a substance abuser is taught to experience and simply notice discomfort without resorting to drinking alcohol to reduce the discomfort. Although the specific problem and population is different in each of these cases, all these interventions are fundamentally aimed at establishing a more general class of behavior, which is to experience private events without engaging in behavior to control their intensity or duration.

In addition to addressing some of the problems with functional analyses, functional diagnostic dimensions could be a useful bridge between traditional structurally oriented assessment and functional analytic behavioral assessment. Although functional diagnostic dimensions differ from traditional disorder-based diagnostic categories by focusing on common functional processes, functional dimensional assessment shares a key goal of traditional assessment, which is to identify individual difference variables that may underlie the etiology of one or more psychological disorders. Yet the functional dimensional approach deviates from category-based assessment by going beyond a description of behavior and focuses on the functions of an entire class of behavior—and it is this functional focus that makes this approach so directly relevant for treatment development.

The incorporation of functional diagnostic dimensions is not without caveats, however. Due to the complexity of functional relations in many behavior problems, identification of functional diagnostic dimensions may prove to be difficult. For example, the function of self-injurious behavior (SIB) of children with severe developmental disabilities is perhaps the most researched dimension, with hundreds of studies examining relevant antecedent and consequent factors. Even though SIB may represent a fairly discrete set of behaviors, often strongly affected by immediate environmental factors, recent articles published in the *Journal of Applied Behavior Analysis* suggest that functional relations often remain unidentifiable. As an extension, when one considers the complexity of a construct as amorphously defined as depression, the difficulty in identifying functional diagnostic dimensions becomes apparent. Thus, functional diagnostic dimensions will likely improve on the limitations of traditional functional analyses, yet some of the problems inherent in the traditional approach may persist.

Focus on Context

In addition to focusing on the function of behavior, behavioral theory purports that behavior is heavily influenced by the context in which it occurs (Bouton, 1993; Bouton & Nelson, 1998). Bronfenbrenner and Morris (1998) defined context as external environmental forces at various levels of analysis that influence behavior. Specifically, the relations among stimuli learned by an individual are dependent upon the context in which they occur. For example, the stimulus "look out!" yelled by another individual will evoke very different responses when in the context of a friendly game of tag (e.g., laughter, evasive movement) compared to the context of a snake-infested cave (e.g., fear, freezing) due to the different contexts within which learning occurred. Therefore, to identify variables maintaining problem behavior, behavioral assessment strategies must consider the context in which the behavior occurs. Context should be considered at the level most appropriate to the specific problem in question. For instance, assessment of maintaining variables of a culture's particular religious behavior should focus on context at the level of society (e.g., social reinforcement for participating in certain rituals), whereas assessment of factors maintaining obsessive-compulsive behavior should focus on context at the level of the individual (e.g., verbal rules related to rituals).

Furthermore, assessment across multiple contexts often is conducted to provide insight into the specific type of contextual control involved in problematic behavior. For instance, a contextual analysis of the anxiety of an individual with panic disorder is likely to show that an increased heart rate within the context of physical exercise will not evoke the same conditioned responses as the same interoceptive stimulus in the context of a crowded mall (Bouton, Mineka, & Barlow, 2001). In other words, an individual with panic disorder is not simply anxious about a fast-beating heart, but is anxious about a fast-beating heart in a particular context where those interoceptive stimuli have previously been associated with false alarms (panic attacks) that signaled danger. This information is directly relevant for designing an intervention strategy in that exposure to interoceptive heart cues is going to be particularly helpful for this individual if this exposure occurs in the relevant context (e.g., in a situation that is functionally related to, or equivalent with, an enclosed crowded place).

A related example concerns persons with noncardiac chest pain and heart-focused anxiety who frequently present to hospital emergency rooms (Eifert, Zvolensky, & Lejuez, 2000b).

For these otherwise healthy individuals, the sensations of a beating heart or chest pain appear to lead to a sequence of verbal and autonomic events that result in the conclusion that one is having a heart attack. Again, a fast or irregular heartbeat is not just felt as a beating heart, but it is an acquired and verbally mediated formulation of what it *means* to have a fast or irregular heartbeat or chest pain (e.g., "I have heart disease" or "I am suffering from a heart attack"). Not only may the person respond to such sensations by rushing to an emergency room, but any other stimulus events (public or private) associated with this response may now acquire similar negative functions (e.g., exercise, smoking, working hard). In addition, persons can condition and recondition themselves in ways not explicitly taught by providing their own language-symbolic experiences that evoke various emotive-reinforcing-directive functions (Staats & Eifert, 1990). By doing so, however, persons also establish these stimulus functions to otherwise neutral stimulus events via higher-order conditioning and transfer of emotional functions (Forsyth & Eifert, 1996).

Conceptually, the problems of these clients are viewed as resulting from deficient and inappropriate verbal-emotional learning that serves as a basis for the development of subsequent problems. Therefore, therapeutic strategies explicitly target the emotive functions of language. This may occur directly through conditioning procedures (Eifert, 1990) or by changing the context in which language occurs (Hayes, Strosahl, & Wilson, 1999). In both cases, the therapist attempts to change the function of language by changing the context in which it occurs. These examples highlight the significance of focusing on contextual variables in assessment.

Multiple Sources of Information

Multiple Modes of Behavior

Behavioral theory suggests that behavior occurs in different forms—that is, behavior is expressed at overt motor, physiological, and cognitive levels. This multiple response mode view of behavior has been very influential and widely accepted in both research and clinical settings (Cone, 1978; Eifert & Wilson, 1991; Evans, 1986). In fact, the notion of multiple response modes has had positive effects on the increased use of more than one type of assessment for most clinical problems. Yet the multiple response mode concept also has led to some conceptual and practical confusion. According to Eifert and Wilson (1991), this confusion is not only due to the problem of confounding the content with the method of assessment, as Cone (1979) suggested, but also because of an imprecise vague use of the cognitive-verbal-subjective mode. It is therefore critical that *content* (what is assessed) is clearly distinguished from the *method* (how the content is being assessed) of assessment. For this purpose, Cone (1978) and Eifert and Wilson (1991) have provided matrices that unambiguously distinguish content from method of assessment. For instance, the behavioral, physiological, and cognitive content areas may be assessed with different methods that include observation, self-report, and technical instruments or other equipment (e.g., pedometers, polygraphs).

Multiple Foci and Instruments

Thorough assessment of behavior includes measurement of multiple content areas with multiple instruments (Cone, 1978; Eifert & Wilson, 1991). The use of multiple instruments that capture unique facets of behavior both within a particular content area as well as across different content areas provides a more thorough understanding of behavior and helps to increase the content validity of an assessment program. For example, unique facets of covert responding to interoceptive arousal can be tapped by using the Anxiety Sensitivity Index (Reiss, Peterson, Gursky, & McNally, 1986) to measure fear of anxiety-related symptoms and the Behavioral Inhibition Scale/Behavioral Activation Scale (Carver & White, 1994) to measure sensitivity to signals of punishment, unfamiliarity, and nonreward (Zvolensky, Feldner, Eifert, & Stewart, 2001). Together these instruments provide a richer picture of potential etiological factors involved in the development of panic attacks than either one of these measures could if used alone. Furthermore, the use of multiple self-report instruments should be complemented by measuring overt behavior (e.g., observing the patient in the natural environment or measuring reaction time/latency in the laboratory; see McNeil et al., 1995) and physiological content through indices such as changes in heart rate and skin conductance (Forsyth & Eifert, 1998). As an example, more of the variance of depressed behavior is captured in the assessment of an individual's depressed behavior if self-report instruments are supplemented with direct observation of patient behavior by the clinician, which captures variance unaccounted for by the inherently biased self-report.

Multiple Informants

Aside from incorporating multiple modes, content areas, and foci/sources of information to enhance the depth of a behavior assessment, the use of multiple informants can reduce levels of error variance, which are inherent to all psychological assessments (Haynes & O'Brien, 2000). For example, a self-report instrument measuring depressive symptoms will

necessarily include error variance resulting from the bias of the respondent. By incorporating multiple respondents, we can collectively tap into different portions of the variability of the behavior. Thus, an assessment strategy incorporating self-report measures, parent ratings, and teacher ratings will capture more of the variability of a behavior of interest relative to an assessment incorporating only self-report instruments.

Focus on Multiple Targets

To assess clinical presentations accurately, it is necessary to consider that clients often present with a number of problem behaviors rather than one discrete narrowly defined problem. For example, individuals experiencing panic attacks often present with depressive behavior, substance abuse, and anxiety-related concerns other than panic attacks. Similarly, is depressed mood a function or a cause, or both, of marital distress, and how do they affect the interactions with an aggressive child, and problems with job performance and excessive alcohol use? In all of these cases, assessment strategies must focus on more than one potential target behavior so that clinicians can identify functional relations between problems and determine which behavior to focus on and in what sequence different behaviors should be targeted. These determinations (clinical judgments) should be guided by an assessment of the functional relations between these behaviors.

At times, the measurement of multiple target behaviors can broadly be guided by our empirical knowledge about the relations among problem behaviors that have been identified in larger groups of people. For instance, comorbidity research has revealed that 15 to 21% of individuals with anxiety disorders also abuse alcohol (for a recent summary of this research, see Lehman, Brown, & Barlow, 1998). These researchers have argued that some patients abuse alcohol to self-medicate. In functional analytic terms, this tension-reduction hypothesis implies that drinking is a negatively reinforced operant response because the anxiolytic properties of the drug temporarily reduce or eliminate aversive affective and physiological states. This analysis provides an explanation for why in some cases alcohol abuse follows the development of anxiety. It does not mean, however, that this functional relation holds true in all cases. Therefore, the relation needs to be examined on an individual case-by-case basis. Nonetheless, knowledge of frequently encountered relations among problem behaviors is likely to point the behavioral assessor (and therapist) in the right direction more quickly and efficiently.

As a functional approach, behaviorism suggests that a goal of behavior therapy is to aid clients in becoming more *functional,* as defined by the client (Hayes et al., 1999; Ollendick & Hersen, 1993) and contribute to the alleviation of human suffering more generally (Hayes, 1997). Thus, behavior therapists need to identify behavior that may be hindering client functioning. Of equal importance is the identification and analysis of a client's resources and strengths to identify and specify positive intervention goals. This constructional approach to behavioral assessment (Evans, 1993) has many advantages. Positive intervention goals may be more acceptable and elicit less discomfort for some clients. A focus on measuring strengths and resources also is likely to encourage the use of positive rather than aversive (e.g., punishment) intervention procedures (Haynes & O'Brien, 2000).

Finally, an important conceptual foundation for the focus on the development of positive goals and values is based on findings that many aversive private events (thoughts, memories, feelings) cannot be successfully controlled or eliminated (Hayes et al., 1996, 1999). In fact, concentrating on their reduction and elimination may cause further problems and exacerbate client suffering (Heffner & Eifert, 2002; Jacobson, Christensen, Prince, Cordova, & Eldridge, 2000). A conceptual and practical solution to this problem is to shift focus to the measurement of behavior that is controllable by the client. For example, we can identify client goals and values in life domains chosen by clients and then help them achieve those goals through overt action during treatment. A succinct way to capture this general assessment and treatment strategy is to paraphrase the popular "serenity prayer": accept what cannot be changed, change what can be changed, and learn to distinguish between the two. We could expand this dictum by saying: accept and *do not* focus measurement and treatment on what cannot be changed, measure and change what can be changed, and learn to distinguish between the two. The conceptual and empirical foundations for adopting this general strategy are becoming increasingly compelling, and we are encouraged by the fact that advancements in the way of measuring such positive treatment targets appear to be on their way (Hayes et al., 1999).

Specificity of Assessment

A broad assessment in the initial stages of therapy is useful in identifying general areas where functioning may be a problem. Subsequently, a funnel approach is adopted that successively narrows the focus of assessment such that specific problem behavior can be identified (Ollendick & Hersen, 1993). This approach allows for the identification of multiple behaviors that may become foci in therapy, yet yields information that is sufficiently specific for direct translatability into clinical strategies.

The specificity of a particular measure refers to the number of sources of variance in a measure, which are positively correlated with the number of facets of a behavior problem subsumed by an assessment. As the specificity of a measure increases, there are fewer alternative explanations for variance observed in measures. Conceptually, empiricism dictates the need to minimize alternative explanations for an observation in order to reduce inferential or rational (as opposed to empirical) explanations of the observation. For example, a highly nonspecific question "Are you happy?" would allow for multiple explanations and inferences for the observed response variance. In this case, people responding "no" may do so because they are of low socioeconomic status, younger, from an extremely hot climate—and speculations could go on ad infinitum. In contrast, a more specific question, such as "Are you happy with your salary?" would leave fewer alternative explanations such that people responding "no" will probably do so because of a discrepancy between what they are paid and what they would like to be paid.

Specific measures identify aspects of a behavior problem with less error variance than nonspecific measures. Thus, specific measures often increase the validity of clinical judgments by more specifically identifying etiological and maintaining factors of a behavior, and, as a consequence, reduce the necessity for clinical inference. Yet more specific measures are not *always* more valid than less specific measures. As an example, consider the measurement of social skills deficits. There is not a great deal of validity in very specifically measuring speech content, eye contact, or latency to responding to verbal prompts. However, ratings of social skills by outside observers, which are less specific, seem to have higher convergent and discriminative validity. Therefore, assessment strategies should use measures that are *optimally* specific for the goals of the assessment—that is, measures that reduce as much error variance as possible.

Finally, when monitoring and documenting treatment progress, specific measures are best able to identify with minimal error variance the components of a treatment package that affect specific aspects of behavior. Taken together, specific assessments are used to reduce inference and thereby improve the empirical foundation of clinical judgment.

Importance of Using Measures With Validation Data

Behaviorism's adoption of an empirical epistemology implies that assessment strategies can reveal "true" knowledge only through the use of measures based on observation. According to Johnston and Pennypacker (1993), an observation is accurate to "the extent to which observed values approximate the 'true' state of nature . . . [and although] perfect accuracy [is] unattainable in any specific instance, [it is] approachable with ever-diminishing error" (p. 138). Behaviorism's emphasis on direct observation of behavior has been succinctly de- scribed by Cone (1998a): "Behavior occurs or it does not. It occurs repeatedly, at different times, and at different places, or it does not" (p. 29). However, direct observation is not always incrementally valid or even possible, as in the case of private behavior (e.g., cognitions, moods) that an outsider cannot directly access or observe. Given that private behav- iors can be important elements in functional relations (e.g., as setting events; see Anderson, Hawkins, & Scotti, 1997), behaviorists are faced with the difficult task of including as- sessment targets in their analyses that are not amenable to direct observation but that should still be congruent with an empirical epistemology.

One way to resolve this dilemma and maintain an incre- mentally valid empirical approach is to ensure that indirect assessment methodologies are supported by empirical vali- dation data. If we are successful in empirical validation ef- forts, behaviorists can claim that knowledge resulting from such assessments closely approximates the *true* state of na- ture. For example, we can compare a self-report instrument of fear of spiders to observed overt behavior and physiolog- ical measures purportedly assessing the same fear. Let us as- sume the self-report instrument suggests that a person is highly afraid of spiders. If the same individual screams and demonstrates increased sweating and heart rate at the presen- tation of a spider, the self-reported measure can be assumed to approximate the *true* fear of spiders for this individual, because it appears to exhibit high levels of convergent valid- ity with motor behavior and measures of physiological arousal.

As another example, the results of an instrument designed to assess level of depressed behavior must be compared to other data based on observation (e.g., direct observation, other previously validated instruments) to determine if the instru- ment is measuring depressed behavior and not capturing clini- cal phenomena other than depression (e.g., anxiety, mania). Unfortunately, the reality of discordance and desynchrony in response systems or different behavior content areas, typically used as indices of anxiety and other constructs, casts a shadow of doubt on even these simple examples (for a detailed dis- cussion of this thorny methodological and conceptual issue, see Cone, 1998b, and Zinbarg, 1998). Suffice it to say that developing valid instruments across different behavioral sys- tems or content areas has proved to be one of the most chal- lenging tasks in behavioral assessment. Cone (1998b) argues that this is because we have neither resolved the underlying conceptual disagreements nor the methodological limitations resulting from low multibehavior-multimethod correlations. We agree with Cone's conclusion that the sheer complexity of this issue may be a reason why the proper synchrony- desynchrony study has not yet appeared.

Beyond these broad implications of an empirical approach for the use of instruments supported by validation data are several specific implications. First, an instrument must be developed based on observations relevant to the individual being assessed. At times, clinicians employ instruments to compare a particular client to a group of other individuals (e.g., "Is client X more anxious than the average person?"). In order to know how a client compares to others, the vali- dation sample must include observations of people similar to the client. Thus, it is necessary to ensure that instruments incorporated in an assessment strategy include, in the vali- dation sample, populations that resemble the client along multiple dimensions, including, but not limited to, sex, age, ethnicity, and type of behavior problem.

A second specific implication of an empirical epistemol- ogy for the use of instruments with validation data is that the instrument itself must have validation data that suggest the measure captures what it purports to capture (construct va- lidity). Although a thorough discussion of construct validity is beyond the scope of the current chapter, we have already indicated why empirical methods (i.e., observation) should be used to determine the validity and reliability of a measure used in behavioral assessment. Thus, some type of observa- tion should underlie any measure used in behavioral assess- ment so that we can be confident the measure is revealing data relevant to a particular client. For these reasons, it is particularly frustrating that we have not yet resolved the methodological problems involved in conducting such cross- validation analyses for instruments that are typically used by behavior therapists to measure common problems such as anxiety and depression (Cone, 1998b).

Time-Series and Change-Focused Measurement

One of the most unique and practical strategies of behavioral assessment is that measurement typically occurs repeatedly across time. Repeated assessment strategies are employed to capture the phasic nature of behavior problems and to moni- tor change in behavior over time. The commitment to re- peated measurements is based on the more general behavioral tenet that behavior is sensitive to contextual variables and adapts to changing environmental contingencies (e.g., Skinner, 1953). This assumption is in contrast to the still popular idea that the central features (*traits*) of a person do not change much over time and can therefore be successfully captured in single measurements (for a more balanced view, see Mischel & Shoda, 1998). One of the core assumptions of behavioral assessment is that the commonly used single measurement pe- riod only captures facets of the behavior problem in its current phase at the specific time of measurement.

In contrast, time-series measurement includes various assessment strategies that analyze variation, and interrelations, among multiple variables across time. Furthermore, such strategies aim to identify the sources of variance across time, rather than between persons. For example, a time-series measurement may aim to identify the environmental changes across time that cause increases in a patient's depressed behavior. In contrast, traditional assessment may seek to determine how a patient's level of depressive symptoms compares to other people similar to the patient. Generally, measurement occurs frequently enough, and at sufficiently short time intervals, to detect relations among the time-series and the dynamic characteristics of measured variables (Haynes & O'Brien, 2000).

Change-focused measurement is similar in that it targets identification of variation in a given variable across time, usually with respect to some intervention (e.g., pre- and post-assessment techniques to monitor change). However, it is important to note that behavioral theory generally does not suggest that the passing of time itself is causal (cf. Bouton, 1993). Rather, time simply allows various causal processes to occur, such as changes in context, contingencies, and developmental growth processes.

As indicated, measurement across time is largely based on behavioral theory's emphasis on context and changing contingencies as determinants of behavior. Historically through current times, behavior therapists have developed questionnaires to document treatment outcome. This purpose required that questionnaires be brief enough to measure behavior efficiently at multiple points in time to monitor changes in relation to treatment. It also means that questionnaires must consist of items that are sensitive to change. Despite the undisputed contributions of these assessments to documenting clinical outcomes in large clinical trials (e.g., Elkin et al., 1989), simply repeating measurements across time may lead to inferential errors, particularly if measurements are only conducted once before and after treatment. As context and resulting behavior are dynamic and often fluctuate in magnitude, rate, and form over time, this approach neglects to account for the dynamic nature of variables across time (Haynes, Blaine, & Meyer, 1995).

More recent efforts at monitoring the variation of behavior within dynamic contexts incorporate nonlinear dynamic mathematical systems theory that accounts for nonlinearity observed in dynamic environments and behavior variability (Heiby, 1995; see also chapter 1). The introduction of these mathematical systems may capture the posited nonlinear relations among behavior and environment more accurately, improve the identification of functional relations, and increase the validity of clinical judgments.

CHALLENGES AND OUTLOOK

As with any theory, behavioral theory is continuously evolving, and because of the inextricable link between the conceptual foundations of behavioral theory and assessment, assessment must adapt to these changes. Unfortunately, assessment strategies not only evolve with advances in theory and empirical findings, but also are heavily influenced by changes in the professional zeitgeist. For instance, behavior therapy's move as a profession toward a more eclectic *cognitive*-behavioral discipline has affected the types of instruments behavior therapists use and what is considered behavioral and acceptable measurement in behavior therapy. As an illustration, anxiety sensitivity (AS) is considered an individual difference variable that is unobservable and inferred from answers to some 16 questions (Anxiety Sensitivity Index [ASI]; Reiss et al., 1986). The question is whether we can consider and conceptually justify the measurement of AS by means of a psychometrically sound instrument as *behavioral* assessment? Our suggestion is: it depends on how you interpret ASI scores and what you do with them. If we view AS as a trait-like relatively stable individual difference variable, it would only be another instrument to measure an inferred construct. In that case, we would not consider measuring AS a case of behavioral assessment. On the other hand, if either individual or groups of answers to questions on this questionnaire help us identify meaningful response units and their controlling variables for the purposes of understanding and changing behavior (Hayes, Nelson, & Jarrett, 1986), then it could be considered behavioral assessment. It remains an open empirical question whether the ASI is indeed such a behavioral assessment instrument.

As another example of an assessment strategy evolving in a particular direction in response to the changing professional zeitgeist, some researchers have changed the theoretical rationale for using measures of overt behavior such as response latency. For instance, the rationale for measuring response latency with a Stroop test often is to infer the absence or presence of cognitive processes and structures assumed to be responsible for producing abnormal behavior. The Stroop test revealing that an individual with social phobia takes longer to name the color of phobia-related words compared to fear-unrelated words (McNeil et al., 1995) frequently is not just observed and recorded but interpreted as a sign of particular idiosyncratic types of cognitive processing styles and biases. In this case, assessors are not interested in the function of the actual behavior but in the processes presumed to underlie the behavior. Although the Stroop test shows acceptable levels of discriminative validity, this instrument still seems to be quite indirect and inferential, and its ultimate clinical utility remains an open question.

As discussed above, behavioral theory's conceptual foundations suggest limiting such inference, because behavior is not viewed as a sign of an underlying problem but as a sample that is worthy of study unto itself (Hawkins, 1986). At a practical level, there is a danger that the regression of some explanations of behavioral measures toward greater inference may further reduce the already low validity of clinical judgment (Haynes & O'Brien, 2000). Thus, it is an ongoing challenge for behavior therapists to minimize shifts in assessment practices that are incompatible with the conceptual underpinnings of behavioral assessment.

A continuing challenge for advancing the conceptual foundations of behavioral assessment is the declining use of observation methods, particularly the observation of overt behavior in the natural environment. This development is important because of the pivotal role of observation as a foundation for behavioral assessment and its role in validity analyses for other measures. Haynes & O'Brien (2000) reported several studies and provided additional data that show an increasing trend for major clinical journals to publish behavior therapy–related articles. At the same time, the percentage of treatment outcome studies published in the *Journal of Consulting and Clinical Psychology* using behavioral observation shows a declining trend from 1968 to 1996, whereas the number of articles using self-report questionnaires has been steadily increasing.

To further examine these trends, we completed a survey of outcome studies published in *Behavior Therapy* for the 5-year period from 1996 to 2000 and found a total of 71 studies evaluating some type of cognitive-behavioral treatment. Although 94% of studies employed self-report questionnaires, only 39% used behavioral observation by others. If self-monitoring is added as behavioral self-observation, the total percentage of studies using some type of observation increases to 62% for this period. Although surveys suggest that a majority of practitioners who are members of the *Association for Advancement of Behavior Therapy* use behavioral observation methods in their work, we wonder how often and pervasively they use such methods given the predominance and strong reliance on self-report instruments (e.g., questionnaires) in even clinical research settings. The demise of the journal *Behavioral Assessment* in 1992 was another indication of this downward trend. In response, the journal *Behaviour Research and Therapy* added a behavioral assessment section in 1993. When we examined the articles published in that section from 1993 to 2000, we found that very few articles dealt with issues of behavioral observation. Instead, the overwhelming majority of articles have focused on

questionnaires (development, reliability, validity, etc.) using principles and criteria of traditional personality assessment.

Rather than simply continuing to call for increases in the use of behavioral assessment strategies, we must ask why past calls have not been heeded to the extent that we may have hoped for during what Hayes and colleagues (1986) called the *honeymoon period* of behavioral assessment in the 1960s and 1970s. A key problem may have been that, like behavior therapy, behavioral assessment often is defined as a specific set of assessment techniques. Yet if we define behavioral assessment as "the identification of meaningful response units and their controlling variables for the purposes of understanding and of altering behavior" (Hayes et al., 1986, p. 464), behavioral assessment is neither a set of techniques nor a content area, let alone a subarea of traditional assessment. Instead, it was meant to be an assessment approach with its own set of assumptions and goals—some of which we have addressed in this chapter. These assumptions and goals need to again become a focus of discussion and research to avoid a continuation of the process that has increasingly blurred the distinction between behavioral and traditional assessment while neglecting to develop the unique strengths of behavioral assessment.

A number of years ago, Hayes and others (1986) identified the lack of developing its own goals and standards as the main culprit responsible for behavioral assessment's *disillusionment period* that started in the early 1980s. At that time already, these authors warned that we risk losing the unique opportunity that the behavioral assessment approach presents to the clinical community. We believe that this risk is even greater today, and the disillusionment has become deeper.

Instead of pushing forward with new goals and standards such as developing a functional approach to evaluate assessment quality by making treatment utility the gold standard for behavioral assessment (e.g., Hayes et al., 1987), we have continued to adopt criteria of traditional personality assessment to evaluate measures used in behavior therapy. For instance, rather than developing functional dimensional diagnostic systems, many of us have moved back to accepting the discrete category trait-like approach that underlies the *DSM-IV* (APA, 1994). The more general and basic problem here is that just as advances in behavior therapy are closely linked to advances in behavioral theory (e.g., improved behavioral models of psychological problems), advances in behavioral assessment strategies are linked to advances in behavioral theory. Unfortunately, such advances have been lacking. Although many articles (e.g., Forsyth, 1997; Hayes, 1997) and books (e.g., Plaud & Eifert, 1998) have discussed different facets of this topic, the relative neglect of conceptual compared to technical advances in behavior therapy is virtually undisputed.

By extension, behavioral assessment has suffered in a way similar to behavior therapy.

A key challenge for behavioral assessment will be to keep up with the advances in behavioral theory that *are* being achieved. A pertinent example is the recent interest in rule-governed and verbal behavior (Anderson et al., 1997). How can behavioral assessment strategies with their emphasis on specific observable behavior deal with the assessment of verbal rules and other more general, not directly observable, classes of behavior and functional dimensions? Similarly, the highly idiographic nature of conducting functional analyses of individual behaviors needs to be complemented with the assessment of functional diagnostic dimensions that may be found in groups of people suffering from a number of functionally related psychological problems. Although these are challenges, the tasks are not impossible to accomplish. If we accept that behavioral assessment is not defined as a set of techniques, then we can accept that the same behaviors (e.g., private events) are assessed by both traditional and behavioral assessment, but that different assumptions and goals are brought to the interpretation of these behaviors (Hayes et al., 1986). For instance, behavioral assessment is not primarily concerned with assessing the form or structure of private events but aims to assess their function (Forsyth & Eifert, 1996).

It is this need for assessment to maintain congruence with behavioral theory that offers the greatest challenge and also the greatest hope given that we have made real advances in behavioral theory related to private events (e.g., Wilson & Blackledge, 2000). Finally, with assessment adopting nonlinear models of mathematics to account for behavioral theory's recent assertion that behavior-environment relations are nonlinear, a more positive outlook for assessment may be warranted provided enough people can actually understand these frequently complicated models.

SUMMARY

Behavioral theory and assessment are inextricably linked. Conceptual foundations of behavioral theory and assessment include an empirical epistemology, focus on context, and an emphasis on function. In accordance with these foundations, assessment strategies aim to increase the validity of clinical judgments, resulting in specific behavior assessment strategies that are empirically based and focus on functional contextual variables to maximize the treatment utility of assessment and to increase clinicians' ability to make valid judgments.

The implications of these conceptual foundations are apparent in an examination of particular behavioral assessment strategies. Specifically, behavioral assessment emphasizes functional relations, focuses on context, aims to use empirically validated assessment instruments, incorporates multiple sources of information, focuses on multiple targets, and incorporates specific assessments.

Changes in the professional zeitgeist have presented a formidable challenge for behavioral assessment and led to a rapprochement of behavioral and traditional assessment. These events have impeded the development of behavioral assessment as an assessment approach with its own set of assumptions and goals rather than as a subarea of traditional assessment. As behavioral researchers, educators, and clinicians, it is crucial that conceptual issues are taught, understood, and present in the development of behavioral assessment strategies to maintain the high degree of conceptual integrity for which behaviorism has historically been noted.

REFERENCES

American Psychiatric Association (1994). *Diagnostic and statistical manual of mental disorders* (4th ed.). Washington, DC: Author.

Anderson, C.M., Hawkins, R.P., & Scotti, J.R. (1997). Private events in behavior analysis: Conceptual basis and clinical relevance. *Behavior Therapy, 28,* 157–179.

Asmundson, G.J.G., Sandler, L.S., Wilson, K.G., & Norton, G.R. (1993). Panic attacks and interoceptive acuity for cardiac sensations. *Behaviour Research and Therapy, 31,* 193–197.

Barlow, D.H. (2001). *Anxiety and its disorders.* New York: Guilford Press.

Bouton, M.E. (1993). Context, time, and memory retrieval in the interference paradigms of Pavlovian learning. *Psychological Bulletin, 114,* 80–99.

Bouton, M.E., Mineka, S., & Barlow, D.H. (2001). A modern learning theory perspective on the etiology of panic disorder. *Psychological Review, 108,* 4–32.

Bouton, M.E., & Nelson, J.B. (1998). The role of context in classical conditioning: Some implications for cognitive behavior therapy. In W.T. O'Donohue (Ed.), *Learning and behavior therapy* (pp. 59–84). Boston: Allyn & Bacon.

Bronfenbrenner, U. & Morris, P.A. (1998). The ecology of developmental processes. In W. Damon (Series Ed.) & R.M. Lerner (Vol. Ed.), *Handbook of child psychology* (5th ed., pp. 993–1028). New York: Wiley.

Carver, C.S., & White, T.L. (1994). Behavioral inhibition, behavioral activation, and affective responses to impending reward and punishment: The BIS/BAS scales. *Journal of Personality and Social Psychology, 67,* 319–333.

Cone, J.D. (1978). The behavioral assessment grid (BAG): A conceptual framework and a taxonomy. *Behavior Therapy, 9,* 882–888.

Cone, J.D. (1979). Confounded comparisons in triple response mode assessment research. *Behavioral Assessment, 1,* 85–95.

Cone, J.D. (1998a). Psychometric considerations. In M. Hersen & A.S. Bellack (Eds.), *Behavioral assessment: A practical handbook* (2nd ed., pp. 22–46). New York: Pergamon Press.

Cone, J.D. (1998b). Hierarchical views of anxiety: What do they profit us? *Behavior Therapy, 29,* 325–332.

Eifert, G.H. (1990). The acquisition and treatment of phobic anxiety: A paradigmatic behavioral perspective. In G.H. Eifert & I.M. Evans (Eds.), *Unifying behavior therapy: Contributions of paradigmatic behaviorism* (pp. 173–200). New York: Springer.

Eifert, G.H. (1992). Cardiophobia: A paradigmatic behavioral model of heart-focused anxiety and non-anginal chest pain. *Behaviour Research and Therapy, 30,* 329–345.

Eifert, G.H., Beach, B, & Wilson, P.H. (1998). Depression: Behavioral principles and implications for treatment and relapse prevention. In J.J. Plaud & G.H. Eifert (Eds.), *From behavior theory to behavior therapy* (pp. 68–97). Boston: Allyn & Bacon.

Eifert, G.H., Schulte, D., Zvolensky, M.J., Lejuez, C.W., & Lau, A.W. (1997). Manualizing behavior therapy: Merits and challenges. *Behavior Therapy, 28,* 499–509.

Eifert, G.H., Thompson, R.N., Zvolensky, M.J., Edwards, K., Haddad, J., Frazer, N.L., & Davig, J. (2000a). The cardiac anxiety questionnaire: Development and preliminary validity. *Behaviour Research and Therapy, 38,* 1039–1053.

Eifert, G.H., & Wilson, P.H. (1991). The triple response approach to assessment: A conceptual and methodological appraisal. *Behaviour Research and Therapy, 29,* 283–292.

Eifert, G.H., Zvolensky, M.J., & Lejuez, C.W. (2000b). Heart-focused anxiety and chest pain: A conceptual and clinical review. *Clinical Psychology: Science and Practice, 7,* 403–417.

Elkin, I., Shea, T., Watkins, J.T., Imber, S.D., Sotsky, S.M., Collins, J.F., Glass, D.R., Pilkonis, P.A., Leber, W.R., Docherty, J.P. Feister, S.J., & Parloff, M.B. (1989). National Institute of Mental Health treatment of depression collaborative research program: General effectiveness of treatments. *Archives of General Psychiatry, 46,* 971–982.

Evans, I.M. (1986). Response structure and the triple-response-mode concept. In R.O. Nelson & S.C. Hayes (Eds.), *Conceptual foundations of behavioral assessment* (pp. 131–155). New York: Guilford Press.

Evans, I.M. (1993). Constructional perspectives in clinical assessment. *Psychological Assessment, 5,* 264–272.

Evans, I.M., & Eifert, G.H. (1990). Unifying behavior therapy from a paradigmatic behaviorism perspective. In G.H. Eifert & I.M. Evans (Eds.), *Unifying behavior therapy: Contributions of paradigmatic behaviorism* (pp. 3–13). New York: Springer.

Evans, I.M., & Wilson, F.E. (1983). Behavioral assessment as decision making: A theoretical analysis. In M. Rosenbaum, C.M. Franks, & Y. Jaffe (Eds.), *Perspectives on behavior therapy in the eighties* (pp. 35–53). New York: Springer.

Forsyth, J.P. (1997). In the name of the "advancement" of behavior therapy: Is it all in a name? *Behavior Therapy, 28,* 615–627.

Forsyth, J.P., & Eifert, G.H. (1996). The language of feeling and the feeling of anxiety: Contributions of the behaviorisms toward understanding the function-altering effects of language. *The Psychological Record, 46,* 607–649.

Forsyth, J.P., & Eifert, G.H. (1998). Response intensity of systemic alarms in content-specific fear conditioning: Comparing 20% versus 13% CO_2-enriched air as unconditioned stimuli. *Journal of Abnormal Psychology, 107,* 291–304.

Forsyth, J.P., Lejuez, C., Hawkins, R.P., & Eifert, G.H. (1996). A critical evaluation of cognitions as causes of behavior. *Journal of Behavior Therapy and Experimental Psychiatry, 27,* 369–376.

Franks, C.M. (1998). Foreword: The importance of being theoretical. In J.J. Plaud & G.H. Eifert (Eds.), *From behavior theory to behavior therapy* (pp. ix–xviii). Boston: Allyn & Bacon.

Friman, P.C., Hayes, S.C., & Wilson, K.G. (1998). Why behavior analysts should study emotion: The example of anxiety. *Journal of Applied Behavior Analysis, 31,* 137–156.

Hawkins, R.P. (1986). Selection of target behaviors. In R.O. Nelson & S.C. Hayes (Eds.), *Conceptual foundations of behavioral assessment* (pp. 331–385). New York: Guilford Press.

Hayes, S.C. (1997). Technology, theory, and the alleviation of human suffering: We still have such a long way to go. *Behavior Therapy, 28,* 517–525.

Hayes, S.C., Hayes, L.J., Reese, H.W., & Sarbin, T.R. (1993). *Varieties of scientific contextualism.* Reno, NV: Context Press.

Hayes, S.C., Nelson, R.O., & Jarrett, R.B. (1986). Evaluating the quality of behavioral assessment. In R.O. Nelson & S.C. Hayes (Eds.), *Conceptual foundations of behavioral assessment* (pp. 463–503). New York: Guilford Press.

Hayes, S.C., Nelson, R.O., & Jarrett, R.B. (1987). The treatment utility of assessment: A functional approach to evaluation assessment quality. *American Psychologist, 42,* 963–974.

Hayes, S.C., Strosahl, K.D., & Wilson, K.G. (1999). *Acceptance and commitment therapy.* New York: Guilford Press.

Hayes, S.C., Wilson, K.G., Gifford, E.V., Follette, V.M., & Strosahl, K. (1996). Experiential avoidance and behavioral disorders: A functional dimensional approach to diagnosis and treatment. *Journal of Consulting and Clinical Psychology, 64,* 1152–1168.

Haynes, S.N. (1998). The changing nature of behavioral assessment. In M. Hersen & A.S. Bellack (Eds.), *Behavioral assessment: A practical handbook* (2nd ed., pp. 1–21). New York: Pergamon Press.

Haynes, S.N., Blaine, D., & Meyer, K. (1995). Dynamical models for psychological assessment: Phase space functions. *Psychological Assessment, 7,* 17–24.

Haynes, S.N., Leisen, M.B., & Blaine, D.B. (1997). Design of individualized behavioral treatment programs using functional analytic clinical case models. *Psychological Assessment, 9,* 334–348.

Haynes, S.N., & O'Brien, W.H. (2000). *Principles and practice of behavioral assessment.* New York: Kluwer/Plenum.

Heffner, M., & Eifert, G.H. (2002). *The effects of acceptance versus control contexts on avoidance of panic-related symptoms.* Manuscript submitted for publication.

Heiby, E.M. (1995). Chaos theory, nonlinear dynamical models, and psychological assessment. *Psychological Assessment, 7,* 5–9.

Jacobson, N.S., Christensen, A., Prince, S.E., Cordova, J., & Eldridge, K. (2000). Integrative behavioral couple therapy: An acceptance-based, promising new treatment for couple discord. *Journal of Consulting and Clinical Psychology, 68,* 351–355.

Johnston, J.M., & Pennypacker, H.S. (1993). *Strategies and tactics of behavioral research* (2nd ed.). Hillsdale, NJ: Erlbaum.

Lehman, C.L., Brown, T.A., & Barlow, D.H. (1998). Effects of cognitive-behavioral treatment for panic disorder with agoraphobia on concurrent alcohol abuse. *Behavior Therapy, 29,* 423–433.

McNeil, D.W., Ries, B.J., Taylor, L.J., Boone, M.L., Carter, L.E., Turk, C.L., & Lewin, M.R. (1995). Comparison of social phobia subtypes using Stroop tests. *Journal of Anxiety Disorders, 9,* 47–57.

Mischel, W., & Shoda, Y. (1998). Reconciling dynamics and dispositions. *Annual Review of Psychology, 90,* 394–402.

Nelson, R., & Hayes, S.C. (1986). The nature of behavioral assessment. In R.O. Nelson & S.C. Hayes (Eds.), *Conceptual foundations of behavioral assessment* (pp. 3–41). New York: Guilford Press.

Ollendick, T.H., & Hersen, M. (1993). Child and adolescent behavioral assessment. In T.H. Ollendick & M. Hersen (Eds.), *Handbook of child and adolescent assessment* (pp. 3–65). New York: Guilford Press.

Plaud, J.J., & Eifert, G.H. (Eds.). (1998). *From behavior theory to behavior therapy.* Boston: Allyn & Bacon.

Rapee, R.M. (1994). Detection of somatic sensations in panic disorder. *Behaviour Research and Therapy, 32,* 825–831.

Reese, H. (1994). The data/theory dialectic: The nature of scientific progress. In S.C. Cohen & H.W. Reese (Eds.), *Life-span developmental psychology: Methodological contributions* (pp. 187–222). Hillsdale, NJ: Erlbaum.

Reiss, S., Peterson, R.A., Gursky, M., & McNally, R.J. (1986). Anxiety, sensitivity, anxiety frequency, and the prediction of fearfulness. *Behaviour Research and Therapy, 24,* 1–8.

Schmidt, N.B., Lerew, D.L., & Trakowski, J.H. (1997). Body vigilance in panic disorder: Evaluating attention to bodily perturbations. *Journal of Consulting and Clinical Psychology, 65,* 214–220.

Scotti, J.R., Morris, T.R., McNeil, C.B., & Hawkins, R.P. (1996). DSM-IV and disorders of childhood and adolescence: Can structural criteria be functional? *Journal of Consulting and Clinical Psychology, 64,* 1177–1191.

Skinner, B.F. (1953). *Science and human behavior.* New York: Macmillan.

Staats, A.W. (1996). *Behavior and personality.* New York: Springer.

Staats, A.W., & Eifert, G.H. (1990). A paradigmatic behaviorism theory of emotion: Basis for unification. *Clinical Psychology Review, 10,* 539–566.

Wilson, K.G., & Blackledge, J.T. (2000). Recent developments in the behavioral analysis of language: Making sense of clinical phenomena. In M.J. Dougher (Ed.), *Clinical behavior analysis* (pp. 27–46). Reno, NV: Context Press.

Zinbarg, R.E. (1998). Concordance and synchrony in measures of anxiety and panic reconsidered: A hierarchical model of anxiety and panic. *Behavior Therapy, 29,* 301–323.

Zvolensky, M.J, & Eifert, G.H. (2001). A review of psychological factors/processes affecting anxious responding during voluntary hyperventilation and inhalations of carbon dioxide-enriched air. *Clinical Psychology Review, 21,* 375–400.

Zvolensky, M.J., Feldner, M.T., Eifert, G.H., & Stewart, S.H. (2001). Evaluating differential predictions of anxiety-related reactivity during repeated 20% carbon dioxide–enriched air challenge. *Cognition and Emotion, 15,* 767–786.

CHAPTER 7

Principles of Behavioral Observation

DONALD P. HARTMANN, BILLY A. BARRIOS, AND DAVID D. WOOD

"You can see a lot by just watching."
—attributed to Yogi Berra

INTRODUCTION

Behavior observation is the recording of the observable responses of individuals by human observers (e.g., Hartmann & Wood, 1990). It differs from related procedures in the following ways:

- From narrative recording by its systematic use of definitions, codes, sampling of behavior, and the like;
- From retrospective reports by its temporal linking of observing and recording;
- From ratings by its emphasis on counts and time budgeting information; and
- From "mechanical" recording methods by the critical role it affords human observers.

Citing Meyer et al. (1998), Mash and Foster (2001) state that "the direct observation of clients in clinical contexts is universal and transcends all theoretical frameworks and methods of assessment involving face-to-face contact between therapist and client" (p. 86). Despite the ubiquity of observational assessment, its association with behaviorism is unique. The work by Watson and his students (e.g., Jones, 1924; Watson & Raynor, 1920) provided an important early stimulus to observational studies, particularly with children (Arrington, 1939, 1943). Compared with other assessment methods, direct observation is more consistent with behaviorism's epistemological emphasis on overt behavior, public events, quantification, low levels of inference, and assumptions of environmental causality (e.g., Hartmann, Roper, & Bradford, 1979). Indeed, behavior observation often has been cited as the hallmark of the behavioral approach to assessment (e.g., Suen & Ary, 1989).

Apart from ideologically based appeals, direct observation has other strengths that cause it to be preferred to alternative assessment methods. The strengths of behavior observation include flexibility, relative simplicity, and applicability across a wide range of populations, behaviors, and settings. Observations can be particularly useful for understanding social process (Cairns & Green, 1979) and for assessing young children and other verbally deficient or unsophisticated subjects. They also can provide measures of responses that most individuals cannot accurately describe (such as expressive movements) and for events that participants may be unwilling to report or else may distort as a function of the event's social undesirability or of the effort required for adequate description (Hartmann & Wood, 1990; also see Mischel, 1968, and Wiggins, 1973).

Recent reviews and surveys indicate that observational methodologies continue to be popular in clinical studies of children as well as in clinical investigations of families and adults (e.g., Hops, Davis, & Longoria, 1995). Haynes and O'Brien (2000, p. 227) report that observational methods are used in nearly one third of outcome studies published in the *Journal of Consulting and Clinical Psychology,* and that when behavioral journals are surveyed, over half of the treatment outcome studies employed behavior observations. The use of formal observation procedures in typical clinical practice is less common and, according to Mash and Foster (2001, p. 87) "their use in the foreseeable future is likely to be even less."[1]

When they are employed in clinical settings, observational assessment data assist with case formulation—including identifying target behaviors and their controlling variables—with designing interventions, as well as with monitoring treatment progress and outcome (e.g., Cone, 1998a; Haynes, 2001a). Their role in identifying controlling variables, particularly as a result of performing a *functional analysis,* has assumed renewed interest in recent years (Haynes & O'Brien, 2000). The use of functional analysis is illustrated in the work by Iwata et al. (1994), who developed a standardized protocol to identify the function of self-injurious behavior. In separate phases, each client's self-injurious behavior was observed when followed by social attention, tangible rewards, and escape from an aversive task and under conditions of social isolation. This assessment information was then used to assign the client to corresponding treatment procedures.[2] As Barrios (1988) has compellingly argued, observational data do not speak to this—or other clinical issues—directly. In the case of a functional analysis, the treatment assignments were accomplished by comparing the client's target behavior obtained in one phase with that obtained in a different phase—the idiographic approach. In other cases, meaning is wrestled from observations by comparing them with similar data obtained for other individuals—the normative approach. Finally, the assessment data might be compared with the performance required to achieve some criterion—the criterion-referenced approach.

In serving these functions, certain assumptions are frequently made about behavior, its assessment, and its maintaining conditions (see, e.g., the integrative review by Hartmann et al., 1979; also see Cone, 1998a; Haynes & O'Brien, 2000; and Silva, 1993). Certainly the foremost assumption is that behavior is important in its own right—rather than being merely a reflection of enduring underlying states or traits. Another assumption is that behavioral observation requires less inference and thus is less prone to error—or at least certain types of error (cf. Stone et al., 2000). Finally, it is assumed that behavior is controlled by the context within which it occurs. As a result, both situational and temporal consistency are considered empirical questions. Nonetheless, it is further assumed that a "correctly" observed sample of behavior will generalize to some larger population of interest.

This chapter focuses on principles or considerations relevant to selecting or developing behavioral observation systems that aspire to produce clinically useful samples of behavior. Major topics include the dozen or so factors important in designing an observation system, selecting and training observers, and assessing the quality of observation data. Our discussion of these issues focuses on observations conducted in naturalistic settings by independent observers, when the descriptions of behavior require little inference and the recordings are made during the time the events—or a replica of the events—occur. However, much of this material is applicable to other circumstances, such as observations conducted in contrived settings by participant-observers.

DESIGNING AN OBSERVATION SYSTEM

An observation system is a more-or-less formalized set of rules for extracting information from the stream of behavior. These rules specify the target behaviors, the observation settings, and the observers; they also specify how the behaviors are defined and sampled and the dimensions or properties of the events that are assessed. The rules also indicate the frequency and duration of observations and how the data are recorded and combined to form scores.

These scores are evaluated to determine their scientific adequacy—their reliability and validity—as well as their clinical utility. The rules followed and the results of the evaluative process determine the cost, detail, and generality of the resulting information, as well as the clinical questions for which the information is relevant.

Developing Behavioral Categories

Because it is so easy to go awry at this first technical step of designing an observational system—to become mired in an unwieldy code—an early warning seems apropos: Begin with a clear question, conduct pilot observations, and keep the behavioral code simple (e.g., Bakeman and Gottman, 1997).

The Question

The information provided by an observational system presumably is directed by the purpose or goals of the observations (e.g., Haynes & O'Brien, 2000). Without a clear purpose, "the essentially infinite variety of potential events muddling along in the passing stream of behavior almost always proves overwhelming" Bakeman and Gottman (1987, p. 821).

Barrios (1993, pp. 142–143) offers a useful perspective for clarifying *the* question and its complexity with his concept of "windows of observation." He distinguishes three levels of complexity based upon the number of behaviors included in the code and whether the focus is on a single target individual or on multiple interactants. At the simplest level, a code is defined by a *symptom,* such as tantrumming. The *syndrome* level targets multiple behaviors for inclusion in the code—for example, the interrelated behaviors that might compose a diagnostic category such as autism. At the *system* level, the behaviors of multiple interactants, such as domestic partners or members of a parent-child dyad, form the basis of the code. Whichever window is appropriate for the questions to be answered with the data produced by the code, conducting pilot observations facilitates code development.

Pilot Observations

Pilot observations assist in code development in a variety of ways. For example, they may aid in identifying relevant properties of the target behaviors, generate hypotheses about controlling variables, and indicate limits of the observational setting. Useful paradigms for conducting pilot observations have been described by child clinicians (e.g., Gelfand & Hartmann, 1984) as well as by investigators with an ethological perspective (e.g., Hutt & Hutt, 1970).

The general procedure is initially to obtain *narrative accounts* of the behavior of interest in the assessment setting. Because this may prove demanding, observers should use the simplest descriptive symbols (with the least number of syllables) possible for accurately describing potential target behaviors and their potentially controlling stimuli. These narrative data can then be reviewed with the intent of developing a more restrictive list of events to be recorded. Subsequent pilot observations may be conducted as indicated. When important observation targets have been identified, the investigator can then generate the behavioral codes and their operational definitions.

The Behavioral Codes

Because the behavioral categories determine the clinical questions that can be addressed, they should be selected with care (e.g., Reid, Baldwin, Patterson, & Dishion, 1988). Category or taxonomic systems differ in a number of ways, the most important of which include the breadth of information they provide, the "size" of the behaviors they address, the level of inference they require from observers, and their exclusiveness and exhaustiveness.

Observation systems that provide information on a broad set of categories—broad-bandwidth (Cronbach, 1960) observation systems—often do so by sacrificing measurement precision or fidelity. Simultaneous breadth and precision of observations are possible in those unusual settings where observers are abundant and clients are both accessible and tolerant of extensive observation (e.g., Paul & Lentz, 1977). Generally, the use of broad-bandwidth observation categories is restricted to such situations as the preliminary phases of assessment, when the information they provide is used for generating hypotheses that subsequently will be tested with more precise information (e.g., Bijou, Peterson, & Ault, 1968). More narrowly focused observation categories are appropriate for formal hypothesis testing, as when performing a functional analysis, or when one or more target behaviors are monitored for the purpose of establishing the causal effects of a treatment intervention (e.g., Gelfand & Hartmann, 1984).

Categories in behavioral observation systems may be either molar or molecular. Molar categories are used to code global units of behavior, such as "aggresses" or "plays," that often define functional response classes.[3] Molecular categories are used to code more narrowly defined units of behavior, such as "bites" or "smiles," that are often defined in terms of specific sequences of motor movements (e.g., Johnston & Pennypacker, 1993).[4]

Molar categories are intended to code events into psychologically meaningful categories, but it is important to demonstrate that they do so effectively (see Foster & Cone, 1986, p. 261, for examples of carefully validated molar observation categories). Information exists to suggest that molar codes may be preferable when developmental transformations or cultural variations in the meaning of behavior may be expected as well as when molar outcomes are to be predicted (e.g., Markman, Leber, Cordova, & St. Peters, 1995). However, molar codes may be troublesome since they require observers to make inferences about events, and they can be expected to be more costly in terms of training time and more susceptible to bias.

In contrast, molecular observation categories may be more difficult to interpret subsequent to data collection, but they are relatively easy for observers to use (e.g., Hollenbeck, 1978; Markman et al., 1995). Molecular categories also can be collapsed into molar categories for summary data analyses, but—unlike Humpty-Dumpty—molar categories cannot be broken down into smaller, more molecular units. Because of the advantages of molecular categories—their ease of use and the flexible manner in which they can be collapsed into molar categories after the data are collected—it may seem advisable to collect data at a more molecular level than the intended level of analysis (e.g., Bakeman & Gottman, 1997). Nonetheless, the continued lively discussion about the appropriate level of molarity to employ in observational codes suggests that this issue is far from resolved (e.g., Alexander, Newell, Robbins, & Turner, 1995; Cairns & Green, 1979; Floyd, 1989; Mash & Terdal, 1997). Furthermore, Floyd (1989) notes that measurement correspondence may be poor when the same constructs are observed with both molar and molecular codes that are applied to the same data.

Codes also differ in terms of their exclusivity and exhaustiveness. With codes that are mutually exclusive, only one code can be assigned to each event or behavior; for exhaustive codes, some code in the system applies to each observation event. For example, in a system that coded two partners' attentiveness to one another, the codes would be mutually exclusive if separate codes were given to A attends to B, B attends to A, and A and B attend to each other. The codes would also be exhaustive if we included a fourth category: Neither A nor B attend to one another. While neither characteristic is required for a coding system, certain advantages accrue to both characteristics involving the effort required of observers and the suitability of the resulting data for various types of analyses (e.g., Bakeman & Gottman, 1987, 1997). Whichever coding decisions are made, the next, and closely related, task required of the investigator is to develop operational definitions for the code categories.

Operational Definitions

Hawkins and Dobes (1977) suggested that adequate operational definitions should (1) refer to directly observable components of the target; (2) be clear, unambiguous, and easily understood; and (3) require little or no inference on the part of observers. Barrios (1993) suggests a multistep process for preparing operation definitions. The process begins by investigating how the behavior has been operationalized in the past. Many investigators may be able to adopt or easily modify behavior observation codes already reported in the literature. See Haynes (1978, pp. 119–120) for a sample listing of observational codes, as well as topic-area reviews in Bellack and Hersen (1998), Mash and Terdal (1997), and Ollendick and Hersen (1993). Next, prepare a draft definition, and subject that definition to knowledgeable critics—including potential observers. Finally, rewrite the definition based upon these recommendations.

According to Hawkins (1982), the final definitions should ideally include a descriptive name, a general definition (as in a dictionary), an elaboration that describes the critical components of the behavior, typical examples of the behavior, and questionable instances—borderline or difficult examples

of both occurrences and nonoccurrences of the behavior. One test for the adequacy of operational definitions is to provide naive observers with a written copy of the definitions. Then, without any formal training, observers should use the definitions to independently observe the same participants for one or more observation sessions. The extent of observer consistency obtained by this method is an index of the relative adequacy of the operational definitions (Hawkins & Dobes, 1977). Related considerations in developing operational definitions and behavior codes have been described, for example, by Arrington (1939) and by Gelfand and Hartmann (1984); also see Adams, Doster, and Calhoun (1977).

During the development of operational definitions, it is also helpful to specify response dimensions that are relevant and can be accurately and easily monitored.

Response Dimensions

Responses can be measured in an array of dimensions, including counts, duration, latency, interresponse time, intensity, and direction (e.g., Gelfand & Hartmann, 1984; Johnston & Pennypacker, 1993). The choice of response dimension(s) is ordinarily based on the purpose of the investigation, the nature of the response, the availability of suitable measurement devices, and perhaps other considerations, such as the developmental status of the client (e.g., Barrios, 1993; Cone, 1998a). Novice behavior observers sometimes record the wrong response characteristic, as when "attending" is targeted for intervention but frequency rather than duration of eye contact is recorded (Hartmann & Wood, 1990).

Typical rules of parsimony and simplicity are reasonable guidelines when determining response dimensions of target behaviors (e.g., Saudargas & Lentz, 1986). Moreover, in most investigations, the appropriate response characteristic will be apparent. When it is not, the examination of decision flowcharts provided by Alevizos, Campbell, Callahan, and Berck (1974) and by Gelfand and Hartmann (1984) may be useful. When meaningful observation targets and their dimensions (or relevant published observation codes) are selected, the investigator also should determine the context or sampling of settings where the observations will be conducted.

Selecting Observation Settings

The settings used for conducting clinical behavioral observations range from natural settings such as schools, homes, and bars to various contrived or analogue settings. The latter settings are heterogeneous, including role play, simulated work sites, behavioral approach tests, and functional analytic experiments. The selection of observation settings—their number, locale, added structure, and correspondence with important natural environments—deserves careful consideration.

Sampling of Settings

Observations conducted in a single setting are appropriate when problems are limited to a specific environment, such as school problems, or when the rate of problem behavior is uniform across settings, as may be the case with some forms of seizure activity. Because many behaviors are dependent on specific environmental stimuli, behavior rates may well vary across settings containing different stimuli (e.g., Haynes & O'Brien, 2000; Kazdin, 1979). More representative data may therefore be obtained by conducting observations in a number of relevant settings (e.g., Ayllon & Skuban, 1973). Sampling of observational settings also is critical if variation in setting control is to be used to suggest stimuli that might effectively be used to generate control over responding, or if setting generalization of treatment effects is to be assessed (Gelfand & Hartmann, 1984).[5]

Control of Settings

The correspondence between observation and naturalistic settings varies as a function of similarities in their physical characteristics, in the persons present, and in the control exerted by the observation process (Nay, 1979). Observations may be conducted in contrived settings of minimal naturalistic importance to most clients, or they may be conducted in primary living environments. Even if observations are conducted in naturalistic settings, the observations may produce variations in the cues that are normally present in these settings (e.g., Oei & Mewett, 1987).

Setting cues may vary when structure is imposed on observation settings. Structuring may range from presumably minor restrictions in the movement and activities of family members during home observations to the use of highly contrived situations such as those employed with standard behavioral avoidance tests (e.g., Barrios & Hartmann, 1997). Cone (1998a) describes the types of restrictions that have been employed, as well as their advantages and disadvantages. The advantages of structuring observational settings include enhanced opportunities for target behavior performance, measurement sensitivity, and cost-effectiveness (also see Hartmann & Wood, 1990). The primary disadvantages involve the resulting scores' uncertain generalizability and questionable social validity. Haynes (2001b), commenting on the articles in a special section of *Psychological Assessment* devoted to clinical applications of analogue behavior observations, provides a penetrating analysis of these methods,

including their inadequate content validity and potential validity erosion over time. In the same volume, Mash and Foster (2001) suggest how use of these methods can be made more compatible with the needs of clinical applications. Their suggestions include determining the conditions under which these methods provide incrementally valid information and increasing their accessibility and cost effectiveness (e.g., through the use of regional assessment centers).

Final Considerations

In deciding upon the number and nature of the settings in which observations will occur, Barrios (1993) offers the metaphor of selecting items for a test. The first consideration is relevance—which we have already noted: The settings selected should be relevant to the natural setting in which the problematic behavior occurs. The second consideration is salience: The setting should be salient for evoking the target behavior. One would not, for example, use a sterile laboratory setting for assessing fear of open spaces—unless, of course, one could create a virtual open space in the laboratory that corresponded with real open spaces. The third consideration is consistency: Will a "standard" setting be available for the various occasions when the target behavior needs to be assessed (e.g., prior to and following treatment)?

Settings are just one of a number of technical aspects of observations that involve sampling issues. Although sampling of observation settings is an important issue, investigators also must determine how best to sample or schedule observations within these settings.[6]

Scheduling Observations

Behavior cannot be observed and recorded continuously unless the targeted behaviors are low-frequency events occurring in captive settings such as homes or schools, and participant-observers record them. Otherwise, partial records must suffice, and the time in which observations are conducted must be sampled. If sampling is required, decisions must be made about the number of observation sessions to be scheduled and the basis for scheduling. More samples are required when behavior rates are low, variable, and either increasing or decreasing; when events controlling the target behaviors vary substantially; when observers are asked to employ complex coding procedures; and when more than a single individual is observed (e.g., Alevizos, DeRisi, Liberman, Eckman, & Callahan, 1978; Haynes, 1978, 2001b).

Observation sessions may be scheduled on the basis of time, or on the occurrence of particular stimuli. When complex observation codes are employed or if the target behavior is not tightly discriminated (e.g., smoking), observations are often scheduled on a temporal basis. If time is the basis for scheduling, the observations may be scheduled at fixed intervals, at random intervals, or on a stratified random basis. For discriminated behaviors, such as responding to requests, observations are scheduled during some or all occurrences of the controlling (discriminative) stimuli (e.g., Gelfand & Hartmann, 1984).[7] Finally, observation sessions may occur without regard to scheduling rules. Such ad lib scheduling (Altmann, 1974) is probably appropriate only for observations conducted during the formative stages of an assessment study.

Once a choice has been made about how frequently and on what basis to schedule sessions, session duration must be decided. Session duration should be a function of the duration of the stimulus situation, the variability of the behavior, and the demands of the data collection procedure (e.g., Barrios, 1993; Tryon, 1998). In general, briefer sessions are necessary to limit observer fatigue—when a complex coding system is used, when coded behaviors occur at high rates, and when more than one client must be observed simultaneously—and when observing individuals from special populations, such as infants (e.g., Hartmann & Wood, 1990). Ultimately, however, session duration as well as the number of observation sessions should be chosen to minimize costs and to maximize the representativeness and reliability of the data as well as the output of information per unit of time (see Arrington, 1943; also see Hartmann, 2002).

If observations are to be conducted on more than one client, decisions must be made concerning the length of time and the order in which individuals will be observed. As one might expect, observing individuals for brief periods in a previously randomized, rotating order is superior to fewer but longer observations or to haphazard sampling (e.g., Thomson, Holmberg, & Baer, 1974). If pilot observations are available, these data used with formulas based on generalizability theory (described later) can be used to estimate optimum values for the frequency and duration of observations (e.g., Hartmann & Wood, 1990).

Selecting a Recording Technique

Decisions about sampling dimensions also should take into account the type of recording technique best suited to the purposes of the investigation. Altmann (1974) and others (e.g., Suen & Ary, 1989) have described a variety of different recording procedures (traditionally called *sampling procedures*), at least five of which seem particularly relevant to clinical assessors.[8] Selection of one of these procedures also will help determine which response characteristic is assessed

as a function of how the behavioral stream is segregated or divided.

Ad lib sampling hardly deserves formal recognition because of its unsystematic nature. As we earlier suggested, such casual method of informal note taking may be particularly suitable for the preliminary mapping of a behavioral domain, for obtaining a crude estimate of the frequency or duration of the target responses, for identifying potential problems in implementing a more formal recording procedure, and for developing preliminary definitions (e.g., Hartmann & Wood, 1990). Although this method may serve pilot observation functions well, it is not recommended as a method for gathering formal data in the course of a structured assessment.

Although the ad-lib method is the least rigorous observation procedure, *real-time observations* are the most rigorous and powerful. With these latter procedures, both event frequency and duration are recorded on the basis of their occurrence in the uninterrupted time flow. Data from real-time recording are the most flexible: They provide measures derived from either duration or frequency (e.g., rate), and they can be used for a variety of purposes such as sequential analysis that may not be well served by other methods (e.g., Bakeman & Gottman, 1997). Real-time sampling has become more feasible in clinical settings with the introduction of computerized devices that automatically record behavior in real time whenever the observer depresses a key during the occurrence of a target behavior (e.g., Greenwood, Carta, Kamps, Terry, & Delaquardi, 1994). Nevertheless, real-time data can be both expensive and time consuming. Furthermore, real-time—or any other event-based—recording can pose problems with regard to segregating the stream of behavior into codeable units. Alexander et al. (1995) describe three levels of coding units based upon the amount and nature of meaning and context involved in establishing the unit. At the low end, units are defined, for example, by speech acts; thought units exemplify the next level; and at the high end are phenomenon-based units. For a complex coding system, it may be necessary to initially segregate the stream of behavior into codeable units and then apply the content codes to these units.

Event recording is used when frequency is the response dimension of interest. With event recording, initiations of the target behavior are scored for each occurrence in an observation session. Event recording is a commonly used method in published clinical research (Haynes & O'Brien, 2000; Kelly, 1977). Because event sampling breaks up the continuity of behavior—as Bakeman & Gottman (1987, p. 832) note, "sequences not accounted for in the coding scheme might pass by unseen like ships in the night"—event sampling is sometimes supplemented with narrative recording. Supplementary narrative recordings may be particularly helpful in the early phases of assessment to assist in identifying antecedent and consequent stimuli that may exert some control over the target behavior. Cone and Foster (1982) describe other advantages, as well as limitations, of event recording. For example, event recording may be difficult with infrequent events of low salience and when the initiation and termination of behaviors are difficult to discriminate (also see Bakeman & Gottman, 1997).

Scan sampling is particularly useful with behaviors for which duration—or related measures of time budgeting—is a more meaningful dimension than is frequency. With scan sampling, the observer periodically scans the target individual and notes whether the behavior is occurring at that instant. The duration of observed responses is then estimated on the basis of the proportion of scan samples during which occurrences of the target behaviors are noted. This method of recording—sometimes called momentary time sampling—has been used to code the location, facial expressions, activities, and a variety of appropriate and inappropriate behaviors of individuals (e.g., Paul, 1986).

An alternative to scan sampling for assessing duration is *duration recording*. Duration recording may require nothing more than a watch, or similar timing device, to time the duration of target responses. In addition to being well suited for measuring other, more complex temporal aspects of responding, such as response latency and interresponse time, duration recording may involve fewer sources of sampling error than does scan sampling, but it does so with greater expenditure of observer time.

The final procedure, *interval recording*, is at the same time one of the most popular recording methods (Kelly, 1977) and one of the most troublesome (e.g., Mann, Ten Have, Plunkett, & Meisels, 1991; Suen & Ary, 1989). With this technique, an observation session is divided into brief observe-record intervals, and the observation category is scored if the relevant target behavior occurs within all (whole-interval) or any part of the observation interval (partial-interval) (Powell, Martindale, & Kulp, 1975). Even though interval-recording procedures have been recommended for their ability to measure both response frequency and response duration, research as well as logical analysis indicates that this method may provide distorted estimates of both of these response characteristics (see reviews by Hartmann & Wood, 1982, 1990; Suen & Ary, 1989).

According to work by Ary and Suen (summarized in Suen & Ary, 1989), as a measure of frequency, the rate of interval-recorded data *varies* depending on the duration of the observation interval. As a measure of response duration, the interval method provides a good estimate of duration only when the observation intervals are very short in comparison with the mean duration of the target behavior.[9]

In view of the numerous liabilities of interval recording, clinicians would be well advised to consider alternative observation procedures. If real-time sampling is not required or is not available, adequate measures of response duration can be obtained from scan sampling or duration recording, and response frequency from event recording. Economical measures of both response frequency and duration can result from combining the scan-sampling and event-recording techniques. However, data produced by combining these two methods may be redundant in some circumstances (Suen & Ary, 1989) and do not have the same range of applications as data obtained by real-time recording (e.g., Bakeman & Gottman, 1997).

As with any of the other aspects of observational methodology, in deciding upon a recording technique, the recommendations by Haynes and O'Brien (2000, p. 234) deserve our consideration: The method selected should generate data that are generalizable to relevant constructs and settings, should maintain a balance of psychometric integrity against the practical constraints of clinical settings, and the ratio of information gained must be weighed against the costs involved in implementation.

Human observers using one of these recording methods will undoubtedly continue to serve as the primary "apparatus" for obtaining observational data. However, various technologies are available to aid or even supplant observers in recording behavioral data.

Selecting Technological Aids

The technologies available to assist in observational assessment range from simple pencil-and-paper recording forms to complicated computer-assisted sensing, recording, and retrieval systems. Selection from among existing technologies can determine the obtrusiveness and efficiency of data collection, the representativeness of sampling, and the feasibility of conducting various statistical analyses (Hartmann & Wood, 1990).

Technology promises to lower the cost of direct observations—by using virtual realities for training observers, by enabling observers to record multiple responses in real-time through the use of handheld computers, and by simplifying data storage and retrieval (see, e.g., Cone, 1998a). Other adjunctive equipment such as timing devices, video recorders, one-way mirrors, stop-action playback, and time-lapse photography also permits more complex coding. Still other devices provide data supplementary to that obtained by human observers by recording dimensions of behavior that produce measurable changes in a variety of energy systems, including photic, mechanical, thermal, electrochemical, and electromagnetic (e.g., Haynes & O'Brien, 2000). Kahng and Iwata (1998) provide a review of computerized observation systems, and Tryon (1991, 1998) describes technological aids that supplement data gathered by human observers. Mash and Foster (2001, p. 95) also provide an interesting set of references that discuss the role of technological aids in clinical decision making.

Despite the considerable merits of technology for behavior observation, this equipment does have its downside. Major limitations include considerable investment in both equipment and in training individuals in its use, increased downtime and data loss because of equipment failure, data overload caused by injudiciously adding performance measures,[10] and limited generality within and across studies because of poor standardization of procedures and nomenclature (see Hartmann & Wood, 1990). Despite its simplicity, Bakeman and Gottman (1987) continue to see an important role for paper and pencil in collecting observational data, and Gelfand and Hartmann (1984) provide suggestions for optimizing this humble approach.

OBSERVERS: ERRORS AND TRAINING

Although observers are a critical component of most observation systems, their performance is fallible and may result in seriously flawed data. Many investigators, however, have assumed that most potential observer effects may be overcome or at least acceptably limited by adequate training. Not all have been quite so sanguine. Tryon (1998), for example, states that

> behavioral observation is not easy to carry out and has significant limitations even when adequate resources are available. Human observers tend to be reactive . . . thereby changing the behavior of interest. Observers can be biased by their expectations and prejudices. Observers drift and need to be retrained periodically. . . . Human observers have a finite information processing capacity that can rapidly be exceeded. . . . Human observers violate the client's right to privacy to some degree. . . . Few clinical facilities can afford to hire, train, and continuously retrain observers (pp. 88–89).

These concerns were sufficiently worrisome to Tryon that he suggested that whenever technological aids are available, they should be used instead of human observers.

Sources of Observer Error

Observer error represents a conglomerate of directional and unsystematic errors in behavior observations that may result from using human observers. This discussion highlights the important sources of errors identified in previous reviews of the literature (e.g., Cone, 1998a; Hartmann & Wood, 1990).

Reactivity

Behavior observation often is an intrusive assessment procedure and can evoke atypical responses from the observed subjects. This reaction to observation is the basis for the term *reactivity* (Lambert, 1960). The outcomes of research conducted on the potential reactive effects of observation have not been uniform; nevertheless, five factors appear to contribute to reactivity (for reviews, see Harris & Lahey, 1982; and Haynes & Horn, 1982). These factors include

• The valence or social desirability of target behaviors: Socially desirable or appropriate behaviors may be facilitated, while socially undesirable or "private" behaviors may be suppressed when individuals are aware of being observed. The suppression of socially undesirable behaviors would seem to be more likely if the purpose of assessment has threatening implications to the client;

• Client characteristics: Young children and individuals who are open and confident or perhaps merely insensitive may react less to direct observation than individuals who do not share these characteristics;

• Conspicuousness of observation. Factors that increase the conspicuousness of observers increase reactivity, including the activity level of participant-observers, instructions that alert individuals to the observation conditions, the observer's proximity to the individual observed, and the presence of observation instrumentation;[11]

• Observer attributes: The observer's gender, responsiveness, and age appear to influence reactivity in children. Appearance, tact, public-relations skills, and socioeconomic status also may contribute to reactivity; and

• The rationale for observation. Johnson and Bolstad (1973) recommended providing a thorough rationale for observation procedures in order to reduce client concerns and potential reactive effects that are due to the observation process.

Methods for lessening the salience and intrusiveness of the observation setting include employing participant observers, enforcing rules for observer dress and etiquette, using an adaptation period that precedes the gathering of formal data, and employing covert assessments—though the latter can pose obvious ethical concerns (e.g., Hartmann & Wood, 1990).

Observer Bias

Observer bias is a systematic error in assessment usually associated with the observers' expectancies and prejudices as well as their information-processing limitations.[12] Other systematic errors due to observer expectancies include explicit or implicit hypotheses about the purposes of an investigation, how individuals should behave, or perhaps even what might constitute "appropriate" data (e.g., Haynes, 1978; Nay, 1979). Several studies have been specifically designed to evaluate the role of observer expectancies in contributing systematic bias to behavioral assessments (see Foster & Cone, 1986; also see Cone, 1998a). These studies suggest that the accuracy of quantitative measures is not much affected by observer expectancies when stringent training criteria are coupled with a precise, low-inference observation code.

Other methods have been proposed for controlling biases in observational reporting (e.g., Hartmann, 1984), including the use of professional observers and cautioning observers about the potential lethal effects of bias. When observers are used to assess the effects of treatment interventions, maintaining experimental naïveté among observers and videotaping the target events and rating the assessment sessions in random order also might reduce bias. If there is any reason to doubt the effectiveness with which observer bias is being controlled, investigators should assess the nature and extent of bias by systematically probing their observers.

Observer Drift

Another source of observer error is measurement decay in observer performance. Observer consistency and accuracy may decrease, sometimes precipitously, from the end of training to the beginning of formal data collection (e.g., Taplin & Reid, 1973). When interobserver consistency remains high yet observer accuracy fails, the phenomenon is labeled *consensual observer drift* (Johnson & Bolstad, 1973). Consensual observer drift occurs when a recording-interpretation bias has gradually evolved over time or when response definitions or measurement procedures are informally altered to suit novel changes in the topography of some target behavior. Reduction in observer consistency (drift) also can result from observer satiation or boredom or even simple inattention. Drift can be limited or its effects reduced by providing continuing training throughout a project, by training and recalibrating all observers at the same time, and by inserting random and covert reliability probes throughout the course of an investigation.[13]

Observer Cheating

Outright observer fabrication of data has been reported occasionally (Azrin, Holz, Ulrich, & Goldiamond, 1961), and observers have been known to calculate inflated reliability coefficients (O'Leary, Kent, & Kanowitz, 1975). Precautions against observer cheating include making random, unannounced data quality spot-checks, collecting data forms immediately after an observation session ends, restricting data analysis and reliability and agreement calculations to individuals who did not collect the data, and by repeatedly warning observers that cheating will bring about dire consequences. Collateral sources, such as nurses in the observation setting, might be asked to report periodically on observer behavior and to verify observations, thereby providing the clinician with both valuable feedback and the confidence of the institutional staff (also see McCall, 1984).

Other Factors Related to Degraded Observer Performance

In his review of the literature, Cone (1998a) identifies a number of additional factors associated with reductions in observer performance. These include factors associated with the observers themselves (their motivation); the code they employ (its complexity); observer training procedures (training contingencies and other forms of feedback, retraining and recalibration, and similarity between training stimuli and observational stimuli); the structure of the observational setting (whether observations are obtained by constant or rotating pairs); and the conduct of reliability assessments (announced versus unannounced).

Selecting and Training Observers

The preceding discussion considered sources of error in observation data, many of which may be limited by adequate observer training. Surprisingly little effort has been devoted to the systematic evaluation of observer characteristics that may help or hinder such training.

Selecting Observers

Certain aptitudes and perceptual motor skills of observers may be directly relevant to training efficiency and to the maintenance of desired levels of observer performance (see, e.g., the reviews by Barrios, 1993; and by Hartmann & Wood, 1990). These include above-average verbal and clerical skills and motivational characteristics such as high morale. Yarrow and Waxler (1979) suggested that good observers have the ability to sustain attention without habituation and manage high levels of environmental stimulation without confusion, have a compulsive regard for detail and precision and an overriding commitment to scientific detachment, and are "intense," analytical, and introspective.

In addition to differing in personal characteristics, potential observers can vary in their level of participation with the observed. At one extreme are nonparticipant (independent) observers whose only role is to gather data. At the other extreme are participant observers such as parents, peers, siblings, spouses, teachers, aides, and nurses, who are normally present in the setting where the observations take place (e.g., Bickman, 1976). The advantages and disadvantages accruing to the use of participant observers are described by Nay (1979) and by Cone (1998a). The major advantages of participant-observers result from their presence at times that may otherwise be inconvenient for independent observers, the possibility that their presence may be less obtrusive, cost, and their access to infrequent behaviors. On the other hand, they may be less dependable, more subject to biases, and more difficult to train and evaluate than independent observers.[14]

Training Observers

Unusually thorough models of observer training aimed at reducing timing and interpretation errors have been available for approximately 70 years (e.g., Arrington, 1932). Based upon previous reviews of the observer-training literature, Hartmann and Wood (1990) suggest a seven-step general model for observer training (also see Barrios, 1993).

- Orientation: Prior to training, observers might be exposed to the observation setting and attempt to record behaviors without the benefit of formal instruction or the aid of coding schema. This procedure may be useful in convincing observers of the need for training and the value of a structured observation system. As part of their orientation, potential observers should be sensitized to relevant clinical and research issues (American Psychological Association, 1992). A suitable rationale and introduction should emphasize the need for objectivity and confidentiality. And, of course, the client's permission should be obtained as with most all observation.

- Learning the observational manual: Trainees should learn the operational definitions and scoring procedures of the observation system as presented in a formal observation training manual (suggestions for observation manuals are discussed by Nay, 1979, p. 237). Observer trainees at this step are required to memorize the operational definitions as well as to learn examples and the rules for scoring the target behaviors. Investigators should utilize appropriate instructional principles in teaching the observer trainees desired observation, recording, and interpersonal skills.

- First criterion check: After studying the observational manual, observers should pass a pencil-and-paper test or score a written protocol presenting sample target events. In this phase, the trainee is required to have a working knowledge of the observation system in order to code the test items accurately.

- Analogue observations: Having passed the written test, observers should next be trained to criterion accuracy on a series of analogue assessment samples, such as film clips, virtual client performance enactments, or role-plays. If response topographies can be expected to change over the course of the investigation, then the trainees should be exposed to both earlier and later response variants. Film or videotape is particularly useful in this regard (Arrington, 1939), especially if sample vignettes meet several important requirements. These vignettes should present rather complex interaction sequences, the interaction sequences should be unpredictable and variable in response patterning, and the observers should be overtrained on these difficult vignettes in order to minimize decrements in performance from training to in vivo observations. Feedback should be abundant, and discussion of procedural problems and confusions should be encouraged throughout this training phase. All observers should be informed of such discussions and the resulting clarifications, and decisions should be posted in an observer log or noted in the observation manual that each observer carries. This phase of training can require substantial time. Research clinicians at the Oregon Social Learning Center (Maerov, Brummett, & Reid, 1978), for example, reported training their observers for 10–15 hours on videotaped examples before exposing them to field experience.

- In situ practice: Observers should next attain some high level of agreement with a "criterion" rater, such as 90%, during "live" practice in the observation setting. Practice in the observation setting can serve the dual purpose of desensitizing observers to fears about settings, such as inpatient psychiatric units, and allowing the client to habituate to the observation procedures. In addition, regular accuracy feedback should be provided throughout training. House (1980) has described a quick and convenient statistical procedure for monitoring systematic errors in observation data; this procedure may be useful in monitoring observer performance during training and could serve as a useful format to provide feedback to observers. It is important to remember that feedback about accuracy improves accuracy, whereas feedback about consistency (e.g., interobserver agreements during coding) improves consistent scoring tendencies but not necessarily accuracy (DeMaster, Reid, & Twentyman, 1977). Observers should be informed that all observation sessions will be checked for quality or that quality will be checked covertly at unannounced times. Reliance on periodic overt checks should be avoided (see Kazdin, 1977).

- Retraining-recalibrating sessions: During the course of the investigation, periodic retraining and recalibration sessions should be conducted with all observers (Johnson & Bolstad, 1973; Kazdin, 1977); recalibration could include spot tests on the observation manual (see Paul, 1986; Paul & Lantz, 1977) and reviews of sample observation events. Perhaps an alternate set of criterion vignettes on film or videotape might be developed for these retraining purposes. Nay (1974) suggested that observers attain predetermined criteria for consistency across multiple partners, and Haynes (1978) recommended that observers be rotated to constitute various teams or pairs during the investigation. Another strategy is to train a second, independent observer group to provide crosschecks of data quality (Kent et al., 1974).

• Postinvestigative debriefing: At the end of the investigation, observers should be interviewed to assess any biases or potential mistakes that may have influenced their observations (Hartmann et al., 1979; Johnson & Bolstad, 1973). Following these interviews, observers should be extended the professional courtesy of being informed about the nature and results of the investigation.[15]

Training observers can be a lengthy and time-consuming process, particularly with complex, clinical-research-based codes. Rueter and Conger (1995), for example, trained observers for 200 hours over a 10-week period.

THE DEPENDABILITY OF OBSERVERS' SCORES

Issues of data *dependability, consistency, generalizability, reliability,* or *agreement* are relevant to scores from any assessment method, including direct observations. The most critical dimension for observations is the observers, although the temporal stability and internal as well as situational generalizability of behaviors also may be relevant (e.g., Wiggins, 1973). Undependable observer data can doom a project, and inconsistent data of any kind—for example, across time—limit the extent to which the observation scores can safely be generalized.

There are at least three distinct viewpoints on dealing with the dependability of scores produced by observers, each with its own range of applicability, vocabulary, conceptual basis, and summary statistics: generalizability, traditional psychometrics, and agreements (e.g., Hartmann, 1982; Suen & Ary, 1989). This section employs the vocabulary and some of the conceptions of the generalizability position and alludes to the traditional psychometric approach. However, it focuses on the agreements between observers on individually coded events or intervals, because this approach seems most relevant to clinical applications of observational data.

Generalizability Theory

The theory of generalizability offers a detailed conceptual analysis of the components of a score, methods for analyzing those components, statistics for summarizing the analysis, and an interpretive framework for evaluating the limits of score generalizability, including methods for determining the optimum combination of settings, observers, and the like (Cronbach, Gleser, Nanda, & Rajaratnam, 1972). The components of a score are determined by the specific conditions under which the score was obtained, including time, context, scoring system, and observer. The contributions of these conditions of measurement, called *facets* in generalizability theory, are determined by analysis-of-variance procedures. The results of the analysis are summarized by estimates of variance components, intraclass correlation coefficients, and error statistics. Large variance components associated with a facet or an interaction of facets is a warning that the generalizability of the observations may be limited along those dimensions. For example, a large variance component associated with the facet of observers may suggest that a replication of similar results is unlikely with a change in observers.

The conceptualization and applied procedures of generalizability theory are readily accessible to assessors who employ direct observations. Despite the availability of nontechnical descriptions of the theory and illustrations of its applicability to observational data (e.g., Hartmann & Wood, 1990; and Suen & Ary, 1989), the generalizability approach is relatively infrequently used in clinical work. Although Berk (1979) provides 11 advantages of the generalizability perspective for assessing the quality of observational data, others have been less sanguine about its application, particularly in small sample clinical investigations in which the data may be autocorrelated and some important variance components cannot be well estimated (e.g., Jacob, Tennenbaum, & Krahn, 1987; Mitchell, 1979; but see Suen & Ary, 1989).

Interobserver Consistency

Since early discussions of the methodology of behavior analysis (e.g., Baer, Wolf, & Risley, 1968), behavioral interventionists have focused on the facet of observers' consistency or generalizability (Kelly, 1977).[16] Despite this attention, assessment of the dependability of data across observers has been plagued by a number of problems. These problems include disagreements about the definition of basic concepts (e.g., Suen, 1988), decisions regarding the level of data at which observer generalizability should be assessed, and methods of summarizing these data. These problems are not new; they have a long and often overlooked history dating back in psychology almost 60 years (e.g., Arrington, 1943). Our discussion here focuses primarily on definitions of basic concepts, the pragmatics of observer consistency, and summary statistics and guidelines for their interpretation.

Definitions

Observer agreement, observer reliability, and *observer accuracy* are the three terms that have been used with some frequency to describe the dependability of observers' scores. Observer agreement and observer reliability are often used interchangeably to describe the consistency of ratings among two or more observers who score the same behavior independently. When the terms are distinguished, observer agreement refers to consistency indexed by an agreement statistic that measures the degree to which observers assign the same score to an event or interval (and sometimes a person). Observer reliability refers to consistency indexed by a correlation coefficient. These coefficients index the proportion of obtained score variance that is due to the variation of true scores and are based upon traditional psychometric theory (e.g., Nunnally, 1978). When observations require dichotomous judgments (occurrence/nonoccurrence), distinctions between these two approaches sometimes blur, as the agreement and reliability statistics may be transformable (e.g., Suen & Ary, 1989).

Observer accuracy, sometimes called criterion-referenced agreement (Frick & Semmel, 1978), refers to consistency between the observations of an observer and *criterion* observations.[17] Cone (e.g., 1981, 1998a) has been the foremost proponent of accuracy assessments (also see Johnston & Pennypacker, 1993). Foster and Cone (1995), Nay (1979), and Boykin and Nelson (1981) provided useful suggestions for the construction of accuracy criteria, particularly criterion videotapes, which are standard for assessing accuracy. Although accuracy is an attractive concept, the nonpareil status accorded accuracy assessments by Cone remains controversial. For example, the development of criterion ratings may be infeasible in many situations. Even when feasible, accuracy assessments may provide unrepresentative estimates of what Cone (e.g., 1998b) terms *application* or field accuracy, particularly if observers can discriminate between these assessments and more typical observations. Furthermore, the status of accuracy criteria as *incontrovertible* is certainly questionable. As Silva (1993, p. 498) states, "It is rare when we feel we have 'incontrovertible' measures of anything, and in a philosophical sense incontrovertible standards simply do not exist. No matter how fine-grained the measurement, we always only approximate reality." Despite these criticisms, the correspondence between the coding performed by an observer and some form of criterion coding can be a useful part of the armamentarium for judging the quality of observational data.[18]

Pragmatics of Observer Consistency

Bakeman and Gottman (1987, p. 835) argue that the focus on observer consistency serves three critical goals:

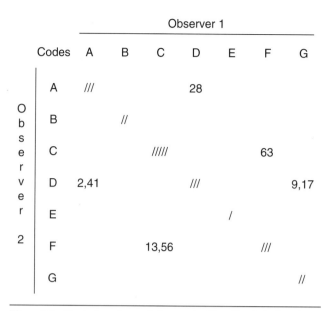

Figure 7.1 Illustration of a confusion matrix. *Note.* The dashed marks refer to intervals or events about which the observers agreed. The numbered entries refer to specific intervals or events about which the observers disagreed. Note that the observers had some tendency to confuse codes C and F, codes A and D, and codes D and G.

1. To ensure that observers are coding events according to definitions given in the coding manual (assessed with agreement with a standard or criterion);

2. To provide observers feedback so as to improve their performance (using a confusion matrix or some other method of explicating specific observer errors; see Figure 7.1); and

3. To assure others that observers are producing replicable data (assessed with a measure of observer agreement or reliability).

While these goals typically are served by focusing on observer data obtained from individual events or intervals (see Figure 7.1), the quality of observational data might also be assessed at some higher level of data aggregation, such as the total scores obtained during entire observational sessions. Such would be the case if the aggregate or session scores were the focus of statistical or visual analysis. Although it is always appropriate to assess the quality of data at the level at which the scores are analyzed (see, for example, Hartmann, 1982), it generally can be assumed that if the quality of observational data is adequate at a more microscopic level, then the aggregation of such data will be of even higher quality.[19]

Summary Statistics

There are well over 20 statistical measures available for summarizing interobserver agreement assessed at the level of the intervals or events that are coded (e.g., Berk, 1979; also see Suen & Ary, 1989). However, only two of these statistical summaries are used with any frequency: proportion (or percent) of agreement and kappa. The proportion-of-agreement statistic has been the most common index for summarizing interobserver agreement (Kelly, 1977). Proportion of agreement is the ratio of the number of agreed-upon events or intervals (called observations) to the total number of observations (agreed upon plus disagreed upon). This agreement statistic has been repeatedly criticized, especially since inflated estimates may result when the target behavior occurs at an extreme rate, and many agreements may be due to chance (e.g., Mitchell, 1979). These inflated estimates may give consumers a false sense of the adequacy of the data reported. For example, Suen and Lee (1985) found that had a chance-corrected agreement been used in a sample of past published data, 25 to 75% of the data sets would have been judged as having unacceptably low agreement!

Of the statistical techniques that have been suggested to remedy the problem of chance agreements, the most popular seems to be Cohen's (1960) kappa. Kappa corrects both the numerator and denominator of the proportion of agreement statistic for chance agreements. It thus is interpreted as the ratio of observed nonchance agreements to the maximum number of nonchance agreements that could occur in the observed data (see, e.g., Hartmann, 1977, 1982; Johnston & Pennypacker, 1993; and Suen & Ary, 1989). Kappa's advantages are that it corrects for chance agreements, provides a metric that can be compared across studies and a stringent assessment of the quality of the observers' data, and can be tested for significance (e.g., Bakeman & Gottman, 1987). Kappa also may be used for summarizing observer accuracy, for determining consistency among many raters, and for evaluating scaled (partial) consistency among observers (see, e.g., Hartmann & Wood, 1990). Hubert (1977) gives a useful technical bibliography on kappa-like statistics, while Uebersax (1988) reviews the limitations of kappa. Kappa's failings are that it may overcorrect for chance agreements and that it is sensitive to base rates of the target behavior (Langenbucher, Labouvie, & Morgenstern, 1996). Nevertheless, kappa remains the "interobserver agreement index of choice" (Suen & Ary, 1989, p. 113).

Interpreting Observer Consistency Statistics

Given the variety of available statistics for summarizing observer agreement—with various statistics based on different conceptions and employing different metrics—and the diverse clinical purposes to which observational data can be put, a common standard of adequacy is impossible. In general, however, values closer to the maximum value of the statistic are preferred over other values. Recommended minimum values for proportion of agreement range from .80 to .90 (Gelfand & Hartmann, 1984; Kelly, 1977); however, Jones, Reid, and Patterson (1975) suggested .70 agreement as an acceptable level of observer agreement when using complex coding schemes. For kappa, Gelfand and Hartmann (1984) recommended a minimum value of .60; Fleiss (1981) characterizes kappas of .60 to .75 as good and those over .75 as excellent.

Other Facets of Generalizability

Other generalizability facets apparently have not engaged the attention of investigators interested in observation systems, as writings on behavior observation typically limit their reliability considerations to observer generalizability (e.g., Hartmann & Wood, 1990; Mitchell, 1979). However, as we have previously argued (Hartmann & Wood, 1990), at least one additional generalizability facet should concern clinical investigators: the adequacy of the sample of behavior that is observed. If the sample of behavior is inadequate—for example, because each observation session is too short or observations are not obtained in enough sessions—any conclusions based upon the resulting data may be suspect.[20] A crude estimate of the adequacy of a behavioral sample can be obtained by procedures analogous to those used to assess the internal consistency of traditional measures (e.g., Nunnally, 1978).

VALIDITY

For a time, the validity litany was expanding as rapidly as the unvalidated uses of observational procedures. The pendulum has swung back to a more unified conception of validity, subsumed by the concept of construct validity (e.g., Messick, 1994). Silva's (1993, p. 69) five points nicely summarize current notions of validity as well as highlight the inadequacies of earlier formulations:

1. Validity is associated with each inference made from assessment information such as observational scores.

2. It is not the instrument that is validated, but rather the interpretation of scores obtained from the instrument.

3. Validity is an integrative judgment, reached after considering all of the information—both empirical evidence and theoretical rationales. It is not reducible to a coefficient or set of coefficients.

4. Types and classes of validity are misnomers for types and classes of *arguments*. The concept of validity is essentially unitary.

5. There is no limit to the range of data used to estimate validity. Any information may be relevant in the validation process—which is simply the process of hypothesis construction and testing.

Until recently, validity had not received the attention it deserves in observation research—but see the recent works that conceptualize validity in a manner uniquely for observations and/or review recent relevant validity studies (Cone, 1998; Foster & Cone, 1995; Haynes & O'Brien, 2000; Silva, 1993). As Hartmann and Wood (1990) indicated, this relative neglect of validity issues is ironic, because behavioral assessors have repeatedly criticized traditional assessment methodologies for their limited reliability and validity. In fact, observations have been considered inherently valid insofar as they are based on direct sampling of behavior and require minimal inferences on the part of observers. Observation data have been excused from the requirements of external validation, yet they often serve as the criteria for validating other types of assessment data.[21]

Clearly, the assumption of inherent validity in observations involves a serious epistemological error (e.g., Haynes, 1978). The data obtained by human observers may not be veridical descriptions of behavior (e.g., Silva, 1993). Accuracy of observations can be attenuated by definitional and sampling inadequacies, and it can be contaminated by reactivity effects and other sources of measurement bias and error as we have indicated earlier (also see Kazdin, 1979). The occurrence of such measurement-specific sources of variation provides convincing evidence for the need to validate interpretations based upon observation scores.

While few, if any, writers currently argue that behaviorally based interpretations should be excused from validation, some still seem to imply that the need for validation is lessened somehow because behaviors rather than "constructs" are assessed. Silva (1993) criticizes this position by arguing that "response classes," which have played such a critical role in behavioral formulations (e.g., Skinner, 1938), are themselves constructs (also see Barrios, 1988; and Barrios & Hartmann, 1986). This section takes the position that it is not the source of assessment information, but rather the interpretation made of assessment data, that determines the requirements for validation.

Messick (1994, p. 2) raises at least a score of questions about the validity of the interpretation of any score (also see Foster & Cone, 1995). The questions concern issues of content, internal and external structure, possible sources of con-

tamination and rival interpretations, generalizability (e.g., across contexts and participants), value implications, utility, and side effects of the score-based interpretation. And except for those dealing with value implications and side effects—what Messick (1994) calls consequential validity—these questions typically are addressed by a variety of arguments or sources of information subsumed under the traditional validity types (see Foster & Cone, 1995; Haynes, 2001b).

Not all score interpretations require all forms of validity information. It is, as Messick (1994, p. 3) indicates, the "relation between the evidence and the inference to be drawn that should determine the validation focus." However, because observations may participate in theories of behavior of varying subtlety and complexity, and because observations are unlimited in the issues that their inferences may address, the variety of forms of validation data that may be relevant to observations may itself be without limits.[22] This chapter will direct its discussion of validity concerns to two that are particularly relevant in clinical applications: Content and treatment-related concerns.

Content Concerns

Concerns with content, unlike other form of validity information, provide important, *instrument-focused* background factors relevant to score interpretation (e.g., Messick, 1994). These factors concern the degree to which the elements of the instrument are relevant to and representative of the construct of interest (e.g., Haynes, Richard, & Kubany, 1995).

Haynes (2001b), following the earlier analysis by Linehan (1980), offered an array of carefully considered content-related principles that, while directed specifically to the construction of analogue behavioral observations, have more general applicability. Perhaps most important among these are that the domain of relevant events must be completely and unambiguously enumerated, carefully defined, and then represented in the instrument. Depending on the nature and purposes of an observation system, these demands may apply to the behaviors of the target subject, to antecedent and consequent events provided by other persons, or to settings and temporal factors.[23] Once these response class members have been enumerated, they should be suitably defined and then included—either exhaustively or in some representational manner—in the instrument. Haynes's (2001b) specification requirements then go on to include response modes and dimensions that are to be measured, situations of observation, and instructions to the participant. In considering these varied aspects of content, Haynes emphasizes the importance of their match with the goals of assessment, of contacting the relevant literature on the topic, and of pilot testing. He also notes the importance of individual difference factors, such as age, gender, ethnicity, and culture. The potential importance of these factors would be obvious in the case of a response class such as peer aggression, where age, gender, and possibly broader sociocultural issues help define relevant forms of behaviors to be included. Finally, the method of combining observations to form scores should be specified.

Most observation systems have generally conformed to the operational requirements of content validity by specifying sampling and analysis procedures. However, less attention has been devoted to enumeration and definitional requirements, particularly in the case of analogue observation procedures (e.g., Haynes, 2001b).

Treatment-Related Concerns

The treatment-related concerns of observation scores refer to the ability of these scores to aid in selecting and individualizing treatment and to assess the effectiveness of treatment. The first issue is the determination of the utility of observations when they are used to identify problem behaviors and controlling stimuli and to select treatment interventions as discussed by Nelson and her associates (e.g., Evans & Nelson, 1977; Hayes, Nelson, & Jarrett, 1989; Nelson, 1988). The utility of observations for such classification decisions has been studied, for example, by Paul and his associates in the validation of observation systems used to assess long-term hospitalized psychiatric patients (e.g., Paul, Mariotto, & Redfield, 1986). Other important work in this area has been conducted by Iwata and colleagues (1994) as previously noted in the discussion of functional analysis. A summary of related work can be found in Haynes and O'Brien (2000, pp. 242–245); also see the commentary on this work by Horner (1994).

Studies assessing the utility of observations are susceptible to numerous methodological difficulties (e.g., *Journal of Consulting and Clinical Psychology,* 1978). Thus, investigators should be sensitive to issues of sampling, control of irrelevant variables, cross-validation, methods of establishing incremental validity, and clinical utility (e.g., Haynes, 2001b). As Haynes, Leisen, and Blaine (1997) have argued, the clinical utility of observations is highly conditional—for example, on the degree to which the variables controlling the client's behavior are not identifiable based on readily available information, such as the client's diagnosis; on the modifiability of these variables; on the power of relevant intervention strategies; and on the need to individualize standardized treatment programs.

A second treatment-related issue is the degree to which one source of observations can be substituted for another—

particularly in evaluating treatment outcomes. Such might occur, for example, when observations in a contrived setting are substituted for observations in the natural environment. Although the literature on the consistency between alternative sources of assessment data is modest, it seems safe to conclude that the cross-method generalizability of observations is variable (e.g., Cone & Foster, 1982). The highest convergence is found when precisely the same behavior at the same level of specificity is assessed by the methods being compared with direct observations (Cone, 1998b). These results underscore the desirability of assessing intermethod generalization (variously referred to as concurrent or convergent validity) when substitute observations are used to assess treatment outcome (cf. Chamberlain & Reid, 1987; Hoge, 1985).

To conclude, it is important to realize that validity is not a general or absolute property of an assessment instrument. Observations may have impressive validity for evaluating the effectiveness of behavioral interventions, but they may be only moderately valid or even invalid measures for other assessment purposes. Observations may be used for various assessment functions, and the validity of observation data for each of these functions must be independently verified (e.g., Hartmann & Woods, 1990).

CONCLUSIONS

This chapter has described the important considerations in developing, employing, and evaluating observational assessment systems. The procedures are complex and time demanding.[24] Although the basic elements of this technology have been available for more than half a century (see, e.g., Arrington, 1939, 1943), it is apparent that many current investigators are not contacting either the earlier or more recent literatures. Haynes, Richard, and Kubany (1995) examined all articles published in the 1993–1994 issues of the *Journal of Applied Behavior Analysis* that reported on the clinical application of a new behavior observation coding system. Of the 18 behavioral observation studies rated,

> . . . 7 did not provide information about how the behavior codes or observation system were developed. Only three studies reported systematic approaches to assessment instrument development. . . . In most cases, idiosyncratic behavior codes were constructed . . . apparently without reference to existing codes and without evidence that the codes selected were the most relevant and representative for a particular target or for a particular assessment function (p. 245).

These results are reminiscent of those reported earlier by Peterson and Hartmann (1975) in their discussion of reliability issues in observational assessment: Reinventing a technology does little to advance a field of investigation and is wasteful of time and effort—though it may be temporarily personally rewarding.

This chapter has omitted a number of important issues that deserve to be addressed, the most important of which is the ethics of conducting observations. Let us end then in noting at least two ethical issues that command our attention: informed consent and anonymity of the resulting data. Informed consent requires telling clients what specific behaviors will be observed, who will be observing them, and under what conditions (Cone, 1998a). In addition, potential clients should be told the purposes their data will serve as well as specific steps that will be taken to protect the anonymity of their data. For additional enlightened discussion of these issues in observational assessment, see Barrios (1993) and Nay (1979).

NOTES

1. Observational approaches to assessment are by no means limited to clinical work. Observational methodologies have an extensive history of use in research in the social and behavioral sciences, including anthropology, child development, education, ethology, and social psychology. See Suen and Ary (1989, p. 9), for pivotal observational assessment references from these and other substantive areas of investigation.

2. Results indicated that 80% of the treatments based on functional analytic experimental results were successful, whereas treatments not so based were reported as having minimal effects.

3. See Foster and Cone (1995, p. 254) for an interesting discussion of the concept of response class and related distinctions between causal and effect indicators (cf. Bollen & Lennox, 1991). Also see the discussion by Bakeman and Gottman (1997) of "splitting and lumping."

4. Very closely related to the distinction between molecular and molar categories is whether the targeted behaviors refer to physically-based or social-based behaviors. According to Bakeman and Gottman (1997), the former "classify behavior with clear and well-understood roots in the organism's physiology," whereas the latter "follow from cultural tradition or simply negotiation among people as to a meaningful way to view and categorize the behavior" (pp. 17–18).

5. We noted earlier (Hartmann & Wood, 1990) that the infrequency with which settings are typically sampled suggests that therapists must either be assessing targets that do not require the sampling of settings or they are disregarding possible situational specificity in their data.

6. See Suen and Ary (1989) for a serious attempt to apply sampling *theory,* including the notion of systematic and random error, to behavior observations.

7. Haynes (1978) refers to this method as "critical event-recording," and Bakeman and Gottman (1987, 1997) to a related procedure as "cross classification." If the discriminative stimulus was a fight, various aspects of the fight, such as its initiator, its verbal or physical nature, and the method of its resolution, might be coded using one of the recording techniques described in the next section.

8. Various attempts have been made to provide a concise organizational scheme for these recording techniques. The dimensions employed include whether the recording occurs continuously or intermittently, whether events or intervals are recorded, and whether the observation intervals are instantaneous or longer (see, e.g., Bakeman & Gottman, 1997).

9. Using sampling theory, Suen and Ary (1989) described how the error in interval-recorded data may be estimated. They also suggest methods for assessing the a priori probability that interval recording will provide accurate information on response frequency and duration. Also see Quera (1990).

10. Bakeman, Cairns, and Applebaum, (1979) refer to this latter phenomenon as *data tyranny.*

11. Perhaps most disquieting—from a research, but not necessarily a clinical perspective—is the finding reported by Harris and Lahey (1982) that conspicuous conditions of observation can interact with treatment phases to produce a form of reactivity that mimics a treatment effect.

12. Campbell (1958), in a rare *conceptual* review of observer bias described a number of cognitively based distortions, including a "bias toward central tendency," in which observers may impose patterns of regularity and orderliness on otherwise complex and unruly behavioral data (e.g., Hollenbeck, 1978).

13. One can evaluate the presence of observer drift by having observers periodically rate prescored videotapes (sometimes referred to as *criterion* videotapes), by conducting quality (e.g., reliability) assessment across rotating members of observation teams, and by using independent quality assessors.

14. Margolin (1987), for example, reports that differences occur surprisingly often between the data obtained from participant observers (spouses) and independent observers.

15. In technical reports, observers should receive footnote acknowledgment and their characteristics described, including how they were selected, their length and type of training to attain criterion, and their criterion-level accuracy and consistency.

16. Cone (1998b) traces the focus on observer consistency or generalizability back to Watson (1919), who argued that events for which consensus could not be established were outside the realm of psychology!

17. Some authors prefer to view accuracy as a form of validity, either criterion-related (Suen & Ary, 1989, p. 172) or representational (Foster & Cone, 1995), rather than as a form of consistency analysis.

18. A high level of accuracy may be best viewed as a necessary, though not sufficient, condition of adequate observer performance.

19. Exceptions occur when positively correlated scores are differenced or negatively correlated components are summed.

20. This requirement is analogous to that imposed on traditional psychometricians to develop tests of adequate length.

21. Traditional measurement specialists have long struggled with the error-proneness of criteria—whatever the composition of the criteria—and have addressed these concerns under the rubric of "the criterion problem" (e.g., Pedhazur & Pedhazur-Schmelkin, 1991).

22. Haynes and O'Brien (2000) address 18 varieties of validation data, and others have extended this list (e.g., Cone, 1998; Messick, 1994).

23. The task confronting the investigator is analogous to that involved in performing a task analysis (e.g., Gelfand & Hartmann, 1984).

24. The process may be shortened by selecting all or parts of existing systems (see Barrios, 1993, pp. 158ff for suggestions for identifying existing measures).

REFERENCES

Adams, H.E., Doster, J.A., & Calhoun, K.S. (1977). A psychologically based system of response classification. In A.R. Ciminero, K.S. Calhoun, & H.E. Adams (Eds.), *Handbook of behavioral assessment* (pp. 47–78). New York: Wiley.

Alevizos, P., Campbell, M.D., Callahan, E., & Berck, P.L. (1974). Communication. *Journal of Applied Behavior Analysis, 7,* 472.

Alevizos, P., DeRisi, W., Liberman, R., Eckman, T., & Callahan, E. (1978). The behavior observation instrument: A method of direct observation for program evaluation. *Journal of Applied Behavior Analysis, 11,* 243–257.

Alexander, J.F., Newell, R.M., Robbins, M.S., & Turner, C.W. (1995). Observational coding in family therapy process research. *Journal of Family Psychology, 9,* 355–365.

Altmann, J. (1974). Observational study of behavior: Sampling methods. *Behavior, 49,* 227–267.

American Psychological Association. (1992). *Ethical principles of psychologists and code of conduct.* Washington, DC: Author.

Arrington, R.E. (1932). Interrelations in the behavior of young children. *Child Development Monograph,* No. 8.

Arrington, R.E. (1939). Time-sampling studies of child behavior. *Psychological Monographs, 5*(2), 37–67.

Arrington, R.E. (1943). Time-sampling in studies of social behavior: A critical review of techniques and results with research suggestions. *Psychological Monographs, 40,* 81–124.

Ayllon, T., & Skuban, W. (1973). Accountability in psychotherapy: A test case. *Journal of Behavior Therapy and Experimental Psychiatry, 4,* 19–30.

Azrin, N.H., Holz, W., Ulrich, R., & Goldiamond, I. (1961). The control of the content of conversation through reinforcement. *Journal of the Experimental Analysis of Behavior, 4,* 25–30.

Baer, D.M., Wolf, M.M., & Risley, T.R. (1968). Some current dimensions of applied behavior analysis. *Journal of Applied Behavior Analysis, 1,* 91–97.

Bakeman, R., Cairns, R.B., & Applebaum, M. (1979). Note on describing and analyzing interactional data: Some first steps and common pitfalls. In R.B. Cairns (Ed.), *The analysis of social interactions: Methods, issues, and illustrations.* Hillsdale, NJ: Erlbaum.

Bakeman, R., & Gottman, J.M. (1987). Applying observational methods: A systematic view. In J.D. Osofsky (Ed.), *Handbook of infant development* (2nd ed., pp. 818–854). New York: Wiley.

Bakeman, R., & Gottman, J.M. (1997). *Observing interaction: An introduction to sequential analysis* (2nd ed.). New York: Cambridge University Press.

Barrios, B.A. (1993). Direct observation. In T.H. Ollendick & M. Hersen (Eds.), *Handbook of child and adolescent assessment* (pp. 140–164). Boston: Allyn & Bacon.

Barrios, B.A. (1988). On the changing nature of behavioral assessment. In A.S. Bellack & M. Hersen (Eds.), *Behavioral assessment: A practical handbook* (3rd ed.). New York: Pergamon Press.

Barrios, B.A., & Hartmann, D.P. (1986). The contribution of traditional assessment: Concepts, issues, and methodologies. In R.O. Nelson & S.C. Hayes (Eds.), *Conceptual foundations of behavioral assessment* (pp. 81–110). New York: Guilford Press.

Barrios, B.A., & Hartmann, D.P. (1997). Fears and anxieties. In E.J. Mash & L.G. Terdal (Eds.), *Assessment of childhood disorders* (3rd ed., pp. 230–327). New York: Guilford Press.

Bellack, A.S., & Hersen, M. (Eds.). (1998). *Behavioral assessment: A practical handbook* (4th ed.). Boston: Allyn & Bacon.

Berk, R.A. (1979). Generalizability of behavioral observations: A clarification of interobserver agreement and interobserver reliability. *American Journal of Mental Deficiency, 83,* 460–472.

Bickman, L. (1976). Observational methods. In C. Selltiz, L.S. Wrightsman, & S.W. Cook (Eds.), *Research methods in social relations.* New York: Holt, Rinehart & Winston.

Bijou, S.W., Peterson, R.F., & Ault, M.H. (1968). A method to integrate descriptive and experimental field studies at the level of data and empirical concepts. *Journal of Applied Behavior Analysis, 1,* 175–191.

Bollen, K., & Lennox, R.L. (1991). Conventional wisdom on measurement: A structural equation perspective. *Psychological Bulletin, 110,* 305–314.

Boykin, R.A., & Nelson, R.O. (1981). The effects of instructions and calculation procedures on observers' accuracy, agreement, and calculation correctness. *Journal of Applied Behavior Analysis, 14,* 479–489.

Cairns, R.B., & Green, J.A. (1979). How to assess personality and social patterns: Observations or ratings? In R.B. Cairns (Ed.), *The analysis of social interactions: Methods, issues and illustrations* (pp. 209–226). Hillsdale, NJ: Erlbaum.

Chamberlain, P., & Reid, J.B. (1987). Parent observation and report of child symptoms. *Behavioral Assessment, 9,* 97–109.

Cohen, J. (1960). A coefficient of agreement for nominal scales. *Educational and Psychological Measurement, 20,* 37–46.

Cone, J.D. (1981). Psychometric considerations. In M. Hersen & A.S. Bellack (Eds.), *Behavioral Asssessment: A practical handbook* (2nd ed., pp. 38–71). New York: Pergamon Press.

Cone, J.D. (1998a). Observational assessment: Measure development and research issues. In A.S. Bellack & M. Hersen (Eds.), *Behavioral assessment: A practical handbook* (4th ed., pp. 183–223). Boston: Allyn & Bacon.

Cone, J.D. (1998b). Psychometric considerations: Concepts, contents, and methods. In A.S. Bellack & M. Hersen (Eds.), *Behavioral assessment: A practical handbook* (4th ed., pp. 22–46). Boston: Allyn & Bacon.

Cone, J.D., & Foster, S.L. (1982). Direct observation in clinical psychology. In J.N. Butcher & P.C. Kendall (Eds.), *Handbook of research methods in clinical psychology*. New York: Wiley.

Cronbach, L.J. (1960). *Essentials of psychological testing* (2nd ed.). New York: Harper & Row.

Cronbach, L.J., Gleser, G.C., Nanda, H., & Rajaratnam, N. (1972). *The dependability of behavioral measurements*. New York: Wiley.

DeMaster, B., Reid, J., & Twentyman, C. (1977). The effects of different amounts of feedback on observer's reliability. *Behavior Therapy, 8,* 317–329.

Evans, I.M., & Nelson, R.O. (1977). Assessment of child behavior problems. In A.R. Ciminero, K.S. Calhoun, & H. Adams (Eds.), *Handbook of behavioral assessment* (pp. 603–681). New York: Wiley.

Fleiss, J.L. (1981). *Statistical methods for rates and proportions*. New York: Wiley.

Floyd, F. (1989). Segmenting interactions: Coding units for assessing marital and family behaviors. *Behavioral Assessment, 11,* 23–29.

Foster, S.L., & Cone, J.D. (1986). Design and use of direct observation systems. In A. Ciminero, K. Calhoun, & H.E. Adams (Eds.), *Handbook of behavioral assessment* (2nd ed., pp. 253–324). New York: Wiley.

Foster, S.L., & Cone, J.D. (1995). Validity issues in clinical assessment. *Psychological Assessment, 7,* 248–260.

Frick, T., & Semmel, M.I. (1978). Observer agreement and reliabilities of classroom observational measures. *Review of Educational Research, 48,* 157–184.

Gelfand, D.M., & Hartmann, D.P. (1984). *Child behavior analysis and therapy* (2nd ed.). New York: Pergamon Press.

Greenwood, C., Carta, J.J., Kamps, D., Terry, B., & Delaquardi, J. (1994). Development and validation of standard classroom observation systems for school practitioners: Ecobehavioral assessment systems software (EBASS). *Exceptional Children, 61,* 197–210.

Harris, F.C., & Lahey, B.B. (1982). Subject reactivity in direct observation assessment: A review and critical analysis. *Clinical Psychology Review, 2,* 523–538.

Hartmann, D.P. (1977). Considerations in the choice of interobserver reliability estimates. *Journal of Applied Behavior Analysis, 10,* 103–116.

Hartmann, D.P. (1982). Assessing the dependability of observational data. In D.P. Hartmann (Ed.), *New directions for the methodology of behavioral sciences: Using observers to study behavior* (pp. 51–65). San Francisco: Jossey-Bass.

Hartmann, D.P. (1984). Assessment strategies. In D.H. Barlow & M. Hersen (Eds.), *Single case experimental designs* (2nd ed., pp. 107–139). New York: Pergamon Press.

Hartmann, D.P. (in press). Selected measurement and design issues. In D. Teti (Ed.), *Handbook of research methods in developmental psychology*. Williston, VT: Blackwell.

Hartmann, D.P., & Wood, D.D. (1982). Observational methods. In A.D. Bellack, M. Hersen, & A.E. Kazdin (Eds.), *International handbook of behavioral modification and therapy,* (pp. 109–138). New York: Plenum.

Hartmann, D.P., & Wood, D.D. (1990). Observational methods. In A.S. Bellack, M. Hersen, & A.E. Kazdin (Eds.), *International handbook of behavioral modification and therapy,* (2nd ed., pp. 107–138). New York: Plenum.

Hartmann, D.P., Roper, B.L., & Bradford, D.C. (1979). Some relationships between behavioral and traditional assessment. *Journal of Behavioral Assessment, 1,* 3–21.

Hawkins, R.P. (1982). Developing a behavior code. In D.P. Hartmann (Ed.), *Using observers to study behavior: New directions for methodology of social and behavioral science* (pp. 21–35). San Francisco: Jossey-Bass.

Hawkins, R.P., & Dobes, R.W. (1977). Behavioral definitions in applied behavior analysis: Explicit or implicit. In B.C. Etzel, J.M. LeBlanc, & D.M. Baer (Eds.), *New developments in behavioral research: Theory, method and application. In honor of Sidney W. Bijou* (pp. 167–188). Hillsdale, NJ: Erlbaum.

Hayes, S.C., Nelson, R.O., & Jarrett, R.B. (1989). Treatment utility of assessment: A functional approach to evaluating the quality of assessment. *American Psychologist, 42,* 963–974.

Haynes, S.N. (1978). *Principles of behavioral assessment*. New York: Gardner Press.

Haynes, S.N. (2001a). Introduction to the special section on clinical applications of analogue behavioral observation. *Psychological Assessment, 13,* 3–4.

Haynes, S.N. (2001b). Clinical applications of analogue behavioral observation: Dimensions of psychometric valuation. *Psychological Assessment, 13,* 73–85.

Haynes, S.N., & Horn, W.F. (1982). Reactivity in behavioral observation: A review. *Behavioral Assessment, 4,* 369–385.

Haynes, S.N., Leisen, M.B., & Blaine, D.D. (1997). Dynamical models for psychological assessment: Phase-space functions. *Psychological Assessment, 7,* 17–24.

Haynes, S.N., & O'Brien, W.H. (2000). *Principles and practice of behavioral assessment*. New York: Kluwer Academic/Plenum.

Haynes, S.N., Richard, D.C. S., & Kubany, E.S. (1995). Content validity in psychological assessment: A functional approach to concepts and methods. *Psychological Assessment, 7,* 238–247.

Hoge, R.D. (1985). The validity of direct observation measures of pupil classroom behavior. *Review of Educational Research, 55,* 469–483.

Hollenbeck, A.R. (1978). Problems of reliability in observational research. In U.P. Sackett (Ed.), *Observing behavior: Vol. 2. Data collection and analysis methods* (pp. 79–98). Baltimore: University Park Press.

Hops, H., Davis, B., & Longoria, N. (1995). Methodological issues in direct observation: Illustrations with the living in familial environments (LIFE) coding system. *Journal of Clinical Child Psychology, 24,* 193–203.

Horner, R.H. (1994). Functional assessment: Contributions and future directions. *Journal of Applied Behavior Analysis, 27,* 401–404.

House, A.E. (1980). Detecting bias in observational data. *Behavioral Assessment, 2,* 29–31.

Hubert, L. (1977). Kappa revisited. *Psychological Bulletin, 84,* 289–297.

Hutt, S.J., & Hutt, C. (1970). *Direct observation and measurement of behavior.* Springfield, Ill.: Charles C. Thomas.

Iwata, B.A., Pace, G.M., Dorsey, M.F., Zarcone, J.R., Vollmer, B., & Smith, J. (1994). The function of self injurious behavior: An experimental-epidemiological analysis. *Journal of Applied Behavior Analysis, 27,* 215–240.

Jacob, T., Tennenbaum, D.L., & Krahn, G. (1987). Factors influencing the reliability and validity of observation data. In T. Jacob (Ed.), *Family interaction and psychopathology: Theories, methods, and findings* (pp. 297–328). New York: Plenum.

Johnson, S.M., & Bolstad, O.D. (1973). Methodological issues in naturalistic observation: Some problems and solutions for field research. In L.A. Hamerlynck, L.C. Handy, & E.J. Mash (Eds.), *Behavior change: Methodology, concepts, and practice* (pp. 7–67). Champaign, Ill.: Research Press.

Johnston, J.M., & Pennypacker, H.S. (1993). *Strategies and tactics of behavioral research* (2nd ed.). Hillsdale, NJ: Erlbaum.

Jones, M.C. (1924). The elimination of children's fears. *Journal of Experimental Psychology, 7,* 383–390.

Jones, R.R., Reid, J.B., & Patterson, G.R. (1975). Naturalistic observation in clinical assessment. In P. McReynolds (Ed.), *Advances in psychological assessment* (Vol. 3, pp. 42–95). San Francisco: Jossey-Bass.

Journal of Consulting and Clinical Psychology. (1978). 46(4).

Kahng, S., & Iwata, B.A. (1998). Computerized systems for collecting real-time observational data. *Journal of Applied Behavior Analysis, 31,* 253–261.

Kazdin, A.E. (1977). Artifact, bias, and complexity of assessment: The ABCs of reliability. *Journal of Applied Behavior Analysis, 10,* 141–150.

Kazdin, A.E. (1979). Situational specificity: The two-edged sword of behavioral assessment. *Behavioral Assessment, 1,* 57–75.

Kelly, M.B. (1977). A review of the observational data-collection and reliability procedures reported in the *Journal of Applied Behavior Analysis. Journal of Applied Behavior Analysis, 10,* 97–101.

Lambert, W.W. (1960). Interpersonal behavior. In P.H. Mussen (Ed.), *Handbook of research methods in child development* (pp. 854–917). New York: Wiley.

Langenbucher, J., Labouvie, E., & Mongenstern, J. (1996). Measuring diagnostic agreement. *Journal of Consulting and Clinical Psychology, 64,* 1285–1289.

Linehan, M.M. (1980). Content validity: Its relevance to behavioral assessment. *Behavioral Assessment, 2,* 147–159.

Maerov, S.L., Brummett, B., & Reid, J.B. (1978). Procedures for training observers. In J.B. Reid (Ed.), *A social learning approach to family intervention: Vol. 2. Observation in home settings* (pp. 37–42). Eugene, OR: Castalia Press.

Mann, J., Ten Have, T., Plunkett, J.W., & Meisels, S.J. (1991). Time sampling: A methodological critique. *Child Development, 62,* 227–241.

Margolin, G. (1987). Participant observation procedures in marital and family assessment. In T. Jacob (Ed.), *Family interaction and psychopathology: Theories, methods, and findings* (pp. 391–426). New York: Plenum.

Markman, H.H., Leber, B.D., Cordova, A.D., & St. Peters, M. (1995). Behavioral observation and family psychology—Strange bedfellows or happy marriage? Comment on Alexander et al. (1995). *Journal of Family Psychology, 9,* 371–379.

Mash, E.J., & Foster, S.L. (2001). Exporting analogue behavioral observation from research to clinical practice: Useful or cost-defective? *Psychological Assessment, 13,* 86–98.

Mash, E.J., & Terdal, L.G., (Eds.). (1997). *Assessment of childhood disorders* (3rd ed.). New York: Guilford Press.

McCall, G.J. (1984). Systematic field observation. *Annual Review of Sociology, 10,* 263–282.

Messick, S. (1994). Foundations of validity: Meaning and consequences in psychological assessment. *European Journal of Psychological Assessment, 10,* 1–9.

Meyer, G.J., Finn, S.E., Eyde, L.D., Kay, G.G., Kubiszyn, T.W., Moreland, K.L., Eisman, E.J., & Dies, R.R. (1998). *Benefits and costs of psychological assessment in healthcare delivery: Report of the Board of Professional Affairs Psychological Assessment Work Group, Part 1.* Washington, DC: American Psychological Association.

Mischel, W. (1968). *Personality and assessment.* New York: Wiley.

Mitchell, S.K. (1979). Interobserver agreement, reliability, and generalizability of data collected in observational studies. *Psychological Bulletin, 86,* 376–390.

Nay, W.R. (1974). Comprehensive behavioral treatment in a training school for delinquents. In K. Calhoun, H. Adams, & K. Mitchell

(Eds.), *Innovative treatment methods in psychopathology* (pp. 203–243). New York: Wiley.

Nay, W.R. (1979). *Multimethod clinical assessment.* New York: Gardner Press.

Nelson, R. (1988). Relation between assessment and treatment within a behavioral perspective. *Journal of Psychopathology and Behavioral Assessment, 10,* 155–170.

Nunnally, J. (1978). *Psychometric theory* (2nd ed.). New York: McGraw-Hill.

Oei, T.P., & Mewett, A. (1987). The role of alcohol-dependent self-statements on drinking behavior in a public bar. *British Journal of Addiction, 82,* 1125–1131.

O'Leary, K.D., Kent, R.N., & Kanowitz, J. (1975). Shaping data collection congruent with experimental hypotheses. *Journal of Applied Behavior Analysis, 8,* 43–51.

Ollendick T.H., & Hersen, M., (Eds.). (1993). *Handbook of child and adolescent assessment.* Boston: Allyn & Bacon.

Paul, G.L. (Ed.). (1986). *Assessment in residential treatment settings.* Champaign, IL: Research Press.

Paul, G.L., & Lentz, R.J. (1977). *Psychological treatment of chronic mental patients: Milieu versus social-learning programs.* Cambridge, MA: Harvard University Press.

Paul, G.L., Mariotto, M.J., & Redfield, J.P. (1986). Assessment purposes, domains, and utility for decision making. In G.L. Paul (Ed.), *Assessment in residential treatment settings* (pp. 1–25). Champaign, IL: Research Press.

Pedhazur, E.J., & Pedhazur-Schmelkin, L.P. (1991). *Measurement, design, and analysis: An integrated approach.* Hillsdale, NJ: Erlbaum.

Peterson, L., & Hartmann, D.P. (1975). A neglected literature and an aphorism. *Journal of Applied Behavior Analysis, 8,* 331–332.

Powell, J., Martindale, A., & Kulp, S. (1975). An evaluation of time-sample measures of behavior. *Journal of Applied Behavior Analysis, 8,* 463–469.

Quera, V. (1990). A generalized technique to estimate frequency and duration in time sampling. *Behavioral Assessment, 12,* 409–424.

Reid, J.B., Baldwin, D.V., Patterson, G.R., & Dishion, T.J. (1988). Observations in the assessment of childhood disorders. In M. Rutter, A.H. Tuma, & I. Lann (Eds.), *Assessment and diagnosis in child psychopathology* (pp. 156–195). New York: Guilford Press.

Rueter, M.A., & Conger, R.D. (1995). Antecedents of parent-adolescent disagreement. *Journal of Marriage and the Family, 57,* 435–448.

Saudargas, R.A., & Lentz, F.E. (1986). Estimating percent of time and rate via direct observation: A suggested observational procedure and format. *School Psychology Review, 15,* 36–48.

Silva, F. (1993). *Psychometric foundations and behavioral assessment.* Newbury Park, CA: Sage.

Skinner, B.F. (1938). *The behavior of organisms.* New York: Appleton-Century-Crofts.

Stone, A.A., Turkkan, J.S., Bachrach, C.A., Jobe, J.B., Kurtzman, H.S., & Cain, V.S. (Eds.). (2000). *The science of self-report: Implications for research and practice.* Mahwah, NJ: Erlbaum.

Suen, H.K. (1988). Agreement, reliability, accuracy, and validity: Toward a clarification. *Behavioral Assessment, 10,* 343–366.

Suen, H.K., & Ary, D. (1989). *Analyzing quantitative behavioral observation data.* Hillsdale, NJ: Erlbaum.

Suen, H.K., & Lee, P.S.C. (1985). Effects of the use of percentage agreement on behavioral observation reliabilities: A reassessment. *Journal of Psychopathology and Behavioral Assessment, 7,* 221–234.

Taplin, P.S., & Reid, J.B. (1973). Effects of instructional set and experimental influences on observer reliability. *Child Development, 44,* 547–554.

Thomson, C., Holmberg, M., & Baer, D.M. (1974). A brief report on a comparison of time-sampling procedures. *Journal of Applied Behavior Analysis, 7,* 623–626.

Tryon, W.W. (1991). *Behavioral measurement in psychology and medicine.* New York: Plenum.

Tryon, W.W. (1998). Behavioral observation. In A.S. Bellack & M. Hersen (Eds.), *Behavioral assessment: A practical handbook* (4th ed., pp. 79–103). Boston: Allyn & Bacon.

Uebersax, J.S. (1988). Validity inferences from interobserver agreement. *Psychological Bulletin, 104,* 405–416.

Watson, J.B. (1919). *Psychology from the standpoint of a behaviorist.* Philadelphia: Lippincott.

Watson, J.B., & Rayner, R. (1920). Conditioned emotional reactions. *Journal of Experimental Psychology, 3,* 1–12.

Wiggins, J.S. (1973). *Personality and prediction: Principles of personality assessment.* Reading, MA: Addison-Wesley.

Yarrow, M.R., & Waxler, C.Z. (1979). Observing interaction: A confrontation with methodology. In R.B. Cairns (Ed.), *The analysis of social interactions: Methods, issues, and illustrations* (pp. 37–65). Hillsdale, NJ: Erlbaum.

CHAPTER 8

Individual Differences and Behavioral Assessment

JUNKO TANAKA-MATSUMI

The goal of behavioral assessment is the specification of the relationship between contextual and situational variables and behavior with the purpose of developing an individualized treatment program (Haynes & O'Brien, 2000). In the age of worldwide migrations and cultural diversity, we need to find effective ways to assess contributions of specific individual difference variables to the process and outcome of behavioral assessment and therapy. The purpose of this chapter is to examine the role of individual difference variables in behavioral assessment, particularly when conducting functional analysis of specific behaviors within the client's cultural context.

Historically, psychology of individual differences has included assessment of dimensions of human cognitive abilities, personality, and vocational interests. These dimensions have been found to contribute to important behaviors and outcomes such as educational achievement, work performance, health maintenance behaviors, and creativity (Lubinski, 2000). In psychotherapy research, great efforts have been made to investigate relationships between client variables and psychotherapy outcome. Beutler and Martin (2000) evaluated the contribution of "patient predisposing variables" to the assessment of individual differences in treatment outcome based on their models of the Systematic Treatment Selection and an Aptitude Treatment Interaction. Their purpose was to identify

which patient predisposing variables are the most promising for selecting specific therapeutic techniques. In behavior therapy, Acierno, Hersen, and Van Hasselt (1998) referred to the utility of assessing the potentially interactive effects of "subject characteristics" (p. 57) with treatment variables in conducting "prescriptive assessment." In multicultural assessment and case formulation, clinicians have proposed guidelines to accommodate the complexities of client cultural characteristics (e.g., Dana, 1998; Hays, 2001; Pedersen, 1997). Cross-cultural researchers are studying the relationships between specific cultural dimensions and patterns of maladaptive behaviors, culture-specific ways of communicating distress to others, and responses to clinical interventions (Draguns & Tanaka-Matsumi, in press; Tanaka-Matsumi, 2001). Epidemiological studies have uncovered cultural similarities and differences in the prevalence of major psychological disorders (e.g., schizophrenia, major depression, and anxiety disorders), frequencies of reported symptoms, and their correlates of individual difference variables such as sex, age, and ethnicity (Lopez & Guarnaccia, 2000; Tanaka-Matsumi & Draguns, 1997). Cultural dimensions reflect individual differences such as the degree to which the individual adopts specific behavioral characteristics of individualism or collectivism according to different situations across family, work, and school (Hofstede, 2001).

Behavioral assessment prizes empiricism, flexibility, functionalism, and an individualized approach. These characteristics suit the accommodation of individual differences in behavioral case formulation. In this chapter, I attempt to demonstrate the contextual basis of individual differences in target behavior selection and the assessment of their antecedents and consequences, their interrelationships, and the interactive effects of client and clinician cultures.

CULTURE, DIVERSITY, AND INDIVIDUAL DIFFERENCES

In principle, behavioral assessment is always conducted within the client's culture, which creates a potential source of individual differences among clients. In addition, if the client and the clinician are of different cultural backgrounds—as in multicultural or cross-cultural therapy—the clinician is faced with complex clinical judgments about the client's presenting problems. Noting the paucity of research on the reliability of target behavior identification in behavior therapy, Sturmy (1996, p. 209) stated, "determining target behaviors is a social process whereby the clinician and other people attempt to reach consensus on the target behavior." In fact, as Ullmann and Krasner (1975) and Evans (1997) noted, clinical judgment involves value judgments. Selecting a target behavior is a social process with a variety of contingencies operating on the clinician. Without training (Yutrzenka, 1995), the clinician may have limited cultural knowledge of what constitutes maladaptive behaviors in the client's culture. In this case, unless the clinician adopts a social-influence model of intervention, negotiating with the client and significant others, the clinician may have poor environmental support and fail to achieve a desired behavior change due to the selection of a culturally inappropriate target behavior.

Definitions of Culture and Individualized Behavioral Assessment

Of noteworthy development in the study of culture and psychopathology is the attempt to "unpack" culture by asking more functional questions instead of treating individual attributes as categories to be classified (Lopez & Guarnaccia, 2001; Tanaka-Matsumi, 2001). Herskovits's (1948) early definition of culture was the "human-made part of the environment." More recent definitions of culture have included "behavioral products of others who preceded us as well as values, language, and way of life" (Segall, Dasen, Berry, & Poortinga, 1999) or "the set of attitudes, values, beliefs, and behaviors, shared by a group of people, communicated from

one generation to the next via language or some other means of communication" (Matsumoto, 1994, p. 4). Pedersen (1997) asserts that all psychotherapies are culture centered: "By defining culture broadly—to include demographic (age, gender, place of residence, etc.), status (social, educational, economic, etc.), and affiliation (formal and informal) variables along with ethnographic variables (nationality, ethnicity, language, religion, etc.)—the construct "multicultural" becomes generic to all counseling relationships. . . . Persons from the same ethnic or nation group may still experience cultural differences" (p. 5). Pedersen emphasized that "the broad definition of culture is particularly important in preparing counselors to deal with the complex differences among clients from every cultural group" (p. 5). The broad definition of culture suits behavioral assessment as it aims to identify relationships among complex controlling variables of multiple behavior problems of the individual within cultural context. Functional assessment of culture is, therefore, consistent with the goal of behavioral assessment.

Behavior therapists ask important questions with regard to the functional relationship between the expression of distress and cultural values, or the impact of client ethnicity and religiosity on coping with distress such as depression and anger (Carter, 2000; Haaga, 1999; Propst, Ostrom, Watkins, Dean, & Mashburn, 1992) or anxiety (Chambles & Williams, 1995; Paradis, Friedman, Hatch, & Ackerman, 1996; Zoellner, Feeny, Fitzgibbons, & Foa, 1999) in cognitive behavioral treatment. Given the enormous cultural context for everything humans do, it is easy to appreciate the importance of cultural underpinning of the client's presenting problem, verbal and nonverbal modes of communicating the presenting problem, and the interaction of specific cultural factors with various aspects of the clinical judgment and diagnosis (Draguns & Tanaka-Matsumi, in press).

Perspectives on the Assessment of Culture and Maladaptive Behaviors

Researchers have studied the questions of how culture influences the formation of maladaptive behaviors and how its members exhibit and communicate maladaptive behaviors from two contrasting theoretical perspectives (Draguns & Tanaka-Matsumi, in press; Tanaka-Matsumi, 2001). Cultural universalists focus on the comparability or even globally applicable dimensions or categories such as the *DSM-IV* disorder categories of schizophrenia and major depressive disorder and their symptom patterns. On the other hand, culture relativists focus on the local context of a phenomenon (e.g., panic attacks) within a culture. They use culture-specific idioms of distress (e.g., ataque de nervios)—that is, the culturally reinforced way of expressing and labeling the distress. The two contrasting perspectives of culture and human behavior can be readily applied to behavioral assessment and individual differences. From the universalistic perspective, the major question is whether the principles of behavior change are universal. From the culture relativistic perspective, the pressing question is how to identify and describe specific maladaptive behaviors and their relationships with the client's specific social environment. Integrating both universalistic and relativistic perspectives, our main concern is the cultural reliability and validity of behavioral assessment and prediction of individual differences in treatment outcome.

Behavioral scientists concerned with the question of the universality of behavioral principles have all answered in the strong affirmative and stated that they are applicable to diverse populations and contexts (e.g., Bandura, 1969; Hayes & Toarmino, 1995; Skinner, 1953, 1971; Ullmann & Krasner, 1975). Specifically, behavior development, modification, maintenance, and generalization can be explained by positive and negative reinforcement, modeling, feedback, discrimination, extinction, punishment, and other generic principles (Kazdin, 2001). These behavioral principles are universally applicable to all human beings across diverse cultures and over many generations (Skinner, 1953). At the same time, there are large cross-cultural differences in culturally appropriate behaviors and social contingencies of those behaviors. Furthermore, beyond the immediate social environment of the client, differences in cultural practices and larger cultural context of specific behavioral contingencies are worthy of evaluation for lasting behavior modification of certain targets such as smoking and child maltreatment (Biglan, 1995). Cultural practices are "the incidence or prevalence of behaviors or the actions of groups and organizations" (Biglan, 1995, p. 12). Furthermore, cultural practices are "analyzed in terms of contextual features that affect the social propagation and maintenance of these behaviors" (Hayes & Toarmino, 1995, p. 21). Specifically, individual behaviors such as smoking or alcohol abuse have been propagated and maintained by the societal and organizational contingencies of tobacco and alcohol industries in many countries, hence these substances are easily available.

Behavioral assessment seeks to identify interlocking contingencies of multiple target behaviors and multiple causal variables (Haynes, Leisen, & Blaine, 1997). Content of specific assessment is culture relevant. For example, an increase of culturally appropriate topographies of assertiveness can be accomplished with skill training and reinforcement of acquired skill across cultures. However, what specific behaviors are deemed culturally appropriate in a given situation and context is culturally variable. Consequences for exhibiting an assertive behavior vary according to power distance, sex, age, and social status. Similarly, identification of effective reinforcers to increase assertiveness requires knowledge of both the individual client's reinforcement history and culture's consequences for assertion. Therefore, what works as an effective reinforcer is individually determined within cultural context.

I have stressed the importance of conducting behavioral assessment within the cultural context of the client. I reviewed various studies from related academic fields that have investigated the relationships between culture and human behavior. I now turn to more specific, conceptual bases of cultural accommodation in behavioral assessment.

BEHAVIORAL ASSESSMENT AND INDIVIDUAL DIFFERENCES

Conceptual Foundations of Behavioral Assessment Within Cultural Context

Structural Versus Functional Approaches

Behaviorists have addressed the question of cultural differences in behavior therapy (Kanfer & Schefft, 1988). Franks (1969) stressed the need to consider "the impact of cultural and allied differences upon the behavior therapist" (p. 21). Skinner (1971) emphasized that culture is an integral part of the context of behavior and should be evaluated carefully through functional analysis. Skinner (1988) equated culture with the social environment, stating that "individuals shape each other's behavior by arranging contingencies of reinforcement, and what contingencies they arrange and hence what behavior they shape are determined by the evolving social environment, or culture, responsible for their behavior" (p. 48). Contextualists (e.g., Biglan, 1995) emphasize the importance of larger social structures, including societal values and norms that maintain the individual's behavior. These ideas of functionalism show a marked departure from syndromal approaches to classification and diagnosis in behavior therapy (Tanaka-Matsumi, Higginbotham, & Chang, 2002). Thus, even though the relevance of cultural considerations is recognized in the classification of behavior disorders (e.g., *DSM-IV*), the syndromal approach cannot identify functions of various symptom patterns and predict individualized treatment based on assessment data.

Functional Analysis

In contrast, behavioral assessment and therapy is founded upon the use of empirical single-subject designs and assessment of functional relationships between the person's behavior and the environment (Baer, Wolf, & Risley, 1968; Kazdin, 1993). This assessment is achieved by functional analysis whose goal is the "identification of important, controllable, causal functional relationships applicable to a specified set of target behaviors for an individual client" (Haynes & O'Brien, 1990, p. 654). Kanfer and Phillips (1970) stressed that assessment should have "practical clinical utility" (p. 504). They proposed that functional analysis could provide information directly applicable to the formulation of a behavior therapy strategy and that a functional analysis of behavior was "part and parcel of treatment" (p. 509).

Behavioral assessment is an ongoing process by which the therapist monitors treatment variables and target behaviors throughout the duration of therapy (Kazdin, 1993). Functional analysis involves the formulation and testing of hypotheses regarding variables that are determining the behavior of concern.

Cultural Accommodation of Diversity Variables

The functional analysis is conducted within the client's social network, and hypotheses are formulated using the client's language. Behaviors that deviate from the client's cultural norms are probed to determine causal functional relationships. As a client's culture increases in diversity, behavior therapists need to consider the relevance of ethnic and cultural variables in clinical decision making, and recognize that their clinical judgments are influenced by their own value judgments and cultural assumptions in addition to cognitive and behavioral principles (Evans, 1997). Among the pretreatment errors associated with the clinician's biases, Haynes and O'Brien (2000) are judgments inappropriately influenced by the age, sex, sexual orientation, disability status, and ethnicity of the client. The cross-cultural and multicultural literature on psychopathology and its assessment and intervention describes serious pitfalls of failure to accommodate diversity variables into case formulation (e.g., Boyd-Franklin, 1989; Evans & Paewai, 1999; Friedman & Paradis, 1991; Harper & Iwamasa, 2000; Nagayama Hall, 2001; Sue & Sue, 1999; Tanaka-Matsumi, Higginbotham, & Chang, 2002). These problems include: (a) communication difficulties between the clinician and the client, (b) assessment errors such as over and under diagnoses of the presenting problem, (c) selection of culturally inappropriate targets of intervention, (d) lack of compliance with treatment guidelines by clients, and (e) premature termination of therapy. To remedy these problems, how do we know which diversity variables to accommodate in assessment and intervention? What inferences can we draw from assessment of diversity variables such as cultural iden-

tity and acculturation? In the age of culturally diverse populations, behavior therapists need to be aware of cultural differences in problem behaviors and their implications for facilitating and impeding the effectiveness of interventions.

For example, within a multicultural society, assessment of the interactive effects of the client's level of acculturation with his or her problem behavior contributes to the development of a culturally sensitive assessment and intervention. Acculturation refers to changes that occur as a result of continuous first-hand contact between individuals of differing origins (Redfield, Linton, & Hersokovits, 1936). One of the most fundamental changes occurring during the process of acculturation relates to cultural identity. Ethnic and cultural identification involves broad areas of human functions, including language preference, social affiliation, self-construal, and observation of traditional values and customs (Ward, 2001). In immigrant families, parents and children may hold different values as a result of intergenerational value differences. Parents may hold on to the values of the culture of their ethnic origin while their children may adopt the values of the peer culture outside home (Szapocznik & Kurtines, 1993). In this case, one set of behaviors (e.g., conformity to authority) may be reinforced within the family based on parents' cultural values, while the same set of behaviors may be extinguished or punished outside the family by the peer culture. In this case, the adolescent's peer culture may reinforce a conflicting set of other behaviors, such as rule breaking and defiance against authority figures. This example demonstrates that the same topographies of behaviors can be reinforced or sanctioned by different social contingencies operating within the multicultural and multigenerational environment.

Behavioral assessment predicts individual differences in relationships between target behaviors and their controlling cultural environments and accommodates to differences in cultural contingencies of social behaviors (Forehand & Kotchick, 1996). As Cone (1997) noted, assessment procedures with good discriminant validity will identify the circumstances under which different contingencies are effective, "not merely tell us two functions are involved and leave it at that" (p. 265).

MULTIPLE DETERMINANTS OF BEHAVIOR

History, Cultural Contingencies, and Individual Differences

I illustrate multiple causalities of problem behaviors with a variety of examples. A major function of culture is to select and reinforce those behaviors and skills that are deemed important for survival and success (Ogbu, 1981; Skinner, 1971).

The child development literature shows the importance of assessing context variables in behavioral assessment. Let us use parent training as an example.

Cultural Contingencies of Parenting and Child Development

Parent training is considered one of the most successful and effective behavioral interventions. There is substantial evidence that parents can be trained to manage difficult child behaviors such as aggression and noncompliance with parental instructions (Patterson, Chamberlain, & Reid, 1982). However, reviewing the behavioral parent training literature, Forehand and Kotchick (1996) cautioned that "behavior therapists have traditionally stopped short of culture and ethnicity in their conceptualization of parenting behavior" (p. 188). The chances of success in changing parental behavior without consideration for the parents' cultural background are limited, because cultural factors may facilitate or hinder the success of parent training. Factors such as parents' socioeconomic status, maternal depression, and marital problems have been found to limit parents' access to or full participation in training (Biglan, 1995).

In a telling example of the cultural transmission of skills, Greenfield, Maynard, and Childs (2000) reported a longitudinal field investigation of the cultural transmissions of a set of weaving skills in a Zinacantec Maya community of Chiapas, Mexico. Their field research focused on the interactional processes involved in the transmission of weaving skills of girls from one generation to the next. Weaving instruction in 1970 was informal and was characterized by a "relatively error-free scaffolding process based on observation of models, obedience to developmentally sensitive commands, and use of help when needed" (Greenfield et al., 2000, p. 355). By 1991 when the researchers returned to the Zinacantec, they found that ecocultural changes and the development of weaving commerce had altered the cultural goals of socialization to those of innovation and independent trial-and-error learning, As shown in the Zinacantec example, knowledge of history, culture, and learning is necessary to conduct accurate assessment of target behavior and its changing contingencies.

Another good example of cultural relevance of child development can be found in a series of U.S.-Japan comparative studies of educational achievement and practices. Differences in mother-child interaction patterns are due to differing cultural goals of nurturing interdependent versus independent children in Japan and the United States, respectively. Japanese mothers of preschool children have been found to expect obedient, self-controlled behavior from their children at an earlier age than U.S. mothers, whereas U.S. parents have been found to value assertive, socially skilled, and independent behavior in their children (Stevenson, Azuma, & Hakuta, 1986). Japanese mothers have been found to adopt less direct and forceful behavioral strategies than U.S. mothers (Conroy, Hess, Azuma, & Kashiwagi, 1980). Research on maternal expectations for their children demonstrates cross-cultural differences in maternal concepts of desirable and undesirable child behavioral characteristics in the United States and Japan. Social insensitivity and uncooperative behaviors were of serious concern to Japanese mothers, whereas aggressive and disruptive behaviors were of serious concern to U.S. mothers (Olson, Kashiwagi, & Crystal, 2001).

These cross-cultural differences would naturally influence the selection of target behaviors and cooperation of parents who have different expectations for specific child behaviors (Harper & Iwamasa, 2000; Tharp, 1991). Thus, behavior therapists study the client's cultural norms and expectations when selecting target behaviors. In addition, Forehand and Wierson (1993) stress the need to assess developmental factors in planning behavioral interventions for children. For example, in developing a behavioral training program for a child with attention and conduct problems, the clinician trains parents when the child is in preschool based on the amount of time the child spends at home with his or her parents. However, when the child enrolls in school and begins to spend more time with peers and teachers, the training target shifts to teacher training and generalization of training across settings. In the constructive assessment, the clinician selects alternative behaviors that are developmentally compatible and can be reinforced naturally within the client culture (Evans, 1993).

Parent training research also suggests universal effectiveness of certain parenting behavior categories (Biglan, 1995; Forehand, Miller, Dutra, & Chance, 1997). For example, parental monitoring of adolescents helps reduce deviance. Specific behaviors include monitoring of where the adolescent went at night, how the adolescent spent his or her time, where the adolescent went after school, and who the adolescent's friends were. These behaviors have been found to be effective in preventing deviance for both Black American and Hispanic American adolescents in three U.S. locations. Behavior therapists should identify specific parent monitoring behaviors in parent training programs to prevent or reduce adolescents' maladaptive behavior problems of school suspension, jailing, drinking, and carrying weapons. For each home, behavior therapists inquire about specific parent monitoring behaviors that are functionally associated with the reduction or prevention of target behaviors of adolescents. Individual differences among families can be probed while testing the universal importance of parental monitoring.

In order to increase the cultural effectiveness of parent training, Forehand and Wierson (1993) endorsed several important research agenda. These include assessment of: (a) cultural definitions of problem behaviors, (b) acceptability of parenting skills training, (c) culture-specific disciplinary strategies and control techniques, (d) the role of family variables such as depression or alcoholism in the effectiveness of parent training. These agenda, in fact, apply to all behavioral case formulations.

GUIDELINES FOR ASSESSING INDIVIDUAL DIFFERENCES AND DIVERSITY IN BEHAVIORAL ASSESSMENT

Only a few years ago, Cone (1997) was still commenting that "the viability of functional approach to assessment in the current era of reorganized health care delivery has not been tested" (p. 272). Similarly, Acierno et al. (1998) stated that "most of these data—including socioeconomic status, ethnicity, age, level of social support, previous psychiatric history, length of current illness, and familial status are not utilized in a manner that would isolate their interactive effects with treatment" (p. 57). Bernal and Scharrón-del-Río (2001) were quite pessimistic about the prospect of establishing generality of "empirically supported psychotherapy techniques" identified by the American Psychological Association Division 12 Task Force on Promotion and Dissemination of Psychological Procedures (Chambles et al., 1996) with ethnic minority clients. Most of these techniques belong to the cognitive-behavior therapy domain and are yet to be tested for their effectiveness in controlled studies with ethnic minority populations. Validation research involving diversity variables is lagging behind the need for providing empirically supported therapies to diverse populations (Cone, 1997; Haynes & O'Brien, 1990; Iwamasa, 1997; Sue, Zane, & Young, 1994). Hayes and Toarmino's (1995) response to this situation was that functional analysis, if properly applied, is so thoroughly individualized that one does not need to give separate attention to cultural diversity.

A number of cognitive behavior therapists have proposed guidelines to gather empirical assessment data and analyze the influence of diversity variables on the identification of specific, observable, and causally linked contextual variables for target behaviors (e.g., Evans & Paewai, 1999; Hansen, Zamboanga, & Sedlar, 2000; Matthews, 1997; Tanaka-Matsumi, Seiden, & Lam, 1996). The Association for Advancement of Behavior Therapy (AABT) has made special efforts to study multicultural issues in cognitive behavior therapy. For example, AABT's journal *Cognitive and Behavioral Practice* (1996) published "The special series: ethnic and cultural diversity in cognitive and behavioral practice" with Gayle Iwamasa as guest editor. Diversity considerations were evident in reports of cognitive behavior therapies with African Americans (Fudge, 1996), Latinos (Organista & Munoz, 1996), African American children (Neal-Barnett & Smith, 1996), women (McNair, 1996), lesbians and gay men (Martell, 2001; Purcell, Campos, & Perilla, 1996), and the elderly (Zeiss & Steffen, 1996). Within the behavioral assessment framework, diversity variables are treated as contextual variables rather than structural variables (as in demographic variables) influencing behavior (Nelson-Gray, Gaynor, & Korotitsch, 1997). For example, Toyokawa and Nedate's (1996) report of a cognitive behavioral therapy with a Japanese female client presenting interpersonal difficulties traced Japanese cultural themes throughout assessment and treatment content.

Development of Specific Guidelines

Culturally Informed Functional Assessment (CIFA) Interview

Utilizing a semistructured interview format, Tanaka-Matsumi, Seiden, and Lam (1996) proposed the Culturally Informed Functional Assessment (CIFA) Interview, which is designed to gather information from the client, the client's family and/or significant others, and the social network. The CIFA goals are to define problems accurately, accommodate the client's cultural background and context, and through negotiation plan treatment strategies that are acceptable to all parties concerned. The therapist gathers data in eight successive steps: (a) assessment of cultural identity and acculturation, (b) assessment of presenting problems, (c) elicitation of the client's conceptualization of problems and possible solutions, (d) functional assessment of the antecedent-target-consequence sequence, (e) negotiation of similarities and differences between the functional analytic model and the client's causal explanation of the problem, (f) treatment plan, (g) format of data gathering, and (h) assessment of expected outcome and negotiation of treatment schedule.

Model of Bicultural Evaluation Criteria in Cognitive Behavior Therapy

Evans and Paewai's (1999) comprehensive model of bicultural evaluation of a case conceptualization aims at ensuring culture fairness, rapport building, and multiple sources of data. They proposed psychometric criteria to evaluate the quality of bicultural case conceptualization. Thus, face validity, reliability, and content validity are sequentially assessed to ensure cultural sensitivity of the assessment process. For outcome evaluation, utility and validity questions are probed to achieve therapeutic success. Specifically, for utility, the therapist asks if the case conceptualization suggests specific treatment strategies and targets that are culturally sensitive and appropriate. For validity, the clinician establishes the relationship between treatment and successful outcome and its social acceptance by the client community. In order to enhance positive outcome, Evans and Paewai developed a list of 15 possible criteria that can be applied to cross-cultural case formulation. These criteria include: (a) assessment of the client's cultural identity, (b) use of the client's own idiom of distress, (c) assessment of family support, (d) identification of affected family members, (e) identification of problem-triggering stimuli, (f) specification of the cultural context of triggers, (g) assessment of culturally appropriate or idiosyncratic automatic thoughts, (h) identification of accepted alternative behavior, (i) assessment of value correlates of desirable and undesirable target behavior, (j) assessment of the social implication of changing the client's behavior, (k) assessment of access to social support networks for sources of natural reinforcement, (l) assessment of conflicting demands from the client's social environment, (m) explanation of the change process in local language and metaphors, (n) inclusion of the client's cultural and ancestral heritage in treatment description, and (o) assessment of the client's motivation for change within the cultural context of therapy.

Multicultural Counseling Models

As shown, culture creates relevant context variables at each assessment step and treatment (Pedersen, 1997). The therapist keeps monitoring the function of these variables throughout the therapy process. There are other helpful guidelines in the counseling psychology and clinical psychology literature. Readers are referred to Dana (1998); Sue & Sue (1999); Hays (2001); Paniagua (1998); Pedersen, Draguns, Lonner, and Trimble (2002); and Sue (1998) for excellent ideas and practical guidelines when conducting multicultural and cross-cultural assessment and therapy. In conclusion, the recent literature contains overlapping criteria aiming at an accurate assessment of individual differences. We await empirical evaluations of the adequacy of these criteria, particularly of reliability and validity of functional analysis.

BEHAVIORAL ASSESSMENT RESEARCH AND DIVERSITY

Clinical Judgment Bias and Behavioral Case Formulation

Much has been written about the need to develop culturally sensitive case formulations for diverse clients. Some guidelines are also available to conduct culturally informed behavioral assessment. Behavioral assessment methods may be considered less biased than more traditional forms of psychological assessment. Paniagua (1998) rank ordered assessment strategies according to bias-causing tendencies. Among the strategies causing the least bias were direct behavioral observation, self-monitoring, and behavioral checklists. Norm-based tests and unstructured tests were considered to produce more bias. When the method of data gathering is direct and requires low inference, it should be accurate and socially relevant to the target phenomenon. Such a method should contribute to effective clinical decision making. The functional analysis strategy produces individualized data from multiple sources and situations and monitors the target behavior on an ongoing basis throughout baseline and intervention phases. The clinician makes multiple clinical judgments during the process of functional analysis. Major decisions involve the selection of target behaviors and their modifiabilities according to obtained information. When the presenting problem has multiple causal antecedents and multiple consequences, the clinician again makes important clinical judgments about which antecedent-behavior-consequence to intervene. Furthermore, as Heiby (1995) cautioned, clinicians should be alerted to unstable behaviors whose prolonged baselines fail to demonstrate stability, as in severe mood fluctuations.

Given the task of making multiple clinical judgments, functional analysis is "conditional and subjective" (Haynes et al., 1997) and is also "social" (Sturmy, 1996) in nature. These characteristics imply that it may be difficult to arrive at a uniform behavioral case formulation if multiple therapists assessed the same client. More specifically, to what extent do behavior therapists agree with each other in the selection of target behavior, and do they identify the same antecedents and consequences in a cross-cultural assessment context?

Measuring Reliability of Behavioral Assessment

Haynes and Jensen (1979) stated that "the behavioral interview should be conceptualized as an assessment instrument and subjected to the same demands for adequate description and for empirical investigations of reliability and validity as other assessment devices (e.g., questionnaires or behavioral observation)" (p. 98). To illustrate, Felton and Nelson (1984) had six clinical psychologists interview three students who had been trained to role-play actual patients. The interviewers were told beforehand of the client's problem behaviors and were asked to conduct a behavioral assessment. They rated the client on data sheets to: (a) identify all controlling variables (antecedents, consequences, etc), (b) rank the importance of each controlling variable, and (c) specify a treatment plan. Results indicated that the mean interclinician agreement ranged from a low of .24 for organism variables, to a high of .59 for treatment variables. Agreements for antecedents were .38 and .42 for consequence variables. Felton and Nelson (1984) concluded that "inter-assessor agreement in hypothesizing controlling variables and in formulating proposals was quite poor" (p. 26). In a cross-cultural or multicultural situation in which the clinician and the client differ in cultural background, one can easily imagine that reliability indices would be much lower.

Sturmy (1996) reviewed the literature on reliability and functional analysis and stated that "the role of clinical judgment in conducting a functional analysis has not been sufficiently acknowledged. . . . However, clinical judgment issues can be found at every juncture in the process of functional analysis" (p. 219). To enhance the utility of functional analysis with culturally diverse clients, it is important to evaluate this idiographic tool empirically with specific acceptance criteria.

Reliability of Cross-Cultural Functional Assessment Decisions

Seiden (1999) conducted the first comprehensive evaluation of cross-cultural functional assessment. His research goal was to evaluate the reliability of cross-cultural behavioral case formulation of four Chinese clients according to a set of functional assessment guidelines probing for antecedents, problem behavior(s), consequences, and interrelationships among them. The four patients met the criteria for the Chinese culture-bound syndrome "neurasthenia" and had multiple somatic problems. Persistent mental or physical fatigue is an essential symptom of neurasthenia. Each client was interviewed by a Chinese behavior therapist in Chinese based on the guidelines adapted from the CIFA interview (Tanaka-Matsumi, Seiden, & Lam, 1996). Each videotaped interview took close to 60 minutes. Eighteen Chinese American and 31 European American behaviorally oriented clinicians individually watched an English subtitled videotape

of a functional assessment interview. The clinician watching the videotape wrote clinical decisions regarding antecedent-problem-consequence sequences and treatment recommendations. Seiden had the descriptive responses classified according to cross-culturally validated codes with high reliability. Results demonstrated that, for three of four clients, there was majority consensus within each clinician group on specific categories of target problems, target antecedents, target consequences, and treatment modalities. For the other client, majority consensus was not reached for target problems.

Seiden found significant differences in clinical judgments between Chinese American and European American therapist groups. Significantly greater proportions of Chinese American therapists targeted more somatization-related problems, stress-related antecedents, and social environmental or medical intervention consequences than the European American therapists, who focused more on cognitive antecedents. In this study, following the functional analytic model of Haynes et al. (1997), clinicians rated the problem severity and modifiability of antecedents and consequences on 10-point scales. Interestingly, the two groups of clinicians did not differ significantly in their ratings of the severity and modifiability. These results show that rated severities and modifiabilities may be similar across different clinicians, but the selected targets and controlling variables differ depending on both client and clinician.

As shown in cross-cultural behavioral case formulation data, even though the clinicians saw the identical stimulus video interviews, their clinical decisions were far from uniform. Consistent with cross-cultural research on diagnosis (Lopez, 1989; Tanaka-Matsumi, 1999; Thakker & Ward, 1998), Seiden's functional assessment results revealed variability for both clients and clinicians at different clinical decision points. Even though the clinicians observed the identical functional assessment material, Chinese American and European American clinician groups each selected 4 to 12 different target behaviors, antecedents, consequences, and five or six treatment recommendations. The result also indicates that clients with the same psychiatric diagnosis had multiple problems, antecedents, and consequences. Furthermore, consistent with the idiographic assessment model, the specific areas agreed upon as targets for intervention varied from client to client. A client's specific neurasthenic problems (e.g., headaches and fatigue) may be maintained by functional interrelationships with different contextual variables for different clients. Functional assessment generates clinical hypotheses for further evaluation. It permits tracking sources of individual differences and developing an individualized treatment plan.

Treatment Utility

According to the perspective of "treatment utility of assessment" (Haynes & O'Brien, 2000), there should be a relationship between contextual variables and selected intervention. Seiden (1999) found relationships between the selection of family-related antecedents or consequences and recommendations of modifying family variables in treatment. These interrelationships were obtained despite the fact that the majority of clinicians, regardless of their cultural backgrounds, reported that they would refer the client to other therapists.

Functional assessment may reduce clinician biases in identifying causal relationships due to its contextual emphasis (Evans & Paewai, 1999; Tanaka-Matsumi, Seiden, & Lam, 1996). Although the functional approach is a promising approach for distinguishing individual differences, research has yet to demonstrate that behavioral case formulation is valid for culturally different groups of clients with regard to treatment outcome that is acceptable to the client's reference group. Specifically, the treatment validity is concerned with answers to: (a) Does behavioral assessment identify diversity variables that are functionally related to behavior change? (b) What types of antecedents and consequences are related to the target behavior? (c) Are there differences in functional relationships among antecedents and consequences for the same target behavior? (d) Do clinicians of the same cultural background reach consensus with regard to functional analysis decisions? (e) To what extent do clinicians of different cultural backgrounds differ in their clinical judgments? (f) What are the specific sources of variations in clinical judgments?

Case Formulation Methods

Presently, answers to these questions depend on the availability of clear guidelines for conducting individualized assessment and replicating assessment across diverse clients using single-subject designs. At multiple clinical decision points, the clinician-researcher can develop hypotheses for individual clients and probe for the contribution of contextual variables. Case formulation methods from the behavioral (e.g., Nezu, Nezu, Friedman, & Haynes, 1997) and cognitive-behavioral (CB) (e.g., Persons & Tompkins, 1997) standpoints spell out necessary types of generic clinical judgments. The clinician's role is to gather appropriate idiographic data from the client and other informants. Persons and Tompkins (1997) asserted, "We cannot think of a case in which a CB Case Formulation is not helpful" (p. 321), particularly for difficult cases with multiple, complex problems. The step-by-step approach helps the clinician with clinical judgments in seven domains: (1) the problem list, (2) core beliefs, (3) precipitating

and activating situations, (4) the working hypothesis, (5) origins or early history of the problem, (6) the treatment plan, and (7) predicted outcome to treatment.

The journal *Cognitive and Behavioral Practice* has started the "Cognitive Behavioral Case Conference" to examine alternative case formulations by several contributing scientist-practitioners of similar theoretical persuasions. This forum may help discover the nature of potential biases as well as reliability and treatment utility of individual case formulation. A major advantage of the case formulation approach is its process orientation and individualized approach. The bicultural and cross-cultural guidelines reviewed in this chapter should be of value when using the case formulation approach with all clients.

CONCLUSION

Behavioral assessment is noted for its idiographic, dynamic, and empirical method of case formulation and hypothesis testing. Drawing upon research on the impact of cultural context on behavior problems, I examined whether the conceptual basis of the functional analytic approach in behavioral assessment is capable of addressing and evaluating individual differences. I reviewed the available guidelines and criteria to assess the interaction of contextual variables with identification of problems in order to develop individualized behavioral interventions. The literature on reliability and validity studies of the behavioral case formulation method demonstrates the importance of studying clinician variables, including clinician values and assumptions, as well as the client variables in context. The functional analytic approach has a built-in mechanism to gather important contextual data to evaluate the clinical utility of individualized assessment and treatment of diverse clients.

REFERENCES

Acierno, R., Hersen, M., Van Hasselt, V.B. (1998). Prescriptive assessment and treatment. In A.S. Bellack & M. Hersen (Eds.), *Behavioral assessment: A practical handbook* (pp. 47–62). Boston: Allyn & Bacon.

Baer, D.M., Wolf, M.M., & Risley, T.R. (1968). Some current dimensions of applied behavior analysis. *Journal of Applied Behavior Analysis, 1,* 91–97.

Bandura, A. (1969). *Principles of behavior modification.* New York: Holt, Rinehart, & Winston.

Bernal, G., & Scharrón-del-Río, M.R. (2001). Are empirically supported treatments valid for ethnic minorities? Toward an alternative approach for treatment research. *Cultural Diversity & Ethnic Minority Psychology, 7,* 328–342.

Beutler, L.E., & Martin, B.R. (2000). Prescribing therapeutic interventions through strategic treatment selection. *Cognitive and Behavioral Practice, 7,* 1–16.

Biglan, A. (1995). *Changing cultural practices: A contextualist framework for intervention research.* Reno, NV: Context Press.

Boyd-Franklin, N. (1989). *Black families in therapy: A multisystems approach.* New York: Guilford Press.

Carter, M.M. (2000). Response paper: Ethnic awareness in the cognitive behavioral treatment of a depressed African American female. *Cognitive and Behavioral Practice, 6,* 273–278.

Chambles, D.L., Sanderson, W.C., Shoham, V., Johnson, S.B., Pope, K.S., Crits-Christoph, P., Baker, M., Johnson, B., Woody, S.R., Sue, S., Beutler, L., Williams, D.A., & McCurry, S. (1996). An update on empirically validated therapies. *Clinical Psychologist, 49,* 5–18.

Chambles, D.L., & Williams, K.E. (1995). A preliminary study of African Americans with agoraphobia: Symptom severity and outcome of treatment with in vivo exposure. *Behavior Therapy, 26,* 501–515.

Cone, J.D. (1997). Issues in functional analysis in behavioral assessment. *Behaviour Research and Therapy, 35,* 259–275.

Conroy, M., Hess, R.D., Azuma, H., & Kashiwagi, K. (1980). Maternal strategies for regulating children's behavior: Japanese and American families. *Journal of Cross-Cultural Psychology, 11,* 153–172.

Dana, R.H. (1998). *Understanding cultural identity in intervention and assessment.* Thousand Oaks, CA: Sage.

Draguns, J.G., & Tanaka-Matsumi, J. (in press). Assessment of psychopathology across and within cultures: Issues and findings. *Behaviour Research and Therapy.*

Evans, I.M. (1993). Constructional perspectives in clinical assessment. *Psychological Assessment, 3,* 264–272.

Evans, I.M. (1997). The effect of values on scientific and clinical judgment in behavior therapy. *Behavior Therapy, 28,* 483–493.

Evans, I.M., & Paewai, K. (1999). Functional analysis in a bicultural context. *Behaviour Change, 16,* 20–36.

Felton, J.L., & Nelson, R.O. (1984). Inter-assessor agreement on hypothesized controlling variables and treatment proposals. *Behavioral Assessment, 6,* 199–208.

Forehand, R., & Kotchick, B.A. (1996). Cultural diversity: A wake-up call for parent training. *Behavior Therapy, 27,* 187–206.

Forehand, R., Miller, K.S., Dutra, R., & Chance, M.W. (1997). Role of parenting in adolescent deviant behavior: Replication across and within two ethnic groups. *Journal of Consulting and Clinical Psychology, 65,* 1036–1041.

Forehand, R., & Wierson, M. (1993). The role of developmental factors in planning behavioral interventions for children: Disruptive behavior as an example. *Behavior Therapy, 24,* 117–141.

Franks, C.M. (Ed.). (1969). *Behavior therapy: Appraisal and status.* New York: McGraw-Hill.

Friedman, S., & Paradis, C. (1991). African American patients with panic disorder and agoraphobia. *Journal of Anxiety Disorders, 5,* 35–41.

Fudge, R.C. (1996). The use of behavior therapy in the development of ethnic consciousness: A treatment model. *Cognitive and Behavioral Practice, 3,* 317–336.

Greenfield, P.M., Maynard, A.E., & Childs, C.P. (2000). History, culture, learning and development. *Cross-Cultural Research: The Journal of Comparative Social Science, 34,* 351–374.

Haaga, D.A. (1999). Treatment options for depression and anger. *Cognitive and Behavioral Practice, 6,* 289–292.

Hansen, D.J., Zamboanga, B.L., & Sedlar, G. (2000). Cognitive-behavior therapy for ethnic minority adolescence: Broadening our perspectives. *Cognitive and Behavioral Practice, 7,* 54–60.

Harper, G.W., & Iwamasa, G.Y. (2000). Cognitive-behavioral therapy with ethnic minority adolescents: Therapist perspectives. *Cognitive and Behavioral Practice, 7,* 37–53.

Hayes, S.C., & Toarmino, D. (1995). If behavioral principles are generally applicable, why is it necessary to understand cultural diversity? *Behavior Therapist, 18,* 21–23.

Haynes, S.N., & Jensen, B.J. (1979). The interview as a behavioral assessment instrument. *Behavioral Assessment, 1,* 97–106.

Haynes, S.N., Leisen, M.B., & Blaine, D.D. (1997). Design of individualized behavioral treatment programs using functional analytic clinical case models. *Psychological Assessment, 9,* 334–348.

Haynes, S.H., & O'Brien, W.H. (1990). Functional analysis in behavior therapy. *Clinical Psychology Review, 10,* 649–668.

Haynes, S.N., & O'Brien, W.H. (2000). *Principles and practice of behavioral assessment.* New York: Kluwer Academic/Plenum.

Hays, P. (2001). *Addressing cultural complexities in practice: A framework for clinicians and counselors.* Washington, DC: American Psychological Association.

Heiby, E.M. (1995). Assessment of behavioral chaos with a focus on transition in depression. *Psychological Assessment, 7,* 10–16.

Herskovits, M.J. (1948). *Man and his works.* New York: Knopf.

Hofstede, G. (2001). *Culture's consequences: Comparing values, behaviors, institutions, and organizations across nations* (2nd ed.). Thousand Oaks, CA: Sage.

Iwamasa, G.Y. (1997). Behavior therapy and a culturally diverse society: Forging an alliance. *Behavior Therapy, 28,* 347–358.

Kanfer, F.H., & Phillips, J.S. (1971). *Learning foundations for behavior therapy.* New York: Wiley.

Kanfer, F.H., & Schefft, B.K. (1988). *Guiding the process of therapeutic change.* Champaign, IL: Research Press.

Kazdin, A.E. (1993). Evaluation in clinical practice: Clinically sensitive and systematic methods of treatment delivery. *Behavior Therapy, 24,* 11–46.

Kazdin, A.E. (2001). *Behavior modification in applied settings* (6th ed.). Pacific Grove, CA: Brooks/Cole.

Lopez, S.R. (1989). Patient variable biases in clinical judgment: Conceptual overview and methodological considerations. *Psychological Bulletin, 106,* 184–204.

Lopez, S.R., & Guarnaccia, P.J. (2000). Cultural psychopathology: Uncovering the social world of mental illness. *Annual Review of Psychology, 51,* 571–598.

Lubinski, D. (2000). Scientific and social significance of assessing individual differences: "Sinking shafts at a few critical points." *Annual Review of Psychology, 51,* 405–444.

Martell, C.R. (2001). Including sexual orientation issues in research related to cognitive and behavioral practice. *Behavior Therapist, 24,* 214–216.

Matsumoto, D. (1994). *Cultural influence on research methods and statistics.* Pacific Grove, CA: Brooks/Cole.

Matthews, A.K. (1997). A guide to case conceptualization and treatment planning with minority group patients. *Behavior Therapist, 20,* 35–39.

McNair, L.D. (1996). African American women and behavior therapy: Integrating theory, culture, and clinical practice. *Cognitive and Behavioral Practice, 3,* 337–349.

Nagayama Hall, G. (2001). Psychotherapy research with ethnic minorities: Empirical, ethical, and conceptual issues. *Journal of Consulting and Clinical Psychology, 69,* 502–510.

Neal-Barnett, A.M., & Smith, J.M. (1996). African American children and behavior therapy: Considering the Afrocentric approach. *Cognitive and Behavioral Practice, 3,* 31–370.

Nelson-Gray, R., Gaynor, S.T., & Korotitsch, W.J. (1997). Commentary on "Behavior therapy and a culturally diverse society: Forging an alliance." *Behavior Therapy, 28,* 359–361.

Nezu, A.M., Nezu, C.M., Friedman, S.H., & Haynes, S.N. (1997). Case formulation in behavior therapy: Problem solving and functional analytic strategies. In T.D. Eells (Eds.), *Handbook of psychotherapy case formulation* (pp. 368–401). New York: Guilford Press.

Ogbu, J.U. (1981) Origins of human competence: A cultural-ecological perspective. *Child Development, 52,* 413–429.

Olson, S.L., Kashiwagi, K., & Crystal, D. (2001). Concepts of adaptive and maladaptive child behavior: A comparison of U.S. and Japanese mothers of preschool-age children. *Journal of Cross-Cultural Psychology, 32,* 43–57.

Organista. K.C., & Munoz, R.F. (1996). Cognitive behavioral therapy with Latinos. *Cognitive and Behavioral Practice, 3,* 255–270.

Paniagua, F.A. (1998), *Assessing and treating culturally diverse clients: A practical guide.* Thousand Oaks, CA: Sage.

Paradis, C.M., Friedman, S., Hatch, M.L., & Ackerman, R. (1996). Cognitive and behavioral treatment of anxiety disorders in Orthodox Jews. *Cognitive and Behavioral Practice, 3,* 271–288.

Patterson, G.R., Chamberlain, P., & Reid, J.B. (1982). A comparative evaluation of a parent-training program. *Behavior Therapy, 13,* 638–650.

Pedersen, P.B. (1997). *Culture-centered counseling interventions: Striving for accuracy.* Thousand Oaks, CA: Sage.

Pedersen, P.B., Draguns, J.G., Lonner, W.J., & Trimble, J.E. (Eds.). (2002). *Counseling across cultures* (5th ed.). Thousand Oaks, CA: Sage.

Persons, J.B. & Tompkins, M.A. (1997). Cognitive-behavioral case formulation. In T.D. Eells (Ed.), *Handbook of psychotherapy case formulation* (pp. 314–339). New York: Guilford Press.

Propst, L.R., Ostrom, R., Watkins, P., Dean, T., & Mashburn, D. (1992). Comparative efficacy of religious and nonreligious cognitive behavioral therapy for the treatment of clinical depression in religious individuals. *Journal of Consulting and Clinical Psychology, 60,* 84–103.

Purcell, D.W., Campos, P.E., & Perilla, J.L. (1996). Therapy with lesbians and gay men: A cognitive behavioral perspective. *Cognitive and Behavioral Practice, 3,* 391–415.

Redfield, R., Linton, R., & Herskovits, M. (1936). Memorandum on the study of acculturation. *American Anthropologist, 38,* 149–152.

Segall, M.H., Dasen, P.R., Berry, J.W., & Poortinga, Y.H. (1999). *Human behavior in global perspective: An introduction to cross-cultural psychology* (2nd ed.). Boston: Allyn & Bacon.

Seiden, D.Y. (1999). *Cross-cultural behavioral case formulation with Chinese neurasthenic patients.* Unpublished doctoral dissertation, Hofstra University, Hempstead, New York.

Skinner, B.F. (1953). *Science and human behavior.* New York: Macmillan.

Skinner, B.F. (1971). *Beyond freedom and dignity.* New York: Bantam Vintage.

Skinner, B.F. (1988). Selection by consequences. Commentaries and responses. In A.C. Catania & S. Harnad (Eds.), *The selection of behavior: The operant behaviorism of B.F. Skinner* (pp. 11–76). New York: Cambridge University Press.

Stevenson, H., Azuma, H., & Hakuta, K. (Eds.). (1986). *Child development and education in Japan.* New York: Freeman.

Sturmy, P. (1996). *Functional analysis in clinical psychology.* New York: Wiley.

Sue, D.W. & Sue, S. (1999). *Counseling the culturally different: Theory and practice* (3rd ed.). New York: Wiley.

Sue, S. (1998). In search of cultural competency in psychotherapy and counseling. *American Psychologist, 53,* 440–448.

Sue, S., Zane, N., Young, K. (1994). Research in psychotherapy with culturally diverse populations. In A.E. Bergin & S.L. Garfield (Eds.), *Handbook of psychotherapy and behavior change* (4th ed., pp. 783–820). New York: Wiley.

Szapocznik, J., & Kurtines, W.M. (1993). Family psychology and cultural diversity. *American Psychologist, 48,* 400–407.

Tanaka-Matsumi, J. (1999). Whatever happened to comparisons of mental health diagnosis across cultures? *Cross-Cultural Psychology Bulletin, 33,* 22–25.

Tanaka-Matsumi, J. (2001). Abnormal psychology and culture. In D. Matsumoto (Ed.), *The handbook of culture and psychology* (pp. 265–286). New York: Oxford University Press.

Tanaka-Matsumi, J., & Draguns, J.G. (1997). Culture and psychopathology. In J. Berry, M. Segall, & C. Kâgitçibaçi (Eds.), *Handbook of Cross-Cultural Psychology: Vol. 3. Social Psychology, Personality and Psychopathology* (2nd ed., pp. 449–491). Boston: Allyn & Bacon.

Tanaka-Matsumi, J., Higginbotham, H.N., & Chang, R. (2002). Cognitive-behavioral approaches to counseling across cultures: A functional analytic approach for clinical applications. In P.B. Pedersen, W.J. Lonner, J.G. Draguns, & J.E. Trimble (Eds.), *Counseling across cultures* (5th ed., pp. 337–354). Thousand Oaks, CA: Sage.

Tanaka-Matsumi, J., Seiden, D., & Lam, K. (1996). The Culturally Informed Functional Assessment (CIFA) Interview: A strategy for cross-cultural behavioral practice. *Cognitive and Behavioral Practice, 3,* 215–233.

Thakker, J., & Ward, T. (1998). Culture and classification: The cross-cultural application of the DSM-IV. *Clinical Psychology Review, 18,* 501–529.

Tharp, R.G. (1991). Cultural diversity and treatment of children. *Journal of Consulting and Clinical Psychology, 59,* 799–812.

Toyokawa, T., & Nedate, K. (1996). Application of cognitive behavior therapy to interpersonal problems: A case study of a Japanese female client. *Cognitive and Behavioral Practice, 3,* 289–302.

Ullmann, L.P., & Krasner, L. (1975). *A psychological approach to abnormal behavior* (2nd ed.). Englewood Cliffs, NJ: Prentice-Hall.

Ward, C. (2001). The A, B, Cs of acculturation. In D. Matsumoto (Ed.), *The handbook of culture and psychology* (pp. 411–445). New York: Oxford University Press.

Yutrzenka, B. (1995). Making a case for training in ethnic and cultural diversity in increasing treatment efficacy. *Journal of Consulting and Clinical Psychology, 63,* 197–206.

Zeiss, A.M., & Steffen, A. (1996). Treatment issues with elderly clients. *Cognitive and Behavioral Practice, 3,* 371–390.

Zoellner, L.A., Feeny, N.C., Fitzgibbons, L.A., & Foa, E.B. (1999). Responses of African American and Caucasian women to cognitive behavioral therapy for PTSD. *Behavior Therapy, 30,* 581–595.

METHODS OF BEHAVIORAL ASSESSMENT

CHAPTER 9

Naturalistic Observation of Relationship Processes

THOMAS J. DISHION AND ISABELA GRANIC

OVERVIEW

Much of behavioral science involves measurement based on conscious, verbal recall of behavioral events or psychological states by using interviews, ratings, and questionnaires. In contrast, direct observation refers to the use of trained observers to "code" behavioral events or psychological states, irrespective of the participants' reports or perceptions.

As Barkely (1997) noted, "direct observation has remained the most effective way of obtaining ecologically valid information on behavior." One clear advantage to direct observation is that it provides data on the functional dynamics of relationship behaviors. It is likely that individual participants are often unaware of the momentary dynamics of the relationships within which they play a major role (Patterson & Reid, 1984; Patterson, Reid, & Dishion, 1992). Individuals in distressed marriages and distressed parenting relationships often report that they have communication problems, but clinically seem to have a limited understanding of the patterns of their disrupted relationships. Similarly, parents seeking clinical help for child behavior problems are often unaware of the extent to which their reactions to their child exacerbate the problem behavior. Parents' reports often tell a story about their children's negative traits, or they may blame other family members or circumstances for the problem behavior.

Observing interactions as they unfold over time provides a basis for studying the relationship dynamics independently of participant accounts of who said what and why. In this chapter, we largely focus on the utility of naturalistic observation in rendering data relationship patterns and discuss how to record and analyze so that is useful to that end. For a broad extensive coverage of direct observations methodology, the reader is referred to reviews by Kerig and Lindahl (2001), Skinner, Dittmer, and Howell (2000), Skinner, Rhymer, and McDaniel (2000), and Cone (1999).

Most "naïve" consumers of behavior science research using direct observation express concern that this research is based on behavior performed under strange and unusual conditions. The conventions of science, however, refer to observations that occur outside the laboratory setting as "naturalistic." In this sense, observations that occur among peers on the playground, among family members in the home, or among friends in the home are considered naturalistic, regardless of the presence of an observer or recording equipment.

Observations span a continuum of contrived to naturalistic. For example, asking individuals to interact with strangers in a hypothetical task (e.g., prisoner's dilemma) in a laboratory setting is contrived. Directly observing a parent in the home in the process of parenting his own child is naturalistic. Both contrived and naturalistic observations have unique advantages and disadvantages.

Many researchers videotape relationship interactions in the natural environment for later analysis. The use of videotaping in observing behavior has changed how the behavior is coded. Progress in technology is radically improving the possibilities in direct observation research. For example, the widespread use of digital recording technology improves the behavioral scientist's ability to control the recording and quantification of behavior as it unfolds over time. For this reason, the bulk of observation research is based on recorded interactions among individuals.

The recording of interactions for later coding raises the issue of what constitutes a naturalistic observation. For obvious ethical reasons, those who are subjected to direct observations need to be informed as such. For instance, a married couple, friends, family members, or children playing are often aware of the presence of either an observer or camera recording their behavior.

In general, naturalistic observations usually refer to studying behavior in the real world. However, much of what occurs in the real world does not provide interesting information about the functional dynamics contributing to individual differences in adjustment. For example, observing couples throughout their day may not reveal much about how they interact in conflict situations because many distressed couples (and families) avoid interactions they see as leading to conflict.

Early research on distressed marriages showed that giving distressed couples analogue interaction tasks in the laboratory did not pull for the dynamics contributing to their distress either (Birchler, Weiss, & Vincent, 1975). Distressed couples looked like nondistressed couples when given these tasks that were irrelevant to their relationship. However, when asked to discuss conflicts in their relationship in a laboratory setting, the dynamics that contribute to distress and divorce were easy to observe (e.g., Gottman 1979).

Similarly, direct observations of adolescents and parents in the home may be less revealing than structured conflict resolution tasks in a laboratory setting. Therefore, it is imperative for the research to provide some structure to relationship interactions that elicit those relationship patterns underlying adjustment. The focus of this review is on naturalistic observations but also will include some observation research that occurs in the laboratory setting and involves structuring interactions presumed indicative of real world relationship processes.

Structured Observations

Often naturalistic observations are structured by the researcher in such a way as to elicit relationship patterns that are meaningful (Haynes & O'Brien, 2000). For example, the following home observations included a female observer, under established conditions with the family (Reid, 1978):

1. No television or other distracting entertainment.
2. Family members stay in the room in which the observation is taking place.
3. No telephone calls.

Another example is provided by Shaw, Keenan, & Vondra (1994), in their study of parent–toddler interaction. They used a high-chair task where they videotaped the child in a high chair while the parent was assigned to complete questionnaires. The parent's management of that situation enabled coding of parent responsiveness, which was found to predict the early emergence of behavior problems (Shaw et al., 1994, 1996; Shaw, Winslow, & Flanagan, 1999).

To study the utility of parental use of proactive structuring on reducing behavior problems, Gardner and colleagues (1999) contrived a tightly controlled clean-up task, then carefully differentiated between parent reactive and preemptive strategies. Preemptive structuring was found to reduce the immediate occurrence of behavior problems and was related negatively to behavior problems two years later, controlling for earlier problem behavior in 3-year-olds.

In our own work, we provided a series of structured interaction tasks in the homes of families with adolescents to provide a direct assessment of family management, and to provide a basis for directly observing monitoring practices. Parents and adolescents were asked to engage in the following seven tasks:

1. Planning an activity for the next week.
2. Parents encouraging a positive behavior in the adolescent.
3. Parent-child discussion of monitoring peer activities.
4. Parent discussion of limit setting within the last month.
5. Family (including siblings) attempt to discuss and solve an identified family problem.
6. Family (including siblings) discussion of norms for using substances.
7. Plan a family celebration (including siblings), not involving birthdays or holidays.

The tasks were designed to directly assess relationship quality, positive reinforcement, parental monitoring, limit setting, problem solving, and substance use norms (tasks 1 through 6, respectively). The observed family management interactions clearly differentiated a multiethnic sample of successful and high-risk students (Dishion and Bullock, 2001). Structured tasks are sometimes the most direct and efficient means of tapping the most meaningful aspects of interpersonal interactions (Haynes & O'Brien, 2000).

The above tasks pull for parents to engage in family management practices with adolescents. However, it is often difficult to manage children and adolescents when there are multiple siblings. We have known for some time that siblings contribute to social development (e.g., Dunn, 1992). In fact, Patterson (1986) described sibling interaction in his model for aggression as "fellow travelers within a coercive system." Negative exchanges among siblings do predict physical aggression and peer rejection (Patterson, Dishion, & Bank, 1984). Bullock and Dishion (2002) examined collusive interactions among siblings when discussing problem-solving issues with their parents. All families videotaped in their homes engaged in semistructured discussion tasks. Sibling interactions rated as collusive were those where two or more of the brothers or sisters: (a) joked about problem behavior; (b) engaged in verbal and nonverbal behaviors that undermine parental attempts to socialize; and (c) used diversionary tactics in family discussions.

In contrasting high-risk families with successful young-adolescent families with more than one child, macroratings of sibling collusion were found to discriminate quite well between the two groups, with sibling interactions in high-risk families being more collusive than those in successful families. Also of interest, high-risk families engaged in higher levels of *both* positive and negative affect, in contrast to successful families.

Another example of structuring a naturalistic setting for observations comes from the recent work of Driver and Gottman (2001a, 2001b). Their work suggests that observing couples as they organize their lives throughout the day can be as useful as it is arduous. These researchers designed a quasi-apartment setting where recently married couples were videotaped from 9:00 A.M. to 9:00 P.M. every day, with periodic breaks and short walks. The challenge with massive interaction data such as these is the researcher needs to conceptualize the processes in such a way as to reliably code and quantify the data. The studies by Gottman testify to the utility of spending time looking at relationship processes as they unfold and attempting to describe salient relationship processes.

The Driver and Gottman (2001a, 2001b) studies are important for two reasons. Methodologically, these studies raise the issue of censoring in naturalistic observation research. That is, researchers must be aware of how their observation methodology censors relationship interactions that may be relevant to understanding broader outcomes such as psychopathology or marital satisfaction. Second, these studies suggest that naturalistic observations may need to be less "microsocial" in the future, since the "patterns" of interest actually may unfold over longer time periods than seconds within an observation hour. We discuss the relative benefits

and limitations of micro- versus macrocoding later in this chapter.

An argument might be made that structured conditions are far from naturalistic. Family members can avoid interacting, for example, by watching television, talking on the telephone, using the Internet, or going to their room. Having a person observe their interaction may inhibit some behaviors like consumption of alcohol and drugs, physical aggression, or other behaviors perceived as embarrassing by the person being observed. These issues suggest that observed individuals "fake good" and do not reveal the behaviors characteristic of their relationship. The classic study of reactivity (Johnson & Bolstad, 1975) suggests that in distressed relationships, faking good is difficult at best. In fact, it appears that a hallmark of a distressed relationship is the inability to fake good under the watchful eye of outside observers.

One way of examining the degree to which naturalistic observations capture real relationship dynamics is to vary the "intrusiveness" of the observation protocol and evaluate the impact on interaction patterns. Jacob, Tennenbaum, Seilhamer, Bargiel, & Sharon (1994) compared audiotaped recordings of family interactions when an observer was present and when she was not. Results showed only trivial differences under these two conditions.

PERFORMANCE, PROCESS, AND GLOP

Performance and Process

It is unlikely that a science of behavior could proceed without a foundation of direct observation of relationship processes within the natural environment (Dishion & Patterson, 1999; Fiske, 1986). Observing relationship interactions within the natural environment affords the opportunity to study and understand behavior performance. A performance model focuses on accounting for individual differences in the display of specific behaviors. Research on children's aggressive and antisocial behavior reveals the utility of such an approach in the development of the coercion perspective on antisocial behavior (Patterson, 1982; Patterson, Reid, & Dishion, 1992).

This program of research, initiated by Patterson and colleagues, suggested that a great deal of children's aggressive acts with peers (e.g., Patterson, Littman, & Bricker, 1967) and with parents (Patterson, 1982) involves escape conditioning. Responding aggressively to peer intrusions reduces the likelihood of future attacks. Responding aversively to caregiver demands reduces the control and leadership of the caregiver. Careful observation of children within the natural environment (preschools and home) provided the data to understand the process surrounding aggression in the peer and family environment.

After observing parent-child interactions, codes were developed that reflected what the researchers saw in the natural environment. Additionally, antecedents and consequences to aggressive acts were studied by systematically comparing conditional probabilities as indices of performance. For example, what is the likelihood of an aggressive child responding aversively given a caregiver command? Comparing clinic-referred children (e.g., stealers, aggressors, and so forth) to nonreferred children provided the basis for the original coercion model for antisocial behavior (Patterson, 1982).

The "Glop" Problem

The "glop" problem refers to the problem of ambiguity introduced by method variance when trying to understand behavior. When only one method is used, one introduces a mono-method bias (Cook & Campbell, 1979). With the innovations in multivariate approaches to modeling, we can more precisely isolate the extent of "method variance" in our research findings. In structural equation modeling of antisocial behavior, Bank, Dishion, Skinner, & Patterson (1990) refer to this as the "glop problem." For an idea of how serious the glop problem is, in comparing parent, child, and staff reports of five parenting practices, Dishion, Burraston, and Li (2002) found that, on average, 50% of the observed variation in the parenting data was due to method effects; much of this variation was presumed to be secondary to idiosyncratic perspectives and reporting styles of various respondents. In this sense, a science that ignores the observed performance of behavior under various conditions will yield a cloudy depiction of reality at best.

Naturalistic observations or, more specifically, the use of observed indices of behavioral performance can significantly decrease the glop problem in developmental and intervention research. For example, based on parent reports, some researchers have concluded that siblings within the same family were so different, it was hard to believe that "shared" family environments had any influence on their emergent personality (Plomin & Daniels, 1987). Hoffman (1991) accurately pointed out that these conclusions might be overly dependent on the assessment methods used to evaluate similarity among siblings. Lewin, Hops, Davis, and Dishion (1993) found that teacher ratings of siblings at school indicated high levels of similarity between siblings on antisocial and prosocial behavior. Importantly, Leve and colleagues (Leve, Winebarger, Fagot, Reid, & Goldsmith, 1998) found that direct observations of genetically related siblings in parent-child interactions yielded substantial indices of similarity among siblings

and, accordingly, higher estimates of the effect of shared environment on children's antisocial behavior.

A number of scholars have elaborated the psychometric issues involved in observational procedures (Cone, 1999; Haynes, Nelson, & Blaine, 1999). Another challenge includes method effects in general, and global reports in particular, which can obfuscate conclusions drawn about intervention research (Eddy, Dishion, & Stoolmiller, 1998). Direct observations are ideal with respect to reducing the likelihood of assessment by intervention interactions (Campbell & Stanley, 1963). For example, it is entirely possible that individuals "report" symptom reductions as a function of their involvement in an intervention study. Dishion and Andrews (1995), for example, found that parents reported large reductions in their young adolescent's problem behavior regardless of the random assignment to control or active intervention conditions. When examining direct observations of parent-adolescent interaction, however, reductions in observed conflict were specific to interventions that actively encouraged behavior change. Thus, the use of observational data is critical if method effects as well as reporters' biases are to be minimized.

It is also true that direct observations of children's behavior produce relatively low intraclass correlations within the context of prevention research. One problem in evaluating efforts to prevent difficulties in the natural environment is that it is necessary to focus interventions on communities that involve an aggregation of individuals. For instance, to prevent antisocial behavior, it may be necessary to focus on schools as an intervention unit. Research shows that antisocial behavior varies as a function of schools (Rutter, 1978). Schools are also a convenient system for testing interventions. Evaluating the impact of such interventions, however, is problematic because data on individuals within each school has a higher level of intraclass correlation. However, using direct observations, compared to teacher ratings, for example, addresses this issue. Stoolmiller, Eddy, and Reid (2000) suggest that the intraclass correlations for direct observations of children's behavior are trivial in contrast to that produced by teacher ratings.

In this sense, both developmental and intervention science need data from direct observations for a foundation for inquiry. In addition to reducing bias, observing relationships affords two important scientific advantages. First, observation data provide a ratio measurement on behavior. That is, when directly observing behavior, it is possible to estimate in real time the relative occurrence of specific behaviors of interest. For example, in observing parent-adolescent interaction, high-risk families were found to engage in a rate-per-minute of aversive behavior of about .5 for mothers and 1.2 for adolescents (Dishion, Andrews, & Crosby, 1995). That roughly translates to one aversive statement every 2 minutes for distressed mothers, and one per minute for adolescents. In this sample, one adolescent female had a negative behavior rate-per-minute of 20 (every minute, she made 20 statements coded as aversive in the coding system). Thus, ratio scale measurement provides a rich description of interpersonal behavior.

QUANTIFYING THE BEHAVIOR STREAM

Microsocial Coding

This term refers to the coding of interpersonal transactions as they unfold over seconds. Codes, which categorize behavior, can be entered as either events or time is sampled and the behaviors that occur during that time are indicated (i.e., time sampling). Many behavior science researchers use a 6-second time frame for defining events at the microsocial level (Reid, 1978). As of this writing, that time frame is a common but an arbitrary scientific convention.

Event coding often focuses on the relationship behaviors of two or more people. There are various approaches to event coding. Researchers interested in relationship processes use event coding to capture interactional behaviors; events are coded much as notes on a score as they unfold in real time (for an example, see Figure 9.1).

Time sampling, on the other hand, is an easier approach than event coding with which to train coders. Observers are asked to indicate whether a behavior occurred within a specified time period. Table 9.1 summarizes the different types of time-sampling approaches and specifies the most common use for each procedure. Cone (1999) reviews these approaches in more detail, discussing the advantages and limitations of each approach.

One advantage of time sampling in direct observation is reduced time in observer training. However, information may be lost if the time sample is too large and behaviors during that time window need to be summarized into one code. Time sampling with relatively brief recording frames (e.g., 10 to 15 seconds), however, retains the microsocial quality of the interaction and is consistent with the original intent of using this type of system. The longer the recording frame, the more the data become "macrosocial."

Macroratings

Of late, some investigators have used macroratings that summarize behavior over an entire observation period (Conger, Patterson, & Ge, 1995; Dishion & Bullock, 2001). Historically such macroratings were called observer impressions and were used to complement microsocial coding (Weinrott, Bauske, & Patterson, 1979). Because of the relative validity, reliability, and cost effectiveness of data collection, macroratings are usually used as the sole measure of relationship behaviors. Cairns and Green (1979) noted this trend in an appendix to a volume on social interaction over 20 years ago

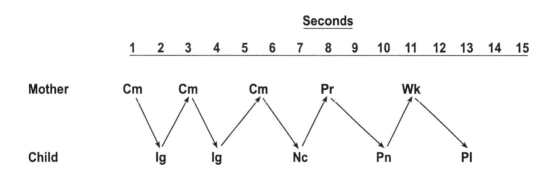

Cm = Command
Ig = Ignore
Pr = Provoke
Nc = Noncomply
Pn = Physical negative
Wk = Work
Pl = Play

Figure 9.1 Event-specific coding of relationship process between a mother and her preschool child: A hypothetical example.

TABLE 9.1   Time-Sampling Methods and Definitions

Time-sampling Method	Definition	Applicability
Frequency-within-interval	Frequency of particular behaviors are recorded	Best for observing a small number of behaviors with easily defined onset and offset periods
Whole Interval	Requires a behavior to occur throughout the designated interval length	When behavior duration is of interest
Partial Interval	Requires that a behavior occurs any time during the designated interval length	When frequency counts are of interest
Momentary Time Sampling	Requires that a behavior occurs at a specific part of the time interval (e.g., at beginning or end)	When frequency counts are of interest
Continuous	Behavior is recorded in a continuous stream, second by second	When behavior duration is of interest; when small changes in behavior need to be captured

and suggested that macro- and microsocial measures may have unique and often complementary scientific utilities.

Several programs of research demonstrate that macro-ratings of relationship process in the natural environment provide unique information about events that unfold over longer time intervals, or they capture relevant outcomes to extended processes. For example, Gottman (1983) considered the co-variation between microsocial exchanges among 5-year-old, unacquainted children and whether they "hit it off as friends." Similarly Gardner (1989) combined a more macrocode of "winning" a conflict bout with a microsocial measure of parenting to capture the negative reinforcement mechanism defining the coercion model. Finally, Hops, Davis, and Longoria (1995) created a multilevel coding system in which macro-categories of affect and content subsume a multitude of microcodes of response types. Their results suggested that microsocial codes were highly correlated with global ratings made by both trained observers and the parents who participated in the study.

Macrolevel coding also could be used to observe relationship events that unfold over the course of the day. Driver and Gottman (2001a, 2001b) examined how newlyweds initiated and responded to bids for intimacy, and then related those patterns to conflict resolution. These analyses provide useful insights about the larger dynamics of how couples self-organize within a context of affection and communication, which provides a motivational stance for solving relationships problems.

Several investigators are using macroratings for summarizing overall patterns of interaction captured on videotape. Conger and colleagues (1992) used macrorating observations of Iowa farm families to understand how economic hardship disrupts parenting and affects child adjustment. An interesting development in both observation and data transduction is the Social Events Coding protocol developed by Petit and

Bates (1990). These family researchers sent coders to families' homes for observations of 2 to 3 hours, where they "narrated" social events that were later transcribed and coded. This procedure has the advantage of incorporating contextual information into the definition of events and also the ability to render both micro- and macrosocial events within a family observation session.

From a functional perspective, both microsocial interactions and macrolevel factors are important to consider. For example, Gardner (1987) examined the macro-outcomes related to parent-child discipline episodes and found that children with conduct disorders often "win" (i.e., the parent often acquiesces to the child's demands or withdraws her own). In studying conflicts among primates, an important macrolevel outcome is the cohesion of the troop over the course of the day. In observation research with chimpanzees, de Waal (2000) found that conflict bouts often function to increase group cohesion in the troop: Conflict served as both an individual function (perhaps coercive) and a group function. Clarification of dominance hierarchies and leadership through microsocial conflict episodes enhances the potential for the group's survival on a macrolevel. Thus, macrocoding of overall patterns of conflict and cohesion can provide a perspective that microsocial coding misses. Similar issues are important in considering, for example, the influence of marital conflict on children's adjustment. The overall resolution of conflict, rated as a macrofactor, has been found to reduce the negative impact of parental arguments on children (Cummings, Simpson, & Wilson, 1993).

Coding Schemes

Coding is a pre-established system of labels that divide the behavior stream into categories. An example of a coding scheme is presented in Figure 9.2. This Relationship Process

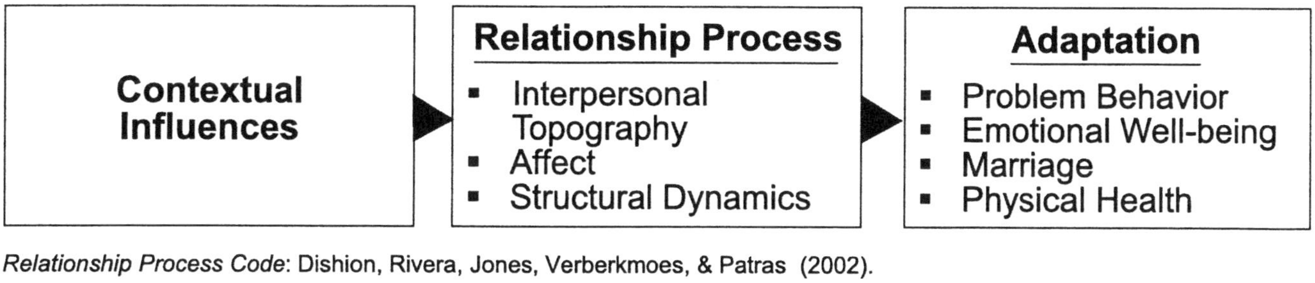

Contextual Influences

Relationship Process
- Interpersonal Topography
- Affect
- Structural Dynamics

Adaptation
- Problem Behavior
- Emotional Well-being
- Marriage
- Physical Health

Relationship Process Code: Dishion, Rivera, Jones, Verberkmoes, & Patras (2002).

Figure 9.2 An overview of the Relationship Process Code. From *Relationship Process Code,* by T.J. Dishion, E.K. Rivera, L. Jones, S. Verberkmoes, and J. Patras, 2002, unpublished coding manual, available from Child and Family Center, University of Oregon, 195 West 12th Avenue, Eugene, OR 97401-3408.

Code (Dishion, Rivera, Jones, Verberkmoes, & Patras, 2002) was developed to provide a basic description of the interactions between family members and within friendships. It consists of 13 coding categories divided into three broadband areas, including verbal behavior (conversation and behavior change), vocal behavior, physical behavior, and compliance. Within each category are a number of codes that are defined a priori as negative, neutral, or positive, based on their presumed interpersonal impact.

This particular coding scheme was derived from multiple generations of coding systems, beginning with the Family Interaction Coding System (Reid, 1978), the Family Process Code (Dishion et al., 1983), the Peer Process Code (Dishion et al., 1989), and the Interpersonal Process Code (Rusby, Estes, & Dishion, 1990). Beginning with the Family Process Code, we approached the behavior stream using a grid to sample codes. Our experience is that there is an optimal balance for the number of codes to use in any system, although there are no hard and fast rules. Coding systems with as many as 60 codes, for instance, may be difficult to achieve reliability and may make data analysis unwieldy.

The coding system presented is only one example among many. One critical point to consider at the outset of a research project is the research question, which should drive priorities on what to code in the behavior stream. For example, when we began our research on friendship process, we coded 200 friendship interaction videotapes with the Peer Process Code (Dishion et al., 1989). We were interested in the friendships of antisocial boys with respect to their social skills and influence on deviance. Our initial analyses of this extensive data set revealed few differences among the friendships of adolescent antisocial boys and those deemed normal. Positive interpersonal behaviors with a friend were uncorrelated with multiagent and multimethod antisocial construct scores (Dishion, Andrews, & Crosby, 1995). The only difference we did find was that antisocial boys were somewhat more likely to use "directives" and to reciprocate negative behaviors. Pe-

rusal of the data, however, revealed that 75% of the interactions between boys and their friends was coded simply "talk."

A cultural anthropologist joined our observation team and began watching the videotapes for discussion content. Specifically, we became interested in the expression of deviant values and developed the Topic Code (Poe, Dishion, Griesler, & Andrews, 1990). We divided the discourse into two broadband topics, referred to as "rule break" and "normative." We added two reactions, "laugh" and "pause." The four-category coding system far exceeded our original hopes for defining an influence dynamic that differentiated boys on a deviant trajectory from well-adjusted boys (Dishion et al., 1995, 1996, 1997; Patterson, Dishion, & Yoerger, 2000). Specifically, the observed deviant friendship process, characterized by reciprocal rule-break talk and laughter, was associated with escalation in alcohol, marijuana, and tobacco use from early-to-middle adolescence. In later analyses, we found this peer process was associated with escalation in self-reported delinquency and violent behavior in adolescence (Dishion, Spracklen, Andrews, & Patterson, 1996; Dishion, Eddy, Haas, Li, & Spracklen, 1997).

This example is illustrative of two issues in observational research. First, it is important to approach the behavior stream with a question in mind. With this question in mind, appropriate codes that capture the relationship dynamic should be generated and refined (see also Patterson, 1982). Then the code definitions can be refined so that two or more individuals can reliably use the code. Second, it is helpful to record relationship processes by conducting multiple passes through the data. With the use of digital coding, it is now possible to do so, so that codes are layered and synchronized in time for later analyses.

Reliability

In order for observational data to be valid and generalizable, reliable coders are essential. Typically, observers are trained to use a pre-established coding system to reliably render quantitative estimates of behavior. A team of observers is trained until they reach conventional criteria of reliability.

Training a group of individuals to see and code behavior similarly is often a challenging task—and training is the operative term. Depending on the coding systems, training may range from a few days to six months to reach reliable coding criteria.

Reliability is assessed in several ways, using a simple index of agreement (as in percent agreement), intraclass correlation coefficients, or an index of nominal agreement that corrects for chance agreement (i.e., kappa). Direct observational coding can be differentiated from ethological approaches to observation by its emphasis on reliability analysis. The latter approach tends toward detailed narrative recording of human interactions, with abundant interpretation during the observation session. Both approaches to observation are direct, but naturalistic observation is concerned with agreement among diverse observers, with the presumption that agreement among coders distills bias in perceptions that are inherent in individual interpretations.

Analyzing Process

One of the basic questions in process research is whether two observed events are contingently related. Because we are interested in function, we want to estimate the extent to which an antecedent is followed by the predicted consequence. For example, in our past research, we were interested in the lag 1 relations (two temporally adjacent events) in order to examine the extent to which deviant talk was followed by laughter.

Observation researchers have developed quantitative indices to determine whether a contingency is statistically reliable by use of an index such as a z score (Gottman & Roy, 1990). It is critical, however, to consider the marginal distribution of the coding scheme and the inherent limitations of a coding scheme in estimating z scores of contingency. For example, in an event duration coding scheme (e.g., the Relationship Process Code), events cannot follow themselves. According to Bakeman and Quera (1995), if statistical adjustments are not made, one can overestimate the contingency between two events. This is especially problematic if the researcher is interested in low frequency events.

One solution to the problem of evaluating contingency between nominal events is to create "streams of behavior" for each interacting partner. This is accomplished by coding each person separately within an interaction, most likely by use of videotape (see Gottman, 1979). Codes can be weighted for interpersonal impact and then summed over prespecified time frames (e.g., 10 seconds) to create a summary score.

Thus, a time series is created for each individual. Statistical associations can subsequently be evaluated using repeated measures techniques such as time series analysis or generalized estimation equations (Zeger & Liang, 1986). These statistical models allow inferences regarding the influence of one person's behavior on another.

More recently, investigators have begun exploring relationship patterns that are nonlinear and involve sudden shifts that are difficult to predict using stochastic models of influence. Gottman (1991) initially provided a conceptual framework for thinking about the nonlinear dynamics of close relationships. Gottman and his colleagues have developed a dynamic systems framework for understanding influence in marriages, referred to as mathematical modeling of relationships (Ryan, Gottman, Murray, Carrere, & Swanson, 1999). The framework focuses on the descriptive analysis of the influence dynamics within individual relationships and yields influence parameters for relationship partners. These parameters can then be used to design interventions or as individual difference parameters in inferential research on marriages.

The dynamic systems (DS) perspective recently led to a number of innovations in the representation and analysis of direct observations of relationship processes. One particular methodology, state space grids (Lewis, Lamey, & Douglas, 1999), holds significant promise. DS theorists use the concept of a *state space* to represent the range of behavioral habits, or attractors, for a given system. In real time, behavior is conceptualized as moving along a trajectory on this hypothetical landscape, being pulled toward certain attractors (stable behavioral patterns) and freed from others. Based on these abstract formalizations, Lewis and colleagues (1999) developed a graphical approach that utilizes direct observational data and quantifies these data according to two ordinal variables that define the state space for any particular system. These researchers have primarily studied intraindividual behavioral patterns that emerge and change in the early years of life (e.g., Lewis et al., 1999; Lewis, Zimmerman, Lamey, & Hollenstein, in press).

State space grids also have been developed to represent dyadic behavior (e.g., parent-child interactions, peer relations; Granic, Dishion, Hollenstein, & Patterson, in press; Granic & Hollenstein, in press; Granic & Lamey, 2002). The dyad's trajectory (i.e., the sequence of behavioral states) is plotted as it proceeds in real time on a grid representing all possible behavioral combinations. Much like a scatter plot, one dyad member's (e.g., parent) coded behavior is plotted on the x-axis, and the other member's (e.g., child) behavior is plotted on the y-axis. Each point on the grid represents a two-event sequence, or a simultaneously coded parent-child event (i.e., a dyadic state). A trajectory is drawn through the

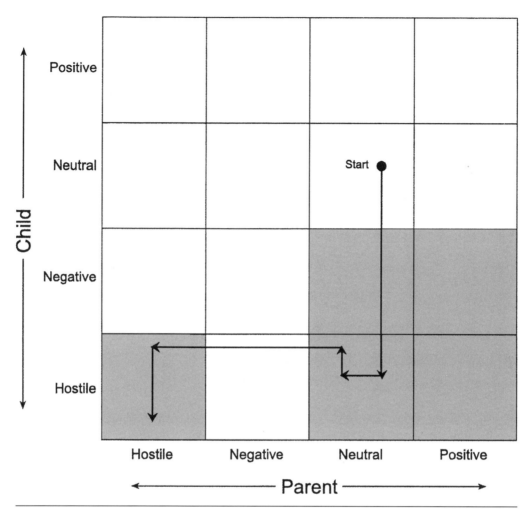

Figure 9.3   Example of a state space grid with a hypothetical trajectory representing the following seven events: Child neutral, parent neutral, child hostile, parent neutral, child hostile, parent hostile. From "Dynamic Systems Methods for Models of Developmental Psychopathology," by I. Granic and T. Hollenstein, in press, *Development and Psychopathology.*

successive dyadic points in the temporal sequence they were observed. For example, a hypothetical trajectory representing seven conversational turns is presented in Figure 9.3. Seven successive events are plotted: parent neutral, child neutral, parent hostile, child neutral, parent hostile, child hostile, parent hostile.

With this temporally sensitive technique, we can examine whether behavior clusters in few or many states (i.e., cells) or regions (i.e., a subset of cells) of the state space. We also can track how long the trajectory remains in some cells but not others, and how quickly it returns or stabilizes in particular cells. We can identify attractors as those cells to which behavior is drawn repeatedly, in which it rests over extended periods, or to which it returns quickly. Moreover, a range of quantitative variables that capture the relative stability of particular attractors may be derived from state space grids, and

these values can be tested statistically for changes in real and developmental time (Lewis et al., 1999, Granic & Hollenstein, in press).

A major advantage of state space grids is that they provide an intuitively appealing way to view complex, interactional behavior; thus, they are first and foremost a useful preliminary tool for exploratory analysis. Another strength of this technique is its inherent flexibility. Researchers can use continuous time-series, as well as categorical and ordinal data for this type of analysis. Also, the grids are malleable in that they can represent systemic behavior on the individual as well as dyadic level. Changes in peer, romantic couples, and sibling interactions, for example, can easily be tracked using this technique. Finally, unlike sequential analysis, this technique does not rely on base rates of behavior to identify important interactional patterns.

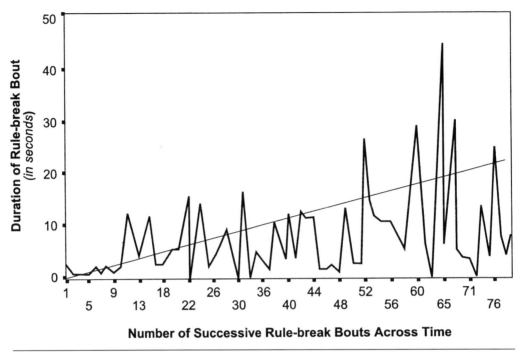

Figure 9.4 Example of a time series for an antisocial youth with a positive rule-break slope.

State space grids have been used to explore differences in the parent-child interactions of "pure" externalizing (EXT) children and children comorbid (MIXED) for externalizing and internalizing problems (Granic & Lamey, 2002). In this study, parents and clinically referred children discussed a problem for 4 minutes and then tried to "wrap up" in response to a signal (or a perturbation). The perturbation was intended to increase the emotional pressure on the dyad, triggering a reorganization of their behavioral system. Consistent with the hypothesis, as a function of differences in the underlying structure of their relationships, EXT and MIXED dyads were differentially sensitive to the perturbation and reorganized to different parts of the state space. Prior to the perturbation, however, dyads' interactions were similar. Separate grids were constructed for the pre- and post-perturbation interaction sessions, and the results were clear: Both EXT and MIXED dyads tended toward the permissive region of the state space grid *before* the perturbation. Afterward, however, EXT dyads stabilized in the permissive region in contrast to MIXED dyads, who shifted toward the mutual hostility region of the state space grid. These graphical observations were subsequently supported by case-sensitive and multivariate statistical analyses including log-linear modeling.

The mutual hostility pattern may be called an absorbing state for the MIXED dyads—behavior is drawn toward this type of interaction and is held there for extended periods. The concept of an "absorbing" state (or attractor) is undoubtedly

going to be useful in future observation studies of relationship processes. Raush (1965), in his observation of troubled children, noted the presence of "absorbing chains" associated with more severe psychopathology. The sense of being "caught" in a destructive cycle certainly fits with both scientific and clinical accounts of troubled families (Patterson, 1982) and troubled marriages (Gottman, 1979).

We recently completed a study that examined the extent to which deviant talk functions as an absorbing state for antisocial peers (Granic, Dishion, Hollenstein, & Patterson, in press). This study highlights the fact that important functional relations can be detected in observational data not only with the use of categorical data (and calculating conditional probabilities) but also by using measures of intensity and duration. In this study, peers were videotaped problem-solving, and the duration of each dyadic deviant talk bout (mutual talk about rule-breaking, lying, stealing, etc.) was recorded. A time-series plot was created from these successive deviant talk bouts, and the slope of that time-series (i.e., the standardized beta) was calculated using simple regression analysis. This was a straightforward measure that indicated whether, over the course of an interaction, deviant talk bouts became longer and longer. It was intended to capture a temporal pattern indicative of a dyad getting "stuck" in the deviant talk process.

Youth with clinically elevated problems showed significantly higher slope values than normal adolescents. An example of an antisocial and normal dyad are presented in

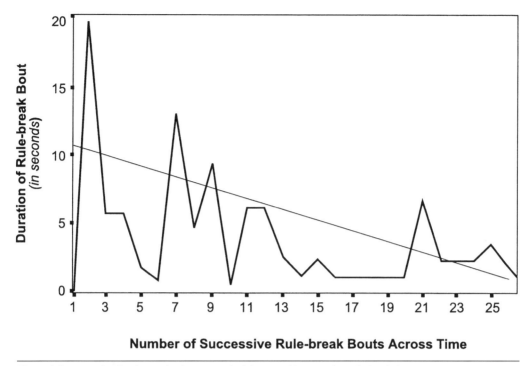

Figure 9.5   Example of a time series for a normal adolescent with a negative rule-break slope.

Figures 9.4 and 9.5. More impressively, this slope value positively predicted delinquency ($R^2 = .41$) and drug abuse ($R^2 = .30$) three years later, *after controlling for previous levels of delinquency, family coercion, and deviant peer affiliation.* The application of dynamic systems' graphical and quantitative tools to capture absorbing states is an important development for process researchers.

INTERVENTION SCIENCE

Overview

In addition to the early studies of development, directly observing behavior in the natural environment is the keystone to the design and evaluation of effective intervention. Direct observation can help in the design of interventions by identifying the behavioral antecedents and consequences of target behaviors that, if modified, can change the occurrence of the response. Early stimulus control studies on aggressive behavior, as a matter of course, would alter an antecedent and evaluate whether there was a subsequent reduction in the consequence (Patterson, 1974a).

The researchers interested in behavioral analysis soon transitioned into conducting between subject research and began using behavior observations in the natural environment as outcome measures. Careful methodological work clarified some of the issues such as generalizability (Jones, Reid, &

Patterson, 1975), observer drift (Reid, 1978), and observer training (Reid, 1982).

Early coding systems, such as the Family Interaction Coding System, used a 6-second time-sampling framework, where observers would record (with pencil and paper) the interactant and codes sequentially within a pre-established time frame. A beep on the clipboard prompted coders to stop and start coding. These observations were used to evaluate the effectiveness and factors affecting outcomes in parent training for children with behavior problems (Dishion & Patterson, 1992; Dumas & Wahler, 1983; Forehand, Furey, & McMahon, 1984; Johnson & Christensen, 1975; Johnson & Lobitz, 1975; Patterson, 1974b; Patterson, Chamberlain, & Reid, 1982). Behavior observations in the natural environment began to be used as individual difference factors in the context of the general linear model (ANOVA, regression, correlation).

The use of behavioral observations as individual difference scores has led to significant progress in intervention science, including the evaluation of universal, selected, and indicated interventions and the analysis of the therapy process itself. Intervention research that uses naturalistic observations has been conducted in diverse settings. This body of research is reviewed below.

School Observations

The first setting in which natural observations have been extensively used is the playground, where children's play in free time can be tracked. We developed a system for coding interactions across contexts that has been used on the playground, among other contexts (Rusby et al., 1991). With this event duration coding system, behavior codes are entered much as shown in Figure 9.1. Each child is targeted, and his or her interactions with a playmate are recorded in real time using code categories that capture the interpersonal process of play.

This coding system was recently used to assess a school-based intervention, the Linking Interests of Families and Teachers (LIFT) program. In an elegant exemplar of multivariate data analysis, Stoolmiller, Eddy, and Reid (2000) examined the effect of the LIFT intervention on playground behavior, specifically physical aggression. A major component of the LIFT intervention was the design of a "good behavior game" on the playground (Barrish, Saunders, & Wolf, 1969; Dolan, Kellam, Brown, & Werthamer-Larsson, 1993; Kellam, Rebok, Ialongo, & Mayer, 1994). Stoolmiller and colleagues (2000) used structural equation modeling to handle two pernicious problems of observation data on the playground. One is the problem of data that are non-normal in distribution, as a function of the low base rate events that are typically informative to intervention research. Second, the rarely acknowledged problem of censoring was statistically addressed. Censoring is an issue, for example, when children are observed on the playground for only 15 minutes of time and some behaviors do not have time to emerge. In these cases, many scores of zero on, for instance, physical aggression are simply a function of limited observation time. Assuming that many children would engage in physical aggression if the observation period were extended, then one corrects for this censoring error.

This report documented change in children's physical aggression on the playground associated with random assignment to the LIFT intervention (Stoolmiller et al., 2000). It is important to note that the direct observation score on the playground was the only indicator among a plethora of data that was sensitive to the intervention. Data were collected at the same time for parent, teacher, and peer reports of the same behaviors. The sensitivity of behavior observations to intervention conditions has been considered to be a major scientific advantage of this methodology (Eddy, Dishion, & Stoolmiller, 1998).

Research by Pepler and colleagues represents a significant innovation in naturalistic observations (Craig & Pepler, 1995; Pepler & Craig, 1995). They too observed children's behavior on the playground, but they used long-distance microphones (hidden in the children's backpacks) and video cameras to record elementary school–aged children's physical and verbal behaviors. From the long-distance vantage point, they unobtrusively observed how children organize themselves into groups during recess. The use of this innovative technique allowed them to examine peer processes associated with aggression and bullying. A key factor seems to be the function of aggression in coalition formation. Their findings revealed that bullying does not occur in isolation—there is often an audience, a system of children that directly and indirectly encourage group aggression. To date, this approach has not been applied to evaluating the effectiveness of programs to prevent bullying in school.

Another setting within the school environment that is rich for naturalistic observations is the classroom. Walker and colleagues (1986; Walker, Colvin, & Ramsey, 1993) developed a direct observation measure for the public school setting that tapped the time spent engaged in academic activities. The coding system was a beautiful illustration of the possible simplicity and cost effectiveness of behavior observation in the natural environment. The data were collected with a stopwatch. The stopwatch was turned on when the student was engaged in an academic activity in the classroom as directed by the teacher. When the student is engaged in other behaviors besides those assigned by the teacher, the stopwatch was turned off. Time spent academically engaged was calculated as a proportion of the total time observed. One can easily imagine that such a coding system would be extremely useful for interventions that target teaching practices that promote academic achievement. This measure was included in the LIFT prevention trial, but the impact of the intervention on academic achievement has not yet been reported.

Therapy Process

Given that most therapy is conducted in a clinic room in a highly structured setting, it is surprising that there is not more observation research on therapy process. Despite our rich tradition of using the talking cure, surprisingly little research has examined the relationship process between the therapist and client that promotes change, or lack thereof. The observations of therapist-client process can expand our understanding of change processes, and can provide the foundation for intervention innovation and improved clinical training.

Although scarce, some important studies have used direct observations to tap the therapeutic process. For example, to study the process by which parent training changes children's aggressive behavior, Chamberlain designed a microsocial coding system that captured momentary changes in client resistance during behavior family therapy (Chamberlain, Patterson, Reid, & Kavanagh, 1984). Client verbal statements such as "I can't," "yes, but," and other locutions implying disagreement or the unwillingness to change were coded as resistance.

The next step was to develop a therapy process code that assessed therapists' skill in reducing resistance to change. Code categories such as "reframe," "support," "confront," "teach," and others described therapist behaviors that could either mobilize or reduce client resistance (Chamberlain et al., 1985).

A series of programmatic studies have demonstrated the utility of this microsocial approach to understanding therapy process. For example, Patterson and Forgatch (1985) demonstrated experimentally that systematically increasing behaviors such as "teach" or "reframe" increased the level of client resistance. Therapist behavior such as "support," in contrast, reduced client resistance. Patterson and Chamberlain (1994) described in detail the functional relations between therapist and client behavior. Stoolmiller, Duncan, Bank, & Patterson (1993) applied latent growth curve analyses to client resistance over the entire course of therapy to real life changes in parenting behavior, finding some evidence in support of a quadratic pattern of client resistance (i.e., the work struggle hypothesis) to be prognostic of a family benefiting from behavior family therapy. In the initial stage of therapy, there is little client resistance as the therapist works to build a relationship. When the work begins, client resistance increases. Presumably, client resistance again reduces during the end of therapy, when the parents have experienced benefits from the therapy process. It is noteworthy that the results from direct observations of therapy process by Patterson and colleagues inspired innovations in behavior therapy leading to motivational interviewing (Miller & Rollnick, 1991). Motivational interviewing for alcohol use was based on therapy process research showing that confronting clients about their drinking or denial decreased the likelihood of future change in problematic drinking.

Direct observations also can shed light on interpersonal processes within group interventions that promote or detract from change. In our research on the effectiveness of a cognitive behavioral group intervention, we found that aggregating high-risk adolescents led to overall increases in problem behavior compared to youngsters in a control group (Dishion, Andrews et al., 1995; Dishion, McCord, & Poulin, 1999; Poulin, Dishion, & Burraston, 2001). Videotaping each of the group interventions afforded the opportunity to study the group dynamics associated with the iatrogenic effects. As expected, subtle forms of deviancy training among the youth in the group was statistically associated with individual differences in youths' increased problem behavior (Dishion, Poulin, & Burraston, 2001).

We also studied the experiences within parent groups that led to observed improvements in parent-child interactions for high-risk adolescents. Hogansen and Dishion (2001) examined a variety of therapist behaviors and parent interactions that were statistically associated with change, based on videotapes of parent groups. In this analysis, we found that the therapist's skills in reframing parent's complaints into positive change statements were most likely to facilitate change. We also found that too-strict adherence to the curriculum guiding the parent groups *inhibited* change (Dishion, Spracklen, & Kavanagh, 1995).

In studying the factors that enhance structural family therapy with troubled adolescents, Robins, Alexander, Newell, and Turner, (1996) directly observed the use of reframing. Based on videotaped observations of the initial family therapy sessions, they found that the therapist's positive reframing of the adolescent's problem behavior was an important determinant of the adolescent remaining engaged in therapy. Most therapists who work with adolescent families realize there is a fine line between building the executive function in a family through parent support and keeping adolescents involved in therapy. Positive reframing of the adolescent's behavior provides a therapeutic perspective conducive to supporting both the adolescent and parents and minimizing the prevalent dropout risk in treatment of adolescents and families (Dishion & Patterson, 1992).

Interestingly, the types of behaviors that have been identified as critical for change from direct observations of therapy may generalize to other settings as well. For example, Hollaway and Wampold (1983) examined interactions between a supervisor and trainee. Their process analyses showed that, similar to therapeutic interactions, support, reframe, and sensitivity in the supervision process when training new clinicians were key factors for success.

Clearly, videotaping therapeutic interactions and conducting microsocial study of the change process is a fruitful approach to clinical research. The work is inherently naturalistic in that the interaction process is representative of that which occurs naturally in the change process.

Naturalistic observations are not only critical for the clinical researcher for analyzing change in therapy, but this methodology has additional uses as a clinical tool. Although videotaped feedback has been used extensively as an intervention tool, it has not been used within a motivational interviewing framework (Miller & Rollnick, 1991). In this framework, videotaped interactions are reviewed, and patterns of interaction that are prognostic of both positive and negative outcomes are delineated in the form of feedback to the parent. The therapist reviews the entire assessment findings with the parent, including the scored videotaped home observation, and engages in a process of supporting motivation to change. It is safe to say that much of the relationship process is based on overlearned patterns of behavior that spin off automatically (Patterson, 1982; Patterson & Reid, 1984). As such, it is often difficult for parents to "see" their own contribution to maladaptive interactions with an adolescent.

Using a random assignment design, Rao (1998) found videotaped feedback to be effective in changing parenting practices and reducing problem behavior, without the addition of more intensive parent training. We found that incorporating this method within the Family Check-Up, an intervention program based in a middle school context, resulted in significant reductions in substance use by the first year of high school (4-year follow-up period; Dishion, Kavanagh, Schneiger, Nelson, & Kaufman, 2002).

In general, in child and family therapy, it is good practice to share assessment results with parents (e.g., Sanders & Lawton, 1993); videotaped feedback may be an especially powerful tool for building motivation to change. We are currently using videotapes of friendship interactions of adolescents in a Teen Check-Up procedure that attempts to build motivation for prosocial planning. Future clinical research may benefit from systematic evaluations of the application of naturalistic observations as a clinical tool to promote change.

FUTURE DIRECTIONS

Cultural Relativity

A major issue in research on naturalistic observations is the role of culture in determining and defining social interaction. Until recently most observation researchers were comfortable with the "objectivity" of direct observation. The idea was that multiple observers using the same coding system provided a third-person perspective on the social interaction. This is both true and potentially misleading. It is clear that extensive observer training is necessary because observers naturally define relationship processes in very different ways. Anyone who has trained a group of observers in a coding system that has more than 10 codes quickly realizes that even a group of culturally homogeneous people can understand the same event very differently. To this extent, observer training removes some method variance from the equation. Thus, it may seem that objective coding can provide powerful information about cultural differences in behavior and perception.

The clearest example of the utility of cross-cultural behavioral observation is the research by Weisz, Weiss, Han, Granger, & Morton (1995), which compared Thai and American children. The comparative teacher rating data suggested that Thai children showed more problem behavior than American children at school. This was exactly the opposite of what was expected. However, when comparing direct observations

of Thai and American children, the exact opposite results were found: American children showed significantly more aggressive behavior than Thai children. Research comparing two cultural groups are replete with potential confounds. Nevertheless, there is theoretical value in the use of direct observation in the context of a multiagent, multimethod data collection.

Findings from socialization research suggest that, indeed, there are important cultural differences that need to be addressed in future observation research. For example, Deater-Deckard and Dodge (1997) found that physical discipline had differential predictive validity depending on family ethnicity. In African American families, physical discipline was associated with positive adjustment in contrast to European American families, where physical discipline was associated with negative adjustment. One possibility is that the meaning of physical punishment varies as a function of ethnicity. This was indeed found, where African American children rated physical discipline as fair, in contrast to European American children. What is unknown in this study was whether the quality of the physical discipline varied as a function of ethnicity. In cultures where physical discipline is deemed acceptable, perhaps it is used more contingently in response to misbehavior and not as an emotive response to a conflict episode.

Dishion and Bullock (2001) examined direct observations of family interactions in the home for African American and European American families, selected as both successful (better than passing grades, no discipline contacts or referrals) and as high risk (teacher ratings of problem behavior). Observers made macroratings on videotapes of these family interactions. In general, we found several interesting interactions. For example, we found a group by ethnicity interaction for observed limit setting. Oddly enough, successful African American families were scored lower than high-risk African American families. The data have yet to be analyzed to determine whether the coder's ethnicity contributed to these findings. We are inclined to believe that the ratings were biased in favor of a European American definition of limit setting. A very similar pattern resulted for the macrorating of relationship quality from the videotaped family interactions.

An interesting finding, however, is that the global family management score did not show any biasing effect for ethnicity. The aggregated score of family management discriminated between successful and high-risk families in the expected direction for both groups. Perhaps the inclusion of more items improved reliability, in that the statistically reliable but relatively trivial differences among ethnic groups were eliminated.

It is critical to pursue further research in the possibility of systematic cultural bias in naturalistic observations. There are two levels of potential bias. The first is the possibility of differential response to the assessment as a function of ethnicity. Note, however, that some careful observation research has been conducted with primarily minority families with rich empirical and theoretical yield (Snyder, West, Stockemer, Givens, & Almquist-Parks, 1996). The second level of potential bias is the use of coding systems that quantify relationship process across cultural groups.

The manner in which researchers structure assessments may be culturally insensitive. For example, in assessing a parent's skill in positive reinforcement, we ask caregivers to discuss positive behaviors they would like to encourage in the adolescent: "In the next 5 minutes we would like you to talk about Jerome doing homework, and how you would like to encourage homework in the future." Interestingly enough, most parents turn this discussion into a lecture or discipline conversation. So the assessment is ideal for assessing exposure to our intervention. On the other hand, Native American families and colleagues do not welcome these direct discussions of positive reinforcement and discipline. More traditional Native American families in many tribes relied on different strategies for socializing young adolescents. One important strategy was the use of stories as a context for discussing behavior and values.

In observation assessments with Native American families, Ball and Ball (1999) include a task called "Coyote Dances with the Stars." In this task, caregivers and adolescents watch a videotape of a story about Coyote and his tendency to seek intense pleasure, without regard to consequences, and his foolish sense of invulnerability. The researchers then ask the caregiver(s) to discuss how this story is relevant to the adolescent. Informally perusing the videotapes, this task elicits parenting strengths in families oriented toward Native American cultural practices. European American families, on the other hand, struggle with turning this story into a useful discussion.

The second potential ethnicity confound in observational research is the use of coding systems that quantify relationship process across cultural groups. Although extensive training coalesces coders' perspectives, we do not know how these coding systems fit within the perspective of families across cultural groups. The research cited above suggests that, indeed, the perspective of some families may differ radically from those of the scientist (Deater-Deckard & Dodge, 1997). Some researchers have obtained subjective ratings of the aversiveness of various coding categories. Typically, behaviors are listed that are prototypic of each code, and undergraduate students rate on a bipolar dimension of pleasant and aversive. Aggregate scores are used to weight the overall summary scores derived from a family's observation data. By

and large, these weightings typically render scores that are consonant with the perspective of the researchers and do not dramatically improve the performance of the coding system to discriminate or predict (Hoffman, Fagot, Reid, & Patterson, 1987).

Future research should focus on getting behavior ratings from individuals who are demographically similar to those under investigation. For example, a community sample of European American families might perceive behavior differently than college undergraduates. We know that measures of discipline are highly correlated with socioeconomic status (Patterson, Reid, & Dishion, 1992). One can imagine a research design that includes both objective coding and participant ratings for high-risk and successful families across two or more ethnic groups. At a basic level, the participant ratings may provide a context for understanding the cultural differences in the display of behaviors.

Collecting multiagent, multimethod data and finding differences in perceptions of behavior does not imply that objective coding does not predict equally well across cultural groups, as this is a separate empirical question. For example, the value system that suggests that smoking marijuana is okay among middle- to upper-class families does not change the fact that onset of marijuana smoking by age 15–16 is highly prognostic of substance use problems in adulthood. In another example, the study by Weisz et al. (1994) suggested that Thai teachers had lower perceptual thresholds in their definition of problem behavior than did U.S. teachers, presumably responding vigilantly to minor problem behaviors and therefore creating contexts with overall lower levels in Thai schools compared to U.S. schools. In this sense, naturalistic observations can be critical for unraveling the processes in which culture makes a difference.

Summary

We cannot understand human behavior without directly observing it. Yet it is puzzling that, as the field of behavioral science develops, proportionally few studies are published that convey findings from observation of relationship processes. Perhaps this trend is due to the collective change in interest in behavior science from patterns of behavior to biological mechanisms of influence. Of course, pragmatic limitations of cost preclude some researchers from conducting naturalistic observations. Also, psychology has traditionally been a science of intrapersonal processes, not interpersonal processes. Those of us who inhabit the boundary areas in the science of behavior in relationships may, on occasion, fall out of step with the zeitgeist of funding and publication. Nonetheless, scientifically, the analysis of micro- and macrosocial

processes will continue to broaden our descriptive understanding of the human condition and suggest realistic remedies to some forms of suffering.

REFERENCES

Bakeman, R., & Quera, V. (1995). Log-linear approaches to lag-
sequential analysis when consecutive codes may and cannot repeat. *Psychological Bulletin, 118,* 272–284.

Ball, T., & Ball, A.J. (1999). Coyote dances with the stars.
Videotape.

Ball, T., & Ball, A.J. (1999). *Coyote Dances with the Stars.* Unpublished task. (Available at Oregon Social Learning Center, 160
East 4th Avenue, Eugene, OR 97401–2426.)

Bank, L., Dishion, T.J., Skinner, M., & Patterson, G.R. (1990).
Method variance in structural equation modeling: Living with
"Glop." In G.R. Patterson (Ed.), *Aggression and depression in
family interactions* (pp. 247–279). Hillsdale, NJ: Erlbaum.

Barkely, R.A. (1997). Attention-deficit/hyperactivity disorder. In
E.J. Mash & L.G. Terdal (Eds.), *Assessment of childhood disorders* (3rd ed., pp. 71–129). New York: Guilford Press.

Barrish, H.H., Saunders, M., & Wolf, M.M. (1969). Good behavior
game: Effects of individual contingencies for group consequences on disruptive behavior in a classroom. *Journal of Applied Behavior Analysis, 2,* 119–124.

Birchler, G.R., Weiss, R.L., & Vincent, J.P. (1975). Multimethod
analysis of social reinforcement exchange between maritally distressed and nondistressed spouse and stranger dyads. *Journal of
Personality and Social Psychology, 31*(2), 349–360.

Bullock, B.M., & Dishion, T.J. (2002). Sibling collusion and problem behavior in early adolescence: Toward a process model for
family mutuality. *Journal of Abnormal Child Psychology, 30,*
143–153.

Cairns, R.B., & Green, J.A. (1979). How to assess personality and
social patterns: Observations or ratings? In R.B. Cairns (Ed.),
*The analysis of social interaction: Methods, issues, and illustra-
tions* (pp. 213–230). Hillsdale, NJ: Erlbaum.

Campbell, D.T., & Stanley, J.C. (1963). Experimental and quasi-
experimental designs for research on teaching. In N.L. Gage
(Ed.), *Handbook of research teaching* (pp. 171–246). Chicago:
Rand McNally.

Chamberlain, P., Davis, J.P., Forgatch, M., Frey, J., Patterson, G.R.,
Ray, J., Rothschild, A., & Trombley, J. (1985). *The therapy pro-
cess code: A multidimensional system of observing therapist and
client interaction.* Unpublished coding manual. (Available at
Oregon Social Learning Center, 160 East 4th Avenue, Eugene,
OR 97401–2426.)

Chamberlain, P., Patterson, G.R., Reid, J., & Kavanagh, K. (1984).
Observation of client resistance. *Behavior Therapy, 15,* 144–155.

Cone, J. (1999). Observational assessment: Measure development
and research issues. In P.C. Kendall, J.N. Butcher, & G.N.

Holmbeck (Eds.), *Handbook of research methods in clinical psychology* (2nd ed., pp. 183–223). New York: Wiley.

Conger, R.D., Conger, K.J., Elder, G.H. Jr., Lorenz, F.O., Simons,
R.L., & Whitbeck, L.B. (1992). A family process model of eco-
nomic hardship and adjustment of early adolescent boys. *Child
Development, 63,* 526–541.

Conger, R.D., Patterson, G.R., & Ge, X. (1995). A mediational
model for the impact of parents' stress on adolescent adjustment.
Child Development, 66, 80–97.

Cook, T.D., & Campbell, D.T. (1979). *Quasi-experimentation: Design and analysis issues for field settings.* Boston: Houghton
Mifflin.

Craig, W.M., & Pepler, D.J. (1995). *Naturalistic observations and
bullying and victimization in the schoolyard.* Unpublished manuscript, Queens University, Kingston, Ontario, Canada.

Cummings, E.M., Simpsom, K.S., & Wilson, A. (1993). Children's
responses to interadult anger as a function of information about
resolution. *Developmental Psychology, 29,* 978–985.

Deater-Deckard, K., & Dodge, K.A. (1997). Spare the rod, spoil the
authors: Emerging themes in research on parenting and child
development. *Psychological Inquiry, 8,* 230–235.

de Waal, F.B. (2000). Primates: A natural heritage of conflict resolution. *Science, 290*(5494), 1096–1097.

Dishion, T.J., & Andrews, D.W. (1995). Preventing escalation in
problem behaviors with high-risk young adolescents: Immediate
and 1-year outcomes. *Journal of Consulting and Clinical Psychology, 63,* 538–548.

Dishion, T.J., Andrews, D.W., & Crosby, L. (1995). Antisocial boys
and their friends in early adolescence: Relationship characteristics, quality, and interactional process. *Child Development, 66,*
139–151.

Dishion, T.J., & Bullock, B. (2001). Parenting and adolescent problem behavior: An ecological analysis of the nurturance hypothesis. In J.G. Borkowski, S. Ramey, & M. Bristol-Power (Eds.),
*Parenting and the child's world: Influences on intellectual, ac-
ademic, and social-emotional development* (pp. 231–249). Mahwah, NJ: Erlbaum.

Dishion, T.J., Burraston, B., & Li, F. (2002). A multimethod and
multitrait analysis of family management practices: Convergent
and predictive validity. In W. Bukoski & Z. Amsel (Eds.), *Handbook for drug abuse prevention theory, science, and practice.*
New York: Plenum Press.

Dishion, T.J., Crosby, L., Rusby, J.C., Shane, D., Patterson, G.R.,
& Baker, J. (1989). *Peer Process Code: Multidimensional system
for observing adolescent peer interaction.* Unpublished training
manual. (Available from Oregon Social Learning Center, 160
East 4th Avenue, Eugene, OR 97401.)

Dishion, T.J., Eddy, J.M., Haas, E., Li, F., & Spracklen, K. (1997).
Friendships and violent behavior during adolescence. *Social Development, 6,* 207–223.

Dishion, T.J., Gardner, K., Patterson, G.R., Reid, J.R., Spyrou, S.,
& Thibodeaux, S. (1983). *The Family Process Code: A multi-*

dimensional system for observing family interaction. Unpublished coding manual. (Available from Oregon Social Learning Center, 160 East 4th Avenue, Eugene, OR 97401.)

Dishion, T.J., Kavanagh, K., Schneiger, A., Nelson, S., & Kaufman, N. (2002). Preventing early adolescent substance use: A family-centered strategy for the public middle-school ecology. In R.L. Spoth, K. Kavanagh, & T.J. Dishion (Eds.), *Universal family-centered prevention strategies: Current findings and critical issues for public health impact* [Special issue]. *Prevention Science, 3,* 191–201.

Dishion, T.J., McCord, J., & Poulin, F. (1999). When interventions harm: Peer groups and problem behavior. *American Psychologist, 54,* 755–764.

Dishion, T.J., & Patterson, G.R. (1992). Age effects in parent training outcome. *Behavior Therapy, 23,* 719–729.

Dishion, T.J., & Patterson, G.R. (1999). Model-building in developmental psychopathology: A pragmatic approach to understanding and intervention. *Journal of Clinical Child Psychology, 28,* 502–512.

Dishion, T.J., Poulin, F., Burraston, B. (2001). Peer group dynamics associated with iatrogenic effects in group interventions with high-risk young adolescents. In D.W. Nangle & C.A. Erdley (Eds.), *The role of friendship in psychological adjustment* (pp. 79–92). San Francisco: Jossey-Bass.

Dishion, T.J., Rivera, E.K., Jones, L., Verberkmoes, S., & Patras, J. (2002). *Relationship Process Code.* Unpublished coding manual. (Available from Child and Family Center, University of Oregon, 195 West 12th Avenue, Eugene, OR 97401-3408.)

Dishion, T.J., Spracklen, K.M., Andrews, D.M., & Patterson, G.R. (1996). Deviancy training in male adolescent friendships. *Behavior Therapy, 27*(1), 373–390.

Dishion, T.J., Spracklen, K., & Kavanagh, K. (1995, November). *Analyses of change in group parent training with high-risk adolescents.* Paper presented at the Annual Meeting of the Association for the Advancement of Behavior Therapy, Washington, DC.

Dolan, L.J., Kellam, S.G., Brown, C.H., & Werthamer-Larsson, L. (1993). The short-term impact of two classroom-based preventive interventions on aggressive and shy behaviors and poor achievement. *Journal of Applied Developmental Psychology, 14*(3), 317–345.

Driver, J.L. and Gottman, J.M. (2001a). Daily marital interactions during dinner time in an apartment laboratory and positive affect during marital conflict among newlywed couples. Manuscript in preparation.

Driver, J. and Gottman, J. (2001b). Dysfunctional marital conflict in everyday marital interaction in an apartment laboratory. Manuscript in preparation.

Dumas, J.E., & Wahler, R.G. (1983). Predictors of treatment outcome in parent training: Mother insularity and socioeconomic disadvantage. *Behavioral Assessment, 5,* 301–313.

Dunn, J. (1992). Sisters and brothers: Current issues in developmental research. In F. Boer & J. Dunn (Eds.), *Children's sibling relationships: Developmental and clinical issues* (pp. 1–17). Hillsdale, NJ: Erlbaum.

Eddy, J.M., Dishion, T.J., & Stoolmiller, M. (1998). The analysis of change in children and families: Methodological and conceptual issues embedded in intervention studies. *Journal of Abnormal Child Psychology, 26,* 53–69.

Fiske, D.W. (1986). Specificity of method and knowledge in social science. In D.W. Fiske & R.A. Shweder (Eds.), *Metatheory in social science* (pp. 61–82). Chicago: University of Chicago Press.

Forehand, R., Furey, W.M., & McMahon, R.J. (1984). The role of maternal distress in a parent training program to modify child non-compliance. *Behavioural Psychotherapy, 12,* 93–108.

Gardner, F.E.M. (1987). Positive interaction between mothers and conduct-problem children: Is there training for harmony as well as fighting? *Journal of Abnormal Child Psychology, 15,* 283–293.

Gardner, F.E.M. (1989). Inconsistent parenting: Is there evidence for a link with children's conduct problems? *Journal of Abnormal Child Psychology, 17,* 223–233.

Gottman, J.M. (1979). *Marital interaction: Experimental investigations.* New York: Academic Press.

Gottman, J.M. (1983). How children become friends. *Monograph of the Society for Research in Child Development, 48*(3, Serial No. 201).

Gottman, J. (1991). Chaos and regulated change in families: A metaphor for the study of transitions. In P.A. Cowan, & M. Heatherington (Eds.), *Family transitions* (pp. 247–372). Hillsdale, NJ: Erlbaum.

Gottman, J.M., & Roy, A.K. (1990). *Sequential analysis: A guide to behavioral researchers.* New York: Cambridge University Press.

Granic, I., Dishion, T.J., Hollenstein, T., & Patterson, G.R. (in press). The family ecology of adolescence: A dynamic systems perspective on normative development. In G.R. Adams & M. Berzonsky (Eds.), *The Blackwell handbook of adolescence.* Oxford, England: Blackwell.

Granic, I., & Hollenstein, T. (in press). Dynamic systems methods for models of developmental psychopathology. *Development and Psychopathology.*

Granic, I., & Lamey, A.V. (2002). Combining dynamic systems and multivariate analyses to compare the mother-child interactions of externalizing subtypes. *Journal of Abnormal Child Psychology, 30,* 265–283.

Haynes, S.N., Nelson, K., & Blaine, D.D. (1999). Psychometric issues in assessment research. In P.C. Kendall, J.N. Butcher, & G.N. Holmbeck (Eds.), *Handbook of research methods in clinical psychology* (2nd ed., pp. 125–154). New York: Wiley.

Haynes, S.N., O'Brien, W. Hayes (2000). Principles and practice of behavioral assessment. Dordrecht, Netherlands: Kluwer.

Hoffman, L.W. (1991). The influence of family environment on personality: Accounting for sibling differences. *Psychological Bulletin, 110,* 187–203.

Hoffman, D.A., Fagot, B.I., Reid, J.R., & Patterson, G.R. (1987). Parents rate the family interaction coding system comparisons of problem and nonproblem boys using parent-derived behavior composites. *Behavior Assessment, 9,* 131–140.

Hogansen, J., & Dishion, T.J. (2001, June). *Promoting change in parent group interventions for adolescent problem behavior.* Poster presented at the 10th Scientific Meeting of the International Society for Research in Child and Adolescent Psychopathology, Vancouver, British Columbia, Canada.

Hollaway, E.L., & Wampole, B.E. (1983). Patterns of verbal behavior and judgements of satisfaction in the supervision interview. *Journal of Counseling Psychology, 30,* 227–234.

Hops, H., Davis, B., & Longoria, N. (1995). Methodological issues in direct observation: Illustrations with the LIFE coding system. *Journal of Clinical Child Psychology, 24*(2), 193–203.

Jacob, T., Tennenbaum, D., Seilhamer, R.A., Bargiel, K., & Sharon, T. (1994). Reactivity effects during naturalistic observation of distressed and nondistressed families. *Journal of Family Psychology, 8,* 354–363.

Johnson, S.M., & Bolstad, O.D. (1975). Reactivity to home observation: A comparison of audio recorded behavior with observers present or absent. *Journal of Applied Behavior Analysis, 8,* 181–185.

Johnson, S.M., & Christensen, A. (1975). Multiple criteria follow-up of behavior modification. *Journal of Abnormal Child Psychology, 3,* 135–154.

Johnson, S.M., & Lobitz, G.K. (1975). The personal and marital adjustment of parents as related to observed child deviance and parenting behaviors. *Journal of Abnormal Child Psychiatry, 2*(3), 192–207.

Jones, R.R., Reid, J.B., & Patterson, G.R. (1975). Naturalistic observations in clinical assessment. In P. McReynolds (Ed.), *Advances in psychological assessment* (Vol. 3, pp. 42–95). San Francisco: Jossey-Bass.

Kellam, S.G., Rebok, G.W., Ialongo, N., & Mayer, L.S. (1994). The course and malleability of aggressive behavior from early first grade into middle school: Results of a developmental epidemiologically-based preventive trial. *Journal of Child Psychology and Psychiatry, 35,* 259–281.

Kerig, P.K., & Lindahl, K.M. (Eds.). (2001). *Family observational coding systems: Resources for systemic research.* Mahwah, NJ: Erlbaum.

Leve, L.D., Winebarger, A.A., Fagot, B.I., Reid, J.B., & Goldsmith, H.H. (1998). Environmental and genetic variance in children's observed and reported maladaptive behavior. *Child Development, 69,* 1286–1298.

Lewin, L.N., Hops, H., Davis, B., & Dishion, T.J. (1993). Multimethod comparison of similarity in school adjustment of siblings in unrelated children. *Developmental Psychology, 29,* 963–969.

Lewis, M.D., Lamey, A.V., & Douglas, L. (1999). A new dynamic systems method for the analysis of early socioemotional development. *Developmental Science, 2,* 457–475.

Lewis, M.D., Zimmerman, S., Lamey, A.V., & Hollenstein, T. (in press). Dynamic systems analysis of a socioemotional transition in the middle of the second year. *Developmental Science.*

Miller, W.R., & Rollnick, S. (1991). *Motivational interviewing: Preparing people to change addictive behavior.* New York: Guilford Press.

Patterson, G.R. (1974a). A basis for identifying stimuli which control behaviors in natural settings. *Child Development, 45,* 900–911.

Patterson, G.R. (1974b). Interventions for boys with conduct problems: Multiple settings, treatments, and criteria. *Journal of Consulting and Clinical Psychology, 42,* 471–481.

Patterson, G.R. (1982). *Coercive family process.* Eugene, OR: Castalia Press.

Patterson, G.R. (1986). The contribution of siblings to training for fighting: A microsocial analysis. In D. Olweus, J. Block, & M. Radke-Yarrow (Eds.), *Development of antisocial and prosocial behavior* (pp. 235–261). New York: Academic Press.

Patterson, G.R., & Chamberlain, P. (1994). A functional analysis of resistance during parent training therapy. *Clinical Psychology: Science and Practice, 1,* 53–70.

Patterson, G.R., Chamberlain, P., & Reid, J.B. (1982). A comparative evaluation of parent training procedures. *Behavior Therapy, 13,* 638–650.

Patterson, G.R., Dishion, T.J., & Bank, L. (1984). Family interaction: A process model of deviancy training. *Aggressive Behavior, 10,* 253–267.

Patterson, G.R., Dishion, T.J., & Yoerger, K. (2000). Adolescent growth in new forms of problem behavior: Macro- and micro-peer dynamics. *Prevention Science, 1,* 3–13.

Patterson, G.R., & Forgatch, M.S. (1985). Therapist behavior as a determinant for client resistance: A paradox for the behavior modifier. *Journal of Consulting and Clinical Psychology, 53*(6), 846–851.

Patterson, G.R., Littman, R.A., & Bricker, W. (1967). Assertive behavior in children: A step toward a theory of aggression. *Monographs for the Research in Psychology and Child Development, 32,* 1–43.

Patterson, G.R., & Reid, J.B. (1984). Social interactional processes within the family: The study of moment-by-moment family transactions in which human development is embedded. *Journal of Applied Developmental Psychology, 5,* 237–262.

Patterson, G.R., Reid, J.B., & Dishion, T.J. (1992). *Antisocial boys.* Eugene, OR: Castalia Press.

Pepler, D.J., & Craig, W.M. (1995). A peek behind the fence: Naturalistic observations of aggressive children with remote audio-visual recording. *Developmental Psychology, 31,* 548–553.

Petit, G.S., & Bates, J.S. (1990). Describing family interaction patterns in early childhood: A "social events" perspective. *Journal of Applied Developmental Psychology, 11,* 395–418.

Plomin, R., & Daniels, D. (1987). Why are children in the same families so different from one another? *Behavioral and Brain Sciences, 10,* 1–60.

Poe, J., Dishion, T.J., Griesler, P., & Andrews, D.W. (1990). *Topic Code.* Unpublished coding manual. (Available from Child and Family Center, University of Oregon, 195 West 12th Avenue, Eugene, OR 97401-3408.)

Poulin, F., Dishion, T.J., & Burraston, B. (2001). 3-year iatrogenic effects associated with aggregating high-risk adolescents in preventive interventions. *Applied Developmental Science, 5,* 214–224.

Rao, S.A. (1998) *The short-term impact of the Family Check-Up: A brief motivational intervention for at-risk families.* Unpublished doctoral dissertation, University of Oregon, Eugene.

Raush, H.L. (1965). Interaction sequences. *Journal of Personality and Social Psychology, 2,* 487–499.

Reid, J.B. (1978). The development of specialized observation systems. In J.B. Reid (Ed.), *A social learning approach to family intervention: Vol. 2. Observation in home settings* (pp. 43–49). Eugene, OR: Castalia.

Reid, J. (1982). Observer training in naturalistic research. In D.P. Harmann (Ed.), *Using observers to study behavior: New methodologies of social and behavioral science* (No. 14). San Francisco: Jossey-Bass.

Robins, M.S., Alexander, J.F., Newell, R.N., & Turner, C.W. (1996). The immediate effect of reframing on client attitude and family therapy. *Journal of Family Psychology, 10,* 28–34.

Rusby, J., Estes, A., & Dishion, T. (1990). *School observations and Family Interaction Task: Interpersonal Process Code (IPC).* Unpublished coding system. (Available from Oregon Social Learning Center, 160 East 4th Avenue, Eugene, OR 97401-2426.)

Rutter, M. (1978). Family, area and school influences in the genesis of conduct disorders. In L.A. Hersov, M. Berger, & D. Schaffer (Eds.), Aggression and antisocial behavior in childhood and adolescence. *Journal of Child Psychology and Psychiatry, Book Series No. 1.* Oxford, UK: Pergamon. (pp. 95–111).

Ryan, K.D., Gottman, J.M., Murray, J.D., Carrere, S., & Swanson, C. (1999). Theoretical and mathematical modeling of marriage. In M.D. Lewis & I. Granic (Eds.), *Emotion, development and self-organization: Dynamic systems approaches to emotional development* (pp. 349–373). Cambridge, England: Cambridge University Press.

Sanders, M.R., & Lawton, J.M. (1993). Discussing assessment findings with families: A guided participation model of information transfer. *Child and Family Behavior Therapy, 15,* 5–33.

Shaw, D.S., Keenan, K., & Vondra, J.I. (1994). Developmental precursors of externalizing behavior: Ages 1 to 3. *Developmental Psychology, 30,* 355–364.

Shaw, D.S., Owens, E.B., Vondra, J.I., Keenan, K., & Winslow, E.B. (1996). Early risk factors and pathways in the development of early disruptive behavior problems. *Development & Psychopathology, 8,* 679–699.

Shaw, D.S., Winslow, E.B., & Flanagan, C. (1999). A prospective study of the effects of marital status and family relations on young children's adjustment among African American and European American families. *Child Development, 70,* 742–755.

Skinner, C.H., Dittmer, K.I., & Howell, L.A. (2000). Direct observation in school settings: Theoretical issues. In E.S. Shapiro & T.R. Kratochwill (Eds.), *Behavioural assessment in schools: Theory, research, and clinical foundations* (2nd ed., pp. 19–45). New York: Guilford Press.

Skinner, C.H., Rhymer, K.N., & McDaniel, E.C. (2000). Naturalistic direct observation in educational settings. In S.N. Elliott and J.C. Witt (Series Eds.) & E.S. Shapiro & T.R. Kratochwill (Vol. Eds.), *The Guilford school practitioner series: Conducting school-based assessments of child and adolescent behavior* (pp. 21–54). New York: Guilford Press.

Snyder, J., West, L., Stockemer, V., Givens, S., & Almquist-Parks, L. (1996). A social learning model of peer choice in the natural environment. *Journal of Applied Developmental Psychology, 17,* 215–237.

Stoolmiller, M. Duncan, T., Bank, L. & Patterson, G. (1993). Some problems and solutions in the study of change: Significant patterns of client resistance. *Journal of Consulting and Clinical Psychology, 61,* 920–928.

Stoolmiller, M., Eddy, J.M., & Reid, J.B. (2000). Detecting and describing preventative intervention effects in a universal school-based randomized trial targeting delinquent and violent behavior. *Journal of Consulting and Clinical Psychology, 68,* 296–306.

Walker, H.M. (1986). The assessments for integration into mainstream settings (AIMS) assessment system: Rationale, instruments, procedures, and outcomes. *Journal of Clinical Child Psychology, 15,* 55–63.

Walker, H.M., & Colvin, G., & Ramsey, E. (1993). *Antisocial behavior in school: Strategies and best practices.* New York: Brooks/Cole.

Weinrott, M., Bauske, B., & Patterson, G.R. (1979). Systematic replication of a social learning approach to parent training. In S.L. Bates, P.O. Sjoden, & W.S. Dockens, III (Eds.), *Trends in behavior therapy* (pp. 331–351). New York: Academic Press.

Weisz, J.R, Weiss, B., Han, S.S., Granger, D.A., & Morton, T. (1995). Effects of psychotherapy with children and adolescents revisited: A meta-analysis of treatment outcome studies. *Psychological Bulletin, 117,* 450–468.

Zeger, S.L. & Liang, K. (1986). Longitudinal data analysis for discrete and continuous outcomes. *Biometrics, 42,* 21–130.

CHAPTER 10

Analogue Behavioral Observation

RICHARD E. HEYMAN AND AMY M. SMITH SLEP

Analogue behavioral observation (ABO) involves a situation designed, manipulated, or constrained by an investigator (or clinician) that elicits a measured behavior of interest (i.e., dependent variable). Observed behaviors comprise both verbal and nonverbal emissions (e.g., motor actions, verbalized attributions, observable facial reactions).

There is probably no better introduction to ABO than through its most well-known variant: reality television. How reflective of "reality" is *Survivor*, where contestants are placed in a remote location and forced to vote one another out? Although more natural, MTV's *The Real World*—where people live together but are able to go to work and see others (albeit with a camera crew in tow the entire time)—is still manufactured (i.e., hand-picked young people placed in a wired group house). Like all ABOs, *The Real World* and its ilk are not the real world; they're an approximation of how real people behave when placed in situations that are only analogous to those in the real world.

A similar shadow world flickers across the video screens of research laboratories around the globe. Like their more popular entertainment cousin, research and clinical ABOs

place people in situations that replicate aspects of the real world; they do not, however, record behavior without constraints, without artificially imposed situations, or without participants knowing that they are being observed. Like reality television, ABO exists on a continuum of reality, ranging from highly contrived situations (e.g., how quickly do people walk down the hallway after being exposed to subconsciously presented words about aging? Bargh, Chen, & Burrows, 1996) to naturalistic situations arranged in unnatural ways or settings (e.g., how do couples talk with one another when told, in an observational laboratory, to discuss their top problem topic? Heyman, 2001) to naturalistic situations with some (but minimal) experimenter-dictated restrictions (e.g., Reid, 1978).

This chapter will provide a brief introduction to ABO, including methods, psychometric considerations, strengths, and weaknesses. We also will provide a clinical case study to elucidate how ABO principles can guide hypothesis-driven clinical assessment.

We plan to take a slightly different approach in our coverage of ABO than that of many of the other chapters in this volume. Whereas standard clinical psychology assessment often focuses on issues such as psychometrics, norms, and the application of measures to clinical populations, ABO is mainly a hypothesis testing tool. Although ABO can be highly useful for clinical assessment of functional relations

Note: Preparation of this chapter was supported by the National Institutes of Mental Health (Grant R01MH57779) and National Center for Injury Prevention and Control, Centers for Disease Control and Prevention (Grant R49CCR218554-01).

and treatment effects, we believe that it has far fewer "off-the-shelf" uses than many other types of assessment. We will discuss psychometrics, but our emphasis will be on how to capitalize, whether in basic research or in clinical assessment, on ABO's ability to illuminate important relations.

WHY USE ABO?

Although it might be obvious why television producers use ABO (i.e., high ratings and large returns on investment), it may be less obvious why scientists and clinicians use ABO and what the empirical and practical considerations are for its use.

As we will discuss in more detail below, ABO is used as a hypothesis-testing tool for three purposes: (a) to observe otherwise unobservable behaviors, (b) to isolate the determinants of behavior, and (c) to observe dynamic qualities of social interaction. Although naturalistic observation might be preferable (i.e., generalizability inferences are minimized), the first two purposes require controlled experimentation, necessitating ABO; for the third purpose, ABO is often preferable because it allows the observer to "stack the deck" to make it more likely that the behaviors (and/or functional relations) of interest will occur when the assessor can see them (Haynes, 2001).

Although ABO paradigms are not always practical for use by clinicians (Mash & Foster, 2001), clinicians can still be informed by the implications of basic ABO research (e.g., behavior can be automatically elicited from the environment with no cognitive mediation; Bargh, 1997) as well as find ways to adapt research-based ABO methods for practical clinical application (e.g., Heyman, 2001; Mash & Foster, 2001). Such an approach has been labeled by Haynes and O'Brien (2001, p. 89) as a "scholarly, empirical, hypothesis-testing approach to assessment."

DOMAINS

Although all ABO methods use constrained, artificially induced, or contrived situations that are in some way analogous to situations in the natural environment, "analogous" is a highly plastic concept. As noted above, the types of ABO used in translational research range from situations that are mostly controlled by the investigator (e.g., social psychology experiments with confederates) to those that are fairly naturalistic (e.g., laboratory-based marital conflicts). ABO comprises two main assessment domains: individual/situation interactions and social situations. The goals of individual/

situation interaction experiments are to manipulate the setting and test individual differences in response. (Think of *Candid Camera.*) This domain comprises an extremely wide variety of tasks in developmental psychology (e.g., strange situation experiments, Ainsworth, Blehar, Waters, & Wall, 1978; visual cliff experiments, Sorce, Emde, Campos, & Klinnert, 1985), social psychology (e.g., prosocial behavior experiments, Darley & Bateson, 1973; emotion regulation experiments, Tice, Bratslavsky, & Baumeister, 2001), and clinical psychology (e.g., functional analysis of self-injurious behavior, Iwata et al., 1994; social anxiety assessment, Norton & Hope, 2001).

The social situation domain employs ABO mostly as a convenience in assessing quasi-naturalistic interaction. The goal of such assessment is typically to understand behavior and its determinants in dynamic, reciprocally influenced systems (e.g., groups, families, couples). (Think of *Big Brother* or *The Real World.*) Understanding generalizable factors that promote or maintain problem behaviors in such systems typically requires more naturalistic approaches than those used in the other domain. Thus, although experimentation is often extremely useful in understanding causal relations in social situations (e.g., whether exciting activities improve couples' interactions, Aron, Norman, Aron, McKenna, & Heyman, 2000; whether maternal attributions affect mother-child interactions, Slep & O'Leary, 1998), most such ABO investigations aim for quasi-naturalism.

RESEARCH APPLICATIONS OF ANALOGUE BEHAVIORAL OBSERVATION TECHNIQUES

Examples of ABO appear in nearly all areas of the empirical psychology literature, addressing an enormous range of research questions and content areas. In the following section, we have chosen to highlight some of the important issues in selecting or designing ABO assessments by describing a variety of specific examples from the literature. We will highlight some of the types of questions that have been successfully addressed using ABO assessment methods and what made the analogues selected particularly appropriate assessment devices. Despite the enormous differences in situations, behaviors, and research questions apparent in the studies reviewed below, the design of each study reveals that the analogue situation was carefully constructed to answer the specific question.

Quasi-Naturalistic Observation

ABO is perhaps most typically used to assess behaviors hypothesized to differ naturally between groups of people (e.g., couples high and low in relationship satisfaction). One might wonder why, if the behaviors differ naturally, it is prudent to use ABO rather than naturalistic observations. ABO is used to focus the observation and to facilitate the sampling of behaviors that are of highest interest (e.g., verbally abusive comments). Often, naturalistic observation of clinically relevant behaviors would require so much observation that it would be untenable (e.g., avoidance behaviors make observation of anxiety-producing situations nearly impossible). Using ABO, the assessor can set up contexts likely to prompt the behavior of interest and can constrain the context enough to minimize unwanted, unstandardized influences. The large literatures describing marital and parent-child observation would most typically fall into this category of ABO (see Heyman, 2001; Roberts, 2001 for recent reviews).

For quasi-naturalistic ABO, the generalizability of ABO behavior to that in natural settings is of highest concern. The work of the Oregon Social Learning Center (OSLC) team is a model of how to design a scientific, clinically relevant quasi-naturalistic ABO paradigm. According to Patterson (1982), his group wanted to conduct naturalistic behavior observations but quickly learned that the natural world was not conducive to cost-effective science. Family members typically disappeared or sat transfixed in front of the TV when observers arrived. Out of necessity, eight rules were imposed on families during their in-home observation sessions. Although some of this work is also discussed in this volume by OSLC associate Dishion in his chapter (with Granic) on naturalistic observation, Patterson himself has noted that the rules transformed the natural environment into an analogue: "the rules that were being implemented for observations produced an unnatural situation" (p. 49; rules appear in Table 10.1).

OSLC developed its analogue paradigm through trial and error, guided by both the preexisting empirical literature and by its theoretical model. The center was organized to observe children's aversive and aggressive behaviors and their parents' responses to these behaviors (and to use these obser-

TABLE 10.1　Rules for Quasi-Naturalistic Family Observation Sessions

1. Everyone in the family must be present.
2. No guests.
3. The family is limited to two rooms.
4. The observers will wait only 10 minutes for all to be present in the two rooms.
5. Telephone: no calls out; briefly answer incoming calls.
6. No TV.
7. No talking to observers while they are coding.
8. Do not discuss anything with the observers that relates to your problems or the procedures you are using to deal with them.

Note. From Reid, 1978.

vations in the designing and testing of interventions). The dinner hour was chosen as the setting because earlier studies had identified the hours before lunch and dinner as the times when mothers reported the most conflict with their children (Goodenough, 1931). The coding system and observation task were designed hand-in-hand to increase the likelihood that the ABO would generate enough behavior for hypothesis testing. This iterative strategy produced a coding system that focused on the negative and positive behaviors of highest interest, maintained the sequence of behavior, and defined codes at a level that promoted interobserver agreement (Reid, 1978; Patterson, 1982). Next, they tested observer influences on the data to identify whether any adjustments to their protocol were indicated. For example, if data indicate that families need to habituate to observation, with more socially desirable behavior in early sessions, then warm-up sessions would be indicated—but the data did not support that hypothesis (Patterson, 1982). They examined the frequency of key behaviors and based the protocol's fixed number of observation sessions on how much observation over how many sessions were needed to get a stable index of the behaviors of interest. They found that that 60 to 100 minutes of data sampled in 5-minute blocks over the course of several sessions provided minimally stable estimates of boys' coercive behavior. Finally, by using observations in a multitrait, multimethod assessment strategy (e.g., parent reports, global observer impressions, and school or arrest data), OSLC provided evidence for the validity of the ABO paradigm and coding system.

Patterson and colleagues' efforts to investigate and refine the psychometric properties of their ABO techniques set the bar for how researchers interested in using ABO to assess naturally occurring and widely generalizable behavior patterns should approach ABO protocol and measure development. They carefully thought through their hypotheses, the behaviors they wanted to observe, the level of precision needed to detect the relations of interest, and the level of precision coders were capable of producing and maintaining. They then went about empirically determining how to collect reliable and valid observational data. No doubt their care regarding their ABO data is, in part, why their work on the etiology of conduct disorder has been so fruitful.

Isolating Determinants of Behavior

ABO also is used creatively to isolate determinants of behavior. ABO is far more amenable than naturalistic observation to testing hypotheses about specific relations because only in ABO can the assessor exercise the level of control necessary to identify causal relations. Typically, this application requires that people's behavior is observed in different analogue conditions. Manipulations can be surprisingly simple, such as studies that ask families to interact as they normally do in one condition and to "look good" or "look bad" in the other conditions (e.g., Lobitz & Johnson, 1975), with the instruction to look good serving to test hypotheses about demand characteristics.

ABO also can provide straightforward methods to isolate the relative importance of extremely complex situational influences on behavior, such as how much having a child with a conduct problem influences parenting. Anderson, Lytton, and Romney (1986) used a clever application of ABO to ask how mothers would parent if they had different children. Mothers and their conduct-disordered or non–conduct-disordered 6- to 11-year-old sons interacted in a series of three 15-minute structured observation sessions in the lab (5-minute clean-up, 5-minute free play, and 5-minute math problems). Mothers completed interactions with their own sons, with boys of the same diagnostic classification as their sons but who were not their own, and boys who were of the other diagnostic classification than their sons. By crossing interaction partners, researchers were able to separate parenting, disorder status, and "ownness." Rather than try to train a child to serve as a confederate and act conduct disordered or not (seemingly quite challenging), or asking mothers to verbally indicate how they would respond to different child behavior scenarios (probably dubiously valid), this simple switching allowed the natural behavior of the children to provide a very complex (but realistic) set of stimuli. It is difficult to imagine how naturalistic observation, self-report, or interview methods could have been used to address this research question as well or as easily as ABO methods did.

ABO To Observe Otherwise Unobservable Behaviors

Frequently, ABO is used to allow the researcher or clinician to observe something that otherwise would be impossible to observe (e.g., mothers' attributions for their children's misbehavior). Although not often discussed in ABO reviews (e.g., Haynes, 2001; Nay, 1986), experimental research represents a large proportion of ABO studies. This work comprises studies that (a) enlist the participant in carrying out the analogue as part of the experimental condition or (b) manipulate the situation or context without the conscious awareness of the participant. Analogue assessments in experiments are often designed around the experimental question rather than selected from more widely used analogue protocols and are quite frequently both clever and simple.

Manipulation of Persons

Some experimental studies manipulate the participant directly. For example, Leith and Baumeister (1996) were interested in whether people made riskier decisions when they were in bad moods. The investigators induced angry, anxious, sad, neutral, positive, and simple arousal states in a series of studies in the lab (to create analogues of naturally occurring mood states) by having participants watch videotapes, anticipate doing something embarrassing, recall emotion eliciting events, or exercise. ABO was then used to assess risk-taking behavior. Participants were asked to choose between two lotteries: one with a 70% chance of winning a $2 prize and one with a 4% chance of winning a $25 prize; losing either lottery meant participants would be subjected to listening to a 3-minute tape of the amplified sound of fingernails scratching across a blackboard. Participants' choice behavior was considered analogous to peoples' willingness to take risky chances more generally. Choosing among lottery alternatives is a particularly attractive and flexible analogue. Researchers can easily modify the size and odds of the payoff and the cost of losing. Either one or many parameters can differ among choices and differences can vary from small to large. Because participants actually chose, ABO was a more valid assessment of decision making than asking for responses to hypothetical situations would have been.

Manipulation of Situations

ABO is a useful tool in isolating situational influences on behavior. Often, the relations being investigated require both experimentation and behavioral observation to detect the hypothesized relations. For example, Cole, Zahn-Waxler, and Smith (1994) were interested in how sensitive preschool boys and girls with and without behavior problems were to social cues to suppress expression of negative emotion. To induce negative emotion in the children, they had each child rank order eight possible prizes (with items ranging from attractive [e.g., new toys] to unattractive [e.g., broken toys]) prior to a cognitive task. At the end of the task, the child was given the last choice prize by an experimenter, who then gathered papers for 1 minute and left the child alone for 1 minute. The child's emotionally expressive behavior was coded after the prize was awarded. The manipulation of the situation was the presence or absence of the experimenter, with the hypothesis being that socially skilled children would mask their disappointment while the experimenter was present, but express it when alone.

Turning Private Events Into Behavior

Finally, ABO of otherwise unobservable behavior typically involves asking participants to make usually private events (e.g., thoughts, feelings) public in the context of an analogue stimulus. One of us designed an ABO protocol to assess parents' thoughts about why children misbehave. In the first study (Smith & O'Leary, 1995), the analogue assessment strategy involved showing mothers videotaped scenes of child misbehavior. We then asked mothers to write their thoughts and respond to an attributional probe. Attributions were then coded for who was the locus of the cause and then were rated on several dimensions. This ABO method provided a valid assessment of child-centered, but not parent-centered, attributions. We designed a different protocol, this time assessing attributions to videos of their own, not actors', responses to child misbehavior. This second strategy seemed to produce adequately representative measures of both child-centered and mother-centered attributions (Slep & O'Leary, 1996, 1998). Should one conclude, however, that the second approach is superior? No. The second approach, by virtue of not employing the same stimuli for all participants, potentially confounds attributions and child behavior. Thus, both approaches have strengths and weaknesses that must be matched to the precise research question. In both cases, however, private events (attributions) were researchable via ABO.

Treatment Outcome Studies

Treatment outcome studies of disorders that include a behavioral facet (e.g., social phobia, attention deficit hyperactivity disorder) frequently include ABO in a multifaceted assessment of outcome. ABO allows researchers to set a standardized context within which to observe behavior for all participants before and after treatment. Actual behavior may be less sensitive to the subjective reporting biases and demand characteristics that can influence self-reports of outcome (e.g., a mother who enjoyed her parent training group might indicate that it had helped a great deal, but may interact with her son in nearly the same way she had prior to treatment). Further, basic research has revealed that for some disorders (e.g., anxiety), behavioral, affective, and physiological symptoms may be only modestly related, thereby necessitating assessment of behavior in evaluating treatment effects (Bradley & Lang, 2000).

For example, ABO is frequently useful in assessing behavioral avoidance in people with social anxiety disorders (e.g., Heimberg et al., 1990; Mattick, Peters, & Clarke, 1989). Typically, the assessor develops a hierarchy of anxiety-eliciting stimuli that the client reports avoiding. Avoidance, anxiety levels, and (sometimes) physiology are assessed during the hierarchy-derived ABOs at pre- and posttreatment. Several aspects of functioning can be incorporated in outcome operationalizations: avoidance, performance quality, reported subjective anxiety, observer-rated anxiety, and physiology. When multiple indices are assessed in the context of the

ABO, complex questions about predictors of differential patterns of treatment response can be addressed.

ABO is included far less often in treatment studies of disorders with less behavioral presentations (e.g., major depressive disorder) or disorders where the behavioral symptoms are less amenable to pre-post analogue observation (e.g., alcohol dependence). Nevertheless, ABO can still be employed to great advantage in these domains (e.g., Allen, Columbus, & Fertig, 1995; Persons, & Fresco, 1998; Rychtarik & McGillicuddy, 1998).

Clinical Assessment

ABO is an extremely useful tool in clinical assessment, although relatively few ABO paradigms have been developed specifically with this application in mind. To be clinically useful, ABO must efficiently provide reliable, valid, nonredundant (but cost-effective) information (Mash & Foster, 2001). Patterson and colleagues' assessment of parent-child aggressive interaction can clearly provide reliable and valid information about negative child behaviors and parent responses. However, to properly conduct these assessments, clinicians would need to be trained and reliable coders, and they would need to observe the family at home at dinner time at least three times (Patterson, 1982). Even before managed care constraints, few, if any, clinicians would go to such lengths in assessment.

An apt analogy for research-protocol based assessment versus field-realistic assessment might be found in the treatment literature. In recent years a distinction has evolved between efficacy studies (i.e., those studying interventions under tightly controlled, idealized circumstances, such as a trial of treatment for major depressive disorder that eliminates all potential participants with comorbid disorders) and effectiveness studies (i.e., those studying interventions under real-world conditions). Because we do not have an adequate research body of efficacy studies, clinicians in the field, urged to use empirically-validated treatments, are expected to adapt such protocols to meet real-world demands. Similarly, clinicians should be urged to use empirically-validated ABO when appropriate, but they should be expected to adapt ABO protocols in a cost-effective but still clinically informative manner. In the next section, we present a clinical case study that demonstrates how such adaptations can be made.

CLINICAL CASE STUDY

Behavioral Clinical Case Formulation

All therapeutic intervention involves an implicit or explicit model of what is causing or maintaining the presenting problems. Every clinician, with every client, must decide to intervene in some things and not others. This decision-making process typically is called *case formulation* or *case conceptualization* and is defined as "a general model . . . to understand problems and generate solutions to them, based on this understanding, in a coherent, systematic way" (Persons, 1989, p. xiii). Whether the assessment and case formulation process is formal and uses empirically supported models or is less formal, intervention is always founded on some approach to understanding dysfunction and preventing or ameliorating it.

A behaviorally focused case formulation can include a *functional analysis,* defined as "the ideographic assessment of an observable problematic target behavior and the observable antecedent and consequent environmental events deemed relevant to the target behavior. . . . Following such an assessment, treatment focus[es] on altering or rearranging the antecedent and consequent stimuli that elicited or reinforced the problematic behavior" (Mash & Hunsley, 1990, p. 90). Notice the focus on "observable" target, antecedent, and consequent behaviors. Such a focus fits naturally with ABO, because observing clients will almost always involve some structuring of situations or environments by the observing clinician.

In some settings, a high degree of precision can be obtained in manipulating or observing setting events and in observing antecedent and consequent behaviors (e.g., functional analysis of self-injurious behaviors—Carr, Robinson, & Palumbo, 1990; Durand, 1990). In many, if not most, clinical populations and settings, however, complete, content valid functional analyses are difficult (Haynes, 2001) or not cost-effective (Mash & Foster, 2001) to conduct.

The case study below is intended to exemplify the way we use ABO in clinical practice. We concur with Haynes and O'Brien (2000, p. 93) that "observations not only can provide strong evidence about functional relations and intervention effects, they can be a rich source of data for clinical hypotheses. . . . Although there are many sources of error in behavioral observation, observation is less susceptible to many errors and biases associated with self-report interviews and questionnaires." ABO allows the clinician to test initial hypotheses generated from the questionnaire and interview assessments; as will be seen below, ABO data often provide concrete evidence disconfirming or enriching the initial hypotheses.

Case Study

Joe and Allison, married seven years, presented for couples treatment following several years of increasing arguments. Joe was 40 years old and employed as a laborer. Allison, 38 years old, was a homemaker who cared for their four children

(ages 8, 5, 3½, and 1). Joe and Allison met at a local bar and dated for 9 months prior to Allison getting pregnant. They moved in together after the birth of their first child, and got married 9 months later.

During the intake session, Joe and Allison were interviewed separately and privately completed a packet of questionnaires. The questionnaires included a free-format question about presenting problems and several reliable and valid measures of the most important constructs in typical couples case conceptualizations: overall relationship satisfaction (Quality of Marriage Index [QMI], Norton, 1983); physical, sexual, and emotional aggression (the Revised Conflict Tactics Scale [CTS2], Straus, Hamby, Boney-McCoy, & Sugarman, 1996); degree and breadth of desired changes from partner (Areas of Change Questionnaire [ACQ], Weiss, Hops, & Patterson, 1973); and thoughts about/steps toward divorce (the Marital Status Inventory, Weiss & Cerreto, 1980).

The questionnaires indicated that both Joe and Allison were quite unhappy (Joe's QMI was 17, Allison's was 19; a clinical cut-off of 29 is equivalent to the Dyadic Adjustment Scale's [Spanier, 1976] widely used cutoff of 97; Heyman, Sayers, & Bellack, 1994). Both reported on the CTS2 that physical aggression had never occurred in this relationship, nor had severe emotional aggression. Both reported minor emotional aggression (e.g., yelling, stomping out of the room). Each spouse sought some change from the other, but the amount indicated by each on the ACQ was below the average for clinical couples (Margolin, Talovic, & Weinstein, 1983). Finally, each reported that he/she had thought about divorce and had discussed it with others, but neither reported pursuing separation or legal proceedings.

The individual interviews began with a structured clinical assessment of distress and abuse (Heyman, Feldbau-Kohn, Ehrensaft, Langhinrichsen-Rohling, & O'Leary, 2001) and of current substance abuse and dependence. This was followed by a discussion of top presenting problems. Converging with questionnaire reports, both spouses were diagnosed as maritally distressed but non-physically abusive. Joe indicated that he would have liked Allison to argue with him less, to discipline the children more, to have sex more often, to leave him more time to himself, and to show more appreciation for things that he does. Allison also wanted fewer arguments (specifically, fewer about money), for Joe to communicate his needs and feelings more clearly (and less angrily), and for them to do more fun things together as a couple. Both indicated that they found their family responsibilities (child care, housecleaning, shopping, car and house maintenance) exhausting, and that they no longer behaved or felt like a couple.

From these data, the initial clinical hypotheses could have easily generated a case conceptualization within the mainstream of marital therapy. First, this couple needs to increase their ratio of positive/supportive behaviors to negative behaviors (e.g., Gottman, 1994), perhaps through "Love Days" (e.g., Jacobson & Margolin, 1979), tracking exercises to counter selective attention (e.g., Baucom & Epstein, 1990), and communication skills training (e.g., Markman, Stanley, & Blumberg, 1994). Next, by failing to support and appreciate each other's hard work and sacrifices, they had allowed life to erode their satisfaction; exercises to increase support and understanding would be indicated (e.g., Perry & Weiss, 1986). Finally, because both spouses complained of frequent arguments, problem solving training would be useful (e.g., Jacobson & Margolin, 1979).

Although this case conceptualization would have been supported by the vast majority of couples therapists, the ABO (excerpted below) indicated that this formulation was incomplete and shallow. Neither the questionnaires nor the interviews indicated the functional relations of the reported conflict behaviors. Without ABO, it was difficult to get a handle on what went on during their conflicts, whether each person played a similar role in conflict initiation and escalation, and what was maintaining the conflicts, upsetting as they might be. ABO offered the opportunity to witness a sample of these relations.

We incorporate ABO routinely in our clinical practices when the presenting problem warrants it (e.g., marital problems, parent-teen conflicts, anxiety problems). In Joe and Allison's case, conflict was the primary presenting problem, so the ABO chosen was a marital conflict task. Had their presenting problem been difficulty supporting each other during infertility treatments, a social support task, rather than a conflict task, would have been more appropriate.

The ABOs were set up as follows. From the ACQ and the discussion of their top problem topics, a topic from each spouse was chosen. (Past research has shown that the sex of the complainant influences both spouses' observed behavior; Christensen & Heavey, 1990; Heavey, Layne, & Christensen, 1993.) Order was decided by the flip of a coin. Allison went first. With both spouses in the room, they were told that to get a better idea of what it looks like when they discuss problems, they would discuss each problem. Allison would bring up the first topic, they would discuss it for about 7 minutes, and then Joe would discuss his. After each conversation, Allison and Joe filled out a short questionnaire about the generalizability of the discussion (Foster, Caplan, & Howe, 1997). These procedures are an adaptation of our standard research protocol (see Table 10.2).

Allison's top problem topic was that she wanted Joe to communicate his needs and feelings more clearly. Allison started by outlining her request. When Joe asked her to be more specific, the following dialogue ensued:

Allison: Sometimes when you come home from work, I say do you want—

Joe: (interrupts) Is that after working 11 hours a day?

Allison: Well—

Joe: (interrupts) Being up since 5:00 in the morning? Is that when you're asking the question? When I come home from work?

Allison: But I'm not—

Joe: (interrupts) *or* when I'm sitting down relaxed? When is the question asked?

Allison: But I'm—

Joe: (interrupts) As soon as I walk in the door.

Joe's frequent interruptions are taking on the belligerent quality of a district attorney (cf. Gottman, 1995). Such behavior is associated with verbal and physical abuse (e.g., Jacobson et al., 1994) and is classified as psychological abuse in the Rapid Marital Interaction Coding System (Heyman & Vivian, 1997).

Allison: I might ask you a simple question, like do you want cheese on your hamburger, and you'll scream, "Who's thinking about food?"

Joe: Why would you ask a question when I always take cheese on my hamburger? Why would you ask something so stupid like that: (derisively) "Do you want cheese on your hamburger?"

Allison's calmly delivered problem description was followed by Joe's angrily delivered psychological abuse. This sequence is not typically found in nonabusive distressed couples.

Allison: I just wish that when you came home from work you'd just say, "I had a really rotten"—

Joe: (interrupts) I have a really rotten day every day. Then you'll come up and ask me a really stupid question to tick me off, like do I want cheese on my burger. If someone comes home from work and they're boiling already, why do you have to add fuel to the fire? Isn't it nice for you to just not say anything when I come home? But no, you want me to scream more, to express myself more. You want to hear more hollering and more screaming.

TABLE 10.2   Couples Conflict Discussion Procedures Used to Elicit "Best Versus Typical" and "Wife-Topic Versus Husband-Topic" Interactions

1. Order of Interactions
   a. Wife's topic: both "at their best"
   b. Wife's topic: typical interaction
   c. Husband's topic: typical interaction

2. Setup (prior to first interaction)
   a. Look at couple's Areas of Change Questionnaire (ACQ) ratings. Pick wife's top two areas of desired changed and the husband's top area. In cases of ties, use random number sheet to determine order. If both spouses pick the same topic, choose a different topic (i.e., three different topics must be selected).
   b. If husband's top topic is the same as one of the wife's top two topics, pick another one of equal value for him.
      i. If there are no topics of equal value, see if the wife has a third topic that is tied with the topic in question.
      ii. If the wife has no tied topic, pick the husband's next highest topic as his topic.

3. First Interaction (wife's topic, "at their best" instructions)
   a. Initial instructions (given to spouses in separate rooms)
      i. To wife, begin with, "You wrote that you'd like to see your husband [ACQ topic] . . ."
      ii. To husband, begin with, "Your wife wrote that she'd like to see you [ACQ topic] . . ."
      iii. "We'd like you to have a conversation with [name] about that topic for 10 minutes and try to get somewhere with it. In this conversation, we'd like you to communicate as you do at your best. By that, I mean, when you think you're handling things as well as you possibly can. I want you to think for a moment about the things you do during a discussion that help it go well, so you can keep those in mind during the interaction here. [pause] Okay, now I want you to think to yourself about the things that sometimes go wrong during your discussions and think of some strategies you could use to help keep things on the right track. Okay, we're just about ready. The last thing is to make sure that you know how you will start. Think to yourself about what you would do if you were to do the best job of bringing up [ACQ topic] at home. Do you know how you would start?" [Check to make sure that they have some way to start and that they understand what "best" means.]
   b. Bring both spouses into video studio, clip on lavaliere microphones, and repeat instructions: "We'd like you to have a conversation about [topic] for 10 minutes and try to get somewhere with it. [Wife's name] will start the conversation. Remember, in this conversation, we'd like you to communicate as you do at your best. By that, I mean, when you think you're handling things as well as you possibly can. You can start when I leave the room. Do you have any questions before we begin?"

4. Second and Third Interactions
   a. Say, "The next interaction will be the two of you talking just like you normally do at home."
   b. To the person with topic, begin with, "You wrote that you would like to see your spouse [ACQ topic] . . ."
   c. To partner, begin with, "Your partner wrote that he/she would like to see you [ACQ topic] . . ."
   d. To both, "We'd like you to have a conversation with [name] about that topic for 10 minutes and try to get somewhere with it. We'd like to see you demonstrate how you typically discuss problems when you are at home. We've already seen what it's like when you're at your best, and this time we'd like to see what it's like when you're *not* at your best, but you're just being yourselves. Remember, for this discussion, just try to discuss the problem like you might normally do at home."

Note. From NIMH grant MH57779, "Anger Escalation and De-Escalation in Aggressive Men," Principal Investigators Richard E. Heyman and Amy M. Smith Slep.

Allison: No.

Joe: That's what you love. You love more screaming and hollering. When someone has a bad day, you should just leave them alone, [bitterly sarcastic] but nooooooo, you want to hear more and more. You get me going, like you're doing right now. You're getting me going. [glares]

Allison's calmly delivered problem solution was followed by Joe's blaming her for his abusive behavior. This is now the second time that Joe has gotten angrier following Allison's apparent attempts at soothing and de-escalating Joe.

Allison: I don't know what to say to you. I want you to talk about what's really bothering you, not—

Joe: (interrupts) You've already heard that a million times. My job. What I am and what I've become, and how I cannot provide for the family. Why do you need to hear that over and over and over? Do you think that I'm happy every day going to work? No, but it pays the bills. So I'm a miserable type person, so don't ask me the same stupid questions over and over.

They then spend less than a minute discussing whether he could get training for a different job.

Allison: I don't know. I just feel like we have to make things a little bit better.

Joe: I don't see any problems. I'm the same as when you met me. You're the one who fell in love with me, you're the one that wanted all this. So you got everything that you wanted, and now you're complaining? Now you're complaining?

Allison: You keep—

Joe: (interrupts) I've always been this way and I will always be this way. This is me.

Allison: You say that—

Joe: (interrupts) There are a million other guys out there that you could have married, but you met me, and you got what *you* wanted, and now you're complaining. I'm the same guy.

Allison: (quietly) No you're not.

Joe: Maybe I'm not the same, because when I first met you, we didn't have a house full of kids, we didn't have a mortgage, we didn't have two cars to pay for, we didn't have all these bills, all the medical problems, we didn't have anything. So yeah, I was a young guy, and I didn't have problems, so yeah, [bitterly] I was different back then, yes. I had a little apartment to rent, I was very happy, and now, now, you expect me to be the same guy as nine years ago?

Allison: I—

Joe: (interrupts) Nine years ago? You expect me to be the same person? (Very sarcastically, waving hands) Sorry, those newlywed days are long gone. This is reality.

Joe's version of what reality is shifts dramatically from "I don't see any problems" to his last statement. Such rapidly shifting definitions of reality could qualify as "gaslighting" (e.g., Heyman & Vivian, 1997), named after the 1944 Ingrid Bergman–Charles Boyer movie in which a husband tries to drive a wife crazy by making her doubt her grasp on reality.

Allison: But you're so nasty.

Joe: I'm so nasty?

Allison: You are.

Joe: Why do you continue to stay with me then? I've always asked you that. If I'm so nasty and so abusive, then why are you still with me?

Allison: Because—

Joe: (interrupts) [Belligerently, challengingly] Break yourself free.

Because expressed anger was so salient in this interaction, each spouse was asked to rate their experienced anger on a scale from 0 (completely calm) to 100 (the angriest they've ever been). Although Allison had behaved calmly, and Joe apoplectic, during most of the interaction, she rated her anger during the conversation at 100; he rated his at 50.

Both spouses reported on the post-ABO questionnaire that this conversation was highly generalizable to their typical discussions. During the second ABO (husband's topic), behaviors and sequences were similar, indicating that neither the topic nor the sex of the person whose topic was being discussed were prime environmental factors in eliciting behaviors.

Although both spouses' questionnaires and interviews implied "garden variety" marital problems, the ABO provided data leading to a very different case conceptualization and treatment plan. First, although no psychological abuse was reported, the ABO revealed that it was common and would likely interfere with the potential interventions discussed above. Because space limits a full discussion of the case formulation and treatment plan, we will present only the portion that affected the plan for the first several sessions: (a) Given the detrimental physical and psychological impact of psychological abuse (e.g., Marshall, 1999), and the power imbalance that it creates and maintains, Joe's psychological abuse would be the prime target behavior to reduce; (b) Joe's hostility and belligerence appear to be overlearned (i.e., minor cues activate immediate, high intensity hostile behavior; Bandura, 1986; Lazarus, 1991), indicating that habit reversal training that breaks the cue-response connection (e.g., Azrin & Nunn, 1973, Foa, Steketee, Grayson, Turner, & Latimer, 1984) would perhaps be more fruitful than dyadic couple interventions; and (c) Because Joe's hostile, abusive behavior likely prevented Allison from expressing her experienced anger, individual work with her on increasing assertive (but not aggressive) behavior would likely be a necessary complement to decreasing Joe's expressed anger. The plan for the first phase of treatment involved separate sessions (e.g., Halford, Sanders, & Behrens, 1994) for approximately one month, with at-home tracking of the antecedents and setting events for angry confrontations assessing progress and an in-session ABO assessing mastery before moving on to additional interventions.

ABO DATA COLLECTION PARADIGMS

As discussed above, it is unrealistic to suggest a straightforward application of many of the more commonly used ABO paradigms in clinical settings. However, that does not suggest that modified versions of some of the paradigms used in research would not be clinically valuable. One of the strengths of ABO is its usefulness in allowing clinicians, as well as researchers, to evaluate hypotheses. Unlike in research applications, however, clinicians are evaluating case-specific hypotheses, and thus do not need to use a standard, off-the-shelf ABO paradigm with every child, adult, or couple who walks into his or her office. In the following section, we take as a starting point some well-developed and validated ABO paradigms, provide references for more details about how they are typically implemented, and go on to discuss how to begin thinking through how to modify standard paradigms when they are not sufficient to isolate the clinical question at hand.

Child Paradigms

The Strange Situation

The Strange Situation is perhaps the most widely investigated and validated ABO paradigms designed for children. It was developed by Ainsworth and colleagues (Ainsworth, Blehar, Waters, & Wall, 1978) and was designed to assess infants' attachment style vis-à-vis their primary caregivers. It consists of eight episodes (described in Table 10.3), during which children's behavior is coded, and then the coding is scored to classify children as securely or insecurely attached (i.e., anxious/ambivalent, avoidant, disorganized). Infants' coded attachment styles based on Strange Situations have been a staple in the developmental literature, and at least one study found that attachment in infancy (assessed with the Strange Situation) predicted interview measures of adult attachment more than 20 years later (Waters, Merrick, Treboux, Crowell, & Albersheim, 2000).

However, unless clinicians are housed within a well-equipped and well-staffed agency that focuses on children likely to have attachment problems (e.g., maltreated children), conducting Strange Situations and coding and then scoring the interactions in the office likely exceeds the limits of practicality. Fortunately, many of the most important facets of the Strange Situation assessment are more amenable to use in typical clinical settings. Of note, attachment is not typically scored from the child's behavior during periods of separation (e.g., how upset the child gets when the mother leaves) or relative to the stranger (e.g., how outgoing the child is). Rather, attachment is indexed by how the child behaves during the reunions with his or her mother (e.g., how well the child attends to the mother's return, how much the child allows him- or herself to be comforted). Further, attachment must be assessed relative to someone the child should be attached to. If a child has not seen her biological father for a year, using a Strange Situation to assess her attachment to him would not make sense. Clinicians who are well informed about attachment theory and the general validity of the Strange Sit-

TABLE 10.3 Strange Situation Episodes

1. Parent and infant are introduced to the experimental room.
2. Parent and infant are alone. Parent does not participate while infant explores.
3. Stranger enters, converses with parent, then approaches infant. Parent leaves inconspicuously.
4. First separation episode: Stranger's behavior is geared to that of infant.
5. First reunion episode: Parent greets and interacts with infant, then leaves again.
6. Second separation episode: Infant is alone.
7. Continuation of second separation episode: Stranger enters and gears behavior to that of infant.
8. Second reunion episode: Parent enters, greets, and interacts with the infant; stranger leaves inconspicuously.

uation and have done some reading on coding attachment styles (e.g., Crowell & Feldman, 1991) can serve as both the stranger and the observer, asking the parent or caregiver to briefly leave the room. Further, other therapists or support staff can serve as strangers if the clinician wants to observe the infant's reactions to multiple caregivers (e.g., biological mother, foster mother). Once the clinician has begun working with a family, informal Strange Situations can be reenacted periodically to help gauge progress.

Parent-Child Interaction

ABO is particularly appealing to clinicians who work with children. Many treatment strategies include both the parent and the child (e.g., Mash & Barkley, 1998), which heightens the importance of all aspects of how the parent and child interact. Although children and parents may have difficulty conveying verbally the kind of detailed information that clinicians often need to develop treatment plans, most child disorders include behavioral symptoms that the clinician can observe directly via ABO. With children older than two, a variety of parent-child interactions ABO paradigms appear in the literature. Free play, more structured play, and compliance tasks are the most widely used ABO paradigms. Although not as standardized as the Strange Situation, these tasks all have been used extensively and their strengths and weaknesses for clinical applications well articulated (see Roberts, 2001).

What is perhaps more challenging for the clinician is selecting the most efficient parent-child interaction to set up. As with research applications, the structure of the ABO paradigm should be guided by the hypotheses (or the clinical conceptualization) of the problem. Is the child presenting specifically with externalizing problems or more generalized family dysfunction? Are the problems specific to a parent or a context (e.g., getting ready for school) or are they across settings? How old is the child? What are the likely maintaining influences? The answers to these questions will help guide the use of ABO. The older the child, the more the clinician needs to load the paradigm to make it likely the behaviors of interest will be observed and the longer the interaction will likely need to be. With a preschooler, nearly any limit is likely to be met with some testing. With a 7-year-old, a more complex situation with competing demands for the parent's attention and requirements for the child to not play computer games and instead complete challenging math problems may be necessary to elicit noncompliance and parental discipline strategies. Further, developmental norms need to be considered. That an 11-year-old boy and his mother are less easily immersed into engaging mutual free play than a 3-year-old boy and his mother may not be as meaningful as if it were peer rather than parent-child interaction. When observing a child with possible oppositional defiant disorder, clinicians want to see how the parent and child deal with a variety of situations, including "don't" demands (e.g., don't touch the computer, don't throw the blocks), "do" demands (e.g., clean up, finish the math problems), teaching situations, and interaction with no demands (e.g., free play). When observing a child with possible attention deficit hyperactivity disorder, teaching situations and situations that require a child to wait or deal with competing demands become even more central.

Carefully constructed ABO will reveal what kinds of situations the child is likely to have the most difficulty with, the parent's skill in setting up tasks to minimize their difficulty for the child (e.g., breaking down instructions rather than giving them all at once), the parent's skill in responding to child noncompliance and misbehavior, and the parent's functioning during potentially positive contexts (e.g., the parent's ability to enjoy the child's company, to pull for positive and enriching interactions). Generally, an entire session may revolve around ABO for older children, while less than a session may be required with younger children.

Peer Interaction

Although ABO of children's peer interactions has not been the norm in clinical settings, the utility of these paradigms in the research literature makes their clinical application appealing. Many child disorders have a peer or socialization component (e.g., peer rejection of aggressive children, social skills deficits in anxious children). Although no standardized ABO paradigms have been systematically investigated across a range of samples, two simple but clever ABO applications may be particularly amenable to clinical work.

The first is the peer interaction task developed by Dishion and colleagues (Dishion, Spracklen, Andrews, & Patterson,

TABLE 10.4   Peer Interaction Task

1. Plan an activity together (one they might do together during the next week).
2. Solve a problem related to getting along with parents, which had come up for the research participant during the previous month.
3. Solve a problem related to getting along with peers, which had come up for the research participant during the previous month.
4. Solve a problem related to getting along with parents, which had come up for the friend during the previous month.
5. Solve a problem related to getting along with parents, which had come up for the friend during the previous month.

1996; Patterson, Reid, & Dishion, 1992). They had their adolescent research participants bring a friend to the lab and asked the boys to talk for 25 minutes. The topics are listed in Table 10.4. The researchers observed what the boys talk about, whether the topic involves breaking the rules or other normative content, and whether these topics are ignored or elicit laughter from the friend. Imbedded in this paradigm is a simple notion: It may be difficult to observe boys engaging in antisocial behavior with their friends, but it's easier to see if boys enjoy and get attention for talking about antisocial behavior. Clinicians might find it useful to have preadolescent and adolescent clients bring in a friend and discuss topics similar to those used by Dishion and colleagues. Do they give each other attention for antisocial comments? Or depressive affect? Or talk of eating disordered behavior? This can help the clinician gauge the potential role of peers in maintaining the behaviors of interest.

The second peer interaction ABO paradigm is somewhat more challenging to bring into the office than asking clients to talk with their best friends, but for some clients it may be worth the additional effort. At times, it is difficult to determine how generalized a child's problematic behavior (e.g., aggression, anxiety) is. At times, it seems likely that problematic behavior is a function of a statistical interaction between the child and whomever he or she is interacting with. How much (a) the client, (b) the peer, and (c) the interaction each contribute to aggression, for example, is a difficult question from a methodological perspective. One powerful and appealing method that enables the quantification of each of these elements is the round robin design (Kenny, 1990; Lashley & Bond, 1997). In a round robin design, each child engages in an ABO task with every other child. Tasks used in this design typically fall on the more naturalistic end of the ABO continuum, but tasks like planning an activity together or making something together would all be amenable to ABO.

Although an ABO assessment this extensive might be untenable for some clinicians, settings where groups are common could support such a protocol. Applying this technique to the assessment of child or adult social anxiety might be particularly interesting. If clients/participants were instructed to introduce themselves and make small-talk for five minutes before moving on, the observing clinicians would be able to observe (depending on the size of the group and the variation among group members) how social proficiency varied as a function of the sex of the partner, their physical attractiveness, their outward status, the social adeptness of the partner, etc., all assessed in a single session. Similar scenarios can be imagined to assess determinants of children's aggression toward peers (see Coie et al., 1999, for an excellent application of this method to children's aggression). Clearly, clinicians would not employ the sophisticated analytic techniques used in research applications of this method. However, for problem behaviors that are likely not solely a function of the client, a round robin style ABO assessment might prove worth the necessary effort.

Adult Paradigms

Couples

The standard couples ABO paradigm can be used in either research or clinical assessment. In research contexts, investigators ask couples to discuss one or two conflict areas for 10 to 15 minutes each; in clinical contexts, about 5 to 7 minutes each is minimally sufficient (e.g., Gottman, 1999). Although in research contexts no one is in the room except for the partners, in clinical contexts the therapist usually instructs the couple to act as if she were not there, stays in the room, and takes notes about the communication process to provide feedback later (O'Leary, Heyman, & Jongsma, 1998). Within these general parameters is wide variability in exactly how the ABO conversations are structured. A typical protocol is presented in Table 10.2; other approaches range from a detailed "play-by-play" interview to narrow the discussion topic (Gottman, 1995) to providing a list of general topics from which top problem areas are selected, either by the investigator (e.g., Markman, Floyd, Stanley, & Storaasli, 1988) or the couple (e.g., Snyder & Wills, 1989), to standardized, role-played topics that may not relate to the couples' own problems (e.g., Olson & Ryder, 1970) to reenactment of prior conflicts (Margolin, Burman, & John, 1989). Nonconflict ABOs also have been developed, including assessments of social support (e.g., Pasch & Bradbury, 1998; Roberts & Linney, in press) and shared exciting activities (Aron et al., 2000).

The standard ABO paradigm appears to elicit reasonably generalizable (externally valid) behavior. First, behavioral frequencies in ABOs in home and laboratory settings are substantially similar, with laboratory interactions a bit less neg-

ative (Gottman, 1979; Gottman & Krokoff, 1989). Second, couples judge laboratory ABO behavior as typical of at-home behavior; when not acting typically, partners were far more likely to be judged as being more supportive and less undermining than usual (Foster et al., 1997). Third, spouses' self-consciousness and reactivity while being observed are relatively low (Christensen & Hazzard, 1983; Jacob, Tennenbaum, Seilhamer, Bargiel, & Sharon, 1994). Finally, although there are no empirical studies, it is our impression that reactivity in treatment-seeking couples' ABOs is lower than that of research-only couples; treatment couples appear to be motivated to let the therapist see just how bad things are and to unmask their partners. If this is true, then the ABO behavior of distressed couples in clinical ABO is even more negative and discernable than the literature on nontreatment participants would suggest. To summarize, even if typical interaction samples researchers have collected are not quite as negative as they are at home, they still reveal detectable differences in affect, behavior, physiology, and interactional patterns and processes (Gottman, 1979, 1994, 1999). (See the case study and Heyman, 2001, for discussion of how ABOs can be applied in clinical practice.)

Adult Social Behavior

For many adult disorders, social functioning deficits are either integral to the diagnosis (e.g., social phobia) or are primary associated symptoms (e.g., social withdrawal of people with major depressive disorder or schizophrenia). Depending on the presenting problems, nonstandardized ABO usage in clinical settings includes observing people with social phobia interact in groups, speak publicly, or eat in public; people with schizophrenia role-play making and refusing requests; and people with depression role-play assertiveness. Standardized ABO has been used widely to assess interpersonal behavioral domains such as assertiveness, interpersonal problem solving, and social skills. For example, the Behavioral Assertiveness Test-Revised (Eisler, Hersen, Miller, & Blanchard, 1975) comprises 32 situations for role-playing with confederates of both sexes. For content validity, the situations vary in both assertiveness skills required (e.g., requesting, praising, refusing, and complaining) and target of assertive behavior (e.g., close others, waiter). A situation vignette is first read to the client (to set the scene), after which a confederate emits a scripted behavior; the client's behavior is then coded. A much less structured ABO is the Social Skill Behavioral Assessment System (Caballo & Buela, 1988), an unscripted protocol to assess heterosocial interaction skills. Clients interact for 5 minutes with an unfamiliar partner of the opposite sex, with the instruction to "get to know each other." To increase standardization and to place more of the focus on the client, confederates "are trained to adhere to specific requirements, such as waiting 20 sec before initiating a conversation, and are told the frequency with which to look at the client or engage in socially reinforcing behaviors such as nodding or smiling" (Norton & Hope, 2001, p. 69). For a detailed review of social behavior ABOs, see Norton and Hope's (2001) recent summary, which includes extensive psychometric information and detailed descriptions of five standardized protocols.

OTHER ABO APPLICATIONS

Space limitations preclude a summary of the wide variety of ABO applications. We note, however, literatures on fear (e.g., McGlynn & Rose, 1998), self-injurious behavior in those with developmental disabilities (e.g., Iwata et al., 1994), the effect of alcohol consumption on family interaction (e.g., Leonard & Roberts, 1998), cooperation and competition (e.g., the prisoner's dilemma paradigm, Sheldon, 1999), and aggression (e.g., Bandura, 1986).

Psychometric Considerations

Traditionally, relatively little attention has been paid to evaluating the psychometric properties of ABO assessments. Issues such as stability and construct validity seem to garner more attention for paper-and-pencil measures (e.g., Child Behavior Checklist, Achenbach, 1991) and psychological tests (e.g., Wechsler Adult Intelligence Scales, Weschler, 1997). There seems to be the impression that whereas scales and tests measure something indirectly, making psychometrics of measures extremely important, ABO (along with all forms of observation) elicits real behavior. But ABO is also an indirect measure. The act of observing can change the behaviors of interest (i.e., reactivity). The paradigms used may not result in behavior that is perfectly representative of naturally occurring behavior. The coding systems filter the behavior observed, which can either strain out the nonessential information (highlighting the important behaviors and sequences) or can strain out indiscriminately (leaving the observer with little useful information). Thus, understanding the psychometrics of ABO assessment is critically important to both researchers and clinicians.

Haynes and O'Brien (2000) provide an extremely useful framework within which to consider the psychometrics of ABO: "Each psychometric evaluative dimension, such as temporal stability, is differentially useful for estimating the validity of obtained measures, depending on the goals of as-

sessment, the assessment settings, the methods of assessment, the characteristics of the measured variable, and the inferences that are to be drawn from the obtained measures." (p. 201). Thus, ABO paradigms and their accompanying coding systems are not reliable or unreliable, valid or invalid, or useful or useless. Rather, the reliability, validity, and utility of an ABO paradigm are conditional. They depend on not only properties of the particular paradigm, but also on whose behavior is being observed for what purpose and in the context of what other measures. Psychometrics are conditional because each component of an ABO protocol (e.g., participant instructions, setting characteristics, interval duration, coding system) is a source of variance that may affect the observed results. This caution applies to all assessment measures, not just ABO; however, with ABO it is especially important to remember that psychometric soundness "is inferred from the cumulative results regarding *what* measure, administered *when*, is an accurate measure of *this* construct with *that* population and under *which* set of circumstances" (Heyman, 2001, p. 24).

Validity

Validity refers to how precisely and accurately a tool measures what it is supposed to measure. Many specific types of validity are evaluated and discussed in the literature (see Haynes & O'Brien, 2000). Of particular relevance to ABO are construct validity (the extent to which the tool measures the construct of interest and not other, perhaps related, constructs), discriminative validity (the extent to which the tool sensitively discriminates individuals known to differ on a particular construct), predictive validity (the extent to which the measure accurately predicts future behavior), and external validity (the extent to which the behavior observed with a particular ABO measure is generalizable to real world behavior).

The validity of ABO paradigms and coding systems has received little direct attention. This is because an ABO paradigm itself is difficult to validate except for face validity (does this tool appear to measure what it is intended to measure?) and, to some extent, external validity (e.g., do participants rate their behavior as representative of their real world behavior? See Foster et al., 1997).

Instead, the validity of the ABO paradigms is implied by the coded results of studies using that paradigm. Coding of coercive interchanges between parents and children relates to arrest when the children reach adolescence (Patterson, Reid, & Dishion, 1992). This finding speaks to not only the substantive content, but also to the psychometric properties of the ABO paradigm and coding system used in the initial assessments. Most potential clinical users of ABO technology would be better served by evaluating what the substantive ABO research findings imply about that protocol than by seeking out literature that specifically addresses the psychometrics of an ABO paradigm or coding system per se. Papers focusing on the psychometric properties of ABO paradigms and coding systems are relatively rare, in part because of the conditional nature of psychometrics. The recent special section on ABO in the February 2001 issue of *Psychological Assessment* and the occasional book or chapter are exceptions.

Clinical Utility

Clinical utility refers to the extent to which a tool contributes to treatment. This is a deceptively simple description of a multifaceted judgment. Subsumed under clinical utility are subdimensions (Haynes & O'Brien, 2000): treatment utility (Does it have direct implications for treatment planning, process, or outcome?), incremental utility (Does it meaningfully add to the information provided by other aspects of the assessment?), sensitivity to change (Can it detect small but clinically important changes in functioning?), cost-effectiveness (Given the time and other resources necessary to conduct this assessment, will the information it provides be worth it?), and user-friendliness (Given the amount of time and other resources for the assessor to become competent with a particular assessment, will the information it could provide across his or her research career/client base be worth it?). Clearly, ABO paradigms can be relatively high on some dimensions (e.g., Patterson and colleagues' assessments of parent-child interaction are high in treatment and incremental utility) while being relatively low on other dimensions (e.g., one could argue that they are not particularly cost effective or user-friendly). The challenge is achieving the optimal balance of all dimensions. Modifying Patterson and colleagues' parent-child ABO paradigm such that it became extremely cost-efficient and user-friendly (e.g., watch the parent and child interact for a few minutes in the waiting area prior to their appointment) would likely render the resulting information far less useful.

CODING AND ANALYZING OBSERVED BEHAVIOR

Coding

As implied in previous sections, the very richness of ABO makes it an extraordinarily useful research tool and an extraordinarily neglected clinical assessment tool in the real world. Although questionnaires and structured interviews can be administered and scored in a standardized, quick, and inexpensive fashion, ABO's products are not scores but behav-

ior, the stuff of life itself. Whereas entertainment ABOs are an end in themselves, scientific (including clinical) ABOs must involve deriving meaning from the behavior stream. For there to be any distinction between the former and latter forms of ABO, the latter should be replicable (i.e., reliable; the behavior observed should reveal information about the clients, not about extraneous factors such as situational behavioral instability or disagreement across judges) and should tell us something valuable about the clients (i.e., be valid).

Deriving meaning from the behavior stream requires coding the behavior. Coding of many ABO target behaviors is difficult to do in a reliable, valid, and cost-effective manner. This exposes the "ABO: useful/cost-defective" dialectic (see Mash & Foster, 2001, for a thoughtful discussion of the opposing tensions and suggestions for clinical applications). In this section we will briefly touch on ABO coding issues. Interested readers should consult several excellent resources for more complete coverage (e.g., Bakeman & Gottman, 1997; Haynes & O'Brien, 2000; Mash & Foster, 2001).

Although we have described ABO as a hypothesis testing tool, in reality it is a set of hypothesis testing tools (i.e., setting, instructions, temporal manipulations, coding). Whereas the other tools involve structuring the observation, coding is perhaps the most important factor in using ABO to test hypotheses. Along these lines, Bakeman and Gottman (1997, p. 16) have emphasized that the creation or use of a coding system is a theoretical act: "There are an infinite number of behaviors that [can] be coded. Without the focus provided by a clear question, it is hard to know just where to look and it is very easy to be overwhelmed." This is equally important in either designing or using coding systems. Why are you observing? What do you hope to learn? How will it impact your hypotheses (i.e., either research questions or case conceptualization questions)?

Concrete Observation Versus Social Informant–Inferred Coding

Some behaviors are so concrete that the observer serves more as a recorder than a coder. For example, did the child touch the forbidden toys in a compliance task? Did the client make eye contact in the assertiveness task? How much time elapsed before the male client spoke to the unfamiliar female confederate in the social conversation task? Other behaviors require at least some degree of inference. For example, in the case study above we used established coding systems to label the husband's behavior as hostile, belligerent, or psychologically abusive. Such coding necessitates the use of culturally sensitive raters, using specified decision rules, to infer that a combination of situational, linguistic, paralinguistic, or contextual cues amounts to a codeable behavior. If concrete coding tends to be simpler, cheaper, and more reliable, why would one ever use social informant–inferred coding? Because "[w]e may not be interested in a description such as the following: 'At 5:19, the husband lowered his brows, compressed his lips, lowered the pitch of his voice, disagreed with his wife, while folding his arms in the akimbo position.' Instead, we may simply wish to describe the husband as angry" (Bakeman & Gottman (1997, p. 23).

Thus, concrete codes are not necessarily better than social informant–inferred codes; sometimes one allows for a more valid measurement of a construct, sometimes the other does. In accord with Occam's razor, coding should be as simple as possible to reliably capture the behavioral constructs of interest. One need not code a child as "inattentive" if the construct of interest is the frequency or duration of his getting out of his chair without permission. On the other hand, as long as interrater agreement can be established, coding "anger" in Bakeman and Gottman's example may more parsimoniously record the emotion than coding each of the cues that are imperfectly associated with anger.

Sampling Strategies

Regardless of whether concrete or social-informant coding is used, ABO coding data must be recorded (sampled) in a format that facilitates analysis. The major sampling strategies are event sampling (the occurrence of behavior is coded, ideally in sequential fashion), duration sampling (the length of each behavior is recorded), interval sampling (the ABO period is divided into time blocks; during each time block, the occurrence of each code is noted), and time sampling (intermittent observations are made, typically in a duration or interval sampling manner). Advantages and disadvantages of each sampling strategy are discussed in Bakeman and Gottman (1997) and Haynes and O'Brien (2000). With each strategy, quality of data issues (e.g., retaining the sequential unfolding of events, reliability, validity) must be weighed against practical issues (e.g., expense, time, availability or practicality of recording devices, difficulty obtaining reliability).

Molar Versus Molecular Units

Global (i.e., molar) coding systems (e.g., Rapid Couples Interaction Scoring System; Krokoff, Gottman, & Haas, 1989) make summary ratings for each code over the entire ABO (or across large time intervals). Codes tend to be few, representing behavioral classes (e.g., negativity). Microbehavioral (i.e., molecular) systems code behavior as it unfolds over time and tend to have many fine-grained behavioral codes (e.g., eye contact, criticize, whine). Despite their specificity, the large number of codes in many microbehavioral systems (e.g., 30 to 40) frequently make them not only impractical in clinical settings, but also inefficient in research settings. This is because (a) coders can almost never get or maintain adequate interrater agreement on such a large number of codes, and (b) the codes occur too infrequently in ABO to make them all useful even if they were reliably coded. Thus, researchers resort to grouping codes, often boiling down a 40-code system into positive, negative, and neutral classes (see review in Heyman, 2001).

Global systems are simpler and faster, and can sometimes represent the construct of interest better (e.g., an overarching construct such as overreactive parenting may be better coded with a global code, where context can better be taken into account, than with microbehavioral coding). However, adequate reliability can sometimes be difficult to obtain due to the lack of anchoring of ratings to specific behaviors and coders' heuristic biases activated by being asked to produce summary scores (Weiss, 1989). Further, global coding systems do not maintain sequential relations, making them less useful for functional analytic purposes. Microbehavioral systems are more complicated and more expensive to use, but may be more appropriate for producing frequencies or sequential relations. The rules of thumb above are necessarily crude, due to the conditional nature of reliability and validity; the optimal choice of coding system depends on a host of factors, from the goals of the assessment to the research question to the ABO protocol used to the skillfulness of the coders.

Topographical Versus Dimensional Scales

Topographical coding systems measure the occurrence of a behavior in a binary fashion (i.e., occurred/didn't occur). Such systems also can incorporate duration of behaviors that occurred. Dimensional coding systems measure the intensity of the behavior in a continuous fashion. Microbehavioral systems tend to be topographical; although global systems tend to use rating scales, they typically summarize frequency rather than intensity. Dimensional coding of intensity, especially on a point-by-point basis, rarely has been used in ABO. Because many models have implicit or explicit intensity × time predictions (e.g., Patterson's [1982] Coercive Family Process model posits that reinforcement of escalating negativity contributes to the development of antisocial behavior in boys), the overreliance on topographical systems is unfortunate. Informal coding by clinicians using ABO typically involves dimensionality (e.g., escalating anger or anxiety intensity);

we hope that research-oriented coding will find ways to take more advantage of it.

Summary

In clinical practice, no formal systems—global or micro-behavioral, topographical or dimensional—are practical to use in many contexts. Extracting meaning from clinical ABOs is frequently closer to global coding; however, as Haynes and O'Brien (2000) point out, knowledge of formal systems, their validity, and their findings can still be extremely useful when conducting any assessment (including ABO) in clinical practice.

Analyses

Analytic strategies will depend on the questions being asked and the format of the data being collected. Thus, a detailed discussion of analytic strategies is beyond the scope of this chapter. An excellent primer on both idiographic and functional analytic approaches can be found in Haynes and O'Brien (2000). However, we will briefly touch on several analytic strategies used.

ABO frequently uses single-subject multiple-baseline designs. Analyses are typically conducted by plotting the data and visually inspecting it for trends (Kazdin, Hayes, Henry, Schacht, & Strupp, 1992). Haynes and O'Brien (2000, pp. 252–253) summarized the pros and cons of this approach: "The primary strengths associated with this method are that it requires modest investment of time and effort on the part of the clinician, it is heuristic—it can promote hypothesis generation, and it is well suited for evaluating complex patterns of data. . . . The validity of intuitive evaluation procedures, however, can be problematic. This is particularly true when the assessor attempts to intuitively estimate co-variation between target behavior and causal variables [and when] multiple behaviors, multiple causes, and multiple interactions [are] evaluated."

When combining data across subjects in research settings, statistical analysis of ABO data uses standard statistical tools. Between-groups hypotheses about behavioral frequencies are tested with analysis of variance, whereas continuous association hypotheses are tested with correlations or regressions. Such tools are widely understood by consumers of research journals and can be used to answer nomothetic research questions. However, in clinical practice, questions tend to be idiographic; furthermore, the expense of collecting samples large enough to warrant such analyses and the time required to manage and analyze large data sets make them impractical for use in most clinical settings.

When functional relations are of interest, testing how interactions unfold over time becomes important (see Bakeman & Gottman, 1997 for an excellent introduction to methods and analyses). Functional relation hypotheses can be addressed with conditional probabilities (see Haynes & O'Brien, 2000) or with sequential analysis, which is similar to conditional probability analysis but which allows for significance testing (e.g., Gottman & Roy, 1990). Dimensional data assessed continuously would use time-series analysis (e.g., Gottman, 1981) instead of sequential analysis.

CONCLUSIONS

Kurt Lewin (1951) wrote that there is "nothing so practical as a good theory" (p. 169); clinical case conceptualization is essentially theory building about the functional relations causing or maintaining the problems of a presenting person or family. Because ABO excels at both the identification of problem behaviors worth theorizing about and the testing of the accuracy of functional theories of what is causing the problem behaviors (e.g., Haynes & O'Brien, 2000), one could also add that there's nothing so practical as a good theory testing tool.

ABO can be a good theory testing tool because (depending on exactly how it is employed), it minimizes inferences needed to assess behavior, it can facilitate formal or informal functional analysis, it can provide the assessor with experimental control of situational factors (thus helping to isolate the determinants of behavior), it can facilitate the observation of otherwise unobservable behaviors, and it can provide an additional mode of assessment in a multimodal strategy (e.g., questionnaires, interviews, observation). Finally, because the assessor can set up a situation that increases the probability that behaviors of interest will occur during the observation period, ABO can be high in clinical utility and research efficiency.

Like any tool, however, ABO's usefulness depends on its match to the resources and needs of the person considering using it. ABO can be a time-consuming, labor-intensive, and expensive assessment strategy; the use of research-tested protocols/coding is often impractical in clinical settings; adaptations of empirically supported ABO methodology in clinical settings may render them unreliable and of dubious validity; the conditional nature of validity may make it difficult to generalize ABOs to the broad variety of real world settings; and, finally, the less naturalistic the ABO situation, the more nagging the concerns about external validity.

We believe that in many research and clinical situations, ABO is indeed a practical, theory-testing tool. Although not as easy to use as questionnaires, as exemplified in our clinical case study, ABO can often provide important, nonredundant information for researchers and clinicians alike.

REFERENCES

Achenbach, T.M. (1991). *Manual for the child behavior checklist/ 4–18 and 1991 profile.* Burlington: University of Vermont, Department of Psychiatry.

Ainsworth, M.D.S., Blehar, M.C., Waters, E., & Wall, S. (Eds.). (1978). *Patterns of attachment: A psychological study of the strange situation.* Hillsdale, NJ: Erlbaum.

Allen, J.P., Columbus, M., & Fertig, J.B. (1995). Assessment in alcoholism treatment: An overview. In J.P. Allen & M. Columbus (Eds.), *Assessing alcohol problems: A guide for clinicians and researchers* (NIAAA treatment handbook series 4, pp. 1–15). Bethesda, MD: National Institute on Alcohol Abuse and Alcoholism.

Anderson, K.E., Lytton, H., & Romney, D.M. (1986). Mothers' interactions with normal and conduct-disordered boys: Who affects whom? *Developmental Psychology, 22,* 604–609.

Aron, A., Norman, C., Aron, E., McKenna, C., & Heyman, R.E. (2000). Couples' shared anticipation in novel and arousing activities and experienced relationship quality. *Journal of Personality and Social Psychology, 78,* 273–284.

Azrin, N.H., & Nunn, R.G. (1973). Habit reversal: A method of eliminating nervous habits and tics. *Behaviour Research and Therapy, 11,* 619–628.

Bakeman, R., & Gottman, J.M. (1997). *Observing interaction: An introduction to sequential analysis* (2nd ed.). New York: Cambridge University Press.

Bandura, A. (1986). *Social foundations of thought and action: A social cognitive theory.* Englewood Cliffs, NJ: Prentice-Hall.

Bargh, J.A. (1997). The automaticity of everyday life. In R.S. Wyer (Ed), *The automaticity of everyday life: Advances in social cognition, Vol. 10.* (pp. 1–61). Hillsdale, NJ: Erlbaum.

Bargh, J.A., Chen, M., Burrows, L. (1996). Automaticity of social behavior: Direct effects of trait construct and stereotype activation on action. *Journal of Personality and Social Psychology, 71,* 230–244.

Baucom, D.H., & Epstein, N. (1990). *Cognitive behavioral marital therapy.* New York: Brunner/Mazel.

Bradley, M.M., & Lang, P.J. (2000). Measuring emotion. Behavior, feeling, and physiology. In R.D. Lane & L. Nadel (Eds.), *Cognitive neuroscience of emotion.* Series in affective science. Oxford, England: Oxford University Press.

Caballo, V.E., & Buela, G. (1988). Molar/molecular assessment in an analogue situation: Relationships among several measurements and validation of a behavioral assessment instrument. *Perceptual and Motor Skills, 67,* 591–602.

Carr, E.G., Robinson, S., & Palumbo, L.R. (1990). The wrong issue: Aversive versus nonaversive treatment; The right issue: Functional versus nonfunctional treatment. In A.C. Repp & S. Nirbhay (Eds.), *Perspectives on the use of nonaversive and aversive interventions for persons with developmental disabilities* (pp. 361–379). Sycamore, IL: Sycamore Publishing.

Christensen, A., & Hazzard, A. (1983). Reactive effects during naturalistic observation of families. *Behavioral Assessment, 5,* 349–362.

Christensen, A. & Heavey, C.L. (1990). Gender and social structure in the demand/withdraw pattern of marital conflict. *Journal of Personality and Social Psychology, 59,* 73–81.

Coie, J.D., Cillessen, A.H.N., Dodge, K.A., Hubbard, J.A., Schwartz, D., Lemerise, E.A., & Bateman, H. (1999). It takes two to fight: A test of relational factors and a method for assessing aggressive dyads. *Developmental Psychology, 35,* 1179–1188.

Cole, P.M., Zahn-Waxler, C., & Smith, K.D. (1994). Expressive control during a disappointment: Variations related to preschoolers' behavior problems. *Developmental Psychology, 30,* 835–846.

Crowell, J.A., & Feldman, S.S. (1991). Mothers' working models of attachment relationships and mother and child behavior during separation and reunion. *Developmental Psychology, 27,* 597–605.

Darley, J.M., & Batson, C.D. (1973). "From Jerusalem to Jericho": A study of situational and dispositional variables in helping behavior. *Journal of Personality and Social Psychology, 27,* 100–108.

Dishion, T.J., Spracklen, K.M., Andrews, D.W., & Patterson, G.R. (1996). Deviancy training in male adolescents friendships. *Behavior Therapy, 27,* 373–390.

Durand, V.M. (1990). The "aversives" debate is over: And now the work begins. *Journal of the Association for Persons with Severe Handicaps, 15,* 140–141.

Eisler, R.M., Hersen, M., Miller, P.M., & Blanchard, E.B. (1975). Situational determinants of assertive behaviors. *Journal of Consulting and Clinical Psychology, 29,* 330–340.

Foa, E.B., Steketee, G., Grayson, J.B., Turner, R.M., & Latimer, P. (1984). Deliberate exposure and blocking of obsessive-compulsive rituals: Immediate and long-term effects. *Behavior Therapy, 15,* 450–472.

Foster, D.A., Caplan, R.D., & Howe, G.W. (1997). Representativeness of observed couple interaction: Couples can tell, and it does make a difference. *Psychological Assessment, 9,* 285–294.

Goodenough, F.L. (1931). *Anger in young children.* Minneapolis: University of Minnesota Press.

Gottman, J.M. (1979). *Marital interaction: Experimental investigations.* New York: Academic Press.

Gottman, J.M. (1981). *Time-series analysis.* New York: Cambridge University Press.

Gottman, J.M. (1994). *What predicts divorce?* Hillsdale, NJ: Erlbaum.

Gottman, J.M. (1995). *What predicts divorce? The measures.* Hillsdale, NJ: Erlbaum.

Gottman, J.M. (1999). *The marriage clinic: A scientifically-based marital therapy.* New York: Norton.

Gottman, J.M., & Krokoff, L.J. (1989). Marital interaction and satisfaction: A longitudinal view. *Journal of Consulting and Clinical Psychology, 57,* 47–52.

Gottman, J.M., & Roy, A.K. (1990). *Sequential analysis: A guide for behavioral researchers.* New York: Cambridge University Press.

Halford, W.K., Sanders, M.R., & Behrens, B.C. (1994). Self-regulation in behavioral couples' therapy. *Behavior Therapy, 25,* 431–452.

Haynes, S.N. (2001). Clinical applications of analogue behavioral observation: Dimensions of psychometric evaluation. *Psychological Assessment, 13,* 73–85.

Haynes, S.N., & O'Brien, W.H. (2000). *Principles and practice of behavioral assessment.* New York: Kluwer.

Heavey, C.L., Layne, C., & Christensen, A. (1993). Gender and conflict structure in marital interaction: A replication and extension. *Journal of Consulting and Clinical Psychology, 61,* 16–27.

Heimberg, R.G., Dodge, C.S., Hope, D.A., Kennedy, C.R., et al. (1990). Cognitive behavioral group treatment for social phobia: Comparison with a credible placebo control. *Cognitive Therapy and Research, 14,* 1–23.

Heyman, R.E. (2001). Observation of couple conflicts: Clinical assessment applications, stubborn truths, and shaky foundations. *Psychological Assessment, 13,* 5–35.

Heyman, R.E., Feldbau-Kohn, S.R., Ehrensaft, M.K., Langhinrichsen-Rohling, J., & O'Leary, K.D. (2001). Can questionnaire reports correctly classify relationship distress and partner physical abuse? *Journal of Family Psychology, 15,* 334–346.

Heyman, R.E., Sayers, S.L., & Bellack, A.S. (1994). Global marital satisfaction versus marital adjustment: An empirical comparison of three measures. *Journal of Family Psychology, 8,* 432–446.

Heyman, R.E., & Vivian, D. (1997). *RMICS: Rapid Marital Interaction Coding System: Training manual for coders.* Unpublished manuscript, State University of New York at Stony Brook (Available at http://www.psy.sunysb.edu/marital).

Iwata, B.A., Pace, G.M., Dorsey, M.F., Zarcone, J.R., Vollmer, B., & Smith, J. (1994). The functions of self-injurious behavior: An experimental-epidemiological analysis. *Journal of Applied Behavior Analysis, 27,* 215–240.

Jacob, T., Tennenbaum, D., Seilhamer, R.A., Bargiel, K., & Sharon, T. (1994). Reactivity effects during naturalistic observation of distressed and nondistressed families. *Journal of Family Psychology, 8,* 354–363.

Jacobson, N.S., Gottman, J.M., Waltz, J., Rushe, R., Babcock, J., & Holtzworth-Monroe, A. (1994). Affect, verbal content, and psychophysiology in the arguments of couples with a violent husband. *Journal of Consulting and Clinical Psychology, 62,* 982–988.

Jacobson, N.S. & Margolin, G. (1979). *Marital therapy: Strategies based on social learning and behavior exchange principles.* New York: Brunner/Mazel.

Kazdin, A.E., Hayes, S.C., Henry, W.P., Schacht, T.E., & Strupp, H.H. (1992). Case study and small sample research. In A.E. Kazdin (Ed.), *Methodological issues and strategies in clinical research* (2nd ed., pp. 475–535). Washington, DC: American Psychological Association.

Kenny, D.A. (1990). Design issues in dyadic research. In C. Hendrick & M.S. Clark (Eds.), *Research methods in personality and social psychology: Review of personality and social psychology* (Vol. 11, pp. 164–184). Thousand Oaks, CA: Sage.

Krokoff, L.J., Gottman, J.M., & Hass, S.D. (1989). Validation of a global rapid couples interaction scoring system. *Behavioral Assessment, 11,* 65–79.

Lashley, B.R., Bond Jr., C.F. (1997). Significance testing for round robin data. *Psychological Methods, 2,* 278–291.

Lazarus, R.S. (1991). *Emotion and adaptation.* New York: Oxford University Press.

Leith, K.P., & Baumeister, R.F. (1996). Why do bad moods increase self-defeating behavior? Emotion, risk taking, and self-regulation. *Journal of Personality and Social Psychology, 71,* 1250–1267.

Leonard, K.E. & Roberts, L.J. (1998). The effects of alcohol on the marital interactions of aggressive and nonaggressive husbands and their wives. *Journal of Abnormal Psychology, 107,* 602–615.

Lewin, K. (1951). *Field theory in social science.* Chicago: University of Chicago Press.

Lobitz, W.C., & Johnson, S.M. (1975). Parental manipulation of the behavior of normal and deviant children. *Child Development, 46,* 719–726.

Margolin, G., Burman, B., & John, R. (1989). Home observations of married couples reenacting naturalistic conflicts. *Behavioral Assessment, 11,* 101–118.

Margolin, G., Talovic, S., & Weinstein, C.D. (1983). Areas of change questionnaire: A practical approach to marital assessment. *Journal of Consulting and Clinical Psychology, 51,* 944–955.

Markman, H.J., Floyd, F.J., Stanley, S., & Storaasli, R.D. (1988). Prevention of marital distress: A longitudinal investigation. *Journal of Consulting and Clinical Psychology, 56,* 210–217.

Markman, H.J., Stanley, S., & Blumberg, S.L. (1994). *Fighting for your marriage: Positive steps for preventing divorce and preserving a lasting love.* New York: Brunner/Mazel.

Marshall, L.L. (1999). Effects of men's subtle and overt psychological abuse on low-income women. *Violence and Victims, 14,* 69–88.

Mash, E.J., & Barkley, R.A. (1998). *Treatment of childhood disorders* (2nd ed.). New York: Guilford Press.

Mash, E.J., & Foster, S.L. (2001). Exporting analogue behavioral observation from research to clinical practice: Useful or cost-defective? *Psychological Assessment, 13,* 86–98.

Mash, E.J., & Hunsley, J. (1990). Behavioral assessment: A contemporary approach. In A.S. Bellack, M. Hersen, & A.E. Kazdin (Eds.), *International handbook of behavior modification and therapy* (2nd ed., pp. 87–106). New York: Plenum,

Mattick, R.P., Peters, L., & Clarke, J.C. (1989). Exposure and cognitive restructuring for social phobia: A controlled study. *Behavior Therapy, 20*, 3–23.

McGlynn, F.D., & Rose, M.P. (1998). Assessment of anxiety and fear. In A.S. Bellack & M. Hersen (Eds.), *Behavioral assessment: A practical handbook* (4th ed., pp. 179–209). Needham Heights, MA: Allyn & Bacon.

Nay, W.R. (1986). Analogue measures. In A.R. Ciminero, C.S. Calhoun, & H.E. Adams (Eds.), *Handbook of behavioral assessment* (pp. 223–252). New York: Wiley.

Norton, P.J., & Hope, D.A. (2001). Analogue observational methods in the assessment of social functioning in adults. *Psychological Assessment, 13*, 59–72.

Norton, R. (1983). Measuring marital quality: A critical look at the dependent variable. *Journal of Marriage and the Family, 45*, 141–151.

O'Leary, K.D., Heyman, R.E., & Jongsma, A.E. (1998). *The couples therapy treatment planner.* New York: Wiley.

Olson, D.H., & Ryder, R.G. (1970). Inventory of Marital Conflicts (IMC): An experimental interaction procedure. *Journal of Marriage and the Family, 32*, 433–448.

Pasch, L.A., & Bradbury, T.N. (1998). Social support, conflict, and the development of marital dysfunction. *Journal of Consulting and Clinical Psychology, 66*, 219–230.

Patterson, G.R. (1982). *Coercive family process.* Eugene, OR: Castalia.

Patterson, G.R. Reid, J.B., & Dishion, T.J. (1992). *Antisocial boys.* Eugene, OR: Castalia.

Perry, B.A., & Weiss, R.L. (1986). *Interactive couples therapy: A couple's guide.* Eugene, OR: Oregon Marital Studies Program.

Persons, J.B. (1989). *Cognitive therapy in practice: A case formulation approach.* New York: Norton.

Persons, J.B., & Fresco, D.M. (1998). Assessment of depression. In A.S. Bellack & M. Hersen (Eds.), *Behavioral assessment—A practical handbook* (4th ed., pp. 210–231). Boston: Allyn & Bacon.

Reid, J.B. (Ed.). (1978). *A social learning approach: Vol. 2. Observation in home settings.* Eugene, OR: Castalia.

Roberts, L.J., & Linney, K.D. (in press). Observing intimacy process behavior: Vulnerability and partner responsiveness in marital interaction. *Journal of Personality and Social Psychology.*

Roberts, M.W. (2001). Clinic observations of structured parent-child interaction designed to evaluate externalizing disorders. *Psychological Assessment, 13*, 46–58.

Rychtarik, R.G., & McGillicuddy, N.B. (1998). Assessment of appetitive disorders: Status of empirical methods in alcohol, tobacco, and other drug use. In A.S. Bellack & M. Hersen (Eds.), *Behavioral assessment—A practical handbook* (4th ed., pp. 271–292). Boston: Allyn & Bacon.

Sheldon, K.M. (1999). Learning the lessons of tit-for-tat: Even competitors can get the message. *Journal of Personality and Social Psychology, 77*, 1245–1253.

Slep, A.M.S., & O'Leary, S.G. (1996, November). *Maternal attributions and discipline style.* Paper presented at the 30th Annual Meeting of the Association for Advancement of Behavior Therapy, New York.

Slep, A.M.S., & O'Leary, S.G. (1998). The effects of maternal attributions on parenting: An experimental analysis. *Journal of Family Psychology, 12*, 234–243.

Smith, A.M., & O'Leary, S.G. (1995). Attributions and arousal as predictors of maternal discipline. *Cognitive Therapy and Research, 19*, 345–357.

Snyder, D.K., & Wills, R.M. (1989). Behavioral versus insight-oriented marital therapy: Effects on individual and interspousal functioning. *Journal of Consulting and Clinical Psychology, 57*, 39–46.

Sorce, J.F., Emde, R.N., Campos, J.J., & Klinnert, M.D. (1985). Maternal emotional signaling: Its effect on the visual cliff behavior of 1-year-olds. *Developmental Psychology, 21*, 195–200.

Spanier, G.B. (1976). Measuring dyadic adjustment: New scales for assessing the quality of marriage and similar dyads. *Journal of Marriage and the Family, 38*, 15–28.

Straus, M.A., Hamby, S.L., Boney-McCoy, S., & Sugarman, D.B. (1996). The revised Conflict Tactics Scales (CTS2): Development and preliminary psychometric data. *Journal of Family Issues, 17*, 283–316.

Tice, D.M., Bratslavsky, E., & Baumeister, R.F. (2001). Emotional distress regulation takes precedence over impulse control: If you feel bad, do it! *Journal of Personality and Social Psychology, 80*, 53–67.

Waters, E., Merrick, S., Treboux, D., Crowell, J., & Albersheim, L. (2000). Attachment security in infancy and early adulthood: A twenty-year longitudinal study. *Child Development, 71*, 684–689.

Wechsler, D. (1997). *Wechsler Adult Intelligence Scale* (3rd ed.). San Antonio, TX: Psychological Corporation.

Weiss, R.L. (1989). The circle of voyeurs: Observing the observers of marital and family interactions. *Behavioral Assessment, 11*, 135–147.

Weiss, R.L., & Cerreto, M.C. (1980). The Marital Status Inventory: Development of a measure of dissolution potential. *American Journal of Family Therapy, 8*, 80–85.

Weiss, R.L., Hops, H., & Patterson, G.R. (1973). A framework for conceptualizing marital conflict: A technology for altering it, some data for evaluating it. In L.D. Handy & E.L. Mash (Eds.), *Behavior change: Methodology concepts and practice* (pp. 309–342). Champaign, IL: Research Press.

CHAPTER 11

Clinical Interviewing

KRISTA A. BARBOUR AND GERALD C. DAVISON

INTRODUCTION AND OVERVIEW

One of the most valuable tools for gathering data used by clinical psychologists and other clinicians is the clinical interview. Its format may vary widely, from informal (unstructured) to structured diagnostic. The purpose of a given interview also varies, from rapport-building to guiding diagnostic decision making. In addition, the interview may be conducted in either a clinical or research context (Wiens & Brazil, 2000).

As we have stated elsewhere:

The paradigm within which an interviewer operates influences the type of information sought, how it is obtained, and how it is interpreted. A psychoanalytically trained clinician can be expected to inquire about the person's childhood history. He or she is also likely to remain skeptical of verbal reports because the analytic paradigm holds that the most significant aspects of a disturbed or normal person's developmental history are repressed into the unconscious. Of course, how the data are interpreted is influenced by the paradigm. By the same token, the behaviorally oriented clinician is likely to focus on current environmental conditions that can be related to changes in the person's behavior—for example, the circumstances under which the person becomes anxious. Thus the clinical interview does not follow one prescribed course but varies with the paradigm adopted by the interviewer. Like scientists, clinical interviewers in some measure find only the information for which they are looking (Davison & Neale, 2001, p. 79; emphasis in original).

The aims of the present chapter are to (1) review the most widely used structured interviews, including a brief description of the instrument and the psychometric properties of each; (2) consider the use of structured interviews in special populations (i.e., ethnic minorities, children, and older adults) and for specific disorders/problem areas; (3) describe the use of semistructured interviews in cognitive-behavioral assessment, along with an illustrative case study; (4) explore alternative data gathering techniques available to clinicians and researchers; and (5) provide conclusions and recommendations regarding the future use of clinical interviews in the assessment of psychological phenomena.

COMMONLY UTILIZED STRUCTURED INTERVIEWS FOR GENERAL PURPOSES

Due to the complexity of the current diagnostic systems, such as the *Diagnostic and Statistical Manual of Mental Disor-*

ders, 4th Edition (DSM-IV; American Psychiatric Association, 1994), structured interviewing has become a necessary tool in the assessment of psychological problems. Indeed, without such systematic assessment, it would be difficult for the clinician to consider all of the relevant criteria of possibly multiple diagnoses for one patient (Helzer & Robins, 1988). In addition, the use of structured interviews has generally been shown to improve diagnostic reliability (see Segal, 1997, for a review of the most commonly utilized methods for assessing the reliability of structured interviews) and may allow for the development of rapport between the interviewer and client (see Helzer & Robins, 1988, for a review). In the following section, some of the more commonly utilized structured interviews in clinical psychology are briefly described. Where available, information will also be provided regarding their psychometric properties.

Structured Clinical Interview for *DSM-IV* (SCID)

This widely used interview covers the Axis I psychological disorders included in the *DSM* (Spitzer, Williams, Gibbon, & First, 1992). The SCID is a branching interview—that is, the patient's response to a given question determines the next question that is asked. It also contains detailed instructions to the interviewer about when and how to probe further and when to shift to another line of questioning about a different diagnosis. For example, a question concerning obsessive-compulsive disorder is asked—for example, whether the patient has been bothered by intrusive thoughts. If the person says yes, then further questions are asked about these thoughts. If the person says no, the interviewer moves on to another domain, like post-traumatic stress disorder. Because the SCID also includes open-ended prompts to allow for clarification of ambiguous responses, this interview is meant to be administered only by people with clinical training (i.e., the interviewer must possess a basic knowledge of psychopathology and the *DSM*), and has an administration time of approximately 60 to 90 minutes.

The SCID possesses adequate psychometric properties. For example, in a sample of patients with substance abuse, the interview was found to have good-to-excellent concurrent, discriminant, and predictive validity (Kranzler, Kadden, Babor, & Tennen, 1996). The SCID also has demonstrated adequate reliability for most disorders (for a review, see Segal, Hersen, & Van Hasselt, 1994). It is available in several languages and offers additional versions for use with a variety of populations (e.g., a brief screening version, and a version for nonpatients to be used in community settings). The SCID-II (First, Spitzer, Gibbon, & Williams, 1995), intended for the assessment of Axis II (i.e., personality) disorders, is similar

in structure to the SCID and has been demonstrated to possess generally satisfactory psychometric properties (Maffei et al., 1997).

Anxiety Disorders Interview Schedule (ADIS)

The ADIS (Di Nardo, O'Brien, Barlow, Waddell, & Blanchard, 1983) was developed in an effort to distinguish among the *DSM* anxiety disorders, as well as rule out other possibly comorbid disorders (e.g., psychosis, substance use). Because of the need to discriminate among similar diagnoses, the ADIS should be administered only by those with clinical interviewing experience and a working knowledge of the *DSM* criteria. Approximate administration time is 90 minutes. Interrater agreement for each of the ADIS diagnoses is generally good (with the exception of generalized anxiety disorder; see Di Nardo, Moras, Barlow, Rapee, & Brown, 1993, for more details).

Diagnostic Interview Schedule (DIS)

The DIS was developed for use in the Epidemiologic Catchment Area (ECA) survey, a large, multisite examination of the prevalence and incidence of psychiatric disorders in the general population of the United States (see Regier et al., 1984, for a description of the study). The DIS was intended for use by nonclinicians (following a brief period of training), and as such it is highly structured, with administrators asking the questions verbatim. A unique aspect of this interview is the manner in which questions are asked. In contrast to interviews that ask only certain questions depending on the preceding responses, the DIS interviewer asks all questions, regardless of endorsement of symptoms on previous questions. The advantage of this technique is the nature of the data collected on the interviewee. That is, upon completion of the DIS, the interviewer has gathered information on each symptom covered by the DIS. Thus, the information obtained during the interview is unaffected by any subsequent changes in the definitions of psychological disorders (Helzer & Robins, 1988).

Although agreement between lay persons administering the DIS and psychiatrist ratings is generally adequate, reliability has been demonstrated to be lower for some diagnoses, such as obsessive compulsive disorder and major depression (Helzer & Robins, 1988; Robins, Helzer, Croughan, & Ratcliff, 1981). The DIS takes approximately 45 to 90 minutes to administer. Computer administration and scoring are available. The DIS has been translated into over 20 languages and thus provides an opportunity for cross-cultural comparisons in diagnoses. It is intended for use with adults 18 and older, and there is also a version for children (DISC-IV; see Shaffer, Fisher, Lucas, Dulcan, & Schwab-Stone, 2000, for a description).

Composite International Diagnostic Interview (CIDI)

The CIDI (World Health Organization, 1990), a structured interview designed to assess general psychopathology, was developed from the DIS and incorporates diagnostic criteria from both the ICD and the *DSM*. Like the DIS, the CIDI is intended to be administered by a layperson with appropriate training (i.e., one week in a World Health Organization training center). The CIDI has been translated into 16 languages and may be used in both clinical and research settings. In addition, the interview possesses adequate psychometric properties across a variety of populations (e.g., medically ill depressed patients; Booth, Kirchner, Hamilton, Harrell, & Smith, 1998). For a review of the psychometric data available for the CIDI, see Wittchen (1994).

Schedule for Affective Disorders and Schizophrenia (SADS)

This interview is based on the Research Diagnostic Criteria, which was a forerunner of the *DSM* criteria. It assesses psychotic and affective disorders, as well as substance abuse and anxiety disorders. Because the SADS is fairly lengthy (approximately 90 to 150 minutes to complete) and requires considerable training to learn to administer, it may be more appropriate for use in a research rather than a clinical context. The SADS is available in several languages and versions (e.g., one for the assessment of the presence of disorders across the respondent's lifetime versus one intended to assess a change in symptom profile upon repeated administration).

There is also a version available for use with children, known as the Schedule for Affective Disorders and Schizophrenia for School Age (the K-SADS; see Ambrosini, 2000; Chambers et al., 1985, for a review of the instrument).

Choosing the Interview

In sum, there exist several highly structured interview options for clinicians and researchers who are interested in the reliable diagnosis of psychopathology (in both adults and children). In fact, choosing the most appropriate interview can be challenging. According to Page (1991), the selection of a structured interview depends on several factors: the disorders and diagnostic systems covered by the interview, the psychometric properties of the instrument, the level of training required of the interviewers (i.e., a clinician skilled in the

diagnosis of psychopathology versus a layperson), and administration time. Finally, consideration should be given to the popularity of a given interview. Selection of a widely used instrument allows for comparison of the data obtained (e.g., prevalence rates of major depression) across studies (although prevalence rates for a disorder, such as depression, may still vary widely; see Brugha, Bebbington, & Jenkins, 1999).

COMMONLY USED STRUCTURED INTERVIEWS FOR SPECIFIC PURPOSES

When the focus of assessment is on a particular diagnosis versus screening for general psychopathology, an interview developed for the measurement of a specific disorder may be preferred. In the following section, interviews available for use in the assessment of eating and substance abuse disorders are highlighted to provide examples of interviews with a more narrow focus.

The Eating Disorders Examination (EDE; Fairburn & Cooper, 1993), a structured interview appropriate for use in both clinical and community settings, allows for the assessment of overeating and the efforts utilized by the respondent to control weight (e.g., vomiting) over the previous 4 weeks, as well as the diagnosis of eating disorders. Currently in its 12th edition, the EDE consists of four subscales (Restraint, Eating Concern, Shape Concern, and Weight Concern), is shorter in length than prior versions, and has been shown to be valid and reliable (Fairburn & Cooper, 1993). This interview requires training to conduct and is available in chapter 15 of Fairburn and Cooper (1993).

The Structured Interview for Anorexic and Bulimic Syndromes for Expert Rating (SIAB-EX; Fichter, Herpertz, Quadflieg, & Herpetz-Dahlmann, 1998) also allows for the diagnosis of eating disorders based on *DSM-IV* and *International Statistical Classification of Diseases and Related Health Problems, 10th Edition* (*ICD-10*) criteria. This 87-item interview can be distinguished from the EDE by its focus on symptoms of general psychopathology that are frequently comorbid with eating disorders (e.g., anxiety and depression), in addition to assessment of symptoms specific to disordered eating. The psychometric properties of the SIAB are acceptable, including internal consistency and interrater reliability. In addition to English, the SIAB is available in Spanish, German, and Italian. Interviewers are trained via a 90-page manual (available from Manfred M. Fichter, M.D., Professor of Psychiatry, Department of Psychiatry, University of Munich, Nußbaumstr. 7, 80336 Munich, Germany).

Interviews are also available for the specific assessment of alcohol/substance abuse disorders. For example, the Alcohol

Use Disorder and Associated Disabilities Interview Schedule (AUDADIS) allows trained nonclinicians to assess both current and previous alcohol and drug use disorders (see Hasin, Carpenter, McCloud, Smith, & Grant, 1997, for a description of the instrument and reliability data). The AUDADIS is suitable for use in both clinical and community samples, as well as with Spanish-speaking populations (Canino et al., 1999). A second interview, the Semi-Structured Assessment for the Genetics of Alcoholism (SSAGA; Hesselbrock, Easton, Bucholz, Schuckit, & Hesselbrock, 1999), assesses alcohol abuse and dependence disorders as well as possible comorbidity with other disorders and can be administered by lay interviewers.

Another frequently utilized interview method in the area of alcohol use, the Time-Line Follow-Back (TLFB; Sobell, Sobell, Maisto, & Cooper, 1985), allows for the retrospective assessment of an individual's drinking pattern over a specific period of time (generally covering one month to one year). The daily drinking data from the TLFB are obtained through the use of a calendar to facilitate recall of alcohol use (e.g., by linking drinking patterns to nondrinking events that have occurred over the same period of time). The TLFB has been demonstrated to be psychometrically sound in a variety of samples, including patients undergoing alcohol treatment (Maisto, Sobell, Cooper, & Sobell, 1982), psychiatric outpatients (Carey, 1997), and the general population (Sobell, Sobell, Leo, & Cancilla, 1988).

In sum, clinicians and researchers have many viable interview options when the goal is the assessment of psychopathology in general, as well as when the focus is on diagnosis of one particular psychological disorder. In addition to those disorders covered in the *DSM* and *ICD* diagnostic systems, interviews have been developed for assessment of problem behaviors that lie outside of these diagnostic systems. Two such phenomena, the Type A Behavior Pattern (TABP) and family functioning, are areas of interest to clinicians and researchers alike. Thus, the Structured Interview for the assessment of the TABP (SI) and the Darlington Family Interview Schedule (DFIS) will be discussed in the next sections.

Interviewing and Other Variables of Interest

The Structured Interview (SI; Rosenman, 1978) was designed to assess the constellation of characteristics known as the Type A Behavior Pattern. The TABP, the name given to behaviors linked to the development of coronary heart disease and coronary artery disease (CHD, CAD, sometimes referred to more generally as cardiovascular disease or CVD; Friedman & Rosenman, 1974), includes behaviors such as impatience, hostility, and competitiveness. Via the SI, information is gathered regarding the interviewee's manner of responding to a variety of challenging situations designed to elicit Type A behaviors, such as hostility and impatience. The interviewer's questions are often intentionally delivered in a provocative, almost insulting manner so as to elicit a Type A response if the disposition is present. The focus is more on the style than on the content of the person's responses.

The SI has been used in numerous research protocols examining the correlation between TABP and later development of heart disease. Interrater reliability regarding the presence of the TABP is adequate (Rosenman, Swan, & Carmelli, 1988). Recently, focus has gradually shifted to the *hostility* component of TABP (Siegman, 1994), because research has generally shown that specific components of the SI (i.e., potential for hostility) may be more predictive of CVD than a global TABP score (e.g., Booth-Kewley & Friedman, 1987; Dembroski, MacDougall, Costa & Grandits, 1989). The SI has been translated into Spanish (e.g., Perez, Meizoso, & Gonzalez, 1999) and has also been used with adolescents (e.g., Siegal, Matthews, & Leitch, 1981).

Turning to clinical interviewing of families, the FDIS (Wilkinson, Barnett, Delf, & Pirie, 1988) was developed as part of a comprehensive assessment package designed to be conducted with an entire family (the package also included questionnaire measures and the behavioral observation of family interaction). This interview is composed of 24 sections, tapping into 16 problem dimensions (e.g., family closeness/distance, parenting, psychological health, child development). The purpose of the FDIS is to allow the clinician to develop a treatment plan based on family member responses to the various problem areas.

The administration time for this family interview is approximately 60 to 90 minutes. Interviewers undergo an 18-hour training course that includes viewing videotaped interviews of families and rating the relevant problem areas (for further details regarding the training process, see Wilkinson, 2000). The FDIS has been found to possess moderate interrater agreement among the problem areas assessed, and may hold promise in discriminating between clinical and "healthy" families (Wilkinson & Stratton, 1991).

SEMISTRUCTURED INTERVIEWING

The aforementioned structured interviews are quite valuable in diagnostic decision making. However, clinicians more frequently utilize a less formal type of interview when assessing client difficulties. Although not structured in the sense that particular questions are asked in a predetermined fashion, clinicians frequently conduct "semistructured" interviews—that is, interviews guided by her or his specific theoretical orientation but not constrained by as much structure as the interviews just described. Sometimes semistructured interviews are referred to simply as "clinical interviews." No interview, however, is truly *unstructured,* because, as noted at the outset of this chapter, the interviewer cannot help but ask questions within a particular paradigm or model, even if only a poorly formed one. (Truly unstructured interviews are, in our opinion, unprofessional.)

A clinician operating within a behavioral or cognitive-behavioral paradigm would, for example, conduct an intake interview that includes a functional analysis and an effort to operationalize the patient's difficulties. A functional analysis aims to determine the conditions under which particular behaviors occur or do not occur, and whether they are followed by reinforcing or punishing events. Operationally defining the patient's problems entails obtaining examples and clear definitions of any labels the patient uses to describe his or her difficulties. This approach to interviewing also provides an opportunity to form hypotheses regarding possible causal factors that may account for problem behaviors. For example, a behavior therapist may emphasize contemporaneous environmental variables (e.g., positive reinforcement from a family member) as playing a causal role in many presenting complaints (e.g., Haynes, 2000).

Other goals of this initial interaction would be to obtain relevant information regarding the patient's social learning history, strengths, and previous efforts to solve his or her difficulties. In addition, the interviewer assesses expectations of therapy and treatment goals (an overview of these interviewing guidelines is provided in Goldfried & Davison, 1994). In this way, cognitive-behavioral interviews are intimately related to any subsequent intervention that is undertaken.

An example of a cognitive-behavioral assessment interview is provided below. It is taken from a videotape of the second author interviewing a patient as part of a series produced in 1989 by Everett Shostrom (Psychological & Educational Films, 1989). The transcript begins with the opening of the interview. Notice the situationalist perspective that is a defining feature of (cognitive) behavior therapy. Notice also how the therapist gradually reframes the client's presenting problem of shyness as sensitivity to criticism and how he encourages her to attend to her thoughts about stressful interpersonal situations, a reflection of the cognitive model that the therapist is employing. Note in particular how, toward the end of the excerpt, the therapist contrasts the patient's cognitive reactions to two different kinds of interpersonal events in an effort to achieve a useful construction of the problem.

Davison: Let's start by inviting you to tell me things that are problematic, things that you might like changed. We'll go from there.

Client: Okay. Lately there are a couple things that are really standing out right now for me. The primary thing is probably my lack of a social life, my lack of really any friendships, and I see that in shyness, 'cause I feel like I am a shy person and I feel like that's part of the reason why I don't have any friends. I do not know how to make friends. And that's real prevalent right now and I'm feeling that, a lot, in my life, the lack and loneliness.

Davison: How long has that been going on?

Client: Pretty much as far back as I can remember, back to probably high school. Once I got out of high school I noticed just that it wasn't easy for me to make friends.

Davison: So, you were more cut off, more isolated from other kids your age?

Client: I think so. Yes.

Davison: You didn't feel too terrific about that, or did you find other things to do?

Client: I kind of, I feel like I kind of found other things to do, and I still do this. I make it okay that I don't have friends, in that I read a lot, I do a lot of alone things so it's okay that I don't have anyone to do those things with. That it's a lack in my life that I feel even though I choose to fill my time with other things.

Davison: Would you like to be a little more outgoing, a little more social?

Client: Yes.

Davison: Tell me a little about the home situation, whom you live with, what's that situation?

Client: Okay. Well I have my husband and my two-year-old son. My husband and I have been married for three years and we've been together for almost ten years. . . .

Some discussion ensues about tensions in the marriage, but because of the very short-term demonstrational nature of the interview, those sections are omitted here.

Davison: Let's, if we could, move back to the shyness dimension for a few minutes. This existed prior to your meeting your husband? [Patient nods.] This is a pattern of being that preceded your relationship with your husband and it's continuing to exist now? [Patient nods.] I want to look at that a little bit and ask you a few questions about shyness. When you're in a social gathering where you don't know many people and you see someone you might like to talk to, and you're moving sort of to say hello to this person. What does it feel like, as best as you can reconstruct?

Client: I feel my adrenaline pumping and it just feels very scary, like I can't do it.

Davison: Get really nervous?

Client: Very nervous.

Davison: Fearful? [Patient nods.] So you're aware of what we call autonomic activity: sweating, dry throat, heart pounding. Your body's doing that.

Client: There's a physical change, yes.

Davison: What about in your mind? Are there things that go through your mind in a situation like this that you can recollect?

Client: Usually I tell myself that I can't do it or don't want to do it.

Davison: Do you ever worry that you won't do it *right* [emphasis in original]? Do you have worries or concerns about their reaction to you? How they're going to respond to you initiating a hello or something like that?

Client: All the time.

Davison: Tell me about that if you can. What goes through your mind about that?

Client: Well I just feel like people aren't going to respond to me. That they're going to think that I'm stupid for saying hello or a conversation I might be able to talk with them about they are not going to respond or think it's not interesting or they're not going to like me.

Davison: So, they're going to be rejecting? Is that too strong a term? Or does rejection make sense to you?

Client: Yes.

Davison: They might criticize you. Do you feel that you might be inferring criticism from them? They don't like you or they don't like what you've said. Does that ever go through your mind?

Client: Yes. I always fantasize that they're saying things in their mind about "Oh gosh, how could she have said that." I do that.

Davison: Let's assume for the moment that this person you're about to talk to, this hypothetical person—let's assume it's a woman. Let's assume she has listened to what you have said, and she's saying something like "Where's she coming from with that?" [Therapist, in role, frowns disapprovingly.] What just happened when I said that?

Client: Oh, just that I'd probably get mad and just think, "Well what does she know anyway" and walk away.

Davison: And this is something that we're saying might be going on in her mind. She's not saying it to you, but you're thinking she might be saying, "What is this per-

son? What did she say? What does that mean?" Now, what would you do internally if you were thinking that that's what they're thinking? What might you be saying to yourself?

Client: Well that I was right. She's really not interested or she thinks that I'm stupid.

Davison: And that would be? What would that mean? What would that be? Would that be, what adjective? Would that be great? Would that be bad?

Client: It would be terrible.

Davison: Is catastrophe too strong a term?

Client: That's too strong.

Davison: Too strong, but it would be really bad. You could definitely do without that. [smiles]

Client: Yes. [smiles]

Davison: So, we have a situation here that we've created, hypothetically, where there's someone you approach. You don't know this person. You might make an overture. As you're thinking of making an overture, you might think that they are criticizing you, that they are about to reject you. They're thinking poorly of you and that's really bad. That would be a bad thing to happen?

Client: Yes.

Davison: Now, even though we've been talking about a very specific situation, I'd like to see how generally useful it is to think of part of your shyness in these terms. In other words, I'd like to ask you whether what we just worked with together tells us about at least part of your shyness, your withdrawal from people. Does it relate to, does it have something to do in general with what goes on more than just in a social situation? Could it go on in a friendship situation or could it go on in a shopping center when you're asking the salesperson for help? Would these things be happening?

Client: I don't think so much [it would happen] in a shopping center situation.

Davison: Why might it not happen, do you think? [Therapist sees an opportunity to enhance the functional analysis—find contrasting conditions under which a target behavior/cognition/emotion does and does not occur.]

Client: Because in that situation I'm the buyer. It doesn't matter to me what the salesperson thinks. So, I'm in control.

Davison: It sounds as though you're protected somehow. They can't really hurt you.

[Client nods.]

Davison: Okay, I'm going to ask you about another hypothetical situation. Let's pretend that that attitude that you are able to have with the salesperson could be transferred to a social situation, like the one we just worked with. Just pretend that can happen now. What would that feel like? How would you like that? What would that kind of change do for you?

Client: Well, when I'm in a position of control or strength, when I feel confident, then I feel like I am much more friendly because I'm not concerned about failing in that situation.

Davison: Would this be a plus for you? This would be a preferable situation?

Client: Definitely.

Davison: Let's just move to another facet of shyness and talk about what psychologists sometimes refer to as social skills. How do you view yourself as having certain necessary social skills, knowing how to do various things with people in social situations? Are you aware of what to do or do you sometimes have no idea what's called for?

Client: When it comes to listening skills, I think I'm really good at that. And I know, I think, how to be a good listener and show people that I'm really interested and attentive. But when it comes to talking myself, then I feel like I don't have the skills because I don't know what to say. I don't know how to just carry on a chit-chat conversation.

Davison: So you see yourself, in part, as lacking certain skills in interacting with others. We're talking on a fairly casual level. There are things . . . you might like to learn . . . if there were things that could be taught to you. Do you think this sort of thing makes sense to you? Do you feel like you could stand to learn some things about engaging in social interaction with others?

Client: Definitely.

Davison: I'm going to summarize a bit and correct me if I'm off the mark. It seems as though there's some inhibitions operating in you even if you know what to say or what to do. You might not do it because you're fantasizing, you're thinking, guessing that this other person might be reacting cognitively in their minds in a negative way towards you and they're going to push you away and they're going to reject you, and that would be bad. So, it sounds like a combination of a skills deficit, what we refer to as a deficit in skills, and some inhibitions. [Note: The therapist was in fact doubtful about the extent of her lack of social skills, and that is the reason he emphasized behavioral inhibition. In-

formation gained later on confirmed that the client had more interpersonal know-how than she gave herself credit for.] Okay? And these things have gone on for a while.

[Clients nods.]

(Transcribed from *Integrative psychotherapy—A six-part series: Part 3. A demonstration with Dr. Gerald Davison.* Produced by Psychological and Educational Films, Corona Del Mar, CA, 1989. Reproduced by permission).

INTERVIEWING SPECIAL POPULATIONS

Ethnic Minorities

The use of structured interviewing often can aid in the diagnosis of psychological disorders in ethnic minorities. For example, Paradis and colleagues (1992) found that panic disorder was underdiagnosed in a sample of ethnic minorities (primarily African American and Latino patients) in an urban, outpatient setting. Presumably, the way these patients described their panic attacks (e.g., "not natural," "like a curse") led the staff to diagnose psychotic disorders instead of panic attacks. The use of the ADIS, with its emphasis on cognitive and physiological symptomology, resulted in either a primary or secondary diagnosis of panic disorder in 23 of these patients. The authors suggested that the use of a structured interview like the ADIS may reduce the effects of cultural bias on psychiatric diagnosis (see also Friedman & Paradis, 1991).

However, the use of structured interviews also can result in the misdiagnosis of certain disorders within particular ethnic groups. For example, Villasenor and Waitzkin (1999) found that a sample of Latino patients was frequently misdiagnosed with a somatoform disorder. It appeared that the clinicians interpreted the somatic complaints of these patients as psychological, despite the presence of medical illnesses that were either not sufficiently articulated by the patient or were misunderstood/undetected by the interviewer because of language barriers. This finding underscores the need for clinicians to recognize the influence of a patient's cultural background and current social context during assessment (Lopez, 1989).

In the event clinicians and researchers are unfamiliar with the ethnic groups with whom they are working, they should make every effort to learn as much as possible about the social and cultural factors that may be relevant to diagnosis. Many resources are available to educate clinicians and researchers on the topic of interviewing and ethnicity (e.g., Dunbar, Rodriguez, & Parker, 2001; Puente & Garcia, 2000; Tanaka-Matsumi, Seiden, & Lam, 1996).

Children

Historically, assessment of psychopathology in childhood relied on information gathered from sources other than the child her or himself, primarily parents or teachers, due to the belief that children are not able to provide accurate reports of their own thoughts, feelings, and behaviors (Edelbrock & Bohnert, 2000). More recently, however, the value of child reports has been recognized and these data are routinely included in the assessment of childhood psychological difficulties.

Many of the structured interviews described earlier for use with adults are available in child versions (for a review of these interviews, see Edelbrock & Bohnert, 2000). For example, the ADIS-C (Child) and the ADIS-P (Parent) are both used to assess and diagnose anxiety disorders in children. In addition, diagnoses may be made using a combination of the Child and Parent scores. The ADIS-C generally possesses adequate test-retest reliability over a 2-week period (Silverman & Rabian, 1995), although reliability may vary according to the age of the child being tested (Silverman & Eisen, 1992). A child version of the SADS, the K-SADS, allows for the assessment of psychotic and affective disorders in childhood. Thus, many structured interviews have been modified for use with children. Other interviews, such as the SI (for the assessment of TABP), have been successfully administered to children in unchanged form.

Clearly, there are unique variables to consider when interviewing children (see Allen & Gross, 1994, for a review). First, attention must be paid to relevant developmental issues. For example, it has been recognized that the symptoms of psychopathology are often more varied among children than in adults (e.g., depression manifested more as an irritable mood than as sadness). Second, interviewers must consider the child's life in context (e.g., family and peer relationships), and thus should meet with parents whenever possible to get a feel for the nature of family interaction, as well as to obtain information regarding the presenting complaint and the child's history. It is also often worthwhile to obtain information from teachers regarding the child's behavior and friendships within the school environment.

Older Adults

As is the case with children, age is a salient variable when interviewing older adults. As one might expect, interviewers are more likely to encounter individuals with sensory impairments (e.g., vision and hearing) in this population. In addition, attention must be paid to the high likelihood of the presence of comorbid medical illnesses (e.g., cardiovascular disease) in older adulthood, which may have a negative effect on cognitive functioning. Clinicians and researchers also should be able to recognize any cognitive decline (e.g., dementia) in older patients and refer any such cases to the appropriate health care provider (e.g., a geriatric neuropsychologist, who may be able to differentiate between memory difficulties associated with the normal aging process and a possible dementing illness; see Koltai & Welsh-Bohmer, 2000, for more information on this topic).

Diagnostic decision-making also may be more complex in older adults than it is in younger adults. For example, current diagnostic systems may not capture depression in older adults, because the disorder may manifest as primarily somatic complaints in these individuals (Patterson & Dupree, 1994). In addition, depression in older adulthood can present with cognitive impairment that may mimic that seen in dementia (i.e., a pseudodementia). However, the cognitive difficulties associated with depression are likely to reverse themselves once the depression has been treated (hence the need for a differential diagnosis between depression and dementia).

In sum, interviewing in a geriatric population can be complicated, with many issues to consider (e.g., the effects of a chronic medical illness on psychological functioning). Clinicians and researchers interviewing older adults should have at least a basic knowledge of the unique characteristics of this population (e.g., the higher rate of suicide in older adults relative to other age groups). For further information regarding older adults and interviewing, see Wenger, 2001.

PRACTICAL ISSUES IN INTERVIEWING

In addition to the characteristics of diverse populations that should be considered when conducting structured interviews are several practical issues that must be addressed. We discuss four of these: generalizability across cultures, choice of informant, order effects, and interviewer training.

Generalizability Across Cultures

As already mentioned—and this holds for all assessment methods—one should use caution in assuming that interviews (and thus the data obtained) generalize across cultures. For example, although translations of many of the instruments described within this chapter are available, potential language difficulties remain (Lesser, 1997), and the phenomena measured using these translated versions may not have the same meaning across all cultures (for a review of issues relating to cultural considerations in psychopathology, see Lopez & Guarnaccia, 2000). Thus, although structured interviews have been found to improve diagnostic precision in samples of ethnic minorities (e.g., Friedman & Paradis, 1991; Paradis, Friedman, Lazar, Grubea, & Kesselman, 1992), interviewers must not ignore the social and cultural factors that might limit the usefulness of the results obtained (Villasenor & Waitzkin, 1999).

Choice of Informant

Because a primary goal of a clinical interview is to gather the most reliable information possible, the interviewer must make a choice regarding the source of the information. That is, should the interviewer rely on the patient's report or instead make use of a knowledgeable informant who may provide more objective information regarding the patient's behavior?

This question was examined by Bernstein and colleagues (1997), who utilized a sample of patients who were undergoing assessment for *DSM* Axis II disorders, along with an individual close to each patient who served as an informant regarding the patient's behavior. Each patient and her or his corresponding informant (usually a family member or friend) were interviewed about the personality disorder symptoms demonstrated by the patient (interestingly, 27 out of 89 patients refused to provide a name of an informant).

Although there was no significant difference in the prevalence of Axis II disorders between the patients and the informants, agreement on the specific diagnoses of these disorders was low. In fact, only three disorders (Schizotypal, Borderline, and Histrionic) reached statistically significant agreement. Thus, it appears that the diagnosis of personality disorders (and likely other psychological disorders) depends on the source of the information.

Order Effects

A third consideration when interpreting interview data involves the order in which questions are presented. For example, during the administration of a structured interview, there may be a reduction of symptom reporting by the patient as the interview progresses. To examine this issue, Jensen, Watanabe, and Richters (1999) administered the Attention Deficit Hyperactivity Disorder (ADHD) and Depression sections of the DISC to two groups of children in counterbalanced order. It was found that, as predicted, respondents reported fewer symptoms during the section that was administered second, regardless of disorder (i.e., ADHD or Depression). Researchers and clinicians should be aware of this order effect, referred to as "symptom attenuation," when conducting structured interviews (for further details regarding this issue, see Lucas et al., 1999; Piacentini et al., 1999).

Interviewer Training

A third practical issue to consider is the phenomenon of "rater drift." Ventura and colleagues (1998) addressed this problem in the context of training people to administer structured interviews. These researchers established a quality assurance program in an effort to monitor the reliability of SCID interviewers across time. As part of this program, interviewers administered SCID interviews that were co-rated by training mentors both during training and following the end of training (i.e., the quality assurance period). It was found that reliability was significantly higher for the interviews administered during the training period relative to those given during the quality assurance period (although reliability remained adequate throughout). These data suggest that the reliability of interviewers varies over time, and researchers may need to provide occasional "booster" training sessions to ensure continued reliability.

ALTERNATIVE METHODS OF GATHERING RELEVANT DATA

Although the interview is an invaluable means of obtaining information regarding relevant clinical variables (e.g., antecedents and consequences associated with the problem behavior), the interviewer relies heavily on the respondent's retrospective reports of events, behaviors, cognitions, and emotions. A technique that allows for assessment of cognition and emotion "in the moment" may provide a better means for obtaining information from the patient that may be difficult for her or him to retrieve from memory during the clinical interview.

One such paradigm, called Articulated Thoughts in Simulated Situations (ATSS), was developed by Davison, Robins, and Johnson (1983). This "think aloud" cognitive assessment procedure allows for open-ended, verbal reports of the thoughts that occur during emotional arousal (for a review of studies utilizing the ATSS paradigm, see Davison, Vogel, & Coffman, 1997). In this procedure, participants listen to emotion-eliciting audiotaped scenarios and are asked to imagine that the situations they are hearing are actually occurring. Each scenario introduced to participants is divided into several brief segments. At the end of each segment, a tone sounds and participants are asked to articulate their thoughts and feelings into a tape recorder during a 30-second pause. After each pause, the scenario continues with another brief segment, followed by another pause for articulation, and so on. The tape-recorded articulations are later transcribed and content analyzed along a number of dimensions by trained coders.

Several scenarios can be presented to the respondent, including control scenes (e.g., nonstressful situations). The content varies with the interests of the investigator and the purposes of the inquiry, constrained only by the ingenuity of the researcher/clinician in creating real-life scenes, the willingness of respondents to involve themselves in the imaginal role-playing, and the ethical propriety of presenting particular scenario content.

The ATSS procedure has been utilized with numerous populations (e.g., participants with depression, social anxiety, high blood pressure, and anger), and its validity has been demonstrated in numerous investigations (e.g., Bates, Campbell, & Burgess, 1990; Davison, Feldman, & Osborn, 1984). As with interviewing, the possibility remains that participants will censor socially undesirable responses during the ATSS procedure (e.g., the desire to verbally aggress against a character portrayed on the audiotape). However, it is believed that this tendency may be minimized somewhat due to the requirements of the task (i.e., the participant is instructed to respond immediately upon hearing the scenario and is typically left alone in the room with the tape recorder in an effort to encourage more open responding). In sum, ATSS may be a useful alternative to an interview when gathering data regarding psychological functioning.

CONCLUSIONS AND FUTURE DIRECTIONS

As demonstrated by the number of structured interviews reviewed in this chapter, researchers and clinicians have many options readily accessible for the assessment of a variety of psychological phenomena (both within and outside of the realm of psychopathology) in both children and adults. Despite the popularity of these manualized interviews, particularly for diagnostic decision-making, semistructured interviews are the more frequently utilized tool of clinicians. These interviews are, like structured ones, shaped by a particular paradigm and therefore follow a set of explicit or implicit "rules." That is, inherent in these interviews are beliefs about the etiology of psychopathology, decisions regarding what information is important to obtain about the client's previous and current difficulties, and formulation of the case. They are, however, much less scripted than structured interviews like the SCID and the ADIS, allowing the interviewer more latitude in the questions asked and the domains explored.

The semistructured form of clinical interviewing will likely continue to be the most widely used method of interviewing by clinicians. However, both researchers and clinicians may also consider alternatives to clinical interviewing, such as the

ATSS paradigm described earlier, to assess the client's difficulties in a way that does not rely solely on the accuracy of the respondent's (or another informant's) retrospective reporting of their typical cognitions, emotions, and behaviors across time.

Lastly, it should not come as much of a surprise that clinical researchers may increasingly turn to the Internet (both web-based and e-mail surveys) to conduct epidemiological studies in clinical psychology (e.g., Houston et al., 2001). Preliminary evidence suggests that the Internet may be a useful research medium. For example, Krantz, Ballard, and Scher (1997), in a study investigating the perception of female attractiveness, found that the responses they obtained from participants in a college setting and those obtained from online participants were highly correlated. In addition, other researchers have replicated the results of a traditional paper-and-pencil study in a sample of Internet participants (see Houston et al., 2001). In sum, it appears that the Internet is a viable way to assess variables of interest to research psychologists. In addition, this mode of communication has the benefits of cost and time-efficiency. For more information about interviewing and the use of the Internet, see Mann and Stewart (2001), Smith (1997), and Wiens and Brazil (2000).

REFERENCES

Allen, J.B., & Gross, A.M. (1994). Interviewing children. In M. Hersen and S.M. Turner (Eds.), *Diagnostic interviewing* (pp. 305–326). New York: Plenum Press.

Ambrosini, P.J. (2000). Historical development and present status of the schedule for affective disorders and schizophrenia for school-age children. *Journal of the American Academy of Child & Adolescent Psychiatry, 39,* 49–58.

American Psychiatric Association (1994). *Diagnostic and statistical manual of mental disorders* (4th ed.). Washington, DC: Author.

Bates, G.W., Campbell, I.M., & Burgess, P.M. (1990). Assessment of articulated thoughts in social anxiety: Modification of the ATSS procedure. *British Journal of Clinical Psychology, 29,* 91–98.

Bernstein, D.P., Kasapis, C., Bergman, A., Weld, E., Nfitropoulou, V., Horvath, T., Klar, H.M., Silverman, J., & Siever, L.J. (1997). Assessing axis II disorders by informant interview. *Journal of Personality Disorders, 11,* 158–167.

Booth, B.M., Kirchner, J.E., Hamilton, G., Harrell, R., & Smith, G.R. (1998). Diagnosing depression in the medically ill: Validity of a lay administered structured diagnostic interview. *Journal of Psychiatric Research, 32,* 353–360.

Booth-Kewley, S., & Friedman, H.S. (1987). Psychological predictors of heart disease: A quantitative review. *Psychological Bulletin, 101,* 343–362.

Brugha, T.S., Bebbington, P.E., & Jenkins, R. (1999). A difference that matters: Comparisons of structured and semi-structured psychiatric diagnostic interviews in the general population. *Psychological Medicine, 29,* 1013–1020.

Canino, G., Bravo, M., Ramirez, R., Febo, V.E., Rubio-Stipec, M., Fernandez, R.L., & Hasin, D. (1999). The Spanish alcohol use disorder and associated disabilities interview schedule (AUDADIS): Reliability and concordance with clinical diagnoses in a Hispanic population. *Journal of Studies on Alcohol, 60,* 790–799.

Carey, K.B. (1997). Reliability and validity of the time-line followback interview among psychiatric outpatients: A preliminary report. *Psychology of Addictive Behaviors, 11,* 26–33.

Chambers, W.J., Puig-Antich, J., Hirsch, M., Paez, P., Ambrosini, P.J., Tabrizi, M.A., & Davies, M. (1985). The assessment of affective disorders in children and adolescents by semistructured interview. *Archives of General Psychiatry, 42,* 696–702.

Davison, G.C., Feldman, P.M., & Osborn, C.E. (1984). Articulated thoughts, irrational beliefs, and fear of negative evaluation. *Cognitive Therapy and Research, 8,* 349–362.

Davison, G.C., Robins, C., & Johnson, M.K. (1983). Articulated thoughts during simulated situations: A paradigm for studying cognition in emotion and behavior. *Cognitive Therapy and Research, 7,* 17–40.

Davison, G.C., Vogel, R.S., & Coffman, S.G. (1997). Think-aloud approaches to cognitive assessment and the articulated thoughts in simulated situations paradigm. *Journal of Consulting and Clinical Psychology, 65,* 950–958.

Dembroski, T.M., MacDougall, J.M., Costa, P.T., & Grandits, G.A. (1989). Components of hostility as predictors of sudden death and myocardial infarction in the Multiple Risk Factor Intervention Trial. *Psychosomatic Medicine, 51,* 514–522.

Di Nardo, P.A., Moras, K., Barlow, D.H., Rapee, R.M., & Brown, T.A. (1993). Reliability of DSM-III-R anxiety disorder categories: Using the anxiety disorders interview schedule-revised (ADIS-R). *Archives of General Psychiatry, 50,* 251–256.

Di Nardo, P.A., O'Brien, G.T., Barlow, D.H., Waddell, M.T., Blanchard, E.B. (1983). Reliability of DSM-III anxiety disorder categories using a new structured interview. *Archives of General Psychiatry, 40,* 1070–1074.

Dunbar, C., Rodriguez, D., & Parker, L. (2001). Race, subjectivity, and the interview process. In J.F. Gubrium & J.A. Holstein (Eds.), *Handbook of interview research* (pp. 279–298). Thousand Oaks, CA: Sage.

Edelbrock, C., & Bohnert, A. (2000). Structured interviews for children and adolescents. In G. Goldstein & M. Hersen (Eds.), *Handbook of psychological assessment* (3rd ed., pp. 369–386). New York: Pergamon-Elsevier Science.

Fairburn, C.G., & Cooper, Z. (1993). The eating disorder examination (12th ed.). In C.G. Fairburn & G.T. Wilson (Eds.), *Binge eating: Nature, assessment, and treatment* (pp. 317–360). New York: Guilford Press.

Fichter, M.M., Herpertz, S., Quadflieg, N, & Herpetz-Dahlmann, B. (1998). Structured interview for anorexic and bulimic disorders for DSM-IV and ICD-10: Updated (3rd) edition. *International Journal of Eating Disorders, 24,* 227–249.

First, M.B., Spitzer, R.L., Gibbon, M., & Williams, J.B.W. (1995). The structured clinical interview for DSM-III-R personality disorders (SCID-II): Part I. Description. *Journal of Personality Disorders, 9,* 83–91.

Friedman, M., & Rosenman, R. (1974). *Type A behavior and your heart.* New York: Knopf.

Friedman, S., & Paradis, C. (1991). African-American patients with panic disorder and agoraphobia. *Journal of Anxiety Disorders, 5,* 35–41.

Goldfried, M.R., & Davison, G.C. (1994). *Clinical behavior therapy* (expanded ed.). New York: Wiley.

Hasin, D., Carpenter, K.M., McCLoud, S., Smith, M., & Grant, B.F. (1997). The alcohol use disorder and associated disabilities interview schedule (AUDADIS): Reliability of alcohol and drug modules in a clinical sample. *Drug and Alcohol Dependence, 44,* 133–141.

Haynes, S.N. (2000). Behavioral assessment of adults. In G. Goldstein & M. Hersen (Eds.), *Handbook of psychological assessment* (3rd ed., pp. 471–502). New York: Pergamon-Elsevier Science.

Helzer, J.E., & Robins, L.N. (1988). The diagnostic interview schedule: Its development, evolution, and use. *Social Psychiatry and Psychiatric Epidemiology, 23,* 6–16.

Hesselbrock, M., Easton, C., Bucholz, K.K., Schuckit, M., & Hesselbrock, V. (1999). A validity study of the SSAGA—A comparison with the SCAN. *Addiction, 94,* 1361–1370.

Houston, T.K., Cooper, L.A., Vu, H.T., Kahn, J., Toser, J., & Ford, D.E. (2001). Screening the public for depression through the Internet. *Psychiatric Services, 52,* 362–367.

Jensen, P.S., Watanabe, H.K., & Richters, J.E. (1999). Who's up first? Testing for order effects in structured interviews using a counterbalanced experimental design. *Journal of Abnormal Child Psychology, 27,* 439–445.

Koltai, D.C. & Welsh-Bohmer, K.A. (2000). Geriatric neuropsychological assessment. In R.D. Vanderploeg (Ed.), *Clinician's guide to neuropsychological assessment* (2nd ed., pp. 383–415). Mahwah, NJ: Erlbaum.

Krantz, J., Ballard, J., & Scher, J. (1997). Comparing the results of laboratory and world wide web samples on the determinants of female attractiveness. *Behavior Research Methods, Instruments, and Computers, 29,* 264–269.

Kranzler, H.R., Kadden, R.M., Babor, T.F., & Tennen, H. (1996). Validity of the SCID in substance abuse patients. *Addiction, 91,* 859–868.

Lesser, I.M. (1997). Cultural considerations using the structured clinical interview for DSM-III for mood and anxiety disorders assessment. *Journal of Psychopathology and Behavioral Assessment, 19,* 149–160.

Lopez, S.R. (1989). Patient variable biases in clinical judgment: Conceptual overview and methodological considerations. *Psychological Bulletin, 106,* 184–203.

Lopez, S.R., & Guarnaccia, P.J.J. (2000). Cultural psychopathology: Uncovering the social world of mental illness. *Annual Review of Psychology, 51,* 571–598.

Lucas, C.P., Fisher, P., Piacentini, J., Zhang, H., Jensen, P.S., Shaffer, D., Dulcan, M., Schwab-Stone, M., Regier, D., & Canino, G. (1999). Features of interview questions associated with attenuation of symptom reports. *Journal of Abnormal Child Psychology, 27,* 429–437.

Maffei, C., Fossati, A., Agostoni, I., Barraco, A., Bagnato, M., Deborah, D., Namia, C., Novella, L., & Petrachi, M. (1997). Interrater reliability and internal consistency of the structured clinical interview for DSM-IV axis II personality disorders (SCID-II), version 2.0. *Journal of Personality Disorders, 11,* 279–284.

Maisto, S.A., Sobell, L.C., Cooper, A.M., & Sobell, M.B. (1982). Comparison of two techniques to obtain retrospective reports of drinking behavior from alcohol abusers. *Addictive Behaviors, 7,* 33–38.

Mann, C., & Stewart, F. (2001). Internet interviewing. In J.F. Gubrium & J.A. Holstein (Eds.), *Handbook of interview research* (pp. 603–627). Thousand Oaks, CA: Sage.

Page, A.C. (1991). An assessment of structured diagnostic interviews for adult anxiety disorders. *International Review of Psychiatry, 3,* 265–278.

Piacentini, J., Roper, M., Jensen, P., Lucas, C., Fisher, P., Bird, H., Bourdon, K., Schwab-Stone, M., Rubio-Stipec, M., Davies, M., & Dulcan, M. (1999). Informant-based determinants of symptom attenuation in structured child psychiatric interviews. *Journal of Abnormal Child Psychology, 27,* 417–428.

Paradis, C.M., Friedman, S., Lazar, R.M., Grubea, J., & Kesselman, M. (1992). Use of a structured interview to diagnose anxiety disorders in a minority population. *Hospital and Community Psychiatry, 43,* 61–64.

Patterson, R.L., & Dupree, L.W. (1994). Older adults. In M. Hersen and S.M. Turner (Eds.), *Diagnostic interviewing* (pp. 373–397). New York: Plenum Press.

Perez, A.D.P., Meizoso, M.T.G, & Gonzalez, R.D. (1999). Validity of the structured interview for the assessment of type A behavior pattern. *European Journal of Psychological Assessment, 15,* 39–48.

Psychological & Educational Films (Producer). (1989). *Integrative psychotherapy—A six-part series: Part 3. A demonstration with Dr. Gerald Davison* [Motion picture]. Psychological & Educational Films, Corona Del Mar, CA.

Puente, A.E. & Garcia, M.P. (2000). Psychological assessment of ethnic minorities. In G. Goldstein & M. Hersen (Eds.), *Handbook of psychological assessment* (3rd ed., pp. 527–551). New York: Pergamon-Elsevier Science.

Reiger, D.A., Myers, J.K., Kramer, M., Robins, L.N., Blazer, D.G., Hough, R.I., Eaton, W.W., & Locke, B.Z. (1984). The NIMH epidemiologic catchment area program: Historical content, major objectives, and study population characteristics. *Archives of General Psychiatry, 41,* 934–941.

Robins, L.N., Helzer, J.E., Croughan, J., & Ratcliff, K.S. (1981). National institute of mental health diagnostic interview schedule. *Archives of General Psychiatry, 38,* 381–389.

Rosenman, R.H. (1978). The interview method of assessment of the coronary-prone behavior pattern. In T.M. Dembroski, S.M. Weiss, J.L. Shields, S.G. Haynes, & M. Feinlab (Eds.), *Coronary-prone behavior* (pp. 55–70). New York: Springer-Verlag.

Rosenman, R.H., Swan, G.E., & Carmelli, D. (1988). Definition, assessment, and evolution of the Type A Behavior Pattern. In B.K. Houston and C.R. Snyder (Eds.), *Type A behavior pattern: Research, theory, and intervention* (pp. 8–31). New York: Wiley.

Segal, D.L. (1997). Structured interviewing and DSM classification. In S.M. Turner and M. Hersen (Eds.), *Adult psychopathology and diagnosis* (3rd ed., pp. 24–57). New York: Wiley.

Segal, D.L., Hersen, M., & Van Hasselt, V.B. (1994). Reliability of the structured clinical interview for DSM-III-R: An evaluative review. *Comprehensive Psychiatry, 35,* 316–327.

Shaffer, D., Fisher, P., Lucas, C.P., Dulcan, M.K., & Schwab-Stone, M.E. (2000). NIMH diagnostic interview schedule for children version IV (NIMH DISC-IV): Description, differences from previous versions, and reliability of some diagnoses. *Journal of the American Academy of Child & Adolescent Psychiatry, 39,* 28–38.

Siegal, J.M., Matthews, K.A., & Leitch, C.J. (1981). Validation of the type A interview assessment of adolescents: A multidimensional approach. *Psychosomatic Medicine, 43,* 311–321.

Siegman, A.W. (1994). From type A to hostility to anger: Reflections on the history of coronary-prone behavior. In A.W. Siegman & T.W. Smith (Eds.). *Anger, hostility, and the heart* (pp. 1–21). Hillsdale, NJ: Erlbaum.

Silverman, W.K., & Eisen, A.R. (1992). Age differences in the reliability of parent and child reports of child anxious symptomatology using a structured interview. *Journal of the American Academy of Child and Adolescent Psychiatry, 31,* 117–124.

Silverman, W.K., & Rabian, B. (1995). Test-retest reliability of the DSM-III-R childhood anxiety disorder symptoms using the anxiety disorders interview schedule for children. *Journal of Anxiety Disorders, 9,* 139–150.

Smith, C. (1997). Casting the net: Surveying an Internet population. *Journal of Computer-Mediated Communication, 3.* Available at http://www.ascusc.org/jcmc/vol3/issue1/smith.html.

Sobell, L.C., Sobell, M.B., Leo, G.I., & Cancilla, A. (1988). Reliability of a timeline method: Assessing normal drinkers' reports of recent drinking and a comparative evaluation across several populations. *British Journal of Addictions, 83,* 393–402.

Sobell, L.C., Sobell, M.B., Maisto, S.A., & Cooper, A.M. (1985). Time-line follow-back assessment method. In D.J. Lettieri, M.A. Sayers, & J.E. Nelson (Eds.), *NIAAA treatment handbook series: Vol. 2. Alcoholism treatment, assessment, research instruments* (DHHS Publication No. 85–1380, pp. 530–534). Washington, DC: National Institute on Alcoholism and Alcohol Abuse.

Spitzer, R.L., Williams, J.B.W., Gibbon, M., & First, M.B. (1992). The structured clinical interview for DSM-III-R (SCID). Part I: History, rationale, and description. *Archives of General Psychiatry, 49,* 624–629.

Tanaka-Matsumi, J., Seiden, D.Y., & Lam, K.N. (1996). The culturally informed functional assessment interview: A strategy for cross cultural behavioral practice. *Cognitive and Behavioral Practice, 3,* 215–233.

Ventura, J., Liberman, R.P., Green, M.F., Shaner, A., & Mintz, J. (1998). Training and quality assurance with structured clinical interview for DSM-IV (SCID-I/P). *Psychiatry Research, 79,* 163–173.

Villasenor, Y., & Waitzkin, H. (1999). Limitations of a structured psychiatric diagnostic instrument in assessing somatization among Latino patients in primary care. *Medical Care, 37,* 637–646.

Wenger, G.C. (2001). Interviewing older people. In J.F. Gubrium & J.A. Holstein (Eds.), *Handbook of interview research* (pp. 259–278). Thousand Oaks, CA: Sage.

Wiens, A.N., & Brazil, P.J. (2000). Structured clinical interviews for adults. In G. Goldstein & M. Hersen (Eds.), *Handbook of psychological assessment* (3rd ed., pp. 387–410). New York: Pergamon-Elsevier Science.

Wilkinson, I. (2000). The Darlington family assessment system: Clinical guidelines for practitioners. *Journal of Family Therapy, 22,* 211–224.

Wilkinson, I., Barnett, M.B., Delf, L., & Pirie, V. (1988). Family assessment: Developing a formal assessment system in clinical practice. *Journal of Family Therapy, 10,* 17–32.

Wilkinson, I., & Stratton, P. (1991). The reliability and validity of a system for family assessment. *Journal of Family Therapy, 13,* 73–94.

Wittchen, H.U. (1994). Reliability and validity studies of the WHO-Composite International Diagnostic Interview (CIDI): A critical review. *Journal of Psychiatric Research, 28,* 57–84.

World Health Organization (1990). Composite International Diagnostic Interview (CIDI): a) CIDI-interview (version 1.0), b) CIDI-user manual, c) CIDI-training manual, d) CIDI-computer programs. Geneva, Switzerland: Author.

World Health Organization (1993). *The ICD-10 classification of mental and behavioral disorders.* Geneva, Switzerland: Author.

CHAPTER 12

Self-report Questionnaires

ROCÍO FERNÁNDEZ-BALLESTEROS

INTRODUCTION

Self-reports are the most common assessment procedures for collecting data in psychology, as well as being important instruments for the social sciences in general (Fernández-Ballesteros & Marquez, 2003; Schwartz, Park, Knauper, & Sudman, 1998; Stone, Turkkan, Bachrach, Jobe, Kurtzman, & Cain, 2000). Self-reports provide information about thousands of types of events, from sociodemographic ("How old are you?") and historical circumstances ("When and where did you go to school?") to present situation ("Do you sleep well?") and even to future plans ("Are you planning to get divorced?" or "Do you think this treatment will work?"). Thus, human beings are able to report on their private, unobservable, subjective world, their thoughts, their emotions ("Are you feeling sad?" "Are you thinking of Mary?"), as well as public observable events ("Did you take your pills?").

In clinical contexts, client self-reports frequently represent the starting point and conclusion of a professional relationship. Thus, the first information received by the clinician refers to the client's complaints, needs, and demands—"I feel terribly depressed," "I can't stand my marriage any more," "I need your help," "I'm thinking of committing suicide"— while the client usually ends his or her relationship with the psychologist by means of self-reports—"I feel so good!" "I do not need your help anymore!".[1]

Strictly speaking, the term "self-report" refers to the act of a person giving a detailed account or statement that describes his or her actions or any personal event. Therefore, as Zuriff (1985) emphasized, the self-report is a very broad category of verbal response given by a subject in the first person in any circumstance. From this point of view, self-reports are present in any human communication, but we are dealing here with the self-report as a procedure for data collection. Even when self-reports are used as formal procedures for data collection they remain a broad methodological category, because self-reports are also present in many other assessment methods: *interviews* always contain self-reports and *self-observation,* and *self-monitoring* also requires self-reports. Finally, self-reports can be obtained through *questionnaires,* which contain a set of relevant statements and a variety of response formats, including true-false options, checklists, scaled responses, etc. A self-report questionnaire has the purpose of helping the client to answer specific relevant questions and recording and scoring his or her answer in a systematic fashion.

It is commonly recognized that self-reports are fallible sources of data. Whatever the type of event reported—from objective events to subjective ones—human beings cannot be considered highly precise observers of themselves and their circumstances. Several internal and external conditions, such as time of the question, formulation of the question, type of answer and response requested, the subject's characteristics, and many other conditions, strongly affect the fidelity of self-reports. This is the main methodological reason why self-reports have been criticized within behavioral psychology and why other more objective methods have been considered more valuable, at least in collecting overt responses or physiological reactions that can be measured directly with specific equipment.

But there is also strong theoretical criticism of self-reports from within general psychology. The main reason for such criticism is that self-reports are at the heart of the heated mentalism-physicalism debate, and because they were a central method in the study of consciousness as the scientific subject of psychology (e.g., Skinner, 1938; Watson, 1913, 1920; also see Boring, 1953).

Also, not only are social scientists in general and clinical psychologists in particular interested in collecting data through self-reports, but they usually perform several statistical manipulations with them (e.g., items aggregation, item anchoring in new scales, etc.) in order to test theoretical hypotheses, and they interpret them as indices of internal structures or processes, such as attitudes, personality characteristics, motives, and other intrapsychic concepts developed from social psychology, trait theory, or psychoanalysis. Thus, from the very beginning of scientific psychology, aggregates of self-reports assessed via questionnaires through intersubjects designs (subjects aggregates) have been used as one of the main assessment methods for describing, classifying, predicting, and even (tautologically) explaining human behavior. For example, the Minnesota Multiphasic Personality Inventory (MMPI, Hathaway & McKinley, 1940) and the California Psycholog-

ical Inventory (CPI, Gough, 1975) are examples of those types of questionnaires.

Self-reports, as indicators of intrapsychic constructs or as the product of introspection, were rejected as unscientific by first- and second-generation behaviorism (Staats, 1975, 1996). It was not until the 1960s, when a third generation of behaviorists (Bandura, 1969; Mischel, 1968; Staats & Staats, 1963; Wolpe, 1964) developed a new conception of behavioral psychology (social learning theory, social behaviorism, cognitive-behavioral psychology) and, as a consequence, behavioral assessment was born and self-reports were accepted as a method for data collection. Questionnaires assessing specific behavioral constructs' links to behavioral intervention techniques—such as the Rathus Assertiveness Schedule (Rathus, 1973) and the Fear Survey Schedule (Wolpe & Lang, 1964)—developed for selecting behavioral targets, were accepted as behavioral instruments.

In summary, human beings are able to report on a myriad of events and are an important source of information. Several assessment methods (such as interviews and self-monitoring) are based on self-reports and questionnaires. Even though self-reports can introduce an important source of errors, it is commonly accepted that self-report questionnaires can be optimized through various strategies and that their fidelity can be maximized. This chapter deals with the diversity of relevant conditions that affect self-report questionnaires and the conditions in which they can serve as rigorous assessment methods (for a review, see Turkkan, 2000).

SELF-REPORT QUESTIONNAIRES IN BEHAVIORAL ASSESSMENT LITERATURE AND PRACTICE

Since the very beginning of behavioral assessment, self-report questionnaires have been an ever-present methodological category in behavioral assessment publications, as well as in clinical practice. Let us review the evidence from these two fields.

Self-report Questionnaires in Behavioral Assessment Publications

Because it is commonly accepted that behavioral assessment was founded in 1965 as a result of the seminal work of Kanfer & Saslow (1965, 1969) and that it was consolidated in the 1970s (the decade Nelson [1983] refers to as "the honeymoon of behavioral assessment"), it is relatively easy to assess the evolution of behavioral self-report questionnaires over the last 30 years by reviewing published books and journals on behavioral assessment.

The Appendix lists 28 books on behavioral assessment. It is important to stress that growth was constant throughout the 1970s and 1980s. Nevertheless, only two books were published during the 1990s, and this fact seems to reflect a crisis in behavioral assessment (Hayes, Nelson, & Jarrett, 1986; Nelson, 1983). However, also during the 1990s, and for the first time in psychological assessment history, behavioral assessment appeared as a chapter or section in general books on psychological assessment (Cohen, Swerdik, & Phillips, 1996; Goldstein & Hersen, 1984, 1990, 2000; Groth-Marnat, 1990), with the same status or role as the assessment of personality or intelligence, or even as the MMPI or the Rorschach. As has been emphasized elsewhere (Fernández-Ballesteros, 1993), the conceptual nature of behavioral assessment has been diluted, and it has been accepted by the psychological assessment community as a set of techniques in which, precisely, self-report questionnaires are prominent (e.g., Groth-Marnat, 1990).

The Appendix also shows that the majority of these books include a chapter or section on self-report questionnaires. It is important to mention that no chapters on self-report questionnaires (nor on self-monitoring or self-observation) are present in the last two editions of Bellack and Hersen's handbooks (1988, 1998)[2] as well as in other more recent books on behavioral assessment.

Among these books, the *Dictionary of Behavioral Assessment Techniques* (Hersen & Bellack, 1988) deserves special mention. As the authors state, as they worked on the *Dictionary of Behavior Therapy Techniques* they were "impressed with the wide range of modalities that behaviorists use to evaluate their clients, patients and subjects" (p. xix): behavioral observations, self-reports, rating by others, physiological assessment, biological assessment, interviews, and analogue tests. The *Dictionary* extensively reviews 287 behavioral assessment instruments and provides information about purposes, development, psychometrics, clinical use, future directions, and references.

Table 12.1 shows frequencies and percentages of the several types of methods reviewed: self-report, observation, rating by others, physiological measures, interviews, and others. Around 53% of all techniques included in the *Dictionary* are self-report questionnaires, inventories, or scales. It can be concluded that self-report instruments are the most widespread methodological category, more than twice as common as observation, which is considered the most representative method in behavioral assessment.

TABLE 12.1   Types of Methods in the *Dictionary of Behavioral Assessment Techniques*

Type of Method	Frequency	Percentage
Self-reports	154	53.47
Observation	75	26.04
Rating by Others	25	8.69
Physiological Measures	18	6.25
Interviews	13	4.51
Other	2	1.04

Note. From Hersen & Bellack, 1988; in Fernández-Ballesteros, 1993, p. 64.

Self-reports in *Behavioral Assessment* and in the *Journal of Behavioral Assessment*

The dissemination of behavioral assessment research over the last 30 years has not only been through books. One of the most important indicators of the maturity and productivity of behavioral assessment occurred in 1979, when two journals devoted to behavioral assessment were published: *Behavioral Assessment* (BA) (Pergamon Press, 1979–1992) and the *Journal of Behavioral Assessment* (JBA) (Plenum Press, 1979–1984, converted in 1985 into the *Journal of Psychopathology and Behavioral Assessment,* JPBA). This is not the place to analyze the reasons why *Behavioral Assessment* had such a short 14-year life (see Cone, 1992) or why the *Journal of Behavioral Assessment* changed its name (see Fernández-Ballesteros, 1994b). Our purpose here is to analyze the impact of self-reports within these two journals by considering how many articles dealt with self-reports. It is important to emphasize that only articles devoted to methods were selected; that is, in BA only 34.36% were analyzed, and in the JBA, 64.03%.

Table 12.2 shows the frequency and percentage of articles dealing with the seven most frequently utilized methods in behavioral assessment: observation, self-reports, interviews,

TABLE 12.2   Number and Percentage of Articles Dealing with Different Types of Methods in *Behavioral Assessment* (1979–1992) and the *Journal of Behavioral Assessment* (1979–1984)

	Behavioral Assessment (N = 410)		*Journal of Behavioral Assessment* (N = 165)	
	Number of Articles	Percentage	Number of Articles	Percentage
Observation	50	12.3	21	12.7
Self-reports	41	10.0	41	24.8
Interview	10	2.4	2	1.2
Rating by Others	11	2.7	9	5.4
Analogue	9	2.2	11	6.6
Self-monitoring	4	0.1	5	3.0
Other	16	3.9	7	10.3

rating by others, analogue observation, self-monitoring, and others. Observation has a similar impact in the two journals (12.9% in BA and 12.7% in the JBA), while self-reports have a greater impact in the JBA (24.8%) than they do in BA (10%). In summary, self-reports have had an important presence in both behavioral assessment journals.

Self-reports in PsycLIT Behavioral Assessment Literature

Cone (1993) reviewed behavioral assessment articles abstracted in PsycLIT during two periods—1980–1982 and 1990–1992—classifying them into six categories (according to the Behavioral Assessment Grid, BAG). As shown in Figure 12.1, direct observation is the most frequently utilized method in the behavioral assessment literature in both periods, but it decreases significantly from 53.3% in 1980–1982 to 38.8% in 1990–1992. Nevertheless, the self-report method increased its presence from 9.2% in 1980–1982 to 13.7% in 1990–1992.

Behavioral Self-reports as Psychological Tests

The *Mental Measurements Yearbook* (MMY), edited by Buros (1941–1978), is a very well-known source of information about psychological tests, from 1941 to 1998 (Murphy, 1992). Moreover, through the evolution of the MMY's sections, we are able to examine the evolution of psychological assessment. Despite the fact that behavioral assessment emerged as an alternative to traditional assessment, and in clear opposition to tests, behavioral assessment is being incorporated into psychological assessment literature. It is therefore interesting to examine the presence of behavioral self-reports in the last MMY as a final avenue of literature-based inquiry.

The 11th MMY (Murphy, 1992) contains descriptive information on 369 tests, as well as 693 test reviews. These reviewed tests generated 3,222 references gathered since 1995. With regard to behavioral assessment and self-reports, two important facts should be considered:

1. *Behavioral Assessment* appeared in the classified subject index with 21 instruments, 81% of them new tests. Since the keyword *behavior* appears to be the criterion for classification, not all tests introduced in this category are behavioral (for example: Adult Attention Deficit Disorders Behavior Rating Scale or Test of Variables of Attention).

2. Several questionnaires and inventories usually considered as behavioral self-reports (as well as other rating-by-others instruments) have been introduced in other subjects. For example, the Beck Depression Inventory (the most fre-

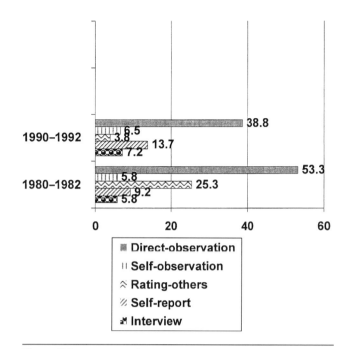

Figure 12.1   Percentage of articles by five types of methods for two periods: 1980–1982 and 1990–1992. From "The Current State of Behavioral Assessment," by J.D. Cone, 1993, *European Journal of Psychological Assessment, 9,* p. 178. Reprinted with permission.

quently cited test, with 1,026 references) was included in the Personality section.

In summary, behavioral assessment and self-report questionnaires are present in one of the most comprehensive compendiums of psychological tests, and some self-report questionnaires are even the most cited instruments.

Self-reports in Clinical Training and Practice

As already emphasized, self-reports have been one of the most commonly used methods throughout the history of psychological assessment. Here we consider two important roles of self-reports in behavioral assessment: the use of self-reports in clinical training and the use of self-reports by clinical psychologists.

Self-reports in Clinical Training

With the aim of emphasizing the relative importance of training in the different types of behavioral assessment methods, several surveys have been conducted within graduate training programs over the last 20 years. In an attempt to replicate the survey conducted in 1982 by Piotrowski and Keller (1984b), in 1991, Piotrowski and Zalewski (1993) assessed the importance of behavioral and nonbehavioral methods in PhD

TABLE 12.3   Assessment Instruments Considered Important by AABT Members (Percentage of Members Who Select Some Instruments Among Five Mentioned)

Behavioral	%	Objectives	%	Projectives	%
Observation	20	MMPI	70	TAT	38
Self-reports	24	CPI	15	Rorschach	34
Self-monitoring	9	Wechsler	12	Drawing a Person	16
Interview	7	16-PF	10	Sentence Completion	15
Role-playing	4	EPPS	6	CAT	6
Physiological	4	EPI	5	Bender-Gestalt	4

Note. Modified from Piotrowski & Keller, 1984b.

and PsyD programs accredited by the American Psychological Association (51% of total accredited programs, $N = 80$). It is important to point out that 57% of these programs were considered eclectic, followed by 13% that were considered behavioral; nevertheless, training in behavioral assessment techniques was required in 50% of the programs.

In those programs that provide training in behavioral assessment, the following six techniques are ranked highest in terms of training emphasis: behavioral observation (39.1%), interview (16.3%), self-monitoring (12.6%), self-reports (10.1%), physiological measures (8.9%), role-playing assessment (6.3%). The remainder of the techniques were mentioned by less than 5% of the sample.

When respondents were asked about the extent to which projective, objective, and behavioral assessment use is warranted in various applied clinical settings, behavioral assessment received the highest affirmative expectancy: 78.6% answered yes (26% projective personality assessment and 69% objective personality assessment).

Although it is extremely difficult to make international comparisons among clinical and/or psychological training, surveys conducted in Europe yield similar results (see *Evaluación Psicológica/Psychological Assessment*, 1991).

Self-reports in Clinical Practice

One of the first surveys on the practice of behavioral assessment was conducted by Piotrowski and Keller in 1984. Table 12.3 shows those instruments mentioned by the Association for Advancement of Behavior Therapy (AABT) members, classified into three categories of behavioral, objective, and projective. Among behavioral methods were several self-report questionnaires and inventories (Beck Depression Inventory, Assertiveness Scales, the Fear Survey Schedule, and anxiety self-reports measures), so a new self-reports category has been included.[3]

Without doubt, self-report questionnaires (both behavioral and objective, or traditional) are the most cited instruments among AABT members. Of course, the mixture of instruments yielded by this first survey contradict any behavioral rationale.

Fifteen years later, Guevremont and Spielgler (1990, cited by Haynes, 1998) surveyed 988 AABT members. On the basis of this second survey, Haynes (1998) arrived at the following conclusions: (1) the interview is the most common assessment method, used by 91% of AABT members; (2) objective personality questionnaires and self-reports inventories are used by 50% to 80% of AABT members; (3) the use of self-monitoring (also a self-report method) has increased to 50%; and (4) observation is decreasing, with only 15% to 25% of clinicians reporting this method.

Data from European countries and other international studies reveal similar results regarding the importance of self-report measurement techniques. In 1995, Bomholt (1996) surveyed members of the European Association of Psychological Assessment (EAPA) ($N = 37$, 27% of membership) and the International Association of Applied Psychology (IAAP) Division 2 on Psychological Assessment & Evaluation ($N = 90$, 34% of membership). Respondents were asked what types of measurement devices, techniques, or instruments they used in their professional work. Psychometric (which includes most objectives questionnaires) was the most chosen methodological category (94% EAPA, 88% Division 2), followed by direct observation (47% EAPA and 56% Division 2), behavioral instruments (36% EAPA, and 33% Division 2), and, finally, neuropsychological devices, projective techniques, and physiological measures (25% EAPA, and 10% Division 2).

In summary, whatever the avenue of inquiry reviewed, self-report questionnaires (as well as other types of self-reports, such as interviews, self-monitoring, or self-observation) are frequently used methods in behavioral assessment.

CHARACTERISTICS OF BEHAVIORAL SELF-REPORT QUESTIONNAIRES

One of the conclusions from the last section is that behavioral assessment involves a prototypical set of methods—interview, direct observation, observing and/or rating by others, self-monitoring or self-observation, and role-playing and/or observation in analogue situations—and that among them are self-report questionnaires. Of course, the ranking of some methods over others depends on the source of information reviewed, but all of them can be considered behavioral methods. Thus, we must ask what are the main characteristics of these methods.

As has been repeated throughout the behavioral assessment literature (Barrios & Hartmann, 1986; Goldfried & Kent, 1972; Hartmann, Roper, & Bradford, 1979), several assumptions underlie behavioral assessment methods; there are also some misconceptions underlying these assumptions that should be clarified.

Direct Versus Indirect Methods

Direct and *indirect* are two adjectives that have been applied to distinguish between traditional and behavioral methods (including self-reports) and constructs, as well as between different types of behavioral methods. Let analyze the different meanings of these adjectives.

Despite the fact that behavioral assessment emerged in the 1960s linked to the third generation of behaviorism, its roots were mainly in radical behaviorism. Thus, characteristic assumptions from radical behaviorism were transferred to behavioral assessment. Because Skinnerian functional analysis has the purpose of analyzing overt target behaviors as well as their environmental control conditions, the priority method of behavioral assessment is, necessarily, direct observation (Skinner, 1953). Thus, several behavioral assessors have emphasized that direct methods are prototypical of behavioral assessment. Without doubt, direct observation is the best method for assessing overt behaviors and environmental conditions, but when other behaviors (physiological, emotional, cognitive, etc.) are to be assessed, what do direct and indirect methods (as opposing terms) mean?

Mischel (1968, 1972) was one of the first authors (within the behavioral assessment context) to deal with the concepts of direct and indirect methods. His conceptualization of indirect and direct has certain parallelisms with the interpretation the assessor gives to a particular test (so that a test can be interpreted in both ways), including self-report questionnaires. Also, Mischel refers to direct items or questions when assessed behaviors are close to the content assessed (e.g., current grades are a direct measure of long-term achievement) and indirect when the behavior assessed has a minor relationship to the construct assessed (e.g., response to the Thematic Apperception Test (Murray, 1938) is an indirect measure of school achievement motivation.

In this discussion, Mischel criticizes behavioral psychologists who are opposed to self-reports in all cases. He emphasizes the importance of self-reports when behavioral data are *directly* reported or when the subject reports on stimuli conditions or his or her perceptions about events. For Mischel, the only restriction on self-reports is that they should not be used to make *indirect* inferences (or as signs) of underlying personality attributes. In sum, Mischel (1968, 1972) introduced a new conceptualization in this field, accepting self-reports as behavioral methods when used as direct measures of clients' behavior. This conceptualization has a parallel assumption: that direct observation is not necessarily a direct method because overt behavior observations (e.g., a smile) can be considered as indirect measures of other variables (e.g., sociability).

Despite Mischel's conceptualization, other behavioral assessors continued with the above-mentioned Skinnerian conceptualization. Thus, Cone (1978, 1981a) proposed a taxonomy of behavioral methods based on two criteria: source of information (oneself or others) and accessibility (public or private behaviors). He classified self-reports and interviews as "oneself/private," self-observation as "oneself/public," rating by others as "others/public," and direct observation as "others/public." Finally, Cone proposed a continuum of directionality, from direct to indirect, placing on this continuum five of the most common behavioral methods: direct observation, self-observation, rating by others, self-reports, and interviews.

Several objections can be made to Cone's taxonomy: (1) Accessibility is related not to the method but to the event assessed. Self-reports, interviews, and self-observations can assess overt and covert events, and, therefore, self-observation cannot be considered (in Cone's terminology) as a direct method when the self-observed behavior is a covert event. At the same time, self-reports and interviews cannot be considered only as methods for assessing private events. (2) When private events are assessed and no method could be considered direct—for example, feelings, thoughts, etc.—the most direct ones are, precisely, interviews, self-reports, and self-observations. (3) Finally, rating by others is highly indirect when others observe and rate a client's private events; assessment of covert behaviors through rating by others involves interpretation of clients' behavior, so this method can be considered highly indirect.

A final conceptualization of the direct versus indirect debate comes from social behaviorism (Burns, 1989; Staats, 1975). The rationale for accepting self-reports as scientific methods is based on two different arguments (Staats & Fernández-Ballesteros, 1987). The first argument refers to a reconceptualization of personality as basic behavioral repertoires defined by Staats (1975) as a complex constellation of stimulus-response associations learned through a long-term cumulative-hierarchical learning processes. Basic behavioral repertoires could be cognitive-linguistic, sensory-motor, or emotional-motivational. These basic behavioral repertoires are an effect of the past environmental conditions and can be conceptualized as causes of target behaviors, and they can be modified by training methods (e.g., social skills, locus of control, pleasant activities, etc.). In other words, basic behavioral repertoires should be observable by both sides of the causal chain. Along the same line, the second argument arises from the scientific need to consider internal events not only as responses to external events but as independent variables. From a methodological point of view, the method for studying both types of behavioral constructs is called *indirect observation* (Staats & Staats, 1963). As Minke (1990) pointed out,

> the logic of indirect observation protects science against errors of inference by arguing that before an inferred implicit event can be used in an explanatory fashion, the existence of two sets of independent causal relationships must be demonstrated, one relating the implicit events to observable antecedent events and the second relating observable consequent events to the implicit event. In other words, it must be demonstrated that the inferred implicit event has both dependent and independent properties within the context of observable variables in the situation. . . . Only after the two sets of causal relationships have been demonstrated to operate independently can the inferred event be given explanatory properties (p. 66).

In order to have observable behavior on both sides of the causal chain, it is necessary to not only operationalize a given construct (as in traditional personality and cognitive assessment), but also for experimental methods to support both internal (cognitive) events and skills, competence, constellation of responses, or basic behavioral repertoires. From psychological behaviorism, we should have at least two types of evidence: experimental evidence about how an internal event or a basic behavioral repertoire has been learned and experimental evidence that a given treatment or manipulating variable can control this internal event and/or this basic behavioral repertoire.

In conclusion, direct versus indirect alternatives have several meanings in behavioral assessment. Assessment methods are as direct as the content assessed can be directly observed. When internal events or basic behavioral repertoires are taken into account, indirect observation is compatible with both experimental methodology and a behavioral model. Therefore, self-reports (like the other behavioral assessment methods) are not a priori indirect methods.

Sample Versus Sign Interpretation

As stated above, the issue of direct versus indirect methods in some way relates to the interpretation of data collected. From the very beginning, behavioral assessors pointed out that the interpretation of responses to a given behavioral method should involve a low *level of inference* (Goldfried and Kent, 1972). This low level of abstraction means that assessed behaviors should be considered *samples* of the subject's behaviors, and not as *signs* of intrapsychic constructs or genotypical characteristics (Mischel, 1968, 1972). "A behavioral sample measures nothing beyond itself" (Kirkland, 1978, p. 14). For example, using a heart rate monitor yielded a sample of the client's heart rate and not a sign (an index) of psychological arousal. An extension of this assumption is that behavioral assessors are interested in what the patient *does* (behavior) and not what the patient *is* or *has* (underlying causal personality condition).

Nevertheless, over the history of behavioral assessment, this radical and quite simplistic opposition between the response taken as sample or as sign has become modulated by conceptual developments. As Sundberg, Tyler, and Taplin (1973) emphasized, in the process of interpretation of a set of collected responses we can distinguish three levels of inference: sample, correlate, and sign. At Level I (response as sample) are descriptive data relating to life history or the current situation. However, when during an interview or after the administration of a given questionnaire a client reports intense depressed mood, diminished interest or pleasure in almost all activities, significant weight loss, insomnia nearly every day, loss of energy, feelings of worthlessness, diminished ability to concentrate, and recurrent thoughts of death, the clinician not only takes this set of behaviors as a *sample,* but makes a *generalization.* He or she thus concludes that, at the time of assessment, the client presents a series of behaviors that *correlate,* and that taken together describe a mood disorder. In other words, the clinician concludes that the case could be classified as major depression without interpreting any underlying causal entity. But, in the conceptualization of Sundberg et al. (1973), Level II refers to a *hypothetical construct* that is more than a pure description or generalization when the assessor considers that this set of behaviors implies an intervening variable or even a causal condition (see MacCorquodale & Meehl, 1948). Finally, for Sundberg et al., Level III refers to a situation in which data collected are taken as a *sign* implying a consistent theory of person-situation and requiring a coherent theoretical system of hypotheses and deductions.[4]

Behavioral assessment and, especially, self-report methods collect information about several types of events at several steps of the assessment process; the level of interpretation of data collected cannot be a theoretical precondition, but should depend on the type of event assessed and of the question required by the process step. For example, during case formulation, self-reported target behaviors (motor, physiological, and cognitive) should be collected and interpreted as a *sample* or as a *correlate*. However, also at this step of the process, maintaining conditions (causal conditions) should be hypothesized and tested. In other words, as recognized by several authors (even at the very beginning of the behavioral assessment approach, Ferster, 1965), functional analysis implies a theoretical link between target responses and causal variables. Nevertheless, at the first step of the assessment process, functional relationships between these variables can be considered as *correlates* between two types of events: any observation about stimulus-response interactions, at a first stage, implies association. Self-reported and other behavioral data may be interpreted not only as a sample of verbal or motor behavior in a similar situation, but as a correlate. Along the same line, targets and basic behavioral repertoires are interpreted as correlates at this point of the process when we assume that they act as intervening or causal conditions of target behaviors (e.g., Fernández-Ballesteros & Staats, 1992; Staats & Staats, 1963).

Moreover, the main goal of behavioral assessment is behavioral change, and, therefore, experimental method is at the root of the behavioral assessment model. This means that after a first assessment phase, hypothesized causal variables should be manipulated through treatment, and, before treatment implementation, it may be necessary to administer assessment methods in order to provide data for treatment evaluation as well as for controlling intervening variables. At this stage, functional relationships among variables imply a theoretical level of inference.

Finally, one of the most important characteristics of behavioral assessment is ongoing assessment through the assessment-treatment-and-evaluation process. Predicted changes of relevant variables (target behaviors, causes, and intervening conditions) assessed by means of self-reports and other behavioral methods can be interpreted as proof of the hypothesized link between targets, causal variables, and intervening and/or manipulating conditions. In other words, responses to self-reports and other behavioral methods also could be interpreted as *signs* of an underlying theory fulfilled in the particular case assessed, treated, and evaluated (e.g., Haynes, 1988).

Depending on the type of conditions assessed, the step in the assessment process, and the purpose of the assessment data collected by behavioral methods, including self-report questionnaires, clients' responses can be interpreted at a high level of inference. However, in order to interpret responses to behavioral methods, it is necessary to address an important question: What guarantees are required? Since behavioral assessment is supported by an experimental design (in the process of assessment-treatment-evaluation), any response interpretation is supported by the logic and inference of experimental methodology.

Idiographic Versus Nomothetic Approach

Behavioral assessment has been described as an idiographic approach, in contrast to the traditional nomothetic assessment. Both conceptualizations originated from Windelbland (1878), a post-Kantian philosopher who, at the end of the nineteenth century—inspired in the opposition stated by Dilthey between Nature Sciences (including biology) and Spirit Sciences (including psychology)—made a distinction between nomothetic (from Greek, *nomos* = norm) and idiographic (from Greek, *idios* = individual) sciences. The former types were devoted to the search for general principles, and the latter were concerned with specific phenomena of a particular individual. Windelbland stated that psychology—given its objective and conceptual structure—is a nomothetic science, but it is idiographic if we consider its content and applications.

Behavioral assessors took these concepts not from the old philosophers but from the interpretations of others, such as Allport (1963), who argued that the aim of the science of personality was to seek general principles applicable to personality and study the configuration of these characteristics in a specific individual. Underlying this conceptualization are differential epistemological and methodological characteristics: objectives (search for laws or search for individuality), concepts (general or specific constructs), methods (general or specific methods), and designs (group or single-case designs).[5]

In psychological assessment, idiographic refers to the study of the *single case* (it is not possible to infer general laws from a single case), studying the situation and needs of the client, and trying to assess his or her specific problem and explain its causes or how general principles and general constructs are expressed in this particular individual. Thus, psychological assessment and therapy usually employ an idiographic position because they deal with a single subject (an individual or a specific group of individuals), assessing his or her demands, needs, and complaints, setting up idiographic hypotheses about the case, testing these hypotheses, implementing and evaluating an intervention, and following up the case. Nevertheless, it should be stressed that this idiographic position is possible because of principles from general psychology that allow us to deduce these hypotheses and treat the case through well-known and valid interventions. In other words, the two perspectives are compatible in practice. As stated elsewhere (Fernández-Ballesteros, 1980, 1994c; West-meyer, 2001), behavioral assessment (as well as therapy) is a subdiscipline derived from scientific psychology and is therefore supported by a network of general concepts and principles (classical and operant conditioning, social-learning, and cognitive behavioral principles). Nevertheless, its essential objective concerns a single case, and it analyzes how general principles are fulfilled in this particular single case (Jaccard & Dittus, 1990).

However, within behavioral assessment and therapy there have been some misunderstandings, and the meanings of the terms idiographic and nomothetic have shifted. The term nomothetic is applied to general constructs and standard tests developed from group designs, while the term idiographic is used for those specific (nonstandard) methods developed or adapted for a specific individual, such as self-monitoring and self-observation. What are the characteristics of these idiographic methods—including self-report questionnaires? First, they have no standard materials; protocols for data collection are specially prepared for a particular client in a specific situation. Second, the raw score derived usually cannot be converted into a standard score; since there are no standard materials, norms cannot be derived. Third, they are immersed in a process of change led by an experimental design, and, therefore, the predictions that can be made from these scores relate not to intersubject differences but to intrasubject change.

Despite this conceptualization, behavioral assessment (and therapy) is also interested and involved in general concepts (such as reinforcement, interaction, social skills, etc.), in general methods (such as general observation codes, standard self-report questionnaires, etc.) developed through group designs, and in the accumulation of results coming from $N = 1$ designs that provide basic knowledge of behavioral science and methods.

Behavioral assessors extend both concepts in an attempt to set nomothetic-traditional assessment in opposition to idiographic-behavioral assessment.[6] Thus, nomothetic assessment is the type that uses general concepts (extroversion, intelligence, etc.) with high levels of inference, measured by *standard methods* that permit interindividual comparisons, require *aggregates of behaviors,* and use group designs (therefore, testing those concepts in subjects' *aggregates*). In contrast, idiographic-behavioral assessment uses *specific concepts* with low levels of inference, measured by *specific methods* (e.g., self-monitoring) that do not require aggregates of heterogeneous behaviors, applied to the *single case.*

As stated above, the majority of polarities used for distinguishing between behavioral and traditional assessment are

highly inconsistent and should be harmonized, taking into account the nature of the *content* assessed, the level of *inference* used, and the *step of the process.* For example, Cautela's (1977) Cues for Tension and Anxiety Survey Schedule for assessing target behaviors can be considered highly idiographic, because it assesses possible targets and does not require aggregates—neither behavior aggregates nor subject aggregates. For example, Item 1 asks, "You feel tense in: a) your forehead, b) back of your neck, c) chest, d) shoulder, e) stomach, f) face, g) other parts (specify where)." But other idiographic techniques such as the Goal Attainment Scaling (Kiresuk, in press; Kiresuk, Smith, & Cardillo, 1994), the Repertory Grid Technique (Bannister & Maier, 1968), or the role-play methodology (Kern, 1991) can be standardized using aggregates.

Therefore, a combination of methods can be used in behavioral assessment. For example, in a case of depression, a client's target behaviors should be assessed idiographically through specific idiographic methods such as self-monitoring, role-playing, or defining change objectives through Goal Attainment Scaling. But, other standardized self-reports can be used for making group comparisons. Also, if in a case of depression the assessor hypothesizes that depressive behaviors are functionally related to the accumulation of unpleasant events and/or to a deficit in social skills (both hypotheses already tested in group designs, see Heiby, 1978; Heiby & Staats, 1990; Lewinsohn, 1974), in both cases nomothetic behavioral concepts should be assessed, and nomothetic self-reports (or other nomothetic behavioral methods) should be used that yield item aggregates and present psychometric guarantees yielded in group designs. Also, if after testing this functional relationship—the association between the target response (e.g., depression) and causal variables (e.g., social skills) is tested—and a treatment on social skills provided, we can expect a change in these nomothetic self-reports (or other behavioral measures) after treatment.

In sum, the idiographic versus nomothetic assessment debate is an oversimplification of the situation with regard to these concepts. Although several idiographic self-report methods have been developed from a behavioral perspective, behavioral self-report inventories and questionnaires—as well as other behavioral methods—can be used from an idiographic or nomothetic perspective depending on the type of variable assessed and the purpose of the assessment.

Use of Multiple Methods/Multiple Contents Versus Use of Monomethod/Monocontent

Behaviorism developed out of logical positivism, and, therefore, throughout the history of behavioral psychology, *objectivity* has been one of the most important characteristics of any measurement device. This was the main reason why introspection, subjective events, and self-reports were rejected by the first and second generations of behaviorism. Because overt behaviors and external stimuli and their functional relationships were the only relevant variables for these early behaviorists, the method considered most appropriate was observation.

As described above, behavioral assessment developed as a product of the evolution of behavioral psychology with the third generation of behaviorism. Its development also was linked and parallel to epistemological and methodological criticisms of logical positivism. As Cook (1985) points out, during the 1960s and 1970s, philosophers, historians, sociologists of science, and methodologists criticized most of the characteristics of logical positivism and the application of its reductionism to the social and psychological sciences. On the basis of these criticisms there emerged a new methodological and epistemological proposal, *multiplism.* Although this issue is relevant, a full discussion here is not possible. The most important point to emphasize is that behavioral assessment was developed at the same time the social and behavioral sciences were strongly criticizing logical positivism and its reductionist assumption that involved taking as scientific subjects only external events and employing only one method of inquiry: observation.

Thus, from the very beginning, behavioral assessment considered three different response systems or response modes—motor, cognitive, and physiological—as well as several research methods—observation, self-report, and physiological equipment measures—and several informants (e.g., Cone, 1978, 1979; Evans, 1986; Kanfer & Saslow, 1965). However, being open to three response modes and to different methods and informants did not solve one of the main problems with behavioral assessment: Because each of the three response modes are assessed by one of the three methods proposed, contents are confused with methods (Cone, 1979). A test by Campbell and Fiske (1959) demonstrated that multitrait-multimethods matrices yielded higher correlations due more to method than to content, and the same results occurred when multi-response-mode multimethods were studied in behavioral assessment (Evans, 1986; Fernández-Ballesteros, 1994d; Fernández-Ballesteros et al., 1981). Nevertheless, the use of multimethods is one of the most characteristic aspects of behavioral assessment. In other words, self-reports questionnaires must be used as part of a set of methods.

Experimental Versus Correlational Designs

The main goal of behavioral assessment is *behavioral change,* and this distinguishes behavioral assessment from other types of assessment. Cronbach (1957, 1975) proposed

correlational and experimental approaches to scientific psychology. The correlational approach searches for associations between variables in natural environments. The experimental approach investigates the effect of the manipulation of an independent (causal) variable on a dependent variable. From this point of view, behavioral assessment is part of an experimental situation in which assessment, experimental manipulations (treatment), and evaluation are steps in the same process (Fernández-Ballesteros, 1979, 1994d; Haynes, 1978). Therefore, behavioral assessment is embedded in an experimental design, but typical self-report questionnaires emerged from intersubject correlational designs.

Nevertheless, in the first phase of the behavioral assessment process, when the case is analyzed, observational and correlational measures must be administered in order to test a hypothetical case formulation (Fernández-Ballesteros, 1980; Haynes, 1992, 1998). This is a precondition for planning an intervention and testing more plausible hypotheses through an experimental design. In other words, as will be described in the next section, the process of assessment, treatment, and evaluation—prototypical of behavioral assessment—combines the correlational and experimental approaches. As Silva (1989, 1993a) emphasized, the correlational and observational phases of behavioral assessment are within the *context of discovery,* and this comes before the experimental approach, which is within the *context of justification.*

However, as mentioned above, first- and second-generation behaviorism and logical positivism reject constructs as units of study in psychology. This important matter also falls outside the scope of the present chapter, but it should be underlined, first, that there are no sciences that operate without constructs, and, second, the point is not an a priori rejection of constructs but rather to establish precisely under what circumstances and with what scientific criteria constructs can be used. These circumstances and criteria are linked to the above sections. In short, behavioral constructs should be operationalized through multimethods and should be able to be manipulated through experimental designs. As Staats (Staats & Staats, 1963) argued, self-reports should be able to be "indirectly" observed (see discussion of direct versus indirect methods above; also see, e.g., Fernández-Ballesteros & Staats, 1992; Staats & Fernández-Ballesteros, 1987).

Let us consider an example with self-report questionnaires. A client complains through a first interview about a problematic situation with her husband: She never reaches orgasm during intercourse with him and has never had sex with anyone else. After several interviews with the client and her husband, functional hypotheses were set up referring to her sexual information, her emotional responses to sexual stimuli (attitudes in traditional vocabulary), and her (and her husband's) sexual interactions (also assessed by her husband).

Several self-report instruments were administered in order to test her problem situation (potential target behaviors and potential causal variables). Among the multiple instruments used, the following self-reports were administered: the Sexual Knowledge Inventory (McHugh, 1967), the Heterosexual Attitude Scale—Female Form (Robinson & Annon, 1975; assessed also through physiological responses to sexual stimuli), and the Survey of Heterosexual Interaction (Twentyman & McFall, 1975; assessed also through hetero-observational procedures). Since, at this step of the assessment process, the objective lies in assessing the extent to which behavioral targets exist (occurrence, frequency, duration, etc.) and which could be causal variables, instruments are administered from a correlational or observational perspective, and hypotheses can be tested only from this correlational strategy—that is, through questionnaires and other physiological and observational methods. Thus, these instruments should have similar psychometric properties to those used in traditional psychological assessment, at least when they are assessing behavioral constructs.

However, as soon as this first correlational analysis has been made and the self-reports (and other measurement devices) have yielded conclusive results that verify (or contradict), with certain probability levels, the hypotheses, an experimental phase begins. To continue with the same case example, self-report questionnaires and scales (as well as other instruments) yielded results allowing us to hypothesize that the client has an inappropriate knowledge (cognitive-language behavioral repertoires) about human sexuality. We can also hypothesize that she has developed negative emotional reactions (or negative attitudes or emotional-motivational behavioral repertoires; see ARD system by Staats, 1975) to sexual stimuli. And, finally, we hypothesize that both basic behavioral repertoires affect her interactions with her husband. This complex set of hypotheses should be tested experimentally; in principle, sexual knowledge and negative emotional reactions are the independent variables, which should be manipulated. A set of dependent variables refers to her sexual interactions with her husband (assessed through self-report questionnaires and hetero-observation applied to her and to her husband) and sexual intercourse without orgasm (assessed through self- and hetero-observation applied to her and to her husband). As Evans (1985) points out, target behavior can be conceptualized not necessarily as the most important behavior to change (in this case, intercourse with orgasm), but as the behavior most specifically under the influence of the therapeutic intervention at any given point in time. It can be predicted that the treatment selected to manipulate sexual knowledge will act through the causal channel.

This second set of hypotheses operationalized through self-report questionnaires (as well as other relevant behavioral methods) is tested through experimental methods. This experimental step not only has the purpose of evaluating target change through treatment, it also provides the means for evaluating the assessment hypotheses, and therefore the assessment process.

In sum, the use of experimental designs is not in opposition to the use of correlational designs. The two alternatives are complementary within the behavioral assessment process. Although it is true that experimental methods represent the core of behavioral assessment when treatment hypotheses are tested, the correlational approach is also necessary at the first step of the process in order to operationalize and measure targets and relevant variables within a discovering framework.

Specific Versus General Information

The final characteristic of behavioral methods to examine concerns the type of items used. As stressed by several authors (Barrios & Hartmann, 1986; Hartmann et al., 1979), behavioral self-report questionnaires (and other behavioral methods) should contain specific items. In other words, while personality questionnaire items are general, behavioral questionnaire items should be specific both in description of stimuli and in response alternatives.

Nevertheless, not all behavioral questionnaires fulfill these conditions, and sometimes items refer to general content and general time. For example, the question "do you feel comfortable in a social situation?" (extremely comfortable/very comfortable/reasonably comfortable/not very comfortable/not at all comfortable), implies unspecified situation and unspecified time. This quasi-general question refers to the present time, and in order to report this information the client must make several speculations, trying to convert what he or she feels in a variety of group situations, and also trying to adjust what he or she feels to the five response categories.

Without doubt, specificity (situation, time, and response) should be a characteristic fulfilled by behavioral questionnaires in order to maximize their fidelity. As Ericsson and Simon (1984) state: "The variety of inference and memory processes that might be involved in producing (general) reports make them extremely difficult to interpret or to use as behavioral data" (p. 27).

SELF-REPORT CONTENT CONDITIONS

A self-report questionnaire implies a verbal question about oneself that should be answered through fixed response alternatives. This answer requires several internal operations related to thinking, language, memory, and learning, all of which depend on certain neurological structures. Despite the fact that behavioral psychologists have sufficiently considered cognitive and neuropsychological research in the study of self-reports, such research has been of great help in establishing the conditions in which self-reports can be considered as scientific data (e.g., Cavanaugh, 1998; Ericsson & Simon, 1980, 1984; Fernández-Ballesteros, 1991; Nisbett & Wilson, 1977; Staats & Fernández-Ballesteros, 1987; Wilson, Hull, & Johnson, 1981). Ericsson and Simon (1980, 1984) developed a model to aid understanding of self-reports and to identify the circumstances in which self reports can be used as verbal data. Let us consider some of the most important findings that support the conditions in which self-reports may be acceptable.

Response Components

As already stated, a first characteristic of self-report methods depends upon the *behavioral components* or response mode system reported. Self-report questions aim to gather different types of information. Bellack and Hersen (1976) classified self-reports following the triple response systems in motor, physiological, and cognitive behavioral modes (How many cigarettes do you smoke? Do you have a high heart rate? Do you feel depressed?). But self-report questions can also refer to the individual's subjective experience or evaluation of these three primary response systems (e.g., Are you a heavy smoker? Is your heart rate abnormal? Why do you feel anxious?). Finally, self-reports also refer to stimuli or complex external events (In what circumstances do you sweat?) or the way these stimuli are perceived (Is this situation threatening you?).

This simple classification divides self-reports into those that refer to objective events (external stimuli or public or observable events or internal events—such as physiological responses—that can be directly assessed) and those that refer to unobservable, subjective (or private) activities. The most important condition that differentiates objective from subjective self-report content is *verifiability*. Content can be verified if there is a criterion or a true measure for such content that allows the testing of correspondence between self-report and criterion. Therefore, objective self-reports can be verified with other methods, but subjective ones cannot. However, in behavioral assessment it is not only important to gather information about objective data (which can be assessed by other methods); subjective information is also extremely relevant (Evans, 1986; Hollon & Bemis, 1981). In any case, this simplistic classification refers merely to the possibility of checking or testing self-reports, but is this sufficient? Let us consider other relevant sources of self-report differentiation.

Accessibility

Another characteristic that self-report content (applying to both objective and subjective information) should have is that the information requested is *accessible* to the subject. By accessibility we usually understand the extent to which a reported event is known or can be known by the reporter (Genest & Turk, 1981). As Eriksson and Simon (1984) emphasized, "Self-report X need not be used to infer that X is true, but only that the subject was able to say X" (p. 7). For example, if subjects are asked how many times they braked when driving to the office that morning, they will not be able to answer the question, because driving is a mechanical activity, and they will not have been conscious of the precise quantity of such behavior.

How can subjects report this type of information? As pointed out by Tverski and Kahneman (1973), when subjects are asked about inaccessible events they will answer with the "available heuristic" or with the most probable or truthful response (Meichenbaum & Buttler, 1979). In sum, behavioral self-report questionnaires should include only accessible information.

Transformation

The self-report can be used as a procedure for gathering information about objective events and subjective experiences that may require certain *transformation* of primary information. Thus, accuracy of self-reports differs according to the level of transformation the question requires. For example, "Did you enjoy school?" "How did you arrive at this decision?" or "Why do you usually think about death?" demand transformation of facts: going to school, making decisions, or thinking about death. In other words, self-report questions can refer to facts and to inferences about facts.

Just as behavioral assessors can interpret client's self-reports at different levels of inference, they also can ask questions requiring subjects to make high-level inferences of internal or external events. As mentioned above, self-reports can deal with *facts* or events (whether the subject went to the theater yesterday), or may require an *interpretation* (why the client went to the theater), with different levels of inference.

Following the model developed by Eriksson and Simon (1980), in order to use self-reports as verbal data, it can be predicted that when information is reproduced in the form in which it was heeded, it can be considered as a direct (or Level I) verbalization, because it is postulated that these events are not modified by these verbal reports. When one or more mediating process occurs between the information requested and its delivery, very high-level transformation (Level 2 or 3) takes place. In accordance with the model, it can be stated that self-report questionnaires involve very high levels of transformation—first because they usually contain questions about evaluations, interpretations, or expectations not already coded, and also because questionnaires usually have a closed response format, so that subjects must transform the required information to the response format by adjusting internal information to adjective or adverb scales.

Nevertheless, it should be emphasized that, for clinical purposes, sometimes it could be important that self-report questions require high levels of transformation. For example, a client's theory about the cause of his or her behavioral problem is relevant because when theories contain irrational beliefs they should be considered as targets for treatment. In any case, behavioral assessors should be aware of the level of transformation required by self-report questionnaires, and when their aim is to assess accurate information already stored, transformation levels should be kept to a minimum.

Time

Self-reports can include information in various tenses: for example, descriptions of past historical events (How old were you when you started school? What were your grades in high school? Describe the first dog that ever frightened you); interpretations of and/or inferences about past behaviors (Why were you afraid of that dog? How did you feel when your mom punished you for getting low grades?); future expectations, perspectives, or plans (Do you think the treatment is going to be successful? Are you planning to go on holiday?); descriptions of past overt behavior (How many cigarettes did you smoke today? How many friends did you meet yesterday?); interpretations of such behaviors (Did you enjoy meeting those people? How many hours of sleep do you need?); and past internal events such as thoughts, feelings, emotions, experiences, and physiological responses (When you were a child, did you think about death? Did you love skiing? How did you feel when your mother criticized you? Did you have a high heart rate?); as well as interpretations of those events (Why do you think you feel so sad?).

Ericsson and Simon (1980, 1984) establish two main forms of verbal report: concurrent verbal reports and retrospective verbal reports. They conclude that present information coded by the subject at the same level of inference as the request is more accurate than information from the past, which usually requires a high level of transformation. Retrospective self-reports are based in long-term memory, and

the process of retrieval may result in several types of error and incompleteness.

Moreover, retrospective self-reports can contain questions about objective or subjective events. For example, if clients report the first time they avoided a dog, this is an objective situation that could equally be reported by other family members. Nevertheless, if clients are asked about their interpretation of an event, it may be that they have never thought about a causal explanation of the behavior in question. "Hence, if subjects are requested to report information that was never heeded, they cannot possibly base their responses on direct memory . . . [and possibly] they will infer and generate an answer based on information provided in the question and other accessible information" (Ericsson & Simon, 1984, p. 20).

Finally, self-report questionnaires can refer to subjects' expectations or plans. Providing this information requires speculation; general predictions about future behavior or situations are frequently inaccurate (Fernández-Ballesteros, 1991). Nevertheless, self-reports seem to be the best instruments for assessing expectation. Even if plans, expectations, or predictions require high levels of inference and transformation, research has shown that self-reports about the future are good predictors of clients' future behavior, at least when a subject is predicting his/her performance in well-known situations. For example, self-efficacy is the best predictor of treatment success (Bandura, 1977, 1997). Although research on self-reports expectancy is promising, much more research must be carried out to increase understanding of such self-reports.

Self-reports contain questions about several types of events and behaviors, as well as inferences related to them. Behavioral assessors should be aware of the type of internal operations required by the information demanded and how certain conditions of the information requested can reduce the accuracy of the self-report.

USE OF SELF-REPORT QUESTIONNAIRES THROUGHOUT THE ASSESSMENT, INTERVENTION, AND EVALUATION PROCESS

Behavioral assessment (and all other types of assessment) is part of a problem-solving process in which the assessor makes decisions about a particular case. As mentioned above, a main objective of behavioral assessment is behavioral change; therefore, assessment has a direct relationship with treatment and evaluation (Barrios & Hartmann, 1986; Goldfried & Kent, 1972; Goldfried & Pomeranz, 1968; Hartmann et al., 1979; Kanfer, 1972; Westmeyer, 2003). Thus, behavioral assessment becomes part of the experimental design, in which the behavioral psychologist, after analyzing the case, selects and implements treatment/s, before proceeding to evaluation and follow-up (e.g., Fernández-Ballesteros, 1979, 1993; Fernández-Ballesteros & Staats, 1992; Haynes, 1978, 1986; Haynes & O'Brien, 1992). This assessment process can be reduced to a set of tasks ordered in a specific sequence in accordance with the scientific method.

Because any process can be devised as an indefinite number of sequential activities and steps, several authors have proposed a limited number of such steps (Fernández-Ballesteros, 1993; Hayes & Follette, 1993; Haynes, 1978, 1992; Haynes, Uchigakiuchi, Meyer, Orimoto, & Blaine, 1993; Kanfer & Saslow, 1965, 1969; Schulte, 1976). Recently, the European Association of Psychological Assessment (Fernández-Ballesteros et al., 2001) developed and published a set of Guidelines for the Assessment Process (GAPs). The GAPs are deduced from a hierarchical framework with four basic steps (developed in several substeps): (1) analyzing the case, (2) organizing and reporting results, (3) planning the intervention, and (4) evaluation and follow-up. Let us introduce the use of self-reports in these steps and substeps relevant for data collection (despite its importance in behavioral assessment and therapy, the second step of organizing and reporting results has not been included here because self-reports are not administered in that step). Table 12.4 shows the assessment process steps and substeps, the potential variables to be assessed, and examples of self-report questionnaires.

It should be emphasized once more that, although our purpose here is to exemplify the use of self-reports at different steps of the assessment, intervention, and evaluation process, questionnaires should be complemented by other assessment methods in order to achieve the *triangulation* of a given variable.

Analyzing the Case

Within the framework of *discovery,* analyzing the case is a complex step in which the assessor should: (1) arrive at a preliminary description of the problematic situation based on initial information provided by the subject/client; (2) hypothesize the nature of the target behaviors and the controlling, maintaining, or explaining conditions (also called "case formulation" by Haynes, 1992; "theoretical functional analysis" by Ferster, 1965; and "behavioral analysis" by Schulte, 1992), operationalizing all of these variables through instruments and other data-collection procedures; and (3) collect and analyze information to test these hypotheses.

Therefore, the first step of any assessment requires the assessor to begin *analyzing the client's complaints and/or the client's goals,* and gathering information in order to obtain

an initial idea about the nature of the problematic situation, the target behaviors, and the controlling conditions.[7] As several authors have stressed, the client's complaints may be converted into targets, or the case may require more in-depth investigation for the selection of targets for change (e.g., Hawkins, 1986).

With the purpose of collecting general information about clients, their sociodemographic context, historical antecedents, complaints or needs, and/or other potential targets, several self-report questionnaires and inventories have been developed. The Life History Questionnaire, the Behavioral Analysis History Questionnaire and the Self-rating Behavioral Scale by Cautela (1977) are good examples. Moreover, at this stage other information regarding self-report questionnaires may be useful in order to gather information about other potential targets, such as the Fear Survey Schedule by Geer (1965), for screening for other frequent target behaviors and/ or problematic situations. Self-report questionnaires at this stage can be considered "primary" (Cautela & Upper, 1976) or "first level" instruments (Fernández-Ballesteros, 1994d).

Continuing with the analysis of the case, after this first data collection a second substep begins, with the goal of testing *hypothetical formulations about the case.* The main objective is to formulate and test hypothetical functional relationships between target responses and potentially causal environmental, personal (basic behavioral repertoires), or biological variables. All variables involved should be operationalized through multiple measurement instruments.

During this subphase, self-report questionnaires play an important role in the description, measurement, and classification of targets, as well as in the identification and measurement of controlling, maintaining, or explaining variables. At this time, within the discovery framework, the assessor should measure the frequency, duration, and other response dimensions of motor, cognitive, or physiological targets, as well as the hypothetical controlling variables that (in this step) correlate with targets.

Among the hypothetical causal factors, we should distinguish those observable *external conditions* that have functional relationships with targets, as well as the *basic behavioral repertoires,* theoretically and empirically linked to target behaviors. As noted above, for a behavioral construct to be considered, it should: be capable of being operationalized through measurement devices; provide empirical proof of its relationship with target behaviors in group designs; provide empirical evidence of learning conditions; and be capable of manipulation through an intervention technique (Fernández-Ballesteros & Staats, 1992). Finally, hypotheses may refer to the *biological conditions* that potentially have a mediating or causal role in target behaviors.

TABLE 12.4   Self-report Questionnaires in Different Steps of the Assessment Process

Process Step	Substeps	Variables Assessed	Examples
Analyzing the Case	Analyzing demands and complaints	Sociodemographics, historical conditions and screening targets, and potential controlling conditions	BAHQ, SRBS (Cautela & Upper, 1976)
	Formulating and testing hypotheses (case formulation, functional analysis)	Assessing/measuring targets	TSSS, CTASS (Cautela & Upper, 1976), BDS (Beck et al., 1961), Self-rating Depression Scale (Zung, 1965), State-Trait Anxiety Inventory (STAI, Spielberger, 1975)
		Assessing functional relationships	Sociotropy-Autonomy Scale (Beck et al., 1983) Frequency of Self-Reinforcement (Heiby, 1982) Pleasant Event Schedule & Unpleasant Event Survey (MacPhillamy & Lewinsohn, 1982)
		Assessing potential causal variables	RAS (Rathus, 1973)
Planning the Intervention	Selecting and operationalizing intervention and outcome variables	Selecting and measuring outcomes	Could be the same as above
		Selecting and measuring causal variables	Could be the same as above
	Reviewing and selecting intervention procedures	Assessing relevant and/or mediating variables	Reinforcement Survey Schedule (RSS) Imagery Survey Schedule (ISS) Relaxation Data Sheet Motivation for Behavior Change Scale (MBCS)
	Selecting and assessing relevant variables for monitoring	Selecting or assessing for monitoring	DACL (Depression Adjective Check-List)
Evaluation and Follow-up	Collecting data about effects of intervention	Client/subject/relatives contentment	Treatment Evaluation Inventory (Kazdin, 1977; Kelley, et al., 1989)
	Changes in targets	Same	Same
	Analyzing intervention outcomes	Same	Same
	Following-up	Same	Same

Self-report questionnaires are important measurement devices for operationalizing hypotheses, and they play a central role in measuring targets, assessing functional relationships between target and external conditions, and assessing basic behavioral repertoires hypothetically linked with targets. It is important to stress that, although self-report questionnaires assessing motor and physiological responses should be complemented through multimethods (observational and physiological measures), cognitive responses and subjective appraisal cannot be complemented in this way. Nevertheless, these cognitive and subjective conditions also could be triangulated through other self-observational procedures (e.g., self-observation, self-monitoring). In other words, behaviors that cannot be tested independently can be examined through other, "subjective" methods, such as self-observation and self-monitoring, arriving at an *intrasubject* evaluation of the client's problem (see Fernández-Ballesteros, 1980, 1994c).

Let us consider some examples related to the diverse use of self-report questionnaires in this step. Self-report questionnaires can be used as measures of targets (see Table 12.4). For example, a client who complains about depressive and anxiety behaviors could be assessed through the Thought Stopping Survey Schedule (Cautela, 1977) for identifying and measuring patients' negative thoughts, while the Cues for Tension and Anxiety Survey Schedule (Cautela, 1979) can be used for identifying and measuring potential physiological responses. Both instruments can be used from an idiographic perspective in order to select and measure the subjective and physiological responses that might constitute targets for modification.

Also, if it is necessary to arrive at a classification or diagnosis of the case, self-report questionnaires on depression and anxiety—such as the Beck Depression Schedule (Beck, Ward, Mendelson, Mock, & Erbaugh, 1961), the Self-rating

Depression Scale (Zung, 1965), or the State-Trait Anxiety Inventory (Spielberger, 1975)—could be used from a nomothetic perspective, using the total score to classify the case by comparing a client's score in intersubjects designs or by using total scores as a measure of depression as an aggregate target behavior. However, these questionnaires also can be used item-by-item, identifying behavioral, somatic, or motor targets and also using these items as targets. Thus, as already stated, the same self-report questionnaire can be used from an idiographic or nomothetic perspective.

Self-report questionnaires are also useful for assessing variables that hypothetically control, maintain, or explain target behaviors. When external conditions are involved, self-reports are only auxiliary methods. To continue with the depression case example, if the hypothesis postulates that depressive behaviors are positively reinforced by family members, then observation procedures (direct and rating-by-others observations) are the best methods. However, self-report questionnaires can be helpful for assessing functional relationships (Haynes, Spain, & Oliviera, 1993). For example, two questionnaires could be used for measuring the interpersonal and achievement concerns of depressed patients: the Sociotropy-Autonomy Scale (Beck, Epstein, Harrison, & Emery, 1983) and the Frequency of Self-Reinforcement Questionnaire (Heiby, 1982).

But if it is postulated that basic behavioral repertoires can explain depressive behaviors, then self-report questionnaires can be used, in the form of aggregate measures, as indicators of these basic behavioral repertoires. For example, if the hypothesis postulates a decline in pleasant events and an increase in unpleasant events, questionnaires such as the Pleasant Events Schedule (MacPhillamy & Lewinsohn, 1982) or the Unpleasant Events Schedule (Lewinsohn & Talkington, 1979) may be used. It also could be postulated that depressive behaviors are functionally related to a deficit in social skills, so that, for example, Rathus's Schedule for Assessing Assertive Behaviors could be used (Rathus, 1973). All of these questionnaires assessing basic behavioral repertoires should present psychometric and experimental guarantees.

During this first phase of the process, from a discovery perspective, hypotheses can be correlationally tested through behavioral instruments and measures, among which self-report questionnaires are important instruments for assessing target behaviors and hypothesized functional relationships.

Planning the Intervention

Following the assessment process, after the behavioral psychologist has *organized the information and reported it* to the subject/client, an intervention is decided upon and a new phase begins. Based on previous analysis, planning the intervention is a fundamental step that requires formulating treatment hypotheses and—from a *justification perspective*—testing them through an experimental design.

It is important to emphasize that two types of relationships should be tested: functional relationships between the target behavior and causal condition and the effect of the intervention on the hypothesized causal condition (Evans, 1985, Fernández-Ballesteros, 1994d; Fernández-Ballesteros & Staats, 1992; Haynes, Spain, & Oliviera, 1993). These two relationships should be taken into consideration when the intervention is planned.

As Table 12.4 shows, planning the intervention involves three main substeps: (1) selecting and/or operationalizing outcome (dependent) and causal (independent) variables; (2) reviewing and selecting intervention procedures; and (3) selecting and assessing relevant variables for monitoring. Let us consider very briefly the nature of these three subphases, with examples of the use of self-report questionnaires.

Selecting and/or Operationalizing Outcome and Causal Variables

From the previous phase, the assessor selects measures among the already-tested targets and functionally related variables in order to evaluate whether the hypothetical relationships, yielded in the functional analysis through tests, receive experimental support after intervention. That is, two types of variables were to be selected: dependent (target) and independent (causal). It is important for both types to be assessed, but the behavioral assessment literature refers mainly to the selection of treatment goals (dependent variables), rather than of independent causal conditions (e.g., *Behavioral Assessment,* 1985; Evans, 1993; Hawkins 1986). Nevertheless, in order to test intervention hypotheses, the effect of intervention procedures on causal (or independent) conditions is a necessary step. Equally, we need to test whether the manipulation (through intervention techniques) of causal variables has the predicted effect on target behaviors (dependent variables). Although both types of variables can be measured by self-report questionnaires, it should again be emphasized that the use of multimethods is a precondition for planning and evaluating behavioral interventions.

At this step of the process, as pointed out in the evaluation and behavioral assessment literature (e.g., Haynes, 1986; Schulte, 1997), there are criteria for selecting the best measures: (1) Bearing in mind that the value observed by means of the chosen instruments after treatment is the basis for inferring intervention success, as Schulte (1997) points out, it is possible to distinguish comparison with the *pretreatment measure* in a pre-/posttest design and comparison with a *stan-*

dard criterion. (2) In both cases, a new condition for the measures selected for assessing change is *sensitivity.* In other words, the selected measures' susceptibility to modification by the intervention is a prerequisite for self-report questionnaires when they are to be used for measuring change. (3) Also, it is important to distinguish between intrasubject comparison and normative change. When the purpose is to produce normative change, normative self-reports (standard questionnaires) should be selected.

Recently, tests batteries for measuring changes after intervention have been developed (for a review, see Strupp, Horowitz, & Lambert, 1997) that contain self-report questionnaires for assessing change in depression, anxiety, and other mood disorders.

Reviewing and Selecting Intervention Procedures

Selecting intervention techniques obviously depends on target behaviors, causal variables, and available treatments. As several authors have pointed out (Fernández-Ballesteros, 1994c; Haynes, 1986; Haynes et al., 1993a, 1993b), in addition to the assessment of dependent and independent variables, at this stage of the process other *intervening or mediating*[8] variables play an important role and should be assessed. Two broad types of intervening variables can be distinguished: the *specific subject conditions* required by the intervention and the general *motivational approach of the subject* to the intervention. Let us briefly consider the nature of these intervening variables and some examples of self-report questionnaires of both types.

Any behavioral intervention techniques used on the basis of the client's imagery require basic imagery skills, so the behavioral assessor and/or therapist should assess those skills. Likewise, any behavioral techniques based on reinforcement require knowledge of the client's potential reinforcements, so his or her reinforcements should be assessed. Finally, any treatment that requires relaxation involves relaxation skills in the client, so these skills should be assessed.

Motivational variables are also extremely important for any intervention; thus, expectations about treatment and/or resistance to treatment can be important factors in treatment outcome. Bandura (1969, 1977, 1997) emphasized the importance of outcome expectation and perceived self-efficacy in treatment outcomes. Self-reports are the most common measures for assessing treatment expectancy, as well as being the best predictors of treatment outcomes (for a review, see Bandura, 1997). Table 12.4 shows examples of the relevant variables that may be assessed before implementing the most common interventions.

Selecting and Assessing Relevant Variables for Monitoring

When an $N = 1$ baseline design is selected, target behaviors to be followed should have specific characteristics, since time series determine specific sources of variability and inferential errors (Barlow, Hayes, & Nelson, 1984; Haynes & Waialae, 1994). Several authors have suggested four principal characteristics for measures placed in temporal series: sensitivity to treatment, as molecular as possible, low variability, and non-reactivity to continued administration (Fernández-Ballesteros, 1994c; Haynes & Waialae, 1994; Kelley, Heffer, Gresham, & Elliot, 1989). Therefore, when self-report questionnaires are taken as aggregates, they are not in principle suitable measures for use in time series designs; only specific self-reports might be used. For example the Depression Adjective Check-List (Lubin, 1965) is a good self-report measure in single-case experimental designs.

Evaluation and Follow-up

From a scientific point of view, evaluation has two main purposes: (1) testing the effect of treatment (so-called treatment validity and/or utility[9]), and (2) testing hypotheses or, in other words, testing assessment process validity (Fernández-Ballesteros, 1980, 1994d). Both objectives will mainly be fulfilled by means of the scores yielded by those tests, instruments, or measures that were selected in the previous process step. Therefore, the same instruments as those administered or selected in order to assess dependent and independent variables should be readministered in this step. Changes after intervention will be the key to making inferences about treatment effects and hypothesis fulfillment.

Nevertheless, from an applied point of view, if a client's complaints (and/or client referral) are what motivate a client to see a psychologist and start an assessment/treatment/evaluation process, then appraisals of treatment effects by the client and his or her context (client, family members, doctors or other professionals) are key indicators of subjective evaluation, or *social validity* (Kazdin, 1977; Kazdin & Wilson, 1978; Wolfe, 1978). Since our concern here is limited to self-report questionnaires, the adequacy of this term and concept will not be addressed. Social validity is a subjective concept, and without doubt self-reports are excellent procedures for assessing such perceptions. As Table 12.4 shows, several evaluation questionnaires have been developed, among them the Treatment Evaluation Inventory (Kazdin, 1977; Kelly et al., 1989), the Intervention Rating Profile (Witt, Moe, Gutkin, & Andrews, 1984) and the Therapy Attitude Inventory (Eyberg & Johnson, 1974).

In summary, the assessment process leads to the use of instruments as well as to the appropriate conditions for those instruments.

THE QUALITY OF SELF-REPORT QUESTIONNAIRES

During the short history of behavioral assessment there has been a fundamental debate about how to evaluate the quality of behavioral assessment and of behavioral assessment methods. While several authors maintain that behavioral assessment methods should be supported by psychometric and generalizability theories (e.g., Fernández-Ballesteros et al., 1982; Haynes, 1998; Silva, 1989, 1993a, 1993b), others maintain that these principles "do not provide an adequate theoretical basis for evaluating the quality of behavioral assessment" (Hayes, Nelson, & Jarrett, 1986; see also Cone, 1981a, 1981b, 1988). This is not the place to enter into this debate; our concern is to present an overview of how to evaluate the quality of self-report questionnaires and how to optimize quality.

This concern has three principal starting points: (1) Self-report questionnaires are procedures for collecting data and measurement devices, and psychometric principles should therefore be applicable to them (because chapter 3 is devoted to these principles, they will not be discussed here). (2) Self-report questionnaires represent a very broad and diversified methodological category with a certain set of characteristics, and it is important to review quality requirements as a function of these characteristics. (3) Finally, self-report questionnaires have specific biases; a review of these distortions is also important for optimizing quality.

What Type of Psychometric Criteria for What Decision?

As Messik (1994, 1995) points out, a score means any coding or summarization of observed behaviors or performance in a given test situation. From scores, inferences and decisions are made and social consequences derived. Scores from behavioral methods—among them self-report questionnaires—should be tested through certain scientific standards that guarantee, with certain levels of probability, inferences, decisions, or likely consequences.

Reliability, validity, and level of generalizability are scientific principles and are accepted as social values whenever judgments and decisions are made (Messik, 1995, p. 742). How can behavioral assessment methods be freed of these evaluative principles? The main question is not whether these principles are applicable to behavioral assessment methods, but which of them are most suitable for which purposes (Silva, 1989, 1993a, 1993b). Evaluative criteria refer to the *circumstances* in which a test can be used for making certain *inferences* and *decisions*. Thus, no criterion can guarantee a measurement device per se; therefore, it is important to link any psychometric criterion to inferences or decisions that will be made (American Educational Research Association, American Psychological Association, & National Council on Measurement in Education, 1999). Let us briefly review the most important sources of evidence for self-report questionnaires.

Because it can be assumed that any score includes a component of error,[10] despite criticism from behavioral assessors (e.g., Cone, 1998), information about measurement error is essential to correct evaluation and use of an instrument. Information about *reliability* includes the major sources of errors (American Educational Research Association, American Psychological Association, & National Council on Measurement in Education, 1999) a given test may have. *Stability* (test-retest reliability), *observer accuracy* (objectivity), and *internal consistency* are the most common categories of reliability accepted in the scientific literature and in practical work. They also can be described, within generalizability theory (Cronbach, Gleser, Nanda, & Rajaratnam, 1972), as generalizable to time, observers, and items. When a self-report is to be used within an experimental design (in time series, in pre-/post-tests, and/or in preexperimental designs), in order to assess changes without confusing time with treatment effects, it is extremely important to know whether a score can be generalized across time (called baseline stability in time-series designs). Therefore, test-retest reliability should be a criterion for testing self-report questionnaires.

Although questionnaires are usually considered objective measures, they also may be self-administered and administered by the assessor through interview (alternate-form coefficient). When assessors administer questionnaires, agreement among assessors and between two parallel administration forms should be provided. In other words, the universe of test administrators or forms of administration should be evaluated.

Finally, as stated earlier, some self-report questionnaires assessing behavioral constructs (assertiveness, pleasant events, etc.)—both during the case formulation and in planning treatment and evaluation steps—are used in aggregate. These questionnaires should provide information about internal consistency or about the extent to which test items can be generalized.

Validity refers to the extent to which empirical evidence supports the interpretations of test scores. Although traditionally three forms of validity are the most commonly accepted (content, criterion, and construct), validity theory has been extended during the last 10 years to include, for example, several forms of validity such as content, substantive, structural, generalizability, external, and consequential (Messik, 1995). These sources of validity led the new APA Standards (American Educational Research Association, American Psychological Association, & National Council on Measurement in Education, 1999) and inspired Cone's (1998, in press) description of three forms: consequential, representational, and elaborative validity. It is premature to evaluate the impact of these new conceptions of validity, but let us briefly review the most important sources of validity evidence for questionnaires.

During the last 30 years, most behavioral assessors have emphasized the importance of evidence based on questionnaire *content;* thus, the extent to which the items of a given questionnaire represent the universe of behaviors in the domain measured is a relevant question in evaluating the quality of the questionnaire.[11]

As already pointed out, one of the most important characteristics of behavioral assessment is the use of multimethods—that is, behavioral questionnaires should present evidence based on their convergent relations with the same content as assessed by other methods, as well as on the extent to which they diverge from nonrelated content or variables assessed by the same and by other methods. This condition has important implications for testing *criterion* and *construct* validity (as well as variants of these) and for testing the *accuracy* of a given instrument for which there exists a true criterion.

Behavioral assessment is part of a behavioral change process, and this means there are two important sources of evidence. First, *experimental* evidence that a given behavioral construct assessed by a certain questionnaire can be manipulated through intervention procedures is a required condition. In other words, when a self-report questionnaire is taken as one of the measures for a key construct (or independent variable), it should provide experimental evidence that it can be manipulated. This is one of the guarantees of indirect observation of behavioral constructs. Second, as already stated, one of the characteristics of behavioral questionnaires should be their *sensitivity;* thus, a test that is going to be used as a dependent variable should be modifiable by the intervention procedures. Both characteristics could be considered as external sources of validity evidence.

The concept receiving attention in recent years is the *consequences* of testing, which (in Messik's terms and according to APA Standards) combine both validity and *utility.* Although some developments have been made (Cone, 1998; Hayes et al., 1986, 1993; Haynes, 1998; Silva, 1989, 1993a, 1993b), our concern here is to summarize the most relevant issues concerning consequences and utility of self-report questionnaires. Three critical points arise in relation to this

kind of validity: (1) Behavioral assessors' developments of the concept of utility in opposition to psychometric standards, and even to decision theory (Cronbach & Gleser, 1957), should be reconsidered within a broader theory of consequential validity. (2) Consequential validity and utility refer also to an economic principle with social repercussions. Self-report questionnaires are undoubtedly less costly procedures for collecting data, and in this sense they have positive consequences. But less costly does not mean more efficient, because the concept of efficiency is related to not only cost but also equal benefit produced with respect to other measurement procedures—and we have no data on this aspect. (3) Self-reports have several important sources of bias (social desirability, faking, etc.). When several contents are assessed through self-reports, they necessarily share the same source of error, and, therefore, it is easy to confuse content with method (Haynes and Waialae, 1994). This is a source of invalidity that influences test utility and, therefore, social consequences (Messik, 1995). (4) Finally, self-reports usually assess subjective events that are not testable by any other type of method (physiological devices, observation, rating by others). When this is the case, the only possibility for assessing quality is to proceed to an intrasubject validation with other self-reports (e.g., self-observation). Unfortunately, however, this method shares several sources of bias with self-report questionnaires. Much more research on consequential validity, treatment utility, and incremental validity of self-reports should be conducted in order to illuminate these important matters.

Self-report questionnaires are the key measures for assessing social validity. Nevertheless, the problem here is not the extent to which self-report contributes to assessing clients' contentment, but rather the extent to which social validity is related to other types of treatment validity—that is, the extent to which social validity is a scientific type of validity.

Self-report Questionnaire Characteristics and Quality Evaluation

Self-report questionnaires constitute a broad and diverse method for collecting and measuring information. Self-report characteristics and use also depend on the process steps. Table 12.5 shows a consideration of self-report characteristics that differentiates quality evaluation[12] as a function of the assessment process steps.

The quality of self-report questionnaires depends on several of the conditions presented in Table 12.5. Quality should be optimized and/or guaranteed depending on the step of the process: *level of inference* should be low in the first step but

TABLE 12.5   Self-report Characteristics, Process Steps, and Substeps and Quality Evaluation

Process Phase	Analyzing the Case			Planing the Intervention		Evaluation and Follow-up	
Sub-Phases Self-Reports Characteristics	Assessing/ measuring historical events and targets	Assessing potential causal variables	Functional relationships	Assessing relevant, functional relationships and/or mediating variables	Selecting or assessing for monitoring	Client/Subject/ Relatives Contentment	Other effects on targets and causal condition measures
Direct/Indirect	Direct	Indirect	Direct	Direct/Indirect	Direct	Direct	Direct, Indirect
Level of inference: Sample/Sign	Sample	Correlate	Correlate	Sample, Sign, Theory	Sample	Sample	Sample, Sign, Theory
Aggregate/ Non-Aggregate	Non-aggregate	Aggregate	Non-aggregate	Aggregate	Non-aggregate	Non-aggregate	Aggregate
Multimethods	Multi	Multi	Multi	Multi	Multi	Multi	Multi
Correlational/ Experimental	Correlational	Correlational	Correlational	Experimental	Experimental	Experimental	Experimental
Specific/ General	Specific	General	Specific	Specific/ general	Specific	Specific	Specific/general
Response modalities	Several	Several	Several	Several	Several	Several	Several
Transform.	Low	Low	Low	Low	Low	Low	Low
Past/Present/ Future	Past, Present	Present	Present	Present	Present	Present, Future	Present, Future

high when functional hypotheses are going to be tested; items should be as *direct* as possible but when constructs are assessed *indirect* evaluation should be provided; low inference variables could be tested through *nonaggregates* analysis, but high-level variables should be evaluated in *aggregate; multimethods* should be employed anytime; *correlational* methods should be complemented with *experimental* design; questions should be *specific* about the three response systems; *level of transformation* of the information requested should be as low as possible; and, finally, the information requested should refer, preferably, to the *present*. We already identified the circumstances in which—and with what guarantees— high inference level, indirect self-reports, nomothetic questionnaires, correlational designs, cognitive self-reports, and reports about the past can be used in behavioral assessment.

Distortion of Self-report Responses

The quality of self-report questionnaires also depends on clients' cooperation, which is usually maximized by their motivation and can be increased by assessor instructions that emphasize the importance of giving fair responses. Nevertheless, self-report accuracy is threatened by several types of response distortions (also called response sets, response bias, or test-taking attitudes), although these can, at least partially, be measured and controlled (Bradburn & Sudman, 1979).

Baer, Rinaldo, and Berry (2003) describe the most important self-report distortions:

Negative impression management, described as over-reporting symptoms, malingering, or faking bad, is a deliberate attempt to create an impression of disturbance or impairment by exaggerating or fabricating problems and negative characteristics. *Positive impression management,* also described as underreporting of symptoms, defensiveness, *socially desirable* response, or *faking good,* is a deliberate attempt to create a favorable impression by falsely denying problems and endorsing positive characteristics. *Random responding,* in which the test-taker responds independently of the content of the items, can result from poor reading or language skills, lack of cooperation, carelessness, poor concentration, or confusion. *Acquiescence* and naysaying are tendencies to respond indiscriminately in the "true" or "false" directions, respectively, without consideration of item content (p. 3).

On the supposition that the base rate of response bias is very low among behavioral therapy clients, response bias has not been a focus of behavioral assessment research, and validity scales (for detecting and/or controlling some response biases) are not systematically administered. Nevertheless, self-report questionnaires (such as Rathus's Assertiveness Scale or Spielberger's State-Trait Anxiety Inventory) are also strongly related to positive impression management (Fernández-Ballesteros, Díaz, Izal, Maciá, & Pérez, 1981; Fernández-Ballesteros & Zamarrón, 1996).

It can be concluded that none of these response distortions invalidate the results of self-report questionnaires. Nevertheless, it is extremely important that behavioral researchers pay more attention to self-report response bias and that behavioral practitioners be alert, through multimethods (and multi-informants), to the possibility of self-report distortion.

FUTURE DIRECTIONS AND CONCLUSIONS

Self-report questionnaires are one of the most frequently used methodological categories within behavioral assessment methods. Nevertheless, they have important flaws, and several channels are open for improving and maximizing their quality. Much more research should be carried out in the following areas: (1) From a methodological point of view, as measurement devices, self-report questionnaires should present psychometric guarantees. Test-retest reliability, inter-rater agreement, and content- and criterion-related validity should be demonstrated. When self-reports are assessing behavioral constructs, other forms of construct validity such as multitrait-multimethod continue to constitute an important way of evaluating self-report questionnaires, and norms should be developed and provided. In other words, self-report questionnaires are not free of the need for psychometric guarantees. (2) Research on the contribution of self-report questionnaires to the intervention is extremely important. Incremental validity is a problematic issue not only for self-report questionnaires but for all behavioral methods. Differences in incremental validity among methods is a pending issue in behavioral assessment. With regard to social validity—bearing in mind that social validity is mainly assessed through questionnaires—it is extremely important to assess the extent to which there is agreement among several informants and on clients' contentment with treatment and other validity indicators. (3) Response bias is an important area of research and practice. Attempting to measure and control self-report distortion should be common practice, and the extent to which a questionnaire is affected by response bias (and the type of bias involved) should be included in the information of all instruments. Basic research in response distortion is without doubt a pending issue in behavioral assessment. (4) From a conceptual point of view, the behavioral assessor should take advantage of and work in collaboration with cognitive neuroscience in order to discover the processes behind self-reports. This is an important avenue for optimizing the quality of self-reports in general and of questionnaires in particular.

Behavioral assessment is a product of the third generation of behaviorism, emerging when reductionism was overcome and subjective responses were also accepted as a subject of inquiry. From this perspective, self-reports should be used without reservations by behavioral psychologists, bearing in mind that they have flaws but that these flaws can be overcome, controlled, or minimized. Three conclusions emerge from this chapter: (1) Polarization—such as sample versus sign interpretation, direct versus indirect methods, idiographic versus nomothetic approach, or correlational versus experimental methodology—is inappropriate, since each extreme at each polarity can be helpful and useful for behavioral assessment and self-report questionnaires, depending on the step of the process and the relevant question answered. (2) Self-report questionnaires should never be administered as the sole method of behavioral assessment. Multicontent/multimethod assessment is both a principle and a methodological guarantee of behavioral assessment. (3) Finally, it is clear that much more research is needed in order to improve this widely used method of behavioral assessment.

APPENDIX: CHAPTERS OR SECTIONS ON SELF-REPORT QUESTIONNAIRES IN THE MOST IMPORTANT BEHAVIORAL ASSESSMENT BOOKS

Year, Publisher	Book Title	Book Authors	Chapter/Section and Pages	Chapter Author/s
1976, Munich: Urban & Scharzenberg	*Diagnostik in der Vehaltensetherapie*	D. Schulte, (Ed.)	Appendix with four questionnaires	
1976, New York: Brunner/Mazel	*Behavioral Assessment: New Directions in Clinical Psychology*	J.D. Cone & R.P. Hawkins (Eds.)	Self-report Inventories in Behavioral Assessment (pp. 52–76)	A.S. Bellack & M. Hersen

Year, Publisher	Book Title	Book Authors	Chapter/Section and Pages	Chapter Author/s
1976, New York: Springer	*Behavior Therapy Assessment. Diagnosis, Design, and Evaluation*	E.J. Mash & L.G. Terdal (Eds.)	Section III: Self-report Measures	
			Prestructuring Behavior Therapy through Precounseling Assessment (pp. 141–149)	R.B. Stuart & F. Stuart
			The Development of a Scale to Measure Fear (pp. 150–156)	J.H. Geer
			Measurement of Social-Evaluative Anxiety (pp. 156–166)	D. Watson & R. Friend
			The College Self-Expression Scale: A Measure of Assertiveness (pp. 167–185).	J.P. Galassi, J.S. DeLo, M.D. Galassi, & S. Bastien
1976, New York: Pergamon	*Behavioral Assessment: A Practical Handbook*	M. Hersen & A.S. Bellack (Eds.)	The Behavioral Inventory Battery: The Use of Self-report Measures in Behavioral Analysis and Therapy (pp. 77–111)	J.R. Cautela & D. Upper
1977, Champaign, IL: Research Press	*Behavior Analysis Forms for Clinical Intervention*	J.R. Cautela		
1977, New York: Wiley	*Handbook of Behavioral Assessment*	A.R. Ciminero, K.S. Calhoun, & H.E. Adams (Eds.)	Self-report Schedules and Inventories (pp. 153–194)	D.L. Tasto
1978, New York: Gardner Press	*Principles of Behavioral Assessment*	S.N. Haynes	Questionnaires in Behavioral Assessment	Same authors
1978, New York: Springer	*A Practical Guide to Behavioral Assessment*	F.J. Keef, S.A. Kopel, & S.B. Gordon	No chapter on self-report questionnaires	
1979, Stuttgart, Germany: Kohlammer	*Praxis der Verhaltensanalyse (Behavioral analysis praxis)*	R. Sachse	No chapter on self-report questionnaires	
1979, San Francisco: Jossey-Bass	*Behavioral Assessment. Recent Advances in Methods, Concepts, and Application*	S.N. Haynes & C.C. Wilson	Behavioral Questionnaires (pp. 241–321)	Same authors
1979, Madrid, Spain: P. del Río De	*Los métodos en evaluación conductual (Methods in Behavioral Assessment)*	R. Fernández-Ballesteros	Section on self-reports	Same author
1981, New York: Pergamon	*Behavioral Assessment: A Practical Handbook* (2nd ed.)	M. Hersen & A.S. Bellack (Eds.)	Self-report and the assessment of cognitive functions (pp. 125–175)	S.D. Hollon & K.M. Bemis
1981, New York: Guilford	*Behavioral Assessment of Childhood Disorders*	E.J. Mash & L.G. Terdal (Eds.)	Section on child self-reports and chapter 1 (pp. 51–53)	E.J. Mash & L.G. Terdal
1981, New York: Guilford	*Behavioral Assessment of Adult Disorders*	D.H. Barlow (Ed.)	No chapter or section on self-reports	
1981, Champaign, IL: Research Press	*Organic Dysfunction Survey Schedules*	J.R. Cautela		

(continued)

Year, Publisher	Book Title	Book Authors	Chapter/Section and Pages	Chapter Author/s
1981, Madrid, Spain: Pirámide	*Evaluación conductual (Behavioral Assessment)*	R. Fernández-Ballesteros & J.A.I. Carrobles (Eds.)	Los auto-informes	C. Vizcarro & J.A. García Marcos
1983, Gottingen: Hogrefe	*Verhaltensdiagnostik* In: *Enzyklopadie der Psychologie. Psychologishe Diagnostik (Behavioral Assessment)*	K.J. Groffmann & L. Michel (Eds.)	No chapter on self-report questionnaires	
1984, New York: Pergamon	*Child Behavioral Assessment*	T.H. Ollendick & M. Hersen (Ed.)	Self-report Instruments	A.J. Finch & T.R. Rogers
1986, New York: Wiley	*Handbook of Behavioral Assessment* (2nd ed.)	A.R. Ciminero, K.S. Calhoun, & H.E. Adams (Eds.)	Self-report Questionnaires and Inventories (pp. 150–176)	B.J. Jensen & S.N. Haynes
1986, New York: Guilford	*Conceptual Foundations of Behavioral Assessment*	R.O. Nelson & S.C. Hayes	Two sections in two chapters: Response Structure and the Triple Response-Mode Concept (pp. 129–151) Assessing the Effects of Therapeutic Interventions (pp. 430–457)	I. Evans S.C. Hayes
1988, New York: Pergamon	*Behavioral Assessment: A Practical Handbook* (3rd ed.)	M. Hersen & A.S. Bellack (Eds.)	No chapter on self-reports	
1988, New York: Guilford	*Behavioral Assessment of Childhood Disorders* (2nd ed.)	E.J. Mash & L.G. Terdal (Eds.)	Section on child self-reports and chapter 1 (pp. 40–41)	Same authors
1988, New York: Pergamon	*Dictionary of Behavioral Assessment Techniques*	M. Hersen & A.S. Bellack		
1989, Madrid, Spain: Pirámide (published in 1993 by Sage)	*Evaluación conductual y criterios psicométricos (Psychometric Foundations and Behavioral Assessment)*	F. Silva	No chapter on self-reports	
1994a, Madrid, Spain: Pirámide	*Evaluación conductual hoy (Behavioral Assessment Today)*	R. Fernández-Ballesteros (Ed.)	No chapter on self-report questionnaires	
1998, Boston: Allyn & Bacon	*Behavioral Assessment: A Practical Handbook* (4th ed.)	A.S. Bellack & M. Hersen (Eds.)	No chapter on self-report questionnaires	
2000, New York: Kluwer/Plenum	*Behavioral Assessment: A Functional Approach to Psychological Assessment*	S.N. Haynes & W.H. O'Brien	No chapter on self-report questionnaires	
2000, Munich, Germany: CIP-Medien	*Verhaltensdiagnostik und Fallkonzeption (Behavioral Assessment and the Case Formulation)*	S.K.D. Sulz	No chapter on self-report questionnaires	

NOTES

1. Also, throughout the therapeutic process, the client's self-reports lead the whole process, being an important part of the entire communication system between client and therapist. In clinical settings, not only are self-reports formal procedures for data collection, but they also may be considered the core of the therapeutic process.

2. It is also important to mention that, at the same time, in the *Dictionary of Behavioral Assessment Techniques,* the majority of instruments listed are self-reports.

3. The category behavioral analysis (12%) has been deleted because it cannot be considered as a class of instrument.

4. For a review and extension of Sundberg, Tyler, and Taplin's (1973) model of response interpretation, see Fernández-Ballesteros (1994c).

5. Despite the fact that behavioral principles (classical and operant conditioning, social learning and cognitive behavioral principles) have been developed mainly through single designs, behavioral assessors have equated group designs with the nomothetic approach, setting them in opposition to single cases, which correspond to the idiographic approach.

6. Cone (1986, 1988) even formulated two models of behavioral assessment: idiographic-behavioral assessment and nomothetic-behavioral assessment.

7. In clinical contexts, the subject and client are usually the same person, but sometimes a psychiatrist, judge, or specific agent asks the psychologist to assess a given subject and is considered to be the "client." In these cases, the client's demands or questions should be considered as an agent separate from the subject.

8. When independent variables are constructs, Nelson and Hayes (1986a) call them Keystone Target Behaviors.

9. As Silva (1989, 1993a) pointed out, treatment validity has been confused with treatment utility, and treatment utility has been partially confused with assessment process validity.

10. No differences between classical test theory and Item Response Theory shall be presented. In fact, reliability information can be reported in terms of variances or standard deviations of measurement errors, in terms of one or more coefficients, or in terms of IRT-based test information functions.

11. Content validity is, moreover, close to "criterion-reference test," which has been accepted by behavioral assessors, as opposed to "norm-referenced test" (e.g., Livingston, 1976; Hambleton, 2003; Hambleton & Rogers, 1990.)

12. Some of these conditions, such as "monomethods versus multimethods" and "accessibility," have not been included because they are not sources of self-report variance.

REFERENCES

Allport, G. (1963). *Pattern and growth in personality.* New York: Holt, Rinehart & Winston.

American Educational Research Association, American Psychological Association, & National Council on Measurement in Education (1999). *Standards for educational and psychological Testing.* Washington, DC: American Educational Research Association.

Baer, R.A., Rinaldo, J.C., & Berry, D.T.R. (2003). Response distortion in self-report assessment. In R. Fernández-Ballesteros (Ed.), *Encyclopedia of psychological assessment.* London: Sage.

Bandura, A. (1969). *Principles of behavior modification.* New York: Holt, Rinehart & Winston.

Bandura, A. (1977). Self-efficacy: Toward a unifying theory of behavioral change. *Psychological Review, 84,* 191–215.

Bandura, A. (1997). *Self-efficacy. The exercise of control.* New York: Freeman.

Bannister, D., & Maier, J.M.M. (1968). *The evaluation of personal constructs.* New York: Academic Press.

Barlow, D.H., Hayes, S.C., & Nelson, R.M. (1984). *The scientist practitioner.* New York: Pergamon Press.

Barrios, B., & Hartmann, D.P. (1986). The contribution of traditional assessment: Concepts, issues, and methodologies. In R.M. Nelson & S.N. Hayes (Eds.), *Conceptual foundation of behavioral assessment.* New York: Guilford Press.

Beck, A.T., Epstein, N., Harrison, R., & Emery, G. (1983). *Development of the Sociotropy-Autonomy Scale.* Unpublished manuscript, University of Pennsylvania, Philadelphia.

Beck, A.T., Ward, C.H., Mendelson, M., Mock, J., & Erbaugh, J. (1961). An inventory for measuring depression. *Archives of General Psychiatry, 4,* 561–571.

Behavioral Assessment (1985). Mini series on Target Behavior Selection. *Behavioral Assessment, 7,* 1–79.

Bellack, A.S., & Hersen, M. (1976). Self-report inventories in behavioral assessment. In J.D. Cone & R.P. Hawkins (Eds.), *Behavioral assessment: New directions in clinical psychology.* New York: Brunner/Mazel.

Bellack, A.S., & Hersen, M. (1988). *Behavioral assessment. A practical handbook* (3rd ed.). New York: Pergamon Press.

Bellack, A.S., & Hersen, M. (1998). *Behavioral assessment. A practical handbook* (4th ed.). Boston: Allyn & Bacon.

Bomholt, N.L. (1996). A tale of two surveys—A comparison between results of two opinion surveys. *European Journal of Psychological Assessment, 12,* 169–173.

Boring, E.G. (1953). A history of introspection. *Psychological Bulletin, 50,* 169–189.

Bradburn, N.M., & Sudman, S. (1979). *Improving interview method and questionnaire design.* San Francisco: Jossey-Bass.

Burns, G.L. (1989). Indirect measurement and behavioral assessment: A case for social behaviorism psychometrics. *Behavioral Assessment, 2,* 197–206.

Buros, O.K. (Ed.). (1941–1978). *The mental measurements yearbooks.* Highland Park, NJ: Gryphone Press.

Campbell, D.T., & Fiske, D.W. (1959). Convergent and discriminant validation by the multitrait-multimethod matrix. *Psychological Bulletin, 56,* 81–105.

Cautela, J.R. (1977). *Behavior analysis forms for clinical intervention.* Champaign, IL: Research Press.

Cautela, J.R., & Upper, D. (1976). The Behavioral Inventory Battery: The use of self-report measures in behavioral analysis and therapy. In M. Hersen & A.S. Bellack (Eds.), *Behavioral assessment: A practical handbook.* New York: Pergamon Press.

Cavanaugh, J.C. (1998). Metamemory as social cognition: Challenges for (and from) survey research. In N. Schwartz, D. Park, B. Knauper, & S. Sudman (Eds.), *Cognition, aging, and self-reports.* Ann Arbor, MI: Psychology Press.

Cohen, R.J., Swerdik, M.E., & Phillips, S.M. (1996). *Psychological testing and assessment.* Mountain View, CA: Mayfield.

Cone, J.D. (1978). The Behavioral Assessment Grid (BAG): A conceptual framework and a taxonomy. *Behavior Therapy, 9,* 882–888.

Cone, J.D. (1979). Confounded comparisons in triple response mode assessment. *Behavioral Assessment, 1,* 57–77.

Cone, J.D. (1981a). Psychometric considerations. In A.S. Bellack & M. Hersen (Eds.), *Behavioral assessment: A practical handbook* (2nd ed.). Boston: Allyn & Bacon.

Cone, J.D. (1981b). Algunas observaciones sobre las comparaciones entre métodos de evaluación conductual. In R. Fernández-Ballesteros & J.A.I. Carrobles (Eds.), *Evalución conductual.* Madrid, Spain: Pirámide.

Cone, J.D. (1986). Idiographic, nomothetic, and related perspectives in behavioral assessment. In R.M. Nelson & S.N. Hayes (Eds.), *Conceptual foundation of behavioral assessment.* New York: Guilford Press.

Cone, J.D. (1988). Psychometric considerations and the multiple models of behavioral assessment. In A.S. Bellack & M. Hersen (Eds.), *Behavioral assessment: A practical handbook* (4th ed.). Boston: Allyn & Bacon.

Cone, J.D. (1992). That was then! This is now. *Behavioral Assessment, 14,* 219–228.

Cone, J.D. (1993). The current state of behavioral assessment. *European Journal of Psychological Assessment, 9,* 175–181.

Cone, J.D. (1998). Psychometric considerations: Concepts, contents, and methods. In A.S. Bellack & M. Hersen (Eds.), *Behavioral assessment: A practical handbook* (5th ed.). Boston: Allyn & Bacon.

Cone, J.D. (2003). Theoretical perspective: Behavioral assessment. In R. Fernández-Ballesteros (Ed.), *Encyclopedia of psychological assessment.* London: Sage.

Cone, J.D., & Hawkins, J.P. (Eds.). (1976). *Behavioral assessment: New directions in clinical psychology.* New York: Brunner/Mazel.

Cook, T.D. (1985). Positivist critical multiplism. In L. Shotland & M. Mark (Eds.), *Postpositivist critical multiplism.* London: Sage.

Cronbach, L.J. (1957). The two scientific disciplines of scientific psychology. *American Psychologist, 12,* 671–687.

Cronbach, L.J. (1975). Beyond the two disciplines of scientific psychology. *American Psychologist, 22,* 116–127.

Cronbach, L.J., & Gleser, G.C. (1957). *Psychological tests and personnel decisions.* Urbana: University of Illinois Press.

Cronbach, L.J., Gleser, G.C., Nanda, H., & Rajaratnam, N. (1972). *The dependability of behavioral measurements: Theory of generalizability for scores and profiles.* New York: Wiley.

Ericsson, K., & Simon, H. (1980). Verbal reports as data. *Psychological Review, 87,* 215–251.

Ericsson, K., & Simon, H. (1984). *Protocol analysis.* Cambridge, MA: MIT Press.

Evaluación Psicológica/Psychological Assessment (1991). *Special Issue: Psychological Assessment in Europe, 7*(1), 5–113.

Evans, I.M. (1985). Building systems models as a strategy for target behavior selection in clinical assessment. *Behavioral Assessment, 7,* 21–32.

Evans, I.M. (1986). Response structure and the triple-response-mode concept. In R.M. Nelson & S.N. Hayes (Eds.), *Conceptual foundation of behavioral assessment.* New York: Guilford Press.

Evans, I.M. (1993). Dynamic response relationships: The challenge for behavioral assessment. *European Journal of Behavioral Assessment, 9,* 206–212.

Eyberg, S.M., & Johnson, S.M. (1974). Multiple assessment of behavior modification with families: Effects of contingency contracting and order of treated problems. *Journal of Consulting and Clinical Psychology, 42,* 594–606.

Fernández-Ballesteros, R. (1979). *Los métodos en evaluación conductual.* Madrid, Spain: Pablo del Río.

Fernández-Ballesteros, R. (1980). *Psicodiagnóstico. Concepto y Metodología.* Madrid, Spain: Kapelusz.

Fernández-Ballesteros, R. (1991). Anatomía de los autoinformes. *Evaluación Psicológica/Psychological Assessment, 7,* 263–290.

Fernández-Ballesteros, R. (1993). Behavioral assessment: Dying, vanishing or still running? *European Journal of Psychological Assessment, 9,* 159–174.

Fernández-Ballesteros, R. (Ed.). (1994a). *Evaluación conductual hoy. Un enfoque para el cambio en psicología clínica y de la salud.* Madrid, Spain: Pirámide.

Fernández-Ballesteros, R. (1994b). Evolución histórica de la evaluación conductual. In R. Fernández-Ballesteros (Ed.), *Evaluación conductual hoy. Un enfoque para el cambio en psicología clínica y de la salud.* Madrid, Spain: Pirámide.

Fernández-Ballesteros, R. (1994c). Características básicas de la evaluación conductual. In R. Fernández-Ballesteros (Ed.), *Evaluación conductual hoy. Un enfoque para el cambio en psicología clínica y de la salud.* Madrid, Spain: Pirámide.

Fernández-Ballesteros, R. (1994d). El proceso en evaluación conductual. In R. Fernández-Ballesteros (Ed.), *Evaluación conductual hoy. Un enfoque para el cambio en psicología clínica y de la salud.* Madrid, Spain: Pirámide.

Fernández-Ballesteros, R., De Bruyn, E.E., Godoy, A., Hornke, L., Ter Laak, J., Vizcarro, C., Westhoff, K., Westmeyer, H., & Zacagnini, J.L. (2001). The Guidelines for the Assessment Process (GAP): A proposal for discussion. *European Journal of Psychological Assessment, 17,* 187–200.

Fernández-Ballesteros, R., Díaz, P., Izal, V., Maciá, A., & Pérez, J. (1981). Relaciones entre métodos de evaluación y modalidades de respuesta. In R. Fernández-Ballesteros (Ed.), *Nuevas aportaciones en evaluación conductual.* Valencia, Spain: Alfaplus.

Fernández-Ballesteros, R., Díaz, P., Izal, M., Maciá, A., & Perez, J. (1982). Distorsiones de respuesta en autoinformes conductuales. In R. Fernández-Ballesteros (Ed.), *Nuevas aportaciones en evaluación conductual.* Valencia, Spain: Alfaplus.

Fernández-Ballesteros, R., & Marquez, M.O. (2003). Self-reports (general). In R. Fernández-Ballesteros (Ed.), *Encyclopedia of Psychological Assessment.* London: Sage.

Fernández-Ballesteros, R., & Staats, A. (1992). Paradigmatic behavioral assessment: Assessment, treatment, and evaluation: Answering the crisis in behavioral assessment. *Advances in Behaviour Research and Therapy, 14,* 1–28.

Fernández-Ballesteros, R., & Zamarrón, M.D. (1996). New findings on social desirability and faking. *Psychological Reports, 79,* 612–614.

Ferster, C.B. (1965). Classification of behavioral pathology. In L. Krasner & L.P. Ullman (Eds.), *Research in behavior modification.* New York: Holt, Rinehart & Winston.

Geer, J.H. (1965). The development of a scale to measure fear. *Behaviour Research and Therapy, 3,* 45–53.

Genest M., & Turk, D.C. (1981). Think-aloud approaches to cognitive assessment. In C. Glass & M. Genest (Eds.), *Cognitive assessment.* New York: Guilford Press.

Goldfried, M.R., & Kent, R.N. (1972). Traditional versus behavioral assessment: A comparison of methodological and theoretical assumption. *Psychological Bulletin, 77,* 409–420.

Goldfried, M.R., & Pomeranz, M. (1968). Role of assessment in behavior modification. *Psychological Reports, 23,* 75–87.

Goldstein, G., & Hersen, M. (Eds.). (1984). *Handbook of psychological assessment.* New York: Pergamon Press.

Goldstein, G., & Hersen, M. (Eds.). (1990). *Handbook of psychological assessment* (2nd ed). New York: Pergamon Press.

Goldstein, G., & Hersen, M. (Eds.). (2000). *Handbook of psychological assessment* (3rd ed.). New York: Pergamon-Elsevier.

Gough, H.G. (1975). *California Psychological Inventory* (Rev. ed.). Palo Alto, CA: Consulting Psychologists Press.

Groth-Marnat, G. (1990). *Handbook of psychological assessment* (2nd ed.). New York: Wiley.

Guevremont, D.C., & Spiegler, M.D. (1990). What do behavioral therapists really do? A survey of the clinical practice of AABT members. Paper presented at the 24th Annual Convention of the Association for Advancement of Behavior Therapy, San Francisco, CA.

Hambleton, R.K. (2003). Criterion reference testing: Methods and procedures. In R. Fernández-Ballesteros (Ed.), *Encyclopedia of psychological assessment.* London: Sage.

Hambleton, R.K., & Rogers, H.J. (1990). Advances in criterion-referenced measurement. In R.K. Hambleton & J.N. Zaal (Eds.), *Advances in educational and psychological testing.* London: Kluwer.

Hartmann, D.P., Roper, B.L., & Bradford, D.C. (1979). Some relationships between behavioral and traditional assessment. *Journal of Behavioral Assessment, 1,* 3–21.

Hathaway S.R., & McKinley, J.C. (1940). A multiphasic personality schedule (Minnesota): I. Construction of the schedule. *Journal of Psychology, 10,* 249–254.

Hawkins, R.P. (1986). Selection of behavioral assessment. In R.M. Nelson & S.N. Hayes (Eds.), *Conceptual foundation of behavioral assessment.* New York: Guilford Press.

Hayes, S.C., & Follette, W.C. (1993). The challenge faced by behavioral assessment. *European Journal of Psychological Assessment, 9,* 182–188.

Hayes, S.C., Nelson, R.O., & Jarrett, R.B (1986). Evaluating the quality of behavioral assessment. In R.M. Nelson & S.N. Hayes (Eds.), *Conceptual foundation of behavioral assessment.* New York: Guilford Press.

Haynes, S.N. (1978). *Principles of behavioral assessment.* New York: Gardner Press.

Haynes, S.N. (1986). The design of intervention programs. In R.M. Nelson & S.N. Hayes (Eds.), *Conceptual foundation of behavioral assessment.* New York: Guilford Press.

Haynes, S.N. (1988). Causal models and the assessment-treatment relationships. *Behavior Therapy Journal of Psychopathology and Behavioral Assessment, 10,* 171–183.

Haynes, S.N. (1992). *Models of causality in psychopathology.* New York: Macmillan.

Haynes, S.N. (1998). The changing nature of behavioral assessment. In A.S. Bellack & M. Hersen (Eds.), *Behavioral assessment: A practical handbook* (4th ed.). Boston: Allyn & Bacon.

Haynes, S.N., & O'Brien, W.O. (1990). The functional analysis in behavior therapy. *Clinical Psychology Review, 10,* 649–668.

Haynes, S.N., Spain, H., & Oliviera, J. (1993). Identifying causal relationships in clinical assessment. *Psychological Assessment, 5,* 281–291.

Haynes, S.N., Uchigakiuchi, P., Meyer, K., Orimoto, L., & Blaine, D. (1993). Functional analytic causal models and the design of treatment programs: Concept and clinical applications with childhood behavioral problems. *European Journal of Psychological Assessment, 9,* 189–205.

Haynes, S.N., & Waialae, K. (1994). Fundamentos psicométricos de la evaluación conductual. In R. Fernández-Ballesteros (Ed.), *Evaluación conductual hoy. Un enfoque para el cambio en psicología clínica y de la salud.* Madrid, Spain: Pirámide.

Heiby, E. (1978). Conditions which occasion depression. *Psychological Reports, 45,* 638–714.

Heiby, E. (1982). A self-reinforcement questionnaire. *Behavior Research and Therapy, 20,* 397–401.

Heiby, E., & Staats, A.W. (1990). Depression: Classification, explanation and treatment. In G.H. Eyfert & I.M. Evans (Eds.), *Unifying behavior therapy: Contributions of paradigmatic behaviorism.* New York: Springer.

Hersen, M., & Bellack, A.S. (1988). *Dictionary of behavioral assessment techniques.* New York: Pergamon Press.

Hollon, S.D., & Bemis, K.M. (1981). Self-report and assessment of cognitive functions. In M. Hersen & A.S. Bellack (Eds.), *Behavioral assessment: A practical handbook* (2nd ed.). New York: Pergamon Press.

Jaccard, J., & Dittus P. (1990). Idiographic and nomothetic perspectives on research methods and data analysis. In C. Hendrick & M.S. Clark (Eds.), *Research methods in personality and social psychology.* Newbury Park, CA: Sage.

Kanfer, F.H. (1972). Assessment for behavior modification. *Journal of Personality Assessment, 36,* 418–423.

Kanfer, F.H., & Saslow, G. (1965). Behavioral analysis: An alternative to diagnostic classification. *Archives of General Psychiatry, 12,* 529–538.

Kanfer, F.H., & Saslow, G. (1969). Behavioral diagnosis. In C.M. Frank (Ed.), *Behavioral therapy: Appraisal and status.* New York: McGraw-Hill.

Kazdin, A.E. (1977). Assessing the clinical or applied importance of behavior change through social validation. *Behavior Modification, 1,* 427–452.

Kazdin, A.E., & Wilson, G.T. (1978). *Evaluation of behavior therapy: Issues, evidence, and research strategies.* Cambridge, MA: Ballinger.

Kelley, M.L., Heffer, R.W., Gresham, F.M., & Elliot, S.N. (1989). Development of a modified treatment evaluation inventory. *Journal of Psychopathology and Behavioral Assessment, 10,* 235–247.

Kern, J.M. (1991). An evaluation of a novel role-play methodology: The standardized idiographic approach. *Behavior Therapy, 22,* 13–29.

Kiresuk, T.J. (2003). The Goal Attainment Scaling. In R. Fernández-Ballesteros (Ed.), *Encyclopedia of psychological assessment.* London: Sage.

Kiresuk, T.J., Smith, A., & Cardillo, J.E. (Eds.). (1994). *Goal Attainment Scaling: Application theory and measurement.* Hillsdale, NJ: Erlbaum.

Kirkland, K. (1978). Frequency of dependent measures in two non-behavioral journals. *Behavioral Therapist, 1,* 14–15.

Lewinsohn, P.M. (1974). A behavioral approach to depression. In R. Friedman & M. Katz (Eds.), *The psychology of depression: Contemporary theory and research.* New York: Wiley.

Lewinsohn, P.M., & Talkington, J. (1979). Studies on the measurement of unpleasant events and relationships with depression. *Applied Psychological Measurement, 3,* 83–101.

Livingston, S.A. (1976). Psychometric techniques for criterion-referenced testing and behavioral assessment. In J.D. Cone & J.P. Hawkins (Eds.), *Behavioral assessment: New directions in clinical psychology.* New York: Brunner/Mazel.

Lubin, B. (1965). Adjective checklist for the measurement of depression. *Archives of General Psychiatry, 12,* 57–62.

MacCorquodale, K., & Meehl, P.E. (1948). On a distinction between hypothetical constructs and intervening variables. *Psychological Review, 55,* 95–107.

MacPhillamy, D.J., & Lewinsohn, P.M. (1982). The Pleasant Events Schedule: Studies on reliability, validity and scale intercorrelation. *Journal of Consulting and Clinical Psychology, 50,* 363–380.

McHugh, G. (1967). *Sex Knowledge Inventory: Form X (Revised).* Durham, NC: Family Life Publications.

Meichenbaum, D., & Buttler, L. (1979). Cognitive ethology: Assessing the streams of cognition and emotion. In K. Blankstein, P. Pliner, & J. Polivy (Eds.), *Advances in the study of communication and affect: Assessment and modification of emotional behavior* (Vol. 6). New York: Plenum.

Messik, S. (1994). Foundations of validity: Meaning and consequences in psychological assessment. *European Journal of Psychological Assessment, 10,* 1–9.

Messik, S. (1995). Validity of psychological assessment. *American Psychologist, 50,* 741–749.

Minke, K. (1990). Research foundations of a developing paradigm: Implications for behavioral engineering. In G.H. Eifert & I.M. Evans (Eds.), *Unifying behavior therapy.* New York: Springer.

Mischel, W. (1968). *Personality and assessment.* New York: Wiley.

Mischel, W. (1972). Direct versus indirect personality assessment: Evidence and implications. *Journal of Consulting and Clinical Psychology, 38,* 319–324.

Murphy, L.L. (1992). *The eleventh mental measurement yearbook.* Lincoln, NE: Buros Institute of Mental Measurement Yearbook.

Murray, H.A. (1938). *Exploration in personality.* New York: Oxford University Press.

Nelson, R.M. (1983). Behavioral assessment: Past, present and future. *Behavioral Assessment, 5,* 195–206.

Nelson, R.M., & Hayes S.C. (Eds.). (1986a). *Conceptual foundation of behavioral assessment.* New York: Guilford Press.

Nelson, R.M., & Hayes, S.N. (1986b). The nature of behavioral assessment. In R.M. Nelson & S.N. Hayes (Eds.), *Conceptual foundation of behavioral assessment.* New York: Guilford Press.

Nisbett, R.E., & Wilson, T.D. (1977). Telling more than we can know: Verbal reports on mental processes. *Psychological Review, 84,* 231–259.

Piotrowski, C., & Keller, J.W. (1984a). Psychodiagnostic testing in APA-approved clinical psychology programs. *Professional Psychology: Research and Practice, 20,* 111–119.

Piotrowski, C., & Keller, J.W. (1984b). Attitudes toward clinical assessment by members of the AABT. *Psychological Reports, 22,* 831–838.

Piotrowski, C., & Zalewski, C. (1993). Training in psychodiagnostic testing in APA-approved PsyD and PhD clinical psychology programs. *Journal of Personality, 61,* 394–405.

Rathus, S.A. (1973). A 30-items schedule for assessing assertive behavior. *Behavior Therapy, 4,* 398–406.

Robinson, C.H., & Annon, J.S. (1975). *The Heterosexual Attitude Scale—Female form.* Honolulu, HI: Enabling System.

Schulte, D. (1976). *Diagnostik in der verhaltensanalyse.* Munich: Urban Schwarzenberg.

Schulte, D. (1992). Criteria of treatment selection in behaviour therapy. *European Journal of Psychological Assessment, 8,* 157–162.

Schulte, D. (1997). Dimensions of outcome measurement. In H.H. Strupp, L.M. Horowitz, & M.J. Lambert (Eds.), *Measuring patient changes.* Washington, DC: American Psychological Association.

Schwartz, N., Park, D.C., Knauper, B., & Sudman, S. (1998). Cognition, aging, and self-reports. In N. Schwartz, D. Park, B. Knauper, & S. Sudman (Eds.), *Cognition, aging, and self-reports.* Ann Arbor, MI: Psychology Press.

Silva, F. (1989). *Evaluación conductual y criterios psicométricos.* Madrid, Spain: Pirámide.

Silva, F. (1993a). *Psychometric foundations and behavioral assessment.* London: Sage.

Silva, F. (1993b). Treatment utility: A re-appraisal. *European Journal of Psychological Assessment, 9,* 222–226.

Skinner, B.F. (1938). *Behavior of organisms.* New York: Appleton.

Skinner, B.F. (1953). *Science and human behavior.* New York: Macmillan.

Spielberger, C.D. (1975). *Manual for the State-Trait Anxiety Inventory.* Palo Alto, CA: Consulting Psychologists Press.

Staats, A.W. (1975). *Social behaviorism.* Homewood: IL: Dorsey Press.

Staats, A W. (1996). *Behavior and personality: Psychological behaviorism.* New York: Springer.

Staats, A.W., & Fernández-Ballesteros, R. (1987). The self-report in personality measurement. *Evaluación Psicológica/Psychological Assessment, 3,* 151–191.

Staats, A.W., & Staats, C. (1963). *Complex human behavior.* New York: Holt, Rinehart & Winston.

Stone, A.A., Turkkan, J.S., Bachrach, C.A., Jobe, J.B., Kurtzman, H.S., & Cain, V.S. (Eds.). (2000). *The science of self-reports: Implication for research and practice.* Mahwah, NJ: Erlbaum.

Strupp, H.H., Horowitz, L.M., & Lambert, M.J. (Eds.). (1997). *Measuring patient changes.* Washington, DC: American Psychological Association.

Sundberg, N.D., Tyler, L.E., & Taplin, J.R. (1973). *Clinical psychology: Expanding horizons.* New York: Prentice-Hall.

Turkkan, J.S. (2000). General issues in self-report. In A.A. Stone, J. S. Turkkan, C.A. Bachrach, J.B. Jobe, H.S. Kurtzman, & V.S. Cain (Eds.), *The science of self-reports: Implication for research and practice.* Mahwah, NJ: Erlbaum.

Tverski, A., & Kahneman, D. (1973). Availability. A heuristic for judging frequency and probability. *Cognitive Psychology, 5,* 207–232.

Twentyman, C., & McFall, R. (1975). Behavioral training of social skills in shy males. *Journal of Consulting and Clinical Psychology, 43,* 384–395.

Watson, J.B. (1913). Psychology as the behaviorist views it. *Psychological Review, 20,* 158–177.

Watson, J.B. (1920). Is thinking merely the action of language mechanisms? *British Journal of Psychology, 11,* 87–104.

Westmeyer, H. (2003). On the structure of clinical case formulation. *European Journal of Psychological Assessment, 3.*

Wilson, T.D., Hull, J.G., & Johnson, J. (1981). Awareness and self-perception: Verbal reports on internal states. *Journal of Personality and Social Psychology, 40,* 53–71.

Windelbland, W. (1878). *Die Geschichte der neueren Philosophie* (Vol. 2). Leipzig: Sitzungsberichte.

Witt, J.C., Moe, G., Gutkin, T.B., & Andrews, L. (1984). The effect of saying the same thing in different ways. The problem of language and jargon in school-based consultation. *Journal of School Psychology, 22,* 361–367.

Wolfe, M.M. (1978). Social validity: The case of subjective measurement or how applied behavior analysis is finding its heart. *Journal of Applied Behavior Analysis, 11,* 203–214.

Wolpe, J. (1964). *The practice of behavior therapy.* New York: Pergamon Press.

Wolpe, J., & Lang, P.J. (1964). A Fear Survey Schedule for use in behavior therapy. *Behavior Research and Therapy, 2,* 27–30.

Zung, W.W.K. (1965). A self-rating depression scale. *Archives of General Psychiatry, 12,* 63–70.

Zuriff, G.E. (1985). *Behaviorism: A conceptual reconstruction.* New York: Columbia University Press.

CHAPTER 13

Computers in the Training and Practice of Behavioral Assessment

DAVID C.S. RICHARD AND DEAN LAUTERBACH

The past few years have witnessed a tremendous increase in the use of computers in psychological and behavioral assessment. A hallmark of this development is the tremendous diversity of programs that have been reported in the literature. Programs have been developed for behavioral training, behavioral assessment, as well as behavior therapy. Published reports have described computer-administered behavioral interviews and rating scales, programs that ease coding of real-time or videotaped behavior samples, and a variety of handheld computer applications that assist in the recording of an individual's behavior as it occurs in the natural environment. In addition, applications have been developed to communicate clinical case formulations and functional analyses. Because computers are especially useful for data collection, management, and processing, computer technology can help behavioral assessors understand the complex and functional relations between environmental events and behavioral processes.

Before beginning the chapter, a few terms should be defined. First, we use the term *computerized behavioral assessment* to refer broadly to all computer applications that facilitate behavioral assessment methods. Computerized behavioral assessment applications may be divided according to the form of interaction between the computer, the behavioral assessor, and the client. *Computer-assisted behavioral assessment* refers to any software program that assists an assessor in his or her activities but does not substitute for the assessor in interactions with the client. For example, a program that is designed to help an assessor code behavior during an analogue behavioral assessment session would be considered a computer-assisted behavioral assessment product. *Direct computerized behavioral assessment,* on the other hand, involves computer-client interactions, usually in the context of an interview or self-monitoring procedure. The client interacts with the computer and enters information contingent upon computer-generated queries (e.g., items, prompts, etc.). The queries are sometimes controlled by a software algorithm that presents items most relevant to a given client.

The term *accuracy* refers to how closely behavioral observations, ratings, or other measurements correspond to reality

The authors extend their great appreciation to Beverly Brown for her assistance in the development of this chapter.

222

on the behavioral dimension being measured (e.g., frequency, magnitude, duration, etc.). The term *ecological validity* refers to the degree to which behavioral assessment results reflect behavior as it occurs in the natural environment along an important behavioral dimension. Ecological validity is also a relevant issue not just with regard to observed behavioral dimensions, but with regard to observed functional relations. For example, an analogue assessment strategy may not possess ecological validity if the variables that function to control a behavior in the analogue setting are different than those controlling behavior in the natural environment. Obviously, behavioral assessment data should be both accurate (i.e., relatively free of measurement error when the data are collected) and ecologically valid with regard to both behavioral dimensions and functional relations.

COMPUTERIZED BEHAVIORAL ASSESSMENT: A DYNAMIC AND GROWING FIELD

One way to quantify trends in the extant literature is to examine the content of research reports over time. For example, in a previous review looking at the growing use of computers in psychological assessment, we examined the PsycInfo[1] literature database and counted the annual frequency of dissertations focusing on computerized psychological assessment over the past 20 years. We found a trend of accelerating research in computerized psychological assessment with almost twice as many dissertations from 1997 to 2001 as the previous 5-year period (Richard & Bobicz, in press). However, using the same strategy to quantify trends in the use of computers in behavioral assessment is more daunting because behavioral assessment is composed of a family of assessment methods (e.g., behavioral observation, analogue observation, self-monitoring, etc.). Further, researchers often identify the behavioral assessment method used in a study without explicitly identifying it as such.

For this chapter, we refined our previous strategy by narrowing a PsycInfo literature search to include only those terms commonly associated with computer applications in behavioral assessment. We also expanded the search to include articles, chapters, and books in addition to dissertations. The search was conducted March 1, 2002. The first search string was "*computerized* or *handheld* or *palmtop* or *automated* or *multimedia*." The Boolean operator "and" joined the first search string with the second search string: "*behavioral assessment* or *behavioral observation* or *self-monitoring* or *momentary assessment* or *simulation*."

The literature search returned 654 citations, many of which were not directly related to behavioral assessment (see Table 13.1 for a list of citation categories, examples, frequency counts, and percentage of total citations returned). We considered a citation to be relevant to computerized behavioral assessment if the abstract referred to (a) the use of computer technology in behavioral assessment; (b) the development of behavioral assessment software systems (e.g., observational software, self-monitoring software); (c) the use of computers to assist in the training of behavioral assessors; (d) a discussion of how computers could be (or have been) applied to behavioral assessment; or (e) quantification strategies for analyzing behavioral assessment data collected by a computer. We excluded from our final tally all citations that did not specifically focus on computer applications in behavioral assessment or the training of behavioral assessors. The final search list included 154 citations (23.55% of the total returned citations) over a 40-year period from 1962 to 2001. Consistent with our previous research on dissertation trends in computerized psychological assessment, Figure 13.1 shows an accelerating increase in citations in computerized behavioral assessment over the last 40 years.

Several conclusions may be drawn from these results. First, the increased interest in applying computer technology to behavioral assessment corresponds with technological advances. The first significant increase in citations occurred in the mid-1970s and probably reflects increased access by scholars to mainframe computers in university and health care settings. The trend continues through the early to mid-1980s before receiving another boost in the late 1980s and early 1990s. This second increase probably reflects the development of applications for affordable desktop computers.

Second, there have been large and consistent increases in the literature base since 1967. With the exception of the interval from 1972 to 1976, each succeeding 5-year interval has produced more research reports in computerized behavioral assessment than the previous interval. This provides empirical support for the conclusion that computerized behavioral assessment represents a growing and dynamic field. Indeed, the number of citations for the interval 1997 to 2001 ($n = 49$) exceeded the combined number of citations from 1962 to 1987 ($n = 46$). Relatedly, the graph shows the youth of the literature base. Fully 89 of the 154 reports identified in the PsycInfo database, or 57.79%, have occurred in the last 10 years. Clearly, one of the most vibrant movements in behavioral assessment involves the integration of computer technology.

One reasonable critique of the above findings is that the increase in articles, books, and dissertations in computerized behavioral assessment may reflect a more general increase in psychological assessment reports. Specifically, reports focusing on traditional assessment instruments, whether they in-

TABLE 13.1 Citation Summary from Literature Search

Citation Category	Examples	n	Percent of Studies (N = 654)
Behavioral Assessment	Ecological momentary assessment, observational coding software, training simulations, self-monitoring, behavioral rating scales, etc.	154	23.55
Human Factors	Flight simulations, human-computer interactions, automation bias, simulated workload and fatigue, problem solving in engineering.	96	14.67
Neuropsychology	Cognitive testing in patients with a neurological disease (e.g., Huntington's chorea), assessing functional reorganization of cerebral hemispheres, neuropsychological testing, assessment of cognitive recovery from head injury.	62	9.48
Quantitative, Psychometric, or Statistical	Development of statistical procedures, Monte Carlo studies, adaptive testing, Bayesian networks, item-response theory, rule-based fuzzy decision modeling, modeling.	43	6.57
Industrial-Organizational	Personnel selection simulations, management training, goal orientation, leadership analysis, group teamwork, decision making.	43	6.57
Educational	Classroom training, training of educational personnel, sex education, special education classification procedures.	41	6.27
General Review Chapter or Article	Assessment texts, review articles on computer technology not specifically focused on behavioral assessment.	40	6.12
Animal Research	Computerized animal tracking systems, computer graphic stimulus discrimination in mice, neuroreceptor functioning in animals.	30	4.59
Cognitive Science	Distributed cognitive systems, modeling information retrieval systems, software developments, Stroop tasks, neural networking, modeling confirmation bias.	30	4.59
Not Related to Behavioral Assessment	Reactions to baldness in children with cancer, frustration tolerance, evaluation of stimuli in a social competence test.	18	2.75
Gaming	Game simulations, cross-cultural gaming, role playing, business simulation games, decision-making analyses in gaming, mental health center management simulation game.	13	1.99
Social Psychology	Group efficiency when confronting a common dilemma, effect of feedback on task performance, assessing competition and cooperation.	11	1.68
Military	Command and control simulations, combat game simulations, air attack flight simulator, message processing simulation during combat event.	11	1.68
Clinical, Nonbehavioral Assessment	Computerized MMPI-A and MMPI-2 administrations, WISC-III training tools, computer applications in objective personality assessment.	10	1.53
Sensation and Perception	Auditory discriminations, memory for tones, sound propagation models, simulation of color appearance for dichromats, preattentive vision, rotation tasks, and sonar operation.	7	1.07
Other	Computer science, music, forensics, medical, behavioral treatment, robotics, nursing, psychophysiology, occupational therapy.	30	4.58

Note. Search terms were (*computerized or handheld or palmtop or automated or multimedia*) and (*behavioral assessment or behavioral observation or self-monitoring or momentary assessment or simulation*). The results reported here should be considered a representative sampling of work in the field rather than a definitive cataloging of research reports. It is unlikely that any combination of search terms will successfully capture all computerized behavioral assessment research given the heterogeneity of keyword descriptors and research applications.

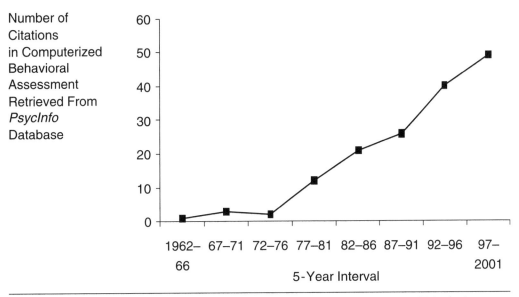

Figure 13.1 PsychInfo search return: Books, articles, and dissertations focusing on computerized behavioral assessment from 1972 to 2001.

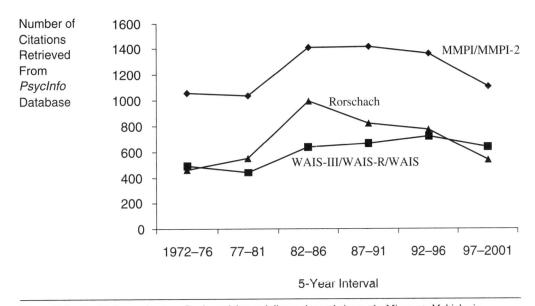

Figure 13.2 PsychInfo search return: Books, articles, and dissertations relating to the Minnesota Multiphasic Personality Inventory (MMPI, MMPI-2), Rorschach, and Weschler Adult Intelligence Scale (WAIS-III, WAIS-R, WAIS) from 1972 to 2001.

volve computer applications or not, may have experienced reporting trends that parallel those in computerized behavioral assessment. To test this alternative hypothesis, we selected three popular psychological assessment instruments in clinical use over the past 30 years (i.e., the Rorschach, the MMPI/MMPI-2, and the WAIS/WAIS-R/WAIS-III). We then searched the PsycInfo database using the names of these instruments as keywords and counted the number of citations from 1972 to 2001. Figure 13.2 aggregates the annual data

into 5-year intervals and shows that, contrary to the trend evidenced in the computerized behavioral assessment literature, there has not been a general increase in reports concerning the comparison instruments. In fact, there is some indication, especially with the Rorschach, that the number of reports may be decreasing. Although we did not track trends in computer applications with the MMPI, Rorschach, or WAIS, the number of citations describing computer applications with these instruments probably has increased over time despite an overall citation trend for each instrument to not change or decrease.

In this chapter, we will review the growing literature surrounding computer applications in the training and practice of behavioral assessment by focusing first on programs that have been developed to train behavioral assessors. After exploring training and quality assurance, we then turn our attention to software that has been written to augment specific behavioral assessment methods. The diversity of computer applications is evident in the varied ways behavioral researchers have applied computer technology. After surveying each behavioral assessment method, we turn our attention to software designed to help behavior therapists develop clinical case formulations from behavioral assessment data. Finally, we close the chapter by considering a variety of issues related to computerized behavioral assessment and suggest a number of directions for future research.

COMPUTERIZED TRAINING PROGRAMS IN BEHAVIORAL ASSESSMENT

Training programs for specific skill development often take the form of course instruction through traditional pedagogical techniques. In this section, we review innovative computerized training programs relevant to behavioral assessment and applied behavior analysis. We close the section with some comments regarding the construction and practicality of these programs.

Simulation Training

A computer simulation is a direct, computerized behavioral assessment tool that attempts to "model reality authentically for the user, thereby providing an opportunity for the user to acquire skills, engage in problem-solving, and attain new concepts" (Gorrell & Downing, 1989, p. 335). Two types of simulations have been reported in the literature that are relevant to behavioral assessment. The first involves simulations that are used in the evaluation and training of behavioral assessors. The second, described later in the chapter, involves simulations clients complete in order for a behavioral assessor to develop hypotheses about client functioning or measure change in a target behavior.

With regard to simulation training for behavioral assessors, the simulations that have been developed in the last 10 to 15 years vary substantially in the degree to which the simulated cases are presented textually (e.g., a written vignette) or visually (e.g., digitized video clips of client behavior). The goal of all simulation training, however, has been to present

realistic clinical cases to either assist instructional objectives or as a means of evaluating a participant's behavioral assessment skills. Although a number of programs have been developed that assist instruction in applied behavior analysis (see Crosbie & Kelly, 1993; Desrochers, 1996; Graf, 1995; Shimoff & Catania, 1995) or in allied fields (e.g., vocational rehabilitation: Chan, Parker, Lam, Mecaskey, & Malphurs, 1987; Chan, Rosen, Wong, & Kaplan, 1993; occupational therapy: Stewart, 2001; counseling: Engen, Finken, Luschei, & Kenney, 1994), our focus here is on programs that create behavioral assessment simulations and assist in the evaluation of a student's assessment skills.

Computerized simulations make it possible to explore unique clinical situations didactically, highlight and display instances of targeted client behaviors on-demand, incorporate algorithmic variations to challenge students, and record trainee responses (Descrochers & Hile, 1993). Computer simulations provide the opportunity for students to consider diverse assessment and treatment strategies when conceptualizing a case and demonstrate their decision-making skills in a context that may possess more ecological validity than traditional essay examinations. Simulation training enhances learning because feedback is presented immediately by the computer (Chan, Parker, Lam, Mecaskey, & Malphurs, 1987). In addition, computerized training eliminates liability issues present when novice students work with real clients.

Computer simulations are not only useful in training students, they also provide instructors with novel ways of assessing student competencies. Specifically, instructors are afforded the opportunity to observe the application of a student's decision-making skills to a potentially wide variety of case simulations that vary in terms of conceptual difficulty, type of presenting problem, appropriateness of assessment strategies, and so forth. Digitized video can be replayed at any point, providing instructors the opportunity to comment on both the simulated client's behavior and provide feedback to the student. Because computer simulations also can include a standardized assessment of skill acquisition, normative evaluations of competencies are possible. Importantly, there is some evidence that computer simulations can identify ways in which students approach clinical problem-solving activities. For example, Peterson (2000) had students complete a simulated clinical case on the computer then analyzed their responses using cluster analysis. He was able to identify four distinct problem-solving strategies students employed when planning assessment activities: *thorough and discriminating* (i.e., efficient assessment planning that took into account all possible useful assessment activities), *shotgun* (i.e., assessment planning that utilized many information sources nondiscriminantly or inefficiently), *constricted* (i.e., conservative assessment planning that underutilized information sources), and *random* (i.e., assessment planning with no discernible strategy or theoretical underpinning). Thus, computer simulations can provide educators the means by which to understand the strategies students use to conceptualize clinical cases.

One of the first simulation programs designed to develop behavioral assessment skills in doctoral students was described by Lambert (1989). Seven clinical psychology doctoral students and 23 master's level social work students completed three text-based clinical simulations. The three simulated cases included clients with agoraphobia, headache, and bulimia. Using the software, students could request different types of behavioral assessment data (e.g., psychophysiological data, behavioral interview data, etc.). The software responded by presenting assessment data, graphically and textually, that was "obtained" from the client. As one would expect in a clinical case, some assessment options produced clinically useful information while others did not. Although Lambert did not assess the degree to which students acquired behavioral assessment skills as a result of the simulation training, students appeared to react favorably to the simulations and considered them useful.

Isaacs, Costenbader, Reading-Brown, and Goodman (1992) described the development of a computer simulation designed for use with school psychologists. Written for Macintosh computers, the simulation allowed users to perform a variety of actions after receiving a simulated teacher referral for a child. The referral described the child and the target behavior problem. Students then selected from a variety of clinical activities: making a simulated phone call to a parent, perusing school records for information about the simulated child, viewing a digitized video of the child's behavior in a simulated classroom, selecting from a variety of simulated standardized test results, and so forth. When the student was satisfied with the amount of information that was collected, the student wrote a case report to a simulated special education committee detailing the case and the student's conclusions. Instructors then have the option of reviewing with the student the choices the student made during the assessment.

More recently, Desrochers, Clemmons, Grady, and Justice (2000) evaluated the *Simulations in Developmental Disabilities* (SIDDS; Descrochers & Hile, 1993) instructional training software with 18 college students. The SIDDS software concentrates on helping users define a target behavior, select assessments, interpret graphed client data, develop functional hypotheses about the causes of the client's problems, and generate a treatment plan. Users view video clips of a simulated client during various phases of treatment (e.g., assessment, follow-up, etc.). To evaluate skill and knowledge acquisition,

Desrochers et al. (2000) tested participants before, after, and 2 weeks following SIDDS training. Outcome measures assessed the degree to which participants could successfully identify the client's problem behavior, suggest valid assessment strategies, analyze the graphed data, and generate useful treatment recommendations. Participants were randomly assigned to experimental (SIDDS) and control (no-SIDDS) groups. Relative to controls, participants receiving the SIDDS training showed greater improvement in their behavioral assessment and case formulation skills from pretest to posttest. In addition, test scores favoring the SIDDS group were significantly different at posttest, suggesting measurably better behavioral assessment skills as a result of the SIDDS training.

Computerized simulations can play an important role not only in the acquisition of initial assessment skills, but also in the retraining of experienced professionals. Specifically, Sailor et al. (2000) pointed out that information technologies can help impart upon special education professionals new research-based intervention strategies without taxing existing school district resources. The same argument may be applied to practicing clinicians—computerized simulations distributed on CD-ROM or via the Internet are efficient ways of communicating new research and practice standards. However, despite the potential broad application of these programs to professionals, most research surrounding computer simulations has focused on undergraduate and graduate students.

Internet-Based Training Programs

The Internet is another avenue through which simulation training in behavioral assessment can be delivered. Researchers outside of behavioral psychology have recognized the potential of the Internet and have used the medium to train assessment skills in nursing students (Thomas, O'Connor, Albert, Boutain, & Brandt, 2001) and small business managers (Blackburn & Athayde, 2000). Although Internet-based training in behavioral assessment has yet to be exploited, a noteworthy first step in this direction has been taken by the federal government. The Office of Special Education established *The Online Academy* (onlineacademy.org), a web site devoted to promoting validated behavioral interventions for educators via the World Wide Web. The site includes resources in positive behavioral support (PBS). The site currently includes seven multimedia modules covering the following topics: foundations of positive behavioral support, functional assessment, development and implementation of PBS plans, intervention strategies (two modules), redesigning environmental lifestyles, and creating positive lifestyles. The site also includes a series of instructor resource files to plan course curriculum in conjunction with site content.

Creating Computer Training Simulations

The increasingly sophisticated multimedia capabilities of desktop computers make it possible for individuals with limited computer experience to produce sophisticated computer simulations. The easiest solution is to use slide presentation software (e.g., Microsoft PowerPoint) and configure it to deliver video clips, training modules, and other relevant stimuli. An additional layer of functionality may be incorporated by writing a simple Visual Basic program that assesses participant decision-making skills and stores responses in a text file or database. Another option is to develop simulations using multimedia authoring programs. Multimedia authoring programs are designed to manage a wide array of audio, visual, and text files in a way that seamlessly integrates their presentation. Authoring programs have been used successfully in business (e.g., development of work training programs) and education (e.g., course modules) for years. Table 13.2 provides a listing of relevant authoring programs and multimedia resources computer simulation developers may wish to consider.

Developers also need to consider the means by which media are delivered to users. The studies reviewed above distributed simulation training programs to users via a diskette and desktop computer. Obviously, this choice reflected the technology of the time (e.g., studies done in the late 1980s and early 1990s did not have the Internet and World Wide Web as an option for media delivery). Today, however, developers may choose from a number of delivery options: diskette, CD-ROM, Internet, interactive videodiscs, and, in the very near future, DVD. While a discussion of the merits of each delivery option is beyond the scope of this chapter, developers should carefully consider the implications of their decisions. For example, computer simulations that incorporate digitized video and utilize the Internet may work well with high-speed connections but perform poorly at lower data transfer rates. If the simulations will be used exclusively in a university computer lab, the issue will not be especially important. If the simulations are designed to be accessed remotely via modem, data transfer rates will be a greater concern.

Methodological Issues and Future Directions

Although the current literature base suggests computerized simulations and instructional courses are effective in training behavioral assessment skills, the data remain sparse with many questions left unanswered. Because of technological limitations, many of the computer simulations did not utilize video clips and relied on written vignettes to describe client behavior.

Issues surrounding the content validity of psychological instruments are also applicable to computer simulation stimulus materials (see Haynes, Richard, & Kubany, 1995). The degree to which a student develops assessment skills through computer simulation training depends in large part on the simulation stimuli parameters (e.g., content, nature of the display, etc.). For example, if the goal of the computer simulation is to train behavioral assessors to discriminate efficient from inefficient assessment strategies, creating a computer simulation that requires the individual to select from a variety of assessment options is essential. However, if the goal of the computer simulation is to train clinical case formulation skills, it may only be necessary for the student to review and interpret simulated client data rather than requiring the student to design an assessment plan. None of the studies reviewed above provided a theoretical rationale for the selected case studies.

The content validity issue is especially important since computer simulations do not exist in an educational vacuum. The relevance of a computer training simulation will depend on the experience of the user. An advanced graduate student may not derive as much benefit from simulations training rudimentary assessment skills as a novice first-year student. Content of training simulations should be tailored to anticipate user experience. Increasingly complex simulations should be developed for individuals with greater clinical experience.

While computer simulations provide unique opportunities for assessing student decision-making skills, useful psychometric principles have largely been ignored in the evaluations of these programs. For example, no study to date has examined the degree to which simulation performance is associated with performance in actual clinical cases (i.e., criterion-related predictive validity). In the few cases where the convergent validity of simulation results has been examined, the results are not always encouraging. For example, Janikowski, Berven, Meixelsperger, & Roedl (1989) found a correlation of .16 between performance in a simulation and grade point average in previous coursework among graduates of a master's degree program in rehabilitation counseling. In addition, researchers generally have not reported the reliability of the measures used to assess student learning, statistics summarizing proportion of correct and incorrect responses during the simulation, and other important results.

Although many studies have assessed student reactions to the simulation experience, positive student reactions do not imply knowledge acquisition or improved performance in clinical assessment contexts. No studies have shown that skills learned in a computer simulation transfer to a student's assessment and treatment of real clients. Researchers should explicitly identify a priori those skills that should change as

TABLE 13.2   Selected Multimedia Authoring Environments and Resources for Simulation Training in Behavioral Assessment

Product	Vendor	Description	Cost
Astound Presentation	Astound (astound.com)	Slide presentation management system, similar in functionality to MS PowerPoint, that can be adapted to suit simulations.	$395.00
CABLES (Computer-Assisted Branching Learning and Examination System)	Reed Hardy, Psychology Dept., St. Norbert College, DePere, WI 54115 (e-mail: *hardrr@ sncac.snc.edu*)	Software teaches basic principles in behavior assessment and analysis through a series of six major online modules. Emphasis is on multimedia presentation of text-based material rather than digitized video simulations. See Desrochers (1996) for review.	Download from *http:// www.snc.edu/psych/rhar.htm* ($20.00 shareware donation for individual users)
Functional Assessment and Intervention Program	Sopris West (sopriswest.com)	Training program to develop in teachers and counselors functional assessment and intervention strategies. Software analyzes acquired skills and provides feedback on assessment and intervention strategies.	$69.00
Functional Behavioral Assessment (2nd Edition)	Sopris West (sopriswest.com)	CD-ROM package training functional behavioral assessment skills. Modules include collecting historical and background data, identifying the target behavior, conducting direct observations, generating and verifying hypotheses, and determining the function of the behavior. Slide show format with case studies and self-tests. Originally developed by Liaupsin, Scott, and Nelson (2000).	$79.00
Hypercard	Apple Computers (apple.com)	Multimedia authoring tool geared toward courseware and computer-based training. Integrates text, video, graphics, sound. No scripting or programming knowledge required.	$99.00
Hyperstudio 4.0	Hyperstudio (hyperstudio.com)	Easy-to-use multimedia creation tool with a long history of utilization in education. Product allows rapid development of multimedia programs and environments and can easily be adapted to simulation training.	$199.00
Macromedia Authorware 6.0	Macromedia (macromedia.com)	Development environment for creation of interactive applications. Can incorporate video, animation, etc. Scripting language available for more sophisticated programming. Can export to multiple operating systems.	$489.95
Macromedia Director 8.5 Shockwave Studio	Macromedia (macromedia.com)	Web-based interactive authoring tool with enormous capabilities. Powerful enough to create web-based simulations.	$1,149.95
Mediator 6.0	Matchware (*matchware.net*)	Multimedia authoring program capable of producing multimedia programs for both stand-alone computers and the Internet.	Mediator 6.0 is bundled for free with ATI Radeon graphics card. Mediator 6.0 Pro costs $399.00. Mediator EXP (programmable version) is $899.00
Metacard	Metacard Corporation (metacard.com)	Similar to Hypercard but for UNIX and MS Windows systems. Uses a "card stacking" metaphor for multimedia creation. Downloadable trial version available for free online.	$995.00
Microsoft PowerPoint	Microsoft (microsoft.com)	Part of Microsoft Office. Program can import video and provides some capabilities adaptive testing. Limited data storage options.	Microsoft Office Standard is $479.00
Microsoft Visual Basic 6.0	Microsoft (microsoft.com)	Not an authoring tool per se, but a programming environment. Visual Basic is a relatively easy language to learn and can create powerful multimedia programs with add-in and third-party products.	$549.00; competitive upgrade is $279.00
Quest	Allencom.com	Runs on 32-bit Windows operating systems (Win 95 and higher). Supports animations, video, and audio.	$2,495.00
QuestionMark	QuestionMark (questionmark.com)	Software designed to conduct computer-based, intranet, or Internet quizzes and tests.	Not available
QuickTime VR Authoring Studio	Apple Computer (apple.com)	Creation of QuickTime movies. Turns photos into virtual reality scenes, can use clickable hot spots in video for programmatic purposes.	$379.95

the result of a computer simulation training program and then select or design measures sensitive to changes in those skills. The targeted assessment skills should be assessed prior to, during, and after simulation training. For example, the rate of student learning, and the *types* of errors students make during simulation training, should be tracked and classified. Researchers should employ a multimethod assessment approach to examine the effectiveness of the simulation in developing targeted skills (e.g., outcome measures could include a knowledge-based test, faculty ratings, current and subsequent supervisor ratings, self-ratings of competencies, subsequent client reactions, etc.).

COMPUTERIZED BEHAVIORAL ASSESSMENT METHODS

A behavioral assessment method is a way of collecting client data through some form of systematic observation. Multiple observations are usually employed so that variability on behavior as a function of changing environmental contingencies may be assessed. Researchers have developed computer programs to facilitate virtually all forms of behavioral assessment. In this section, we will primarily focus on recently developed software programs that facilitate behavioral observation, self-monitoring, and interview methods.

Behavioral Observation

A mainstay of behavioral assessment is direct behavioral observation, either in the natural environment or in an analogue setting. In both cases, the behavioral assessor observes behavior and then utilizes a coding system to quantify his or her observations. Given the large amounts of data that may be collected during a behavioral observation session, and the complexity of analyzing large data sets, it is not surprising that some of the first computer applications in behavioral assessment were designed to facilitate behavioral observations.

Recent descriptive reviews of behavioral observation software have been published by several research teams (e.g., Emerson, Reeves, & Felce, 2000; Kahng and Iwata, 1998, 2000; Sandman, Touchette, Ly, Marion, & Bruinsma, 2000; Tapp & Wehby, 2000). The evolution of behavioral observation software programs has been marked by increasing user-friendliness, more sophisticated data analytic routines, and a migration to handheld computer platforms. Many behavior observation software programs allow simultaneous recording of multiple variables across several behavioral dimensions (e.g., frequency, magnitude, duration, etc.). In addition, many programs include analytic routines that can

calculate central tendencies, statistical significance (e.g., z-score transformations, kappa, and other statistics). Most programs include routines for graphing data, although the sophistication of the graphs varies from program to program. Many programs include an option to export data to a spreadsheet (e.g., Microsoft Excel) for further analysis. While some of the programs are free (e.g., EthoLog 2.2; Ottoni, 2000), prices for most programs range from $50 to $1,700. Kahng and Iwata (2000) provide a very helpful table describing the various programs and sales contact information.

Behavioral observation software has been used to help researchers gain a better understanding of patients' daily behavior. For example, Bowie and Mountain (1993) programmed handheld computers to assist in coding behavior of long-term residential patients diagnosed with dementia. Patients were observed for 300 seconds every hour. A total of 114 hours of data were recorded. They found that patients spent 56.5% of their waking time detached from the environment, engaged in solitary and nonproductive behaviors. VanHaitsma and colleagues (1997) reported a similar study using *The Observer* software system and a handheld computer. They studied the behavior of 157 nursing home residents with dementia and coded the individuals' behavior, physical location, bodily position, and the social environment. They found that residents were found standing or walking only 10% of the time (90% of the time they were sitting or lying down). In addition, passive behaviors (sleeping, null behavior) were observed 24% of the time while patients spent the vast majority of their time, 83%, alone. The overall picture painted by these two studies regarding the behavior of demented patients is one of disengagement and behavioral poverty.

Although behavioral observation software has been designed to code behavior as it occurs in the natural environment, observational software has been used to address fundamental research questions. For example, Tapp and Wehby (2000) described *PROCODER,* an observational software system designed for DOS-compatible computers that interfaces with a tape controller deck to record electronic codes on videotapes. By writing electronic codes directly to the tape, researchers can precisely identify (to 1/30th of a second) occurrences of behavior. This is especially useful when studying contingent interpersonal behaviors. For example, the researchers reported a series of studies in which they used the *PROCODER* system to examine whether parents of developmentally delayed children were as responsive to their children's initiatives to interact as parents of children without delays. The *PROCODER* system was used to electronically code both target child and parent behaviors. Results showed that parents of children with developmental delays were less contingently responsive to their children than the parents of children without delays.

The lack of responsiveness may have been due, in part, to a detection problem—the social signals for interaction emitted by developmentally disabled children were much more difficult to detect by parents than those emitted by other children.

A glimpse of the future of behavioral observation software may be seen in the work of Noldus, Spink, and Tegelenbosch (2001). In a fascinating report, these researchers described EthoVision, an automated and computerized observational tracking system. The EthoVision system utilizes a video camera to record animal movements, usually rats and fish, in a predefined space. The video images are then sent to a desktop computer where the computer extracts from one video frame the location of an animal and then tracks the image across video frames. When the entire series of frames is analyzed, the speed of the animal's movements can be calculated because the rate of video frames is constant.

In addition to the several software packages that focus on facilitating behavioral observation recordings, training software that teaches users how to observe behavior also has been developed. Dickins et al. (2000) described the development of *OBSERVE,* a multimedia course for teaching undergraduate and graduate students how to observe behavior in naturalistic and analogue settings. The modules in their CD-delivered training program cover a wide range of topics: identification of behaviors and behavioral categories, hypothesis construction and testing, sampling methods, inter- and intraobserver agreement, data handling, sequential analysis, and temporal patterns. Blasko, Kazmerski, Corty, and Kallgren (1998) also developed an interactive multimedia software program designed to teach observational research methods. Their *Courseware for Observational Research* includes five in-class lessons used in conjunction with videos, coding sheets, and a projection system. Laboratory assignments also can be completed independently by students. The topics covered by the courseware include planning an observation, recording and sampling methods, interrater reliability, and data analysis. While integrating multimedia technology into the training of behavioral assessors has face validity, the effectiveness of these training methods will likely depend on the user-friendliness of the software and the degree to which the exercises adequately demonstrate important observation concepts and principles. To date, no independent evaluations of these training systems have been conducted.

Although behavioral observation software offers tremendous data collection and analysis potential, we agree with conclusions made by Symons and MacLean, Jr. (2000). Specifically, practical considerations involving staff training, program modifications, and the complexities of data analysis may inhibit the use of observational software. Even with computerization, coding schemes are often complex and dif-

ficult to learn. Overly complex coding schemes inevitably negatively affect recording accuracy—as do a host of other factors that are extrinsic to computerization (e.g., observer bias, observer drift, etc.). Reliability and data checks can be time consuming for the busy professional. Thus, although observational software programs have steadily improved with each revision, many practical issues will constrain their use in applied settings.

Simulation-Based Behavioral Assessment of Client Functioning

Earlier, the use of computer simulations in behavioral assessment training was described. Simulations also have been used to assess and modify client behavior. For example, individuals with significant physical disabilities often require electric, motorized wheelchairs. Learning the manual dexterity skills to manipulate the wheelchair's joystick directional controller is difficult, costly, and potentially unsafe. Hasdai, Jessel, and Weiss (1998) developed a simulation program to help children with progressive muscular dystrophy or cerebral palsy learn how to use the wheelchairs. The program presented computerized mazes corresponding to four possible paths at their school. The mazes differed in their level of complexity (e.g., movement within a simple room to stop and start points in several different rooms). Using an analogue wheelchair joystick that was connected to the computer, the program assessed skill development by recording the number of virtual collisions and time to complete each maze. Participants then completed a training program for 30 to 45 minutes twice per day for 12 weeks. Performance of novice wheelchair users using the simulation improved significantly by the posttest in the twelfth week, although performance remained slightly below that of experienced wheelchair users.

Computer driving simulations also permit the assessment of behaviors that would simply be too dangerous to assess otherwise. For example, Horswill and McKenna (1999) examined drivers' propensities to take risks (e.g., close following distance) when distracted. Participants performed a driving simulation under two conditions: engagement versus nonengagement in a concurrent verbal task. For all risk-taking indices, persons performed significantly worse when distracted and were likely to take greater driving risks during the simulation.

Simulation assessment of more clinically related behavioral phenomena also has been done. For example, Ritchie (1999) used a computer simulation to study maternal reactions to individual instances of child misbehavior and power bouts (i.e., several consecutive instances of child misbehavior). She hypothesized that continued child noncompliance would lead to assertive and progressively more authoritarian responses in mothers, especially if children continued to be noncompliant despite maternal feedback. Participants were mothers of 3-year-old children. The participants completed a computer simulation in which they were presented 28 digitized video segments concerning the same child. Each video segment presented the child engaging in a behavior and a series of response options available to the mother. Ten possible maternal responses were available for the mother to choose from and varied in their degree of assertiveness and authoritarianism. Some scenes involved a single instance of noncompliant behavior by the child while other scenes involved continued noncompliant behavior (six instances) regardless of the parenting strategy chosen by the mother. Participants also were queried regarding their confidence to control the child, the likelihood that the child was testing authority, how likely the child's behavior was due to a "negative personality," the participant's irritation with the child, and estimated firmness of maternal response (see Ritchie, 1999, p. 583). Results indicated that maternal reactions to the video segments portraying a power bout were qualitatively different than reactions to individual episodes of noncompliance: participants reported more negative cognitions about the child during a power bout. Simulation results also showed mothers were more likely to use greater authoritative and assertive responses when managing a power bout than when reacting to an individual instance of misbehavior. Specifically, mothers dealing with a power bout proceeded through a chain of response strategies characterized initially by negotiation, then passive commands, and finally aversive consequences.

Although video and audio clips can enhance simulation assessments, interesting simulations have been developed using text-based simulations. For example, Anbar and Raulin (1994) developed a simulation to assess medical students' social skills. Using CASIP, an authoring tool to create simulation exercises in which participants provide a natural language response to a simulated case (rather than choosing from predetermined response options), the researchers performed a content analysis of medical students' responses to five simulated patient interactions. The five simulation scenarios involved simulated patients who behaved in ways characterized by: (1) an oscillation between militancy and compliance, (2) confrontation, (3) suspicion and aggression, (4) authoritative bullying, and (5) irrationality. Medical student responses were coded for levels of social skill, frustration, submissiveness, combativeness, and negotiation skill. The results suggested that, while the context of the simulated behavior exerted a significant influence on the qualities of the students' responses, it was possible to identify medical students with problematic social skills across the five scenarios.

In our opinion, simulation-based assessment of client functioning has been underutilized as a means of measuring meaningful behavioral change. Simulation-based assessments are relatively easy to develop (especially if they do not include video or audio), may be delivered across several delivery platforms (e.g., desktop computer, Internet, CD-ROM, handheld computer, etc.) and may provide data on treatment progress that possess more ecological validity than traditional self-report data derived from questionnaires. However, simulation-based assessments have largely been confined to the industrial-organizational, gaming, aviation, and military psychology literatures. Behavioral assessors have not invested significant energy in this area despite the fact that simulation-based assessment strategies are consistent with principles of analogue behavioral assessment.

Self-Monitoring

Self-monitoring is a behavioral assessment method that involves "systematically observing and recording one's own behavior and internal and environmental events thought to be functionally related to that behavior" (Cone, 1999, p. 411). In most self-monitoring procedures, the client and therapist design a schedule for recording self-observations. The schedule may involve recording behavior once per day to several times per day depending on the dimensions of the behavior (e.g., frequency, intensity, etc.), the time required to complete the self-observation form, whether the recording is contingent on behavioral instances or occurs after a fixed time interval, and so forth. A recent special section in the journal *Psychological Assessment* (1995) was devoted to self-monitoring issues.

For many years, a common self-monitoring research practice was to use paper-and-pencil journals or diaries for data entry. While self-monitoring diaries are convenient, some important issues surround their use. The first issue involves confidentiality and social desirability. If a diary is lost, its entire contents are available for others to read. Relatedly, diaries are conspicuous and may make clients uncomfortable, especially if the recording must occur in a public venue. Thus, for some clients, noncompliance in completing scheduled recording sessions may reflect an interaction between the method and the setting in which the recordings are completed. As a result, observations may be recorded elsewhere, or at a later time, calling into question the accuracy of the recordings.

A second issue involves the logistics of data aggregation and analysis. Self-monitoring programs can generate enormous amounts of data. For example, a client instructed to make three recordings per day for a week will complete 21 recording sessions in seven days. Assuming full compliance

TABLE 13.3 Handheld Computer Software Programming Tools and Development Environments

Product	Vendor	Functionality	Cost
AppForge	Appforge (appforge.com)	Runs within Visual Basic development environment. Supports all major operating systems.	$699.00 (Palm OS version) to $899.00 (PocketPC version)
CASL (Computer Application Solution Language)	Feras Information Technologies (caslsoft.com)	For Palm and Windows CE programming environment. Similar to Visual Basic and Java Script.	$84.95 to $200.00 (professional version)
CE Toolkit for Visual Basic 6.0	Microsoft (microsoft.com)	Add-in toolkit to Visual Basic 6.0 using ActiveX controls that allows Windows CE program development.	$199.95
CEfusion Professional	Odyssey Software (odysseysoftware.com)	Strong data management tool allowing wireless interactivity and access to large data sets.	$399.95
Codewarrior 8 for Palm OS Platform	Metroworks (metroworks.com)	Integrated editor, project manager, compiler, linker, and target device interface. Good for C/C++ users.	Regularly $499.00; $119.00 for academic version
General Electronic Psychotherapy Diary	Michael Hinkel and O. Bernard Scholz, Dept. of Psychology, University of Bonn, Germany	Software program developed for handheld computers in GNU C++. Program holds a large number of diary questionnaires and stores responses to a database. Response options can include rating scale, bipolar rating scale, dichotomous responses, frequency, and free text.	See Hinkel & Scholz (2001) for more information regarding the program. No pricing available.
HanDBase	DDH Software (handbase.com)	Development environment for survey forms and database management. Compatible with MS Office and other database report utilities.	Not available
MobileBuilder 2.0	PenRight (penright.com)	Development environment for Windows CE, Palm OS, Windows NT, and other operating systems.	$1,595.00
MobileDB	Handmark (handmark.com)	Views and edits spreadsheet information on Palm OS. Can create database forms for data entry and export to Excel or Filemaker.	$29.95
MONITOR	Jochen Fahrenberg, Dept. of Psychology, University of Freiburg, Germany	Software program specifically written to facilitate handheld computer research and ambulatory assessment. User can input rating scales, text, instructions, etc. Allows control of handheld computer beeper, sleep mode, facilitates event/time/contingency sampling. Files can be written to Excel, SPSS formats.	No information regarding price of software currently available. Please see Fahrenberg, Hüttner, & Leonhart (2001) for program details.
NS Basic/Palm and NS Basic/CE	NS Basic Corporation (nsbasic.com)	Development environment for Palm OS and Windows CE in Basic. NS Basic/CE is good for users familiar with VB Script.	$149.95

with the self-monitoring schedule and simultaneous monitoring of one behavior (e.g., smoking) and two variables thought to be functionally related to the behavior (e.g., a mood rating, level of perceived stress), a total of 63 data points must be plotted each week. Thus, data analysis obstacles may make it less likely that some clinicians will, or can, make full use of self-monitoring as an assessment methodology in the absence of technological innovations.

Recently, the self-monitoring literature has seen a surge of interest in mobile computing using a handheld computer to collect self-monitoring data. A *handheld computer* is a small, relatively inconspicuous device usually operated by pressing a stylus onto a small touch-sensitive computer screen. As the name suggests,[2] the devices can be held in one hand and are easily stored in a shirt pocket, purse, or briefcase when not being used. Handheld computer programs can be developed

using a desktop computer and any of a variety of software programs currently on the market (see Table 13.3).

The advent of mobile computing has reinvigorated self-monitoring research efforts for several reasons. First, all of the issues raised above are moderated to some degree using handheld computers. The devices have gained wide acceptance in society as organizational planners and as a means of scheduling daily activities. A person completing a self-monitoring log using a handheld device is indistinguishable from a person using the device for another purpose. If a handheld computer is ever lost, data may be protected using password entry codes. In addition, the handheld device can signal the client by beeping when a recording session should occur. If a recording session is missed, the handheld computer can automatically log the missed session. Some researchers have tracked recording sessions outside of the participants' awareness to measure compliance with recording tasks. For example, Newman, Consoli, and Taylor (1999) found with three individuals diagnosed with generalized anxiety disorder that participant compliance with four daily self-monitoring prompts decreased from a high of 75% during the first seven weeks to a low of 31% by the twelfth week. However, compliance to prompts occurring at the end of the day was much higher (92% during the first seven weeks with a low of 52% by the end of the study). In addition, handheld computers make it possible to collect and analyze large amounts of data. Data can be downloaded from a handheld device to a desktop computer and then plotted in a graph with ease. Because the data are already in tabular form, they can be exported to a statistical program or database for further analysis or archiving.

Behavioral researchers have been quick to recognize the potential research benefits that accrue by using handheld computers. Stone and Shiffman (1994) coined the term *ecological momentary assessment* (EMA) to describe assessment strategies that involved the measurement of participant behavior in their natural environment. While the term originally was associated with the use of ambulatory monitoring devices that measured physiological events (e.g., heart rate, galvanic skin response, blood pressure; see Van Egeren & Madarasmi, 1988; Kamarck et al., 1998, for examples), EMA increasingly has been associated with the use of handheld computers to measure momentary states of behavior in a person's natural environment. Since 1990, researchers have used handheld computers to assess a wide variety of behavior problems and environmental variables hypothesized by researchers to covary with target behavior problems. Table 13.4 is a compendium of handheld computer EMA studies indexed by the type of behavioral problem studied.

For example, researchers have used handheld computers to understand the relationship between binge eating and mood. Greeno, Wing, and Shiffman (2000) asked 41 women with a binge eating disorder and 38 women without the disorder to monitor their eating behavior for a period of one week using a Psion LZ32 handheld computer. Participants were instructed to complete assessments prior to every eating event and again at random intervals signaled by the computer. Dependent measures included eating and mood assessments. Results from this study indicated that women diagnosed with a binge eating disorder evidenced worse mood, were less alert, experienced higher levels of tension, perceived less control over their eating, craved more sweets than did the control group, reported significantly more negative affect than the control group, and averaged nine binges per week.

Several researchers have used handheld computers to assess clients with an anxiety disorder. For example, Herman and Koran (1998) used handheld computers to collect self-report data from 13 participants diagnosed with obsessive-compulsive disorder for 3 days. A computerized version of the Yale-Brown Obsessive Compulsive Scale (Y-BOCS) was administered via a Casio PB-1000 palmtop computer every hour on the hour between 9 A.M. and 9 P.M. If the participant did not complete the scheduled assessment session, the computer would provide a reminder beep after five minutes. In addition to the questionnaire, participants were asked where they were in the past hour (e.g., home, car, work, store, etc.), who was around them during that time (e.g., friends, family, etc.), and their level of stress since the last recording session. The handheld version of the Y-BOCS correlated only moderately with prior clinician ratings in the assessment of obsessive ($r = .46$) and compulsive ($r = .38$) symptoms. In fact, mean clinician ratings of symptom severity on the Y-BOCS were almost one standard deviation higher than mean client ratings on the handheld version of the same instrument. Contrary to self-reports, the researchers also found that patients did not experience less severe or fewer OCD symptoms in the company of others, their symptoms did not correlate with environmental stressors, and there was no relationship between symptom severity and time of day.

Some researchers have explored using handheld computers for both assessment and treatment purposes. Newman, Consoli, and Taylor (1999) designed a six-session treatment program for generalized anxiety disorder (GAD) that included modules incorporating various cognitive-behavior principles. The computer initially conducted a baseline self-monitoring assessment of GAD symptoms using a diary metaphor. During this phase the client was beeped five times per day to complete the momentary assessment questionnaire. Participants continued to complete the momentary assessment questions and completed the online therapy modules. The three modules included relaxation training, cognitive therapy, and imaginal exposure. The results showed that self-reported levels of daily anxiety for three participants who completed the computerized assessment and treatment modules decreased over the course of treatment. While participants responded favorably to the assessments and intervention, compliance with scheduled recording sessions decreased significantly from the beginning of treatment to the end. Earlier studies examining the feasibility of handheld computer-administered treatment programs also have shown some success in the treatment of panic (see Newman, Kenardy, Herman, & Taylor, 1996, 1997).

Ecological Validity and Implications of EMA Studies

Assessment methods and instruments that are not accurate, or possess poor ecological validity, are not likely to be sen-

TABLE 13.4 Ecological Momentary Assessment (EMA) Studies Utilizing Handheld Computers

Behavioral Problem or Disorder	Reference(s) in Chronological Order	Variables Assessed Across Studies
Alcoholism and Drinking Moderation	Collins et al. (1998); Litt, Cooney, & Morse (1998)	Alcohol consumption; drinking restraint; mood when drinking; drinking urges; situation when drinking urge occurred.
Binge Eating	Greeno, Wing, & Shiffman (2000); Le Grange, Gorin, Catley, & Stone (2001)	Binge episode; quality of affect; location during binge; whether alone or accompanied during binge; stress prior to binge; desire to binge; appetite; alertness; perceived eating control; sweets craving.
Borderline Personality Disorder	Stiglmayr, Grathwol, & Bohus (2001)	Self-reported tension levels; increases in rate of tension; sleep cycles.
Chronic Pain and Headache	Sorbi, Honkoop, & Godaert (1996); Stone, Broderick, Porter, & Kaell (1997); Affleck et al. (1998); Catley (2000); Holden et al. (2000); Godaert et al. (2001); Godaert, Sorbi, Peters, Dekkers, & Geenen (2001); Jamison et al. (2001)	Pain intensity for chronic pain disorder, migraines, and rheumatoid arthritis; hourly pain scores; minor stressful events; positive and negative affect; mood; pain aversiveness, pain anxiety; sleep; fatigue; daily hassles; irritability; depression.
Coping Skills	Stone et al. (1998); Perrez, Berger, & Wilhelm (1998); Perrez, Wilhelm, Schoebi, & Horner (2001)	Estimates of coping in the moment; cognitive and behavioral coping; strategies for coping with stress in the family; emotional and somatic state; causal attributions; control expectations; place; setting; conflicts with others; individual stress levels; partner's affective state.
Dieting	Carels et al. (2001)	Dietary temptation and lapse; location; mood state; type of activity; abstinence violation.
Generalized Anxiety Disorder	Newman, Consoli, & Taylor (1999)[a]	Daily and hourly anxiety level; worrisome thinking; catastrophic imagery; behavioral avoidance; muscle tension.
High Blood Pressure	Fahrenberg, Franck, Baas, & Jost (1995)	Estimation of blood pressure; setting variables; self-ratings of subjective state.
Mood States	Fahrenberg et al. (1999); Hank, Schwenkmezger, & Schumann (2001); Kaeppler & Rieder (2001); Wilhelm (2001)	Emotional state; local setting; social contacts; current activity; cognitive performance; diurnal changes in mood and attention; working memory; mood; arousal; comparison of immediate and retrospective reports.
Obsessive-Compulsive Disorder (OCD)	Herman & Koran (1998)	OCD symptom intensity; environmental factors and events; presence of friends or family.
Panic Disorder	Taylor, Fried, & Kenardy (1990); Kenardy, Fried, Kraemer, & Taylor (1992); Newman, Kenardy, Herman, & Taylor (1997)[a]	Panic attacks; anxiety level; sense of control; sense of threat or danger; likelihood of having a panic attack in the next 24 hours; environmental contexts; somatic symptoms.
Smoking and Smoking Cessation	O'Connell et al. (1998); Catley, O'Connell, & Shiffman (2000); O'Connell et al. (2000)	Absentminded lapses during smoking cessation; smoking urges; playfulness; rebelliousness; arousal seeking; coping responses and strategies; location when having smoking urge.

[a]Included a computer-assisted cognitive-behavioral treatment intervention for panic disorder as well as assessment modules.
Note. Review articles and studies using portable ambulatory assessment devices or using nonclinical samples (e.g., personnel decision making, use of handheld computers with workers, etc.) were excluded from this table.

sitive measures of behavior change. As results from EMA studies are published, researchers are increasingly noting the lack of agreement between data from self-report instruments completed retrospectively, clinician rating scales, and data collected using handheld devices. Since many clinicians assume that questionnaires completed retrospectively by clients and interviews/ratings scales administered or completed by clinicians are reasonably accurate measures of a client's behavior in his or her natural environment, these findings have considerable implications. For example, in a study of the relationship between smoking and mood in 158 adolescents, Whalen, Jamner, Henker, and Delfino (2001) reported low to

moderate correlations between surveys administered prior to self-monitoring and data collected over a 4-day period using handheld computers. Specifically, survey data of smoking urges correlated .60 with actual smoking urges, number of cigarettes smoked in the past 30 days correlated .63 with number of cigarettes smoked during the experiment, self-reported levels of stress correlated .44 with self-reports made using the handheld computer, and premonitoring scores on a depression instrument correlated .47 with momentary ratings of sadness. In another study, Schwartz, Neale, Marco, Shiffman, & Stone (1999) found that data from self-report questionnaires of trait-based coping accounted for only 15 to 30% of the variance in momentary reports of how people *actually* cope with stressors in the environment. Findings such as these suggest that data collected using EMA procedures may provide a very different, and perhaps more accurate, picture of client functioning than questionnaires, rating scales, and clinical interviews.

While EMA may help researchers indirectly observe proximal antecedents, researchers should be aware of issues that apply to all self-monitoring studies. For example, the willingness of a client to complete self-monitoring protocols will have a large bearing on the accuracy of the obtained data. Some individuals may not complete EMA assessments either because they are unable (e.g., a severely developmentally disabled client) or because they are unwilling (e.g., an eating disordered client who is reluctant to disclose eating behaviors) to do so. With regard to eating disordered patients, Smyth and colleagues (2001) concluded that EMA is a viable assessment method and that most eating disordered patients are willing to engage in EMA studies. However, their conclusion is most likely conditional and may not accurately predict compliance in eating disordered patients who are resistant to treatment efforts. Further, patients with seriously debilitating mental disorders (e.g., schizophrenia) and patients who, for whatever reason, wish to conceal their behavior (e.g., substance users, batterers, bulimic patients) are not likely to be good self-monitoring candidates.

Behavioral Questionnaires, Interviews, and Rating Scales

Researchers also have examined using computers to administer questionnaires and behaviorally oriented interviews to clients. Many times, the computer adaptations are identical in item content with the parent instruments from which they were derived. Computerized questionnaires and interviews frequently include data storage and reporting routines that are extremely useful for tracking clients over time or producing interpretive reports. In addition, computerized data collection has significant research implications at several levels (e.g., data collection efficiency, standardization, elimination of participant response omissions, speed to data analysis activities, etc.).

For example, Richard (1999) developed the Computerized PTSD Scale (CPS), a computerized adaptation of the Clinician-Administered PTSD Scale structured interview (CAPS-Dx; Blake et al., 1997). The software assessed Criterion A of the PTSD diagnostic criteria as well as the 17 PTSD symptoms and symptoms commonly associated with PTSD. In a sample of 143 treatment-seeking Vietnam veterans, the CPS correlated .87 with the Mississippi Scale for Combat-Related PTSD and .74 with both the Beck Depression Inventory and the Beck Anxiety Inventory. In a subsample of 26 veterans interviewed with the CAPS-Dx, the correlation between the CPS and the CAPS-Dx total severity scores (i.e., an index of overall symptom severity) correlated .91.

In a series of studies, Farrell and colleagues (Farrell 1999a; Farrell 1999b; Farrell, Camplair, & McCullough, 1987) have shown how computerized behavioral questionnaires and interviews can become a routine part of outpatient treatment assessment and planning. The *Computerized Assessment System for Psychotherapy Evaluation and Research* (CASPER) is a software program designed to identify client problems, classify problem severity, generate problem lists, assess client change on identified target problems across sessions, identify areas requiring additional assessment, and assist with treatment planning. The latest version of the interview includes 121 items covering a wide array of cognitive and behavioral domains. Farrell and his colleagues' work is especially exciting because it demonstrates how computerized behavioral assessment can be successfully integrated into ongoing outpatient clinical activities.

In many ways, computerized behavioral questionnaires, interviews, and rating scales serve the same function as their noncomputerized counterparts. Several advantages accrue from computerization, however. First, assessment is more likely to become an ongoing facet of clinical activities when the logistics of administration are automated. And in addition to facilitating the collection of data, computerization permits rapid data aggregation and analysis within and between clients—a significant advantage when evaluating outcomes across therapists, treatment modalities, and clinical treatment delivery systems.

The Internet

Although reports of Internet-based research have been published for the past several years, researchers are only now examining the utility of the Internet with behavioral assessment. Most of the early studies involved either online psychological experiments (e.g., Krantz, Ballard, & Scher, 1997; Welch & Krantz, 1996) or validation of personality inventories that were easily adapted to web page formats (e.g., Buchanan & Smith, 1999a, 1999b; Davis, 1999). Since then, researchers have published a myriad of reports describing the seemingly endless number of ways the Internet can be used for the purposes of psychological assessment and treatment.

Despite the speed with which many clinicians have jumped on the Internet bandwagon, behavioral assessors and therapists have not published many reports that take advantage of the Internet. One reason for this is that behavioral assessment often requires observational data, collected usually by the assessor or the client. While the Internet is useful for collecting large amounts of self-report data quickly and efficiently, it does not offer the same advantages for observational methods. In the case of self-monitoring, handheld computers offer greater programming flexibility and allow self-ratings that are proximal to a target behavior. As a result, Internet-based research frequently focuses on symptom identification and topographic dimensions of behavior while ecological momentary assessment research is useful for identifying environmental covariates and functional relations. For example, using online surveys, Anderson and Ley (2001) were able to estimate the frequency of dyspnea in a sample of 205 patients with panic disorder. Similarly, Cloud and Peacock (2001) used an online survey to screen 2,813 Internet users for alcohol abuse and dependence. Neither study, however, addressed functional relations. In sum, researchers have used the Internet to conduct online experiments and administer surveys. However, the inherent restrictions of the Internet with regard to the collection of observational data has limited its utility for the purposes of behavioral assessment.

THE FUNCTIONAL ANALYSIS AND CLINICAL CASE FORMULATION

Ultimately, data collected during a behavioral assessment must be aggregated, analyzed, and used to support or disconfirm initial hypotheses of client functioning. A functional analysis[3] or clinical case formulation is a working model of the behavior therapist's hypotheses regarding functional relations operating in a client's life. The clinical case formulation is dynamic in that it is expected to change as (a) more assessment data are collected, (b) the client's behavior changes during treatment, and (c) the therapist learns more about factors that mediate a client's behavior. Clinical case formulations are important because they imply both the function of behavior and the direction of treatment. For example, aggressive behavior in a child who is developmentally disabled that has the function of gaining parental and teacher attention may be successfully treated by differentially reinforcing alternative, and more adaptive, behaviors. Alternatively, if the function of the aggressive behavior is to escape a situation in which the child has a behavioral deficit (e.g., grooming) then shaping or chaining procedures to improve the child's behavioral repertoire may be more appropriate.

According to Haynes, Leisen, and Blaine (1997), the importance of an explicit functional analysis has been demonstrated most convincingly in the treatment of self-injurious

behavior. However, for most behavioral problems the treatment utility, or the "degree to which assessment is shown to contribute to *beneficial treatment outcome*" (Hayes, Nelson, & Jarrett, 1987, p. 963, emphasis added) of the functional analysis has been studied infrequently.[4] Indeed, estimating the treatment utility of an assessment method is a complex task involving the operationalization of the term "beneficial treatment outcome" as well as a myriad of mediating and moderating variables (e.g., the power of the treatment, the efficiency with which the treatment is delivered, the sensitivity of measurement instruments in detecting meaningful behavioral change, and so forth). The issue has been complicated by suggestions that treatment utility may be estimated by observing the effect adding an assessment instrument has on treatment outcome. For example, Kratochwill and McGivern (1996) suggested that the treatment utility of the Child Behavior Checklist (CBCL) could be shown if treatment outcomes for children are improved when the CBCL is added to a standardized parent interview. An objection to this approach is that treatment utility is confounded with a narrow definition of treatment outcome. In many cases, an assessment method may have treatment utility even if a patient's behavior does not improve as a result of the assessment (i.e., treatment outcome is unchanged). For example, a positron emission tomography scan of a patient with dementia showing cortical shrinkage should not be expected to result in observable patient behavior change or clinical improvement. However, the results of the assessment may be useful in other important ways (e.g., planning the patient's treatment, helping staff and family understand the etiology of the client's behavior problems). It is probably the case that treatment utility is a multifaceted construct that refers to how an assessment method, assessment instrument, and case formulation work independently and together to influence treatment planning and treatment outcome.

While researchers continue to debate the degree to which an accurate functional analysis possesses treatment utility, Weigle and Scotti (2000) recently demonstrated that explicitly identifying functional relations influences ratings of *treatment acceptability*—or the degree to which a treatment is perceived to be credible or possess social validity.[5] In their study, 55 educators who worked with students with developmental disabilities were given a series of case vignettes describing a child's self-injurious behavior. The vignettes varied in the degree to which information was provided about the attention or escape functions of the child's behavior. When the educators read vignettes that included information identifying the function of behavior, they were more likely to endorse the treatment acceptability of interventions employing differential reinforcement (e.g., praising a student for appropriate rather

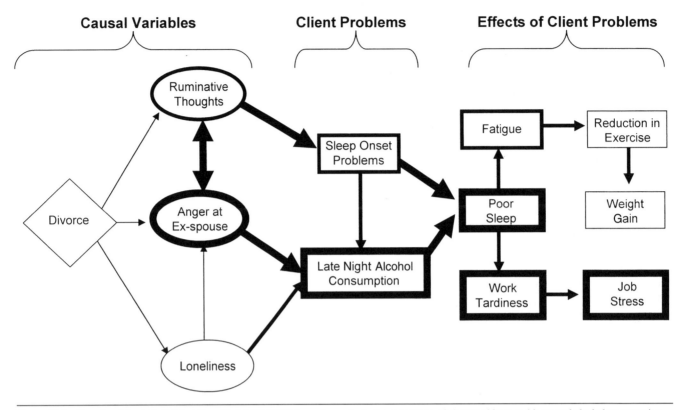

Figure 13.3 Functional Analytic Clinical Case Model (FACCM) for a divorced client complaining of sleep problems and increased alcohol consumption.

than inappropriate behavior) or brief interruptions (e.g., physical or verbal interruptions by the teacher of the student's behavior). Thus, explicitly identifying functional relations may increase the perceived social validity of a treatment.

To our knowledge, only one software program has been developed to help clinicians express hypothesized functional relations in a clinical case. Haynes, Richard, and O'Brien (2000) developed Clinical Case Modeling (CCM) software, a Microsoft Windows program that assists clinicians in the identification of client problems, causal variables, and the effects of client problems. In addition, clinicians can specify the magnitude of both the clinical problems and causal variables, the strength of the relationships among all the variables, and the direction of those relationships (e.g., unidirectional, bidirectional, etc.). The CCM software then suggests treatment avenues by calculating path coefficients for each causal variable and hierarchically organizing the causal variables in terms of their relative importance within the model. The software updates and displays the functional analysis as a vector-graphic diagram, called a *Functional Analytic Clinical Case Model* (FACCM; Haynes, Leisen, & Blaine, 1997), like the one seen in Figure 13.3. The FACCM identifies important variables in a client's life and the relationships between the variables. Variables are of three primary types: *causal variables, client problems,* and *effects of client problems.* For cli-

ent problems and the effects of client problems, the clinical importance of a variable is symbolized by the width of the variable's border (i.e., thicker lines signify more important variables). For causal variables, represented by ovals, the width of the border is an estimate of the modifiability of the variable (i.e., thicker lines signify variables more amenable to therapeutic intervention). The causal variable *divorce* in Figure 13.3 is called an *original causal variable*—it is not modifiable and has influenced variables currently operating in the client's life. Relationships between variables are demarcated by arrows. The thickness of the arrow indicates the strength of the contingent relationship between two variables. Arrowheads symbolize directionality of relationships and may be unidirectional (implying a one-way relationship) or bidirectional (implying a reciprocal relationship). Although no research has been conducted investigating the accuracy, reliability, or treatment utility of FACCMs, they represent a unique way of expressing the complex relationships identified in a functional analysis.

ISSUES IN THE USE OF COMPUTERS IN BEHAVIORAL ASSESSMENT

How computer technology is eventually incorporated into behavioral assessment activities is contingent upon several issues related to training, practice, and ethics. Much of the work described above has been conducted by scholars in academic facilities and research institutions. The routine use of these technologies in clinical practice has been slower to evolve. We agree with Farrell's (1991) conclusion that advances in computerized behavioral assessment will have little overall impact unless they become *regularly* implemented in both research and clinical settings. According to Farrell, major barriers to regular use of contemporary technology involve practical, training, and financial issues (e.g., inadequate time to learn how to use computers, inadequate training or experience with computers, scarce organizational resources). The final section of this chapter addresses possible reasons for the slow transfer of technology to clinical activities in behavioral assessment and proposes some broad systemic remedies with a focus on training.

Training Issues

Less than optimal exposure to computerized behavioral assessment applications in academic training is one of the major reasons why computer applications have not transferred quickly to clinical practice. Graduate courses in behavioral assessment frequently focus on well-established assessment principles and strategies and do not necessarily incorporate computer technology. The focus on tradition over innovation is certainly not limited to the domain of behavioral assessment. However, behavioral assessment possesses perhaps the greatest potential of all assessment paradigms to utilize computer technology because of its emphasis on intensive, and often time-consuming, data collection and analysis. Consequently, we encourage behavioral assessment instructors to facilitate technology transfer by emphasizing computer applications in their courses. We have contended elsewhere that providing clinical students training in rudimentary programming skills using an easy-to-learn programming language like Visual Basic would exploit the extant technology and could be incorporated into coursework (see Richard & Bobicz, 2003). For example, students could develop a handheld computer self-monitoring application and then assess their own behavior over a 7-day period. While some may consider the expense of a handheld computer to be excessive, one can buy several handheld computers for the cost of a single WAIS-III kit.

Graduate-level research design and statistics courses also need to be sensitive to the implications of conducting research using emerging technologies. For example, research design courses frequently focus on group-based ANOVA and regression analyses while neglecting single subject time-series designs. By definition, EMA studies lend themselves to repeated measures time-series designs. Most doctoral programs in clinical psychology provide training in parametric and nonparametric data analysis strategies. However, data from repeated measures and longitudinal designs are more fruitfully understood using time-series analyses, hierarchical modeling, latent growth curves, and structural equation models that can account for nonlinear, and autoregressive, changes in behavior.

Although targeting current graduate training is an important first step, it does not address technology transfer to practicing clinicians. Specialized training, workshops, and symposia at conferences or distributed via CD-ROMs and the Internet can introduce clinicians to the clinical use of emerging technologies. Statistical software manufacturers have long recognized the need to retrain end users in the use of more advanced programs. For example, the statistical software company SPSS provides training through specialized seminars, web-based training, and computer-based training. If behavioral assessors are to incorporate emergent technologies in their clinical activities, it is incumbent upon graduate faculty and software developers to provide graduate students and trained professionals the training required to take advantage of the technologies.

Practical Issues

Researchers have been aware of the issues surrounding the *equivalence* of computerized instruments to their parent instruments for some time (e.g., Skinner & Pakula, 1986). Equivalence is a complicated, multidimensional issue that refers to the degree of agreement between a computerized instrument and its traditionally administered counterpart (Richard & Haynes, 2000). The equivalence of a computerized instrument to its parent instrument may be assessed along several dimensions (e.g., observed data, testing conditions, interactions between testing modalities and sample characteristics, etc.). For example, there is some evidence that one's willingness to disclose sensitive or embarrassing information varies as a function of the interview modality, although the results are mixed. Some studies have shown that, relative to traditionally administered paper-and-pencil instruments or structured interviews, computerized assessments may result in greater disclosure of sensitive or embarrassing symptoms related to sexual functioning (Carr, Ghosh, & Ancill, 1983) and substance abuse (Duffy & Waterton, 1984; Lucas, Mullin, Luna, & McInroy, 1977). However, some studies report contrary findings (see Skinner & Allen, 1983). If level of client disclosure is meaningfully different with a computer, it is reasonable to hypothesize that the change in disclosure will influence a behavioral assessor's understanding of functional relations operating in a client's life and, ultimately, treatment planning.

The effort of many researchers to show the equivalence of computerized instruments to their parent instruments assumes that the computerized version of an instrument is, and should be, identical to its parent instrument. However, computer programs can utilize algorithms impossible for a human interviewer or paper-and-pencil instrument to replicate (e.g., tailored administration of items that is responsive to an individual's pattern of responding). In addition, multimedia and handheld technologies make it possible to present dynamic assessment stimuli and assess behavior in more relevant, naturalistic settings. Obviously, measurement equivalence under these circumstances is even more complex. However, a potential repercussion may be that clinicians will be uncertain about the clinical utility of computerized behavioral assessment instruments in the absence of an empirical literature pertaining to a preexisting parent instrument.

Ethical Issues

In 1986 the American Psychological Association published its *Guidelines for Computer-Based Tests and Interpretations* (APA, 1986). Essentially, these guidelines were an extension and interpretation of the general guidelines regarding testing that had been published by the APA in 1985. Although the guidelines provided a blueprint for the ethical development of computerized tests and assessment instruments, less guidance was provided on how to actualize the ethical principles in practice. More recently, the American Psychological Association's Council of Representatives approved the latest revision of its *Standards for Educational and Psychological Testing,* which is jointly authored by the APA, the American Educational Research Association (AERA), and the National Council on Measurement in Education (NCME). Because these standards are geared toward computerized testing using traditional clinical measures, it is unclear whether the new standards will provide sufficient structure and guidance in the ethical use of computerized behavioral assessment tools.

Obviously, all clinicians and researchers should behave professionally in a manner that conforms to established ethical standards. Unfortunately, the current ethical standards have failed to keep pace with technological advances. For example, the most recent draft of the APA's ethical guidelines makes only a veiled reference to the uses of technology in clinical training and practice. Section 2.01 addresses boundaries of competence and states:

> In those emerging areas in which generally recognized standards for preparatory training do not yet exist, psychologists protect

clients/patients, students, supervisees, research participants, organization clients, and others from harm (APA, 1999, p. 6.).

While this is an important first step that possesses significant face validity, the vagueness of the language does not provide clinicians, academicians, or behavioral assessors with a criterion-based training standard that addresses issues beyond the welfare of the participant or client. Similarly, the section addressing test construction provides little additional guidance:

> Psychologists who develop and conduct research with tests and other assessment techniques use appropriate psychometric procedures and current scientific or professional knowledge for test design, standardization, validation, reduction or elimination of bias, and recommendations for use (APA, 1999, p. 19).

Needless to say, in a rapidly developing field, as is the case with computerized behavioral assessment, ascertaining the appropriateness of an assessment procedure can be challenging at times. For example, we know of no studies or policy reports that have addressed the conditions under which ecological momentary assessment is, or is not, an *appropriate* self-monitoring strategy. One wonders whether ambulatory assessments using beepers and paper-and-pencil diaries are now inappropriate given the advent of handheld computers that can be programmed to eliminate post hoc response entries by research participants. Further, findings from EMA studies have led many to question the accuracy of results garnered from commonly used self-report instruments and clinician-administered structured interviews. Resorting to a priori definitions of the appropriateness of psychometric procedures based on traditional practices has the potential to inhibit the development of new assessment strategies that may result in more accurate, and useful, client data and clinical inferences.

Developers of computerized behavioral assessment tools are advised of the necessity to document all aspects of their software (e.g., conceptual underpinnings, interface, specification of and rationale for variable parameters, scoring algorithms, user demands, psychometric properties, and rationale for strategies to assess psychometric properties, etc.). Further, construct-irrelevant variance pertinent to computer-based tests and measures should be addressed in their design and use. While the current ethical standards provide general guidance, the guidelines provide few specific recommendations on how equivalence of paper-and-pencil and computerized measures should be established. For example, when attempting to establish equivalence, a clear rationale and supporting evidence should be provided for any claim that scores earned on different forms (e.g., paper-and-pencil self-monitoring versus handheld computer) may be used interchangeably. This can include direct evidence of score equivalence or a demonstration that the theoretical assumptions underlying procedures for establishing score comparability have been sufficiently satisfied. Further, the specific rationale and the evidence required will depend in part on the intended uses for which score equivalence is claimed. Detailed technical information should be provided on the method by which equating functions or other linkages were established and on the accuracy of equating functions (APA, 1999).

CONCLUSION

Computerized behavioral assessment is a rapidly evolving and dynamic field that will likely continue to grow in the coming years. Technological advances have been noted with virtually every behavioral assessment method, and we expect behavioral assessors to increasingly incorporate these advances in coming years. However, the pace of the integration will depend on the degree to which graduate instructors incorporate technology in their training programs. Graduate training programs that encourage both the *use* and *development* of computerized behavioral assessment strategies by their students will play a significant role in the more general evolution of behavioral assessment in the future.

NOTES

1. The PsycInfo literature database catalogs publications in psychological journals and books from 1887 to present.

2. Although the terms *handheld, portable, palmtop,* and *personal digital assistant* are sometimes used synonymously, they reflect different types of computing devices. To simplify matters for this chapter, however, we refer to all these instruments as *handheld computers* or *handheld devices.*

3. We use the term *functional analysis* in a way consistent with Haynes and O'Brien's (2000) definition: "the identification of important, controllable, causal functional relations applicable to specified behaviors for an individual" (p. 302). In this context, the terms *functional analysis* and *clinical case formulation* may be used interchangeably.

4. One should note, however, that the same may be said of other assessment paradigms. For example, there is little evidence demonstrating the treatment utility of multiaxial assessment using the *Diagnostic and Statistical Manual.* Results of studies investigating the treatment utility of cognitive case formulation models also have yielded mixed results. For example, Hess (2001) concluded with a sample of seven depressed patients that identification of core cognitive beliefs had no effect on the quality of the therapeutic alliance,

symptom change, readiness for change, or perceived meaningfulness of a session.

5. The term *social validity* refers to the degree to which the goals of the intervention are socially significant, the intervention procedures are appropriate, and the effects of the intervention are meaningful (Wolf, 1978).

REFERENCES

Affleck, G., Tennen, H., Urrows, S., Higgins, P., Abeles, M., Hall, C., Karoly, P., & Newton, C. (1998). Fibromyalgia and women's pursuit of personal goals: A daily process analysis. *Health Psychology, 17*(1), 40–47.

American Psychological Association (1985). *Standards for educational and psychological testing.* Washington, DC: Author.

American Psychological Association (1986). *Guidelines for computer-based tests and interpretations.* Washington, DC: Author.

American Psychological Association (1999). *Standards for educational and psychological testing.* Washington, DC: AERA Publication.

Anbar, M., & Raulin, M. (1994). Psychological assessment using simulations with unrestricted natural language input. *Journal of Educational Computing Research, 11*(4), 339–346.

Anderson, B., & Ley, R. (2001). Dyspnea during panic attacks: An Internet survey of incidences of changes in breathing. *Behavior Modification, 25*(4), 546–554.

Blackburn, R., & Athayde, R. (2000). Making the connection: The effectiveness of Internet training in small business. *Education and Training, 42*(4–5), 289–299.

Blake, D.D., Weathers, F.W., Nagy, L.M., Kaloupek, D.G., Charney, D.S., & Keane, T.M. (1997). *Clinician-administered PTSD scale for DSM-IV: Current and lifetime diagnostic version (CAPS-Dx).* Boston: National Center for Posttraumatic Stress Disorder.

Blasko, D.G., Kazmerski, V.A., Corty, E.W., & Kallgren, C.A. (1998). Courseware for observational research (COR): A new approach to teaching naturalistic observation. *Behavior Research Methods, Instruments, & Computers, 30*(2), 217–222.

Bowie, P., & Mountain, G. (1993). Using direct observation to record the behaviour of long-stay patients with dementia. *International Journal of Geriatric Psychiatry, 8,* 857–863.

Buchanan, T., & Smith, J.L. (1999a). Research on the Internet: Validation of a World-Wide Web mediated personality scale. *Behavior Research Methods, Instruments, & Computers, 31*(4), 565–571.

Buchanan, T., & Smith, J.L. (1999b). Using the Internet for psychological research: Personality testing on the World Wide Web. *British Journal of Psychology, 90,* 125–144.

Carels, R.A., Hoffman, J., Collins, A., Raber, A.C., Cacciapaglia, H., & O'Brien, W.H. (2001). Ecological momentary assessment of temptation and lapse in dieting. *Eating Behaviors, 2*(4), 307–321.

Carr, A.C., Ghosh, A., & Ancill, R.J. (1983). Can a computer take a psychiatric history? *Psychological Medicine, 13,* 151–158.

Catley, D. (2000). Absentminded lapses during smoking cessation. *Psychology of Addictive Behaviors, 14*(1), 73–76.

Catley, D. (2000). Psychological distress in chronic pain: Examination of integrative models of stress, and a cognitive-behavioral mediation model of depression. *Dissertation Abstracts International, 60*(8-B), 4207.

Catley, O'Connell, & Shiffman (2000). Absentminded lapses during smoking. *Psychology and Addictive Behavior, 14,* 73–76.

Chan, F., Parker, H.J., Lam, C.S., Mecaskey, C., & Malphurs, L. (1987). Computer case management simulations: Applications in rehabilitation education. *Rehabilitation Counseling Bulletin, 30*(4), 210–217.

Chan, F., Rosen, A.J., Wong, D.W., & Kaplan, S. (1993). Evaluating rehabilitation caseload management skills through computer simulations. *Journal of Counseling and Development, 71*(5), 493–498.

Cloud, R.N., & Peacock, P.L. (2001). Internet screening and interventions for problem drinking: Results from the www.carebetter.com pilot study. *Alcoholism Treatment Quarterly, 19*(2), 23–44.

Collins, R.L., Morsheimer, E.T., Shiffman, S., Paty, J.A., Gnys, M., & Papandonatos, G.D. (1998). Ecological momentary assessment in a behavioral drinking moderation training program. *Experimental and Clinical Psychopharmacology, 6*(3), 306–315.

Cone, J.D. (1999). Introduction to the special section on self-monitoring: A major assessment method in clinical psychology. *Psychological Assessment, 11*(4), 411–414.

Crosbie, J., & Kelly, G. (1993). A computer-based Personalized System of Instruction course in applied behavior analysis. *Behavior Research Methods, Instruments, & Computers, 25*(3), 366–370.

Davis, R.N. (1999). Web-based administration of a personality questionnaire: Comparison with traditional methods. *Behavior Research Methods, Instruments, and Computers, 31*(4), 572–577.

Desrochers, M.N. (1996). Behavior analysis: A computer-based tutorial. *Computers in Human Services, 13*(4), 70–85.

Desrochers, M.N., Clemmons, T., Grady, M., & Justice, B. (2000). An evaluation of Simulations in Developmental Disabilities (SIDD): Instructional software that provides practice in behavioral assessment and treatment decisions. *Journal of Technology in Human Services, 17*(4), 15–27.

Desrochers, M.N., & Hile, M.G. (1993). SIDDS: Simulation in developmental disabilities. *Behavior Research Methods, Instruments, and Computers, 25*(2), 308–313.

Dickins, D.W., Kwint, M.A.C.G., Magnusson, M.S., Neads, C.M., Noldus, L.P.J.J., & Quera, V. (2000). OBSERVE: A multimedia course on the observational analysis of behavior. *Behavior Research Methods, Instruments, & Computers, 32*(2), 263–268.

Duffy, J.C., & Waterton, J.J. (1984). Under-reporting of alcohol consumption in sample surveys: The effect of computer interviewing in fieldwork. *British Journal of Addiction, 79*(3), 303–308.

Emerson, E., Reeves, D.J., & Felce, D. (2000). Palmtop computer technologies for behavioral observation research. In T. Thompson, D. Felce, and F.J. Symons (Eds.), *Behavioral observation: Technology and applications in developmental disabilities* (pp. 47–60). Baltimore: Brookes.

Engen, H.B., Finken, L.J., Luschei, N.S., & Kenney, D. (1994). Counseling simulations: An interactive videodisc approach. *Computers in Human Services, 11*(3–4), 283–298.

EthoLog 2.2 (n.d.). Available at http://www.geocities.com/ebottoni/ethohome.html or http://members.xoom.com/Etholog/ethohome.html.

Fahrenberg, J., Bruegner, G., Foerster, F., & Kaeppler, C. (1999). Ambulatory assessment of diurnal changes with a hand-held computer: Mood, attention, and morningness-eveningness. *Personality and Individual Differences, 26*(4), 641–656.

Fahrenberg, J., Franck, M., Baas, U., & Jost, E. (1995). Awareness of blood pressure: Interoception or contextual judgement? *Journal of Psychosomatic Research, 39*(1), 11–18.

Fahrenberg, J., Hüttner, P., & Leonhart, R. (2001). MONITOR: Acquisition of psychological data by a hand-held PC. In J. Fahrenberg and M. Myrtek (Eds.), *Progress in ambulatory assessment* (pp. 93–112). Seattle, WA: Hogrefe & Huber.

Farrell, A.D. (1991). Computers and behavioral assessment: Current applications, future possibilities, and obstacles to routine use. *Behavioral Assessment, 13,* 159–179.

Farrell, A.D. (1999a). Development and evaluation of problem frequency scales from Version 3 of the Computerized Assessment System for Psychotherapy Evaluation and Research (CASPER). *Journal of Clinical Psychology, 55*(4), 447–464.

Farrell, A.D. (1999b). Evaluation of the Computerized Assessment System for Psychotherapy Evaluation and Research (CASPER) as a measure of treatment effectiveness in an outpatient training clinic. *Psychological Assessment, 11*(3), 345–358.

Farrell, A.D., Camplair, P.S., & McCullough, L. (1987). Identification of target complaints by computer interview: Evaluation of the Computerized Assessment System for Psychotherapy Evaluation and Research. *Journal of Consulting and Clinical Psychology, 55,* 691–700.

Godaert, G., Sorbi, M., Peters, M., Dekkers, C., & Geenen, R. (2001). Ambulatory monitoring of diurnal changes in pain in chronic pain disorder, migraine and rheumatoid arthritis. In J. Fahrenberg and M. Myrtek (Eds.), *Progress in ambulatory assessment: Computer-assisted psychological and psychophysiological methods in monitoring and field studies* (pp. 123–128). Kirkland, WA: Hogrefe and Huber.

Gorrell, J., & Downing, H. (1989). Effects of a computer-simulated behavior analysis on pre-service teachers' problem solving. *Journal of Educational Computing Research, 5*(3), 335–347.

Graf, S.A. (1995). Three nice labs, no real rats: A review of three operant laboratory simulations. *The Behavior Analyst, 18,* 301–306.

Greeno, C.G., Wing, R.R., & Shiffman, S. (2000). Binge antecedents in obese women with and without binge eating disorder. *Journal of Consulting and Clinical Psychology, 68*(1), 95–102.

Hank, P., Schwenkmezger, P., & Schumann, J. (2001). Daily mood reports in hindsight: Results of a computer-assisted time sampling study. In J. Fahrenberg and M. Myrtek (Eds.), *Progress in ambulatory assessment: Computer-assisted psychological and psychophysiological methods in monitoring and field studies* (pp. 143–156). Kirkland, WA: Hogrefe and Huber.

Hasdai, A., Jessel, A.S., & Weiss, P.L. (1998). Use of a computer simulator for training children with disabilities in the operation of a powered wheelchair. *American Journal of Occupational Therapy, 52*(3), 215–220.

Hayes, S.C., Nelson, R.O., & Jarrett, R.B. (1987). The treatment utility of assessment: A functional approach to evaluating assessment quality. *American Psychologist, 42,* 963–974.

Haynes, S.N., Leisen, M.B., & Blaine, D.D. (1997). Design of individualized behavioral treatment programs using Functional Analytic Clinical Case Models. *Psychological Assessment, 9*(4), 334–348.

Haynes, S.N., & O'Brien, W.H. (2000). *Principles and practice of behavioral assessment.* New York: Kluwer Academic Press.

Haynes, S.N., Richard, D.C.S., & Kubany, E.S. (1995). Content validity in psychological assessment: A functional approach to concepts and methods. *Psychological Assessment, 7*(3), 238–247.

Haynes, S. N., Richard, D.C.S., & O'Brien, W.O. (2000). *Functional analytic clinical case modeling software.* New York: American Psychological Association.

Herman, S., & Koran, L.M. (1998). In vivo measurement of obsessive-compulsive disorder symptoms using palmtop computers. *Computers in Human Behavior, 14*(3), 449–462.

Hess, S.M. (2001). The effects of a case formulation approach on process and outcome in the treatment of depression (Doctoral dissertation, University of Texas at Austin, 2001). *Dissertation Abstracts International, 61,* 6136.

Hinkel, M., & Scholz, O.B. (2001). Development and user's acceptance of the General Electronic Psychotherapy Diary. In J. Fahrenberg and M. Myrtek (Eds.), *Progress in ambulatory assessment: Computer-assisted psychological and psychophysiological methods in monitoring and field studies* (pp. 129–134). Seattle, WA: Hogrefe and Huber.

Holden, B.G., Bearison, D.J., Rode, D.C., Kapiloff, M.F., & Rosenberg, G. (2000). The effects of a computer network on pediatric pain and anxiety. *Journal of Technology in Human Services, 17*(1), 27–47.

Horswill, M.S., & McKenna, F.P. (1999). The effect of interference on dynamic risk-taking judgments. *British Journal of Psychology, 90*(2), 189–199.

Isaacs, M., Costenbader, V., Reading-Brown, M., & Goodman, G. (1992). Using a computer simulation in the research, training, and evaluation of school psychologists. *Behavior Research Methods, Instruments, and Computers, 24*(2), 165–168.

Jamison, R.N., Raymond, S.A., Levine, J.G., Slawsby, E.A., Nedeljkovic, S.S., Srdjan, S., & Katz, N.P. (2001). Electronic diaries for monitoring chronic pain: One year validation study. *Pain, 91*(3), 277–285.

Janikowski, T.P., Berven, N.L., Meixelsperger, M.K., & Roedl, K.E. (1989). A computer-based simulation to assess skill in predicting client behavior. *Rehabilitation Counseling Bulletin, 33*(2), 127–139.

Kaeppler, C., & Rieder, S. (2001). Does the retrospection effect hold as a stable phenomenon? In J. Farenberg (Ed.), *Progress in Ambulatory Assessment* (pp. 113–122). Kirkland, WA: Hogrefe and Huber.

Kahng, S., & Iwata, B.A. (1998). Computerized systems for collecting real-time observational data. *Journal of Applied Behavior Analysis, 31,* 253–261.

Kahng, S., & Iwata, B.A. (2000). Computer systems for collecting real-time observational data. In T. Thompson, D. Felce, & F.J. Symons (Eds.), *Behavioral observation: Technology and applications in developmental disabilities* (pp. 35–45). Baltimore: Brookes.

Kamarck, T.W., Shiffman, S.M., Misthline, L., Goodie, J.L., Thompson, H.S., Ituarte, P., et al. (1998). The diary of ambulatory behavioral states: A new approach to the assessment of psychosocial influences on ambulatory cardiovascular activity. In D.S. Krantz & A. Baum (Eds.), *Technology and methods in behavioral medicine* (pp. 163–193). Mahwah, NJ: Erlbaum.

Kenardy, J., Fried, L., Kraemer, H.C., & Taylor, C.B. (1992). Psychological precursors of panic attacks. *British Journal of Psychiatry, 160,* 668–673.

Krantz, J.H., Ballard, J., & Scher, J. (1997). Comparing the results of laboratory and World-Wide Web samples on the determinants of female attractiveness. *Behavior Research Methods, Instruments, & Computers, 29*(2), 264–269.

Kratochwill, T.R., & McGivern, J.E. (1996). Clinical diagnosis, behavioral assessment, and functional analysis: Examining the connection between assessment and intervention. *School Psychology Review, 25*(3), 342–355.

Lambert, M.E. (1989). Using computer simulations in behavior therapy training. *Computers in Human Services, 5*(3–4), 1–12.

Le Grange, D., Gorin, A., Catley, D., & Stone, A.A. (2001). Does momentary assessment detect binge eating in overweight women that is denied at interview? *European Eating Disorders Review, 9*(5), 309–324.

Liaupsin, C.J., Scott, T.M., & Nelson, C.M. (2000). *Functional behavioral assessment: An interactive tutorial.* Longmont, CO: Sopris West.

Litt, M.D., Cooney, N.L., & Morse, P. (1998). Ecological momentary assessment with treating alcoholics. *Health Psychology, 17,* 48–52.

Lucas, R.W., Mullin, P.J., Luna, C.B., & McInroy, D.C. (1977). Psychiatrists and a computer as interrogators of patients with alcohol-related illnesses: A comparison. *British Journal of Psychiatry, 131,* 160–167.

Newman, M.G., Consoli, A.J., & Taylor, C.B. (1999). A palmtop computer program for the treatment of generalized anxiety disorder. *Behavior Modification, 23*(4), 597–619.

Newman, M.G., Kenardy, J., Herman, S., & Taylor, C.B. (1996). The use of hand-held computers as an adjunct to cognitive-behavior therapy. *Computers in Human Behavior, 12*(1), 135–143.

Newman, M.G., Kenardy, J., Herman, S., & Taylor, C.B. (1997). Comparison of palmtop-computer-assisted brief cognitive-behavioral treatment to cognitive-behavioral treatment for panic disorder. *Journal of Consulting and Clinical Psychology, 65*(1), 178–183.

Noldus, L.P.J.J., Spink, A.J., & Tegelenbosch, R.A.J. (2001). EthoVision: A versatile tracking system for automation of behavioral experiments. *Behavior Research Methods, Instruments, & Computers, 33*(3), 398–414.

O'Connell, K.A., Gerkovich, M.M., Bott, M., Cook, M.R., & Shiffman, S. (2000). Playfulness, arousal-seeking, and rebelliousness during smoking cessation. *Personality and Individual Differences, 29*(4), 671–683.

O'Connell, K.A., Gerkovich, M.M., Cook, M.R., Shiffman, S., Hickcox, M., & Kakolewski, K.E. (1998). Coping in real time: Using ecological momentary assessment techniques to assess coping with the urge to smoke. *Research in Nursing and Health, 21*(6), 487–497.

Ottoni, E.B. (2000). EthoLog 2.2: A tool for the transcription and timing of behavior observation sessions. *Behaviour Research Methods, Instruments, & Computers, 32*(3), 446–449.

Perrez, M., Berger, R., & Wilhelm, P. (1998). Assessment of stress and coping in the family: Self-monitoring as a new approach. *Psychologie in Erziehung und Unterricht, 45*(1), 19–35.

Perrez, M., Wilhelm, P., Schoebi, D., & Horner, M. (2001). Simultaneous computer-assisted assessment of causal attribution and social coping in families. In J. Fahrenberg and M. Myrtek (Eds.), *Progress in ambulatory assessment: Computer-assisted psychological and psychophysiological methods in monitoring and field studies* (pp. 25–44). Seattle, WA: Hogrefe and Huber.

Peterson, D.B. (2000). Clinical problem solving in micro-case management: Computer-assisted instruction for information-gathering strategies in rehabilitation counseling. *Rehabilitation Counseling Bulletin, 43*(2), 84–96.

Richard, D.C.S. (1999). Development and psychometric evaluation of the Computerized PTSD Scale. (Doctoral dissertation, University of Hawaii, 1999). *Dissertation Abstracts International, 60*(5-B), 2364.

Richard, D.C.S., & Bobicz, K. (2003). Computers and behavioral assessment: Five years later. *The Behavior Therapist, 26*(1), 219–223.

Richard, D.C.S., & Haynes, S.N. (2000). Computerized psychological assessment. In W.E. Craighead and C.B. Nemeroff (Eds.), *The Corsini encyclopedia of psychology and behavioral science* (3rd ed., pp. 339–341). New York: Wiley.

Ritchie, K.L. (1999). Maternal behaviors and cognitions during discipline episodes: A comparison of power bouts and single acts of noncompliance. *Developmental Psychology, 35*(2), 580–589.

Sailor, W., Freedman, R., Britten, J., McCart, A., Smith, C., Scott, T., & Nelson, M. (2000). Using information technology to prepare personnel to implement functional behavioral assessment and positive behavioral support. *Exceptionality, 8*(3), 217–230.

Sandman, C.A., Touchette, P.E., Ly, J., Marion, S.D., & Bruinsma, Y.E.M. (2000). Computer-assisted assessment of treatment effects among individuals with developmental disabilities. In T. Thompson, D. Felce, & F.J. Symons (Eds.), *Behavioral observation: Technology and applications in developmental disabilities* (pp. 271–293). Baltimore: Brookes.

Schwartz, J.E., Neale, J., Marco, C., Shiffman, S.S., & Stone, A.A. (1999). Does trait coping exist? A momentary assessment approach to the evaluation of traits. *Journal of Social and Personality Psychology, 77*(2), 360–369.

Shimoff, E., & Catania, A.C. (1995). Using computers to teach behavior analysis. *The Behavior Analyst, 18,* 307–316.

Skinner, H.A., & Allen, B.A. (1983). Does the computer make a difference? Computerized versus face-to-face versus self-report assessment of alcohol, drug, and tobacco use. *Journal of Consulting and Clinical Psychology, 51*(2), 267–275.

Skinner, H.A., & Pakula, A. (1986). Challenge of computers in psychological assessment. *Professional Psychology: Research and Practice, 17*(1), 44–50.

Smyth, J., Wonderlich, S., Crosby, R., Miltenberger, R., Mitchell, J., & Rorty, M. (2001). The use of ecological momentary assessment approaches in eating disorder research. *International Journal of Eating Disorders, 30*(1), 83–95.

Sorbi, M., Honkoop, P.C., & Godaert, G.L.R. (1996). A signal-contingent computer diary for the assessment of psychological patients of the migraine attack. In J. Fahrenberg and M. Myrtek (Eds.), *Ambulatory assessment: Computer-assisted psychological and physiological methods in monitoring and field studies* (pp. 403–412). Kirkland, WA: Hogrefe and Huber.

Stewart, L.S.P. (2001). The role of computer simulation in the development of clinical reasoning skills. *British Journal of Occupational Therapy, 46*(1), 2–8.

Stiglmayr, C., Grathwol, T., & Bohus, M. (2001). States of aversive tension in patients with borderline personality disorder: A controlled field study. In J. Fahrenberg and M. Myrtek (Eds.), *Progress in ambulatory assessment: Computer-assisted psychological and psychophysiological methods in monitoring and field studies* (pp. 135–142). Seattle, WA: Hogrefe and Huber.

Stone, A.A., Broderick, J.E., Poerter, L.S., & Kaell, A.T. (1997). The experience of rheumatoid arthritis pain and fatigue: Examining momentary reports and correlates over one week. *Arthritis Care and Research, 10*(3), 185–193.

Stone, A.A., Schwartz, J.E., Neale, J.M., Shiffman, S., Marco, C.A., Hickcox, M., Paty, J., Porter, L.S., & Cruise, L.J. (1998). A comparison of coping assessed by ecological momentary assessment and retrospective recall. *Journal of Personality and Social Psychology,* 74(6), 1670–1680.

Stone, A., & Shiffman, S. (1994). Ecological momentary assessment (EMA) in behavioral medicine. *Annals of Behavioral Medicine, 16,* 199–202.

Symons, F.J., & MacLean, W.E., Jr. (2000). Analyzing and treating severe behavior problems in people with developmental disabilities. In T. Thompson, D. Felce, & F.J. Symons (Eds.), *Behavioral observation: Technology and applications in developmental disabilities* (pp. 143–157). Baltimore: Brookes.

Tapp, J., & Wehby, J.H. (2000). Observational software for laptop computers and optical bar code readers. In T. Thompson, D. Felce, & F. J. Symons (Eds.), *Behavioral observation: Technology and applications in developmental disabilities* (pp. 71–82). Baltimore: Brookes.

Taylor, C.B., Fried, L., & Kenardy, J. (1990). The use of a real-time computer diary for data acquisition and processing. *Behaviour Research and Therapy, 21,* 93–97.

Thomas, M.D., O'Connor, F.W., Albert, M.L., Boutain, D., & Brandt, P.A. (2001). Case-based teaching and learning experiences. *Issues in Mental Health Nursing, 22*(5), 517–531.

Van Egeren, L.F., & Madarasmi, S. (1988). Blood pressure and behavior: Mood, activity, and blood pressure in daily life. *American Journal of Hypertension, 1,* 1795–1855.

VanHaitsma, K., Lawton, M.P., Kleban, M.H., Klapper, J., & Corn, J. (1997). Methodological aspects of the study of streams of behavior in elders with dementing illness. *Alzheimer Disease and Associated Disorders, 11*(4), 228–238.

Weigle, K.L., & Scotti, J.R. (2000). Effects of functional analysis information on ratings of intervention effectiveness and acceptability. *Journal of the Association for Persons With Severe Handicaps, 25*(4), 217–228.

Welch, N., & Krantz, J.H. (1996). The World-Wide Web as a medium for psychoacoustical demonstrations and experiments: Experience and results. *Behavior Research Methods, Instruments, & Computers, 28*(2), 192–196.

Whalen, C.K., Jamner, L.D., Henker, B., & Delfino, R.J. (2001). Smoking and moods in adolescents with depressive and aggressive dispositions: Evidence from surveys and electronic diaries. *Health Psychology, 20*(2), 99–111.

Wilhelm, P. (2001). A multilevel approach to analyze ambulatory assessment data: An examination of family members' emotional states in daily life. In J. Fahrenberg & M. Myrtek (Eds.), *Progress in ambulatory assessment: Computer-assisted psychological and psychophysiological methods in monitoring and field studies* (pp. 173–189). Kirkland, WA: Hogrefe and Huber.

Wolf, M.M. (1978). Social validity: The case for subjective measurement or how applied behavior analysis is finding its heart. *Journal of Applied Behavior Analysis, 11,* 203–214.

CHAPTER 14

Program Evaluation

KATHERINE M. MCKNIGHT AND LEE SECHREST

INTRODUCTION

This chapter identifies some of the important areas of concern to evaluators when undertaking the evaluation of a program. Our discussion is meant to be sufficiently general to apply to evaluations on all scales, ranging from the evaluation of a small local program to large multisite evaluations. Our purpose is to highlight broad areas of concern in order to stimulate critical thinking about problems that are likely to arise as well as some possible solutions. We introduce program evaluation by defining what a program is and discussing the tasks and role of the evaluator. This discussion occurs within the context of a program's life span; that is, from its inception to its long-term outcomes. More importantly, we address the task of the evaluator, regardless of the purpose of the evaluation, in light of the need to be persuasive with evaluation conclusions.

Although this chapter is part of a larger text focused specifically on behavioral assessment, our focus is more general in order to ensure wide applicability. This chapter will not serve as a "how to" guide for program evaluation, but rather as a discussion of some of the broad concerns associated with the evaluation of social programs. The chapter can be used as a general guide or starting point by clinicians, program administrators, program staff, and other program personnel interested in program planning, development, monitoring, outcomes, and impact.

WHAT CONSTITUTES A PROGRAM?

No formal, widely accepted definition of a program exists, but we believe that the following will suit most purposes: a program is an integrated, systematic arrangement of activities and resources directed at solving some problem or filling some need. The definition includes several terms of specific import. First a program involves integrated and systematic efforts. A conglomeration of activities happening to exist in the same spatial or temporal context would not necessarily constitute a program; they would need to be related to one another—or integrated. Moreover, a program involves systematic efforts in the sense that elements must fit together in a planned, coherent way. A professional center that offers both diagnostic and treatment services would constitute a program only if the two types of services occurred in a useful temporal order and were interrelated—for example, so that treatment services depended in some way on diagnostic services. Programs involve both activities and resources, and resources may be either material or professional or, most likely, both. Finally, programs have direction, they are aimed at doing something that needs to be done; they are not simply a convenient display of resources to be chosen or not, according to the particular interests or whims of an audience or the public.

Any organization or service-providing entity may be regarded as having a program to the extent that it meets the

246

foregoing requirements. Just what the program is, however, will be determined by the way the requirements are met in particular instances. One substance abuse treatment clinic might have been instituted to "meet the need for substance abuse treatment services" in a geographically defined area, and its program would be constituted by its array of services and would be judged by the extent to which it met the needs specified. Another treatment clinic might have been developed to reduce the number of youth at risk for incarceration for drug offenses. That clinic's program might have quite a different array of specific services and would be judged by different criteria.

WHAT CONSTITUTES AN EVALUATION?

It is difficult to get complete agreement on what activities constitute program evaluation. Activities can be as varied as program development, evaluation of needs, monitoring program implementation, and assessment of program outcomes and/or impact. These activities have been summarized as formative and summative (cf. Rossi & Freeman, 1993) and relate to the various stages of a program's life. Evaluation can be incorporated at the earliest stages of a program, even prior to its inception (e.g., during the needs assessment phase), through the latest stages (e.g., evaluation of long-term consequences). During these different phases, program evaluation activities vary depending on the objectives of the evaluation. During the needs assessment phase, for example, evaluators assess the needs of the population for whom the program is being developed in order to design a relevant and useful program. The implementation phase requires evaluators to assess how the program is being delivered so that, among other things, it may be determined whether program personnel are delivering the program as they should and so that understanding of the program (theory) may be advanced—that is, how program X leads to outcome Y. In order to understand the mechanisms of action leading from program interventions to an outcome, it is necessary to know what was delivered as part of the program. If one cannot characterize the program, it becomes a "black box" that can neither be improved in any systematic way nor replicated for wider application.

The activities and goals most obviously associated with program evaluation are those related to outcomes or what is sometimes called "summative" evaluation (Scriven, 1991). An outcomes evaluation is directed toward assessing program effects. Common outcomes evaluation objectives include determining whether a program is successful in meeting its purpose, whether one program outperforms another, and the impact of a program within a community. Evaluators of a behavioral assessment program might be asked to determine whether the program is progressing toward its goal, for example, of reducing problem behaviors for school children diagnosed with attention deficit hyperactivity disorder. Or an evaluator might be asked to compare the outcomes of a behavioral program with those achieved in a program incorporating psychopharmacological treatment along with behavioral interventions. These activities all fall under summative, or outcomes, evaluation.

Program evaluation may be distinguished generally from clinical research by the fact that the former is directed toward assessment of interventions that have generally been judged to be potentially effective, often on the basis of clinical work, and that are being implemented in what may be thought of as "real life" settings (i.e., not under controlled, laboratory conditions). Program evaluation is, therefore, akin to the idea of "effectiveness" research as opposed to "efficacy" research, a distinction often made in biomedical and health research (Figueredo & Sechrest, 2001).

Regardless of the program phase in which an evaluation is carried out, the task of the program evaluator is to design and carry out a research study in such a way as to enhance the persuasiveness of the conclusions (Sechrest, Ametrano, & Ametrano, 1982). Thus, two important issues ought to be considered at the onset of planning an evaluation: (1) who it is who must be persuaded, and (2) what type of evidence is needed to be persuasive. The first issue has to do with the audience for the evaluation while the second has to do with the nature of the evidence. The answers to both of these questions are dictated by the purposes of the evaluation. For example, if federal funds are granted to evaluate the effectiveness of a methadone treatment protocol enhanced by behavioral assessment, the audience and type of evidence required would be quite different from that for an evaluation to meet the needs of a local oversight group. An evaluation for a federal agency might be intended to inform federal drug treatment policy, thus involving a wide range of stakeholders, including but not limited to state and local methadone clinics, clinicians, clinic administrators, methadone clients, lawmakers, the funding agency, taxpayers, and probably many others. The requirements for evidence on which to base national-level policy recommendations for methadone treatment would be quite stringent and subject to debate, particularly by stakeholders who might support a different policy. By contrast, a local oversight board would likely have more circumscribed interests and might well be satisfied with summary statistics and testimonial evidence.

Problems arise when these issues of audience and persuasiveness of evidence are not taken into consideration early on in the planning stage of program evaluation. For most evaluations, there are multiple stakeholders—those who pay for the program, those who administer it, those who benefit from it, etc.—and the different audiences are likely to differ substantially in the ease with which they are persuaded to any conclusions (Sechrest et al., 1982). Thus, which evidence might be regarded as persuasive is intertwined with stakeholder characteristics as well with as the purpose of the evaluation. As the previous example illustrates, making public policy versus making local program decisions demands different types of evidence. Furthermore, some groups of stakeholders might be more easily persuaded than others. For example, it is likely to be difficult to persuade conservative community physicians that methadone doses should be increased, and it is likely to be difficult to persuade proponents of methadone treatment that such treatment should be time-limited.

Problems in evaluation arise when requirements for evidence are markedly discrepant. For example, academic colleagues or professional peers (e.g., editors and peer reviewers) often have stringent requirements for evidence—for example, randomization of cases to treatment conditions, reliability of measures, and/or specific appropriateness of statistical tests in order to be persuaded by the evaluation conclusions. Yet it is highly unlikely that legislators or methadone clients would require such evidence, let alone know what to do with it, in order to be persuaded by evaluation results. In fact, some evidential requirements, especially random assignment to treatment, may be strongly resisted by program personnel or service clients, thus frustrating one of the most fundamental bases for inference available to the researcher/evaluator.

WHO ARE THE STAKEHOLDERS?

Evaluators can enhance the persuasiveness of their conclusions by carrying out a few relatively simple tasks during the planning stages of the evaluation. As noted previously, what is regarded as persuasive depends on the audience. Therefore, after the purpose of the evaluation has been determined, the evaluator ought to identify the audience for the evaluation. Generally the audience will be those who have an interest in the outcomes of the program, or program stakeholders. Identifying relevant stakeholders is not always easy and requires some careful thought. Certainly individuals who are more directly involved with a program are obvious candidates, such as those who pay for the program, administer it or provide services (and receive pay) under its auspices, and those who are expected to benefit from it (after enduring its rigors). Those indirectly involved can also be stakeholders, even though their interests are not always immediately obvious.

For example, for a crime prevention program for at-risk youth, potential stakeholders with indirect involvement include the communities in which the crimes would have taken place, and the police department and local politicians, all of whom might benefit as crime rates decrease. Parents of delinquent youth may be stakeholders in antidelinquency programs, and families of substance abusers are stakeholders in those programs. Programs often have unintended consequences, some of which have an impact on individuals who were never intended to be affected by the program. Crime prevention programs, for example, sometimes have the unintended consequence of shifting crime to nearby communities that are not served by the program. Members of these communities thus become stakeholders in the program owing to its impact on their lives.

Identifying the stakeholders assists the evaluator in identifying the appropriate outcomes on which to focus the evaluation, which should enhance the utility and persuasiveness of conclusions. For example, school administrators might require information about the impact of a behavioral assessment program on classroom management in order to be persuaded of the utility of the program, while teachers might focus more strongly on the academic performance of students. School districts might have a different focus as well, such as the image of the school as being responsive to students with special needs. These different concerns of the various stakeholders reflect a variety of variables on which the evaluator would need to focus in order for evaluation conclusions to be generally useful and persuasive. Omitting relevant stakeholders in planning an evaluation can result in a less-than-optimal evaluation design because outcomes important to some interests will not have been measured. Such omissions decrease the persuasiveness of evidence to those stakeholders and possibly decrease the overall utility of the evaluation. For example, omitting the school district as a potential stakeholder could result in failure to obtain information about community perceptions that would persuade the district of the utility of the school-based behavioral assessment program.

Part of the difficulty in identifying stakeholders is that opinions often differ about the intended purpose of a program. For example, international agencies might view a primary purpose of an HIV/AIDS prevention program in Africa to be the reduction of the need for international intervention, while the local clinicians might view it as the reduction of HIV/AIDS incidence in their specific village. To the international agencies, other nations are identified as primary stakeholders, while to the clinician, the clients and their families are the primary stakeholders. Along with differing opinions regarding purpose, evaluation feasibility is also important. Many more resources would be needed to examine the international impact of the prevention program as opposed to estimating local impact on the villagers. From the perspective of a local HIV/AIDS clinic, such a resource-intensive design would be prohibitively costly and might seem irrelevant in any case.

Difficult questions are involved in the identification of stakeholders when many persons with a potential interest in a program may not even be aware of it. For example, taxpayers often are unaware of the programs they fund, and the interests of program beneficiaries (e.g., Medicaid recipients) may be quite different from those of other groups. Identification of the appropriate audience and the type of evidence they require to be persuaded by evaluation conclusions is relevant to evaluations of any kind, from large-scale evaluations at the national or multinational level to evaluations of small programs. The purpose of the evaluation should dictate who the audience for the evaluation will be, and who the audience is will dictate what type of evidence is necessary to provide persuasive conclusions. Identifying less obvious stakeholders requires careful thought in order to avoid the omission of relevant information upon which to base evaluation conclusions.

IDENTIFYING RELEVANT EVIDENCE

An important, but often neglected, step in planning an evaluation is to determine what evidence would be considered persuasive for the target audience(s) to which the report is addressed. The evaluation should at the very least be structured so it is as persuasive as possible, whatever its conclusions, to its most immediate audiences. Sometimes that is more difficult than it seems. The obvious outcome of interest for the evaluation of a court-mandated drug treatment program, for example, is to show a decrease in drug abuse. Decrease in drug abuse might be measured in fewer days of substance use, reduced frequency of use per day, or reduced amount of substances used. Yet for some audiences, such evidence might not be persuasive of the success of the program. Taxpayers and the criminal justice system, for example, might view a reduction in substance use as meaningless without evidence of fewer drug-related crimes. Program clients and clinicians might want evidence of improved quality of life as a result of decreased substance use as well as proof of long-term abstinence. Program administrators might want evidence that the program could feasibly be administered in other settings with other clients. Finding out from these stakeholders about the types of evidence they would view as persuasive prior to carrying out the evaluation will increase the

likelihood of such evidence being collected and available for the report.

Designing an evaluation to be persuasive involves the selection of measures that will be considered relevant and satisfactory to the audience for the evaluation report (Sechrest et al., 1982). Because a range of indicators can answer questions about the same program objectives, the evaluator must try to determine which indicators would be the most meaningful to the particular evaluation question. In assessing the effectiveness of a school-based behavioral assessment program, for example, outcome indicators might include the student's self-report of feelings and behaviors, classroom observations of student behaviors, parents' report of the student's feelings and behaviors, school grades, and so on. Conclusions based on the student's report might be quite different from those based on school grades or the parents' report. Quite often, reports of parents and their children correlate only minimally. Thus, selecting indicators that reflect only one perspective is not likely to tell the whole story and may produce biased conclusions not acceptable to all parties.

To address this problem of choosing meaningful indicators of an outcome, the usual recommendation is the use of multiple measures, from multiple sources, reflecting different perspectives. The use of multiple measures is part of a process of inquiry known as critical multiplism (Shadish, 1994). The foundation of the critical multiplist strategy is to carry out the various tasks of scientific inquiry using more than one alternative in order to minimize bias.[1] Selecting measures from a variety of sources (e.g., students, teachers, parents), using a variety of methods (e.g., self-report vs. behavioral observation) and measuring constructs that are related but not exactly the same (e.g., measuring not only attention but anxiety, fatigue, confusion, etc. as well), can help to counter the potential bias inherent in the use of only one of these indicators.

As noted previously, programs have multiple stakeholders who usually have different perspectives on program objectives. When possible, evaluators should select indicators to measure these different objectives. For a school-based behavioral assessment program, it is likely that all stakeholders are interested in indicators of academic performance. The most obvious indicator would be standardized test scores. However, including other indicators of academic performance, such as graded homework assignments, teacher evaluations of student work, and parent reports of students' performance at home, would enhance the picture of student achievement. Indicators of still other outcomes, such as markers of improved classroom management, better social functioning of the child, and improved school image in the eyes of the community, would provide an even more complete picture of the impact of the program. The end result would likely be an evaluation providing broad information about the effects of the program and conclusions ultimately persuasive to diverse stakeholders.

FORMATIVE VERSUS SUMMATIVE EVALUATION AND THE ROLE OF THE EVALUATOR

Both what constitutes an evaluation and what role the evaluator serves are primarily dictated by the purpose of the evaluation. Evaluations can take place in various stages of a program and therefore serve very different purposes. Formative evaluations are used in the early stages of a program to guide program development and/or program improvement. Summative evaluations are appropriate when the goal is to assess program outcomes and/or impact and generally occur during the intermediate and later stages of the program. The activities of an evaluation and the evaluator's role vary depending on evaluation objectives.

Program evaluators may be either internal (or in-house) individuals who are part of the regular program staff, or they may be external—brought in from the outside for the sole purpose of conducting an evaluation. Which relationship is preferable depends on the needs of the evaluation. For example, if familiarity with the program is a critical factor in conducting an evaluation, having an internal person would be preferable; if objectivity is the key factor, then an external person might be needed. Although not a hard-and-fast rule, often an internal evaluator who is familiar with the program can be very useful for formative evaluations, while an objective external person is useful for conducting summative evaluations. Sechrest and colleagues (1982) discuss the various conflicts between evaluators and program personnel that can arise as a result of an internal versus external relationship between the program and the evaluator. Although the discussion is outside the scope of the present chapter, it is worthwhile reading for would-be evaluators.

Whether internal or external, the evaluator's role will change throughout the life stages of the program. Programs are constantly changing and developing, generally in a gradual and often informal manner, altering the program from the way in which it was originally conceived. Program directors make changes in staffing, budget, and program priorities, while clinicians make changes in how they deliver services as they become more experienced. Program client characteristics might change over time as well. Despite these ongoing changes, program evaluations are designed to address the program as it was originally intended to be. However, rather than trying to hold programs constant, it is likely to be more effective to monitor changes as they occur, document them, and measure the effects of programs in terms of phases (Weiss, 1972). In other words, evaluation should be an ongoing process in the context of developing and changing programs (cf. Tharp & Gallimore, 1979). It is in this context that we discuss the elements of program evaluation and the evaluator's role.

Program Planning

As Sechrest (1977) noted decades ago, program evaluation has the best chance at succeeding and being utilized when it is built in and planned for from the program's inception. The reality, however, is that evaluations are commonly requested after a program has been operating for some time. Yet the evaluator and the notion of evaluation will be accepted more readily if they are part of the program operation from the onset. The first point at which an evaluator can have an impact is in assessing need for the program. Because programs are designed to address an existing problem (or to improve a given condition), a needs assessment is useful to specify the nature of the problem or condition and document its extent. In other words, the needs assessment establishes baseline conditions. From those baseline conditions, program evaluators and stakeholders can assess the change in those conditions that took place after the onset of the program or intervention.

The needs assessment also should clearly identify the target population for whom the program is intended. This is particularly important in light of our previous discussion about developing and changing programs in which even the target population might change. For example, a substance abuse program might initially be intended only for adults but as referrals for adolescents increase due to lack of resources for that population, the program might come to serve them equally. That would likely result in program changes, some of which might be substantial. Additionally, with a change in clientele, program objectives might also change, which would have an impact on the evaluation plan and, ultimately, the evaluation report.

The evaluator should assess the needs of the target population as they are relevant to the program. For example, with a substance abusing population, it might be important to female clients to have child care during intensive outpatient treatment programs. Similarly, potential clients might not be able to attend a program if there is no available transportation. Knowledge of these needs can assist program developers in the design of a program that will meet the clients' perceived needs in an optimal way with the given resources. Moreover, if the target population does not see the need for the proposed program, they are not likely to make use of it.

Identifying stakeholders and their perspectives regarding program objectives and outcomes of interest is a critical aspect of needs assessment. Involving these different constituents in the planning phases will not only help in defining the problem to be addressed by the program, but it also should increase their commitment to the program and the evaluation.

Another important role of the evaluator in this program planning stage is to specify the types of questions that can be addressed and information that can be obtained via the evaluation, which can be advantageous in many ways. Careful delineation of just what information may result from an evaluation can prevent evaluation consumers from expecting too much from an evaluator and/or evaluation and therefore avoid disappointment with evaluation results. Furthermore, specifying what can and cannot be addressed by a given evaluation can help guide the design of the program and of the evaluation. For example, if it is determined at the onset that a particular question cannot be addressed given the types of measures that have been selected for the evaluation, then changes can be made to the measurement plan if necessary.

Program Implementation

Another stage in the unfolding of a program in which evaluation is useful is the implementation phase. Evaluation of program implementation is sometimes referred to as process evaluation, or more commonly as program monitoring. Process evaluation involves an assessment of program operations or "inputs" that are expected to result in the desired program effects. Without monitoring these inputs, there is little hope that we can know what contributed to the outcomes; there is only knowledge of what was supposed to or what might have contributed. Yet, as previously discussed, programs undergo changes throughout their lifespan and therefore often do not operate exactly as planned. Without monitoring program operations, we cannot know what types of changes occurred in program implementation, and therefore we will not be able to know what it is about a program that worked or did not work.

Program monitoring heavily involves measurement issues, particularly that of construct validity. Construct validity is the ability to generalize from the operationalizations in a particular study to the theoretical constructs those operationalizations are supposed to reflect (see Cook & Campbell, 1979; Shadish, Cook, & Campbell, 2002). As William Trochim (n.d.) notes, construct validity can be viewed as a "labeling" issue. That is, when we implement what we call a "behavioral assessment" program, is our label accurate? Are we really measuring what we term "depression?" With respect to programs or interventions, we operationalize them by clearly

identifying and defining key features or effective treatment components that we suspect contribute to program outcomes. To establish the connection between these program operations and program outcomes, evaluators should assess implementation or treatment integrity or fidelity and the strength of treatment. These two construct validity issues must be considered in assessing programs if evaluation results are to have any meaning.

Treatment Fidelity

The degree to which a program or intervention has been delivered as planned determines treatment fidelity. The failure to produce desirable outcomes may be due to the fact that the program was not delivered as planned. For example, for a school-based behavioral assessment program designed to assess children in a variety of settings, if assessments are not made in each of the required settings, treatment was not delivered as planned and treatment fidelity would be low. Similarly, fidelity is low when clients miss program sessions or do not engage in activities outside of the program setting that are part of the intervention. The authors conducted an evaluation of a reservation-based substance abuse treatment program where it was discovered that, although clients would show up at the treatment setting, many would eat and chat with each other in the clinic kitchen rather than actually attend treatment sessions. If treatment fidelity were not monitored, it would not have been known that those clients had not engaged in the treatment and that their outcomes were not representative of those for individuals who had the treatment delivered as planned.

The evaluator can help enhance treatment fidelity during the program design phase. By addressing the clarity of the description of the intervention, the degree of staff commitment, the degree of supervision, the feasibility of the intervention, and the target population for the intervention at the program planning stage, the evaluator can help program personnel avoid some of the problems that lead to low fidelity. Plans that are described in vague terms leave room for a variety of interpretations on the part of those involved in program delivery. Programs that involve counseling, for example, could clearly specify the theoretical model (e.g., cognitive behavioral), the amount of time and number of sessions, and possibly the topic of particular sessions. This would leave far less room for interpretation than a program that specifies "counseling" as part of the plan. Furthermore, to avoid varying interpretations of the treatment and actual treatment delivery, planning for close supervision of staff is one helpful way to ensure that the program or intervention is delivered as planned.

Similarly, plans that are not feasible to begin with are far less likely to be delivered successfully. Not infrequently, there is greater demand for than supply of program resources, and program components must be cut—such as when clinicians become overburdened by too many clients and therefore cut back on time spent with each client. Designing the program with feasibility issues in mind can help prevent such problems during the implementation phase. Additionally, levels of staff commitment can affect integrity of treatment delivery. If staff are not supportive of and committed to the program, their delivery of services likely will reflect that. Although it is difficult to assess staff commitment prior to program implementation, evaluators can include staff in the decision-making process when designing the program and address their concerns as well as their ideas for the program from the onset.

Consideration of the target population is also important during the design phase, because delivery of services to a different group can certainly affect outcomes. Defining the target population during the design phase of the study will help the evaluator during the implementation phase to know whether the program is being delivered to the intended population and, if not, measure the effect such an alteration might have on program outcomes.

Finally, it is important to build in a program monitoring system during the design phase of the study to improve the integrity of treatment delivery. If a solid monitoring system is well in place during the program implementation phase, feedback can be obtained and used more immediately. If treatment delivery is not going as planned, the information obtained from the monitoring system can be used to alert program personnel, make alterations if need be, and document changes in order to understand what it was about the program that brought about the observed outcomes.

Strength of Treatment

The strength of treatment has been discussed for decades and concerns the a priori likelihood that a treatment could have the intended outcome (e.g., Yeaton & Sechrest, 1981). Unlike medical treatments in which a specific dosage of a medication is prescribed, social interventions are generally negligent in quantifying interventions in terms of strength. For example, how many hours of a particular type of counseling or how many sessions are necessary to obtain a specific outcome are not addressed. In many cases it is assumed that more of the intervention is better, but how much is optimal is usually not addressed. As in the case of treatment fidelity, strength of treatment is an important factor to consider when assessing a program's effectiveness.

The assessment of treatment strength should be included in the design phase of the program if possible. An evaluator who attempts to measure treatment strength has a better chance of accurately assessing the program's effects. Without knowledge of treatment strength, it is unclear whether weak or nonexistent program effects were due to an inappropriate treatment, an intervention that was administered in too weak a form, or the treatment itself being inherently weak (Yeaton & Sechrest, 1981). In fact, as Sechrest and colleagues (1982) note, it is most likely that potentially effective interventions and programs have been abandoned because they were tested at inappropriately low strengths.

Strength of treatment is difficult to measure with social interventions. However, methodologists have made suggestions for possible approaches that we briefly delineate here (see Sechrest et al., 1982). One source of treatment strength is the adequacy of its theoretical basis. Treatments that have clearly delineated causal mechanisms supported by prior research are strong in this dimension. An intervention with questionable causal mechanisms might be inappropriate for the target problem and/or population and therefore might be weak. Strength also could be assessed by having experts rate the intervention, as it is intended to be delivered, in terms of how much change they would expect to occur. Additionally, norms could be developed for a standard by which to compare the intervention being evaluated. For example, a new substance abuse treatment program could be compared to the "standard of care" or even "treatment as usual." Both of these comparison treatments usually specify required program components, such as a certain number and/or type of counseling sessions or patient visits, against which the new intervention can be measured. Finally, experts could rate the proposed intervention against an ideal one for the given problem for evaluators to gain a sense of the strength of the new intervention via that comparison.

As Sechrest and colleagues discussed earlier, regardless of the method by which the assessment of strength is chosen, there are a few dimensions on which interventions ought to be compared (see Sechrest, West, Phillips, Redner, & Yeaton, 1979). For example, intervention intensity is an important dimension, the indicators of which could be frequency of client contacts per week or number of hours per week the client is engaged in a particular intervention activity. The length of intervention is also an indicator of treatment strength, as is the clarity of the intervention plan and the qualifications and/or training of the staff. Additionally, specificity of the intervention focus is an important dimension of strength. For example, a specific problem such as heroin abuse and dependence would reflect greater treatment strength than a broader and less clear focus such as improving self-esteem.

Program Monitoring

The previous discussion addresses how the integrity and strength of program delivery can be dealt with during the program planning stages. Yet additional questions about strength and integrity can only be addressed during program operation and after. Regarding treatment integrity, the evaluator and program personnel should make an a priori determination of the boundaries within, which a program can fluctuate and still be considered the intended program. That is, it is important to establish how far an intervention can deviate from what was intended and still be considered to have been implemented (see Patton, 1978, for a still relevant discussion). The evaluator must be able to determine not only whether the treatment was delivered as intended, but whether it was delivered at all. Regarding strength of treatment, evaluators must assess whether mediating processes expected to occur as a result of the intervention actually did occur. If it is expected that a school-based behavioral assessment program will change the contingencies maintaining a particular problematic learning style, then it must be established that the change in contingencies actually occurred.

There are several methods for monitoring a program in order to address these concerns, only a few of which we discuss here. For one, evaluators can measure the extent to which the target population is utilizing the services. Program records as well as client surveys can tell evaluators exactly who is making use of the program, giving an indication of whether the program is reaching the intended population. Another important method is to collect as much information as possible regarding program operations in order to gain a picture of the daily realities of the program. Evaluators can do so with direct observations of service delivery or indirect measures of how the program or intervention was delivered. Direct observations could include, for example, the evaluator watching program personnel deliver the intervention and documenting what occurs or the use of less reactive measures such as audio- or videotaped intervention sessions in which the program staff and its clients are not immediately aware of being observed. Indirect measures could include, for example, having service delivery staff and/or clients provide reports of how services or interventions are delivered. Additionally, program records such as counts of client visits, service delivery hours, and types of services provided can be used. Many types of evidence can be used to indicate the quality and quantity of program services or the intervention. For example, if a substance abuse program provides van transportation to clients, the van driver can keep daily records of the number of clients transported. Similarly, if bus passes are allotted or massage therapy is offered as part of the pro-

gram, records can be kept of how many bus passes have been given out to clients and how many massages are given per day, week, month, etc. Even program brochures, flyers, or other sources of program media can be collected to document service delivery. In the evaluation of a substance abuse program, the authors collected brochures and flyers and created a "program journal" to document program services such as monthly "clean urinalysis" celebrations, new 12-step meetings, community events, and grand openings. Direct and indirect observations of treatment delivery as well as program records can assist the evaluator in knowing exactly what type of intervention is being delivered. Knowing what actually occurred versus what is supposed to occur is necessary if the evaluator is to be able to link outcomes with specific program factors.

Assessment of Outcomes

Although program development and monitoring are important evaluation tasks, the assessment of program effects usually are the reason an evaluation was called for and certainly are of ultimate interest. Outcomes evaluations do not necessarily occur only at the point of termination of a program, but instead reflect an ongoing process in which short-term, intermediate, and long-term objectives are measured as the program operates, develops, and changes. Activities associated with these types of evaluations include the formulation of program objectives, development of outcome criteria, and identification of appropriate measures. Although it would be optimal if the evaluator were involved in these tasks during the program development phase, that is generally not the case. Therefore, it is important that a clear understanding and statement of objectives exist before the outcomes evaluation gets underway.

One way in which evaluators can obtain a clear understanding of program objectives is to draw up a logic model for the program (Bickman, 1987). The logic model depicts the theory or action of a program in a graphic representation that links program inputs (i.e., resources) to program outputs (e.g., activities, products, services) and eventually to program results (i.e., the results and benefits for individuals, groups, agencies, communities, etc.).[2] The model generally includes a description of the target population, program resources (e.g., personnel, physical resources, finances, etc.), program activities or "action steps," program components (groupings of conceptually related activities such as educating, counseling, social marketing, etc.), outcomes and objectives (including implementation benchmarks, intermediate and long-range), and measures or indicators to be used.

Logic models serve a variety of useful purposes for the evaluator and program personnel. Formulating a logic model requires program personnel to make explicit the program theory of action, which is, in fact, quite often based on implicit assumptions that may or may not be tenable. Creating a logic model forces persons involved in the program to verbalize their assumptions about how program actions and outcomes are linked and how resources will be used, which, in turn, allows these assumptions to be questioned. Logic models also serve as a blueprint for the program, which can guide the design of the evaluation. These models highlight key variables to target for the evaluation, including important benchmarks for program monitoring, as well as variables that are thought to be part of the causal chain between the program actions and the outcomes. The identification of these key variables informs the design of a measurement plan as well as a data collection and analysis plan. Furthermore, a logic model can help program personnel develop strategies for many of the program operations, such as recruiting participants, designing interventions, program monitoring, and so on. And, a note of no small importance, the logic model serves as a useful and simple means by which to communicate the program theory owing to the intuitive appeal of a graphic depiction of complex concepts.

Engaging program stakeholders in the development of the logic model is a useful way to incorporate multiple perspectives and develop program objectives to address concerns of a variety of program stakeholders. As we pointed out earlier, asking these constituents about the program objectives and outcomes in which they are interested can guide the evaluator in identifying key variables, appropriate measures of those variables, and the methods for analyzing the data. Because stakeholders have different values and concerns regarding the program, designing the evaluation at the onset to collect relevant information increases the likelihood that evaluation results will be meaningful and conclusions will be more persuasive to program constituents.

Involving multiple perspectives in the development of program objectives can result in a wide range of outcomes on which to focus the evaluation. Thus, it is the task of the evaluator to prioritize and incorporate these interests. Evaluations cannot be all things to all people without going far beyond the resources likely to be available; the evaluator must, therefore, limit the scope of the evaluation for a variety of reasons, including feasibility, relevance, and purpose of the evaluation. Establishing priorities of interests and stakeholder preferences may be approached in different ways, ranging from quantitative approaches (e.g., assigning weights based on importance and selecting those with the greatest value) to personal preference to "value-free" evaluations

(Scriven, 1991). Evaluation and decision researchers have discussed the pros and cons of a variety of means by which to identify and prioritize interests in a vast literature beyond the scope of the present chapter. (Interested readers are referred to Luce and Raiffa's, 1957, classic discussion of group decision making in which the authors discuss methods by which individual choices are combined to yield social decisions. Additionally, Shadish, Cook, & Leviton, 1991, provide an interesting discussion about the science of valuing and measurement of utilities.)

The effects of program interventions cannot be guaranteed to be limited to those expected by program planners. *Unintended consequences* are common, sometimes good, but often undesirable. Sometimes consequences are unanticipated because program planners are inexperienced; these consequences would have been expected by more experienced professionals. If program planners are known to be new to areas in which they are intending to intervene, evaluators would do well to consult with more experienced planners so as to be able to anticipate and measure all program outcomes. For example, experienced program planners know that the scope of certain kinds of programs is difficult to limit because of the "widening of the net" phenomenon, referring to the tendency of some types of services to attract clients of increasingly marginal eligibility, resulting very often in the overburdening of program resources and dilution of service packages. Evaluators who recognize the risk of that consequence can build that knowledge into their evaluation strategy so that any such effects are detected and taken into account in interpreting outcomes.

Additionally, program effects may be anticipated but not be regarded as within the goals of the program. An assertiveness training program, for example, might be intended to improve the prospects of shy, withdrawing employees, but any improvement in their status would be at the expense of other employees. A fair evaluator should plan to examine such effects, even if they are not the focus of program efforts. Scriven (1991) has discussed the concept of "goal free" evaluation to suggest that evaluations should be open to all program effects, not just those delineated in specific objectives. Undertaking such an approach in its purest form—that is, when the evaluator is completely blind to the specified program objectives—has disadvantages, such as the lack of structure provided by the expectations of assessing specific objectives. Therefore Scriven (1991) recommends a hybrid approach in which evaluators are aware of and plan for the assessment of specific program objectives but also are prepared to assess effects outside the range of specified objectives.

Difficulties arise, in some cases extending into the tragic, when undesirable program effects are not anticipated because of lack of knowledge or, worse, lack of foresight. In a book dedicated to describing a wide range of unintended consequences of twentieth-century ingenuity, Tenner (1996) describes a variety of unforeseen outcomes of well-intended programs and interventions. One such program was the introduction of technologically advanced protective headgear into the sport of collegiate football in order to decrease injuries. Unfortunately, the program had the paradoxical effect of actually increasing serious injuries, particularly spinal fracture and paralysis. When an orthopedic surgeon studied the problem, he concluded that the stronger plastic helmets enabled players to use their headgear like a battering ram in order to stop opponents. As Tenner writes:

> When they bent their heads forward, the spine straightened. Like a freight train hitting an obstacle on the track, the spinal column, propelled by the body's momentum, kept moving after the helmet struck its target. What seemed to be a technological solution had become an extension of the . . . problem (p. 217).

Similarly, social programs and/or interventions can have unintended consequences despite a planner's best efforts and expertise. A frequently cited example is the "deinstitutionalization" of patients with serious mental illness that began to occur in the late 1960s. Although the goals of deinstitutionalization were highly desirable, the net result was to put many, many psychiatric patients into communities that probably could not make proper provision for them so that many ended up on the streets and in jails and prisons. It is critically important for evaluations to document such outcomes if others are to benefit and programs are to be improved. In order to do so, evaluators ought to plan, from the beginning, for mechanisms to detect outcomes that are not part of the prespecified evaluation objectives.

It is useful to think of program outcomes in terms of a multistage model that is akin to one currently widely used in health services research (Figueredo & Sechrest, 2001). The general model may be represented as shown in Figure 14.1.

The model as portrayed in Figure 14.1 differs from the simple model usually used in clinical settings by the addition on the right side of *outcomes* as a variable in the evaluation. Clinical research often concerns itself only with whether an intervention (treatment) produces changes in specified clinical indicators. For example, for quite a few years many behavior therapists used snake phobia as a test-bed for treatment efficacy. The typical outcomes used in assessing treatment were such observations as the "closeness of approach" to a snake before and after treatment and self-reported anxiety about snakes. Measures of that sort may be termed *analogue measures* (Haynes, 2001), being regarded as highly similar

Figure 14.1 Health services outcomes model.

to the sorts of situations that people might meet in their natural environments, although clearly not identical to them. Similarly, in medical research, it is common to test the effects of treatments on such clinical indicators as blood pressure, change in CD4 cell count, or reported frequency of headaches.

Outcomes are assumed to be at least partially dependent on clinical improvement, but they represent the consequences in people's lives of clinical interventions. The same idea applies directly to evaluation of programs aimed at social problems. A school program to improve the self-esteem of children, for example, might actually increase self-esteem scores. The more important question, however, is "so what?" That is, what difference does it make in children's lives if their self-esteem is improved? Will they do better in school? Get into less trouble? Get along better with other kids? Outcomes assessment assumes that the ultimate reason for intervention is to make a difference in people's lives. What is it that people are able to do after an intervention that they could not do before?

Generally speaking, program evaluators are interested in latent variables rather than manifest indicators (Bollen & Lenox, 1991). That is, the variables we observe (measure) are usually of interest because they show something about an underlying variable that is in some sense more fundamental but cannot be directly observed. The model shown in Fig. 14.2 is a latent variable model and one more in accord with the real interests of a program evaluator.

Suppose an intervention aimed at improving employment prospects is being evaluated. The program is supposed to increase the work potential of candidates as a relatively direct and immediate outcome. Work potential, though, is a variable that can only be estimated; it cannot be assessed directly by some measure (e.g., in the way that the length of a field can be measured). The evaluator would have to look for indicators of work potential that might be influenced by the program. In the case illustrated, the job training program was thought to influence work habits, specific work skills, and sense of personal efficacy. Presumably, if those variables were not affected, then there would be no reason to think that employment prospects would have improved. The outcome desired from the program is an improvement in the individual's employment status. Again, that variable is considered latent, but it is reflected in measures of income, adequacy of

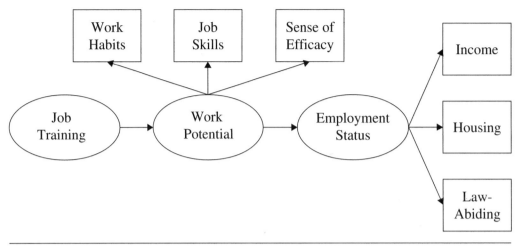

Figure 14.2   Outcomes assessment model for a job training program.

housing, and being a law-abiding member of society. (Many other potential indicators might exist, of course.) The model portrayed is a *mediated* model since the effects of the intervention on the ultimate outcome are mediated by the effects on work potential.

Even outcomes themselves may be related in different ways. The model for the job training program assumed that employment status would be reflected in three indicators (which might or might not be related to one another). Another possibility, however, is that the three outcome indicators might be modeled income leading to improved housing leading to becoming a law-abiding member of society. That is, the effect of improved work potential would result in increased income, which leads to better housing, which in turn leads to law-abiding behavior. According to that model, if income did not result in better housing (e.g., by getting the person out of a bad neighborhood), then the goal of greater law-abiding behavior would not be met.

Many models of outcomes are possible, especially if evaluators think in terms of levels of program effects, multiple effects, and multiple indicators. The important point is that evaluators need to think carefully about what effects may be expected of an intervention and how those effects might be manifested in relation to each other.

Measurement

All program objectives and other potential consequences must be related to specific operational indicators of them. Selection of appropriate outcome indicators is a critical part of the evaluation since, as noted earlier, a variety of indicators can answer questions about the same program objective. The first step for the evaluator is to make judgments about what indicators best reflect program objectives. For example, for a

substance abuse program, although the intermediate goal is to decrease substance use, the ultimate objective usually is to decrease the harmful consequences such as crime, health problems, and so on. Indicators of crime rates and health care usage might be better indicators of program effects than measures of frequency and rate of substance use. Using logic models and working with program planners and stakeholders can help the evaluator to make these judgments. Using multiple indicators in the spirit of critical multiplism can help prevent the biases associated with the use of indicators that reflect a single perspective or a single method of measurement (e.g., gathering only self-report data).

Whatever measures are selected for use in a program evaluation, they should be included with due regard for their psychometric properties. It is not necessarily the case that psychometric expectations can be met any more by simply reporting a reliability coefficient and citing a study or two said to establish validity. To some extent, "new rules of measurement" apply (Embretson, 1996), and more attention is required to document the characteristics of observations as measures. It is becoming increasingly important to show in detail exactly how a given set of observations (e.g., items, problems, behaviors) may be taken to represent a quantity of the variable involved.

Measuring Change

No problem has proven more challenging than the measurement of change. The problem is not actually one of arithmetic—that is, deciding whether the second of two observations is quantitatively different from the first—but rather one of inference about the meaning of any observed difference, or lack thereof. Suppose a child in a behavioral treatment shows a decline over a school term in frequency of disruptive behaviors in the classroom. Assuming that one has a good system of observation and counting, one can be confident that the number of disruptions observed in the last week of the term is smaller than the number observed in the first week. The important questions are whether the change is real (dependable), whether the change is attributable to the treatment, whether the change is linear, and whether the change is important.

Change scores may be considered reliable or dependable if they enable one to distinguish between two persons with respect to amount of change (or between two time periods or between two sets of circumstances). The reliability of change scores depends on the separate reliabilities of the two observations involved. If one or both of the observations is not reliable, then the difference between them cannot be reliable. For example, if a pretest given to children is too difficult so that a large proportion of children score at a chance level, then change from the pretest to a posttest cannot be reliable. Measurement of change starts with selection of good measurement tools.

Measurement of change also starts with careful specification of what is supposed to change and with assurance that measures are appropriate to one's expectations. There is no point in selecting measures that cannot be expected to change as a result of whatever intervention is to be tried. For example, it is not that parental attendance at school functions is an "insensitive" measure of interventions to increase parental involvement in school affairs, but that parental attendance is really difficult to change. By contrast, many types of self-report measures are easy to change, but that does not mean that they are more sensitive. In any case, if one wants in the final analysis to increase parental attendance at school affairs, then it is better to plan an intervention that will actually change attendance and then measure that phenomenon.

One of the difficulties in attributing observed change to program interventions is that any changes resulting from those interventions are likely to occur in the context of many other changes that may either exaggerate or mask program effects. Secular change—change in the broader societal context—is continuous and pervasive. It would be possible, for example, that because of changes in school policies and teacher experience, disciplinary problems would decline generally over the course of a school term, and any change in children in treatment groups would simply reflect those changes. Moreover, groups and people also change individually over time, and a decrease in a child's disruptive behavior might be part of a normal developmental process. The aim of sound scientific research designs is to make attributions of causes for change as certain as possible.

Whether an observed change is important is also a matter of considerable importance. A change must be large enough in magnitude to have implications that are of interest in relation to the resources, effort, and time required to produce the change. As is well known, statistical significance is not a guide to either the magnitude of a change nor its importance (Cohen, 1988; Jacobson & Truax, 1991). To be important, a change must be large enough to make a difference in some outcome of importance. Jacobson and Truax (1991) devised a method of expressing the magnitude of change in terms of the degree to which deviant or abnormal behaviors or characteristics are moved toward "normal" as statistically defined. Sechrest, McKnight, and McKnight (1996) proposed an alternative approach involving calibration of scores or values of observations in terms of their implications or their obviousness to other persons. It is also possible to characterize change in terms of the costs of producing it (e.g., in terms of payments to professionals); a change made only at very great cost would have to be examined carefully to determine its worth.

One final question of great importance is whether change is linear or whether the function relating change to time may have some other form. For example, a common alternative functional form is asymptotic; that is, change occurs rapidly at first and then levels off to a plateau. Another common alternative is that the function is U-shaped (or inverted U-shaped) with change occurring early that is later reversed. The shape of a change function cannot be estimated with only two points of measurement, a situation that is regrettably common in program evaluation (e.g., in simple pre-post designs). With only two data points, even if there is change from the first to the second, one cannot tell whether change might be expected to progress further or whether maximum change has been achieved. Or, if there is no difference between pre and post measures, one cannot be certain that change did not occur only to be lost in a relapse. Studies attempting to assess change over time should, whenever possible, include at least three data points (observations). In that way, the functional form of change can be estimated.[3]

If at least three data points are available, then it is usually possible to express change in terms of a growth function, or growth curve. The slope of a growth curve is the rate of change over time. One may also calculate the intercept, or beginning point. Both of these values can then be used in ordinary statistical analyses, including general linear models, as well as more complex multivariate models such as multilevel models and structural equations models. Predictors of change as well as initial starting point can be included in the model to test theories of change as well as to assess those factors that are most responsible for change.

Assessing Costs and Benefits

With the growing demands for accountability of all sorts, there is an increasing demand for the assessment of benefits of social interventions in relation to the costs of producing them. Successful programs are usually thought of as those whose benefits exceed the costs. Yet defining costs and benefits can be a difficult task for the evaluator, particularly one who is not trained in economics. With respect to assessing the utility or value of a program, costs and benefits are generally expressed in monetary terms. At the simplest level, costs can be defined as the actual amount of money spent on implementing the program, and benefits can be defined as the amount of money saved as a result of the program. However, most program stakeholders are also interested in program costs and benefits to which it is difficult to assign a market value. For example, in a program designed to reduce the number of teacher absences by posting attendance records in the teachers' lounge, monetary costs might include the cost of the materials and staff time for collecting and keeping such records. These are referred to as the direct costs of the program. Nonmonetary or indirect costs might be demoralization or resentment on the part of the teachers, increased workplace stress, and decreased interest and effort in teaching. Monetary benefits might include reduced overtime pay and less expenditure on substitute teacher pay. Nonmonetary benefits could be greater parent satisfaction, improved student performance, and decreased stress on administrators, to all of which it is difficult to assign a monetary value.

To add further difficulty, defining costs and benefits can be quite controversial, particularly when what appears to be a benefit to some might be a cost to others. Referring back to our posting example, although reduced reliance on substitute teachers might be seen as a benefit to school administrators and staff, it is likely that substitutes would not view reduced work hours in a beneficial light. In fact, just as determining program objectives and outcomes can be difficult, some of the difficulty in defining costs and benefits is deciding on whose perspective to take. Stakeholders represent multiple viewpoints that would likely result in multiple opinions about costs and benefits, some of which might even conflict. As noted previously, methods by which to prioritize program constituents' interests exist and ought to be considered carefully when designing and implementing the evaluation.

Another difficulty associated with assessing costs and benefits is expressing them in a meaningful metric by which they can be compared. For example, how many units of parental satisfaction do we need to outweigh the number of lost jobs for substitute teachers in order to conclude that program benefits outweigh the costs? How can we possibly compare

levels of parental satisfaction against levels of teacher resentment and come to a conclusion that one outweighs the other? In formal cost-benefit analyses, costs and benefits are expressed in monetary terms in order for them to be (a) expressed in a meaningful metric and (b) standardized so they can be directly compared. However, placing a monetary value on variables for which no market prices exist (e.g., an unpleasant work environment or parental satisfaction), can create even greater complexity and controversy when assessing costs and benefits than trying to obtain consensus from multiple stakeholders. In a formal cost-benefit analysis, monetary values are assigned either directly (as in dollars saved) or indirectly (as in the "cost" of 1 quality life year). The following summary from the Congressional Research Service (n.d.) Report for Congress highlights the complexity of cost-benefit analysis:

> The difficulty is that most public actions to improve public well-being do not have well established private markets which generate price information on which to judge their value or benefits. To compare the public benefit of such actions to their costs, benefits (and sometimes costs) are indirectly estimated in dollar terms. The objective is to determine the alternative for public action that produces the largest net gain to the society. In this case, gain is not in terms of private sector profit, but rather as an estimated surplus of monetized benefits over estimated costs. Based on this criterion, cost-benefit analysis attempts to identify the most economically efficient way of meeting a public objective.

Thus, the difficulty lies in estimating these dollar values. This is done indirectly by considering the dollar value of indicators associated with the factors of interest. For example, assigning a dollar value to parental satisfaction might include the price of school tuition (happy parents continue sending their children to the school), parental donations to the school, etc. Deciding which indirect costs to include is not a simple task and generally requires the help of an economist. Thus, many program evaluators do not undertake a formal cost-benefit analysis to assess the value of a program. These are very expensive and, as noted, complicated and not without controversy.

Although a formal cost-benefit analysis would probably increase the persuasiveness of evaluation conclusions, it is not necessary in order to compare program costs to benefits. Evaluators can discuss the costs and benefits of a program without focusing on monetary values. Some evaluators carry out this task by discussing all program effects, positive and negative, and leaving it to the stakeholders to arrive at a position regarding whether these effects are costs or benefits. Without discussing monetary values, stakeholders themselves can conclude whether the positive outcomes of the program are worth the negative consequences. Sometimes program benefits are considered to be so great that the costs are irrelevant. For example, in a program designed to teach safe street crossing to young children, nobody would argue against such a program by stating the costs outweigh the benefits. For such programs, the benefit is a moral one upon which nobody cares to make a cost estimate. In such cases, stakeholders and evaluators are more interested in cost-effectiveness. That is, the benefit is given, and therefore the question is whether it can be achieved at a lesser cost. In cost-effectiveness evaluations, two or more methods or programs for obtaining the same objective are compared with respect to their costs. If the programs achieve the outcome equally well, it is generally the case that the least costly program will be selected.

Even if an evaluator does not have the expertise or access to an economist to conduct a formal cost-benefit analysis, different types of program costs discussed in the economics literature can have heuristic value that can be incorporated into an outcomes evaluation. For example, economists discuss programs in terms of "true costs," or costs that are incurred by a program but typically are not considered to be direct output. The cost of cattle ranching, for example, might be defined as the cost of cattle feed, water, land, veterinary expenses, the cattle themselves, and the wages of the ranchers. But this accounting process does not take into account the soil erosion and water pollution that result from cattle ranching. The costs associated with these problems might include clean-up costs, medical bills associated with illnesses that are a result of the polluted water, and so on. These indirect costs are part of the entire package of costs associated with cattle ranching, and thus reflect the "true costs" of that enterprise. Similarly, the cost of a pack of cigarettes does not reflect the true cost of smoking. True costs would include the health care costs associated with smoking-related health problems.

One need not calculate these true costs in actual dollar amounts in order for the concept to be of use for an evaluation. Instead, the notion of true costs can be useful in forcing evaluators and program planners to anticipate possible costs of the program that go beyond the dollars spent on program operations. That is, the notion of true costs includes both the immediate and long-term effects of a program. By considering indirect program costs as well, the evaluator is able to plan for and assess a wider range of program impacts, some of which might not be intended. Thus, the consideration and inclusion of the true costs of the program in an evaluation will improve our understanding of the actual program impact as well as its value.

The following example illustrates the utility of considering true costs. The Violence Policy Center produced a report about the indirect costs of the promotion of gun ownership for the purposes of self-defense (see http://www.vpc.org/studies/uninsum.htm for a summary of the report). The authors of this report state that, contrary to the intentions of the promotion of handguns to allow citizens to protect themselves, the majority of gun owners are either ignorant of or fail to practice basic handgun safety and, worse, do not have the necessary handgun combat marksmanship skills to successfully defend themselves without harming innocent others. Undoubtedly, the costs of consequences such as these are high. An evaluation that focuses only on the direct or immediate effects of this program—that is, increased handgun sales—fails to take into consideration other possible outcomes. In this case, an indirect and unintended consequence of the program is increased mortality due to the improper use of handguns. An evaluation of the program without this important information is limited indeed, and fails to provide program stakeholders (in this case, the general public) with important, relevant information by which to judge the program's utility.

Another useful concept to consider is that of "opportunity cost." To summarize, because we do not have the economic means to satisfy all of our wants and needs, we need to make decisions about how to spend our money and use our time. These decisions involve tradeoffs. When we make a choice about spending our money and our time, we give up an opportunity to do something else.[4] For example, in order to provide behavioral assessment, a clinic might have to give up the salaries of therapists who provide another form of intervention, say family systems therapy. Similarly, when a client purchases behavioral assessment, he or she gives up seeking treatment elsewhere, perhaps from a more suitable modality. The highest-valued alternative we give up is the opportunity cost of our decision.

With programs, opportunity costs are incurred when the decision is made to implement one type of program instead of another. Similarly, opportunity costs are incurred when a client decides on one program over another. The costs are derived from the highest-valued alternative that was given up. Therefore, if a program has great value (which is not necessarily only monetary), the opportunity cost of deciding on that program versus another one would likely be quite low because the alternative does not have as high a value. However, when other programs exist and are of greater value, then opportunity costs can be great. For example, if one type of intervention for classroom conduct problems is known to be more effective than another, there is an opportunity cost to selecting the less effective intervention. The money and time invested in the less successful treatment is lost, and possibly so is the parents', teachers', and/or students' confidence in interventions for classroom conduct problems, as well as their morale. Such costs can be high.

Design Issues

Perhaps the simplest question one can ask about a program is at what level its participants are functioning when they leave. Often, such a question is answered with a single observation, such as "students who completed the behavioral assessment program reduced problem behaviors by 50% or greater." Evaluation, however, goes beyond such simple observation to allow causal inferences that are as unambiguous as possible about a program and its effects. This is a task that is rarely straightforward but is of crucial importance in determining the utility of an evaluation. To the extent that the evaluation design allows one to rule out alternative explanations of causal relationships, it produces clear and useful information. To the extent that it allows alternative explanations of the results, the evaluation is problematic and has failed to fulfill one of its primary objectives.

Of concern is that the evaluation generates a product that is valid, in a general sense. Validity has been conceptualized as consisting of subtypes varying in specificity (cf. Cook & Campbell, 1979; Shadish, Cook, & Campbell, 2002), which are reflected in the various conclusions growing out of a study. Problems with validity will therefore depend on the nature of the statement whose validity is at issue. For example, at the end of an evaluation, we might conclude that children in the experimental group were significantly better off than those in the comparison group with respect to standardized test scores and aggressive behaviors. Or we might conclude that systematic behavioral assessment improved academic performance and behavioral problems. Each of these statements implies that the evaluation was a valid test of some proposition, but the validity implications are somewhat different for each statement. We briefly discuss four validity concepts described in detail by Cook and Campbell (1979) and more recently by Shadish, Cook, and Campbell (2002) to illustrate these types of concerns.

Statistical Conclusion Validity

The confidence one is able to place in the conclusions of an evaluation depends initially on the adequacy of the statistical justification for the conclusions. For example, conclusions would be questionable if they were based on a test for which the data failed to meet important statistical assumptions or if inappropriate statistical tests were used. Frequent potential sources of invalid statistical conclusions are low statistical power, the use of unreliable outcome measures, and "data mining"—or multiple explorations of the data to search out statistical significance. To protect against threats to statistical conclusion validity, obviously one must plan a study carefully so as to have measures of adequate reliability, sufficient sample sizes for the desired statistical power, and a data analysis plan that is appropriate given the evaluation question. Unlike some of the other validity problems, those involving the validity of statistical conclusions are usually easily identified and most are under the control of the evaluator.

Internal Validity

To the extent that an alternative explanation remains possible for the outcome of a study, the research lacks internal validity. Experimental designs are implemented to increase confidence in the internal validity of a study. These designs are intended to allow the investigator to make the claim that the observed difference between the group receiving the intervention and a comparison group are due to the intervention and not the result of some extraneous factor. For example, if assignment to an intervention required parental consent, differences between those in the intervention condition and those in the comparison group might be related to some initial differences in the children rather than to the intervention itself. Lacking random assignment to conditions, internal validity is a concern, which calls into question evaluation conclusions based on the comparison of these two groups.

Construct Validity

Conclusions about interventions or programs assume that the nature of the program is known and described accurately. However, as noted previously, that is not always the case. Often programs are multifaceted and complex, leaving one uncertain as to what the critical elements of the program might be. Additionally, interventions are rarely delivered as planned. Our confidence in the construct validity of our programs is proportional to the adequacy by which they are described, the strength of their underlying rationale, and the extent of the documentation of their implementation (Sechrest et al., 1982).

External Validity

We are rarely interested in the specific outcome of a single research study. Instead, we are interested in how well the results would apply to other settings, populations, resources, and so on. The extent to which study findings are generalizable reflects external validity. There are many reasons why findings from a single study might not be generalizable. For example, if a sample is narrowly defined (e.g., only those with depression who have no comorbid diagnoses), findings might not apply to a broader population (e.g., anyone diagnosed with depression). Similarly, the manner in which an intervention was delivered (e.g., reinforcement) might not be applicable to other versions of that intervention. Additionally, the types of problems addressed by the program might not apply to other populations, and specific measures used (e.g., eye contact and polite requests) might not generalize to the broader concepts we claim to be measuring (e.g., social skills).

Often the greatest limitation on external validity is the reactive nature of research studies. That is, research studies, particularly true experiments, are often carried out in such specialized arrangements that the findings are not generalizable outside of the experimental situation. In fact, the "Hawthorne effect"—the tendency of research participants to respond differently when they believe they are part of an experiment—is one potential threat to external validity. Additionally, conditions of an experiment can produce a pressure for certain types of responses, a phenomenon known by social psychologists as demand characteristics (Orne, 1969).[5]

True Experiments

In general, issues of internal validity can be considered prior to all others because other issues are moot if we are unable to assert that a particular program or intervention produced a particular outcome. True experiments are research designs that are intended to allow investigators to rule out alternative explanations of results. Internal validity concerns are appeased by these designs due primarily to two important features: random assignment and the inclusion of a control group. Random assignment helps prevent initial differences between groups prior to receiving an intervention, which might in turn be responsible for outcomes rather than the intervention itself. Control groups also help to ensure the initial equivalence of research participants so that the only difference between them is that some received the intervention and others did not.

True experiments often are considered the gold standard by which to compare all other study designs. They are highly desirable in terms of their strength in ruling out alternative explanations, and they are persuasive to even the toughest audiences. However, these designs are not without their limitations. Often, the experimental control that is required to rule out possible alternative explanations can be so tight as to render the conditions within the study nonrepresentative of the "real world." That is, low external validity can be the

price for high internal validity. For example, randomly assigning individuals to interventions likely does not reflect the state of affairs outside of the experiment, in which individuals choose interventions for many reasons and therefore do not simply accept whatever is given to them. Moreover, many people are not willing to be assigned to an intervention in which they are not interested. Another potential problem is the inability to randomly assign individuals to interventions due to the nature of the setting, characteristics of the population, the problem of interest, etc. For example, in a tight-knit community it is often impossible to randomly assign one member to one intervention and their friend or relative to another, particularly when one intervention appears to be more attractive than the other.

Similarly, investigators are often concerned about randomly assigning individuals who appear to be in need of assistance to a no-treatment condition or to what might be perceived as a weaker intervention. This is often the case in psychotherapy studies. Objections are often raised to randomization of interventions on the grounds that valuable, or at least potentially valuable, treatments are being withheld from some individuals. Although it is obvious that it would be unethical to withhold an effective treatment from someone who could benefit from it, it also can be argued that an untested intervention, especially one thought to require justification through a research demonstration of its effectiveness, is not in fact a treatment. Evaluations are generally conducted because the effectiveness of the intervention is not yet known, and perhaps in question. Problems arise, however, because that doubt is held in different degrees by different persons involved in delivering the intervention. Clinicians, for example, may not be as doubtful as those who provide funding for the intervention and therefore might be opposed to withholding it to facilitate an evaluation that they regard as superfluous.

It is not always the case that ethical concerns and good research design cannot be compatible. Designs in which treatment is delayed (i.e., a wait-list control design) can be feasible and address ethical concerns to the extent that individuals awaiting treatment must endure distress. A delayed treatment design is most advantageous in settings in which the treatment would naturally be delayed due to the incapacity of the program to handle all of the clients in an immediate fashion. In such cases, determining who receives treatment first via a randomization process would seem to be eminently fair. Other potential ethical alternatives to randomization include offering an alternative treatment in lieu of placebo—one that might be weaker than the experimental intervention. Another possibility is to break down an intervention into its components, if doing so will not destroy its integrity, and then offer the components separately to different groups at different times.

It is important to note that a paradox arises in planning any comparison of interventions that can have important consequences for evaluation conclusions. Specifically, as the condition against which the experimental intervention is to be compared is made stronger, the probability of finding any advantage for the experimental treatment decreases. Thus, decisions based on ethical concerns should take into account the whole spectrum of ethical issues, including the possibility that a poorly planned evaluation study could be risky to participants as well as provide inconclusive findings. In other words, it could be regarded as unethical to involve people in a study out of which no prospects for quality data will emerge. Moreover, it is often the case that innovative interventions prove worse than standard treatments, and therefore thought should be given to the presumption that withholding experimental treatments somehow puts participants at a disadvantage (e.g., see Sechrest, West, Phillips, Redner, & Yeaton, 1979).

Quasi-Experimental Designs

Where true experimental design is not feasible, we must use the next strongest design. Quasi-experimental designs include some of the features of true experiments and therefore can provide information that is of the quality approaching that of an experiment and thus permitting reasonable definitive conclusions (Cook & Campbell, 1979; Shadish et al., 2002). What is important is that the design alternatives be carefully considered and that the strongest possible design consistent with circumstances be chosen. Choice of the best design will require a careful analysis of the threats to validity and of the immediate circumstances that rule out a randomized experiment.

Probably the most commonly used quasi-experimental design is the nonequivalent control group design (NCGD), in which there is a comparison group and individuals get into the comparison group by means other than randomization. Because the comparison group is not chosen randomly, it is assumed to be nonequivalent to the intervention group. Therefore, the challenge with such designs is to make the comparison group as much like the intervention group as possible. To do so, investigators must try to equate individuals who make up the comparison group with those in the intervention group on variables that are assumed to be relevant to the claim that the intervention, and not one of these variables, is responsible for the differences between the groups. For example, a comparison group for children with behavioral problems being treated in a school environment should be other children with highly similar problems and from similar circumstances. The challenge when working with NCGDs is to develop the best possible comparison group. Using the same example, if the school-based intervention is taking a large proportion of the children with behavioral problems, it might be better to find children from other schools with the same types of problems for the comparison group rather than children from the same school whose behaviors are less problematic. The task for the investigator is to anticipate plausible alternative explanations that the treatment is responsible for differences between groups at the conclusion of the study, and weaken them as much as possible using solid research design. NCGDs are useful to the extent that groups are comparable and threats to validity are weakened by other means.

One means by which to weaken alternative explanations is to use multiple comparison groups, each of which helps to weaken one or more alternatives and which, in theory, leave the experimental hypothesis as the best explanation. As long as it does not become too resource-intensive, these multiple comparison groups can be of value. A study of children with behavioral problems, for example, might use as comparison groups children with behavioral problems in other programs, those whose parents refused to enter them into the program, those in a community lacking any program, and perhaps children whose problems are less severe and therefore cannot participate.

Matching is a tactic investigators often use as a means for equating groups, but there are some serious problems that almost always make it an undesirable method. One can probably never match individuals on all relevant variables and would have no way of confirming it anyway. Matching also often increases the potential for regression effects, sometimes resulting in an alternative explanation that did not initially exist in a NCGD. Studies employing matching have great potential for being positively misleading and should be viewed with suspicion (Cook & Campbell, 1979).

Time series designs are another quasi-experimental design that often yields high-quality data and defensible conclusions. The interrupted time series utilizes a series of measures taken before the intervention, during the baseline period, and after the intervention starts. Such designs are common in the evaluation of behavioral interventions with individual subjects but, in that context, usually lack a statistical analysis and depend for their interpretation on tactics such as removal of treatment with subsequent observation of return to baseline. Time series analyses can show that mean levels of the outcome of interest are different before and after an intervention, that the slope of change over time is different, and/or that change at the time of the intervention is abrupt. For example, school records might show a history of behavioral problems for the year prior to the introduction of a school-based behavioral assessment intervention and a decrease in those problems in the year following the onset of the program. Or a time series might show that behavioral problems dropped after the onset of the program and stayed that way. Or it might show that behavioral problems were dropping anyway, but the drop was sharper after the onset of the program.

Time series might be more convincing if a multiple time series design is used, in which several different time series are undertaken at different sites using the same intervention at different times. Therefore, one could evaluate time series data from three different schools offering the same behavioral assessment program, with services beginning at different times. Even the more subtle effects might be convincing if it were shown that the level of behavioral problems in the school dropped in all three settings after the intervention was underway. The multiple time series also can be of use to ruling out alternative explanations by obtaining time series data on other relevant variables that might explain differences in pre- and postintervention tests. For example, a time series for behavior problems might be accompanied by a similar time series for other school-related problems such as attendance rates. The comparison with attendance rates might rule out the possibility that the new administration was reducing problematic behavior generally, regardless of the behavioral assessment intervention.

One advantage of time series designs is that they can be used with existing data so no new data will have to be collected. If adequate records exist, one can map out the outcome of interest as it existed prior to the onset of an intervention as well as after the onset. The key is to have a sufficient number of observations over a substantial time period before and after the intervention in order to make defensible conclusions.

It is often the case that ongoing modifications to the research design are made as the evaluation progresses, particularly for evaluations taking place over a substantial period. Such designs were originally referred to as "patched up" designs (Campbell & Stanley, 1966). As threats to validity become apparent, the evaluator modifies the design, usually by additional comparison groups or series, to decrease or eliminate likely threats. Only the threats viewed as most likely are targeted, with the notion that ruling out as many as possible is better than ruling out none. Such designs are by nature difficult to generalize about because the modifications are specific to the unique characteristics of the evaluation.

Sometimes evaluators are asked to evaluate programs that are delivered at various sites. Multisite designs can help rule out a variety of threats to validity. In multisite studies in which the same intervention is delivered, generalizability is enhanced because the intervention is tested in different settings, under

different circumstances, with different populations. When different interventions are delivered at the different sites, threats to validity associated with participants' awareness of the availability of other, possibly more attractive interventions can be decreased or eliminated. In such cases, participants can become demoralized and/or resentful if they believe they have been assigned to a less attractive condition, or they might become competitive with others assigned to a different condition, both of which can account for outcomes.

One of the tasks associated with multisite designs is determining the unit of analysis for comparison. Comparing site-level data alone, particularly for a small number of sites (e.g., two or three), is not a good use of these designs. That is, comparing the mean for one site on the outcome of interest with the mean for the other site is not compelling with respect to evaluation conclusions. Multisite designs call for a hierarchical or multilevel approach, in which participant-level as well as organizational-level information are taken into account. Because participants are grouped within programs that are grouped within different sites, these studies are conceived of as multilevel or hierarchical, with the participant representing the smallest or micro unit, and the site representing the largest or macro unit (e.g., Bryk & Raudenbush, 1992). In its simplest form, there are two levels within a multilevel study: participants are grouped within sites. In more complex designs, one comparing school districts for example, participants might be grouped within classrooms, which are grouped within schools, which are grouped within school district sites. Thus, information about participants, their classrooms, the schools, and the school district should be accounted for in the evaluation in order to lessen the threat of alternative explanations to study outcomes. For example, it could be the case that differences observed between school districts are due to characteristics associated with the schools rather than due to the effects of a particular intervention. Therefore, information about the schools must be collected in order to tease out those effects.

Multilevel statistical models, referred to by a variety of names such as hierarchical linear models, mixed effects models, and random coefficients models (see Kreft & deLeeuw, 1998), have been designed specifically to address the various levels of information that are available from multilevel designs such as multisite studies. In these analyses, data collected from participants as well as from the more macrounits within the hierarchy, such as classrooms, schools, and school districts, are all entered into the statistical model and therefore level-specific effects can be taken into account and teased apart. Thus, if differences between school sites offering different interventions are actually due to characteristics associated with the schools rather than to the interventions themselves, such effects can be modeled statistically and evaluated. This, of course, presumes that the data were collected in the first place. Thus, the task of the evaluator undertaking a study in which microunits exist or are nested within macrounits (e.g., students within classrooms or patients within clinics) and those macrounits are to be compared (e.g., classrooms with other classrooms or clinics with other clinics), is to collect information at all levels of the hierarchy for relevant variables that could serve as confounds to the study. For example, some school sites might serve children from vastly different socioeconomic backgrounds that might have an effect on school resources that would affect the delivery of the experimental intervention. Available resources is a school-level indicator that should be taken into account when comparing outcomes, as is the average socioeconomic status for each school.

Case studies are another type of research design that can be used for evaluations. However, such designs are not optimal, as they are almost always open to many threats to validity, most notably to internal validity. Case studies are sometimes useful in formative evaluations and might help to convince decision-makers of the need for further investigation. They can also sometimes, albeit rarely, provide valuable information by revealing striking and unexpected phenomena. But in general, these designs do not provide conclusive information, and the audience for the evaluation will be reminded of many alternative explanations of any findings.

Evaluation Synthesis

Almost always the results of an evaluation require some kind of a "summing up," a process often referred to as *synthesis* (Scriven, 1991). Evaluations quite frequently involve multiple issues or questions; not often can the question be phrased quite so simply as "does this program work?" Programs may meet some aims quite well, others not so well, and still others not at all. They may have mostly desirable effects, but some that are undesirable. They may work more or less well with different types of persons or in different sets of circumstances. As Scriven (1991) notes, some evaluators may not believe that it is their responsibility to try to sum things up, but that argument is seriously weakened by considering that the program evaluator surely knows more about the results of the evaluation, and perhaps about the program itself, than anyone else.

Program evaluators cannot be expected, at least not in most cases, to put all results together in a way that can be expressed by a single number. But they do need to pay attention to a wide range of concepts and characteristics of the evaluation setting and develop a narrative summary that will

leave readers with a reasonable comprehension of what it all means. Representativeness of the sample, strength of the intervention, quality of the measures, sizes of the effects, and so on need to be fit together to form a coherent view of the evaluation in relation to program aims. That view should then be elaborated by consideration of the implications of the account for the future of the program, its needs, and its prospects.

All too often, programs are developed, implemented, and then evaluated in isolation, as if no history, background, precedent, or theory related to the program ever existed. A useful evaluation synthesis needs to provide that context. Thus, a synthesis ought to put the program and its evaluation in the perspective provided by an account of the theory underlying it, including making explicit theory that may not have been fully delineated. The synthesis should consider the adequacy of other empirical support for the theory and the results that may have been obtained in evaluations of other similar programs. Interpretation of specific findings often may be informed by Bayesian thinking that takes into account the likelihood of observed findings in relation to what would have been expected on the basis of other information. For example, if a program of behavioral interventions to reduce school discipline problems seems not to be effective even though it has been shown to be effective in other places, then the evaluator should feel compelled to consider why that might be so and to provide at least a tentative and informative explanation. If an intervention is strongly recommended by sound theory and that intervention does not work, then an explanation is needed.

A well-thought-out and well-prepared evaluation synthesis will be maximally informative to all of the stakeholders in the program. Even if stakeholders are not terribly sophisticated, they will almost certainly appreciate and understand a good synthesis better than they will understand a jumble of seemingly unconnected and sometimes conflicting "results." Merely pasting together a series of results in the form of percentages and other descriptive statistics is not useful to anybody—even the least sophisticated audience. Evaluation consumers are looking for what it all means and thus require some context and perspective by which to interpret those statistics in a meaningful way. Ultimately, evaluation results are used for decision making, and if the results are reported in such a way that decisions cannot be made, then the report is useless. Scriven (1991) refers to the presentation of unsynthesized results as "unconsummated evaluation."

Perhaps of nearly equal importance, a well-prepared evaluation synthesis will be a contribution to the fields represented by the program and by the science underlying it. The results of the evaluation will be valuable because they will be readily incorporated into the larger body of knowledge and will fulfill the striving of science toward cumulative knowledge.

Coda

The problems of program evaluation are far more complicated than this chapter might imply. Space and other limitations prevent us from providing more than a brief overview of and introduction to the field. Certainly this chapter cannot serve as a manual by which to plan and carry out evaluations. However, many books, articles, Internet sites, and professional organizations exist that are devoted to program evaluation and specialized topics within the field. Our hope is that the chapter might have illuminated the complexities of program evaluation, as well as excited readers to the available possibilities. Readers will need to seek more technical guidance elsewhere.

SUMMARY

A successful evaluation is one whose findings are persuasive. From the start, the evaluator should be aware of who is to be persuaded and what evidence is required by the various evaluation audiences. Persuasiveness will be determined by the type of information collected and even more so by the ability of the evaluator to rule out alternative explanations for the results. Research design will assist the evaluator in doing so. The selection of the evaluation design will rely heavily on the circumstances of the program, and thus might not allow for the strongest designs that involve random assignment to interventions and a control group. In such cases, the evaluator is obligated to select the best design that will accommodate the circumstances of the program and yet still diminish the threats to validity that are most likely to occur.

The role of the program evaluator varies, depending on the relationship to the program as well as the purpose of the evaluation. In-house evaluators may be more dependent in relation to administrative decisions than external evaluators, and financial decisions might affect them differently as well. To avoid serious conflict and to ensure the quality of the evaluation, it is optimal that the evaluator be involved in the earliest stages of a program, from the planning process through the phases of implementation, monitoring to assure delivery as planned, and through the data collection and outcome assessment.

Many evaluations will involve measuring change. There is a vast literature on the best methods for evaluating change that should be taken seriously. If the knowledge that has been gained over the past few decades about measuring change is not taken into account, evaluators can run into a wide range of serious problems that jeopardize the validity of evaluation conclusions concerning change.

Given the recent climate of accountability with respect to programs and interventions, it is likely that many evaluations will involve some sort of analysis of costs and benefits. In business, cost-benefit ratios can be constructed rather easily. However, it is far more difficult to estimate costs and benefits of social programs for which it is nearly impossible to assign monetary values. However, it is possible to assess cost effectiveness: if one program produces the same benefit as another but at a lower cost, it is more cost effective. It is also important to consider program costs, although they might not be monetized. Costs can include indirect effects and unintended consequences, both of which must be measured in order to obtain a full understanding of the impact of a program. There are also opportunity costs to consider. When there are limited resources to be used and a decision is made to squander them on a poorly conceived program, there is an opportunity cost to that decision. Similarly, there is an opportunity cost to spending valuable resources on a poorly conceived program evaluation. Results will be meaningless and therefore unusable to stakeholders, who will then have fewer resources to spend to obtain a useful product. More regrettably, experience with a poor evaluation might inspire little confidence in evaluation and evaluators and the many benefits of an evaluation well done will not be realized.

NOTES

1. The following web site provides a useful discussion and example of the use of a critical multiplist approach to scientific inquiry: http://www.digitaltempo.com/e-forums/chap3.html#Critical%20multiplism.

2. A useful protocol for the development and display of logic models may be found in www.pmn.net/education/Logic.htm and www.gse.harvard.edu/hfrp/projects/afterschool/resources/learning_logic_models.pdf.

3. The number of observations required depends on the shape of the functional form. More complex shapes—for example, those in which change trajectories shift directions—require more observations for mathematical as well as logical reasons.

4. The web site EconEdLink (http://www.econedlink.org/lessons/index.cfm?lesson = EM51) provides a simple example of opportunity cost.

5. There are many other potential threats to external validity as well as to the other types of validity we have discussed. For the interested reader, Cook and Campbell (1979) detail these threats to validity.

REFERENCES

Bickman, L. (1987). The functions of program theory. In L. Bickman (Ed.), *Using program theory in evaluation: New directions in program evaluation, 33.* San Francisco: Jossey-Bass.

Bollen, K., & Lennox, R. (1991). Conventional wisdom on measurement: A structural equation perspective. *Psychological Bulletin, 110,* 305–314.

Bryk, A.S., & Raudenbush, S.W. (1992). *Hierarchical linear models: Applications and data analysis methods.* Thousand Oaks, CA: Sage.

Campbell, D.T., & Stanley, J.C. (1966). *Experimental and quasi-experimental designs for research.* Skokie IL: Rand McNally.

Cohen, J. (1988). *Statistical power analysis for the behavioral sciences* (2nd ed.). Hillsdale, NJ: Erlbaum.

Congressional Research Service (n.d.). http://cnie.org/NLE/CRS reports/Risk/rsk-4.cfm#What is Cost-Benefit Analysis?

Cook, T.D., & Campbell, D.T. (1979). *Quasi-experimentation: Design and analysis issues for field settings.* Skokie, IL: Rand McNally.

Embretson, S.E. (1996). The new rules of measurement. *Psychological Assessment, 8,* 341–349.

Figueredo, A.J., & Sechrest, L. (2001). Approaches used in conducting health outcomes and effectiveness research. *Evaluation and Program Planning, 24,* 41–59.

Haynes, S.N. (2001). Clinical applications of analogue behavioral observation: Dimensions of psychometric evaluation. *Psychological Assessment, 13,* 73–85.

Jacobson, N.S., & Truax, P. (1991). Clinical significance: A statistical approach to defining meaningful change in psychotherapy research. *Journal of Consulting and Clinical Psychology, 59,* 12–19.

Kreft, I., & de Leeuw, J. (1998). *Introducing multilevel modeling.* London: Sage.

Luce, D.R., & Raiffa, H. (1957). *Games and decisions: Introduction and critical survey.* New York: Wiley.

Orne, M.T. (1969). Demand characteristics and the concept of quasi-controls. In R. Rosenthal & R.L. Rosnow (Eds.), *Artifact in behavioral research.* New York: Academic Press.

Patton, M.Q. (1978). Evaluation of program implementation. In M.Q. Patton (Ed.), *Utilization-focused evaluation.* Beverly Hills, CA: Sage.

Rossi, P.H., & Freeman, H.E. (1993). *Evaluation: A systematic approach* (5th ed.). London: Sage.

Scriven, M. (1991). *Evaluation thesaurus* (4th ed.). London: Sage.

Sechrest, L. (1977). Evaluation results and decision making: The need for program evaluation. In L. Sechrest (Ed.), *Emergency medical services research methodology.* DHEW Publication No. [PHS] 78–3195. Hyattsville, MD.

Sechrest, L., Ametrano, D., & Ametrano, I. (1982). Evaluation of social programs. In J.R. McNamara & A.G. Barclay (Eds.), *Critical issues, developments, and trends in professional psychology* (pp. 129–166). New York: Praeger.

Sechrest, L., McKnight, P., & McKnight, K. (1996). Calibration of measures for psychotherapy outcome studies. *American Psychologist, 15,* 1065–1071.

Sechrest, L., West, S.G., Phillips, M.A., Redner, R., & Yeaton, W. (1979). Some neglected problems in evaluation research: Strength and integrity of treatments. In L. Sechrest, S.G. West, M.A. Phillips., R. Redner, & W. Yeaton (Eds.), *Evaluation studies review annual, 4.* Beverly Hills, CA: Sage.

Shadish, W.R. (1994). Critical multiplism: A research strategy and its attendant tactics. *New Directions for Program Evaluation, 60,* 13–57.

Shadish, W.R., Cook, T., & Campbell, D. (2002). *Experimental and quasi-experimental designs for generalized causal inference.* Boston: Houghton-Mifflin.

Shadish, W.R., Cook, T.D., & Leviton, L.C. (1991). *Foundations of program evaluation: Theories of practice.* Thousand Oaks, CA: Sage.

Tenner, E. (1996). *Why things bite back: Technology and the revenge of unintended consequences.* New York: Knopf.

Tharp, R.G., & Gallimore, R. (1979). The ecology of program research and evaluation: A model of evaluation succession. In L. Sechrest, S.G. West, M.A. Phillips., R. Redner, & W. Yeaton (Eds.), *Evaluation studies review annual, 4.* Beverly Hills, CA: Sage.

Trochim, W. (n.d.). http://trochim.human.cornell.edu/kb/constval.htm.

Weiss, C.H. (1972). *Evaluation research: Methods of assessing program effectiveness.* Englewood Cliffs, NJ: Prentice-Hall.

Yeaton, W.H., & Sechrest, L. (1981). Critical dimensions in the choice and maintenance of successful treatments: Strength, integrity, and effectiveness. *Journal of Consulting and Clinical Psychology, 49,* 156–167.

APPLICATIONS OF BEHAVIORAL ASSESSMENT

CHAPTER 15

Behavioral Assessment in the Measurement of Treatment Outcome

GIAO Q. TRAN AND JOSHUA P. SMITH

OVERVIEW

The behavioral approach has played a leading role in developing assessment strategies for psychological disorders. In particular, the Lang's (1993) three-response-systems approach that includes observational, self-report, and physiological assessment has been used to study the multiple dimensions of psychopathology and treatment outcome.

This chapter will focus on the principles and procedures guiding behavioral assessment of an individual intervention's efficacy and effectiveness. The chapter will begin with a review of issues specific to treatment outcome: efficacy versus effectiveness in treatment outcome, types of treatment efficacy studies, and methods of assessing treatment change. The chapter will then cover the following behavioral assessment modalities and provide a conceptual basis for each modality: structured interviews, clinician-administered scales, self-report questionnaires, behavioral assessment tests, and physiological measures. To illustrate the applications of these methods, assessment measures for adult social anxiety will be described in some detail, and a

well-designed treatment outcome study illustrating the use of these measures for social anxiety disorder (SAD) or social phobia will be presented. The chapter will close with conclusions on the applications of different assessment modalities to the measurement of treatment outcome in research and clinical settings.

TREATMENT OUTCOME ISSUES

An extensive body of literature has been devoted to investigating treatments of specific psychological disorders. These investigations have relied heavily on efficacy study designs and statistical significance tests to address the questions, "Does treatment have any effect on the targeted symptoms?" and "How well does this treatment work compared to a controlled condition or an alternative intervention?" The advancement of intervention research requires consideration of treatment effectiveness and clinical significance in addition to treatment efficacy and statistical significance. Thus, all four issues are covered in this section.

Treatment Efficacy Versus Effectiveness

The publication of the Consumer Reports data (Seligman, 1995) on treatment effectiveness has increased consciousness among researchers and clinicians on the relevance of treatment efficacy versus treatment effectiveness in the measurement of client's treatment outcome. Many have debated about whether treatment efficacy or effectiveness is the true indicator of an intervention's effects. Treatment efficacy addresses the question, "has the treatment been shown to be beneficial in a controlled research study?" (Chambless & Hollon, 1998). Treatment effectiveness, on the other hand, taps into the question, "is treatment useful in applied clinical settings?" (Chambless & Hollon, 1998). By design, internal validity is emphasized in treatment efficacy studies, while external validity is emphasized in treatment effectiveness studies. Although the issues have been debated, treatment efficacy and treatment effectiveness studies typically have differed on sample (diagnostic comorbidity) and treatment (treatment assignment, flexibility, and dosage) characteristics. To increase internal validity in testing the benefits of a specific intervention for a specific disorder, patients are selected to have a primary psychological disorder and are randomly assigned to treatment conditions. The delivered treatment also is based on a treatment manual that typically outlines the specific interventions session by session. On the other hand, patients in an effectiveness study self-select to treatment, and their treatments can vary in terms of duration, intensity, and contents. One issue that continues to be at the center of the debate is the complexity of presenting problems in efficacy versus effectiveness studies. Investigators have disagreed and presented contrasting evidence on whether research participants enrolled in efficacy studies are as complex in terms of severity and comorbidity of disorders as patients in effectiveness studies (Chambless & Hollon, 1998; Seligman, 1995). A positive outcome of the many discussions that followed the Seligman's (1995) publication of the Consumer Reports study is greater communication on how efficacy studies can be designed to increase generalizability and transportability to clinical settings. The most noted example of the efforts to link treatment efficacy to treatment effectiveness is the National Institute on Drug Abuse's funding of the Clinical Trial Network research. The purpose of the study is to establish an infrastructure for research in community treatment centers and to test the effectiveness of psychosocial and pharmacological interventions that were developed in research settings.

Types of Treatment Efficacy Study

The first step in developing a new treatment is an uncontrolled study in which participants receiving the experimental treatment are assessed before and after the intervention to determine whether the treatment had any effects at all. The primary concern with an uncontrolled study is that what appears to be a treatment effect may only be a natural resolution of the problem during the passage of time. The next step after treatment development is a controlled and randomized treatment efficacy study. The efficacy of a new treatment is typically examined by comparing an experimental treatment group with a control treatment group in a clinical trial where participants are randomly assigned to treatment conditions. There are three types of control treatment conditions to which the experimental treatment could be compared: no-treatment, wait-list treatment, and credible placebo condition. In addition to being contrasted with a control treatment condition, the treatment of interest can be compared to another active treatment condition in a comparative treatment design. Testing of a new treatment typically is conducted in sequential order. First, the treatment is compared to a no-treatment or wait-list control condition to answer the question "does the treatment have any effect on symptoms after considering symptom reduction from just the passage of time and repeated assessments?" The next step is to compare the new intervention to a treatment that controls for the nonspecific factors of therapy such as supportive therapy or another credible treatment condition that has shown no efficacy for the targeted problem. The latter is a more stringent test of the efficacy of the experimental treatment. A new treatment is often designed because it has a proposed advantage over an existing active treatment as a result of a specific intervention strategy. Thus, the comparison to another active treatment for the targeted problem addresses the question, "does the new treatment have a specific advantage over an existing treatment?"

In the no-treatment condition, the experimental treatment group is compared to a group of individuals with the targeted problem who do not get any intervention during the course of treatment. This treatment design faces the ethical concern of not providing service to individuals with clinical needs. These clients typically are referred to standard clinical treatment after the assessment phase of the study and do not receive treatment provided by the researchers. The wait-list control condition undergoes a procedure similar to the no-treatment condition during the study period. However, after the study terminates, the wait-list condition is offered the experimental treatment but is typically not evaluated any further for research purposes. Because individuals with the target clinical disorder do not receive treatment for a period of time (typically three months) existing data on the psychopathology and the course of the disorder need to demonstrate that this waiting period will not likely result in deterioration or harm to the research participants. In both the credible placebo and the comparative treatment conditions, participants are offered some form of intervention between pretreatment and posttreatment assessment. The main difference is that the credible placebo is expected to have less of an effect than a comparative treatment condition. The credible placebo is designed to control for the nonspecific effects of therapy, while the active comparison treatment is designed to examine the effect of specific intervention techniques or mechanisms of action. To identify mechanisms of change, assessment would need to include potential causal variables in addition to the target treatment behaviors.

METHODS OF ASSESSING TREATMENT CHANGE

The dynamic nature of many behaviors requires periodic assessment. Sufficiently frequent assessment of relevant variables facilitates timely detection of differential treatment effects and possibly their mechanisms of change. Published treatment outcome results usually highlight assessments conducted at pretreatment, posttreatment, and follow-up. Most clinical trials also collect data (often unpublished) throughout the course of the active intervention phase to track more closely the course of symptom changes. More intensive data collection during the treatment phase helps to address the client's clinical needs and monitor internal validity of the study. Because earlier chapters in this volume have addressed in some detail the guidelines for periodic assessment based on behavioral principles, the emphasis here is on methods of assessing treatment change.

A number of methods have been proposed and used to assess treatment change. These methods can be broadly classified as statistical and clinical significance tests. Like other quantitative psychological research, psychotherapy research relies primarily on the use of statistical methods to determine whether treatment results in any change (Kazdin, 1998). Statistical evaluation tells us whether the difference obtained on a dependent measure is likely to occur by chance, typically defined as p-value $< .05$. This p-value tells us that there is less than a 5% chance that the difference we observed would likely occur by chance. However, finding a statistical significance does not tell us whether this effect is meaningful in terms of the patient's distress and impairment level. Clinical significance tests were developed as a means to provide additional information to statistical tests and to indicate whether the change observed after treatment has any practical implications for the patient's functioning. Described below are the most relevant issues to consider regarding statistical and clinical significance.

Statistical Significance

Statistical significance tests are employed to address the presence of within- and between-group effects. Treatment change can be examined via raw gain (difference) scores or residualized gain scores. A raw difference score is simply the difference between pretreatment and posttreatment scores and does not control for individual differences in a patient's symptom severity at treatment onset. A t-test or a nonparametric equivalent (typically a Mann-Whitney test) is used to determine whether a statistically significant change occurred in the raw score. A residualized gain score, on the other hand, controls for individual differences in symptom severity at pretest in calculating the effect of treatment on symptom change (Cronbach & Furby, 1970). Most clinical researchers prefer to use the residualized gain method. Statistical procedures that compare residualized gains from different treatments essentially compare the rates of symptom change in patients from different treatment conditions. The most common procedure for examining the rate of change is analysis of covariance (ANCOVA) or multivariate analysis of covariance (MANCOVA) controlling for differences in pretreatment scores. Either planned or post hoc pairwise comparisons controlling for familywise error would follow significant ANCOVA and MANCOVA results when there are more than two comparison groups (Keppel, 1991; Kirk, 1995).

Random-effects regression is a newer method that some clinical researchers have begun using to examine treatment effects (Gibbons et al., 1993; Gibbons, Hedeker, Waternaux, & Davis, 1988; Nich & Carroll, 1997). This method uses a combination of the random changes at an individual level and the fixed effects of the independent variable. Proponents of random-effects regression have suggested that it has at least two advantages compared to traditional ANOVA models. First, it enables the investigators to use all collected data from all participants because this method allows missing observations to become estimable by plotting the regression line through the model parameter estimates. Second, this approach can better reflect the clinical reality of data collection in a treatment outcome study because it allows real time (when the data are actually collected) rather than scheduled time (when the data are scheduled to be collected) to be used for each participant. Thus, random-effects regression appears to be a very promising approach for assessing differential treatment effects for longitudinal clinical trials.

In addition to comparing the efficacy of two treatments, some investigators are interested in examining predictors of treatment outcome. If an investigator is interested in examining how individual patient and treatment variables are related to group change (e.g., Chambless, Tran, & Glass, 1997;

Steketee, Chambless, & Tran, 2001), then partial correlation in regression analysis is used. Partial correlation shows the strength and direction of an independent variable's (e.g., treatment expectancy) effects on treatment outcome, and is thus useful to identify individual variables that may differentially influence treatment change within a particular intervention. The cognitive-behavioral approach to assessment has been at the forefront of developing and validating measures that tap into symptom severity, maladaptive beliefs, and coping responses that are frequently proposed as moderators and mediators of psychopathology development, maintenance, and recovery. Such cognitive and behavioral indicators of vulnerability have played prominent roles in psychopathology models of depression (Beck, Rush, Shaw, & Emery, 1979), anxiety (Beck & Emery, 1985; Rapee & Heimberg, 1997) addictive disorders (Abrams & Niaura, 1987), and eating disorders (Fairburn, 1985). Further research on moderators and mediators of treatment outcomes may help match patients to beneficial treatments.

Noteworthy in this discussion on statistical significance is the issue of effect size. Effect size is part of the computation of statistical significance. Effect size refers to the magnitude of difference between two or more treatment conditions using a common metric that is expressed in standard deviation units (Kazdin, 1998). Clinical researchers are encouraged to report effect sizes to allow cross-study comparison of results, as well as to facilitate meta-analysis of a large sample of studies to examine the overall effects of the same or similar treatments (e.g., group cognitive-behavioral therapy of social phobia). An advantage of effect size over statistical significance is that the former is not dependent on the sample size. A frequent limitation in treatment outcome studies is that limited power due to small sample sizes prevents important treatment differences from being detected by statistical methods.

Clinical Significance

Jacobson, Follette, and Revenstorf's (1984) landmark article provided both the conceptual basis for assessing clinical significance of treatment outcome and the needed calculation procedure to put this recommendation into practice. In addition to the observation that a statistical significance has little practical implication about how well a patient will function, it also has been observed that the symptom or functioning level attained at the end of therapy is a better predictor of long-term functioning for many clinical disorders than the magnitude of change measured by statistical tests. Because many domains affect a person's functioning, clinical significance involves a range of possible outcomes. Several methods have been suggested to assess clinical significance: dysfunc-

tional comparison, normative comparison, and high-end-state functioning.

Dysfunctional and Functional Comparison

The most commonly used clinical significance assessment method is comparison of the patient's posttreatment scores to the scores of the dysfunctional group (the untreated individuals with the target disorder) and the functional group (normal individuals who do not have psychiatric problems) (Jacobson et al., 1984). A patient must meet two criteria to achieve clinically significant change. First, his or her score must be outside the range of the dysfunctional group's scores and fall within the range of the functional or normal group's scores. Similar to most symptom measures, higher scores indicate greater symptomology or dysfunctionality. C, the clinical significance cutoff, is selected to fall halfway between the dysfunctional group's clinical cutoff at two standard deviations below its mean and the functional group's clinical cutoff at two standard deviations above the functional group's mean. Selecting the clinical cutoff to fall between the dysfunctional and the functional cutoffs is based on the assumption that, for many clinical disorders, the data distributions for the dysfunctional and functional groups overlap.

The second criteria for clinically significant change involves whether the patient has made enough of a change that we can confidently say that such a chance is outside the limit of measurement error. In essence, the change between pretreatment and posttreatment scores must indicate a reliable change. Jacobson et al. (1984) proposed that the reliable change index (*RC*) is calculated by dividing the difference between pretreatment and posttreatment scores by the standard error of measurement: $RC = (X_2 - X_1)/SE$. Standard error of measurement (*SE*) is the spread of the data distribution that would be expected if no actual change has occurred. An *RC* larger than $+1.96$ would be unlikely to occur ($p < .05$) without any actual change, and would thus indicate a reliable change.

Several factors should be considered in using Jacobson et al.'s (1984) clinical significance criteria. The major drawback of this approach is that the *RC* is dependent on the reliability of the measure. If a measure were highly reliable, then the *RC* would appear as large even when little change has occurred between pre- and posttreatment. In this case, having a clinically significant cutoff value *C* provides some protection from elevated *RC* due to the measure's high reliability. Furthermore, the clinical significance value is highly dependent on the samples selected for the dysfunctional and the functional groups. To reduce potential bias in setting the *C* value, dysfunctional and functional groups must be carefully selected to reflect representative samples. Jacobson et al's (1984) clinical significance method is a complex one that has been subjected to both appropriate and inappropriate uses in psychotherapy research. Jacobson, Roberts, Berns, and McGlinchey (1999) discussed representative applications and provided helpful recommendations against misapplication.

Normative Comparison

Another option to obtain practical interpretation of treatment results is to compare the patient's pretreatment and posttreatment scores to the mean of a normative sample (Kendall & Grove, 1988). Here, the estimate of clinically significant change becomes a function of the group used as a normative sample. Like dysfunctional and functional groups, normative samples are selected to be nontreatment seekers and any bias in the selection of a nontreatment group would bias the practical interpretation of the patient's scores. College and community samples are the most used normative samples.

High Endstate Functioning

High endstate functioning defines clinical improvement as reaching normality on a combination of outcomes by setting a priori cutoff scores for each outcome measure. Jacobson, Wilson, and Tupper (1988) proposed several methods of defining high endstate functioning. Expert opinions are typically used to determine cutoff scores. As with the selection of the criterion group(s) in normative and dysfunctional/ functional methods of comparison, expert opinions can be dependent on their targeted normal sample. Past research has shown wide variability in expert opinions on psychopathology depending on their exposure to different clinical populations and how high they set the bar for normal functioning.

Clearly, there are many options for assessing statistical and clinical significance of treatment change. Optimal application of these methods hinges on the availability of unbiased data. Thus, researchers have devoted much time and effort into developing reliable and valid measures that have promising clinical utility. The next section highlights the major issues to consider in evaluating psychometric properties of a behavioral measure.

MEASUREMENT ISSUES

The quality of an assessment measure is critical for obtaining accurate results and consequently the meaningful conclusions drawn from them. An instrument should demonstrate adequate reliability and validity before it is used as a treatment outcome measure. Reliability is an indicator of a test's consistency in the results that it yields. Validity indicates the extent to which a test measures what it is intended to measure. For instruments used to assess treatment outcome, clinical utility based on both treatment sensitivity and time efficiency is also important. A measure needs to be sensitive enough to detect specific changes that occur during the course of treatment as well as time efficient enough to enhance the patient's compliance with assessment completion. Given the importance of clinical utility in the assessment of treatment outcome, the conceptual bases of this psychometric property are discussed in some detail here. However, only a brief review of reliability and validity concepts in behavior assessment will be presented below, because a more extensive discussion of these psychometric principles is available elsewhere in this volume.

Reliability

In determining an instrument's consistency in measurement, there are four types of reliability: test-retest, internal consistency, alternate-form, and interrater. The first three types of reliability are applicable to both self-report and clinician-administered instruments, but interrater reliability is used only with measures that involve an interviewer's rating of the patient's behavior, symptoms, and functioning. For most types of reliability, a reliability coefficient in the .80s or .90s is preferred (Annatassi, 1988), and coefficients in the .70s are usually acceptable. As demonstrated in the determination of a clinically significant change, a measure's reliability is very important in the determination of treatment outcome. In order to conclude that treatment change has occurred, it must be demonstrated that the observed change is greater than the scoring fluctuations due to error variance in measurement.

Validity

The validity of a test indicates how well a test measures what it is designed to measure. Content validity and face validity are typically built into the construction of a psychological test but are often not assessed systematically for most psychological measures. Content validity refers to the measure's adequacy in covering a representative behavior domain. Face validity, on the other hand, refers to what the test "appears" to measure, not necessarily what it actually measures. Face validity is important for eliciting a patient's compliance with completing the test and for facilitating wider use of the particular instrument in other clinical and research settings. Construct and criterion validity are the categories most relevant to psychological tests because they tap into what a test is supposed to measure with reference to theoretical constructs and criteria currently accepted as the "gold standard" in the field. Construct validation procedures indicate the extent to which a test measures a theoretical construct or trait. It is important to consider both a measure's convergent and discriminant abilities in assessing its measurement of a concept or trait. Criterion validation procedures for psychological measures indicate how effective an instrument is in predicting an individual's performance in the criterion at the current or later time. The criterion should be carefully selected because reliability and validity problems with the criterion measures will limit accurate conclusions to be drawn about the criterion validity of the instrument under investigation. Common criteria in clinical research include diagnostic category and treatment relapse.

Clinical Utility

How clinically useful a measure is depends on both its ability to detect actual changes in symptoms as well as the time efficiency of its administration. Achieving the balance between efficiency and sensitivity is a key challenge for assessment that requires repeated measurements. Stability of the target behavior is a critical determinant of how often its assessment should occur. For example, personality characteristics that the Minnesota Multiphasic Personality Inventory II is empirically derived to measure are not expected to change within a short time duration; thus, a large time lapse should be allowed between repeated administrations of this personality measure. However, state-dependent measures such as the Beck Depression Inventory are assessed weekly in some treatment outcome studies because fluctuations in depression symptoms may influence the patient's treatment response.

Time Efficiency

Brevity in assessment is particularly important for measures that require multiple assessments. Clients are more likely to comply with completing the same measure if it can be done quickly, typically within five minutes. However, assessment brevity is not useful if the brief instrument is not able to detect symptom change. Ratings of target anxiety symptoms that are the foci of treatment are a good example of a brief measure that has demonstrated treatment sensitivity (e.g., Chambless & Steketee, 1999). Although individuals with social phobia are routinely asked to rate their anxiety in social situations, target ratings have not been used as primary measures of treatment outcome.

Treatment Sensitivity

Treatment sensitivity can be thought of as a higher-order psychometric property contingent on good reliability and validity properties. An instrument must be able to give consistent measurement on a construct of interest before it can be used to reflect the changes resulting from therapy. There is evidence that measures differ reliably in their sensitivity to treatment change (Lambert & Hill, 1994). For example, results of a study by Taylor, Woody, McLean, and Koch (1997b) suggest that the Social Phobia and Anxiety Inventory (Turner, Beidel, Dancu, & Stanley, 1989) is more sensitive to treatment change than briefer measures such as the Fear Survey's Social Phobia Scale (Marks & Matthews, 1979) and the Social Interaction and Anxiety Scale (Mattick & Clarke, 1998). Again, the question returns to the balance between the sensitivity level required and the assessment time available.

REVIEW OF SPECIFIC INSTRUMENTS TO ASSESS SOCIAL ANXIETY DISORDER

Behavioral measures used in clinical psychology vary along many dimensions including modality or type of measure, rating specificity, stability of characteristic measured, breadth of domain, and format of responses (Kazdin, 1998). The characteristic that may distinguish these measures the most is modality or type of measure. The major categories are structured interviews, clinician-administered scales, self-report questionnaires, behavioral assessment tests, and psychophysiological measures. This section will address the specific applications of these modalities for the assessment of adult social anxiety disorder (SAD) or social phobia.

SAD is selected as the application disorder for several reasons. First, SAD is characterized by an intense fear of negative evaluation that is reflected in subjective experiences of anxiety, physiological reaction, and observable behaviors. Second, the disorder is complicated by comorbid depression and anxiety disorders. Thus, assessment needs to be sensitive to symptoms specific to social anxiety rather than general anxiety or depression. Many authors view SAD as a condition that exists on the same continuum of normal to pathological social anxiety. There has been a burgeoning of clinical tools for assessment of adult social phobia in the past 10 years, and these tools have been subjected to investigation in treatment outcome studies. The purpose, scoring method, psychometric properties, clinical utility, and relative strengths and weaknesses of the primary measures of social anxiety are reviewed below. The review is not intended to be an exhaus-

TABLE 15.1   Primary Behavioral Measures of Social Anxiety and Social Phobia

Modality	Measure
Structured Interviews	Structured Clinical Interview for *DSM-IV* (SCID-IV)
	Anxiety Disorders Interview Schedule-IV (ADIS-IV)
Clinician Administered Scales	Liebowitz Social Anxiety Scale (LSAS)
	Brief Social Phobia Scale (BSPS)
Self-Report Measures	Social Interaction Anxiety Scale (SIAS)
	Social Phobia Scale (SPS)
	Social Phobia and Anxiety Inventory (SPAI)
	Social Avoidance and Distress Scale (SAD)
	Fear of Negative Evaluation (FNE)
	Fear Questionnaire-Social Phobia Subscale (FQ-SP)
	Personal Report of Confidence as a Speaker (PRCS)
Behavioral Assessment Tests	Simulated Social Interaction Test (SSIT)
	Individually tailored extended role-plays
	Standardized extended role-plays
Physiological Measures	Heart rate
	Electrodermal response
	Cortisol level

tive discussion of the many measures of social anxiety, but rather a highlight of the major measures to illustrate the principles of behavior assessment. Table 15.1 provides an overview of the behavioral measures that will be detailed below.

Structured Interviews

Structured interviews are the most common method of clinical assessment. These interviews guide clinicians through the systematic assessment of diagnostic criteria and provide an established method by which reliable and accurate diagnoses may be obtained. By ensuring adequate coverage of critical areas of functioning and by standardizing the interview, structured interviews enhance diagnostic reliability and interview validity (Rogers, 1995; Wiens, 1990). Given their breadth of assessment and known psychometric properties, this method of assessment is preferred to unstructured interviews in research settings. One caveat regarding the utility of these measures is that proper training must be assured. Further, this type of assessment can be costly and time-consuming. The structured interviews most often used in social phobia research are the Structured Clinical Interview for *DSM-IV*, Axis I (SCID-IV; First, Spitzer, Gibbon, & Williams, 1994) and the Anxiety Disorders Interview Schedule for *DSM-IV*, Lifetime Version (ADIS-IV-L; DiNardo, Brown, & Barlow, 1994).

Structured Clinical Interview for DSM-IV

The SCID-IV is a semistructured interview for making the major *DSM-IV* Axis I diagnoses. The SCID-IV was designed to increase diagnostic reliability through standardization of the assessment process, as well as increase diagnostic validity by facilitating the application of the operational criteria from *DSM-IV*. Certainly, use of this interview provides research clinicians with significant benefits. Aside from systematically probing symptoms that otherwise might be overlooked, the SCID-IV is a broad-ranging, time-efficient instrument that contributes an algorithm for arriving at a final diagnosis. In addition, the SCID allows researchers to tailor a diagnostic assessment to fit the needs of a particular research protocol (Spitzer, Williams, Gibbon, & First, 1992). Since its inception, it has enjoyed widespread popularity that is largely due to these characteristics.

The SCID-IV was originally designed to meet the needs of both researchers and clinicians. However, each consumer group desires different levels of detail for their respective purposes. For this reason, separate clinical (SCID-CV) and research (SCID-RV) versions were developed. The research version differs from the clinical version in that it is longer and includes ratings for subtypes, severity and course specifiers, and additional disorders not of general interest to clinicians. Both versions, however, require training to ensure proper administration and interpretation.

The SCID-IV has demonstrated desirable psychometric properties. The interview has exhibited high interrater reliability on assessments of symptoms across a variety of disorders (Ventura, Liberman, Green, Shaner, & Mintz, 1998). For the diagnosis of social phobia in particular, Tran and Haaga (2002) obtained acceptable interrater reliability (kappa = .60). Data pertaining to the utility of the SCID-IV as an outcome measure are sparse, however. This may be due to lack of depth in coverage, a sacrifice made to provide breadth without being overly time-consuming. The measure was developed for and primarily used in the context of diagnosis, which is reflected in the fact that the items are concerned mostly with only the presence or absence of symptoms. The possibility of using the SCID-IV for treatment outcome is not entirely reduced, though, as a researcher could utilize differences in severity ratings as a change indicator.

It must be noted that the vast majority of studies engaging this instrument used an earlier version that was designed to coordinate with the *DSM-III-R*. Yet, due to the high degree of similarity between the SCID-IV and this earlier version, the potential differences in psychometric properties are most likely negligible. Overall, the SCID-IV is a useful research tool, albeit primarily as a diagnostic instrument. The SCID-IV is an efficient, broad-ranging, user-friendly, and psychometrically sound instrument that allows for differential diagnosis.

Anxiety Disorders Interview Schedule-IV, Lifetime

DiNardo et al. (1994) designed the semistructured ADIS-IV to reliably and validly assess current and lifetime anxiety disorders, consistent with *DSM-IV* criteria. The instrument contains modules for disorders that commonly co-occur or overlap with the anxiety spectrum (mood, substance, somatoform disorders) as well as screening questions for other major disorders. An especially favorable aspect of the ADIS-IV-L is that it obtains useful data beyond the basic information required for diagnosis. For example, the measure gathers knowledge about the history of the problem, situational and cognitive factors influencing anxiety, and detailed symptom ratings of fear and avoidance. Also, it yields clinical severity ratings (0 to 8) and collects information on anxiety symptoms of all individuals, including those who do not meet full diagnostic criteria. These characteristics provide a database for clinical investigation that is especially useful in evaluating social phobia.

Brown, DiNardo, Lehman, and Campbell (2001) evaluated the reliability of the ADIS-IV-L. In their analysis, good to excellent reliability was obtained for the majority of DSM-IV categories. Likewise, evaluation of clinical severity ratings indicated favorable interrater agreement for the dimensional features of *DSM-IV* anxiety and mood disorders. Adequate reliability (kappa = .64) also has been found for the diagnosis of social anxiety disorder specifically (DiNardo, Brown, Lawton, & Barlow, 1995). Moreover, with the range of information provided, this interview has been amenable for use in clinical studies of treatment outcome of patients with social phobia (e.g., Heimberg et al., 1999). In sum, the ADIS-IV-L is very useful to researchers studying social anxiety; the anxiety-focused measure provides a wealth of information suitable for differential diagnosis, treatment planning, and outcome studies. The administration of the interview is time-consuming, but this is offset by its other, more desirable aspects.

Clinician-Administered Scales

These measures, developed for administration by knowledgeable interviewers, can be very helpful for the purposes of treatment planning and outcome research. The primary advantage of this method of assessment is that the researcher is given latitude to query the interviewee's responses and adjust the ratings accordingly. In general, application of clinician-

administered scales is relatively straightforward and scoring presents little difficulty. Two regularly used scales are the Liebowitz Social Anxiety Scale (LSAS; Liebowitz, 1987) and the Brief Social Phobia Scale (BSPS; Davidson et al., 1991). Notably, these measures are most often employed in pharmacological studies, though they are not limited to such use.

Liebowitz Social Anxiety Scale

The LSAS was the first clinician-rated scale developed for the assessment of social phobia. Composed of 24 items, the test is subdivided into two component scales that gauge social/interaction situations (13 items) and performance situations (11 items). Each item is separately rated on a 4-point Likert scale for both fear and avoidance, yielding seven scale scores: an overall severity rating (total score), total fear, total avoidance, social fear, social avoidance, performance fear, and performance avoidance. Heimberg et al. (1999) introduced data regarding the reliability and validity of the LSAS. Internal consistency was high for the total score and subscales (kappas = .81–.96), while the test also demonstrated convergent and discriminant validity. However, high correlations among the scale scores were also found, indicating that the actual factor structure of the LSAS may not match its subscale structure. In fact, the LSAS overall severity rating was so highly correlated with the total fear and total avoidance scores (both $rs = .98$) that they may be considered interchangeable. The validity of the theoretically derived LSAS subscales has been examined, and Safren et al. (1999) provides a valuable discourse regarding this issue. The LSAS has been widely used to detect treatment effects and has generated effect sizes comparable to other measures (Davidson et al., 1993; Heimberg et al., 1998; Montgomery, 1998). Despite the possibility that the factor structure of this measure may be suspect, it has remained the most commonly used clinician-administered instrument to assess the severity of social anxiety and change as a result of treatment.

Brief Social Phobia Scale

Davidson et al. (1991) developed the BSPS during the course of clinical studies of social phobia as a brief measure of severity. The 11-item scale asks respondents to rate the severity of fear and avoidance about seven social situations in addition to the intensity of four autonomic symptoms. All ratings are made on 5-point Likert scales. Research exploring the psychometric aspects of the BSPS has been favorable. High test-retest reliability, adequate internal consistency, very high interrater reliability, and demonstrated convergent validity indicate that the measure is reliable and valid (Davidson et al.,

1991). Further evidence for the psychometric competence of the instrument has been obtained in a sample of 275 patients with social phobia (Davidson et al., 1997). Also, the BSPS total score has demonstrated sensitivity to the effects of pharmacological treatment, though limited data exist regarding its use with psychological treatment (Davidson et al., 1993; Stein, Fyer, Davidson, Pollack, & Wiita, 1999; Van Ameringen, Mancini, & Oakman, 1999). In all, the BSPS is a promising development in social phobia research. The measure is psychometrically sound, concise, easy to administer, and sensitive to treatment effects.

Self-Report Measures

A wide array of instruments tapping social anxiety and phobia has been developed for self-administration. Scholing and Emmelkamp (1990) noted that these self-report measures can be divided into those that are targeted directly toward symptoms of social phobia and those that are more general measures of anxiety and fear. Practically speaking, these scales are efficient and require little time to score, affording the research clinician ease of repeated administration. A multitude of these measures are currently available, but only those most important in terms of their impact on the field will be highlighted in this chapter.

Social Interaction Anxiety Scale and Social Phobia Scale

The Social Interaction Anxiety Scale (SIAS) and Social Phobia Scale (SPS) were developed concurrently as companion measures of social phobia. The SIAS items describe an individual's cognitive, behavioral, or affective responses to situations that require social interaction, while the SPS items pertain to situations that involve being observed by others. Each instrument contains 20 items rated on a 5-point Likert scale, and the two can be regarded as subscales of one larger measure that may be most useful when used together. Details of the construction of the SIAS and SPS are outlined by Mattick and Clarke (1998).

Both scales have demonstrated strong psychometric properties. Across five patient and control groups, test-retest reliability ($rs = .91–.93$) and internal consistency (alphas = .88–.94) were excellent (Mattick & Clarke, 1998). Heimberg, Mueller, Holt, Hope, and Liebowitz (1992) reported similar results in a study with undergraduates, community volunteers, and patients with social phobia. Moreover, the validity of these measures has been acceptable, because the SIAS and SPS have shown discriminative abilities and significant positive correlations with other standard measures (Heimberg et al., 1992; Mattick & Clarke, 1998). In addition, the SIAS was

more highly correlated with a similar measure of interaction anxiety relative to the SPS, while the SPS correlated significantly only with a measure of fear and avoidance of performance situations (Heimberg et al., 1992). Both scales also have established utility as outcome measures sensitive to cognitive-behavioral treatment (Mattick & Clarke, 1998; Mattick, Peters, & Clarke, 1989), performing well relative to other standard tests (Cox, Ross, Swinson, & Direnfield, 1998). In sum, the SIAS and SPS are reliable and valid instruments that appear to measure different, though related, aspects of social anxiety.

Social Phobia and Anxiety Inventory

Turner et al. (1989) systematically constructed the Social Phobia and Anxiety Inventory (SPAI) according to the behavioral-analytic model of Goldfried and D'Zurilla (1969). The scale is an empirically derived 45-item instrument designed to assess cognitions, somatic symptoms, and avoidance and escape behaviors in situations that people with social phobia typically find distressing. The SPAI includes two subscales: Social Phobia (32 items) and Agoraphobia (13 items). A 7-point Likert scale format is used to gauge functional impairment and severity of distress. The SPAI is innovative such that separate ratings for strangers, authority figures, opposite sex, and people in general are obtained for several of the Social Phobia items.

A potential drawback with the SPAI is that scoring, when compared to other social phobia self-report measures, is rather complex and time-consuming. A separate score is obtained for each subscale, and a difference score is derived by subtracting the Agoraphobia scale score from the Social Phobia score. In fact, a lively debate has ensued regarding which of the SPAI scores is the best measure of social phobia. Herbert, Bellack, and Hope (1991) argued that the unadjusted Social Phobia scale score may be a better measure than the difference score, positing that the strong correlation between them ($r = .91$) and lack of assumptions regarding the relationship between social phobia and agoraphobia implies little benefit for use of the latter. Beidel and Turner (1992), in turn, have maintained that the difference score, which controls for the anxiety associated with agoraphobia situations, is the most useful measure. However, the debate itself may be moot, as each score performs similarly well in assessing patients with social phobia (Ries et al., 1998), and the better measure may actually depend on the intended use of the instrument (Herbert, Bellack, Hope, & Mueser, 1992).

The SPAI has been deemed appropriate for research purposes, as many high quality studies of reliability and validity have been favorable (Beidel, Borden, Turner, & Jacob, 1989;

Herbert et al., 1991; Turner et al., 1989; Turner, Stanley, Beidel, & Bond, 1989). The measure also has demonstrated utility in differentiating subtypes among social phobics in a clinical sample (Ries et al., 1998). Furthermore, the SPAI has reliably measured clinically significant changes following treatment in a number of studies, performing well relative to other standard measures (Beidel, Turner, & Cooley, 1993; Cox et al., 1998). Despite the fact that the test requires a total of 109 responses and scoring is potentially somewhat complex, the quantity and specificity of the information coupled with the psychometric strength of the test is compelling.

Social Avoidance and Distress Scale and Fear of Negative Evaluation Scale

The Social Avoidance and Distress Scale (SAD) and Fear of Negative Evaluation Scale (FNE), developed simultaneously by Watson and Friend (1969), are among the most widely used measures of social anxiety. The SAD scale consists of 28 true-false items about anxiety and avoidance associated with social interactions, while the FNE includes 30 true-false questions assessing one's expectation of being evaluated negatively by others. A brief, 12-item Likert-type version of the FNE has been developed (Leary, 1983) that correlates highly with the original scale ($r = .96$) and demonstrates good test-retest reliability and internal consistency. The brief FNE is especially useful because its brevity facilitates repeated administrations, and the Likert-type format may make it more sensitive to treatment effects.

Through three experimental studies and one correlational study with undergraduates, Watson and Friend (1969) reported that the measures demonstrated sufficient concurrent validity and adequate test-retest reliability after a 1-month interval (SAD: $r = .68$, FNE: $r = .78$). Further, a KR-20 reliability coefficient of .94 was found for both instruments in a sample of anxiety patients (Oei, Kenna, & Evans, 1991). Criterion validity for the SAD has been demonstrated as scores have been found to be significantly related to peer ratings and specific behavioral measures of social skills (Arkowitz, Lichtenstein, McGovern, & Hines, 1975). Also, the concurrent validity has been suggested by significant positive correlations with other social anxiety questionnaires (Wallander, Conger, Mariotto, Curran, & Farrell, 1980). These scales also have been used as outcome measures, showing sensitivity to change (Baldwin, 2000; Mattick & Peters, 1988; McCann, Woolfolk & Lehrer, 1987). Changes detected with the FNE, however, have typically been small (Heimberg, 1994), and both scales are further limited by the true-false format.

The use of the SAD and FNE scales for social phobia patients has not been free of criticism; its appropriateness has

been debated in the literature. In particular, Turner, McCanna, and Beidel (1987) have criticized these instruments for lacking discriminative validity and correlating too highly with general measures of emotional distress. Alternatively, others have argued that social anxiety may be an important component of trait anxiety and general emotional distress, and that the results obtained by Turner et al. (1987) should not be interpreted as evidence against the discriminative validity of these measures (Heimberg, Hope, Rapee, & Bruch, 1988). Regardless, these scales have been used for some time and remain quite popular among researchers.

Fear Questionnaire

A 15-item Total Phobia scale is included in the Fear Questionnaire (FQ; Marks & Matthews, 1979). The measure yields scores on three 5-item subscales representing categories of phobias: Agoraphobia (FQ-AG), Social Phobia (FQ-SP), and Blood/Injury Phobia (FQ-BI). Total Phobia scale scores can be derived from the sum of all items, though the three subscales have been more frequently used (Arrindell, Emmelkamp, & van der Ende, 1984). The FQ-SP has been commonly used in social phobia research and has shown strong correlations with analogue measures of social anxiety (Van Zurren, 1988). The factor-analytically derived items of the FQ-S represent social anxiety/phobia situations and are rated on a 0 to 8 scale for severity of avoidance.

The FQ has fared well in assessment of its psychometric properties. Based on a thorough evaluation, Arrindell and colleagues (1984) concluded that the FQ dimensions are suitable for research purposes. Along these lines, high test-retest reliability and acceptable internal consistency have been reported in the literature (Marks & Matthews, 1979; Van Zurren, 1988). Moreover, individuals with agoraphobia and social phobia have been amply discriminated by their respective subscales, suggesting discriminant validity (Cox, Swinson, & Shaw, 1991; Van Zurren, 1988). Since its inception, the FQ-S has developed a reputation as something of a gold standard in social phobia assessment (Cox & Swinson, 1995). When used as a measure of treatment outcome, however, it has produced effect sizes smaller than those gained with other measures of social phobia (Taylor et al., 1997a). In addition, the measure is further limited as the scale's five items are only rated for avoidance and thus do not provide the amount of clinical information necessary for treatment planning.

Personal Report of Confidence as a Speaker

The original Personal Report of Confidence as a Speaker (PRCS; Gilkinson, 1942) was designed to assess both fear and confidence before, during, and after public speaking.

Consisting of 104 items, however, the test proved to be cumbersome when used as a screening tool. Paul (1966) addressed this difficulty by modifying the PRCS into a 30-item scale, and this version has since been more popular among researchers. The current version of the test retains the original version's true-false format and contains a mixture of fear and confidence items across the three temporal dimensions. Normative data for the PRCS are available, though there remains no standard method to determine whether a person has public-speaking phobia based on derived scores (Phillips, Jones, Rieger, & Snell, 1997).

The PRCS has been examined with respect to its reliability and validity, and this literature has supported its continued use. Daly (1978) found that the PRCS was positively correlated with a number of other measures of speech and social anxiety ($rs = .52-.97$) and had high internal consistency (Cronbach's alpha $= .91$). In addition, higher PRCS scores have been associated with less effective speech performance (Tarico, van Velzen, & Altmaier, 1986). Validity data are also available from Lombardo (1988). The scale has also frequently been used as a measure of treatment effectiveness (Altmaier, Ross, Leary, & Thornbrough, 1982; Kirsch & Henry, 1977; Mannion & Levine, 1984). Overall, the PRCS is important in social anxiety research as the major instrument for use in assessing public speaking fear.

Behavioral Assessment Tests

The assessment of overt behavior in social phobia research is essential in gaining a complete understanding of social functioning. Although interviews and self-report questionnaires provide valuable information, behavioral measurements yield revealing samples of the activities of interest. Naturalistic observations would be ideal, yet they are difficult to implement for practical and ethical reasons. As a result, researchers have created alternative assessment strategies designed to capture social behavior in controlled settings. The logic underlying these evaluations is based upon the notion that people's behavior while performing the requisite tasks in laboratory or therapy settings corresponds with their behavior in real-life settings.

Behavior Assessment Tests (BATs) are frequently used in the comprehensive assessment of social phobia. A typical BAT may involve a situation patients routinely encounter in everyday life, such as talking with a stranger. Often, role-play procedures are utilized, and the possibility of implementing a multimodal assessment (e.g., recording behavioral, self-report, and physiological responses) within the BAT is very appealing to research clinicians. Due to wide variability among these instruments, though, they may be more accu-

rately delineated as an assessment strategy rather than as a particular type of test.

Primary among these variations is the distinction between standardized and idiographic (individually tailored) BATs. Although standardized BATs yield results that may be comparable across studies, the idiographic variety affords researchers the most flexibility. Scores for BATs often are collected on the Subjective Units of Discomfort Scale (SUDS), which are subjective discomfort ratings on a scale ranging from 0 (no anxiety) to 100 (panic or extreme anxiety). Also, values may be derived for measures of avoidance and escape (e.g., Hofmann, Newman, Ehlers, & Roth, 1995). Moreover, results derived from physiological and self-report assessment are readily implemented as well (e.g., Turner, Beidel, & Townsley, 1992). Other noteworthy variations of BATs include differences in the number of items used, presence of sequential steps, instruction sets, duration, familiarity of interaction partners, and the use of role-play procedures. Indeed, role-play procedures have been a staple, playing a prominent role in many BATs.

In a typical role play, patients confront one or more fear-eliciting social situations in a controlled setting. Although many varieties of role-play tests exist, each is characterized by the enactment of simulated social interactions to elicit responses that are indicative of the participant's level of social skill. Often, patients will role-play with confederates or respond to standard stimuli presented on tape. Role-play procedures also vary along the lines of duration (brief vs. extended) and degree of structure (structured vs. unstructured). Aside from being shorter, brief role-play tests are typically more structured than extended tests. The structured approach typically involves presenting the subject with a series of descriptions of social situations, with a confederate reciting a prompt at the end of each description. This method is sometimes preferred to less structured alternatives in research settings because they employ standard stimuli. However, a tradeoff exists as the use of unstructured role-play tests has been shown to enhance the external validity of the assessment (Torgrud & Holborn, 1992). Role-play tests also differ with respect to degree of specificity (general vs. specific). For example, while some assess general social skills (Curran, 1982), others focus specifically on heterosocial or dating situations (e.g., Perri & Richards, 1979).

The Simulated Social Interaction Test (SSIT; Curran, 1982; Curran et al., 1980) is an example of a structured role-play test. It examines behavior in eight brief social interactions (e.g., heterosexual contact; disapproval or criticism). These items are based, in part, on earlier work by Richardson and Tasto (1976). Four of the simulations involve a male confederate, while the others incorporate a female confederate. Each simulation requires that a narrator read a script describing the situation, after which a confederate provides a verbal prompt. After each interaction, subjects rate their level of anxiety and skill on separate 11-point Likert scales. Higher points represent either high anxiety or high social skill. In addition, responses are videotaped and evaluated by trained, independent judges using the same 11-point scales. Research investigating the psychometric properties of this test has indicated that it is both reliable and valid. Specifically, the measure has demonstrated good interrater reliability, high test-retest reliability, and high internal consistency (Curran, 1982; Curran et al., 1980; Fingeret, Monti, & Paxson, 1985). The construct validity of the SSIT has been evidenced in various populations, including psychiatric patients and college students (Curran et al., 1980; Monti, Wallander, Ahern, Abrams, & Munroe, 1983). Also, Tran and Haaga (2002) showed the ability of the SSIT to discriminate between individuals with social phobia and those in a control group. The convergent validity of the instrument has been called into question, however, in a Dutch sample of people with social phobia (Mersch, Breukers, & Emmelkamp, 1992). Finally, research involving training group and treatment outcome studies has revealed that the SSIT is sensitive to change (Mersch, Emmelkamp, & Lips, 1991). One note of caution regarding this test, nonetheless, is that the research evaluating it has been limited by primary use of males as subjects.

The brief role-play tests, exemplified by the SSIT, are contrasted with the extended variety of role-play procedures. While traditionally imposing less structure on the fabricated social situation, examples of these longer tests have been shown to distinguish confident from shy students, while also displaying sensitivity to changes associated with treatment in individuals with dating anxiety (Arkowitz et al., 1975; Twentyman & McFall, 1975). For a more detailed analysis of an example of these tests, refer to Gershenson and Morrison (1988). Regardless of the format of the role-play procedure, however, three levels of measurement have typically been employed: molecular, midi-level, or molar. As reviewed by Scholing and Emmelkamp (1990), these coding systems differ primarily in terms of their degree of specificity (Becker & Heimberg, 1988). While molecular ratings include highly specific behaviors such as pauses and dysfluencies, molar ratings involve gauging complex groups of actions to yield a more global rating of social skill. So-called midi-level ratings attempt to bridge the gap by collapsing molecular and molar ratings into a single category (e.g., rate and pressure of speech). Presently there are no widely accepted standards regarding which rating level to use, resulting in difficulty with cross-study comparisons.

BATs have been shown to be psychometrically sufficient. The reliability of multiple response-system measures taken during a BAT has shown adequacy (Beidel, Turner, Jacob, &

Cooley, 1989), while Coles and Heimberg (2000) reported excellent interrater reliability (kappa = .94) in a sample of individuals with social phobia. In terms of validity, Bellack (1983) suggested that research assessing the validity of BATs supports their continued use. Furthermore, BATs have been effectively used as a sensitive measure of treatment outcome (Chambless et al., 1997; Mattick & Peters, 1988). Becker and Heimberg (1988) posit that BATs that maximize patient involvement, are individually tailored, and instruct the patient to reproduce a specific behavioral event may have the greatest utility and external validity. Although questions of generalizability persist with this type of assessment, it has proven to be of value to clinicians and researchers as an efficient and effective method for multimodal measurement.

Physiological Measures

An important alternative in the behavioral assessment of anxiety is the use of physiological measures. Autonomic arousal is a key characteristic of anxiety, and a growing body of research addresses the measurement of these processes. The autonomic nervous system is divided into two complementary systems, both of which can be involved in anxiety reactions: sympathetic and parasympathetic. The vast majority of work has involved sympathetic arousal. Elevated activity in this subsystem produces physiological changes such as increased heart rate, respiration, muscle tension, and galvanic skin response and decreased peripheral blood flow and gastrointestinal processes. The decrease in peripheral blood flow, such as in the hands and face, and the increase in blood flow to the heart and muscles are responsible for the fact that anxious people often have pale faces, cool hands, and an advancing heart rate. Essentially, the net effect of the sympathetic response to threat is to prepare for the so-called fight-or-flight response. The effects of sympathetic arousal are substantially neutralized by parasympathetic reactions, which are largely opposite to those of the former and usually occur after sympathetic activation. Leary and Kowalski (1995) contend that these processes also may be involved in anxiety-related responses, such as embarrassment.

The assessment of physiological processes in general applications has demonstrated adequate psychometric properties. These measurements have been shown to be stable and suitable for use in research (Waters, Williamson, Bernard, Blouin, & Faulstich, 1987). However, results derived from physiological assessment may not be consistent with those found in self-report measures (e.g., Rudestam & Bedrosian, 1977). Comparisons among self-report, overt behavior, and physiological data may be problematic given the relative independence of these response systems. Three common types of physiological assessment are measures of heart rate, electrodermal response, and cortisol levels.

Heart Rate

As noted previously, the increase in sympathetic activity resulting from a perceived threat in an anxiety-inducing situation produces a corresponding escalation in heart rate. For some time, researchers have used heart rate as an indicator of anxiety and have found that it is easily accessible and relatively insensitive to measurement artifacts (Nietzel & Bernstein, 1981). In fact, measurement of cardiovascular processes is the most common method of psychophysiological assessment in social phobia research. These activities are recorded either continuously with a plethysmograph or by assessing the pulse rate at regular intervals across a specified period of time. One advantage of heart rate assessment is that it can be recorded easily at relevant points (e.g., before, during, and after a role-play procedure or an impromptu speech) while the individual engages in other tasks.

Heart rate measurements have evidenced psychometric properties that render them suitable for research purposes. There are data suggesting good test-retest reliability during an impromptu speech task (Beidel, Turner, Jacob, & Cooley, 1989). Results from a variety of studies also suggest that heart rate is useful in differentiating individuals with social phobia and those in control groups (e.g., Beidel, Turner, & Dancu, 1985; Hofmann et al., 1995) when engaged in anxiety-related tasks. Furthermore, heart rate also has displayed utility in distinguishing subtypes of social phobia (Heimberg, Hope, Dodge, & Becker, 1990; Levin et al., 1993). Interestingly, the results of these studies have generally indicated an incongruence between heart rate and subjective anxiety. Specifically, individuals with "generalized" social phobia report greater subjective anxiety during the task, while those with "discrete" social phobia exhibit higher heart rates. Heart rate recordings also have been shown to be sensitive to treatment effects in social phobia outcome studies (Emmelkamp, Mersch, Vissia, & Van Der Helm, 1985; Jerremalm, Jansson, & Ost, 1986; Turner, Beidel, Long, & Greenhouse, 1992). It is important to note that, although consensus exists as to the importance of baseline measurement, there is no accepted standard for the parameters of these recordings.

Electrodermal Response

Assessment of dermatologic electrical activity has been incorporated in social phobia research, because it is expected that skin response can be a useful indicator of anxiety. Electrodermal response can be assessed by both skin conductance and skin resistance. Palmar Sweat Prints is a classic example

of an electrodermal assessment. Common measurements include change in skin conductance, magnitude of first response, habituation rate, and spontaneous fluctuations.

Electrodermal responses have exhibited the ability to distinguish individuals with social phobia from those in a control group. Skin conductance responses of individuals with social phobia have been shown to habituate more slowly and to have more spontaneous fluctuations than responses of those in the control group (Lader, 1967). Additionally, slower habituation and greater magnitude of response are related to the degree of social anxiety in the presence of social stimuli (Dimberg, Fredrikson, & Lundquist, 1986). Electrodermal recordings have also been used in treatment outcome studies for social phobia (e.g., Rudestam & Bedrosian, 1977). One should be aware, however, that electrodermal activity is susceptible to both psychological and environmental artifacts.

Cortisol Level

In primates, social stress has been associated with activation of the hypothalamic-pituitary-adrenal (HPA) axis (Sapolsky, 1982; Sassenrath, 1970). One extrapolation of this result is the expectation that those with social phobia will exhibit higher cortisol level due to hyperarousal when compared to people in normal control groups. To obtain the necessary recordings of cortisol level, researchers most commonly utilize plasma or urine samples. A noteworthy development in this literature is that, despite being similar in methodological quality, some studies have found no connection between cortisol and social phobia while others have. For example, when cortisol levels from samples of individuals with social phobia are compared to those from normal groups outside of any behavioral or pharmacological challenge, no differences were revealed (Potts, Davidson, Krishnan, Doraiswamy, & Ritchie, 1991; Uhde, Tancer, Gelernter, & Vittone, 1994). In contrast, a study involving a pharmacological challenge demonstrated an augmented cortisol response in women with social phobia (Hollander et al., 1998). Moreover, research involving behavioral challenges such as a role-play interaction or a speech has shown elevated cortisol levels during these tasks (Houtman & Bakker, 1991; McCann et al., 1997). These findings indicate that there may be a state-dependent effect of anxiety on cortisol level, and it is here that a connection between social phobia and cortisol may exist. The extent to which the HPA axis is elevated in patients with pathological anxiety remains controversial (Cameron & Nesse, 1988; Uhde, Joffe, Jimerson, & Post, 1988). Cortisol assessment also has been used in pharmacotherapy research (DeVane et al., 1999).

There has been considerable controversy regarding the degree of importance to place on psychophysiological assessment of social anxiety. While some advocate its use as an integral component of behavioral assessment (Lang, 1968, 1993), others disagree (Scholing & Emmelkamp, 1990). Those who do not support the utility of this type of assessment raise concerns about test-retest reliability and the overall lack of specificity in arousal patterns across the various anxiety disorders. Furthermore, a motoric confound may be present in a number of studies because many social situations involve tasks that may interfere with physiological measurement (McNeil, Vrana, Melamed, Cuthbert, & Lang, 1993). Lastly, the conceptual validity of physiological responses and their relation to treatment outcome remain unclear. Turpin (1991) provides a useful discourse on these areas of uncertainty.

It is difficult to draw any general conclusions pertaining to the physiology of social phobia, because small samples, lack of uniformity in study procedures, and inconsistent results plague this literature. However, one must not immediately discount the utility of physiological assessment in social phobia research. Indeed, physiological measurements are useful in that they can be recorded within the context of other tasks, they may uncover subtypes, and they have demonstrated some utility in the measurement of treatment outcome. In sum, physiological assessment is a key addition to behavioral measurement when used appropriately and with attention given to its methodological limitations.

Summary

To date, use of the three-response-systems approach (i.e., self-report, overt behavior, and physiology) has been embraced in social anxiety research. However, each response system is relatively independent of the others, which may be cause for concern. This lack of harmony may reflect methodological inadequacies though (Cone, 1979), and more work must be done to determine the relationships between them. The independence of these systems also may reflect important individual differences in response manifestation. Nevertheless, each response system has some advantages over the others, and none of the strategies alone provides the breadth of measurement necessary for comprehensive behavioral assessment of social anxiety. It is recommended that researchers reflect upon the purpose of their studies to determine which methods will yield the information necessary.

APPLICATION OF BEHAVIOR ASSESSMENT IN A TREATMENT EFFICACY STUDY FOR SOCIAL ANXIETY DISORDER

The availability of psychometrically sound measures of social anxiety and social phobia has facilitated the conduct of

well-designed studies on psychosocial and pharmacological treatments of SAD. Of particular relevance to this chapter are the investigations of cognitive-behavioral therapies (CBT) for social phobia that have made extensive use of multimodal behavior assessment. Many good examples of the application of behavioral assessment in measuring CBT outcomes for social phobia have been conducted in the past two decades. This section provides an overview of CBT studies for SAD and a critique of an illustrative study that uses behavioral assessment.

Overview of Behavioral Assessment in Cognitive-Behavioral Treatment Studies of Social Phobia

The variants of SAD psychosocial treatments are typically classified as exposure therapy or CBT that combines exposure therapy and cognitive restructuring. Among the psychosocial treatments, cognitive-behavioral group therapy (CBGT; Heimberg, 1991) has enjoyed the most empirical investigations and support indicating both short-term and long-term efficacy (Heimberg et al., 1990a; Heimberg, Saltzman, Holt, & Blendell, 1993). Many studies were conducted to compare exposure therapies and CBTs in the 1980s and 1990s (Butler, Cullington, Munby, Amies, & Gelder, 1984; Hope, Heimberg, & Bruch, 1995; Mattick & Peters, 1988; Mattick et al., 1989; Taylor et al., 1997a). Interest in comparing exposure therapy and CBT appears to have decreased with the finding from multiple studies, including Feske and Chambless' (1995) meta-analysis, that both treatment modalities were equally effective at producing improvement on measures of social anxiety, cognitive symptoms, or general depressed/anxious mood in participants with social phobia. When differences were found between behavior therapy and CBT in an individual clinical trial, CBT appeared to have better outcomes during follow-up because CBT patients continued to make gains after treatment (Mattick & Peters, 1988; Mattick et al., 1989). Attention has now turned toward comparing the efficacy of psychosocial and pharmacological treatments of SAD. Studies comparing the effects of CBTs and pharmacotherapies have presented rich opportunities for incorporating well-developed behavioral measures into pharmacological research (Clark & Agras, 1991; Gelernter et al., 1991; Heimberg et al., 1998; Otto et al., 2000; Scholing & Emmelkamp, 1993; Turner, Beidel, & Jacob, 1994).

Critical Analysis of Behavioral Assessment Used in an Illustrative Treatment Comparison Study

Turner et al.'s (1994) clinical trial has stood out among the well-designed and well-executed studies for its comprehensive assessment as well as its integration of statistical significance and clinical significance in assessing treatment outcome at posttreatment and during 6 months of follow-up. This study compared two active treatment conditions, flooding (an intensive exposure therapy) and atenolol (a beta blocker pharmacotherapy), to each other and to a placebo control in the treatment of social phobia. Behavior assessment included multiple measures from each assessment modality: structured diagnostic interview, clinician-administered symptom scales, self-report measures of social anxiety and general functioning, behavior assessment test, and physiological measures. Self-report, behavior test, and psychophysiological data were collected at all assessment time points. Clinical symptom ratings were available before and after treatment. As done in most treatment outcome studies, a structured diagnostic interview was conducted only at pretreatment. Table 15.2 provides a listing of the measures and their assessment time points in Turner et al.'s study.

Behavioral Assessment Choices

All patients were carefully diagnosed with the Anxiety Disorders Interview Schedule-Revised to select for individuals with primary diagnoses of social phobia. Twenty-five percent of the interviews were videotaped and later rated independently by an additional clinician to confirm the primary diagnosis. Obtaining confirmation of the primary diagnosis is a critical control of internal validity in psychopathology and treatment investigations because this helps to enhance the likelihood that the disorder of interest is being studied in the given sample. Another notable strength of this study was the use of independent evaluators to rate the participants' symptomology to remove potential bias in the therapists' assessments of their patients' treatment progress. The independent evaluators rated each patient's clinical status using the following rating scales: Clinical Global Impression Scale Severity of Illness Rating and Improvement Rating (Guy, 1976), Hamilton Rating Scale for Anxiety (Hamilton, 1959), and a 9-point Likert-type rating scale of social avoidance. Ideally, independent evaluators also should be blind to the participants' treatment conditions and assessment time points, so that these factors would not influence their ratings. The article did not indicate whether the evaluators in this study were in fact unaware of the participants' treatment status. A third strength of this study was the inclusion of a behavioral assessment test (BAT) that challenged the participant to engage in a speech task during which physiological and cognitive measures were completed. Physiological data included blood pressure and pulse rate; cognitive data consisted of positive and negative thoughts assessed with a form of the Social

TABLE 15.2 Behavioral Assessment Conducted in Turner, Beidel, and Jacob's (1994) Treatment Efficacy Study

Measure	Pre	Post	Follow-Up[a]
Clinician-Administered Interviews and Scales			
Anxiety Disorders Interview Schedule-Revised	X		
Clinical Global Impression Scale	X	X	
Hamilton Rating Scale for Anxiety	X	X	
Self-Report Measures			
Social Phobia and Anxiety Inventory	X	X	X
Social Anxiety and Distress Scale	X	X	X
Fear of Negative Evaluation	X	X	X
Fear Questionnaire	X	X	X
State-Trait Anxiety Inventory-State Form	X	X	X
State-Trait Anxiety Inventory-Trait Form	X	X	X
Behavioral and Physiological			
10-minute Speech[b]	X	X	X
Subjective Unit of Distress Rating	X	X	X
Social Interaction Self-Statement Test	X	X	X
Pulse Rate	X	X	X
Blood Pressure	X	X	X
Composite Clinical Significance Measure			
Social Phobia Endstate Functioning Index[c]	X	X	

[a]Follow-up assessments were conducted at 1, 3, and 6 months after treatment termination.
[b]Multimodal data were collected during the speech, including a cognitive measure.
[c]Endstate functioning is a composite measure based on an expert-rating system that combines clinician, self-report, and behavioral test data.

Interaction Self-Statement Test developed by Beidel et al. (1985). Despite the recognition that physiological arousal plays an important role in maintenance of social avoidance, psychophysiological assessment is rarely used in treatment efficacy research. Fourth, the study made very good use of both newly developed and more traditional measures of social anxiety. The newer Social Phobia and Anxiety Inventory provided better treatment sensitivity (Taylor et al., 1997b), while the older Social Avoidance and Distress Scale, Fear of Negative Evaluation Scale, and Fear Questionnaire–Social Phobia allowed comparison of this study's results with prior investigations' results that used these measures. Fifth, the study adequately assessed the effect of the treatments on symptoms of general distress and functioning using both clinician-administered and self-report measures. In addition to the measures administered by independent evaluators, the participants also completed the self-report State-Trait Anxiety Inventory that taps into general anxiety at both state and trait levels (Spielberger, Gorsuch, & Lushene, 1970). Finally, follow-up data were collected 1, 3, and 6 months after treatment termination, thus allowing ample opportunities to track clinical changes, especially relapse, during the early posttreatment phase. Such periodic measurement of target behaviors using standardized measures is a distinguishing feature of behavioral assessment.

Along with its numerous assessment strengths, this study also has some limitations. One issue that appeared to confound the results was the use of a very lengthy 10-minute behavior task with an escape option, which may have resulted in smaller treatment effects than those obtained in other social phobia treatment studies. This task diverged from BATs used in other investigations (e.g., Heimberg et al., 1990; Hope et al., 1995; Taylor et al., 1997a) that typically lasted 4 to 5 minutes and did not give the participant an opportunity to terminate the task early at a fixed time duration. It was also striking that a study as comprehensive in its assessment battery as Turner et al.'s (1994) did not track the participants' depression symptoms. Because depression is a common comorbidity among SAD patients and pretreatment depression has predicted negative outcome in patients with social phobia, depression is often assessed at major time points and sometimes routinely tracked during the course of treatment (e.g., Brown, Heimberg, & Juster, 1995; Chambless et al., 1997). Recently there has also been a growing interest in incorporating quality of life assessment into SAD treatment research (e.g., Cottraux et al., 2000) due to psychotherapy research's increasing attention on assessing general functioning in addition to disorder-specific symptom changes.

Data Analyses and Results

Turner and colleagues (1994) attended to both statistical and clinical significance in analyzing their data. The authors conducted standard statistical procedures to examine statistical differences among the treatment conditions on behavioral outcome indicators. BAT data were analyzed with repeated measures multivariate analysis of covariance (MANCOVA) that controlled for pretreatment differences in symptom severity. Self-report data were also analyzed with MANCOVA that included pretreatment symptoms as covariates. Each significant univariate analysis of covariance (ANCOVA) in the MANCOVAs was followed up with Tukey's tests that examined post hoc differences on outcome measures. The selection of Tukey's post hoc tests rather than planned comparison tests appeared to reflect the fact that no specific, directional hypothesis was made in the comparison between exposure therapy and pharmacotherapy. The conduct of univariate tests following an omnibus multivariate test was appropriate because the different outcome indicators were conceptually re-

lated and the comparison of the active treatments appeared exploratory in nature (Huberty & Morris, 1989). Furthermore, the use of the omnibus multivariate test is a common practice in clinical research based on the assumption that it helps to control Type I errors. Yet statisticians have debated on whether this method actually controls for Type I errors for all result patterns (Huberty & Morris, 1989).

Consistent with the current recommendations by experts in psychotherapy research (Feske & Chambless, 1995; Jacobson et al., 1999; Kazdin, 1998), effect sizes and clinical significance of treatment change were also examined. Turner et al. (1994) provided effects sizes for the primary outcome measures in self-report (SPAI), clinician rating (CGI), and behavioral performance during the speech tasks that allowed the results from this study to be compared to those from other clinical trials. The authors used the Social Phobia Endstate Functioning Index as a measure of clinical significance to compare the patients' clinical status to that of a control group. This measure based on five criteria established by social phobia experts was developed in the authors' research program (Turner, Beidel, Long, Turner, & Townsley, 1992). The scoring of this index was based on data from a battery of measures designed to depict different aspects of social phobia syndrome and to utilize different modes of assessment (self-report, clinician ratings, and behavioral assessment). The composite index appeared to be comprehensive and clinically sound. Turner and Beidel's reputation as leading investigators in SAD research lent credibility to their expert-based measure of clinical significance. Like other expert-based measures, this composite index was dependent on the experts' exposure to clinical populations and their standard for normal functioning.

Turner et al.'s (1994) methodological rigor in selecting assessment instruments facilitated the production of results that were clear and interpretable. The results showed that flooding was generally better than placebo and atenolol in reducing social phobia symptoms and yielded higher endstate functioning at posttreatment. However, the atenolol group did not show significant differences from the other groups on any assessment modality. The use of both social anxiety and general anxiety measures showed that flooding was more effective at reducing social anxiety than general anxiety symptoms in individuals with primary diagnoses of social phobia. Similar patterns of results were obtained with self-report, clinician-administered, and BAT data. Furthermore, the endstate functioning data bolstered the statistical differences found on pairwise comparisons of the three groups' self-report and independent evaluation data. These results showed that by termination 30% of the flooding patients achieved high endstate functioning compared to 22% and 6% of the participants in the atenolol and placebo control conditions, respectively.

Among participants who provided follow-up data (71% flooding and 57% atenolol), flooding patients continued to improve between posttreatment and follow-up while atenolol patients remained unchanged or deteriorated slightly.

Physiological results were presented in cursory manner, perhaps because they were not clearly related to other outcomes, and their relevance to understanding psychopathology of SAD remains questionable. Similarly, the authors made limited use of the cognitive data collected during BATs. Given that neither active treatment showed a clear comparative advantage, it might be useful to test cognitive and physiological variables as moderators of patients' responses to pharmacological and behavior treatments. For example, a participant with high physiological response to a social fear may benefit more from taking a beta blocker and thus may be more compliant with medication prescription than a participant with low physiological responder when facing a social fear. Hence, the research question may need to shift from "which treatment is more efficacious?" to "for which patient groups are the treatments efficacious?" Much remains to be examined in the area of patient-treatment matching research, including whether this line of research should be conducted with efficacy studies, effectiveness studies, or both types (Donovan, 1999).

Critique Conclusion

In conclusion, Turner and colleagues' (1994) study is an excellent example of the important and facilitating roles of behavioral assessment in CBT and pharmacological treatment outcome studies. The authors' cautious interpretation of their data paralleled their methodological rigor in behavioral assessment. Rather than being complacent with the positive findings of their behavioral treatment, they clearly addressed this study's limitations and directed readers toward an understanding of the data within the context of its strengths and limitations.

CONCLUSIONS

Behavioral assessment is central to the measurement of treatment outcome in both research and clinical settings. Much advancement has been made in this assessment domain, especially for the measurement of adult social anxiety. The application of behavioral assessment in treatment efficacy studies on social anxiety disorder provides a useful model for using multimodal behavioral assessment to study other psychological disorders and to expand the investigation of treatment outcome to effectiveness studies in community clinics. The

different assessment modalities—clinician-administered interviews, self-report questionnaires, behavior assessment tests, and physiological measures—have their individual advantages and limitations. Self-report scales, which are dependent on the participant's self-report reliability, are used most frequently because of their cost-efficiency and transportability across settings. Interview measures allow assessment of a patient's psychopathology and functioning by trained professionals, but they require more training to administer and need to be monitored regularly for rating integrity. More time and cost consuming are the direct measures of observable behaviors and physiological functioning. Further research is needed on the meaning associated with physiological measures, especially as they are related to treatment outcomes. The available data suggest variable correspondence among the different modalities of behavioral assessment. Different results from different data sources may reflect both measurement variances across instruments and complementary data from these different sources.

REFERENCES

Abrams, D.B., & Niaura, R.S. (1987). Social learning theory. In H.T. Blane & K.E. Leonard (Eds.), *Psychological theories of drinking and alcoholism* (pp. 131–178). New York: Guilford Press.

Altmaier, E., Ross, S., Leary, M., & Thornbrough, M. (1982). Matching stress inoculation's treatment components to clients' anxiety mode. *Journal of Counseling Psychology, 29,* 331–334.

Annatassi, A. (1988). *Psychological testing* (6th ed.). New York: Macmillan.

Arkowitz, H., Lichtenstein, E., McGovern, K., & Hines, P. (1975). The behavioral assessment of social competence in males. *Behavior Therapy, 6,* 3–13.

Arrindell, W.A , Emmelkamp, P.M.G., & van der Ende, J. (1984). Phobic dimensions: I. Reliability and generalizability across samples, gender and nations. *Advances in Behavior Research and Therapy, 6,* 207–254.

Baldwin, D.S. (2000). Clinical experience with paroxetine in social anxiety disorder. *International Clinical Psychopharmacology, 15* (supplement), 19–24.

Beck, A.T., & Emery, G. (1985). *Anxiety disorders and phobias: A cognitive perspective.* New York: Basic Books.

Beck, A.T., Rush, A.J., Shaw, B.F., & Emery, G. (1979). *Cognitive therapy of depression.* New York: Guilford Press.

Becker, R.E., & Heimberg, R.G. (1988). Assessment of social skills. In A.S. Bellack & M. Hersen (Eds.), *Behavioral assessment: A practical handbook* (3rd ed). New York: Pergamon Press.

Beidel, D.C., Borden, J.W., Turner, S.M., & Jacob, R.G. (1989). The Social Phobia and Anxiety Inventory: Concurrent validity with a clinic sample. *Behavior Research and Therapy, 27,* 573–576.

Beidel, D.C. & Turner, S. M. (1992). Scoring the Social Phobia and Anxiety Inventory: Comments on Herbert et al. (1991). *Journal of Psychopathology and Behavioral Assessment, 14,* 377–379.

Beidel, D.C., Turner, S.M., & Cooley, M.R. (1993). Assessing reliable and clinically significant change in social phobia: Validity of the Social Phobia and Anxiety Inventory. *Behaviour Research and Therapy, 31,* 149–158.

Beidel, D.C., Turner, S.M., & Dancu, C.V. (1985). Physiological, cognitive, and behavioral aspects of social anxiety. *Behaviour Research and Therapy, 23,* 109–117.

Beidel, D.C., Turner, S.M., Jacob, R.G., & Cooley, M.R. (1989). Assessment of social phobia: Reliability of an impromptu speech task. *Journal of Anxiety Disorders, 3,* 149–158.

Bellack, A.S. (1983). Recurrent problems in the behavioral assessment of social skill. *Behaviour Research and Therapy, 21,* 29–41.

Brown, E.J., Heimberg, R.G., & Juster, H.R. (1995). Social phobia subtype and avoidant personality disorder: Effect on severity of social phobia, impairment, and outcome of cognitive behavioral treatment. *Behaviour Therapy, 26,* 467–486.

Brown, T.A., DiNardo, P.A., Lehman, C.L., & Campbell, L.A. (2001). Reliability of DSM-IV anxiety and mood disorders: Implications for the classification of emotional disorders. *Journal of Abnormal Psychology, 110,* 49–58.

Butler, G., Cullington, A., Munby, M., Amies, P., & Gelder, M. (1984). Exposure and anxiety management in the treatment of social phobia. *Journal of Consulting and Clinical Psychology, 52,* 642–650.

Cameron, O.G., & Nesse, R.M. (1988). Systemic hormonal and physiological abnormalities in anxiety disorders. *Psychoneuroendocrinology, 13,* 287–307.

Chambless, D.L., & Hollon, S.D. (1998). Defining empirically supported therapies. *Journal of Consulting and Clinical Psychology, 66,* 7–18.

Chambless, D.L., & Steketee, G. (1999). Expressed emotion and behavior therapy outcome: A prospective study with obsessive-compulsive and agoraphobic outpatients. *Journal of Consulting and Clinical Psychology, 67,* 658–665.

Chambless, D.L., Tran, G.Q., & Glass, C.R. (1997). Predictors of response to cognitive-behavioral group therapy for social phobia. *Journal of Anxiety Disorders, 11,* 221–240.

Clark, D.B., & Agras, W.S. (1991). The assessment and treatment of performance anxiety in musicians. *American Journal of Psychiatry, 148,* 598–605.

Coles, M.E., & Heimberg, R.G. (2000). Patterns of anxious arousal during exposure to feared situations in individuals with social phobia. *Behaviour Research and Therapy, 38,* 405–424.

Cone, J.D. (1979). Confounded comparisons in triple response mode assessment research. *Behavioral Assessment, 1,* 85–95.

Cottraux, J., Note, I., Albuisson, E., Yao, S.N., Note, B., Mollard, E., Bonasse, F., Jalenques, I., Guerin, J., & Coudert, A.J. (2000). Cognitive behavior therapy versus supportive therapy in social phobia: A randomized controlled trial. *Psychotherapy and Psychosomatics, 69,* 137–146.

Cox, B.J., Ross, L., Swinson, R.P., & Direnfield, D.M. (1998). A comparison of social phobia outcome measures in cognitive-behavioral group therapy. *Behavior Modification, 22,* 285–297.

Cox, B.J., & Swinson, R.P. (1995). Assessment and measurement. In M.B. Stein (Ed.), *Social phobia: Clinical and research perspectives.* Washington, D.C.: American Psychiatric Press.

Cox, B.J., Swinson, R.P., & Shaw, B.F. (1991). Value of the Fear Questionnaire in differentiating agoraphobia and social phobia. *British Journal of Psychiatry, 159,* 842–845.

Cronbach, L.J., & Furby, L. (1970). How should we measure "change"—or should we? *Psychological Bulletin, 74,* 68–80.

Curran, J.P. (1982). A procedure for the assessment of social skills: The Simulated Social Skills Interaction Test. In J.P. Curran & P.M. Monti (Eds.), *Social skills training: A practical handbook for assessment and treatment.* New York: Guilford Press.

Curran, J.P., Monti, P.M., Corriveau, D.P., Hay, L.R., Hagerman, S., Zwick, W.R., & Farrell, A.D. (1980). The generalizability of a procedure for assessing social skills and social anxiety in a psychiatric population. *Behavioral Assessment, 2,* 389–401.

Daly, J. (1978). The assessment of social-communicative anxiety via self-reports: A comparison of measures. *Communication Monographs, 45,* 204–218.

Davidson, J.R.T., Miner, C.M., DeVeaughGeiss, J., Tupler, L.A., Colket, J.T., & Potts, N.L.S. (1997). The Brief Social Phobia Scale: A psychometric evaluation. *Psychological Medicine, 27,* 161–166.

Davidson, J.R.T., Potts, N.L.S., Richichi, E.A., Ford, S.M., Krishnan, K.R.R., Smith, R.D., & Wilson, W. (1991). The Brief Social Phobia Scale. *Journal of Clinical Psychiatry, 52* (supplement), 48–51.

Davidson, J.R.T., Potts, N.L.S., Richichi, E.A., Krishnan, K.R.R., Ford, S.M., Smith, R.D., & Wilson, W.H. (1993). Treatment of social phobia with clonazepam and placebo. *Journal of Clinical Psychopharmacology, 13,* 423–428.

DeVane, C.L., Ware, M.R., Emmanuel, N.P., Brawman-Mintzer, O., Morton, W.A., Villareal, G., & Lydiard, R.B. (1999). Evaluation of the efficacy, safety and physiological effects of fluvoxamine in social phobia. *International Clinical Psychopharmacology, 14,* 345–351.

Dimberg, U., Fredrikson, M., & Lundquist, O. (1986). Autonomic reactions to social and neutral stimuli in subjects high and low in public speaking fear. *Biological Psychology, 23,* 223–233.

DiNardo, P.A., Brown, T.A., & Barlow, D.H. (1994). *Anxiety Disorders Interview Schedule for DSM-IV: Lifetime Version (ADIS-IV-L).* San Antonio, TX: Psychological Corporation.

DiNardo, P.A., Brown, T.A., Lawton, J.K., & Barlow, D.H. (1995). *The Anxiety Disorders Interview Schedule for DSM-IV Lifetime Version: Description and initial evidence for diagnostic reliability.* Paper presented at the 29th Annual Conference of the Association for Advancement of Behavior Therapy, Washington, DC.

Donovan, D.M. (1999). Efficacy and effectiveness: Complementary findings from two multisite trials evaluating outcomes of alcohol treatments differing in theoretical orientations. *Alcoholism: Clinical and Experimental Research, 23,* 564–572.

Emmelkamp, P.G., Mersch, P.P., Vissia, E., & Van Der Helm, M. (1985). Social phobia: A comparative evaluation of cognitive and behavioral interventions. *Behaviour Research and Therapy, 23,* 365–369.

Fairburn, C.G. (1985). Cognitive-behavioral treatment for bulimia. In D.M. Garter & P.E. Garfinkel (Eds.), *Handbook of psychotherapy for anorexia nervosa and bulimia* (pp. 160–192). New York: Guilford Press.

Feske, U., & Chambless, D.L. (1995). Cognitive behavioral versus exposure only treatment for social phobia: A meta-analysis. *Behavior Therapist, 26,* 695–720.

Fingeret, A.L., Monti, P.M., & Paxson, M.A. (1985). Reliability of social skills and social anxiety ratings with different sets of raters. *Psychological Reports, 57,* 773–774.

First, M.B., Spitzer, R.L., Gibbon, M., & Williams, J.B.W. (1994). *Structured Clinical Interview for Axis I DSM-IV Disorders, Non-Patient Edition.* New York: Biometrics Research Department, New York State Psychiatric Institute.

Gelernter, C.S., Uhde, T.W., Cimbolic, P., Arnkoff, D.B., Vittone, B.J., Tancer, M.E., Bartko, J.J. (1991). Cognitive-behavioral and pharmacological treatments of social phobia: A controlled study. *Archives of General Psychiatry, 48,* 938–945.

Gershenson, B., & Morrison, R.L. (1988). Social Interaction Test. In M. Hersen & A.S. Bellack (Eds.), *Dictionary of behavioral assessment techniques.* New York: Pergamon Press.

Gibbons, R.D., Hedeker, D., Elkin, I., Waternaux, C., Kraemer, H.C., Greenhouse, J.B., Shea, M.T., Imber, S.D., Sotsky, S.M., & Watkins, J.T. (1993). Some conceptual and statistical issues in analysis of longitudinal psychiatric data. *Archives of General Psychiatry, 50,* 739–750.

Gibbons, R.D., Hedeker, D., Waternaux, C., & Davis, J.M. (1988). Random regression models: A comprehensive approach to analysis of longitudinal data. *Psychopharmacology Bulletin, 24,* 438–443.

Gilkinson, H. (1942). Social fears as reported by students in college speech classes. *Speech Monographs, 9,* 131–160.

Goldfried, M.R. & D'Zurilla, T.J. (1969). A behavioral-analytic model for assessing competence. In C.D. Speilberger (Ed.), *Current topics in clinical psychology* (Vol. 1). New York: Academic Press.

Guy, W. (1976). *ECDEU assessment manual for psychopharmacology.* Washington, DC: Department of Health, Education, and Welfare.

Hamilton, M. (1959). The assessment of anxiety states by rating. *British Journal of Medical Psychology, 32,* 50–55.

Heimberg, R.G. (1991). Cognitive-behavioral treatment of social phobia in a group setting: A treatment manual. (Available from R. Heimberg, Department of Psychology, Temple University, 1701 N. 13th Street, Philadelphia, PA 19122-6085.)

Heimberg, R.G. (1994). Cognitive assessment strategies and the measurement of outcome of treatment for social phobia. *Behaviour Research and Therapy, 32,* 269–280.

Heimberg, R.G., Dodge, C.S., Hope, D.A., Kennedy, C.R., Zollo, L.J., & Becker, R.E. (1990a). Cognitive behavioral group treatment for social phobia: Comparison with a credible placebo control. *Cognitive Therapy & Research, 14,* 1–23.

Heimberg, R.G., Hope, D.A., Dodge, C.S., & Becker, R.E. (1990b). DSM-III-R subtypes of social phobia: Comparison of generalized social phobics and public speaking phobics. *Journal of Nervous and Mental Disease, 178,* 172–179.

Heimberg, R.G., Hope, D.A., Rapee, R.M., & Bruch, M.A. (1988). The validity of the Social Avoidance and Distress Scale and the Fear of Negative Evaluation Scale with social phobic patients. *Behaviour Research and Therapy, 26,* 407–410.

Heimberg, R.G., Horner, K.J., Juster, H.R., Safren, S.A., Brown, E.J., Schneier, F.R., & Liebowitz, M.R. (1999). Psychometric properties of the Liebowitz Social Anxiety Scale. *Psychological Medicine, 29,* 199–212.

Heimberg, R.G., Liebowitz, M.R., Hope, D.A., Schneier, F.R., Holt, C.S., Welkowitz, L., Juster, H.R., Campeas, R., Bruch, M.A., Cloitre, M., Fallon, B., & Klein, D.F. (1998). Cognitive-behavioral group therapy versus phenelzine in social phobia: 12-week outcome. *Archives of General Psychiatry, 55,* 1133–1141.

Heimberg, R.G., Mueller, G., Holt, C.S., Hope, D.A., & Liebowitz, M.R. (1992). Assessment of anxiety in social interaction and being observed by others: The Social Interaction Anxiety Scale and the Social Phobia Scale. *Behaviour Therapy, 23,* 53–73.

Heimberg, R.G., Saltzman, D.G., Holt, C.S., & Blendell, K.A. (1993). Cognitive-behavioral group therapy for social phobia: Effectiveness at five-year follow-up. *Cognitive therapy and Research, 17,* 325–339.

Herbert, J.D., Bellack, A.S., & Hope, D.A. (1991). Concurrent validity of the Social Phobia and Anxiety Inventory. *Journal of Psychopathology and Behavioral Assessment, 13,* 357–369.

Herbert, J.D., Bellack, A.S., Hope, D.A., & Mueser, K.T. (1992). Scoring the Social Phobia and Anxiety Inventory: Reply to Beidel and Turner. *Journal of Psychopathology and Behavioral Assessment, 14,* 381–383.

Hofmann, S.G., Newman, M.G., Ehlers, A., & Roth, W.T. (1995). Psychophysiological differences between subgroups of social phobia. *Journal of Abnormal Psychology, 104,* 224–231.

Hollander, E., Kwon, J., Weiller, F., Cohen, L., Stein, D.J., DeCaria, C., Liebowitz, M., & Simeon, D. (1998). Serotonergic function in social phobia: Comparison to normal controls and obsessive-compulsive disorder subjects. *Psychiatry Research, 79,* 213–217.

Hope, D.A., Heimberg, R.G., & Bruch, M.A. (1995). Dismantling cognitive-behavioral group therapy for social phobia. *Behaviour Research and Therapy, 33,* 637–650.

Houtman, I.L.D., & Bakker, F.C. (1991). Individual differences in reactivity to and coping with the stress of lecturing. *Journal of Psychosomatic Research, 35,* 11–24.

Huberty, C.J., & Morris, J.D. (1989). Multivariate analysis versus multiple univariate analyses. *Psychological Bulletin, 105,* 302–308.

Jacobson, N.S., Follette, W.C., & Revenstorf, D. (1984). Psychotherapy outcome research: Methods for reporting variability and evaluating clinical significance. *Behaviour Therapy, 15,* 336–352.

Jacobson, N.S., Roberts, L.J., Berns, S.B., & McGlinchey, B. (1999). Methods for defining and determining the clinical significance of treatment effects: Description, application, and alternatives. *Journal of Consulting and Clinical Psychology, 67,* 300–307.

Jacobson, N.S., Wilson, L., & Tupper, C. (1988). The clinical significance of treatment gains resulting from exposure-based interventions for agoraphobia: A re-analysis of outcome data. *Behaviour Therapy, 19,* 539–554.

Jerremalm, A., Jansson, L., & Ost, L.G. (1986). Cognitive and physiological reactivity and the effects of different behavioral methods in the treatment of social phobia. *Behaviour Research and Therapy, 24,* 171–180.

Kazdin, A.E. (1998). *In research design in clinical psychology.* Needham Heights, MA: Allyn & Bacon.

Kendall, P.C., & Grove, W.M. (1988). Normative comparisons in therapy outcome. *Behavioral Assessment, 10,* 147–158.

Keppel, G. (1991). *Design and analysis: A researcher's handbook* (3rd ed.). Englewood Cliffs, NJ: Prentice-Hall.

Kirk, R.E. (1995). *Experimental design: Procedures for behavioral sciences* (3rd ed.). Pacific Grove, CA: Brooks/Cole.

Kirsch, I., & Henry, D. (1977). Extinction versus credibility in the desensitization of speech anxiety. *Journal of Consulting and Clinical Psychology, 45,* 1052–1059.

Lader, M.H. (1967). Palmer skin conductance measures in anxiety and phobic states. *Journal of Psychosomatic Research, 11,* 271–281.

Lambert, M.L., & Hill, C.L. (1994). Assessing psychotherapy outcomes and processes. In A.E. Bergin & S.L. Garfield (Eds.), *Handbook on psychotherapy and behavior change.* New York: Wiley.

Lang, P.J. (1968). Fear reduction and fear behavior: Problems in treating a construct. In J.M. Shlien (Ed.), *Research in psycho-*

therapy (Vol. 3). Washington, DC.: American Psychological Association.

Lang, P.J. (1993). The three-system approach to emotion. In N. Birbaumer & A. Ohman (Eds.), *The structure of emotion.* Seattle, WA: Hogrefe & Huber.

Leary, M.R. (1983). A brief version of the Fear of Negative Evaluation Scale. *Personality and Social Psychology Bulletin, 9,* 371–375.

Leary, M.R., & Kowalski, R.M. (1995). *Social anxiety.* New York: Guilford Press.

Levin, A.P., Saoud, J.B., Strauman, T., Gorman, J.M., Fyer, A.J., Crawford, R., & Liebowitz, M.R. (1993). Responses of "generalized" and "discrete" social phobics during public speaking. *Journal of Anxiety Disorders, 7,* 207–221.

Liebowitz, M.R. (1987). Social phobia. *Modern Problems of Pharmacopsychiatry, 22,* 141–173.

Lombardo, T.W. (1988). Personal Report of Confidence as a Speaker. In M. Hersen & A.S. Bellack (Eds.), *Dictionary of behavioral assessment techniques.* New York: Pergamon Press.

Mannion, N. & Levine, B. (1984). Effects of stimulus representation and cue category level on exposure (flooding) therapy. *British Journal of Clinical Psychology, 23,* 1–7.

Marks, I.M. & Mathews, A.M. (1979). Brief standard rating for phobic patients. *Behaviour Research and Therapy, 17,* 263–267.

Mattick, R.P. & Clarke, J.C. (1998). Development and validation of measures of social phobia scrutiny fear and social interaction anxiety. *Behaviour Research and Therapy, 36,* 455–470.

Mattick, R.P., & Peters, L. (1988). Treatment of severe social phobia: Effects of guided exposure with and without cognitive restructuring. *Journal of Consulting and Clinical Psychology, 56,* 251–260.

Mattick, R.P., Peters, L., & Clarke, J.C. (1989). Exposure and cognitive restructuring for severe social phobia: A controlled study. *Behaviour Therapy, 20,* 3–23.

McCann, B.S., Woolfolk, R.L., & Lehrer, P.M. (1987). Specificity in response to treatment: A study of interpersonal anxiety. *Behaviour Research and Therapy, 25,* 129–136.

McCann, U.D., Morgan, C.M., Geraci, M., Slate, S.O., Murphy, D.L., & Post, R.M. (1997). Effects of the 5-HT antagonist, ondansetron, on the behavioral and physiological effects of pentagastrin in patients with panic disorder and social phobia. *Neuropsychopharmacogy, 17,* 360–369.

McNeil, D.W., Vrana, S.R., Melamed, B.G., Cuthbert, B.N., & Lang, P.J. (1993). Emotional imagery in simple and social phobia: Fear vs. anxiety. *Journal of Abnormal Psychology, 80,* 206–210.

Mersch, P.P.A., Breukers, P., & Emmelkamp, P.M.G. (1992). The Simulated Social Interaction Test: A psychometric evaluation with Dutch social phobic patients. *Behavioral Assessment, 14,* 133–151.

Mersch, P.P.A., Emmelkamp, P.M.G., & Lips, C. (1991). Social phobia: Individual response patterns and the long-term effects of behavioral and cognitive interventions. A follow-up study. *Behaviour Research and Therapy, 29,* 357–362.

Montgomery, S.A. (1998). Implications of the severity of social phobia. *Journal of Affective Disorders, 50* (supplement), 17–22.

Monti, P.M., Wallander, J.L., Ahern, D.K., Abrams, D.B., & Munroe, S.M. (1983). Multi-modal measurement of anxiety and social skills in a behavioral role-play test: Generalizability and discriminant validity. *Behavioral Assessment, 6,* 15–25.

Nich, C., & Carroll, K. (1997). Now you see it, now you don't: A comparison of traditional versus random-effects regression models in the analysis of longitudinal follow-up data from a clinical trial. *Journal of Consulting and Clinical Psychology, 65,* 252–261.

Nietzel, M.T., & Bernstein, D.A. (1981). Assessment of anxiety and fear. In M. Hersen & A.S. Bellack (Eds.), *Behavioral assessment: A practical handbook* (2nd ed.). New York: Pergamon Press.

Oei, T.P.S., Kenna, D., & Evans, L. (1991). The reliability, validity and utility of the SAD and FNE scales for anxiety disorder patients. *Personality and Individual Differences, 12,* 111–116.

Otto, M.W., Pollack, M.H., Gould, R.A., Worthington, J.J., III, McArdle, E.T., Rosenbaum, J.F., & Heimberg, R.G. (2000). A comparison of the efficacy of clonazepam and cognitive-behavioral group therapy for the treatment of social phobia. *Journal of Anxiety Disorders, 14,* 345–358.

Paul, G. (1966). *Insight versus desensitization in psychotherapy: An experiment in anxiety reduction.* Palo Alto, CA: Stanford University Press.

Perri, M.G., & Richards, C.S. (1979). Assessment of heterosocial skills in male college students: Empirical development of a behavioral role-playing test. *Behavior Modification, 3,* 337–354.

Phillips, G.C., Jones, G.E., Rieger, E.J., Snell, J.B. (1997). Normative data for the Personal Report of Confidence as a Speaker. *Journal of Anxiety Disorders, 11,* 215–260.

Potts, N.L.S., Davidson, J.R.T., Krishnan, K.R.R., Doraiswamy, P.M., & Ritchie, J.C. (1991). Levels of urinary free cortisol in social phobia. *Journal of Clinical Psychiatry, 52* (supplement), 41–42.

Rapee, R.M., & Heimberg, R.G. (1997). A cognitive-behavioral model of anxiety in social phobia. *Behaviour Research and Therapy, 8,* 741–756.

Richardson, F.C., & Tasto, D.L. (1976). Development and factor analysis of a social anxiety inventory. *Behaviour Therapy, 7,* 453–462.

Ries, B.J., McNeil, D.W., Boone, M.L., Turk, C.L., Carter, L.E., & Heimberg, R.G. (1998). Assessment of contemporary social phobia verbal report instruments. *Behaviour Research and Therapy, 36,* 983–994.

Rogers, R. (1995). *Diagnostic and structured interviewing.* Odessa, FL: Psychological Assessment Resources.

Rudestam, K.E., & Bedrosian, R. (1977). An investigation of the effectiveness of desensitization and flooding with two types of phobias. *Behaviour Research and Therapy, 15,* 23–30.

Safren, S.A., Heimberg, R.G., Horner, K.J., Juster, H.R., Schneier, F.R., & Liebowitz, M.R. (1999). Factor structure of social fears: The Liebowitz Social Anxiety Scale. *Journal of Anxiety Disorders, 13,* 253–270.

Sapolsky, R.M. (1982). The endocrine stress-response and social status in the wild baboon. *Hormones and Behavior, 16,* 279–292.

Sassenrath, E.N. (1970). Increased adrenal responsiveness related to social stress in rhesus monkeys. *Hormones and Behavior, 1,* 283–298.

Scholing, A., & Emmelkamp, P.M.G. (1990). Social phobia: Nature and treatment. In H. Leitenberg (Ed.), *Handbook of social and evaluation anxiety.* New York: Plenum Press.

Scholing, A., & Emmelkamp, P.M.G. (1993). Cognitive and behavioural treatments of fear of blushing, sweating or trembling. *Behaviour Research and Therapy, 31,* 155–170.

Seligman, M.E. (1995). The effectiveness of psychotherapy: The Consumer Reports study. *American Psychologist, 50,* 965–974.

Spielberger, C.D., Gorsuch, R.L., & Lushene, R.E. (1970). *The State-Trait Anxiety Inventory: Test manual for form X.* Palo Alto, CA: Consulting Psychologists Press.

Spitzer, R.L., Williams, J.B., Gibbon, M., & First, M.B. (1992). The Structured Clinical Interview for DSM-III-R (SCID): History, rationale, and description. *Archives of General Psychiatry, 49,* 624–629.

Stein, M.B., Fyer, A.J., Davidson, J.R.T., Pollack, M.H., & Wiita, B. (1999). Fluvoxamine treatment of social phobia (social anxiety disorder): A double-blind, placebo-controlled study. *American Journal of Psychiatry, 156,* 756–760.

Steketee, G.S., Chambless, D.L., & Tran, G.Q. (2001). The effects of Axis I and Axis II comorbidity on behavior therapy outcome for obsessive-compulsive disorder and agoraphobia. *Comprehensive Psychiatry, 42,* 76–86.

Tarico, V., van Velzen, D., & Altmaier, E. (1986). Comparison of thought-listing rating methods. *Journal of Counseling Psychology, 33,* 81–83.

Taylor, S., Woody, S., Koch, W.J., McLean, P., Paterson, R.J., & Anderson, K.W. (1997a). Cognitive restructuring in the treatment of social phobia. *Behavior Modification, 21,* 487–511.

Taylor, S., Woody, S., McLean, P.D., & Koch, W.J. (1997b). Sensitivity of outcome measures for treatments of generalized social phobia. *Assessment, 4,* 181–191.

Torgrud, L.J., & Holborn, S.W. (1992). Developing externally valid role-play for assessment of social skills: A behavior analytic perspective. *Behavioral Assessment, 14,* 245–277.

Tran, G.Q. & Haaga, D.A.F. (2002). Coping responses and alcohol outcome expectancies in alcohol abusing and non-abusing social phobics. *Cognitive Therapy and Research, 26,* 1–17.

Turner, S.M., Beidel, D.C., Dancu, C.V., & Stanley, M.A. (1989). An empirically derived inventory to measure social fears and anxiety: The Social Phobia and Anxiety Inventory. *Psychological Assessment, 1,* 35–40.

Turner, S.M., Beidel, D.C., & Jacob, R.G. (1994). Social phobia: A comparison of behavior therapy and atenolol. *Journal of Consulting and Clinical Psychology, 62,* 350–358.

Turner, S.M., Beidel, D.C., Long, P.J., & Greenhouse, J. (1992). Reduction of fear in social phobics: An examination of extinction patterns. *Behaviour Therapy, 23,* 389–403.

Turner, S.M., Beidel, D.C., Long, P.J., Turner, M.W., Townsley, R.M. (1993). A composite measure to determine the functional status of treated social phobics: The social phobia endstate functioning index. *Behaviour Therapy, 24,* 265–275.

Turner, S.M., Beidel, D.C., & Townsley, R.M. (1992). Social phobia: A comparison of specific and generalized subtypes and avoidant personality disorder. *Journal of Abnormal Psychology, 101,* 326–331.

Turner, S.M., McCanna, M., & Beidel, D.C. (1987). Validity of the Social Avoidance and Distress and Fear of Negative Evaluation Scales. *Behaviour Research and Therapy, 25,* 113–115.

Turner, S.M., Stanley, M.A., Beidel, D.C., & Bond, L. (1989). The Social Phobia and Anxiety Inventory: Construct validity. *Journal of Psychopathology and Behavioral Assessment, 11,* 221–234.

Turpin, G. (1991). The psychophysiological assessment of anxiety disorders: Three-systems measurement and beyond. *Psychological Assessment, 3,* 366–375.

Twentyman, C.T., & McFall, R.M. (1975). Behavioral training of social skills in shy males. *Journal of Consulting and Clinical Psychology, 43,* 384–395.

Uhde, T.W., Joffe, R.T., Jimerson, D.C., & Post, R.M. (1988). Normal urinary free cortisol and plasma MHPG in panic disorder: Clinical and theoretical implications. *Biological Psychiatry, 23,* 575–585.

Uhde, T.W., Tancer, M.E., Gelernter, C.S., & Vittone, B.J. (1994). Normal urinary free cortisol and postdexamethasone cortisol in social phobia: Comparison to normal volunteers. *Journal of Affective Disorders, 30,* 155–161.

Van Ameringen, M., Mancini, C., & Oakman, J.M. (1999). Nefazodone in social phobia. *Journal of Clinical Psychiatry, 60,* 96–100.

Van Zurren, F.J. (1988). The fear questionnaire, some data on validity, reliability, and layout. *British Journal of Psychiatry, 153,* 659–662.

Ventura, J., Liberman, R.P., Green, M.F., Shaner, A., & Mintz, J. (1998). Training and quality assurance with the Structured Clinical Interview for DSM-IV (SCID-I/P). *Psychiatry Research, 79,* 163–173.

Wallander, J.L., Conger, A.J., Mariotto, M.J., Curran, J.P., & Farrell, A.D. (1980). Comparability of selection instruments in studies of heterosexual-social problem behaviors. *Behaviour Therapy, 11,* 548–560.

Waters, W.F., Williamson, D.A., Bernard, B.A., Blouin, D.C., & Faulstich, M.E. (1987). Test-retest reliability of psychophysiological assessment. *Behaviour Research and Therapy, 25,* 213–221.

Watson, J., & Friend, R. (1969). Measurement of social-evaluative anxiety. *Journal of Consulting and Clinical Psychology, 33,* 448–457.

Wiens, A.N. (1990). Structured clinical interviews for adults. In G. Goldstein & M. Hersen (Eds.), *Handbook of psychological assessment.* Elmsford, NY: Pergamon Press.

CHAPTER 16

Behavioral Assessment of Children in Outpatient Settings

SARAH E. FRANCIS AND BRUCE F. CHORPITA

Behavioral assessment seeks to identify specific behaviors occurring within a particular context, determine the antecedents of those behaviors, and describe the consequences that follow them. Such strategies have been used across a wide range of clinical populations, including children and adolescents. Child behavioral assessment has been defined as "an exploratory, hypothesis-testing process in which a range of procedures is used in order to understand a given child, group, or social ecology, and to formulate and evaluate specific intervention strategies" (Ollendick, 1995, p. 100). Essentially, child behavioral assessment seeks to understand a child at the level of the individual through a systematic application of scientific principles across a broad range of life domains, including familial, educational, and peer settings. Findings obtained via behavioral assessments can then be used to craft customized interventions designed to alter a specified target behavior. These intervention strategies are then continually monitored in order to evaluate their effectiveness specific to those intervention goals designated for a particular child. Be-

cause children fulfill numerous roles (i.e., son or daughter, student, friend) across multiple environments (i.e., home, school, community), yet are often dependent on caregivers and parents in a manner dissimilar to that of most other populations, conducting behavioral assessments with children and their families often presents the assessor with a set of unique challenges and considerations. However, because of children's involvement in their family system, many additional sources of information become available to behavioral assessors, helping to expand their conceptualizations of childhood difficulties in ways unique from those available when working only with adults.

As will be evident throughout this chapter, the basic underlying tenets of behavioral assessment with outpatient child populations are identical to those of behavioral assessment conducted with any other clinical population. However, for each component of the behavioral assessment paradigm, strategic considerations specific to children and their families abound.

BASIC TENETS OF BEHAVIORAL ASSESSMENT STRATEGIES

Of particular importance for child behavioral assessment strategies is the recognition that the child functions within the context of a hierarchical series of domains, such that a child exists within a family, which exists within a neighborhood, which exists within a larger community (Bronfenbrenner, 1979). Recognition of the broader context within which a child and his or her behaviors operate allows for the examination of relationships among family members as well as those relations between the family and the socioecological system within which they exist. Specifically, if a child was observed to frequently hit his younger sibling at home as well as younger classmates at school, the behavioral assessor might examine (a) contingencies in place across the child's environments, at home and in the classroom, for aggressive behavior, (b) behaviors that the child is observing in the home, school, peer environment, and the larger community within which the child operates, and (c) the idiosyncratic rules for socially appropriate behavior that prevail in each context.

Given the role of behavioral assessment strategies in evaluating the effectiveness of an intervention (Ollendick & King, 1999), behavioral assessment is viewed as an ongoing process (Mash & Terdal, 1997). Child behavioral assessment practices are continually changing and self-correcting processes (Ollendick & King, 1999). They allow for the revision of treatment strategies, such that a given intervention can be best suited to a child's current difficulties, and also enable a child's treatment goals to expand and include more applicable or relevant behavioral targets as individual progress is made or as environmental circumstances are altered. When treating children with anxiety, once the therapist has identified a specific domain of fear or worry, children are then assisted in the identification of a list or hierarchy of feared situations, which are rank-ordered according to their current fearfulness, thus assisting the clinician in the development of intervention designed to target those areas of concern most relevant to the child. Although this method of assessment may mark the beginning of treatment, the child is asked to provide a rating of fear for each item at the beginning of each treatment session, allowing for the monitoring of treatment progress, while simultaneously allowing the clinician to modify the treatment program to address domains of fear or worry that do not improve or that change in intensity over time.

Another fundamental component of child behavioral assessment strategies is the use of multiple methods and measures of assessment (Mash & Terdal, 1997), allowing for various types of information to be obtained from numerous informants (Ollendick & King, 1999), each of whom might have different experiences or relationships to the child. Such multimethod multi-informant assessment strategies also allow for the comparison of data across informants, settings, and time, thus enabling the assessor to discern behavioral patterns, antecedents, and consequences that may not be readily apparent when examining the child from a single point of view at one point in time or with a single method of assessment. For instance, if a child is experiencing difficulty attending school on a consistent basis, he might report, during the course of an interview, that he simply does not like attending school. However, the assessor's formulation of the child's attendance difficulties might be altered upon obtaining observational reports from the child's parents indicating that the child cries and experiences stomachaches each morning before school and interview data from the child's teacher suggesting that the child is teased everyday by classmates during recess. Thus, employing multiple methods of assessment, as well as obtaining information from multiple informants, allows for a more complete and comprehensive perspective of the presenting area of concern.

Focusing on the strengths and resources inherent in a child and his or her family is an important component of any behavioral assessment strategy, given that such a focus identifies existing protective factors within the family system, assists in treatment planning, and increases the ecological validity of the treatment interventions (Henggeler, Schoenwald, Borduin, Rowland, & Cunningham, 1998). Strengths can be identified across multiple individuals and domains in the child's environment—including the child, parents, extended family network, peers, the school, and the neighborhood and surrounding community—and used to increase the likelihood that changes that occur during treatment will be maintained over time (Henggeler et al., 1998). Regardless of how thoughtfully constructed an intervention strategy is, if there are no supports or resources available in the child's natural environment to implement such a plan, the intervention has a low likelihood of succeeding. The availability of such family and community resources is particularly important for clinicians in outpatient settings to consider, given that the effectiveness of their interventions often depends upon individuals outside of the clinic. For instance, in assessing a child who is engaging in delinquent acts in the community, were the assessor to discover that the child's parents worked during the day and did not return home until late in the evening, an intervention in which the parents were to play a major role in implementation would not be optimal for the family. However, if the assessment revealed that the child excels in sports and lives in a community with a recreational center, part of the subsequent intervention might involve enrolling the child in after-school athletic activities, thus drawing on both the child's own strengths as well as those resources available within the community.

Although many child behavioral assessment strategies often may be perceived to be time-consuming and labor intensive on the part of the assessing clinician working in an outpatient setting, behavioral techniques remain unrivaled in their ability to provide comprehensive information about a child's functioning across a number of life domains, about the specific behaviors that are of concern to a child and family, and about those intervention strategies best suited to meeting a particular child's needs in that specific environment. Furthermore, behavioral techniques often can be modified in order to work within the unique constraints present in many outpatient settings while continuing to provide the clinician with a detailed and problem-specific profile of a particular child's current difficulties in functioning and the ways in which such difficulties might be addressed through treatment.

COMMON PURPOSES OF CHILD BEHAVIORAL ASSESSMENT

Child behavioral assessment strategies lend themselves to several applications, including the identification of target behaviors or diagnosis, prognosis, treatment design and recommendations, and evaluation of treatment outcomes (Mash & Terdal, 1997; Nelson, 1987).

Target Behavior Identification

Behavioral assessment strategies are often paramount in the first step of treatment planning and development: target behavior identification. Determining the problems that are interfering most with a child's functioning or that are creating the highest levels of distress for a child not only provides the clinician with a point at which to implement the specified intervention, but also indicates those variables by which treatment success will be measured. For example, in their design of a treatment intervention for a young boy with attention deficit hyperactivity disorder, McCain and Kelley (1993) obtained reports from the child's teacher indicating that the child was "inattentive, impulsive, distractible, and disruptive" at school. Although such labels are appropriately descriptive of the child's behavior, they are limited in the extent to which they specify behaviors that can be monitored, targeted for intervention, and measured for change. Thus, direct observation was conducted to identify three target behaviors, on-task behavior, disruptive behavior, and number of activity changes, which were able to be assessed during a baseline

period as well as monitored throughout the intervention to assess for treatment effects.

Prognosis

Behavioral assessment strategies are also useful in terms of making predictions regarding the outcome of a specific behavioral or emotional difficulty. Prognostic information can assist clinicians in determining whether a specific behavior or set of behaviors requires treatment, such that some problematic behaviors may be indicative of a particular developmental stage and are difficulties that the child will outgrow, whereas other behaviors may be indicators of more severe later difficulties and should be treated more intensely (Mash & Terdal, 1997). Specifically, nighttime fears in a very young child are fairly typical and often can be alleviated with a relatively brief and specific intervention. However, delinquent behaviors, such as aggression or truancy in a young child represent nonnormative behaviors that have a greater likelihood of persisting over time and of placing the child at risk for developing future difficulties of a more serious nature, such as causing harm to others or involvement with the legal system. Behavioral assessment techniques also provide information concerning short-term and long-term child outcomes, collecting information about those factors that place children at risk for, as well as those factors that protect children from, developing specific mental illnesses (Mash & Terdal, 1997). Assessing a child with oppositional tendencies and a history of hyperactive behavior might suggest that the child is at risk of developing subsequent conduct difficulties (Bagwell, Molina, Pelham, & Hoza, 2001), just as the presence of excessive worry in a young child might place him or her at risk for later disturbances of mood (Masi, Favilla, Mucci, & Millepiedi, 2000; Muris, Meesters, Merckelbach, Sermon, & Zwakhalen, 1998).

Treatment Design and Recommendations

Child behavioral assessment techniques often assist the clinician in identifying behavioral antecedents, evaluating the resources available for change within the family and their environment, assessing the child's and the family's motivation for behavioral change, compiling a list of potential reinforcers for change, identifying treatment objectives that are operationally defined and realistic given the child's currently displayed capabilities, and determining the treatment methods that would be optimally acceptable to and effective for the child and the family (Mash & Terdal, 1997). For a child presenting to an outpatient clinic with recurrent temper tantrums, the assessor might seek to determine specific situational or contextual cues that preceded the tantrums, such as being asked to comply with parental directives, the availability of the child's parents to assist in the intervention (i.e., determining whether both parents work outside the home, the number of other siblings in the household and their needs, and other variables that may impact caregiver resources), and choosing a list of specific behavioral modifications that would be most beneficial for the family to implement, such as getting the child to bed in a timely manner or eating dinner without behavioral outbursts. The child's current capabilities might then be assessed to ensure that he is physically and cognitively able to comply with the behavioral criteria chosen. Specifically, whereas a 14-year-old could be expected to "be in bed by nine o'clock" with only a warning from his parents, a 6-year-old might require considerably more assistance with bedtime routines. Further, when designing such interventions, the therapist's determination of family acceptability also should take into consideration physical family resources, such as the availability of a caregiver during a child's bedtime; a parent's outside job or the demands of younger siblings may make such apparently "simple" treatment recommendations unfeasible.

Treatment Evaluation

Behavioral assessment techniques are used continually to evaluate treatments and their effects on identified behavioral concerns. Such continual evaluation throughout treatment allows the clinician to determine whether specific treatment objectives are being fulfilled, whether changes observed during the course of treatment have long-term implications for the client and will generalize to other problematic behaviors, whether a treatment is economically viable for the child's family, and whether the specific treatment and its resultant outcomes are acceptable to the child and the family (Mash & Terdal, 1997). For example, while treating an extremely depressed child in an outpatient setting, it would be of particular importance to continually assess the child and his or her progress, given that ongoing treatment that is perceived by the child to be unhelpful might result in disengagement in treatment, such that the child ceases to come to the clinic for appointments. Conversely, being able to provide the child and family with documented evidence of treatment progress that might not always be readily apparent to the child or family can be a motivating factor to continue participation in treatment. Thus, outlining behaviorally defined treatment goals allows the clinician to continually monitor the child's progress throughout treatment, such that both the clinician and the child are able to observe gains made over time. Further, continual evaluation via behavioral methods allows the cli-

nician to modify intervention strategies that are not yielding improvements, making the treatment more applicable to the client and his or her current situation (Nelson-Gray & Farmer, 1999).

INTEGRATION OF TRADITIONAL AND BEHAVIORAL ASSESSMENT PRACTICES

Traditional and behavioral methods of assessment differ along several dimensions (Barrios & Hartmann, 1986; Ollendick & Greene, 1990). However, there are many ways in which these two approaches can be combined to complement one another. For instance, standardized instruments, a central component of traditional assessment methods, can be employed during the initial stages of a behavioral assessment in order to develop testable hypotheses, which are then examined idiographically. Similarly, idiographic data collected via behavioral assessment techniques can be used to guide the selection of nomothetic instruments, which can then be used to screen for broad areas of impairment or distress (Mash & Terdal, 1997). Combining these two methods of assessment can be of particular value in outpatient settings, given that using such strategies simultaneously or sequentially often results in a more efficient method of data collection. For example, in the former scenario, a standardized self-report measure, such as the Revised Fear Survey Schedule for Children (Ollendick, 1983), might be administered to a child to screen for the presence of specific fears or phobias; on the basis of the child's report on the FSSC-R, several Behavioral Avoidance Tests (BATs), specific to fears reported on the FSSC-R, might be devised to be administered to the child in order to assess the extent to which specific stimuli and circumstances elicit fearful responses in that particular child. Conversely, in the latter scenario, an assessor may discern through the course of a behavioral observation that a child displays many clinging behaviors and becomes tearful upon even brief separations from her mother; this observational data might then guide the assessor toward the selection of several broad screening measures of anxiety (i.e., the Anxiety Disorders Interview Schedule for *DSM-IV*, Silverman & Albano, 1996; the Revised Child Anxiety and Depression Scale; Chorpita, Yim, Moffitt, Umemoto, & Francis, 2000) to assess for the presence of other anxiety related concerns.

Normative comparisons also may be used to identify areas of functioning in which a child displays behaviors that are deficient or in excess of those typically displayed by children of similar ages or developmental levels (Mash & Terdal, 1997). Normative comparisons can be used to determine the extent to which a parent's expectations are acceptable, such that a problem behavior observed in a child is not overlooked because of a lack of concern on the part of the parents, as well as that a typical behavior is not targeted for treatment because parental expectations are too high (Mash & Terdal, 1997). Specifically, if a mother is concerned that her child is much more fearful of being separated from her than are most children of the same age, part of a behavioral assessment might include the administration of an instrument designed to assess separation anxiety in youth, on which normative data have been collected from a large sample of children (e.g., the Revised Child Anxiety and Depression Scale, RCADS; Chorpita et al., 2000). Should the child obtain a standardized score on the measure much higher than would the majority of other children possessing similar demographic features, a more thorough assessment of the child's worries might then be pursued. Further, in attempts to maximize the efficiency of behavioral interviews for use in outpatient settings, the therapist might use normative information to assist in the selection of portions of an interview schedule to administer. Specifically, should a child score above the normative range on only the worrying portion of a broad-based self-report measure of anxiety, the entire Generalized Anxiety Disorder portion of the interview might be administered. However, for other sections of the interview, only general screening questions might be asked rather than detailed questions about areas that do not appear to be of concern for the child at that time (i.e., separation anxiety, obsessional thoughts).

Further, although idiographic measures may provide a unique profile of a specific child and his or her problematic behaviors, the initial identification of the need for further assessment is often determined through the use of broadband assessment techniques, such as normative comparisons. This idea has been illustrated by the behavioral assessment funnel approach in which broad areas of concern are examined first, with assessment strategies narrowing upon the attainment of initial assessment information, to examine more discrete and specific areas of concern (Nelson-Gray & Farmer, 1999; Barrios & Hartmann, 1986). This approach allows clinicians to screen several domains of behavior for problems in functioning and to examine molecular levels of behavior in an informed manner, rather than guessing about those areas that might benefit from more intensive investigation, or in which significant difficulties might exist.

One example of applying the funnel approach to the assessment of children in an outpatient setting is illustrated by Chorpita, Albano, Heimberg, and Barlow (1996) who used a semistructured diagnostic interview to evaluate a 10-year-old girl refusing to attend school. Upon determining that this child met diagnostic criteria for separation anxiety disorder and social phobia, the clinician administered several self- and

parent-report measures to the child and her mother, including the School Refusal Assessment Scale (SRAS; Kearney & Silverman, 1993). Data yielded from the SRAS suggested that the child was refusing to attend school because she was seeking attention and was fearful of separating from her mother. Thus, once the primary sources of the child's emotional distress (separation anxieties and social fears) and her school refusal behaviors (attention and separation concerns) were identified, both she and her mother were requested to monitor the child's behavior; however, as a result of information yielded from the SRAS suggesting that the child might be refusing to attend school because of attention-seeking behaviors, the child's mother was instructed to monitor her daughter's behaviors in an unobtrusive manner in order to avoid giving her child attention for her behaviors and to reduce the risk of inadvertently reinforcing such behaviors in her child. Information yielded from the parent monitoring indicated four separate domains to target during the course of treatment, including somatic complaints, anger and tantrums, tears, and other complaints. In addition to providing a list of behaviors to target during the course of treatment, parent monitoring also provided for a list of behaviors to monitor during the initial assessment period as well as for a list of behaviors by which to evaluate progress during the course of treatment (Chorpita et al., 1996). In this case, a behavioral interview identified general areas of concern, self-report measures revealed more specific domains of difficulties, and parent monitoring yielded a precise list of target behaviors to monitor and address throughout treatment.

Despite the many valuable uses of standardized, broadband assessment measures in behavioral assessment, in some instances, caution should be taken when administering a battery of standardized self- or parent-report measures. Although any assessment should be comprehensive in terms of the areas of a child's functioning that are examined, an investigation of all situations and areas of interest would require an impractically large number of assessment measures (Mash & Terdal, 1997) and would require an unrealistic amount of time to administer in an outpatient setting. As such, normative instruments should be chosen carefully with particular consideration given to their applicability to the individual child and family being assessed. Further, normative data should not be used without keeping practical considerations in mind, such as realizing that normative data cannot be taken to imply that any behavior exhibited by a large number of children is "normal" (Ollendick & King, 1991). Conversely, simply because the majority of children do not display a particular behavior, when such behaviors are observed among selected groups of children, their presence should not be indiscriminately classified as "pathological." Instead the situational, societal, and developmental characteristics surrounding the behavior must also be considered when making determinations about the clinical significance of any observed behavior or behavioral constellation. Specifically, although most school-aged children would not report seeing ghosts or spirits, and the presence of such reports might suggest cognitive deficits or dysfunctions of thinking, in some cultures being able to visualize such figures is a relatively common occurrence and a valued characteristic and might not be classified as a target for intervention.

DEVELOPMENTAL SENSITIVITY

Development, or those "systematic and successive changes [that occur] over time in an organism" (Lerner, 1986, p. 41), greatly influences the selection and application of behavioral assessment strategies among children. Cognitive, social, and emotional changes during development take place within given contexts and often operate in a bidirectional relationship with the environment in which a child functions (Mash & Terdal, 1997; Ollendick, 1995; Ollendick & King, 1991). For example, a young child who observes aggression as a means to achieve desired outcomes will soon begin engaging in disruptive behaviors when he has needs that he wants to fulfill. However, as that child is developing a method of negotiating his environment, the adults in his environment will also change their behaviors in order to reduce the frequency of his aggressive behaviors, leading the child to misbehave more often and to devise perhaps more manipulative and effective means of obtaining desired outcomes. In such a case the child will have developed a set of behaviors, which in turn shaped his environment, which further influenced his behavioral development (Patterson & Reid, 1984).

Consideration of the influence of developmental differences over the selection, application, and interpretation of specific assessment strategies, however, need not preclude the use of normative measures as part of a behavioral assessment approach. The normative-developmental perspective, one conceptual framework guiding the appropriate application of normative and developmental considerations in assessment, places particular emphasis on the need for normative criteria by which to make clinical judgments when assessing children (Mash & Terdal, 1997; Ollendick & King, 1991). Taking developmental norms into consideration allows the assessor to view a child relative to other children in the same age or developmental group, assisting in the determination of those behaviors that are appropriate or inappropriate among a particular age group. One example of a norm-referenced measure is the Child Behavior Checklist (CBCL; Achenbach,

1991), which allows for comparisons across age groups by providing standardized scores, derived from large-scale normative investigations, for each of eight narrowband subscales. Behavioral assessors also should use information about those qualitative changes in the nature of childhood emotional and behavioral problems that occur over time when choosing assessment materials (Mash & Terdal, 1997), as well as when conceptualizing the nature of behavioral or emotional difficulties that are reported during the assessment process. Specifically, problematic or delinquent behaviors occurring first during early childhood may have a more stable course throughout development, whereas those occurring at later stages of development (e.g., adolescence) may be viewed as more situationally determined and transient over time.

Developmental considerations are also a critical component of behavioral assessment strategies when applying diagnoses to children on the basis of their ability or inability to successfully negotiate the normative developmental expectations and demands posed to them (Mash & Terdal, 1997). For example, taking developmental considerations into mind, the therapist of a 14-year-old child who displays feelings of anxiousness upon being separated from his parents might consider this child to be experiencing more difficulties in functioning than a 5-year-old who cannot be separated from his parents.

USING PSYCHOMETRICALLY SOUND ASSESSMENT MEASURES

A general objective of all assessment techniques is to obtain data to inform clinical decisions (Barrios & Hartmann, 1986). In order to make the most informed clinical decisions, it is imperative that those measures and methods used during the course of behavioral assessment are carefully evaluated in order to ensure the use of instruments that are psychometrically sound.

Comprehensive Assessment Strategies

Conducting comprehensive assessments need not indicate simply the inclusion of more assessment instruments (Mash & Terdal, 1997), as it is often the case that more assessment measures are not necessarily better. Specifically, the incremental validity of additional instruments should be considered, such that the information each measure will add to the conceptualization of a given case must be in some manner significant to warrant its inclusion (Mash & Terdal, 1997). For instance, administering an interview schedule to obtain information about a child's specific phobia of dogs might provide a sufficient amount of information to design an intervention, such that administering additional assessment instruments might have very little incremental validity. Conversely, asking interview questions about a child's obsessive thoughts and compulsive tendencies may only alert the assessor to the presence of obsessive-compulsive features. However, using a more thorough assessment instrument, such as the Leyton Obsessional Inventory-Child Version (Berg, Rapoport, & Flament, 1986), which uses a large number of cards on which obsessive-compulsive symptom categories are written, may add considerable incremental validity to the information obtained through assessment. Specifically, the Leyton identifies not only obsessions and compulsions experienced by the child, but also provides an indication of the resistance experienced by the child in trying to stop the obsessions or compulsions, and the extent to which these symptoms interfere in his or her daily functioning.

Idiographic Versus Standardized Measures

Instrument selection often involves a tradeoff between the psychometric quality of the measures used and the extent to which the assessment data obtained are directly relevant to the child and his or her presenting difficulties (Mash & Terdal, 1997; King, Ollendick, & Tongue, 1995). Specifically, whereas idiographic instruments provide child-, situation-, and time-specific data, such unstandardized measures are of unknown psychometric quality, sometimes making decisions about the validity of the data obtained questionable. Furthermore, developing an integrated understanding of the nature and developmental progression of childhood disorders becomes more challenging as idiographic measures of assessment are used (Ollendick & King, 1999). Such instruments tend to focus on molecular rather than molar behaviors, making it more difficult to ascertain those global factors that might be responsible for the development or maintenance of a perceived behavioral difficulty. However, some instruments can be standardized with respect to their form but idiographic with respect to their content. Specifically, one way in which children's fears and worries have been monitored in outpatient settings during a baseline phase before treatment and during active treatment sessions is through the use of a Fear Ladder (e.g., Chorpita, 1998) or a list of the child's feared stimuli, which is then used to guide the nature and sequence of subsequent exposure-based exercises. Although Fear Ladders incorporate the same format and structure across all children, the items that each individual child is asked to provide fear ratings for vary according to each child's specific area of concern (e.g., separation fears, social anxieties, generalized worries). Thus, the assessor is able to efficiently obtain

information specific to each child within a given context at a given point in time while simultaneously using an instrument design that has been shown to provide clinically meaningful data.

Norm-Referenced Tests

Norm-referenced tests allow the assessor to make inferences about a child's performance on a measure with respect to the performance of other children on an identical measure (Barrios & Hartmann, 1986). However, using broadband norm-referenced testing approaches often does not assist the assessor in determining whether a problem area is in need of further investigation (Barrios & Hartmann, 1986). Instead, such approaches are only able to inform a clinician about where a child falls along a continuum of performance or development; they do not indicate those specific areas that require direct intervention or those that would be most meaningful to the child to modify. For example, the Child Behavior Checklist (CBCL; Achenbach, 1991) is an instrument commonly used in outpatient settings for which normative standards have been determined for behaviors across gender, age, and multiple cultural and ethnic groups. Determining that a child has received a standardized score in the clinical range of impairment on the Delinquent Behaviors scale informs the assessor that this child is engaging in a significant number of delinquent behaviors compared with other children of the same age and gender. However, the child's standardized score on this scale does not indicate that the child is in need of treatment services. Specifically, the score, out of context, does not take into account the level of interference or distress associated with such behaviors or any potential biases of the caregiver respondent. The score, further, does not direct the assessor toward specific treatment recommendations given that it does not yield information concerning the specific behaviors exhibited, the frequency with which they are displayed, the contexts in which they occur, or the functional purposes of these behaviors for the child.

Criterion-Referenced Tests

In contrast to norm-referenced testing approaches are criterion-referenced testing approaches, which allow for the assessor to make direct interpretations of results, without requiring data from other individuals, and facilitate the identification of specific areas of concern (Barrios & Hartmann, 1986). Further, criterion-referenced methods of assessment allow the assessor to alter the criterion with respect to the individual child's presenting level of ability (Wilson & Bornstein, 1984). Specifically, in order to determine the child's capabilities with respect to fearfulness of the dark, the assessor might set the criterion for the child to spend 30 seconds in a dark room by him- or herself. If the child initially experiences difficulty meeting this criterion, the goal can be modified until the child's present ability is determined. In order to evaluate treatment progress, this criterion can be repeatedly increased allowing the clinician to determine whether the child's fear of the dark is indeed declining. Further, employing a criterion-method of assessment allows treatment goals to be created individually for each child, taking into consideration factors such as personal goals on the part of the child, parental goals for the child, and the child's current developmental level and inherent capabilities and limitations.

Construct-Referenced Tests

In contrast to both norm-referenced and criterion-referenced assessment instruments are construct-referenced measures. The premise of such measures is to assess for problem behaviors associated with the primary clinical area of concern, but not the presenting problem itself. These measures target potential covariates that have been demonstrated to maintain the target behavior, thus suggesting testable hypotheses (Barrios & Hartmann, 1986). Although construct-referenced measures cannot indicate the specific nature of the treatment intervention needed, such measures can facilitate further assessment, indicating which variables may be causing the perpetuation of a given problem area (Barrios & Hartmann, 1986). Specifically, a construct-referenced measure postulates potential reasons for a particular child's scores on standardized measures and suggests the ways in which scores on standardized assessment measures may fit together to represent a given construct. For example, a construct often thought to underlie school refusal is social anxieties with respect to peers at school. Measuring a child's social fears prior to treatment would provide a more comprehensive view of the child's presenting difficulties and might direct the course of treatment for school attendance difficulties. Although social anxiety measures would provide information about a causal variable hypothesized to underlie the child's refusal to attend school, such measures would provide little information about the child's school attendance or feelings of distress or concern specific to the school environment.

Multidimensional Assessment Strategies

Given that behavioral problems seldom occur in isolation, multiple assessment techniques, applicable across several domains, are often of greatest benefit (Barrios & Hartmann,

1986). Multidimensional assessment strategies are also advantageous because behaviors often serve multiple functions for a child, such as when a child who throws a tantrum every morning before school not only receives additional attention from her mother, but also misses part of the school morning and gets driven, rather than bussed, to school. Further, causal factors of a given behavior will necessarily vary across individual children, and will vary in their salience across individuals, as well as over time for a single individual (Haynes, 1988). For example, although two children may display similar difficulties going to bed cooperatively in the evening and staying in their rooms after bedtime, one child might experience fears of the dark and be unable to stay in bed because of heightened levels of anxiety, whereas the other child might be refusing to go to sleep in order to obtain additional attention from his parents. Additionally, the child who was initially fearful of the dark might later find staying up past bedtime intrinsically rewarding and begin to refuse to stay in bed for attentional reasons, although this causal factor might not have initially been responsible for her observed behaviors.

METHODS EMPLOYED IN BEHAVIORAL ASSESSMENT STRATEGIES

A great variety of specific techniques comprise the tools available to clinicians conducting behavioral assessments, including direct observation, participant observation, analogue observation, behavioral interviews, self-report measures, self-monitoring, parent/other paper-and-pencil report measures, family/systems assessment, physiological tests, and laboratory-based measures. A description of each of these assessment strategies is provided below with specific examples and suggestions for implementation.

Direct Observation

Direct observation, long considered the hallmark of behavioral assessment (Mash & Terdal, 1997; Ollendick & Greene, 1990), typically entails the recording of a behavior at the time and in the setting in which it occurs (Mash & Terdal, 1997). Given the close proximity between the time of the occurrence of the behavior and its recording, direct observational methods are often perceived as the least inferential and most direct method of assessment (King, Ollendick, & Murphy, 1997; Ollendick, 1995). Direct observational methods can fulfill many goals of assessment, including assisting in the construction of comprehensive and integrative theories of childhood behavioral problems, the provision of recommendations to treating clinicians regarding the services best suited for a given child, and the creation of applicable and clinically relevant measures of treatment outcomes (Mash & Terdal, 1997). Direct observational techniques are often considered best suited for those behaviors that are overt in nature or occur at a relatively low frequency (Baird & Nelson-Gray, 1999), such as tantrums, clinging behaviors, or waking up during the night.

Implementation

Direct observation is applicable in a variety of settings, including the home, a clinic, or the child's school or classroom environment (Mash & Terdal, 1997). Specific behaviors are typically first identified and targeted for change, defined operationally, and then systematically recorded by an observer trained in the appropriate use of the given behavioral observational protocol (King, Ollendick, & Murphy, 1997). When choosing a setting in which to conduct direct observation of a target behavior, the assessor must initially determine the degree of control which will be placed on the situation. Forcing as little structure as is feasible on a direct observational setting allows the target behavior to occur most similarly to the way it would in the natural environment (Mash & Terdal, 1997), given that more structured methods of observation also tend to be those that are most obtrusive into the child's environment (King, Ollendick, & Murphy, 1997). However, the behavioral assessor also must be careful to avoid the use of insufficient structure in a direct observational assessment, given that inadequate structure may not yield valid samples of a child's behavior.

Subtypes

Behavioral assessment strategies often distinguish between "natural" and "artificial" observation, typically referring to observation that occurs in the environment in which a child "naturally" resides, as opposed to observation that occurs in a structured environment, such as a clinic or office setting, in which a child is thought to respond in ways that are "artificial." However, this distinction is often arbitrary, given that observations in natural environments can yield artificial reactions to events, just as observations in artificial settings can yield quite natural reactions to simulated situations and events (Mash & Terdal, 1997). It is thus recommended that the type of observation chosen by the assessor be that which is most suited to the purposes of the given assessment (Mash & Terdal, 1997).

Data

Observational data typically provide the assessor with summaries of a child's behavior over time, as well as the responses to his or her behavior that the child receives from others in the environment. The use of observational data further assumes that the antecedents and consequences of observed behaviors function as controlling events relative to the target behavior (Mash & Terdal, 1997).

Precautions

Perhaps the greatest threat to the utility of observational data is that of reactivity, in which the child being observed changes his or her behavior as a result of being observed by others (Ollendick & Greene, 1990). For example, when engaging in behavior such as hair pulling or talking out of turn in the classroom, a child who becomes aware that he is being observed may be very conscious of his behavior and cease to engage in such actions. Other factors that influence the objectivity and reliability of observational data include the coding system created by the assessor, the behavior targeted for observation, characteristics of the observer, and the ways in which observational data are summarized and interpreted (Mash & Terdal, 1997). Among the factors that often prevent the application of direct observational procedures in real-world outpatient settings are time constraints, a lack of trained observers, and an insufficient amount of resources to conduct the observation in a scientific and psychometrically sound manner (Ollendick & Greene, 1990). For instance, when conducting behavioral observations in a classroom, the assessor must take many considerations into account, such as coordinating the schedules of the observers with that of the classroom (i.e., not scheduling observational sessions during recess or lunchtime), obtaining the appropriate observational materials—ranging from stop watches to video cameras, which might be costly as well as difficult to transport—and remaining inconspicuous in a classroom environment. Specifically, an observer might not be noticed amidst a high school class of 30 students but would most surely be highly visible in a kindergarten special education classroom of four students. In addition to each of these practical considerations, the assessor must also keep in mind those difficulties associated with finding qualified and competent observers who are able to learn and use an observational coding system with high rates of reliability. Thus, despite the valuable contributions of direct observational methods to behavioral assessment, clinicians might wish to carefully consider the feasibility of such assessment techniques in outpatient settings.

Examples

One example of an observational rating system, designed to provide the assessor with a detailed account of behaviors occurring at a relatively high frequency, is the Family Interaction Coding System (FICS; Patterson, 1977b), which evaluates both aggressive and prosocial behaviors exhibited among family members. Using the FICS, the observer watches familial interactions at 30-second intervals over a period of 5 minutes. During each interval, the observer records the behaviors observed using a list of 29 behavioral categories. An additional example of a direct observational tool used with children and families is the Maternal Observation Matrix (Tuteur, Ewigman, Peterson, & Hosokawa, 1995), which is designed to rate the quality and intensity of a range of maternal behaviors occurring during a 10-minute time period, subdivided into twenty 30-second intervals. Each of these forms of direct observation provides observers with a structured rating format, thus yielding frequency counts for similar behaviors across different children. However, the assessor can also define a list of behaviors to observe for each individual child on the basis of reports obtained from other sources (i.e., parent reports, interview findings, teacher checklists).

Participant Observation

Participant observation involves the observation and recording of behaviors of interest by individuals who are already present in the child's natural environment, whether at home, at school, or elsewhere in the community (Nelson-Gray & Farmer, 1999). In many cases, participant observers are preferred to nonparticipant observers, because they are often less costly and more likely to be in the child's environment when the target behaviors of interest occur than are nonparticipant observers (Hay, Nelson, & Hay, 1977). Specifically, teachers or after-school care providers tend to be present during a large proportion of a child's waking hours, thus providing them with more opportunities to witness targeted behaviors than an observer who is able to set aside only 1 hour of his or her day to observe the child. Participant observers are of particular value to assessments conducted in outpatient clinics, given that the clinician is able to gather highly relevant information about the child that in other instances would be too difficult for the assessor to efficiently obtain.

Implementation

Given that participant observers are present in the child's natural environment on a consistent basis over time, their role in observation is the same as that of direct observers, with the exception that participant observers do not require the addition of outside individuals into a child's daily activities. Furthermore, participant observers can, in some cases, function as mediators, ameliorating reactive changes in the child's behaviors that are often attributed to the unusual presence of observers who are artificially introduced into a child's environment (Hay et al., 1977). For instance, a child who is unable to stay in his seat every day during math class is much less likely to cease this behavior when his teacher begins to use a monitoring form than when an outside observer is brought into the classroom.

Precautions

Despite the inherent utility of participant observers, as well as their ability in some circumstances to reduce threats to validity posed by behavioral reactivity, participant observers may sometimes fail to comply with data collection procedures, such as when observers are unable to fulfill their role because of conflicts with their original roles in the environment. For example, a parent of more than one child may have to cease observing the target child in order to fulfill child-rearing responsibilities, or a teacher may be unable to monitor a child's behaviors consistently because of the demands of other students in the classroom. Participant observers also may yield unreliable data or may elicit unwanted reactions in the child's or other observer's behavioral responses (Nelson-Gray & Farmer, 1999).

It must also be noted that observations by individuals in a child's environment may alter the behaviors exhibited by a child over time, as well as the responses elicited from others in the environment by the child's behavior. Participant observers, in such cases, may act as a form of treatment, given that the very act of observation may yield an increase or decrease in the target behavior. In such cases, the assessor must be cognizant of the stage of assessment during which participant observation methods are employed, such that reactivity does not interfere with the data obtained during interventions (Hay et al., 1977).

Example

One example of having parents engage in participant monitoring in the context of an outpatient setting is illustrated by Mackay, McLaughlin, Weber, and Derby (2001), who asked parents to keep simultaneous but independent records of the frequency of their child's noncompliant behavior at home. Such monitoring allowed not only for a record of the child's behavioral patterns at home, but also served as a reliability check on the accuracy of each parent's report. Similarly, Ronen (1991) requested that two parents keep a diary of their child's sleep behavior. Given that sleeping behavior is typically a difficult area for outside observers to rate, participant monitoring was particularly well suited to this case. Further, requesting that both caregivers in the child's environment keep monitoring logs allows the assessor to obtain a detailed picture of the child's specific behavior at specific times, while simultaneously providing a measure of the parents' accuracy in reporting on such behaviors.

Analogue Observation

Analogue observation, or the measurement of behaviors in an environment contrived for the purposes of assessment, attempts to derive valid and cost-effective estimates of children's behavioral, affective, and cognitive processes, their emotional and physiological functioning, and their interactions with others in their typical environment (Haynes, 2001). Analogue assessment is particularly well suited to outpatient settings, because it allows the clinician to observe a child in a variety of situations while remaining within the clinic environment. Analogue observational procedures are intended to assist clinicians in the formulation of hypotheses about those variables that maintain a child's behavioral problems, as well as those factors that will affect the outcome of intervention efforts (Haynes, 2001).

Subtypes

Among the different techniques of analogue assessment available to behavioral assessors are role plays, experimental functional analyses, enactment analogues, contrived situation tests, think-aloud procedures, family interaction tasks, response generation tasks, and behavioral avoidance tasks (Haynes, 2001). Despite the many different types of analogue assessment techniques available, they all share several common characteristics. All analogue assessment strategies seek to measure a child's overt behaviors, or those that can be readily observed and recorded. Similarly, the situations developed for analogue assessments are all intended to be analogous to those in which the child normally functions and in which the target behaviors of interest typically occur (Haynes, 2001).

Data

Analogue assessment strategies can be a particularly useful component of any behavioral assessment because they identify functional relationships that are particularly relevant to a child's idiosyncratic behavioral difficulties (Haynes, 2001). Analogue methods further incorporate observation into the assessment process, offering valuable and pertinent information in cases in which a child is not able to report on his or her own behavior or in which reliable and valid reporters are not available in the child's natural environment to report on the child's behavior. Analogue assessment strategies are also of particular value when target behaviors occur infrequently or tend to be exhibited in the absence of others (Haynes, 2001).

Precautions

The simulated environment, the clarity of instructions to participants, and the nature of the eliciting stimuli all influence the probability that the target behaviors will be observed during the period of analogue assessment. Such factors also increase the likelihood that clinically important behaviors and functional relations will be observed (Haynes, 2001). Specifically, the greater degree of similarity between the natural and simulated environments, the more unambiguous the instructions to assessors, and the more the analogue stimuli closely resemble those present in the child's natural environment, the more likely it is that analogue assessment procedures will provide clinically relevant and applicable information about the target behavior, its antecedents, and its consequences.

Example

One way in which analogue observation can be of particular use among child outpatient populations is through the use of role plays within the context of assessment (Baird & Nelson-Gray, 1999). Specifically, if the assessor is unable to access the target behavior in the natural environment and the behavior does not lend itself to clinic-based assessment, the target behavior can be elicited in a clinical setting by constructing a role play in which the behaviors of interest are assessed. For example, if evaluating the extent to which a socially anxious child is able to engage in conversations with others, the assessor might design a role play in which confederates interact with the child. Such an analogue assessment would enable the assessor to not only observe the child interacting with others, but would also provide a point from which the clinician could identify additional targets of treatment (i.e., eye contact, facial expressions) more specific than those labeled broadly "social interaction." In conjunction with such analogue assessment, the clinician also might administer a self-report measure designed to elicit the presence or frequency of specific cognitions during the situation. One example of such a self-report measure is the Social Interaction Self-Statement Test (Glass, Merluzzi, Biever, & Larsen, 1982; Johnson & Glass, 1989). This instrument is designed for use following a behavioral assessment and asks the child to rate the frequency of specific self-statements before, during, and immediately following the situation. Children indicate their ratings along a 5-point scale, and the instrument yields both Positive Thoughts and Negative Thoughts scores (Mash & Terdal, 1997). Innovative assessors also may find it useful to videotape such analogue observations to later critique and review with the child. By viewing a videotape of this exercise, the child would be able to also identify areas of concern and targets for later intervention, and the assessor can note those behaviors by which treatment gains might later be measured.

An additional example of a contrived or analogue situation designed to test specific behaviors associated with fearfulness is the Behavioral Avoidance Test (BAT). Using a BAT, the child is typically presented with a stimulus to which he or she is reported to exhibit a fearful response. The degree to which the child subsequently approaches or avoids the fearful stimulus is then measured (Baird & Nelson-Gray, 1999). BATs can be used with fear ratings, such that at different points during the BAT, subjective units of distress ratings are obtained from the child. Clinicians also can conduct BATs using videotaped stimuli, such as in the cases of those specific phobias that do not easily lend themselves to clinic-based assessment, including fears of snakes, blood, or shots.

The Behavioral Interview

Behavioral interviews focus on the target behavior exhibited by a child, and the antecedents and consequences related to that behavior in a predetermined situational context (Ollendick, 1995; Ollendick & Greene, 1990). Behavioral interviews seek to identify and delineate behaviors that are problematic to and of concern for the individual (Nelson-Gray & Farmer, 1999). One advantage of using an interview schedule with children is that the interview can simultaneously provide a guide for the assessor to query about the existence of particular concerns and behaviors and allow for considerable flexibility with respect to the way in which questions are asked, such as by paraphrasing or using language geared toward each child's level of understanding (Korotitsch & Nelson-Gray, 1999). For example, when assessing for the presence of generalized anxiety disorder, if a child does not understand the concept of "worrying," alternative phrases or words can be used, such as "upset," "thinking a lot about something," or "having lots on your mind." Further, an interview schedule provides a guide of the questions that need to be asked such that the clinician has a sufficient amount of information to determine whether the client meets diagnostic criteria for a specific disorder. However, once the individual has endorsed

the presence of certain worries, the clinician can then follow up such responses by asking for further details about the content of the worry, when it occurs, for how long it has been occurring, and any antecedents and consequences associated with the worries.

Data

Data obtained during behavioral interviews are often used in the formulation of specific treatment plans. The inherent flexibility of behavioral interviews provides opportunities for the behavioral assessor to establish rapport with the child as well as the family, thus making available valuable information that may not be accessible through other methods of assessment (King, Ollendick, & Tongue, 1995). The data derived via behavioral interviews can also be used to construct theoretical formulations of a client's behavioral difficulties, examining the interrelationships among behaviors by taking into account behavioral similarities in those variables that contributed to the etiology of the behaviors as well as those factors that acted as predisposing (i.e., putting one at risk for), precipitating (i.e., occurring immediately prior to), and maintaining (i.e., sustaining the behavior over time) factors (Nelson-Gray & Farmer, 1999). Behavioral interviews also can be useful in the determination of specific diagnoses (Nelson-Gray & Farmer, 1999) as well as yield information concerning prognostic outcomes.

Conducting behavioral interviews often fulfills multiple assessment purposes (Mash & Terdal, 1997). Behavioral interviews can be used to gather information about the parents' concerns, their expectations, and their goals for their child, as well as to assess parental perceptions of their child's presenting difficulties (Mash & Terdal, 1997). Behavioral interviews also help the behavioral assessor to identify those variables that serve to maintain or elicit the observed problematic behaviors, to obtain historical information about the child's behavioral difficulties and any types of intervention previously implemented, and to discern possible reinforcers in the child's environment that may be perpetuating the occurrence of the problematic behaviors (Mash & Terdal, 1997; Ollendick, 1995). For example, if a parent endorses questions indicating the presence of oppositional difficulties with respect to his or her child, the assessor would then be able to inquire about the specificity of the situations or events that trigger the behavior (i.e., math homework versus every situation that comes up for the child), how long such behaviors have been occurring (i.e., since the beginning of fourth grade or since age two), and the consequences for such behaviors currently in place (i.e., time out versus ice cream to make the child happier). Obtaining more information via the interview regarding each of these variables greatly influences the clinician's conceptualization of the child's case, leading to perhaps further assessments for difficulties with school, or to a closer examination of familial interactions within the home. Behavioral interviews also ideally provide the clinician with the opportunity to educate parents about the nature of their child's difficulties and provide them with information about the prevalence, etiology, and prognosis of such behavioral concerns (Mash & Terdal, 1997). The interview session may be used to inform parents about the rationale for treatment and to assess the family's resources to engage in treatment, such as the parents' affective states, their motivation to participate in the modification of their child's behavior, and their ability to be active participants in the treatment of their child (Mash & Terdal, 1997). The information obtained during behavioral interviews also allows assessors to communicate directly with parents and set attainable goals for treatment (Mash & Terdal, 1997). Behavioral interviews also enable assessors to ascertain the sociocultural context within which the child's problematic behaviors occur (Ollendick, 1995) by obtaining information from children and their parents about the contexts within which a child functions and the key elements in those environments that might influence the child's behavior.

Specific Considerations

When conducting behavioral interviews, clinicians obtain information in a systematic, standardized and efficient manner by using structured and problem-specific interviews that seek disorder- and context-specific information about the presenting problem from both the parent and child (Mash & Terdal, 1997). In addition to providing support and encouragement to the child in order to increase his or her likelihood of appropriate responding during the interview (Ollendick, 1995), it is often helpful to use a child's own words describing difficulties when asking questions or discussing the presenting problem areas (King, Ollendick, & Tongue, 1995; Ollendick, 1995). However, open-ended questions should be used with some caution, given that such questions often yield vague responses from reticent children (King, Ollendick, & Tongue, 1995). The child's developmental stage also should be taken into consideration, such that questions posed to a child during the interview should be stated in simple terms, using words that are easily understood by the child (King, Ollendick, & Tongue, 1995; Ollendick, 1995). It is also often helpful to interview not only the child, but the parents and other caregivers in the child's environment, given that reporters often disagree about the problem areas (Ollendick, 1995), thus making it optimal for the assessor to obtain reports from as many different informants as is feasible. Further, many children experiencing difficulties often present with both internal symptoms of distress (about which the child is often the best reporter) and overt symptoms of interference (about which the parent is often able to provide the best report). One way to increase the reliability of information obtained through behavioral interviews is to ask individuals about only currently occurring behaviors or difficulties and the conditions under which such difficulties occur. Asking children and families to focus only on those behaviors, antecedents, and consequences that occur in the present increases the likelihood of obtaining information that is valid and clinically useful in assessment and treatment planning (King, Ollendick, & Murphy, 1997).

Precautions

Despite their widespread use, behavioral interviews have several limitations, including their often lengthy administration time and their sometimes threatening nature to children (Ollendick, 1995). Further, although all individuals tend to have difficulty recalling events retrospectively, such recall is often particularly challenging for children (Korotitsch & Nelson-Gray, 1999). For these reasons, it is often best to ask children questions that are more direct and concrete with respect to time. Instead of asking, "Do you remember when this first became a concern?" asking, "Was this happening at the beginning of this school year; what about at the end of last school year?" provides the child with specific time markers for past events. Furthermore, children also may withhold information from the clinician because it might be embarrassing. Given such concerns, it is often beneficial to normalize concerns by stating to the child, for example, "Other children have told me . . ." or "When most children feel this way they say that. . . ." Further, given that many children may not disclose information when they are worried about getting into trouble, it is often necessary to seek additional reports from others close to the child, such as parents, teachers, or other care providers.

Despite their broad scope and wide-ranging applicability, behavioral interviews are often not feasible for use in an outpatient setting because of the length of time they require to administer and score. Clinicians assessing children in outpatient settings may therefore want to consider (a) using only selected portions of an interview schedule once general areas of concern have been identified by other means of assessment (i.e., self- or parent-report instruments, participant observation), or (b) asking only general screening questions from the interview and following up with more detailed questions if difficulties are indicated in response to more general questions. However, it must be noted that data do not yet exist regarding the use of selected portions of behavioral interviews, thus making the psychometric quality of such interviews applied in an altered manner unknown.

Example

Many structured and semi-structured interview schedules have been designed for use among child and adolescent populations, including the Anxiety Disorders Interview Schedule for *DSM-IV*, Child and Parent Versions (ADIS-IV-C/P; Silverman & Albano, 1996); the Diagnostic Interview for Children and Adolescents, Revised (DICA-R; Reich & Welner, 1989), designed to correspond to *DSM-III*-R diagnostic criteria; the Diagnostic Interview Schedule for Children, Version IV, developed by the National Institute of Mental Health (NIMH DISC-IV; Shaffer, Fisher, Lucas, Dulcan, & Schwab-Stone, 2000); and the Schedule for Affective Disorders and Schizophrenia for School-Age Children (K-SADS; Orvaschel & Puig-Antich, 1987), a diagnostic structured/semistructured interview designated to tap approximately 50 symptom areas. Behavioral interviews can often comprehensively assess the presence of symptoms associated with a broad range of difficulties, including anxiety, mood disturbances, attentional deficits, hyperactivity, opposition, and delinquency.

Self-Report Measures

Self-report measures are typically instruments completed by the child that ask the child to rate, rank, or otherwise indicate the extent of their own experience of particular thoughts, feelings, or behaviors. Such instruments allow for the attainment of information specific to a given situation that is related to the occurrence of the target behavior, as well as to the subjective experiences of the individual that are linked to the target behavior (Ollendick, 1995). Given that self-report measures provide information about subjective experiences, they allow the assessor access to information that is qualitatively different from that obtained through observational methods (Mash & Terdal, 1997), as well as from interviews, given that a child might be more willing to disclose personal information in a written format than in an interpersonal context. Self-report measures represent one way in which behavioral assessment techniques have expanded to include an examination of the cognitive and affective components that accompany observable behaviors. Theories of assessment also have been extended to include the child as a viable reporter of his or her own actions and environment, as self-report findings increasingly suggest that children are able to provide accurate reports of their own actions, thoughts, and feelings (Mash &

Terdal, 1997). Because self-report measures are inexpensive to administer and do not require extensive investments of time on the part of the clinician or the child, they are particularly well suited to outpatient clinical settings.

Data

In addition to providing a more detailed profile of a child, balancing observations of others with reports from the individual child, self-report measures also benefit behavior therapists (Collins & Thompson, 1993) in that a child's perceptions of his or her own behavior may exert as much influence as the behavior itself in achieving behavioral change (Ollendick & Greene, 1990). Similarly, self-report measures can provide therapists with an efficient index by which to measure changes in behaviors, affect, and cognition following the implementation of a treatment program (Ollendick & Greene, 1990). For example, when working in an outpatient setting with a child with social anxiety, the therapist might administer the Social Anxiety Scale, Child and Adolescent Versions, Revised (SAS-C/A-R; La Greca & Stone, 1993) prior to beginning treatment as well as during treatment in order to obtain an index of changes that might be occurring in the degree of social fears experienced by the child across situations.

Specific Considerations

Self-report measures also can be used to assess the degree to which information yielded via this method converges with verbal reports obtained from the child and his or her caregivers as well as to obtain normative information about the child's areas of concern. Specifically, self-report measures on which normative data have been generated allow the clinician to compare the child with other children his or her age and gender, assisting in the determination of whether the behavior is engaged in to a significantly greater or lesser degree than is generally the case for most other children belonging to the same group (Korotitsch & Nelson-Gray, 1999).

Example

Self-report measures can be employed in different capacities at different points in the assessment process. One example of using self-report measures in an outpatient clinical setting is illustrated by Ollendick, Hagopian, and Huntzinger (1991), who assessed the nighttime fears of two girls, ages 10 and 11, by administering several self-report measures to each child, including the State-Trait Anxiety Inventory for Children (STAIC; Spielberger, 1973). In addition to providing a baseline measure of child anxiety levels that could later be referenced to assess for treatment gains, the assessors also administered the State Form of the STAIC to each child before each treatment session. Before each administration of the State Form, each girl received modified completion instructions, requesting her to answer the inventory while imagining her feelings upon going to sleep each night. The repeated administration of a self-report measure in this instance provided the clinicians with an additional index of the course of each child's anxiety levels during treatment, thus maximizing the ability of a self-report measure to provide continuous assessment data.

Self-Monitoring

Self-monitoring is a process through which an individual begins by first observing and then systematically recording and evaluating his or her own behaviors that are targeted for change (King, Ollendick, & Murphy, 1997; Mash & Terdal, 1997). Self-monitoring is often used to assess covert behaviors or cognitions that are known only to the individual, such as obsessional thoughts (Baird & Nelson-Gray, 1999). In many cases, self-monitoring may act as its own form of intervention, because simply bringing a child's behaviors into his or her awareness can affect the frequency with which such behaviors occur. Specifically, Tombari, Fitzpatrick, and Childress (1985) reported that a boy who self-monitored the frequency with which he engaged in out-of-seat behaviors was able to manage his classroom behavior to the extent that such behaviors ceased to be problematic within the classroom setting. Self-monitoring is another example of a behavioral assessment method that is very feasible to employ in outpatient settings. Specifically, the child can be provided with instructions to monitor a specific behavior outside of sessions; data yielded from the self-monitoring can then be used to guide the content of treatment sessions.

Implementation

Self-monitoring practices have been found to be both simple to implement and an efficient way to collect data about the behaviors of a given child in clinical settings. Furthermore, self-monitoring techniques can be successfully employed across a range of behavior problems (i.e., habit behaviors such as hair pulling, fears, worries, social anxieties, separation fears, social skills difficulties) in a wide variety of domains in which a child functions (i.e., home, school, peer groups, extracurricular activities) (Ollendick & Greene, 1990). In order to self-monitor, a child must be capable of noting the occurrence of a behavior and subsequently recording that behavior as it occurs (King, Ollendick, & Tongue, 1995;

Ollendick, 1995; Ollendick & Greene, 1990). Self-monitoring typically requires a child to be aware that he or she is engaging in the behavior and to have a timely and efficient means of noting the occurrence of the behavior, such as frequency marks, a handheld counter, checkmarks on a behavioral checklist, or tokens that represent occurrences of the behavior. Grandy and Peck (1997), in their investigation of the application of behavioral self-management techniques with a first-grade student, instructed the child to place an X on either a happy face or a neutral face to indicate whether he was engaging in working/listening behaviors or disruptive behaviors, respectively. These self-monitoring instructions were easy for the child to understand and provided immediate feedback about his performance during a specific period of time; the child could quickly determine from his monitoring sheet whether he had spent more time engaging in on-task or off-task behaviors (Grandy & Peck, 1997).

Specific Considerations

Despite concerns that children are not able to accurately monitor their own thoughts and feelings, research has indicated that, under appropriate conditions, children can be reliable and accurate reporters of their own behaviors, thoughts, and feelings (Ollendick & Greene, 1990). Considerations that increase the reliability and validity of child self-monitoring include explicitly defined behaviors, prompts for monitoring, and rewards for appropriate self-monitoring (King, Ollendick, & Tongue, 1995; Ollendick & Greene, 1990). When behaviors are chosen for the child to self-monitor, each must be explicitly defined, such that there is little doubt about whether the target behavior has occurred. The child also should be provided with prompts or reminders to monitor, and rewards should be given when the child remembers to monitor (King, Ollendick, & Tongue, 1995; Ollendick & Greene, 1990), thus serving to increase the probability that the child will continue to monitor effectively. Examples of external prompts to monitor might include a timer set to go off at predetermined intervals, a cassette tape that emits a tone when the child is supposed to monitor, or a pager that alerts the child when it is time to monitor.

Changes in a target behavior during the course of self-monitoring but prior to treatment are fairly common (King, Ollendick, & Murphy, 1997). Studies examining the utility of self-monitoring procedures for use with children have demonstrated that during the course of self-monitoring procedures, the rate of desired behaviors often increases while the rate of undesirable behaviors often decreases (Ollendick & Greene, 1990). For example, if a child is asked to monitor the frequency with which she bites her nails as opposed to keeping her hands folded neatly in her lap, the very act of self-monitoring such behaviors might result in an increased frequency of folded hands and a decreased frequency of nail-biting.

Subtypes

Methods of self-monitoring are highly variable and often depend on the behavior being observed as well as the context in which the observation occurs (Ollendick & Greene, 1990). Self-monitoring can take many forms, such as recording mood ratings, writing down distressing thoughts, or recording the number of occurrences of a behavior within a specific period of time. The format of self-monitoring varies greatly with the behaviors or thoughts to be monitored, and thus should be designed to be most applicable to the child and his or her area of concern.

Data

Data from self-monitoring procedures prior to intervention often can be used to provide information regarding the frequency of the target behavior as well as information pertaining to those antecedents and consequences functionally related to the target behavior (King, Ollendick, & Murphy, 1997). Self-monitoring procedures also may provide information pertaining to the child's cognitions associated with the behavior problem (King, Ollendick, & Murphy, 1997).

Precautions

A primary concern with self-monitoring procedures is the ability of the child to accurately monitor and record his or her behaviors (King, Ollendick, & Murphy, 1997). A child's ability to self-monitor accurately often can be increased by instructing the child in the use of self-monitoring procedures prior to the beginning of formal assessment. Explanation and examples of the specific self-monitoring procedures to be employed also should be provided to the child. Further, many clinicians have found telephone contact with the child's family between sessions and praise for the children's monitoring efforts to be helpful (King, Ollendick, & Murphy, 1997). The act of self-monitoring also has been shown to yield behavioral changes due to reactivity (Ollendick & Greene, 1990). Although researchers are uncertain as to the direct causes of reactivity, children who employ self-monitoring techniques appear to be using a method of behavioral self-management (King, Ollendick, & Murphy, 1997), whereby heightening their awareness of a problem increases their ability to regulate their behavior. Should assessors wish to avoid reactivity,

several methods of self-monitoring are available that reduce the risk of behavior change during observational periods (Ollendick & Greene, 1990). Such techniques include providing the child with specific instructions concerning the process of self-monitoring, ensuring that the child's motivation to self-monitor appropriately is high by providing rewards, setting specific behavioral goals, and providing the child with self-recording devices that are easily understood and employed (Ollendick & Greene, 1990). In many cases, very young children experience difficulty carrying out self-monitoring instructions accurately, thus making it necessary to carefully consider the age of a child when deciding whether to employ self-monitoring techniques during a behavioral assessment (King, Ollendick, & Murphy, 1997). It also has been found that methods of self-monitoring that require the most disruption in the natural environment or those that are most noticeable to a child will result in the most behavioral change, or reactivity effects (Ollendick & Greene, 1990).

Example

Diaries represent a subset of self-monitoring techniques. When keeping a behavioral or cognitive diary, the child is asked to record the frequency with which a target behavior or behaviors occur (Baird & Nelson-Gray, 1999). In addition, the child may be asked to record those antecedents and consequences associated with the target behavior, as well as any other information that may give the clinician an indication of the nature of the behavior targeted for intervention, such as the intensity of the behavior or its duration. When requesting that children keep diaries, the clinician must provide the child with explicit instructions and examples. Similarly, in order to avoid situations in which a child's diary does not provide a sufficient amount of information to establish a baseline, parents should be asked to keep a diary concurrently with that kept by their child (Chorpita et al., 1996).

In accordance with suggestions that children often require very structured and specific diaries in which to self-monitor, Beidel, Neal, and Lederer (1991) devised a diary in which children were instructed to monitor their anxiety levels. Children were asked to indicate the date, time, location, and situation of their anxiety as well as their subsequent behavioral response to their experience of anxiety. In order to make this method of self-monitoring applicable for both younger and older children, a printed and a pictorial version of this diary were created (Beidel et al., 1991). The Self-Monitoring Log (McNamara, 1988) represents another method of self-monitoring developed specifically for use with children. This log requires children to record dates of school attendance and the number of classes attended on each occasion. The child then provides a self-confidence rating ranging from 0 ("dreadfully upset") to 100 ("completely at ease"), thus providing both the child and the assessor with an objective and subjective record of an observable behavior (school attendance) and a feeling (confidence) by which to mark progress over time.

Parent/Other Paper-and-Pencil Report Measures

Paper-and-pencil report measures completed by parents or other adults familiar with the child are typically used to provide information about the child's behaviors and functional relationships among behaviors as they occur in the child's natural environment (Mash & Terdal, 1997) by asking such individuals to provide information about the intensity, duration, or frequency of particular behaviors or to otherwise rate the child and his or her behaviors on a written-response format. Parent-report scales are particularly well suited for use in outpatient settings because they are efficient in terms of the amount of time required to obtain data, and inexpensive with respect to the use of materials needed to complete them. Whereas parent-report scales can provide assessors with information pertaining to a child's overall behavioral and emotional functioning, they also are often used in order to examine specific behaviors, antecedents, and consequences that converge to create problematic childhood behaviors (King, Ollendick, & Murphy, 1997).

Data

Questionnaire data obtained from parents and other caregivers and adults in the child's environment allow for a standardized and comprehensive means of collecting data relevant to a child's presenting difficulties (King, Ollendick, & Murphy, 1997). Parent-report measures can be used to assess parental motivation to engage in methods of behavioral change. Similarly, parent-report scales also provide information relevant to a child's behavior in the child's home environment, as well as inform clinicians regarding the effectiveness of those interventions implemented (Mash & Terdal, 1997).

Obtaining parental perceptions of a child's behavior is particularly relevant to determining the course of treatment to take with respect to a child's presenting concerns (Mash & Terdal, 1997). Objective parent questionnaires are also of particular use given that a clinician's judgments about a child's difficulties may be biased by a parent's report during an interview. For instance, during an interview, a parent may not indicate that the child engages in disruptive behaviors more than most children his age; however, on a checklist such as the Child Behavior Checklist (Achenbach, 1991), the same parent might endorse a sufficient number of behaviors at a

high level of intensity to indicate that the child's behavior indeed is excessive relative to other boys his age. Parent-report measures may thus provide the assessor with more objective information about a child's presenting difficulties than will parents' verbal reports (Mash & Terdal, 1997). Parent-report measures also can inform others who interact with the child about specific skills or deficits demonstrated by the child, serving to instruct significant individuals in the child's environment about means by which observation and other behavioral recording may yield information that is later beneficial for the purposes of treatment planning and monitoring (Ollendick & Greene, 1990).

Specific Considerations

Parent- and other-reports can provide the clinician with behavioral information about a child in a more timely manner than is often possible through other means of assessment (Mash & Terdal, 1997), and are thus often more economical with respect to cost, effort, and time (Mash & Terdal, 1997), making them quite applicable in outpatient clinical settings. Employing parents, teachers, and other adults as informants of the child's behavior helps such adults acquire particular skills in observing, tracking, and monitoring the child's behavior (Mash & Terdal, 1997).

Subtypes

Several types of parent-report scales exist that ask parents about a broad range of domains. Questionnaires may ask parents to describe specific parenting behaviors, such as their use of discipline, rewards, and punishment. Other parent questionnaires may query about parents' attitudes toward parenting and childrearing, asking parents about their satisfaction with their parental roles, their own self-esteem, and their expectations for their child (Mash & Terdal, 1997). Parent self-rating forms can also provide assessors with information about the manner in which parents react to specific difficulties that their child may exhibit (Mash & Terdal, 1997), thus indicating parental behaviors that may be functionally related to difficulties displayed by the child.

Precautions

One concern specific to the use of parent-report measures, mother-father agreement, is often influenced by the specific instrument used, as well as the way in which interrater agreement is calculated (Mash & Terdal, 1997). Assessors also must take into consideration that parental recordings of behaviors yield reactive effects, such that the behavior being rated or observed by parents may increase or decrease in frequency when the child notices that his or her behavior is being monitored (Mash & Terdal, 1997). Data obtained from parental report scales also may be unrepresentative, because it is obtained from only one perspective, typically in one environmental context (Mash & Terdal, 1997), thus emphasizing the importance of obtaining reports from multiple informants in the child's environment.

Example

Several parent-report measures have been designed to obtain information from the parent about the extent to which a given behavior is present, or the degree to which the behavior is considered to be problematic. These instruments include the Child Behavior Checklist (CBCL; Achenbach, 1991); the Behavior Assessment System for Children, Parent Rating Scale (Reynolds & Kamphaus, 1992); the Conners Parent Rating Scale (Conners, 1990); the Parent Attitudes Test (Cowen, Huser, Beach, & Rappaport, 1970); and the Behavior Problem Checklist (Hinshaw, Morrison, Carte, & Cornsweet, 1987). In addition to completing checklists that inquire about a broad range of child behaviors, parents also can be requested to complete forms designed to monitor the intensity and frequency of behaviors that have been targeted for treatment, as well as the antecedents and consequences associated with these behaviors. Such forms can be designed by the therapist to include only those behaviors that will be targets of intervention, but to also allow for the identification of those parent behaviors that might precede or follow the child's behavior. For example, if a child throws tantrums whenever she is requested to do her math homework, her parents might be asked to record their behavior before the tantrum and the way in which they responded to the child's behavior. Such a method of data collection might then reveal that the child's mother repeatedly tells the child to do her homework, and then comforts the child with hugs and kisses after the tantrum, thus suggesting two parental behaviors that might be addressed when working to reduce the frequency of the child's tantrums.

Family/Systems Assessment

Notions that a child manifests behavioral or emotional difficulties in isolation of the context in which he functions are often faulty. Families typically display patterns, clusters, or constellations of behavior that tend to be relatively stable and persistent over time (Mash & Terdal, 1997). As such, behavioral assessment techniques conceptualize the child as existing in the context of a family with parents and siblings,

instead of focusing only on the target child. Thus, behavioral difficulties must be treated as events that result from reciprocal interactions between the child and others in that child's environment (Mash & Terdal, 1997).

Family assessment techniques can occur on two levels. On the first level, information is obtained from the family, which allows the assessor to understand the ways in which each member of the family relates to other members of the family, within the family structure. The second level is the functional or structural organization of the family, in which the family is viewed as a comprehensive system (Mash & Terdal, 1997) that fulfills a particular set of functions and is structured in a manner designed to optimally achieve these functions. Conceptualizing a family from an ecologically oriented systems approach allows for the assessment of whole family variables (Mash & Terdal, 1997), such as communication patterns among family members, attachment patterns among parents and children, or differences between mothers and fathers with respect to their patterns of interaction with their children.

Specific Considerations

Difficulties in family interactions often are observed to exist among the families of children with behavioral and emotional problems. Further, relational difficulties between parents or intrapersonal parental difficulties may contribute to the development or maintenance of problematic behaviors among children (King, Ollendick, & Murphy, 1997). Given that such family challenges may affect the success with which treatment is implemented, it is of particular importance to conduct an assessment that examines the family system as a whole.

Methods of family assessment can have immediate and significant effects on the behaviors of individuals within the family system (Ollendick & King, 1999). Conducting family-based assessments allows the assessor to observe both verbal and nonverbal behaviors that occur within the family in response to external cues, as well as in each family member's response to one another (King, Ollendick, & Tongue, 1995). When assessing a family, it is often crucial to assess not only parent-child interactions, but to also examine parental perceptions of their own and each other's interactions with their children (King, Ollendick, & Tongue, 1995; Ollendick & Greene, 1990).

Family-based assessment techniques often provide the assessor with a much more comprehensive clinical picture than can be obtained from any single reporter. However, despite the valuable contributions of such methods to child behavioral assessments, clinicians in outpatient settings might wish to carefully consider the feasibility of assessing families or familial patterns of interaction. Specifically, it is often diffi-cult to arrange for more than one additional family member to accompany a child to a treatment session, and arranging to meet with families in their own homes is often challenging as well. Additionally, given that many forms of family as-sessment involve behavioral observation methods, such as-sessment is often time-consuming with respect to both data collection and data interpretation. However, if it appears that information concerning family functioning would be of par-ticular importance to a given assessment, the clinician might wish to administer paper-and-pencil measures of the family environment or familial relationships that can be completed by other family members outside of session and returned to the clinic at a later time (i.e., the Family Environment Scale, Moos & Moos 1976, 1983; the Family Functioning Scales, Bloom, 1985; the Family Adaptability and Cohesion Evalu-ation Scales-III, Crowley, 1998).

Subtypes

Behavioral observation is one method frequently employed to assess a family's functioning and interactions. Among those objective measures most commonly used to assess families and systems are the Self-Administered Dependency Questionnaire (SADQ; Berg, 1974), the Family Assessment Measure (FAM-III; Skinner, Steinhauer, & Santa-Barbara, 1983), and the Family Beliefs Inventory (FBI; Roehling & Robin, 1986).

Example

Applying the principle of examining child behaviors as they occur within the context of a child's family to assessment, Greene, Kamps, Wyble, and Ellis (1999), in their investiga-tion of noncompliance among school-aged children, examined not only child behaviors but also assessed child interactions with parents and siblings. Specifically, these assessors ob-served children and rated their behavior at 10-second inter-vals, coding their interactions with those around them as "positive," "negative," or "neutral." The data yielded during these observations were later used to assist parents in the modification of their child's behavior through the use of posi-tive instructions. On the basis of their style of interaction observed during the assessment, parents were able to be pro-vided with modeling and feedback on a number of effective parenting skills. Thus, observations of interactions between children and parents allowed not only for therapist knowl-edge of the interaction between the child and his or her en-vironment, but also directed the clinician in working toward altering those interactions to effect treatment gains.

Physiological Tests

Physiological testing represents yet another component of be-havioral assessment. Physiological responses can be of partic-ular importance given that physiological arousal is a primary feature of many behavioral and emotional responses (King, Ollendick, & Murphy, 1997).

Subtypes

It is currently possible to record a variety of different phys-iological responses as a result of technological advances in the instrumentation available for such assessment (King, Ollendick, & Murphy, 1997). Two of the most common types of physiological assessment are cardiovascular response measures and electrodermal response measures (Ollendick, 1995), although blood pressure and muscle tension are also frequently assessed during physiological measurement strat-egies (King, Ollendick, & Murphy, 1997). Such physiologi-cal measures are used to make inferences about a child's behavioral responses in particular situations and are often best for behaviors that are otherwise difficult to observe or record, such as a fast-beating heart or difficulty breathing. In those cases in which children present with internalizing symp-toms of distress (i.e., nervousness, fear, worry), behavioral observation is often more challenging, given that fear or panic responses that do not involve leaving a situation are typically difficult to observe. As such, physiological assess-ment strategies are of incremental value with respect to as-sessing children with internalizing concerns because they provide the assessor with data about physical sensations of fear or worry that are not accessible to observers and may be difficult for a child to describe accurately via self-report measures.

Specific Considerations

Although measures of physiological arousal can be obtained through self-report and self-monitoring, direct measurement of physiological variables can generate both discrete and con-tinuous data that are highly sensitive to physiological processes often outside of the child's awareness. Further, physiological assessment typically requires only passive participation on the part of the individual being assessed, thus particularly lending itself to situations in which a child might experience difficulty providing detailed accounts of his or her physio-logical processes during anxious or upsetting events. Physi-ological assessment measures also may be better suited to detect small but significant changes in physiological responses that might not be detected by self-report measures (Korotitsch & Nelson-Gray, 1999).

Precautions

Although cardiovascular measures provide information that can be relevant to many bodily functions, studies have found that heart rate may be influenced by motor and perceptual activity, and also may be confounded with stress (Ollendick, 1995). Furthermore, heart rate is a very idiosyncratic variable, which varies greatly not only within the individual child, but across children as well (Ollendick, 1995). It is thus of particular importance to use multiple measures of physiological arousal because no single measure is likely to be representative of an individual's physiological responding. Further, in many cases, responding across multiple systems of physiological arousal is seldom synchronous (King, Ollendick, & Murphy, 1997). Despite the potentially interesting nature of data yielded via physiological assessment strategies, such precautions suggest that these measures might benefit from further evaluation before being employed as a typical component of behavioral assessment strategies. Additionally, physiological measures are also often time-consuming and expensive (Ollendick, 1995), and thus may not be well suited to many outpatient settings.

Example

One example of a physiological assessment measure used with phobic children is the Computer Instruments Heart Watch (Silverman & Rabian, 1994), an electronic device resembling a wristwatch. When placed on the child's wrist, this instrument measures changes in the child's heart rate during exposure to fear-provoking stimuli, thus gathering data beyond that obtainable via self-report measures or behavioral observations (Silverman & Rabian, 1994). Because a physiological measure such as the Heart Watch is relatively unobtrusive and easily transportable, it and similar instruments may be more feasible to use for outpatient assessments.

Laboratory-Based Measures

Techniques designed to assess information processing in individuals provide data relevant to the existence of information processing biases, response latency, processing speed, and related behaviors. One area in which children have been shown to exhibit information processing biases is in their response to threat cues. Such biases toward threatening stimuli are important to measure because they can provide the assessor with clues about those factors that may maintain fears and phobias (King, Ollendick, & Murphy, 1997) as well aggressive responses to stimuli (Barrett, Rapee, Dadds, & Ryan, 1996; Dadds, Barrett, Rapee, & Ryan, 1996). Another domain in which laboratory measures have been widely used

has been in the assessment of attention deficit hyperactivity disorder (ADHD).

Laboratory measures often can provide assessors with information not obtainable through methods such as self-report or behavioral interviewing. However, the feasibility of these measures in outpatient clinics can be limited because they often require computerized equipment that may be expensive to purchase as well as to maintain. Further, because such equipment is often difficult to transport, relying on laboratory-based assessment measures may limit the clinician to conducting assessments only in the clinic rather than in schools or other community facilities.

Data

Information processing methods of assessment provide details regarding an individual's information processing capabilities. Such data can be helpful in treatment planning, as well as in treatment outcome research (King, Ollendick, & Murphy, 1997). Specifically, these measures can be used to detect cognitive biases or misattributions, which can then be targeted during the course of treatment. Further, laboratory-based measures of assessment can be used after treatment to determine whether the intervention was effective to the extent that it reduced those biases observed during assessment (King, Ollendick, & Murphy, 1997). Although it may initially be presumed that laboratory-based measures of assessment leave less room for interpretation or ambiguity with respect to assessment results, it must be noted that the clinician must be able to knowledgably interpret the assessment data yielded. Thus, although such forms of assessment may be efficient with respect to administration time, the time required to interpret and integrate these data into a functional formulation must also be considered.

Example

In assessing for the presence of attentional deficits commonly associated with ADHD, assessors often employ continuous performance tests (CPTs), a laboratory-based assessment instrument that assesses both attention span and vigilance. CPTs typically present the child with stimuli rapidly projected onto a computer monitor and require the child to press a button when the target stimulus or stimuli series appears (Mash & Terdal, 1997). CPTs yield data regarding the number of correct responses, the number of trials on which the target stimulus was missed (errors of omission), and the number of trials on which an incorrect stimulus was responded to affirmatively (errors of commission). The number of correct responses and errors of commission is then used to provide an index of sustained attention and impulse control. Among those CPTs with normative data available for use among clinicians are the Continuous Performance Test (Conners, 1995), the Gordon Diagnostic System (Gordon, 1983), and the Test of Variables of Attention (Greenberg & Waldman, 1992).

SPECIALIZED TOOLS FOR BEHAVIORAL ASSESSMENT

Even with a well-founded knowledge in the techniques of behavioral assessment, it is often difficult in outpatient clinical child assessment to identify a starting point with a new case from which hypothesized variables can be generated and functional relationships tested. Assessment is an ongoing process throughout which different maintaining and eliciting variables can be repeatedly tested until a working functional model of a child's behavior has been constructed. However, some measures have been found to facilitate this testing process by providing information about the function of specific behaviors prior to testing hypothesized functional relationships or specific intervention strategies. Such instruments inform the clinician of the function of the child's observed behaviors, thus suggesting not only potential means of intervention, but also additional more specific or idiographic methods of assessment.

One instrument developed to identify maintaining variables for specific problematic behaviors is the Motivation Assessment Scale (MAS), designed by Durand and Crimmins (1988) to assess for the presence of four possible maintaining variables of self-injurious behavior. Durand and Crimmins (1988) demonstrated that the MAS, completed by children's teachers, enabled clinicians to determine those motivating conditions responsible for the maintenance of self-injurious behaviors among children. The MAS was also useful in the identification of the appropriate mode of treatment to be applied to the targeted behaviors (Helmstetter & Durand, 1991).

Another instrument designed to identify variables that are functionally related to an observable behavior is the School Refusal Assessment Scale (SRAS; Kearney & Silverman, 1993), intended to assess those factors and their functional relations that maintain school refusal behaviors in children. Specifically, the SRAS, on the basis of an objectively derived set of data, seeks to classify school refusal behaviors into discrete functional categories, thus linking the child's behaviors to treatment strategies that might be most appropriate and that are prescribed specifically for those variables determined to be maintaining school refusing behaviors (Kearney & Silverman, 1993). This measure is particularly easy to add to an outpatient assessment protocol because it is a paper-

and-pencil measure that can be quickly completed by the child and his or her parent, yet it provides highly relevant clinical information to the assessor.

The SRAS proposes that school refusal behaviors can be conceptualized as existing along four functional dimensions, each of which is hypothesized to represent a behavioral continuum. The child's score on each of these four dimensions yields a profile of his or her school refusal behaviors, which is subsequently used to assist in the development of treatment plans (Kearney & Silverman, 1993). The SRAS thus suggests treatment modalities in an individualized, prescriptive manner, determining treatment on the basis of the functional condition of school refusal behaviors identified by the questionnaire (Kearney & Silverman, 1993). In this manner, the SRAS enables the clinician to more efficiently conceptualize the case as well as make specific decisions regarding treatment.

The SRAS also provides an example of the interface between assessment and treatment for child clinical populations, given that it accurately predicts prescriptive, individualized treatment strategies for children exhibiting school refusal behaviors (Kearney & Silverman, 1993). This instrument has provided preliminary support for the hypothesis that a theory-driven model of assessment can enhance the efficacy of those interventions implemented (Kearney & Silverman, 1993). Specifically, implementing an a priori assessment approach assists clinicians in the choice of treatment strategies that are most efficacious for each type of school refusal behavior, as has been indicated by findings demonstrating that six out of seven clients were able to successfully return to school, and levels of specific fearfulness, general anxiety, and other internalizing and externalizing behaviors were also reduced (Kearney & Silverman, 1990) when interventions were developed on the basis of results obtained from the SRAS.

CASE ILLUSTRATION

Heather, a 9-year-old girl, was referred by her parents to an outpatient center for anxiety. An initial telephone screening interview indicated that, according to Heather's parents, her primary areas of concern centered around intense fears and worries, difficulties interacting with peers, and tantrum behavior exhibited when she became upset. Heather's parents indicated that their daughter's worries and disruptive behaviors were creating significant difficulties for the family at home and were impairing Heather's ability to function comfortably at school among her peers. Although Heather had been receiving counseling services from a school-based therapist, this individual had been unable to identify the specific source of Heather's emotional and behavioral difficulties.

An initial intake evaluation was scheduled for the family at the clinic. Heather and her parents were first requested to complete several paper-and-pencil assessment measures and were then administered a semistructured interview. Among the parent-report measures administered to Heather's parents were several broad-based questionnaires requesting background and medical history information relevant to Heather, as well as information regarding the extent to which Heather engaged in specific behaviors. Maternal reports on these instruments indicated that Heather had been displaying heightened levels of worry since the age of three or four, at which time Heather became very upset when she discovered that her father had sold his old car and bought a new one. At this time, Heather reportedly continued to persistently question her father for six months, asking about where the car was and when it was coming back. Although Heather's behaviors were reported to initially be of some concern to her parents, these behaviors did not prevent Heather from engaging in activities with other family members, nor did they initially interfere with Heather's ability to attend school and achieve satisfactory grades. However, when Heather entered the second grade, her parents reported that her school work became more challenging for her, and she began to experience difficulties attending school. Heather's mother further indicated that she observed Heather becoming very upset if she did not do well in school, and noted that Heather often placed a great deal of pressure on herself to excel in her school work.

During the autumn of her second grade year, Heather's mother reported that she and Heather's teacher noted that Heather had failed to establish friendships in her class and was experiencing difficulties maintaining friendships with other children both at school and in her neighborhood. Heather's parents reported that during this time they became increasingly concerned about their daughter's distress related to attending school, as well as her apparent lack of close peer relationships with children her age. Parent reports on the background history questionnaire further indicated that during Heather's second grade year, she began to display heightened levels of problematic behaviors, including (a) extreme feelings of distress when confronted with change or loss, (b) a tendency to hoard unnecessary items and to experience great degrees of distress when instructed to throw them away, and (c) acts of noncompliance and argumentativeness toward her parents when she was instructed to engage in activities in which she did not want to participate. It was at this time that Heather's parents brought Heather to the clinic for an evaluation.

To obtain more specific information pertaining to Heather's display of behavioral difficulties, the Child Behavior Checklist (CBCL; Achenbach, 1991), a parent-report measure that

reflects a range of child behavior problems, was administered to Heather's parents. This parent-report measure provides both broad- and narrowband scores, indicating general and specific areas of behavioral concern. Maternal and paternal reports on the CBCL indicated that Heather scored in the clinical range on the Internalizing (T = 72; T = 70, respectively) and Externalizing (T = 73; T = 71, respectively) broadband scales, suggesting that Heather was concurrently experiencing both emotional and behavioral difficulties. Heather's narrowband scale scores on the CBCL were then examined. Her mother's report yielded scores in or near the clinical range on the Anxious/Depressed (T = 65), Social Problems (T = 77), Thought Problems (T = 76), Attention Problems (T = 70), and Aggressive Behavior (T = 76) scales. The paternal report on the CBCL concurred; Heather scored in the clinical range on the Withdrawn (T = 68), Somatic Complaints (T = 67), Social Problems (T = 77), Thought Problems (T = 82), Attention Problems (T = 81), and Aggressive Behavior (T = 70) scales. Those items endorsed by Heather's parents on the CBCL appeared to be indicative of difficulties in thought processes and were conceptualized as being related to Heather's experience of worries and her tendency to have a great deal of difficulty throwing unnecessary items away (e.g., mind wandering off, engaging in strange acts, and repeating acts). Heather's elevated scores on the aggressive behavior scale were hypothesized to be related to Heather's parents' reports indicating that Heather would become distressed and at times aggressive when she was requested to comply with actions that were contrary to her wishes.

To further assess those areas of concern reported by Heather's parents on the parent-report measures, several self-report instruments were administered to Heather, including the Revised Children's Anxiety and Depression Scale (RCADS; Chorpita et al., 2000), a self-report measure of general anxiety, and the Children's Depression Inventory (CDI; Kovacs, 1980/1981), a self-report measure of depressive symptoms. Examination of the subscales of the RCADS indicated that Heather scored in the clinical range of the Obsessive Compulsive Disorder scale (T = 72), and endorsed items including "I can't seem to get bad or silly thoughts out of my head," "I have to think of special thoughts (like numbers or words) to stop bad things from happening," and "I have to do some things over and over again (like washing my hands, cleaning or putting things in a certain order." Heather's raw score on the CDI was within the clinical range for her age group, as indicated by her T-score of 71 on this instrument. On the CDI, Heather endorsed items such as "I never have fun at school," "I do not want to be with people at all," "I have to push myself all the time to do my schoolwork," and "I can never be as good as other kids," converging with Heather's reports indicating that she was experiencing difficulties with peers, concentration, and school work. Heather's scores on the RCADS and CDI suggested further assessment of her feelings of depression as well as of her repeated experience of unwanted thoughts and feelings that she had to engage in particular actions.

A semistructured behavioral interview, the Anxiety Disorders Interview Schedule for *DSM-IV,* Child and Parent Versions (ADIS-IV, C/P; Silverman & Albano, 1996), was then administered to Heather and her parents as a general screening tool to assist in the diagnosis of childhood anxiety, mood, behavioral, and attentional disturbances. Given that children are typically good informants with respect to their experience of internalizing symptoms of distress, such as anxiety and depression, Heather and her parents were each administered separate diagnostic interviews.

During the initial interview, Heather avoided eye contact and was restless and fidgety, playing with objects in the interview room. Heather was reluctant to participate in the assessment process and ignored requests to enter the interview room until coaxed by her mother and father. She cried upon being separated from her parents, and became upset when questioned about things that may have been bothering her. In attempts to alleviate Heather's distress associated with speaking with the assessor, the interview was set aside for several minutes during which the interviewer attempted to engage Heather in conversation and provided her with some paper and pencils to keep Heather seated at the table. When Heather displayed difficulty responding to the questions, the interviewer began paraphrasing the interview questions and solicited Heather's preferred words to discuss her current difficulties (i.e., "worries" rather than "unwanted thoughts"). To reward Heather's subsequent compliance with the interviewer, two brief breaks were taken during which Heather was allowed to walk around the waiting room and obtain a drink of water. Because several of the areas of concern about which Heather was questioned inquired about the duration of such worries or fears, Heather was first prompted to recall the onset of her worries and fears by her grade in school or by her age at that time. For more recent events, Heather was provided with a calendar on which memorable events were marked (i.e., holidays, birthdays, recent trips) to aid her memory, because children often have difficulty recalling the time course of past events accurately (Korotitsch & Nelson-Gray, 1999). Following the administration of the ADIS-IV-C to Heather, the ADIS-IV-P, a parallel interview schedule, was administered to her parents.

On the basis of interview information obtained from Heather and her parents, Heather's presenting symptoms were hypothesized to stem from her persistent worries that "things would not be right" if she were unable to perform certain ritualized behaviors, such as (a) hoarding and collecting trivial items; (b) ordering and arranging items such as toys, blocks, and shoes; (c) asking the same question repeatedly and persistently; (d) having to touch things in a special way; and (e) eating only certain foods. Heather and her parents endorsed obsessional items such as (a) repeating songs over and over, accompanied by a need to start over at the beginning if interrupted; (b) hoarding items, such as shreds of napkins or used paper cups; and (c) symmetry and exactness, accompanied by a need to line up shoes outside the house, arrange stuffed animals, and erase and rewrite her class work. At the time of the evaluation, Heather's rituals and compulsions occupied between 4 and 6 hours per day. However, if her rituals were successfully completed, they interfered less than if they were not. Heather and her parents indicated that when Heather was prevented from performing her rituals, or from completing them once started, she subsequently would feel unable to persist in her daily activities. Although Heather reported symptoms associated with feelings of depression on self-report measures, when this area of concern was assessed via the behavioral interview, such concerns did not meet diagnostic criteria for a diagnosis of a disturbance of mood; further, Heather's expressed feelings of sadness were conceptualized as stemming from her anxiety and the social difficulties created by her behaviors.

An additional area of concern identified during the interview surrounded Heather's tendency to become upset and display tantrum-like behaviors, including crying, yelling, kicking, and hitting, when she was prevented from engaging in behaviors such as hoarding, ordering, or repeated questioning, or when she was asked by her parents to engage in activities in which she did not want to participate. Heather's parents further reported that Heather often (a) was argumentative with her parents, (b) was easily annoyed by others, (c) became upset when she did not get her way, and (d) blamed others around her when things did not work out for her. Although Heather's tendency to engage in such argumentative and noncompliant behaviors began approximately one and a half years prior to the time of her evaluation, such behaviors had reportedly escalated in intensity and frequency during the six months prior to Heather's assessment. Based on reports obtained from Heather and her parents, she met all of the diagnostic criteria required for a diagnosis of obsessive-compulsive disorder and oppositional defiant disorder (OCD and ODD, respectively; *DSM-IV*).

Approximately 1 week after Heather's intake evaluation, Heather and her family were provided with feedback on the assessment results, and treatment was offered to Heather through the clinic. However, at the time of the feedback session, Heather's mother reported that Heather's avoidance of certain foods had escalated to the point where Heather was gagging or vomiting several times daily when attempting to eat food. An extensive physical examination by Heather's physician to investigate a possible medical explanation for her frequent vomiting had revealed no medical or physical reason for Heather's recurrent vomiting. Therefore, to obtain a behavioral indicator of the extent of this behavior, Heather's parents were requested to monitor the frequency of their daughter's gagging and vomiting behavior, as well as those events that preceded and followed Heather's eating difficulties. This list of specific behaviors to monitor was derived from parental reports indicating those most pronounced areas of concern. Heather's parents were given a set of participant observation, or monitoring, forms that asked them to record the time of the behavior, the place in which it occurred, the food that triggered the behavior, and the actions or reactions that followed these behaviors (i.e., whether the meal was concluded, how Heather and her parents responded to the vomiting, the way in which the incident was discussed among family members). The therapist reviewed these forms with Heather's parents and helped them fill out one monitoring form during the session, such that questions about how to monitor could be answered immediately. Heather's parents were called two days later to check in on their use of the forms and to answer any further questions about the monitoring. Heather's teacher was also asked to monitor Heather's eating and vomiting behaviors at school, such as during snack and lunch times, and was given similar monitoring forms to complete.

Parent monitoring reports indicated that Heather was vomiting after eating approximately two to three times per day. A great variety of foods triggered gagging or vomiting, and foods that were one day acceptable to Heather could not be tolerated on another day. The monitoring forms completed by Heather's parents further revealed that following Heather's gagging or vomiting behaviors, her parents would accommodate her needs by allowing her to avoid the remainder of the meal, bringing her drinks to calm her stomach, and reading her a story to stop her crying and distressed behaviors. Teacher reports revealed that at school Heather vomited when she attempted to eat cafeteria food, and was subsequently moved away from the other children at lunch time and seated in an isolated area of the cafeteria close to the student bathroom. Teacher observations also indicated that over time Heather began to gag while walking to the cafeteria, stating that the smell of the cafeteria food was bothering her very much. Observational reports obtained from Heather's teacher further indicated that Heather's classmates often paid a great

deal of attention to Heather's gagging and vomiting behaviors, discussing and asking questions about their classmate. Given the findings yielded by observational reports, it was determined that Heather was being reinforced for her responses to food through attention from others. Given previous findings suggesting that parental involvement enhances outcome in the treatment of childhood OCD (Knox, Albano, & Barlow, 1996), Heather's therapist subsequently instructed Heather's parents on the techniques of differential reinforcement of alternative behaviors. Results obtained from monitoring 2 weeks subsequent to this intervention revealed that Heather was gagging approximately once per week at school, while her vomiting during mealtimes at home had ceased, indicating a significant change in Heather's behavior from the baseline observational period to the active treatment phase.

Approximately 4 weeks following the initial intake evaluation and subsequent to the implementation of techniques designed to reduce the frequency of Heather's vomiting, Heather and her parents came to the clinic for their first treatment appointment. Heather's therapist first worked with Heather and her family to construct a fear ladder, or a list of her feared stimuli. Specifically, Heather worked with her therapist to identify particular events or situations that led to heightened feelings of distress for her. Heather was then provided with the Feelings Thermometer from the ADIS-IV-C (Silverman & Albano, 1996), which presents children with a series of nine thermometers, each of which depicts an increasingly higher "temperature." Heather was then asked to indicate a thermometer most closely corresponding to her level of distress associated with each situation or event, ranging from 0 ("not at all") to 8 ("very, very much"). These items were rank ordered from those situations associated with the most to the least amount of distress. Items on Heather's fear ladder included "Mom or Dad will not answer your questions," "You have to go somewhere you don't want to," "Throwing away the trash in your shoebox," and "Eating something that you don't know what it is or where it came from." Both Heather and her parents provided initial ratings on the fear ladder, and both were requested to provide ratings for the fear ladder items once during the week and at the beginning of each treatment session. Ratings obtained from both Heather and her parents on many of these items were 6 or above, indicating very elevated levels of fear and distress.

During Heather's fourth treatment session, her mother reported that Heather had been experiencing heightened levels of distress associated with her need to hoard items of trivial value. Heather's mother reported that Heather kept a special box under her bed where she would collect items such as shreds of paper and other nonpurposeful items. Heather reportedly experienced so much difficulty throwing things away that she gave the objects to her parents to either hold or throw away without her knowledge. An additional phone interview with Heather's teacher also indicated that Heather often became extremely distressed when her teacher attempted to throw away an old portfolio and replace it with a new one. Although allowed to keep her old folder, Heather cried and continued to appear anxious and upset for quite some time after the incident had ended.

Heather was subsequently asked to self-monitor her hoarding behavior by recording the items she collected as well as her levels of distress when asked to throw such things away. Heather was given explicit instructions on how to use the monitoring form, and examples were reviewed with her such that she was able to record the item she was unable to throw away, her thought when asked to throw it away, and her level of distress if required to get rid of the item (as indicated on the Feelings Thermometer, ranging from 0 to 8). Heather's parents also were informed of Heather's self-monitoring exercises, and it was agreed that Heather would be rewarded for each day that she complied with her self-monitoring with items such as choosing what the family ate for dinner, an extra half hour of television before bedtime, or an additional half hour of time at the computer. Heather's therapist also made a brief phone call to Heather on alternate days to remind Heather to continue monitoring and to reinforce her success at this practice.

After one week of consistent self-monitoring, it was determined that Heather experienced heightened levels of distress when she needed to throw away things she had used, including tissues, napkins, pieces of paper, notebooks, and labels. Heather reported that when she was asked to throw away these items, she "felt that things would not be right" and noted that this feeling made her scared. Heather's therapist then requested that Heather's parents bring her box of collected items into the clinic for Heather's next session. An analogue observation was then conducted in which Heather was asked by her mother to throw certain objects away and Heather's reaction to these requests was recorded. On the basis of the information collected via self-monitoring and the analogue observation, it was determined that Heather might benefit from exposure exercises in order to become habituated to her fears surrounding throwing away nonpurposeful items. Heather and her parents were assigned practice exercises to complete at home that involved Heather having to throw away certain items while refraining from engaging in compulsive acts or rituals designed to reduce her feelings of anxiety. During this time Heather was asked to continue monitoring the occurrence of hoarding behaviors and her feelings surrounding such behaviors. Two weeks after the implementation of the exposure exercises, Heather's fre-

quency of hoarding behaviors was significantly reduced. An analogue observational session conducted by Heather's therapist in the clinic revealed that Heather was able to throw away any item requested by the therapist without experiencing visible signs of distress or discomfort, and with no apparent urge to engage in compulsive behaviors.

An additional area of concern, identified during the initial intake evaluation and that occurred during the course of Heather's treatment, interfering not only with Heather's relationship with her parents but also with her ability to engage in practice exercises outside of session and come to her appointments on time, was Heather's display of argumentative and noncompliant behaviors toward her parents. When asked to go to places that she did not want to go, such as after-school activities, or to engage in activities in which she did not want to participate, Heather's resistance to attending such activities would escalate into whining, crying, screaming, throwing tantrums, and hiding. These noncompliant behaviors made it difficult for Heather's parents not only to get Heather to complete her chores at home, but also to get Heather to practice those exercises given to her by her therapist during session. Heather's parents also indicated that Heather was unable to remain in school groups or clubs for any duration of time, given that Heather would, soon after joining, refuse to attend meetings with her peers.

Heather's parents were again asked to observe and monitor the frequency, duration, antecedents to, and consequences of Heather's tantrum behavior. Examination of the data yielded from these observations indicated that Heather would cry, kick, and scream when she did not want to go somewhere or do something that her parents had requested. Further, observations by Heather's parents indicated that after the display of such tantrum-like behavior, Heather was reinforced for the performance of such behaviors by being allowed to avoid the activity in which she did not want to participate, or by having her parents complete her chores for her. On the basis of previous work indicating the significant role parents can play in shaping their child's behavior within the home environment (Patterson, 1977a), Heather's parents were subsequently instructed in the use of time-out, whereby Heather was removed from the situation in which she was throwing a tantrum, placed into a time-out zone for a specified amount of time, and then returned to the previous activity, such that she was not allowed to escape from aversive situations or activities because she had thrown a tantrum. Heather's parents were asked to continue monitoring the occurrence of Heather's tantrums during the implementation of the time-out procedures. Following one month of using time-out for Heather's argumentative behaviors and tantrums, her parents reported that the frequency with which such behaviors occurred was greatly reduced, as was the duration of tantrums when they did occur. Heather's parents also indicated that they found it much easier to get Heather to comply with her practice exercises at home, as well as to get her to participate in after-school activities with her peers.

After 4 months of treatment, a follow-up assessment was conducted with Heather and her parents, at which time the ADIS-IV-C and ADIS-IV-P were administered, along with the same battery of self- and parent-report measures initially given. Interview results indicated that Heather was no longer engaging in hoarding behaviors, had ceased to repeatedly question her parents about things that she did not want to change or felt uncomfortable not knowing, and was significantly more compliant in terms of her behaviors at home, thus suggesting that at the end of treatment, she no longer met diagnostic criteria for either OCD or ODD. Heather also had been able to successfully develop close friendships with two other girls in her class at school and participated in an art club two afternoons each week at school. Heather reported being much happier about attending school and was able to eat lunch with and play during recess with her peers. Heather's self-reports on the RCADS and CDI indicated standardized scores falling within the nonclinical range, and maternal and paternal reports on the CBCL yielded standardized Internalizing (T = 55, T = 59, respectively) and Externalizing (T = 49, T = 51, respectively) scores within the nonclinical range.

Heather's case thus illustrates the use of several behavioral assessment techniques that assisted in Heather's initial evaluation—including an interview, self-report instruments, and parent-report instruments—as well as techniques that were used later to obtain further information about Heather's functioning at home and at school as well as to monitor treatment progress and outcomes—including participant observation, self-monitoring, and analogue observations. Employing this range of behavioral assessment strategies not only allowed for an enhanced knowledge base from which to conceptualize Heather's presenting difficulties, but also provided an empirically based, clinically relevant way to measure Heather's progress throughout treatment.

FUTURE DIRECTIONS

Many advances have occurred in recent years in the development of behavioral assessment measures for use among children. However, much work remains to be done. Although many behavioral assessment strategies include the use of measures designed to be used with children of a given age, developmental factors must play a larger role in the selection and evaluation of child behavioral assessment procedures

(Ollendick & Greene, 1990). Further, increased assessment efforts must be directed toward cognitive and emotional assessment, such that behavioral assessors work toward the construction of developmentally sensitive and empirically validated procedures that assess often covert cognitive processes in children, rather than merely observing overt behaviors (Ollendick & Greene, 1990). Greater attention also must be focused on the incremental validity of assessment procedures when used as part of a comprehensive behavioral assessment battery for children for varying ages. Specifically, certain assessment procedures may be found to be less reliable or valid when used with children of varying ages, thus precluding the use of the instrument across children of different ages and developmental levels (Ollendick & Greene, 1990).

Behavioral assessors also must be aware of the ways in which different assessment procedures vary in terms of their contribution to a treatment's efficacy. Specifically, the degree to which assessment strategies are shown to contribute to beneficial treatment outcomes may be influenced by the type of assessment strategies employed, thus making decisions guiding the selection of assessment instruments and strategies of particular importance. Assessment efforts also should concentrate on the role of the child in the assessment strategy, such that the child's place in his or her environment is emphasized, rather than merely testing, rating, or observing the actions of a child in isolation (Ollendick & Greene, 1990).

Functional models of assessing and treating behavioral difficulties among children appear at present to be a sound foundation for continued research (Kearney & Silverman, 1990). Future developments must continue to focus on constructing theory-driven assessment instruments that aim to measure the functional relationships among behaviors exhibited by a child in order to more skillfully apply prescriptive treatments (Kearney & Silverman, 1990). Of particular relevance to child outpatient assessment might be the development of better decision rules to guide clinicians in the selection and sequencing of assessment instruments. Although clinicians currently have access to a great wealth of information concerning the psychometric properties or normative standards of given assessment instruments, comparatively little is known about when to select more intensive methods of assessment in favor of less intensive methods, or for whom particular assessment instruments are best suited. Research must therefore continue to explore the manner in which clinicians should assemble various assessment components to achieve the most cost-efficient yet clinically comprehensive assessment that is feasible within the unique context of outpatient assessment services. Once such detailed information has been collected concerning how to select and sequence assessment methods, clinicians will be better able to make more informed decisions about which instruments to administer to whom as well as what parts of relatively complex measures (i.e., structured interviews) might be of use in outpatient contexts.

REFERENCES

Achenbach, T.M. (1991). *Manual for the Child Behavior Checklist/ 4–18 and 1991 Profile.* Burlington: University of Vermont, Department of Psychiatry.

Bagwell, C.L., Molina, B.S.G., Pelham, W.E., & Hoza, B. (2001). Attention-deficit hyperactivity disorder and problems in peer relations: Predictions from childhood to adolescence. *Journal of the American Academy of Child & Adolescent Psychiatry, 40,* 1285–1292.

Baird, S., & Nelson-Gray, R.O. (1999). Direct observation and self-monitoring. In S.C. Hayes, D.H. Barlow, & R.O. Nelson-Gray (Eds.), *The scientist practitioner* (pp. 353–386). Boston: Allyn & Bacon.

Barrett, P.M., Rapee, R.M., Dadds, M.R., & Ryan, S.M (1996). Family enhancement of cognitive style in anxious and aggressive children. *Journal of Abnormal Child Psychology, 24,* 187–203.

Barrios, B., & Hartmann, D.P. (1986). The contributions of traditional assessment: Concepts, issues, and methodologies. In R.O. Nelson & S.C. Hayes (Eds.) *Conceptual foundations of behavioral assessment* (pp. 81–110). New York: Guilford Press.

Beidel, D.C., Neal, A.M., & Lederer, A.S. (1991). The feasibility and validity of a daily diary for the assessment of anxiety in children. *Behavior Therapy, 22,* 505–517.

Berg, I. (1974). A Self-Administered Dependency Questionnaire (S.A.D.Q.) for use with the mothers of schoolchildren. *British Journal of Psychiatry, 124,* 1–9.

Berg, C.J., Rapoport, J.L., & Flament, M. (1986). The Leyton Obsessional Inventory—Child Version. *Journal of the American Academy of Child Psychiatry, 25,* 84–91.

Bloom, B.L. (1985). A factor analysis of self-report measures of family functioning. *Family Process, 24,* 225–239.

Bronfenbrenner, U. (1979). *The ecology of human development: Experiments by nature and design.* Cambridge, MA: Harvard University Press.

Chorpita, B.F. (1998). *Modular cognitive behavior therapy for child and adolescent anxiety disorders.* Unpublished treatment manual, University of Hawaii at Manoa.

Chorpita, B.F., Albano, A.M., Heimberg, R.G., & Barlow, D.H. (1996). A systematic replication of the prescriptive treatment of school refusal behavior in a single subject. *Journal of Behavior Therapy & Experimental Psychiatry, 27,* 281–290.

Chorpita, B.F., Yim, L., Moffitt, C., Umemoto, L.A., & Francis, S.E. (2000). Assessment of symptoms of DSM-IV anxiety and depression in children: A Revised Child Anxiety and Depression Scale. *Behaviour Research and Therapy, 38,* 835–855.

Collins, F.L., & Thompson, J.K. (1993). The integration of empirically derived personality assessment data into a behavioral conceptualization and treatment plan. *Behavior Modification, 17,* 58–71.

Conners, C.K. (1990). *Conners Rating Scales.* North Tonawanda, NY: Multi-Health Systems.

Conners, C.K. (1995). *The Conners Continuous Performance Test.* North Tonawanda, NY: Multi-Health Systems.

Cowen, E.L., Huser, J., Beach, D.R., & Rappaport, J. (1970). Parental perceptions of young children and their relation to indexes of adjustment. *Journal of Consulting and Clinical Psychology, 34,* 97–103.

Crowley, S.L. (1998). A psychometric investigation of the FACES-III: Confirmatory factor analysis with replication. *Early Education & Development, 9,* 161–178.

Dadds, M.R., Barrett, P.M., Rapee, R.M., & Ryan, S. (1996). Family process and child anxiety and aggression: An observational analysis. *Journal of Abnormal Child Psychology, 24,* 715–734.

Durand, V.M., & Crimmins, D.B. (1988). Identifying the variables maintaining self-injurious behavior. *Journal of Autism & Developmental Disorders, 18,* 99–117.

Glass, C.R., Merluzzi, T.V., Biever, J.L., & Larsen, K.H. (1982). Cognitive assessment of social anxiety: Development and validation of a self-statement questionnaire. *Cognitive Therapy and Research, 6,* 37–55.

Gordon, M. (1983). *The Gordon Diagnostic System.* DeWitt, NY: Gordon Systems.

Grandy, S.E., & Peck, S.M. (1997). The use of functional assessment and self-management with a first grader. *Child & Family Behavior Therapy, 19,* 29–43.

Greenberg, L.M., & Waldman, I.D. (1992). *Developmental normative data on the Test of Variables of Attention (T.O.V.A.).* Minneapolis: University of Minnesota Medical School, Department of Psychiatry.

Greene, L., Kamps, D., Wyble, J., & Ellis, C. (1999). Home-based consultation for parents of young children with behavioral problems. *Child & Family Behavior Therapy, 21,* 19–45.

Hay, L.R., Nelson, R.O., Hay, W.M. (1977). The use of teachers as behavioral observers. *Journal of Applied Behavior Analysis, 10,* 345–348.

Haynes, S.N. (1988). Causal models and the assessment-treatment relationship in behavior therapy. *Journal of Psychopathology and Behavioral Assessment, 10*(2), 171–183.

Haynes, S.N. (2001). Clinical applications of analogue behavioral observation: Dimensions of psychometric evaluation. *Psychological Assessment, 13,* 73–85.

Helmstetter, E., & Durand, V.M. (1991). Nonaversive interventions for severe behavior problems. In L.H. Meyer & C.A. Peck (Eds.), *Critical issues in the lives of people with severe disabilities.* Baltimore: Paul H. Brookes.

Henggeler, S.W., Schoenwald, S.K., Borduin, C.M., Rowland, M.D., & Cunningham, P.B. (1998). Multisystemic treatment of antisocial behavior in children and adolescents. In D.H. Barlow (Series Ed.), *Treatment manuals for practitioners.* New York: Guilford Press.

Hinshaw, S.P., Morrison, D.C., Carte, E.T., & Cornsweet, C. (1987). Factorial dimensions of the Revised Behavior Problem Checklist: Replication and validation within a kindergarten sample. *Journal of Abnormal Child Psychology, 15,* 309–327.

Johnson, R.L., & Glass, C.R. (1989). Heterosocial anxiety and direction of attention in high school boys. *Cognitive Therapy and Research, 13,* 509–526.

Kearney, C.A., & Silverman, W.K. (1990). *A preliminary analysis of a functional model of assessment and treatment for school refusal behavioral, 14,* 340–366.

Kearney, C.A., & Silverman, W.K. (1993). Measuring the function of school refusal behavior: The School Refusal Assessment Scale. *Journal of Clinical Child Psychology, 22,* 85–96.

King, N.J., Ollendick, T.H., & Murphy, G.C. (1997). Assessment of childhood phobias. *Clinical Psychology Review, 17,* 667–687.

King, N.J., Ollendick, T.H., & Tongue, B.J. (1995). *School refusal: Assessment and treatment.* Boston: Allyn & Bacon.

Knox, L.S., Albano, A.M., & Barlow, D.H. (1996). Parental involvement in the treatment of childhood obsessive compulsive disorder: A multiple-baseline examination incorporating parents. *Behavior Therapy, 27,* 93–114.

Korotitsch, W.J., & Nelson-Gray, R.O. (1999). Self-report and physiological measures. In S.C. Hayes, D.H. Barlow, & R.O. Nelson-Gray (Eds.), *The Scientist Practitioner* (pp. 320–352). Boston: Allyn & Bacon.

Kovacs, M. (1980/1981). Rating scales to assess depression in preschool children. *Acta Paedopsychiatry, 46,* 305–315.

La Greca, A.M., & Stone, W.L. (1993). Social Anxiety Scale for Children-Revised: Factor structure and concurrent validity. *Journal of Clinical Child Psychology, 22,* 17–27.

Lerner, R.M. (1986). *Concepts and theories of human development* (2nd ed.). New York: Random House.

Mackay, S., McLaughlin, T.F., Weber, K., & Derby, K.M. (2001). The use of precision requests to decrease noncompliance in the home and neighborhood: A case study. *Child & Family Behavior Therapy, 23,* 43–52.

Mash, E.J., & Terdal, L.G. (1997). Assessment of child and family disturbance: A behavioral-systems approach. In E.J. Mash & L.G. Terdal (Eds.), *Assessment of childhood disorders* (pp. 3–68). New York: Guilford Press.

Masi, G., Favilla, L., Mucci, M., & Millepiedi, S. (2000). Depressive comorbidity in children and adolescents with generalized anxiety disorder. *Child Psychiatry & Human Development, 30,* 205–215.

McCain, A.P., & Kelley, M.L. (1993). Managing the classroom behavior of an ADHD preschooler: The efficacy of a school-home note intervention. *Child & Family Behavior Therapy, 15,* 33–44.

McNamara, E. (1988). The self-management of school phobia: A case study. *Behavioral Psychotherapy, 16,* 217–229.

Moos, R.H., & Moos, B.S. (1976). A typology of family social environments. *Family Process, 15,* 357–372.

Moos, R.H., & Moos, B. S. (1983). Adaptation and the quality of life in work and family settings. *Journal of Community Psychology, 11,* 158–170.

Muris, P., Meesters, C., Merkelbach, H., Sermon, A., & Zwakhalen, S. (1998). Worry in normal children. *Journal of the American Academy of Child & Adolescent Psychiatry, 37,* 703–710.

Nelson, R.O. (1987). DSM-III and behavioral assessment. In C.G. Last & M. Hersen (Eds.), *Issues in diagnostic research* (pp. 303–328). New York: Plenum.

Nelson-Gray, R.O., & Farmer, R.F. (1999). Behavioral assessment of personality disorders. *Behaviour Research and Therapy, 37,* 347–368.

Ollendick, T.H. (1995). Assessment of anxiety and phobic disorders in children. In K.D. Craig & K.S. Dobson (Eds.), *Anxiety and depression in adults and children* (pp. 99–124). Thousand Oaks, CA: Sage.

Ollendick, T.H. (1983). Reliability and validity of the Revised Fear Survey Schedule for Children (FSSC-R). *Behaviour Research and Therapy, 21,* 685–692.

Ollendick, T.H., & Greene, R. (1990). Behavioral assessment of children. In G. Goldstein & M. Hersen (Eds.), *Handbook of psychological assessment* (2nd ed., pp. 403–422). New York: Pergamon Press.

Ollendick, T.H., Hagopian, L.P., & Huntzinger, R.M. (1991). Cognitive-behavior therapy with nighttime fearful children. *Journal of Behavior Therapy & Experimental Psychiatry, 22,* 113–121.

Ollendick, T.H., & King, N.J. (1991). Developmental factors in child behavioral assessment. In P.R. Martin (Ed.), *Handbook of behavior therapy and psychological science: An integrative approach* (pp. 57–72). New York: Pergamon Press.

Ollendick, T.H., & King, N.J. (1999). Child behavioral assessment and cognitive-behavioral interventions in schools. *Psychology in the Schools, 36,* 427–436.

Orvaschel, H., & Puig-Antich, J. (1987). *Schedule for Affective Disorders and Schizophrenia for School-Age Children* (4th ed.). Unpublished manuscript, University of Pittsburgh, Western Psychiatric Institute for Clinic.

Patterson, G.R. (1977a). *Living with children: New methods for parents and teachers.* Champaign, IL: Research Press.

Patterson, G.R. (1977b). Naturalistic observation in clinical assessment. *Journal of Abnormal Clinical Psychology, 5,* 309–322.

Patterson, G.R., & Reid, J.B. (1984). Social interactional processes within the family: The study of the moment-by-moment family transactions in which human social development is imbedded. *Journal of Applied Developmental Psychology, 5,* 237–262.

Reich, W., & Welner, Z. (1989). *Diagnostic Interview for Children and Adolescents—Revised.* St. Louis, MO: Washington University, Division of Child Psychiatry.

Reynolds, C.R., & Kamphaus, R.W. (1992). *Behavior Assessment System for Children (BASC)*. Circle Pines, MN: American Guidance Service.

Roehling, P.V., & Robin, A.L. (1986). Development and validation of the Family Beliefs Inventory: A measure of unrealistic beliefs among parents and adolescents. *Journal of Consulting & Clinical Psychology, 54,* 693–697.

Ronen, T. (1991). Intervention package for treating sleep disorders in a four-year-old girl. *Journal of Behavior Therapy & Experimental Psychiatry, 22,* 141–148.

Shaffer, D., Fisher, P., Lucas, C., Dulcan, M., & Schwab-Stone, M. (2000). NIMH Diagnostic Interview Schedule for Children version IV (NIMH DISC-IV): Description, differences from previous versions, and reliability of some common diagnoses. *Journal of the American Academy of Child and Adolescent Psychiatry, 39,* 28–38.

Silverman, W.K., & Albano, A.M. (1996). *Anxiety Disorders Interview Schedule for DSM-IV, Child and Parent Versions.* San Antonio, TX: Psychological Corporation.

Silverman, W.K., & Rabian, B. (1994). Specific phobia. In T.H. Ollendick, N.J. King, & W. Yule (Eds.), *International handbook of phobic and anxiety disorders in children and adolescents* (pp. 87–109). New York: Plenum.

Skinner, H.A., Steinhauer, P.D., & Santa Barbara, J. (1983). The Family Assessment Measure. *Canadian Journal of Community Mental Health, 2,* 91–105.

Spielberger, C.D. (1973). *Manual for the State-Trait Anxiety Inventory for Children.* Palo Alto, CA: Consulting Psychologists Press.

Tombari, M.L., Fitzpatrick, S.J., & Childress, W. (1985). Using computers as contingency managers in self-monitoring interventions. *Computers in Human Behavior, 1,* 75–82.

Tuteur, J.M., Ewigman, B.E., Peterson, L., & Hosokawa, M.C. (1995). The maternal observation matrix and the mother-child interaction scale: Brief observational screening instruments for physically abusive mothers. *Journal of Consulting and Clinical Psychology, 24,* 55–62.

Wilson, G.L., & Bornstein, P.H. (1984). Paradoxical procedures and single-case methodology: Review and recommendations. *Journal of Behavior Therapy & Experimental Psychiatry, 15,* 195–203.

CHAPTER 17

Behavioral Assessment of Psychiatric Patients in Restrictive Settings

MARK R. SERPER, BRETT R. GOLDBERG, AND KURT SALZINGER

INTRODUCTION

Nat Schoenfeld used to tell the story of how he responded to the question, "you're a behaviorist?" by saying, "yeah, and you, you're a *nonbehaviorist;* you study *nonbehavior?*" We can only add to this that behavior is all we have when we assess people psychologically. The fact of the matter, however, is that we all study behavior at varying distances and with varying needs for interpretation. Thus, sometimes we study behavior in the raw, so to speak; we observe it by looking and listening, counting both its frequency and duration after having established that more than one person can arrive at the same counts and temporal judgments. At other times we use rating scales to specify how aggressive or how often a person was aggressive, say, over the course of a day. These observations have the problem of being affected by the rater's memory as well as not providing information about exactly how often and on what occasion the behavior occurred. Definitions must apply to domains as well as to the specific behaviors considered to represent that domain—for example, aggression as the domain, with hitting, cursing, and ironic

statements serving as increasingly peripheral representatives of that domain or response class.

BASIC ISSUES IN BEHAVIORAL ASSESSMENT

The word *symptom* has become generally accepted in psychopathological or abnormal behavior descriptions even by behavior analysts. The word does, however, bring with it the theoretical freight of the medical model. In this chapter we will restrict its meaning to signify abnormal behavior that needs to be assessed and altered with no necessary implications about its provenance. Once we do talk about behavior, of course, we also must take note of the fact that operant behavior (and the behavior to be discussed will be that only) comes in classes. Individual members of each class are not identical but are members of the same class because they are functioning under the same reinforcement contingency, meaning they are evoked by the same discriminative stimulus and/ or are strengthened by the same or similar reinforcer. Because responses that are members of the same response class differ from one another topographically, the assessment tools that we generate must be sensitive to that circumstance. That is, we must describe behavior in terms of its functional significance rather than its topographical similarity.

The first step in assessment then becomes one of identifying behaviors that constitute functional response classes. The second step is to identify what is problematic about the response class in question as shown below:

1. Behaviors performed in excess of normal limits (e.g., positive symptoms of psychosis; aggressive behavior directed at other clients or hospital staff)
2. Behavioral deficits (flattened affect; social withdrawal; failure to participate in community meetings; failure to take medicine)
3. Behaviors inappropriate in particular settings (e.g. taking a shower with one's clothing on; wearing an overcoat on a very hot summer day in front of a swimming pool)
4. Behaviors that are pathological by their very nature, such as self-injurious, suicidal behaviors, or stereotypic behavior.

Additionally, assessment of the environmental contexts themselves also can be the focus of behavioral assessment and intervention, because the severity and frequency of psychosis can vary as a function of the environment as a whole (McInnis & Marks, 1990; Mirsky, Silberman, Latz, & Nagler, 1985; Paul & Lentz, 1977; Salzinger, 1991; Zarlock, 1966). Within the restrictive setting, many authors have found that the severity of psychotic symptoms displayed by patients could be increased or decreased by altering environmental stimuli (Ayllon & Haughton, 1964; Paul & Lentz, 1977; Salzinger, Pisoni, Portnoy, & Feldman 1970; Zarlock, 1966). Salzinger and colleagues (1970), for example, were able to increase or decrease the occurrence of symptomatic verbal response classes by presenting or omitting reinforcing events. Similarly, Ayllon and Haughton (1964) decreased patients' aberrant verbal behavior by making it contingent on social reinforcement. Zarlock (1966) also provided an example of the effect of inpatient context on the occurrence of bizarre speech and behavior. Over a 10-day period Zarlock manipulated the environment in the activity room on an inpatient unit. When the activity room was filled with posters and pamphlets containing only medical information, over 300 occurrences of bizarre speech and behavior were recorded. When the room, however, was modified to include only occupational, social, or recreational materials, the frequency of bizarre speech and behavior occurrences dropped drastically in all three environments. Results of Zarlock's and other studies indicate the effect of environment in the expression of abnormal behavior and illustrate the importance of including

environmental factors when assessing behavior in the restrictive setting. Additionally, when choosing target behaviors to modify, it is important for the clinician to identify the settings the behavior occurs in and determine to what degree the behavior is elicited by the context and the degree to which the behavior will be generalized across contexts (Kohlenberg & Tsai, 1991). This is a salient issue in hospital settings where certain behaviors may be specific to an inpatient setting and absent in the community environment.

CONCEPTUAL ISSUES: ORIGIN OF MALADAPTIVE BEHAVIORS

Although it is widely recognized that many aspects of psychotic illnesses may be biologically mediated in part, the origin of any maladaptive behavior does not differ in principle from any other learned behavior. That is, psychotic behavior, like all behavior, is determined, in part, by its antecedent conditions and maintained by its reinforcement contingencies. It is also now widely accepted that psychotic behavior frequently occurs across many psychiatric illnesses, including schizophrenia, schizoaffective disorder, and bipolar and other mood disorders (Bentall, Jackson, & Pilgrim, 1988; Pope & Lipinski, 1978; Salzinger, 1986) borderline and schizotypal personality disorders (Dowson, Sussams, Grounds, & Taylor, 2000; Serper et al, 1993), and patients entering the hospital with substance-induced psychosis (Serper & Chou, 2000). Although most of the assessment techniques outlined in this chapter focus on severely disabled psychiatric patients, our discussion can be applied to many different populations and not limited to any one diagnostic category.

The notion that many psychotic individuals suffer a disruption in the normal relationship between their learning history and current sensory input has received much support over the years (e.g., Gray et al., 1995; Hemslcy, 1996; Lubow & Gurwitz, 1995; Salzinger, 1984; Salzinger, Portnoy, & Feldman, 1966). According to the Immediacy Hypothesis (Salzinger, 1984; Salzinger et al., 1966), behavior of an individual with schizophrenic disorder is controlled by the most immediate environmental stimuli available. More remote or distal stimuli and their contingencies are less effective in controlling behavior than are the immediate, proximal stimuli. The implications of this are that an individual may be acting psychotic because he or she is responding to only a subset of the total stimuli (i.e., the most immediate) surrounding him or her. Behavior under control of immediate stimuli and contingencies makes remote stimuli and reinforcement history less effective in the control of behavior. Consequently, the individual prone to making immediate responses is less capable of adapting to meet the needs of the dynamic contextual and sometimes abstract environment in which we live, thus presenting as disorganized and psychotic to others.

For example, individuals with schizophrenia become less comprehensible the longer they speak. Salzinger (1984) hypothesizes that this may be due to the disturbed speaker's verbal behavior being influenced by the immediate sounds of the contiguous words rather than the more distal contextual and semantic meaning of sentence strings. With stimulus control of behavior limited to the most immediate stimuli, the task of stringing words together becomes guided by acoustical immediacy rather than by the more abstract semantic content. Consequently, the verbal response-produced stimulus control is disrupted, resulting in difficult to understand speech.

Another example of effect of immediacy control includes a patient's delusional beliefs, which are responses to current events that fail to take into account past events or current contexts. Misattribution occurs when the same stimuli occur in different contexts. For example, paranoid ideation may be elicited when an individual reacts to the more immediate stimuli without taking into account other, remote stimuli that may negate a long-held threat or belief system.

Classical conditioning theories concerning the origin of psychotic symptoms also have been advanced (Ellson, 1941; Hefferline, Bruno, & Camp, 1974; Hefferline & Perrera, 1963; Lubow & Gurwitz, 1995). Ellson (1941), for example, speculated that hallucinations are the result of sensory conditioning. After repeated pairings of a tone (the unconditioned stimulus) with a light (conditioned stimulus), Ellson (1941) found subjects reliably "hallucinated," hearing the tone when the light was presented alone. These findings have been replicated over the years using more sophisticated methodologies (Hefferline & Perrera, 1963; Hefferline et al., 1974; Kot & Serper, 2002). Kot and Serper (2002), for example, applied the sensory conditioning procedure to hallucinating and nonhallucinating schizophrenic inpatients. Consistent with the sensory conditioning model, Kot and Serper found hallucinating patients more quickly acquired and maintained their sensory-conditioned hallucinations than their nonhallucinating counterparts. This finding suggested that hallucinators have a heightened susceptibility to form sensory-conditioned associations (Kot & Serper, 2002).

Similarly, researchers examining latent inhibition have found that psychotic individuals do not benefit from conditioned stimulus preexposure and rapidly acquire associations during conditioning trials. Latent inhibition failure, in turn, causes disorganized thinking and psychotic behavior (Gray et al., 1995; Hemsley, 1995, 1996; Lubow & Gurwitz, 1995). Combining latent inhibition and immediacy theories, it may

be the case that psychotic behavior occurs when conditioned associations to immediate stimuli are not inhibited because adaptive latent inhibitory mechanisms have failed. That is, individuals who experience psychosis may be more prone to form deviant associations to immediate stimuli, because they fail to benefit from the latent inhibitory mechanisms that prevent the learning of these abnormal associations. The resulting behavior appears irrational because it is elicited by immediate and nonmeaningful discriminative stimuli and strengthened by idiosyncratic and nonadaptive reinforcement contingencies.

OPERANTS AS MALADAPTIVE BEHAVIORS

From the theoretical conceptualizations of the behavioral origins of psychosis described above, investigators have consistently found that psychotic behavior is subject to operant control (for reviews in specific symptom domains, see Burns, Heiby, & Tharp, 1983; and Layng & Andronis, 1984). By modifying environmental factors such as increasing competing and attention-engaging stimulation, and/or increasing or reducing the attainability of reinforcement, investigators have controlled the onset of psychotic and maladaptive behavior in individuals with severe mental disorders. The manipulation of multiple environmental variables has been found to control the frequency of occurrence for psychotic behaviors, including hallucinations (Alford & Turner, 1976; Slade, 1976), delusional ideation (Chadwick & Lowe, 1994; Leibman & Salzinger, 1998), deviant verbal behavior (Higgs, 1970; Salzinger et al., 1970), as well as a variety of maladaptive social behaviors exhibited by clients in restricted environments (Paul & Lentz, 1977). Behavioral interventions have met with success via their identification and manipulation of antecedent conditions that trigger the onset of maladaptive behavior and/or through the use of contingency management programs.

Assessment of Stimulus Control and Competing Behaviors

Stimulus control and competing behavior procedures are ways by which manipulation of antecedent variables can reduce the occurrence of a response class comprising particular psychotic or maladaptive behaviors often exhibited by clients in restricted environments. Identification and manipulation of antecedent conditions can reduce the occurrence of psychotic symptoms and help clients identify the discriminative stimuli that signal the onset of psychotic behavior. Interestingly, many schizophrenic individuals are able to identify external antecedent stimuli that trigger the onset of their psychotic symptoms with no prior behavior analytic training, but appear to be poor at identifying internal arousal cues that may precede the onset of psychotic behavior and poor functioning (Tarrier, Harwood, Yusopoff, & Beckett, 1990; Tarrier & Turpin, 1992). Relatedly, others have found that certain schizophrenic individuals' were able to devise their own competing behavioral strategies to interfere with the onset of some psychotic symptoms (Falloon & Talbot, 1981; McCandless-Glimcher, McKnight, Hamera, & Smith, 1986). Effective coping strategies reported by these clients included increased interpersonal contact, resting/sleeping, and ignoring/not attending to the hallucinated voices (Falloon & Talbot, 1981). Consequently, identification of external and internal determinants that trigger the onset of maladaptive behavior will produce control over the occurrence of symptomatic response classes.

Falloon and Talbot (1981), for example, designed their study to explore the relationship between auditory hallucinations and patients' coping mechanisms. They selected a group of chronically ill patients who were experiencing auditory hallucinations on a daily basis. Open-ended questions were used to assess various aspects of the strategies patients' utilized to cope with their hallucinations. Assessment focused the frequency, variety, and effectiveness of coping strategies as well as any information volunteered about the thoughts or feelings surrounding hallucinations for each study patient. The interviewer recorded the statements made by each patient verbatim. Patients' daily functioning and coping ability were then rated as "good," "fair," or "poor." Results of their study indicated a distinct pattern between the types of coping methods utilized by higher and lower functioning patients. Patients functioning more effectively in their daily environment, for example, were more likely to use a majority of different strategies, including reduced attention, sleep/relaxation, posture change, and prescribed medication when experiencing auditory hallucinations.

Yet many symptoms of psychosis, even in restrictive environments, can be difficult to assess. For example, delusional ideation and the hallucinatory experience cannot be observed directly. Clinical evidence, however, shows that heightened arousal accompanies these behaviors (e.g., Freeman & Garety, 1999). Hallucinations, for example, are often triggered by stress (Baker & Morrison, 1998; Slade, 1972, 1973) and abnormally high levels of arousal (Cooklin, Sturgeon, & Leff, 1983; Toone, Cooke, & Lader, 1981). Cooklin and colleagues (1983), for example, examined the relationship between arousal state and the development of auditory hallucinations. Arousal state was measured via skin conductance recordings over a long baseline assessment period and

throughout the experiment. Patient self-report and observational techniques were used to gauge subjects' hallucinatory behavior. Rapid eye flickers up and to one side, abrupt cessation of speech, accompanied by cocking of the head into a listening pose, laughter/smiling for no observable reason, and conversing with their voices were indicators that subjects were actively hallucinating. To manipulate arousal level throughout each 30-minute recording period, subjects were switched back and forth between isolation and interpersonal conditions where they engaged in conversation with a single interviewer. Two independent raters coded all video records separately. To be considered evidence that a patient was hallucinating, both raters were required to be in agreement (i.e., within 15 seconds of each other) about the onset and cessation of the observable signs of hallucinatory behavior. Thirty-five seconds with no self-reported or observed signs of hallucinations was set as the standard for marking a period as "hallucination absent." Results indicated that patients' underreported the occurrence of their hallucinatory behaviors. Observations of the behavioral indices were more reliable markers of hallucinations than was self-report. Specifically, eye movements to the side were the most frequently observed behavior during a hallucination. Increased arousal also was found to be highly related to hallucinatory behavior. Spontaneous fluctuations of skin conductance rate coincided with auditory hallucinations as measured by coinciding self-report and the behavioral markers of hallucinations. The authors concluded that future clinicians could improve their sensitivity to hallucination assessment through greater awareness of the observable behaviors that occur with hallucinations.

Relatedly, anxiety appears to play a crucial mediating role in latent inhibition failure and the resulting experience of psychosis (Braunstein-Bercovitz, Rammsayer, Gibbons, & Lubow, 2002). It may be the case that individuals prone to hallucinate form deviant conditioned associations to immediate stimuli in the environment and also to high internal arousal states. Internal arousal, which may normally be subject to latent inhibition mechanisms, may serve for hallucinating schizophrenics as a conditioned emotional stimulus (acquired through associations with external stimuli or thoughts) that elicits hallucinations. Anxiety can be measured by a number of techniques (e.g., self-report, psychophysiological assessment), and indications of it can be directly observed and modified. In his case study, Slade (1972), for example, determined that onset of a subject's hallucinations was triggered by observable indices of situational anxiety. Employment of systematic desensitization significantly reduced the occurrence of situational anxiety that preceded the onset of the client's auditory hallucinations (Slade, 1972). Similarly, anxiety and arousal may have a key role in the maintenance of delusional beliefs (Freeman & Garety, 1999) and may be subject to the same operant control as hallucinations.

Other stimulus control procedures evoke incompatible responses such as thought stopping, assertion training, and relaxation to reduce the frequency of paranoid ideation and other positive symptoms in stressful situations. They have had mixed success in controlling psychosis (e.g., Erickson & Gustafson, 1968; Nydegger, 1972; Serber & Nelson, 1971). Serber and Nelson (1971), for example, examined the effectiveness of assertion training and systematic desensitization on treatment of phobias and deficiency of effective interactive skills/assertiveness in a sample of inpatients diagnosed with schizophrenia. A 1-hour interview was conducted for each potential patient, and a mental status examination was used to screen for hallucinations and delusions, which were exclusionary criteria for this study. Patients who met full criteria for inclusion in the study were then briefed about the study, including the treatments and rationale for the study. Therapy was conducted for no less than 1 week, and no more than 6, in 30- to 45-minute sessions, three times a week. To be included in the study, participants had to agree to report monthly for assessment should they be discharged from the hospital. As inpatients, hospital staff provided the behavioral information. Treatment success was evaluated based upon self-report and observations of patients' engaging in operationally defined assertive behavior. Behavior was reassessed at a 6-month follow-up. Results indicated that these treatments did not work effectively in the sample of schizophrenic inpatients.

Investigators also have attempted to reduce psychotic behavior by using external auditory stimulation to interfere with the onset of hallucinations. This approach is based on the notion that auditory hallucinations can be decreased by increasing external auditory input (Slade, 1976), conceptualized as reducing auditory input to the nondominant hemisphere (Green, 1997) or the prevention of subjects from responding to their more immediate subvocal generated speech (Bick & Kinsbourne, 1987; Salzinger, 1984).

Bick and Kinsbourne (1987) designed two experiments to test the premise that auditory hallucinations would be reduced or eliminated after implementing an exercise task designed to preclude subvocalizations, hypothesized to be accompanying or possibly aiding in the generation of hallucinations. In experiment 1, subjects were selected based upon diagnosis of schizophrenia and verbalizations of current auditory hallucinations during the initial interview. Then they were counterbalanced into three conditions: opening their mouths wide (experimental), closing their eyes tight (control), and squeezing their fists (control). All treatments were maintained for a 1-minute period. A rater blind to the hypothesis of the study

recorded the patient's report indicating whether the voices they heard increased, decreased, or remained at the previous level. As per the initial hypothesis, only the mouth-opening condition resulted in decreased report of voices.

In experiment 2, Bick and Kinsbourne (1987) tested whether hallucinations by normal and nondiagnosed subjects could be eliminated by the same technique. College students were hypnotized with the suggestion that they would hear voices. Twenty-one college students were successfully hypnotized and rapidly reported hearing voices. Implementation of the same procedures as in experiment 1 revealed the same effect; that is, the mouth-opening condition resulted in significantly greater reduction of hallucinations than the control conditions.

Margo, Hemsley, and Slade (1981) found that they could alter the occurrence of hallucinations by manipulating the hallucinator's exposure to external stimuli. Feder (1982), in a case study, reported a reduction in the frequency of hallucinations when a client used headphones to listen to the radio. Additionally, earplug "therapy" to the nondominant hemisphere alone or with competing behaviors directed to the dominant side (e.g., object naming, reading, sentence completion) also has resulted in reducing hallucinations (Birchwood, 1986; Done, Frith, & Owens, 1986; McInnus & Marks, 1990).

McInnis and Marks (1990) examined the efficacy of using audiotape therapy for reduction of depressive, auditory hallucinations. The audiotape was made by the patient and consisted of "pleasant memories of his family, work and holidays." In their single-subject design, the day was divided into two conditions, alternating by 6-hour intervals. Headphones were worn during hallucinatory experiences regardless of condition. In condition A, the participant was instructed to activate the tape if hallucinations began. For condition B, the tape was not to be used at all, regardless of hallucinations. The participant was instructed to record frequency and duration of hallucinatory experiences, as well as descriptions about their intensity. Experimenters periodically reviewed the records with the participant as a manipulation check. Participant records also were compared to staff records of observed behavior and were judged to be reliable. Records were maintained over the course of 35 days, and follow-up was conducted 15 months later. Results of the study indicated that use of the audiotape significantly reduced the duration, but did not affect the frequency, of reported hallucinations. Review of staff records indicated that motor agitation and verbalizations of suicidal ideation also decreased during the audiotape periods. The participant maintained usage of the audiotape 15 months later. McInnis and Marks concluded that modification of environmental contingencies was effective in reducing psychotic behavior.

Identifying Reinforcement Contingencies

Investigators have identified and manipulated salient external contingencies in psychiatric patients in order to decrease their maladaptive behaviors, while increasing a variety of appropriate behaviors. Ayllon and Haughton (1964), for example, decreased clients' aberrant verbal behavior by making it contingent on social reinforcement. Introduction of social reinforcement (Alford & Turner, 1976) and negative reinforcement contingencies (Belcher, 1988; Fonagy & Slade, 1982) also have been shown to reduce the frequency of reported hallucinatory behavior.

Belcher (1988) targeted the hallucinatory behavior of a single subject who was selected based on a long history of hallucinations, recent elevations in symptoms, and neuroleptic treatment nonresponse. Staff collected baseline data over a 6-week period, and the participant was monitored at all times. Frequency and duration of verbalizations of hallucinatory episodes were recorded during the baseline and experimental conditions, but intensity was not measured. In this study, the negative reinforcement contingency administered, following baseline, consisted of contingent exercise, unpopular with the subject, paired with inappropriate verbal outbursts, such as yelling, screaming, or cursing. Such outbursts were common reactions to the subject's hallucinations. Removal of the aversive stimulus was paired with cessation of the inappropriate behaviors. Results revealed significant decreases in verbalizations related to hallucinations. Although overall hallucinations were not directly measured, reduction in inappropriate verbalizations were found in follow-up to have led to greater functioning for the client in a variety of areas, including general social interactions.

TRADITIONAL METHODS OF DATA COLLECTION, REDUCTION, AND ANALYSES

The methods of data collection, reduction, and analysis in restricted environments are the same as in more naturalistic settings, although the manner in which they are applied can differ. In many ways, it is easier to implement many of these techniques in restricted environments than elsewhere. By definition, captive audiences are continuously observable, with few means of avoiding observation. The restricted environment can be subject to control and manipulation within the bounds of ethical considerations. Because restricted settings often become a primary residence for the individual (e.g., a nursing home; a long-term psychiatric care residential facility), extended observational periods for determination of baseline behaviors to be targeted are possible.

Toward this end, direct observation in the restricted setting is one of the most effective assessment tools available. Direct observation can be performed by an outside observer or the clients themselves, resulting in measurement (counting and timing) or estimation (rating) type assessments. Unstructured observation can be used to determine the types of behaviors that merit more detailed observation. Each behavior must be operationally defined in such a way that all raters can be trained to recognize and accurately assess target behaviors when they are emitted. There are many different methods of observation; a few of the most useful ones will be discussed here.

Even in restricted environments, it is unreasonable, impractical, and intrusive to monitor clients continuously. Behavioral assessment techniques have been developed into systems whereby accurate measures of behavior can be obtained with less than continuous observation. One such technique is time sampling, in which a number of short periods of observation are used to assess a target behavior. The observer records each time the target behavior occurs during an entire observation period (whole interval time sampling), records whether the behavior occurred at all during the observation period (partial interval time sampling), or records whether the behavior occurred at precise moments, such as the first second of each minute (momentary time sampling).

One of the best known instruments for the assessment of psychiatric patients in restricted settings is the Time-Sample Behavioral Checklist (TSBC; Paul, 1987). The TSBC assesses a wide range of behaviors via direct observation by the examiner. The TSBC contains nine higher order scores and two global scores that can be calculated—(1) total appropriate activity and (2) total inappropriate activity—and seven component scores—(1) amusement/leisure time activity; (2) bizarre motor activity; (3) bizarre facial and verbal activity; (4) hostile/belligerent behavior; (5) instrumental activity; (6) interpersonal interaction; and (7) self-maintenance ability (Paul, 1987). TSBC observations are made on a standard timetable during all waking hours for patients, which comprise a weekly average of about 100 observations per person.

The TSBC requires training for the clinician to learn how to conduct the observations and gain a working knowledge of the operational definitions for all the TSBC categories and the procedures for recording observations over the sampling periods (Paul, 1987). The TSBC has been utilized frequently over the years in restricted settings to assess patient treatment response (for examples, see Beck et al., 1997; Menditto, Beck, Stuve, & Fisher, 1996; Pestle, Card, & Menditto, 1998).

Two related observational instruments developed by Gordon Paul and colleagues are the Clinical Frequencies Recording System (CFRS; Paul & Lentz, 1997) and the Staff-Resident Interaction Chronograph (SRIC; and also available as part of the Computerized TSBC/SRIC Planned-Access Observational Information System—Paul & Licht, 1988). The CFRS is also an observational scale, but it uses event-sampling procedures to record the occurrence of clinically relevant behaviors (e.g., aggressive outbursts) per occurrence. The SRIC is a time-sampling instrument designed to measure the content, frequency, and the functional nature of interactions between patients and hospital staff. The importance of assessing the staff's interaction with patients comes from research that has found that the number and quality of therapeutic contacts with patients (rather than just the overall staff-to-patient ratio) incrementally increases patient discharge rates and adjustment and tenure in the community after discharge above the variance accounted for by patient-to-staff ratio alone (Coleman & Paul, 2001; Paul & Lentz, 1977).

The SRIC is composed of a 5×21 matrix sheet, in which five global categories are used to gauge aspects of patient behavior (e.g., appropriate, inappropriate/failure, inappropriate/crazy, request, neutral) and 21 category rows used to gauge aspects of staff behavior (e.g., reflect/clarify, attend/record/observe, positive verbal, negative nonverbal, ignore/no response, negative statement, instruct/demonstrate). Each of the SRIC cells is comprised of ten 1-minute observation periods during which all behavior of a single staff member is recorded in relation to the functional behavior of all patients present at the time of assessment. The SRIC contains 94 cells to record staff-patient interactive behaviors and three cells to record noninteractive staff behaviors. An attention-received index can be calculated from the SRIC by dividing the sum of the 94 interactive cells by the number of clients present from all observations over the assessment period (Paul, Licht, & Engel, 1988). Collateral information also can be obtained during each observation, including the time and frequencies of departures a staff member makes from specified treatment procedures.

Jones, Menditto, Geeson, Larson, and Sadewhite (2001) used the SRIC, for example, to evaluate paraprofessional staff behavior and staff-patient interactions on a maximum security inpatient psychiatric unit both before and after intensive training on social learning program techniques designed by Paul, McInnis, and Mariotto (1973). Baseline SRIC recordings were conducted for 2 weeks. After intensive social learning program training, SRIC observations were made over a 3-month period. After training, significant increases were found in overall staff activity (greater than 100% increase) and amount of time staff interacted with patients (greater than 200%) as well as decreases in the amount of time spent by staff in job-irrelevant activities (more than 85%) from their baseline assessment. Jones and colleagues concluded that, after social learning based technical training, paraprofessional staff demonstrated dramatic increases in their application of social learning principles in their treatment program (designed after Paul & Lentz, 1977, 1997) in the forensic psychiatric inpatient setting.

Two other techniques used in traditional behavioral assessment are event sampling and duration measurement. Event sampling is a simple technique, whereby the number of times each specific behavior occurs throughout a time period, such as a day, is recorded. With duration measurement, each instance of the target behavior is timed, providing an additional measure of strength. Duration measurement can be used to record such sustained behaviors as temper tantrums, compulsive hand-washing, or crying. This is appropriate for any behavior that typically occurs for a length of time, rather than as brief instances. The magnitude of the behavior also can be monitored. Simply recording whether a behavior occurred reveals little useful information in some instances. For example, aggressive verbal behavior (cursing, verbally threatening others) recorded as an instance for a time interval merely indicates some form of verbal aggression occurred during that period. There is a difference, however, between uttering a single curse word to nobody in particular and screaming a series of extremely vulgar words and threats directed at a particular individual. By recording the strength or severity of the behavior, more information is obtained. The term latency refers to the amount of time between the presence of the antecedent stimuli and the start of the contingent behavior associated with that stimulus. Latency measurement can be useful for determining the strength of the suspected antecedent in evoking the target, maladaptive behavior.

Indirect measurement (by interview and questionnaire) is another common method of assessment for maladaptive behavior. Unfortunately, clinicians too often rely on global, retrospective self-report for assessing symptomatic behavior. Along with global retrospective self-report accounts come biases, responding to make a good or bad impression, and a multitude of inaccuracies and misinterpretations. Clients frequently use self-report to evoke reassuring statements from the examiner. Additionally, self-report often reveals more about clients' perceptions of their symptoms than valid estimates of the frequency of occurrence, functional determinants, and life consequences of dysfunctional behavior (Hamera, Schneider, Potocky, & Casebeer, 1996). In addition, global self-report assessment may be a client's attempt to control and manipulate his or her environment. Overall, self-report has great utility as a screener for quickly learning about a range of symptoms and clients' subjective complaints with relative ease and speed.

In contrast, self-monitoring (measurement or estimation) is an effective tool to use across many therapies and with many assessment techniques. It involves clients monitoring their own target behaviors and recording them as they occur in their natural contexts. This brings the target behaviors to the continuous attention of the clients, and has the clients actively scrutinizing their own behavior, its antecedent conditions, and its consequences. Another characteristic that makes this technique useful is that observations occur continuously and cross-situationally.

Recently, Myin-Germeys, Nicolson, and Delespaul (2001) employed a variation of time-sampling and self-monitoring techniques to examine the contextual antecedents in patients' daily environment that might influence the occurrence of delusional thinking. This study was interesting because it attempted to assess the variability of delusional thinking ("delusional moments") over the hours and days of the study period. Although employed in a community setting, the technique appears to be highly adaptable for assessing captive audiences in restricted environments.

This study used a variation of time sampling assessment called the experience sampling method (ESM). The investigators gave each participant a digital wristwatch and standardized ESM assessment forms collated into a booklet for each study day. Ten times a day over 6 consecutive days the watch emitted a signal at unpredictable times between the hours of 7:30 A.M. and 10:30 P.M. After every signal the participant recorded thoughts, moods, current context (activity, persons present, location) and severity of symptoms. To assess delusions, participants described their current thoughts in their ESM booklets, and the research staff coded these qualitative responses into predetermined categories for statistical analysis. Participants were also required to rate on 7-point Likert scales. Their delusions on several dimensions, including "preoccupation," "suspicion," and "feeling controlled." To assess the validity of the ESM procedure, participants' delusional ideations also were rated independently by researchers using the Brief Psychiatric Rating Scale (BPRS; see below for a discussion of this instrument). It should be noted that, prior to initiation of ESM assessment, the participants were trained by the research staff and underwent ESM practice sessions, although the authors report several patients dropped out of the study and that some data were not usable due to misunderstanding of instructions.

Results of the study revealed that the ESM procedure was a valid assessment of delusional ideation. The ESM-defined delusions correlated highly with the independent coding of delusions and the participants' BPRS delusions scale score. Although the authors caution that causal direction of temporal associations in ESM data cannot be resolutely estab-

lished, analysis of the ESM data revealed that participants' momentary delusional ideation increased during periods of inactivity and decreased while in the presence of acquaintances and family members. Study results indicated that the ESM time-sampling technique was effective at identifying situational antecedents to fluctuations in psychotic processes. The authors also suggested that ESM assessment could provide a context for a clinician to discuss a client's delusional thinking as it occurs in the client's day-to-day or even hour-to-hour experiences (Myin-Germeys et al., 2001).

SUPPLEMENTS TO BEHAVIORAL ASSESSMENT TECHNIQUES

Multidimensional and Cognitive Assessment Strategies

The efficacy of traditional behavioral assessment and treatment of patients in restricted settings has met with much success, but traditional behavioral assessment also suffers some shortcomings as well. The ability to perform a behavioral analysis (e.g., direct observation) by highly trained personnel on every inpatient is beyond the resources available in most restricted care settings. As noted above, harnessing the ability of clients to self-monitor and using hospital staff and other nonprofessionals as collateral sources of information may help conserve professional time. But it is still of limited value in acute inpatient care settings because many individuals may not consent to direct observation and/or are unable or unwilling to self-monitor or perform ESM time sampling for a variety of reasons (e.g., cognitive deficits/disorganization, uncooperativeness, lack of insight).

Another limitation to traditional approaches is that many of the response classes targeted for intervention (i.e., hallucinations and delusions) are private events and not subject to direct observation. As mentioned above, many behavioral approaches focus on assessment and modification of verbal behavior (e.g., antecedents of deluded speech, bizarre behavior, responding to internal stimuli) thought to correlate with or reflect patients' perceptual and cognitive experiences. However, using client self-report of symptoms may, at times, lack validity and suffer from low reliability (Junginger & Frame, 1985). For example, traditional approaches often use extinction schedules to treat hallucinations and delusions. Since extinction procedures are contingent on emission of verbal behavior, it may be that patients continue to "hear" their voices and harbor their delusional beliefs, but simply learn not to report symptomatic behavior to their therapist. This process may reduce the reliability between patients' verbal reports of symptomatic behavior and their psychotic experiences.

In addition, a drawback of traditional assessment approaches is that symptomatology is typically measured dichotomously or on a single dimension of severity and may not capture the multifactorial nature of psychotic behavior. That is, traditional assessment approaches are based on either a present or absent conceptualization of symptomatic behavior or a Likert-type rating of a symptom (absent to severe) on a single dimension or continuum. To overcome some of these limitations, researchers have developed innovative strategies using scales that assess multidimensional aspects of the psychotic experience (e.g. Chadwick, Lees, & Birchwood, 2000; Haddock, McCarron, Tarrier, & Faragher, 1999).

For example, over the past decade there has been a growing interest in the assessment of cognitive mediators of psychotic experience. Multidimensional cognitive assessment strategies rely on direct observation but also on the assessment of a variety of cognitive mediators that underlie and/or maintain dysfunctional behavior. This multidimensional approach enables clinicians to identify numerous domains of behavior to target for intervention. Multidimensional approaches are also ideally suited for assessment of clients in captive settings. In the following sections, we review some recent cognitive multidimensional assessment approaches for symptom domains typically targeted for treatment in clients residing in restricted environments.

Assessment of Delusions

Many innovative assessment scales have been developed in recent years that measure various aspects of a person's delusional experience. Studies have shown that hospitalized individuals are capable of reliably rating a wide variety of belief characteristics (e.g., Garety, Everitt, & Hemsley, 1988). Garety & Hemsley (1987), for example, used a visual analogue scale method of assessing delusions that included 11 belief characteristics rated by clients on a scale of 1 to 10. Dimensions of delusional ideation assessed included the pervasiveness of the delusional belief, its perceived absurdity, resistance to change, its dismissibility, the extent to which a belief is self-evident, reassurance-seeking behavior, the extent of worry and unhappiness, as well as cultural acceptability of the belief. The delusions subscale of the Psychotic Symptom Ratings Scale (PSYRATS; Haddock et al., 1999) is comprised of six items that assess dimensions of delusions rated on a five-point ordinal scale (0 to 4). The items include preoccupation, distress, duration, conviction, intensity of distress, and disruption. Preliminary analysis of the PSYRATS indicates that it has adequate reliability and validity (Haddock et al., 1999). Similarly, Jones & Watson (1997) developed a self-report questionnaire designed to assess deluded individ-

uals' religious, paranoid, schizophrenic, and anorexic beliefs. Subjects were asked to rate several beliefs on 12 characteristics represented by pole opposites, including: (a) conviction: "believe absolutely—believe not at all"; (b) influence on behavior: "makes a big difference to what I do"—"makes no difference to what I do"; (c) influence on cognition: "has a major impact on my thinking"—"has no impact on my thoughts"; (d) truthfulness: "is absolutely true"—"is not true at all"; (e) importance: "is very important to me"—"is not at all important"; (f) frequency: "think about it all the time"—"never think about it at all"; (g) acceptability: "acceptable to everyone"—"acceptable to no one"; (h) use of imagination: "requires great imagination"—"requires no imagination"; (i) speed of formation: "forms very quickly"—"forms very gradually"; (j) perceptual evidence: "is based largely on perception"—"is not based on perception at all"; (k) focused thought: "requires a lot of thought"—"requires no thought at all"; and (l) affective content: "evokes strong feelings"—"involves no feelings at all."

Leibman and Salzinger (1998) targeted the delusional statements made by long-term psychiatric inpatients using the Personal Questionnaire (PQ; Garety, 1985). The PQ method rates fixity, intensity, and anxiety associated with each delusional belief statement. Importantly, the PQ method requires individual development and reflects each patient's own statements to describe his or her beliefs and feelings. Consequently, the PQ is very sensitive to detecting changes over the course of treatment. In their study Leibman and Salzinger devised PQ's weekly throughout the baseline, and again during the 4th, 6th, and 8th weeks of the study's treatment phase, as well as during a follow-up assessment. Mean scores on the PQ for conviction for delusional beliefs at each assessment was used to gauge treatment response. Frequency measures of symptoms also were assessed three times each week, for the same weeks as the administration of the PQ, and were rated on an 8-point scale, ranging from "not at all" to "all the time." The means of each of the three weekly frequency measures were used to measure outcome. Intervention focused on training subjects to use stimulus control self-management strategies to interfere with onset of disturbing symptoms. In the latter treatment phases, subjects were trained to combine stimulus control procedures with learning to make more adaptive responses to more remote stimuli and to then generalize their responses to an array of situations.

Chadwick & Lowe (1994) also used the personal questionnaire method to assess three belief dimensions in their treatment outcome study—consisting of Likert scale ratings of conviction that the belief was true, preoccupation with the belief, and anxiety associated with the belief—devised for each patient. The PQ appeared to be an effective gauge to mark reductions in various aspects of delusional ideation during cognitive-behavioral treatment. This study was noteworthy because the authors were able to establish some independence in treatment response to the various dimensions of the delusional experience. For example, for some clients, cognitive behavioral treatment appeared to significantly reduce delusional conviction independently of preoccupation or anxiety. Also important, these authors employed a scale that measured participants' hypothetical reaction to contradiction of delusional ideation. This scale rated a participant's estimation of their own ability to lessen their delusional conviction if presented with contradictory information. The hypothetical reaction to contradiction scale appeared to be somewhat sensitive to reductions in delusional thinking that occurred as a result of treatment for some of the participants in the study. It should be noted that investigators should be prepared to make assessments at multiple time points because the various dimensions of the delusional experience (e.g., delusional conviction, affective content) have been found to change over time (Brett-Jones, Garety, & Hemsley, 1987; Fowler & Morley, 1989; Freeman & Garety, 1999; Garety, 1985; Haddock et al., 1999; Walkup, 1990).

Although the self-report scales described above have shown good psychometric properties, the relative importance of a particular dimension to the origin and maintenance of delusional thinking is still unclear. Additionally, it is unclear how orthogonal each of the various dimensions of delusional behavior comprising each scale is. Relatedly, the scales provide no way to evaluate which dimensions may be most relevant to target for treatment intervention. Multidimensional assessment of delusions offers new insights into the full range of patients' experiences, but more work needs to be done to validate each dimension and determine their overlap and importance and interdependence on other cognitive constructs (Bentall, 1999).

Assessment of Hallucinations

Typically, multidimensional assessment of hallucinations focuses on the frequency of voices, distress caused by the voices (pleasant to hostile), the physical characteristics of the voices (e.g., loudness, tone, accent), as well as voice content and source attribution (Bentall, Baker, & Havers, 1991). Others have focused on cognitive variables that may help maintain hallucinatory behavior (Chadwick & Birchwood, 1994; Himadi & Curran, 1995). The PSYRATS (Haddock et al., 1999) auditory hallucinations subscale (AH) is comprised of 11 items that measure several dimensions, including frequency, duration, severity, and intensity of distress caused by hallucinations, but also contains symptom specific dimensions of controllability, loudness, location, negative content, degree of negative content, beliefs about origin of voices, and disruption of functioning. The AH subscale is a five-point ordinal scale used to rate symptom scores from 0 to 4. Despite limitations, the authors point out that the PSYRATS may be useful for clinicians in an initial assessment and provide a sensitive measure of dimensional ratings over the course of treatment along with other traditional behavioral measures.

Similarly, Chadwick and Birchwood (1994) proposed that persistence of auditory hallucinations is in part due to the meaning given to the voices. They argue that the importance of beliefs about identity, purpose, omnipotence, and the consequences of compliance or resistance to voices determines the intensity and chronicity of a patient's hallucinations. Assessment of such factors includes the subject's engagement—how willingly a subject complies with a voice and does things to elicit an hallucination; resistance—defined as the degree of noncompliance or avoidance of cues that trigger voices; indifference—defined as the degree to which a hallucinator ignores a voice; and power and authority of voices—defined as the degree of perceived omnipotence of the voices. Based on this notion, Chadwick and Birchwood (1995, 2000) developed the Beliefs about Voices Questionnaire and more recently the revised version (BAVQ-R). The BAVQ-R assesses various beliefs that an individual may hold about their voices. Changes included in the BAVQ-R include five additional items that assess for the omnipotence of hallucinated voices compared with the original version. The BAVQ-R contains 35 items that assess four dimensions of beliefs about voices (benevolence, malevolence, engagement, and resistance) in a self-report format. All responses of the BAVQ-R are rated on a 4-point scale: 0 ("disagree"); 1 ("unsure"); 2 ("agree slightly"); 3 ("agree strongly"). The overall scale and its four subscales showed good retest reliability and validity.

Although the scales discussed above have excellent psychometric characteristics, many inpatients may lack awareness of their symptoms. Consequently, clients, at times, may be unreliable at self-monitoring or self-reporting their psychotic experiences (Amador et al., 1996; Cooklin et al., 1983; Johns et al., 2001; Junginger & Frame, 1985). Junginger and Frame (1985), for example, found that the greater the reliability with which participants were able to identify the perceived location of their hallucinations, the worse they were able to perceive the clarity of their voices. Because hallucinators are the sole experiencers and observers of their voices, self-report assessment used alone may be unreliable and should be supplemented with other assessment techniques (e.g., direct observation of individuals who appear to be talking to themselves or responding to internal stimuli).

Assessment of Depression and Suicidal Behavior

The suicide risk for individuals with severe mental illness is 20 to 40 times higher than that observed in the general population (Black, 1988; Moscicki et al., 1988; Tsuang, 1978). Moreover, patients at various times are at elevated risk to commit suicidal or self-destructive acts even while residing in psychiatric or general hospital restricted inpatient environments (e.g., Appleby et al., 1999; Hung et al., 2000). Appleby et al. (1999), for example, conducted a large-scale survey in England and found that 16% of psychiatric patients committed suicide while residing on a psychiatric inpatient service (13% completed suicide on the ward itself) and a quarter of these patients committed suicide while under some type of observation (3% under constant suicide watch and 16% under suicide watch every 5 to 30 minutes). Consequently, assessment and prevention of suicide for psychiatric patients residing in restricted settings is no less crucial than in less restrictive environments and community settings.

Assessment of suicidal behavior in restricted settings often focuses on assessment of high-risk social and clinical factors, including a history of substance misuse, homelessness, poor social support systems (i.e., living alone), and past suicide attempts (Appleby et al., 1999; Currier & Serper, 1996; Tsuang, 1978). Suicide risk also has been reported to increase during the first week of admission and during discharge planning (Appleby et al., 1999). But illness duration, severity, and frequency of relapse and rehospitalization also have been found to be associated with increased suicide risk in patient groups (Drake, Gates, Whitaker, & Cotton, 1985; Westermeyer, Harrow, & Marengo, 1991).

Additionally, some investigators have found that the presence of active psychosis increases suicide risk. For example, an association has been found between delusional ideation and suicidality in patients hospitalized with either psychotic depression (e.g., Grunebaum et al., 2001; Miller & Chabrier, 1988; Thakur, Hays, Ranga, & Krishnan, 1999) or schizophrenia (Amador et al., 1996). Grunebaum and colleagues (2001) caution that the risk for suicidal behavior due to delusions in both mood-disordered and schizophrenic groups may be confounded by patients' severity of depression. Young and colleagues (1998) found severity of depression to correlate with current suicide ideation in schizophrenic patients, but they reported that only past occurrences of suicide ideation predicted suicide ideation or attempts over a 3-month period. Taiminen and colleagues (2001) compared schizophrenic patients who had committed suicide to living matched control subjects in developing the Schizophrenia Suicide Risk Scale (SSRS). Using medical chart information, police records, and interviews with patients' families and health pro-

fessionals, the authors assessed the sensitivity and specificity of the SSRS in predicting which patients' committed suicide. Although the scale did not demonstrate adequate sensitivity and internal consistency (and thus is currently not useful as a clinical suicide screener), consistent with previous studies, they found predictors of successful suicide included expressed suicide planning, a history of suicide attempts, and depression. Along with past suicidal behavior, Grunebaum and colleagues (2001) suggested that depression severity may be the most important factor associated with risk for suicide, and they underscored the need for assessment and treatment of depression regardless of patients' primary diagnoses.

Toward this end, assessment of suicidal ideation in the restricted environment should include the use of direct observational techniques of behavior. For example, the aggression directed against self subscale of the Overt Aggression Scale (Yudofsky, Silver, Jackson, Endicott, & Williams, 1986; see below for a discussion) has been used effectively to assess patients' risk of suicide in hospital settings (e.g., Steinert, Wiebe, & Gebhardt, 1999). Also, use of components of the TSBC can provide a functional analytic assessment of antecedents and maintaining variables associated with the changes in patients' social, entertainment, instrumental, and self-maintenance activities and can be useful to detect signs of social withdrawal and depression.

Phenomenological scales commonly used to assess depression among inpatients include the Hamilton Depression Rating Scale (HDRS; Hamilton, 1960), which is most often used to assess severity of depression in patients with unipolar mood disorder diagnoses, but has been found to be useful with other groups. The HDRS includes 17 symptoms of depression that are rated on a 5-point scale. One study found HDRS scores distinguished between schizophrenic patients with and without a history of suicide (Jones, Stein, Stanley, & Guido, 1994). Addington, Addington, and Atkinson (1996) have suggested, however, that HDRS items may be poor at distinguishing between schizophrenic negative and extrapyramidal symptoms and depressive symptomatology. But others have found the severity of schizophrenic patients' HDRS-rated depression did not correlate with their negative symptom severity or other demographic factors (Zisook et al., 1999).

The Calgary Depression Scale for Schizophrenia (CDSS; Addington, Addington, & Maticka-Tyndale, 1993; Addington, Addington, & Schissel, 1990) is a univariate 9-item rating scale designed to differentiate positive, negative, and extrapyramidal symptoms from depressive symptoms (Addington et al., 1996; Lancon, Auquier, Reine, Bernard, & Addington, 2001). The CDSS has been found to show good interrater and internal reliability, as well as concurrent validity with the

HDRS (Lancon, Auquier, Reine, Bernard, & Toumi, 2000). Although some investigators have found the CDSS to discriminate between negative symptoms and depression (Kontaxakis et al., 2000), others have found the CDSS to correlate with schizophrenic patients' positive and extrapyramidal symptoms (e.g., Lancon et al., 2000).

Assessment of Aggressive Behavior

Aggressive or violent behavior committed by patients in restricted settings is also a significant issue for behavioral assessment and intervention (Steinert et al., 1999). Clients residing in restricted settings frequently engage in verbally threatening behavior, as well as acts of physical aggression (Lavoie, Carter, Danzi, & Berg, 1988). An instrument frequently used to measure multidimensional aspects of aggressive behavior committed by patients in restricted environments is the Overt Aggression Scale (OAS; Yudofsky et al., 1986), which measures aggressive behaviors operationally defined into four categories: physical aggression directed at others, physical aggression directed at self, verbal aggression, and physical aggression against objects in the environment. Within each of the four categories, the aggression is further broken down into clearly operationalized levels, from a rating of 1 ("least severe") to 4 ("most severe"). The OAS also provides a record of the frequency of aggressive acts based on direct observation on an incident-by-incident basis, and operationalized verbal descriptions of aggressive behavior are used to weight each point on the four rating scales, which enhances reliability and validity of the scale. Using this tool, staff can record aggressive incidents in a manner that allows for quick review and comparison over time, which is very useful for evaluating aggression over the course of treatment on the inpatient service.

Over the years, several variations of the OAS have been developed (e.g., Alderman, Knight, & Morgan, 1997; Kay, Wolkenfeld, & Murrill, 1987; Sorgi, Ratey, Knoedler, Markert, & Reichman, 1991). In the retrospective version of the original scale (ROAS; Sorgi et al.,1991), a trained rater reviews medical chart notes of aggressive incidents that occurred over the preceding week. However, a limitation of the ROAS (and all retrospective assessment scales) is that it relies on the diligence of the staff to record past instances of aggression in the client's chart. A recent study has found staff underreported and underdocumented the number of violence incidences committed on the inpatient service (Ehmann et al., 2001). Consequently, retrospective assessment of violence committed by inpatients on the psychiatric unit may underestimate actual incidents.

Alderman and colleagues (1997) adapted the OAS to reflect the type of aggressive acts committed by patients with brain injury undergoing neurorehabilitation (OAS-MNR) in the United Kingdom. The authors added items to the OAS-MNR to include the basic elements for clinicians to provide a functional analysis of aggressive behavior. Interestingly, the authors added 18 categories of antecedent events observed to precede the onset of aggressive incidents for use with traditional behavioral assessment methods. The OAS-MNR has been found to possess good interrater reliability, and preliminary studies suggest it is a valid indicator of the types and severity of aggression seen in brain-injured populations in the United Kingdom (Alderman et al., 1997; Alderman, Davies, Jones, & McDonnell, 1999).

Like the OAS, the Staff Observation Assessment Scale (SOAS; Palmstierna & Wistedt, 1997) and its revision (SOAS-R; Nijman et al., 1999) is an observer rating instrument that assesses the severity and frequency of aggressive behavior of captive audiences in restricted settings. The scale assesses physical assaults, verbal assaults, and assaults against property. Like the OAS, assessment is performed by the hospital staff's observation and recording of aggressive incidents onto a standardized form. The SOAS-R has been used to classify violent behaviors into five subscales: (1) provocation, (2) means used by the patient, (3) aim(s) of aggression, (4) resulting damage or injury, and (5) measures to stop aggression. Each item of the three central aspects of aggression (means, aims, and consequences) is rated on a 0- to 4-point scale, and their sum yields a global score indicative of the severity of the event (ranging from 0 to 12). Preliminary studies of the SOAS and SOAS-R have shown the scale to have good psychometric properties, including adequate reliability and validity (Nijman et al., 1999; Steinert, Wölfe, & Gebhardt, 2000). Steinert and colleagues (2000) examined violent behavior committed by patients with psychosis on the inpatient unit and found the OAS and SOAS-R correlated very highly with each other, indicating they measure very similar behaviors.

Assessment of Adaptive Functioning

People with psychiatric disorders often suffer impairment in their general living skills. Many questionnaires, observational systems, and structured interviews are used to assess this domain of functioning. In this section we briefly discuss a few scales that have been used to evaluate a client's level of care and ability to transition from the inpatient service to less restricted or community-based settings. The Independent Living Skills Survey (ILSS; Vacarro, Pitts, & Wallace, 1992) was designed to assess normal living skills among a group of chronic mentally ill individuals. The ILSS is comprised of 188 items that assess performance in 12 areas of functioning (e.g., personal hygiene, personal appearance, food preparation, money management, transportation, and job-maintenance skills). Both self-report and staff-rated versions of the ILSS have been created. This scale is easy to use and is useful for determining level of functioning in chronic psychiatric patients.

A related functional assessment measure is the Independent Living Skills Inventory (ILSI) (Menditto et al., 1999). Like the ILSS, the ILSI was designed to measure a client's ability to perform a wide range of skills needed for independent living in the community. A distinctive aspect of the ILSI is that each item is rated on two related factors. One factor is the degree to which the skill can be performed, and the other is the amount of assistance required to perform the skill. This scoring technique aids in treatment planning because it distinguishes between skills deficits and performance deficits, which require different types of treatment interventions. Like the ILSS, the ILSI is comprised of 12 subscales, each representing a different area of community functioning ability (e.g., money management; personal hygiene). Menditto and colleagues (1999) compared the ILSS to the ILSI (and also included components from the TSBC to examine concurrent validity) and concluded that both functional assessment instruments have a high degree of shared variance, reliability, validity, and sensitivity for detecting treatment effects during psychosocial rehabilitation programs designed for individuals with chronic psychiatric difficulties.

Another functional assessment inventory is the Social Adaptive Functioning Evaluation scale (SAFE; Harvey, Davidson, Mueser, Parrella, & Davis, 1997). The SAFE was specifically designed for skills assessment of geriatric patients in restricted settings. The SAFE is a 17-item scale that assesses an individual's social-interpersonal, instrumental, and impulse control skills. The scale is designed to be rated by an evaluator after observation of and interaction with a client, an interview with the subject's caregiver, and review of medical chart notes. The scale has demonstrated good reliability, convergent and predictive validity, and, importantly, has successfully discriminated between geriatric clients requiring full-time hospital or nursing home care and those able to be discharged to less restricted environments (Harvey et al., 1997).

Psychiatric Rating Scales

Interviewer-based rating scales that assess symptom severity are commonly used to assess a wide range of psychiatric symptoms and responses to psychological and pharmacolog-

ical treatment in the restricted setting. Examples of rating scales commonly used in inpatient hospital settings include the Brief Psychiatric Rating Scale (BPRS; Overall & Gorham, 1962), the Positive and Negative Symptom Scale (PANSS; Kay, Fiszbein, & Opler, 1987), the Schedule for the Assessment of Negative Symptoms (SANS; Andreasen, 1982a), and the Schedule for the Assessment of Positive Symptoms (SAPS; Andreasen, 1982b).

Perhaps the best known tool for the assessment of general psychopathology used in restricted settings is the BPRS. The BPRS was originally developed to gauge inpatients' symptomatic response to neuroleptic treatment. The BPRS is comprised of 16 items that are rated in interview format using Likert scale ratings from 1 ("absent") to 7 ("very severe"). The BPRS anchored version (BPRS-A; Woerner, Mannuzza, & Kane, 1988) describes expected symptoms and problems for each of the seven rating options for each item. As such, it is thought that the BPRS-A anchor points provide an increased level of standardization and relies more on clinical competence than the original version and as a result may improve rater reliability (Woerner et al., 1988).

Investigators have found that the original five factors of the BPRS—Thought Disturbance, Anergia, Hostility, Activation, and Anxiety/Depression—fit the data poorly (Harvey, Davidson, White, & Keefe, 1996; Mueser, Curran, & McHugo, 1997). One report also found the original BPRS five-factor structure varied depending on a client's medication status at the time of assessment (Czbor & Volavka, 1996). These authors advised caution when interpreting BPRS factor scales in longitudinal assessment over the course of pharmacological treatment.

A few investigators have found various BPRS four-factor solutions provided a better fit than the original five-factor model. For example, Lachar and colleagues (2001) reported a BPRS-A factor analytic solution consisting of Resistance, Positive Symptoms, Negative Symptoms, and Psychological Discomfort subscales. A recent study demonstrated predictive validity of the BPRS-A subscales. It was found that acutely admitted inpatients' scores on the Resistance, Positive Symptoms, and Psychological Discomfort scales were robust predictors of which patients would require extended periods of inpatient services (Hopko, Lachar, Bailley, & Varner 2001). Another BPRS factor solution consisted of Thought Disturbance, Anergia, Affect, and Disorganization (Mueser et al., 1997). Additionally, unlike the five-factor solution, it has been reported that the four-factor solution was stable across medication status (Harvey et al., 1996) and that the four factors were relatively stable over a 3-year assessment period (Long & Brekke, 1999).

Also, with the increased attention given to negative symptomatology over the last few decades, investigators have developed more comprehensive scales with a greater emphasis on the assessment of negative symptoms than the BPRS provides (e.g., PANSS; SANS). The PANSS is an anchored 30-item psychiatric rating scale presented in interview format and is scored in a similar Likert fashion to the BPRS. The instrument retains the original BPRS items, and most of the additional items on the PANSS not included in the BPRS appear to measure symptoms distinct from those measured by the BPRS (Bell, Milstein, Beam-Goulet, Lysaker, & Cicchetti, 1992). The PANSS is composed of a negative symptom scale, a positive symptom scale, and a general symptom scale, but this three-scale structure has not received empirical support from PANSS factor analytic studies. Most investigations examining the factor structure of the PANSS have relied primarily on information obtained from individuals with schizophrenia residing in acute or long-term care restricted settings. These studies typically have found a five-factor solution to the PANSS consisting of Negative Symptoms, Positive Symptoms, Dysphoric Mood, Activation, and Autistic Preoccupation (e.g., Bell, Lysaker, Beam-Goulet, Milstein, & Lindenmayer, 1994; Lindenmayer, Grochowski, & Hyman, 1995; Marder, Davis, & Chouinard, 1997; White et al., 1997). Other investigators, less commonly, have found that the PANSS contains as many as seven or eight factors (e.g., Kay & Sevy, 1990; Peralta & Cuesta, 1995).

A few researchers have attempted to validate the utility of psychiatric rating–based assessment of positive and negative symptoms by comparing them to behaviorally based assessment techniques (e.g., Dingemans, 1990; Farrell & Mariotto, 1982; Gilbert et al., 2000; Lewine, Fogg, & Meltzer, 1983) with varying degrees of success. In an innovative study, Gilbert and colleagues (2000) investigated the concurrent validity of interviewer-based ratings of negative symptoms by comparing the negative symptom ratings using the BPRS and the PANSS to negative symptom behavior assessed via direct observation using the TSBC. The researchers found a significant relationship between the BPRS and PANSS negative symptom factors and the TSBC component score that measured participants' social activity on the inpatient ward. No relationship, however, was found between TSBC observations of patients' entertainment, instrumental, or self-maintenance activities and their BPRS or PANSS negative symptom ratings. The authors concluded that these results partially support the notion that interviewer-based ratings of negative symptoms correspond to direct observation of a patient's interpersonal activity in the restricted setting. But the results also seem to suggest that cross-sectional interviewer-based ratings may be insensitive to detecting specific behavioral

domains of interpersonal difficulty on the inpatient service. It should be noted that the authors speculated that their failure to find a relationship between observer-rated instrumental and self-care behavior, and interviewer ratings also might have been due to a token-economy program on the ward that was ongoing during their study. It was noted that the token-economy program specifically rewarded grooming, personal hygiene, and recreational and work activities, but not interpersonal engagement. Consequently, the lack of relationship between the BPRS and PANSS negative symptom ratings to the TSBC instrumental and self-care component scores may have been confounded by the ongoing treatment regimen. Additionally, important for this discussion, Gilbert and colleagues also concluded that since social opportunities in the restricted setting vary greatly from the interpersonal opportunities in the community, replication of studies in other environments would help elucidate the validity of interviewer-based ratings of psychiatric symptoms and of negative symptoms in particular.

In addition, some psychiatric rating scales contain items and statistically derived factors that assess an individual's cognitive status (e.g., Vadhan, Serper, Harvey, Chou, & Cancro, 2001). On the PANSS, for example, such cognitive symptom items require the interviewer to clinically rate items such as the client's abstract reasoning, attention, stereotyped thinking, and disorientation. The interpretation of clinically rated cognitive dysfunction, however, has been difficult because few studies have examined the validity of these cognitive symptom ratings (Vadhan et al., 2001).

To address this issue, a few investigators have begun to examine the concurrent validity of cognitive symptom ratings by examining the relationship between patients' performance on formal neuropsychological testing and clinicians' ratings of similar cognitive constructs using psychiatric rating scales like the PANSS. Harvey and colleagues (2001) found mixed results regarding the validity of PANSS-based cognitive symptom ratings. A comparison of patients' ratings on five PANSS cognitive symptom factor solutions to their performance on a wide variety of neuropsychological assessment tasks revealed that cognitive performance was poorly correlated with clinicians' cognitive symptom rating of the same psychological constructs (e.g., memory; distractibility).

The SANS, in contrast, is an interviewer-based rating scale that measures a wide variety of negative symptoms, including Flat Affect, Anhedonia/Asociality, Avolition/Apathy, and Inattention subscales. Unlike the wide ranging cognitive factors derived from the PANSS, the SANS rating scale limits cognitive symptoms to attentional dysfunction, and factor-analytic studies have generally supported the coherence of the SANS Attention subscale (Keefe, Harvey, Lenzenweger,

Davidson, & Davis 1992; Peralta & Cuesta, 1995). Unlike the PANSS cognitive symptom factors, a recent study has found the SANS attention subscale correlated well with neuropsychological performance measures of attentional functioning in individuals with schizophrenia (Vadhan et al., 2001). The authors concluded that SANS attention symptom–based assessment may be useful as an adjunct to traditional cognitive screening instruments (e.g., the Mini-Mental Status Exam, Folstein, Folstein, & McHugh, 1975) and formal performance-based neuropsychological assessment. Overall, psychiatric rating scales such as the BPRS and the PANSS are convenient to use but require training, can be time-consuming to administer, and are susceptible to rater drift (Morlan and Tan, 1999; Ventura, Green, Shaner, & Liberman, 1993). Alternatively, psychiatric rating scales provide quantitative information about the topography of many symptoms and are perhaps the most widely used assessment instrument in restricted settings. Despite their ubiquity in the hospital setting, psychiatric rating scales continue to pose significant methodological and psychometric challenges for researchers wishing to continue to establish their reliability and validity (Hopko & Hopko, 1999).

FUTURE DIRECTIONS

New approaches to assessment have incorporated aspects of nonlinear dynamic systems theory (chaos theory), catastrophic theory, and topological theory. These theories work under the assumption that psychopathology is the result of variations in a dynamic system and not simply the result of an increase or decrease in neurological and/or psychological functioning.

Dynamical Systems Assessment

Chaotic theories of psychopathology seek to assess complex patterns of dysregulated behavior and quantify the disorganization using dynamical system models of behavioral sequences (Ciompi, 1997). A major tenet of chaos theory is that functional relationships and response organization only appear to be chaotic, but are in fact deterministic (i.e., "deterministic chaos"). Ciompi (1997) theorizes that many of the productive symptoms of schizophrenia are in fact generated by a chaotic dynamic system. Topological theory attempts to explain more gradual types of human changes over time, while catastrophic theory delves into rapid social changes that occur after a long period of delay (Cangemi, Payne, Kowalski, & Snell, 1999). Several researchers have postulated that when the mathematical models become better elucidated, these dy-

namic theories will increase our understanding and prediction of psychotic behavior.

Several researchers, for example, have attempted to use chaos theory to explore the relationship between functional behavior and psychiatric symptomatology. In a series of studies (Paulus, Geyer, & Braff, 1990; Paulus, Geyer, & Braff, 1996; Paulus, Perry, & Braff, 1999), Paulus and colleagues used methods from nonlinear dynamical systems theory to examine schizophrenic patients' organizational behavior. Paulus and colleagues (1996), for example, asked schizophrenic individuals and control subjects to predict whether an object would appear on the left or the right side of a computer screen. Subjects' binary response (e.g., left side or right side) was analyzed by nonlinear dynamical techniques that quantified the interdependency between consecutive responses on the task. Results revealed that schizophrenic individuals showed a higher degree of interdependency between consecutive responses, less consistency in their response selection and ordering than the comparison group. The researchers noted, however, no overall group differences between most of the qualitative characteristics of sequences. Group differences, therefore, could not be explained by interindividual differences (e.g., aberrant responding by a subgroup). Instead the authors suggested that schizophrenic individuals' dysfunctional behavior organization is characterized by a high degree of interdependency and overreliance on previous responding. The pattern suggested that the organizational difficulties in schizophrenic patients may be due to their interdependence of responses over many trials and suggests that patients' response history contributes to their disorganization rather than a global deficit in their organizational ability. Paulus and colleagues (1999) concluded that the behavior of schizophrenic patients relative to comparison subjects is pathologically dependent on previous behavior and is characterized by the allocation of fewer processing resources to external stimuli than control subjects.

Snyder (1999) also attempted to apply chaos theory to explain schizophrenic symptomatology. She reanalyzed archival data from subjects diagnosed with dementia praecox. The investigation originally assessed their performance on an operant conditioning model with variable interval reinforcement delivered contingent on their responses. Vocalizations by the inpatients also were recorded, and, because they were not relevant to the task, they were hypothesized to be linked to symptomatology. Using nonlinear dynamical systems analysis techniques, and various analyses, the relationship between symptoms, responses, and vocalizations were analyzed. Snyder concluded that the symptoms, responses, and vocalizations by the psychotic inpatients represented a chaotic, nonlinear system. Snyder determined that these behaviors were controlled by two factors: one causing an increase in behavior and one causing a decrease. She concluded that her findings had implications for determining the relationship of functional behavior and symptomatology for inpatients suffering from chronic psychosis. Ciompi (1997) and others point out, however, that the mathematical models of a chaos theory for severe disorganized behaviors seen in major psychopathology have yet to be fully elucidated for clinical use.

Survival Analysis

Another outgrowth of traditional behavioral assessment comes from survival analysis. As noted above, suicide in schizophrenic or depressed clients, for example, is one of the major risk factors that must be periodically assessed and monitored, even in inpatient settings. Survival analysis is one method that researchers have used to better determine who is at risk for suicide. Researchers, for example, have conducted a study examining suicidal individuals and searched for functional relationships that contributed to future suicidal attempts, successful and not (Tejedor, Diaz, Castillon, & Pericay, 1999). Tejedor and colleagues (1999) examined 150 inpatients admitted to a psychiatric hospital after attempting suicide. These patients were then monitored over a 10-year period to predict behaviors associated with future suicide attempts. A multitude of possible predictive functioning domains were examined, including psychological and socioeconomic factors. Two variables emerged as important in the survival analysis: Global Adaptive Functioning (GAF) score and the patients' number of previous suicide attempts. A high GAF score was the factor most related to increased survival time, while survival time decreased and the number of suicide reattempts increased the greater the number of past suicidal behaviors.

Performance-Based Assessment Strategies

Although verbal report is essential for communicating clients' perceptual experiences and thought processes, future strategies may combine self-report and observational-based strategies with laboratory and performance-based measures of functioning. For example, a recently developed performance-based measure of functional living skills called the UCSD Performance-Based Skills Assessment (UPSA; Patterson, Goldman, McKibbin, Hughs, & Jeste, 2001) uses role-play to measure patients' performance in five domains of functioning: household chores, communication, finance, transportation, and planning recreational activities. In contrast to previous measures that use self-report and observational methods of functional skills, use of performance measures may provide new insights by offering clinicians interactive in vivo assessment of severely disabled psychiatric patients' everyday functioning ability. While performance-based measures of living skills provide a unique perspective, it is always important to assess and distinguish between patients' skills deficits and performance deficits, because each requires different types of treatment interventions.

Assessment of performance indicators of psychological constructs that underlie symptom formation may yield both insights into both the etiology of symptoms as well as provide operationalized targets for treatment intervention. Bentall, Corcoran, Howard, Blackwood, & Kinderman (2001), for example, proposed an integrative model of the development of paranoid symptoms based on causal attributions and theory of mind (ToM) deficits. Assessment of deluded patients' attributional style and ToM can offer a point of entry for treatment. Acoustic measures of voice prosody also have been used effectively to measure thought disturbance and certain types of negative symptoms (e.g., flat affect, pause duration) and also have been shown to be more sensitive than clinician-based ratings of negative symptoms over the course of neuroleptic treatment (Alpert, Pouget, Sison, Yahia, & Allan, 1995). Methodological and psychometric challenges remain, however, in terms of establishing reliability and validity of psychological constructs thought to underlie symptoms, as well as determining the ways in which they cause and maintain various aspects of maladaptive behavior, interact with each other, and change over time and treatment course.

Learning Potential Assessment Strategies

Instead of assessing a patient's cognitive deficits, learning potential–based assessment techniques are geared toward ascertaining a client's ability to benefit from instruction reinforcement contingencies and/or repeated practice. Although several studies have shown that schizophrenic patients' failure to learn or benefit from repeated practice is related to increased severity of illness and treatment nonresponsivity (e.g., Harvey, Moriarity, & Serper, 2000; Serper, Bergman, & Harvey, 1990), learning potential assessment techniques have been infrequently employed for use with patients in restrictive settings. The few studies conducted to date in this area, however, have shown that learning potential–based assessment techniques may aid in designing treatment programs for clients based on their ability to benefit from instruction and repeated practice. Studies conducted to date have been able to discriminate "learner" from "nonlearner" patient groups. These studies have found that inpatients who were able to learn the organizing principle of a particular test, like the Wisconsin Card Sorting Task, could be distinguished from patients who had difficulty learning and benefiting from instruction and reinforcement contingencies (Green, 1997; Hellman, Kern, Neilson, & Green, 1998; Wiedl & Weinhobst, 1999; Wiedl, Weinhobst, Schottke, Green, & Nuechterlein, 2001). Use of these strategies may help tailor treatment interventions to the specific needs based on a patient's learning potential (Wiedl et al., 2001). To date, however, learning potential assessment, like many of the assessment techniques described above, has not been widely used, despite the fact that many aspects of cognitive functioning (e.g., verbal memory performance, executive functioning performance) have been found to be related to treatment outcome (Green, 1997; Keefe, 1995; Silverstein, 2001; Spaulding, 1997).

Combining biological and behavioral approaches, moreover, offers the potential for new avenues for treatment in patients with persistent and severe mental illness. There have been successful attempts, for example, to quantify biologic and neural activity coincident with the experience of psychotic symptoms by combining neuroimaging, neural network models with psychological constructs (e.g., Blackwood, Howard, Bentall, & Murray, 2001). Due to advances in neuropsychiatry, future investigators may be able to enhance behavioral assessment by incorporating measures of neuronal activity and neuropsychological functioning, which will yield greater insights into the mechanisms that underlie psychosis and result in increased assessment precision.

OBSTACLES TO IMPLEMENTATION

Despite empirical validation, use of behaviorally based assessment and treatment strategies for psychiatric residents in restrictive environments remain vastly underutilized (Brewin, Wing, Mangen, & Brugha, 1988; Hayes, 1996; Paul & Menditto, 1992; Paul, Stuve & Cross, 1997). One set of factors that impedes the implementation of behavioral strategies on the inpatient service involves the culture and philosophy of many psychiatric institutions. Most psychiatric facilities are committed to medical, psychoanalytic, eclectic, and/or custodial models of care and are overburdened with mandated administrative responsibilities. A recent survey of psychologists working with severely mentally ill patients in state hospitals across the midwestern United States found, for example, that psychologists in these settings spent the most amount of their work day (27%) doing paperwork (e.g., documentation of their activities, writing treatment plans—but not writing up test protocols). In contrast, 18% of their time was utilized for treatment services. While the psychologists in the survey stated that they used some behavioral assessment approaches, the majority of psychologists reported they also

added psychoanalytic theories to their case formulations (Corrigan, Hess & Garman, 1998).

Relatedly, the centralized organizational structure of the hospital may impede the delivery of behaviorally based interventions. Stuve and Menditto (1999) point out that many psychiatric facilities are organized by disciplinary departments with supervisors that have little to no daily patient contact making treatment and staffing decisions. In describing the development of creating a "rehabilitation-ready" hospital environment, Stuve and Menditto (1999) provide an example that illustrates the difficulties in implementing a behaviorally based program because of the organizational structure of the inpatient service:

> A program manager attempting to add a skills training group to the schedule of a particular staff member was likely to encounter resistance to changing the status quo duties, both from the staff member and the supervisor. With primary supervisory authority lying so far away from the actual treatment team, the program manager was reduced largely to the role of "cheerleader" in an effort to organize effective programs and treatment teams (p. 37).

This scenario is typical of the organizational structure of many psychiatric facilities. Replacing a centralized hierarchy with a model that allowed final decision-making authority to trained staff with day-to-day direct patient responsibilities may result in better integration of delivery of behavioral services to patients (Stuve & Menditto, 1999). Hayes (1996, 1997) goes a step further and argues that implementation of scientifically validated interventions should be mandatory rather than the current focus on licensing clinicians to provide care based on their subjective assessments of a patient's difficulties.

Another obstacle to the implementation of behavioral assessment and intervention in restrictive settings is that these approaches require specialized training and intensive resources. Conducting a comprehensive behavioral assessment and treatment program, for example, may require weeks of academic instruction, role play, in vivo demonstrations, modeling, feedback, and practice of the social-learning techniques under direct supervision in order for staff members to reliably apply social learning and behavioral principles and techniques (e.g., Jones et al., 2001; Paul et al., 1973). The shortage of adequately trained hospital staff is an important issue because, as noted above, both the quality of patient-staff interaction and the patient-staff ratio have been found to be important predictors of treatment response and adjustment in the community after discharge (e.g., Coleman & Paul, 2001). Consequently, adequate funding is needed to implement behavioral programs, train staff to administer and maintain their integrity, as well as monitor and assess treatment outcome at multiple time points both in and out of the hospital. However, it has been reported that, since the introduction of managed care over the past decade, there have been significant reductions in mental health service resources and delivery as well as shorter treatment duration for individuals in the public psychiatric system (Burnam & Escarce, 1999; Mechanic & McAlpine, 1999). Such reductions serve to impede the ability for providers to meaningfully apply behavioral principles and techniques as well as implement follow-up assessment on the inpatient service and in community settings.

CASE STUDY (BASED ON COMPOSITES OF A FEW CASES)

Mr. Q. is a 44-year-old homeless male. He has a long history of mental illness, with many prior hospitalizations going back into his early twenties. He was diagnosed with chronic schizophrenia at age 24. Mr. Q. has been living in a halfway house for the last 8 years and has only one living relative, his mother. Over the last few months, however, Mr. Q.'s level of functioning had deteriorated from his baseline. For example, while normally Mr. Q. had enjoyed socializing with others after work and on weekends, he began to spend increasing amounts of time alone. It was also noted that he began talking to himself ("responding to internal stimuli") in the days prior to hospitalization. He became increasingly agitated and grew suspicious of his roommate, other residents, and his coworkers. Two days before his hospital admission, he accused his roommate of stealing from him and conspiring to kill him. It was also noted at this time that he began to consume large amounts of water and lost 15 pounds. A subsequent medical examination, however, revealed that there was no organic basis for his excessive thirst and weight loss. Although his antipsychotic medication dose was increased at this time, his functioning continued to worsen, and Mr. Q. was admitted to a local psychiatric hospital. His presenting symptoms included persecutory delusions, auditory hallucinations, and polydipsia (excessive drinking of water). Review of his chart indicated that he has been admitted to the hospital on many previous occasions suffering from similar symptoms, including delusions of persecution, agitation, and auditory hallucinations.

Setting

An inpatient unit at a psychiatric center to which Mr. Q. was completely restricted but within which he could move around freely.

Measures and Procedure

Clinicians at the psychiatric center interviewed Mr. Q. and obtained background information from his mother and his outpatient psychologist. From information gathered, target symptoms were identified over the first few days of hospitalization and served as a baseline assessment. Treatment goals included elimination of excessive drinking behavior and reductions in delusional ideation and auditory hallucinations to levels that do not interfere with his ability to function in his community setting.

All psychological assessment techniques were implemented directly by the staff psychologists, psychology interns, and medical students and in conjunction with pharmacotherapy.

Paranoid Ideation

Mr. Q.'s delusions consisted of beliefs that the government was trying to have him killed because he had the ability to "read people's minds" and consequently represented a threat. Whole interval time sampling, with intervals of 1 hour, were used to monitor his delusional beliefs. Positive delusional states were recorded based upon self-report by Mr. Q., who was instructed to verbalize to staff when he started to experience paranoid ideation. Staff, however, also made regular inquiries as a secondary measure to assess frequency of delusional ideation. Mr. Q. reported experiencing delusional ideation 21 times over the baseline period, and staff inquiries resulted in 7 additional instances in which Mr. Q. engaged in delusional ideation. Overall, delusional ideation was reported to occur on average, three times a day for an average of 25 minutes each time before Mr. Q. reported he could redirect his attention. Delusional moments occurred most frequently after he experienced an auditory hallucination, in the evening hours, during unstructured periods, or when alone in his room.

The personal questionnaire (PQ) was used to measure the multidimensional aspects of the degree of conviction, preoccupation, and anxiety associated with his paranoid beliefs. Baseline assessment revealed that his conviction and anxiety associated with his delusional ideation during these episodes were high because he suspected that many people were involved in the conspiracy, including his roommate and several coworkers. Despite high conviction and frequency of delusional ideation, his preoccupation with these beliefs, however, was found to be in the moderate range. This suggested that while Mr. Q. believed in the authenticity of his beliefs, they did not preclude his ability to participate in ward activities, nor did they consume all his attentional resources.

The evidence supporting Mr. Q.'s beliefs centered on hallucinated voices that told him that they were "going to get him" and it was "only a matter of time." He believed these voices were initiated by the government to harass him and make him anxious. His score on the Hypothetical Reaction to Contradiction Scale (Chadwick & Lowe, 1994) indicated that if it could be proven that (1) the voices were internally generated, (2) his roommate was not working against him, and/or (3) he could not read people's minds, it would lessen his conviction, anxiety, and preoccupation with his suspicious beliefs.

Auditory Hallucinations

Hallucinatory behaviors were also self-monitored by Mr. Q., who was instructed to record each hallucinatory experience. The Psychotic Symptom Rating Scales (Haddock et al., 1999) auditory hallucinations subscale (AH) was given weekly during baseline and treatment periods to assess the multidimensional aspects of Mr. Q.'s auditory hallucinations (e.g., intensity, distress, controllability) and the relationship to his paranoid thinking.

Over the baseline assessment, Mr. Q. reported hearing the voices three to four times per day every day, especially during the evening when he was alone in his room. Each episode lasted between 5 and 10 minutes. The voices threatened his physical safety, and AH subscale assessment indicated that they were very loud and experienced as outside his control. He also was convinced about the authenticity of the voices as coming from the government. The voices also appeared to be functionally related to his subsequent paranoid episodes.

Polydipsia

Measures of frequency and duration were recorded by Mr. Q. himself, who was trained to carefully self-monitor his drinking behavior and record the time of day he started and ended drinking, the amount of water consumed, and any corresponding feelings of anxiety and ways he coped with these feelings. Mr. Q. was given a cup marked with liquid measurements, and instructed to use the cup for all drinking, regardless of source (water fountain, bottled water, etc.). Staff worked closely with him for 2 days to train him for this self-monitoring. Day one consisted of staff recordings while Mr. Q. observed, and day two consisted of Mr. Q. self-monitoring with staff guidance.

In addition, trained raters utilized the Virginia Polydipsia Scale (VPS; Shutty, Hundley, Leadbetter, Vieweg, & Hill, 1992). The VPS is a functional analytic assessment scale consisting of three subscale measures. The first measure is an observation scale designed to be completed at the end of each 15 minutes observed. General activities, such as specific patient location, activities engaged in, and quantity of water consumed, are measured. The second measure is specific to the drinking behavior and focuses on quantity, source, rate, and time of occurrence, defined as the interval between first beginning to consume water until it is completely consumed. The third subscale of the VPS is an assessment of 20 functional behaviors that are related to polydipsia, including such behaviors as tremors and shakes, unkempt appearance, staring into space, shouting, and yelling. These 20 relevant behaviors are rated on a 4-point scale, ranging from 1 (not observed at all) to 4 (behavior approaching constancy). The use of this scale provides general information about the patient's actions and interactions on the ward, behavioral assessment of drinking behaviors, and the behavioral assessment of related functional, social, and psychological behaviors in as naturalistic a method as possible.

Results of baseline assessment revealed Mr. Q. drank from the water fountain 8 to 12 times a day, for a period of between 5 and 15 minutes each time. Once to twice a day he would become agitated at another patient using the water fountain when he wanted to drink from it. The VPS indicated that he seemed to want to use the water fountain more when another patient was already using it, rather than when it was unattended. Drinking behaviors were engaged in evenly across the day, with significantly less of the behavior observed during the evening and night.

With baseline recordings completed, behavioral treatment was initiated. He was monitored and reassessed weekly on the PQ and PSYRATS AH and VPS subscales.

Results and Discussion

In addition to antipsychotic medication, cognitive-behavioral therapy (based on Chadwick & Lowe, 1994) was employed to treat Mr. Q.'s delusional ideation. Treatment consisted of twice-per-week sessions over a 4-week period. Outcome was assessed using the PQ after each treatment session, as well as continued observation assessment for frequency of delusional ideation occurrences on the unit. Treatment focused on verbal disputation and empirical testing that challenged the authenticity of his voices and his ability to read people's minds. Mr. Q. stated that it would lessen his delusional conviction if it could be proven that he could not read other people's thoughts. To challenge this belief, Mr. Q. participated in group sessions where a member was asked to think of a number, and write it down on a piece of paper. Mr. Q was then asked to read the person's mind and ascertain the number.

Another aspect of treatment focused on the source of his voices. He stated that he would be less convinced of the authenticity of his voices and his delusional beliefs if the voices could be "drowned out." He stated that this would make him feel he had more control over his voices. Mr. Q. was given a radio and headset and asked to play the radio loud whenever he heard the voices. Mr. Q. was initially doubtful of this procedure, stating that the government-sent voices would "overpower" any electronic device.

Over the course of his twice-weekly treatment sessions, PQ results indicated a steady decline in his conviction and anxiety associated with his paranoid ideation. Mr. Q.'s delusional preoccupation, however, remained relatively unchanged over the treatment period. Time sampling data also revealed significant reductions in the frequency of Mr. Q.'s delusional ideation on the ward—averaging six paranoid episodes per week over the treatment period.

Auditory hallucinations also decreased in frequency over the treatment period. Mr. Q. reported experiencing one to two hallucinatory episodes per week. Additionally, the average duration had decreased from 5 to 10 minutes at baseline to an average of approximately 1 minute per episode. However, he attenuated his hallucinatory experience by putting on the headsets. On his AH weekly ratings he reported reductions in the amount distress caused by hallucinations, their controllability, loudness, location, and also beliefs about the origin of voices and questioned whether they did in fact originate from "government transmissions."

Excessive Drinking Behaviors

Polydipsia was treated for the first few days exclusively by restricting fluid intake by means of limiting the amount of time he had access to water. By the end of the first week, staff and Mr. Q. had worked together to design his token economy to supplement the restriction in fluid intake. Reinforcement was contingent on daily measurements of weight gain, as well as periodic measurements of urine specific gravity and serum sodium level. Compliance with the token economy was positively reinforced with praise from staff.

Four weeks into treatment, Mr. Q.'s excessive drinking behaviors had decreased in both frequency and duration. Mr. Q. drank from the water fountain 8 to 10 times per day, for a period of usually less than 2 minutes each time. He drank no more than 4 liters of water per day. On the few occasions that Mr. Q. was observed drinking for greater than 4 minutes, staff would approach him and remind him of the incentives he was working toward. Over the last several weeks of his hospitalization, when he was moving toward discharge to a less restrictive environment, the token economy was phased out, as was the monitoring of his fluid restrictions. Positive reinforcement was still administered for low levels of fluid intake. Mr. Q. was able to maintain a healthy consumption rate during this period. Overall, assessment revealed that, along with antipsychotic medication, behavioral treatment produced successive gains in reducing various aspects of the target behaviors. Once treatment goals were reached, the patient was discharged to his community residence.

After discharge, a 1-month follow-up assessment was conducted at Mr. Q.'s residence. PQ results revealed slight increases in his anxiety and delusional convictions, along with mild increases in his PSYRATS AH score from his last treatment session. Additionally, the VPS revealed that his excessive drinking behaviors, although periodically disproportionate, were no longer in a range of medical concern after successful implementation of the inpatient token reinforcement program. Since effective intervention requires a strategy of multiple assessment and follow-ups (Paul & Menditto, 1992), Mr. Q. will continue to be monitored and provided booster therapy sessions to reinforce treatment gains. Despite the mild increase in some behaviors, Mr. Q. had effectively transitioned back to community living.

REFERENCES

Addington, D., Addington, J., & Atkinson, M. (1996). Psychometric comparison of the Calgary Depression Scale for Schizophrenia and the Hamilton Depression Rating Scale. *Schizophrenia Research, 19,* 205–212.

Addington, D., Addington, J., & Maticka-Tyndale, E. (1993). Assessing depression in schizophrenia: The Calgary Depression Scale. *British Journal of Psychiatry, 16*(Suppl. 22), 39–44.

Addington, D., Addington, J., & Schissel, B. (1990). A depression rating scale for schizophrenics. *Schizophrenia Research, 3,* 247–251.

Alderman, N., Davies, J.A., Jones, C., & McDonnel, P. (1999). Reduction of severe aggressive behaviour in acquired brain injury: Case studies illustrating clinical use of the OAS-MNR in the management of challenging behaviours. *Brain Injury, 13,* 669–704.

Alderman, N., Knight, C., & Morgan, C. (1997). Use of a modified version of the Overt Aggression Scale in the measurement and assessment of aggressive behaviours following brain injury. *Brain Injury, 11,* 503–523.

Alford, G.S., & Turner, S.M. (1976). Stimulus interference and conditioned inhibition of auditory hallucinations. *Journal of Behavior Therapy and Experimental Psychiatry, 7*(2), 155–160.

Alpert, M., Pouget, E.R, Sison, C., Yahia, M., & Allan, E. (1995). Clinical and acoustic measures of the negative syndrome. *Psychopharmacological Bulletin, 31,* 321–326.

Amador, X.F., Friedman J.H, Kasapis, C., Yale, S.A., Flaum, M., & Gorman, J.M. (1996). Suicidal behavior in schizophrenia and its relationship to awareness of illness. *American Journal of Psychiatry, 135,* 1241–1243.

Andreasen, N.C. (1983a). *Scale for the Assessment of Negative Symptoms (SANS).* Iowa City: University of Iowa.

Andreasen, N.C. (1983b). *Scale for the Assessment of Positive Symptoms (SAPS).* Iowa City: University of Iowa.

Appleby, L., Shaw, J., Amos, T., McDonnell, R., Harris, C., McCann, K., Kiernan, K., Davies, S., Bickley, H., & Parsons, R. (1999). Suicide within 12 months of contact with mental health services: National clinical survey. *British Medical Journal, 318,* 1235–1239.

Ayllon, T., & Haughton, E. (1964). Control of the behavior of schizophrenic patients by food. *Journal of the Experimental Analysis of Behavior, 5*(3), 343–352.

Baker C.A., & Morrison, A.P. (1998). Cognitive processes in auditory hallucinations: Attributional biases and metacognition. *Psychological Medicine, 28*(5), 1199–1208.

Beck, N.C., Greenfield, S.R., Gotham, H., Menditto, A.A., Stuve, P., & Hemme, C.A. (1997). Risperidone in the management of violent, treatment-resistant schizophrenics hospitalized in a maximum security forensic facility. *Journal of the American Academy of Psychiatry and the Law, 25,* 461–468.

Belcher, T.L. (1988). Behavioral reduction of overt hallucinatory behavior in a chronic schizophrenia. *Journal of Behavior Therapy and Experimental Psychiatry, 19*(1), 69–71.

Bell, M.D., Lysaker, P.H., Beam-Goulet, J.L., Milstein, R.M., & Lindenmayer, J. (1994). Five-component model of schizophrenia: Assessing the factorial invariance of the positive and negative syndrome scale. *Psychiatry Research, 52,* 295–303.

Bell, M., Milstein, R., Beam-Goulet, J., Lysaker, P., & Cicchetti, D. (1992). The Positive and Negative Syndrome Scale and the Brief Psychiatric Rating Scale. Reliability, comparability, and predictive validity. *Journal of Nervous and Mental Disease, 180,* 723–728.

Bentall, R.P. (1999). Commentary on Garety & Freeman III: Three psychological investigators and an elephant. *British Journal of Clinical Psychology, 38*(3), 323–327.

Bentall, R.P., Baker, G.A., & Havers, S. (1991). Reality monitoring and psychotic hallucinations. *British Journal of Clinical Psychology, 30,* 213–222.

Bentall, R.P., Corcoran, R., Howard, R., Blackwood, N., & Kinderman, P. (2001). Persecutory delusions: A review and theoretical integration. *Clinical Psychology Review, 21,* 1143–1192.

Bentall, R.P., Jackson, H.F., & Pilgrim, D. (1988). Abandoning the concept of "schizophrenia": Some implications of validity arguments for psychological research into psychotic phenomena. *British Journal of Clinical Psychology, 27,* 329–331.

Bick, P.A., & Kinsbourne, M. (1987). Auditory hallucinations and subvocal speech in schizophrenic patients. *American Journal of Psychiatry, 144,* 222–225.

Birchwood, M.J. (1986). Control of auditory hallucinations through occlusion of monaural auditory input. *British Journal of Psychiatry, 149,* 104–107.

Black, D.W. (1988). Mortality in schizophrenia—The Iowa Record-Linkage Study: A comparison with general population mortality. *Psychosomatics, 29,* 55–60.

Blackwood, N.J., Howard, R.J., Bentall, R.P., & Murray, R.M. (2001). Cognitive neuropsychiatric models of persecutory delusions. *American Journal of Psychiatry, 158,* 527–539.

Braunstein-Bercovitz, H., Rammsayer, T., Gibbons, H., & Lubow, R.E. (2002). Latent inhibition deficits in high-schizotypal normals: Symptom-specific or anxiety-related? *Schizophrenia Research, 53,* 109–121.

Brett-Jones, J.R., Garety, P.A., & Hemsley, D.R. (1987). Measuring delusional experiences: A method and its application. *British Journal of Clinical Psychology, 26,* 257–265.

Brewin, C.R, Wing, J.K, Mangen, S.P, & Brugha, T.S. (1988). Needs for care among the long-term mentally ill: A report from the Camberwell High Contact Survey. *Psychological Medicine, 18,* 457–468.

Burnam, M.A., Escarce, J.J. (1999). Equity in managed care for mental disorders. *Health Affairs 18,* 22–31.

Burns, C.E., Heiby, E.M., & Tharp. R.G. (1983). A verbal behavior analysis of auditory hallucinations. *Behavior Analyst, 6,* 133–143.

Cangemi, J.P., Payne, K.E., Kowalski, C.J., & Snell, J. (1999). Chaos theory, catastrophic theory and topological theory: Examples and perspectives. *Psychology: A Journal of Human Behavior, 36,* 11–20.

Chadwick, P., & Birchwood, M. (1994). The omnipotence of voices: A cognitive approach to auditory hallucinations. *British Journal of Psychiatry, 164,* 190–201.

Chadwick, P., & Birchwood, M. (1995). The omnipotence of voices: II. The Beliefs About Voices Questionnaire (BAVQ). *British Journal of Psychiatry, 166,* 773–776.

Chadwick, P., Lees, S., & Birchwood, M. (2000). The revised Beliefs about Voices Questionnaire (BAVQ-R). *British Journal of Psychiatry, 177,* 229–232.

Chadwick, P., & Lowe, C.F. (1994). A cognitive approach to measuring and modifying delusions. *Behaviour Research and Therapy, 32,* 355–367.

Ciompi, L. (1997). Non-linear dynamics of complex systems: The chaos-theoretical approach to schizophrenia. In H.D. Brenner & W. Boeker (Eds.), *Toward a comprehensive therapy for schizophrenia.* Kirkland, WA: Hogrefe and Huber.

Coleman, J.C, & Paul, G.L. (2001). Relationship between staffing ratios and effectiveness of inpatient psychiatric units. *Psychiatric Services, 52,* 1374–1379.

Cooklin, R.S., Sturgeon, D., & Leff, J.P. (1983). The relationship between auditory hallucinations and spontaneous fluctuations of skin conductance in schizophrenia. *British Journal of Psychiatry, 142,* 47–52.

Corrigan, P.W., Hess, L., & Garman, N.L. (1998). Results of a job analysis of psychologists working in state hospitals. *Journal of Clinical Psychology, 54,* 11–18.

Currier, G., & Serper, M.R. (1996). Emergency assessment and treatment of substance abuse and co-occurring psychiatric illness. In M. Allen (Ed.), *New directions in mental health service: Advances in emergency psychiatry.* San Francisco: Jossey-Bass.

Czbor, P., & Volavka, J. (1996). Dimensions of the Brief Psychiatric Rating Scale: An examination of stability during haloperidol treatment. *Comprehensive Psychiatry, 37,* 205–215.

Dingemans, P.M. (1990). The Brief Psychiatric Rating Scale (BPRS) and the Nurses' Observation Scale for Inpatient Evaluation in the evaluation of positive and negative symptoms. *Journal of Clinical Psychology, 46,* 168–174.

Done, D.J., Frith, C.D., & Owens, D.C. (1986). Reducing persistent auditory hallucinations by wearing an ear-plug. *British Journal of Clinical Psychology, 25,* 151–152.

Dowson, J.H., Sussams, P., Grounds, A.T., & Taylor, J. (2000). Associations of self-reported past "psychotic" phenomena with features of personality disorders. *Comprehensive Psychiatry, 41,* 42–48.

Drake, R.E., Gates, C., Whitaker, A., Cotton, P.G. (1985). Suicide among schizophrenics: A review. *Comprehensive Psychiatry, 26,* 90–100.

Ehmann, T., Smith, J.N., Yamamoto, A., McCarthy, N., Ross, D., Au, T., Flynn, S.W., Altman, S., & Honer, W.G. (2001). Violence in treatment resistant psychotic inpatients. *Journal of Nervous and Mental Disease, 189,* 716–721.

Ellson, D.G. (1941). Hallucinations produced by sensory conditioning. *Journal of Experimental Psychology, 28,* 1–20.

Erickson, G.D., & Gustafson, G.J. (1968). Controlling auditory hallucinations. *Hospital and Community Psychiatry, 19,* 327–329.

Falloon, I.R., & Talbot, R.E. (1981). Persistent auditory hallucinations: Coping mechanisms and implications for management. *Psychological Medicine, 11,* 329–339.

Farrell, A.D., & Mariotto, M.J. (1982). A multimethod validation of two psychiatric rating scales. *Journal of Consulting and Clinical Psychology, 50,* 273–280.

Feder, R. (1982). Auditory hallucinations treated by radio headphones. *American Journal of Psychiatry, 139,* 1188–1190.

Folstein, M.F., Folstein, S.E., & McHugh, P.R. (1975). "Mini-mental state." *Journal of Psychiatric Research, 12,* 189–198.

Fonagy, P., & Slade, P.D. (1982). Punishment versus negative reinforcement in the aversive conditioning of auditory hallucinations. *Behaviour Research and Therapy, 20,* 483–492.

Fowler, D., & Morley, S. (1989). The cognitive-behavioural treatment of hallucinations and delusions: A preliminary study. *Behavioural Psychotherapy, 17,* 267–282.

Freeman, D, & Garety, P.A. (1999). Worry processes and dimensions of delusions: An exploratory investigation of a role for anxiety processes in the maintenance of delusional distress. *Behavioural and Cognitive Psychotherapy, 27,* 47–62.

Garety, P.A. (1985). Delusions: Problems in definition and measurement. *British Journal of Medical Psychology, 58,* 25–34.

Garety, P.A., Everitt, B.S., & Hemsley, D.R. (1988). The characteristics of delusions: A cluster analysis of deluded subjects. *European Archives of Psychiatry and Neurological Sciences, 237,* 112–114.

Garety, P.A., & Hemsley, D.R. (1987). Characteristics of delusional experience. *European Archives of Psychiatry and Neurological Sciences, 236,* 294–298.

Gilbert, E.A., Liberman, R.P., Ventura, J., Kern, R., Robertson, M.J., Hwang, S., & Green, M.F. (2000). Concurrent validity of negative symptom assessments in treatment refractory schizophrenia: Relationship between interview-based ratings and inpatient ward observations. *Journal of Psychiatric Research, 3,* 443–447.

Gray, J.A., Joseph, M.H., Hemsley, D.R., Young, A.M.J., Warburton, E.C., Boulenguez, P., Grigoryan, G.A., Peters, S.L., Rawlins, J.N.P., Taib, C.T., Yee, B.K., Cassaday, H., Weiner, I., Gal, G., Gusak, O., Joel, D., Shadach, E., Shalev, A., Trasch, R., & Feldon, J. (1995). The role of mesolimbic dopaminergic and retohippocampal afferents to the nucleus accumbens in latent inhibition: Implications for schizophrenia. *Behavioural Brain Research, 71,* 19–31.

Green, M.F. (1997). What are the functional consequences of neurocognitive deficits in schizophrenia? *American Journal of Psychiatry, 153,* 321–330.

Grunebaum, M.F., Oquendo, M.A., Harkavy-Friedman, J.M., Ellis, S.P., Li, S., Haas, G.L., Malone, K.M., & Mann, J. (2001). Delusions and suicidality. *American Journal of Psychiatry, 158,* 742–747.

Haddock, G., McCarron, J., Tarrier, N., & Faragher, E.B. (1999). Scales to measure dimensions of hallucinations and delusions: The psychotic symptom rating scales (PSYRATS). *Psychological Medicine, 29,* 879–889.

Hamera, E.K., Schneider, J.K., Potocky, M., & Casebeer, M.A. (1996). Validity of self-administered symptom scales in clients with schizophrenia and schizoaffective disorders. *Schizophrenia Research, 19,* 213–219.

Hamilton, M. (1960). A rating scale for depression. *Journal of Neurology, Neurosurgery and Psychiatry, 23,* 56–62.

Harvey, P.D., Davidson, M., Mueser, K.T., Parrella, M., & Davis, K.L. (1997). Social-Adaptive Functioning Evaluation (SAFE): A rating scale for geriatric psychiatric patients. *Schizophrenia Bulletin, 23,* 131–145.

Harvey, P.D., Davidson, M., White, L., & Keefe, R. (1996). Empirical evaluation of the factorial structure of clinical symptoms in schizophrenia: Effects of typical neuroleptics on the Brief Psychiatric Rating Scale. *Biological Psychiatry, 40,* 755–760.

Harvey, P., Moriarity, P., & Serper, M. (2000). Practice-related improvement in information processing with novel antipsychotic treatment. *Schizophrenia Research, 46,* 139–148.

Harvey, P.D., Serper, M.R., White, L., Parrella, M.J., McGurk, S.R., Moriarty, P.J., Vadhan, N., Friedman, J., & Davis, K.L. (2001).

The convergence of neuropsychological testing and clinical ratings of cognitive impairment in patients with schizophrenia. *Comprehensive Psychiatry, 42,* 306–313.

Hayes, S. (1996). Creating the empirical clinician. *Clinical Psychology—Science & Practice, 3,* 179–181.

Hayes, S. (1997). Why managed care is ripe for market-oriented behavior therapy: Commentary on "Since the operant chamber: Is behavior therapy still thinking in boxes?" *Behavior Therapy, 28,* 585–587.

Hefferline, R.F., Bruno, L.J., & Camp, J.A. (1974). Hallucinations: An experimental approach. In F.J. McGuigan & R.A. Schoonover (Eds.), *Psychophysiology of Thinking.* New York: Academic Press.

Hefferline, R.F., & Perrera, T.B. (1963). Proprioceptive discrimination of a covert operant without its observation by the subject. *Science, 139,* 834–835.

Hellman, S.G., Kern, R.S., Neilson, L.M., & Green, M.F. (1998). Monetary reinforcement and Wisconsin Card Sorting performance in schizophrenia: Why show me the money? *Schizophrenia Research, 34,* 67–75.

Hemsley, D.R. (1995). Associative learning in acutely ill and recovered schizophrenic patients. Comment. *Schizophrenia Research, 17,* 287–288.

Hemsley, D.R. (1996). Schizophrenia: A cognitive model and its implications for psychological intervention. *Behavior Modification, 20,* 139–169.

Higgs, W.J. (1970). Effects of gross environmental change upon behavior of schizophrenics: A cautionary note. *Journal of Abnormal Psychology, 3,* 421–422.

Himadi, B., & Curran, J.P. (1995). The modification of auditory hallucinations. *Behavioral Interventions, 10,* 33–47.

Hopko, D.R., & Hopko, S.D. (1999). What can functional analytic psychotherapy contribute to empirically-validated treatments? *Clinical Psychology and Psychotherapy, 6,* 349–356.

Hopko, D.R., Lachar, D., Bailley, S.E., & Varner, R.V. (2001). Assessing predictive factors for extended hospitalization at acute psychiatric admission. *Psychiatric Services, 52,* 1367–1373.

Hung, C.I., Liu, C.Y., Liao, M.N., Chang, Y.H., Yang, Y.Y., & Yeh, E.K. (2000). Self-destructive acts occurring during medical general hospitalization. *General Hospital Psychiatry, 22,* 115–121.

Johns, L.C., Rossell, S., Frith, C., Ahmad, F., Hemsley, D., Kuipers, E., & McGuire, P.K. (2001). Verbal self-monitoring and auditory verbal hallucinations in patients with schizophrenia. *Psychological Medicine, 31,* 705–715.

Jones, E., & Watson, J.P. (1997). Delusion, the overvalued idea and religious beliefs: A comparative analysis of their characteristics. *British Journal of Psychiatry, 170,* 381–386.

Jones, J.S., Stein, D.J., Stanley, M., & Guido, J.R. (1994). Negative and depressive symptoms in suicidal schizophrenics. *Acta Psychiatrica Scandinavica, 89,* 81–87.

Jones, N.T., Menditto, A.A., Geeson, L.R., Larson, E., & Sadewhite, L. (2001). Teaching social-learning procedures to paraprofessionals working with individuals with severe mental illness in a maximum-security forensic hospital. *Behavioral Interventions, 16,* 167–179.

Junginger, J., & Frame, C.L. (1985). Self-report of the frequency and phenomenology of verbal hallucinations. *Journal of Nervous and Mental Disease, 173,* 149–155.

Kay, S.R., Fiszbein, A., & Opler, L.A. (1987). The Positive and Negative Syndrome Scale (PANSS) for schizophrenia. *Schizophrenia Bulletin, 13,* 261–274.

Kay, S.R., & Sevy, S. (1990). Pyramidical model of schizophrenia. *Schizophrenia Bulletin, 16,* 537–544.

Kay, S.R., Wolkenfeld, F., & Murrill, L.M. (1988). Profiles of aggression among psychiatric patients. I. Nature and prevalence. *Journal of Nervous and Mental Disease, 176,* 539–546.

Keefe, R.S.E. (1995). The contribution of neuropsychology to psychiatry. *American Journal of Psychiatry, 152,* 6–15.

Keefe, R.S.E., Harvey, P.D., Lenzenweger, M.F., Davidson, M., & Davis, K.L. (1992). Empirical assessment of the factorial structure of clinical symptoms in schizophrenia negative symptoms. *Psychiatry Research, 44,* 153–165.

Kohlenberg, R.J., & Tsai, M. (1991). Functional analytic psychotherapy: Creating intense and curative relationships. New York & London: Plenum.

Kontaxakis, V.P., Havaki-Kontaxaki, B.J., Stamouli, S.S., Margariti, M.M., Collias, C.T., & Christodoulou, G.N. (2000). Comparison of four scales measuring depression in schizophrenic inpatients. *European Psychiatry, 15,* 274–277.

Kot, T., & Serper, M.R. (2002). Susceptibility to sensory conditioning in hallucinating schizophrenic patients. *Journal of Nervous and Mental Disease, 190,* 282–288.

Lachar, D., Bailley, S.E., Rhoades, H.M., Espadas, A., Aponte, M., Cowan, K.A., Gummattira, P., Kopecky, C.R., & Wassef, A. (2001). New subscales for an anchored version of the Brief Psychiatric Rating Scale: Construction, reliability, and validity in acute psychiatric admissions. *Psychological Assessment, 13,* 384–395.

Lancon, C., Auquier, P., Reine, G., Bernard, D., & Addington, D. (2001). Relationships between depression and psychotic symptoms of schizophrenia during an acute episode and stable period. *Schizophrenia Research, 47,* 135–140.

Lancon, C., Auquier, P., Reine, G., Bernard, D., & Toumi, M. (2000). Study of the concurrent validity of the Calgary Depression Scale for Schizophrenics (CDSS). *Journal of Affective Disorders, 58,* 107–115.

Lavoie, F., Carter, G., Danzi, D., & Berg, R. (1988). Emergency department violence in United States teaching hospitals. *Annals of Emergency Medicine, 17,* 1227–1233.

Layng, T.J., & Andronis, P.T. (1984). Toward a functional analysis of delusional speech and hallucinatory behavior. *Behavior Analyst, 7,* 139–156.

Leibman, M., & Salzinger, K. (1998). A theory-based treatment of psychotic symptoms in schizophrenia: Treatment successes and obstacles to implementation. *Journal of Genetic Psychology, 59,* 404–420.

Lewine, R.R., Fogg, L., & Meltzer, H.Y. (1983). Assessment of negative and positive symptoms in schizophrenia. *Schizophrenia Bulletin, 9,* 368–376.

Lindenmayer, J.P., Grochowski, S., & Hyman, R.B. (1995). Five factor model of schizophrenia: Replication across samples. *Schizophrenia Research, 14,* 229–234.

Long, J.D., & Brekke, J.S. (1999). Longitudinal factor structure of the Brief Psychiatric Rating Scale in schizophrenia. *Psychological Assessment, 11,* 498–506.

Lubow, R.W., & Gerwitz, J.C. (1995). Latent inhibition in humans: Data, theory, and implications for schizophrenia. *Psychological Bulletin, 117,* 87–103.

Marder, S.R., Davis, J.M., & Chouinard, G. (1997). The effects of risperidone on the five dimensions of schizophrenia derived by factor analysis: Combined results of the North American trials. *Journal of Clinical Psychiatry, 58,* 538–546.

Margo, A., Hemsley, D.R., & Slade, P.D. (1981). The effects of varying auditory input on schizophrenic hallucinations. *British Journal of Psychiatry, 139,* 122–127.

McCandless-Glimcher, L., McKnight, S., Hamera, E., & Smith, B.L. (1986). Use of symptoms by schizophrenics to monitor and regulate their illness. *Hospital and Community Psychiatry, 3,* 929–933.

McInnis, M., & Marks, I. (1990). Audiotape therapy for persistent auditory hallucinations. *British Journal of Psychiatry, 157,* 913–914.

Mechanic, D., & McAlpine, D.D. (1999). Mission unfulfilled: Potholes on the road to parity. *Health Affairs, 18,* 7–21.

Menditto, A.A., Beck, N.C., Stuve, P., & Fisher, J.A. (1996). Effectiveness of clozapine and a social learning program for severely disabled psychiatric inpatients. *Psychiatric Services, 47,* 46–51.

Menditto, A.A., Wallace, C.J., Liberman, R.P., Vander Wal, J., Jones, N.T., & Stuve, P. (1999). Functional assessment of independent living skills. *Psychiatric Rehabilitation Skills, 3,* 200–219.

Miller, F.T., & Chabrier, L.A. (1988). Suicide attempts correlate with delusional content in major depression. *Psychopathology, 21,* 34–37.

Mirsky, A.F., Silberman, E.K., Latz, A., & Nagler, S. (1985). Adult outcomes of high-risk children: Differential effects of town and kibbutz rearing. *Schizophrenia Bulletin, 11,* 150–154.

Morlan, K.K., & Tan, S.Y. (1998). Comparison of the brief psychiatric rating scale and the brief symptom inventory. *Journal of Clinical Psychology, 54,* 885–894.

Moscicki, E.K., O'Carroll, P., Rae, D.S., Locke, B.Z., Roy, A., Regier, D.A. (1988). Suicide attempts in the Epidemiologic Catchment Area Study. *Yale Journal of Biological Medicine, 61,* 259–268.

Mueser, K.T., Curran, P.J., & McHugo, G.J. (1997). Factor structure of the Brief Psychiatric Rating Scale in schizophrenia. *Psychological Assessment, 9,* 196–204.

Myin-Germeys, I., Nicolson, N.A., & Delespaul, P.A.E.G. (2001). The context of delusional experiences in the daily life of patients with schizophrenia. *Psychological Medicine, 31,* 489–498.

Nijman, H.L., Muris, P., Merckelbach, H.L.G.J., Palmstierna, T., Wistedt, B., Vos, A.M., van Rixtel, A., & Allertz W. (1999). The Staff Observation Aggression Scale-Revised (SOAS-R). *Aggressive Behavior, 25,* 197–209.

Nydegger, R.V. (1972). The elimination of hallucinatory and delusional behavior by verbal conditioning and assertive training: A case study. *Journal of Behavior Therapy and Experimental Psychiatry, 3,* 225–227.

Overall, J.E., & Gorham, D.R. (1962). The brief psychiatric rating scale. *Psychological Reports, 10,* 799–812.

Palmstierna, T., & Wistedt, B. (1987). Staff Observation Aggression scale, SOAS: Presentation and evaluation. *Acta Psychiatrica Scandinavica, 76,* 657–673.

Patterson, T.L., Goldman, S., McKibbin, C.L., Hughs, T., & Jeste, D.V. (2001). USCD performance-based skills assessment: Development of a new measure of everyday functioning for severely mentally ill adults. *Schizophrenia Bulletin, 27,* 235–245.

Paul, G.L. (1987). *The Time-Sample Behavior Checklist.* Champaign, IL: Research Press.

Paul, G.L., & Lentz, R.J. (1977). *Psychosocial treatment of chronic mental patients: Milieu vs. social learning programs.* Cambridge, MA: Harvard University Press.

Paul, G.L., & Lentz, R.J. (1997). *Psychosocial treatment of chronic mental patients: Milieu versus social-learning programs* (2nd ed). Champaign, IL: Research Press.

Paul, G.L., & Licht, M.H. (1988). Staff-Resident Interaction Chronograph computer summaries and intended uses. In G.L. Paul (Ed.), *Observational assessment instrumentation for service and research: The Staff-Resident Interaction Chronograph: Assessment in residential treatment settings.* Champaign, IL: Research Press.

Paul, G.L., Licht, M.H., & Engel, K.L. (1988). The Staff-Resident Interaction Chronograph observer manual. In G.L. Paul (Ed.), *Observational assessment instrumentation for service and research: The Staff-Resident Interaction Chronograph: Assessment in residential treatment settings.* Champaign, IL: Research Press.

Paul, G.L., McInnis, T.L., & Mariotto, M.J. (1973). Objective performance outcomes associated with two approaches to training mental health technicians in milieu and social-learning programs. *Journal of Abnormal Psychology, 82,* 527–532.

Paul, G.L., & Menditto, A.A. (1992). Effectiveness of inpatient treatment programs for mentally ill adults in public psychiatric facilities. *Applied and Preventive Psychology, 1,* 41–63.

Paul, G.L., Stuve, P., & Cross, J. (1997). Real-world inpatient programs: Shedding some light—A critique. *Applied and Preventive Psychology, 6,* 193–204.

Paulus, M.P., Geyer, M.A., & Braff, D.L. (1990). Long-range correlations in choice sequences of schizophrenic patients. *Schizophrenia Research, 35,* 69–75.

Paulus, M.P., Geyer, M.A., & Braff, D.L. (1996). Use of methods from chaos theory to quantify a fundamental dysfunction in the behavioral organization of schizophrenic patients. *American Journal of Psychiatry, 153,* 714–717.

Paulus, M.P., Perry, W., & Braff, D.L. (1999). The nonlinear, complex sequential organization of behavior in schizophrenic patients: Neurocognitive strategies and clinical correlations. *Biological Psychiatry, 46,* 662–670.

Peralta, V., & Cuesta, M.J. (1995). Negative symptoms in schizophrenia. A confirmatory factor analysis of competing models. *American Journal of Psychiatry, 152,* 1450–1457.

Pestle, K., Card, J., & Menditto, A. (1998). Therapeutic recreation in a social-learning program: Effect over time on appropriate behaviors of residents with schizophrenia. *Therapeutic Recreation Journal, 32,* 28–41.

Pope, H.G., & Lipinski, J.F. (1978). Diagnosis in schizophrenia and manic-depressive illness: A reassessment of the specificity of schizophrenic symptoms in the light of current research. *Archives of General Psychiatry, 35,* 811–828.

Salzinger, K. (1984). The immediacy hypothesis in a theory of schizophrenia. In W.D. Spaulding & J.K. Cole (Eds.), *Nebraska Symposium on Motivation: Theories of Schizophrenia and Psychosis.* Lincoln: University of Nebraska Press.

Salzinger, K. (1986). Diagnosis: Distinguishing among behaviors. In T. Millon & G.L. Klerman (Eds.), *Contemporary directions in psychopathology: Toward the DSM-IV.* New York: Guilford Press.

Salzinger, K. (1991). The road from vulnerability to episode: A behavioral analysis. *Psycoloquy, 2,* NP.

Salzinger, K., Pisoni, D.B., Portnoy, S., & Feldman, R.S. (1970). The immediacy hypothesis and response-produced stimuli in schizophrenic speech. *Journal of Abnormal Psychology, 76,* 258–264.

Salzinger, K., Portnoy, S., & Feldman, R.S. (1966). Verbal behavior in schizophrenics and some comments toward a theory of schizophrenia. In P. Hoch & J. Zubin (Eds.), *Psychopathology of schizophrenia.* New York: Grune & Stratton.

Serber, M., and Nelson, P. (1971). The ineffectiveness of systematic desensitization and assertive training in hospitalized schizophrenics. *Journal of Behavior Therapy and Experimental Psychiatry, 2,* 107–109.

Serper, M.R., Bergman, R.L., & Harvey, P.D. (1990). Neuroleptic medication is required for automatic information processing in schizophrenia. *Psychiatry Research, 32,* 281–288.

Serper, M.R., Bernstein, D.P., Maurer, G., Horvath, T., Coccoro, E., & Siever, L. (1993). Psychological test profiles of patients with borderline and schizotypal personality disorders. *Journal of Personality Disorders, 7,* 144–154.

Serper, M.R, & Chou, J. (2000). Cognitive functioning and substance use disorders in schizophrenia. In T. Sharma & P.D. Harvey (Eds.), *Cognition in schizophrenia. Impairments, importance, and treatment strategies.* New York: Oxford University Press.

Shutty, M.S., Jr., Hundley, P.L., Leadbetter, R.A., Vieweg, V., & Hill, D. (1992). Development and validation of a behavioral observation measure for the syndrome of psychosis, intermittent hyponatremia, and polydipsia. *Journal of Behavior Therapy and Experimental Psychiatry, 23,* 213–219.

Silverstein, S.M. (2001). Psychiatric rehabilitation of schizophrenia: Unresolved issues, current trends and future directions. *Applied and Preventive Psychology, 9,* 227–248.

Silverstein, S.M., Menditto, A.A., & Stuve, P. (2001). Shaping attention span: An operant conditioning procedure to improve neurocognition and functioning in schizophrenia. *Schizophrenia Bulletin, 27,* 247–257.

Slade, P.D. (1972). The effects of systematic desensitization on auditory hallucinations. *Behaviour Research and Therapy, 10,* 85–91.

Slade, P.D. (1973). The psychological investigation and treatment of auditory hallucinations: A second case report. *British Journal of Medical Psychology, 46,* 293–296.

Slade, P.D. (1976). An investigation of psychological factors involved in the predisposition to auditory hallucinations. *Psychological Medicine, 6,* 123–132.

Snyder, J.A. (1999). Nonlinear dynamic relationships between functional behavior and symptomatology in people with chronic psychosis. Unpublished Dissertation.

Sorgi, P., Ratey, J., Knoedler, D.U., Markert, R.J., & Reichman, M. (1991). Rating aggression in the clinical setting: A retrospective adaptation of the overt aggression scale: Preliminary results. *Journal of Neuropsychiatry, 3,* S52–S56.

Spaulding, W.D. (1997). Cognitive models in a fuller understanding of schizophrenia. *Psychiatry, 60,* 341–346.

Steinert, T., Wiebe, C., & Gebhardt, R.P. (1999). Aggressive behavior against self and others among first-admission patients with schizophrenia. *Psychiatric Services, 50,* 85–90.

Steinert, T., Wölfe, M., & Gebhardt, R.P. (2000). Measurement of violence during in-patient treatment and association with psychopathology. *Acta Psychiatrica Scandinavia, 102,* 107–112.

Stuve, P., & Menditto, A.A. (1999). State hospitals in the new millennium: Rehabilitating the "not ready for rehab players." *New Directions for Mental Health Services, 84,* 35–46.

Taiminen, T., Huttunen, J., Heilae, H., Henriksson, M., Isometsae, E., Kaehkoenen, J., Tuominen, K., Loennqvist, J., Addington, D., & Helenius, H. (2001). The Schizophrenia Suicide Risk Scale (SSRS): Development and initial validation. *Schizophrenia Research, 47,* 199–213.

Tarrier, N., Harwood, S., Yusopoff, L., & Beckett, R. (1990). Coping Strategy Enhancement (CSE): A method of treating residual schizophrenic symptoms. *Behavioural Psychotherapy, 18,* 283–293.

Tarrier, N., & Turpin, G. (1992). Psychosocial factors, arousal and schizophrenic relapse: The psychophysiological data. *British Journal of Psychiatry, 161,* 3–11.

Tejedor, M.C., Diaz, A., Castillon, J.J., & Pericay, J.M. (1999). Attempted suicide: Repetition and survival—Findings of a follow-up study. *Acta Psychiatrica Scandinavica, 100,* 205–211.

Thakur, M., Hays, J., Ranga, K., & Krishnan, R. (1999). Clinical, demographic and social characteristics of psychotic depression. *Psychiatry Research, 86,* 99–106.

Toone, B.K., Cooke, E., & Lader, M.H. (1981). Electrodermal activity in the affective disorders and schizophrenia. *Psychological Medicine, 11,* 497–508.

Tsuang, M.T. (1978). Suicide in schizophrenics, manics, depressives, and surgical controls. A comparison with general population suicide mortality. *Archives of General Psychiatry, 35,* 153–155.

Vacarro, J.V., Pitts, D.B., & Wallace, C.J. (1992). Functional assessment. In R.P. Liberman (Ed.), *Handbook of psychiatric rehabilitation* (pp. 56–77). New York: Macmillan.

Vadhan, N.P., Serper, M.R., Harvey, P.D., Chou, J.C.-Y., & Cancro, R. (2001). Convergent validity and neuropsychological correlates of the Schedule for the Assessment of Negative Symptoms (SANS) Attention Subscale. *Journal of Nervous and Mental Disease, 189,* 837–641.

Ventura, J., Green, M.F., Shaner, A., & Liberman, R.P. (1993). Training and quality assurance with the Brief Psychiatric Rating Scale: "The drift buster." *International Journal of Methods in Psychiatric Research, 3,* 221–224.

Walkup, J. (1990). On the measurement of delusions. *British Journal of Medical Psychology, 63,* 365–368.

Westermeyer, J.F., Harrow, M., & Marengo, J.T. (1991). Risk for suicide in schizophrenia and other psychotic and non-psychotic disorders. *Journal of Nervous and Mental Disease, 179,* 259–266.

White, L., Harvey, P.D., Opler, L., Lindenmayer, J.P., Bell, M., Caton, C., Davidson, M., Dollfus, S., Parrella, M., & Powchick, P. (1997). Empirical assessment of the factorial structure of clinical symptoms in schizophrenia. *Psychopathology, 30,* 263–274.

Wiedl, K.H., & Weinhobst, J. (1999). Intraindividual differences in cognitive remediation research with schizophrenic patients—Indicators of rehabilitation potential? *International Journal of Rehabilitation Research, 22,* 1–6.

Wiedl, K.H, Weinhobst, J., Schottke, H.H., Green, M.F., & Nuechterlein, K.H. (2001). Attentional characteristics of schizophrenia patients differing in learning proficiency on the Wisconsin Card Sorting Test. *Schizophrenia Bulletin, 27,* 687–695.

Woerner, M.G., Mannuzza, S., & Kane, J.M. (1988). Anchoring the BPRS: An aid to improved reliability. *Psychopharmacology Bulletin, 24,* 112–117.

Young, A.S., Nuechterlein, K.H., Mintz, J., Ventura, J., Gitlin, M., & Liberman, R.P. (1998). Suicidal ideation and suicide attempts in recent-onset schizophrenia. *Schizophrenia Bulletin, 24,* 629–634.

Yudofsky, S.C., Silver, J.M., Jackson, W., Endicott, J., & Williams, D. (1986). The overt aggression scale for the objective rating of verbal and physical aggression. *American Journal of Psychiatry, 143,* 35–39.

Zarlock, S.P. (1966). Social expectations, language, and schizophrenia. *Journal of Humanistic Psychology, 6,* 68–74.

Zisook, S., McAdams, L.A., Kuck, J., Harris, M.J., Bailey, A., Patterson, T.L., Judd, L.L., & Jeste, D. (1999). Depressive symptoms in schizophrenia. *American Journal of Psychiatry, 156,* 1736–1743.

CHAPTER 18

Assessment in Work Settings

KEVIN R. MURPHY

INTRODUCTION

Although public perceptions of psychological testing some-times focus on clinical applications, the great majority of all psychological tests and assessments are done in one of two settings: the classroom or the workplace. Testing for person-nel selection and placement is a huge undertaking. For ex-ample, one widely used test, the Wonderlic Personnel Tests (Wonderlic Inc., Libertyville, IN; for a review, see Murphy, 1984b) has been administered to over 130 million examinees in over 50,000 organizations over its 55-year history. The military and civil service commissions administer millions of tests each year; the Armed Services Vocational Aptitude Bat-tery (Welsh, Kucinkas & Curran, 1990; for a review, see Murphy, 1984a) is given annually to well over a million ex-aminees. If you think of the term "assessment" broadly, to include employment interviews, performance evaluations, and the like, it is safe to say that the great majority of adults have participated in testing and assessment in work settings.

Tests and assessment are used for a variety of purposes in organizations, most of which focus on enhancing fit, perfor-mance, and effectiveness. Most of the research literature deal-ing with assessment in organizations focuses on individual assessment (evaluating job applicants' fit to the job or eval-uating incumbents' current or past performance), but assess-ments at the level of work teams, departments, and divisions

and assessments of organizational effectiveness are also im-portant. This chapter will cover a wide range of assessments of job-related abilities and skills, and of performance and ef-fectiveness, but it is important to acknowledge that these do not necessarily exhaust the domain of assessments carried out in work settings. Assessments of physical and mental health, attitudes and beliefs, and interests and preferences also might occur in work settings, but they will not be discussed in depth in this chapter. Rather, I will discuss assessments that are di-rectly related to job performance or effectiveness.

APPLICATIONS OF ASSESSMENT METHODS IN WORK SETTINGS

Assessments in work settings can be divided into those that are done with the purpose of forecasting future performance and those that are done with the purpose of assessing past and present performance. The most common example of future-oriented assessment occurs in the context of selecting among applicants for entry-level jobs. It is common for or-ganizations to receive many applications for each job to be filled, and it is also common for organizational decision mak-ers to have little direct knowledge of the applicants' charac-teristics. Finally, entry-level applicants often have little directly relevant experience with the job in question. As a result, assessments used in entry-level selection often focus on broad abilities (e.g., standardized tests of general mental ability are widely used) or on skills that might reasonably be obtained by individuals with relatively little job experience (e.g., assessments of basic clerical skills). The selection of specific tests and assessments is likely to be guided by the results of a careful analysis of the duties, activities, and responsibilities that the job involves, and assessments are generally chosen on the basis of some evidence that they measure attributes that will predict performance in training and on the job itself (Cascio, 1982; McCormick, 1979).

Assessments of applicants for skilled jobs are likely to encompass a wider range of abilities. While assessments of basic abilities are still quite useful, evaluations of applicants at this level will often include assessments of experience, knowledge, skills, and performance in previous jobs. Assessments of internal candidates will probably examine different factors than assessments of external applicants (e.g., in evaluating internal job candidates, it is common to obtain information about previous job performance that may not be available or readily interpretable for external candidates), but in most cases, information about performance in similar jobs or positions will form one basis for evaluating applicants for skilled jobs.

The second major category of assessments involves evaluations of job performance or effectiveness. These evaluations are rarely done on the basis of standardized tests (although some licensing and certification tests might provide information about job performance), but rather are likely to be based on the judgments of supervisors, or of subordinates and customers (as in 360-degree performance feedback systems; Bracken, Timmreck & Church, 2001). As these performance assessments move from the individual to small teams to evaluations of the performance of organizational units or of organizations themselves, the focus is likely to shift from subjective judgment to objective indicators (e.g., sales figures, output data) as the most reliable and relevant performance indices.

CONCEPTUAL BASES OF WORKPLACE ASSESSMENTS

Tests and assessments of job applicants usually attempt to determine the fit between demands and requirements of jobs and the attributes of applicants, although as noted below, a large family of assessments follows quite different conceptual models. The standard model for workplace testing starts with an analysis of the job. The term "job analysis" refers to systematic efforts to define the duties, responsibilities, and re-

quirements of jobs or positions (Fine & Cronshaw, 1999; Harvey, 1991; Whetzel & Wheaton, 1997). This can be done using objective questionnaires, participant observation, or structured interviews of subject matter experts. The Position Analysis Questionnaire (McCormick & Jenneret, 1988) is one of the most widely used standardized job analysis questionnaires; it can be used to describe a wide range of jobs on a common set of worker-oriented characteristics (e.g., information-processing demands of a job).

The principal aims of job analysis are identifying and measuring sets of "can do" and/or "will do" factors that are likely to be related to job performance. Abilities, knowledge, skills, and experience all represent potential "can do" factors that tell us something about the applicant's likelihood of successfully learning and executing important job tasks. A distinction is often made between maximal and typical performance (DuBois, Sackett, Zedeck, & Fogli, 1993; Sackett, Zedeck, & Fogli, 1988); abilities, knowledge, and skills are thought to be especially relevant to predicting maximal performance—that is, performance under circumstances in which the employee is devoting maximum levels of attention and effort to the task at hand. Measures of personality dimensions, values, and preferences have the potential to tell us whether individuals "will do"—that is, whether they will be motivated, satisfied, interested, etc. in performing the job up to their capabilities. Typical levels of job performance are probably a function of both ability and motivation (Campbell, McCloy, Oppler, & Sager, 1992).

The "can do–will do" framework represents one way of thinking about the fit between individuals and jobs. Another strategy for structuring personnel selection is to examine the similarities between applicants and current or past employees who are regarded as either successes or as failures. A number of assessment methods are built upon the premise that people who are similar, in important ways, to successful employees are likely themselves to succeed. Similarly, people who share many characteristics with employees who have failed may themselves be at greater risk of failure. As noted below, assessments based on these principles have shown consistent evidence of validity.

Finally, we might look at fit in terms of consistency between the values, preferences, or interests of the individual and the characteristics of the organization (rather than focusing on fit between the person and the job). This is essentially the same strategy that underlies vocational interest testing and vocational counseling, in which the fit between persons and occupations is of greatest interest (instruments such as the Strong Interest Inventory and the Kuder Occupational Interest Survey are exemplars of tests that reflect this approach to assessment), but it also has been advocated as a strategy for personnel selection (Schneider, 1987). There are significant challenges to the conceptualization and measurement of person-organization fit (Guion, 1998), but the general idea of considering the fit between a person and an organization when making selection decisions seems reasonable.

As noted above, evaluations of job performance usually are based on the judgments of supervisors, although peers, subordinates, customers, and other stakeholders are increasingly being used as sources of information in evaluating job performance (Bracken et al., 2001). Regardless of the source of performance information, the conceptual model is the same—that is, raters are treated as measurement instruments, and it is assumed that raters are willing and able to provide ratings that reflect the performance of the individuals being evaluated. There is compelling evidence that this assumption is wrong (Murphy & Cleveland, 1995); performance appraisals are affected by a number of biases, political pressures, rater attitudes and beliefs, and other rating context factors (Tziner, Murphy, & Cleveland, 2001). Performance ratings have long been the subject of criticism and complaint in organizations and in the literature; Murphy and Cleveland (1995) suggest that the root of this problem is a mismatch between the model that assumes that raters are passive measurement instruments and the reality that rater behavior is influenced by a number of factors that have little to do with the performance of the individual being evaluated.

ASSESSMENT METHODS IN PERSONNEL SELECTION

Five types of structured assessments are widely used in personnel selection and evaluation: (1) assessments of experience and background, (2) structured interviews, (3) standardized tests, (4) simulations and work samples, and (5) assessment centers. One of the key conclusions coming out of this research is that well-developed tests, interviews, and other structured assessments can contribute significantly to the quality and fairness of selection decisions and can be highly cost-effective, even in contexts where jobs are constantly changing.

Assessments of Experience and Background

Information about an individual's experiences, background, and life experiences can provide a basis for valid predictions about future job performance and effectiveness. This information, often referred to as "biodata," is relatively easy to collect and can provide a very useful basis for assessment. The uses of biodata range from simple scans of resumes to highly sophisticated systems for scoring and validating empirically keyed biodata forms.

Resume Screening

Virtually every applicant for most jobs will complete an application or provide a resume, and these documents contain a wealth of information that can be useful for evaluating applicants. Resume screening methods can range from automated techniques (e.g., software that screens resumes for particular keywords) to methods that involve expert evaluations of the information presented in each resume. The appropriateness and utility of each method depends on a number of factors, the most important of which might be the sheer number of resumes that must be evaluated.

The use of electronic resumes and Internet-based recruiting is increasingly common in many sectors of the economy (Quible, 1995, 1998). Vaas, Chen, and Hicks (2000) note that the number of job-related web sites is growing rapidly, and the number of resumes posted already exceeds 16 million. The use of electronic resumes is especially common in the information technology (IT) industry, and it is not unusual to receive thousands of resumes in the process of filling desirable IT jobs.

Hough (1984) described the development of "accomplishment records," which may provide a more valid and fair assessment than simple keyword screens or screens based solely on self-descriptions. Methods for developing accomplishment records vary, but they usually follow a content-validation strategy, in which the sorts of accomplishments evaluated are based on a careful analysis of the job. Accomplishment records require organizations to identify the key dimensions of performance on each job and to develop specific behavioral examples of performance at the level required in that job (e.g., the behavioral examples that describe adequate performance on the dimension of oral communication would be different for a university professor than for members of a team involved in assembling automobile engines). Applicants then rate themselves in reference to these dimensions and exemplars.

Brown and Campion (1994) studied the processes and strategies used by recruiters in evaluating resumes. They suggest that recruiters evaluate resumes both in terms of the information they provide about the candidate's abilities (e.g., language, math, physical) and in terms of the information they provide about attributes usually classed as "soft skills" (e.g., interpersonal, leadership, motivation). Both types of attributes can be judged with high reliability, but these evaluations can be time-consuming. Smith (1995) describes a more elaborate multistep system for screening applicant resumes that involves: (1) analyzing both the "can do" criteria (functional skills) and the "will do" criteria (e.g., ability to work under pressure) that underlie successful performance, (2) identifying resumes that state a job objective that matches with the available position, and (3) a close review of resumes to evaluate the length and breadth of experience and to evaluate concrete achievements and identifiable skills. Again, this method may be time-consuming, especially in contexts in which there is a large number of resumes to evaluate.

Empirical Methods of Using Biodata To Predict Performance or Success

Resume screening methods, even those that involve careful expert reviews of applicants' strengths, weaknesses, etc., represent a very limited use of biographical and background information to evaluate candidates. A stream of research going back at least 50 years suggests strong and systematic links between the information presented on application blanks and resumes and future job performance and success (Mumford, Uhlman, & Kilcullen, 1992; Owens, 1976; Reilly & Chao, 1982). Well-constructed biodata measures often achieve validity coefficients in the .30 to .45 range. This research suggests that the methods by which this information is evaluated and scored are critical to the success of assessments based on biodata. The resume screening methods described below sometimes do little more than scratch the surface in terms of getting useful information from biodata. Empirically based strategies for evaluating and scoring biodata have the potential to provide highly valid predictions of future performance and success.

There are two different empirically based strategies for using background data in the selection of suitable job candidates: (1) the development of empirical keys, or data-based systems for scoring resumes and application blanks and (2) the classification of applicants into groups that are homogeneous with respect to biographical information but differ in terms of expected job performance. The empirical keying strategy is the older of the two; to date, much of the research reporting substantial correlations between background data and job performance has followed this strategy. However, more recent research on the use of background data in predicting job performance has moved in the direction of theories that classify persons on the basis of their patterns of past behavior and that predict future performance on the basis of those classifications (Mael, 1991; Mumford et al., 1992, Owens & Schoenfeldt, 1979; Stokes, Mumford, & Owens, 1994).

The empirical method of scoring biographical information blanks rests on the assumption that successful workers (defined in terms of performance, tenure on the job, salary, etc.) systematically differ from unsuccessful workers in a number of ways and that at least some of the variables on which they differ can be measured by standard application blanks and resumes. If an applicant's responses to a biographical item are highly similar to those of successful workers and dissimilar to those of unsuccessful workers, the likelihood that the applicant will also succeed increases. On the other hand, a person whose responses are highly similar to those of the unsuccessful group is on the whole more likely to fail. Thus, it is possible to assign scores to each person's set of responses to a standard application blank or resume that measures the degree to which responses to the entire set of items are similar to those given by successful workers, as opposed to those given by unsuccessful workers. There is considerable evidence that biodata scores of this type can be used to predict both job performance and turnover (Cascio, 1976; Reilly & Chao, 1982).

One critique of the empirical method described above is that it is based solely on consistencies in the data and does not reflect any underlying theory of how or why biographical items predict success. In recent years, there has been considerable interest and progress in identifying the constructs that underlie responses to biodata items (Mael, 1991; Mumford et al., 1992). Stokes and colleagues (1994) suggest that biodata systems can provide useful measures of introversion versus extroversion, social leadership, independence, achievement motivation, maturity, adjustment, academic achievement, health, scientific/engineering pursuits, work values, organizational commitment, professional skills, and career development (this list is far from exhaustive; there is evidence that many additional attributes can be measured using biodata).

Empirically validated systems for evaluating and scoring biodata hold a great deal of promise as assessment tools. Biodata inventories are consistently identified as among the most valid and cost-effective methods of assessment for personnel selection (Reilly & Chao, 1982; Stokes et al., 1994), showing validities comparable to those of the most valid objective tests (e.g., correlations in the .50s with measures of job performance). However, some difficulties arise in applying this method of assessment. First, biodata scoring schemes are usually custom-developed for each job, organization, etc. One reason for this is that the content of resumes or applications for different jobs or organizations often varies. More fundamentally, the links between biodata and success are not always the same across jobs or organizations. Aspects of a person's background and experience that predict failure in one organization may predict success in another. There is evidence that biodata scoring systems developed in one organization can hold up well in others (Carlson, Scullen, Schmidt, Rothstein & Erwin, 1999), but the limits to the generalizability of biodata scoring systems are not yet well understood. Organizations may find it difficult to obtain valid and useful biodata scoring systems off the shelf, and may have to invest time and resources to develop appropriate and valid scoring systems.

Structured Interviews

Although there is considerable diversity in the types of tests and assessments used in making personnel selection decisions, the one nearly universal component of all systematic personnel selection strategies is the interview. Surveys suggest that well over 95 percent of all employers use interviews as part of the selection process and that the number of interviews conducted yearly may run as high as 20 per person hired (Landy & Trumbo, 1980). More recent studies (e.g., Ahlburg, 1992) attest to the continuing popularity of the interview. It is therefore no surprise that the employment interview has been the focus of a tremendous amount of research.

From the 1940s to the 1980s, research on the reliability and validity of the employment interview portrayed a consistently negative picture (Arvey & Campion, 1982). Validity coefficients for interviews (i.e., the correlations between interview ratings and measures of performance or success) rarely exceeded the teens and were often embarrassingly close to zero (Hunter & Hunter, 1984; Reilly & Chao, 1982). Indeed, one of the most interesting research questions in the early 1980s was why organizations continued to rely so heavily on such an invalid method of making selection decisions (Arvey & Campion, 1982).

More recent research suggests that interviews can indeed be a useful and valid method of selecting employees, as long as structure is imposed (Campion, Pursell, & Brown, 1988; Wiesner & Cronshaw, 1988). Most of the interview research cited in earlier reviews had focused on unstructured interviews, in which different interviewers might ask different sets of questions, or in which the same interviewer might ask different applicants different questions. Interviews of this sort are widely regarded as poor predictors of future performance (although as McDaniel, Whetzel, Schmidt, and Maurer, 1994, note, they can show higher levels of validity than was suggested in earlier reviews). However, when care is taken to develop a consistent set of job-related questions and a consistent method for scoring or evaluating responses, interviews can show very respectable levels of validity. Schmidt and Hunter (1999) suggest that structured interviews show correlations in the .50s with measures of job performance.

Latham, Saari, Pursell, and Campion (1980) recommended an extremely structured interview format, referred to as a "situational interview," in which examinees are asked to describe how they would behave in several hypothetical but critical situations. For example, an applicant for a baker's job might be asked what he or she would do if two oven thermometers gave readings that varied widely. Responses to these interviews are often independently rated by multiple interviewers, and composite ratings are typically used to make decisions about examinees. Although this structure may not be optimal in all settings, it represents a clear advance over the unconnected series of spontaneous questions that an untrained interviewer tends to ask (Wiesner & Cronshaw, 1988).

An alternative is to structure interviews around discussions of past behavior on the job (Janz, 1982). Rather than asking what a person might do in a hypothetical situation, interviewers might ask what he or she did do in specific situations encountered previously on the job. For example, applicants for a sales job might be asked to describe a situation in the past where they were required to deal with a dissatisfied customer or client, and to describe how they handled this situation. McDaniel and colleagues (1994) suggest that such job-related interviews show higher levels of validity than unstructured interviews, but lower validity than the situational interview method described above.

Campion, Palmer, and Campion (1997) note that, while adding structure to an interview generally improves its reliability and validity, there are many ways that one might add structure. They review the effects of 15 components of structure (e.g., standardizing the set of questions, tying questions to a job analysis, rating each answer on a fixed scale, using multiple interviewers). Just about all methods of adding structure seem to help, and there is no professional consensus about which methods of structuring interviews are best or worst.

Interviews are probably most useful when they cover areas not already covered by paper-and-pencil tests or other assessment devices. A number of researchers have suggested that interviews should focus on behaviors rather than attitudes or skills (Janz, 1982; Motowidlo et al., 1992). There is evidence that a clear focus on behavioral information increases the reliability and criterion-related validity of measures obtained on the basis of interviews. Structured interviews might prove particularly useful for assessing soft skills. First, the interview is itself a social interaction, which allows the interviewer to obtain a sample of behaviors that may accurately predict future behavior in work settings. Applicants who are unwilling or unable to communicate clearly with the interviewer or who cannot interact productively with interviewers may show similar behaviors on the job. Second, situational or behavioral interviews can be tailored to focus on the sorts of social interactions, teamwork skills, or leadership skills required for successful performance on the job.

Standardized Tests

Standardized tests of abilities, skills, and personality characteristics are extensively used in personnel assessment and have been the focus of a very substantial body of research (Murphy & Davidshofer, 1998; Schmidt & Hunter, 1999). Approximately two-thirds of all companies use written tests as aids in making hiring and promotion decisions; standardized tests are especially common in evaluating applicants for clerical and administrative jobs, but they are used across a broad spectrum of occupations.

Cognitive Ability Tests

Research in personnel selection has focused most heavily on tests of cognitive ability (sometimes called intelligence tests). Hundreds of studies dealing with the relationship between scores on ability tests and performance on the job, success in training, and other organizationally relevant criteria have led to a consistent set of conclusions. Scores on standardized tests of cognitive ability are related to measures of performance and success in virtually every job studied (see Schmidt and Hunter, 1999, for a review). Furthermore, the relationship between measures of ability and measures of performance and success is stronger in jobs that are more complex and demanding (e.g., computer programmer, systems analyst) than in jobs that are relatively simple and repetitive (e.g., assembly line worker).

If evaluated solely in terms of their validity and practicality, cognitive ability tests would almost certainly be the preferred method for evaluating job applicants. Compared with other methods of assessment, cognitive ability tests are relatively inexpensive, are easy to obtain (well-validated tests can be purchased and used off the shelf), have a clear track record of validity, and they need not be time-consuming (e.g., the Wonderlic Personnel Test can be administered in 12 minutes and scored in a matter of seconds). However, some features of cognitive ability tests limit their attractiveness to organizations.

First, average scores on cognitive ability tests are likely to vary as a function of race and ethnicity (Gottfredson, 1986; Jensen, 1980; Neisser et al., 1996). The causes and the meaning of differences in average test scores across groups have been among the most widely researched and contentious issues in the field of psychological testing, and no ready resolutions of these controversies are in sight. The practical implications of these differences, however, are clear. Organizations that rely heavily on cognitive ability tests to screen applicants are likely to discriminate against members of a number of protected groups. It is often possible to mount a successful defense of such tests, especially when they are part of a thorough program that includes a careful job analysis, judicious selection of tests, careful validation, and deliberate consideration of alternatives. Nevertheless, organizations often prefer to avoid discriminating in the first place, or being forced to defend what appear to be discriminatory procedures, and may opt not to use standardized ability tests.

A second factor that may limit the appeal of these tests is that applicants may react negatively to them. Tests of general cognitive ability vary widely in their content and format, and there is not always an obvious link to the content of the job. The weaker the manifest link between the test and the job, the greater the likelihood that the test will be perceived as invalid and irrelevant.

Personality Inventories

The use of personality inventories as predictors of job performance has been a subject of controversy for nearly 30 years. An influential review by Guion and Gottier (1965) concluded that the research available at that time did not support the validity of personality measures as selection instruments. As a result of several recent reviews of research on the validity and practicality of personality inventories (Barrick & Mount, 1991; Hough, Eaton, Dunnette, Kamp, & McCloy, 1990; Tett, Jackson, & Rothstein, 1991), this view has changed.

There is evidence that a variety of personality characteristics are consistently related to job performance. In particular, measures of agreeableness, conscientiousness, and openness to experience appear to be related to performance in a wide range of jobs. Average validities for measures of these traits are typically not as high as validities demonstrated by cognitive ability tests (correlations with job performance measures are typically in the .10 to .20 range), but the evidence does suggest that personality inventories can make a worthwhile contribution to predicting who will succeed or fail on the job.

One potential drawback to the use of personality inventories in personnel selection is the fact that many of these inventories are susceptible to faking (e.g., job applicants may distort their responses to appear more dependable or agreeable than they really are). Research on the effects of response distortion suggests that it does not substantially affect the validity of personality inventories as predictors of performance (Hough et al., 1990), but that it can have an influence on which candidates are accepted or rejected (Rosse, Stecher, Miller, & Levin, 1998).

A potentially more serious drawback to the use of personality tests in hiring is that some of the most popular and widely used tests have little proven validity and utility. For example, the Myers-Briggs Type Indicator (for a review of this test, see Pittenger, 1992) is one of the more popular tests in industry, even though there is very little evidence that this test can be used to predict success or failure on the job. Similarly, projective tests (e.g., the Rorschach Inkblot Test; Exner, 1974) or tests of psychopathology (e.g., the Minnesota Multiphasic Personality Inventory, Minneapolis: University of Minnesota) are sometimes used in industry, despite decades of research questioning their validity and usefulness. The choice of a particular inventory may be critically important when using personality tests in personnel selection.

Integrity Tests

A number of tests are designed to assess integrity, dependability, honesty, etc. These tests have been the subject of considerable controversy, but research over the last 10 to 15 years has consistently supported their usefulness. Sackett and his colleagues have conducted several reviews of research on the reliability, validity, and usefulness of integrity tests (Sackett, Burris, & Callahan, 1989; Sackett & Decker, 1979; Sackett & Harris, 1984, 1985); Ones, Viswesvaran, and Schmidt (1993) and McDaniel and Jones (1988) have subjected some of the same studies to meta-analyses, a statistical method designed to quantitatively summarize the outcomes of multiple validity studies. O'Bannon, Goldinger, and Appleby (1989) also have reviewed this research and, additionally, have given attention to a variety of practical issues that surround the administration and use of integrity tests. Although each review raises different concerns, and most reviews lament the shortcomings of research on the validity of integrity tests, the general conclusion of the more recent reviews is positive. A reasonable body of evidence now shows that integrity tests have some validity for predicting a variety of criteria that are relevant to organizations (correlations with measures of both counterproductivity and overall job performance are typically in the .30s). This research does not say that tests of this sort will eliminate theft or dishonesty at work, but it does suggest that individuals who receive poor scores on these tests tend to be less desirable employees.

Work Samples and Simulations

It has long been argued that predictions of future behavior that are based on samples of present behavior are likely to be more accurate than predictions that are based on measures of specific skills, ability, or knowledge (Wernimont & Campbell, 1968). Reviews by Asher and Sciarrino (1974) and Reilly and Chao (1982) provide at least partial support for this argument. Scores on work samples have been used to predict performance in a wide range of jobs, especially jobs that involve production or the manipulation of objects, and correlations between scores on work samples and measures of job performance are often in the .40 to .50 range. This research suggests that one way to predict a person's future performance is to obtain a sample of their current work.

Work-sample tests range from those that involve relatively simple tasks, such as a 5-minute typing sample, to those involving complex samples of performance, such as those obtained using flight simulators. There are two common features to all work-sample tests that should be examined when evaluating these tests. First, every work-sample test puts the applicant in a situation that in some essential way is similar to a work situation and measures performance on tasks reasonably similar to those that make up the job itself. Second, every work sample differs in important ways from the job in which it will be used. Even when the tasks are identical to those required on the job, it is reasonable to expect that examinees who are trying to impress prospective employers will show higher levels of motivation in work-sample tests than they will on the job. Thus, it is most reasonable to regard a work sample as a measure of maximal performance rather than a measure of typical performance. This is an important distinction, because measures of maximal performance are not necessarily correlated with measures of typical performance (Dubois et al., 1993; Sackett et al., 1988). Referring to the earlier distinction between "can do" and "will do" factors in predicting job performance, job applicants who perform well in work samples *can* do the job, but factors such as low motivation, lack of access to the tools, materials, information etc. needed to perform well, or workgroup norms that limit performance might lead to substantial differences between what they can do and what they will do on the job.

A work-sample test is most likely to be successful if the tasks that comprise the job are well understood, can be done by a person working alone, and can be done with minimal job-specific training. For example, work samples for computer programming jobs might involve asking applicants to write the code needed to carry out specific tasks or functions. Work samples have been used most often in jobs that are not highly complex (e.g., clerical jobs, semiskilled manufacturing jobs), but this technique can also be adapted and applied in managerial and professional jobs, as described in the following section.

Work Samples in Managerial and Professional Jobs

Although it is more difficult to develop a comprehensive and valid work-sample test in managerial or professional jobs than in many less complex jobs, the potential payoff of a valid work-sample test in jobs of this sort is considerable. Effective performance in these jobs is often not the simple result of possessing one or two key traits or abilities, but rather the result of a complex interaction between characteristics of the individual and characteristics of the situation. Samples of behavior in situations that seem to capture many of the salient characteristics of day-to-day work might therefore be particularly valuable in predicting performance as a manager or in a professional setting (Cascio, 1982). A substantial body of research examines the use of work-sample methods for predicting performance in managerial jobs. Fewer studies examine this technique in professional jobs, but it seems likely that some generalizations can be drawn from research on managerial applications.

Probably the most frequently used type of managerial work-sample test is the in-basket test (Fredericksen, 1962). This simulation presents the applicant with the types of memos, letters, notes, and other materials typically found in a manager's in-basket. The applicant is given background information on the job and is instructed to play the role of a new manager in the job. The applicant is required to write letters, memos, agendas, and so forth in response to the information in the in-basket. Although in-basket tests vary considerably in content, generally being tailored to individual jobs and organizations, there is considerable consistency in the results achieved using this type of test (Brass & Oldham, 1976; Wollowick & McNamara, 1969; see, however, Schippman, Prien, & Katz, 1990).

Another popular managerial work-sample test is the leaderless group discussion. This is an exceedingly simple simulation, yet one that has considerable potential for measuring characteristics of potential managers important for successful job performance that are not readily measured using other types of tests. In a leaderless group discussion, a group of participants is asked to carry on a discussion of a specific, usually job-related topic for a period of time. For example, a group of applicants might be told to conduct a 45-minute discussion of career planning. By design, there is no formal discussion leader. Several raters may observe the discussion, but these raters do not participate in any way. Group members are therefore responsible for initiating, maintaining, and directing the group discussion. This technique also has been used to assess characteristics such as persuasiveness, self-confidence, resistance to stress, oral communication ability, and interpersonal skills (Wollowick & McNamara, 1969).

Thornton and Cleveland (1990) reviewed the use of simulation methods in management development. All work samples involve simulating some aspects of the job, but such simulations differ considerably in their complexity and fi-

delity. For example, complex business games, in which individuals assume various roles and make numerous decisions over periods of hours or even days with regard to a simulated business problem, are popular for both assessing and developing managerial competencies. Although at an operational level such games are a far cry from the leaderless group discussion, at a conceptual level they represent the same strategy for measurement—that is, observing behavior in a setting that reflects some aspect of the job itself. Thornton and Cleveland's (1990) review suggests that a wide range of methods for simulating key portions of the job performed by managers and professionals hold potential for predicting future success in these roles.

In theory, complexity and fidelity of simulations should be directly related to the validity of managerial work samples. It has long been argued that the higher the correspondence between the work sample and the actual work situation, the stronger the link between work sample performance and job performance (Asher & Sciarrino, 1974). However, there is surprisingly little empirical support for this prediction. That is, complex, realistic work samples (e.g., elaborate business games and simulations) do not show consistently higher validities than simpler simulations, such as in-basket tests. In part, this is probably due to the difficulty in standardizing and scoring complex simulations, in which the performance of any one participant depends in part on the performance of others involved in the simulation, and in which performance can be defined in terms of a complex range of behaviors that might be difficult to specify a priori. More generally, the lack of empirical support for the hypothesis that higher complexity and fidelity translates into better prediction of performance raises important questions about how and why simulations work. As noted below in the discussion of assessment centers, there is some question about which features of simulations are or are not critical to their success.

Assessment Centers

The assessment center is not, as its name might imply, a place; nor is it a single, unified method of predicting job performance. Rather, an assessment center is a structured combination of assessment techniques that is used to provide a wide-ranging, holistic assessment of each participant. This technique is most likely to be used in making managerial selection and promotion decisions, although assessment centers are also employed for many other jobs.

The assessment center as it exists today is a lineal descendant of the multiple assessment procedures used by German and British psychologists in World War II and adopted by the American Office of Strategic Services (OSS) as aids in selecting agents and operatives (OSS, 1948). By the early 1970s, over 1,000 companies had experimented with this method, prompting Hinrichs (1978) to refer to the assessment center as one of the more phenomenal success stories of applied psychology. Although the assessment centers used in different organizations differ widely in terms of content and organization, there are several features that nearly all assessment centers share and that are distinctive to this approach (Bray, Campbell, & Grant, 1974; Finkle, 1976). They include the following:

1. *Assessment in groups.* In an assessment center, small groups of participants are assessed simultaneously. Because group activities and peer evaluations are an integral part of most assessment centers, it would be impossible to use this technique to its fullest advantage in assessing a single individual.

2. *Assessment by groups.* The assessment team may be made up of managers, psychologists, consultants, or some mix of these three groups. Each participant's behavior is observed and evaluated by a number of different assessors, and the final ratings represent the assessment team's consensus regarding the individual being evaluated.

3. *The use of multiple methods.* Assessment center activities might include ability tests, personality tests, situational tests, interviews, peer evaluations, and performance tests. The central assumption of this method is that each test has its strengths and weaknesses and that a combination of diverse tests is necessary to capitalize on the strengths of each individual test.

4. *The use of situational tests.* Although the specific tests used vary from organization to organization, nearly every assessment center uses some type of work-sample or situational test. Both the in-basket and the leaderless group discussion tests are popular, as are other role-playing exercises.

5. *Assessment along multiple dimensions.* The end result of an assessment center is a consensus rating along each of several dimensions. For example, candidates going through an assessment center at AT&T are rated on 25 dimensions, including organizational planning, resistance to stress, energy, and self-objectivity. Each exercise in the assessment center typically provides information relevant to one or more dimensions, and ratings of a specific dimension (e.g., energy) might reflect data obtained from several different exercises.

Empirical evaluations of assessment centers are generally quite favorable (Borman, 1982; Finkle, 1976; Gaugler, Rosenthal, Thornton, & Bentson, 1987; Thornton, 1992). Assessment center ratings have been shown to predict future job performance, even when there is a substantial lag between assessment and the subsequent evaluation of employee performance and success (however, the predictive validity of

assessment center ratings has rarely been as high as the validity of cognitive ability tests for making similar predictions; Schmidt & Hunter, 1999). For example, the AT&T Management Progress Study documented the validity of assessment center ratings, taken at the beginning of managers' careers, for predicting career progress decades later. In addition, assessment centers appear to be fair and relatively unbiased methods of making selection and promotion decisions.

Assessment centers have emerged as an especially important tool in managerial development. Because of the complexity and cost of assessment centers, they are not always practical for employee screening (although they are sometimes used in selection for high-level jobs), but they might provide a practical and valuable tool for assessing managers' strengths and weaknesses and for guiding efforts at managerial development. There are reasons, however, to be skeptical about the value of assessment center ratings for this purpose. More than 25 years ago, Klimoski and Strickland (1977) raised the question of why assessment centers work, and this question has never been fully addressed (Lance et al., 2000; Sackett & Decker, 1982). The most probable hypothesis for the predictive validity of assessment centers is that people who make a positive impression in the assessment center context also make a generally favorable impression in other settings, and thus receive generally favorable ratings from both assessors and from their supervisors and managers. Assessment center ratings show impressive predictive validity, but much less impressive construct validity.

The particular pattern of findings that has proven most troublesome in interpreting assessment center ratings is the dominance of exercise effects over dimension effects. In a typical assessment center, each exercise or assessment method is used to measure multiple dimensions or attributes, and each attribute is measured in multiple exercises. So, for example, one might obtain evaluations of "leadership" from a group discussion, from a business game, and from a structured interview. The data quite consistently show that evaluations of leadership are not highly correlated across exercises (Lance et al., 2000; Sackett & Decker, 1982). Rather, there is a general factor emerging from each exercise. So a person who does well in a leaderless group discussion will be rated high on all of the dimensions that exercise is designed to measure, and if that same person does poorly in a business game (even though he or she showed leadership behaviors), ratings of the various dimensions (including leadership) that game is supposed to measure will all be low. On the whole, there is little evidence that assessment centers provide valid indications of the relative strengths and weaknesses of the people being assessed. Rather, they tend to do a good job identifying those who will be generally successful or generally unsuccessful.

This makes them very useful (albeit impractical) for personnel selection, but possibly less useful for guiding employee development.

ASSESSMENTS OF JOB PERFORMANCE

Three general classes of data might be used, singly or in combination, to measure the performance of an individual worker. First, and most obvious, are data arising from some sort of production count. It might be possible to count the number of bricks laid by a mason, the number of calls answered by an operator, the number of parts produced by a machinist, or the number of arrests carried out by a police officer and to use this production count to measure job performance. A second type of data that might be used in measuring performance is personnel data. It can be argued that workers who are frequently late or absent or who frequently lose time due to accidents produce at a significantly lower level than workers who put in 8 hours every day. Finally, it is possible to use judgmental methods, such as supervisory performance ratings or rankings, or peer nominations, which depend on the judgment of a specific person or set of persons, to measure an individual worker's performance.

Of the three, judgmental methods are by far the most widely used; over 80 percent of studies published in the last 35 years have used judgmental ratings or rankings as the primary, if not the sole, method of measuring job performance (see Austin & Villanova, 1992, for a review of the history of criterion research). This preference for subjective measures of performance is largely explained by the fact that objective data such as production counts, absenteeism, etc. rarely capture the complex domain that the term "job performance" represents. An additional problem with using personnel data to measure job performance lies in their low levels of reliability. For example, Latham and Pursell (1975) and Hammer and Landau (1981) report reliability coefficients of approximately .30 for a variety of absence measures over time spans ranging from 12 weeks to 30 months. Similarly low levels of test-retest reliability have been noted for many other indexes that are based on personnel data. The lack of reliability places some rather obvious limits on the value of personnel measures as indicators of job performance.

Rating scales represent the single most common measure of job performance (Landy & Farr, 1980, 1983). As opposed to ranking techniques, which call for comparisons between persons, rating scales require the supervisor to evaluate each worker with regard to a particular standard that may be vaguely described (e.g., good, average, poor) or that may be described in concrete behavioral terms (e.g., "This teacher could be expected to miss class frequently"). Whereas ranking methods require supervisors to decide on a relative basis which of two workers is a better performer, rating scales require supervisors to evaluate and describe the level of each individual worker's performance.

Rating scale formats range from scales that are quite simple and straightforward to those that involve complex scoring rules or extremely concrete behavioral anchors. The most common and the simplest form of rating instrument is the graphic rating scale. This format asks the rater to make a direct judgment about the quality of each worker's performance and to indicate this judgment on a specific response scale (e.g., 1 = "Poor," 3 = "Average," 5 = "Good"). Unfortunately, the simplicity of a graphic rating scale is also the source of considerable ambiguity. First, there is a good deal of ambiguity with regard to the precise meaning of the performance dimensions being rated. Graphic scales are typically used to measure somewhat broad dimensions of performance, such as "Quality of Work," "Oral Communication," or "Planning." It is never clear precisely what behaviors are included in a dimension such as "Quality," and it is therefore likely that different raters will have different ideas regarding the aspects of employee performance that they should consider when rating the "quality" of each employee's work.

Second, there is often a good deal of ambiguity in the interpretation of the scale anchors. Supervisors almost certainly have different interpretations of what is meant by good or average performance, and in most cases scale anchors do not really provide a concrete, detailed description of the behavior that best represents good, average, or poor performance. Behavior-based scales were developed in an attempt to remove several sources of ambiguity in rating.

One of the most heavily researched rating scale formats, behaviorally anchored rating scales (BARS), were developed to deal with the two principal sources of ambiguity that plague graphic rating scales: (1) ambiguity in the dimensions being rated and (2) ambiguity in the scale anchors. BARS provide concrete behavioral statements that are used to identify particular levels of performance and that, taken together, provide a series of clear behavioral exemplars of the performance dimension under consideration (Smith & Kendall, 1963).

The development of behaviorally anchored rating scales typically involved extensive input from the supervisors and workers who use the scale (Landy, 1985). The goal of this input is to develop behavioral anchors that have three properties. First, they should be relevant to the work setting. Second, they should provide good illustrations of the dimension being measured. Thus, a police officer who is not sure exactly what is meant by "job knowledge" could consult the scale shown in the table for behavioral examples. Third, they should provide a good illustration of a particular level of performance. Thus, an officer who consults the scale shown in the table should have a good idea of what is meant by good, average, and poor performance.

Various aspects of the literature on behaviorally anchored rating scales have been reviewed by Bernardin and Smith (1981), Jacobs, Kafry, and Zedeck (1980), Kingstrom and Bass (1981), and Landy and Farr (1980). There is general agreement that BARS have not lived up to their promise; ratings obtained using BARS do not appear to be substantially more accurate or less prone to bias than ratings obtained using simpler graphic scales (Borman, 1991). However, the process of developing BARS may itself be highly beneficial to an organization, and it may very well justify the investment of the organization's time and resources.

First, as the result of developing BARS, the organization arrives at fairly precise, agreed-upon behavioral definitions of performance in specific aspects of the job (Landy & Farr, 1980). This outcome contrasts sharply with that achieved by organizations that employ graphic rating scales, in which every supervisor might have a unique definition of average performance. Second, the process of scale development involves many members of the organization (Borman & Vallon, 1974). A good deal of evidence indicates that participation in the scale development process itself contributes to the acceptance of performance appraisal systems and to the perception that these systems are fair and accurate (Dipboye & de Pontbriand, 1981; Landy & Farr, 1980).

Landy and Farr (1980) suggest that 30 years of research on scale formats have failed to produce an alternative that is demonstrably more efficient or more psychometrically sound than simple graphic rating scales. On this basis, they called for a moratorium on format-related research. Although this recommendation may represent a somewhat extreme reaction, their review does bring into focus the relatively minor impact of rating scale formats on the outcomes of rating. A good graphic scale is probably adequate for measuring the performance of one's workers, and the use of a complex behavioral format is unlikely to improve the quality of rating data.

CASE STUDY: THE DEVELOPMENT AND VALIDATION OF A SELECTION TEST BATTERY

A medium-size manufacturer that produces specialty boxes (e.g., boxes for high-speed film) was interested in improving its selection of employees for several manufacturing jobs, in particular corrugated box constructors, folder-gluers, and die cutters. They contacted a nearby university, and faculty in the area of industrial and organizational psychology helped them develop and validate a selection system. The first step in this process involved a series of structured interviews with job incumbents and supervisors, along with a series of plant visits in which members of the research team observed the jobs being performed. Next, a structured job analysis questionnaire (the Position Analysis Questionnaire (PAQ); McCormick & Jeanneret, 1988) was used to examine the duties, activities, and requirements of these jobs.

The PAQ analyses led the research team to two conclusions. First, although the levels of various activities and abilities required to carry out those activities vary from job to job, the overall patterns were quite similar across all six jobs. Therefore, the same abilities and the same selection tests appeared to be appropriate for all jobs. Second, on the basis of research on the abilities required to perform successfully in a variety of jobs and tasks, the abilities most relevant to successful performance in these jobs were identified as: (a) general mental ability—which includes abilities to analyze situations and problems and learn new techniques and methods, (b) numeric ability—which includes ability to work with abstract numeric concepts, and (c) spatial ability—which includes the ability to visualize objects and object relations in a three-dimensional space.

On the basis of this analysis, three tests were chosen as potential selection tools, the Wonderlic Personnel Test, the Differential Aptitude Test–Numeric, and the Differential Aptitude Test–Space Relations, respectively. Over a period of approximately 6 months, these tests were administered to job applicants and applicants for intercompany transfers, and measures of the job performance (supervisory ratings) were obtained for about half of these individuals. These results were used to evaluate the validity of these tests.

This validity study confirmed the value of the Wonderlic Personnel Test and the Differential Aptitude Test–Numeric; scores on both of these showed significant correlations with job performance ($r = .32$ and $.47$, respectively), but the Differential Aptitude Test–Space Relations showed lower validity ($r = .05$). However, all three tests contributed significantly in a multiple regression; scores on the three tests combined accounted for over 25% of the variance in performance ratings. It was concluded that the selection test battery was successful in predicting job performance, and these three tests were retained by the organization as part of their selection process.

RELIABILITY AND VALIDITY OF WORKPLACE ASSESSMENTS

Selection tests and other assessments used to predict future performance are typically more structured and more objective than measures of job performance, and the literature on the reliability and validity of these two classes of measures has led to some different conclusions about the psychometric quality of these measures. The two classes of measures are discussed below.

Evaluating Selection Tests

Thousands of studies have examined the relationship between scores on tests, interviews, and other methods of assessment and measures of job performance, work effectiveness, and other organizationally relevant criteria (e.g., awards, patents, turnover). The results of these studies provide a clear picture of which methods work well and poorly as predictors of future performance and effectiveness.

The availability of paper-and-pencil tests, interviews, biographical information blanks, work samples, and assessment centers as alternative methods of predicting job performance leads to the question of which method is best. Reilly and Chao's (1982) review provides an excellent starting point for this comparative assessment. They examined research on alternatives to standard ability tests and focused on eight alternative methods of predicting future job performance: biodata, interviews, peer evaluations, self-assessments, reference checks, academic performance, expert judgments, and objective tests. They evaluated each technique in terms of its criterion-related validity, practicality, and likelihood of providing unbiased predictions of future performance. Their review suggests that only biodata and peer evaluations show levels of validity that are in any way comparable to the validity of paper-and-pencil tests. They also suggest that none of the alternatives show comparable levels of validity with less adverse impact against minority applicants than standardized cognitive ability tests, and that when the issue of practicality is considered, paper-and-pencil tests are by far the best single selection device. A report by the National Academy of Sciences (Wigdor & Garner, 1982) reached a similar conclusion, that in employment testing there are no known alternatives to standard ability tests that are equally informative, equally fair, and of equal technical merit (see also Hartigan & Wigdor, 1989; Hunter, 1986; Hunter & Hunter, 1984).

Schmidt and Hunter (1999) summarize the practical and theoretical implications of 85 years of research on the validity and utility of selection tests. Their meta-analysis examines the validity of 19 selection procedures for predicting job performance and training. Table 18.1 summarizes some of their key findings.

The statistics shown in Table 18.1 include a number of statistical and psychometric corrections that are controversial (Hartigan & Wigdor, 1989; Murphy & DeShon, 2000), and that probably lead to inflated estimates. For example, esti-

TABLE 18.1   Estimates of the Validity of Widely Used Tests and Assessments (from Schmidt & Hunter, 1999)

	Job Performance	Performance in Training
Cognitive Ability Tests	.51	.56
Work Samples	.54	—
Integrity Tests	.41	.38
Conscientiousness Measures	.31	.30
Structured Interviews	.51	.35[a]
Assessment Centers	.37	—
Reference Checks	.26	.23
Job Experience (Years)	.18	.01
Years of Education	.10	.20
Graphology	.02	—

[a]Structured and unstructured combined.

mates of the validity of cognitive ability tests that use more conservative corrections typically suggest that the correlation between scores on these tests and measures of job performance are probably in the .35 to .40 range rather than the .51 cited in this table (See Hartigan & Wigdor, 1989). Nevertheless, there does seem to be clear and compelling evidence that selection tests can show substantial validity as predictors of performance, and conclusions about the relative validity of these tests (e.g., ability tests show similar levels of validity to situational interviews) appear reasonable.

The results presented in Table 18.1 suggest that structured interviews, work samples, and cognitive ability tests are all highly valid predictors of future performance and of success in training. These results also suggest that assessment centers, personality inventories (particularly those that provide a measure of the trait Conscientiousness) and integrity tests provide useful predictors of performance in the job and in training. However, some widely used methods of assessment do not appear to be very effective. For example, reference checks show some validity, but they are less valid and more costly than many alternatives (e.g., standardized tests). Candidates with more years of experience or more years of education are often favored by recruiters and hiring managers, but there is actually very little relationship between experience or education and job performance or performance in training. Finally, graphology (handwriting analysis) is widely used in Europe and Israel and is being aggressively promoted in the United States as a tool for assessing job candidates. Graphologists' ratings turn out to have virtually no relationship to peoples' subsequent job performance. Organizations that use this method in personnel selection might be better served by simply flipping a coin.

Schmidt and Hunter (1999) and others (e.g., Murphy & Shiarella, 1997) note that organizations rarely use a single test as a basis for making decisions. Schmidt and Hunter's (1999) review suggests that using combinations of tests can lead to high degrees of accuracy in predicting job performance. For example, combining general mental ability tests with a work sample test could yield a validity coefficient as high as .63; the same level of validity that might be attained by combining a structured interview and an ability test. Ability tests combined with integrity tests might do even better (an estimated validity of .65).

Although standard ability tests appear to be the best aids available for making selection decisions, it is unrealistic to expect that ability tests will be used as the sole method of making selection decisions. Managers' distrust of paper-and-pencil tests and their attachment to alternative selection devices (e.g., the interview) are not likely to be significantly affected by reviews of the research literature. Alternatives to paper-and-pencil tests are here to stay; the question is not whether they should be used but, rather, how they might best be combined with standard ability tests to maximize accuracy in predicting performance.

Surveys of personnel managers (Ahlburg, 1992; Dankin & Armstrong, 1989) reveal two depressing findings. First, personnel and human resource professionals are often unaware of the most basic findings of research on the validity of various personnel assessment and selection methods. For example, personnel managers in several countries, including the United States, consistently rank cognitive ability tests as among the least valid and useful tools for selection, and they rank interviews as among the most valid and useful tools for selection. The available body of research, which includes thousands of studies conducted in a wide variety of settings, shows that the opposite is true. Second, even those who know which techniques have been shown to have the most or the least validity (e.g., individuals holding recent graduate degrees, who would have had extensive exposure to this research) do not seem to translate their knowledge into concrete action. That is, even when they are aware of the relevant evidence, well-trained personnel managers are more likely to use techniques such as the interview or assessments of experience, which they know are less valid in most settings than ability tests or other relatively objective assessment methods. It appears that personnel managers' habit of using less valid methods is a difficult one to break.

Personnel researchers long believed that the validity and usefulness of tests varied substantially across organizations and that every testing program would require its own validity study. Over the last 25 years, this view has been challenged; research on validity generalization suggests that the major classes of tests tend to perform similarly across organizations, jobs, and industries (Callender & Osburn, 1980, 1981, 1982; Hartigan & Wigdor, 1989; Hunter, Schmidt, & Pearlman, 1982; Schmidt, Hunter, Pearlman, & Shane, 1979). Although some inconsistency in the results is obtained when different models for evaluating validity generalization are applied, the general trend suggested by the model is unmistakably clear. Research on validity generalization suggests that in almost every case, test validities are (1) substantially larger and (2) much less variable than psychologists have traditionally believed.

Although the validity of selection tests is both higher and more uniform than a casual scan of the literature would suggest, it is unlikely that the validity of these tests will be invariant. For example, there is considerable evidence that the validity of selection tests is higher for complex, higher-level jobs than for simpler, lower-level jobs (Gutenberg, Arvey, Osburn, & Jenneret, 1983). It is also likely that validities are different in stable jobs than in jobs where change is frequent and unpredictable (Murphy, 1989).

In addition to these substantive factors, it is likely that procedural variables systematically influence the practical utility of tests and assessments. Tests, interviews, behavioral observation methods, etc. work best when they are administered in a consistent way, with minimal disruptions or distractions. Testing and assessment practices in organizations are not likely to achieve the same level of reliability and consistency as is typical for high-stakes testing (e.g., the SATs), and variation in the quality of test administration, scoring, and reporting will almost certainly degrade the validity of selection tests. Unfortunately, we know little about how organizations actually administer and use tests (Murphy & Bartram, in press), and it is unwise to assume that all field applications of a particular class of tests will achieve comparable levels of standardization, reliability, or validity.

Evaluating Performance Ratings

The goals and uses of performance appraisals in organizations can often have a profound impact on the quality of the data obtained from performance ratings (Murphy & Cleveland, 1995), and psychometric criteria might not always be the best bases for assessing the success or failure of a performance appraisal system. Nevertheless, it is useful to consider criteria such as reliability and validity in evaluating the adequacy of supervisory ratings as measures of job performance.

Reliability

Different models for defining reliability have led to very different judgments about the reliability and validity of these measures. For example, when evaluated in terms of internal consistency criteria (e.g., coefficient alpha), ratings seem highly reliable. Viswesvaran, Ones, and Schmidt's (1996) meta-analysis suggests that the mean of the coefficient alpha values reported in the literature is .86. However, when evaluated in terms of interrater agreement, performance ratings have fared much worse.

Viswesvaran et al. (1996) and others (e.g., Rothstein, 1990) have shown that interrater reliabilities for job performance measures are rarely much higher than .50; Viswesvaran et al. (1996) estimate the mean interrater correlation for supervisory ratings to be .52. Conway and Huffcutt's (1997) meta-analysis shows that subordinates showed the lowest level of interrater reliability. On average, subordinate ratings of job performance show correlations in the low .30s; average interrater correlations are slightly higher for peers (.37). Supervisors show slightly higher levels of agreement (.50,) but, again, similarly situated raters tend to provide evaluations that are only moderately consistent. Viswesvaran et al. (1996) report similar estimates. In their review, average interrater correlations were .42 for peers.

A number of studies have examined agreement in ratings obtained from different sources (e.g., agreement between supervisory and peer ratings). For example, Harris and Schaubroeck's (1988) meta-analysis reported that the average correlation between peer and supervisor ratings was .53, the average self-supervisory correlation was .31, and the average self-peer correlation was also .31. They note many reasons why different sources should *not* agree, including the effects of egocentric biases (self-evaluations often differ from evaluations received from others; Thornton, 1980), differences in opportunities to observe (Murphy & Cleveland, 1995), and differences in organizational level. A more recent meta-analysis (Conway & Huffcutt, 1997) suggested that correlations between ratings obtained from different sources (e.g., supervisors, peers, subordinates) are even lower than this. This analysis suggests that the mean correlation between ratings obtained from a supervisor and a single peer is .34, and all other correlations between ratings obtained from different sources are in the .20s or lower.

Validity of Performance Ratings

There is no simple way to determine or to demonstrate the validity of most measures of job performance. Consider, for example, supervisory performance ratings. Ideally, the validity of ratings might be determined by correlating these ratings with other measures of job performance (Kavanaugh, 1971). The problem with this approach is that ratings are often the only available measure of the worker's performance; there is rarely any other acceptable standard against which ratings can be compared. In short, there are rarely "criteria for criteria" such that a particular measure of job performance is, in fact,

a valid measure of the performance of individual workers. Because there are typically no standards against which most criterion measures can be compared, it is difficult to use the predictive or concurrent validity strategies in assessing the validity of criteria.

Recognizing that the strategy of determining the validity of a criterion measure directly by comparing that measure to some standard is often impossible, a number of authors have suggested indirect strategies for assessing the validity of criterion measures. For example, it is often possible to determine the extent to which raters discriminate among individuals or differentiate among performance dimensions in their ratings of job performance (Kavanaugh, MacKinney, & Wolins, 1971; Saal, Downey, & Lahey, 1980). It is assumed that raters who are sensitive to differences in their subordinates' levels of performance are more accurate than those who give everyone similar ratings. Other authors suggest that interrater agreement be used as an indirect indicator of the validity of ratings (Bernardin, Alveres, & Cranny, 1976). Although it is true that valid ratings also should be reliable, several authors have noted that reliability does not necessarily imply validity and on this basis have questioned the use of interrater agreement as an indicator of valid ratings (Buckner, 1959; Freeberg, 1969; Wherry & Bartlett, 1982).

Finally, James (1973) has proposed the most comprehensive approach to assessing the validity of criterion measures—the construct validity approach. He notes that performance can be thought of as a construct and that the relationships between a measure of performance and a number of other observable behaviors could be compared to the pattern of relationships implied by the theoretical network in which the construct performance is embedded to assess the validity of a criterion measure.

Research on the construct validity of performance ratings has progressed significantly in recent years. For example, the research teams involved in U.S. Armed Forces Project A relied on careful explications of the construct domain of job performance to develop concrete performance measures (see *Personnel Psychology*, Vol. 43, No. 2, for a detailed description of this project). Kraiger and Teachout (1990) illustrated ways in which analyses of the generalizability of ratings could be used to assess construct validity. Other authors (e.g., Lance, Teachout, & Donnelly, 1992; Murphy & Shiarella, 1997) have suggested methods for identifying dimensions that underlie the performance domain.

A report by the National Research Council (Milkovich & Widgor, 1991) examined performance appraisal validity in the context of the debate over pay for performance. They concluded that performance appraisals show reasonably high levels of reliability and moderate evidence of validity. They further concluded that the goal of performance appraisal should be to "support and encourage informed managerial judgment and not to aspire to the degree of standardization, precision, and empirical support that would be required of, for example, selection tests" (Milkovich & Wigdor, 1991, p. 151).

FUTURE DIRECTIONS

A large and robust literature deals with the use of tests and assessments in personnel selection; Schmidt and Hunter's (1999) review captures the current state of this literature nicely. The general theme of this review is that we can do a relatively good job of predicting performance, especially if attention is paid to the empirical literature on test validity. In particular, they suggest that systems that include measures of cognitive ability along with measures of other job-related attributes can show substantial levels of validity.

Historically, personnel psychologists have been skeptical of the validity and utility of personality inventories in personnel selection, but there is growing willingness to consider measures of personality in developing selection batteries. Influential reviews (e.g., Barrick & Mount, 1991; Tett et al., 1991) have documented the potential usefulness of these measures, and scales such as the Hogan Personality Inventory are increasingly being considered as candidates for use in selection testing. Important issues (e.g., the influence of faking of selection) still need to be resolved before personality inventories will be fully embraced by selection researchers, but it appears that progress is being made in addressing most of these concerns.

A second trend involves validation research rather than testing and assessment per se, but it has clear implications for testing. Selection systems almost always involve multiple components (e.g., interviews combined with tests, tests combined with simulations, etc.), but most of the available validity research is univariate in focus. Several recent studies have attempted to estimate the validity of different combinations of tests (Murphy & Shiarella, 1997; Schmidt & Hunter, 1999), and increasing attention is being paid to the incremental validity of tests when combined with commonly used predictors, but this research is still in its early development. It does seem safe, however, to suggest that more and more attention will be devoted to identifying tests and assessments that fill the gaps between the classes of tests described in this chapter.

Performance appraisals are often obtained from a single rater (i.e., the direct supervisor), making it difficult to determine the extent to which ratings reflect ratee performance as opposed to raters' preconceptions and biases. Many companies have attempted to address this problem by obtaining evaluations from supervisors, subordinates, peers, customers, etc. in an effort to arrive at a broad and representative evaluation of each employee's performance. These systems are more widely used for feedback than for administrative decision-making (Bracken et al., 2001), but it is not hard to imagine that an employee who receives poor ratings from his or her peers, supervisors, subordinates, and customers will be in trouble when it comes time to decide on merit increases and promotions. Multirater systems do indeed solve some of the problems typically encountered in performance appraisal, but they also may bring new problems to the surface. One of the most significant challenges to these systems is raters' disagreement in evaluations of performance (Murphy, Cleveland, & Mohler, 2001). These systems are designed to provide useful and credible feedback, but the high levels of interrater disagreement that are found in many 360-degree rating systems may in fact tend to heighten ratees' concerns that performance ratings are subjective and unreliable.

Performance ratings are often the target of well-founded criticisms and complaints, and unfortunately, little meaningful progress has been made in improving the quality or the usefulness of supervisory performance ratings. Recent models suggest (e.g., Murphy & Cleveland, 1995) that traditional strategies involving rating training, scale development, behavior diaries, etc. are not likely to succeed, in part because raters are often motivated to provide ratings that reflect things other than the ratee's performance. These authors suggest some ways of changing performance appraisal systems to match the social and political realities of performance appraisal, but little research has been done on the effectiveness of these remedies.

SUMMARY

Most of the testing and assessment that is done in work settings focuses on two broad themes, predicting future performance and effectiveness and measuring past or present levels of performance. Testing for personnel selection and placement has been an active area of research and application for over 90 years, and a wide range of tests are available for this purpose. These include assessments of experience and background, interviews, standardized tests, work samples, and multimethod assessments (e.g., assessment centers). There is substantial empirical support for using all of these techniques in selection, and clear evidence that combinations of these methods can contribute substantially to the quality of selection decisions.

A number of measures of job performance are available, but, in most cases, performance measures rely on the judgments of supervisors. Companies are increasingly seeking additional sources of information about performance (e.g., 360-degree rating systems), and while systems that involve multiple inputs have many advantages, interrater disagreements can undercut the value and credibility of such systems. Unfortunately, such disagreements are the norm rather than the exception. Although some research supports the construct validity of performance ratings, measures of job performance have not achieved the level of psychometric sophistication or precision that characterize selection tests. A review by the National Academy of Sciences (Milkovich & Wigdor, 1991) suggests that performance appraisals will not and should not be held to this standard, and this conclusion seems a very reasonable one. Nevertheless, it is likely that the measurement of past and present job performance will continue to be done on a more subjective and a less reliable basis than the prediction of future job performance.

REFERENCES

Ahlburg, D.A. (1992). Predicting the job performance of managers: What do the experts know? *International Journal of Forecasting, 7,* 467–472.

Arvey, R.D., & Campion, J.E. (1982). The employment interview: A summary and review of recent research. *Personnel Psychology, 35,* 281–322.

Asher, J.J., & Sciarrino, J.A. (1974). Realistic work sample tests: A review. *Personnel Psychology, 27,* 519–553.

Austin, J.T., & Villanova, P. (1992). The criterion problem: 1917–1992. *Journal of Applied Psychology, 77,* 836–874.

Barrick, M.R., & Mount, M.K. (1991). The Big Five personality dimensions and job performance: A meta-analysis. *Personnel Psychology, 44,* 1–26.

Bernardin, H.J., Alveres, K.M., & Cranny, C.J. (1976). A recomparison of behavioral expectation scales to summated scales. *Journal of Applied Psychology, 61,* 564–570.

Bernardin, H.J., & Smith, P.C. (1981). A clarification of some issues regarding the development and use of behaviorally anchored rating scales (BARS). *Journal of Applied Psychology, 66,* 458–463.

Borman, W.C. (1982). Validity of behavioral assessment for predicting military recruiter performance. *Journal of Applied Psychology, 67,* 3–9.

Borman, W.C. (1991). Job behavior, performance, and effectiveness. In M. Dunnette & L. Hough (Eds.), *Handbook of industrial and organizational psychology* (2nd ed., Vol. 2, pp. 271–326). Palo Alto, CA: Consulting Psychologists Press.

Borman, W.C., & Vallon, W.R. (1974). A view of what can happen when behavioral expectation scales are developed in one setting and used in another. *Journal of Applied Psychology, 59,* 197–201.

Bracken, C., Timmreck, C., & Church, A. (2001). *Handbook of multisource feedback.* San Francisco: Jossey-Bass.

Brass, D.J., & Oldham, G.R. (1976). Validating an in-basket test using an alternative set of leadership scoring dimensions. *Journal of Applied Psychology, 61,* 652–657.

Bray, D.W., Campbell, R.J., & Grant, D.L. (1974). *Formative years in business: A long-term AT&T study of managerial lives.* New York: Wiley.

Brown, B.K., & Campion, M.A. (1994). Biodata phenomenology: Recruiters' perceptions and use of biographical information in resume screening. *Journal of Applied Psychology, 79,* 897–908.

Buckner, D.N. (1959). The predictability of ratings as a function of interrater agreement. *Journal of Applied Psychology, 43,* 60–64.

Callender, J.C., & Osburn, H.G. (1980). Development and test of a new model for validity generalization. *Journal of Applied Psychology, 65,* 543–558.

Callender, J.C., & Osburn, H.G. (1981). Testing the constancy of validity with computer-generated sampling distributions of the multiplicative model variance estimate: Results for petroleum industry validation research. *Journal of Applied Psychology, 66,* 274–281.

Callender, J.C., & Osburn, H.G. (1982). Another view of progress in validity generalization. *Journal of Applied Psychology, 67,* 846–852.

Campbell, J.P., McCloy, R.A., Oppler, S.H., & Sager, C.E. (1992). A theory of performance. In N. Schmitt & W. Borman (Eds.), *Personnel selection in organizations* (pp. 35–70). San Francisco: Jossey-Bass.

Campion, M.A., Palmer, D.K., & Campion, J.E. (1997). A review of structure in the selection interview. *Personnel Psychology, 50,* 655–702.

Campion, M.A., Pursell, E.D., & Brown, B.K. (1988). Structured interviewing: Raising the psychometric properties of the employment interview. *Personnel Psychology, 41,* 25–42.

Carlson, K., Scullen, S., Schmidt, F., Rothstein, H., & Erwin, F. (1999). Generalizable biographical data validity can be achieved without multi-organizational development and keying. *Personnel Psychology, 52,* 731–756.

Cascio, W.F. (1976). Turnover, biographical data, and fair employment practice. *Journal of Applied Psychology, 61,* 576–580.

Cascio, W.F. (1982). *Applied psychology in personnel management* (2nd ed.). Reston, VA: Reston.

Conway, J.M., & Huffcutt, A.I. (1997). Psychometric properties of multisource performance ratings: A meta-analysis of subordinate, supervisor, peer, and self-ratings. *Human Performance, 10,* 331–360.

Dankin, S., & Armstrong, J.S. (1989). Predicting job performance: A comparison of expert opinion and research findings. *International Journal of Forecasting, 5,* 187–194.

Differential Aptitude Tests. San Antonio, TX: Psychological Corporation.

Dipboye, R.L., & de Pontbriand, R. (1981). Correlates of employee reactions to performance appraisals and appraisal systems. *Journal of Applied Psychology, 66,* 248–251.

DuBois, C., Sackett, P.R., Zedeck, S., & Fogli, L. (1993). Further exploration of typical and maximum performance criteria: Definitional issues, prediction, and white-black differences. *Journal of Applied Psychology, 78,* 205–211.

Exner, J.E. (1974). *The Rorschach: A comprehensive system.* New York: Wiley.

Fine, S., & Cronshaw, S. (1999). *Functional job analysis: A foundation for human resources management.* Mahwah, NJ: Erlbaum.

Finkle, R.B. (1976). Managerial assessment centers. In M. Dunnette (Ed.), *Handbook of industrial and organizational psychology.* Chicago: Rand McNally.

Fredericksen, N. (1962). Factors in in-basket performance. *Psychological Monographs, 76*(22, Whole No. 541).

Freeberg, N.E. (1969). Relevance of rater-ratee acquaintance in the validity and reliability of rating. *Journal of Applied Psychology, 53,* 518–524.

Gaugler, B.B., Rosenthal, D.B., Thornton, G.C., & Bentson, C. (1987). Meta-analysis of assessment center validity. *Journal of Applied Psychology, 72,* 493–511.

Gottfredson, L. (1986). Societal consequences of the g factor in employment. *Journal of Vocational Behavior, 29,* 379–410.

Guion, R.M. (1998). *Assessment, measurement and prediction for personnel decisions.* Mahwah, NJ: Erlbaum.

Guion, R.M., & Gottier, R.F. (1965). Validity of personality measures in personnel selection. *Personnel Psychology, 18,* 135–164.

Gutenberg, R.L., Arvey, R.D., Osburn, H.G., & Jenneret, P.R. (1983). Moderating effects of decision-making/information processing job dimensions on test validities. *Journal of Applied Psychology, 68,* 602–608.

Hammer, T.H., & Landau, J. (1981). Methodological issues in the use of absence data. *Journal of Applied Psychology, 66,* 574–581.

Harris, M.H., & Schaubroeck, J. (1988). A meta-analysis of self-supervisory, self-peer, and peer-supervisor ratings. *Personnel Psychology, 41,* 43–62.

Hartigan, J.A., & Wigdor, A.K. (1989). *Fairness in employment testing: Validity generalization, minority issues, and the General Aptitude Test Battery.* Washington, DC: National Academy Press.

Harvey, R.J. (1991). Job analysis. In M.D. Dunnette & L.M. Hough (Eds.), *Handbook of industrial and organizational psychology* (2nd ed., Vol. 2, pp. 71–164). Palo Alto, CA: Consulting Psychologists Press.

Hinrichs, J.R. (1978). An eight-year follow-up of a management assessment center. *Journal of Applied Psychology, 63,* 596–601.

Hogan Personality Inventory. Tulsa, OK: Hogan Assessment Systems.

Hough, L. (1984). Development and evaluation of the "accomplishment record" method of selecting and promoting professionals. *Journal of Applied Psychology, 69,* 135–146.

Hough, L.M., Eaton, N.K., Dunnete, M.D., Kamp, J.D., & McCloy, R.A. (1990). Criterion-related validities of personality constructs and the effect of response distortion on those validities. *Journal of Applied Psychology, 75,* 581–595.

Hunter, J.E. (1986). Cognitive ability, cognitive aptitudes, job knowledge, and job performance. *Journal of Vocational Behavior, 29,* 340–362.

Hunter, J.E., & Hunter, R.F. (1984). The validity and utility of alternative predictors of job performance. *Psychological Bulletin, 96,* 72–98.

Hunter, J.E., Schmidt, F.L., & Pearlman, K. (1982). History and accuracy of validity generalization equations: A response to the Callender and Osburn reply. *Journal of Applied Psychology, 67,* 853–856.

Jacobs, R., Kafry, D., & Zedeck, S. (1980). Expectations of behaviorally anchored rating scales. *Personnel Psychology, 33,* 595–640.

James, L.R. (1973). Criterion models and construct validity for criteria. *Psychological Bulletin, 80,* 75–83.

Janz, T. (1982). Initial comparisons of patterned behavior description interviews versus unstructured interviews. *Journal of Applied Psychology, 67,* 577–582.

Jensen, A. (1980). *Bias in mental testing.* New York: Free Press.

Kavanaugh, M.J. (1971). The content issue in performance appraisal: A review. *Personnel Psychology, 24,* 653–668.

Kavanaugh, M.J., MacKinney, A., & Wolins, L. (1971). Issues in managerial performance: Multitrait–multimethod analysis of ratings. *Psychological Bulletin, 75,* 34–49.

Kingstrom, P.O., & Bass, A.R. (1981). A critical analysis of studies comparing behaviorally anchored rating scales (BARS) and other rating formats. *Personnel Psychology, 34,* 263–289.

Klimoski, R.J., & Strickland, W.J. (1977). Assessment centers—Valid or merely prescient? *Personnel Psychology, 30,* 353–361.

Kraiger, K., & Teachout, M.S. (1990). Generalizability theory as construct-related evidence of the validity of job performance ratings. *Human Performance, 3,* 19–36.

Kuder Occupational Interest Survey. Chicago: Science Research Associates.

Lance, C.E., Newbolt, W.H., Gatewood, R.D., Foster, M.R., French, N.R. & Smith, D.E. (2000). Assessment center exercise factors represent cross-situational specificity, not method bias. *Human Performance, 13,* 323–353.

Lance, C.E., Teachout, M.S., & Donnelly, T.M. (1992). Specification of the criterion construct space: An application of hierarchical confirmatory factor analysis. *Journal of Applied Psychology, 77,* 437–452.

Landy, F.J. (1985). *The psychology of work behavior* (3rd ed.). Homewood, IL: Dorsey Press.

Landy, F.J., & Farr, J.L. (1980). Performance rating. *Psychological Bulletin, 93,* 72–107.

Landy, F.J., & Trumbo, D.A. (1980). *Psychology of work behavior* (rev. ed.). Homewood, IL: Dorsey Press.

Latham, G.P., & Pursell, E.D. (1975). Measuring absenteeism from the opposite side of the coin. *Journal of Applied Psychology, 60,* 369–371.

Latham, G.P., Saari, L.M., Pursell, E.D., & Campion, M.A. (1980). The situational interview. *Journal of Applied Psychology, 65,* 422–427.

Mael, F.A. (1991). A conceptual rationale for the domain of attributes of biodata items. *Personnel Psychology, 44,* 763–792.

McCormick, E.J. (1979). *Job analysis: Methods and applications.* New York: Amacom.

McCormick, E.J., & Jeanneret, P.R. (1988). Position Analysis Questionnaire (PAQ). In S. Gael (Ed), *The job analysis handbook for business, industry and government* (Vol. 1, pp. 825–842). New York: Wiley.

McDaniel, M.A., & Jones, J.W. (1988). Predicting employee theft: A quantitative review of the validity of a standardized measure of dishonesty. *Journal of Business and Psychology, 2,* 327–345.

McDaniel, M.A., Whetzel, D.L., Schmidt, F.L., & Maurer, S.D. (1994). The validity of employment interviews: A comprehensive review and meta-analysis. *Journal of Applied Psychology, 79,* 599–616.

Milkovich, G.T., & Wigdor, A.K. (1991). *Pay for performance.* Washington, DC: National Academy Press.

Motowidlo, S.J., Dunnette, M.D., Carter, G.W., Tippins, N., Werner, S., Griffiths, J.R., & Vaughan, M.J. (1992). Studies of the behavioral interview. *Journal of Applied Psychology, 77,* 571–587.

Mumford, M.D., Uhlman, C.E., & Kilcullen, R.N. (1992). The structure of life history: Implications for the construct validity of background data scales. *Human Performance, 5,* 109–137.

Murphy, K. (1984a). *Review of the Armed Services Vocational Aptitude Battery. Test Critiques* (Vol. 1). Kansas City, MO: Test Corporation of America.

Murphy, K. (1984b). *Review of Wonderlic Personnel Test. Test Critiques* (Vol. 1). Kansas City, MO: Test Corporation of America.

Murphy, K. (1989). Is the relationship between cognitive ability and job performance stable over time? *Human Performance, 2,* 183–200.

Murphy, K., & Bartram, D. (in press). Recruitment, personnel selection and organizational effectiveness. In I. Robertson, D. Bartram, & M. Callinan (Eds.), *The role of individual performance in organizational effectiveness.* Chichester, England: Wiley.

Murphy, K., & Cleveland, J. (1995). *Understanding performance appraisal: Social, organizational and goal-oriented perspectives.* Newbury Park, CA: Sage.

Murphy, K., Cleveland, J., & Mohler, C. (2001). Reliability, validity and meaningfulness of multisource ratings. In D. Bracken, C. Timmreck, and A. Church (Eds.), *Handbook of multisource feedback* (pp. 130–148). San Francisco: Jossey-Bass.

Murphy, K., & Davidshofer, C. (1998). *Psychological testing: Principles and applications* (4th ed). Englewood Cliffs, NJ: Prentice-Hall.

Murphy, K., & DeShon, R. (2000). Inter-rater correlations do not estimate the reliability of job performance ratings. *Personnel Psychology, 53,* 873–900.

Murphy, K., & Shiarella, A. (1997). Implications of the multidimensional nature of job performance for the validity of selection tests: Multivariate frameworks for studying test validity. *Personnel Psychology, 50,* 823–854.

Neisser, U., Boodoo, G., Bouchard, T.J., Boykin, A.W., Brody, N., Ceci, S., Halpern, D.F., Loehlin, J.C., Perloff, R., Sternberg, R.J., & Unbina, S. (1996). Intelligence: Knowns and unknowns. *American Psychologist, 51,* 77–101.

O'Bannon, R.M., Goldinger, L.A., & Appleby, J.D. (1989). *Honesty and integrity testing: A practical guide.* Atlanta, GA: Applied Information Resources.

Office of Strategic Services (OSS) Assessment Staff. (1948). *Assessment of men: Selection of personnel for the Office of Strategic Services.* New York: Rinehart.

Ones, D.S., Viswesvaran, C., & Schmidt, F.L. (1993). Comprehensive meta-analysis of integrity test validities: Findings and implications for personnel selection and theories of job performance. *Journal of Applied Psychology, 78,* 679–703.

Owens, W.A. (1976). Background data. In M. Dunnette (Ed.), *Handbook of industrial and organizational psychology* (pp. 609–644). Chicago: Rand McNally.

Owens, W.A., & Schoenfeldt, L.F. (1979). Toward a classification of persons. *Journal of Applied Psychology, 65,* 569–607.

Pittenger, D.J. (1992). The utility of the Myers-Briggs Type Indicator. *Review of Educational Research, 63,* 467–488.

Quible, Z.K. (1995). Electronic resumes: Their time is coming. *Business Communication Quarterly, 58,* 5–9.

Quible, Z.K. (1998). The electronic resume: An important new job-search tool. *Journal of Education for Business, 74,* 79–82.

Reilly, R.R., & Chao, G.T. (1982). Validity and fairness of some alternate employee selection procedures. *Personnel Psychology, 35,* 1–67.

Rosse, J.G., Stecher, M.D., Miller, J.L., & Levin, R.A. (1998). The impact of response distortion on preemployment personality testing and hiring decisions. *Journal of Applied Psychology, 83,* 634–644.

Rothstein, H.R. (1990). Inter-rater reliability of job performance ratings: Growth to asymptote level with increasing opportunity to learn. *Journal of Applied Psychology, 75,* 322–327.

Saal, F.E., Downey, R.G., & Lahey, M.A. (1980). Rating the ratings: Assessing the psychometric quality of rating data. *Psychological Bulletin, 88,* 413–428.

Sackett, P.R., Burris, L.R., & Callahan, C. (1989). Integrity testing for personnel selection: An update. *Personnel Psychology, 42,* 491–529.

Sackett, P.R., & Decker, P.J. (1979). Detection of deception in the employment context: A review and critique. *Personnel Psychology, 32,* 487–506.

Sackett, P.R., & Decker, P.J. (1982). Constructs and assessment center dimensions: Some troubling empirical findings. *Journal of Applied Psychology, 67,* 401–410.

Sackett, P.R., & Harris, M.M. (1984). Honesty testing for personnel selection: A review and critique. *Personnel Psychology, 37,* 221–245.

Sackett, P.R., & Harris, M.M. (1985). Honesty testing for personnel selection: A review and critique. In H.J. Bernardin & D.A. Bownas (Eds.), *Personality assessment in organizations.* New York: Praeger.

Sackett, P.R., Zedeck, S., & Fogli, L. (1988). Relationship between measures of typical and maximal job performance. *Journal of Applied Psychology, 73,* 482–486.

Schippman, J.S., Prien, E., & Katz, J.A. (1990). Reliability and validity of in-basket performance measures. *Personnel Psychology, 43,* 837–859.

Schmidt, F.L., & Hunter, J.E. (1999). The validity and utility of selection methods in personnel psychology: Practical and theoretical implications of 85 years of research findings. *Psychological Bulletin, 124,* 262–274.

Schmidt, F.L., Hunter, J.E., Pearlman, K., & Shane, G.S. (1979). Further tests of the Schmidt–Hunter Bayesian validity generalization procedure. *Personnel Psychology, 32,* 257–281.

Schneider, B. (1987). The people make the place. *Personnel Psychology, 40,* 437–453.

Smith, P., & Kendall, L. (1963). Retranslation of expectations: An approach to the construction and unambiguous anchors for rating scales. *Journal of Applied Psychology, 47,* 149–155.

Smith, R. (1995). A 6-step program is detailed to help human resource personnel successfully screen resumes to select the right person for the right job. *HRFocus, 72,* 24.

Stokes, G.S., Mumford, M.D., & Owens, W.A. (1994). *Biodata handbook.* Palo Alto, CA: Consulting Psychologists Press.

Strong Interest Inventory. Palo Alto, CA: Consulting Psychologists Press.

Tett, R.P., Jackson, D.N., & Rothstein, M. (1991). Personality measures as predictors of job performance: A meta-analytic review. *Personnel Psychology, 44,* 703–745.

Thornton, G.C. (1980). Psychometric properties of self-appraisals of job performance. *Personnel Psychology, 33,* 351–354.

Thornton, G.C., III (1992). *Assessment centers in human resource management.* Reading, MA: Addison-Wesley.

Thornton, G.C., III, & Cleveland, J.N. (1990). Developing managerial talent through simulation. *American Psychologist, 45,* 190–199.

Tziner, A., Murphy, K.R., & Cleveland, J.N. (2001). Relationships between attitudes toward organizations and performance appraisal systems and rating behavior. *International Journal of Selection and Assessment, 9,* 226–239.

Vaas, L., Chen, A., & Hicks, M. (2000). Web recruiting takes off. *PC Week,* January 17, 57–68.

Visweswaran, C., Ones, D.S., & Schmidt, F.L. (1996). Comparative analysis of the reliability of job performance ratings. *Journal of Applied Psychology, 81,* 557–574.

Welsh, J., Kucinkas, S., & Curran, L. (1990). *Armed Services Vocational Aptitude Battery: Integrative review of validity studies.* San Antonio, TX: Brooks Air Force Base.

Wernimont, P.F., & Campbell, J.P. (1968). Signs, samples, and criteria. *Journal of Applied Psychology, 52,* 372–376.

Wherry, R.J., & Bartlett, C.J. (1982). The control of bias in ratings: A theory of rating. *Personnel Psychology, 35,* 521–551.

Whetzel, D.L., & Wheaton, G.R. (1997). *Applied measurement methods in industrial psychology.* Palo Alto, CA: Davies-Black.

Wiesner, W.H., & Cronshaw, S.F. (1988). A meta-analytic investigation of the impact of interview format and degree of structure on the validity of the interview. *Journal of Occupational Psychology, 61,* 275–290.

Wigdor, A.K., & Garner, W.R. (1982). *Ability testing: Uses, consequences, and controversies,* Part I: Report of the committee. Washington, DC: National Academy Press.

Wollowick, H.B., & McNamara, W.J. (1969). Relationship of the components of an assessment center to management success. *Journal of Applied Psychology, 53,* 348–352.

CHAPTER 19

The Application of Behavioral Assessment Methodologies in Educational Settings

ELISA STEELE SHERNOFF AND THOMAS R. KRATOCHWILL

INTRODUCTION AND OVERVIEW

Although traditionally there has been a limited focus on behavioral assessment with children and adolescents in educational settings, this situation has changed over the past decade. For example, several books and chapters are primarily devoted to behavioral assessment with children in educational settings (see Breen & Fiedler, 1996; Kratochwill, Sheridan, Carlson, & Lasecki, 1999; Shapiro & Kratochwill, 2000a, 2000b). Several factors account for the growing interest in and reliance on behavioral assessment strategies in psychological and educational practice. First, contemporary behavioral assessment strategies are now used across diverse settings, with diverse clients, to develop treatment programs for a variety of academic and behavioral problems (Kratochwill et al., 1999). Second, behavioral assessment techniques and strategies are used as an alternative or adjunct to traditional academic and social-emotional assessment techniques (i.e.,

standardized cognitive assessment, projective tests, and psychoeducational tests). In recent years, many of these traditional assessments have been called into question due to concerns over norms, reliability, and validity issues and especially in their link to the design of treatment programs (Kratochwill & Shapiro, 2000; Mash & Terdall, 1997). Behavioral assessment strategies, for example, have been highlighted in recent years because of their treatment utility (Hayes, Barlow, & Nelson-Gray, 1999).

Interest in behavioral assessment also has increased due to the development of specific measures in treatment outcome research for child and adult disorders (Cone, 2001; Kratochwill & Shapiro, 2000). For example, behavioral assessment measures such as direct observation, self-monitoring, and behavioral interviews have helped standardize the assessment and intervention process and increase the knowledge base regarding which assessments and interventions are well matched to specific childhood problems. Behavioral assessment strategies especially have played a critical role in documenting the outcomes in the evidence-based treatment movement (e.g., Chambless & Ollendick, 2001; Kratochwill & Stoiber, 2000; Stoiber & Kratochwill, 2000). Behavioral assessment has provided researchers with a variety of outcome measures that can be used to test the effectiveness of specific interventions. This contribution comes at a critical time when the field of education is being held accountable for producing better student outcomes.

GENERAL DEFINITION OF BEHAVIORAL ASSESSMENT

Because behavioral assessment represents a diverse set of procedures and techniques, there is no single definition of behavioral assessment. It is broadly defined as "a hypothesis-testing process about the nature of problems, causes of problems, and evaluation of treatment programs" (Kratochwill & Shapiro, 2000, p. 5). Various behavioral assessment models also have been used—including applied behavioral analysis, cognitive behavior modification, and social learning theory. The primary difference between these models is what constitutes "behavior;" therefore, the focus of the assessment varies based on the theoretical model that is implemented. A behavioral approach to academic and social/emotional assessment broadly assumes that a student's learning and behavior are a function of the relationship between individual student characteristics, dimensions of the task, and characteristics of the environment (Gettinger & Seibert, 2000). Although there is *no single technique* that defines an assessment as behavioral in nature, there are unifying concepts regarding the methods, goals, and purposes of behavioral assessment.

COMMON FEATURES AND UNDERLYING ASSUMPTIONS OF BEHAVIORAL ASSESSMENT

These common features include: measuring observable behaviors across a variety of settings and situations, considering the reciprocal nature between behavior and the environment, evaluating the functional links between behaviors and the environment, relying on multimethod assessment strategies, embracing a nomothetic and idiographic approach to assessment and intervention, using assessment strategies that require low levels of inference about a child's functioning, using ongoing and repeated measurement, adhering to evidence-based assessments, and ensuring psychometric evaluation of assessment methods.

Focuses on Measuring Behaviors That Occur in Different Situations

A core assumption regarding behavioral assessment is that measurement needs to focus on observable behaviors in a variety of situations (Kratochwill & Shapiro, 2000). Thus, evaluation occurs across multiple settings because environmental and ecological variables are assumed to have a direct influence on a person's thoughts, behaviors, and feelings. These different environmental characteristics help the psychologist develop hypotheses about the development and maintenance of different behaviors. From a behavioral orientation, behavior is assessed within the context of the environment, rather than viewing behavior as a global, underlying, stable trait (Mash & Terdal, 1988, 1997).

Considers Multiple Factors That Affect Behavior

Historically, there has been a misconception that behavioral assessment strategies assume that behavior is exclusively a product of the interaction between a person and his or her environment. However, conventional behavioral assessment strategies take a balanced approach that emphasizes the importance of the environment *and* the individual's reaction to it. Stanger (1996) suggests that the goal of behavioral assessment is to assess the multiple contributing and controlling factors that influence behavior. These factors include the environment, the family, and the individual child characteristics (e.g., affective responses, thoughts, and physical responses).

Describes Behavior and Situational Variables and Selects and Evaluates Intervention

The primary purpose of behavioral assessment is to describe and evaluate the functional links between targeted behaviors and environmental events. As such, functional assessment and analysis are viewed as primary tools within behavioral assessment. A functional approach focuses on identifying the environmental antecedents, consequences, and setting events viewed as important factors that may be functionally linked to specific behaviors. By altering the conditions that are thought to be maintaining behavior, the practitioner is able to evaluate the functional properties of the child's behavior in an explicit manner (Schill, Kratochwill, & Gardner, 1996; Stoiber & Kratochwill, in press). Once the function of the behavior is understood, a program of positive behavioral support or academic instruction are designed to help the student meet his or her needs in a more adaptive and appropriate manner.

Relies on Multimethod Strategies

A hallmark of a behavioral assessment approach is that it uses multimethod assessment strategies. This focus includes gathering data from multiple sources, such as parents, teachers, peers, and the target child. It also involves using multiple assessment methodologies, including observational data, self-report, standardized rating scales, and behavioral interviews. Relying on only one method of assessment (i.e., self-report) or one source of information (i.e., one teacher) may increase measurement error. Thus, one way of reducing this error is to use multiple methods of data collection as corroborating evidence (Stoiber & Kratochwill, 2001).

Is Nomothetic and Idiographic

Cone (1986) argued that within the field of psychology, there has historically been a debate about the relative contributions of taking an idiographic versus a nomothetic approach to understanding human behavior. However, more recent developments within the field of behavioral assessment point to the use of a wide range of both idiographic and nomothetic assessment approaches (Kratochwill & Shapiro, 2000). Idiographic approaches assess behavior on the individual level and are concerned with intraindividual variation. As such, assessment focuses on identifying the most effective interventions for a given individual with a specific problem. For example, when a student is referred to a psychologist because of disruptive classroom behavior, an idiographic approach would focus on observing the student in the context of the classroom and attempting to identify the specific functions that are linked to the child's behavior. Idiographic approaches would also focus on planning, monitoring, and evaluating interventions. Nomothetic approaches, on the other hand, focus on general principles and theories about behavior (Cone, 1986). Thus, the focus is on interindividual differences and comparing individuals to a normative group. For instance, for the student who engages in disruptive classroom behavior, a nomothetic approach includes identifying target problems based on how the student's behavior is different from his or her peers, selecting target behaviors based on the clinical significance of the problem, and evaluating the effectiveness of interventions to treat the disruptive behavior problem.

Reduces Levels of Inference

Unlike traditional assessment approaches (e.g., projective techniques), behavioral assessment strategies rely on low levels of inference about individual functioning. Assessment focuses on describing and evaluating observable behaviors and events, including the form and shape of the current behavior. Assessment also focuses on the situational factors that may influence behavior. For example, in using functional assessment to assess disruptive classroom behavior, the conclusions that are drawn are based on data used in hypothesis testing regarding the function of a behavior in a specific context. A more traditional assessment approach may focus on the innate characteristics of the individual or personality as the primary cause for disruptive behavior.

Involves Ongoing and Repeated Measurement

Behavioral assessment often involves an evaluation of behavior as ongoing, rather than a one-time event. As such, repeated measurement is an important means of monitoring a student's response to an intervention. Therefore, behavioral assessment approaches typically involve ongoing, repeated measurement before, during, and after the intervention is put into place (Kratochwill et al., 1999). Assessment should occur throughout the various stages or phases of the treatment process with outcomes evaluated across single-participant design structure (Hayes et al., 1999) or case study approaches (Stoiber & Kratochwill, 2001).

Should Be Evidence Based

Behavioral assessment strategies focus on the explicit specification of the problems that are assessed and use multiple methods for gathering data. These strategies might include direct assessment of the child, integrating data from informants who see the child under different conditions, and systematically documenting variation in behavior across different settings (Achenbach & McConaughy, 1996). Like all assessment measures, behavioral assessment methods must meet appropriate psychometric standards, such as validity of the interpretation and proposed use of assessment data (AERA, APA, NCME, 1999). Behavioral assessment measures also should display adequate test-retest reliability, internal consistency, content, and concurrent validity. Measures also should meet the standards of behavioral assessment, such as interobserver agreement, treatment validity, and social validity (Shapiro, 1996).

Is Subject to Psychometric Evaluation

Behavioral assessment methods are subject to the same psychometric standards in terms of reliability and validity as traditional assessment methods. Reliability refers to the "consistency of scores obtained by the same persons when reexamined with the same assessment device under systematically changing circumstances (e.g., different time, different items, or different examiners)." Validity of an assessment device refers to the degree to which accumulated evidence supports specific interpretations of that measure. Evaluating the quality of behavioral assessment data using traditional psychometric criteria can also be challenging. While reliability and validity assess the consistency and stability of measurement, behavior itself is often changing. Hayes, Nelson, and Jarrett suggest that it is plausible that low reliability and validity coefficients in behavioral assessment can be a function of behavior change, rather than systematic mismeasurement (see Hayes et al., 1986, for a more thorough discussion of these issues).

PHASES OF BEHAVIORAL ASSESSMENT

Traditionally, assessment has been conceptualized as occurring prior to and after an intervention is implemented. A common feature of behavioral assessment is that evaluation procedures are used throughout each stage or phase of the evaluation process. Although designation of certain phases is somewhat arbitrary, specification of phases assists in conceptualizing the assessment procedures that will be useful at certain times. The phases or steps of the assessment process presented here (see Figure 19.1) are modeled on *Outcomes: Planning, Monitoring, Evaluating* (Outcomes: PME; Stoiber & Kratochwill, 2002). The five phases include (1) describing the concern and establishing baseline, (2) setting meaningful goals and benchmarks, (3) planning the intervention, (4) monitoring progress and analyzing data, and (5) evaluating intervention outcomes. Although these phases provide structure for the assessment process, they are by no means distinct, linear stages. Instead, assessment is conceptualized as a fluid, cyclical process in which the different phases may overlap (Stoiber & Kratochwill, 2002). For example, a practitioner may return to Step 1 to further clarify the nature of the problem, or may return to Step 3 to adjust an intervention. In addition, different procedures and methods can be used during the different stages of assessment.

Describe the Concern, Identify the Context, and Establish Baseline

In the first step, the problem(s) to be solved are specified. A problem is defined broadly as a discrepancy between observed behavior and desired behavior (Shapiro & Kratochwill, 2000a). A primary objective in this phase is defining the scope and nature of the problem. This process includes iden-

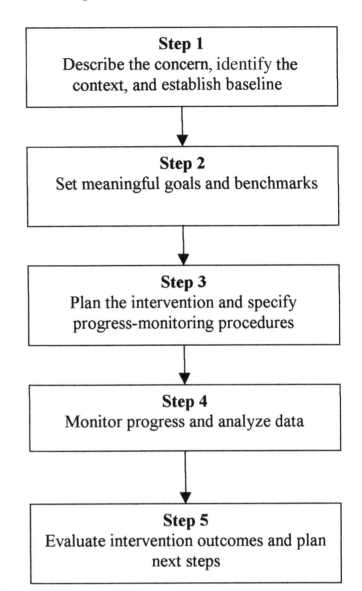

Figure 19.1   Outcomes: PME procedural process.

tifying and defining the challenging behavior(s); estimating the frequency of the behavior, identifying the conditions surrounding the behavior; and initiating baseline data collection. During Step 1, various assessment methodologies can be used. Kratochwill and McGivern (1996) review some of these strategies, which include (a) traditional diagnosis using the *Diagnostic and Statistical Manual of Mental Disorders-Fourth Edition* (*DSM-IV*), (b) empirically based assessment (e.g., standardized rating scales), or (c) behavioral assessment approaches that involve keystone target behavior selection, template matching, and functional analysis.

Over the course of the assessment, the form of the problem may shift or expand. For example, a student may be referred to a school psychologist because he knows only 3 of the 26 letters in the alphabet. The psychologist may ask the teacher, as part of a multimethod behavioral assessment, to complete the Behavioral Assessment System for Children (BASC; Reynolds & Kamphaus, 1992), a rating scale that evaluates behavior and functioning across a variety of domains. With this additional information, the teacher and psychologist together may determine that the child is also experiencing a lot of anxiety at school, which may be impacting early literacy skill development. As a result, both identified problems are the focus of additional assessment.

The purpose of this analysis is to identify the variables that facilitate a problem solution and to develop a plan to solve the problem specified in Step 3. This phase emphasizes identifying environmental factors that are contributing to the student's behavior. This process includes assessing antecedent and consequent events related to the challenging behavior in addition to ecological conditions and setting variables contributing to the problem. Assessment activities during this phase include using baseline data to establish goals, possibly conducting a functional assessment (see Stoiber & Kratochwill, in press), and designing a treatment plan. Assessment methodologies can include but are not limited to direct observations, self-monitoring, and analogue assessment (Kratochwill et al., 1999) For example, in the letter learning situation, the practitioner and the teacher may consider some behavioral principles that are effective in teaching the letters of the alphabet. For example, it may be determined that feedback and reinforcement needs to be presented in a consistent fashion or that a discrimination procedure should be developed using similar letters. Subsequently, a specific plan would be developed to implement the suggested procedures, including the conditions, time, place, and factors that facilitate generalization. Through data generated from the functional assessment, the teacher and psychologist may conclude that the student's anxiety level increases when he is asked to publicly perform academic tasks that are complex and challenging. As such, the teacher and psychologist may jointly develop a plan where the student is asked to perform academic activities for tasks that are less challenging and tasks for which he will be able to achieve a high degree of success.

Set Meaningful Goals and Benchmarks

During Step 2, the psychologist establishes a goal for treatment and the context for those goal(s). An important part of this step is developing benchmarks for evaluating the student's progress in academic and social performance. Social validity criteria are specified in this step. This process involves establishing and socially validating criteria to determine whether the behavior changes achieved during the intervention are educationally/clinically meaningful and socially acceptable. In the context of evaluating intervention outcomes, social validation consists of two procedures (Kazdin, 1977). The first is subjective evaluation, which involves the evaluation of the importance of the level and significance of a behavior change by individuals in direct contact with the student. The second includes social comparison, whereby the behavior of the student is normatively compared to the performance of a peer. The success or clinical significance of the intervention is evaluated by comparing the typical peer behavior to the targeted child's behavior at baseline, intervention, and follow-up phases to determine whether the target child's level of behavior is socially acceptable. Outcome: PME, for example, embraces a goal-attainment strategy for evaluating intervention outcomes (see Cone, 2001, and Stoiber & Kratochwill, 2002, for a discussion of goal-attainment scaling).

Plan the Intervention and Specify Progress Monitoring

During the intervention planning step, a treatment is planned and progress procedures are established. The interventions in this stage are generated from several possible sources, including, for example, functional assessment, empirical research, those identified as "evidence based" from professional task forces, and from ideas generated through collaborative teams of professionals brainstorming solutions. Data collection continues to facilitate evaluation of the effectiveness of the treatment plan. During this phase, the psychologist collaborates with the teacher to answer any questions regarding implementation of the intervention and deal with unforeseen implementation problems.

Monitor Progress and Analyze Data

Once an intervention has been implemented, it must be evaluated to understand its effectiveness in addressing the challenging behavior or academic concern. Treatment evaluation provides an accountability system for evaluating child outcomes. Evaluation activities include assessing goal-attainment scaling, evaluating intervention integrity, and determining whether the intervention was responsible for the observed changes. Assessment methodologies during this step can include direct observational measures, rating scales, or interviews established in Step 3. Within a behavioral assessment paradigm, direct measures of behavior (i.e., direct observation, self-monitoring) are used with indirect methods (i.e., rating scales or interviews), with the indirect methods being used as corroborating evidence of the intervention's success.

Evaluate Intervention Outcomes and Plan Next Steps

The fifth stage in behavioral assessment is assessing outcomes and planning the next steps. In most cases, an intervention program that results in positive change in a significant behavior will also result in changes in other behaviors. For example, it is possible that an intervention program that reduces aggressive incidents in the classroom will also reduce such aggression on the playground, if it was occurring there. More likely, however, generalization will need to be programmed to maximize the transfer of newly acquired skills and behaviors. Nevertheless, it is insufficient to assess the primary target behaviors because the effects of the total intervention program must be judged by their pervasive influence on behavior beyond the target behavior(s).

The dimensions to be assessed during this phase include both situations and individuals. As such, the psychologist evaluates the degree to which this transfer occurs across different situations and with other individuals. Sometimes it is desirable to assess behavior changes other than those targeted for intervention. For example, an intervention that focused on one child in the classroom may have effects on peers, and therefore should be assessed. Assessment strategies used during the generalization phase of behavioral assessment should primarily focus on direct measures of behavior in naturalistic settings. Thus, self-monitoring and direct observations are preferred, but other assessment methods might well be used depending on time, cost, and practical considerations.

Like generalization, follow-up represents an important aspect of behavioral assessment. Although follow-up is sometimes thought of as a passive phenomenon, it can be viewed as one dimension of generalization over time. In this regard, it represents a form of maintenance across time and is subject to the same factors that can be used to facilitate generalization across settings and individuals. Follow-up can occur at many different times. It is recommended, however, that follow-up assessment be conducted soon after the activities of the intervention program are terminated. Thereafter, measures can be taken over weeks, months, or even years, depending on the student and the nature of the problem. The measures obtained are typically narrow in focus and are similar to those used during the treatment evaluation phase. Like generalization assessment, direct methods in natural environments are preferred. However, various considerations such as cost and time may lead the assessor to use interview, self-report, and rating scale measurement.

Case Study Application to Outcomes: PME

This case study illustrates the development of a treatment plan for a kindergarten girl, Paula, experiencing selective mutism in the classroom. Selective mutism is a childhood problem characterized by not speaking in select situations and/or to certain people. Paula was brought to the attention of the building consultation team (BCT) at Brooks Elementary School by Paula's teacher, who is interested in and willing to try an intervention in the classroom and has spoken to Paula's parents about the need for services. Paula's academic skills are well developed, and she appears to have no other problems other than the social phobia related to speaking in the school and, according to her parents, in the community.

The BCT, consisting of the classroom teacher, the school psychologist, the speech and language specialist, and the building principal, have decided to meet and develop an intervention program focused on Paula's speech in the classroom. Outcomes: PME was chosen as the structure for the case. Figure 19.2 includes a completed record form that illustrates the application of the five steps of Outcomes: PME to one major goal of the intervention program designed for Paula.

METHODS USED IN ASSESSMENT

Techniques within behavioral assessment can be categorized on a dimension of directness. Specifically, behavioral assessment methods may be ordered along a continuum of directness representing the extent to which they (a) measure clinically and educationally relevant behavior and (b) measure behavior at the time and place of its natural occurrence. In this conceptualization, the various behavioral assessment methods are categorized as either direct or indirect (see Figure 19.3). Interviews and rating scales that involve self-report and informant report would be classified as indirect methods of assessment. In both of these strategies, a particular behavior is observed or reported, but that behavior is a verbal representation of a clinically/educationally relevant activity taking place at some other time or place. Rating behaviors using standardized rating scales takes place after the behavior occurs, rather than at the same time and place of its occurrence.

In contrast, direct methods involve measuring behavior at the time that it is actually occurring. The most common form of direct assessment occurs when individuals are assessed in the natural environment where their behavior is free to vary without imposed contingencies from the practitioner or teacher. Assessing a child's behavior in the classroom or at home would be an example of this form of assessment. This approach often requires minimal inferences to interpret what is being observed (Shapiro & Kratochwill, 2000c). Because certain behaviors are challenging to observe in the natural en-

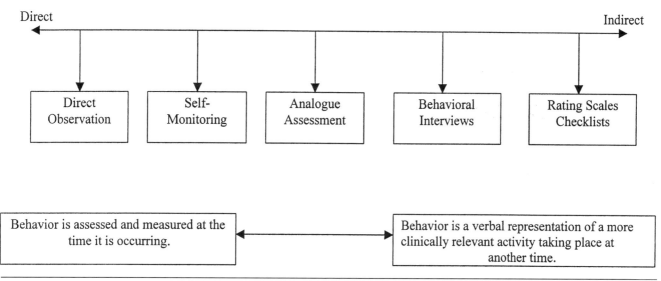

Figure 19.2   Outcomes: PME record form.

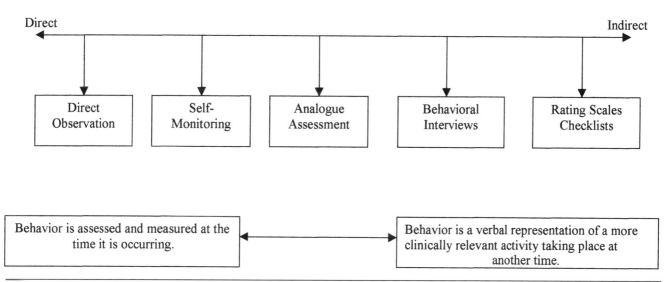

Figure 19.3   Behavioral assessment methods ordered along a continuum of directness.
Note. From *Handbook of Behavior Modification With the Mentally Retarded,* by E.S. Shapiro and J.L. Browder, 1990, pp. 93–120. New York: Plenum Press. Copyright 1990 by Plenum Press. Adapted with permission.

vironment, such as low frequency events, a practitioner may assess the student in a setting or situation that is analogous to, but not the same as, the natural environment. This situation, which has been contrived to facilitate assessment of some clinically relevant behaviors, is referred to as an analogue setting. For example, a clinic office may include a playroom that is similar to a play situation in the natural environment, or the psychologist may have the child and significant others respond as they normally would in a situation similar to the "real" or natural environment.

A third form of direct assessment includes self-monitoring. This form of assessment occurs when the observer and the observee are the same person. It should be emphasized that self-monitoring differs from self-report in that self-monitoring is an observation of a clinically or educationally relevant behavior, which is assessed at the time of its occurrence by the individual. The student may keep a journal, mark a card, complete a checklist, or use a mechanical counter to record behavior. Self-report, on the other hand, is an indirect measure in which behavior is described retrospectively.

METHODS OF BEHAVIORAL ASSESSMENT

The remainder of this chapter will focus on the most common methods used in behavioral assessment in educational settings: (1) direct observation, (2) behavioral interviews, (3) behavioral checklists and rating scales, (4) self-monitoring, and (5) analogue assessment.

Direct Observation

One of the most prominent features of behavioral assessment is the collection of data regarding overt behaviors and performance (Kazdin, 1981; Ollendick & Cerney, 1981). As such, direct observation is one of the most widely used behavioral assessment procedures with a substantial literature base (e.g., Daly & Murdoch, 2000; Mash & Terdal, 1997; Skinner, Rhymer, & McDaniel, 2000). Reid, Baldwin, Patterson, and Dishion (1988) noted that best practice in the domain of direct observation includes recording behaviors in their natural settings, at the time they occur, using trained impartial observers, and using descriptions of behavior that require little if any inference. Typically, when using direct observation systems, the target behaviors have already been determined during earlier phases of the assessment. Based on the comprehensiveness of the observation system, other student behaviors and the behavior of other individuals (i.e., peers, teachers, siblings) may be recorded to determine the functional links between the problem behaviors and environmental variables (Stoiber & Kratochwill, in press).

Differentiating Between Observation Procedures and Observation Instruments

One important issue in direct observation approaches is differentiating observation procedures from observational instruments (Kratochwill et al., 1999). Most professionals have used some type of observational procedures in their assessment work. This assessment may take the form of direct observation of a child in a classroom or asking a parent or teacher to record the occurrence of some behavior. Although observational measurement procedures may vary on a number of dimensions (e.g., the observer, the target response, the sophistication and complexity of the rating form), they are most commonly used as part of the general observational assessment. In contrast to these observational procedures are observational instruments, which typically focus on a narrow range of problems and have standardized coding systems that accompany them. An important consideration in the decision to use an observation instrument or system is the extent to which it is appropriate and has been validated for a specific

situation or problem (Kratochwill et al., 1999; Mash & Terdal, 1988).

Observation Procedures

When considering the different observation procedures that are available, it is critical to first determine the type of information to collect about the target behavior. Those dimensions of behavior include rate, duration, latency, topography, and intensity. The type of information a psychologist wants to gather will guide the choice of the numerous observational procedures that are available. Although a detailed review of those procedures is beyond the scope of this chapter, interested readers may consult Saudergas and Lentz (1986), Schloss and Smith (1998), and Shapiro (1996). Table 19.1 illustrates some of the inherent strengths and limitations of different observation procedures.

Narrative Recording. Narrative or anecdotal recording involves the observation and noting of behaviors in a descriptive fashion. Events are typically recorded in a chronological order, as they occur, with a particular emphasis on critical

TABLE 19.1 Strengths and Limitations of Different Observation Procedures

Procedure	Strengths and Limitations
Narrative Recording	Provides rich information about behaviors and can help evaluate the function of behaviors. These procedures are time consuming, difficult to quantify, and challenging to interpret.
Event Recording	Appropriate when target behaviors have a discrete beginning and ending. Provides important information about frequency. It is difficult to rate continuous, long-lasting, or inconsistent behaviors using event recording procedures. Does not provide information on opportunity to exhibit behavior.
Duration/ Latency Recording	Appropriate when assessing behaviors in which duration of response is the target of intervention. Useful in measuring the effects of classroom-wide interventions. Difficult to implement while teaching because observer is required to attend to time and behavior. Behaviors without a clear beginning and end should not be rated using this procedure.
Interval Recording	Provides frequency and duration data, which can be used when behaviors do not have discrete beginnings and endings. Facilitates observer training and reliability estimates. More time efficient than duration/latency recordings. Accuracy may be decreased because of overestimates or underestimates of the occurrence of specific behaviors.
Time Sampling Recording	Can be used for observing multiple students or multiple behaviors simultaneously. More time efficient than interval recording procedures. Accuracy may be decreased because of overestimates or underestimates of the occurrence of specific behaviors.

incidents that emerge. Schloss and Smith (1998) review four major purposes of narrative recording: (a) confirming that a hypothesized problem exists, (b) revealing antecedent and setting events that are linked to the problem, (c) evaluating events that reinforce or consequate the behavior, and (d) identifying replacement behaviors for disruptive responses. *Antecedent behavior consequence* recording is a widely used method for structuring narrative recording, and, as noted above, it is part of the functional assessment process. In this type of recording, the observer notes the antecedents, or events that immediately precede the behavior; the target behavior itself; and the consequences, or events that follow the behavior. Antecedent behavior consequence analysis is often useful in establishing the plausible function(s) of the target behavior. Narrative recording procedures are often used as an initial recording procedure because they do not require a precise behavioral definition. Drawbacks of narrative recording procedures are that they are time consuming, difficult to quantify, and, without structure, they can be relatively difficult to interpret (Schloss & Smith, 1998).

Event Recording. Event recording procedures measure the number of occurrences of a behavior during a specific time period. *Frequency recording* involves counting the occurrence of a specific behavior over a period of time. For example, a problem behavior might be defined as a student who grabs food from other students during lunchtime. *Percentage occurrence* is another form of event recording that should be used when the opportunity to perform a behavior varies across an environment or situation. In this case, data are expressed as a ratio that can be converted into a percentage. An example includes a student who exhibits noncompliance with teacher directions and is observed during recess complying with 5 out of 10 directives (50%) versus math class, when he complies with 4 out of 5 directives (83%). *Rate data* is another form of event recording that can produce more educationally and clinically meaningful data than frequency and percentage occurrence methods. Rate data involve dividing frequency counts by the time observed (Skinner, Rhymer, & McDaniel, 2000). In the example above, three instances of noncompliant behavior within a 10-minute time interval is suggestive of a more serious problem than three instances of noncompliant behavior during a 60-minute interval. Event recording procedures are most appropriate when the target behavior has a discrete beginning and ending (e.g., completing math problems or raising one's hand to be called on). Behaviors that are continuous or occur for a longer duration of time are more difficult to rate using an event recording procedure (Hintze & Shapiro, 1995).

Duration/Latency Recording. Unlike event recording procedures, which focus on how often a behavior occurs, duration/latency procedures measure increases or decreases in the amount of time a child is engaged in a behavior (Schloss & Smith, 1998). *Duration recording procedures* measure the length of time a behavior occurred (e.g., Bobby studied his social studies for 15 minutes). *Latency recording procedures,* on the other hand, measure the length of time between an event and the onset or completion of a behavior (e.g., the teacher told Sue to put her book away and get out her reading; 5 minutes later Sue was ready with her reading materials). In duration or latency recording, the observer needs a clear definition of when the behavior begins and ends. Duration measures are helpful when assessing behaviors in which duration of the response is likely to be the target of the intervention. Examples of those behaviors include temper tantrums, social isolation, or aggression (Hintze & Shapiro, 1995).

Interval Recording. Interval recording measures the number or percentage of intervals within which a behavior occurred (e.g., John was working on his math for 14 of the 30 intervals observed). In this type of procedure, the observer determines the observation session and interval length based on the approximate length of the behavior. In *whole interval recording procedures,* the behavior must be occurring or not occurring for the entire interval in order for the behavior to be scored as present or absent. In contrast, *partial interval recording procedures* require that any single or multiple occurrence of the behavior during the time interval constitutes coding the behavior as present (Hintze & Shapiro, 1995). When using interval recording procedures, observations are completed in an "observe-record" sequence where an amount of time is prespecified.

Time Sampling. Time sampling, also known as momentary time sampling procedures, measures the number of times a behavior occurs at a prespecified point in time. An example of this would be "when observed once every 5 minutes, Lynn was attending to her work for 12 of 15 observations." Using this type of recording procedure, observations are divided into a series of shorter time intervals. Time sampling is often used to rate behaviors that do not have a clear beginning or ending or when time or practical issues preclude continuous observation.

Example Observational Instruments

In the past, direct observation recording systems have been relatively simplistic. However, recent trends in the field of behavior analysis have established the need for more complex recording systems. Advances in laptop computer technology have made these computers ideal for collecting observational data in applied settings. The EcoBehavioral Assessment System Software (EBASS) and the State-Event Classroom Observation System (SECOS), both of which use laptop computers and a more complex recording system, will be reviewed because of their particular relevance to conducting behavioral assessment in applied settings.

EcoBehavioral Assessment System Software (EBASS).
EBASS is a series of observation instruments designed to assess instructional and student academic outcomes (Greenwood, Carta, Kamps, Terry, & Delquadri, 1997). The EBASS system includes a computer software system for three classroom observation instruments. The Code for Instructional Structure and Student Academic Response (CISSAR) is most appropriate for observing general education settings, the Mainstream Version of CISSAR (MS-CISSAR) is used to assess students with special needs, and the Ecobehavioral System for Complex Assessments of Preschool Environments (ESCAPE) is designed for assessing preschool or kindergarten students. The EBASS system provides a detailed analysis of various classroom and instructional characteristics, including the instructional subject, curricular materials used, grouping practices, and teacher proximity to the students. The EBASS system also codes student behaviors, such as response format and engagement (Greenwood et al., 1997). EBASS provides percentage occurrence data, level of academic engagement, and variability in student behavior across different settings. The EBASS is used by psychologists to assess students' responses to different instructional programs and to evaluate intervention outcomes. In addition, it can be used to conduct a functional assessment and to evaluate system-wide change (Kratochwill et al., 1999).

State-Event Classroom Observation System (SECOS).
The SECOS (Saudargas, 1992; Saudargas & Creed, 1980) is another observational instrument commonly used in educational settings. This instrument allows a psychologist to gather data on multiple behaviors simultaneously. The SECOS divides observed student behaviors into two categories: "states" and "events." A state is defined as a behavior that a student can engage in for different lengths of time (i.e., completing schoolwork) and is coded using a momentary time sampling procedure. Events are discrete occurrences of a particular behavior (i.e., calling out of turn). The SECOS also records teacher behavior, including proximity, use of praise, and use of consequences. Both of these instruments have educational

and research applications but require intensive training of observers.

Strengths and Limitations of Direct Observation

The direct nature of observation gives this method a clear advantage over other procedures that require higher levels of inference. In addition, direct observation provides invaluable information about the rate, frequency, and duration of behavior, in addition to the functional links between setting events and the behavior. Research has also shown that direct observation has greater face validity for assessing intervention outcomes than more indirect methods (Barton & Ascione, 1984). Direct observational methods also do a better job of evaluating the social validity of interventions. By using local norms and peer comparisons, an observer can establish whether the behavior warrants intervention and whether the intervention produces changes that are clinically meaningful (Kazdin, 1977).

Issues of reliability often emerge when considering data gathered through direct observation. Several variables, such as observer bias, drift, location, and presence can confound the data gathered through direct observation (Barton & Ascione, 1984). Observer bias is present when the observer is systematically influenced by sources of data other than the occurrence of the target behavior. These variables include knowledge of the expected outcomes or feedback from the psychologist regarding the target behavior. Expectancy errors or the tendency to identify anticipated changes regardless of the actual occurrence of the behavior also introduces error into observation procedures (Schloss & Smith, 1998). Observer drift includes the gradual altering of the definition of the target behavior(s), the standards for defining the behavior, or changes in vigilance of observations. For example, over time, an observer may become more or less stringent in his or her definition of the problem behavior. These systematic sources of error can be minimized through periodic training, monitoring, and random reliability checks.

One of the most serious limitations to direct observation procedures is the reactivity associated with the presence of an observer in an applied setting. Suggestions for increasing the reliability and validity of direct observational data include the following: (1) using less obtrusive observation methods such as observers who are already present in the setting or using analogue observations, (2) increasing the number of observation sessions as reactive effects are most likely to occur during the initial sessions, (3) increasing the number of observers, (4) withholding from the observers information about intervention plans, and (5) using standardized observational procedures. Methods for evaluating the reliability of observation data involve calculating interobserver agreement, which is the extent to which independent observers agree on the occurrence or duration of a behavior. See Schloss and Smith (1998) for a detailed explanation of how to calculate interobserver agreement based on the observational procedure used.

Behavioral Interviews

Interviewing parents, teachers, and the child is common practice in educational settings. At times, it may be the only mechanism for obtaining information from individuals who have intimate knowledge of the problem behavior under investigation. The interview is often the first contact point for obtaining information about the problem, as well as the antecedents and consequences controlling those behaviors. Interviews are the primary methodology for behavioral or problem solving models of psychological consultation in educational settings (see Bergan & Kratochwill, 1990; Kratochwill & Bergan, 1990). Despite the popularity of interviews, there is a paucity of research related to behavioral interviewing and the informal strategies by which behavioral interviews are commonly conducted (Beaver & Busse, 2000; Kratochwill et al., 1999). In addition, while some systems present a conceptual framework for conducting a behavioral interview, few formal guidelines and standardized protocols exist in the area of behavioral interviewing (Kanfer & Grimm, 1977).

Characteristics

Two primary characteristics of behavioral interviews are their level of structure and their level of focus. Behavioral interviews vary in their level of structure, which can be defined as the overall flexibility with which the interview is conducted. This structure includes the order in which items are administered, the question and response format, and the degree to which the examiner structures the interview process. *Unstructured interviews* do not follow a standardized format; instead the interviewee responds freely to questions and leads the discussion. In practice, unstructured interviews are quite common. Because unstructured interviews are highly flexible and tailored to the individual situation, they can yield richer data regarding the child's functioning. A major drawback of unstructured interviews is that it is more difficult to measure reliability and validity. For example, it is difficult to compare information across different interviewees because different topics may have been covered.

Semistructured interviews have a standard format that allows for flexibility in questioning and responding. For example, the interviewee has the discretion to change the order of the questions or may ask follow-up questions as needed. The Behavioral Consultation Interview (Bergan & Kratochwill, 1990) and the Semistructured Clinical Interview for Children and Adolescents (McConaughy & Achenbach, 1994) are examples of semistructured behavioral interviews. The strength of semistructured interviews is that they are flexible, while maintaining a structured format. *Structured* interviews have a standardized method for asking questions along with fixed response options. Structured interviews are most often used in research and tend to have stronger psychometric properties because of their standardized format.

In addition, interviews can be characterized in terms of their level of focus. Behavioral consultation interviews, for example, have a high degree of focus. These interviews are usually narrow in focus and scope, and a limited number of problems are typically assessed. Problem-solving interviews often begin with a broad focus, as the interviewee discusses and explores his or her concerns. However, as the interview progresses, it becomes more focused, with the goal of identifying a problem and generating a plan for intervention. Interviews with a low degree of focus include case histories, in which general developmental information is obtained in many different domains of the child's functioning.

Behavioral Consultation Interviews

The Behavioral Consultation Model (Bergan & Kratochwill, 1990) provides a method for formalizing the verbal interactions occurring during the behavioral interview. The problem-solving model is designed to assist teachers and parents in defining problem behaviors, formulating and implementing plans to solve the identified problems, and evaluating various intervention goals and the effectiveness of educational programs. The consultation interview format is a conceptual system for intervening with a variety of problems through interview methodology. In this regard, the approach is particularly useful in assessing and intervening with learning and behavior problems. Consultative problem solving may focus on the achievement of long-range developmental goals, or it may center on the specific concerns of immediate importance to the child, parent, or teacher.

Behavioral consultation is procedurally standardized through semistructured interviews during the three stages of the consultation process: problem identification, problem analysis, and intervention evaluation. The goals of the Problem Identification Interview (PII) include defining the problem in behavioral terms, tentatively identifying setting variables, establishing the strength of the behavior, and establishing data collection procedures. The goals of the Problem Analysis Interview (PAI) include reviewing baseline data, validating the existence of the problem, analyzing the problem in terms of variables that are influencing it, designing an intervention plan, and establishing behavioral goals. The final stage of the Behavioral Consultation Model is the Treatment Evaluation Interview, which focuses on evaluating the student's progress in meeting his or her goals, evaluating the effectiveness of the intervention plan, and making plans for post-implementation.

Problem Identification Interview (PII) Example

The case presented in Figure 19.4 is an excerpt from a Problem Identification Interview that is occurring conjointly between a parent, a teacher, and a consultant. The child in the case is "Mark," a 6-year-old boy referred to a psychologist by his teacher because of her concerns regarding his excessive fearfulness of monsters and spiders. This excerpt illustrates the process of discussing a presenting problem and narrowing the focus to a target behavior that is measurable and manageable (Sheridan, Kratochwill, & Bergan, 1996).

Strengths and Limitations of Behavioral Interviews

Behavioral interviews have several important strengths. First, interviews help assess an interviewee's beliefs and perceptions about the problem behavior or concern. Second, variation in the informant's verbal and nonverbal behavior can be examined in relation to the interviewer's questions, thereby allowing an analysis of responding and lines of further inquiry. Third, interviews help the evaluator assess motive, function, and low-frequency events, in addition to resolving ambiguity and clarifying misunderstandings that may emerge during the interview process. Fourth, behavioral interviews, and especially the Behavioral Consultation Interviews can have a high degree of treatment utility because the assessment process is clearly linked to intervention (Kratochwill et al., 1999). Finally, interviews, because of their interactive nature, help establish rapport and promote the development of a personal relationship with the informant. This is in contrast to direct observation, for example, where there is limited interaction between the interviewer and the informant.

Although behavioral interviewing, like all assessment methods, should be subject to psychometric scrutiny, one of the major obstacles in evaluating behavioral interviews is the absence of a coherent literature base (Busse & Beaver, 2000). Bias, or systematic mismeasurement, is one of the most serious limitations to interview methodology. Bias is related to the interviewee in the form of distortion, selective memory, or demand characteristics. The interviewer can also encourage or discourage certain responses in an interview. In addition, recording errors can introduce mismeasurement into

the interview process (Sattler, 1992). Validity issues that must be evaluated in the context of behavioral interviewing include concurrent validity (i.e., do interview data correspond with data obtained from other methods?), treatment validity (i.e., do interview data effectively map onto the design of appropriate interventions and successful outcomes?) and predictive validity (i.e., does the information from an interview predict an intervention or outcome?) (Sattler, 1992).

Behavioral Rating Scales

Behavioral rating scales are an indirect assessment procedure because individuals retrospectively describe clinically relevant behavior that occurred at another time and place (Merrell, 2000). Rating scales provide a standardized format for summarizing and evaluating behavior and are often used to gather information about behaviors that are infrequent or difficult to observe. Currently, rating scales are an integral part of the assessment process in schools and applied settings. It is important to make the distinction between checklists and rating scales. Checklists use dichotomous ratings to indicate the presence or absence of a specific behavior. Rating scales, however, are structured so that responses fall on an ordinal scale. This structure provides more information about the nature and degree of the problem (Kratochwill et al., 1999). Behavioral rating scales will be the focus of discussion in this chapter.

Characteristics

Rating scales vary on several important dimensions. The first dimension is the informant. The parent, the teacher, the clinician, a naïve observer, or the target child can complete rating scales. Although some behavioral rating scales are developed for use with specific informants, most include parallel forms to be completed by multiple informants. Rating scales also vary in the scope or range with which they assess behavior. A common distinction made between different scales is whether they are broadband or narrowband measures. Broadband rating scales are comprehensive measures of general behavior that assess a wide variety of problems. These instruments help identify behavioral assets and weaknesses in addition to identifying specific behaviors worthy of further assessment. Some examples of broadband ratings scales frequently used in practice include the Child Behavior Checklist (Achenbach, 1991a, 1991b, 1991c; Achenbach & Edelbrock, 1980), the Behavioral Assessment System for Children (BASC; Reynolds & Kamphaus, 1992); and the Behavioral Evaluation Scale-2 (McCarney & Leigh, 1990).

Consultant: What are some of the things that you're concerned about?

Parent: Well, actually, the only thing that I'm concerned about with Mark is the fact that he does not like or want to go to bed in his own room by himself at night.

Consultant: Mm Hmm.

Parent: As I've told his teacher, he seems to have a genuine fear of something or someone, you know, monsters, I mean. He has even rigged up these elaborate traps in his room.

Consultant: Mm. hmm.

Parent: You know, string going all over the place to catch the monsters.

Consultant: Mm.

Parent: That really is my only concern with him, and . . .

Teacher: He actually told me that one time something actually grabbed his ankle from under the bed.

Parent: Oh.

Teacher: That he knew it was real because it grabbed him and it wasn't, he said, "It's not my imagination, something grabbed me."

Parent: Really?

Teacher: Yeah.

Parent: I, I just, I don't know what to do. I've done all kinds of things, you know . . . we've had our little chart, and, "Gee, if you go to bed tonight and sleep in your bed . . . all night, if you stay there . . ."

Consultant: Mm hmm. Mm hmm.

Parent: ". . . you get up in the morning, then you'll get a star and if you get . . ." You know, first we start out with just one day at a time, okay, if he did it for that night he got a star, or . . . something special that night, okay, then we try two days and then we try three days . . .

Consultant: Mm hmm.

Parent: . . . and after a week, you know, he'd get something special but it never got to a week.

Consultant: Mm hmm. How far did you get with him?

Parent: Oh, I don't remember, I think we got four or five days . . . I think we got like five days, and then probably what happened was the weekend came and we are much less structured on the weekend. . . . On the weekend we just kind of, you know, hang loose and we don't have a set bedtime and things like that. And then that maybe broke the cycle. But like I say, he seems to have a genuine fear.

Later in the interview:

Consultant: Okay, another example [of irrational fears] is that he sets traps in his room to catch the monster?

Parent: Yes.

Consultant: And comes to school and talks about tarantulas?

Parent: When it's a little spider.

Consultant: Okay. I guess there's a few different directions that we could go. One would be . . . it sounds like the bedtime routine is the one you're most concerned with.

Parent: Mm hmm. And then staying, you know, in bed, if he awakens at night.

Consultant: Okay, so staying in bed would be the goal that you might have.

Parent: Going to bed in his bed and staying there, yes.

Consultant: Okay. I think that would be a real manageable kind of thing to try to work out, because it's specific and we'd know if he's doing it or not.

Parent: Oh yes, yeah.

Consultant: So rather than trying to address this global kind of fear that he has . . .

Parent: Mm hmm.

Figure 19.4   Example of a Problem Identification Interview (PII) conducted conjointly with a parent, teacher, and consultant.
Note. From *Conjoint Behavioral Consultation,* by S.M. Sheridan, T.R. Kratochwill, and J.R. Bergan, 1996, pp. 116–117. New York: Plenum Press. Copyright 1996 by Plenum Press. Reprinted with permission.

Narrowband behavioral rating scales, on the other hand, include an in-depth assessment of a specific aspect of behavior. These are often used to assess infrequent behaviors, identify target behaviors and intervention goals, and monitor intervention outcomes. Narrowband behavioral rating scales are available to assess a wide variety of behaviors, including problems with attention and hyperactivity (e.g., Conners' Rating Scales-Revised; Conners, 1997), social skills (e.g.,

Social Skills Rating System; Gresham & Elliott, 1990), academic competence (e.g., Academic Competence Evaluation Scales, DiPerna & Elliott, 2000), depression (e.g., Reynolds Child Depression Scale; Reynolds, 1989, & Reynolds Adolescent Depression Scale; Reynolds & Richmond, 1987), and anxiety (Revised Children's Manifest Anxiety Scale; Reynolds & Richmond, 1985). A comprehensive review of these measures can be found in several sources (e.g., Barkley, 1988; Breen & Fiedler, 1996; Mash & Terdal, 1997).

Behavioral rating scales boast a wide range of uses. It is suggested that because rating scales are relatively low cost in terms of time and training, in addition to having strong psychometric qualities, they are an ideal tool for screening (Merrell, 2000). These instruments can be used to identify students within a school or school district who are exhibiting moderate to high levels of a problem behavior and are in need of additional assessment and intervention. Although behavioral rating scales should not be used as a single form of evidence for making diagnostic or classification decisions, they are often an important source for making these decisions. Merrell argues that best practice in using rating scales to make classification or diagnostic decisions dictates the use of multiple raters across multiple settings as converging evidence.

Behavioral ratings scales also can be used to select interventions. For example, the Academic Competence Evaluation Scales (DiPerna & Elliott, 2000) assesses a student's level of competency in specific academic domains, which provides a framework for initial decisions regarding the types of skills in need of intervention. Behavioral rating scales also lend themselves to monitoring progress and evaluating outcomes. For example, repeated measures of behavior using standardized rating scales can help evaluate the child's progress in meeting intervention goals. Continuous measurement is also useful because it facilitates the alteration of interventions that have not been successful in helping students reach desired goals (Merrell, 2000). Rating scales are also used as part of follow-up, to measure the degree to which behavioral change is maintained and generalized over time and across different settings.

Rating scales also have been developed to evaluate treatment acceptability, or the degree to which interventions are perceived as fair, appropriate, and effective (Elliott & Busse, 1993; Kazdin, 1980). Treatment acceptability is an important aspect of monitoring consultation-based interventions because it can have a strong impact on the use and possible effects of an intervention (Elliott, 1998). Figure 19.5 is an example of the Intervention Rating Profile (IRP-15), which is a rating scale that evaluates treatment acceptability.

Strengths and Limitations

Important advances in the research and development of rating scales have made them a popular and widely used behavioral assessment tool (Merrell, 2000). First, they have a broad range of uses, which makes them particularly attractive. Second, they are an economical, efficient assessment tool in terms of time, cost, and the amount of training required to administer and score them. Third, many rating scales utilize multiple informants, which helps reduce measurement error and provide a more complete picture of the child's functioning across multiple settings. Fourth, behavioral rating scales often provide normative comparisons to measure deviance or severity of behaviors. Fifth, rating scales are often relatively easy to quantify, which facilitates evaluation and comparison of data gathered using other measures. Sixth, rating scales can be used to collect data on the social validity of interventions or the degree to which an intervention is socially acceptable (Kazdin, 1977; Wolf, 1978). For example, several rating scales ask raters to indicate the importance of the behavior and the significance of behavior change (e.g., Social Skills Rating System, Gresham & Elliott, 1990; Academic Competence Evaluation Scales, DiPerna & Elliott, 2000).

Some cautions should be considered when using and interpreting data derived from behavioral rating scales. First, because rating scales are an indirect form of assessment in which data are gathered retrospectively, they require higher levels of inference. Second, behavioral rating scales provide a summary of observations of the relative frequency of specific behaviors, rather than being more objective accounts of behavior (Kratochwill et al., 1999). Third, although they provide data on situational differences in behavior, most behavioral rating scales do not adequately assess the function of behaviors, which has important implications for selecting appropriate interventions. Fourth, rating scales are often vulnerable to reporting bias, including halo effects, reporting extremes, and reporting central tendencies. Modifications to the scale construction can help alleviate these problems—for example, by including 4-point scales instead of 3-point scales. In addition, several newer rating scales (e.g., BASC, Reynolds & Kamphaus, 1992) include measures that allow a practitioner to evaluate the general quality of the data generated from a rating scale. Specific indexes also help determine the degree to which a respondent tended to systematically rate behaviors in a positive or negative manner. Kratochwill et al. (1999) argue that many of these limitations can be addressed by using standardized behavioral rating scales within the context of a multidimensional and multimethod framework, which would include parental, teacher, and child reports; cognitive

The purpose of this questionnaire is to obtain information that will aid in the selection of classroom interventions. These interventions will be used by teachers of children with behavior problems. Please circle the number which best describes your agreement or disagreement with each statement.

	Strongly Disagree	Disagree	Slightly Disagree	Slightly Agree	Agree	Strongly Agree
1. This would be an acceptable intervention for the child's problem behavior.	1	2	3	4	5	6
2. Most teachers would find this intervention appropriate for behavior problems in addition to the one described.	1	2	3	4	5	6
3. This intervention should prove effective in changing the child's problem behavior.	1	2	3	4	5	6
4. I would suggest the use of this intervention to other teachers.	1	2	3	4	5	6
5. The child's behavior problem is severe enough to warrant use of this intervention.	1	2	3	4	5	6
6. Most teachers would find this intervention suitable for the behavior problem described.	1	2	3	4	5	6
7. I would be willing to use this intervention in the classroom setting.	1	2	3	4	5	6
8. This intervention would *not* result in negative side-effects for the child.	1	2	3	4	5	6
9. This intervention would be appropriate for a variety of children.	1	2	3	4	5	6
10. This intervention is consistent with those I have used in classroom settings.	1	2	3	4	5	6
11. The intervention was a fair way to handle the child's problem behavior.	1	2	3	4	5	6
12. This intervention is reasonable for the behavior problem described.	1	2	3	4	5	6
13. I liked the procedures used in this intervention.	1	2	3	4	5	6
14. This intervention was a good way to handle this child's behavior problem.	1	2	3	4	5	6
15. Overall, this intervention would be beneficial for the child.	1	2	3	4	5	6

Figure 19.5   The Intervention Rating Profile (IRP-15).
Note. From *Advances in school psychology,* by J.C. Witt and S.N. Elliott, 1985, pp. 251–288. Hillsdale, NJ: Erlbaum. Copyright 1985 by Lawrence Erlbaum Associates, Inc. Reprinted with permission.

assessment; physical assessment; and direct observation of the child.

Self-Monitoring

Self-monitoring refers to assessing or recording one's own behavior. It requires that an individual identify and then record occurrences of the targeted behavior. This procedure is re-

garded as a direct assessment procedure because the behavior is recorded at the time of its occurrence. Self-monitoring is often used in the context of assessment and intervention with various behaviors, including academic tasks, engagement, and social skills. When self-monitoring is used as an assessment method, a student would collect data on a particular behavior. Cole, Marder, and McCann (2000) assert that self-monitoring may occur in the context of the functional assess-

Ordinal Self-Rating Form

Rate yourself on a scale from 0 to 2 on how well you paid attention during math class.

   0 = I did not pay attention
   1 = I paid attention fairly well
   2 = I paid attention extremely well

	Math 9:00–10:00 A.M.	Reading 10:00–11:00 A.M.
Monday		
Tuesday		
Wednesday		
Thursday		
Friday		

Frequency Self-Monitoring Form

Make a mark beside each day for the number of math problems completed during math class.

	Math 9:00–10:00 A.M.
Monday	////
Tuesday	//// ///
Wednesday	//// ////
Thursday	///
Friday	//// //// ///

Interval Self-Monitoring Form

Each time a signal is given, place a ✔ beside the signal number if you were working at your desk since the last time you heard the signal.

Monday	Tuesday	Wednesday	Thursday	Friday
1	1	1	1	1
2	2	2	2	2
3	3	3	3	3
4	4	4	4	4
5	5	5	5	5
6	6	6	6	6
7	7	7	7	7
8	8	8	8	8

Figure 19.6   Examples of self-monitoring recording devices.

ment process, to collect baseline data, or to assess antecedents and consequences of a particular behavior. The majority of recording devices and methods used for self-monitoring in educational settings include paper-and-pencil procedures, such as record booklets, checklists, calendars, timers, and scales (Cole et al., 2000). Self-monitoring can include frequency ratings (i.e., Sally tallies the number of math problems she completed during math class), ordinal ratings (i.e., John rates himself on a scale of 0 to 3 on how well he paid attention during math class), and interval ratings (i.e., when signaled, Sue rates whether she remained seated in her desk since the last signal). Examples of these recording devices are illustrated in Figure 19.6.

When self-monitoring is used as an intervention method, the goal is to teach students to change, maintain, or control their own behavior (Shapiro & Cole, 1994). Several theories have emerged in the literature that explain the positive effects of self-monitoring. First, self-information provides immediate feedback, which can function as positive reinforcement. In addition, there are reactive effects of self-monitoring, whereby the act of observing and recording one's own behavior, or increasing attention to one's own behavior, causes behavior to change. Self-monitoring used as an intervention often has the broad goal of helping students regulate their own learning and behavior independently.

Strengths and Limitations

The advantages of self-monitoring have been noted in the literature (see Cole & Bambara, 2000; Kern, Marder, Boyajian, Elliot, & McElhattan, 1997; Shapiro & Cole, 1994). An important strength of self-monitoring procedures is that they reduce immediate external contingencies associated with conventional behavioral management approaches. Moreover, these procedures are perceived as advantageous because of the reduction in demands made on teachers (Shapiro & Cole, 1994). In addition, with a decreasing reliance on external contingencies, self-monitoring procedures increase the likelihood that students will develop self-management skills and portable coping strategies with the potential to generalize to other settings (Kern et al., 1997).

The limitations of self-monitoring procedures relate to accuracy and reactivity. The utility of self-monitoring assessment and intervention strategies depends on the accuracy with which students are able to monitor their own behavior. To date, research has been inconclusive in determining the accuracy of children's ability to monitor their own behavior. For example, several studies have found that students presenting with a variety of behaviors and levels of functioning are able to accurately self-monitor specific target behaviors (see Carr & Punzo, 1993; Cole & Bambara, 2000). However, other studies have found children and adolescents to vary in the degree to which they were able to accurately self-monitor target behaviors (see McDougall & Brady, 1995). Reactivity is a second problem that emerges in self-monitoring assessment methods. Reactivity is a problem when unintended or unwanted influences result from self-recording, and the data are not representative of data that would have occurred had self-monitoring not been used. The use of independent observers to collect baseline and intervention data help control for the effects of reactivity.

Analogue Assessment

Analogue assessment is conceptualized as indirect measurement procedures that demonstrate how an individual might react or behave in a real life situation (Hintze & Shapiro, 1995). Broadly speaking, analogue measures assess behavior in an artificial or hypothetical situation with the goal of mimicking the real-life situation in which the target behavior occurs. For example, analogue assessment is often used as an alternative to direct observation measures as a means of gathering data. Although Cone (1978) argued that direct observation within the natural setting provides the most ecologically valid form of data within the domain of behavioral assessment, certain behaviors are difficult to observe directly (Hintze, Stoner, & Bull, 2000). These include low-frequency events, behaviors that occur in settings to which the psychologist does not have access (i.e., school bus), and complex constructs (Kratochwill et al., 1999). Similar to the other behavioral assessment approaches reviewed in this chapter, analogue assessment procedures emphasize evaluating how children learn, how they will benefit from changes to the instructional or social environment, and why the student is experiencing those problems (Gettinger & Seibert, 2000). As such, there is a fundamental emphasis on linking the assessment procedures with an intervention.

Example of Analogue Assessment Procedures for Evaluating Academic Skills Problems

Many forms of traditional assessment, such as cognitive and achievement measures, can be considered analogue measures. Such tools assess behavior under controlled conditions, which may occur in other settings. The analogue assessment procedures for evaluating academic skills problems that will be reviewed in this chapter include criterion-referenced measures and curriculum-based assessment methods.

Criterion-Referenced Measures. Criterion referenced measures are one method for conducting behavioral assessments within an analogue framework. These measures are used to compare a student's performance against an established standard of performance that reflects mastery of a skill rather than a normative comparison used in norm-referenced testing (Shapiro, 1996). Criterion-referenced measures are usually precise measures of discrete skills and competencies used to identify an individual's level of mastery in a specific domain (e.g., math). These measures are a form of analogue assessment that is closely aligned with, but not limited to, a behavioral orientation (Kratochwill et al., 1999).

Curriculum-Based Assessment. Curriculum-based assessment (CBA) is another method for conducting an analogue behavioral assessment. CBA is considered an alternative to more traditional, norm- or criterion-referenced assessments because, even though it generates numerical data, these data are not compared with national norms or any external criterion (Joshi, 1995). These approaches involve direct, continuous assessment of a performance that is tied to the current curriculum. Several models are associated with CBA, including, for example, the resource teaching model (Idol-Maestas, 1981), data-based program modification (Deno, Marston, & Tindal, 1986), and the problem-solving model (Shinn, 1995). Although a thorough review of the different CBA models is beyond the scope of this chapter, interested readers should consult the original sources, in addition to Fuchs and Fuchs (2000), Shapiro (1996), Shapiro and Elliott (1999), and Shinn (1989). The standardized formats of CBA procedures are referred to as Curriculum Based Measurement (Shapiro, 1989). The advantage of the standardized procedures is that validity and reliability indices are available (Joshi, 1995).

The multiple uses of CBA methods include screening, classification, instructional planning, and progress monitoring (Gickling & Rosenfield, 1995). Most importantly, CBA methods should focus on providing meaningful data to guide instructional intervention. One benefit of CBA methods is that they are closely aligned with the local curriculum, are cost and time efficient, allow for frequent administration in order to monitor progress, and are sensitive to changes in skill level over time (Stoiber & Kratochwill, 2002). CBAs are also advantageous to use in the context of behavioral assessment because they can be administered across time for purposes of progress monitoring (Kratochwill et al., 1999). Thus, pre- and postintervention data can be graphed in a time-series fashion to help systematically evaluate progress on goals and to make decisions regarding intervention.

Over the years, several criticisms of CBA methods have emerged. The first issue is the lack of normative data provided in this type of assessment. CBA methods also have limitations in terms of goal setting and outcome assessment. For example, because CBA methods evaluate academic skills, this approach may not provide a comprehensive picture of the broader context of the instructional environment and domains to target for remediation (Shapiro, 1996). As such, CBA methods should be supplemented with assessment data that provide a more comprehensive picture of the student's functioning in multiple contexts (e.g., behavioral rating scales, behavioral consultation interviews, direct observation).

Authentic or Performance Assessment

Performance assessment provides students with real-life problem solving and decision-making situations, which require them to "develop solutions that involve the application and integration of multiple skills and strategies" (Fuchs & Fuchs, 2000, p. 182). Performance assessment is often seen as a form of authentic assessment in which a student's behavior and performance is observed directly. The primary goal of performance assessment is to inform an evaluator (who is usually a teacher) about the different strategies and processes invoked by the student, versus only providing information about isolated skills. Performance assessment requires students to construct responses rather than select them (Fuchs & Fuchs, 2000). Another important goal of performance assessment is to encourage instruction that includes learning activities that extend into real-life situations.

Assessment methods subsumed under performance assessment include portfolio assessment, performance-based grading benchmarks, and self-assessment (Kratochwill et al., 1999). *Portfolio assessment* is based on a collection of a student's work selected by the student and/or teacher. Marzano (1994) recommended that portfolio assessment should (a) include nonschool items, such as extracurricular projects completed at home or in the community, (b) be used to evaluate performance on curricular and personal goals, and (c) be individualized to meet the unique learning needs of the students. *Performance-based grading benchmarks* replace traditional grades (where performance is compared with normative standards, such as peer performance) with predetermined criteria, which determines mastery (Kratochwill et al., 1999). *Self-assessment* is another method used in performance assessment, in which students review and analyze their own work based on explicit learning objectives and outcomes. Self-assessment is often accomplished through rubrics, which are statements that specify the criteria associated with different levels of proficiency for evaluating performance (McTighe, 1997).

Fuchs and Fuchs (2000) outline some of the major advantages of using performance assessment: (a) measuring skill

application and integration that closely reflects desired educational outcomes, (b) relying on assessment strategies that have authentic, real-world, meaningful implications, and (c) providing information on student strategies and processing of learning. Because performance assessment is relatively new, it still needs to be evaluated systematically. Fuchs and Fuchs (2000) also outline some fundamental limitations of this type of assessment. First, the degree to which performance assessment provides adequate information regarding skill acquisition is still unknown. Second, performance assessment does not provide adequate information regarding the reasons why a skill was not acquired. For example, performance assessment does not provide insight into the function of the behavior and whether the child's failure to demonstrate a particular skill was the result of a performance or skill deficit. This lack of information limits an educator's ability to design and evaluate an intervention. Third, this form of assessment is neither time nor cost efficient, which has direct implications for the acceptability of this assessment method. Teachers must devote a great deal of time to designing and administering the assessment, in addition to developing unique strategies for assessing performance and evaluating accuracy.

FINAL PERSPECTIVES

In this chapter we have provided an overview of the common behavioral assessment methodologies used in schools and other applied settings. Because behavioral assessment represents a diverse set of procedures and techniques, there is no single definition of behavioral assessment. However, there are unifying concepts that underlie these procedures. Behavioral assessment procedures are often used as an alternative or adjunct to more traditional assessment methodologies. Behavioral assessment procedures allow a psychologist to assess behavior across diverse settings and with diverse clients. In addition, these methods are popular because of their treatment utility. Future research in the area of behavioral assessment must continue to advance the knowledge base regarding the psychometric qualities of these procedures. Specifically, more research needs to be conducted on the reliability and validity of these assessment methodologies. It is likely that these procedures will continue to gain popularity as empirical advances in behavioral assessment are made.

REFERENCES

Achenbach, T.M. (1991a). *Integrative guide for the 1991 CBCL/4– 18, YSR, and TRF profiles.* Burlington: University of Vermont Department of Psychiatry.

Achenbach, T.M. (1991b). *Manual for the Child Behavior Checklist/ 4–18 and 1991 Profile*. Burlington: University of Vermont Department of Psychiatry.

Achenbach, T.M. (1991c). *Manual for the Teacher's Report Form and the 1991 Profile*. Burlington: University of Vermont Department of Psychiatry.

Achenbach, T.M., & Edelbrock, C. (1980). *Child Behavior Checklist of Ages 4–16*. Burlington: University of Vermont Department of Psychiatry.

Achenbach, T.M., & McConaughy, S.H. (1996). Relations between *DSM-IV* and empirically based assessment. *School Psychology Review, 25,* 329–342.

American Educational Research Association, American Psychological Association, and National Council on Measurement in Education. (1999). *Standards for educational and psychological testing* (3rd ed.). Washington, DC: Author.

American Psychiatric Association (1994). *Diagnostic and statistical manual of mental disorders* (4th ed.). Washington, DC: Author.

Barkley, R.A. (1988). Child behavior rating scales and checklists. In M. Rutter, A.H. Tuma, & I.S. Lann (Eds.), *Assessment and diagnosis in child psychopathology* (pp. 113–155). New York: Guilford Press.

Barton, E.J., & Ascione, F.R. (1984). Direct observation. In T.H. Ollendick & M. Hersen (Eds.), *Child behavioral assessment: Principles and procedures*. New York: Pergamon Press.

Beaver, B.R., & Busse, R.T. (2000). Informant reports: Conceptual and research bases of interviews with parents and teachers. In E.S. Shapiro & T.R. Kratochwill (Eds.), *Behavioral assessment in schools: Theory, research, and clinical foundations* (pp. 257–287). New York: Guilford Press.

Bergan, J.R., & Kratochwill, T.R. (1990). *Behavioral consultation and therapy*. New York: Plenum Press.

Breen, M.J., & Fiedler, C.R. (1996). *Behavioral approach to assessment of youth with emotional/behavioral disorders: A handbook for school-based practitioners*. Austin, TX: Pro-ed.

Busse, R.T., & Beaver, B.R. (2000). Informant report: Parent and teacher interviews. In E.S. Shapiro & T.R. Kratochwill (Eds.), *Conducting school-based assessments of child and adolescent behavior* (pp. 235–273). New York: Guilford Press.

Carr, S.C., & Punzo, R.P. (1993). The effects of self-monitoring of academic accuracy and productivity on the performance of students with behavior disorders. *Behavior Disorders, 18,* 241–250.

Chambless, D.L., & Ollendick, T.H. (2001). Empirically supported psychological interventions: Controversies and evidence (Electronic version). *Annual Review of Psychology, 52,* 685–716.

Cole, C.L., & Bambara, L.M. (2000). Self-Monitoring. In E.S. Shapiro & T.R. Kratochwill (Eds.), *Behavioral assessment in schools: Theory, research, and clinical foundations* (pp. 202–232). New York: Guilford Press.

Cole, C.L., Marder, T., & McCann, L. (2000). Self-monitoring. In E.S. Shapiro & T.R. Kratochwill (Eds.), *Conducting school-based assessments of child and adolescent behavior* (pp. 121–149). New York: Guilford Press.

Cone, J.D. (1978). The behavioral assessment grid (BAG): A conceptual framework and a taxonomy. *Behavior Therapy, 9,* 882–888.

Cone, J.D. (1986). Idiographic, nomothetic, and related perspectives in behavioral assessment. In R.O. Nelson & S.C. Hayes (Eds.), *Conceptual foundations of behavioral assessment* (pp. 111–128). New York: Guilford Press.

Cone, J.D. (2001). *Evaluating outcomes: Empirical tools for effective practice*. Washington, DC: American Psychological Association.

Conners, C.K. (1997). *Conners' Rating Scales-Revised Technical Manual*. North Tonawanda, NY: Multi-Health Systems.

Daly, E.J., & Murdoch, A. (2000). Direct observation in the assessment of academic skills problems. In E.S. Shapiro & T.R. Kratochwill (Eds.), *Behavioral assessment in schools: Theory, research, and clinical foundations* (pp. 46–77). New York: Guilford Press.

Deno, S.L., Marston, D., & Tindal, G. (1986). Direct and frequent curriculum-based measurement: An alternative for educational decision making. *Special Services in the Schools, 2,* 5–27.

DiPerna, J.C., & Elliott, S.N. (2000). *The Academic Competence Evaluation Scales (ACES)*. San Antonio, TX: Psychological Corporation.

Elliott, S.N. (1998). Acceptability of behavioral treatments in educational settings. In J.C. Witt & S.N. Elliott (Eds.), *Handbook of behavior therapy in education* (pp. 121–150). New York: Plenum Press.

Elliott, S.N., & Busse, R.T. (1993). Effective treatments with behavioral consultation. In J.E. Zins, T.R. Kratochwill, & S.N. Elliott (Eds.), *Handbook of consultation services for children* (pp. 179–203). San Francisco: Jossey-Bass.

Fuchs, L.S., & Fuchs, D. (2000). Analogue assessment of academic skills: Curriculum-based measurement and performance assessment. In E.S. Shapiro & T.R. Kratochwill (Eds.), *Behavioral assessment in schools* (pp. 168–201). New York: Guilford Press.

Gettinger, M., & Siebert, J.K. (2000). Analogue assessment: Research and practice in evaluating academic skills problems. In E.S. Shapiro & T.R. Kratochwill (Eds.), *Behavioral assessment in schools: Theory, research, and clinical foundations* (pp. 139–167). New York: Guilford Press.

Gickling, E.E., & Rosenfield, S. (1995). Best practices in curriculum-based assessment. In A. Thomas & J. Grimes (Eds.), *Best practices in school psychology* (Vol. 3, pp. 587–595). Washington, DC: National Association of School Psychologists.

Greenwood, C.R., Carta, J.J., Kamps, D., Terry, B., & Delquadri, J. (1997). *EcoBehavioral Assessment System Software (EBASS) practitioner's manual*. Kansas City, KS: Juniper Gardens Children's Project.

Gresham, F.M., & Elliott, S.N. (1990). *Social Skills Rating System manual*. Circle Pines, MN: American Guidance Service.

Hayes, S.C., Barlow, D.H., & Nelson-Gray, R.O. (1999). *The scientist practitioner: Research and accountability in the age of managed care*. Boston: Allyn & Bacon.

Hintze, J., & Shapiro, E.S. (1995). Best practices in the systematic observation of classroom observation. In A. Thomas & J. Grimes (Eds.), *Best practices in school psychology III* (pp. 651–660). Washington, DC: National Association of School Psychologists.

Hintze, J.M., Stoner, G., & Bull, M.H. (2000). Analogue assessment: Research and practice in evaluating emotional and behavioral problems. In E.S. Shapiro & T.R. Kratochwill (Eds.), *Behavioral assessment in schools: Theory, research, and clinical foundations* (pp. 104–138). New York: Guilford Press.

Idol-Maestas, L. (1981). A teacher training model: The resource consulting teacher. *Behavioral Disorders, 6,* 108–121.

Joshi, R.M. (1995). Assessing reading and spelling skills. *School Psychology Review, 24,* 361–375.

Kanfer, F.H., & Grimm, L.G. (1977). Behavior analysis: Selecting target behaviors in the interview. *Behavior Modification, 1,* 7–28.

Kazdin, A.E. (1977). Assessing the clinical or applied importance of behavior change through social validation. *Behavior Modification, 1,* 427–452.

Kazdin, A.E. (1980). Acceptability of alternative treatments for deviant child behavior. *Journal of Applied Behavior Analysis, 13,* 259–273.

Kazdin, A.E. (1981). Behavioral observation. In M. Hersen & A.S. Bellack (Eds.), *Behavioral assessment: A practical handbook* (pp. 101–124). New York: Pergamon Press.

Kern, L., Marder, T.J., Boyajian, A.E., Elliot, C.M., & McElhattan, D. (1997). Augmenting the independence of self-management procedures by teaching self-initiation across settings and activities. *School Psychology Quarterly, 12,* 23–32.

Kratochwill, T.R., & Bergan, J.R. (1990). *Behavioral consultation in applied settings: An individual guide.* New York: Plenum Press.

Kratochwill, T.R., & McGivern, J.E. (1996). Clinical diagnosis, behavioral assessment, and functional analysis: Examining the connection between assessment and intervention. *School Psychology Review, 25,* 342–355.

Kratochwill, T.R., & Shapiro, E.S. (2000). Conceptual foundations of behavioral assessment in schools. In E.S. Shapiro & T.R. Kratochwill (Eds.), *Behavioral assessment in schools: Theory, research, and clinical foundations* (pp. 3–18). New York: Guilford Press.

Kratochwill, T.R., Sheridan, S.M., Carlson, J., & Lasecki, K.L. (1999). Advances in behavioral assessment. In C.R. Reynolds & T.B. Gutkin (Eds.), *The handbook of school psychology* (pp. 350–382). New York: Wiley.

Kratochwill, T.R., & Stoiber, K.C. (2000). Empirically-supported interventions and school psychology: Conceptual and practical issues—Part II. *School Psychology Quarterly, 15,* 233–253.

Marzano, R.J. (1994). Commentary on literacy portfolios: Windows on potential. In S.W. Valencia, E.H. Hiebert, & P.P. Afflerbach (Eds.), *Authentic reading assessment: Practices and possibilities* (pp. 41–45). Newark, DE: International Reading Association.

Mash, E.J., & Terdal, L.G. (Eds.). (1988). *Behavioral assessment of childhood disorders* (2nd ed.). New York: Guilford Press.

Mash, E.J., & Terdal, L.G. (Eds.). (1997). *Assessment of childhood disorders* (3rd ed.). New York: Guilford Press.

McCarney, S.B., & Leigh, J.E. (1990). *The Behavior Evaluation Scale* (2nd ed.). Columbia, MO: Hawthorne Educational Services.

McConaughy, S.H., & Achenbach, T.M. (1994). *Manual for the Semistructured Clinical Interview for Children aged 6–11.* Burlington: University of Vermont Department of Psychiatry.

McDougall, D., & Brady, M.P. (1995). Using audio-cued self-monitoring for students with severe behavior disorders. *Journal of Educational Research, 88,* 309–317.

McTighe, J. (1997). What happens between assessments? *Educational Leadership, 54(4),* 6–12.

Merrell, K.W. (2000). Informant reports: Theory and research in using child behavior rating scales in school settings. In E.S. Shapiro & T.R. Kratochwill (Eds.), *Behavioral assessment in schools: Theory, research, and clinical foundations* (pp. 233–256). New York: Guilford Press.

Ollendick, T.H., & Cerney, J.A. (1981). *Clinical behavior therapy with children.* New York: Plenum Press.

Reid, J.B., Baldwin, D.V., Patterson, G.R., & Dishion, T.J. (1988). Observations in the assessment of childhood disorders. In M. Rutter, A.H. Tuma, & I.S. Lann, *Assessment and diagnosis in child psychopathology* (pp. 156–195). New York: Guilford Press.

Reynolds, C.R. (1989). *Professional manual for the Reynolds Child Depression Scale.* Odessa, FL: Psychological Assessment Resources.

Reynolds, C.R., & Kamphaus, R.W. (1992). *Behavior assessment system for children.* Circle Pines, MN: American Guidance Service.

Reynolds, C.R., & Richmond, B.O. (1985). *Revised Children's Manifest Anxiety Scale.* Los Angeles: Western Psychological Services.

Reynolds, C.R., & Richmond, B.O. (1987). *Professional manual for the Reynolds Adolescent Depression Scale.* Odessa, FL: Psychological Assessment Resources.

Sattler, J.M. (1992). *Assessment of children: Revised and updated third edition.* San Diego: Author.

Saudargas, R.A. (1992). *State-Event Classroom Observation System (SECOS).* Knoxville: University of Tennessee, Department of Psychology.

Saudargas, R.A., & Creed, V. (1980). *State-Event Classroom Observation System.* Knoxville: University of Tennessee, Department of Psychology.

Saudargas, R.A., & Lentz, F.E. (1986). Estimating percent of time and rate via direct observation: A suggested observational procedure and format. *School Psychology Review, 15,* 36–48.

Schill, M.T., Kratochwill, T.R., & Gardner, W.I. (1996). Conducting a functional analysis of behavior. In M.J. Breen & C.R. Fiedler (Eds.), *Behavioral approach to assessment of youth with emo-*

tional/behavioral disorders: A handbook for school-based practitioners (pp. 83–180). Austin, TX: Pro-ed.

Schloss, P.J., & Smith, M.A. (1998). *Applied behavior analysis in the classroom.* Boston: Allyn & Bacon.

Shapiro, E.S. (1989). *Academic skills problems: Direct assessment and intervention.* New York: Guilford Press.

Shapiro, E.S. (1996). *Academic skills problems: Direct assessment and intervention.* New York: Guilford Press.

Shapiro, E.S., & Browder, J.L. (1990). Behavioral assessment: Applications for persons with mental retardation. In J.L. Matson (Ed.), *Handbook of behavior modification with the mentally retarded* (pp. 93–120). New York: Plenum Press.

Shapiro, E.S., & Cole, C.L. (1994). *Behavior change in the classroom: Self-management interventions.* New York: Guilford Press.

Shapiro, E.S., & Elliott, S.N. (1999). Curriculum based assessment and other performance-based assessment strategies. In C.R. Reynolds & T.B. Gutkin (Eds.), *The handbook of school psychology* (pp. 383–408). New York: Wiley.

Shapiro, E.S., & Kratochwill, T.R. (Eds.). (2000a). *Behavioral assessment in schools: Theory, research and clinical foundations.* New York: Guilford Press.

Shapiro, E.S., & Kratochwill, T.R. (Eds.). (2000b). *Conducting school-based assessments of child and adolescent behavior.* New York: Guilford Press.

Shapiro, E.S., & Kratochwill, T.R. (2000c). Introduction: Conducting a multidimensional behavioral assessment. In E.S. Shapiro & T.R. Kratochwill (Eds.), *Conducting school-based assessments of child and adolescent behavior* (pp. 1–20). New York: Guilford Press.

Sheridan, S.M., Kratochwill, T.R., & Bergan, J.R. (1996). *Conjoint behavioral consultation.* New York: Plenum Press.

Shinn, M.R. (1989). *Curriculum-based measurement: Assessing special children.* New York: Guilford Press.

Shinn, M.R. (1995). Best practices in curriculum-based measurement and its use in a problem-solving model. In A. Thomas & J. Grimes (Eds.), *Best practices in school psychology* (Vol. 3, pp. 547–567). Washington, DC: National Association of School Psychologists.

Skinner, C.H., Rhymer, K.N., & McDaniel, E.C. (2000). Naturalistic direct observation in educational settings. In E.S. Shapiro & T.R. Kratochwill (Eds.), *Conducting school-based assessments of child and adolescent behavior* (pp. 21–54). New York: Guilford Press.

Stanger, C. (1996). Behavioral assessment: An overview. In M.J. Breen & C.R. Fiedler (Eds.), *Behavioral approach to assessment of youth with emotional/behavioral disorders: A handbook for school-based practitioners* (pp. 3–22). Austin, TX: Pro-ed.

Stoiber, K.C., & Kratochwill, T.R. (2000). Empirically supported interventions and school psychology: Rationale and methodological issues—Part I. *School Psychology Quarterly, 15,* 75–105.

Stoiber, K.C., & Kratochwill, T.R. (2002). *Outcomes: Planning, monitoring, evaluating.* San Antonio, TX: Psychological Corporation.

Stoiber, K.C., & Kratochwill, T.R. (in press). *Functional assessment and intervention system.* San Antonio, TX: Psychological Corporation.

Witt, J.C., & Elliott, S.N. (1985). Acceptability of classroom intervention strategies. In T.R. Kratochwill (Ed.), *Advances in school psychology* (pp. 251–288). Hillsdale, NJ: Erlbaum.

Wolf, M.M. (1978). Social validity: The case for subjective measurement or how applied behavior analysis is finding its heart. *Journal of Applied Behavior Analysis, 11,* 203–214.

CHAPTER 20

Behavioral Neuropsychology

MICHAEL D. FRANZEN

There are gross commonalities between neuropsychological and behavioral assessment. Broadly stated, neuropsychological assessment involves the evaluation of cognitive, behavioral, and emotional variables related to central nervous system function. Behavioral assessment is the evaluation of observable psychological phenomena for the purposes of delineating the influence and control of environmental variables. By examining these two definitions we can see that the overlap or interface between the two would be in the phenomena under consideration, rather than in the constructs underlying the process.

As a part of qualifying the definition, we can also ask what is a neuropsychological test and what is a behavioral assessment instrument? In what may be an apocryphal anecdote, a famous clinical neuropsychologist replied in response to the former question that a neuropsychological test is a test that a neuropsychologist uses. When we ask more broadly, what is a test? we are reminded of the statement from Cronbach that a test is a systematic method of comparing behavior across persons, situations, or time. Viewed in that way, there would seem to be much in common between traditional neuropsychological assessment and behavioral assessment. However, given the different paths along which these two forms of assessment have diverged, such a view of commonality also requires that we keep one eye closed and cock our heads to the side. It is the purpose of this chapter to highlight the commonalities and to describe some fruitful venues for col-

laboration, but to do so in a way that utilizes level-headed and open-eyed perception. Furthermore, it is proposed that the two areas would be improved by consideration of each others' conceptions and operations. This chapter will not be an exhaustive review of either neuropsychological or behavioral assessment. Instead this chapter will present an overview of commonalities and differences between the two forms of assessment. It will also present a clinical paradigm for the fruitful collaboration of the two areas. Earlier publications either reviewed applications of behavioral treatment to individuals with acquired brain impairment (Franzen, 1991) or reviewed application of assessment to the treatment of these individuals (Franzen & Smith-Seemiller, 1998). This chapter will discuss methodological and conceptual differences and similarities while also describing some fruitful interaction between the two.

Two misconceptions need to be dispelled before proceeding. The first misconception is that neuropsychological tests are meant to be interpreted blindly, and the second is that neuropsychologists are involved only in assessment and not in treatment. Despite being commonly held, the first misconception is egregiously untrue. Perhaps because research regarding the validation of neuropsychological tests frequently involves blind diagnosis using only test data, it is frequently thought that neuropsychological assessment comprises the interpretation of standardized test data. Certainly, standardized test data are an important component in many neuropsychological assessments. However, every clinical neuropsychological assessment additionally involves either a review of history or a personal interview in which historical factors are elicited. Furthermore, neuropsychological assessment also frequently includes consideration and interpretation of qualitative data. In fact, the conduct of a clinical neuropsychological assessment can also include behavioral observation and use of a behavioral coding system. That which makes a clinical neuropsychological assessment is the relation of the data or their interpretation to physiological and structural aspects of the central nervous system.

The second unfounded misconception is that neuropsychologists are concerned only with assessment, and not concerned with treatment. While that had been true when the field was in its nascent stages, it is not true currently. Clinical neuropsychologists are now involved in treatment in rehabilitation facilities; providing psychotherapy to patients with closed head injury, stroke, tumor, and dementia; and teams that use pharmacological treatment for dementia and seizure disorder. A corollary of the misconception is that behavioral assessment is only worthwhile in the context of an applied treatment setting, when actually behavioral assessment is also useful in diagnosis of different neurocognitive conditions as well as in furthering our understanding of these conditions.

Similarly, behavioral assessment is probably better characterized by its level of inference than by its methods. Although the hallmark of behavioral assessment is usually direct behavioral observation in real time, multiple modalities are currently available, including behavioral checklists using information from collateral sources, behavioral products, physiological monitoring, and portable computers (Haynes, 1998). There is some overlap between neuropsychological instruments and behavioral instruments in the form of behavioral checklists, physiological instruments, and collateral sources, so where is the difference between the two? Actually, large differences exist between the two systems of assessment, such that an individual trained in one is unlikely to be able to competently use the other. Yet it is not the technology that separates the two types of practitioners; it is the conceptualization and the knowledge base needed to complete the respective assessments.

One obvious commonality of the two approaches is that general psychological processes underlie the constructs being assessed in both. This point may seem so obvious as to be trite or even tautological, but, in fact, keeping this in mind is helpful in working with both sets of data. There may be central mechanisms that exert influence over these two realms of psychological assessment data. For example, neurocognitive, functional/adaptive, and behavioral decline are all related to changes in the quantitative spectral EEG in patients

with early Alzheimer's disease (Claus et al., 1998). As further evidence that psychological/behavioral and cognitive variables are related, the presence of cognitive impairment and the presence of behaviors related to depression are associated with greater mortality in the elderly (Arfken, Lichtenberg, & Tancer, 1999), presumably because both depression and cognitive impairment reflect central nervous system dysfunction and decline.

Another fascinating, but less well understood, phenomenon is that poor performance on the clock-drawing test (Freedman et al., 1994) is associated with paranoid and delusional ideation in patients with Alzheimer's disease (Heinik et al., 2001). Because this correlation is not seen with paranoid ideation and other forms of cognitive function, it is likely that some central mechanism is responsible for both. Identifying cognitive tests that are related to extra-test behavior is an increasing focus for neuropsychology as the field becomes more focused on ecological validity (Franzen & Wilhelm, 2000). The identification of these tests will not supplant functional assessment, but will instead help screen patients for the need for the assessment of adaptive living skills. McGinty, Podell, Franzen, Baird, and Williams (2002) report that, of a battery of clinical neuropsychological measures, the Trail Making Test B and the Wisconsin Card Sorting Test predicted functional status in older adults, whereas other neuropsychological tests—including tests of memory—did not.

Yet another similarity between neuropsychological assessment and behavioral assessment (though one that is not well recognized) is that both types of assessment attempt to bridge two general realms of phenomena. Neuropsychological assessment attempts to bridge the psychological and physiological realms, and behavioral assessment attempts to bridge psychological and environmental realms. Both of these attempts are ambitious in design and far-reaching in scope.

COMPARISON OF THEORIES OF MEASUREMENT

Michell (1986) discussed three general theories of measurement as applied to psychological assessment. Under classical theory, the numbers resulting from the measurement process are thought to reflect some underlying concept. Representational theory posits that the numbers are useful for describing empirical relations among the objects of measurement. Here it is not important whether the numbers reflect some abstract construct, only that the numbers are accurate in depicting lawful relations among phenomena. In the third major theory of measurement, operational theory, the numbers are the result of the operations involved in the measurement process, and they neither have an inherent meaning nor reflect an abstract construct. Franzen (2000) has discussed the implications of neuropsychological assessment having as its basis the classical theory. Suffice it to say here that numbers in clinical neuropsychological assessment are thought to reflect a position along a continuum of skill. A T-score of 50 on the Word page of the Stroop Color Word Test (Golden, 1978) indicates a skill level that is exactly average.

On the other hand, the theory of measurement inherent in behavioral assessment is operational. The numbers produced by the measurement operation signify nothing, and their meaning is discernable only in the context of assessment. The number of deep sighs produced by the subject of a behavioral assessment has no meaning until we consider that the number decreased under conditions of self-monitoring and increased under conditions of conspicuous observers.

This set of differences is not absolute. In neuropsychological assessment, the consideration of qualitative features and pathognomonic signs is clearly from the operational theory. In behavioral assessment, the comparison of obtained numbers to normative information is sometimes useful as would be the case when behavioral checklists are interpreted or self-report instruments are used to determine appropriate treatment targets. Furthermore, both neuropsychological and behavioral assessment sometimes seem to function under the representational theory.

However promising the similarities, the presence of this type of difference is fairly fundamental and represents a significant disjunction between the two areas. The numbers in the two types of assessment are conceptualized very differently. It is partly for this reason that the combination of neuropsychological and behavioral assessment is not more common.

COMPARISON OF LEVELS OF INFERENCE

It is usually stated that behavioral assessment involves a lower level of inference, and this is sometimes misunderstood as indicating that behavioral assessment does not involve the use of abstract constructs. In fact, there are constructs involved in behavioral assessment, but these constructs are highly related to observable phenomena. For example, a behavioral assessment coding system for evaluating hyperactive behaviors in school children may utilize the construct of "in-seat behavior" as one of its targets. This concept of "in-seat behavior" is still abstract in that it is comprised of reading at one's desk, listening to a teacher's explanation while seated in the chair, and may or may not include standing with one foot in the aisle and one foot on the seat of the chair or talking with one's neighbor while seated in the chair at the desk. On

the other hand, neuropsychological assessment may include a more discrete and less abstract behavior such as correctly repeating a list of seven words that had been presented orally, but the interpretation includes inferences about the integrity of certain brain structures and the action of certain neurochemical operations as well as psychological functions.

DIAGNOSIS AND TREATMENT TARGET SELECTION

Neuropsychological assessment traditionally has been used in a consultative diagnostic manner. Behavioral assessment has been used to identify target behaviors and to specify the relation of targets to environmental events and processes. As a practical concern, most clinical situations will require some form of diagnosis and some method of identifying treatment targets. The diagnosis may not be sufficient to develop a treatment plan, but it will help limit the choices to be evaluated. For example, once the neuropsychological assessment determines the diagnosis of Alzheimer's disease, the clinician can focus on the areas of memory impairment, personal safety, and wandering behavior as possible targets for treatment. Other areas such as delusions, depression, or irritability may be in need of treatment, but the diagnosis carries with it a collection of problem areas with associated probabilities that these problems may be present in the current situation.

The methods of assessment can be similar across both neuropsychological and behavioral assessment. Both forms of assessment may use observer ratings or self-report. There may be a general relation between the content of the area of interest and the method of assessment. For example, the assessment of cognitive skills is more likely to utilize observer ratings, whereas the evaluation of cognitive processes or affective state is more likely to use self-report. Furthermore, this relation is common to both neuropsychological and behavioral assessment.

Because it is in the theories of measurement that the two types of assessment are different, and it is in the methods that the two types of assessment are similar, it would seem that the greatest arena for combination of the two would be in the clinical realm. In the clinical setting it is frequently important to provide a diagnosis as well as to identify treatment targets and provide a baseline of pretreatment levels of the target. Here, despite the differences, neuropsychological assessment and behavioral assessment can be fruitfully combined. This combination may be complementary or supplementary; it may be sequentially or concurrently applied. But in the clinical arena, if the best interest of the patient is pursued, both types of assessment may be necessary. Let us examine the interaction between neuropsychological assessment and behavioral assessment in individuals with closed head injury, in individuals with progressive dementia, and in individuals with developmental disorders.

OVERVIEW OF APPLICATIONS

The first application of combined assessment models is in the delineation of relative strengths and weaknesses. The clinical neuropsychological assessment can show whether verbal memory or visual-spatial memory is a greater strength for the patient. The behavioral assessment can identify those situations in which impaired memory is resulting in disability for the patient so that a program of substituting visual memory for verbal memory increases the adaptation of the patient to that environment.

A second application is in matching skill levels to environmental demands. Let's consider the example of a patient who has experienced a moderate closed head injury with resulting attentional deficits. In a work setting it may be important for the patient to maintain attention on a drill press while ignoring background noise. Furthermore, more than one task at a time may be required in this particular work setting—for example, the patient may need to monitor the rate of speed of production in order to make decisions about accessing other workers to the project. All of this information is acquired through the functional analysis, which is matched with the neuropsychological test data, which indicate that sustained attention is not a deficit although the abilities to multitask and to screen extraneous distractions are deficits. The environment can be modified to reduce the demands on this particular worker and provide a better match with the worker's skills.

As part of understanding these forms of assessment we can compare and contrast behavioral and traditional neuropsychological assessment activities (dependent measures of intensity, frequency, accuracy, absence/presence) in assessment. In clinical neuropsychological assessment, an individual may be asked to generate a list of words that begin with a single letter. The dependent measure is the number of accurate responses in a given amount of time (frequency). The patient may also be asked to squeeze a dynamometer with one hand at a time (intensity). The patient may be shown a simple line drawing of geometric forms and be asked to reproduce that design in an immediate recall condition and after a 30-minute delay. The dependent measure uses a standardized scoring system to produce a quantitative index of similarity of the reproduced design to the original stimulus (accuracy). Additionally, the reproduction is examined for instances of perseveration, simplification of the design, or visual-spatial construction errors (absence/presence).

The behavioral assessment of the same individual may include a measure of the number of times the patient emits self-derogatory comments in a given time period (frequency). The rater may assign an index related to observations of level of effort expended by the patient during the task (intensity). The finished product in a work task may be compared to a model (accuracy). In each instance a similar index or measurement was used, but to slightly different purposes, in the same person.

Rehabilitation of Brain-Impaired Individuals

Improvement in Skills Areas

The cognitive deficits resulting from closed head injury include memory impairment, attentional difficulties, and executive dysfunction. The behavioral deficits include social skills, initiation deficits, and planning. Not all of these deficits are present in all patients. Furthermore, depending upon the degree of impairment and the demands from the patient's environment following acute treatment, even if some deficits are present, treatment might be more fully directed to some other area. An important consideration is the set of demands from the environment and the capacity of the patient to independently meet those demands.

In many instances there might be an association between cognitive impairment and functional limitations following closed head injury (McPherson, Berry, & Pentland, 1997). In these cases, the standard neuropsychological assessment might identify the cognitive deficits, thereby alerting the clinician to likely problem areas. In other areas of cognitive limitations following closed head injury, there may be limitations in specific behavioral skills that are manifested because of the cognitive impairment, but they would not be precisely identified using traditional neuropsychological assessment methods. For example, impairment in cross-modal sensory integration, documented by neuropsychological assessment, may result in difficulty interpreting the meaning of social communication when that communication depends upon the interplay of verbal content, tone of voice, and facial expression. However, even if the cognitive deficits are identified, the specific skills deficits need to be evaluated before treatment can proceed. In this case, the identification of cognitive deficits might be followed by the use of an instrument such as the Behaviorally Referenced Rating System of Intermediate Social Skills (Flanagan, McDonald, & Togher, 1995). In this situation, neuropsychological assessment identifies spatial analysis deficits in facial expression. The decision can be made whether to train the patient to request more direct verbal elaboration of the communicated information or to train toward the view of improving spatial analysis. The behavioral assessment will help identify situations in which communication skills are not sufficient and need to be rehearsed.

Development of Adaptive Strategies and Behaviors

In many cases, it may not be the presence of specific skills deficits that result in maladaptive behavior. Instead there may be impairment in the capacity to utilize different cognitive skills in a concerted and reiterative fashion, responding to feedback from the environment and modifying the behavioral plan accordingly. This set of activities is known as executive functions. Patients with closed head injury often demonstrate deficits in the ability to plan, predict, evaluate, and modify their behavior, all under the collective rubric of executive functions. Deficits here may be manifested in inappropriately silly behavior or statements that transgress normal social mores. Development of an effective rehabilitation effort must take into account deficits in this area. While cognitive skill areas such as memory can be evaluated using standardized tests of cognitive function, executive function is relatively free of specific cognitive areas and as such may be more fruitfully assessed using behavioral assessment techniques. Standard instruments such as the Stroop Color Word test, the Trail Making test (Reitan & Wolfson, 1993), and the Wisconsin Card Sorting test (Heaton, Chelune, Talley, Kay, & Curtiss, 1993) are suggested for the assessment of executive function. But these instruments are relatively focused on only one aspect of executive function (e.g., response inhibition). The Behavioral Assessment of the Dysexecutive Syndrome is an example of an instrument that instead utilizes reliable observations and behavioral coding (Wilson, Evans, Emslie, Alderman, & Burgess, 1998). Although preliminary data indicate that interobserver and temporal reliability are adequate, researchers examining a Dutch translation of the instrument found significant practice effects (Jelicic, Henquet, Derix, & Jolles, 2001). Future research will need to focus on discriminative and predictive validity. Here, as in other areas, neuropsychological and behavioral assessment may be supplementary where the cognitive test data help predict organizational and problem solving skills and behavioral assessment helps predict risk-taking and impulsive behaviors (Ready, Stierman, & Paulsen, 2001). There is also a behavioral checklist for executive functions in children (Gioia, Isquith, Guy, & Kenworthy, 2000).

Modulation of Emotional/Behavioral Dyscontrol

Aggressive behavioral outbursts are so frequently seen in individuals with acquired brain impairment that central nervous system dysfunction is often hypothesized to be the etiologic agent in the production of aggressive behavior. Although the possible presence of frontal lobe dysfunction can be determined through the use of cognitive instruments such as the Wisconsin Card Sorting Test or the Stroop Color Word Test, these instruments would need to be supplemented by behavioral assessment techniques that could identify high-risk situations as well as identify the possible antecedents or consequences. Additionally, behavioral assessment would be necessary to evaluate any treatment effects. Alderman, Davies, Jones, and McDonnel (1999) report that the Overt Aggression Scale–Modified for Neurorehabilitation could serve as both a source of hypotheses regarding treatment methods as well as a dependent measure to evaluate treatment effects.

The final stage in developing an intervention would be performing the functional analysis to identify the initiating and maintaining factors that may vary across individuals even when the necessary condition (cognitive impairment) and the situational aspects (e.g., in small groups vs. in one-to-one settings) may be the same. For example, Richman, Wacker, Asmus, Casey, and Andelman (1999) reported that, of three individuals exhibiting aggressive behavior, two showed response class characteristics while the third demonstrated differential reinforcement effects that were identifiable via the functional analysis. The relation between cognitive impairment and behavioral dyscontrol may not be that simple. Simpson, Tate, Ferry, Hodgkinson, and Blacszcynski (2001) have demonstrated that, for sexual acting out, neither cognitive performance nor premorbid personality characteristics discriminated between traumatic brain injury patients with sexually inappropriate behavior and the same type of patients who did not show that behavior.

It is difficult to see how traditional neuropsychological assessment would be useful in determining the effect of treatment for emotional dyscontrol resulting from central nervous system dysfunction, especially when that treatment involved application of some behaviorally based technology. In Carr et al.'s (2000) review of the use of noncontingent reinforcement to reduce emotionally disturbed behavior, traditional measures of emotionality provided only a gross depiction of the effect of treatment. However, in certain disorders, the change in behavioral functioning and cognitive functioning may be correlated due to a central neurological mechanism. For example, when elderly patients with frontal lobe dementia were given neuropsychological and behavioral assessments, changes in executive functioning and behavioral changes (impulsivity, poor planning) were seen together with emotional functioning (especially elation, flat affect, or exaggerated emotionality), indicating that the cognitive and behavioral changes had a shared etiology in the physical localized changes in brain function. The extent to which treatment targeting one area—such as emotional functioning—can affect another area—such as cognitive functioning—is unknown and represents an area for future research. In general, for depressed individuals, improvement in emotional functioning is frequently accompanied by improvement in attention and memory, but the generalization of this observed relation to other emotional states and cognitive functions remains unknown.

Treatment of Cognitively Impaired Elderly

The assessment and treatment of older individuals with cognitive impairment involves an understanding of the cognitive skills and deficits of the individual as well as an understanding of the environmental demands and sources of support for the individual. As more and more of the population enters the range of elderly, more clinical services are being aimed at these individuals. It is important to have information regarding the correct diagnosis before planning an intervention effort.

Assessment for Diagnosis and Prognosis

Typically, older individuals are diagnosed as having dementia on the basis of neuropsychological data, but these same individuals are hospitalized on the basis of behavioral data. Although in the past the diagnosis of dementia has presented a bleak prognosis, recent advances in both pharmacology and behavioral interventions have resulted in more optimistic views. The positive outcome in such interventions, however, is not the reversal of cognitive decline but is instead the maintenance or relearning of behavioral adaptive skills. Stewart, Hiscock, Morgan, Murphy, and Yamamoto (1998) describe an assessment system, the Environment-Behavior Interaction Code, that involves critical event sampling as well as interval sampling to record target behaviors and which possesses sufficient reliability to be recommended as an outcome measure in treatment efforts. Because of the extent and effect of cognitive impairment in individuals with dementia, behavioral assessment is frequently the only valid outcome measure (Perrin, 1998). From a consumer point of view, the behavior is the most relevant aspect related to disability or impairment in an individual with dementia. Although forgetfulness may be problematic, relatives become especially concerned and seek treatment when the patient displays maladaptive or unsafe behavior.

In diagnosing certain subtypes of dementia, such as dementia of the frontal lobe type, it is important to be able to demonstrate evidence of frontal dysfunction both in terms of neuropsychological test data and behavioral data (Venneri, Grassi, & Caffarra, 1996). The broader category of Alzheimer's disease may contain subtypes, which are discriminable

on the basis of neuropsychological test data and regional cerebral blood flow studies and which have behavioral signs of emotional dysfunction as group membership criteria, as was reported by Lebert and colleagues (1994) in an examination of Alzheimer's patients with and without manic behavioral signs. Here, the combination of behavioral data and standardized psychometric test data increases our understanding of the clinical condition and aids in classifying similar sets of patients. Bozeat, Gregory, Ralph, and Hodges (2000) reported that stereotypic behavior and changes in eating behavior along with loss of social awareness discriminated Alzheimer's patients from patients with frontal compromise when using both psychometric test data and the results of caregivers' reports on a standardized questionnaire.

Individuals with dementia also may show behavioral signs of apathy sufficient to suggest a syndrome. In Alzheimer's disease, the presence of apathy symptoms is associated with greater cognitive impairment, lesser independent functioning, and depression (Starkstein, Petracca, Chemerisnki, & Kremer, 2001).

Treatment Planning (Identification of Strengths and Weaknesses)

Plaud, Moberg, and Ferraro (1998) discuss the relation between standardized cognitive assessment and behavioral assessment in the diagnosis of dementia and also suggest that behavioral assessment can be fruitfully applied to research into normal healthy aging. This application would involve development of normative information regarding behaviors and skills and points to the fluidity of the distinction between behavioral and traditional assessment. Although traditional assessment is usually construed as involving assessment of fairly abstract constructs, it has at its core an assumption of a meaningful average performance. This assumption also can be applied to instances where the construct of interest is fairly low on the abstraction hierarchy or where the construct is described close to the construct-method unit. For example, performance on a check-writing skill task can be construed in terms of mathematico-deductive reasoning (traditional assessment) or in terms of being able to write checks independently (behavioral assessment) and handle one's own finances. In either case, it would be useful to know how the average nonimpaired community-dwelling elderly individual performs on the task in order to compare the performance of the patient in the clinical setting and make predictions about the degree of independence possible if that same patient were in the open environment.

Benedict, Goldstein, Dobraski, and Tennenhaus (1997) report that neuropsychological test performance, specifically tests of visual-spatial processing, predict adequate performance on kitchen tasks as measured by naturalistic behavioral assessment. However, these same authors make the point that, because there is not a perfect correlation between the two realms of variables, cognitive testing should be viewed as complementary to behavioral assessment in this situation. Similarly, although neuropsychological cognitive test performance helped explain the performance of patients with Alzheimer's disease on a route-learning task in an analogue behavioral assessment, the test scores did not suffice to predict presence or degree of deficits in learning a new route.

Behavioral and neuropsychological assessment might complement each other when used as dependent measures in evaluating treatment effects. This is especially true in testing the effects of drugs designed to improve the situation of patients with dementia. Early studies had assumed that the cholinergic enchancers would improve memory and cognition, but results indicated that, although memory at best stayed stable with these medications, adaptive behaviors and independent functioning improved. As a result, subsequent studies have included behavioral and cognitive measures, such as the study by Greene and colleagues (2000), which investigated the effect of donepezil in patients with multiple sclerosis and demonstrated positive effects on cognitive and adaptive behavior. Behavioral responses also have been used to study the effect of donepezil on functioning in patients with Alzheimer's disease in which the effect of the medication seems to have been on behavioral functioning rather than on cognition (Mega, Masterman, O'Connor, Barclay, & Cummings, 1999).

Designing the Environment

The identification and assessment of problematic behaviors for purposes of diagnosis or to evaluate the effects of treatment is only one application of behavioral assessment. In addition, direct behavioral observation can be helpful in designing environments that are most conducive to maximal independence in elderly patients with dementia. It was direct observation of the wandering behavior of patients with Alzheimer's disease that led architects to design Alzheimer's units with circular halls so that wandering patients always ended up where they started. Furthermore, direct observation of Alzheimer's patients resulted in care facilities whose bedrooms were designed such that the door to the bathroom could be seen from every part of the bedroom. Direct observation of inpatient behavior is a daunting task unless a specific coding system and a reasonable sampling process are in place. In order to meet these demands, systems have been designed using handheld computers and data recording implements. One such system known simply as "The Observer" records behaviors, contexts, positions, and locations for later

analysis (Van Haitsma, Lawton, Kleban, Klapper, & Korn, 1997). The sampling periods and techniques can be adjusted according to the design of the assessment.

Informant Report of Observable Behaviors Related to Neurobehavioral Symptoms

Progressive dementias have cognitive decline as their hallmark. However, the decrease in ability to perform independent living behaviors is at the heart of the disability attendant upon dementia. Memory impairment and attention difficulties play a role in this behavioral decline, but it may be the decrease in executive functioning that is the main force behind decreases in self-care. As such, it is important to obtain an evaluation of independent functioning skills as well as executive functioning and other cognitive areas such as memory. Two fairly broad instruments to do just that are the Behavioral Rating Scale for dementia, which is part of the Center for the Establishment of a Registry in Alzheimer's Dementia, and the Cohen-Mansfield Agitation Inventory, which may give relatively equivalent information (Weiner et al., 1998).

Because of the unreliability of self-report in individuals with cognitive impairment, there is an increased role for behavioral assessment in identifying problematic internal states. However, this approach has its limitations as well. Allen, Esser, Tyriver, and Striepling (2000) found that a behavioral observation system was inadequate to the task of separating individuals with dementia from individuals with dementia and depression. Many of the behaviors associated with depression are shared with dementia, and a more precise behavioral assessment system may be helpful here. It cannot be ruled out that the very nature of depression, being largely related to internal states, makes the condition less reliably identifiable by observation.

Historically, there has been a dynamic tension between self-report and observer ratings in assessment psychology regardless of whether the underlying ethos of the assessment was behavioral or nomothetic. Behavioral assessment has the additional dialectic between observer report and direct behavioral assessment. Although asking for data from informants may be a more practical and less costly form of assessment as well as being more timely in cases of an emergent need for information, direct behavioral observation may offer greater accuracy. A recent study (Yarbrough & Carr, 2000) involving the identification of problem behaviors in adolescents with mental retardation indicated that informants were very accurate in identifying situations in which the problem behavior occurred (sensitivity), but not accurate in identifying situations in which the behavior was less likely to occur (specificity).

The uses to which the information is put may moderate the utility of the assessment information. Hadwin and Hutley (1998) report that a teacher questionnaire demonstrated discriminative validity in evaluating students with severe learning disabilities either with or without concomitant autism. Farther up the continuum of confidence in accuracy may be some tradeoff when observer ratings are used instead of objective testing. Of course, observer ratings are probably more accurate when they are taken from trained professionals rather than relatives, but at least one study has indicated that we should have more confidence in ratings provided by relatives. Cipolli, Bolzani, Pinelli, and Neri (1998) reported high concordance between dementia severity ratings when taken from objective test data or from relative's ratings as taken from a structured interview. Furthermore, the ratings of relatives correlated with the objective test data as related to everyday functioning. However, the population of interest and the relation of the informants to the subjects may affect the accuracy of the informant ratings. For example, parents may overestimate the cognitive ability of their own children (Dewey, Crawford, Creighton, & Suave, 2000).

Rather than viewing the different assessment modalities as competitive, it might be fruitful to see them as complementary and to understand the conditions under which one might possess greater utility or the information derived from one modality might be modulated by information from another. Monteiro, Auer, Boksay, and Reisberg (2000) discuss how the different modalities can interact in the assessment of behaviors associated with dementia. These authors conclude that informant report via telephone is an efficient means of complementing direct behavioral observation. Without devaluing the contribution of direct behavioral observation, Lefroy, McHale, Hyndman, and Hobbs (1996) promote the utility of using behavioral rating scales in evaluating individuals with dementia in an inpatient setting. In another application of the interaction of behavioral and neurocognitive assessment, Hall, Halperin, Schwartz, and Newcorn (1997) used a computerized continuous performance test, a solid-state actigraph, and a neuropsychological response incompatibility task to compare children with attention deficit hyperactivity disorder with and without reading disability. They found no differences between the two groups on the actigraph or the continuous performance task, but the children without reading disability showed deficient performance on the response incompatibility task.

Identification of Relevant Behaviors

One area in which the modalities of behavioral and neuropsychological assessment interact is in the diagnosis of de-

mentia. On the basis of the *DSM-IV* TV, a diagnosis of dementia is considered when evidence of cognitive decline is sufficient to cause impairment in vocational or adaptive functioning. The neuropsychological assessment would provide the evidence of cognitive skill inconsistent with hypothesized levels based on the individual history. The behavioral assessment would provide the evidence of decline in vocational or adaptive functioning. Additionally, different forms of dementia may have characteristic patterns of cognitive impairment and behavioral disturbance. For example, Lewy Body disease is more likely than Alzheimer's dementia to be associated with waxing and waning of symptoms over the course of days. Reisberg and colleagues (2000) report on the use of a behavioral assessment instrument to classify dementia syndromes, but this promising start is in need of replication as well as more basic work to provide greater understanding of what the distinct syndromes may be. Kunik and colleagues (2000) report that, although behavioral agitation did not differ across different forms of dementia, patients with vascular dementia were often hospitalized with equivalent behavioral disturbances but less cognitive impairment. Even if the different types of dementia do not provide different behavioral profiles, the examination of behavioral pathology can be useful in understanding the patient, and evidence suggests that the degree of behavioral pathology as measured by the Behavioral Pathology in Alzheimer's Disease Scale may have a correlation with the degree of cognitive impairment as measured by the Folstein Mini-Mental State Exam (Harwood, Ownby, Barker, & Duara, 1998).

At the current time, there has been greater success reported in the development of instruments to assess the presence and degree of specific target behaviors without concern for the diagnosis. Obviously, making diagnostic-level decisions would require more training for the observers and a higher level of inference for the assessment interpretation. As an example of the latter approach, Whall and colleagues (1999) have shown that it is possible to train nurses' aides to reliably code the presence and severity of behavioral agitation in patients with dementia. The accurate assessment of target behaviors by paraprofessional staff requires adequate definitions that do not rely on assumptions regarding cause (Shah & Allen, 1999). Additionally, there must be adequate training of the observers in the coding system, which itself must be specific with sufficient behavioral anchors. Finally, there should be intermittent checks against observer drift. In order to design an effective intervention, it would be necessary to conduct a functional analysis (Fisher & Swingen, 1997).

There are multiple observer report instruments, such as the Brief Psychiatric Rating Scale, the Consortium to Establish a Registry in Alzheimer's Disease, and the Neuropsychiatric Inventory (Tariot, Porsteinsson, Teri, & Weiner, 1996). However, all of these instruments rely on retrospective judgments or global impression and may not be well suited to the particulars of fine-grain behavioral analysis. These instruments can be helpful in focusing the observations of caregivers to those behaviors most likely to be problematic in cases of dementia or which might be the target of psychological or psychiatric interventions.

As well as being useful in the development of treatment plans and in the diagnosis of impaired individuals, information about specific behaviors can be helpful in other contexts. For example, Vieweg, Blair, Tucker, and Lewis (1995) reported the use of the Agitation Behavior Mapping Instrument, an observer report of the incidence and frequency of target behaviors, to identify behaviors that were likely to lead to inpatient hospital admissions in elderly patients with dementia. They determined that aggressive behavior was the most frequently reported behavioral disturbance leading to hospital admission. This result points out the need for early identification of aggressive behavioral trends in community-dwelling elderly in order to provide less costly and earlier interventions. Although aggressive behaviors were more likely to occur in patients with dementia, these behaviors also occurred in patients with affective disorders, and diagnosis did not necessarily predict the occurrence of the problem behavior. Gordon, Powell, and Rockwood (2000) argue that traditional psychometric methods may be inadequate to the task of measuring aggressive behavior and that a more individualized approach is necessary. However compelling their arguments, the final question is best answered with data.

Earlier it was stated that certain behaviors associated with neurocognitive conditions may vary with changes in cognitive status. This may not be true for all behaviors and cognitions. Edgerly and Donovick (1998) report that, although level of activity and amount of wandering were significantly related to performance on tests of neurocognitive functioning, there was not a relation to the number of attempts to exit the facility.

Many disorders, such as Alzheimer's, have a constellation of cognitive, behavioral, and emotional changes associated with them. The simplistic view of these progressive disorders is that symptoms appear roughly around the same time and proceed uniformly. McCarty and colleagues (2000) provide evidence that not only do these sets of symptoms progress unevenly, it appears that the relation between progression of the illness and behavioral decline is curvilinear rather than linear. Under that condition, both cognitive and behavioral assessment would be independently necessary in order to accurately assess the individual. Padoani and De Leo (2000) report on three older individuals who demonstrated decline in independent behaviors without change in cognitive status over a period of 5 years. It was presumed that a psychiatric condition was responsible, but one was not identified. Regardless of the etiology, cognitive testing without behavioral assessment would be insufficient to evaluate the patient's need for supervision or environmental accommodation.

At least for caregivers of patients with dementia, the association between caregiver report and actual behavioral observation in assessing activities of daily living depends partly upon the amount of stress experienced by the caregiver and the amount of assistance required by the patient (Zanetti, Geroldi, Frisoni, Bianchetti, & Trabucchi, 1999).

Assessment of Individuals with Developmental Disabilities

Persons with developmental disabilities have often been the subject of behavioral assessment. Because their developmental problems have observable behavioral consequences that are unpleasant or dangerous for themselves and others, there have been efforts to evaluate and treat the behaviors within the context of the cognitive limitations. This requires some knowledge of the actual cognitive skills of the individuals in question.

Cognitive Assessment of Memory and Learning Skills

Although intervention with individuals with developmental disabilities is almost always behavioral in nature, the assessment and diagnosis of those same individuals is almost always neuropsychological. The diagnosis necessary for such individuals to receive state-funded services requires IQ scores below a certain range or a *DSM-IV* diagnosis of mental retardation, in which case IQ below a certain level in conjunction with evidence of limitations in adaptive functioning is required. Once the diagnosis is obtained, further assessment may be necessary to develop an effective intervention plan. There is no definitive consensus regarding the optimal method of developing an intervention plan. McDaniel (2001) describes an assessment procedure in which examination of the response of the patient to simple observational learning, instrumental conditioning, and object discrimination can provide information related to both the patient's neuropsychological skills and the optimal components of an intervention program once the target behaviors are identified via other means. This method is in need of empirical evaluation, but it certainly seems sensible as a way of bridging the chasm between neuropsychological and behavioral assessment in developing treatment for this population.

In Vivo and Analogue Assessment of Behavioral and Community Skills

The value of applied behavioral assessment has been recognized in the treatment of individuals with developmental disabilities (Figuero, Davis, & Smith, 1995). Here, as in other areas of clinical practice, although the neuropsychological assessment paradigm can offer much to the identification and treatment of these individuals, the realms of neuropsychological and behavioral evaluation do not seem to interact.

The use of analogue assessment procedures frequently has been used with intact individuals, but has been less common in assessing individuals with cognitive impairment, perhaps because of concerns regarding their ability to respond in the analogue setting in the same way as in the in vivo setting. There is little data to support either viewpoint, although given the limitations in abstraction in impaired individuals, fairly strong theoretical arguments support the emphasis on in vivo assessment. One study investigating the relation between social context and the elicitation of self-injurious or aggressive behavior in individuals with severe developmental disabilities seems to indicate that, although analogue assessment situations may be appropriate, individuals with cognitive impairment may be especially sensitive to the social meaning of the events leading up to the assessment period (O'Reilly, Lancioni, & Emerson, 1999).

Anderson, Freeman, and Scotti (1999) examined the generalizability of analogue assessment in individuals with developmental disabilities and found that, for the three subjects in the study, the results were generalizable and the resulting treatments were valid (effective). Yet another problem in the treatment of individuals with developmental disabilities is the identification of reinforcing stimuli to be used as rewards in training programs. Although this procedure can be accomplished straightforwardly by simply asking individuals with average intelligence, individuals with developmental disabilities present challenges either because their communication skills are limited or because they cannot conceptualize the question. Roane, Vollmer, Ringdahl, and Marcus (1998) describe a short procedure that assesses individual preferences that can then be used in designing a reinforcement program. Similarly, behavioral assessment procedures were necessary to identify what was reinforcing elopement behavior in three children with developmental disabilities (Piazza et al., 1997). It is not necessary to start from scratch with each patient and problem. There are programs in the literature that can be modified and applied to the given situation. For example, Kohler and Strain (1997) describe a method for assessing social interaction in terms of magnitude, function, reciprocity, and duration of the behavior.

In a survey of clinicians, the most frequently used method of assessment for individuals with developmental disorders was the functional assessment, although behavioral interviews and standardized instruments also played a role (Ellingson, Miltenberger, & Long, 1999). Standard neuropsychological assessment has significant limitations in its ability to design an intervention program. It is not so much that the neuropsychological data are irrelevant, but that they are insufficient. Feldman and Griffiths (1997) present what they call an ecobehavioral model for the assessment of problem behaviors in individuals with developmental disabilities. Here all possible aspects of the environment, the individual, and the hierarchy of behaviors are considered in order to design an intervention and then evaluate its effectiveness.

In some instances, while the demonstration of cognitive impairment may be necessary for the diagnosis of certain disorders, the more important consideration in the diagnosis is the determination of relative strengths and weaknesses. For example, autism may have associated cognitive impairment, but it is the behaviors such as self-stimulation, repetitive stereotypies, and abhorrence for change that actually characterize the individual with autism. Adrien and colleagues (2001) report on the use of a behavioral rating instrument for individuals with developmental disabilities with a focus on behaviors associated with autism. The Behavior Function Inventory was able to identify individuals with autism and quantify features of the core characteristics of autism even in individuals with different diagnoses.

As yet another indication of the importance of behavioral assessment in understanding developmental disorders, Ross, Yu, Dickie, and Kropla (1998) investigated stereotyped behaviors in a variety of developmental disorders in order to determine whether the behaviors demonstrate periodicity or rhythmicality. Interestingly, rocking alone showed periodicity, indicating that environmental variables may play a greater role in eliciting or maintaining the other stereotyped behaviors. Yet another examination of stereotypy resulted in the development of a behavioral assessment methodology called Stereotypy Analysis (Pyles, Riordan, & Bailey, 1997). The method analyzes the relation of environmental events to different forms of stereotypy in order to uncover relations between the two and help guide design of interventions to reduce such target behaviors.

Informant Assessment of Skill and Competence

In behavioral assessment, an important informant is the client. In fact, self-report has a long and venerable tradition in psychological assessment in general. When the subject is an individual with cognitive limitations, new issues arise with regard to the design and utility of self-report instruments. Although self-report instruments need not be entirely discarded, they need to be modified and adapted to the level of cognitive skill of the population under consideration. Individuals with mental retardation is one example of a population for whom modifications to typical self-report methods are needed.

Finlay and Lyons (2000) have discussed some of the exigencies in applying self-report methods to patients with mental retardation. Of course there is great variability in the level of skill in the broad population of individuals with mental retardation. The first step would be to define the characteristics of the population of interest. For example, if one is designing a self-report instrument for individuals in the early stages of a progressive dementia, the level of reading skill and general cognitive skill would need to be specified first. The content of the items—including vocabulary, diction, phrasing, and grammatical and syntactic complexity—would need to be matched to the target population's skill level. Quantitative judgments and estimates of time may present particular challenges for these individuals. Questions related to direct comparison may be difficult, and instead it may be better to ask separately for ratings on the two items to be compared. Abstract concepts and questions of generalized information (e.g., what is typical or what do you usually do?) may be difficult for an individual with cognitive impairment to answer. The passive voice and negative wording should be avoided. Open-ended questions may result in limited answers in this population. Excess verbiage should be avoided, but examples should be provided whenever possible.

Case Study

Ms. A. is a 73-year-old woman referred for a neuropsychological assessment by her family physician. In fact, this physician has come into contact with Ms. A only in the past 2 years, because Ms. A. has never been hospitalized except during the birth of her children. She completed the eleventh grade successfully but had to quit school because her father was killed in an industrial accident, and, as the oldest child, she had to help her mother care for the six younger children. She was widowed 11 years ago. She continues to live in the same house in which she and her husband raised their five children. She never learned to drive, and after her husband died, she learned to use public transportation. Her husband had handled the family finances. She took over with no apparent problems until recently, when her children noticed errors in the checking account and late notices for bills. Her family also reports finding outdated food containers in the refrigerator. She denies any problems, but she admits that her

memory has become less reliable lately and ascribes that to "old age." Family history is significant for an aunt who died in a nursing home at age 69 and reportedly had "hardening of the arteries."

During the interview, Ms. A. is friendly and cooperative. She describes what life was like in the city when she was growing up. At times she cannot remember details such as the names of some of her grandchildren. She reports that she previously enjoyed crossword puzzles but currently doesn't "have time for them." She described her previous participation in activities at her church but that she quit because "That's for younger people." She still helps launder and iron the altar vestments. Her children or grandchildren have daily contact.

Test Results

Folstein Mini-Mental Status Exam: Total score was 23 (borderline performance). She was oriented to person, day, place, and situation, but was incorrect in year (2 years off) and month (3 months off).

Clock Drawing Test: Score of 5 out of 10. Errors of placement of the hands and numbers.

Boston Naming Test (Goodglass & Kaplan, 1983): 38 of 60 correct, numerous examples of semantic paraphasic errors and word finding difficulties

Wechsler Memory Scale-III (Wechsler, 1997): Impaired performance on tests of verbal learning, verbal narrative recall, and visual reproduction. Performance is more severely impaired for delayed recall. Recognition memory is also impaired.

Trail Making Test: Adequate performance on the task of simple sequencing, but significantly impaired on the double alternating sequence aspect of the task.

Wisconsin Card Sorting Test: Impaired performance on problem solving, numerous perseverative errors and responses.

Geriatric Depression Scale: Total score of 8 (nonclinical range).

Overall, the test results indicate significant impairment in memory, semantic relations, and visual-spatial construction—a constellation associated with Alzheimer's dementia. Although the diagnosis of a progressive dementia would require subsequent assessments, the history is suggestive of a progressive decline. Because this cognitive impairment carries a high chance of functional impairment, an assessment of living skills was conducted. The clinical interview indicated that Ms. A. denied any significant impairment in living skills, but she agreed to an in vivo assessment of living activities at the behest of her family. A clinician came to her house and spent 3 hours observing her in daily activities. The clinician recorded each instance of forgetfulness or poor judgment that occurred in that time. By use of a notebook, descriptions of the behaviors were recorded and a later conference among the observing recorder and the neuropsychologist determined whether the behaviors were counted as examples of forgetfulness or danger. There were instances of memory lapses at the rate of three per hour, but relatively few examples of unsafe behavior. Additionally, the Independent Living Scales (Loeb, 1996) was administered. Impairment was seen on the Memory/Orientation and Managing Money scales. Ms. A. showed relatively adequate performance on the Managing Home and Transportation, Health and Safety, and Social Adjustment scales.

As a result of the evaluation, the following recommendations were made. Any important information Ms. A. needed to learn or remember was repeated to her several times in the same occasion and across occasions. She agreed to have her son-in-law, an accountant, take over her financial affairs. She had power of attorney assigned to her son. The family set up a schedule of daily visits to Ms. A. in order to check on her. She was referred to a neurologist for a medical evaluation and to initiate treatment with Aricept. A reevaluation was scheduled in 9 months.

In this case example, the neuropsychological evaluation indicated the presence of cognitive deficits and additionally pointed to the diagnosis of Alzheimer's dementia. The behavioral assessment indicated the impact of the cognitive impairment. Additionally, the areas of financial affairs and memory were identified as being in need of intervention. A baseline of cognitive test scores and functional capacity were recorded for future comparisons following implementation of the medical treatment and possible progressive decline with time.

Strengths and Weaknesses

Psychometric Considerations

A typical way to compare assessment methods is to examine the psychometric qualities of the instruments in question. This type of comparison is useful mainly when the assessment instruments share intended use, method, and design. For example, the temporal reliability of an instrument intended to measure a stable trait might be compared to an instrument that was intended to measure fluctuations in mood. The difficulties are magnified when the assessments to be compared differ in terms of epistemology, theories of measurement, and levels of inference. What then of validity? Would an index

of validity make a better point of comparison between the two assessment methods?

Validity carries its own limitations. Although many psychologists think of validity as a binary decision process—yes or no—validity actually can be determined only for the use of certain instruments in certain contexts and populations to answer certain clinical questions. So here, too, a validity index is not a good point of comparison. Ecological validity may be an index of behavioral specificity of neuropsychological assessment results. Here we come the closest to being able to directly compare the two assessment results, but again, because of the different levels of inference, we fall short.

The method-construct unit has been suggested as a reasonable way to conceptualize the science of psychological assessment (Fiske, 1976). The measurement of clinical entities might also utilize this conceptualization. Instead of asking whether an assessment method has validity, we would instead ask whether a method of measuring a psychological phenomenon has utility for the task for which it is being used. Of course, this complicates the comparison between neuropsychological and behavioral assessment, but then the two forms of assessment are complicated in themselves.

Can behavioral and neuropsychological assessment be compared in a meaningful way in a single setting? Are they complementary or independent? Is clinical utility the key to resolving issues of validity? These questions deserve answers, but they cannot be answered at the present time. In the clinical model, the two forms of assessment are complementary. Can either behavioral or neuropsychological assessment be used to improve the results of the other? How can they be combined? The utility of both neuropsychological and behavioral assessment data can be improved by consideration of the other. Gabrieli and colleagues (1999) report that an experimental behavioral technique—namely, cueing in category exemplar identification tasks—can enhance the information gained from the standard visual confrontation naming task used in clinical neuropsychology. The results of one form increase the utility of the other form, and both are directed toward the improvement of the patient's condition.

To what task is each better suited? It is not useful to think of functional assessment as unidimensional. If the behavioral zeitgeist has taught us anything, it is that the clinical approach to the person requires individual tailoring of the assessment and the intervention. Group data can tell us which approaches might be more useful and which could be tried first, but group data cannot tell us which specific approach will work with a given individual. Informant report, experimental, and descriptive approaches to functional analysis may result in different hypotheses and conclusions (Toogood & Timlin, 1996). Perhaps the best coordination of behavioral and neuropsychological assessment will occur in the individually designed instance, such as that described by Peters, Koller, and Holliday (1995).

FUTURE DIRECTIONS

Need for Theoretical Framework to Organize Interactions

Pyles, Muniz, Cade, and Silva (1997) describe a paradigm for integrating two disparate models of behavior and the variables that control it: behavior analysis and psychopharmacology. Here the fertile meeting ground is in the realm of treatment. The scientific substrate of both helps provide an underpinning and a set of common assumptions and ways of evaluating data. Similarly, cognitive neuroscience and psychopharmacology have made great contributions to the understanding of each other. Whether clinical neuropsychology and behavioral assessment can do the same is an open question.

Need for Cross-Education of Proponents

If proponents of these two approaches to assessment are to enjoy a rapprochement, there must be greater understanding of the underlying theoretical underpinnings and the manifest methods. This can be accomplished only through education and training that teaches both approaches. It is not necessary for all behavioral clinicians to be trained in clinical neuropsychology and for all neuropsychologists to receive thorough training in functional assessment. However, it would be beneficial for all individuals training in one of the areas to receive rudimentary training in the other if they intend to work in the treatment of patients with brain impairments.

New Methods and Instruments

There has been some development in the area of behaviorally based neuropsychological assessment instruments. A major impetus for these developments comes from the attempts of neuropsychologists to examine and increase the ecological validity of their assessments. When the clinical questions posed of neuropsychologists were related to localization of the tumor or diagnosis of stroke or toxic encephalopathy, the behavioral referents and correlates of the test-related task were unimportant. However, when the clinical questions posed were related to prediction about independence of functioning or return to work, the extra-test behaviors rose to preeminence. As a result, we have seen the development of tests such as the Rivermead Behavioral Memory Test (RBMT), which assesses memory by posing challenges similar to those

in real life (e.g., remembering the time of an appointment or the location of a health provider's office). Some evidence suggests that the RBMT may provide clinical information but not identify specific memory deficits (Martin, West, Cull, & Adams, 2000). Similarly, the Loewenstein Direct Assessment of Functional Status (Loewenstein et al., 1989) provides a naturalistic assessment of behaviors such as writing a check, dressing, and grooming using standard coding measurements.

The interaction of neuropsychological and behavioral assessment will be aided and changed by the development of new assessment technologies. In addition to handheld computers and electronic data recording devices, there is also work being done to develop virtual reality as an assessment technology (Rizzo, Buckwalter, Neumann, Kesselman, & Thiebaux, 1998). These approaches may utilize either a desktop environment or an immersive environment (Elkind, 1998). The earliest applications are in the assessment of visual and spatial perception and memory, but behavioral tasks such as route learning also can be modified to fit the virtual reality paradigm. The early stages will face significant generalization issues to be addressed because cognitively impaired and older patients will experience the virtual reality situation as novel and may be reactive to the task as a result. However, as virtual reality permeates our culture, these issues will likely fade.

SUMMARY

There exists awareness that both behavioral and cognitive features may be important in the identification and treatment of neurologic disorders. What is needed is greater awareness of the differences and similarities between the two approaches of behavioral and neuropsychological assessment. These two approaches arise from very different traditions and theories of measurement, but they have much to offer each other, especially in the clinical arena. The two methods can probably be successfully combined to provide more successful treatment; the degree of complementarity is still a question. Answering that question will require greater empirical evidence.

REFERENCES

Adrien, J-L., Roux, S., Couturier, G., Malvy, J., Guerin, P., Debuly, S., Lelord, G., & Barthelemy, C. (2001). Towards a new functional assessment of autistic dysfunction in children with developmental disorders: The Behavior Function Inventory. *Autism, 5,* 249–264.

Allen, B., Esser, W., Tyriver, C., & Striepling, A. (2000). The behavioral diagnosis of depression for people with dementia. *American Journal of Alzheimer's Disease, 15,* 303–307.

Alderman, N., Davies, J.A., Jones, C., & McDonnel, P. (1999). Reduction of severe aggressive behaviour in acquired brain injury: Case studies illustrating clinical use of the OAS-MNR in the management of challenging behaviours. *Brain Injury, 13,* 699–704.

Anderson, C.M., Freeman, K.A., & Scotti, J.R. (1999). Evaluation of the generalizability (reliability and validity) of analog functional assessment methodology. *Behavior Therapy, 30,* 31–50.

Arfken, C.L., Lichtenberg, P.A., & Tancer, M.E. (1999). Cognitive impairment and depression predict mortality in medically ill older adults. *Journals of Gerontology Series A: Biological Sciences & Medical Sciences, 54A,* M152–M156.

Benedict, R.H.B., Goldstein, M.Z., Dobraski, M., & Tennehaus, J. (1997). Neuropsychological predictors of adaptive kitchen behavior in geriatric psychiatry patients. *Journal of Geriatric Psychiatry and Neurology, 10,* 146–153.

Bozeat, S., Gregory, C.A., Ralph, M.A.L., & Hodges, J.R. (2000). Which neuropsychiatric and behavioural features distinguish frontal and temporal variants of frontotemporal dementia from Alzheimer's disease? *Journal of Neurology, Neurosurgery, and Psychiatry, 69,* 178–186.

Carr, J.E., Coriaty, S., Wilder, D.A, Gaunt, B.T., Dozier, C.L., Britton, L.N., Avina, C., & Reed, C.L. (2000). A review of "noncontingent" reinforcement as treatment for the aberrant behavior of individuals with developmental disabilities. *Research in Developmental Disabilities, 21,* 377–391.

Cipolli, C., Bolzani, R., Pinelli, M., & Neri, M. (1998). Assessing behavioural and cognitive impairment in dementia using an informant's report: Evidence from the CAMDEX interview. *Perceptual and Motor Skills, 87,* 404–406.

Claus, J.J., Kwa, V.I., Teunisse, S., Walstra, G.J., van Gool, W.A., Koelman, J.H., Bour, L.J., & Ongerboer de Visser, B.W. (1998). Slowing on quantitative spectral EEG is a marker for rate of subsequent cognitive and functional decline in early Alzheimer disease. *Alzheimer Disease and Associated Disorders, 12,* 167–174.

Dewey, D., Crawford, S.G., Creighton, D.E., & Suave, R.S. (2000). Parent's ratings of everyday cognitive abilities in very low weight birth children. *Journal of Developmental and Behavioral Pediatrics, 21,* 37–43.

Edgerly, E.S., & Donovick, P.J. (1998). Neuropsychological correlates of wandering in persons with Alzheimer's disease. *American Journal of Alzheimer's Disease, 6,* 317–329.

Elkind, J.S. (1998). Use of virtual reality to diagnose and habilitate people with neurological dysfunctions. *CyberPsychology and Behavior, 1,* 263–273.

Ellingson, S.A., Miltenberg, R.G., & Long, E.S. (1999). A survey of the use of functional assessment procedures in agencies serving individuals with developmental disorders. *Behavioral Interventions, 14,* 187–198.

Feldman, M.A., & Griffiths, D. (1997). Comprehensive assessment of severe behavior problems. In N.N. Singh (Ed.), *Prevention and treatment of severe behavior problems: Models and methods in developmental disabilities* (pp. 23–48). Pacific Grove, CA: Brooks/Cole.

Figiero, R.G., Davis, B.E., & Smith, K.H. (1995). Behavior analysis. In B.A. Thyer (Ed.), *Developmental disabilities: A handbook for interdisciplinary practice* (pp. 32–59). Cambridge, MA: Brookline Books.

Finlay, W.M.L., & Lyons, E. (2000). Methodological issues in interviewing and using self-report questionnaires with people with mental retardation. *Psychological Assessment, 13,* 319–335.

Fisher, J.E., & Swingen, D.N. (1997). Contextual factors in the assessment and management of aggression in dementia patients. *Cognitive and Behavioral Practice, 4,* 171–190.

Fiske, D.W. (1976). Can a personality construct have a singular validational pattern?: Reply to Huba and Hamilton. *Psychological Bulletin, 83,* 87.

Flanagan, S., McDonald, S., & Togher, I. (1995). Evaluating social skills following traumatic brain injury: The BRISS as a clinical tool. *Brain Injury, 9,* 321–338.

Franzen, M.D. (1991). Behavioral assessment and treatment of brain-impaired individuals. In M. Hersen, R.M. Eisler, & P.M. Miller (Eds.), *Progress in behavior modification* (Vol. 27, pp. 56–85). New York: Academic Press.

Franzen, M.D. (2000). *Reliability and validity in neuropsychological assessment* (2nd ed.). New York: Kluwer Academic/Plenum.

Franzen, M.D., & Smith-Seemiller, L. (1998). Behavioral neuropsychology. In A.S. Bellack & M. Hersen (Eds.), *Behavioral assessment: A practical handbook* (pp. 407–417). Boston: Allyn & Bacon.

Franzen, M.D., & Wilhelm, K.L. (2000). Conceptual foundations of ecological validity in neuropsychological assessment. In R. Sbordone & C.J. Long (Eds.), *The ecological validity of neuropsychological testing* (pp. 91–112). Winter Park, FL: GR Press.

Freedman, M., Leach, L., Kaplan, E., Winocur, G., Shulman, K., & Delis, D. (1994). *The clock drawing test: A neuropsychological analysis.* New York: Oxford University Press.

Gabrieli, J.D., Vaidya, C.J., Stone, M., Francis, W.S., Thompson-Schill, S.L., Fleischman, D.A., Tinklenberg, J.R., Yeasavage, J.A., & Wilson, R.S. (1999). Convergent behavioral and neuropsychological evidence for a distinction between identification and production forms of repetition priming. *Journal of Experimental Psychology, 128,* 479–498.

Gioia, G.A., Isquith, P.K., Guy, S.C., & Kenworthy, L. (2000). Behavior rating inventory of executive function. *Child Neuropsychology, 6,* 235–238.

Golden, C.J. (1978). *Stroop color and word test: A manual for clinical and experimental use.* Chicago: Stoelting.

Goodglass, H., & Kaplan, E. (1983). *The assessment of aphasia and related disorders.* Philadelphia: Lea and Fibiger.

400 Behavioral Neuropsychology

Gordon, J., Powell, C., & Rockwood, K. (2000). "Is improvement possible in the measurement of behaviour disturbance in dementia?" Comment. *International Journal of Geriatric Psychiatry, 15,* 664–665.

Greene, Y.M., Tariot, P.N., Wishart, H., Cox, C., Holt, C.J., Schwid, S., & Noviasky, J. (2000). A 12-week, open trial of donezepil hydrochloride in patients with multiple sclerosis and associated cognitive impairments. *Journal of Clinical Psychopharmacology, 20,* 350–356.

Hadwin, J., & Hutley, G. (1998). Detecting features of autism in children with severe learning difficulties: A brief report. *Autism, 2,* 269–280.

Hall, S.J., Halperin, J.M., Schwartz, S.T., & Newcorn, J.H. (1997). Behavioral and executive functions in children with attention-deficit hyperactivity disorder and reading disability. *Journal of Attention Disorders, 1,* 235–247.

Harwood, D.G., Ownby, R.L., Barker, W.W., & Duara, R. (1998). The Behavioral Pathology in Alzheimer's Disease Scale (BEHAVE-AD): Factor structure among community-dwelling Alzheimer's disease patients. *International Journal of Geriatric Psychiatry, 13,* 793–800.

Haynes, S.N. (1998). The changing nature of behavioral assessment. In A.S. Bellack and M. Hersen (Eds.), *Behavioral assessment: A practical handbook* (pp. 1–17). Boston: Allyn & Bacon.

Heaton, R.K., Chelune, G.J., Talley, J.L., Kay, G.G., & Curtiss, G. (1993). *Wisconsin card sorting test manual: Revised and expanded.* Odessa, FL: Psychological Assessment Resources.

Heinik, J., Solomesh, I., Shein, V., Mester, R., Bleuch, A., & Becker, D. (2001). Correlation between clock-drawing test and paranoid and delusional ideation in dementia of the Alzheimer's type. *International Journal of Geriatric Psychiatry, 16,* 735–736.

Jelicic, M., Henquet, C.E.C., Derix, M.M.A., & Jolles, J. (2001). Test-retest reliability of the behavioral assessment of the dysexecutive syndrome in a sample of psychiatric patients. *International Journal of Neurosciences, 110,* 73–78.

Kohler, F.W., & Strain, P.S. (1997). Procedures for assessing and increasing social interaction. In N.N. Singh (Ed.), *Prevention and treatment of severe behavior problems: Models and methods in developmental disabilities* (pp. 49–59). Pacific Grove, CA: Brooks/Cole.

Kunik, M.E., Huffman, J.C., Bharani, N., Hillman, S.L., Molinari, V.A., & Orengo, C.A. (2000). Behavioral disturbances in geropsychiatric inpatients across dementia types. *Journal of Geriatric Psychiatry and Neurology, 13,* 49–52.

Lebert, F., Pasquier, F., Danel, T., Steinling, M., Petit, H., & Cabaret, M. (1994). Psychiatric, neuropsychologic, and SPECT evidence of elated mood in dementia of Alzheimer's type. *Neuropsychiatry, Neuropsychology, and Behavioral Neurology, 7,* 299–340.

Lefroy, R.B., McHale, P., Hyndman, J., & Hobbs, M.S.T. (1996). Understanding the behaviour of people in special dementia units: The contribution of rating scales. *Australian Journal on Ageing, 15,* 105–110.

Loeb, P.A. (1996). *Independent living scales manual.* San Francisco: Harcourt, Brace Jovanovich.

Loewenstein, D.A., Amigo, D.A., Duara, R., Guterman, A., Hurwitz, D., Berkowitz, N., Wilkie, F., Weinberg, G., Black, B., Gittleman, B., & Eisdorfer, C. (1989). A new scale for the assessment of functional status in Alzheimer's and related disorders. *Journal of Gerontology: Psychological Sciences, 44,* 114–121.

Martin, C., West, J., Cull, C., & Adams, M. (2000). A preliminary study investigating how people with mild intellectual disabilities perform on the Rivermead Behavioural Memory Test. *Journal of Applied Research in Intellectual Disabilities, 13,* 186–193.

McCarty, H.J., Roth, D.L., Goode, K.T., Owen, J.E., Harrell, L., Donovan, K., & Haley, W.E. (2000). Longitudinal course of behavioral problems during Alzheimer's disease: Linear vs. curvilinear patterns of decline. *Journals of Gerontology Series A: Biological Sciences & Medical Sciences, 55A,* M200–M206.

McDaniel, W.F. (2001). A simple strategy for the qualitative assessment of learning capacity of clients with mental retardation or other severe cognitive deficits. *Developmental Disabilities Bulletin, 29,* 1–22.

McGinty, S., Podell, K., Franzen, M.D., Baird, A.D., & Williams, M.J. (2002). Standard measures of executive function in predicting instrumental activities of daily living in older adults. *International Journal of Geriatric Psychiatry, 17,* 828–834.

McPherson, K., Berry, A., & Pentland, B. (1997). Relationships between cognitive impairments and functional performance after brain injury as measured by the Functional Assessment Measures (FIM + FAM). *Neuropsychological Rehabilitation, 7,* 241–257.

Mega, M.S., Masterman, D.M., O'Connor, S.M., Barclay, T.R., & Cummings, J.L. (1999). The spectrum of behavioral responses to cholinesterase inhibitor therapy in Alzheimer disease. *Archives of Neurology, 56,* 1388–1393.

Michell, J. (1986). Measurement scales and statistics: A clash of paradigms. *Psychological Bulletin, 100,* 398–407.

Monteiro, I.M., Auer, S.R., Boksay, I., & Reisberg, B. (2000). New and promising modalities for assessment of behavioral and psychological symptoms of dementia. *International Psychogeriatrics, 12,* 175–178.

O'Reilly, M.F., Lancioni, G.E., & Emerson, E. (1999). A systematic analysis of the influence of prior social context on aggression and self-injurious behavior within analogue analysis assessments. *Behavior Modification, 23,* 578–596.

Padoani, W., & De Leo, D. (2000). Severe and persistent regressive behaviors in three elderly subjects without cognitive decline. *International Journal of Geriatric Psychiatry, 15,* 70–74.

Perrin, T. (1998). Single-system methodology: A way forward in dementia care? *British Journal of Occupational Therapy, 61,* 448–452.

Peters, R.H., Koller, J.R., & Holliday, G.A. (1995). A functional assessment approach to strategy development and implementation for a person with a specific learning disability: A case study. *Journal of Applied Rehabilitation Counseling, 26,* 30–35.

Piazza, C.C., Hanley, G.P., Bowman, L.G., Ruyter, J.M., Lindauer, S.E., & Saiontz, D.M. (1997). Functional analysis and treatment of elopement. *Journal of Applied Behavior Analysis, 30,* 653–672.

Plaud, J.J., Moberg, M., Ferraro, F.R. (1998). A review of Alzheimer's disease and dementia: Applied behavioral assessment and treatment approaches. *Journal of Clinical Geropsychology, 4,* 269–300.

Pyles, D.A.M., Muniz, K., Cade, A., & Silva, R. (1997). A behavioral diagnostic paradigm for integrating behavior-analytic and psychopharmacological interventions for people with a dual diagnosis. *Research in Developmental Disabilities, 18,* 185–214.

Pyles, D.A.M., Riordan, M.M., & Bailey, J.S. (1997). The stereotypy analysis: An instrument for examining environmental variables with differential rates of stereotypic behavior. *Research in Developmental Disabilities, 18,* 11–38.

Ready, R.E., Stierman, L., & Paulsen, J.S. (2001). Ecological validity of neuropsychological and personality measures of executive functions. *Clinical Neuropsychologist, 15,* 314–323.

Reisberg, B., Monteiro, I., Boksay, I., Auer, S., Torossian, C., & Kenowsky, S. (2000). Do many of the behavioral and psychological symptoms of dementia constitute a distinct clinical syndrome? Current evidence using the BEHAVE-AD. *International Psychogeriatrics, 12,* 155–164.

Reitan, R.A., & Wolfson, D. (1993). *The Halstead-Reitan Neuropsychological Battery: Theory and clinical interpretation.* Tucson, AZ: Neuropsychology Press.

Richman, D.M., Wacker, D.P., Asmus, J.M., Casey, S.D., & Andelman, M. (1999). Further analysis of problem behavior in response class hierarchies. *Journal of Applied Behavior Analysis, 32,* 269–283.

Rizzo, A.A., Buckwalter, J.G., Neumann, U., Kesselman, C., & Thiebaux, M. (1998). Basic issues in the application of virtual reality for the assessment and rehabilitation of cognitive impairment and functional disabilities. *CyberPsychology and Behavior, 1,* 59–78.

Roane, H.S., Vollmer, T.R., Ringdahl, J.E., & Marcus, B.A. (1998). Evaluation of a brief stimulus preference assessment. *Journal of Applied Behavior Analysis, 31,* 605–620.

Ross, L.L., Yu, S., Dickie, Y., & Kropla, W.C. (1998) *Behavior Modification, 22,* 321–334.

Shah, A., & Allen, H. (1999). Is improvement possible in the measurement of behaviour disturbance in dementia? *International Journal of Geriatric Psychiatry, 14,* 512–519.

Simpson, G., Tate, R., Ferry, K., Hodgkinson, A., & Blacszcynski, A. (2001). Social neuroradiologic, medical, and neuropsychological correlates of sexually aberrant behavior after traumatic brain injury. *Journal of Head Trauma Rehabilitation, 16,* 556–572.

Starkstein, S.E., Petracca, G., Chemerisnki, E., & Kremer, J. (2001). Syndromic validity of apathy in Alzheimer's disease. *American Journal of Psychiatry, 158,* 872–877.

Stewart, N.J., Hiscock, M., Morgan, D.G., Murphy, P.B., & Yamamoto, M. (1998). Development and psychometric evaluation of the Environment-Behavior Interaction Code (EBIC). *Nursing Research, 48,* 260–268.

Tariot, P.N., Porsteinsson, A., Teri, L., & Weiner, M.F. (1996). Measurement of behavioral disturbance in chronic care populations. *Journal of Mental Health and Aging, 2,* 213–229.

Toogood, S., & Timlin, K. (1996). The functional assessment of challenging behaviour: A comparison of informant-based, experimental, and descriptive methods. *Journal of Applied Research in Intellectual Disabilities, 9,* 206–222.

Van Haitsma, K., Lawton, M.P., Kleban, M.H., Klapper, J., & Korn, J. (1997). Methodological aspects of the study of streams of behavior in elders with dementing illness. *Alzheimer's Disease and Associated Disorders, 11,* 228–238.

Venneri, A., Grassi, F., & Caffarra, P. (1996). Dementia of the frontal lobe type: Report of the neuroimaging and neuropsychological results of a case study. *Dementia, 7,* 155–160.

Vieweg, V., Blair, C.E., Tucker, R., & Lewis, R. (1995). A geropsychiatric hospital survey to determine behavioural factors leading to hospital admission. *Journal of Clinical Geropsychology, 1,* 305–311.

Wechsler, D. (1997). *Wechsler Memory Scale—Third edition.* San Antonio, TX: Psychological Corporation.

Weiner, M.F., Koss, E., Patterson, M., Jin, S., Teri, L., Thomas, R., Thals, L.J., & Whitehouse, P. (1998). A comparison of the Cohen-Mansfield Agitation Inventory with the CERAD behavioral rating scale for dementia in community-dwelling persons with Alzheimer's disease. *Journal of Psychiatric Research, 32,* 347–351.

Whall, A.L., Black, M.E.A., Yankou, D.J., Groh, C.J., Kupferschmid, B., Foster, N.L., & Little, R. (1999). Nurse aides' identification of onset and level of agitation in late stage dementia patients. *American Journal of Alzheimer's Disease, 14,* 202–206.

Wilson, B.A., Evabs, J.J., Emslie, H., Alderman, N., & Burgess, P. (1998). The development of an ecologically valid test for assessing patients with dysexecutive syndrome. *Neuropsychological Rehabilitation, 8,* 213–228.

Yarbrough, S.C., & Carr, E.G. (2000). Some relationship between informant assessment and functional analysis of problem behavior. *American Journal of Mental Retardation, 105,* 130–151.

Zanetti, O., Geroldi, C., Frisoni, G.B., Bianchetti, A., & Trabucchi, M. (1999). Contrasting results between caregivers' report and direct assessment of activities of daily living in patients affected by mild and very mild dementia: The contribution of the caregiver's personal characteristics. *Journal of American Geriatrics Society, 47,* 196–202.

CHAPTER 21

Case Formulation in Cognitive-Behavior Therapy

ARTHUR M. NEZU, CHRISTINE MAGUTH NEZU, MICHELLE A. PEACOCK, AND CANDACE P. GIRDWOOD

> When a man does not know what harbor he is making
> for, no wind is the right wind.
>
> —Seneca

INTRODUCTION

Over two millennia ago, the Roman philosopher Seneca eloquently underscored the importance of determining one's goals prior to articulating specific means by which to achieve them. He also implied in this quote that one needs additionally to identify the obstacles to such goals in order to develop an effective "traveling route." In a psychotherapy context, this translates into the need to first develop a veridical case formulation of a given individual's problems prior to helping him or her overcome them.

What Is Case Formulation?

Case formulation can be viewed as a set of hypotheses, generally framed by a particular personality theory or psycho-

therapy orientation, regarding what variables serve as causes, triggers, and/or maintaining factors of an individual's emotional, psychological, interpersonal, and behavior problems (Eells, 1997). It is a description of a patient's complaints and symptoms of distress, as well as an organizing mechanism to help the clinician understand how such complaints came into being, how various symptoms coexist, what environmental or intrapersonal stimuli trigger such problems, and why such symptoms persist. A case formulation can also help to determine how various *nomothetic* information (about such problems, symptoms, complaints) found in the professional and empirical literature can be *idiographically* relevant to a given patient. Finally, it helps guide the clinician when deciding how to best help the patient overcome such complaints. In other words, it helps to answer the type of question that Paul (1969) first asked over 30 years ago (as paraphrased by Nezu & Nezu, 1989, p. 30)—"What procedures should be implemented, with this specific patient, who has this particular disorder, given these unique characteristics and circumstances?"

Problems in Case Formulation

Case formulation requires a plethora of clinical decisions. Unfortunately, human decision making in general has been demonstrated to be frequently unreliable and invalid due to various cognitive impediments (Kahnemann & Tversky, 1973). Moreover, decisions made by health and mental health professionals have also been consistently shown to be vulnerable to errors in clinical reasoning (Arkes, 1981; Nezu & Nezu, 1989).

Tversky and Kahneman (1974) identified three judgmental heuristics or strategies that can negatively affect the veracity of the reasoning process when people make decisions. The *availability heuristic* is invoked when people attempt to estimate the frequency of a class or the probability of an event based on the *facility or ease* with which instances of that class or event come to mind. As an example related to clinical assessment, the availability heuristic might affect a therapist's prediction of a new patient's risk for suicide if a recent case involved a person who actually committed suicide when the initial risk was thought to be low. The *representativeness heuristic* occurs when attempting to assess the degree to which certain events are related to each other (e.g., "What is the probability that A is associated with B or that A is a member of class B?" "What is the likelihood that event A caused event B or that B caused A?") based on the perceived degree to which A resembles B. From a cognitive perspective, a major problem caused by representativeness thinking occurs when a schema is accessed by a given characteristic to the exclusion of other schemas. For example, if a particular diagnostic schema (e.g., major depression) is accessed automatically as a function of this heuristic on the basis of a given symptom (e.g., feelings of sadness), once this schema is accessed, the search for new information is likely to cease. The probability of viewing the patient's problems from the perspective of other conceptual or diagnostic schemas (e.g., bipolar illness, medically related mood difficulties, personality disorder) becomes substantially reduced, thus restricting the range of possible causal hypotheses that might be considered.

The third heuristic, *anchoring,* occurs when a shortcut method of estimation or prediction is used whereby ultimate decisions are based more on initial impressions than on subsequent information, even though this new information is conflicting. For example, two thirds of a sample of more than 300 behavior therapists indicated that less than two sessions were required to conceptualize a patient's problem (Swan & MacDonald, 1978). Thus, if the depressed patient only discusses issues of interpersonal difficulties during these two sessions, unless the therapist ensures that a broad spectrum of other problem areas are explored, the anchoring heuristic might influence the clinician to select poor social skills as the predominant reason why this patient is depressed without the benefit of a more extensive case formulation.

In addition to those heuristics identified by Tversky and Kahenmann (1974), other problems in clinical reasoning have been reported (see Nezu & Nezu, 1989). First, the strategy itself used to obtain information when making decisions often inadvertently leads to erroneous conclusions. For example, selective attention to certain types of information can lead to biased perceptions of the degree of covariation between two events. Second, confirmatory search strategies have been shown to be ubiquitous means by which people attempt to verify inferences and make predictions. These strategies involve procedures that seek only to obtain information that supports one's initial impressions; attempts to seek disconfirming evidence are rare. In addition, being overconfident in one's abilities can serve as a source of systematic error in clinical reasoning, as confidence has been found to be unrelated to clinical accuracy.

These judgmental biases can lead to a situation, for example, in which a patient who complains of depressive feelings is automatically taught to change his or her negative cognitions (or to cope with stressful problems or increase positive experiences or become more assertive) without the benefit of a more detailed and comprehensive case formulation. Put another way, how a clinician conceptualizes a patient's problems may depend to a large degree on these heuristics rather than on a careful case formulation. Because such conceptualizations can influence the therapist's behavior (e.g., which problems become targeted, which assessment procedures are applied, which interventions become implemented), formal guidelines to develop valid case formulations are crucial.

Case Formulation and Behavior Therapy

Historically, the major thrust behind the empirical efforts extended by behavior therapists was aimed at developing, improving, and validating assessment and treatment protocols rather than at the process of clinical judgment and decision making invoked when applying such assessment and treatment protocols to a particular patient (Nezu, Nezu, Friedman, & Haynes, 1997). For example, whereas significant advancements have occurred during the past several decades regarding the empirically based assessment of psychological problems, few scholarly attempts have addressed the translation of such assessment data into treatment design recommendations.

This is especially salient when considering that there are few "textbook cases" whereby any patient matches exactly the subject sample contained in a given outcome investigation addressing that patient's presenting problem (Nezu & Nezu, 1989). Differences in age, sex, race, cultural background, severity of symptomatology, presence of comorbid disorders, historical background, current socioeconomic status, and nature of one's social support network are probably likely to exist. As Hersen (1981) stated, "complex problems require complex solutions." Moreover, a multitude of causal hypotheses within a cognitive-behavioral perspective exist for the same psychological disorder. Major depression, for example, has been found to be causally related to a wide variety of psychosocial variables, including cognitive distortions, ineffective social skills, deficient problem-solving ability, inaccurate attributions, and poor self-control skills (Nezu, 1987). However, studies have also demonstrated that no one cause ubiquitously characterizes all people experiencing depression (Nezu & Nezu, 1993). This lack of consistency for any given clinical disorder leaves substantial room for error when attempting to articulate idiographically a case formulation for a specific patient.

As such, there is a need for systematic models that help guide behavior therapists when conducting assessment and treatment. The purpose of this chapter is to present several models of case formulation within a broad-based behavioral perspective that have been articulated as a means of enhancing this decision-making process. We begin with a description of our own model, which is based on a problem-solving paradigm (e.g., Nezu & Nezu, 1989), followed by descriptions of three additional approaches. The first is that of Persons (e.g., Persons & Tompkins, 1997), who attempts to synthesize elements of cognitive therapy and functional analysis. The second model has been articulated by Linehan (e.g., Koerner & Linehan, 1997) and focuses on the case formulation process specific to dialectical behavior therapy. The last model to be described has been developed by Haynes and his colleagues (e.g., Haynes, 1994; Haynes et al., 1993) and provides for a more quantitative approach to functional analysis.

NEZU AND NEZU'S PROBLEM-SOLVING MODEL OF COGNITIVE-BEHAVIORAL CASE FORMULATION

Our model of cognitive-behavioral case formulation (Nezu & Nezu, 1989; 1993; Nezu, Nezu, Saad, & Good, 1999) characterizes the therapist as an active problem solver. In this role, clinicians are faced with a series of "problems to solve" whenever conducting assessment and treatment. This clinical situation represents various problems because of the inherent discrepancy between the individual's current state (i.e., pres-

ence of complaints, problems, symptoms) and his or her desired state (i.e., achievement of his or her goals). According to this problem-solving framework, numerous impediments or obstacles exist that prevent patients from reaching their goals without the therapist's aid. Such variables may be related to the patients themselves (e.g., behavioral, cognitive, affective, or physiological excesses or deficits) or to the environment (e.g., lack of resources, presence of aversive stimuli). Cognitive-behavioral assessment and treatment, therefore, represent a therapist's attempt to solve these problems. To achieve such goals, we advocate adopting a problem-solving perspective of clinical decision making. Simply put, our model recommends using various problem-solving operations in order to effectively address such clinical problems, which includes identifying salient treatment targets and goals, developing an efficacious treatment protocol, and evaluating the outcome of a given implemented intervention (Nezu & Nezu, 1995).

The Problem-Solving Process

Our approach to case formulation draws heavily from the prescriptive model of social problem solving developed by D'Zurilla, Nezu, and their colleagues (e.g., D'Zurilla & Nezu, 1999; Nezu, Nezu, Friedman, Faddis, & Houts, 1998) but focuses specifically on two major problem-solving components—problem orientation and rational problem-solving skills. *Problem orientation* refers to the set of orienting responses (e.g., general beliefs, assumptions, appraisals, and expectations) one engages in when attempting to understand and react to problems in general. To a large degree, this can be viewed as one's world view regarding problems. A world view refers to the underlying philosophical framework that contributes to a person's understanding of how the world works (Pepper, 1942). Relevant to the present discussion, a clinician's world view provides the cohesive framework that guides his or her attempts to understand, explain, predict, and change human behavior. In this case, the overarching world view would be one that is in keeping with a cognitive-behavioral perspective. We previously defined our world view of cognitive-behavior therapy as falling

within an experimental-clinical framework and incorporates a broad definition of behavior that includes overt actions, internal cognitive phenomena, and the experience of affect or emotions. These components range in complexity from molecular (i.e., lower-level) events (e.g., smoking a cigarette, hyperventilation, a critical comment in a dyadic interaction) to molar (i.e., higher-level) pluralistic and multidimensional constructs (e.g., complex social skills, solving a difficult calculus problem, major depressive disorder) (Nezu et al., 1997, pp. 368–369).

TABLE 21.1   Specific Tasks Associated with Rational Problem-Solving Skills

Defining Problems
- Gathering facts about the problem
- Describing these facts in clear and unambiguous terms
- Differentiating between facts and assumptions
- Identifying factors (e.g., obstacles) that make the situation a problem
- Setting realistic problem-solving goals

Generating Alternatives
- Generating multiple alternative solutions
- Deferring initial critical judgment until a later time
- Thinking of general strategies, as well as specific tactics, when generating alternatives

Making Decisions
- Evaluating alternatives according to (a) the likelihood that the alternative, if implemented optimally, will achieve the desired goals and (b) the value of that alternative in terms of personal, social, short-term, and long-term consequences
- Developing solution plans that have the highest utility

Evaluating Solution Outcome
- Carrying out the chosen plan as optimally as possible
- Monitoring the consequences of the implemented solution
- Comparing the predicted and actual consequences
- Recycling through the process if the outcome is unsatisfactory

Whereas one's problem orientation is primarily a cognitive activity, *rational problem-solving skills* entail specific cognitive and behavioral tasks and operations that are used to solve a problem effectively. These include: (a) defining problems; (b) generating alternatives; (c) making decisions; and (d) evaluating the solution outcome. Table 21.1 lists the specific activities associated with each of these problem-solving tasks. Although not all of these problem-solving operations are directly relevant to case formulation, the model encourages their use where appropriate when addressing any clinical decisions that are encountered during the course of treatment.

Phases of Therapy

As depicted in Figure 21.1, behavior therapy can be viewed as incorporating three major interrelated phases, each of which is associated with certain important clinical decisions (Nezu & Nezu, 1989): (a) *case formulation* (also termed "problem analysis" by Nezu & Nezu, 1989; e.g., What are this patient's problems, how did they come to be this way, and what are meaningful and reasonable treatment goals for this particular patient?); (b) *treatment design* (e.g., What treatment strategies and clinical interventions should be implemented to achieve these goals?); and (c) *outcome evaluation* (e.g., What are the effects of this treatment plan, and does it need to be adjusted?).[1]

As Figure 21.1 suggests, the flow of these treatment phases are not linearly unidirectional. Rather, the outcome of one phase can lead to the need to revisit a previous phase. For example, if the outcome of a particular intervention strategy is unsatisfactory (e.g., a patient's depression level is not attenuating), the therapist needs to review whether errors were made during the case formulation phase (e.g., the "cause" of the depression for this patient was not properly identified) or the treatment design phase (e.g., a particular intervention was not optimally implemented).

In addition to the major clinical tasks generally associated with these three therapy phases, other problems that affect treatment success may arise during the course of therapy (e.g., poor patient motivation, scheduling difficulties, identification or emergence of new patient problems). The effectiveness of a clinician's decision making when such problems emerge plays an important role in the success of any intervention plan. Therefore, this model advocates using the various problem-solving operations to effectively address the multiple clinical tasks and decisions encountered during the course of treatment.

Goals of Case Formulation

According to our model (Nezu & Nezu, 1989, 1993), during this initial treatment phase, the therapist seeks to (a) obtain a detailed understanding of the patient's presenting problems, (b) identify variables that are functionally related to such difficulties in order to select salient intervention targets, and (c) delineate general treatment goals and objectives. General treatment goals have been characterized by Rosen and Proctor (1981) as *ultimate outcomes* or outcomes "for which treatment is undertaken and reflect the objectives toward which treatment efforts are to be directed" (p. 419). These are differentiated from *instrumental outcomes,* which are changes or effects that "serve as the instruments for the attainment of other outcomes" (Rosen & Proctor, 1981, p. 419). Instrumental outcomes, depending on their functional relationships to other variables, may have an impact on ultimate outcomes (e.g., increasing one's self-esteem can reduce the severity of depressive behaviors) or on other instrumental outcomes within a hypothesized causal chain (e.g., improving a patient's coping ability can increase his or her self-esteem, which in turn may decrease depressive severity).

Clinically, instrumental outcomes (or "intermediate goals," Mash & Hunsley, 1993) can reflect the therapist's hypotheses concerning the variables that are believed to be pathogenically related to (i.e., causal variables that affect) the ultimate outcome(s). Experimentally, instrumental outcomes can be viewed as independent variables (IVs), whereas ultimate

TREATMENT PHASES

RELATED SAMPLE CLINICAL DECISIONS

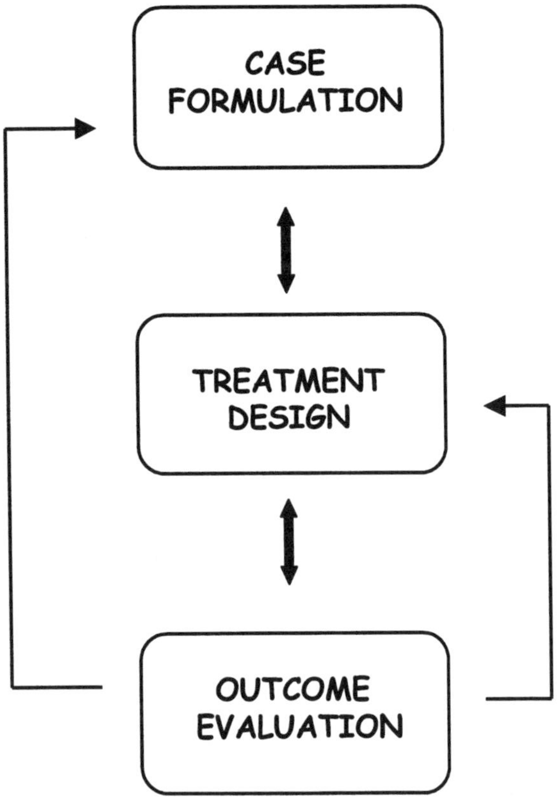

What areas of this patient's life should be assessed?
What methods should I use to gather more information?
Should I obtain information from other sources?
What targets should be chosen?
What general goals should be specified?

What problems should be targeted first?
What are effective treatments for these problems?
What intervention strategies should be employed?
Should I include others in treatment?
What intervention should be conducted first?

What methods do I use to evaluate outcome?
How long should treatment continue without change before I alter strategies?
When should treatment stop?

Figure 21.1 Phases of therapy and sample-related clinical decisions.

outcomes represent dependent variables (DVs). Instrumental outcome variables can serve as mediators, which are those variables that account for or explain the relationship between two other variables, similar to a causal mechanism (i.e., the mechanism by which the IV impacts or influences the DV). They can also serve as moderators, or those types of factors that can influence the strength and/or direction of the relationship between two or more other variables (Haynes & O'Brien, 2000). In this manner, instrumental variables denote potential targets for clinical interventions. For example, Nezu and his colleagues (Nezu, Nezu, Saraydarian, Kalmar, & Ronan, 1986; Nezu & Ronan, 1985) found that social problem-solving ability serves to moderate the relationship between negative life stress and depression. More specifically, under equivalently high levels of negative life stress, individuals characterized as effective problem solvers report lower levels of depression than their ineffective problem-solving counterparts. Such findings suggest that interventions geared to improve one's problem-solving ability to cope with stressful

events leads to the attenuation of depression, a hypothesis subsequently supported by outcome investigations (e.g., Nezu, 1986; Nezu, Nezu, & Perri, 1989; Nezu & Perri, 1989).

In this manner, making the distinction between instrumental and ultimate outcomes can help guide the process of treatment planning, implementation, and evaluation (Kanfer & Schefft, 1988; Nezu et al., 1997). In addition, it can also help to identify when treatment is *not* working. Mash and Hunsley (1993), for example, indicate that within the context of clinical practice, a primary goal of assessment is early corrective feedback, rather than a simple evaluation at the "endpoint" of the successful or unsuccessful achievement of a patient's ultimate goal. For example, if a cognitive therapy intervention is found to be ineffective in engendering changes in a depressed patient's negative self-schemas, then such an evaluation provides for immediate feedback that this particular treatment may not be working. Therefore, in order to reduce the likelihood of treatment failure, assessment of success in achieving instrumental outcomes or goals should precede evaluation of reaching one's ultimate goals, in this case, a decrease in depression.

In sum, according to this model, to effectively address the three major objectives associated with the case formulation process (i.e., better understanding the patient's problems, identifying and selecting salient instrumental outcomes or intervention targets, delineating general treatment goals), the therapist should apply the various problem-solving operations as described next.

Applying the Problem-Solving Model: Problem Orientation

Relevant to case formulation, as a means of minimizing the likelihood that the cognitive-behavioral therapist will engage in the judgmental biases described earlier, the current model advocates adopting a problem orientation that emphasizes two additional perspectives: (a) behavior can be multiply caused, and (b) behavior generally occurs within various systems.

The multiple causality framework is derived from a planned clinical multiplism philosophy. This methodological approach to the conduct of science advocates the use of multiple operations (Cook, 1985). In the context of clinical assessment, this framework suggests numerous paths by which the same set of symptoms can manifest across different patients. Further, within a multiple causality framework, variables that act and interact in the initiation and maintenance of an individual's symptoms may be biological, psychological, or social. These factors may contribute to the presence of a symptom or disorder in either a proximal (i.e., immediate antecedent, such as the presence of a phobic object) or a distal (i.e., developmental history, such as the occurrence of a traumatic event) manner.

A *systems perspective* emphasizes the notion that instrumental and ultimate outcome variables can relate to each other in mutually interactive ways, rather than in a simple unidirectional and linear fashion (Kanfer, 1985). For example, Nezu, Nezu, and Lombardo (2001) outline how biological, psychological, and social factors all interact with each other in initiating and maintaining various nonbiologically caused distressing physical symptoms (e.g., noncardiac chest pain, fibromyalgia). For example, early imitative learning within a family where a parent responds to stress with undue physical symptoms can serve as a psychological vulnerability factor that influences the manner in which a child interprets the experience of physical symptoms (i.e., gastrointestinal distress) under stressful circumstances. Such cognitive factors then can influence his or her behavior (e.g., avoid stressful circumstances, seek out his or her parents for reassurance, focus undue attention on the distress "caused" by the symp-

toms). This behavior in turn can lead to parental reinforcement of such behavior and an exacerbation of the symptoms, which in turn can lead to an intensification of the child's schema concerning appropriate behavior under certain circumstances, and so forth. In this manner, the reciprocal relationships among the various cognitive, behavioral, environmental, and biological/physical factors comprise a unique constellation of causal chains within an overall network that can change over time and under different circumstances for a given individual.

Our model, then, advocates assessing the manner in which such pathogenically involved variables reciprocally interact with one another in order to obtain a more complete and comprehensive picture of a patient's unique network. Using a systems perspective allows the behavior therapist to better identify the instrumental outcome variables that play a central role in order to prioritize such variables as initial treatment targets. In other words, those instrumental variables that appear to be either functionally related to a wide range of other instrumental variables in the network or related to ultimate outcome variables in a significant manner (i.e., the strength of the relationship is significant, as in a high correlation coefficient), would appear to be important initial treatment targets, as changes in such key variables are likely to engender maximal change in both intermediate and ultimate outcome factors. An additional advantage of identifying the interacting variables in an individual's system is that it enables the therapist to delineate numerous potential targets, thereby increasing the likelihood of success if all such variables are the targets of effective interventions.

Applying the Problem-Solving Model: Defining Problems

Using problem-solving language, the focus at this point involves gathering information, separating facts from assumptions, and identifying the factors that contribute to the problem situation while using clear and unambiguous language. With regard to the case formulation process, the first step is to investigate a wide range of areas of the patient's life (e.g., interpersonal relationships, job, finances, sex, physical health) in order to ensure a broad understanding of his or her current functioning. This leads to the delineation of various ultimate outcome goals. It should be noted that, whereas ultimate outcomes are often patient defined in a direct manner (e.g., "I'm feeling really sad and I want to feel better," "I have a lot of difficulty having good relationships with the opposite sex"), at times they are the therapist's translations of a patient's presenting complaints. Such translations can be in the form of formal diagnostic categories (e.g., obsessive-compulsive disorder, major depression) or a series of statements regarding specific problem situations (e.g., "to improve interpersonal relationships," "to increase self-confidence and self-esteem," "to reduce pain"). Further, as a function of changes that occur due to treatment, certain ultimate outcome goals may be discarded, modified, or new ones added by the patient or the therapist.

Of particular importance during this phase is the identification of instrumental outcome variables that are potentially causally related to the articulated ultimate outcome goals. The important concern here relates to the issue of content validity (Haynes, personal communication, 2001), where the clinician needs to identify the representative elements that are contained in the domains of the universe of important causal variables potentially impacting a patient's problems (called a "problem space" by Nezu & Nezu, 1989). To help facilitate this search, two guides can be used by the therapist to better identify potential problems and related causal variables: a theory-driven strategy and a diagnosis-driven strategy. A *theory-driven strategy* recommends that the empirically based literature linking various instrumental outcomes to ultimate outcomes be used to guide the therapist's search for meaningful clinical targets. For example, if one ultimate outcome goal is to reduce anger, the empirical literature containing multiple theories attempting to explain, for example, why people get angry or have difficulties controlling anger, would be an important source to search for potentially important causally related variables. This pool of nomothetically derived instrumental outcome variables may then be evaluated idiographically based on its applicability to a particular patient.

A *diagnosis-driven strategy* may also facilitate the identification of treatment targets. Diagnostic guidelines, such as the *DSM-IV* (American Psychiatric Association, 1994), may provide a useful means of understanding response clusters and response covariations (Haynes, 1986). Symptoms of clusters that have been found to covary and that have been categorized within particular diagnostic categories can guide the therapist's assessment. In other words, this type of search would be guided by a patient's diagnosis—for example, major depressive disorder—whereby the literature on the treatment of depression can identify potentially relevant causal variables.

Whereas theory-driven and diagnosis-driven approaches can foster the identification of relevant instrumental outcome variables, it is incumbent on the therapist to be guided by the multiple causality framework previously described. For example, exclusive use of a single theory to guide one's assessment strategy increases the likelihood of judgmental errors. Likewise, labeling and categorizing patients into a diagnostic category may erroneously imply that their behavior problems are always related to similar underlying variables.

To better understand the specific nature of these variables, we recommend the use of a multidimensional framework (Nezu & Nezu, 1989, 1993). The first assessment dimension of this model relates to the patient him- or herself (i.e., behavior, affect, cognition, biology), as well as his or her environment (i.e., physical environment, social environment). For the purposes of the case formulation process, problem behaviors can be globally categorized as either behavioral deficits or excesses (Kanfer & Schefft, 1988). Examples of behavioral deficits include poor social skills, deficits in daily living skills, or poor self-control. Behavioral excesses might include compulsive behavior, avoidance of anxiety-provoking stimuli, frequent negative self-evaluation, or aggressive actions. Problematic affect involves the wide array of negative emotions and mood states, such as anxiety, depression, hopelessness, fear, anger, and hostility. With regard to psychopathology-related cognitive factors, it is useful to distinguish between cognitive deficiencies and cognitive distortions (Kendall, 1985). Cognitive deficiencies are absences in one's thinking processes (e.g., failure to contemplate the consequences of one's actions). Cognitive distortions refer to errors in cognitive processing (e.g., misinterpretations of certain events based on dichotomous thinking). Biological variables include the wide range of physiological, medical, and physical factors that are problems by themselves or functionally related to a patient's psychosocial problems or goals. These can include such factors as a medical illness, physical limitation or disability, side effect of medication, or biological vulnerability to heightened arousal under stress. Physical environmental variables can include housing, climate, and living conditions. Social environmental factors can include a patient's relationships with friends and family.

The second assessment dimension involves time. Specifically, this temporal factor suggests that gathering information regarding a patient's current and past functioning can contribute to a more accurate case formulation. Current or proximal factors often serve as potential stressors that can trigger various maladaptive behaviors, cognitions, and affective states. In addition, those variables that are temporally distant from current problems often contribute to a better understanding of a patient's current difficulties (e.g., early trauma can engender posttraumatic stress disorder symptoms years later); understanding a patient's family history can provide information concerning how the patient developed certain beliefs about the world. Identifying these distal variables provides another opportunity to investigate the causal mechanisms that may contribute to the patient's major problems. Note that inclusion of such variables in this model is different than other theoretical construct systems (e.g., psychodynamic psychotherapy) that focus heavily on past events.

The function of each of these variables with respect to the identified ultimate outcome constitutes the final assessment dimension. Function here refers to the covariation that exists between two or more variables. In many cases, this covariation signifies causation (i.e., that A "caused" B), whereas in others, there may be no need to invoke the concept of causality (i.e., that A simply changes when B changes and visa versa). In this latter case, the covariation can describe a functional relationship whereby one variable serves as a maintaining factor of the second variable. For example, B may not be the "original cause" of A, but is a reason why A continues to persist or exist either because B serves as a stimulus leading to A or because B increases the probability of A persisting because of its reinforcing properties in relation to A.

Nezu and Nezu (1989) use the acronym *SORC* to summarize various functional relationships with regard to a specific response or problem. For example, if the presenting problem (e.g., depression) is identified as the response to be changed (i.e., the ultimate outcome), then assessment can determine which variables function as the antecedents, which serve as consequences, and which function as mediators of the response. In this framework, a given variable can be identified as a *stimulus* (S; intrapersonal or environmental antecedent), *organismic variable* (O; biological, behavioral, affective, and cognitive variables that mediate or moderate the effects of the stimulus), *response* (R), or *consequence* (C; intrapersonal, interpersonal, or environmental effects engendered by the response).

Given the complexity of human behavior, it is likely that several important and relevant SORC chains within a larger causal network can be identified for a given patient that collectively help to explain the initiation and persistence of his or her problems. Moreover, these chains are likely to interact with each other, whereby for one particular causal chain a given variable may serve as a stimulus, and in another chain the same variable serves as a consequence. For example, a particular consequence may not only increase the probability that a behavior will recur in the future (via positive reinforcement), but it may also increase the likelihood that a particular stimulus will be elicited (i.e., serve as a stressor or discriminative stimulus). However, changes in a particular variable can lead to changes in the functional relationship between two other variables. For example, positive changes in coping ability (an "O" variable), which can serve as a moderator of the relationship between stressful events (an "S" variable) and depressive affect (an "R" variable), can thus change the strength of the relationship between stress and depression such that stressful events for a given person no longer rep-

resent a major trigger. As such, a given SORC chain represents a "snapshot" of the manner in which certain factors are functionally related to each other at a given point in time. A comprehensive understanding of a patient's problems, as well as his or her unique obstacles to goal attainment, will likely be best described by an interacting set of SORC chains within an overall causal network (i.e., a comprehensive, but idiographic, causal model of how a series of variables are functionally related to such problems).

Using SORC nomenclature to identify the functional relationships certain variables have with the ultimate outcome provides information regarding potential target problems and suggests interventions that may be used to address them. For example, intervention strategies might possibly be identified that are geared to change the stimulus variables, organismic mediating variables, or consequential variables in order to impact the ultimate outcome. In this manner, the emphasis on the integral relationship between case formulation and treatment design placed by Nezu and Nezu's model can be observed.

Applying the Problem-Solving Model: Generating Alternatives

To achieve the goal of ultimately identifying the most clinically salient and empirically derived treatment targets, the therapist should engage in this next problem-solving activity. The goal of this process is to identify a comprehensive list of potential target problems, thereby maximizing the probability that the most effective ones will be ultimately identified. This objective can be met by utilizing the brainstorming method of idea production, which advocates the use of three general problem-solving principles: (a) *the quantity principle* (i.e., the more ideas that are produced, the more likely that the potentially most effective ones are generated, (b) *the deferment-of-judgment principle* (i.e., more high quality alternatives can be generated if evaluation is deferred until after a comprehensive list of possible solutions has been compiled), and (c) *the strategies-tactics principle* (i.e., thinking of solution strategies, or general approaches, in addition to specific tactics, increases idea production). Relevant to the case formulation process, this last principle is similar to the notion underscoring the need to focus on functional response classes when attempting to identify relevant treatment targets (Haynes, 1992), because many behaviors may be different in topography but can be similar in their function with regard to their relationship to ultimate outcome variables. In this manner, more ideas (or treatment targets) can be identified.

At this point, the therapist uses the problem-solving principles in concert with theory-driven and diagnosis-driven

TABLE 21.2   Potential Instrumental Outcomes Regarding Depression

- Increase pleasant activities
- Decrease unpleasant activities
- Increase future expectation of positive outcomes
- Increase focus on positive rather than negative events
- Increase coping abilities
- Increase problem-solving ability
- Increase assertive behavior
- Increase time management skills
- Increase communication skills
- Facilitate marital relationship
- Facilitate various interpersonal relationships
- Decrease negative automatic thoughts
- Decrease negative self-evaluations
- Decrease negative ruminations
- Decrease associated anxiety
- Reduce unrealistically high expectations
- Increase positive self-reinforcement
- Decrease self-punishment
- Increase cognitive flexibility and perspective taking
- Facilitate positive orientation to problems in living
- Decrease cognitive distortions
- Decrease errors in logic
- Decrease irrational thinking
- Decrease self-blame
- Decrease negative attributions
- Decrease stress
- Increase social skills
- Decrease importance of unattainable goals
- Increase tolerance of negative images and memories

Note. Adapted from "Unipolar Depression," by C.M. Nezu and A.M. Nezu, in *Clinical Decision Making in Behavior Therapy: A Problem-Solving Perspective,* A.M. Nezu and C.M. Nezu (Eds.), 1989, Champaign, IL: Research Press. Copyright 1989 by A.M. Nezu and C.M. Nezu. Adapted with permission.

search strategies and within the context of the multidimensional assessment matrix to generate a list of possible instrumental outcome variables that might be selected as treatment targets for a patient. As an example, based on the empirical literature, Table 21.2 lists instrumental outcome variables that can serve as intervention targets for a depressed individual.

Applying the Problem-Solving Model: Making Decisions

The process of selecting instrumental outcomes from the comprehensive list that has been generated occurs during the decision-making process of the overall problem-solving model. The goal of this process is to select instrumental outcomes that, when targeted, will maximize treatment success for a given patient.

According to the problem-solving model, decision making should be based on an evaluation of the utility of the various alternatives. The alternative or group of alternatives with the highest degree of utility should then be chosen. Utility is determined by both (a) the likelihood that an alternative will achieve a particular goal and (b) the value of that alternative.

Using problem-solving language, estimates of likelihood involve assessing the probability that an alternative will, in fact, facilitate goal attainment, as well as the probability that the person implementing the alternative will be able to do so optimally. These general principles are applied to the case formulation process by taking into account the probability that (a) the particular target problem is amenable to treatment (i.e., On the basis of the literature, can *this* instrumental outcome be achieved successfully?), (b) this particular therapist is able to treat the given target problem (i.e., Is *this* therapist competent to implement the interventions that are geared toward targeting this problem?), (c) the treatment necessary to facilitate change for the patient is available, and (d) addressing this problem will help the patient meet his or her goals (i.e., Will achieving this instrumental outcome lead to the desired ultimate outcome either directly or by means of achieving another related instrumental outcome?). Answers to many of these types of questions (e.g., Will achieving this instrumental outcome positively impact on this patient's ultimate outcome?) require first accessing the empirical literature to determine nomothetically the *strength* of such relationships between specific instrumental outcome–ultimate outcome pairs (e.g., zero-order correlation between depressive symptom severity and cognitive distortions; percentage of suicidal patients who score high on a hopelessness scale) and, second, consistent with a multiple causality orientation, to determine whether such nomothetic information is relevant to the specific patient at hand.

The value of an idea is estimated by assessing four specific areas. Specific to case formulation, the first area includes the *personal consequences* to the therapist and to the patient. These may include (a) the time, effort, or resources necessary to reach the instrumental outcome, (b) the emotional cost or gain involved in reaching this outcome, (c) the consistency of this outcome with one's ethical values, (d) the possible physical or life-threatening effects involved in changing this target problem, and (e) the effects of changing this problem area on other target problems. *Social consequences* for other people such as a significant other, family, friends, or community that are involved in achieving this instrumental outcome should also be examined. In addition, *short-term effects* on the patient's other problem areas, as well as short-term iatrogenic effects related to achieving the instrumental outcome, should be assessed. Finally, *long-term effects* of changing these instrumental outcomes on future psychological functioning should be considered. Once again, answers to these questions require idiographically applying the nomothetic empirical literature to a specific patient.

By using these types of criteria to judge utility, the clinician can conduct a cost-benefit analysis for each potential target problem that was previously generated. Table 21.3 provides a more detailed list of the types of questions the therapist should ask when conducting this analysis. In essence, instrumental outcomes with a high likelihood of maximizing positive effects and minimizing negative effects are then selected as initial target problems. Thus, the likelihood and value criteria are used to guide the selection of target problems and to prioritize which areas to address early in therapy.

Given the fluid nature of therapy, it is likely that simultaneous with identifying and selecting instrumental outcome variables, the therapist and patient might also develop a list to articulate those ultimate outcome goals that the patient initially came to therapy to achieve (e.g., to become less depressed, eliminate phobia, improve marital relationship). If so, as is the case in selecting target problems, the therapist should use the various problem-solving operations to delineate specific and realistic therapeutic goals. Doing so involves generating a list of possible goals and objectives via brainstorming, evaluating and rating each potential idea along the major decision-making criteria, and selecting, in conjunction with the patient, those goals that appear to have the greatest utility (highest likelihood and value ratings). The questions presented in Table 21.3 for evaluating the consequences of change with regard to potential target problems may be readily adapted for judging the utility of potential ultimate outcome goals.

Applying the Problem-Solving Model: Evaluating Solution Outcomes

Continuing to use problem-solving language, the next operation involves implementing the solution response, monitoring the outcomes, and evaluating the match between the predicted consequences and the actual consequences. During case formulation, this process involves developing a Clinical Pathogenesis Map (CPM; Nezu & Nezu, 1989). A CPM is a graphic depiction of the variables hypothesized to contribute to the initiation and maintenance of the patient's overall difficulties, specifying the functional relationships using SORC nomenclature. It can be viewed as an example of a path analysis or causal modeling diagram idiographically developed for a single patient (Nezu et al., 1997). More importantly, the CPM provides an important basis upon which to design a treatment plan and offers a concrete statement of the therapist's initial hypotheses against which to test alternative hypotheses. As new information is obtained, and various predictions are confirmed or disconfirmed, the CPM can be altered. The development of the CPM is essentially the implementation of

TABLE 21.3 Decision-Making Criteria for Evaluating Utility: Sample Questions the Therapist Should Ask

I. Likelihood Criteria
- What is the likelihood that this particular target problem is amenable to cognitive-behavioral treatment?
- What is the likelihood that this target problem is amenable to the treatment the particular therapist can provide?
- What is the likelihood that the treatment necessary to effect change for this problem is available?
- What is the likelihood that any treatment designed to ameliorate this problem will be effective?
- What is the likelihood that this problem can be resolved?
- What is the likelihood that addressing this problem will achieve the patient's overall goals? Or what is the likelihood that achieving this instrumental outcome will have a positive impact on this patient's ultimate outcome?

II. Value Criteria
A. Personal Consequences
- How much time and other resources will be involved in resolving this problem?
- How much effort will be required by the patient to ameliorate this problem? By the therapist?
- What will the emotional cost or gain of addressing this problem be for the patient? For the therapist?
- Is resolving this problem consistent with the morals, values, and ethics of the patient? Of the therapist?
- What are the physical side effects associated with resolving this problem (i.e., is the problem life-threatening)? Concerning the patient? Concerning the therapist?
- What impact will addressing this problem have on the patient's personal growth?
- What are the effects of resolving this problem on other patient problem areas?

B. Social Consequences
- What effects would ameliorating this problem have on the patient's family? On friends? On the community?
- Is resolving this problem consistent with the values of others?
- Will addressing this problem engender support or antagonism from others?

C. Short-term Consequences
- Will resolving this problem have a positive or negative effect on the patient's motivation?
- Will resolving this problem have an immediate positive or negative impact on the patient's other problems?
- Are there any immediate iatrogenic effects, even though long-term consequences are predicted to be positive?

D. Long-term Consequences
- Will the long-term consequences of resolving this problem be to achieve the patient's goal(s)?
- Will ameliorating this problem prevent or minimize the need for future psychological intervention?

Note. Adapted from "Clinical Decision Making in the Practice of Behavior Therapy," by A.M. Nezu and C.M. Nezu, in *Clinical Decision Making in Behavior Therapy: A Problem-Solving Perspective,* A.M. Nezu and C.M. Nezu (Eds.), 1989, Champaign, IL: Research Press. Copyright 1989 by A.M. Nezu and C.M. Nezu. Adapted with permission.

TABLE 21.4   A Partial List of Strategies, Tactics, and Methods for Treating Depressed Mood

Overall Goal: To Decrease Depressive Symptoms

Potential Strategies
1. Decrease self-defeating thoughts
2. Increase rational thinking
3. Increase problem-solving skills
4. Increase pleasurable activities
5. Decrease unpleasurable activities
6. Increase tolerance to negative memories
7. Increase tolerance to negative visual images
8. Facilitate existing interpersonal relationships
9. Increase new relationships
10. Increase amount of time spent with others
11. Increase self-control skills
12. Decrease negative attributional style
13. Decrease cognitive distortions
14. Refer patient to physician for medication

Potential Tactics: Relevant to Strategy #1 above (i.e., decrease self-defeating thoughts)
1. Cognitive restructuring
2. Systematic rational restructuring
3. Thought stopping
4. Hypnosis
5. Bibliotherapy
6. Values clarification
7. Implosive therapy
8. Covert desensitization
9. Covert stimulus control
10. Positive mood induction
11. Systematic desensitization
12. Problem-solving therapy
13. Induction of positive self-statements
14. Meditation
15. Encouragement of religious/spiritual beliefs
16. Reinforcement for positive self-statements
17. Punishment for negative self-statements
18. Use of unconditional positive regard

Potential Methods: Relevant to Tactic #1 above (i.e., cognitive restructuring)
1. Bibliotherapy
2. Modeling
3. Mild refutation
4. Overt confrontation
5. Didactics
6. Relevant homework assignments
7. Use of family members as adjunct therapists
8. Use of friends as adjunct therapists
9. Visualization
10. Use of diagrams and pictures
11. Use of cartoons/humorous material
12. Reversed advocacy role plays

Note. Adapted from "Clinical Decision Making in the Practice of Behavior Therapy," by A.M. Nezu and C.M. Nezu, in *Clinical Decision Making in Behavior Therapy: A Problem-Solving Perspective,* A.M. Nezu and C.M. Nezu (Eds.), 1989, Champaign, IL: Research Press. Copyright 1989 by A.M. Nezu and C.M. Nezu. Adapted with permission.

the solution plan outlined in the decision-making process. An example of a CPM is provided later when we describe a clinical case.

In addition, it is useful to construct a Goal Attainment Map (GAM; Nezu & Nezu, 1989), similar to the CPM, in order to provide a visual representation of "where the patient is currently" and "where he or she wants to go." At this point, the GAM would include both the instrumental outcome (i.e., "obstacles" to goal attainment, such as deficient social skills, presence of cognitive distortions) and ultimate outcome (i.e., treatment objectives, such as anxiety reduction) goals that were previously selected during the decision-making process and is largely based on the patient's unique CPM. At a later phase, the GAM can then serve as the basis upon which possible intervention strategies can be identified that ultimately lead to goal attainment. In other words, the GAM is the "treatment map" or plan that visually describes a patient's current state (i.e., presence of symptoms or problems), the treatment goals that have been mutually selected (i.e., ultimate outcomes), as well as the specific means (i.e., intervention strategies) by which to overcome those obstacles (i.e., instrumental outcome variables or causal mechanisms of action) necessary to reach such goals.

Given the above process, it should be apparent how treatment design flows directly from an individual's unique CPM or case formulation. Given that the literature is replete with multiple interventions that address the same goal, as well as several different means by which to implement each of these differing interventions, the need to apply the systematic problem-solving model for this therapy phase is further underscored. As an example, Table 21.4 contains a partial list of various intervention strategies that address various instrumental outcomes related to the ultimate outcome goal of reducing depressive symptoms, as well as various tactics related to just one of these strategies. Also included on this list are various methods to implement one of these tactics. Such a list of possible intervention strategies, tactics, and implementation methods would be the product of the generation-of-alternatives process early in the treatment design phase of therapy and would be subsequently narrowed via the decision-making process.

Determining whether the outcome of the problem-solving process thus far (i.e., the development of a CPM and initial GAM) is effective may be accomplished through several means. First, social validation involves the clinician sharing the initial CPM and GAM with the patient (and significant others if they are involved). Patient feedback can be sought regarding the relevance, importance, and salience of the selected target problems and goals. Second, testable hypotheses based on the original case formulation also may be used to verify the CPM. Specifically, the therapist can evaluate the outcome by attempting to confirm and disconfirm hypotheses that are based on the CPM. For example, if a CPM indicates that a patient's major presenting problem involves anxiety related to interpersonal difficulties and fears of social rejection, the therapist can delineate certain predictive statements. One prediction might suggest that the patient will have high scores on a self-report measure of social avoidance and distress. Another hypothesis might suggest that during a structured role play involving a social situation (e.g., meeting new people), the patient will experience anxiety, display visible signs of tension, and report feeling distressed. Confirmations and disconfirmations of such predictions can help the clinician to evaluate the veracity and relevance of the original CPM.

A third approach involves evaluating the effects of the treatment plan that is developed on the basis of the CPM and GAM. In other words, interventions that successfully achieve a particular instrumental outcome that engenders positive movement toward an ultimate outcome would confirm the initial CPM and GAM. Conversely, change in a hypothesized mechanism of action that does *not* effect change in the ultimate outcome would suggest that that part of the CPM was not veridical. Monitoring treatment effects is an important source of feedback despite the fact that it is several steps removed from the case formulation phase of therapy.

These three methods of evaluation, then, determine whether any problems exist with the most current versions of the CPM and GAM. If so, the clinician must then reinitiate the problem-solving process and attempt to determine the source(s) of the mismatch (e.g., Were insufficient target problems generated? Was the cost-benefit analysis inconclusive?). If, however, the evaluation supports the veracity and relevance of the uniquely derived CPM and/or GAM for this patient, the therapist may continue to the next phase of therapy, that of treatment design.

Because this chapter is primarily focused on the case formulation phase of therapy, a detailed explanation of how to apply the problem-solving model to clinical tasks associated with the next two phases of therapy—treatment design and outcome evaluation—is beyond our current purpose. Readers are directed to other sources for such a description (e.g., Nezu & Nezu, 1989, 1995; Nezu et al., 1999). However, we do provide, in the next section, a clinical case example to illustrate the process of case formulation using the problem-solving model.

Clinical Case Example

Wendy, recently diagnosed with breast cancer, was referred by her oncologist to a psychotherapist—Dr. B.—for evalua-

tion and treatment. Several weeks prior to her first psychotherapy visit, she underwent surgery and received a partial mastectomy. She currently was receiving adjunctive radiotherapy and her medical prognosis was considered excellent. She planned to return to her work shortly as a special education teacher. The incidents that led to a psychotherapy referral included complaints to her physician of feeling extremely sad and lonely. Her medical records indicated a history of depression and medically unexplained chronic pain. Specifically, her first symptoms of depression began approximately 5 years previously, following a miscarriage. Wendy reported that she never fully recovered from this miscarriage and that marital difficulties ensued. She reported frequent thoughts of hopelessness and overwhelming sadness during this time and admitted to thoughts of "wanting to die." She also reported several instances of alcohol abuse during the months following her miscarriage. At one point, she considered suicide by drinking alcohol and ingesting sleeping pills. This was the first time that Wendy reported experiencing thoughts of suicide. However, she reported that she did not follow through with this suicidal plan due to religious beliefs.

Wendy lacked a history of psychiatric hospitalization. However, she reported that she spoke to a counselor when attending college about an incident of sexual molestation that occurred during her teenage years when she was babysitting for a neighbor. When Wendy told her parents about the neighbor's sexual advances, she reported that her parents reacted by telling her to avoid the neighbor in the future, indicating that they "just wanted to forget" that the incident ever occurred. Wendy was the only child of parents who were deceased. Her mother died when she was in college following a long and debilitating illness (chronic lung disease), and her father died of cancer several years earlier. Wendy stated that, although she spent much time caring for her mother, she was never "close" with either of her parents.

Wendy also described difficulties sleeping through the night. She complained that upon awakening in the morning, she "feels exhausted" with little motivation for activities that she previously enjoyed. Her current use of alcohol was limited to occasional wine with meals, but she had experienced recent urges to drink more. Wendy denied any changes in her appetite, but stated that many foods did not "agree" with her due to the radiation treatments that she currently received.

Wendy further reported experiencing anxiety throughout her life. She described this as "tightness in the chest," physical tension, and vague fears that "something bad will happen." She reported coping with this anxiety in various ways, including crying, verbally "lashing out" at others, listening to music, or taking a walk to "cool down." At various times, her primary care physician had prescribed anxiolytic and antidepressant medications, which Wendy described as "not very helpful."

When Wendy came for her first appointment, she arrived late and appeared somewhat tired and distressed. When asked about her reasons for coming to therapy, she stated she could no longer "deal with everything on my own." She was frightened by recent thoughts about ending her life and stated that she was "in need of support during this difficult time." She reported that she and her husband had seen a marital therapist a few times, but that they had stopped going when she was diagnosed with cancer. She reported that, although her husband had been financially supportive throughout her treatment, he had not helped with the household responsibilities and he had been "emotionally distant." When questioned about what her husband did to make her describe him this way, Wendy was unable to provide any examples or clear descriptions, stating, "I just feel like he doesn't want to hear my problems." An actual description of household responsibilities indicated that Wendy did a majority of the housework. However, while exploring possible changes in the workload, she experienced an increase in anxiety, stating that giving up chores made her uncomfortable because she wanted to be sure that things were "done right." Wendy also reported that worrying about her marriage contributed to current sleep problems. She reported no desire for sexual intimacy with her husband, but stated that she did feel guilty about "not having sex because he wants it."

Applying the Problem-Solving Model: Problem Orientation

Approaching treatment from a clinical world view that characterizes symptoms of pain, depression, and anxiety as potentially multiply determined, Dr. B.'s goal was to explore the various psychological, biological, and social factors that may be contributing to Wendy's current symptom picture. According to a systems perspective, the interactions of these variables are thought to be particularly relevant. Thus, Dr. B.'s analysis of Wendy's problems and identification of relevant treatment targets was based on an individualized assessment of Wendy, rather than a "standard treatment" for depression or anxiety for persons diagnosed with cancer.

Applying the Problem-Solving Model: Problem Definition

Dr. B., by engaging in a broad-based assessment of Wendy's current life, identified several potential ultimate outcome goals: (a) decrease depression, anxiety, anger, pain, and suicidal thoughts; and (b) improve marital and other interpersonal in-

teractions. Next, Dr. B. surveyed the literature regarding possible instrumental outcome variables that might be related to these ultimate outcome goals. She next conducted a detailed analysis of each problem identified in this search by examining various patient-related and environmental-related variables, as well as their developmental and proximal relationship to the ultimate outcomes. Her assessment incorporated multiple means of gathering data, including self-report (i.e., depression and anxiety inventories, pain questionnaire, measures of coping and social problem-solving skills, anger, diary of sleep problems, relationship satisfaction questionnaire), as well as ratings by others, behavioral observation procedures, and interviews with significant others. For example, Wendy's husband also completed a relationship satisfaction questionnaire and participated in an interactional marital role-play assessment. These multiple sources of data provided Dr. B with greater confidence in her case formulation and represented a quantitative baseline to which she could later compare changes in both instrumental and ultimate outcomes.

According to the problem-solving case formulation model, the first dimension of Dr. B.'s assessment focused on a broad range of patient and environmental variables. These included behavioral (e.g., crying spells, lack of assertiveness skills, episodes of verbal aggression, deficient problem-solving skills, avoidance of social interaction, reduced interest in sex), affective (e.g., sadness, anxiety, anger, loneliness), cognitive (e.g., cognitive distortions of self-blame, belief in herself as defective, worry, low expectation of help or support from others, sense of hopelessness), biological (e.g., cancer diagnosis and treatment, past miscarriage, current reduced fertility, pain symptoms, fatigue), physical environmental (e.g., lack of "private space," cluttered home environment), and social environmental (e.g., social isolation, perceived lack of support from husband, loss of all immediate family members) factors.

The second dimension of Dr. B.'s case formulation focused on the importance of current or proximal factors (e.g., stressful medical condition, current thoughts of suicide, functional marital difficulties), as well as developmental or more distal considerations regarding Wendy's problems. With regard to distal factors, Wendy had grown up as an only child in a family that "didn't show emotions very much" and in which she held the major caregiving role for her mother. She experienced resentment concerning this role which was frequently accompanied by self-statements of guilt and perception of herself as selfish. Anger toward her parents increased, however, when they provided minimal support and understanding when she was the victim of sexual molestation by a neighbor. Such distal interpersonal learning experiences appeared to both initiate and reinforce cognitive schemas of hopeless expectations regarding help or nurturance from others. Discussions regarding her current cancer-related problems identified anger toward her medical team for "not caring about what I'm going through." Wendy viewed such responses from others as inevitable.

At 18, Wendy took steps to "do something for myself" by entering college. Her mother's death occurred almost simultaneous with her attempt to leave home. She learned to avoid painful emotions of anger, guilt, and sadness by focusing her attention on schoolwork and other accomplishments. Her experience with chronic, medically unexplained pain symptoms (e.g., gastrointestinal and chest pains) also began to emerge at this time. Years later, a similar avoidance strategy was evident at the time of her miscarriage. However, as she was unsuccessful in completely avoiding the feelings of guilt and loss, she felt hopeless concerning her ability to cope.

In reviewing the assessment data that she obtained through various sources (e.g., scores on standardized measures of depression, anxiety, pain, sleep difficulties, measures of coping ability, martial satisfaction ratings, behavioral martial roleplay), Dr. B. noted a discrepancy among the results. Specifically, Wendy's perception of her husband as emotionally distant was in contrast to initial interviews with him that revealed that, although somewhat unassertive, he was quite eager to understand her difficulties and acknowledge her feelings and concerns. Moreover, he expressed concern that his wife seemed to mistrust other people and often "comes across like she will take care of everything and doesn't need anyone's help." Further, this behavioral style appeared to be fueled by Wendy's unrealistically high expectations of herself. For example, despite having information that fatigue was a predictable consequence of cancer treatment, she viewed her loss of energy as a personal failure. Scores from a marital adjustment scale indicated that this was an area of difficulty for both partners, and observations of their interactions showed that Wendy was often successful in avoiding topics of conflict and disagreement. Moreover, items on the self-rating scales that Wendy completed indicated a high degree of avoidance and schemas of mistrust in general. Finally, a problem-solving inventory indicated that Wendy had a pronounced style of problem avoidance, corroborated by her own report of avoidance of sex because she didn't "want to be reminded" of her cancer treatment. Finally, Wendy admitted that she also experienced difficulty expressing her feelings to Dr. B., concerned that she would not be able to help.

Based upon this information, Dr. B. sought next to identify how different aspects of Wendy's problems were functionally related to each other (i.e., which variables served as stimuli, organismic mediators, responses, or consequences?). With regard to one causal chain, Wendy's pain was identified as the response. Examination of the stimuli that occurred prior to the pain noted the following variables: loss of energy, proximity to her husband at bedtime, thoughts about sex or intimacy, and anxiety. Consequences of the pain, as well as her behavioral reactions to them, included her husband's response of comforting her (positive reinforcement), decreased attempts of sexual intimacy (negative reinforcement), decreased physical demands (negative reinforcement), and avoidance of affect through increased attention on physical pain (negative reinforcement) (see Nezu et al., 2001, for a cognitive-behavioral analysis of medically unexplained symptoms, such as chronic pain). This led to the observation that the only time Wendy would accept help with housework and social support from her husband was when she was experiencing pain. Thus, one instrumental outcome goal would be to motivate Wendy to accept such support prior to such episodes of pain or as part of an overall pain prevention strategy. In another causal chain, Wendy's schemas of mistrust and problem-solving deficits were viewed as important cognitive responses in need of change. Triggering stimuli included situations in which she perceived impending loss. Aversive consequences of such thoughts included increased anger and depressive symptoms. Negatively reinforcing consequences led to anxiety reduction.

In this manner, Dr. B., according to our model, properly conceptualized several causal chains as interacting in important ways within an overall causal network. For example, as stated previously, Wendy's pain symptoms were often triggered when she experienced physical demands (i.e., housework) and sexual performance concerns when she was near her husband. Consequences of her pain symptoms, which included her husband's decreased attempts at intimacy, decreased physical demands, and anxiety reduction, then served as stimuli for other behavioral problems. These included the distortion of her husband's decreased attempts at intimacy as being emotionally distant and unwilling to be supportive, which was then followed by anger and further anxiety and other emotional avoidance strategies. Lowered expectations of help and support then led her to try to complete all housework by herself. When the experience of pain forced her to relinquish and accept her husband's help, she would remain resentful that it required her experience of pain "to finally get some support."

Applying the Problem-Solving Model: Generating Alternatives

Dr. B. constructed a list of potential variables in order to identify the most salient or meaningful instrumental treatment goals, attempting to initially defer judgment and increase the probability that she would discover the most effective targets.

Her initial list included Wendy's cognitive distortions of herself and others, chronic beliefs or schemas of mistrust and low expectations of others, emotional avoidance, problem-solving deficits, anger toward others, and unrealistic expectations of herself regarding physically demanding tasks.

Applying the Problem-Solving Model: Making Decisions

In order to construct a Clinical Pathogenesis Map and make decisions regarding target behavior selection, a cost-benefit analysis of each target area was conducted next. The potential targets were rated regarding (a) the probability that they would improve Wendy's ability to better manage her current stressful situation, (b) the impact they would have on other problem areas and on ultimate goal attainment, (c) the accessibility of the intervention, (d) the amount of time and effort that would be required to modify the symptoms, (e) required expertise, (f) the possibility of change, and (g) short-term and long-term consequences. Cycling through the decision-making process for each potential target problem, Dr. B. decided to focus on Wendy's current social problem-solving skills deficits, modification of maladaptive schemas, decreasing unrealistic expectations, and improving her marital social support system as initial treatment targets.

Applying the Problem-Solving Model: Evaluating Solution Outcome

Dr. B. then organized her hypotheses regarding how several variables related to each other in the form of a CPM. Depicting the variables of interest graphically, Dr. B. first included the ultimate goals of therapy for Wendy. These were translated from her initial complaints and listed as symptoms of depression, anxiety, anger, suicidal thoughts, chronic pain, and alcohol urges and considered as reactions to her current major life stressors (diagnosis and treatment of breast cancer, marital difficulties, and cancer-related pain). Using the results of her previous decision-making process concerning the importance and primacy of specific instrumental goals, Dr. B. generated several hypothetical paths (or SORC chains) regarding these variables in relation to Wendy's current situation.

Dr. B.'s completed CPM depicted these variable paths that were hypothesized to contribute to the initiation and maintenance of Wendy's problems. This CPM is depicted in Figure 21.2 and provides a visual picture of the various elements or factors, which included (but were not limited to) physical demands, negative affective states, distorted and negative internal statements concerning herself and others, schemas of abandonment and loneliness, multiple actual and perceived

losses, and problem-solving coping deficits. It is important to note that a SORC model of assessment provides useful categories or headings with which to depict a CPM: distal (developmental) factors, mediating organismic factors, proximal stressful events, and current functional stimuli (cues regarding symptomatic complaints). However, it is not always possible to clearly depict the paths of *all* considered functional chains of behavioral, cognitive, emotional, and biological factors. In Dr. B.'s case formulation concerning Wendy, instrumental factors that appear in frequent clinical pathways and as functionally relevant to multiple systems are highlighted in bold. These factors were Dr. B.'s primary initial targets of treatment and included (a) the consequences of pain (e.g., increased attention and support), (b) decreased physical demands, (c) anxiety reduction (emotion avoidance), (d) social isolation, and (e) specific coping deficits. Coping skills deficits included problem-solving skills deficits, cognitive distortions of self-blame, and schemas of mistrust. This last area, which consisted of pervasive and long-held beliefs, also represented a significant treatment obstacle.

To evaluate the outcome of her attempt to select target variables, Dr. B. shared the CPM with Wendy and requested her feedback. Wendy agreed with the selection of improving her coping abilities (e.g., problem solving) and changing cognitive distortions as initial target problems, stating that she often saw herself as "weak and unable to cope" but "needing to be strong because I have no one to count on." Although she agreed that it would be helpful to increase her support system and increase her trust of others, she predictably expressed reservations regarding the likelihood that her husband would become involved in treatment. However, she agreed to have Dr. B. invite him to attend sessions in order to observe the result. Confronted with disconfirming evidence regarding her husband's lack of motivation or ability to help, Wendy agreed to keep "an open mind" concerning her beliefs of mistrust.

Dr. B.'s final step in the case formulation process consisted of the development of a Goal Attainment Map that provided her with a more concise and direct roadmap for planning treatment. As such, Dr. B. listed the instrumental outcome goals (i.e., changing cognitive distortions, increasing anxiety management skills, increasing problem-solving skills, decreasing physical expectations, and increasing emotional awareness and tolerance), chief obstacles (cognitive-emotional schemas of mistrust), and ultimate outcome goals (improve management of chronic pain, decrease anger, decrease depression, decrease suicidal thoughts, decrease behavioral impulse to drink, improve management of anxiety), based upon Wendy's CPM. The GAM could now serve as the basis upon which possible treatment strategies could be

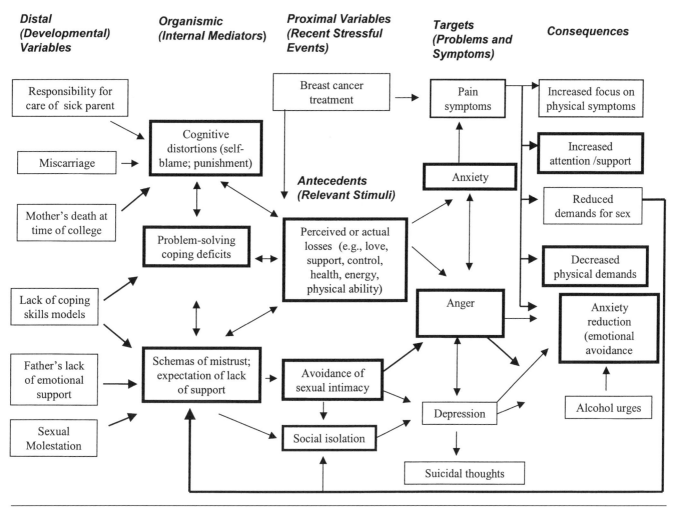

Figure 21.2   Example of a Clinical Pathogenesis Map.

identified. Dr. B.'s actual selection of treatment strategies was conducted through application of the problem-solving model to the treatment design phase of clinical intervention. This task was approached using the same problem-solving operations that she applied to the case formulation endeavor.

PERSONS' COGNITIVE-BEHAVIORAL CASE FORMULATION MODEL

Cognitive-behavioral case formulation, as described by Persons and her colleagues, involves the construction of a clinical hypothesis regarding underlying mechanisms of each patient's reported problems (Persons, 1989, 1993). Similar to the other models described in this chapter, a core goal of this model is to maximize treatment utility. As such, Persons underscores the philosophy that a formulation that guides the choice of treatment and improves treatment outcome should

arise directly from one's hypothesized beliefs about the underlying cause of a patient's problems (Persons & Tompkins, 1997).

This model of case formulation is rooted in both cognitive therapy and in functional analysis. This joint foundation requires the synthesis of both the structural (i.e., topography and underlying causal mechanisms of problematic behaviors) as well as the functional (i.e., focusing on the function of a given behavior) aspects of patient problem areas in order to develop a working hypothesis of underlying behavioral mechanisms. From its cognitive roots, this case formulation model emphasizes a diathesis-stress model, whereby a stressful situation interacts with one's cognitions to initiate underlying core beliefs and schemas. Persons' model places significant primacy on the importance of core beliefs that are learned via early life experiences. This model also follows a functional analytic tradition of identifying important and controllable causal relationships that are relevant to the problematic behavior under scrutiny. The identification and measurement of overt problems and specification of functional hypotheses concerning these overt behaviors are included as important elements toward the treatment utility of Persons' model.

Levels of Cognitive-Behavioral Case Formulation

Persons' model provides a clinical case conceptualization at both the case and situational levels. The *case formulation* refers to all the problems that a patient presents in therapy. It also includes relationships among these problems and the mechanisms that maintain them. A *situational formulation* is much less generalized and focuses on specific problems and the underlying mechanisms of only those problems. Whereas the situational formulation level guides therapy sessions, the case formulation level helps the therapist conceptualize the case as a whole.

Persons also distinguishes between *overt problems* and the *underlying mechanisms* that maintain these problems. Overt problems are surface problems or those for which the client seeks therapy. Examples of these "real life" overt problems may include depression, anxiety, or relationship difficulties. Underlying mechanisms can be defined as psychological processes that operate less visibly but are very powerful in causing and maintaining overt problems. Moreover, overt problems are described at both macro and micro levels. At the macro level, clients describe their difficulties as problems in living (e.g., obesity, depression), whereas at the micro level problems are manifested less obviously via cognitions (e.g., automatic thoughts, images, memories or dreams), behaviors (e.g., verbal, overt, physiological), and/or emotions (e.g., moods). Persons further states that the relationship among these three systems are generally synchronous and interdependent. Interventions are therefore directed toward one system with the intention of influencing all three systems.

A central proposition of this model is that negative schemas, core beliefs, and automatic thoughts are the basic psychological mechanisms underlying one's problems. These beliefs are viewed as underlying vulnerabilities that interact with negative life stress to produce overt problems. As mentioned previously, these underlying mechanisms may manifest themselves overtly as cognitions, behaviors, or emotions. However, at their core, they are internal constructs that are not measurable via direct or objective tools. Although this model suggests that one underlying central problem causes and maintains overt problems, Persons does not dismiss the possibility that more than one underlying mechanism can cause psychological difficulties. She also acknowledges the possibility of one underlying problem causing many overt problems. The model also incorporates the role of other fac-

tors, such as biology and physiology, that may predispose a client to have problems such as alcoholism or obesity. In such cases, Persons maintains that pharmacological interventions may act adjunctively to cognitive-behavioral therapy.

Components of the Case Formulation

Persons (1993) delineates seven steps in the process of conducting a case conceptualization. The first two steps address the therapist's hypotheses regarding the overt difficulties and underlying psychological mechanism(s) causing and maintaining the problems. The remaining five steps focus on understanding how the underlying mechanisms relate to the patient's problems and deciding upon the best treatment intervention course. Each of the components are described briefly below.

Problem List

The goal of generating a problem list is to find clues that assist in proposing a hypothesis regarding a client's core beliefs and to develop a working formulation regarding a client's problems. The problem list is a comprehensive list of 5 to 8 (with no more than 10) reported problems generated collaboratively within the initial session of therapy. The list begins with the patient's central complaint and continues to include all psychological, medical, interpersonal, occupational, legal, housing, and/or leisure difficulties. In addition, careful behavioral observation is important in order to reveal any problems that the individual is avoiding, neglecting to mention, or unaware of. Treatment success can be negatively impacted if clients and therapists cannot agree on the problems to be addressed in therapy.

Hypothesizing Underlying Mechanisms

In this step, the therapist looks at the interrelationships among the problems on the list with the intention of identifying the underlying core belief(s) that is causing and maintaining these problems. During this stage, the therapist is also advised to consider behavioral and/or biological influences that could contribute to the client's problems, although cognitive mechanisms are highlighted as the primary mechanism of action in this model.

Precipitants and Activating Situations

During this step, clients are asked to describe events that preceded the onset of their problems with the intention of identifying external situations that either caused the underlying mechanism(s) to be triggered or reinforced the current problems.

Working Hypothesis

This represents the core of the clinical conceptualization in Persons' model. In this phase, therapists attempt to test their hypothesized underlying mechanisms by telling a "story" that meaningfully explains how an activating event elicits the hypothesized underlying mechanisms and causes overt problems to emerge. The therapist's explanation should include each of the problems on the problem list and should tie them together either directly or indirectly to the underlying core belief. Persons recommends that decisions to modify or reject a working hypothesis be based on whether interventions ensuing from the working hypothesis are conducive to the client's treatment goals. If they are not, a revised formulation may be necessary.

Origins of the Underlying Mechanisms

This element of the formulation process involves a historical analysis of a patient's social, familial, and interpersonal life. Relationships with parents, caregivers, or others in the patient's life that may have been influential to the development of schemas concerning self, others, and the world are viewed as significant.

Treatment Plan

The treatment plan is not a part of the case formulation per se, but is derived directly from the working hypothesis and should address the problems on the problem list. Persons recommends explicitly stating goals for treatment before beginning any intervention; hence, the first step in creating a treatment plan should be to generate a list of therapy goals followed by another list of intervention strategies.

Predicted Obstacles to Treatment

During this final stage, the therapist troubleshoots any potential obstacles to successful treatment outcome. Potential obstacles are generated from the lists of problems, hypothesized underlying beliefs, and working hypothesis (Persons & Tompkins, 1997). By addressing these areas before they become problems themselves, the therapist is better able to solve problems as they emerge in therapy and is better able to prevent circumstances such as early termination, client-therapist power struggles, or other potential setbacks to therapy.

LINEHAN'S CASE FORMULATION MODEL FOR DIALECTICAL BEHAVIOR THERAPY

Linehan and her colleagues (Koerner & Linehan, 1997; Linehan, 1993) have outlined a model for case formulation specific to Dialectical Behavior Therapy (DBT), a cognitive-behavioral approach to treating persons diagnosed with borderline personality disorder (BPD). DBT provides guidelines for working with a difficult and frustrating clinical population for whom suicide, self-injurious behavior, and emotional lability are frequent and expected problems. The ultimate goal of DBT is to reduce emotional pain while teaching clients to adaptively regulate their own emotions (see Linehan, 1993, for a more complete description of DBT).

DBT Components

The following five components of DBT are crucial to the process of case conceptualization: (a) stage theory of treatment, (b) behavioral learning principles, (c) biosocial origins of BPD, (d) BPD behavioral patterns, and (e) philosophical guiding principles. Linehan offers the analogy of these five approaches as the "lenses" through which a therapist can best view problematic behavior(s).

Stage Theory

The stage theory approach assumes that individuals must successfully pass through one stage of development before progressing to a subsequent stage. In each of the treatment stages of DBT, Linehan suggests that problems relevant to each stage be matched to an appropriate treatment intervention. For example, the priority in Stage 1 of treatment is to address suicidal, homicidal, and self-injurious behaviors; treatment interfering behaviors; behaviors that decrease a patients' quality of life; and behavioral deficits. In Stages 2 and 3, treatment goals include improvement of patients' self-esteem, quality of life, and generalizing treatment gains to the outside world. Treatment often overlaps in various stages and it is not unusual for problems of earlier stages to reemerge throughout treatment. Utilizing DBT stage theory allows therapists to conceptualize cases based on the level of behavioral instability presented at a given treatment stage.

Learning Principles

Behavioral learning principles allow the therapist to understand how dysfunctional behaviors emerged, what function they serve, and the consequences of the behavior(s) for each patient. Such principles also can explain why a patient failed to learn more adaptive behaviors and emotional responses during his or her development. Treatments are matched to the relevant functional analysis for each patient.

Biosocial Origins of BPD

The biosocial theory of BPD suggests that a genetic predisposition to emotional dysregulation (i.e., high sensitivity to emotional cues, high reactivity, and slowed response to return to a "normal" emotional state), coupled with an "invalidating environment" results in behavioral and emotional responses characteristic of BPD. The term *invalidating environment* depicts an atmosphere of rejection and punishment that teaches individuals to believe that their emotional reactions are pathological or incorrect. Over time, patients with BPD internalize the messages received from this history of negative social consequences—that their reactions are wrong and not to be taken seriously.

BPD Behavior Patterns

A frequent behavioral difficulty observed in such patients is the extreme vacillation between over- and underregulation of emotional responses. One consequence of this imbalance is that both intrapersonal and social problems are likely to occur. Because the therapy relationship is part of a patient's social context, the DBT case model conceptualizes these extreme behavioral and emotional patterns as *therapy-interfering behaviors* and other obstacles to effective treatment.

Philosophical Guiding Principles

The dialectical principles underlying DBT play an important role in case conceptualization. A "dialectic philosophy" assumes that the "whole" individual is made up of interrelated, but polarized, parts. A successful case conceptualization is designed to view behavioral and emotional problems within the context of all these interrelated patient factors, including the patient's social world (e.g., the relationship with his or her therapist). In addition, dialectic philosophy assumes that these parts are constantly changing; therefore, the case formulation needs to be a dynamic and constantly revising process.

Behavioral Analysis

Linehan views all disordered behaviors and emotional dysregulation as "problems to be solved" collaboratively by the therapist and client. As such, similar to Nezu and Nezu's approach described earlier, DBT case conceptualization has a strong problem-solving component. Linehan (1993) suggests that the first step in DBT problem solving is conducting a thorough behavioral analysis during the initial assessment sessions. This allows the therapist to answer the following questions: What is the problem? What causes or elicits the problem? What is the best intervention strategy to solve the problem? A meticulous behavior analysis is viewed as paramount to an accurate and succinct conceptualization. Linehan denotes three tenets of behavioral analysis: (a) the examination of target behaviors should be a collaborative process between the therapist and client; (b) the analysis should offer sufficient information to explain both internal and external factors involved in the problem under investigation; and (c) the outcome of the behavioral analysis should be refutable if disconfirming evidence indicates that it is inaccurate.

Steps in DBT Case Formulation

Koerner and Linehan (1997) offer three steps in formulating a DBT case. They first recommend gathering information regarding the target behavior, then organizing the information in a purposeful way, and, last, revising the conceptualization as needed.

Gathering Information Regarding the Target Behavior

During this initial step, the therapist utilizes information regarding the stage of treatment to guide his or her choice of problems to address. For example, for an individual in Stage 1 of treatment, target behavior should address suicidality. As such, the first behavioral analysis should be conducted on major suicidal and/or parasuicidal incidents. Once the problem has been identified, it should be conceptualized in terms of its influence on the client's thoughts, feelings, and behaviors. Stating the client's reaction to the problem (e.g., attempting suicide) and not the problem itself (e.g., relationship difficulties) is an important focus.

Next, a chain analysis is recommended in order to understand how a specific target behavior is maintained. Moreover, when a chain analysis is conducted, no one system (e.g., emotional, biological, environmental, cognitive, physiological) is always presumed to have primacy or considered more influential in eliciting and maintaining behaviors. To conduct a valid and accurate chain analysis, the therapist should assess the following areas: situations that automatically elicit emotional or behavioral responses; skills deficits that may have contributed to the problem; circumstances (e.g., beliefs, rules, fears) that may have prevented adaptive learning to take place; and the process by which the client decided upon the problematic behavior as the best choice of action. Clinicians should discontinue the chain analysis when the function that the targeted behavior serves is identified. Once the function of the targeted behavior has been identified, the conceptualization can focus on how to interrupt the dysfunctional links from continuing in the behavioral chain. Further, Linehan suggests that replacing dysfunctional links with more adaptable behaviors requires a task analysis. Much like the chain analysis, this approach aims to identify the chain of behaviors and situations needed to interrupt or replace the targeted behavior.

Organizing Information in a Purposeful Way

This step recommends that each target behavior be descriptively illustrated with a flow chart so that therapists can best understand their conceptualization. Depicting the formulation in this way guides the choice of other targeted behaviors as well as further assessment and treatment. The information given in this description should summarize all five components that aided in case formulation (i.e., stage theory, principles of learning and behavior therapy, biosocial origins of BPD, behavioral patterns of BPD, and dialectical philosophies guiding DBT) into an explanation of the causal and maintaining factors, and the recommended behavior with which to replace the disordered behavior.

Revising the Conceptualization as Needed

Given the dynamic nature of DBT, new or disconfirming information regarding the target behavior(s) can require the DBT formulations to be adjusted or revised. Reevaluation of the formulation should also be made when therapy is not progressing as originally predicted. Therapists should explore alternative explanations via written notes, chain analyses, by eliciting feedback from others on the treatment team, and by looking at how they themselves may have created interpersonal obstacles to treatment. Identifying and rectifying these oversights is imperative to treatment success.

HAYNES' FUNCTIONAL ANALYTIC CLINICAL CASE MODEL (FACCM)

Haynes' model provides a systematic approach to organizing and visually displaying patient information when developing a behavioral case formulation (Haynes, Leisen, & Blaine, 1997; Haynes & O'Brien, 2000; Haynes et al., 1993). The FACCM, which provides a method of illustrating functional analysis, utilizes a vector-graphic representation based partially on structural equation modeling and vector geometry

to illustrate and quantify the elements of a functional analysis (Haynes, 1998; Haynes & O'Brien, 2000). Similar to Nezu and Nezu's Clinical Pathogenesis Map and Linehan's recommendation to descriptively illustrate the analysis of target behaviors via a flowchart, the FACCM visually organizes information concerning target behaviors and their antecedents, causal mechanisms, and maintaining factors. Haynes' model strongly recommends utilizing a systems-oriented approach (i.e., the reciprocal interactions among biological, psychological, and environmental factors that maintain a patient's behavior problems) when constructing a FACCM. However, while the importance of biological factors is acknowledged, his model emphasizes the specific cognitive and environmental antecedents and consequences. One unique feature of this model is that it allows the clinician to mathematically estimate the strength and direction of causal and noncausal functional relationships relevant to a patient's behavior problems (i.e., hypothesized antecedents, consequents, covariates, mediating variables, and maintaining factors). In addition, it provides an estimate of the amenability of causal variables to treatment and the relative importance of modifying behavior problems. The main goal of the FACCM is to assist clinicians in treatment-planning decisions by mathematically weighing the advantages and disadvantages of focusing on each causal variable in treatment and to aid them in the decision-making process.

The FACCM can be useful and instructive to therapists in several ways. First, the FACCM requires the therapist to separate and analyze the variables and clinical judgments (e.g., the relative importance of a patient's behavior problems) involved in the development of a functional analysis and case conceptualization. Most patients present with multiple behavioral problems. As such, the FACCM allows the therapist to attend to and integrate a plethora of information when working with a complex case. Furthermore, it aids the experienced clinician who may rely inadvertently on judgmental heuristics, as well as the student being trained in functional analysis, to approach case conceptualization in a sequential and systematic manner, thereby reducing potential errors in the clinical decision-making process. In addition, the FACCM facilitates the communication of a clinical case formulation, including treatment decisions, to other mental health care and non–mental health care professionals, such as third-party payers and patients themselves. Finally, quantification of clinical judgments encourages empirical investigation of clinical decision making.

Quantifying Elements of the FACCM

The FACCM consists of the functional variables hypothesized by the therapist to be important because they are variables whose modification is estimated to have the greatest benefits for the patient. Accurately identifying the functional, causal variables and their relations regarding behavior problems is essential, because the focus of treatment is based upon these determinations. The type and direction of relationships among hypothesized functional variables may be causal, correlational but not causal, moderating, mediating, unidirectional, or bidirectional. After specifying the hypothesized functional variables and their relationships, the clinician subjectively assigns numerical values to the paths or links between variables, which provides an estimate of the magnitude of treatment effects. Thus, case formulation developed through construction of an FACCM includes path coefficients, quantification of the modifiability of causal variables, the relative importance of behavior problems, mediators or causal sequela and chains, and moderating variables. Figure 21.3 illustrates a hypothetical FACCM regarding the earlier outpatient case example of Wendy.

FACCM path coefficients represent the clinician's best estimate of the degree of correlation or covariance between two variables. The therapist, utilizing information obtained during a multimodal, multisource assessment, assigns a numerical value between 0 and 1 to indicate the degree to which a change in the causal variable is hypothesized to result in a change in the behavior problem. The greater the strength or higher path coefficient between two variables, the more likely goal attainment will be met. Although the path coefficient is determined subjectively, a review of the nomothetic literature can sometimes assist the clinician in estimating the strength of relationships among variables (Haynes, 1994). The estimated correlation represented by a FACCM path coefficient is dynamic across time for a patient and can represent a causal or noncausal relationship between two variables. Although a path coefficient in a causal path represents the estimated degree to which a change in the causal variable will result in change in the behavior problem, a correlated, noncausal behavior problem will not change unless a causal variable affecting both behavior problems are treatment targets. Haynes notes that, although correlated, noncausal relationships do not impact upon the estimated magnitude of effect of treatment targets, these relationships are important to consider in assessment planning, because one variable may be easier to evaluate and measure than another. Reciprocal causal relations are especially important treatment targets because they have effects that reverberate over time. For example, as shown in Figure 21.3, targeting schemas of mistrust affects cognitive distortions, which further impacts upon depressive symptoms.

The clinician must also take the modifiability of causal variables into account when formulating an effective treatment plan. Static variables, such as having a developmental

disability or a history of physical abuse, cannot be changed through therapeutic interventions. Although static variables may be causal in nature and have high path coefficients, attempts to modify them would be ineffective. For example, sexual molestation, as symbolized in Figure 21.3, can be considered such a static variable, because it is historic and cannot be changed. As such, the therapist must select treatment variables that are dynamic or potentially changeable. Dynamic factors often include the sequela associated with static factors that mediate relationships between current behavior problems and historical causal variables. Relevant to the example in Figure 21.3, a maladaptive problem-solving style moderates the relationship between anxiety symptoms, as sequela of early molestation and pain.

The clinician's estimate of the relative importance of the behavior problems is also quantified on the FACCM and taken into consideration during treatment planning. When making these judgments, the clinician evaluates the severity and frequency of the problem behaviors, the impact the behavior problem has on the patient's quality of life, and the degree to which the behavior problem is harmful or dangerous to the patient and others. Although the clinician assigns a weight that is somewhat arbitrary regarding the importance of the behavior problem, the value given for one behavior problem is relative to the importance assigned to other behavior problems.

After subjectively quantifying all elements of the FACCM, the therapist uses a cost-benefit approach to select treatment targets that will be optimally effective in attaining goals. The values given to the elements of the FACCM are not absolute and should be considered relative to the values of the other elements. If changes are made in the FACCM, the relationships among the causal variables will also change. The variables and estimated strength of relations among variables are dynamic, often changing between sessions and within a session. These changes may be due to factors such as reactive effects of the assessment, new data available to the clinician, or progress from treatment. As such, content validity when constructing the FACCM is imperative. To reduce the judgmental heuristics and biases, it is important to use multiple methods of assessment throughout the therapeutic process. Thus, estimates of the magnitude of effect are conditional as to the accuracy of the proposed model (i.e., the fit of the model). Although measurements obtained during assessment and a review of the nomothetic literature can aid the therapist in estimating values, these values do not necessarily reflect measurements of duration, rate, or magnitude of a behavior problem. As one example, a value of 8 for depression in Figure 21.3 represents the importance of this behavior problem rather than a measure of depression severity. Further-

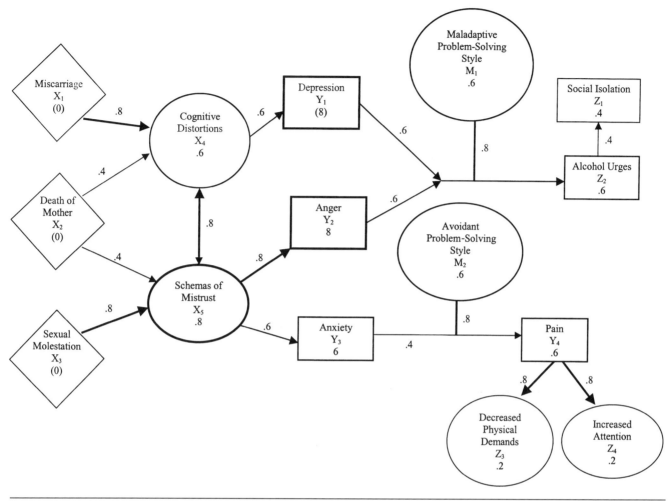

Figure 21.3 Functional Analytic Clinical Case Model of Wendy.
Note that X = Causal variable; Y = Behavior problem; M = Mediating variable; $(\ )$ = Relative importance or modifiability; causal variables in diamond shapes represent static or unmodifiable variables; causal variables in circles represent modifiable variables. The thickness of the arrow represents the strength of the relationship between two variables; the thickness of a geometric shape denotes the evaluation of its importance.

more, a causal variable that is highly related to a behavior problem (i.e., high path coefficient) and is also highly valued as an important behavior to change, but estimated to have low modifiability, may be a less likely focus of treatment than a causal variable that is amenable to treatment but not represented by a high path coefficient or value of importance.

Estimating the Magnitude of Effect

Once values are assigned to all elements of the FACCM, the therapist estimates the magnitude of the effect for each causal variable. When estimating an effect between a causal variable and the patient's behavior problems, the product of the following FACCM elements along the causal path can be calculated by taking into account (a) all path coefficients leading from the causal variable including the correlation coefficients among behavior problems and their sequela, (b) the modifi-

ability of the causal variable, and (c) the importance ratings of all behavior problems and sequela along the causal chain. In most cases, the FACCM will contain causal routes that are indirect or have multiple routes between the causal variable and the patient's behavior problems. When calculating the effect for multiple routes, the clinician multiplies the FACCM elements for *each* and *all* routes that exist between the causal variable and the behavior problem and their sequela (for further discussion and demonstration of the calculation of magnitude of effect estimates, see Haynes et al., 1997; Haynes & O'Brien, 2000).

Differences between the estimated magnitude of effect for each causal path are then compared to help determine the most effective treatment plan for the patient. Due to the subjective and imprecise nature of the predicted values and resulting estimates, more confidence can be placed on large differences between effect sizes than on small differences. To obtain the greatest improvement in the patient's quality of life, the therapist targets variables identified in the FACCM that will modify the most important behavior problem or the greatest number of behavior problems. Furthermore, because estimated magnitudes of effects are idiographic, they are relative only to the FACCM constructed for that individual patient and cannot be compared to other FACCMs for other patients.

Clinicians not familiar with structure equation modeling may find the complexity of the model and the calculation of magnitudes of effects to exacerbate this limitation. However, Haynes, Richard, O'Brien, and Grant (1999) have developed a computer program to assist clinicians in constructing a FACCM and estimating magnitudes of effects, which would ostensibly reduce the time needed to construct a FACCM.

CONCLUDING REMARKS

This chapter began with underscoring the importance of case formulation and highlighting the integral relationship between an accurate case conceptualization and eventual treatment success. We noted that humans, even trained cognitive-behavioral therapists, are susceptible to certain common judgmental heuristics and biases. In response to such vulnerabilities, in addition to the recognition that the vast majority of clinical cases seen by therapists deviate significantly from the "classic textbook case," we argued that formal models of behavioral case formulation are necessary in order to accurately translate assessment data into effective treatment design recommendations.

Four models of case conceptualization were then presented. We began with our own model (e.g., Nezu & Nezu, 1989), which is based on a problem-solving paradigm. More specifically, our model views the cognitive-behavior therapist as the "problem solver" and the discrepancy between a patient's current state (e.g., psychological distress, marital problems) and his or her goals as the "problem to be solved." A second model, that of Persons (1993), places primacy on cognitive factors when conceptualizing psychopathology and identifying treatment targets. The model by Linehan (e.g., Koerner & Linehan, 1997) specifically addresses the case formulation process when conducting Dialectic Behavior Therapy, a cognitive-behavioral intervention originally designed for the treatment of persons with borderline personality disorder. The fourth model, one developed by Haynes (e.g., Haynes et al., 1993), offers a means to quantify the strength of the relationships among various hypothesized causative factors and psychological problems in order to inform the treatment design process.

Although these four models of case formulation vary in the emphasis they place on various factors, several similarities across models are evident (see also Haynes & O'Brien, 1999). Most significant is the emphasis that all four models place on the importance of a functional analysis. In addition, they all underscore the importance of individualized assessment and offer a set of guidelines on how to process the results of such an assessment for the purpose of (a) better understanding the patient and his or her problems and (b) designing individual treatment protocols. Further, all four models argue that behavior problems are most likely to have multiple causes that are dynamic across time. It is also interesting to note that three of these models (Nezu & Nezu, Linehan, Haynes) underscore the importance of a visual display of the case formulation—for example, Nezu and Nezu's CPM and Haynes' FACCM. Another similarity among models involves the argument that biased clinical judgment can be a negative influence on treatment decisions. Last, all models appear to be amenable to a constructional approach and a focus on positive treatment goals.

Because of the apparent similarities across these models of case formulation, it would seem that the face validity of the shared underlying tenets are particularly strong. However, questions regarding interrater reliability of these approaches and especially their predictive validity and treatment utility have yet to be demonstrated empirically. With debates continuing about the soundness of using randomized clinical trials (RCT) with homogeneous groups of patients to determine the efficacy of a particular treatment intervention coupled with more recent attempts to identify and categorize "empirically supported treatments," we would argue that such research is imperative. In other words, RCTs, by overemphasizing the importance of enhanced internal validity, may not offer a complete answer to the question by Paul (1969) that began this chapter: "What procedures should be implemented, with this specific patient, who has this particular disorder, given these unique characteristics and circumstances?" (see Nezu & Nezu, 1989, p. 30); neither would effectiveness studies. On the other hand, the models described in this chapter may be very time-consuming and only necessary for complex clinical cases or situations where a patient is treatment resistant. A case where the patient has unipolar depression and no other complications may be best treated with an empirically supported treatment. Yet this remains an empirical question and, therefore, given both perspectives, a means by which to better integrate these two approaches appears especially warranted. In lieu of such answers, the models of case formulation presented in this chapter offer significant promise for this endeavor in that they provide systematic guidelines by which to apply nomothetically derived information in an idiographic manner. As such, the validity of any or all of these case formulation models becomes particularly crucial in building better bridges between the art and science of psychotherapy and assessment, as well as between results emanating from RCTs and from effectiveness studies.

NOTE

1. It is possible to add a fourth therapy phase that occurs *prior* to case formulation—that of "screening." In essence, it is during this phase that a therapist needs to determine whether he or she is able and willing to enter into a therapeutic relationship with a patient. Nezu and Nezu (1989) claim that similar to the other therapy phases, this one also entails a variety of clinical decisions that need to be addressed (e.g., Can I help this person? Should I refer this patient to another therapist? Is cognitive-behavior therapy warranted?). Moreover, they advocate the use of the various problem-solving operations to effectively answer such questions.

REFERENCES

American Psychiatric Association (1994). *Diagnostic and statistical manual of mental disorders* (4th ed.). Washington, DC: Author.

Arkes, H.R. (1981). Impediments to accurate clinical judgment and possible ways to minimize their impact. *Journal of Consulting and Clinical Psychology, 49,* 323–330.

Cook, T.D. (1985). Postpositivist critical multiplism. In R.L. Shotland & M.M. Marks (Eds.), *Social science and social policy* (pp. 21–62). Beverly Hills, CA: Sage.

D'Zurilla, T.J., & Nezu, A.M. (1999). *Problem-solving therapy: A social competence approach to clinical intervention* (2nd ed.). New York: Springer.

Eells, T.D. (1997). Psychotherapy case formulation: History and current status. In T.D. Eells (Ed.), *Handbook of psychotherapy case formulation* (pp. 1–25). New York: Guilford Press.

Haynes, S.N. (1986). The design of intervention programs. In R.O. Nelson & S.C. Hayes (Eds.), *Conceptual foundations of behavioral assessment* (pp. 386–429). New York: Guilford Press.

Haynes, S.N. (1992). *Models of causality in psychopathology: Toward synthetic, dynamic, and nonlinear models of causality in psychopathology.* Boston: Allyn & Bacon.

Haynes, S.N. (1994). Clinical judgment and the design of behavioral intervention programs: Estimating the magnitudes of intervention effects. *Psicologia Conductual, 2,* 165–184.

Haynes, S.N. (1998). The assessment-treatment relationship and functional analysis in behavior therapy. *European Journal of Psychological Assessment, 14,* 26–35.

Haynes, S.N., Leisen, M.B., & Blaine, D.D. (1997). Design of individualized behavioral treatment programs using functional an-

alytic clinical case models. *Psychological Assessment, 9,* 334–348.

Haynes, S.N., & O'Brien, W.H. (2000). *Principles and practice of behavioral assessment.* New York: Kluwer Academic/Plenum Publishers.

Haynes, S.N., Richard, D., O'Brien, W.H., & Grant, C. (1999). *Clinical case modeling.* Washington, DC: American Psychological Association.

Haynes, S.N., Uchigakiuchi, P., Meyer, K., Orimoto, L., Blaine, D., & O'Brien, W.H. (1993). Functional analytic causal models and the design of treatment programs: Concepts and clinical applications with childhood behavior problems. *European Journal of Psychological Assessment, 3,* 189–205.

Hersen, M. (1981). Complex problems require complex solutions. *Behavior Therapy, 12,* 15–29.

Kahnemann, D., & Tversky, A. (1973). On the psychology of prediction. *Psychological Review, 80,* 237–251.

Kanfer, F.H. (1985). Target selection for clinical change programs. *Behavioral Assessment, 7,* 7–20.

Kanfer, F.H., & Schefft, B.K. (1988). *Guiding the process of therapeutic change.* Champaign, IL: Research Press.

Kendall, P.C. (1985). Toward a cognitive-behavioral model of child psychopathology and a critique of related interventions. *Journal of Abnormal Child Psychology, 13,* 357–372.

Koerner, K., & Linehan, M.M. (1997). Case formulation in dialectical behavior therapy. In T.D. Eells (Ed.), *Handbook of psychotherapy case formulation* (pp. 340–367)). New York: Guilford Press.

Linehan, M.M. (1993). *Cognitive-behavioral treatment of borderline personality disorder.* New York: Guilford Press.

Mash, E.J., & Hunsley, J. (1993). Assessment considerations in the identification of failing psychotherapy: Bringing the negatives out of the darkroom. *Psychological Assessment, 5,* 292–301.

Nezu, A.M. (1986). Efficacy of a social problem-solving therapy approach for unipolar depression. *Journal of Consulting and Clinical Psychology, 54,* 196–202.

Nezu, A.M. (1987). A problem-solving formulation of depression: A literature review and proposal of a pluralistic model. *Clinical Psychology Review, 7,* 122–144.

Nezu, A.M., & Nezu, C.M. (Eds.). (1989). *Clinical decision making in behavior therapy: A problem-solving perspective.* Champaign, IL: Research Press.

Nezu, A.M., & Nezu, C.M. (1993). Identifying and selecting target problems for clinical interventions: A problem-solving model. *Psychological Assessment, 5,* 254–263.

Nezu, A.M., Nezu, C.M., Friedman, S.H., Faddis, S., & Houts, P.S. (1998). *Helping cancer patients cope: A problem-solving approach.* Washington, D.C.: American Psychological Association.

Nezu, A.M., Nezu, C.M., Friedman, S.H., & Haynes, S.N. (1997). Case formulation in behavior therapy: Problem-solving and functional analytic strategies. In T.D. Eells (Ed.), *Handbook of psychotherapy case formulation* (pp. 368–401). New York: Guilford Press.

Nezu, A.M., Nezu, C.M., & Lombardo, E.R. (2001). Cognitive-behavior therapy for medically unexplained symptoms. A critical review of the treatment literature. *Behavior Therapy, 32,* 537–583.

Nezu, A.M., Nezu, C. M., & Perri, M.G. (1989). *Problem-solving therapy for depression: Theory, research, and clinical guidelines.* New York: Wiley.

Nezu, A.M., Nezu, C.M., Saad, R., & Good, W. (1999). Clinical decision making in behavior therapy: A problem-solving approach to guide case formulation and treatment planning. *Gedragstherapie, 32,* 159–186.

Nezu, A.M., Nezu, C.M., Saraydarian, L., Kalmar, K., & Ronan, G.F. (1986). Social problem solving as a moderating variable between negative life stress and depression. *Cognitive Therapy and Research, 10,* 489–498.

Nezu, A.M., & Perri, M.G. (1989). Problem-solving therapy for unipolar depression: An initial dismantling investigation. *Journal of Consulting and Clinical Psychology, 57,* 408–413.

Nezu, A.M., & Ronan, G.F. (1985). Life stress, current problems, problem solving, and depressive symptoms: An integrative model. *Journal of Consulting and Clinical Psychology, 53,* 693–697.

Nezu, C.M., & Nezu, A.M. (1995). Clinical decision making in everyday practice: The science in the art. *Cognitive and Behavioral Practice, 2,* 5–25.

Paul, G.L. (1969). Behavior modification research: Design and tactics. In C.M. Franks (Ed.), *Behavior therapy: Appraisal and status* (pp. 29–62). New York: McGraw-Hill.

Pepper, S.C. (1942). *World hypotheses.* Berkeley: University of California Press.

Persons, J.B. (1989). *Cognitive therapy in practice: A case formulation approach.* New York: Norton.

Persons, J.B. (1993). Case conceptualization in cognitive-behavior therapy. In K. Kuehlwein & H. Rosen (Eds.), *Cognitive therapies in action* (pp. 33–53). San Francisco: Jossey-Bass.

Persons, J.B., & Tompkins, M.A. (1997). Cognitive-behavioral case formulation. In T.D. Eells (Ed.), *Handbook of psychotherapy case formulation* (pp. 314–339). New York: Guilford Press.

Rosen, A., & Proctor, E.K. (1981). Distinctions between treatment outcomes and their implications for treatment evaluations. *Journal of Consulting and Clinical Psychology, 49,* 418–425.

Swan, G.E., & McDonald, M.L. (1978). Behavior therapy in practice: A national survey of behavior therapists. *Behavior Therapy, 9,* 799–807.

Tversky, A., & Kahnemann, D. (1974). Judgment under uncertainty: Heuristics and biases. *Science, 185,* 1124–1131.

CHAPTER 22

Behavioral Assessment in the Era of Managed Care: Understanding the Present, Preparing for the Future

KIRK D. STROSAHL AND PATRICIA J. ROBINSON

INTRODUCTION

The era of managed health care is nearly two decades old and there is every indication that the principles underpinning this political, economic, and social movement will continue to reshape the U.S. health care system. The behavioral health industry has been no exception to this trend. In almost every conceivable sense, behavioral health providers today engage in different assessment and treatment practices than they did a decade ago. Many traditional assessment strategies have been relegated to secondary status, while other strategies have gained an unprecedented amount of attention. Contemporary behavioral assessment strategies no longer address just the clinical needs of the therapist and client, but are in-creasingly being used to fulfill the requirements of managed care reviewers and the purchasers of health care. Increasingly, managed behavioral care systems view behavioral assessment as a valuable adjunct to the process of managing care. This has led to significant revisions in the types of assessment data sought and how data are used at the clinical, organizational, and system level. From the level of individual clinical provider to system analyst, assessment plays a fundamental role in behavioral health care today.

The purpose of this chapter is to analyze the current status of behavioral assessment in the context of contemporary managed care. This will require a thorough understanding of contemporary managed care practices. First, we will give a brief overview of the origins of managed care so that readers

who are unacquainted with managed care can better understand the basic characteristics of this complicated and controversial movement. The reader will understand contemporary
managed care in a context often not appreciated by practicing
clinicians. Managed care itself is evolving in the face of political, regulatory, clinical, and financial pressures. We will
examine key themes in this evolution, which include the
growing emphasis on quality assessment and performance
accountability, the evolution of the concept of "quality," the
growing dominance of population-based care as the philosophy underpinning health care, and the expansion of clinical
services in different service settings and populations. At the
level of clinical practice, the emergence of evidence-based
care has had a major impact on the utility of behavioral assessment as practitioners strive to address the accountability
requirements of managed behavioral health care systems.
These central characteristics of the new generation of managed care systems will directly bear upon the way behavioral
assessment must be practiced to support the interests of clients, providers, and key external "stakeholders" (i.e., managed
care systems, regulatory and accrediting bodies, financing entities). In anticipation of these changes in managed care, we
will propose a set of guidelines for using behavioral assessment strategies that not only will promote effective clinical
practice, but also will help the clinician prosper in the managed care environment of the future. It is our strong belief
that the core philosophies and practices of behavioral assessment are congruent with the goals and strategies of managed
behavioral health care.

THE GENESIS OF MANAGED CARE

The advent of managed health care can be traced to a prolonged period of double-digit health care inflation between
1970 and 1990, combined with a severe economic recession
in the early 1980s that took many U.S. companies near to or
over the edge of bankruptcy. For example, in the 1980s, the
average annual increase in health care premiums was approximately 19% (Shoor, 1993; Strosahl, 1994). Effectively,
the cost of behavioral health care to the purchaser was dou-
bling every 5 years. A number of factors contributed to this
unsustainable cost spiral. First, mental health and substance
abuse benefits were being added to an increasingly large
number of employer and federally sponsored health plans.
Whereas less than 30% of the population had insurance coverage for mental health services in 1960, nearly 80% had a
mental health benefit by 1980 (Strosahl, 1994). The expansion of behavioral health benefits led to a proliferation of
mental health training programs. For example, the American

Psychological Association promoted the concept of training
programs in professional psychology. This training model was
designed to address what was perceived to be a growing demand for psychologists that could provide insurance-covered
mental health services (Cummings, 1995). Over the years,
these clinically oriented training programs have drastically
increased the supply of psychologists in practice. Unfortunately, this pattern of ratcheting up the supply of mental
health clinicians was repeated for other mental health training
programs as well, leading to a huge oversupply of mental
health providers. As the social stigma associated with seeking
mental health services eased, more people than ever sought
this relatively expensive type of specialty care. In the un-
managed service delivery environment of the time, these
trends led to a skyrocketing bill associated with mental health
benefits.

At the same time access to behavioral health care was
growing, purchasers were generally skeptical about its effectiveness (Trabin & Freeman, 1995). Wide variations in both
diagnostic and treatment practices were commonplace, with
little data available to help purchasers differentiate between
effective and incompetent mental health practitioners. In essence, what had started out as a cottage industry had been
replaced by a major service industry subsidized by private
and public insurance (Cummings & Hayes, 1996; Mechanic,
1996). Faced with an uncontrollable cost spiral, the purchasers of health care (e.g., employers, Medicaid, Medicare,
CHAMPUS) had to make a simple choice. They could eliminate mental health coverage as part of health insurance or
find a way to control the costs of behavioral health care.
Managed care as a movement was and is an attempt by the
purchasers to control the costs of health care. For the behavioral health industry, the shift to managed care signaled the
"industrialization" of behavioral health care (Cummings &
Hayes, 1996). Behavioral health services would thereafter be
treated as commodities and would be subjected to the same
marketplace and regulatory forces that are true of any other
industry.

Generation 1: Managed Cost

The early years of managed care had a profound impact on
the behavioral health industry. First, the supply-side economics model popularized by David Stockman, chief financial
advisor to Ronald Reagan, heavily influenced the early strategies of managed care. Supply-side strategies have two essential features: (1) to reduce accessibility to goods and services
that are being overconsumed and (2) to drive down the unit
cost of services by allowing the marketplace to favor the most
efficient and effective models of production. Applied to be-

havioral health care, supply-side strategies attempt to limit easy access to services and drive down the costs of services for the payer—in this case, employer- and federally sponsored insurance programs (Sobel, 1995). Both employers and insurance companies were generally ambivalent about their ability to effectively regulate the costs of behavioral care. The common belief was that cost control could be achieved only by a segregated and specialized management system. Thus, the "carve out" model was developed with its corporate manifestation, the managed behavioral health organization (MBHO). In the carve out model, separate financing, claims, credentialing, and utilization management systems were established specifically to reduce the cost of behavioral health care. The goal was to place responsibility for managing the behavioral health benefit in the hands of behavioral health experts, who could directly profit from managing costs. Economically speaking, managed care carve out companies began to split profits that previously had been the sole province of providers, psychiatric facilities/outpatient clinics, and insurance companies (Hayes, Barlow, & Nelson-Gray, 1999). This led to an explosion in the number of managed care companies competing for the health care dollar. For example, from 1975 to 1995, the number of health maintenance organizations (HMOs) in the United States increased from 166 to 600 (Group Health Association of American, 1995).

A major initial strategy of MBHOs was to restrict access to an unlimited supply of mental health services. For example, patients seeking behavioral care had to meet stringent "medical necessity" criteria to qualify for insurance coverage. Ordinarily, the patient had to suffer from a diagnosable mental health or chemical dependency disorder to qualify for insurance coverage. Practically speaking, this meant that patients with life circumstance difficulties (i.e., marital dissatisfaction) were often denied care. The provision of services was aggressively managed through a variety of utilization review strategies, the net effect being to reduce the number of mental health treatment sessions any given patient could consume. Another common strategy was to restructure mental health benefits so that the patient bore a larger financial burden when receiving mental health services. Strategies such as copayments or coinsurance were widely employed to decrease the rate of service seeking. Services research clearly showed that, irrespective of clinical need, cost-sharing strategies resulted in decreased service use (Simon, Grothaus, Durham, VonKorff, & Pabiniak, 1996).

Second, MBHOs were able to use the oversupply of mental health providers to drive down professional fees to artificially low levels by having providers compete with one another for a limited number of openings in "preferred provider organizations" (PPOs). Those who refused to work for

below market rate fees were simply excluded from provider networks. If a patient received mental health services from a non–preferred provider, the MBHO could refuse payment for such services. In essence, MBHOs were allowed to structure administration of the mental health benefit so that the financial incentives routed patients to providers who delivered services at artificially low rates. Experts in managed care agree that it is not so much the structure of a health benefit that determines its ultimate cost to the purchaser, but rather how the benefit is interpreted administratively by the managed care entity (Strosahl, 1994; Trabin and Freeman, 1995).

Third, managed care shifted financial risk from the insurer to the provider. Practices such as utilization review were used to deny payment for what was judged to be unnecessary care. MHBOs used billing and utilization review data to profile the practices of contracted behavioral health providers. Providers that took longer to treat patients were selectively weeded out of practice networks. These strategies favored providers with brief assessment and treatment practices and, over time, resulted in greatly abbreviated outpatient regimes of behavioral care.

Fourth, there was a strategic shift away from the widespread use of inpatient psychiatric services, the cost of which was a major factor in the escalating cost of behavioral care. In response, MBHOs required that more patients be treated on an outpatient basis and aggressively managed the average length of stay for inpatients. Psychiatric units that offered treatment programs based on 3- to 4-week stays were contracted to complete treatment in 7 days or less. These strategies resulted in the closure of hundreds of psychiatric inpatient units across the country (Trabin & Freeman, 1995).

Collectively, the strategies of Generation 1 were enormously successful. Between 1985 and 1994, it is estimated that the costs of behavioral health care were reduced by approximately 40% (Strosahl, 1995). Although there are sampling bias issues involved, these reductions appear to have been achieved with little impact on the overall quality of care (Mechanic, 1996). As we shall see, however, the major detrimental impact of MBHOs has been to shift patients from the mental health system into the health care system.

CORE CHARACTERISTICS OF MANAGED CARE SYSTEMS

Although the term "managed care" is often used as if it refers to a monolithic entity, it is instead a summary label used to describe a bewildering variety of strategies (Giles, 1993). These loosely interconnected strategies exist at the level of delivery system design, clinical practice management, and financing/contracting. Table 22.1 summarizes these three levels of managed care. In practice, these three levels of managed care strategies are highly interdependent and difficult to disentangle. Therefore, it is important to understand them in an abstract sense first, and then appreciate their interconnection at the level of application.

Delivery System Design

A delivery system is the overarching structure in which clinical services are provided. Managed care has favored larger systems that can capitalize on the economies of scale. This has led to the development of three primary delivery system methods: preferred provider organization, independent provider association (IPA), and the health maintenance organization.

The PPO is sometimes referred to as a "network model" system because it can involve thousands of independent practitioners who are under contract to provide behavioral health services at a set rate. For example, the Value-Options Healthcare Network contains in excess of 30,000 mental health clinicians, each under contract with the parent company. Many mental health providers are under contract with more than one PPO, which explains one of the most common complaints heard in the practice sector. Specifically, each PPO has its own unique paperwork requirement, practice standards, and clinical practice management strategies. It has been estimated that the average practitioner spends as much as 1 hour of managed care–related paper work for every hour of clinical service delivered!

The IPA is often referred to as a "group practice model" because it is a consortium of independent practitioners that form a common business entity to attract and negotiate favorable managed care contracts. The IPA evolved in part as a protection against the leverage exercised by MBHOs against the solo practitioner. The solo practitioner has no bargaining power in a large system and is forced to accept whatever session rate is offered by the much bigger carve out company. In contrast, the IPA can bargain collectively for more favorable contract terms because it can offer a larger area of coverage, specialized services, and better coordination of care. The IPA itself is a business entity that can provide certain services to its constituents in a more cost effective way. Some examples of this economy of scale are claims and billing, scheduling and appointments, peer review, and outcomes assessment. An IPA can generally provide these services to its members far cheaper than would be the case if each clinician procured these services separately.

The HMO is really the progenitor of managed care delivery systems. In part, this is because HMOs such as Kaiser Permanente and Group Health Cooperative of Puget Sound were the first managed care delivery systems in the United States. These two systems have been in existence since the late 1940s, long before the concept of managed care became popularized. Further, the HMO act of 1974, passed by Congress to institutionalize and legitimize the HMO as a health care entity, is widely regarded as the beginning of the managed care movement in the United States (Strosahl, 1994). Historically, the HMO model is defined by its health care mission rather than by the structure of its provider system. This is an excellent example of how the three levels of managed care strategies interconnect at "ground zero." The HMO is generally based on a prepaid health care approach that emphasizes prevention, early detection, and management of health risk and illness factors over time. Prepaid health care is often referred to as "capitation" financing (see Table 22.1). In capitated systems, payment for services is made before the delivery of services, based on a formula that predicts how much it should cost to provide health care to a defined population. The unit measure of this formula is the cost per member per month to provide the full range of health care services. This is the amount of money the HMO will get each month for each person enrolled in the prepaid health care plan. HMO "bashing" has become a popular exercise in the media, in the professional guilds, and in consumer advocacy groups because of the temptation in prepaid health care environments to deny services to consumers and thereby improve profits. These abuses have largely occurred in many new HMOs that have formed since the advent of managed care. These entities generally lack any real connection or allegiance with the social contracts that characterized the first generation of HMOs. The magnitude of this disconnect is illustrated by the fact that, while consumer protection legislation has been triggered by the abuses witnessed in new HMOs, the more established HMOs consistently rank in the top 20 quality health care systems in the United States.

Clinical Practice Management

A second core characteristic of managed care is the emphasis on managing care at the level of individual clinical practice. Recall that one of the major concerns leading to managed care was the widespread conviction that behavioral health care providers were engaging in highly variable treatment practices across patients and settings. Clinical practice management is a set of strategies designed to control this variability and, in theory, improve clinical outcomes while decreasing the costs associated with unnecessary variability. These clinical practice management strategies are also listed in Table 22.1. Utilization review is a general strategy designed to aggressively manage the type and intensity of services that are de-

TABLE 22.1 Core Managed Care Characteristics and Strategic Effects

Domain	Strategy	Definition	Impact
Delivery System Design	Preferred Provider Organization (PPO)	Network of individual providers under contract to managed behavioral health organization (MBHO); clients directed to provider in care management process	Allows MBHO to negotiate below market session rates; providers agree to be reviewed as part of contract; allows MBHO to control type and amount of services
	Health Maintenance Organization (HMO)	Model of prepaid healthcare; can include a preferred provider organization (PPO), independent provider organization (IPA), hospital physician group (HPG), or Staff model; designed to allow easy access to preventive care, full continuum of primary care and hospital services	Allows health plan to prevent disease, remove barriers to seeking care; goal is to improve health of plan members, allow full range of services in single system; decrease costs
	Independent Provider Association (IPA)	Network of providers in a single business entity; usually smaller individual and group practices; can cover a wide geographic area	Allows patients access to a large system of providers at a fixed cost; MBHO can negotiate lower rate in return for greater volume of clients
	Hospital Physician Group (HPG)	Hospital-based business entity "buys out" primary care and behavioral practices; forms a local network of services owned and operated by the hospital	Offers full continuum of care in a single contract; allows contract requirements to substitute for managed care review; reduces expense to MBHO
	Group Practice	A business entity involving a full range of behavioral health and medical providers; practices are larger with multiple sites	Can contract with MBHO or directly with purchaser; internalizes review processes, volume creates lower cost
Clinical Practice Management	Precertification	Provider must present clinical assessment data in advance of approval; limited number of sessions approved in advance	Allows MBHO to detect improper assessment or treatment plans; can focus and narrow treatment targets, reduce cost of care
	Mandatory Session Reviews	Requires review of treatment at preestablished session intervals (i.e., every fourth contact); provider must demonstrate treatment progress	Allows MHBO to detect and prevent failing or unnecessary treatment; can decertify treatment not in compliance with guidelines
	Treatment Progress Profiling	Requires frequent time series assessment using self-report measure(s); statistical formula predicts expected level of change versus actual level of change; review is based on concordance with expected and actual estimates	Allows MBHO to detect treatment failures and revise treatment plans; establishes asymptote for cost effectiveness of continuing treatment (i.e., point at which further treatment will not increase outcome); provides model for managing treatment and setting session limits
	Provider Practice Profiling	MBHO uses aggregate clinical outcome database to identify high performing and low performing providers in terms of costs and outcomes	Allows MBHO to disenroll low performing providers from PPO; protects consumers from receiving ineffective and expensive treatment
Financing and Contracting	Case Rates	MBHO pays a fixed price for treatment of a certain condition, negotiated with individual provider	Shifts financial risk to provider for delivering treatment under the fixed rate; removes risk of unneeded treatment
	Capitation	MBHO pays a fixed amount in advance, based on per person per month (PPPM) formula; provider entity manages care internally; accountability is driven by service contract	Shifts financial risk to provider, while giving provider flexibility in how resources are allocated; provider absorbs managed care responsibilities; reduces administrative cost to MBHO
	Group or Network Contracting	Favored method for large MBHO; uses oversupply of providers to create demand for entry into a PPO; allows MBHO to negotiate below market rate service contracts	MBHO gets services at a reduced rate, but must manage care externally at some cost; contracts favor MBHO right to restrict or deny payment for service
	Direct Contracting	New method in which group practice negotiates directly with employer; contract is between employer and group practice with no MBHO involved; contracts often performance based; group practice responsible for managing care	Eliminates administrative costs of the MBHO as an intermediary between purchaser and service provider; direct relationship may improve access to care and eliminate abusive MBHO practices
	Administrative Service Organization (ASO)	MBHO-type entity provides utilization review services for a separate system of providers; MBHO does not operate its own delivery system; very popular in Medicaid state carve out models	ASO has sole authority to authorize services; can use any clinical practice review strategy needed; removes conflict of interest of being reviewer and provider of care as in classic MBHO

livered over the course of a treatment regime. There are several utilization review strategies, ranging from precertification to post hoc review. Notice that in any of these strategies, the onus is on the provider of services to demonstrate that the services planned or already delivered are medically necessary. The concept of "medical necessity" is a core element of utilization review because it allows the MBHO to deny payment for services not deemed to be necessary. Especially as it pertains to behavioral health, what is medically necessary is largely a subjective judgment. If the criteria are rigorous, then a large number of people seeking services will be denied insurance coverage, thus increasing the MBHO profit picture. If the criteria are lenient, then many more people will receive mental health services and the MBHO may not be able to demonstrate the overall cost reductions that are expected by the purchaser.

An interesting utilization review strategy that has been used widely in the MBHO environment is the mandatory session limit review. At periodic intervals throughout treatment (i.e., every third session), the provider must present evidence that the treatment is appropriate, the client is making progress, and that further sessions need to be authorized. This strategy is designed to detect inappropriate execution of a treatment plan, treatment failure, or "packing" the treatment with unnecessary additional sessions. Of all the strategies employed in managed behavioral care, this is the one most consistent with the underlying principles of behavioral assessment. Behavioral health care providers may have the option of using their own assessment data, such as that derived from self-monitoring assignments or the completion of empirically validated self-report questionnaires that the utilization reviewer accepts as a valid measure of progress (Persons, 1989). In other systems of care, a system wide assessment tool is administered and re-administered at defined intervals. This allows the delivery system to accumulate a large database regarding clinical outcomes, which can then be used to define performance standards for clinical practice.

Financing and Contracting Strategies

A final core component of managed care is the application of financing and contracting strategies that favor providers and systems that can provide clinically and cost effective services. Most of the financing methods listed in Table 22.1 effectively shift the risk for managing care to the provider. For example, case rates set a preestablished payment for a selected diagnosis. If the provider is able to successfully complete treatment at a cost that is under the case rate, then a profit is made. If the cost of delivering treatment exceeds the case rate, the provider incurs a loss. A similar incentive is

created in capitation financing. When a provider (i.e., group practice, HMO, etc.) is able to manage the behavioral health service needs of a population under the capitation rate, then a profit occurs. If extensive and unnecessary behavioral health services are delivered, the system will experience a significant monetary loss. A new development in managed care financing known as direct contracting is an attempt by health care purchasers to circumvent the administrative costs involved in contracting with a "middleman"—in this case, the MBHO. Instead of contracting with an MBHO to manage care, the contract is directly between the purchaser (i.e., employer, state government) and the provider of services. Typically, direct contracting is performance based. The provider agrees to provide a range of services to a certain percentage of the patients covered in the contract as well as to collect and submit data of clinical outcomes, access to services, consumer satisfaction, and so on. Many experts in managed behavioral health care believe that performance-based contracting will be the dominant financing strategy within managed care in the next decade.

CONTEMPORARY TRENDS IN MANAGED CARE

As is true with any major sociopolitical movement, a correction will always be met with a counter-correction. Such has been the case with managed health care. Admittedly, much of the criticism directed toward managed care practices is the result of professional guilds that are engaging in thinly disguised self-serving behavior. At the same time, there are reasons to be concerned about the long-term viability of a management model that is so completely focused on cost containment. As the risk for providing services has shifted to providers, providers have been forced into an intrinsic conflict of interest between the requirements for making money and the requirements for delivering quality care. In some sad situations, the temptation of the pocketbook has resulted in poor clinical practice. These abuses of some managed care systems have been well documented in the media and have resulted in civil litigation sponsored by such professional associations as the American Medical Association and the American Psychological Association (Mechanic, 1996). Regulatory oversight has also been forthcoming, as evidenced by such initiatives as parity legislation and the patient bill of rights currently being debated in Congress. Some states have passed legislation that makes it easier for patients to sue managed care organizations, not just the providers who work for them (Verhovek, 1997). In any evolving industry, there is a natural evolution that generally moves from monopolistic dominance to the infusion of increased competition, regulatory reform, and legal protections. Managed care itself has begun such an evolution that holds great promise for clinicians who believe in the principles of behavioral assessment.

Generation 2: Managed Care

Apart from the financial conflicts of interest that have been pursued in legal actions, there are structural reasons for being concerned about the long-term viability of the U.S. health care system (of which behavioral health care is a part). A recent Institute of Medicine Report on the status of the U.S. health care system paints an even more disturbing picture. Describing the system as "broken," this report details a wide variety of flaws that make receiving health care a dangerous proposition for the average citizen. These flaws include poor coordination among providers, wide variations in medical decision making, financing methods that encourage highly segregated service delivery, poor health outcomes for patients with both acute and chronic diseases, and a singular lack of emphasis on providing quality health care. Indeed, it appears that managed cost has resulted in the dismantling of the U.S. health care system (National Academy of Science, 2000).

In the behavioral health arena, a similar pattern of results has occurred. When patients are systematically denied access to preventive and/or acute care, the percent of the population suffering from behavioral health conditions increases, and the severity of the behavioral disturbances manifested by those seeking treatment also increases. The results of the Epidemiologic Catchment Area Surveys (Regier et al., 1993) and the National Co-Morbidity Study (Kessler et al., 1994) clearly suggest that the behavioral health of the U.S. population had deteriorated since the advent of managed care. There was approximately a 5–7% increase in the annual incidence of mental disorders in the general population between 1985 and 1995. In 1994, one of us (KS) wrote that while managed cost would initially control health care costs, the "penny wise pound foolish" model of supply-side restriction would inevitably fail and behavioral health care costs would rebound to their pre–managed care levels (Strosahl & Quirk, 1994). One basic reason for this rebound would be the shifting of patients with mental health and substance abuse treatment needs from the specialty treatment sector into the general medical sector. In general medicine, patients in need have far less access to effective mental health services because the systems of care are completely segregated. This population shifting would unleash a large cohort of patients with mental health needs on a system that is primarily designed to deliver basic medical care. As a result, the health care system would begin to "implode" as a result of the financial risk and service burden represented by this class of patients. Inevitably, health care

premiums would begin to rise because health care costs would keep rising. Precisely this outcome has been obtained. While health care premiums were essentially flat between 1992 and 1996, health care inflation reappeared in 1997 and this year is estimated to be in the vicinity of 17%.

Collectively, these factors have provoked the emergence of what is referred to as "Generation 2" of managed care (Cummings, 1997; Hayes, Barlow, and Nelson-Gray, 1999; Strosahl, 1995, 1996a). This generation of managed care will focus on balancing the three essential parameters of quality behavioral health care: clinical/functional outcomes, consumer satisfaction, and cost. No longer is the value of behavioral care determined solely by how much it costs. Rather, value is a multidimensional construct reflecting appropriate clinical care delivered in a cost effective way that is acceptable to the consumer (Strosahl, 1995). The concept of "value-based purchasing" reflects a fundamental change in the philosophy of health care purchasers. Instead of mindlessly awarding managed care contracts to the lowest bidder, purchasers are willing to pay more if it can be shown that increased funding for behavioral care leads to superior clinical outcomes, improved functioning at work and home, and increased consumer satisfaction. This signals that the sponsors of health care are willing to abandon supply-side management strategies if behavioral health systems of care can demonstrate value.

THE EVOLUTION OF BEHAVIORAL ASSESSMENT: FROM PROMISE TO PROBLEMS

Ironically, the genesis and evolution of behavioral assessment mirrors that of the managed care movement. Both of these movements occurred as a response to a status quo that was deemed unacceptable; both movements got off to a quick and promising start; and both movements have struggled in recent years. The genesis of behavioral assessment was in part a response to the needs of behavior therapy as it matured during the 1970s. Behavioral interventions required a different approach to measurement because they often targeted observable behaviors that could not be easily measured using traditional methods. More importantly, behavioral assessment as a paradigm was to the assessment field what behavior therapy was to the psychotherapy field: a fundamental shift in the way human behavior is conceptualized. The behavioral assessment paradigm rejected traditional trait constructs of personality, which advocated measuring underlying, stable behavioral predispositions. Instead, behavioral assessment emphasized the value of direct observation of behavior, with the assumption that behavior can be understood and controlled only through a careful analysis of antecedents and consequences. Clinically significant behaviors are not stable across time or situations, but rather are shaped and maintained by highly localized influences. The principle of "situational specificity" is perhaps the single most influential assumption underpinning the behavioral assessment paradigm. These situation-specific responses could be understood only by conducting a functional analysis of observable behavior. On the continuum of scientific inference, observable behavior is preferred over patient self-reports. Similarly, multiple observations drawn from multiple sources are preferred over single observations. Because clinically relevant behavior varies across time and settings, it is imperative to sample a large enough domain of situations to truly capture the range of possible response classes and controlling variables. The principle of observing the client's behavior across a range of clinically relevant situations is often referred to as content validity (Goldfried & Linehan, 1977; Strosahl & Linehan, 1986).

In a classic treatment of the role of behavioral assessment in clinical psychology, Cone and Hawkins (1977) articulated five roles for behavioral assessment: (1) screening, clinical triage, and case disposition; (2) clinical problem definition and hypothesis formation; (3) target problem intervention design; (4) progress monitoring; and (5) long-term assessment of behavior change. Given the early stage of development of behavioral assessment at the time, it is astonishing to note that this basic assessment template remains very much at the center of managed behavioral health care. More contemporaneous behavioral assessment theorists have dramatically increased the clinical sophistication of this assessment paradigm (Haynes & O'Brien, 2000; Mash & Terdal, 1997). These new approaches emphasize the importance of behavioral assessment in a clinical case formulation paradigm that is highly idiographic, scientifically sound, sensitive to behavior-environment and behavior-behavior relations, and sensitive to multiple, reciprocally interactive causal relations. The targets of clinical interventions are those functional relationships that control the most variation in the behavior of clinical concern (Haynes, Thacher, Kaholokula, & Nelson, 2001).

Whatever Happened to Behavioral Assessment?

Concurrent with the emergence of managed care, behavioral assessment underwent some growing pains of its own. The progenitors of behavioral assessment always regarded indirect methods of assessment (i.e., self-report surveys, clinical interviews) as less informative and less accurate than direct observational assessment. However, as the cognitive revolution in behavior therapy legitimized private events as valid targets for behavioral interventions, there was a need to rethink some of the early notions underpinning behavioral as-

sessment. Strosahl & Linehan (1986) argued that, in principle, the measurement of covert events such as beliefs and attitudes could be accomplished in much the same fashion as the measurement of observable behavior. First, it is necessary to collect a domain of possible beliefs/attitudes that are thought to influence a particular set of clinically relevant responses. Then, it is possible to collect information about beliefs/attitudes using interview and/or self-report methods and empirically validate their clinical utility. In essence, there is nothing sacred about which mode of assessment is used (i.e., behavior observation, self-report, interview, informants, naturalistic data), as long as one can demonstrate both content and predictive validity. In retrospect, this was perhaps one of the most important developments in behavioral assessment, because it opened the door for a new generation of self-report and interview assessment protocols. At the same time, however, this development resulted in a disturbing trend that would eventually cause behavioral assessment to lose its bearings.

As the emphasis on the measurement of private events increased, traditional psychological assessment principles began to dominate the behavioral assessment research agenda. The emphasis in research was to demonstrate the soundness of new instruments and procedures. Traditional psychometric, trait-oriented concepts such as test-retest reliability, internal consistency, and factor structure replaced the principles of idiographic, single case, and functional analytic assessments. In response to federal grant funding requirements, behavior therapy researchers adopted nomothetic research designs in lieu of single subject designs. This required behaviorally oriented researchers to adopt measurement strategies that were, in many ways, the antithesis of behavioral assessment. In a basic way, behavioral assessment was subsumed and permanently altered by the growing behavior therapy outcome research community. One indication of this loss of identity was the collapse of a journal specifically devoted to behavioral assessment; another journal originally designed to promote basic behavioral assessment research was forced to change its name to attract a sufficient readership. In a classic criticism, Hayes, Nelson, and Jarrett (1987) argued that the clinical utility of measurement, not the psychometric soundness of measurement instruments, should be the overarching principle of behavioral assessment. Measurement techniques that demonstrate the ability to identify important treatment targets and are empirically linked to differential outcomes are superior to measurement strategies that have admirable psychometric characteristics but cannot demonstrate clinical utility in the individual case. This important principle was largely ignored by the behavior therapy research community and, to some extent, it still is today. By and large, practitioners in the field have underutilized contemporary behavioral assessment strategies. Those that have managed to proliferate have done so more in response to the demands of managed care than to an intrinsic linkage by practicing clinicians to the core philosophies of behavioral assessment.

TRANSITIONAL THEMES IN MANAGED CARE

Independent of the struggles within the behavioral assessment paradigm, the era of managed care has been a turbulent time for behavioral health providers. There has been a basic shift in the parameters underlying the provision of behavioral care. These parameters are closely tied to how the managed care marketplace has been shaped by various stakeholders in the health care system. These stakeholders include consumers, providers, health care purchasers, insurance companies, accrediting bodies, as well as state and federal regulatory agencies. It should be no surprise that the present and future functions of behavioral assessment have been and will continue to be shaped, maintained, and reinforced by these influences. It is important to first examine some of the key themes emerging in contemporary managed care. It will then be possible to assess the real and projected impact of these influences on contemporary behavioral assessment practices.

Quality and Accountability

It is important to understand that many of the issues that have led to Generation 2 of managed care are at heart assessment issues. How does one define quality and measure it? How can the employer purchaser tell a good managed care system from a bad one? What types of behavioral health services produce the best "bang for the buck"? Questions like this are pervasive in the contemporary managed care environment and can be answered only by conducting systematic assessments of clients, providers, and systems of care. This environment is ripe with opportunities for providers who adhere to the principles of behavioral assessment.

In essence, the shift to value-based purchasing signifies a shift to a data-driven decision-making model. As purchasers require more tangible evidence of value in the behavioral health care product, managed care systems have been forced to develop strategies for measuring quality. This has resulted in an explosion of interest in strategies that can effectively measure clinical outcomes, cost, and consumer satisfaction. This information is being used to manage care at the level of clinical practice. At the system level, MBHOs are seeking to use aggregated clinical outcomes data to demonstrate value to the purchasers. This trend is so pervasive that it has spawned a new behavioral health industry: behavioral informatics.

Behavioral informatics is a field specializing in the applications of computer technology to the information needs of managed behavioral health care systems. These needs include, among other things, methods for assessing and triaging patients, tracking clinical progress, and measuring both intermediate and long-term clinical outcomes. The growth of the behavioral informatics sector has truly been amazing. This industry attempts to use information technology to provide automated support to practitioners in the field resulting in the proliferation of automated assessment methods such as point-of-view boxes, interactive voice response, and FAX technology (Strosahl, 1999, 2000). Behavioral health software vendors have formed a national trade association, with one goal being the development and implementation of national standards for performance benchmarking, including unified systems for describing patients, clinical services, clinical outcomes, and consumer satisfaction. Among the more notable software trends are the proliferation of automated clinical outcomes packages, electronic patient records, and clinical decision support models (Strosahl, 2000). As will be discussed in detail in a later section, many managed behavioral health care systems actively seek providers who employ evaluation strategies designed to assign patients to an appropriate level of care, establish measurable clinical goals, monitor treatment progress in real time, and evaluate both short- and long-term outcomes.

The Redefinition of "Outcome"

In addition to the resurgence of interest in assessing outcomes, we have witnessed the emergence of many new stakeholder groups in the behavioral health service delivery environment. These stakeholders (i.e., clients, professional guilds, employer purchasers, managed care companies, federal and state agencies, accrediting bodies) have specific interests that collectively have produced a revolution in the definition a "clinical outcome." No longer will it suffice for a clinician to point to reduced severity scores on a depression scale as evidence of a positive clinical outcome. The clinician may be required to demonstrate a reduction in days missed at work during the last month (for the employer purchaser); improvement in the patient's social role functioning and general well-being (for the consumer advocates); decreased use of medical service (for the health plan sponsoring the behavioral health benefit); and costs of treatment that fall below a specific "value" benchmark (for the managed care company). The transition from a provider-centered to a stakeholder-centered definition of clinical quality requires that traditional models of behavioral assessment be revised to account for all the parameters incorporated in the new definition of outcome. For example, there are no efficient methods for assessing the functional status of therapy patients. Existing self-report and interview methods not only have questionable construct validity, but are prohibitively time consuming to administer. Protocols will have to be developed for assessing work performance (i.e. absenteeism, lost productivity, work disability), social role functioning, health status, and general well-being in a time- and cost-efficient way. Some stakeholders may not regard symptom reduction, in the absence of demonstrable improvements in functional status, as a positive clinical outcome.

Population-Based Care

Contemporary managed care is characterized by an increasing emphasis on "demand management." Unlike supply-side management, which focuses on restricting access to or reducing the absolute cost of behavioral health services, demand management focuses on raising the behavioral health of the population so that there is less demand for services (Strosahl, 1996a). Population health care has gained ascendancy in general health care and is beginning to take hold in the behavioral health industry as well. In general, population care adopts a public health approach that focuses on the prevention and early detection of disease using an evidence-based care framework. Population health indicators, such as the percentage of community members who have at least one ambulatory medical visit in an index year, the percentage of women who have had a pap smear in the previous year, or the percentage of children under 5 who have all the required immunizations are now used to evaluate the quality of health care plans (cf. Eddy, 1996).

A unique feature of population care is that there is less emphasis on measuring outcomes of a specific case as a "marker" of the performance of an entire system of care. For example, there is considerable debate on which population behavioral health markers to use in the primary care population and how to measure them in a way that promotes effective clinical practice and permits some level of standardization in performance benchmarking. Robinson (in press) has suggested that population markers be associated with specific quality improvement programs. For example, a system might seek to improve recognition of depression in primary care clinics and would assess the percentage of patients diagnosed with depression on a monthly or yearly basis. In this example, the individual clinic could determine the extent to which its identification rates were similar to prevalence rates suggested in national epidemiological studies. Because behavioral health care historically has not been grounded in population health

concepts, there will be great pressure to develop measurement strategies that are sensitive to both population health and clinical change parameters.

Service Integration

In recent years, the limitations of the managed cost model have become increasingly apparent to health care policymakers, in that there is a mismatch between where patients present for behavioral care and where behavioral care is available (Sobel, 1995). Partly in response to consumer preferences and the growing recognition of the service mismatch, managed care philosophies are changing to an emphasis on "one stop shopping" service venues. Applied to behavioral care, this means services will be made available in new settings such as schools, primary medicine, and jails, to name a few. This will require the development of new assessment protocols designed for patients with behavioral health needs who are seen in new service delivery environments. In a primary care system, measuring reductions in medical services use as a function of providing behavioral care to patients in need may be the major outcome of interest. In a school setting, the impact of behavioral interventions on subsequent truancy or referrals for disciplinary action may be central assessment targets. The challenge in integrated service settings will be to apply behavioral assessment principles to measure outcomes that may be highly specific to that setting.

As mentioned previously, epidemiological studies have suggested a decline in the mental health of U.S. citizens, while health care premiums are once again rising. Service utilization research has clearly suggested that primary care is the de facto mental health and chemical dependency treatment system in the United States (Regier et al., 1993). Approximately 70% of all Americans with mental or chemical dependency disorders receive their care exclusively from a general medical care provider (Strosahl, 2001). The primary care setting has become the focus of interest in contemporary managed care because many more patients with behavioral health problems circulate in that setting than in traditional mental health settings. From a population care perspective, it is imperative to address the impact of behavioral factors in general health care. The integration of primary care and behavioral health services is a focal point of contemporary managed care (Strosahl, 1996a, 1996b).

This presents providers who follow the concepts of behavioral assessment a golden opportunity to develop screening, process, and outcome measures that are usable in the primary care environment. A great deal of work has already been accomplished in this arena, with instrumentation ranging from measures of daily and weekly stress (Brantley &

Jeffries, 2000) to condition-specific assessment protocols such as the PRIME-MD (Spitzer et al., 1995). In general, behavioral assessments developed for primary care will have to be more efficient and user friendly. The work pace in primary care is vastly quicker than in traditional mental health settings, and general medical care providers are loath to use procedures that take more than 2 to 5 minutes. The challenge faced by researchers and practitioners is to build instruments and protocols that are both accurate and expedient.

Patient-Centered Care

Managed care has promoted the delivery of services based upon consumer preferences, and this trend is likely to continue. At the system level, major sponsors of care are involving patients in the development of both assessment and treatment approaches. For example, the Health 2000 Outcomes project involved input from multiple consumer advocacy groups. In clinical practice, providers routinely generate patient-centered treatment goals and use methods such as goal attainment scaling (GAS) to assess treatment progress (Lewis, Spencer, Haas, & DiVittis, 1987). In fact, many commercially based clinical outcomes packages, such as the Treatment Outcome Package (ACCESS Measurement Systems, 1998), focus on the patient's description of problems as well as the patient's level of satisfaction with treatment.

The patient-centered care model has indirectly stimulated new areas of assessment not previously of much interest to the provider community, including measures for assessing treatment acceptability/adherence, health-related quality of life, and service quality, to name a few. This newfound emphasis on responding to consumer preferences has resulted in some innovative behavioral assessment strategies. For example, solution-focused therapy models emphasize the use of scaling techniques at all therapy sessions to provide quick and meaningful indications of patient level of investment and confidence in treatment. Miller, Duncan, and Hubblel (1997) describe a brief process evaluation administered at the conclusion of every therapy session to provide information about the adequacy of the therapist-patient relationship. These end-of-session checks typically involve having the patient complete a limited number of rating scales. This allows the patient to quickly indicate the extent to which he or she felt respected or whether treatment goals were developed collaboratively. This approach has been adapted for use in family therapy sessions—where all members respond simultaneously to a brief process check questionnaire—and to primary care—where four process check items appear on the bottom of a chart-note that is signed by the patient and therapist (Robinson, Wischman, & Del Vento, 1996).

The managed care movement has also stimulated the development of unique perspectives on the conceptual targets of assessment. For example, medical sociologists have long suggested that there is a distinction between the concepts of disease as assessed by care providers and illness, suffering, and pain as assessed by patients (Eisenberg & Kleinman, 1981; Twaddle, 1981). This distinction is useful to managers of care, particularly in regard to the assessment of individuals with chronic, serious mental disorders and their families. The families of such patients often have to endure much more than the psychological distress of having a seriously impaired person in their midst. The burden also includes limitations on family activities, financial hardship, and an increased risk of health and mental health problems in family caregivers (Dowart, 1996). These are outcomes that can be measured, and their impact on the cost of health care is substantial. Consequently, measures of family burden are now routinely used as a component of assessment batteries for patients with serious mental illness. This type of measurement focus would not have been possible without the managed care movement.

IMPACT OF MANAGED CARE ON CONTEMPORARY BEHAVIORAL ASSESSMENT PRACTICES

The core transitional themes in managed care discussed in the previous section will have a dramatic impact on clinical assessment practices in general and behavioral assessment in particular. In many cases, these influences are already evident in the research and clinical emphases of managed care. Overall, the salutary impact of managed care on practice evaluation has far exceeded its negative impact. Managed care has prompted behavioral health practitioners to include the consumer's perspective on assessment and shifted the focus of assessment from theoretical constructs and symptoms to functioning and quality of life. Managed care, inadvertently, has furthered the integration of physical and behavioral health concepts in assessment practices and prompted the development of measures of condition-specific symptoms and general functioning. Managed care has clarified the need for understanding normal behavior and healthy functioning. It has required that we include new assessment targets, including consumer and provider satisfaction and cost of treatment. Overall, managed care has had a positive impact on the communication between behavioral health providers and patients, MBHOs, medical providers, and employers. It has also inspired pursuit of new directions in treatment, including stepped models of care, linkage of assessment approaches with practice settings, and use of population-based care markers to evaluate models of care, as well as individual providers, clinics, and even systems of care. Understanding the impact of these diverse influences, both negative and positive, will allow the behavioral clinician to build a set of strategies for adapting clinical practice to the demands of managed care.

Increased Emphasis on Time Series Assessment

A unique feature of the behavioral assessment paradigm has been the emphasis on the use of single subject assessment strategies (Gresham, 1998; Hayes, 1992). Although many single subject designs are not well suited for applied clinical practice, the growing managed care emphasis on individualized clinical practice management has led to the widespread adoption of repeated clinical assessments as a basic managed care strategy. In effect, most managed care systems use a time series approach to assessment, but managed care reviewers lack needed expertise in the interpretation of time series data (Hayes, Barlow, and Nelson-Gray, 1999). Methods for conducting and analyzing time series data are widely available in the behavioral assessment literature (Barlow, Hayes, & Nelson, 1984; Franklin, Allison, & Gorman, 1996; Gaynor, Baird, & Nelson-Gray, 1999; Hayes, Barlow, & Nelson-Gray, 1999). Many behaviorally oriented clinicians now use time series assessment methodology as a basic strategy for addressing the requirements of managed care review (Persons, 1989). Various measurement strategies have been developed that help practicing clinicians overcome the practical difficulties of establishing patient-specific measures of change that can be periodically readministered to assess clinical progress. One such innovation is goal attainment scaling (Lewis et al., 1987), which allows the clinician and patient to formulate behaviorally anchored treatment goals, assess baseline level of attainment, and periodically reassess progress using a Likert scaling strategy.

Increased Application of Self-Monitoring Strategies

Strategies that are brief, individualized, and amenable to repeated administration have gained popularity among managed care systems and behavioral health providers. One of the most prominent strategies is the collection of self-monitoring data to track clinical events that are the focus of treatment. Self-monitoring involves two components. First, the client is asked to notice the occurrence of a target behavior. The target problem may be an action, thought, emotional response, or kinesthetic sensation. Second, the client is asked to produce a quantifiable record of the target behavior and any other information that is relevant to the goals of treatment (Korotitsch & Nelson-Gray, 1999). Self-monitoring strategies are fre-

quently a key component of evidence treatments for adults with depression (Beck, Rush, Shaw, & Emery, 1979), panic and anxiety (Craske & Tsao, 1999), and eating disorders (Wilson & Vitousek, 1999). Self-monitoring methods are a basic component of behavioral medicine interventions for such diverse complaints as headaches, insomnia, obesity, and self-management of chronic diseases (Barton, Blanchard, & Veazy, 1999). In family and child treatment settings, self-monitoring is used extensively to support mental health treatments (Shapiro & Cole, 1999) and behavioral medicine interventions for children with medical problems (Peterson & Tromblay, 1999). As Cone (1999) correctly points out, self-monitoring strategies possess the flexibility in design, application, and clinical relevance to dramatically improve the quality of behavioral care. This fact has not been lost on managed care administrators, and they seek to link ongoing outcomes assessment to the process of care management. When combined with more standardized self-report and/or interview assessments, self-monitoring data can be used to make a powerful case to managed care reviewers (Persons, 1989).

Decreased Application of Direct and Analogue Behavioral Observation

A defining principle of classical behavioral assessment was the strong reliance upon direct observational assessments of clinically relevant behaviors. With childhood disorders, for example, the assessment process may have involved spending time observing family interactions in the home and/or assessing the patient's behavior in the school setting. (Mash & Terdal, 1997). Behavior change targets are generated as a result of observational assessment data, and repeated observations would be employed to determine whether the child was progressing in treatment. In general, direct observation is a time consuming and therefore expensive form of assessment. It may require the clinician to devote several hours to establishing treatment targets, when the reality of managed care is that treatment will be restricted to a limited number of hours. Managed behavioral health care administrators (many of whom are psychologists) have never been convinced that direct observation is incrementally cost effective when other less expensive assessment procedures are available. With few exceptions, direct observational assessments are rarely conducted in the managed care environment.

An alternative methodology has been to employ analogue observational assessments (see Haynes, 2001), which try to elicit clinically relevant behaviors using simulated tasks and/or settings. Analogue behavioral observations have been developed for social skills and social deficits (Norton & Hope, 2001), couples conflict (Heyman, 2001), childhood problems including fear, avoidance, and hyperactivity (Mori & Armendariz, 2001), and parent-child interactions in children with impulsive and disruptive behavior (Roberts, 2001). Unfortunately, analogue behavioral observations have not been widely adopted in managed care or by practicing clinicians (Mash & Foster, 2001). The reasons for this hesitation include a lack of evidence for construct validity and incremental clinical utility. In addition, managed care administrators are concerned about the resource requirements of analogue assessments, as compared with less expensive forms of assessment such as interviews and informant rating scales. In a basic sense, proponents of analogue assessments have not produced convincing data that clinical outcomes are differentially improved when analogue assessments are employed as part of the treatment/assessment process. In large managed behavioral health care systems (with 30,000 or more behavioral health providers), assessment-related costs are generated for several hundred thousand patients in any given year. Without convincing evidence of improved clinical outcomes or decreased treatment costs, it is highly unlikely these methods will ever be sanctioned in any significant way.

A quasi-observational method that is accepted in most managed care systems is the use of informant observational data. For example, childhood assessments may involve eliciting systematic observation data from parents and teachers in the form of structured behavior checklists (Mash & Terdal, 1997). As one might expect, a singular characteristic of these methods is that they allow the clinician to collect clinically relevant assessment data, while shifting the cost of data collection to the parent and/or participant informant. This reflects the omnipresent theme in managed care of sanctioning those assessments that can be cost justified (Groth-Marnat, 1999).

The Death of Personality Assessment

Objective and subjective methods of trait personality assessment have not fared well under managed behavioral health care. With few exceptions, personality assessment devices such as the Minnesota Multiphasic Personality Inventory (MMPI) and the Millon Clinical Multiaxial Inventory are seldom used and almost never paid for within managed behavioral health care. Projective testing protocols such as the Thematic Apperception Test and the Rorschach are even less frequently used in practice. The basic problem with trait-based personality assessment is that it lacks predictive validity for any of the "markers" that are important to managed care. For example, there is no evidence that the feedback from an MMPI evaluation leads to better clinical outcomes; nor does this information appear to increase the efficiency or

outcome of the treatment process. For this reason, personality assessment is not seen as a "value-added" clinical service. In clinical settings that still have access to these assessment methods, master's-level psychology technicians often administer and write up the test results. What used to be one of the principal functions of the licensed psychologist is now perceived as a poor use of that provider's time. In contrast, neuropsychological assessment has gained elevated status in managed care due to the strong content, concurrent, and predictive validity of these test batteries.

Prediction and Prevention of Treatment Failures

It is a well-established fact that some patients fail to benefit from psychotherapy and pharmacotherapy, while others may actually deteriorate in response to treatment (Mash & Hunsley, 1993). This fact has not been lost on managed care administrators, who are generally skeptical of the individual provider's ability to detect impending treatment failure and adjust the treatment plan accordingly. In response to this potential cost containment issue, many managed care systems have developed treatment progress profiling systems. These computerized systems use aggregated clinical outcome data involving thousands of therapy cases to build statistical models of expected change. Using time series measurement strategies, managed care reviewers can match the expected level of change with the actual level of change for any given patient. When the actual level of change is significantly below the predicted level, the clinician is required to revise and submit a new treatment plan for certification. One example of this emerging practice management trend is the computerized scoring system recently released for the Outcomes Questionnaire-45 (OQ-45; Lambert et al., 1996). Utilizing principles for progress tracking developed for the COMPASS Outcome package, Lambert, Okiishi, Johnson, and Finch (1998) developed an automated software package designed to track patient progress and identify potential "treatment failures" before they happen. They used concepts of social validation (Kazdin, 1977; Wolf, 1978) and statistically significant change (Jacobson & Truax, 1991) to develop standards for clinically meaningful patient change. This system calculates two statistical indices for evaluating the reliability of change made by a patient. These include a cutoff point between normal and dysfunctional samples and an evaluation of the reliability of the change score. This innovative assessment methodology allows managed care companies to track the progress of an individual patient on a week-to-week basis and to compare rates of patient recovery between providers and practice settings.

Managed care also has encouraged the development of behavioral assessment strategies for managing process-of-care variables that are directly implicated in treatment outcomes. For example, clinicians are encouraged to assess and quantify the risk related to failure in both medication and behavioral treatment approaches. Robinson, Wischman, and Del Vento (1996) describe a Medication Assessment Questionnaire that was constructed using a content validity approach to the patient's adherence-related beliefs, attitudes, behaviors, and expectancies. This approach involves a structured interview that yields adherence risk ratings in five areas pertinent to successful medication treatment: the patient's history of medication use, current preference concerning use of medication, beliefs about using medications for psychological problems, preferred impact of medication treatment, and concerns about and skillfulness in coping with specific side effects. The clinical utility of this approach was demonstrated in a study showing superior adherence to antidepressant medications by primary care patients who received behavioral assessment and targeted intervention when compared to patients who did not (Katon et al., 1996).

Another well-established process-of-care variable is the completion of home-based practice assignments (Mash & Hunsley, 1993). In the same study, a behavioral assessment protocol examined follow-through with behavior change assignments and patient-provider relationship variables at every treatment session. Results suggested that nearly 92% of patients completed their entire treatment regime for depression, an attrition rate far below what is normally observed in clinical trials examining pharmacological and/or behavioral treatments for depression.

Increased Emphasis on Clinical Effectiveness

A significant service delivery issue is the clinical effectiveness, as opposed to clinical efficacy, of a behavioral health intervention. Clinical effectiveness is a measure of how well a treatment performs in the naturalistic clinical setting, when delivered by a typically trained provider. Treatments with high clinical efficacy, but low clinical effectiveness, will not be allowed to proliferate in population-based health care systems. Therefore, it is imperative to gauge the clinical effectiveness of evidence-based treatments, both at the system level and at the level of individual practice. As managed care has proliferated, the question of the clinical effectiveness of treatments has become a central concern.

Clinical effectiveness is a concept much more closely tied to behavioral assessment methodology than is true for clinical efficacy. Clinical efficacy traditionally has been demonstrated using nomothetic research designs that demonstrate a significant treatment effect relative to a placebo or wait-list control group. As Hayes, Barlow, and Nelson (1999) succinctly point out, group significance testing has an unpredictable re-

lationship to how the individual patient may be faring. The assessment methods required to evaluate clinical effectiveness may be dramatically different than those used to establish clinical efficacy (Seligman, 1996; Strosahl, Hayes, Bergan, & Romano, 1998). Clinical effectiveness may require a highly individualized, time series approach to assessment. The clinical problems and their functional antecedents and consequences may require a much more basic behavioral assessment approach. One example is the tradeoff between the precision and scope of assessment methods we encountered in a study of the effectiveness of Acceptance and Commitment Therapy (ACT) (Strosahl, Hayes, Bergan, & Romano, 1998). Because this was a study of the general clinical effectiveness of ACT in an HMO sample involving patients with an array of presenting complaints, it was not possible to use a single empirically validated clinical survey. Instead, a modified version of goal attainment scaling was used, which allowed study patients to individually define the clinical issue of greatest concern to them. Goal attainment scaling is a classic example of using behaviorally anchored scaling techniques to create idiographic measures of clinical outcome (Kiresuk, Smith, & Cardillo, 1994). Even though the target problems were unique among patients, the GAS system allowed us to construct rating scales that could quantify such parameters as problem severity and successful use of coping strategies. These ratings could then be grouped for analysis, even though the problem statements were unique for each patient. In general, clinical effectiveness assessments will tend to be more idiographic in design, due to the greater heterogeneity of the general mental health population. We may discover that, for certain types of questions, straightforward single subject designs may provide the most useful information.

Assessment of Functional Outcomes

One major benefit of consumer-centered care is the growing realization that physical and behavioral health are difficult, if not impossible, to separate. The interest among consumer advocacy groups in quality of life as a superordinate outcome has resulted in a great deal of emphasis on measures of general health status, social-role functioning, and quality of life. The assessment of health and functional status started in the 1970s in medical, as opposed to mental, health settings. Managed care has given it impetus and emphasized its relevance in the treatment of behavioral health conditions. As Stewart and Ware (1989) state, " The focus on the outcomes of medical care is now shifting to the assessment of functioning, or the ability of the patients to perform the daily activities of their lives, how they feel, and their own personal evaluation of their health in general (p. 51).

A great deal of theoretical and psychometric work has been done in the field of health status assessment (Bergner, 1989; Breslow, 1989; Patrick, 1989; Stewart & Ware, 1992). Stewart and Ware (1992) used the definition of health originally suggested by the World Health Organization (1948): "Health is a state of complete physical, mental, and social well-being and not merely the absence of disease or infirmity." Health includes physical and mental wellness. Therefore, the assessment of the patient's capacity to experience personal growth and change, to care for oneself and one's loved ones, and to participate in productive work is an important aspect of health status (Dickey, & Wagenaar, 1996). Jahoda (1958) suggested 40 years ago that mental health is more than the absence of symptoms; it is the presence of positive beliefs about self and the world. Managed care has helped us restate the goals of behavioral assessment and treatment: "What is it that healthy, normal people do that contributes to their higher quality of life?" "What treatment strategies will permit the patient to engage in these behaviors?"

Proliferation of Condition-Specific Assessment Approaches

In response to the demands of the managed care environment, researchers have worked diligently in recent years to develop brief assessment questionnaires that allow rapid, valid diagnosis of specific disorders amenable to evidence-based treatments. There are brief questionnaires for attention deficit disorders (Barkley, 1998), eating disorders (Stice, Telch, & Rizvi, 2000), posttraumatic stress (Kubany, Leisen, Kaplan, & Kelly, 2000), and pain (Melzack, 1987) just to name a few. Numerous other instruments assess psychotherapy outcome (Froyd, Lambert, & Froyd, 1996), and most have excellent psychometric properties (Ogles, Lambert, & Masters, 1996). However, scales that are designated for use with specific disorders often have limitations when used for the accountability purposes emphasized by managed care. They often are overly focused on measuring symptom severity to the exclusion of other important outcome parameters such as functional status. The degree of specialization itself places a burden on the practicing clinician, who must locate, analyze, and often pay for the privilege of using these instruments in daily practice. An alternative that is attractive to managed care is a generic assessment approach that is sensitive to symptoms, functioning, health status, and quality-of-life variables.

Emphasis on General Measures for Screening and Clinical Outcomes

A major theme in managed care has been to place less emphasis on the clinical "cure" and more emphasis on restoring the client to an acceptable level of general functioning (Strosahl, 1994). This goal is far more achievable, given the limited resources available for behavioral care and the subjective, highly variable definitions of cure that exist among competing theoretical orientations. This has prompted the search for behavioral assessment protocols capable of measuring a range of clinically relevant factors. For example, the OQ-45 was developed by two managed care companies and a university research group (Lambert et al., 1996). It measures three areas of patient functioning: symptomatic distress, interpersonal problems, and social role adjustment. While it measures common mental health symptom complaints (primarily anxiety and depression), it also attempts to measure indicators of general functioning. The benefit of a general screening and outcomes management tool is that it can be used with various patient subpopulations and still be a sensitive measure of clinical progress and outcome. The MOS Short-Form General Health Survey (Stewart, Hays, & Ware, 1988; Ware, Sherbourne, & Davies, 1992) and the MOS 36-Itme Short-Form Health Survey (McHorney, Ware, & Raczek, 1993) are examples of other assessment approaches that were developed with academic and managed care collaboration.

RECOMMENDATIONS FOR BEHAVIORAL ASSESSMENT PRACTICES IN MANAGED CARE: A SCIENTIST-PRACTITIONER APPROACH

Managed care has forced behavioral health providers to provide a data-based rationale for treatment plans and to assess the quality of the services they provide. In contemporary managed care, certification of and payment for clinical services are based upon the adequacy of level of care and clinical response data provided by the practitioner. Of all the changes driven by managed care, this shift to provider-specific accountability has had the greatest impact on the practice of behavioral health care. The concept of practice evaluation, as it is addressed in this section, refers to the strategies used by the clinician to screen and triage patients, generate behavioral treatment targets, design interventions that are closely tied to assessment results, monitor and report on treatment progress using appropriate assessment methods, and demonstrate the eventual clinical benefits of an entire regime of care. In essence, practice evaluation is the process by which the individual clinician demonstrates to a managed care reviewer what treatment is indicated, how treatment will be delivered, how progress will be monitored, and how the eventual clinical and fiscal value of a service will be demonstrated. At another level, practice evaluation is fundamentally linked to a scientist-practitioner model (Hayes, Barlow, & Nelson-Gray, 1999). The goal is to take a scholarly, scientifically sound approach to the process of assessment, case formulation, treatment planning, and service delivery. As managed care review practices become less arbitrary and more closely tied to scientifically based practice guidelines, practitioners who emphasize an evidence-based approach to assessment and treatment are likely to prosper. The purpose of this section is to provide a set of underlying principles for effective behavioral assessment practices in the evolving managed care environment.

Use a Behavioral Assessment Case Formulation Approach

A basic strategy for success in the managed care review process is the ability to quickly identify a clinical target that will have the maximum impact on the client's symptomatic distress and general functioning. In our view, a well-conducted functional analysis and associated case conceptualization are prerequisites for effective, clinical practice. Managed care reviewers generally favor therapists who can develop a specific treatment plan based upon a foundation of clearly delineated assessment practices. An additional feature of behavior therapy and behavioral assessment is that this evolves into a continuous, reciprocal process throughout treatment. This characteristic is also reassuring to managed care reviewers because of their omnipresent interest in tracking treatment progress and assuring clinical outcomes.

One central recommendation for success in managed care is to adopt a behavioral assessment case formulation approach, such as those described by Haynes, Thacher, Kaholokula, and Nelson (2001) and Persons (1989). Persons' case formulation model exemplifies the utility of applying single case design concepts to clinical practice. She provides guidelines for developing a problem list using multiple sources of information, encourages repeated measurement of client progress, and emphasizes frequent updates of the problem list driven by assessment results. She recommends that practitioners measure all target problems using self-report instruments and/or self-monitoring methods. Changes in depression scores and rates of engaging in social activities taken from an activity log can be charted. Persons suggests that, because depression and anxiety are so prevalent in general practice, the clinician should employ multiple measures such as the Beck Depression Inventory (Beck et al., 1979), the Fear Survey Schedule (Wolpe & Lang, 1969), and the Behavioral Avoidance Test (Taylor & Agras, 1981).

Haynes and colleagues (2001) describe a behavioral analytic case formulation model that emphasizes the use of self-report, self-monitoring, analogue behavioral observation, and participant/informant data. The goal of the assessment pro-

cess is to build a model that specifies clinically relevant target problems, controlling variables and reciprocal interactions among problems and controlling variables. Based upon these multisource, multimethod assessments, the clinician can estimate the "effect size" of any particular intervention and choose the intervention with the largest estimated effect size. This method of case conceptualization seems particularly well suited to the cost-sensitive demands of managed care. In an environment of limited resources, picking the clinical target that will have the greatest impact on a client's overall health and well-being is a major goal of the care management process.

Adopt a Scientist-Practitioner Approach

As briefly discussed in a previous section, the scientist-practitioner model is a practice model that is highly attuned to the emerging demands of managed care. The goals of behavioral assessment in clinical practice are to help identify the most important targets for change and to track the effects of an evidence-based clinical intervention. The time series approach provides a model of behavioral assessment that is feasible within the confines of a busy practice, yet provides an indication of the complexity of effective treatment of an individual. For example, Chronis and colleagues (2001) present a case illustrating comprehensive, combined behavioral and pharmacological treatment for a child diagnosed with attention deficit hyperactivity disorder (ADHD) and conduct disorder over a period of 3 years. Treatment components included the Summer Treatment Program (Pellam & Hoza, 1997), behavioral parent training (Cunningham, Bremner, & Secord-Gilbert, 1994), behavioral classroom interventions, individually titrated stimulant medication, and a cognitive-behavioral depression-prevention program for the child's mother. Multiple forms of assessment with multiple sources of input were obtained to evaluate all treatments. Forms of assessment ranged from a daily report card, with data from teachers, to frequency counts of rule violations in an analogue academic classroom observation. This type of single-case design is helpful to managed care providers and researchers. It highlights some of the shortcomings of the current mental health system, including that the system is not geared toward long-term care and not constructed for effective implementation of treatment outside of offices. These problems loom large when one considers that our mental health system, in key ways, does not support effective treatment of a high prevalence childhood disorder like ADHD.

Other single-session case research highlights needs for change in assessment and treatment approaches. Randall, Henggeler, Cunningham, Rowland, and Swenson, (2001) report on an adaptation of multisystemic therapy (MST) for treatment of adolescent substance abuse. MST (Henggeler, Schoenwalk, Borduin, Rowland, & Cunningham, 1998) is an intensive community-based treatment for children and adolescents presenting serious behavioral and emotional problems and their families. While randomized controlled trials have found MST to be effective (Henggeler, 1999), its results were not as successful with substance abusing or dependent juvenile offenders (Henggeler, Pickrel, & Brondino, 1999). Unfortunately, many, if not most, youth with serious emotional disturbance also abuse drugs and alcohol. Randall and colleagues (2001) report on merging of MST with the Community Reinforcement Approach (CRA) to improve outcomes with substance abusing youth with serious emotional problems. The CRA approach requires use of repeated assessments of urine, as well as development and evaluation of functional analyses and self-management plans. The challenge for managers of mental health care will be to coordinate collection of outcomes among the many partners in care, including juvenile courts, schools, and primary care.

Guidelines for Using Behavioral Assessment in Clinical Practice

As illustrated in previous sections, some core behavioral assessment practices have knowingly or unknowingly been adopted by managed behavioral health care systems. This situation presents clinicians with a behavioral assessment focus the opportunity to gain an advantage in the process of managed care review. Table 22.2 presents a set of practice parameters for the optimal use of behavioral assessment methods in the managed care environment. For example, the behavioral assessment paradigm is predicated on a highly idiographic, functionally oriented approach to target problem identification and analysis. Normally, the managed care review process requires the clinician to provide an organized set of assessment data, often involving a combination of functional analytic clinical interviews, self-report, observational, and/or informant data. Done properly, this produces a set of intervention strategies that can be monitored and corrected over time. Many managed care systems use this type of information to establish initial eligibility for services (i.e., medical necessity) and to assign and reassign patients to a specific type and intensity of care. Many managed care systems favor providers who conduct pretreatment baseline assessments as a core component of the treatment-planning process. Most managed care systems require that treatment planning be closely tied to the results of initial assessments. In many systems, clinical services will be "decertified" if treatment is not targeted to the problem areas identified in the assessment—

a process that favors providers who employ a quantifiable method for establishing pretreatment targets and measure level differences. Strategies such as GAS and self-monitoring measurements are very compatible with this patient-centered emphasis.

Another central characteristic of contemporary behavioral assessment models is the use of repeated measurements to track clinical progress over time (Haynes et al., 2001). This effectively amounts to a time series methodology within a single-subject design framework. It is a common practice in managed behavioral care to conduct periodic assessments of a patient's progress in treatment as a way to improve the quality of care. This can involve the readministration of idiographic measures of functioning, the use of empirically validated condition-specific surveys, or general measures of symptoms and functioning. Providers who use a scholarly approach to combine individualized measures with nomothetic scales will be very effective in managed care systems. Finally, the contemporary behavioral assessment paradigm emphasizes measures of both intermediate and ultimate outcomes (Mash & Hunsley, 1993; Rosen & Proctor, 1981). Intermediate outcomes may involve reductions in symptom severity or disruptive classroom behaviors; ultimate outcomes are improvements in end-state functioning such as missed days at work, social adjustment, or general health status. The majority of managed behavioral care systems collect baseline and intermediate outcome data, and there is an increasing emphasis on measuring ultimate outcomes. Practitioners who emphasize the use of assessments that are sensitive to both intermediate and ultimate outcomes will fare well in this new practice environment. Overall, there are many reasons to believe that behavioral assessment strategies can play a major role in supporting clinical practice in the new generation of managed care.

CROSSING THE QUALITY CHASM IN BEHAVIORAL HEALTH CARE: THE POTENTIAL CONTRIBUTION OF THE BEHAVIORAL ASSESSMENT PARADIGM

Managed behavioral health care has achieved a surprising level of success in meeting consumer and payer demands for access to care at a reasonable price (Geraty et al., 1994). In order to achieve this level of success, early care managers encouraged researchers and providers to reshape methods for assessing quality. The individualized care management approach used by managed care depends upon the availability of a full continuum of care and the existence of reliable and valid measures of clinical response. Using what amounted to

TABLE 22.2   Phases of Clinical Service, Managed Care Goals and Practices, and Behavioral Assessment Recommendations

Stage of Treatment	Managed Care Goals and Practices	Behavioral Assessment Functions	Specific Behavioral Assessment Strategies
Initial Clinical Assessment	Assessment data must drive determination of eligibility, match level of service to level of need, and be patient centered; use precertification as primary mechanism	Create a framework for understanding clinically relevant target behaviors; their level of intensity, controlling variables, reciprocal interactions, and derive a focus for treatment planning	Use behavioral case formulation model; include both diagnostic profile and functional analysis of behavior; collect multiple source data (informants, analogue observations, self-monitoring) to provide data supporting clinical impression
Treatment Planning	Establish clear target(s) for treatment using baseline assessments that will both justify treatment and be amenable to tracking over time; treatment plan should focus on both symptom reduction and improving general functioning; pretreatment certification is primary control	Create individualized measures of clinical target problem, focusing on most important target behaviors, establish baseline functioning using different methods; evaluate both symptom-based complaints and relationship to environmental function	Consider use of Goal Attainment Scaling to quantify baseline level; use empirically validated self-report measures for symptom data; consider use of measures of daily functioning (i.e., missed work days) using idiographic assessments or self-report scales (i.e., SF-36); present data as part of treatment planning review
Monitor ongoing Treatment Response	Detect early indications of treatment failure, prevent delivery of unnecessary treatment, adjust services to optimize dose-response curve; primary controls are mandatory review and treatment progress profiling	Conduct assessments on an ongoing basis to determine effects of intervention, detect the influence of new controlling variables, establish new interventions for controlling variables that appear over time, eliminate ineffective treatment	Use time series methodology to conduct session-by-session assessments of relevant target behaviors; conduct response graphs for utilization review; consider use of self-monitoring data, condition-specific self-report indices, goal attainment indices; conduct postsession surveys of treatment alliance and consumer satisfaction; provide process data as part of progress report
Treatment Termination	Define an end point of treatment and adhere to it; eliminate psychiatric symptoms and restore client to previous level of functioning; measurement should clarify when treatment is finished, rather than subjective clinical judgment; primary control mechanisms are session reviews, post hoc utilization review	Measurement focus is on criterion-based outcomes, operationalized in behavioral terms that are relevant to the individual client and directly related to the client's behavioral effectiveness in settings that previously produced problematic responses	Establish clear rules for treatment success and present to reviewer, including levels of symptom reduction (i.e., 50% reduction in symptoms); improved goal attainment (i.e., a score of 4 on a 5 point scale); a threshold change in target event frequency in self-monitoring logs; improved functioning in analogue observations; decrease in missed work days
Improve End State Functioning	Stabilize long term functioning in domains such as work, family and community; lower relapse rates to prevent the costs of repeated treatment; create a specific criteria for re-entry into treatment to avoid "problem hunting"; primary control is provider profiling to eliminate low performing providers	Assess stability of behavior change across settings, time and situations; provide patient with measurement tools for self-assessment and management; create specific re-entry criteria using measurement indices	Provide client with methods and instructions for self self-monitoring of target symptoms; consider mail in surveys of social adjustment or health status; provide reviewers with end state data to support long term effectiveness of treatment

behavioral assessment techniques, managed care researchers demonstrated that patients served by a capitated system of care could be returned to the community and maintained with a significant reduction in costs. Further, they determined that the appropriate use of alternative care settings, such as partial hospitalization or intensive outpatient treatment, does not increase recidivism or adverse occurrences (Baker & Giese, 1992; Canton & Gralick, 1987). Key to these early successes

was the ability to collect valid, clinically useful assessment data and create individualized treatment plans.

Unfortunately, the lessons learned in these early projects have not generalized. Behavioral health providers have not achieved consensus on the issues surrounding the assessment of individualized, clinically relevant variables. In mental health, quality historically has been defined by structure and process of service delivery rather than by assessment data relevant to treatment outcome or the relationship of process of care variables and eventual outcome (Rodriquez, 1988). Often, the quality factors presumed to be relevant to treatment have been based on psychodynamic models with little demonstrated reliability and validity (Klerman, 1990). These conceptual paradigms are deeply antagonistic to basic measurement practices. For example, the American Psychiatric Association Office of Quality Assurance (1988) has argued against use of an outcome-based definition of quality in mental health:

> Quality of care is a determination that the treatment given . . . meets the explicit and implicit standards of care accepted by the profession. However, in psychiatry, the lack of such outcome measures, except of the most general kind, means that the review of quality is based on the process of care and the ongoing response of the patient; that is, measures of process and progress rather than outcome (p. 19).

In their efforts to transition to a quality-oriented system of care, managed care administrators have experienced difficulties enticing behavior health providers to employ empirically validated treatments. Arguments between managed care, clinical providers, and researchers have been complex and costly. Many providers have adopted required behavioral assessment methods with a cavalier attitude and employed empirically validated strategies using a "technique-of-the-month" stance, which has produced an unacceptable level of variation in outcomes among patients with similar behavioral health problems. An honest appraisal of the behavioral health community must conclude that the majority of providers do not integrate behavioral assessment as a routine component of clinical practice. In many cases, there is active resistance to the idea of systematically evaluating the impact of clinical interventions. However, many practicing clinicians are not averse to using behavioral assessment strategies such as time series measurement or self-monitoring to guide their practice. However, the data must be easily interpretable, emphasize clinical action items, and be available in real time (Strosahl, 1999, 2000). In other words, most providers would use behavioral assessment strategies if they were easy to administer, interpret, and implement in general practice. The unfortunate fact is that some behavioral assessment methods are difficult to employ in a fast-paced practice environment, are technically cumbersome, and are beyond the skill and training level of most providers. Adapting laboratory behavioral assessment methods for consumption by field-based clinicians (most of whom have master's degree–level training) is one of the major challenges facing behavioral assessment researchers in the upcoming decade.

Because of this deeply embedded philosophical resistance in the provider community, the data needed for assessing the clinical effectiveness of empirically validated treatments at the level of individual practice have accumulated slowly. These data are needed to justify increases in funding for behavioral health services, to create a more consistent quality orientation in the behavioral health industry, and to inform policy development in such areas as research and training. Consensus on such basic assessment issues will also facilitate the development and implementation of technological solutions that could systematize the types of practice evaluation strategies used, which would subsequently reduce the time burden on clinicians.

A major theme throughout this chapter is to adopt a scholarly, scientist-practitioner approach to assessment, treatment planning, treatment progress monitoring, and clinical outcomes assessment. This requires behavioral health providers to keep current on the assessment and treatment research literature and to integrate new scientifically sound processes into their daily practices. Unfortunately, surveys of mental health professionals indicate that they perceive fewer than 20% of research articles to have applicability to professional educational settings (Cohen, 1976). Sadly, 40% of mental health professionals surveyed in the 1970s thought that no research existed that was relevant to practice. Over the past three decades, the National Institutes of Health budget for research has increased significantly (National Institutes of Health, 2000), and health professionals are barraged with nearly 10,000 randomized controlled trials every year (Chassin, 1998). Still, the mental health care system struggles with translating this knowledge into practice. For example, even though analogue behavioral observations have been clinically applied and researched for nearly 40 years, there is still scant evidence that these methods are used in general clinical practice (Mash & Foster, 2001).

For their part, researchers have selected methods for evaluating psychotherapy treatments that have contributed to translation difficulties with respect to both assessment and treatment issues. The historic overreliance on a nomothetic model of statistical significance testing has resulted in the loss of important information about sources of treatment variation. In their zeal to publish significant findings, researchers have mistakenly operated on the assumption that statistical significance indicates powerful effects, whereas the clinical utility of such findings may be minimal. Despite Meehl's (1978) warning that use of the statistical significance approach to the basic science of psychology would produce findings that were weak, unreliable, and difficult to replicate (given the large intersubject variability), this approach continues to be prominent today. Ironically, the very methods that have legitimized behavioral health as a "science" have caused us to underemphasize the application of such findings to the individual patient.

The Role of Behavioral Assessment in Promoting Scientifically Based Practice

One of the six aims for improvement in the health care system of the twenty-first century identified by the Committee on the Quality of Health Care in America is that of "providing services based on scientific knowledge to all who could benefit and refraining from providing services to those not likely to benefit (avoiding under-use and over-use, respectively)" (National Academy of Sciences, 2000, p. 6). We are faced with a quality crisis in behavioral health care that can be addressed only by employing a scientist-practitioner approach in clinical training and by providing financial incentives.

Migrating behavioral assessment into the field is the only effective way to answer the million-dollar question: What treatments work for what patients under what conditions? Progress toward answering this question occurs with collaboration among all managed care providers (concerned with accountability), clinical service providers (concerned with feasibility, which includes effectiveness), and researchers (concerned with advancement of science). Building an assessment model that is sensitive to individual patient characteristics, cost effective, easy to implement in daily practice, and within the skills of a typically trained behavioral health provider is the critical issue for all stakeholders seeking to answer to this question. Although there is a difference in the level of information needed by providers, researchers, and managed care reviewers, getting behavioral health providers to provide clinically relevant behavioral assessment data is critical to the success of any attempt to improve quality.

The future of behavioral assessment will be closely tied to our ability to link the concepts and strategies of this field with the interests of the key stakeholders in the behavioral health care industry. The opportunities here are enormous, but so are the challenges. Only time will tell whether behavioral assessment can adapt to the changing demands of the health care marketplace. In this regard, we are optimistic. If anything, behavioral assessment has been characterized by a constant growth and maturation since its inception. Equally "traumatic" changes (i.e., the cognitive revolution) have been encountered and successfully integrated within the behavioral assessment framework. If the practice of behavioral assessment continues to evolve with the aim of supporting clinical practice, we are confident that practitioners and managed care administrators alike will see the benefits of disseminating these assessment methods.

REFERENCES

ACCESS Measurement Systems (1998). *Treatment Outcome Package (TOP)*. Ashland, MA: Behavioral Health Products & Services.

American Psychiatric Association, Office of Quality Assurance (1988). *Concepts and definitions in psychiatric quality assurance and utilization review*. Washington, DC: American Psychiatric Association.

Baker, N.J., & Giese, A.A. (1992). Reorganization of a private psychiatric unit to promote collaboration with managed care. *Hospital Community Psychiatry, 42,* 1126–1129.

Barkley, R.A. (1998). *Attention deficit hyperactivity disorder: A handbook for diagnosis and treatment* (2nd ed.). New York: Guilford Press.

Barlow, D.H., Hayes, S.C., & Nelson, R.O. (1984). *The scientist practitioner: Research and accountability in clinical and educational settings*. Boston: Allyn & Bacon.

Barton, K., Blanchard, E., & Veazy, C. (1999). Self-monitoring as an assessment strategy in behavioral medicine. *Psychological Assessment, 11,* 490–497.

Beck, A., Rush, A., Shaw, B., & Emery, G. (1979). *Cognitive therapy of depression*. New York: Guilford Press.

Bergner, M. (1989). Quality of life, health status, and clinical research. *Medical Care, 27*(3), 148–156.

Brantley, P., & Jefferies, S. (2000). Daily Stress Inventory (DSI) and Weekly Stress Inventory (WSI). In M. Maruish (Ed.), *Handbook of psychological assessment in primary care settings* (pp. 373–390). Mahwah, NJ: Erlbaum.

Breslow, L. (1989). Health status measurement in the evaluating of health promotion. *Medical Care, 27*(3), 205–216.

Canton, C.L.M., & Gralick, A. (1987). A review of issues surrounding length of psychiatric hospitalization. *Hospital Community Psychiatry, 38,* 858–863.

Chassin, M.R. (1998). Is health care ready for six-sigma quality? *Milbank Quarterly, 76*(4), 575–591.

Chronis, A.M., Fabiano, G.A., Gnagy, E.M., Wymbs, B.T., Burrows-MacLean, L., & Pelham, W.E. (2001). Comprehensive, sustained behavioral and pharmacological treatment for attention-deficit/hyperactivity disorder: A case study. *Cognitive and Behavioral Practice, 8*(4), 346–359.

Cohen, L.H. (1976). Clinicians' utilization of research findings. *JSAS Catalog of Selected Documents in Psychology, 6,* 116.

Cone, J. (1999). Introduction to the special section on self-monitoring: A major assessment method in clinical psychology. *Psychological Assessment, 11,* 411–414.

Cone, J., & Hawkins, R. (1977). *Behavioral assessment: New directions in clinical psychology* (pp. xiii–xxiv). New York: Bruner Mazel.

Craske, M., & Tsao, J. (1999). Self-monitoring with panic and anxiety disorders. *Psychological Assessment, 11,* 466–479.

Cummings, N. (1995). Behavioral health after managed care: The next golden opportunity for professional psychology. *Register Report, 20,* 30–33.

Cummings, N. (1997). Practitioner-driven IDS groups continue as best hope for the future. *National Psychologist, 6,* 10–11.

Cummings, N., & Hayes, S. (1996). Now we are facing the consequences: A conversation with Nick Cummings. *Scientist Practitioner, 6,* 9–13.

Cunningham, C., Bremner, R., & Secord-Gilbert, M. (1994). *The Community Parent Education (COPE) program: A school based family systems oriented course for parents of children with disruptive behavior disorders.* Unpublished manuscript, McMaster University and Chedoke-McMaster Hospitals, Toronto, Ontario, Canada.

Dickey, B., & Wagenaar, H. (1996). Evaluating health status. In L. Sederer & B. Dickey (Eds.), *Outcomes assessment in clinical practice* (pp. 55–64). Baltimore: Williams & Williams.

Dowart, R.A. (1996). Outcomes management strategies in mental health: Applications and implications for clinical practice. In L. Sederer & B. Dickey (Eds.), *Outcomes assessment in clinical practice* (pp. 45–54). Baltimore: Williams & Williams.

Eddy D.M. (1996). *Clinical decision making from theory to practice: A collection of essays from the Journal of the American Medical Association.* Sudbury, MA: Jones and Bartlett.

Eisenberg, L., & Kleinman, A. (1981). Clinical social science. In L. Eisenberg & A. Kleinman (Eds.), *The relevance of social science to medicine* (pp. 1–26). Boston: Reidel.

Franklin, R., Allison, D., & Gorman, B. (Eds.). (1996). *Design and analysis of single case research* (pp. 1–12). Mahwah, NJ: Erlbaum.

Froyd, J.E., Lambert, M.J., & Froyd, J.D. (1996). A review of practices of psychotherapy outcome measurement. *Journal of Mental Health, 5,* 11–15.

Gaynor, S., Baird, S., & Nelson-Gray, R. (1999). Application of time series (single subject) designs in clinical psychology. In P. Kendall, J. Butcher, & G. Holmbeck (Eds.), *Handbook of research methods in clinical psychology* (2nd ed., pp. 297–329). New York: Wiley.

Geraty, R., Bartlett, J., Hill, E., Lee, F., Shusterman, A., & Waxman, A. (1994). The impact of managed behavioral healthcare on the costs of psychiatric and chemical dependency treatment. *Behavioral Healthcare Tomorrow, 3,* 18–30.

Giles, T. (1993). *Managed mental health care.* Boston: Allyn & Bacon.

Goldfried, M., & Linehan, M. (1977). Basic issues in behavioral assessment. In A. Ciminero, K. Calhoun, & H. Adams (Eds.), *Handbook of behavioral assessment* (pp. 3–23). New York: Wiley-Interscience.

Gresham, F. (1998). Designs for evaluating behavior change: Conceptual principles of single case methodology. In T. Watson & F. Gresham (Eds.), *Handbook of child behavior therapy* (pp. 23–40). New York: Plenum Press.

Groth-Marnat, G. (1999). Financial efficacy of clinical assessment: Rational guidelines and issues for future research. *Journal of Clinical Psychology, 55,* 813–824.

Group Health Association of American. (1995). *Sourcebook on HMO utilization data.* Washington DC: Author.

Hayes, S. (1992). Single case experimental design and empirical clinical practice. In A. Kazdin (Ed.), *Methodological issues and strategies in clinical research* (pp. 491–521). Washington DC: American Psychological Association.

Hayes, S., Barlow, D., & Nelson-Gray, R. (1999). *The scientist practitioner: Research and accountability in the age of managed care.* Boston: Allyn & Bacon.

Hayes, S., Nelson, R., & Jarrett, R. (1987). Treatment utility of assessment: A functional approach to evaluating the quality of assessment. *American Psychologist, 42,* 963–974.

Haynes, S. (2001). Clinical applications of analogue behavioral observation: Dimensions of psychometric evaluation. *Psychological Assessment, 13,* 73–85.

Haynes, S., & O'Brien, W. (2000). *Principles of behavioral assessment: A functional approach to psychological assessment.* New York: Plenum/Kluwer Press.

Haynes, S., Thacher, I., Kaholokula, J., & Nelson, K. (2001). Outpatient behavioral assessment and target selection. In M. Hersen & K. Porzelius (Eds.), *Diagnosis, conceptualization and treatment planning for adults: A textbook.* New York: Erlbaum.

Henggeler, S.W. (1999). Multisystemic therapy: An overview of clinical procedures, outcomes, and policy implications. *Child Psychology & Psychiatric Review, 4,* 2–10.

Henggeler, S.W., Pickrel, S.G., & Brondino, M.J. (1999). Multisystemic treatment of substance abusing and dependent delinquents: Outcomes, treatment fidelity, and transportability. *Mental Health Services Research, 1,* 171–184.

Henggeler, S., Schoenwald, S., Borduin, T., Rowland, R., & Cunningham, S. (1998). *Multisystemic treatment of antisocial behavior in children and adolescents.* New York: Guilford Press.

Heyman, R. (2001). Observation of couple conflicts: Clinical assessment applications, stubborn truths and shaky foundations. *Psychological Assessment, 13,* 5–35.

Jacobson, N.S., & Truax, P. (1991). Clinical significance: A statistical approach to defining meaningful change in psychotherapy research. *Journal of Consulting and Clinical Psychology, 59,* 12–19.

Jahoda, M. (1958). *Current concepts of mental health.* New York: Basic Books.

Katon, W., Robinson, P., Von Korff, M., Lin, E., Bush, T., Ludman, E., Simon, G., & Walker, E. (1996). A multifaceted intervention to improve treatment of depression in primary care. *Archives of General Psychiatry, 53,* 924–932.

Kazdin, A.E. (1977). Assessing the clinical or applied importance of behavior change through social validation. *Behavior Modification, 1,* 427–452.

Kessler, R., Nelson, C., McGonagle, K., Liu, J., Swartz, M., & Blazer, D. (1994). Lifetime and 12-month prevalence of DSM-III-R psychiatric disorders in the United States. *Archives of General Psychiatry, 51,* 8–19.

Kiresuk, T., Smith, A., & Cardillo, J. (Eds.). (1994). *Goal attainment scaling: Applications, theory and measurement* (pp. 173–212). Hillsdale, NJ: Erlbaum.

Klerman, G.L. (1990). The psychiatric patient's right to effective treatment: Implications of Osheroff v. Chestnut Lodge. *American Journal of Psychiatry, 147,* 409–418.

Korotitsch, W., & Nelson-Gray, R. (1999). An overview of self-monitoring research in assessment and treatment. *Psychological Assessment, 11,* 415–425.

Kubany, E.S., Leisen, M.B., Kaplan, A.S., & Kelly, M.P. (2000). Validation of a brief measure of posttraumatic stress disorder: The Distressing Event Questionnaire (DEQ). *Psychological Assessment, 12*(2), 197–209.

Lambert, M.J., Hansen, N.B., Umphress, V., Lunnen, K., Okiishi, J., Burlingame, G.M., & Reisinger, C.W. (1996). *Administration and scoring manual for the Outcome Questionnaire (OQ-45.2).* Stevenson, MD: American Professional Credentialing Services.

Lambert, M., Okiishi, J., Johnson, L., & Finch, A. (1998). Outcome assessment from conceptualization to implementation. *Professional Psychology: Research and Practice, 29,* 63–70.

Lewis, A.B., Spencer, J.H., Haas, G.L., & DiVittis, A. (1987). Goal attainment scaling: Relevance and replicability in follow-up of inpatients. *Journal of Nervous and Mental Disease, 175*(7), 408–417.

Mash, E., & Foster, S. (2001). Exporting analogue behavioral observation from research to practice: Useful or cost-defective? *Psychological Assessment, 13,* 86–98.

Mash, E., & Hunsley, J. (1993). Assessment considerations in the identification of failing psychotherapy: Bringing the negatives out of the darkroom. *Psychological Assessment, 5,* 292–301.

Mash, E., & Terdal, L. (1997). Assessment of child and family disturbance: A behavioral systems approach. In E. Mash & L. Terdal (Eds.), *Assessment of childhood disorders* (3rd ed., pp. 3–68). New York: Guilford Press.

McHorney, C.A., Ware, J.E., & Raczek, A.E. (1993). The MOS 36-Item Short-Form Health Survey (SF-36): II. Psychometric and clinical tests of validity in measuring physical and mental health constructs. *Medical Care, 31*(3), 247–263.

Mechanic, D. (1996). Key policy considerations for mental health in the managed care era. In R. Manderscheid & M. Sonnenschein (Eds.), *Mental health, United States, 1996* (pp. 1–16). Washington, DC: Substance Abuse and Mental Health Services Administration.

Meehl, P.E. (1978). Theoretical risks and tabular asterisks: Sir Karl, Sir Ronald, and the slow progress of soft psychology. *Journal of Consulting and Clinical Psychology, 46,* 806–835.

Melzack, R. (1987). The short-form McGill Pain Questionnaire. *Pain, 30,* 191–197.

Miller, S.D., Duncan, B.L., & Hubblel, M.A. (1997). *Escape from Babel: Toward a unifying language for psychotherapy practice.* New York: Norton.

Mori, L., & Armendariz, G. (2001). Analogue assessment of child behavior problems. *Psychological Assessment, 13,* 36–45.

National Academy of Sciences. (2000). *Crossing the quality chasm: A new health system for the 21st century.* Available at http://www.nap.edu/openbook/0309072808/html/2.html.

National Institutes of Health. (2000). An overview. Online. Available at http://www.nih.gov/about/NIHoverview.html. Last accessed October 28, 2001.

Norton, P., & Hope, D. (2001). Analogue observation methods in the assessment of social functioning in adults. *Psychological Assessment, 13,* 59–72.

Ogles, B.M., Lambert, M.J., & Masters, K., (1996). *Assessing outcome in clinical practice.* New York: Allyn & Bacon.

Patrick, D. (1989). Generic and disease specific measures in assessing health status and quality of life. *Medical Care, 27*(3 Suppl.), 217–232.

Pellam, W.E., & Hoza, B. (1997). *Children's summer treatment program manual.* Buffalo, NY: CTADD.

Persons, J.B. (1989). *Cognitive therapy in practice: A case formulation approach.* New York: Norton.

Peterson, L., & Tromblay, G. (1999). Self-monitoring in behavioral medicine: Children. *Psychological Assessment, 11,* 458–465.

Randall, J., Henggeler, S.W., Cunningham, P.B., Rowland, M.D., & Swenson, C.C. (2001). Adapting multisystemic therapy to treat adolescent substance abuse more effectively. *Cognitive and Behavioral Practice, 8,* 359–366.

Reiger, D., Narrow, W., Rae, D., Manderschied, R., Locke, B., & Goodwin, F. (1993). The de facto US mental and addictive disorders service system: Epidemiologic Catchment Area prospective 1 year prevalence rates of disorders and services. *Archives of General Psychiatry, 50,* 85–94.

Roberts, M. (2001). Clinic observations of structured parent-child interactions to evaluate externalizing disorders. *Psychological Assessment, 13,* 46–58.

Robinson, P. (in press). Adapting evidence-based treatments for the primary care setting: A template for success. In W. O'Donohue (Ed.), *Treatments that work in primary care.* New York: Allyn & Bacon.

Robinson, P., Wischman, C., & Del Vento, A. (1996). *Treating depression in primary care: A manual for primary care and mental health providers.* Reno, NV: Context Press.

Rodriquez, A.R. (1988). An introduction to quality measures in mental health. In G. Striker & A. Rodriquez (Eds.), *Handbook of quality assurance in mental health* (pp. 3–36). New York: Plenum Press.

Rosen, A., & Proctor, E. (1981). Distinctions between treatment outcomes and their implications for treatment evaluation. *Journal of Consulting and Clinical Psychology, 49,* 418–425.

Seligman, M. (1996). Science as an ally of practice. *American Psychologist, 51,* 1072–1079.

Shapiro, E., & Cole, C. (1999). Self-monitoring in assessing children's problems. *Psychological Assessment, 11,* 448–457.

Shoor, R. (1993, November). For mental health cost problems, see a specialist. *Business and Health,* 59–62.

Simon, G., Grothaus, L., Durham, M., VonKorff, M., & Pabiniak, C. (1996). Impact of visit copayments on outpatient mental health utilization by members of a health maintenance organization. *American Journal of Psychiatry, 153,* 331–338.

Sobel, D. (1995). Rethinking medicine: Improving health outcomes with cost-effective psychosocial interventions. *Psychosomatic Medicine, 57,* 234–244.

Spitzer, R., Kroenke, K., Linzer, M., Hahn, S., Williams, J., deGruy, F., Brody, D., & Davies, M. (1995). Health related quality of life in primary care patients with mental disorders. *Journal of the American Medical Association, 274,* 1511–1517.

Stewart, A.L., Hays, R.D., & Ware, J.E. (1988). The MOS Short-Form General Health Survey: Reliability and validity in a patient population. *Medical Care, 26,* 724.

Stewart, A.L., & Ware, J.E. (1989). *The medical outcomes study.* Santa Monica, CA: Rand.

Stewart, A., & Ware, J.E. (Eds.). (1992). *Measuring functioning and well-being.* Durham, NC and London: Duke University Press.

Stice, E., Telch, C.F., & Rizvi, S.L. (2000). Development and validation of the Eating Disorder Diagnostic Scale: A brief self-report measure of anorexia, bulimia, and binge-eating disorder. *Psychological Assessment, 12*(2), 123–131.

Strosahl, K. (1994). Entering the new frontier of managed mental health care: Gold mines and land mines. *Cognitive and Behavioral Practice, 1,* 5–23.

Strosahl, K. (1995). Behavior therapy 2000: A perilous journey. *Behavior Therapist, 18,* 130–133.

Strosahl, K. (1996a). Three gold-mine land-mine themes in generation 2 of managed care. *Behavior Therapist,* 19, 52–54.

Strosahl, K. (1996b). Confessions of a behavior therapist in primary care: The odyssey and the ecstasy. *Cognitive and Behavioral Practice, 3,* 1–28.

Strosahl, K. (1999). Selecting a clinical outcomes system. *Behavioral Healthcare Tomorrow, 8*(6), 48–51.

Strosahl, K. (2000). Using interactive voice response technology to reduce the administrative burden of outcomes management. In K. Coughlin (Ed.), *2000 behavioral health outcomes and guidelines sourcebook* (pp. 172–179). New York: Faulkner and Gray.

Strosahl, K. (2001). The integration of primary care and behavioral health: Type II change in the era of managed care. In N. Cummings, W. O'Donohoe, S. Hayes, & V. Follette (Eds.), *Integrated behavioral healthcare: Positioning mental health practice with medical/surgical practice* (pp. 45–70). New York: Academic Press.

Strosahl, K., Hayes, S., Bergan, J., & Romano, P. (1998). Assessing the field effectiveness of acceptance and commitment therapy: An example of the manipulated training research method. *Behavior Therapy, 29,* 35–63.

Strosahl, K., & Linehan, M. (1986). Basic issues in behavioral assessment. In A. Ciminero, K. Calhoun, & H. Adams (Eds.), *Handbook of behavioral assessment* (2nd ed., pp. 12–60). New York: Wiley.

Strosahl, K., & Quirk, M. (1994, July). The trouble with carve-outs. *Business and Health,* 52.

Taylor, C., & Agras, S. (1981). The therapeutic relationship in behavior therapy. *Clinical Psychology Review, 4,* 253–272.

Trabin, T., & Freeman, M. (1995). *Managed behavioral healthcare: History, models, strategic challenges and future course.* Tiburon, CA.: CentraLink.

Twaddle, A. (1981). Sickness and the sickness career: Some implications. In L. Eisenberg & A. Kleinman (Eds.), *The relevance of social science to medicine* (pp. 111–134). Boston: Reidel.

Verhovek, S. (1997, June 5). Texas will allow malpractice suits against HMOs. *New York Times,* p. 1, col. 6.

Ware, J., Sherbourne, C., & Davies, A. (1992). Developing and testing the MOS 20-item Short-Form Health Survey: A general population application. In A.L. Stewart & J.E. Ware (Eds.), *Measuring functioning and well-being: The Medical Outcomes Study approach.* Chapel Hill, NC: Duke University Press.

Wilson, G., & Vitousek, K. (1999). Self-monitoring in the assessment of eating disorders. *Psychological Assessment, 11,* 480–489.

Wolf, W.M. (1978). Social validity: The case for subjective measurement or how applied behavior analysis is finding its heart. *Journal of Applied Behavior Analysis, 11,* 203–214.

Wolpe, J., & Lang, P.J. (1969). *Fear survey schedule.* San Diego, CA: Educational and Industrial Testing Service.

World Health Organization. (1948). *Constitution.* In basic documents. Geneva, Switzerland: Author.

SECTION FIVE

INTEGRATION BETWEEN BEHAVIORAL AND NONBEHAVIORAL ASSESSMENT METHODS

CHAPTER 23

Projective Techniques and Behavioral Assessment

HOWARD N. GARB, SCOTT O. LILIENFELD, AND JAMES M. WOOD

One of the central controversies in psychology involves the use of projective techniques. Although behavioral psychologists rarely use projective techniques, they have taken an active interest in the controversy. In fact, a number of behavioral psychologists serving as editors at prominent journals have played important roles in the development of the controversy (e.g., David Barlow, Alan Bellack, Stephen Haynes, Alan Kazdin).

Three of the most popular projective techniques are the Rorschach, Thematic Apperception Test (TAT), and human figure drawings. For the Rorschach, clients are shown 10 inkblots, one at a time, and they are asked to say what each blot resembles. For the TAT, they are shown cards depicting ambiguous situations (e.g., a young woman grabbing the shoulders of a young man who appears to be attempting to pull away from her), and they are instructed to tell a story. For human figure drawings, they are given a blank sheet of paper and a pencil, and they are instructed to draw a person (variations on the instructions are used—e.g., they may be instructed to draw a person, tree, and house). The stimuli used in projective techniques tend to be ambiguous, and the nature and number of responses are typically allowed to vary. This chapter focuses on the Rorschach, TAT, and human figure drawings because they remain the most popular and widely used of all projective techniques (Lilienfeld, Wood, & Garb, 2000).

The controversy over projective techniques has received a remarkable amount of attention, in part because there is evidence that the use of projective techniques can sometimes be harmful. Since 1999, debates on the scientific status of the Rorschach and other projective techniques have appeared in the following professional journals: *Assessment, Clinical Psychology: Science and Practice, Harvard Mental Health Letter, Journal of Clinical Psychology, Journal of Forensic Psychology Practice, Journal of Personality Assessment, Psychological Assessment,* and *Psychology, Public Policy, and the Law.* Conclusions critical of projective techniques were reached in many of these articles. For example, Grove and Barden (1999) concluded that expert witness testimony based on the Rorschach should not be found admissible in legal settings (also see Grove, Barden, Garb, & Lilienfeld, 2002; Ritzler, Erard, & Pettigrew, 2002). Similarly, Hunsley and Bailey (1999, p. 266) concluded that, "There is currently no scientific basis for justifying the use of Rorschach scales in psychological assessment." The controversy also has been described in general news and popular science outlets, including the *New York Times* (Goode, 2001) and *Scientific American* (Lilienfeld, Wood, & Garb, 2001).

Given the attention that the controversy has received in professional journals and general news and popular science outlets, it is appropriate that it be acknowledged and addressed in the *Comprehensive Handbook of Psychological*

Assessment. We will describe the projectives controversy and draw conclusions that should prove useful to behavioral psychologists.

Some psychologists believe that projective techniques have been unfairly criticized. They seem to believe that other assessment instruments, including behavioral assessment instruments, could not withstand the same level of scrutiny to which projective techniques have been subjected. For example, Ritzler et al. (2002) asserted that:

> Most of their arguments against the RCS [Rorschach Comprehensive System] apply equally well to the use of the MMPI-2, the MCMI tests, the DSM-IV, clinical interviews, mental status examinations, and, ultimately, any application of clinical psychological principles (p. 29).

It will be helpful for behavioral psychologists to learn more about the controversy surrounding projective techniques so they can decide for themselves whether behavioral assessment instruments are vulnerable to the same criticisms that have been leveled at projective techniques.

Many behavioral psychologists believe that projective techniques have always been controversial. To an extent this is true, but it is also true that their popularity has ebbed and flowed. The Rorschach was a frequent target of scientific criticism from the 1950s to the early 1970s (see summary by Dawes, 1994; Wood, Nezworski, Lilienfeld, & Garb, 2003), but the publication of *The Rorschach: A Comprehensive System* (Exner, 1974) seemed to restore its reputation. Surveys conducted in the 1990s indicated that the Rorschach was widely used in clinical and forensic settings and that the Comprehensive System (CS) was the most popular system for interpreting the Rorschach (Ackerman & Ackerman, 1997; Lees-Haley, 1992; Pinkerman, Haynes, & Keiser, 1993; Piotrowski, 1996; Piotrowski & Keller, 1989).

It may be helpful to describe the types of interpretations made by psychologists who use projective techniques. Whereas behavioral assessment tends to focus on behaviors and environmental variables (e.g., antecedent stimuli, reinforcers), projective techniques generally focus on the assessment of global traits. For example, using the CS (Exner, 1991, 1993, 2001), interpretations are typically made regarding: (a) a client's dominant personality style, including the level of stress the client is experiencing and how effectively the personality style allows the client to tolerate stress; (b) the manner in which a client organizes his or her perceptions (e.g., active, passive, overintellectualization); (c) how a person modulates and expresses affect (e.g., whether the person is likely to be overwhelmed by affective impulses); (d) whether a client is unconventional or overly conventional; (e) the quality and

efficiency with which a client processes information; and (f) a client's interpersonal style (e.g., with regard to needs, attitudes, and coping styles).

Using projective techniques, one will not meet the goals of behavioral assessment. Haynes and O'Brien (2000) have described these goals, which include being able to describe: (a) highly specific, minimally inferential behaviors and variables; (b) observable behaviors and environmental events (as opposed to intrapsychic events or highly inferential latent variables); (c) behaviors and causal relations as they occur in the natural environment; (d) functional relations, including behavior-behavior relations and behavior-environment relations; (e) situational/contextual variables associated with variance in behavior problems; (f) multiple targets in clinical assessment (e.g., main treatment effects, side-effects, generalization); (g) multiple response modes (behavioral, physiological, cognitive); and (h) social systems and extended causal relations. Behavioral assessment is also used for treatment outcome measurement. Interestingly, in a survey of studies published since the 1960s in the *Journal of Consulting and Clinical Psychology,* Haynes and O'Brien (2000, pp. 27–28) reported that projective techniques were rarely used to measure treatment outcome, presumably because research investigators in this area do not find these techniques to be reliable, valid, or useful.

The goal of this chapter is to address whether the use of projective techniques can complement behavioral assessment. We also address whether behavioral principles can help us understand a client's responses on a projective measure. We begin by describing how clients' responses on projective techniques are sometimes related to environmental factors (e.g., reinforcement obtained from the examiner). The second topic we address is the reliability and accuracy of the scoring of projective technique protocols. Next, we describe a serious problem with projective techniques: There is extensive evidence that their use leads to the overperception of psychopathology. We then describe results of using projective techniques to aid in: (a) making diagnoses and (b) detecting child sexual abuse. Next, we describe the overall validity, incremental validity, and treatment utility of projective techniques. We contrast our findings with conclusions reached by the Psychological Assessment Work Group (PAWG)—a work group commissioned by the Board of Professional Affairs of the American Psychological Association to address issues related to the declining popularity of psychological assessment (Kubiszyn et al., 2000). Finally, we discuss issues related to the availability of data and manuscripts, and we conclude that most of the fundamental papers cited by John Exner in his series of books on the CS (Exner, 1974, 1978, 1986, 1991, 1993; Exner & Weiner, 1982, 1995) are often unavailable for scrutiny by scholars, and in many cases have never even been written.

EXAMINER AND SITUATION EFFECTS

As noted earlier, proponents of projective techniques typically assume that the scores on these measures reflect stable underlying dispositions (i.e., traits) rather than the transient situational variables (e.g., reinforcers) often studied by behavioral assessors. Nevertheless, there is evidence that scores on projective techniques can be affected by numerous short-term environmental manipulations, thereby compromising their validity for making trait inferences.

For example, by providing differential reinforcement, examiners can influence responses on projective techniques (Hersen & Greaves, 1971; Magnussen, 1960; Masling, 1966; Simkins, 1960; Simmons & Christy, 1962; Tobias, 1960; Wickes, 1956; for reviews and comments, see Masling, 1960, 1966, 1997). For example, Hersen and Greaves (1971) found that merely saying the word "good" following clients' responses can increase the total number of responses on the Rorschach by as much as 50%. Masling (1965) reported that graduate student examiners led to believe that a higher ratio of animal to human responses was indicative of greater examiner competence elicited Rorschach protocols with a significantly higher proportion of animal responses than graduate student examiners not provided with this information. Interestingly, analyses of taped sessions suggested that this effect was not mediated by verbal conditioning, because examiners provided little or no verbal feedback to examinees. Instead, this effect appears to have been produced by subtle nonverbal behaviors, such as holding the card in front of the subjects for longer periods of time after an animal response had not been made (Masling, 1966).

Just as test examiners can influence clients, clients can influence test examiners. For example, Masling (1957) reported that the sentence completion protocols of participants who behaved in a warm fashion toward the examiner were scored more positively than those of participants who behaved in a cold fashion toward the examiner.

Other studies indicate that situational variables can exert significant effects on clients' responses. For example, Hess, Hess, and Hess (1999) found that exposure to violent stimuli (either videotaped or audiotaped depictions of a heinous crime) produced significant increases in the number of violent responses to inkblots compared with exposure to pastoral stimuli. These results are consistent with the possibility that exposure to violent media preceding testing could lead to high scores on test indicators of violent disposition.

In conclusion, clients' responses on projective measures can be markedly influenced by examiner and environmental factors. This tendency is likely to lead to errors in interpretation because psychologists interpret clients' responses as reflective of needs, conflicts, or traits rather than of short-term situational variables.

RELIABILITY AND ACCURACY OF SCORING

Do most psychologists reliably and accurately score projective technique protocols? In many cases, the answer is no. For example, for human figure drawings, psychologists frequently do not agree on the scoring of a particular indicator (Kahill, 1984; Palmer et al., 2000; Vass, 1998). For the TAT, few psychologists use an objective scoring system (Pinkerman, Haynes, & Keiser, 1993). That is, the vast majority of clinicians interpret the TAT using intuition and subjective impressions. When clinicians interpret a test in this manner, interrater reliability is likely to be poor, particularly when the responses lend themselves to a wide variety of interpretations. Conversely, when clinicians adhere to explicit rules for scoring a protocol, they are likely to be in greater agreement about what the results mean. Thus, when using human figure drawings and the TAT, we cannot conclude that most psychologists reliably and accurately score protocols.

One reason for the popularity of the Rorschach and the CS is that Exner (1993, p. 23) has claimed that interrater reliability is uniformly above .85 for CS variables. The results from several studies indicate that this claim is incorrect (Acklin, McDowell, Verschell, & Chan, 2000; Gronnerod, 1999; Nakata, 1999; also see Meyer, 1997a, 1997b; Shaffer, Erdberg, & Haroian, 1999; Wood, Nezworski, & Stejskal, 1997). In one study (Acklin et al., 2000), ratings were made by two clinical psychology graduate students with advanced training and at least three years of experience in the use of the CS. About half of the CS scores had reliability coefficients below .85. Thus, if one uses Exner's standard, one would conclude that interrater reliability is not satisfactory for many CS scores. However, Acklin and colleagues (2000, p. 34) argued that values greater than or equal to .61 and less than .81 represent "substantial and acceptable levels of reliability." Using this standard, Acklin and colleagues concluded that reliability is generally acceptable. In our opinion, this standard is too lax. It suggests that psychologists using the CS interpret variables that contain a substantial amount of error. By comparison, the intraclass correlation coefficients for the Wechsler Adult Intelligence Scale, Third Edition (WAIS-III) have a median value of .95 and a minimum value of .90 (Psychological Corporation, 1997), and the interrater reliability for scoring the Minnesota Multiphasic Personality Inventory-II (MMPI-2; Butcher, Dahlstrom, Graham, Tellegen, & Kaemmer, 1989) is essentially perfect because answer sheets are nearly always scored using computers.

Scoring accuracy is also a significant problem. Results suggest that clinicians do not score protocols in accordance with the CS rules. In one study (Guarnaccia, Dill, Sabatino, & Southwick, 2001), 21 clinical and school psychology graduate students and 12 licensed psychologists scored Rorschach responses. The graduate students had about 25 hours of scoring instruction and practice in the use of the CS, an amount that is about equal to the average reported by other training programs (Durand, Blanchard, & Mindell, 1988). The licensed psychologists all stated that they had used the Rorschach and the CS at least once a month in their clinical work. Accuracy scores for both graduate students and psychologists were below acceptable levels. For Rorschach responses made by patients, the average scoring accuracy was about 65%, even when the results were analyzed separately for the graduate students and the psychologists. These results suggest that scoring errors frequently occur in clinical practice.

OVERPERCEPTION OF PSYCHOPATHOLOGY

Normative data describe how individuals in the community perform on a test. By comparing a client's test scores to normative data, one can determine whether the client's scores deviate from scores that are typically obtained by relatively normal individuals. This procedure should reduce the risk of inferring psychopathology from responses that are similar to those made by relatively normal individuals. The use of group norms is *not* emphasized in behavioral assessment because behavioral assessors are interested in tracking the behavior of a single person across different situations and periods of time. In contrast, the validity of projective interpretations hinges on the availability of appropriate normative data.

When psychologists use projective techniques, they frequently do not have normative data available. This is almost always true for the TAT and projective drawings (an exception involves the DAP-SPED; Naglieri, McNcish, & Bardos, 1991). The situation is different for the Rorschach; normative data are available, but they appear to be flawed.

As already noted, the most popular system for the Rorschach is Exner's CS. The CS provides norms that can be used to interpret Rorschach results for children and adults. The norms were designed to describe how relatively normal individuals in the community perform on the Rorschach. By comparing a client's scores with the CS norms, one should be able to detect psychopathology.

The 1993 CS adult normative sample was recently revised after Exner learned that he had made an error of enormous magnitude. For many years, it was widely believed that the 1993 adult normative sample was composed of 700 distinct protocols. It actually contained 479 distinct protocols with 221 duplicates (Exner, 2001, p. 172; Exner, personal communication, March, 23, 2001). That is, 221 of the protocols were mistakenly counted twice. Although the adult normative sample has been revised, even the 2001 sample has been found to contain errors. Over the years, Exner revised the CS rules for scoring protocols. However, he did not return to the normative sample and rescore it using the revised rules. As a result, the CS norms for Form Quality are based on the wrong scoring rules and have been seriously in error since 1983 (Meyer & Richardson, 2001).

Perhaps the most serious problem with the Rorschach is that the use of the CS norms is likely to cause psychologists to overperceive psychopathology (Wood, Garb, Lilienfeld, & Nezworski, 2002). The research evidence for this assertion will be described in detail.

Shaffer, Erdberg, and Haroian (1999) administered the Rorschach to 123 "nonpatient" adults using the CS rules for administration and scoring. To ensure that participants were relatively normal, individuals were excluded if they had a major medical illness, a history of psychiatric hospitalization, psychological treatment in the past 2 years, a felony conviction, or psychological testing in the past year. Participants obtained scores that were substantially different from the CS norms. When compared with the norms, the participants tended to appear pathological. If one used the CS norms to make interpretations, one would probably conclude that the participants were seriously disturbed on measures of perceptual inaccuracy and distorted thinking. These results suggest that the use of the CS can make relatively normal individuals appear as though they suffer from serious thought disorder.

There is also evidence that the use of the CS norms for children will lead psychologists to overperceive psychopathology. Hamel, Shaffer, and Erdberg (2000) administered the Rorschach to a group of 100 relatively normal children. To ensure that participants did not have "histories of gross psychopathology or misconduct" (p. 290), the researchers excluded children if they had (a) a history of suspensions from school, (b) been evaluated or treated for attention deficit hyperactivity disorder, or (c) received psychotherapy for emotional or behavioral disorders. The sample of children in this study demonstrated healthier than average behaviors, as measured by the Conners Parent Rating Scale-93 (Conners, 1989). Striking discrepancies from the CS norms were obtained when the Rorschach was administered. Hamel and colleagues concluded that:

If we were writing a Rorschach-based, collective psychological evaluation for this sample, the clinical descriptors would command attention. In the main, these children may be described as grossly misperceiving and misinterpreting their surroundings and having unconventional ideation and significant cognitive impairment. Their distortion of reality and faulty reasoning approach psychosis. These children would also likely be described as having significant problems establishing and maintaining interpersonal relationships and coping within a social context. They apparently suffer from an affective disorder that includes many of the markers found in clinical depression (p. 291).

To determine whether Shaffer, Erdberg, and Haroian's (1999) study could be generalized to other samples, we reviewed Rorschach studies that included groups of nonpatient adults (Wood, Nezworski, Garb, & Lilienfeld, 2001b). In these studies, results for a clinical group (e.g., clients with antisocial personality disorder) were compared with the results for a group of nonpatient adults (e.g., undergraduate students or community volunteers). We found 32 studies and examined the results for the groups of nonpatient adults on the following 14 CS variables: EB style (percent of ambient protocols), Reflection responses, $X+\%$, $X-\%$, Afr, Form-Color responses, Populars, Sum Y, the sum of Texture Responses, WSumC, MOR, WSum6, Lambda, and the total number of Pure Human responses. These 14 indexes are critical to CS interpretation. Results were in the predicted direction, and differences were statistically significant for all 14 scores. The median difference between the nonpatient adult groups and the CS norms was large ($d = .73$).[1] We reached the following conclusion:

If Rorschach scores for a normal adult are interpreted using the CS norms, the adult will appear relatively self-focused and narcissistic (elevated Reflection scores), unconventional with impaired judgment and distorted perceptions of reality (low $X+\%$, low Populars, high $X-\%$), depressed, anxious, tense, and constrained in emotional expression (elevated Morbid responses, elevated *Sum Y*, low *WsumC*), insecure and fearful of involvement (elevated Lambda), vacillating and inefficient (elevated number of ambients), with low empathy (low *Pure H*), a tendency to withdraw from emotions (low *Afr*), and poor emotional control (low *FC*) (Wood et al., 2001b, p. 356).

Not everyone agrees that the use of the CS norms is likely to lead to the overperception of psychopathology. Meyer (2001) presented evidence that supports this countervailing view. He analyzed results from nine international studies on the CS that contained a total of 2,125 nonclinical participants. Instead of focusing on the results for the 14 variables that we examined, he examined the results for 69 Rorschach scores. He found that the international samples were about four-

tenths of a standard deviation more impaired than the CS normative sample. Although Meyer reported a smaller effect size ($d = .38$) than was reported by Wood and colleagues (2001b) ($d = .73$), a value of $d = .38$ is not trivial by any means. Using guidelines proposed by Cohen (1988), a value of $d = .38$ is close to being a medium effect size.

Using the data from the nine international studies that Meyer had analyzed, we (Wood, Nezworski, Garb, & Lilienfeld, 2001a) examined the results for the 14 variables that we had examined in our original review (Wood et al., 2001b). The findings for the international sample were remarkably similar to those obtained in our original review. For these 14 variables, the international sample was about eight-tenths of a standard deviation more impaired than the CS normative sample. In our original review, the aggregated nonpatient sample was only about seven-tenths of a standard deviation more impaired than the CS normative sample. Thus, for these 14 critical variables, the results are even more striking for the international sample than for the aggregated nonpatient sample in our original review.

The research evidence suggests that psychologists using the most popular system for interpreting the Rorschach have been systematically overperceiving psychopathology. Disturbingly, psychologists may have been treating clients for problems they did not have (e.g., a specific mental disorder). Worse yet, psychologists may have convinced patients that they had problems that they did not really have. With regard to forensic practice, it is troubling to realize that the use of the CS norms may contribute to detrimental outcomes. For example, a parent given a Rorschach may be unfairly denied child custody because the results appear pathological when compared with the CS norms. In contrast, it is unlikely that the use of behavioral assessment could lead to the overperception of psychopathology. This is because behavioral assessment involves the careful observation of individual clients over long periods of time, so a few aberrant responses are unlikely to be overinterpreted. Moreover, the emphasis on functional assessment and identifying environmental antecedents of behavior may make the overperception of psychopathology less likely.

PROJECTIVE TECHNIQUES AND DIAGNOSIS

If projective techniques could help clinicians make more accurate diagnoses, this could be of interest to behavioral psychologists. We have reviewed the research literature on projective techniques and diagnosis (Lilienfeld et al., 2000; Wood, Lilienfeld, Garb, & Nezworski, 2000). Results for the Rorschach, TAT, and projective drawings will be described.

Findings indicate serious problems with using the Rorschach as a diagnostic tool. In fact, in research studies, psychologists have become *less* accurate when projective test information has been made available in addition to other information (Garb, 1998). For example, in one study (Whitehead, 1985), when psychologists and advanced psychology graduate students used the MMPI alone or the CS and MMPI together, hit rates averaged across diagnostic tasks were 76% and 74%, respectively.

To aid in making diagnoses, only a few Rorschach indexes appear to be valid. For the CS, poor form quality and deviant verbalizations have been associated with the diagnosis of schizophrenia and may also provide useful information for the diagnosis of bipolar disorder, schizotypal personality disorder, and borderline personality disorder. However, even these indexes are of limited utility because it is unclear whether they can be used to differentiate among the presence of schizophrenia, bipolar disorder, and other disorders in which a thought disorder is often present.

Rorschach scores have not shown a clear relation to major depressive disorder, anxiety disorders, dissociative identity disorder (multiple personality disorder), conduct disorder, psychopathy, or dependent, narcissistic, and antisocial personality disorders, so it is unlikely that they can be helpful for the diagnosis of these disorders. When positive findings have been obtained, they have rarely been replicated by independent investigators (Wood et al., 2000). For example, the most extensively studied Rorschach indicator of depression is the Depression Index (DEPI) (Exner, 1991, 1993). According to Exner (1991, p. 146), scores on the DEPI "correlate very highly with a diagnosis that emphasizes serious affective problems." However, in studies conducted by independent investigators, diagnoses of depression have rarely been related to scores on either the original or revised versions of the DEPI (for a detailed review, see Jorgensen, Andersen, & Dam, 2000). This is true for studies on both adolescents and adults. For the eight studies that were conducted independently of the Rorschach Workshops, seven found no significant relation between the original DEPI and psychiatric diagnoses (Archer & Gordon, 1988; Ball, Archer, Gordon, & French, 1991; Carter & Dacey, 1996; Lipovsky, Finch, & Belter, 1989; Sells, 1990/1991; Silberg & Armstrong, 1992; Viglione, Brager, & Haller, 1988). Results in the eighth study were mixed (Singer & Brabender, 1993). With regard to the revised DEPI, no significant relation was found in five studies (Archer & Krishnamurthy, 1997; Ball et al., 1991; Caine, Frueh, & Kinder, 1995; Ritsher, Slivko-Kolchik, & Oleichik, 2001; Sells, 1990/1991), mixed results were found in two studies (Ilonen et al., 1999; Meyer, 1993), and positive results were found in one study (Jansak, 1996/1997).

Many psychologists believe that Rorschach scores are positively related to diagnoses of antisocial personality disorder (ASPD). For example, Gacono and Meloy (1994, pp. 108–117, 157–169) concluded that individuals with ASPD exhibit a distinctive pattern of pathological scores on the Rorschach. However, their conclusions are highly problematic. In many of the studies they reviewed, Rorschach results for individuals with ASPD were compared with the CS norms. Although the authors reported significant differences, these results are of doubtful validity because many individuals in the community with no known pathology also score in a pathological direction when compared with the CS norms (Hamel et al., 2000; Shaffer et al., 1999; Wood et al., 2001a, 2001b).

If one excludes studies that compared results with the problematic CS norms, it becomes clear that no Rorschach score (except perhaps Pair responses) has shown a well-demonstrated relationship to ASPD (Wood et al., 2000). Positive findings for the following commonly interpreted scores have *not* been replicated: Aggressive Movement (*AG;* Baity & Hilsenroth, 1999; Berg, Gacono, Meloy, & Peaslee, 1994), *T* responses (Berg et al., 1994; Blais, Hilsenroth, & Fowler, 1998; Howard, 1998/1999), Aggressive Content (*AgC;* Berg et al., 1994; Baity & Hilsenroth, 1999), Color responses (Berg et al., 1994; Blais et al., 1998), Diffuse Shading (*Y*) and Vista (*V*) responses (Gacono, Meloy, & Berg, 1992; Howard, 1998/1999), and Space (*S*) and Pure Human responses (Howard, 1998/1999). Similar results have been obtained for the assessment of psychopathy and conduct disorder: attempts to replicate positive Rorschach findings have nearly always failed (Wood et al., 2000; also see a reanalysis of data from Archer & Krishnamurthy, 1997, conducted by Robert Archer and reported in Wood, Lilienfeld, Nezworski, & Garb, 2001, p. 55).

The TAT, like the Rorschach, seems to have limited value for diagnostic purposes. For example, in one study (Sharkey & Ritzler, 1985), TAT measures did not significantly distinguish samples of normal individuals, depressed individuals, and psychotic individuals. Even for the most promising objective scoring system, the Social Cognition and Object Relations Scale (SCORS; Westen, 1991; Westen, Lohr, Silk, Gold, & Kerber, 1990), results have been mixed. For example, in one study (Ackerman, Clemence, Weatherill, & Hilsenroth, 1999), patients with ASPD did not differ significantly from patients with other personality disorders on the Moral Standards variable of the SCORS, even though one would expect individuals with ASPD to have weak moral standards. Paradoxical results were also found for the SCORS Aggression variable. In contrast, provisional research support exists for using the SCORS to detect borderline personality disorder (Gutin, 1997; Malik, 1992; Westen, Lohr, et al. 1990; Westen,

Ludolph, Lerner, Ruffins, & Wiss, 1990; for a review, see Lilienfeld et al., 2000).

As with the Rorschach and the TAT, one cannot help but wonder whether reliance on the use of human figure drawings will lead psychologists astray. Two major approaches for scoring and interpreting human figure drawings can be delineated. Using the sign approach, one draws inferences from isolated drawing features (e.g., pronounced eyes purportedly indicate paranoia). In contrast, using the global approach, one typically examines a number of features of a drawing to obtain a composite score. Results for the sign approach have typically been negative, not only for the task of diagnosis but also for other tasks, including personality description (e.g., Kahill, 1984; Klopfer & Taulbee, 1976; Motta, Little, & Tobin, 1993; Thomas & Jolley, 1998). For virtually all figure drawing signs, there has been a dearth of replicated findings. On the other hand, positive results have sometimes been obtained for the global approach, presumably because reliability increases as the number of items that a score is based on increases. For example, positive results have been obtained for the DAP:SPED, a measure that can be used to screen for global psychopathology (Naglieri & Pfeiffer, 1992). Nevertheless, there is little consistent evidence that the global approach can be used to differentiate among different forms of psychopathology within clinical samples (Lilienfeld et al., 2000).

In conclusion, one must be cautious when using projective techniques to help make diagnoses. The Rorschach may sometimes be helpful for evaluating conditions characterized by thought disorder (e.g., schizophrenia; see Wood et al., 2000). However, there is little reason to believe that the Rorschach can help in diagnosing other disorders, including major depression, conduct disorder, panic disorder, and antisocial and narcissistic personality disorders. In fact, the use of the Rorschach may decrease accuracy when making diagnoses for these disorders. With regard to the TAT, there is modest support for using the SCORS (Westen, 1991) to detect borderline personality disorder, but the validity of the TAT has not been established for the diagnosis of other mental disorders. Finally, with regard to human figure drawings, there is some evidence that global approaches (e.g., the DAP: SPED) can be used to screen for mental disorders among children, but the overwhelming majority of projective drawing signs possess negligible or essentially zero validity.

DETECTION OF CHILD SEXUAL ABUSE

Are projective techniques helpful for determining whether a child has been sexually abused? In one survey (Oberlander,

1995), 54.8% of mental health professionals who specialize in evaluating child sexual abuse said they believe that projective techniques are useful for this task, 25.8% said they are unsure, and only 19.4% said they believe the techniques would not be useful. We discuss this issue here because of its obvious social and clinical importance and because it illustrates how the use of projective techniques can be harmful.

West (1998) conducted a meta-analysis and concluded that "projective techniques have the ability to discriminate between children who have been sexually abused and those who were not abused sexually" (p. 1151). She located 12 studies in which projective techniques had been used for this task.

Nevertheless, the meta-analysis conducted by West (1998) is seriously flawed. Although she never explicitly acknowledged this point in her article, West included only positive results in her meta-analysis. She excluded negative results even when they were reported in the same articles as the positive ones. Furthermore, when results for a particular score were positive in one study but negative in another, she entered only the positive results into the meta-analysis. Thus, only by systematically excluding all negative results was West (1998) able to conclude that projective techniques are valid for the detection of child sexual abuse.

A new meta-analysis was conducted (Garb, Wood, & Nezworski, 2000) using all of the data from the 12 studies located by West (1998). When all of the data are included, the lower bound estimate for overall effect size is $d = .35$ and the upper bound estimate is $d = .46$. West had reported an overall effect size of $d = .81$. We (Garb et al., 2000) concluded that:

> Most of the positive findings on detecting sexual abuse have not yet been replicated. There have been a few exceptions involving the Rorschach and Human Figure Drawings, but even these indicators are in need of further study because the findings that were replicated involved comparisons between sexually abused children and children who were not being seen by a mental health professional (Chantler, Pelco, & Mertin, 1993; Hibbard & Hartman, 1990; Leifer et al., 1991; Zimmerman & Dillard, 1994) (p. 166).

Although a few indicators discriminated between sexually abused children and relatively normal children in the community, these indicators may be measuring general level of distress rather than effects specific to sexual abuse. Thus, they may not be useful for discriminating between sexually abused children and children likely to be seen in a mental health clinic.

We subsequently conducted a meta-analysis that was broader in scope and included results from unpublished manuscripts (Garb, Wood, & Lilienfeld, 2000). With one exception, we found no evidence that projective techniques consistently discriminated between sexually abused children and nonabused children who are receiving mental health treatment. Positive results were obtained for Westen's (1991) TAT SCORS. Specifically, for the Affect-Tone Scale (one of the SCORS scales), positive findings were replicated by independent investigators. For the comparison of sexually abused children and nonabused children receiving mental health treatment, values of d were .36 and .69 (Ornduff, Freedenfeld, Kelsey, & Critelli, 1994; Westen, Ludolph, Block, Wixom, & Wiss, 1990). Although results for the Affect-Tone Scale are promising, adequate normative data are not available.

The relation between the Affect-Tone Scale and sexual abuse may be substantial, but without normative data clinicians cannot be certain what cutoff scores they should use. For example, in one of the studies (Westen, Ludolph, Block et al., 1990), the mean score for sexually abused children was 2.48 and the mean score for nonabused children was 2.64. In the other study (Ornduff et al., 1994), the mean score for sexually abused children was 2.75 and the mean score for nonabused children was 2.96. Without adequate normative data, it would be difficult to infer whether a particular score (e.g., 2.75) indicates that the child has, or has not, been abused.

Additional problems with the SCORS can be described. First, the precise TAT cards and number of cards presented to clients has not been standardized for the SCORS, rendering its present application to clinical settings problematic. That is, if a psychologist presents cards that are different from those presented in research studies, one can question whether the interpretations made by the clinician should be based on findings from the research studies. Second, when presenting results for the detection of child sexual abuse, investigators should not simply report mean scores or effect sizes. The predictive power of the test should also be described. For example, investigators should report the number of sexually abused children with a positive test finding divided by the number of all children with a positive test result (positive predictive power) and the number of nonabused children with a negative test finding divided by the number of all children with a negative test result (negative predictive power). They should also describe sensitivity (the number of sexually abused children with a positive test finding divided by the number of all sexually abused children) and specificity (the number of nonabused children with a negative test finding divided by the number of all nonabused children). In other words, even when modest correlations and effect sizes are obtained, results may be weak for positive predictive power, negative predictive power, sensitivity, and specificity.

In our meta-analysis examining the use of projective techniques to detect child sexual abuse, we found evidence consistent with substantial publication bias, in that published studies yielded markedly higher effect sizes than did unpublished studies. For this analysis, 19 median effect sizes from published studies and 43 median effect sizes from unpublished studies were gathered. The average effect size for unpublished studies was $d = .24$, and the average effect size for published studies was $d = .51$. These results suggest a *file drawer effect:* studies of projective techniques are less likely to be published when results are small in magnitude.

The use of projective techniques for the detection of child sexual abuse can be harmful. If a psychologist incorrectly concludes that a child has been sexually abused, or incorrectly determines that a child has *not* been abused, these errors may cause considerable suffering and pain for the child and the child's family as well as for other persons. A particular concern is that the textbook use of the Rorschach can lead psychologists to make inaccurate and harmful judgments. As noted earlier, normal children can appear maladjusted when their Rorschach results are compared with the CS norms. Our fear is that a psychologist may mistakenly conclude that a child has been sexually abused, not because the child was abused, but because the CS norms are flawed.

OVERALL VALIDITY OF PROJECTIVE TECHNIQUES

Two approaches have been used to describe the overall validity of projective techniques. First, a series of global meta-analyses have been conducted, frequently involving comparisons of results for the Rorschach and Minnesota Multiphasic Personality Inventory-II. A second approach involves examining results separately for individual projective technique scores.

Global meta-analyses have been as controversial as the projective techniques themselves. One of the most recent global meta-analyses (Hiller, Rosenthal, Bornstein, Berry, & Brunell-Neuleib, 1999) has been criticized for a number of reasons (Garb, Wood, Nezworski, Grove, & Stejskal, 2001). For example, although 8,000 to 9,000 articles have been published on the Rorschach (Ritzler et al., 2002), Hiller and colleagues (1999) included the results from only 30 studies on the Rorschach in their meta-analysis. They did not conduct a comprehensive search for the results of any particular score, so it is not clear that they could describe the overall validity for any single Rorschach score, let alone the overall validity of the Rorschach itself. Another problem with their meta-analysis can be described. Two Rorschach experts independently coded the Rorschach studies. Based on their ratings, a result was either included in, or excluded from, the meta-analysis. Yet, interrater reliability for the two coding judges was only .35, as indexed by the coefficient. No coding book was available to help the judges make their ratings. Finally, inappropriate studies have sometimes been included in meta-analyses. For example, in some studies, positive findings were reported when clinical groups differed from the CS norms on key variables. We now know that serious problems exist with the CS norms and that even groups of relatively normal individuals can be expected to differ from these norms.

A second approach to characterizing the overall validity of projective techniques involves examining results separately for different scores (Wood, Nezworski, & Stejskal, 1996b). In a comprehensive review of the research on the validity of projective techniques (Lilienfeld et al., 2000), we used the following three criteria to evaluate the validity of an index: (1) an index must demonstrate a consistent relation to a particular symptom or disorder, (2) results must be obtained in methodologically rigorous studies, and (3) findings must be replicated by independent investigators. Using these criteria, the existence of positive findings did not lead us to conclude that an indicator is valid unless those findings were from sound studies and had been replicated by other researchers.

We concluded that the following projective scores have received at least provisional empirical support (Lilienfeld et al., 2000):

1. *Rorschach:* (a) Thought Disorder Index for the Rorschach in the assessment of thought disorder, (b) Rorschach Prognostic Rating Scale in the prediction of treatment outcome, (c) Rorschach Oral Dependency Scale in the assessment of objective behaviors related to dependency, and (d) deviant verbalizations and poor form quality (as well as the CS Schizophrenia Index and other indexes derived from these variables) in the assessment of schizophrenia (and perhaps schizotypal personality disorder and bipolar disorder) and borderline personality disorder.

2. *TAT:* (a) McClelland, Atkinson, Clark, and Lowell's (1953) scoring system for the need for achievement in the assessment of achievement-related outcomes and (b) Westen's (1991) SCORS in the identification of child sexual abuse history and borderline personality disorder (although in the case of child sexual abuse history, the SCORS Affective-tone scale only) (p. 54).

We also concluded that, for projective drawings, global indexes are moderately correlated with intelligence and can sometimes be used to detect maladjustment (e.g., Naglieri & Pfeiffer, 1992), but that "there are no well-replicated relationships between specific drawing signs and either personality or psychopathology" (Lilienfeld et al., 2000, p. 51).

Finally, scores for a few other projective techniques appear to be valid for certain purposes. It is ironic that perhaps the best validated projective technique, the Washington University Sentence Completion Test (Loevinger, 1976, 1998), is rarely used in clinical practice. Scores on this test are significantly correlated with measures of antisocial behavior and moral development, and have been shown to have substantial levels of incremental validity for predicting personality traits and psychiatric outcome (Lilienfeld et al., 2000; Loevinger, 1993).

INCREMENTAL VALIDITY AND TREATMENT UTILITY

Is it worth the time and money to use the Rorschach and other projective techniques? The Rorschach alone takes 2 to 3 hours to administer, score, and interpret. Equally important, an enormous investment of time and energy is required to become qualified in its use. According to Hilsenroth and Handler (1995):

> At least two courses are necessary to teach the Rorschach, one to teach administration and scoring, and at least one more to teach interpretation, diagnosis, and an integration of both into an assessment report (p. 255).

To help us evaluate whether projective techniques are worth using, we describe results on incremental validity and treatment utility.

Projective techniques are said to possess incremental validity if validity increases when projective protocols are made available in addition to other data. In a study described earlier (Whitehead, 1985), when judgments were made by psychologists and advanced psychology graduate students, the addition of the CS to the MMPI led to a decrease in hit rates. The results for this study are consistent with those from other studies: When describing personality traits and psychopathology, judgments made by psychologists do not become more valid when projective test results are added to other information (Garb, 1998).[2] Results on incremental validity also have been disappointing when statistical prediction rules have been used to make judgments. Positive findings on incremental validity have been found for several projective scores, but these results have not been replicated (Lilienfeld et al., 2000). Overall, incremental validity has not been studied for the vast majority of Rorschach scores, and negative results have been reported for many scores.

There is practically no evidence that the use of projective techniques leads to improved treatment decisions and outcomes. Put another way, we are unaware of any studies that show that clients who received projective testing had improved treatment outcomes. Given the results covered in this review, it seems likely that the use of projective techniques will sometimes lead to deleterious effects. This will be true when the use of projective techniques leads to the overperception of psychopathology and clients are treated for problems they do not have.

COMMENTS ON THE PSYCHOLOGICAL ASSESSMENT WORK GROUP

Our findings on projective techniques differ markedly from those reached by the Psychological Assessment Work Group. PAWG was established by the Board of Professional Affairs of the American Psychological Association to address issues related to the declining popularity of psychological assessment (Kubiszyn et al., 2000). They have published a series of articles that present arguments in favor of psychological testing in general, and projective techniques in particular. In the course of their work, they have received support from the Society for Personality Assessment and Rorschach Workshops. For reasons that are unclear, PAWG has never mentioned the existence of a controversy surrounding projective techniques. Nor have they mentioned that serious problems exist with the CS norms.

According to PAWG, the Rorschach and the TAT are valuable for making diagnoses. For example, they claim that:

Other, more general studies have demonstrated the ability of the Rorschach or the TAT . . . to differentiate among Axis II conditions like borderline, antisocial, narcissistic, and schizotypal personality disorders and Axis I conditions like schizophrenia, major depression, conduct disorder, and panic disorder (Kubiszyn et al., 2000, p. 121).

However, Kubiszyn and colleagues (2000) consistently described positive findings for the Rorschach and TAT, but almost always omitted negative findings. For example, for the diagnosis of depression and antisocial personality disorder, they did not cite a single negative result; earlier in this chapter we cited a number of studies and we concluded that negative results greatly outweigh positive ones. Similarly, narrative reviews were cited in Kubiszyn and colleagues' (2000) article if they supported projective techniques (e.g., Stricker & Healey, 1990) but not if they failed to support them (e.g., Frank, 1990, 1993; Nezworski & Wood, 1995; Wood, Nezworski, & Stejskal, 1996a). For example, for the diagnosis of borderline personality disorder, Kubiszyn et al. (2000) cited a review article that supported the use of the Rorschach (Gartner, Hurt, & Gartner, 1989) but did not cite another review paper (Zalewski & Archer, 1991) that concluded, "It is markedly premature to conclude that a pattern of distinguishing Rorschach characteristics has been reliably identified for the Borderline Personality Disorder patient" (p. 341).

In addition to concluding that the Rorschach and the TAT are valuable for assisting in making diagnoses, PAWG concluded that the "Rorschach or the TAT" are capable of "differentiating patients who have experienced physical or sexual trauma from those who have not" (Kubiszyn et al., 2000, p. 121). However, to support their claim, they cited only one study (Leifer, Shapiro, Martone, & Kassem, 1991). In this study, the Rorschach was used to detect sexual abuse. Positive findings were obtained in this study, but they were obtained for the comparison of sexually abused children with presumably relatively normal children. Thus, these scores may be useful for discriminating between distressed children and nondistressed children, but they are not necessarily useful for discriminating between sexually abused children and children likely to be seen in a mental health clinic. Notably, PAWG did not cite a single study on the detection of physical abuse.[3] For this reason, it is puzzling that PAWG endorsed the use of the Rorschach and TAT for detecting physical abuse.

In an even more recent article (Meyer et al., 2001), PAWG described results from meta-analyses conducted on psychological and medical assessment. Most pertinent to this chapter, they concluded that, "Despite the perceptions held by some, assessments with the Rorschach and TAT do not produce consistently lower validity coefficients than alternative personality tests" (p. 135). Their article is likely to be influential because it was published in *American Psychologist* and featured prominently in the *APA Monitor on Psychology* (Daw, 2001). However, their conclusions are extremely misleading (Garb, Klein, & Grove, 2002). For example, only one meta-analysis (Spangler, 1992) has examined the validity of the TAT. This meta-analysis examined a task that is *not* usually performed in clinical practice (evaluating achievement motivation) using an approach that is very rarely used in clinical practice (using an objective scoring system; scoring responses to a combination of TAT and non-TAT cards; McClelland, Atkinson, Clark, & Lowell, 1953). Similarly, for the Rorschach, no meta-analysis has examined all of the evidence for a single CS score. Yet, PAWG recommended the clinical use of the TAT and Rorschach without qualification.

AVAILABILITY OF DATA AND MANUSCRIPTS

In a series of books, Exner, alone and in collaboration with a colleague, has cited over 100 studies that are claimed to provide a scientific basis for the CS (Exner, 1974, 1978, 1986, 1991, 1993; Exner & Weiner, 1982, 1995). Although these studies might appear to form a substantial body of evidence, most of the research consists of unpublished studies by Exner's Rorschach Workshops. More important, papers describing the studies are often unavailable for scrutiny by independent scholars, and in many cases papers have never been written to describe the studies. The references for the studies that appear in Exner's books suggest that written papers are available. Specifically, they use the following format: Author(s), year, title, and study reference number. When a request was sent to Rorschach Workshops for copies of 27 of the papers, not a single one was made available (Wood et al., 1996a). An official at Rorschach Workshops offered the following explanation:

> During the period from 1968 to 1990 more than 1000 studies were undertaken at Rorschach Workshops to address various issues. The majority of these are not written in a publishable form. Instead, they usually include a brief statement concerning the methodology of the study, which often includes information that we cannot release, such as identifying specific sites, names of participants, etc. (P.M. Greene, personal communication, March 11, 1994).

The provision of only a brief statement is inadequate for describing the design, procedure, and analyses of a study, and would normally preclude acceptance for publication in a journal.

The accessibility of data is also an important issue. Recently, Wood and his colleagues requested a copy of the data for the CS norms (J. Wood, personal communication, August 5, 2000). Exner refused to make these data available (J. Exner, personal communication, December 8, 2000). Subsequently, he reported that the data contain errors (Exner, 2001, p. 172).

DISCUSSION AND RECOMMENDATIONS

The goal of this chapter was to address whether the use of projective techniques can complement behavioral assessment. Our comments are limited to the use of the Rorschach, TAT, and human figure drawings.

It is important to note that most indexes for the Rorschach, TAT, and projective drawings have not satisfied the three criteria described earlier in this chapter: (1) an index must demonstrate a consistent relation to a particular symptom or disorder, (2) results must be obtained in methodologically rigorous studies, and (3) findings must be replicated by independent researchers. Using these three criteria, the follow-

ing indexes have not been found to be empirically supported (Lilienfeld et al., 2000):

> . . . the overwhelming majority of Rorschach indexes, most TAT scoring systems (including the Defense Mechanisms Manual of Cramer, 1991), all isolated signs derived from human figure drawings, and global scoring approaches to human figure drawings that are intended to detect specific conditions (e.g., mood disorders) and child sexual abuse history (p. 54).

In other words, only a very small percentage of the projective indexes commonly used in clinical practice have satisfied the aforementioned criteria.

The projective indexes that we recommend in the following paragraphs are not directly helpful for behavioral assessment because they do not assess specific behaviors or minimally inferential constructs, but they may still be useful to behavioral psychologists. Some indexes are not recommended, not because they are invalid, but because it is doubtful that they would be of interest to behavioral psychologists (e.g., measures of need for achievement, predictors of success in insight-oriented psychotherapy).

First, for the task of detecting emotional disturbance among children, psychologists can administer the Draw-A-Person test and then score the drawings using the DAP-SPED (Naglieri et al., 1991). However, the Child Behavior Checklist (Achenbach, 1978; Achenbach & Edelbrock, 1983) possesses considerably greater empirical support than the DAP: SPED.

As with screening for emotional disturbance, diagnosis is of interest to some behavioral psychologists even though it is not central to behavioral assessment. For this task, clinicians should rely primarily on behavioral observation measures along with history and interview information. Nevertheless, results from psychological tests, including projective techniques, can sometimes be helpful. For example, to assist with the diagnosis of a severe mental disorder, it may be helpful to evaluate a patient for the presence of thought disorder. Using the Rorschach, this can be done by evaluating the form quality of responses and detecting deviant verbalizations. However, as already noted, serious problems exist with the CS norms for deviant thinking and form quality. To avoid using the CS norms, one can instead use the Thought Disorder Index for the Rorschach (Johnston & Holzman, 1979; Solovay et al., 1986). An alternative approach is to use the CS form quality variables but rely on local norms that one collects oneself, but this is an imperfect solution because one will still not have norms for nonimpaired individuals in the community.

With regard to the diagnosis of borderline personality disorder, one can use the SCORS (Westen, Lohr, et al., 1990) to score and interpret a client's TAT protocol. Encouraging results have been obtained when the SCORS has been used to aid in diagnosing this disorder (Lilienfeld et al., 2000). However, the scoring rules are complicated, and adequate norms are not available. Until additional research is conducted, it will not be clear what cutoff scores psychologists should use to interpret the results (i.e., they will not know what cutoff indicates whether a client is likely to have a borderline personality disorder).

Projective techniques are purportedly most helpful for describing personality traits and the nature of psychopathology, not for screening for the presence of psychopathology or for making diagnoses or behavioral predictions. Yet, for this task, the vast majority of indexes have not been consistently supported. The only exception we are aware of is the Rorschach Oral Dependency Scale (ROD; Masling, Rabie, & Blondheim, 1967). The ROD can be used to assess dependency, although it is not known whether the addition of the ROD to interview and history information results in improved validity. In general, the popularity of projective techniques for evaluating personality and psychopathology seems to be based largely on a willingness to accept clinical lore (the experiences of other psychologists) and unreplicated research findings.

Many psychologists report that when they make judgments, they feel comfortable relying on clinical lore, professional experience, and research findings (without specifying that research findings need to be replicated). However, research on *illusory correlations* (Chapman & Chapman, 1967, 1969) demonstrates that the subjective impressions and intuitions of even highly experienced clinicians may be badly mistaken. For example, Chapman and Chapman (1967) conducted a two-part study to learn why psychologists continue to use the Draw-A-Person test despite research documenting no relation between figure drawing characteristics (e.g., large or emphasized head) and personality characteristics (worried about being intelligent). First, psychologists were asked to state which features of drawings are associated with specific traits and symptoms. Second, drawings were presented to undergraduates, and they were instructed to examine each drawing and then to read a statement on the back that described a trait or symptom that the client who had drawn the picture was said to have. Unbeknownst to the undergraduates, the drawings and statements were randomly paired. The results were remarkable: undergraduates reported observing the same relations that had been reported by experienced psychologists. The results suggest that psychologists may use invalid test scores because they believe that they have observed relations between the test scores and symptoms and traits even though the relations do not exist.

The ability of clinicians to learn from experience is an important issue. Controlled research has consistently demonstrated that, for a wide range of tasks, the validity of judgments does not increase with experience (Garb, 1998; Garb & Schramke, 1996; Meehl, 1997). For example, in a range of studies, clinical psychologists have not been more accurate than advanced graduate students who have received didactic training in the use of assessment instruments (Garb, 1989, 1998).

There are many reasons why it can be difficult to learn from professional experience (Garb & Boyle, 2003). Psychologists frequently do not receive accurate feedback. For example, after making a diagnosis, psychologists rarely receive feedback on whether they were right or wrong. Also, fallible cognitive processes can result in the use of suboptimal hypothesis testing and learning strategies.

Behavioral assessors have frequently criticized traditional assessment instruments. For example, according to Haynes (2000):

> Traditional assessment methods, such as projective techniques and global personality trait questionnaires, do not provide data that are sufficiently specific or that reflect the conditional nature of behavior problems. . . . The aggregated, global nature of many constructs measured in traditional clinical assessment rendered traditional instruments insufficiently sensitive to changes across time or situations and insufficiently amenable to individualized assessment. . . . Assessment instruments of questionable psychometric qualities were used to provide indices of highly inferential, unobservable, and situationally insensitive intrapsychic phenomena (p. 473).

These criticisms certainly seem to apply to most projective techniques.

Behavioral principles can help us understand the overall poor performance of most projective techniques. Behaviorists work with minimally inferential constructs and are careful to not overgeneralize from samples of behavior. By performing careful functional analyses that take into account not only overt behaviors but also environmental antecedents of these behaviors, behavioral assessors may be better able to distinguish situational from trait variance. In contrast, projective techniques emphasize the evaluation of constructs that are often ambiguously defined. Furthermore, a basic premise of Rorschach interpretation is that a client's responses represent a sample of behavior and that one can generalize from those responses to determine how the client is likely to behave in other situations. Examples of how psychologists generalize from responses on the Rorschach to behaviors in real-life settings were provided by Groth-Marnat (1997):

For example, persons who broke down their perceptions of an inkblot into small details were likely to behave similarly for perceptions outside the testing situation. . . . Rorschach responses that described threatening objects would suggest persons who perceive their world as similarly threatening (p. 395).

Nevertheless, Groth-Marnat (1997) did not cite studies to support the validity of these interpretations. Instead, he provided these examples to illustrate how the Rorschach can be used. Although the examples make intuitive sense, it is inappropriate to assume that a client will behave a particular way across all, or most, situations based on his or her Rorschach responses.

In conclusion, the popularity of the Rorschach, TAT, and projective drawings is greatly outstripped by the meager research evidence supporting their validity. Psychologists are advised to proceed with considerable caution when using these instruments in clinical practice.

NOTES

1. A value of $d = .73$ indicates that the mean for the nonpatient adult group was .73 of a standard deviation from the mean of the CS norms.

2. In contrast, results have frequently been favorable for self-report tests (Garb, 1984, 1994, 1998).

3. Nor was a single study on the detection of physical abuse cited in the report by Meyer et al. (1998). Furthermore, to support their claim that the Rorschach and TAT are valid, Meyer et al. (1998, p. 26) cited studies by Nigg, Lohr, Westen, Gold, and Silk (1992) and Westen, Ludolph, Misle, Ruffins, and Block (1990), even though no data on the Rorschach or the TAT were reported in either study.

REFERENCES

Achenbach, T.M. (1978). The child behavior profile. I. Boys ages 6–11. *Journal of Consulting and Clinical Psychology, 46,* 478–488.

Achenbach, T.M., & Edelbrock, C. (1983). *Manual for the Child Behavior Checklist/4–18 and Revised Child Behavior Profile.* Burlington: University of Vermont, Department of Psychiatry.

Ackerman, M.J., & Ackerman, M.C. (1997). Custody evaluation practices: A survey of experienced professionals (revisited). *Professional Psychology: Research and Practice, 28,* 137–145.

Ackerman, S.J., Clemence, A.J., Weatherill, R., & Hilsenroth, M.J. (1999). Use of the TAT in the assessment of DSM-IV Cluster B personality disorders. *Journal of Personality Assessment, 73,* 422–448.

Acklin, M.W., McDowell, C.J., Verschell, M.S., & Chan, D. (2000). Interobserver agreement, intraobserver reliability, and the Rorschach Comprehensive System. *Journal of Personality Assessment, 74,* 15–47.

Archer, R.P., & Gordon, R.A. (1988). MMPI and Rorschach indices of schizophrenic and depressive diagnoses among adolescent inpatients. *Journal of Personality Assessment, 52,* 276–287.

Archer, R.P., & Krishnamurthy, R. (1997). MMPI-A and Rorschach indices related to depression and conduct disorder: An evaluation of the incremental validity hypothesis. *Journal of Personality Assessment, 69,* 517–533.

Baity, M.R., & Hilsenroth, M.J. (1999). Rorschach aggression variables: A study of reliability and validity. *Journal of Personality Assessment, 72,* 93–110.

Ball, J.D., Archer, R.P., Gordon, R.A., & French, J. (1991). Rorschach depression indices with children and adolescents: Concurrent validity findings. *Journal of Personality Assessment, 57,* 465–476.

Berg, J.L., Gacono, C.B., Meloy, J.R., & Peaslee, D. (1994). *A Rorschach comparison of borderline and antisocial females.* Unpublished manuscript.

Blais, M.A., Hilsenroth, M.J., & Fowler, J.C. (1998). Rorschach correlates of the DSM-IV histrionic personality disorder. *Journal of Personality Assessment, 70,* 355–364.

Butcher, J.N., Dahlstrom, W.G., Graham, J.R., Tellegen, A., & Kaemmer, B. (1989). *Minnesota Multiphasic Personality Inventory–II (MMPI-2): Manual for administration and scoring.* Minneapolis: University of Minnesota Press.

Caine, S.L., Frueh, B.C., & Kinder, B.N. (1995). Rorschach susceptibility to malingered depressive disorders in adult females. In J.N. Butcher & C.D. Spielberger (Eds.), *Advances in personality assessment* (Vol. 10, pp. 165–174). Hillsdale, NJ: Erlbaum.

Carter, C.L., & Dacey, C.M. (1996). Validity of the Beck Depression Inventory, MMPI, and Rorschach in assessing adolescent depression. *Journal of Adolescence, 19,* 223–231.

Chantler, L., Pelco, L., & Mertin, P. (1993). The psychological evaluation of child sexual abuse using the Louisville Behavior and Checklist and Human Figure Drawing. *Child Abuse & Neglect, 17,* 271–279.

Chapman, L.J., & Chapman, J.P. (1967). Genesis of popular but erroneous psychodiagnostic observations. *Journal of Abnormal Psychology, 72,* 193–204.

Chapman, L.J., & Chapman, J.P. (1969). Illusory correlation as an obstacle to the use of valid psychodiagnostic observations. *Journal of Abnormal Psychology, 74,* 271–280.

Cohen, J.E. (1988). *Statistical power analysis for the behavioral sciences* (2nd ed.). Hillsdale, NJ: Erlbaum.

Conners, K. (1989). *Manual for Conners' rating scales.* North Tonawanda, NY: Multi-Health Systems.

Cramer, P. (1991). *The development of defense mechanisms: Theory, research, and assessment.* New York: Springer-Verlag.

Daw, J. (2001). Psychological assessments shown to be as valid as medical tests. *APA Monitor, 32* (July/August), 46–47.

Dawes, R.M. (1994). *House of cards: Psychology and psychotherapy built on myth.* New York: Free Press.

Durand, V.M., Blanchard, E.B., & Mindell, J.A. (1988). Training in projective testing: Survey of clinical training directors and internship directors. *Professional Psychology: Research and Practice, 19,* 236–238.

Exner, J.E. (1974). *The Rorschach: A comprehensive system. Volume 1.* New York: Wiley.

Exner, J.E. (1978). *The Rorschach: A comprehensive system, Volume 2. Interpretation.* New York: Wiley.

Exner, J.E. (1986). *The Rorschach: A comprehensive system, Volume 1. Basic foundations* (2nd ed.). New York: Wiley.

Exner, J.E. (1991). *The Rorschach: A comprehensive system, Volume 2. Interpretation* (2nd ed.). New York: Wiley.

Exner, J.E. (1993). *The Rorschach: A comprehensive system, Volume 1. Basic foundations* (3rd ed.). New York: Wiley.

Exner, J.E. (2001). *A Rorschach workbook for the Comprehensive System* (5th ed.). Asheville, NC: Rorschach Workshops.

Exner, J.E., & Weiner, I.B. (1982). *The Rorschach: A comprehensive system, Volume 3. Assessment of children and adolescents.* New York: Wiley.

Exner, J.E., & Weiner, I.B. (1995). *The Rorschach: A comprehensive system, Volume 3. Assessment of children and adolescents* (2nd ed.). New York: Wiley.

Frank, G. (1990). Research on the clinical usefulness of the Rorschach: 1. The diagnosis of schizophrenia. *Perceptual and Motor Skills, 71,* 573–578.

Frank, G. (1993). On the validity of hypotheses derived from the Rorschach: The relationship between shading and anxiety, update 1992. *Psychological Reports, 72,* 519–522.

Gacono, C.B., & Meloy, J.R. (1994). *The Rorschach assessment of aggressive and psychopathic personalities.* Hillsdale, NJ: Erlbaum.

Gacono, C.B., Meloy, J.R., & Berg, J.L. (1992). Object relations, defensive operations, and affective states in narcissistic, borderline, and antisocial personality disorder. *Journal of Personality Assessment, 59,* 32–49.

Garb, H.N. (1984). The incremental validity of information used in personality assessment. *Clinical Psychology Review, 4,* 641–655.

Garb, H.N. (1989). Clinical judgment, clinical training, and professional experience. *Psychological Bulletin, 105,* 387–396.

Garb, H.N. (1994). Judgment research: Implications for clinical practice and testimony in court. *Applied & Preventive Psychology, 3,* 173–183.

Garb, H.N. (1998). *Studying the clinician: Judgment research and psychological assessment.* Washington, DC: American Psychological Association.

Garb, H.N., & Boyle, P. (2003). Understanding why some clinicians use pseudoscientific methods: Findings from research on clinical judgment. In S.O. Lilienfeld, S.J. Lynn, & J.M. Lohr (Eds.),

Science and pseudoscience in contemporary clinical psychology (pp. 17–38). New York: Guilford Press.

Garb, H.N., Klein, D.F., & Grove, W.M. (2002). Comparison of medical and psychological tests. *American Psychologist, 57,* 137–138.

Garb, H.N., & Schramke, C.J. (1996). Judgment research and neuropsychological assessment: A narrative review and meta-analyses. *Psychological Bulletin, 120,* 140–153.

Garb, H.N., Wood, J.M., & Lilienfeld, S.O. (2000). *The detection and assessment of child sexual abuse: An evaluation of the Rorschach, Thematic Apperception Test, and projective drawings.* Manuscript in preparation.

Garb, II.N., Wood, J.M., & Nezworski, M.T. (2000). Projective techniques and the detection of child sexual abuse. *Child Maltreatment, 5,* 161–168.

Garb, H.N., Wood, J.M., Nezworski, M.T., Grove, W.M., & Stejskal, W.J. (2001). Towards a resolution of the Rorschach controversy. *Psychological Assessment, 13,* 433–448.

Gartner, J., Hurt, S.W., & Gartner, A. (1989). Psychological test signs of borderline personality disorder: A review of the empirical literature. *Journal of Personality Assessment, 53,* 423–441.

Goode, E. (2001, February 20). What's in an inkblot? Some say, not much. *New York Times,* D1, D4.

Gronnerod, C. (1999). Rorschach interrater agreement estimates: An empirical evaluation. *Scandinavian Journal of Psychology, 40,* 115–120.

Groth-Marnat, G. (1997). *Handbook of psychological assessment* (3rd ed.). New York: Wiley.

Grove, W.M., & Barden, R.C. (1999). Protecting the integrity of the legal system: The admissibility of testimony from mental health experts under Daubert/Kumho analyses. *Psychology, Public Policy, and the Law, 5,* 224–242.

Grove, W.M., Barden, R.C., Garb, H.N., & Lilienfeld, S.O. (2003). Failure of Rorschach Comprehensive System-based testimony to be admissible under *Daubert-Joiner-Kumho* standard. *Psychology, Public Policy, and the Law, 8,* 216–234.

Guarnaccia, V., Dill, C.A., Sabatino, S., & Southwick, S. (2001). Scoring accuracy using the Comprehensive System for the Rorschach. *Journal of Personality Assessment, 77,* 464–474.

Gutin, N.J. (1997). Differential object representations in inpatients with narcissistic and borderline personality disorders and normal controls. *Dissertation Abstracts International, 58* (03-B), 1532.

Hamel, M., Shaffer, T.W., & Erdberg, P. (2000). A study of nonpatient preadolescent Rorschach protocols. *Journal of Personality Assessment, 75,* 280–294.

Haynes, S.N. (2000). Behavioral assessment of adults. In G. Goldstein & M. Hersen (Eds.), *Handbook of psychological assessment* (3rd ed., pp. 471–502). New York: Pergamon Press.

Haynes, S.N., & O'Brien, W.O. (2000). *Principles of behavioral assessment: A functional approach to psychological assessment.* New York: Plenum/Kluwer Press.

Hersen, M., & Greaves, S.T. (1971). Rorschach productivity as related to verbal performance. *Journal of Personality Assessment, 35,* 436–441.

Hess, T.H., Hess, K.D., & Hess, A.K. (1999). The effects of violent media on adolescent inkblot responses: Implications for clinical and forensic assessments. *Journal of Clinical Psychology, 55,* 439–445.

Hibbard, R.A., & Hartman, G.L. (1990). Emotional indicators in human figure drawings of sexually victimized and nonabused children. *Journal of Clinical Psychology, 46,* 211–219.

Hiller, J.B., Rosenthal, R., Bornstein, R.F., Berry, D.T.R., & Brunell-Neuleib, S. (1999). A comparative meta-analysis of Rorschach and MMPI validity. *Psychological Assessment, 11,* 278–296.

Hilsenroth, M.J., & Handler, L. (1995). A survey of graduate students' experiences, interests, and attitudes about learning the Rorschach. *Journal of Personality Assessment, 64,* 243–257.

Howard, W.W. (1998/1999). The utility of selected Rorschach indices of distress and attachment for differential diagnosis in a forensic setting. (Doctoral dissertation, Georgia State University, 1998). *Dissertation Abstracts International, 59,* 5578B.

Hunsley, J., & Bailey, J.M. (1999). The clinical utility of the Rorschach: Unfulfilled promises and an uncertain future. *Psychological Assessment, 11,* 266–277.

Ilonen, T., Taiminen, T., Karlsson, H., Lauerma, H., Leinonen, K.M., Wallenius, E., Tuimala, P., & Salokangas, R. (1999). Diagnostic efficiency of the Rorschach schizophrenia and depression indices in identifying first-episode schizophrenia and severe depression. *Psychiatry Research, 87,* 183–192.

Jansak, D.M. (1996/1997). The Rorschach Comprehensive System Depression Index, depression heterogeneity, and the role of self-schema (Doctoral dissertation, California School of Professional Psychology, San Diego, 1996). *Dissertation Abstracts International, 57,* 6576B.

Johnston, M., & Holzman, P.S. (1979). *Assessing schizophrenic thinking.* San Francisco: Jossey-Bass.

Jorgensen, K., Andersen, T.J., & Dam, H. (2000). The diagnostic efficiency of the Rorschach Depression Index and the Schizophrenia Index: A review. *Assessment, 7,* 259–280.

Kahill, S. (1984). Human figure drawing in adults: An update of the empirical evidence, 1967–1982. *Canadian Psychology, 25,* 269–292.

Klopfer, W.F., & Taulbee, E. (1976). Projective tests. *Annual Review of Psychology, 27,* 543–567.

Kubiszyn, T.W., Meyer, G.J., Finn, S.E., Eyde, L.D., Kay, G.G., Moreland, K., Dies, R., & Eisman, E. (2000). Empirical support for psychological assessment in clinical health care settings. *Professional Psychology: Research and Practice, 31,* 119–130.

Lees-Haley, P.R. (1992). Psychodiagnostic test usage by forensic psychologists. *American Journal of Forensic Psychology, 10,* 25–30.

Leifer, M., Shapiro, J.P., Martone, M.W., & Kassem, L. (1991). Rorschach assessment of psychological functioning in sexually abused girls. *Journal of Personality Assessment, 56,* 14–28.

Lilienfeld, S.O., Wood, J.M., & Garb, H.N. (2000). The scientific status of projective techniques. *Psychological Science in the Public Interest, 1,* 27–66.

Lilienfeld, S.O., Wood, J.M., & Garb, H.N. (2001, May). What's wrong with this picture? *Scientific American, 284,* 80–87.

Lipovsky, J.A., Finch, A.J., & Belter, R.W. (1989). Assessment of depression in adolescents: Objective and projective measures. *Journal of Personality Assessment, 53,* 449–458.

Loevinger, J. (1976). *Ego development: Conceptions and theories.* San Francisco: Jossey-Bass.

Loevinger, J. (1993). Measurement of personality: True or false. *Psychological Inquiry, 4,* 1–16.

Loevinger, J. (1998). *Technical foundations for measuring ego development: The Washington University Sentence Completion Test.* Mahwah, NJ: Erlbaum.

Magnussen, N.G. (1960). Verbal and non-verbal reinforcers in the Rorschach situation. *Journal of Clinical Psychology, 16,* 167–169.

Malik, R. (1992). An exploration of object relations phenomena in borderline personality disorder. *Dissertation Abstracts International, 52*(09B), 4962.

Masling, J. (1957). The effect of warm and cold interaction on the interpretation of a projective protocol. *Journal of Projective Techniques, 21,* 377–383.

Masling, J. (1960). The influence of situational and interpersonal variables in projective testing. *Psychological Bulletin, 57,* 65–85.

Masling, J. (1965). Differential indoctrination of examiners and Rorschach responses. *Journal of Consulting Psychology, 29,* 198–201.

Masling, J. (1966). Role-related behavior of the subject and psychologist and its effect upon psychological data. In D. Levine (Ed.), *Nebraska symposium on motivation* (pp. 67–104). Lincoln: University of Nebraska Press.

Masling, J. (1997). On the nature and utility of projective tests. *Journal of Personality Assessment, 69,* 257–270.

Masling, J., Rabie, L., & Blondheim, S. (1967). Obesity, level of aspiration, and Rorschach and TAT measures of oral dependence. *Journal of Consulting Psychology, 31,* 233–239.

McClelland, D.C., Atkinson, J.W., Clark, R.A., & Lowell, E.L. (1953). *The achievement motive.* New York: Appleton-Century-Crofts.

Meehl, P.E. (1997). Credentialed persons, credentialed knowledge. *Clinical Psychology: Science and Practice, 4,* 91–98.

Meyer, G.J. (1993). The impact of response frequency on the Rorschach constellation indices and on their validity with diagnostic and MMPI-2 criteria. *Journal of Personality Assessment, 60,* 153–180.

Meyer, G.J. (1997a). Assessing reliability: Critical corrections for a critical examination of the Rorschach Comprehensive System. *Psychological Assessment, 9,* 480–489.

Meyer, G.J. (1997b). Thinking clearly about reliability: More critical corrections regarding the Rorschach Comprehensive System. *Psychological Assessment, 9,* 495–498.

Meyer, G.J. (2001). Evidence to correct misperceptions about Rorschach norms. *Clinical Psychology: Science and Practice, 8,* 389–396.

Meyer, G.J., Finn, S.E., Eyde, L.D., Kay, G.G., Moreland, K.L., Dies, R.R., Eisman, E.J., Kubiszyn, T.W., & Reed, G.M. (2001). Psychological testing and psychological assessment: A review of evidence and issues. *American Psychologist, 56,* 128–165.

Meyer, G.J., Finn, S.E., Eyde, L.D., Kaye, G.G., Kubiszyn, T.W., Moreland, K., Eisman, E.J., & Dies, R.R. (1998). *Benefits and costs of psychological assessment in healthcare delivery: Report of the Board of Professional Affairs Psychological Assessment Work Group, Part I.* Washington, DC: American Psychological Association.

Meyer, G.J., & Richardson, C. (2001). *An examination of changes in Form Quality codes in the Rorschach Comprehensive System from 1974 to 1995.* Presented at the Midwinter Meeting of the Society for Personality Assessment, Philadelphia.

Motta, R.W., Little, S.G., & Tobin, M.I. (1993). The use and abuse of human figure drawings. *School Psychology Quarterly, 8,* 162–169.

Naglieri, J.A., McNeish, T.J., & Bardos, A.N. (1991). *Draw-A-Person: Screening Procedure for Emotional Disturbance.* Austin, TX: ProEd.

Naglieri, J.A., & Pfeiffer, S.I. (1992). Performance of disruptive behavior-disordered and normal samples on the Draw-A-Person: Screening Procedure for Emotional Disturbance. *Psychological Assessment, 4,* 156–159.

Nakata, L.M. (1999). Interrater reliability and the Comprehensive System for the Rorschach: Clinical and non-clinical protocols (Doctoral dissertation, Pacific Graduate School of Psychology, 1999). *Dissertation Abstracts International, 60,* 4296B.

Nezworski, M.T., & Wood, J.M. (1995). Narcissism in the Comprehensive System for the Rorschach. *Clinical Psychology: Science and Practice, 2,* 179–199.

Nigg, J.T., Lohr, N.E., Westen, D., Gold, L.J., & Silk, K.R. (1992). Malevolent object representations in borderline personality disorder and major depression. *Journal of Abnormal Psychology, 101,* 61–67.

Oberlander, L.B. (1995). Psycholegal issues in child sexual abuse evaluations: A survey of forensic mental health professionals. *Child Abuse & Neglect, 19,* 475–490.

Ornduff, S.R., Freedenfeld, R.N., Kelsey, R.M., & Critelli, J.W. (1994). Object relations of sexually abused female subjects: A TAT analysis. *Journal of Personality Assessment, 63,* 223–238.

Palmer, L., Farrar, A.R., Valle, M., Ghahary, N., Panella, M., & DeGraw, D. (2000). An investigation of the clinical use of the House-Tree-Person projective drawings in the psychological investigation of child sexual abuse. *Child Maltreatment, 5,* 169–175.

Pinkerman, J.E., Haynes, J.P., & Keiser, T. (1993). Characteristics of psychological practice in juvenile court clinics. *American Journal of Forensic Psychology, 11,* 3–12.

Piotrowski, C. (1996). The status of Exner's Comprehensive System in contemporary research. *Perceptual & Motor Skills, 82,* 1341–1342.

Piotrowski, C., & Keller, J.W. (1989). Use of assessment in mental health clinics and services. *Psychological Reports, 64,* 1298.

Psychological Corporation. (1997). *Wechsler Adult Intelligence Scale, Third Edition. Wechsler Memory Scale, Third Edition, Technical Manual.* San Antonio, TX: Author.

Ritsher, J.B., Slivko-Kolchik, E.B., & Oleichik, I.V. (2001). Assessing depression in Russian psychiatric patients: Validity of MMPI and Rorschach. *Assessment, 8,* 373–389.

Ritzler, B., Erard, R., & Pettigrew, G. (2002). Protecting the integrity of Rorschach expert witnesses: A reply to Grove and Barden (1999) re: the admissibility of testimony under *Daubert/Kumho* analyses. *Psychology, Public Policy, and the Law, 8,* 201–215.

Sells, J.E. (1990/1991). A validity study of the DEPI index: The Rorschach Comprehensive System (Doctoral dissertation, University of Utah, 1990). *Dissertation Abstracts International, 51,* 5590B.

Shaffer, T.W., Erdberg, P., & Haroian, J. (1999). Current nonpatient data for the Rorschach, WAIS-R, and MMPI-2. *Journal of Personality Assessment, 73,* 305–316.

Sharkey, K.J., & Ritzler, B.A. (1985). Comparing diagnostic validity of the TAT and a new picture projection test. *Journal of Personality Assessment, 49,* 406–412.

Silberg, J.L., & Armstrong, J.G. (1992). The Rorschach test for predicting suicide among depressed adolescent inpatients. *Journal of Personality Assessment, 59,* 290–303.

Simkins, L. (1960). Examiner reinforcement and situation variables in a projective testing situation. *Journal of Consulting Psychology, 10,* 107–114.

Simmons, W.L., & Christy, E.G. (1962). Verbal reinforcement of a TAT theme. *Journal of Projective Techniques, 26,* 337–341.

Singer, H.K., & Brabender, V. (1993). The use of the Rorschach to differentiate unipolar and bipolar disorders. *Journal of Personality Assessment, 60,* 333–345.

Solovay, M., Shenton, M., Gasperetti, C., Coleman, M., Daniels, E., Carpenter, J., & Holzman, P. (1986). Scoring manual for the Thought Disorder Index. *Schizophrenia Bulletin, 12,* 483–496.

Spangler, W.D. (1992). Validity of questionnaire and TAT measures of need for achievement: Two meta-analyses. *Psychological Bulletin, 112,* 140–154.

Stricker, G., & Healey, B.J. (1990). Projective assessment of object relations: A review of the empirical literature. *Psychological Assessment, 2,* 219–230.

Thomas, G.V., & Jolley, R.P. (1998). Drawing conclusions: A re-examination of empirical and conceptual bases for psychological evaluations of children from their drawings. *British Journal of Clinical Psychology, 37,* 127–139.

Tobias, S. (1960). Effects of reinforcement of verbal behavior on response changes in a nonreinforced situation. *Dissertation Abstracts, 21,* 964.

Vass, Z. (1998). The inner formal structure of the H-T-P drawings: An exploratory study. *Journal of Clinical Psychology, 54,* 611–619.

Viglione, D.J., Brager, R.C., & Haller, N. (1988). Usefulness of structural Rorschach data in identifying inpatients with depressive symptoms: A preliminary study. *Journal of Personality Assessment, 52,* 524–529.

West, M.M. (1998). Meta-analysis of studies assessing the efficacy of projective techniques in discriminating child sexual abuse. *Child Abuse & Neglect, 22,* 1151–1166.

Westen, D. (1991). Clinical assessment of object relations using the TAT. *Journal of Personality Assessment, 56,* 56–74.

Westen, D., Lohr, N., Silk, K.R., Gold, L., & Kerber, K. (1990). Object relations and social cognition in borderlines, major depressives, and normals: A Thematic Apperception Test analysis. *Psychological Assessment, 2,* 355–364.

Westen, D., Ludolph, P., Block, M.J., Wixom, J., & Wiss, F.C. (1990). Developmental history and object relations in psychiatrically disturbed adolescent girls. *American Journal of Psychiatry, 147,* 1061–1068.

Westen, D., Ludolph, P., Lerner, H., Ruffins, S., & Wiss, C. (1990). Object relations in borderline adolescents. *Journal of the American Academy of Child and Adolescent Psychiatry, 29,* 338–348.

Westen, D., Ludolph, P., Misle, B., Ruffins, S., & Block, J. (1990). Physical and sexual abuse in adolescents with borderline personality disorder. *American Journal of Orthopsychiatry, 60,* 55–66.

Whitehead, W.C. (1985). Clinical decision making on the basis of Rorschach, MMPI, and automated MMPI report data (Doctoral dissertation, University of Texas Southwestern Medical Center at Dallas, 1985). *Dissertation Abstracts International, 46,* 2828.

Wickes, T.A. (1956). Examiner influence in a test situation. *Journal of Consulting Psychology, 20,* 23–36.

Wood, J.M., Garb, H.N., Lilienfeld, S.O., & Nezworski, M.T. (2002). Clinical assessment. *Annual Review of Psychology, 53,* 519–543.

Wood, J.M., Lilienfeld, S.O., Garb, H.N., & Nezworski, M.T. (2000). The Rorschach test in clinical diagnosis: A critical review, with a backward look at Garfield (1947). *Journal of Clinical Psychology, 56,* 395–430.

Wood, J.M., Lilienfeld, S.O., Nezworski, M.T., & Garb, H.N. (2001). Coming to grips with negative evidence for the Comprehensive System for the Rorschach: A comment on Gacono, Loving, and Bodholdt; Ganellen; and Bornstein. *Journal of Personality Assessment, 77,* 48–70.

Wood, J.M., Nezworski, M.T., Garb, H.N., & Lilienfeld, S.O. (2001a). Problems with the norms of the Comprehensive System for the Rorschach: Methodological and conceptual considerations. *Clinical Psychology: Science and Practice, 8,* 397–402.

Wood, J.M., Nezworski, M.T., Garb, H.N., & Lilienfeld, S.O. (2001b). The misperception of psychopathology: Problems with the norms of the Comprehensive System for the Rorschach. *Clinical Psychology: Science and Practice, 8,* 350–373.

Wood, J.M., Nezworski, M.T., Lilienfeld, S.O., & Garb, H.N. (2003). *What's wrong with the Rorschach? Science confronts the controversial inkblot test.* San Francisco: Jossey-Bass.

Wood, J.M., Nezworski, M.T., & Stejskal, W.J. (1996a). The Comprehensive System for the Rorschach: A critical examination. *Psychological Science, 7,* 3–10.

Wood, J.M., Nezworski, M.T., & Stejskal, W.J. (1996b). Thinking critically about the Comprehensive System for the Rorschach: A reply to Exner. *Psychological Science, 7,* 14–17.

Wood, J.M., Nezworski, M.T., & Stejskal, W.J. (1997). The reliability of the Comprehensive System for the Rorschach: A comment on Meyer (1997). *Psychological Assessment, 9,* 490–494.

Zalewski, C., & Archer, R.P. (1991). Assessment of borderline personality disorder: A review of MMPI and Rorschach findings. *Journal of Nervous and Mental Disease, 179,* 338–345.

Zimmerman, D.P., & Dillard, J. (1994). The Rorschach assessment of sexually abused children in residential treatment: A research note. *Residential Treatment for Children & Youth, 12,* 59–72.

CHAPTER 24

Behavioral Assessment and the *DSM* System

ROSEMERY O. NELSON-GRAY AND JAMES F. PAULSON

The purpose of this chapter is to discuss the relationship between behavioral assessment and the *Diagnostic and Statistical Manual of Mental Disorders (DSM)* diagnostic system. Behavioral assessment and psychiatric diagnosis developed on two parallel tracks. The benefits and detriments of diagnosis in general and the *DSM* system in particular (American Psychiatric Association, 1952, 1968, 1980, 1987, 1994, 2000) have been discussed at length, both in general and from a behavioral perspective. Alternative and more behaviorally based classification systems have been proposed. It is nonetheless the thesis of this chapter that the recent versions of the *DSM,* currently *DSM-IV-Text Revision* (American Psychiatric Association, 2000), can be useful to behavioral assessors. Behavioral assessment, however, also provides a necessary and valuable addition to diagnosis.

HISTORY OF TWO PARALLEL TRACKS: BEHAVIORAL ASSESSMENT AND DIAGNOSIS

Behavioral assessment and diagnosis developed on two parallel and very separate tracks. Behavioral assessment began (e.g., Kanfer & Saslow, 1969) as an adjunct to the successful and rapidly burgeoning techniques of behavior therapy. In its early years, behavior therapy was seen within clinical psychology as radical or revolutionary, requiring its own form of assessment. Conversely, diagnosis has a long history and is integral to the medical model, with the *DSM-I* (American Psychiatric Association, 1952) developed to diagnose not physical disorders, but their counterpart of medical disorders.

A Brief History of Behavioral Assessment

Behavioral assessment began informally, as a means of quantifying outcome measures while behavior therapy or behavior modification initially demonstrated its efficacy. The various series of case studies that demonstrated the effectiveness of specific behavior therapy techniques included outcome measures, showing changes in particular target behaviors (e.g., Eysenck, 1976; Ullmann & Krasner, 1965). Even when the case study dealt with a classic diagnosable disorder—for example, depression—behavior therapists were content with selecting a few salient target behaviors to demonstrate improvements that resulted from behavioral interventions (e.g., very slow speech rate in a chronically depressed man; Robinson & Lewinsohn, 1973). Frequently, data collection strategies were borrowed from animal research related to learning theory or from observational measures, initially employed by developmental psychologists in the 1920s and 1930s (e.g., Arrington, 1939). In these early case studies utilizing behavior therapy, no mention was made of formal diagnosis or of changes in covarying behaviors that comprise the diagnostic syndrome.

The development of behavioral assessment was accelerated with a few seminal publications in the 1960s (e.g., Ferster, 1965; Goldfried & Pomeranz, 1968; Kanfer & Saslow, 1969). Behavioral assessment became a formal enterprise in the late 1970s with the publication of various books devoted to behavioral assessment approaches and techniques (e.g., Ciminero, Calhoun, & Adams, 1977; Cone & Hawkins, 1977; Hersen & Bellack, 1976), and with the launching of two journals devoted to behavioral assessment (i.e., *Behavioral Assessment,* published by Pergamon under the auspices of the Association for the Advancement of Behavior Therapy, and the *Journal of Behavioral Assessment,* published by Plenum). Formally, "the goal of behavioral assessment is to identify meaningful response units and their controlling variables for the purposes of understanding and of altering behavior" (Nelson & Hayes, 1979, p. 1).

The central approach used in behavioral assessment was the functional analysis, in which the environmental events controlling the target behavior are identified in behavioral assessment and are subsequently modified in treatment (Goldfried & Pomeranz, 1968). In Ferster's words: "Such a functional analysis of behavior has the advantage that it specified the causes of behavior in the form of explicit environmental events that can be objectively identified and that are potentially manipulable" (Ferster, 1965, p. 11). The functional analysis was extended to include organismic variables, especially physiological variables and past learning history, by Goldfried and Sprafkin (1976). The links between behavioral assessment and treatment were expanded beyond the functional analysis to include assessment of keystone responses and use of diagnoses (Nelson, 1988). The history of behavioral assessment and the differences between behavioral and traditional assessment are elaborated by Ollendick, Blier, & Greene (chapter 2).

The rise and fall of behavioral assessment as a freestanding enterprise has been chronicled by Cone (1992) and by Taylor (1999). In reality, behavioral assessment has simply become more mainstream, as has behavior therapy (and cognitive-behavioral therapy) (Nelson-Gray, Gaynor, & Korotitsch, 1997). To illustrate, many cognitive-behavioral therapy techniques appear on the list of empirically validated therapies compiled by Division 12 of the American Psychological Association (Chambless et al., 1996; Chambless et al., 1998; Chambless & Ollendick, 2001). Behavioral outcome measures are required to demonstrate the efficacy of these ther-

apies. As a further sign of the times, and in an ironic turn of fate, the list of empirically validated therapies is disorder- or diagnosis-based. The behavioral approach to assessment and treatment that originally ignored or eschewed diagnosis now finds itself claiming to be effective in treating various diagnosis-based disorders.

A Brief History of Diagnosis and the *DSM* System

The Greek origins of "diagnosis" are "dia" (through) and "gnosis" (knowledge or investigation); to know something thoroughly includes distinguishing it from other things (Matarazzo, 1983). The diagnostic classification of mental and/or behavioral disorders has had a long history (Matarazzo, 1983; Singerman, 1981) that is notably distinct from the history of behavioral assessment and behavior therapy. Some of the outstanding figures in the history of diagnosis are: Hippocrates, who in the fifth century B.C., created one of the first recorded categorization of mental illnesses; Phillipe Pinel, who in the nineteenth century, devised a classification system for the psychotic states that he observed at La Bicetre Hospital in Paris; Emil Kraepelin, who at the turn of the twentieth century divided mental illnesses into three categories of organic psychoses, endogenous psychoses (including dementia praecox and manic depressive psychosis), and deviations of personality and reactive states; William Menninger, whose work in World War II was incorporated by the American Psychiatric Association into *DSM-I* (1952) and *DSM-II* (1968); J. Feighner, who with Eli Robins at Washington University, developed the Feighner diagnostic criteria for several mental illnesses (Feighner et al., 1972); Robert Spitzer, Jean Endicott, and, again, Eli Robins, who modified the Feighner criteria into the Research Diagnostic Criteria (1978); again, Robert Spitzer, who chaired the American Psychiatric Association's task force that produced *DSM-III* in 1980 and *DSM-III-Revised* in 1987; Allen Frances, who chaired the American Psychiatric Association's Task Force that produced *DSM-IV* in 1994; and Michael First who edited the Text Revision of *DSM-IV* in 2000.

The first two editions of the *DSM* were widely criticized. Very major changes occurred in the *DSM* with the development and publication of *DSM-III,* which set traditions that have been incorporated into *DSM-III-R* and *DSM-IV.* The history of the development of *DSM-III* is detailed in the introduction to the *DSM-III,* as well as in summaries by Kazdin (1983); Matarazzo (1983); Spitzer, Endicott, and Robins (1978); and Taylor (1983). Some of the breaks with past *DSM* tradition in the *DSM-III* include the following. First are the operational criteria, both inclusive and exclusive, provided for each diagnostic category (Kazdin, 1983; Klerman, 1984;

Millon, 1983; Spitzer et al., 1978). These operational criteria were modeled after the Feighner Criteria devised by the Washington University group (Feighner et al., 1972) and the Research Diagnostic Criteria (Spitzer et al., 1978) that had been developed for a limited number of diagnostic categories primarily for research purposes. Second, *DSM-III* was developed by an open process (Spitzer et al., 1978) with many individuals and groups involved in its evolution. Even though the process of development was not always smooth, a more or less acceptable consensus emerged. Third, *DSM-III* was at least somewhat empirically based in that there were field trials that permitted input into *DSM-III* by online clinicians (Klerman, 1984; Spitzer et al., 1978). The final field trial involved hundreds of clinicians across the country and was sponsored by the National Institute of Mental Health. Fourth, the *DSM-III* had demonstrated improved reliability over its predecessors (Spitzer et al., 1978). Diagnostic reliability was evaluated in two phases using kappa, which is a conservative measure that corrects for chance agreement. Overall kappa reliability for Axis I for adults was .68 and .72 in the two phases, respectively, and for children it was .68 and .52 (APA, 1980). Matarazzo (1983) notes that these reliability figures are even more impressive because no standardized method, such as a structured interview, was used to elicit patient information. Fifth, to help portray the complexity of each client, *DSM-III* employed a multiaxial format that has been maintained in subsequent versions (Kazdin, 1983; Klerman, 1984; Millon, 1983; Spitzer et al., 1978). As is now familiar, one or more clinical disorders (or other conditions that may be the focus of clinical attention) are coded on Axis I; personality disorders and mental retardation are coded on Axis II; general medical conditions are coded on Axis III; psychosocial and environmental problems are indicated on Axis IV; and global assessment of functioning is rated on Axis V. Sixth, *DSM-III* is generally atheoretical (Kazdin, 1983), with a focus on presenting symptoms rather than presumed etiology. Seventh, *DSM-III* provides a comprehensive description of individual disorders (Kazdin, 1983; Millon, 1983). Several characteristics of a disorder are described, including its essential and correlated features, age of onset, course, impairment, complications, predisposing factors, prevalence, sex ratio, familial patterns, and criteria for differential diagnosis.

Of chief import here is that the *DSM* system developed independently of behavioral assessment. The *DSM* system is based on a medical model of mental illness that had been eschewed by early behaviorists because of its assumption that behavior has underlying or inner causes, as opposed to the behavioral assumption that behavior has largely environmental causes (Ullmann & Krasner, 1965).

GENERAL BENEFITS AND CRITICISMS OF DIAGNOSIS

The use of diagnoses has become increasingly more pervasive, even among behavioral clinicians, because of some advantages of diagnosis, especially in facilitating communication among professionals. Nonetheless, criticisms remain of diagnosis in general (e.g., the validity of a categorical distinction between normalcy and psychopathology) and of the *DSM* in particular (e.g., the necessity and validity of diagnosing one individual with several comorbid disorders).

General Benefits of Diagnosis

Historically, it may have been considered heretical for behaviorally oriented psychologists to extol the merits of diagnosis. This view, however, is more mainstream today, even among behaviorists. One major advantage of a diagnostic or classification system, organizing data into precise and meaningful concepts, is that it is absolutely necessary for the development of a clinical science (Adams & Haber, 1984). A diagnostic or classification system enhances communication among scientists because it provides labels and precise definitions for the commonalities observed in clinical practice and research: commonalities in behavior or symptoms, etiology, prognosis, and responses to particular types of treatment. Classification systems enhance ease of contributing to the research literature. Data can be compiled and hypotheses generated about phenomena from one generation of scientist-practitioners to the next. The alternative—elaborate individual case descriptions—would be unworkably cumbersome. It is hard to even imagine setting up a database for a clinical science that lacked the organization of a diagnostic system. Relatedly, professionals can more easily access a research literature related to a particular client's presenting problems when the literature is categorized. It would be a near-impossible task to obtain information from a research literature that was not based on shorthand terms, recognizing the commonalities among clients.

Other communication functions are greatly simplified by the use of a widely agreed upon classification system. One benefit is in the process of making referrals from one professional to the next. Simply stating the diagnostic labels assigned to a client facilitates communication between the referring source and recipient and provides a useful shorthand description of the client. Classification systems also assist in record-keeping and statistical compilations, such as epidemiological records or tallies of the types of clients served by different hospitals or agencies. Diagnosis further facilitates communication between service providers and third-party payers of those services (Miller, Bergstrom, Cross, & Grube, 1981). The number of preauthorized sessions may differ greatly depending on the diagnosis of the client and the severity and chronicity of difficulties associated with that diagnosis.

A final and recent advantage of diagnosis is its utility in indexing empirically validated treatments, sometimes called empirically substantiated treatments (Chambless et al., 1996; Chambless et al., 1998; Chambless & Ollendick, 2001). As noted earlier, a task force within Division 12 of the American Psychological Association has identified criteria and specific treatments that meet these criteria at two levels of empirical validation: well-established treatments and probably efficacious treatments. In both cases, treatments are listed by disorder. More is written later in this chapter about the essential role of behavioral assessment in supplementing this list; but in the interim, a diagnosis provides the index to access entries within the list of empirically validated treatments.

General Disadvantages of Diagnosis

Despite the numerous advantages of diagnosis and the obvious improvements in *DSM-III* and its successive editions (compared with *DSM-I* and *II*), diagnosis in general and the *DSM* system in particular has received abundant criticism. First, the iatrogenic effects of labeling have been widely recognized (Hobbs, 1975; Stuart, 1970; Szasz, 1960). Among these iatrogenic effects are the social stigma of being labeled "mentally ill," the passivity of waiting to be cured of one's "mental illness," the pessimistic belief that some or most mental disorders cannot be cured, and the self-fulfilling prophesy resulting in the exaggeration of symptoms consistent with one's diagnosis.

A second concern about the *DSM* system is that it endorses, at least implicitly, a disease model of mental and behavioral disorders. In survey results reported by Smith and Kraft (1983), nearly three-fourths of the 556 respondents (members of Division 29 of the American Psychological Association) agreed that most conditions that the *DSM-III* labels as mental disorders can be best described as nonmedical problems in living. Szasz (1960) prefers a sociobehavioral classification of behavioral disturbances rather than a medical classification. McLemore and Benjamin (1979) believe that the interpersonal basis of diagnosis should be more explicitly recognized.

A third concern is the validity of the categorical basis of classification used in the *DSM*. One general issue with assessing validity is that there is no gold standard by which the

"real diagnosis" of an individual can be determined. Nonetheless, the *DSM* utilizes a categorical basis of classification, with an assumption that a diagnosis is either applicable or not to a particular person. The categorical basis of diagnosis raises numerous issues, detailed by Widiger (1997). One issue is whether there exists a categorical distinction between normalcy and psychopathology. According to Widiger (1997), a mental disorder is believed to differ from normalcy on two grounds: *dyscontrol* or the concept that the behavior of a person with a mental disorder is not within his or her own control; and *impairment*, the concept that a mental disorder causes clinically significant impairment in social, occupational, or other important areas of functioning. Both of these ideas of dyscontrol and impairment in functioning suggest continua rather than categories. With dyscontrol, individuals have neither full volitional control over all behavior nor absolutely no control over their behavior. Similarly, the concept of clinically significant impairment is subjective at best. *DSM-IV* does not attempt to define clinically significant impairment, and simply notes that this "is an inherently difficult clinical judgment" (APA, 1994, p. 7). The blurring between a mental disorder and daily problems in living was noted by Frances, First, and Pincus (1995, p. 15): "The ever-increasing number of new categories meant to describe the less impaired outpatient population raises the question of where psychopathology ends and the wear and tear of everyday life begins." The basic idea here is that it is very difficult to draw a categorical distinction between normalcy and psychopathology or mental disorders. We have all seen clients seeking treatment because of clinically significant distress or impairment, who are also stuck in well-worn paths of behaving that are difficult to change, but who do not meet the criteria for any specific diagnostic category (e.g., separating couples with financial or child custody issues and great emotional distress involving anger, revenge, blaming, and sadness). A diagnosis is neither applicable (except perhaps a V-code, Partner Relational Problem, that is not indicative of a mental disorder) nor helpful in assessing and treating such individuals, despite their difficulty in changing behavioral habits and their daily distress.

A second categorical blurring noted by Widiger (1997) is the boundary between physical and mental disorders—for example, in pain disorders, sexual disorders, and sleep disorders. Of greater interest here is Widiger's third categorical difficulty: the failure of the categorical view to capture the psychopathology of those given multiple diagnostic labels. Individuals are frequently given multiple diagnostic labels, with the assumption that the various disorders are comorbid. Comorbidity is very high, with 56% and 60% in community samples (Kessler et al., 1994; and Robins, Locke, & Regier, 1991, respectively) and similar rates in clinical samples—for example, 65% of patients with dysthymia and 59% of patients with major depression had at least one comorbid Axis I disorder (Sanderson, Beck, & Beck, 1990). In the case of individuals with multiple diagnostic labels, "a fundamental question is whether this apparent comorbidity represents the co-occurrence of multiple mental disorders or the presence of one disorder that is being given multiple diagnoses" (Widiger, 1997, p. 3). We are reminded of a case in our clinic of a client who was difficult to diagnose and very resistant to completing the SCID semistructured diagnostic interview. The client said: "Why are you asking me all these questions? I don't belong in any pigeonhole. Don't you know that I am just plain crazy?" Rampant comorbidity or the use of multiple diagnoses may exist because the *DSM* system does not have sufficient validity.

Similarly, a great many individuals are diagnosed with a mental disorder NOS (not otherwise specified). According to Widiger (1997), whenever NOS is utilized within a research study, it is often the most frequent diagnosis—for example, in cases of mood disorders (Angst, 1992) or personality disorders (Morey, 1992). This overreliance on the NOS specifier again may reflect poorly on the validity of the current *DSM* system, with the existing diagnostic categories an inadequate fit with client reality.

Finally, the validity of the categorical basis of the diagnostic system is brought into question by the several disorders that have been created to fill a gap between two other disorders, such as schizoaffective disorder. The lack of neatness of the diagnostic categories is further seen in the overlap between social phobia generalized and avoidant personality disorder or the classification of hypochondrias as a somatoform disorder instead of a specific phobia of illness.

One alternative view is dimensional, with individuals located on a continuum of a descriptive variable, with some locations indicating more dysfunction than other locations (Kendell, 1975). Widiger (1992) has explicitly proposed that personality disorders are more validly assessed from a dimensional rather than a categorical framework. In fact, the current *DSM-IV-TR* contains several proposed dimensional systems for personality disorders (pp. 689–690). This dimensional viewpoint also has been suggested for other disorders, such as schizophrenic spectrum disorder (described by Rhee, Feignon, Bar, Hadeishi, & Waldman, 2001), autism spectrum disorder, and depressive spectrum disorder. Indeed, Waller and Meehl (1998) have proposed a statistical methodology—multivariate taxometric procedures—to distinguish between types and continua, the practical ramifications of which remain to be seen.

GENERAL IMPROVEMENTS IN *DSM-IV* AND REMAINING CRITICISMS

Successive editions of the *DSM* have been greeted with increasing approval. *DSM-III* provided a marked and positive turning point among the *DSM* editions. The positive features of *DSM-III* have been retained and enhanced in *DSM-IV* and *DSM-IV-TR*. Nonetheless, there remain criticisms of the *DSM-IV*, along with suggestions to improve subsequent editions of the *DSM*.

Improvements in *DSM-IV*

While the completion and publication of *DSM-IV* in 1994 does not skirt the core criticisms of diagnosis, it does provide some needed improvements while retaining assets similar to the previous two *DSM* editions. The *DSM-IV-Text Revision* (2000) was intended to clarify and update the text within *DSM-IV*. Similar to *DSM-III* and *DSM-III-R*, *DSM-IV* was developed through an open process that utilized input from even more psychiatrists, psychologists, social workers, and other mental health professionals (more than 1,500 professionals).

The *DSM-IV* revision process involved specific work groups for different disorder classes that were designated to conduct extensive literature reviews, reanalyze numerous data sets, and evaluate the results of field trials of proposed *DSM-IV* diagnostic criteria (Frances, Pincus, Widiger, Davis, & First, 1990). These field trials involved over 6,000 subjects. With evidence from these sources guiding changes, revisions in *DSM-IV*, while still decided by committee, were more firmly based on a foundation of empiricism.

Structurally, the *DSM-IV* is similar to *DSM-III-R* in that it utilizes operational criteria for each diagnostic category. For most disorders, the defining criteria in *DSM-IV* are greater than required to generate a diagnosis. This polythetic approach to classification permits more flexibility for clinicians in making diagnoses based on the often heterogeneous behavior of individuals.

Further assets of the *DSM-IV* that are retained from *DSM-III-R* include: an atheoretical approach to diagnosis, avoiding any assumptions of etiology underlying listed disorders, and a multiaxial system of classifying the patient's behavior and status on assessment. The multiaxial system introduced in *DSM-III* and utilized in *DSM-IV* allows for the description of a patient's presenting behavior and also permits the classification of patient behavior on several contextual dimensions that may impact his or her current functioning. These axes are thought to be somewhat independent of each other and were designed to describe the complexity of the individual

(Kazdin, 1983; Millon, 1983). With respect to behavioral assessment, these axes permit a more thoroughly textured description of the individual's presentation as well as the biological and environmental conditions that may impact or be a product of the individual's functioning.

From the formation of work groups, the *DSM-IV* has been marked by substantially greater diversity. Many more non-psychiatrist mental health professionals joined work groups along with more women and people from varied ethnic backgrounds (Nathan, 1994). Along with these changes in the professionals behind *DSM-IV*, the manual underwent changes designed to increase its validity when used with diverse populations. Some of these changes included discussion of the presentation of disorders in various cultures, a description of specific culture-bound syndromes (Appendix I), and an outline addressing culturally sensitive diagnostic formulation (also in Appendix I, *DSM-IV-TR*, 2000).

In order to help standardize assessment with the *DSM-IV*, a pair of structured interviews were introduced for Axis I and Axis II psychopathology. The Structured Clinical Interview for *DSM-IV* (SCID) is in two parts: SCID I for Axis I and SCID II for Axis II (Spitzer, Williams, Gibbon, & First, 1990). These structured interviews provide detailed instructions for interviewers and have recently been developed into a computerized version that can be administered and scored with less effort and greater consistency. Also, the SCID has been divided into two versions, a research version and a clinical version (First, Spitzer, Gibbon, & Williams, 1997). Useful information about the SCID, including order information, is available in Segal, Corcoran, and Coughlin (2002).

Remaining Criticisms of *DSM-IV*

Although the *DSM-IV* is characterized by several improvements over previous editions, a number of features of the manual remain open to criticism. Despite the substantive empirical basis bolstering revisions appearing in the *DSM-IV*, the research itself was conducted largely within a *DSM* framework (Clark, Watson, & Reynolds, 1995). Alternative approaches or conceptualization to diagnosis were not considered, with the exception being a dimensional perspective for personality disorders (e.g., Livesley, 1991).

Another limitation of DSM-IV is the assumption that diagnoses are best decided based almost exclusively upon presenting symptomatology (Acierno, Hersen, & Van Hasselt, 1997). In this respect, *DSM-IV* and its atheoretical approach to diagnosis are insensitive to environmental, biological, social, cultural, and other factors that may contribute to treatment selection and outcome. Practitioners from various theoretical perspectives must indeed, however, consider these other factors in making treatment choices. The specific role of behavioral assessment in this regard is described in subsequent sections of this chapter. In fact, a sixth axis (in addition to the five currently in the *DSM*) has been suggested. Schact and Nathan (1977) suggested a "response to treatment" axis, on which could be coded both the treatment offered to the patient and his or her response to it. Karasu and Skodol (1980) suggested "psychodynamic evaluation" as a sixth axis suggesting the psychotherapeutic approach by which the patient is likely to derive benefits and the problems that he or she is likely to encounter with a particular therapeutic venture. Another alternative to the current atheoretical basis of the *DSM* is an etiologically based classification, such as that proposed by Andreasen and Carpenter (1993).

Although the operational diagnostic criteria of *DSM-IV* can simplify diagnosis by providing the diagnostician with a list of specific criteria, it has been argued that the details of diagnostic criteria in *DSM-IV* may be more arbitrary and pseudo-specific than many users of the manual assume (Taylor, 1983). Diagnosticians may find that criteria appear to be specific but may require inference, subjective judgment, and decision making that go beyond the scope of the available evidence.

This concern is compounded by the lack of prescribed methods of assessing *DSM-IV* disorders from individual presentations. Although a practitioner may elect to use a structured interview such as the SCID to assess for a *DSM-IV* disorder, there is neither a directive nor recommendation in the *DSM-IV* to use such a tool for assessment. Without a standard assessment, as was used in its field trials, use of *DSM-IV* can be expected to be variable at best, with some individuals with inadequate training using informal methods to make diagnoses that are then indistinguishable from those made by individuals using the most structured and systematic assessment methods.

Related to this issue is a concern of the reliability of the *DSM-IV* when used in settings not employing the quality control standards in use during field trials and other studies of *DSM-IV*. Although structured instruments such as the SCID have found interrater and internal consistency coefficients often in the high .90s (Maffei et al., 1997), the use of *DSM-IV* in practice and under less optimal conditions can be expected to be much less reliable. This trend toward less reliability was observed in the *DSM-III* field trials, in which individuals interviewed jointly were diagnosed much more reliably than those interviewed separately (Spitzer, Forman, & Nee, 1979).

Even with the increased attention to diversity in the development of *DSM-IV*, there remain questions about its possible gender biases (Hartung & Widiger, 1998). For example, Kaplan (1983) has argued that the *DSM* system uses masculine-based assumptions to determine healthy behaviors and that the diagnoses of particular personality disorders are prejudicial against women (i.e., histrionic and borderline personality disorders).

Beyond general criticisms of *DSM-IV*, there have been concerns raised about the validity of *DSM-IV* classifications in specific subgroups. These include validity of *DSM-IV* in child and adolescent populations (e.g., Achenbach & McConaughy, 1996; Cantwell, 1996) as well as concerns over *DSM-IV*'s classification of personality disorders (e.g., Nelson-Gray & Farmer, 1999). There has also been criticism regarding specificity of diagnoses for both of these subgroups, particularly in light of the high degree of statistical overlap of several childhood disorder classes and personality disorder groupings.

Curiously, the major strength of the *DSM-IV*'s revision—the open process that permitted input from a diverse group of professionals—is also a source of enduring criticism. Because the *DSM-IV* was revised by a group of professionals working in a committee, we are left with a manual for which the "truth" of diagnostic categories and criteria was decided through a political process (Schacht, 1985).

ALTERNATIVE AND BEHAVIORALLY BASED CLASSIFICATION SYSTEMS

Given the long history of criticism of the *DSM* system, including *DSM-IV*, from professionals of various theoretical orientations (including behavior therapists), it is not surprising that alternative and behaviorally based classification systems have been proposed. An initial and now-classic attempt at classification from a behavioral perspective was proposed by Kanfer and Saslow (1969). "Behavioral diagnosis," to use their term, was based on the functional analysis, described earlier in this chapter in the section on the history of behavioral assessment. Succinctly, in a functional analysis, the historical and current environmental variables that are controlling the target behavior are identified in assessment and are modified in treatment. If the controlling variables have truly been identified, then of necessity the target behavior will change as a result of the modification of these controlling variables in treatment. To give the flavor of Kanfer and Saslow's behavioral diagnostic system, here are the main categories to be assessed, as well as some of the prototypical subcategories: (a) initial analysis of the problem situation, including behavioral excesses, behavioral deficits, and behavioral assets; (b) clarification of problem situation, especially any impairment or consequences related to the problem behavior, as well as to its anticipated improvement; (c) motivational analysis, including positive reinforcers, social re-

inforcers, and aversive stimuli; (d) developmental analysis, including biological, sociological, and behavioral changes; (e) analysis of self-control, including situational strengths and weaknesses in self-control; (f) analysis of social relationships; and (g) analysis of the social-cultural-physical environment.

Another classic behaviorally based classification system was proposed by Bandura (1968), also in the context of the functional analysis being the primary tool of behavioral assessment. The essential components of Bandura's system can be summarized as follows: (a) difficulties in the stimulus control of behavior, including defective stimulus control and inappropriate stimulus control; (b) aversive self-reinforcing systems, related to overly high standards of self-reinforcement; (c) deficient behavioral repertoires; (d) aversive behavioral repertoires; and (e) difficulties with incentive systems or reinforcers, including defective or inappropriate incentive systems in individuals, and absence of or inappropriate incentives in the environment.

Another "behavioral diagnostic system" proposed by Tryon (1999) consists of positive and negative behaviors and their consequences that either increase or decrease or maintain these behaviors. According to Tryon, the advantages of his classification system are that: "(a) it is theoretically consistent with behavior therapy, (b) it is etiologically based in that the taxonomy concerns conditions found sufficient to increase and decrease behavior, and (c) behavioral diagnosis leads directly to intervention" (Tryon, 1999, p. 4).

Another functional system, but one based on dimensions rather than categories, has been proposed by Hayes, Wilson, Gifford, Follette, & Strosahl (1996). The main dimension discussed in this article is experiential avoidance that characterizes such disorders as substance abuse, obsessive-compulsive disorder, panic disorder with agoraphobia, and borderline personality disorder. Other functional dimensions that are mentioned, but not elaborated on, in this article are poor rule generation, inappropriate rule following, or socially impoverished repertoires.

A different type of behaviorally based classification system was proposed by Adams, Doster, and Calhoun (1977). Their classification system focused on the classification of responses per se. From their viewpoint, their system that categorized responses differed from the *DSM* system that categorized people. Also, their system differed from other behaviorally based classification systems in its focus on responses per se, rather than on the environmental, historical, and/or organismic variables controlling those responses. In their view, their system is theory-free and based on the assumption that the distinction between normal and abnormal behavior is arbitrary. The main response categories in the Psychological Response Classification System are Motor, Perceptual, Biological, Cognitive, Emotional, and Social. The authors suggest that this response classification system should be accompanied by similar classification systems for stimulus events and for consequences, and that appropriate methods of measurement need to be developed for their classified responses.

Obviously, none of these behaviorally based classification systems became accepted in a mainstream fashion. Nonetheless, behavior therapists and other clinicians maintained their criticisms of the *DSM* system, including its medical model implications. Therefore, the American Psychological Association considered the development of a "descriptive behavioral classification" that could serve as an alternative to *DSM-III*. The project was eventually judged to be infeasible (Horai, 1981).

However, a more limited project directed at the behavioral classification of children's disorders was instead initiated. Achenbach's system is characterized by an empirically based paradigm that uses standardized procedures to assess problems reported by different informants (namely, the Child Behavior Check List which has self-report, parent-report, and teacher-report versions for children in different age groups, e.g., Achenbach, 1995; Edelbrock & Achenbach, 1984). This empirically based approach uses multivariate analyses to derive taxonomic constructs comprising syndromes that are robust across samples and assessment procedures. The taxonomic constructs are operationally defined via scales that are normed in relation to participants' characteristics and sources of data. New cases can be evaluated via the same assessment procedures used to derive and operationalize the constructs. Achenbach proposes this empirically based approach as an alternative to the *DSM*.

In conclusion, despite these noble early and recent attempts at more behaviorally or empirically based approaches to classification, the *DSM,* currently, *DSM-IV,* remains the "only game in town." As reviewed earlier in this chapter, despite the continued concerns generated by the *DSM* taxonomic system, having a common taxonomic system across scientist-practitioners presents numerous advantages, namely, forming a common basis for a clinical science and facilitating communication among professionals.

RELATIONSHIP BETWEEN *DSM-IV* AND BEHAVIORAL ASSESSMENT

Despite theoretical differences between behavioral clinicians and proponents of the medical model, the *DSM* has become more acceptable, as well as more useful, to behavior therapists over the years. Despite its beginnings as a revolutionary and radical new therapeutic approach, currently, behavior therapy is considered to be a mainstream approach to psychological problems (Nelson-Gray et al., 1997). Not only do many cognitive-behavioral therapy techniques appear on the list of empirically validated therapies put together by Division 12 of the American Psychological Association (Chambless et al., 1996; Chambless et al., 1998; Chambless & Ollendick, 2001), but also behavioral outcome measures are required to demonstrate the efficacy of these therapies. Not only has behavior therapy become more widely accepted by scientist-practitioners of various theoretical persuasions, but behavior therapists have also become more tolerant of at least some mainstream assessment and therapy practices, including the use of *DSM* diagnosis, with the implicit proviso that the practices have an empirical basis.

The Utility of a *DSM* Diagnosis Per Se

As mainstream scientist-practitioners, behavior therapists have much to gain by utilizing *DSM* diagnoses. Basically, communication functions are greatly simplified by the use of an agreed-upon classification system. As noted earlier, one benefit of a widely accepted classification system is in the process of making referrals from one professional to the next. Simply stating the diagnostic labels assigned to a client facilitates communication between the referring source and recipient and provides a useful shorthand description of the client. Classification systems also assist in record-keeping and statistical compilations, such as epidemiological records or tallies of the types of clients served by different hospitals or agencies. Diagnosis further facilitates communication between service providers and third-party payers of those services (Miller et al., 1981). A final and recent advantage of diagnosis is its utility in indexing empirically validated treatments, sometimes called empirically substantiated treatments (Chambless et al., 1996; Chambless et al., 1998; Chambless & Ollendick, 2001). More is said later in this chapter about the essential role of behavioral assessment in supplementing this list; but in the interim, a diagnosis provides the index to access entries within the list of empirically validated treatments.

The Necessary and Useful Addition of Behavioral Assessment to Diagnosis

Historically, three goals have been stated for behavioral assessment: (a) to identify target behaviors or treatment goals; (b) to select a treatment strategy; and (c) to evaluate the effectiveness of the treatment strategy (Nelson & Hayes, 1986). Despite the long history of behavioral therapists and assessors eschewing diagnosis, the *DSM-IV* marks the evolution of a number of positive features that help accomplish the goals of behavioral assessment. Nonetheless, various behavioral assessment strategies are also necessary to accomplish these three goals.

The addition of behavioral assessment to the use of diagnosis is necessary because of theoretical differences between the two systems. The *DSM* is a nomothetic system, classifying groups of similar individuals, whereas behavioral assessment and therapy is idiographic, fulfilling the three goals of behavioral assessment for each individual client. The *DSM* is a structural or topographic system, describing how individuals behave—that is, what is the form or topography of the behavior—whereas behavioral assessment and therapy are functional, emphasizing why people behave the way they do. The *DSM* uses a personologist approach, assuming that the causes of behavior lie largely within the individual, whereas behavioral assessment and therapy uses a more contextual or situational approach, assuming the causes of behavior also lie within the environment, both the past learning experiences of the individual as well as the present environment.

A diagnostic approach focuses on the individual, whereas behavioral assessment is more systemic because the environment is broadly conceived to include the individual's various systems (e.g., family and home environment, work or school environment, community, and culture). Also, a diagnostic approach focuses on the individual's weaknesses or psychopathology, whereas a behavioral assessment approach also assesses the individual's strengths and assets.

GOALS OF BEHAVIORAL ASSESSMENT

The following section describes the necessary use of behavioral assessment, along with benefits of diagnosis, to accomplish the three goals of behavioral assessment.

Selection of Target Behaviors or Treatment Goals

Historically, an early step in a program of behavior assessment is to identify a class of target behaviors on which the searchlight of assessment can be focused (Hawkins, 1986). A more contemporary term for target behaviors is treatment goals. Once treatment goals have been selected, further steps can be taken to provide a better-textured picture of the individual's problem behaviors. The *DSM-IV*, while avoiding behavioral language of target behaviors, specifies a class of covarying behaviors in the operational criteria of each diagnosis (Nelson & Barlow, 1981). When the clinician observes a criterion that, in part, characterizes a disorder, he or she is provided with a ready-made list of likely correlated behaviors that can be targeted and observed in greater detail. For example, if a person complains of depressed mood and insomnia, the behavioral assessor should inquire about all nine symptoms or behaviors that comprise a major depressive episode (APA,1994). Thus, when an individual reports some of the responses within a diagnostic category, there is sufficient probability of his or her manifesting other responses within this same category to warrant assessment of these additional responses.

Also, in the spirit of the idiographic focus of behavioral assessment, the *DSM-IV* allows for some individual variation within diagnoses, as recognized by the polythetic nature of *DSM-IV* diagnoses. For example, an individual must exhibit five of nine specific symptoms (including either depressed mood or loss of interest or pleasure) in order for their experience to qualify as a major depressive episode, thus leaving open a multitude of individually different symptom presentations that can be targeted under the rubric of major depression.

Nonetheless, the task of selection of treatment goals is incomplete at this point. The treatment goals of the individual client must be specified. The diagnostic criteria of the *DSM* are relatively specific, but the diagnostic criteria contain only categories of symptoms. It must be determined which of the polythetic diagnostic criteria are applicable to the particular client, and the content within that diagnostic criterion that might form a treatment goal for the individual client must be specified. For example, one diagnostic criterion for depression is indecisiveness. "Improving indecisiveness" is too vague as a treatment goal. Instead, the depressed client who is a single mother may wish to improve decision-making skills in relation to child-rearing. In fact, one of our clients frequently asks for reassurance regarding everyday decisions that she needs to make regarding her child's upbringing. In addition, the client probably has other treatment goals that are not included in the diagnostic criteria for his or her disorder. For example, a client might be seeking treatment for panic disorder, but in addition might want to lose weight and spend more quality time with her husband and children.

The various situations in which the goals are to be accomplished must be specified. For example, depressed mood may vary across situations. The depressed individual may be able to function adequately at work, but come home and feel very sad and isolated and lethargic. The treatment goal might be to increase positive mood at home by increasing pleasant events or by completing gradually more demanding home tasks. In the case of a child diagnosed with attention deficit hyperactivity disorder (ADHD), school is often a more problematic situation/environment than home. Treatment goals for a child with ADHD might be to increase the number of tasks completed at school or improve daily teacher ratings of classroom behavior.

Also, the client's values must be included in the selection of treatment goals. Behavior therapy has long recognized the role of the client in specifying goals: "the practice of behavior therapy is typically guided by a contractual agreement between both client and therapist specifying the goals and methods of intervention" (Davison & Stuart, 1975, p. 755). A more contemporary recognition of the role of client values in the selection of treatment goals is seen in the work of Hayes and his colleagues in Acceptance and Commitment Therapy (ACT).

> ACT is at its core a behavioral treatment. Its ultimate goal is to help the client develop and maintain a behavioral trajectory in life that is vital and valued. All ACT techniques are eventually subordinated to helping the client live in accord with his or her chosen values. . . . Helping the client identify valued life goals . . . and implement them in the face of emotional obstacles . . . both directs and dignifies ACT (Hayes, Strosahl, & Wilson, 1999, p. 205).

ACT's values assessment lists life areas, such as family relations, career/employment, and spirituality. Within valued life areas, the client is asked to identify concrete goals within those areas. This view of clients as humans capable of verbal behavior indicating values and choices does not usually emanate from the *DSM* system.

In addition to selecting treatment goals, in behavioral assessment, the client's strengths are also identified. In the example of the client mentioned above who is concerned about her ability to make good decisions in relation to child-rearing, her strengths are used to provide reassurance to her about her capabilities. Her strengths include her devotion to her child and her ability to maintain stable employment, thereby providing housing, food, and other physical necessities for her child. Note that this strength-based assessment is not included in the diagnostic process, which is pathology based.

When treatment goals are selected through behavioral assessment, a wide range of assessment strategies are usually employed. The range of behavioral assessment techniques used has been neatly summarized by Haynes, Nelson, Thacher, and Kaholokula (2002). The client is typically interviewed, as are significant others (such as a teacher, parents, spouse). Questionnaires may be administered, either self-report questionnaires or those completed by significant others. Parenthetically, a wonderful source for questionnaires and brief information about each of them is a two-volume work by Fischer and Corcoran (2000). There may be direct observations of behavior in school (e.g., of a child presenting with behavioral or academic difficulties in school), a clinic play-

room (e.g., of a mother-child dyad where noncompliance and negative interactions are at issue), or a clinic waiting room (e.g., of a couple in relationship distress). The client may be asked to participate in role-playing—for example, a man with Asperger's disorder might role-play asking his boss for more definitive information about job requirements. The client may be requested to self-monitor—for example, a patient with bulimia might be asked to self-monitor normal food intake, as well as binges and purges. The broad range of methods used in behavioral assessment can be contrasted with the relatively narrow range of methods usually used in reaching a *DSM* diagnosis—typically, a clinical interview and perhaps a computerized semistructured interview such as the SCID (Spitzer et al., 1990).

Selection of a Treatment Strategy

Once the target behaviors or treatment goals have been selected, a second goal of behavioral assessment is the selection of a treatment strategy. The link between assessment and treatment has been recognized as especially important in behavioral assessment. In fact, it has been suggested that various aspects of behavioral assessment be evaluated by the criterion of "treatment utility" (Hayes, Nelson, & Jarrett, 1987). The question asked in treatment utility is: Does this assessment enhance treatment outcome? Three different approaches within behavioral assessment used to select treatment strategies have been summarized by Nelson (1988): (a) the use of diagnosis; (b) identification and modification of critical response classes; and (c) the functional analysis.

Treatment Selection Based on Diagnosis

One way to select a treatment strategy is to base it on the client's diagnosis or diagnoses. A major contribution of *DSM* to behavioral assessors is the list of empirically validated treatments, which are disorder based, compiled by a task force within Division 12 of APA (Chambless et al., 1996; Chambless et al., 1998; Chambless & Ollendick, 2001). These treatments, most of which are behavioral and cognitive-behavioral, are indexed entirely by diagnosis. The use of diagnosis by a behavioral assessor allows easy access to this treatment list, thereby suggesting one or more treatments that may be effective with a particular client. This approach, however, does have many limitations.

For a few disorders, there is more than one empirically validated treatment. For example, recommended treatments for depression include behavior therapy for depression, cognitive therapy for depression, interpersonal therapy for depression, brief dynamic therapy, self-control therapy, and social problem-solving therapy. Behavioral assessment may be useful for determining which treatment to select to optimize effectiveness for a particular client. Even though the research on treatment matching is in a primitive state, there are some suggestions that treatment matched to a particular presenting problem or target behavior is more effective than mismatched treatment (e.g., McKnight, Nelson, Hayes, & Jarrett, 1984; Nelson-Gray, Herbert, Herbert, Sigmon, & Brannon, 1989).

The empirically validated treatments are each described in a treatment manual that allows replication of the treatment across clinicians. The intent is to implement the treatment manual with a particular client on a session-by-session basis. However, many clients poorly tolerate such structured treatment, despite its previous demonstrations of efficacy with other clients. Many of the clients who react negatively to such manualized or structured treatments are those who not only have an Axis I disorder, but who also have a personality disorder. For example, persons diagnosed with borderline personality disorder (BPD) are characterized by a pattern of unstable interpersonal relationships and marked affective impulsivity (e.g., irritability, anxiety, anger episodes). People with BPD are often in a state of crisis, involving mostly life outside of therapy, but perhaps also involving their therapist. These individuals are often too crisis-ridden and emotionally labile to participate in structured or manualized treatment for an Axis I disorder on a week-to-week basis. We also have experienced some difficulties in applying the skills training portion of Dialectical Behavior Therapy (Linehan, 1993), an empirically validated treatment for persons with borderline personality disorder, to some clients with BPD because of either constant life crises or resistance to structured treatments. Behavioral assessment and behavioral principles also may be useful in suggesting how to modify the application of empirically validated treatments to clients with co-occurring personality disorders. For example, utilizing the Premack principle, the session agenda can be arranged so that the first portion is spent on structured treatment and the second portion on the client's crisis.

The same issue as discussed above, how to effectively apply an empirically validated treatment with an individual client, also may occur when clients have normal variations in personality. To illustrate, many of the manualized or structured treatments require completion of weekly therapy homework assignments. A client who is low in conscientiousness (which is a normal variation of personality) may be unlikely to complete weekly therapy homework assignments, and may be also unlikely to even attend therapy sessions on a regular basis. Behavioral assessment also may be useful in suggesting how to modify the application of empirically validated

treatments to clients with co-occurring normal personality variations.

Many disorders do not have empirically validated treatments. These disorders include Axis I disorders like dissociative or somatoform disorders, and most Axis II disorders (excluding Linehan's Dialectical Behavior Therapy for individuals diagnosed with BPD; Linehan, 1993). For the many individuals who present for treatment who have disorders without empirically validated treatments, a behavioral assessment is required to determine target behaviors, controlling variables, treatment strategies, and outcome measures, using perhaps the SORC model. Turkat and Maisto (1985) have suggested some applications of behavioral assessment specifically for the assessment and treatment of personality disorders.

Relatedly, many individuals are diagnosed with mental retardation or a pervasive developmental disorder, diagnoses which are very broad and also without empirically validated treatments. Here again, a behavioral assessment is required to determine target behaviors, controlling variables, treatment strategies, and outcome measures. A good example of this is provided by Carr and Durand (1985), who utilized behavioral assessment to differentiate the controlling variables in tantrums in different children with autism. Some children were displaying tantrums because their work was too hard for them, and others were displaying tantrums because they were seeking more adult attention. The two sets of controlling variables suggested different treatments for different children with autism.

Treatment Selection Based on Response Classes

Most clients present with multiple behavior problems. The problems may be unrelated to each other, or the problems may covary in some systematic fashion. In fact, sets of *DSM* diagnostic criteria can be thought of as lists of behaviors that frequently covary across individuals within a diagnostic category (Nelson & Barlow, 1981). Since the 1980s, behavioral assessors have become more sophisticated in recognizing the complex ways in which responses or problem behaviors relate to each other (e.g., Evans, 1985; Mash, 1985).

Sometimes, when a client has multiple problems, a keystone target behavior can be identified—that is, a target behavior that produces therapeutic response generalization. As an illustration, in a study comparing the relative advantages of selecting one target behavior over another, the reinforcement of academic accuracy altered both academic correctness and on-task behavior, but the reinforcement of on-task behavior had no effect on academic accuracy (Hay, Hay, & Nelson, 1977). Thus, the keystone target behavior is academic difficulties because changes in this target generalize to or covary with classroom social behavior. Similarly, children's oppositional behavior decreased more when they were rewarded for solitary play than when they were rewarded for cooperative parent-child activities (Wahler & Fox, 1980). Thus, the keystone target behavior is solitary play because increases in this target generalize to or covary with children's oppositional behavior.

In the two examples above, the selection of the keystone behavior was *consistent* across the children in these studies. In the two examples presented next, the keystone behavior *differed* across individual clients. In a study by Trower, Yardley, Bryant, and Shaw (1978), patients were assessed as having either a social skills deficit or social anxiety. In a 2 × 2 design, half of each type of patient was administered systematic desensitization, and half received social skills training. The identification of the proper keystone target behavior was important for the patients with social skills deficits, because they improved more when given social skills training than they did when they received systematic desensitization. Identification of the keystone behavior was less important for patients with social anxiety, because they improved under either treatment protocol. In a study by McKnight et al. (1984), women with depression received social skills training and cognitive therapy in an alternating-treatments design. Depressed women with assessed problems in social skills significantly improved more in both social skills and depression after receiving the related treatment of social skills training as compared to the unrelated treatment of cognitive therapy. Depressed women with assessed problems in dysfunctional thinking significantly improved more in both cognitions and depression after receiving the related treatment of cognitive therapy as compared to the unrelated treatment of social skills training.

When a client presents with multiple problems, as most do, there is unfortunately no systematic means of assessment to determine which presenting problem is a keystone behavior for that person. This is true whether the multiple problems are viewed from a diagnostic viewpoint (i.e., the behaviors that are assessed are the behaviors within the diagnostic criterion set) or from a behavior assessment viewpoint (i.e., any type of behavior is "fair game" for assessment, using a multimethod assessment format). There is some scant literature that might provide some guidance in the selection of keystone target behaviors for some clients, but, largely, it is left to client and clinician judgment (e.g., Evans, 1985).

Treatment Selection Based on Functional Analysis

A hallmark of behavioral assessment from its early days has been the functional analysis—the classic strategy that links behavioral assessment and behavioral treatment. The variables presently controlling the target behavior are identified in assessment and are subsequently modified in treatment (Goldfried & Pomeranz, 1968). The antecedent and consequent environmental variables, and sometimes the biological or cognitive variables, of which the problem behavior is a function are identified in assessment. The assumption is that if these maintaining variables are altered in treatment, then the problem behavior will improve. In Ferster's words, "Such a functional analysis of behavior has the advantage that it specified the causes of behavior in the form of explicit environmental events that can be objectively identified and that are potentially manipulable" (1965, p. 11). A more current presentation of the components of the functional analysis has been elaborated by Haynes and colleagues (2002).

DSM-IV can be useful for behavioral assessors in that the text related to each disorder suggests environmental and organismic controlling variables that contribute to the occurrence of the disorder (Nelson & Barlow, 1981). Utilizing the SORC model, the environmental controlling variables are the antecedent and consequent stimuli that contribute to the disorder, and the organismic controlling variables include both biological variables and past learning history that contribute to the disorder. To illustrate, major depressive disorder suggests both environmental variables (e.g., a severe psychosocial stressor such as the death of a loved one or divorce) and organismic variables (e.g., familial pattern of depressive disorder, female gender, inadequate repertoire of social skills to obtain or maintain sufficient social support, depressogenic cognitive style). There is sufficient consistency in controlling variables across individuals within a diagnostic category to merit a behavioral assessment of the controlling variables suggested in the *DSM* chapters. The environmental variables bearing on the presenting problem are summarized, albeit inadequately, in Axis IV, and consequences related to impairment are summarized in Axis V.

There are more contemporary and much more highly elaborated versions of the functional analysis that are known as behavioral case formulation strategies. Succinct and useful summaries of four of these case formulation strategies are presented by Haynes et al. (2002). The first of these case formulation strategies is Nezu and Nezu's problem-solving model (e.g., Nezu, Nezu, Friedman, & Haynes, 1997; Nezu, Nezu, Peacock, & Girdwood, chapter 21), consisting of problem orientation, problem definition and formulation, generation of alternatives, decision making, and solution implementation and verification. A second type of case formulation strategy is Persons and Tompkins' (1997) cognitive-behavioral case formulation, consisting of behavior problem list, core beliefs, precipitants and activating situations, working hypothesis, origins, treatment plan, and predicted obstacles to treatment. A third strategy is the dialectical behavior therapy clinical case formulation (Koerner & Linehan, 1997), which includes three stages: gathering information on potential targets for therapeutic intervention, organization of information to guide therapeutic interventions using a written narrative or flowchart, and frequent revisions of the written case formulation as assessment and treatment continue. A fourth type of behavioral case formulation is the culturally informed functional assessment interview (Tanaka-Matsumi, Seiden, & Lam, 1996), consisting of these steps: assessment of cultural identity and acculturation, specification of presenting problems, elicitation of the client's explanatory model, functional assessment, comparison and negotiation of causal explanatory models, and treatment.

In summary, the functional analytic or case formulation approach to treatment selection focuses on the variables that are believed to be contributing to the client's problems. It is assumed that modification of these controlling variables will help the client accomplish his or her treatment goals.

Selection of Outcome Measures

A final goal of behavioral assessment is the selection of treatment outcome measures. In this age of managed care, it behooves any clinician, and not only scientist-practitioner clinicians, to obtain client outcome measures. The same types of measures that are used in the initial assessment to identify the client's treatment goals may be administered as outcome measures. Haynes and colleagues (2002) and Cone (2001) have provided excellent summaries of the range of these behavioral assessment techniques; and Hayes, Barlow, and Nelson-Gray (1999) have provided an overview of guidelines for the collection of outcome measures.

Frequently, multiple types of measures are utilized with the same client. Dependent measures that are less sensitive to change may be given on a pre-post treatment basis. An example of this might be the SCID semistructured interview (Spitzer et al., 1990) that results in a *DSM* diagnosis. Optimistically, the client may qualify for one or more diagnoses prior to treatment, and not qualify for a diagnosis after treatment, or at least meet fewer diagnostic criteria. Diagnosis, however, is a molar not molecular measure and, hence, is not very sensitive to small but perhaps significant treatment gains. Another example of a molar measure is a personality inventory, such as the Minnesota Multiphasic Personality Inventory (Hathaway & McKinley, 1951). A personality inventory is too global or molar to reflect daily or weekly changes in a client's behavior. Yet a personality inventory may be an adequate pre-post treatment measure, if supplemented by more

specific measures that are more sensitive to daily or weekly change (Nelson, 1981). Although some measures may be taken on a pre-post treatment basis, it is more common in behavioral assessment to use repeated measurement. Some convenient measures, like self-monitoring, may be used on a daily basis, while other convenient measures, like questionnaires, may be used on a weekly basis. Other measures that are less convenient, like psychophysiological measures, role-playing, or naturalistic observation, may be taken on a monthly basis.

Collection of outcome measures is used in daily clinical practice to determine whether the client is making progress toward the accomplishment of his or her treatment goals. Similar measures are used by clinical researchers when contributing to clinical science. Haynes and O'Brien (2000) tracked the types of outcome measures used in articles published in the *Journal of Consulting and Clinical Psychology* from 1962 to 1998 and found that personality inventories and projective measures are infrequently used, compared with a more frequent use of behavioral observation, psychophysiology, and self-monitoring. It seems that molecular measures are used more than molar measures in clinical research.

Another aspect about collecting repeated outcome measures in clinical practice and/or in clinical research is using some type of single-subject or repeated measures design. The various types of time series designs are described by Hayes et al. (1999). The most common of these is the case study, consisting of repeated measures taken during baseline and treatment. Multiple case studies result in a clinical replication series. Other useful time series designs include the multiple baseline design, alternating-treatments design, and the cross-over design.

To accomplish the third goal of behavioral assessment—to evaluate the effectiveness of the selected treatment in helping the client to achieve his or her treatment goals—a variety of outcome measures and repeated-measure designs are used. The use of diagnosis is very limited in the accomplishment of this third goal. At best, diagnosis is a molar measure that might be used in a pre-post fashion with a semistructured interview such as the SCID. Diagnosis is not a sufficiently sensitive measure to be used on a repeated basis, or to reflect small but perhaps significant changes in client functioning.

CONCLUSION: A COMPLEMENTARY SYNTHESIS BETWEEN DIAGNOSIS AND BEHAVIORAL ASSESSMENT

In conclusion, diagnosis, including the present *DSM* diagnostic system, has received perhaps more than its fair share of criticism. Behavioral assessors in the past have been among the critics of diagnosis. Improvements in the *DSM* system, beginning with *DSM-III,* along with the acculturation of behavior therapy and behavioral assessment into contemporary clinical science, have set the stage for the useful synthesis of diagnosis and behavioral assessment.

There are benefits of diagnosis per se for clinicians and clinical researchers. Diagnosis or classification forms the basis of a clinical science. Diagnosis also permits communication among professionals—for example, in making referrals, accessing relevant literature, and negotiating managed care.

The *DSM* is also useful to behavioral assessors in suggesting nomothetic response patterns that occur within a diagnostic category and in suggesting nomothetic environmental and organismic controlling variables for a diagnostic category. The list of empirically validated treatments (Chambless et al., 1996; Chambless et al., 1998; Chambless & Ollendick, 2001) is diagnosis-based, so accessing this list requires a diagnosis.

Despite these various advantages to behavioral assessors of using a *DSM* diagnosis, a diagnosis is an adjunct to and not a replacement for behavioral assessment. The main reason for this status is that the *DSM* is nomothetic, and behavioral assessment is idiographic. Each of the contributions made by *DSM* to behavioral assessors consist of nomothetic suggestions that must be tailored to the individual client through behavioral assessment. Behavioral assessment is necessary to make an idiographic determination of specific symptoms, controlling variables, treatment choice, and treatment outcome measures for an individual client. Individual treatment goals and appropriate treatment outcome measures must be established in the context of the client's presenting problems, covarying responses, and values. Even though the *DSM* does indeed suggest environmental and/or organismic controlling variables for each disorder, a behavioral assessment must be conducted to determine which of these controlling variables or additional controlling variables is applicable for the specific client. Also, the list of empirically validated treatments, although a great contribution to clinical science, is far from being an easy blueprint for treatment selection for all clients. Many disorders do not have empirically validated treatments, while other disorders may have more than one empirically validated treatment. In many cases, clients simply cannot comply with the manualized treatments that characterize the empirically validated treatments. In each of these instances, behavioral assessment may be useful in tailoring or creating a treatment that may be effective for a specific client. This synthesis of diagnosis and behavioral assessment simply works best.

REFERENCES

Achenbach, T.M. (1995). Empirically based assessment and taxonomy: Applications to clinical research. *Psychological Assessment, 7,* 261–274.

Achenbach, T.M., and McConaughy, S.H. (1996). Relations between DSM-IV and empirically based assessment. *School Psychology Review, 25(3),* 329–341.

Acierno, R., Hersen, M., & Van Hasselt, V.B. (1997). DSM-IV and multidimensional assessment strategies. In S.M. Turner & M. Hersen (Eds.), *Adult psychopathology and diagnosis* (pp. 578–594). New York: Wiley.

Adams, H.E., Doster, J.A., & Calhoun, K.S. (1977). A psychologically based system of response classification. In A.R. Ciminero, K.S. Calhoun, & H.E. Adams (Eds.), *Handbook of psychological assessment* (pp. 47–78). New York: Wiley, 1977.

Adams, H.E., & Haber, J.D. (1984). The classification of abnormal behavior: An overview. In H.E. Adams & P.B. Sutker (Eds.), *Comprehensive handbook of psychopathology* (pp. 3–25). New York: Plenum.

American Psychiatric Association (1952). *Diagnostic and statistical manual of mental disorders.* Washington, D.C.: Author.

American Psychiatric Association (1968). *Diagnostic and statistical manual of mental disorders* (2nd ed.). Washington, D.C.: Author.

American Psychiatric Association (1980). *Diagnostic and statistical manual of mental disorders* (3rd ed.), Washington, D.C.: Author.

American Psychiatric Association (1987). *Diagnostic and statistical manual of mental disorders* (3rd ed., rev.). Washington, D.C.: Author.

American Psychiatric Association (1994). *Diagnostic and statistical manual of mental disorders* (4th ed.). Washington, D.C.: Author.

American Psychiatric Association (2000). *Diagnostic and statistical manual of mental disorders* (4th ed., text revision). Washington, D.C.: Author.

Andreasen, N.C., & Carpenter, W.T. (1993). Diagnosis and classification of schizophrenia. *Schizophrenia Bulletin, 19,* 199–214.

Angst, J. (1992). Recurrent brief psychiatric syndromes of depression, hypomania, neurasthenia, and anxiety from an epidemiological point of view. *Neurological, Psychiatric, and Brain Research, 1,* 5–12.

Arrington, R.E. (1939). Time-sampling studies of child behavior. *Psychological Monographs, 51.*

Bandura, A. (1968). A social learning interpretation of psychological dysfunction. In P. London & D. Rosenhan (Eds.), *Foundations of abnormal psychology* (pp. 293–344). New York: Holt, Rinehart, & Winston.

Cantwell, D. (1996). Classification of child and adolescent psychopathology. *Journal of Child Psychology and Psychiatry and Allied Disciplines, 37*(1), 3–12.

Carr, E.G., & Durand, V.M. (1985). The social-communicative basis of severe behavior problems in children. In S. Reiss & R.R.

Bootzin (Eds.), *Theoretical issues in behavior therapy* (pp. 220–254). New York: Academic Press.

Chambless, D.L., Baker, M. J., Baucom, D.H., Beutler, L.E., Calhoun, K.S., Crits-Christoph, P., Daiuto, A., DeRubeis, R., Detweiler, J., Haaga, D.A.F., Bennett Johnson, S., McCurry, S., Muser, K.T., Pope, K.S., Sanderson, W.C., Shoham, V., Stickle, T., Williams, D.A., & Woody, S. (1998). Update on empirically validated treatments II. *Clinical Psychologist, 51*, 3–18.

Chambless, D.L., & Ollendick, T.H. (2001). Empirically supported psychological interventions: Controversies and evidence. *Annual Review of Psychology, 52*, 685–716.

Chambless, D.L., Sanderson, W.C., Shoham, V., Bennett Johnson, S., Pope, K.S., Crits-Cristoph, P., Baker, M., Johnson, B., Woody, S.R., Sue, S. Beutler, L., Williams, D.A., & McCurry, S. (1996). An update on empirically validated therapies. *Clinical Psychologist, 49*, 5–18.

Ciminero, A.R., Calhoun, K.S., & Adams, H.E. (Eds.). (1977). *Handbook of behavioral assessment.* New York: Wiley.

Clark, L.A., Watson, D., & Reynolds, S. (1995). Diagnosis and classification of psychopathology: Challenges to the current system and future directions. In J.T. Spence, J.M, Darley, & D.J. Foss (Eds.), *Annual review of psychology* (Vol. 46, pp. 121–153). Palo Alto, CA: Annual Reviews.

Cone, J.D. (1992). That was then! This is now! *Behavioral assessment, 14*, 219–228.

Cone, J.D. (2001). *Evaluating outcomes: Empirical tools for effective practice.* Washington, D.C.: American Psychological Association.

Cone, J.D., & Hawkins, R.P. (Eds.). (1977). *Behavioral assessment: New directions in clinical psychology.* New York: Brunner/Mazel.

Davison, G.C., & Stuart, R. (1975). Behavior therapy and civil liberties. *American Psychologist, 30*, 755–763.

Edelbrock, C., & Achenbach, T.M. (1984). The teacher version of the child behavior profile: I. Boys aged 6–11. *Journal of Consulting and Clinical Psychology, 52*, 207–217.

Evans, I.M. (1985). Building systems models as a strategy for target behavior selection in clinical assessment. *Behavioral Assessment, 7*, 21–32.

Eysenck, H.J. (Ed.). (1976). *Case studies in behaviour therapy.* London: Routledge & Kegan Paul.

Feighner, J.P., Robins, E., Guze, S.B., Woodruff, R.A., Winokur, G., & Munoz, R. (1972). Diagnostic criteria for use in psychiatric research. *Archives of General Psychiatry, 26*, 57–63.

Ferster, C. (1965). Classification of behavioral pathology. In L. Krasner & L.P. Ullman (Eds.), *Research in behavior modification* (pp. 6–26). New York: Holt, Rinehart, & Winston.

First, M.B., Spitzer, R.L., Gibbon, M., & Williams, J.B.W. (1997). *Structured clinical interview for DSM-IV Axis I disorders–clinical version (SCID-CV).* Washington, DC: American Psychiatric Association Press.

Fischer, J., & Corcoran, K. (2000). *Measures for clinical practice* (3rd ed.). New York: Free Press.

Frances, A.J., First, M.B., & Pincus, H.A. (1995). *DSM-IV guidebook.* Washington D.C.: American Psychiatric Association Press.

Frances, A.J., Pincus, H.A., Widiger, T.A., Davis, W.W., & First, M.B. (1990). DSM-IV: Work in progress. *American Journal of Psychiatry, 147*, 1439–1448.

Goldfried, M.R., & Pomeranz, D.M. (1968). Role of assessment in behavior modification. *Psychological Reports, 23*, 75–87.

Goldfried, M.R., & Sprafkin, J.N. (1976). Behavioral personality assessment. In J.T. Spence, R.C. Carson, & J.W. Thibaut (Eds.), *Behavioral approaches to therapy* (pp. 295–321). Morristown, NJ: General Learning Press.

Hartung, C.M., & Widiger, T.A. (1998). Gender differences in the diagnosis of mental disorders: Conclusions and controversies of DSM-IV. *Psychological Bulletin, 123*(3), 260–278.

Hathaway, S.R., & McKinley, J.C. (1951). *MMPI manual.* New York: Psychological Corporation.

Hawkins, R.P. (1986). Selection of target behaviors. In R.O. Nelson & S.C. Hayes (Eds.), *Conceptual foundations of behavioral assessment* (pp. 331–385). New York: Guilford Press.

Hay, W.M., Hay, L.R., & Nelson, R.O. (1977). Direct and collateral changes in on-task and academic behavior resulting from on-task versus academic contingencies. *Behavior Therapy, 8*, 431–441.

Hayes, S.C., Barlow, D.H., & Nelson-Gray, R.O. (1999). *The scientist-practitioner: Research and accountability in the age of managed care.* Needham Heights, MA: Allyn & Bacon.

Hayes, S.C., Nelson, R.O., & Jarrett, R.B. (1987). Treatment utility: A functional approach to evaluating the quality of assessment. *American Psychologist, 42*, 963–974.

Hayes, S.C., Strosahl, K.D., & Wilson, K.G. (1999). *Acceptance and commitment therapy: An experiential approach to behavior change.* New York: Guilford Press.

Hayes, S.C., Wilson, K.G., Gifford, E.V., Follette, V.M., & Strosahl, K. (1996). Experiential avoidance and behavioral disorders: A functional dimensional approach to diagnosis and treatment. *Journal of Consulting and Clinical Psychology, 64*, 1152–1168.

Haynes, S.N., Nelson, K.G., Thacher, I., & Kaholokula, J.K. (2002). Outpatient behavioral assessment and treatment target selection. In M. Hersen & L.K. Porzelius (Eds.), *Diagnosis, conceptualization, and treatment planning for adults: A step-by-step guide* (pp. 35–70). Mahwah, NJ: Erlbaum.

Haynes, S.N., & O'Brien, W.H. (2000). *Principles and practice of behavioral assessment.* New York: Kluwer Academic/Plenum.

Hersen, M., & Bellack, A.S. (Eds.). (1976). *Behavioral assessment: A practical handbook.* New York: Pergamon Press.

Hobbs, N. (1975). *The futures of children: Categories, labels, and their consequences.* San Francisco: Jossey-Bass.

Horai, J. (1981). A brief history of the descriptive behavioral classification project. Washington, D.C.: American Psychological Association.

Kanfer, F.H., & Saslow, G. (1969). Behavioral diagnosis. In C.M. Franks (Ed.), *Behavior therapy: Appraisal and status* (pp. 417–444). New York: McGraw-Hill.

Kaplan, M. (1983). A woman's view of DSM-III. *American Psychologist, 38,* 786–792.

Karasu, T.B., & Skodol, A.E. (1980). Sixth axis for DSM-III: Psychodynamic evaluation. *American Journal of Psychiatry, 137,* 607–610.

Kazdin, A.E. (1983). Psychiatric diagnosis, dimensions of dysfunction, and child behavior therapy. *Behavior Therapy, 14,* 73–99.

Kendell, R.E. (1975). *The role of diagnosis in psychiatry.* Oxford, England: Blackwell Scientific.

Kessler, R.C., McGonagle, K.A., Zhao, S., Nelson, C.B., Hughes, M., et al. (1994). Lifetime and 12-month prevalence of DSM-III-R psychiatric disorders in the United States: Results from the National Comorbidity Study. *Archives of General Psychiatry, 51,* 8–19.

Klerman, G.L. (1984). The advantages of DSM-III. *American Journal of Psychiatry, 141,* 539–542.

Koerner, K., & Linehan, M.M. (1997). Case formulation in dialectical behavior therapy. In T.D. Eells (Ed.), *Handbook of psychotherapy case formulation* (pp. 340–367). New York: Guilford Press.

Linehan, M.M. (1993). *Skills training manual for treating borderline personality disorder.* New York: Guilford Press.

Livesley, J. (1991). Classifying personality disorders: Ideal types, prototypes, or dimensions? *Journal of Personality Disorders, 5,* 52–59.

Maffei, C., Fossati, A., Agostoni, I., Barraco, A., Bagnato, M., Deborah, D., Namia, C., Novella, L., and Petrachi, M. (1997). Interrater reliability and internal consistency of the Structured Clinical Interview for DSM-IV Axis II Personality Disorders (SCID II) version 2.0. *Journal of Personality Disorders, 11*(3), 279–284.

Mash, E.J. (1985). Some comments on target selection in behavior therapy. *Behavioral Assessment, 7,* 21–32.

Matarazzo, J.D. (1983). The reliability of psychiatric and psychological diagnosis. *Clinical Psychology Review, 3,* 103–145.

McKnight, D.L., Nelson, R.O., Hayes, S.C., & Jarrett, R.B. (1984). Importance of treating individually-assessed response classes in an amelioration of depression. *Behavior Therapy, 15,* 315–335.

McLemore, C.W., & Benjamin, L.S. (1979). What happened to interpersonal diagnosis? A psychosocial alternative to DSM-III. *American Psychologist, 34,* 17–33.

Miller, L.S., Bergstrom, D.A., Cross, H.J., & Grube, J.W. (1981). Opinions and use of the DSM system by practicing psychologists. *Professional Psychology, 12,* 385–390.

Millon, T. (1983). The DSM-III: An insider's perspective. *American Psychologist, 38,* 804–814.

Morey, L.C. (1992). Personality disorders NOS: Specifying patterns of the otherwise unspecified. Paper presented at the annual meeting of the American Psychological Association, Washington, D.C.

Nathan, P.E. (1994). DSM-IV: Empirical, accessible, not yet ideal. *Journal of Clinical Psychology, 50,* 103–110.

Nelson, R.O. (1981). Realistic dependent measures for clinical use. *Journal of Consulting and Clinical Psychology, 49,* 168–182.

Nelson, R.O. (1988). Relationship between assessment and treatment within a behavioral perspective. *Journal of Psychopathology and Behavioral Assessment, 10,* 155–170.

Nelson, R.O., & Barlow, D.H. (1981). Behavioral assessment: Basic strategies and initial procedures. In D.H. Barlow (Ed.), *Behavioral assessment of adult disorders* (pp. 13–43). New York: Guilford Press.

Nelson, R.O., & Hayes, S.C. (1979). Some current dimensions of behavioral assessment. *Behavioral Assessment, 1,* 1–16.

Nelson, R.O., & Hayes, S.C. (1986). The nature of behavioral assessment. In R.O. Nelson & S.C. Hayes (Eds.), *Conceptual foundations of behavioral assessment* (pp. 3–41). New York: Guilford Press.

Nelson-Gray, R.O., & Farmer, R.F. (1999). Behavioral assessment of personality disorders. *Behaviour Research and Therapy, 37,* 347–368.

Nelson-Gray, R.O., Gaynor, S.T., & Korotitsch, W.J. (1997). Behavior therapy: Distinct but acculturated. *Behavior Therapy, 28,* 563–572.

Nelson-Gray, R.O., Herbert, J.D., Herbert, D.L., Sigmon, S.T., & Brannon, S.E. (1989). Effectiveness of matched, mismatched, and package treatments of depression. *Journal of Behavior Therapy and Experimental Psychiatry, 20,* 281–294.

Nezu, A.M., Nezu, C.M., Friedman, S.H., & Haynes, S.N. (1997). Case formulation in behavior therapy: Problem-solving and functional analytic strategies. In T.D. Eells (Ed.), *Handbook of psychotherapy case formulation* (pp. 368–401). New York: Guilford Press.

Persons, J.B., & Tompkins, M.A. (1997). Cognitive-behavioral case formulation. In T.D. Eells (Ed.), *Handbook of psychotherapy case formulation* (pp. 314–339). New York: Guilford Press.

Rhee, S.H., Feignon, S.A., Bar, J.L., Hadeishi, Y., & Waldman, I.D. (2001). Behavior genetic approaches to the study of psychopathology. In P.B. Sutker & H.E. Adams (Eds.), *Comprehensive handbook of psychopathology* (3rd ed.). New York: Kluwer Academic/Plenum.

Robins, L.N., Locke, B.Z., & Regier, D.A. (1991). *An overview of psychiatric disorders in America.* In L.N. Robins & B.Z. Locke (Eds.), *Psychiatric disorders in America* (pp. 328–366). New York: Free Press.

Robinson, J.C., & Lewinsohn, P.M. (1973). Behavior modification of speech characteristics in a chronically depressed man. *Behavior Therapy, 4,* 150–152.

Sanderson, W.C., Beck, A.T., & Beck, J. (1990). Syndrome comorbidity in patients with major depression or dysthymia: Prevalence and temporal relationships. *American Journal of Psychiatry, 147,* 1025–1028.

Schacht, T.E. (1985). DSM-III and the politics of truth. *American Psychologist, 40,* 513–521.

Schacht, T.E., & Nathan, P.E. (1977). But is it good for psychologists? Appraisal and status of DSM-III. *American Psychologist, 32,* 1017–1025.

Segal, D.L., Corcoran, J., & Coughlin, A. (2002). Diagnosis, differential diagnosis, and the SCID. In M. Hersen & L.K. Porzelius (Eds.), *Diagnosis, conceptualization, and treatment planning for adults: A step-by-step guide* (pp. 13–34). Mahwah, NJ: Erlbaum.

Singerman, B. (1981). DSM-III: Historical antecedents and present significance. *Journal of Clinical Psychiatry, 42,* 409–410.

Smith, D., & Kraft, W.A. (1983). DSM-III: Do psychologists really want an alternative? *American Psychologist, 38,* 777–785.

Spitzer, R.L., Endicott, J., & Robins, E. (1978). Research diagnostic criteria. *Archives of General Psychiatry, 35,* 773–782.

Spitzer, R.L., Forman, J.B.W., and Nee, J. (1979). DSM-III field trials: Initial interrater diagnostic reliability. *American Journal of Psychiatry, 136,* 815–817.

Spitzer, R.L., Williams, J.B.W., Gibbon, M., & First, M.B. (1990). *Structured clinical interview for DSM-III-R (SCID).* Washington, D.C.: American Psychiatric Association.

Stuart, R.B. (1970). *Trick or treatment.* Champaign, IL: Research Press.

Szasz, T.S. (1960). The myth of mental illness. *American Psychologist, 15,* 113–118.

Tanaka-Matsumi, J., Seiden, D.Y., & Lam, K.N. (1996). The Culturally Informed Functional Assessment (CIFA) Interview: A strategy for cross-cultural behavioral practice. *Cognitive and Behavioral Practice, 3,* 215–233.

Taylor, C.B. (1983). DSM-III and behavioral assessment. *Behavioral Assessment, 5,* 5–14.

Taylor, S. (1999). Behavioral assessment: Review and prospect. *Behaviour Therapy and Research, 37,* 475–482.

Trower, P., Yardley, K., Bryant, B.M., & Shaw, P. (1978). The treatment of social failure: A comparison of anxiety reduction and skills-acquisition procedures on two social problems. *Behavior Modification, 2,* 41–60.

Tryon, W.W. (1999). Behavioral diagnosis versus the *Diagnostic and Statistical Manual. Behavior Therapist, 22,* 3–4, 19.

Turkat, I.D., & Maisto, S.A. (1985). Personality disorders: Application of the experimental method to the formulation and modification of personality disorders. In D.H. Barlow (Ed.), *Clinical handbook of psychological disorders* (pp. 502–570). New York: Guilford Press.

Ullmann, L.P., & Krasner, L. (Eds.). (1965). *Case studies in behavior modification.* New York: Holt, Rinehart, & Winston.

Wahler, R.G., & Fox, J.J. (1980). Solitary play versus timeout: A family treatment package for children with aggressive and oppositional behavior. *Journal of Applied Behavior Analysis, 13,* 23–39.

Waller, N.G., & Meehl, P.E. (1998). *Multivariate taxometric procedures: Distinguishing types from continua.* Thousand Oaks, CA: Sage.

Widiger, T.A. (1992). Categorical versus dimensional classification: Implications from and for research. *Journal of Personality Disorders, 6,* 287–300.

Widiger, T.A. (1997). Mental disorders as discrete clinical conditions: Dimensional versus categorical classification (pp. 3–23). In S.M. Turner & M. Hersen (Eds.), *Adult psychopathology and diagnosis.* New York: Wiley.

CONCLUSION, SUMMARY, NEW DIRECTIONS

CHAPTER 25

Behavioral Assessment: Sometimes You Get What You Need

ERIC J. MASH AND JOHN HUNSLEY

INTRODUCTION

Historical reviews of the field of behavioral assessment indicate that it failed to develop as a distinct assessment approach as was hoped for by its early advocates in the late 1960s and early 1970s (e.g., Chapter 2; Cone, 1992; Taylor, 1999). For example, during its short-lived history, behavioral assessment was politely distanced by its own professional organizations, developed first-rate journals that could not be sustained under its banner alone, and was branded by many assessment researchers and practitioners as conceptually limited, impractical, or nothing new. Clearly, behavioral assessment did not get the distinct identity (or recognition) as a freestanding assessment approach that it wanted (Chapter 24). Indeed, there is *not a single* reference to "behavioral assessment" in a recent review of clinical assessment strategies that appeared in the *Annual Review of Psychology* (Wood, Garb, Lilienfeld, & Nezworski, 2002). This is so despite the fact that many of the conclusions of the chapter relating to the need for accountability and utility in clinical practice can be directly traced to past and current behavioral work in this area. Herein lies the paradox of behavioral assessment: Despite its rocky beginnings and failure to develop as a distinct approach, as evidenced by the impressive work described in the chapters in this volume, the principles and practices of

behavioral assessment have proven to be extremely resilient, enduring, and influential.

In their lead article in the inaugural issue of the now defunct journal *Behavioral Assessment,* Nelson and Hayes (1979) stated: "The novelty of the field of behavioral assessment lies then, not in its goals or strategies, but rather in its deliberate attempt to improve the identification and measurement of dependent variables, to increase the probability of selecting successful treatment techniques, and to refine the evaluation of those intervention procedures" (p. 2). In today's lingo, the three novel elements identified by Nelson and Hayes (1979) refer to the role of assessment in clinical decision making and the identification of treatment goals, its utility in enhancing treatment outcomes, and its usefulness in evaluating treatment effectiveness. In other words, the central themes in behavioral assessment were, and continue to be, an overriding emphasis on evidence and accountability in clinical practice.

The early behavioral assessment emphasis on accountability was based on behavioral science values and principles, the foremost being the need for scientifically informed assessment and treatment practices, rather than (solely) on economics. This emphasis preceded by many years the economic crunch that fueled the current focus on accountability in health care (Chapter 22; Hayes, Barlow, & Nelson-Gray, 1999; Mash & Hunsley, 1993b). As the chapters in this volume attest to, behavioral assessment approaches, in concert with other important contemporary economic and cultural forces, have led to significant advancements in accountability in treatment, and in doing so have radically transformed the way in which psychological assessments are conceptualized and conducted. The chapters also document the many accomplishments of behavioral assessment, and how far the approach has progressed both conceptually and methodologically since its early emphasis on the quantification of observable target behaviors (Kanfer, 1979; Mash, 1985). Although behavioral assessment may not have achieved the distinct identity that it wanted, with some unanticipated help from economic pressures on the health care system and a concomitant push for evidence-based practice (Berman, Rosen, Hurt, & Kolarz, 1998), it appears to have gotten what it needs—and then some.

In this chapter, we summarize and highlight some of the main features of current approaches to behavioral assessment as reflected in the preceding chapters. We first discuss the evolution of behavioral assessment, from its early days, to later developments, to the present. In considering this evolution we note that in transforming itself, not only has behavioral assessment become more "mainstream" (Nelson-Gray, Gaynor, & Korotitsch, 1997), but it has also altered the way in which mainstream assessments are now conceptualized and implemented. As such, we discuss how the diffusion of behavioral assessment principles and practices can be characterized as a form of social movement. We conclude with a discussion of two pressing interrelated issues and challenges that behavioral assessment is likely to face in the coming decade, specifically incremental validity and clinical and cost utility.

THE EARLY GROWTH OF BEHAVIORAL ASSESSMENT: THE FORMATIVE YEARS

Early behavioral approaches to assessment and treatment involved the specification of target behaviors and their modification through the alteration of antecedent and consequent stimulus events in a manner loosely conforming to learning principles encompassed under the operant, classical, and observational learning paradigms (Ullmann & Krasner, 1965). These applications were characterized by their focus on easily defined and observable events, current behaviors, situational determinants, and the individual client as the primary target for assessment and treatment (O'Donohue & Henderson, 2001). Consistent with this approach, early behavioral assessments consisted essentially of obtaining frequency, rate, and duration measures describing the behaviors of interest and the "pinpointing, recording, and consequating" of target

behaviors. This approach provided a direct and often highly effective method of changing the targeted behaviors.

The significance of these systematic assessments of target behaviors during the early development of behavior therapy cannot be overemphasized. The early work stimulated a broadly empirical approach to clinical practice and by doing so contributed greatly to the current emphasis on empirically supported treatments (Chambless & Ollendick, 2001). It also underscored the importance of creating continuity between assessment and intervention (Antony & Barlow, 2002), emphasized the need to evaluate treatment outcomes using objective measures (Kazdin, 2001), reinforced the need for individualized assessments (Wolpe, 1986), sensitized assessors to the importance of evaluating behavior in context (Evans, 1985), and led to the development of assessment methods with high face validity (Nelson, 1983).

However, along with the early focus on target behavior assessment, some doubt was expressed regarding whether the measurement of unambiguously defined observable behaviors was sufficient for a full account of human behavior in the social/clinical context (Kanfer, 1979). The need for behavioral assessment to develop theories and methods of greater complexity was noted, and several frameworks were presented to accommodate this greater level of complexity, a good example being Kanfer and Saslow's (1969) guidelines for "behavioral diagnosis." As behavior therapy evolved, a greater emphasis was also placed on evaluating ongoing *patterns* of behavior and the client as part of a larger network of interacting social systems and subsystems (Kanfer, 1985). This growing emphasis on systems was consistent with parallel developments in many other areas of psychology and health care. Although assessments continued to be viewed as individualized in relation to the system under consideration (e.g., couple or child-parent subsystem), they did not necessarily occur at the level of the individual. A much wider range of variables encompassing partners, peers, life stress, social support, and community resources, as well as the relationships among these variables and individual patterns of behavior, were often targeted for assessment and treatment. Within the various subsystems, greater attention was given to the assessment of cognition and affect, reciprocal influences, and the role of more distal events in the neighborhood, work or school environment, and community. These developments began to transform behavioral assessment from an approach based on target behavior measurement to one based on a general set of problem-solving strategies encompassing a much wider range of system variables and a greater variety of methods than was previously the case (Kanfer & Nay, 1982; Mash & Terdal, 1997b).

CONTINUING DEVELOPMENTS: BEHAVIORAL ASSESSMENT CIRCA 1990

Over a decade ago we evaluated the status of behavioral assessment and addressed a number of issues related to the purposes, methods, and future of behavioral assessment (Mash & Hunsley, 1990). As we indicated at that time, behavioral assessors had not only developed specific techniques and tools, but had labored to demonstrate the scientific basis of this relatively new assessment approach. By 1990 it was clear that behavioral assessment had changed greatly from its initial roots, and there were growing concerns about the seeming lack of conceptual clarity evident in models of behavioral assessment (McFall, 1986). However, many proponents of behavioral assessment were strongly supportive of the broadening focus of behavioral assessment based on both theoretical and empirically verifiable rationales. As evidenced by the chapters in this volume, there continues to be great diversity and dynamism associated with the growth and spreading influence of behavioral assessment, with applications spanning the gamut from assessments in work settings (Chapter 18) to behavioral neuropsychology (Chapter 20).

In order to better understand the transition from the early days of behavioral assessment to its current forms, we will briefly highlight some of the issues and concerns we previously identified as critical in the development of behavioral assessment (Mash & Hunsley, 1990). From our perspective, there was clear agreement that a hallmark of behavioral assessment was the use of assessment strategies that were individually tailored to meet the needs of specific clients and situations. There was also an emerging consensus that four interrelated purposes could be identified for conducting behavioral assessments, including: (1) diagnosis (determining the nature and/or cause(s) of the presenting problems); (2) prognosis (generating predictions about the course of the problems if left untreated); (3) treatment design (developing and implementing interventions designed to address the problems); and (4) treatment evaluation (determining the acceptability and/or effectiveness of the intervention). Furthermore, by this time, behavioral assessment methods had expanded beyond direct observation of behavior in naturalistic or analogue situations to include structured and unstructured interviews, behavioral checklists and inventories, self-monitoring procedures (both to assess behavioral variability and to assess cognitive and affective components of presenting problems), and psychophysiological methods.

As we and others indicated (e.g., Cone, 1988), the growth of numerous assessment models (including operant-based, response-class, and systems-based models) made it impossible to precisely define the nature of behavioral assessment.

In many ways it was easier to define behavioral assessment by its dissimilarity to traditional psychological assessment, which emphasized trait measurements, required high levels of inference, and was relatively unconcerned with examining contextual influences on dynamic patterns of behavior (cf. Haynes & Uchigakiuchi, 1993). It was becoming clearer, however, that defining behavioral assessment by what it was *not* was becoming unwieldy and untenable. As a result, we suggested that (then) current attempts to conceptualize behavioral assessment could be best understood as relying on systems-based models. In our view the most promising work was being conducted on the nature of the structural and functional relations between situations, behaviors, physiological functioning, thoughts, and emotions. Because each individual is best understood as part of a complex and dynamic system containing many potential controlling variables, problem behaviors and psychological disorders should be assumed to be multiply determined (cf. Haynes, 1986). Therefore, we argued, it was no longer sufficient to focus exclusively on discrete behaviors or environmental events, because complex behavior chains and interrelations must be assessed to fully understand the problem and the context in which it occurs. Moreover, such a perspective must (a) reject a priori assumptions regarding the primacy of controlling variables that affect the problem and (b) recognize that variables that originally led to the development of the problem may not be relevant to the ongoing expression of the problem.

Finally, we highlighted a range of issues that we saw confronting those committed to the development and promulgation of behavioral assessment. These included inconsistencies in the selection of behaviors to target in treatment (Wilson & Evans, 1983), the process of basing clinical decision making on scientific principles and data (Kanfer & Busemeyer, 1982), and the future of computer applications in behavioral assessment (see Chapter 13 for a comprehensive discussion of this area). Additionally, we discussed two general issues critical to the advancement of behavioral assessment. The first issue was the importance of not only coming to terms with test requirements such as standardization, psychometrics, and norms, but to actively embrace these concepts within the scope of behavioral assessment. In order to meet professional standards for psychological assessments, it *was* and *is* imperative that all assessment methods, including observational coding systems, successfully address these issues (Hunsley, Lee, & Wood, 2003). For example, we suggested that measures needed to be standardized in order to facilitate the development of norms, to allow cross-study comparisons, and to increase the applicability of measures to a variety of clinical settings. Moreover, we argued that the frequent dismissal of psychometrics as being tied to trait concepts of behavior or devoid of context was erroneous, and that psychometrically sound measures can and should be used in idiographic assessments (see Chapter 3). The second issue was the importance of evaluating the treatment utility of behavioral approaches to assessment. As originally proposed by Mash (1979) and Hayes, Nelson, and Jarrett (1987), treatment utility involves a focus on the meaningfulness of assessments in terms of their ability to effect desired intervention outcomes. For example, an assessment method would be said to have treatment utility if its use led to a course of action in treatment that was more effective than what would have been done without the information provided by the method. However, rather than replacing the need for psychometrically sound measures as some had argued, we suggested that focusing on the psychometric qualities of assessment strategies and their treatment utility were complementary activities.

THE CURRENT STATUS OF BEHAVIORAL ASSESSMENT

The chapters in this volume provide a truly all-encompassing perspective on the current status of behavioral assessment. The range of topics, issues, and populations served by behavioral assessment strategies has grown to include almost the entire domain of psychological assessment. Clearly the behavioral assessment paradigm has had an important influence on the fields of psychological assessment and psychological intervention. The following sections focus on the common themes and elements underlying current behavioral assessment practices that are evident throughout the chapters in this book. We begin by discussing the general purposes of behavioral assessment and follow with discussions of the features and processes of behavioral assessment.

The Purposes of Behavioral Assessment

Inherent in our view of behavioral assessment as an ongoing problem-solving strategy is the recognition that assessments of clients are always carried out in relation to one or more purposes. Along with the assessor's working assumptions and conceptualizations about behavior and its determinants, these purposes will determine which individuals, behaviors, and settings are evaluated, the choice of assessment methods, the way in which findings are interpreted, the specification of assessment and treatment goals, and how these goals are evaluated. Questions surrounding the assessment of client disturbances can be considered only within the context of the intended assessment purpose(s). Therefore, decisions regarding the appropriateness or usefulness of particular assessment

methods and procedures are always made in relation to the needs of the situation. Discussions concerning the relative merits of information obtained via self-report versus direct observation methods have little meaning outside of the assessment context and purposes. A multicategory observational coding system may be appropriate for assessments designed to identify potential controlling variables to be altered with treatment, but perhaps unnecessary for evaluating the outcome of a highly focused intervention to eliminate a child's bedwetting.

Francis and Chorpita (Chapter 16) nicely captured the essential purpose of behavioral assessment. Behavioral assessors strive to systematically apply scientific principles across an individual's (or a couple's or family's) life domains in order to gather data that can inform decisions made about the nature of problems and possible treatments. Our observation in 1990 of an emerging consensus on four interrelated purposes of behavioral assessment appears to have been borne out in subsequent developments. Indeed, the authors of many of the chapters in this volume identified the gathering of assessment data for purposes of diagnosis/target behavior description, prognosis, treatment design, and treatment evaluation as the central purposes of behavioral assessment. Moreover, as noted by Strosahl and Robinson (Chapter 22), these purposes are not only compatible with current systems of health care provision, but also offer the promise of basing psychological services on a firm empirical footing.

The Defining Features of Behavioral Assessment

As mentioned previously, there was much discussion during the 1980s about the identity problem that behavioral assessment was experiencing. As indicated by its absence in the present volume, this concern has almost disappeared and has been replaced by a focus not on identity but on guiding principles. As Garb, Lilienfeld, and Wood (Chapter 23) make abundantly clear, there is a world of difference between behavioral assessment and projective assessment.

We believe that the depiction of behavioral assessment in contrast with traditional approaches was useful, and perhaps necessary, during the formative stages of the field. However, a focus on this distinction at present may have a number of potentially negative effects. First, the categories behavioral and traditional each encompass a heterogeneous range of conceptual and methodological approaches to assessment, and global comparisons between the two categories inevitably obscure a host of important and subtle distinctions within each. Second, the behavioral versus traditional contrast tends to perpetuate a view of the field as reactionary, when there are many strengths of the behavioral assessment approach that clearly stand on their own merit within mainstream psychological assessments. Third, definitions based on contrasts with traditional views tend to foster the blanket acceptance or rejection of certain ideas (e.g., stable traits) or procedures (e.g., personality tests, psychiatric diagnosis, observational assessment) when such categorical decisions are often unnecessary or undesirable within the problem-solving model of current behavioral approaches. Finally, the practices of clinicians and researchers rarely conform to these global designations. In practice, the use of assessment concepts and practices characterized as traditional or behavioral is often based on a variety of pragmatic considerations that include administrative requirements (e.g., billing practices, research criteria for defining specific disorders), normative assessment practices in a particular clinical or research setting, resources for assessment, and individual preferences and priorities.

We believe that any definition of behavior assessment that requires the presence of certain *essential* ingredients—such as a focus on observable behavior, a natural-science perspective, and criterion-referenced performance (see Cone & Hoier, 1986, for a lucid description of this position)—could result in the rejection of behavioral assessment methods by many clinicians who feel that their practices do not strictly adhere to such a definition and who see no need to exclude concepts and techniques that they have found to be both clinically and empirically useful.

It is perhaps a sign of the maturity of the field of behavioral assessment that we have advanced past the stage in which the activities of behavioral assessors are defined primarily as being different from previous approaches to psychological assessment. Although the vitality of the field makes it unlikely that all would agree on a precise set of defining features, we believe that a prototype-based view can accurately depict the current state of the field (cf. Mash & Terdal, 1997b). The strength of behavioral assessment is not in any single element but rather in the relationships and similarities of concepts, methods, and practices that characteristically occur—in other words, not in any single thread that runs its entire length but in the "overlapping of many fibers" (Wittgenstein, 1968, p. 32).

Within such a framework, behavioral assessment is based on sets of imperfectly correlated features, or prototypes. Assessment strategies having the largest number of general category features would be considered the most typical examples of behavioral assessment. The prototypical view also recognizes that within the broad category of behavioral assessment there can exist a hierarchically but imperfectly nested set of subcategories, such as "behavioral assessment in primary health care settings," "behavioral assessment with adults," or "behavioral assessment with children." Behavioral assess-

ments may take many forms depending on the problem of interest. For example, the prototype for behavioral assessment with a 7-year-old child with attention deficit hyperactivity disorder (Barkley, 1997) will be quite different than that for an adult with depression (Dozois & Dobson, 2002). This view is consistent with the relativistic, contextually based, and idiographic nature of behavioral assessment strategies and with the growing emphasis on the importance of organizing one's assessment strategies and plans for treatment in relation to what we know about specific problems and disorders (Antony & Barlow, 2002; Mash & Terdal, 1997a). In the points that follow, we use the prototype-based view to highlight several of the common conceptual, strategic, and procedural characteristics of behavioral assessment that are discussed throughout this volume.

(1) Behavioral assessment is based on conceptualizations of personality and abnormal behavior that give greater *relative* weight to thoughts, feelings, and behaviors as they occur in specific situations than to global underlying traits or dispositions, although clearly the need to recognize and integrate both views is important. Recently proposed conceptual frameworks and methods have the potential for achieving an integration of these two perspectives (Mischel, Shoda, & Mendoz-Denton, 2002).

(2) Behavioral assessment is predominantly idiographic and individualized (Wolpe, 1986). Greater relative emphasis is given to understanding the individual and her or his social context, than to nomothetic comparisons that describe individuals primarily in relation to group norms.

(3) Behavioral assessment emphasizes the role of situational influences on behavior. It is recognized that the patterning and organization of an individual's behavior across situations is highly idiographic (Mischel, 1968), and it is therefore important to assess behaviors *and* situations. The pragmatic outcomes of the emphasis on situational specificity in behavioral assessment have been a greater sensitivity to the measurement of situational dimensions and a corresponding increase in the range of environments sampled—school, home, work, health care. Nevertheless, our methods and strategies for assessing situations, although much improved, remain far less developed than those for assessing behavior, and there is a need for behavioral measures (e.g., interview, self-report) that include more situational content than is currently the case (e.g., McDermott, 1993).

(4) Behavioral assessment emphasizes both the instability and stability of behaviors over time. This is in contrast to an emphasis on the consistency of behavior over time as a reflection of stable and enduring underlying traits. Conceptually, behavioral assessment would predict either consistency or variability in behavior as a function of stability or variation

in context. However, because externally and internally induced changes are the norm rather than the exception, particularly in behavioral assessments during periods of transition and change (i.e., during treatment), the predominant behavioral assessment view has emphasized change. In this regard, outcomes may vary as a function of the point in time at which they are taken, and the timing of assessments assumes a particularly important role.

(5) As we have noted, behavioral assessments are systems oriented. They are directed at describing and understanding (a) characteristics of the individual and his or her social context, (b) the contexts in which these characteristics are expressed, and (c) the structural organizations and functional relationships that exist among situations, behaviors, thoughts, and emotions.

(6) Behavioral assessment emphasizes contemporaneous controlling variables *relative* to historical ones. However, when information about temporally remote events (e.g., age at onset) can facilitate an understanding of current influences, such information will be sought and used in assessment. For example, observational assessment of attachment patterns may assist in understanding a child's current pattern of social disturbance (Chapter 10).

(7) Behavioral assessment is more often concerned with behaviors, cognitions, and affects as direct samples of the domains of interest rather than as signs of some underlying or remote causes. For example, assessments focusing on cognitive deficiencies or distortions consider these events as functional components of the problem to be modified, rather than as symptoms of some other problem. Nevertheless, an emphasis in behavioral assessment on response-system covariation means that the assessment of some behaviors may be of interest predominantly because of their relation to some other more central aspect of the problem.

(8) Behavioral assessment focuses on obtaining information that is directly relevant to treatment. Relevance for treatment refers to the usefulness of information in identifying treatment goals, selecting targets for intervention, designing and implementing interventions, evaluating the outcomes of therapy, and enhancing treatment outcomes.

(9) Behavioral assessment relies on a multimethod assessment strategy, which emphasizes the importance of using different informants and a variety of procedures, including interviews, questionnaires, and observations. The superiority of one method over another is not assumed; its use should be based on the purposes and needs associated with specific assessments (McFall, 1986). Direct observations of behavior in naturalistic and analogue contexts are more commonly used in behavioral assessment than in other assessment approaches (Chapters 7 and 9). One of the challenges of using multi-

method assessments has and continues to be finding ways to integrate data from different sources or informants, particularly when they are in disagreement.

(10) Behavioral assessments are ongoing and self-evaluative (Mash & Hunsley, 1993a). Instead of assessments being conducted on one or two occasions prior to and after treatment, the need for further assessment and its type is dictated by the effectiveness of the methods in facilitating desired treatment outcomes.

(11) Behavioral assessments are scientifically informed and empirically anchored. The assessment strategy—including the decision regarding what to assess—is guided by (a) knowledge concerning the characteristics of the client being assessed and (b) what we know about the specific disorder(s) being assessed. Where assessments are theoretically driven (e.g., based on one of the cognitive models of depression), as much as possible, guiding theories should be based on data.

The Process of Behavioral Assessment

As indicated by a number of contributors to this volume (e.g., Chapters 2 and 11), what makes behavioral assessment unique among assessment approaches is not the assessment/evaluation methods used, but how the methods are selected, integrated, and interpreted. No other assessment approach emphasizes the systematic evaluation of clinical practice typical of behavioral assessment (e.g., Kazdin, 1993). Furthermore, in contrast to other assessment and intervention approaches, behavioral assessment is an integral aspect of behavioral/cognitive-behavioral treatment for a given patient, as the data obtained from ongoing clinical evaluations are used to formulate and modify treatment.

The multiple purposes for which assessments are conducted suggest that not all clients should be assessed in all possible ways. Usually, the choice of assessment methods in a particular case is based on a variety of factors such as the purpose(s) of the assessment (e.g., screening vs. treatment evaluation), nature of the problem behavior(s), (e.g., overt vs. covert, chronic vs. acute), characteristics of the client (e.g., age, sex, education), the assessment setting (e.g., primary practice setting, diagnostic clinic), characteristics of the assessor (e.g., conceptual preferences, level of training, available time), and characteristics of the method (e.g., reliability, validity, amount of technical resources or training required for use, sensitivity to particular interventions).

Keeping this variety of factors in mind, the hallmark of the process of behavioral assessment is, without a doubt, the functional analysis. Contributors to this volume consistently identified the conceptual and practical reliance on functional analysis as the cornerstone of behavioral assessment. Stemming from the position that behavior is controlled by the context in which it occurs, a functional analysis serves as both a heuristic strategy for collecting and integrating clinical data and a means by which clinical hypotheses/formulations are translated into possible options for intervention.

Historically, functional analysis was associated with a straightforward operant orientation to assessment in which observable antecedent and consequent environmental events were related to the frequency, intensity, and/or duration of the behavior of interest. For example, an observational assessment of parent-child interaction looked for the causes of child behavior in terms of the parent's responses to the child in that situation (e.g., cues and consequences). Developmental-historical information was not deemed particularly important, and the parent's response was viewed as a direct reaction to the child's immediate behavior in the situation rather than the result of the cumulative effects of many prior experiences with the child, or the parents' belief systems. However, numerous findings suggest that the reactions of parents are based on more than their children's immediate behaviors. For example, abusive parents have been found to respond harshly to their children, even when their children are behaving appropriately, suggesting the need to consider other possible controlling variable(s) than the child's behavior (Mash, Johnston, & Kovitz, 1983). Similarly, early behavioral assessment placed minimal emphasis on the broader contextual variables that were related to ongoing behaviors. However, such factors as personality, family climate, peer relations, marital relationships, social support, and community conditions have been shown to be potent sources of influence for client behavior—indeed, as or more important than the reactions of others to the client's behavior at the time of its occurrence.

Thus, in the past two decades, in part due to the recognition of the complex nature of behavior (including the role of mediational variables and complex response-response and response-environmental stimulus chains) and to the availability of research-based information on factors influencing behavior, there has been a growing tendency to recognize that cognitive elements, affective states, neurobiological factors, extended social systems, cultural factors, and even language may play pivotal roles in controlling or eliciting problem behaviors (Chapters 6 and 8). However, as Eifert and Feldner (Chapter 6) noted, there are a host of conceptual and practical problems with current approaches to conducting functional analyses, including the scope and range of factors that should be considered in a functional analysis, the variability in behavioral assessors' approaches to conducting a functional analysis and utilizing the resultant information to plan treat-

ment options, and the ever-present problem of biases and errors in clinical decision making. Although, as noted by Nelson-Gray and Paulson (Chapter 24), the availability of empirically supported treatments may guide assessment efforts in designing and evaluating the outcome of treatment. One of the significant challenges facing behavioral assessors is developing strategies for optimizing the accuracy of functional analyses while balancing factors related to the costs, time requirements, and feasibility of collecting data necessary to the analysis. To this end, the case formulation approaches described by Nezu, Nezu, Peacock, and Girdwood (Chapter 21) are an important step toward the development of strategies for conducting empirically based, reliable, accurate, and clinically useful functional analyses.

THE CONTINUING QUESTION OF THE ROLE OF OBSERVATION IN BEHAVIORAL ASSESSMENT

Behavioral assessment and observational assessment were joined at the hip at birth, and ever since, concerns have been expressed about the viability of direct observation as a method of clinical assessment. These concerns have taken many forms, the foremost being the impracticality of using direct observational methods in clinical practice and the ecological validity and psychometric adequacy (e.g., standardization, reliability, generalizability, utility) of these methods (Mash & Foster, 2001). Despite its long-recognized potential as an assessment method, the systematic use of direct observation has been slow to gain acceptance (Reid, Baldwin, Patterson, & Dishion, 1988). Most clinicians rarely use systematic behavioral observation in their day-to-day practices (Haynes, 1998; Piotrowski, 1999), and recommendations for training in psychological assessment give minimal attention to these methods (American Psychological Association Division 12 Task Force, 1999). Nevertheless, the scope and quality of discussions in this volume indicate that the strategic use of direct observational methods continues to play a central, if not exclusive, role in behavioral assessment (Chapters 7, 9, and 10).

As described in this volume, direct observational methods are designed to obtain samples of behaviors deemed to be clinically important (in relation to diagnosis, design, prognosis, and evaluation) in a naturalistic setting or in an analogue situation that is structured in such a way as to provide information about behaviors and settings comparable to what would have been obtained in situ. Observational methods usually involve the recording of behavior when it occurs; the use of impartial observers trained to follow clearly specified rules and procedures regarding the timing of observations and their context; the use of previously designated categories that require a minimal degree of inference; and some procedure to assess reliability (Chapter 7).

The role given to direct observations of ongoing behavior as the sine qua non by early behavioral assessors (e.g., Johnson & Bolstad, 1973) was so great that observational procedures and behavioral assessment were (erroneously) viewed by many as one and the same. This strong, and perhaps overzealous, early focus on direct observation as the primary data source in behavioral assessment derived from a perceived need for greater objectivity in clinical assessment and from the compatibility of direct (and less inferential) data sources with the nonmediational focus characteristic of the earlier approaches to behavior therapy. However, as indicated by the range of assessment methods discussed in this volume, a lessening emphasis on the exclusive use of direct observational methods in behavioral assessment has occurred along with the growing systems orientation in behavioral assessment and the growing recognition of the need to assess cognition and affect in cognitive-behavior therapy.

The early emphasis in behavioral assessment on direct observational procedures was also part of the general reaction against the indirect and often highly inferential assessments characterizing traditional forms of assessment (Goldfried & Kent, 1972). Ratings by others, personality inventories, self-report measures, and projective tests as they were traditionally used to generate inferences regarding emotional conflict and intrapsychic processes, often seemed far removed from the client's major presenting problems.

It was argued by many early behavioral assessors that direct observation is less subject to bias and distortion than self-report measures. However, this issue cannot be addressed without considering the informant, the client being assessed, and the context and purposes for assessment. Furthermore, support for this argument comes more from studies demonstrating poor reliability and validity associated with verbal report measures than from those showing observational data to be accurate and unbiased. In fact, many studies have shown that observations can be readily distorted by biases on the part of observers and those being observed. In light of the demand characteristics of most situations in which observational assessments are used (e.g., relating to diagnosis of the problem, eligibility for treatment, educational placement, legal adjudication, and evaluation of treatment change), it seems reasonable that most clients may attempt to systematically influence what is being observed.

Although a host of studies have focused on issues associated with the use of observational methods (Chapters 7 and 10), these studies collectively have not been as informative as one would hope. Many of the studies have explored ques-

tions concerning bias and reactivity "in general," and questions of this nature do not address the issues of bias and reactivity under specific conditions for individual clients. Bias and reactivity are likely to vary as a function of the answers to "What is being assessed, who is being assessed, by whom, using what methods, for what purposes, and in what situations?"

The preceding comments are not meant to diminish the usefulness of direct observation as a method of behavioral assessment. Rather, our remarks are intended to caution against a steadfast adherence to any single method (including direct observation) as the preferred method of assessment under all conditions in the face of an increasing conceptual emphasis on cognitive and affective variables, contradictory empirical findings related to possible biases and reactivity, the potential unrepresentativeness of observational data, the relativity of assessment purposes, and the many practical concerns and demands on resources associated with the use of observational methods in clinical practice.

The many positive features and innovative applications of direct observation methods described in this volume suggest the need to find creative ways to overcome some of the challenges that have limited the use of these methods in clinical practice. We and others have suggested that one way to make observational assessments more accessible would be to develop an observational assessment infrastructure or "assessment center" outside of the clinic setting that would operate in a manner similar to medical laboratories (Groth-Marnat, 2000; Mash & Hunsley, 1993a, 1993b). Using this approach, the time and resource demands of conducting observational assessments would shift from individual clinicians to the assessment center. These centers would possess the assessment personnel, technical resources, and measurement expertise needed to code, analyze, and interpret observational data (or for that matter data obtained from a wide variety of methods, informants, and settings) using coding systems suitable to particular purposes and needs. Assessment centers could then provide interactive feedback to clinicians as required regarding a variety of treatment goals. For example, case formulations based on continuous samples of observed behavior could be used in treatment planning, and observational indicators of progress and failure in treatment could be obtained. Over time, assessment centers also could create large databases of norms, so that information obtained from individual clients could eventually contribute to the database, be compared to existing relevant norms, and be used to develop decision-making algorithms to guide clinical interventions (Grove & Meehl, 1996).

However, the challenges involved in developing such an observational infrastructure in a cost-conscious health care environment are considerable, despite the promise of long-term benefit. This reality is evidenced by the fact that such an observational assessment center has yet to emerge. Ultimately, assessment centers would need to demonstrate their financial and clinical worth (Groth-Marnat, 1999). Meanwhile, observational assessments will likely continue to play a useful role in informing clinical practice following some of the suggestions made by Heyman and Smith Slep (Chapter 10).

THE DIFFUSION OF BEHAVIORAL ASSESSMENT PRINCIPLES AND PRACTICES

As we have illustrated, while remaining generally true to the principles that guided the development of behavioral assessment, the current methods of behavioral assessment are far more diverse than was originally intended by those who initially proposed and promoted a uniquely behavioral approach to assessment. Although traditional personality assessment measures are still researched and used by many psychologists, the growth of behavioral assessment has dramatically transformed the practice of psychological assessment. For example, the diverse methods of behavioral assessment that are represented in this volume (including structured/semistructured interviews, symptom-/disorder-specific self-report measures, self-monitoring measures, observational methods, psychophysiological methods, and measures of the patient's general life context and functioning) are now commonly recommended in evidence-based guidelines for assessing psychological disorders and developing appropriate treatment plans (Antony & Barlow, 2002).

Even more importantly, many of the prototypic features of behavioral assessment outlined above have been generally adopted as features of scientifically and ethically informed psychological assessment. For example, guidelines for conducting child custody evaluations emphasize the need for scientifically sound measures, assessing context, obtaining multiple forms and sources of information, and exercising caution in drawing conclusions from the obtained data (American Psychological Association, 1994; Ontario Psychological Association, 1998). Furthermore, in addition to the summary data provided by Fernández-Ballesteros (Chapter 12) on behavioral self-report measures, even a cursory examination of major journals focused on psychological assessment and/or psychological intervention shows that these fields have adopted numerous behavioral measures and principles and have moved away from an almost total reliance on global measures of personality to assess psychological functioning. In other words, although the downside of the spreading influence of behavioral assessment has been a dilution of some of the

initial hopes for behavioral assessment, the upside has been that behavioral assessment, as a movement, has radically altered the basis of psychological assessment.

We use the term "movement" intentionally, because there are many ways in which the field of behavioral assessment can be characterized as a form of social movement. Elements such as the rejection of established practices or values, the development of a collective identity, the development of within-group forms of communications, and the goal of societal or organizational change are commonly found in social movements (Giugni, 1998; Polletta & Jasper, 2001). Anyone familiar with the behavioral assessment literature will be able to quickly identify aspects of the behavioral assessment movement that match these characteristics. The heuristic value in viewing behavioral assessment as a social movement is that there is a large sociological literature that can be used as an aid to understand both (a) the variety of views held by behavioral assessors about the growth and status of the field and (b) possible future challenges for the field.

Sociologists have developed various models to categorize and understand the consequences, both intended and unintended, of social movements. Generally these models include outcomes such as co-optation (i.e., recognition or acceptance by the "establishment"), collapse (i.e., failure), and transformation (i.e., movement participants become part of the establishment and start to influence established policies and practices). By virtue of the publication of the present volume, it is self-evident that behavioral assessment has not collapsed as a movement. Equally evident from the information presented in numerous chapters is that behavioral assessment has been both accepted by the field of clinical psychology and has begun to actively transform the field through the influence of research data and the involvement of many prominent proponents (both early and current) of behavioral assessment in the general realm of clinical psychology. Two important aspects integral to such models are (a) the explicit recognition that participants in social movements and external observers may differ in their views of what constitutes success and failure of the movement and (b) the likelihood that there will *not* be consensus across movement participants regarding the success or impact of the movement (Guigni, 1998). This latter point is particularly relevant to the growing pains experienced by behavioral assessment during the 1980s and the diversity of opinions expressed at that time about the appropriate form that behavioral assessment should take.

Sociological research on the spread or diffusion of strategies and practices promoted by social movement also can yield predictions about the nature of some of the challenges likely to occur in the future development of behavioral assessment. For example, evidence suggests that practices are more likely to spread if (a) there is consensus within the movement about the nature and values of the movement and (b) the practices address issues that are central to current problems and crises in established systems (Giugni, 1998). Consideration of these factors should provide a great deal of optimism about the future of behavioral assessment, as the chapters in this volume indicate a general acceptance of a broad definition of behavioral assessment, and, as Strosahl and Robinson (Chapter 22) indicated, behavioral assessment can effectively meet the needs of a changing health care system. Moreover, Strang and Soule (1998) have argued that practices in accord with the dominant view of appropriate and effective action tend to spread more rapidly than those that are not. As we have suggested previously, there is a good fit between behavioral assessment and therapy and many of the goals and practices of responsible managed health care systems (Mash & Hunsley, 1993b). This also should bode well for the future of behavioral assessment in health care settings.

Diffusion research does, however, hold warnings for the development of behavioral assessment. Perhaps most critically, there is evidence that the process of adopting novel practices may change as the practices become part of established policies and institutions. Specifically, it appears that early adopters of novel practices tend to creatively tailor these practices to fit the needs of their settings, whereas later adopters tend to simply use practices that have gained acceptance, with less attention paid to concerns about the degree of fit with their settings (Westphal, Gulati, & Shortell, 1997). Applied to the context of behavioral assessment, this may lead to the relatively uninformed use of assessment guidelines established by managed care systems or other groups/agencies simply because they are recommended or required by a health care system, rather than because of their actual relevance to a specific patient or treatment plan. Similarly, it also could lead to a watering down of behavioral assessment principles if concerns about simplicity and time efficiency become the dominant determinants of assessment guidelines. A significant challenge will be to maintain the integrity of behavioral assessment while adjusting to calls for cost efficiency and the demands of primary care (cf. Chapter 22).

FUTURE DIRECTIONS AND CHALLENGES

The current volume has fully and explicitly demonstrated the vitality and contributions of behavioral assessment, and as such has done a great service to advancing the field. The contributors to this volume have presented detailed information on the multiple directions that behavioral assessment

is taking and the challenges being encountered. In this final section we will selectively synthesize some of the information presented by the contributors with our own views on two pressing issues facing behavioral assessors in the coming decade: incremental validity and clinical utility/cost utility.

The Incremental Validity of Behavioral Assessment

Several contributors raised concerns about the issue of incremental validity (e.g., Chapters 2 and 12). Put simply, the issue is whether behavioral assessment data add significantly to the understanding of patient problems or to the formulation of treatment options beyond what is possible from other forms of assessment data. As part of responsible and accountable practice, behavioral assessment clearly has a major role to play in evaluating treatment progress and outcome. The ongoing challenge, though, is to determine whether (and when) the various assessment methods available to behavioral assessors have added value beyond more easily obtained data. Given the commitment of behavioral assessors to empirically evaluate their methods and to be guided by the results of such research, incremental validity questions must be considered more fully than has been the case to date.

Behavioral assessment is, by its very nature, a dynamic process that involves the collection of clinical data on an ongoing basis from patients. This is very different from a situation in which, for example, an MMPI-2 is used for diagnostic or treatment planning purposes. It is relatively simple to design a study to determine whether MMPI-2 data add to the accuracy in predicting client diagnosis beyond what is available from other data or how much they contribute to the formulation of a clinically useful treatment plan. The situation with behavioral assessment is substantially more complex, because an assessment method that may contribute little incremental validity at an initial assessment phase may be incredibly important for tailoring treatment at a later phase. For example, direct observation of a client who is reporting social phobic behavior may not be necessary to reach an accurate diagnosis, but it may prove critical for tailoring treatment to the specific needs of the client (e.g., determining whether social skills deficits are evident). Although some have warned that requiring evidence of incremental validity may set a standard that is too high given our current knowledge of psychological assessment (Meyer & Archer, 2001), it is crucial for behavioral assessors to know the conditions under which it is most appropriate to conduct a comprehensive assessment or to conduct a focused, but restricted, assessment.

Much conceptual and empirical work needs to be done before clinical questions such as this can be addressed with scientific evidence. There are, however, some encouraging signs in the field of some areas in which it may be relatively easy to study the incremental validity of behavioral assessment. In this era of empirically supported treatments (cf. Kazdin & Kendall, 1998; Weisz, Hawley, Pilkonis, Woody, & Follette, 2000), an obvious question that requires consideration is whether the efforts involved in conducting a functional analysis add anything beyond what a DSM diagnosis can offer. For example, is the effort involved in gathering multiple measures from multiple informants likely to yield data that significantly improve upon the clinician's case conceptualization and eventual treatment services? If so, are there parameters such as patient age, cultural background, and specific diagnosis that consistently affect the incremental value of these data? The evidence thus far, although relatively limited, does suggest the added value of functional analyses in some treatment contexts (Haynes, Leisen, & Blaine, 1997).

Clinical Utility and Cost Utility

Clinical utility can be defined in three distinct ways (Hunsley & Bailey, 1999). The simplest and least stringent approach to determine the clinical utility of behavioral assessment is to see whether behavioral assessment is found to be useful by practitioners. Without a doubt, evidence presented throughout this volume indicates that behavioral assessment possesses this form of clinical utility. A second approach to clinical utility focuses on whether there is replicated evidence that behavioral assessment data provide reliable and valid information about psychological functioning. Again, the evidence in this volume strongly supports behavioral assessment possessing this form of clinical utility. The third and most stringent definition of clinical utility requires that the use of behavioral assessment improves upon typical clinical decision making and treatment outcome. As with all forms of psychological assessment, the data on this form of clinical utility are rather limited, even though it has been at least 25 years since the need for the meaningfulness of assessment to be judged (at least in part) in terms of its effect on desired intervention outcomes has been identified (Hayes et al., 1987; Mash, 1979).

Consistent with our position in 1990, we continue to believe that clinical (or treatment) utility questions must be addressed by the field. The challenge facing behavioral assessors is that consistent empirical evidence for the validity and incremental validity of behavioral assessment does not guarantee its clinical utility. The importance of functionality is unquestioned in behavioral assessment models, yet the same requirement for functionality in considering behavioral assessment practice means that there must be evidence that

behavioral assessment makes a noticeable and reliable difference in the outcome of services offered to patients. Thus, simply knowing that behavioral assessment methods are reliable and valid is not enough; there must be evidence that practitioners who use these methods are better equipped to help their patients, and that these patients have clinical outcomes that are superior to what would be possible if behavioral assessment was not used (Hunsley & Bailey, 2001).

As Hayes and colleagues (1987) have indicated, the research design strategies to evaluate such questions are relatively straightforward. If such evidence is forthcoming, the next step that must be taken is to examine the extent to which the treatment advantage related to behavioral assessment activities is worth the added time and expense. There are commonly used metrics and standards in evaluating the cost effectiveness and cost utility of health care interventions, such as evaluating the costs of the assessment or intervention in terms of quality-adjusted life years, that could be readily applied to behavioral assessment and intervention practices (Hunsley, 2003). What is needed now to advance our applied knowledge of behavioral assessment *and* other forms of psychological assessment is for researchers to start to conduct research on these issues in order to determine whether the science of psychological assessment truly has the ability to meaningfully inform the provision of psychological interventions.

CONCLUSION

Although behavioral assessment did not become the freestanding assessment approach that was envisioned at the outset, the scope and diversity of behavioral assessment principles and practices described in this volume bear witness to the fact that behavioral assessment is alive and well in the twenty-first century. The compatibility of many fundamental behavioral assessment principles and practices with contemporary forces in health care, particularly the emphases on accountability and scientifically informed practices, has enabled behavioral assessment to transform the way in which psychological assessments are currently conducted. Although falling short of developing a distinct identity, behavioral assessment's influence on the field of assessment more generally seems to have met or exceeded many of the goals for accountability in assessment and treatment that early proponents of the approach were hoping to achieve. The continuing advancements in behavioral assessment theory and practice, and their likely future influence on the field of assessment, is well documented by the contributors to this important volume.

REFERENCES

American Psychological Association, Committee on Professional Practice and Standards (1994). Guidelines for child custody evaluations in divorce proceedings. *American Psychologist, 49,* 677–680.

American Psychological Association, Division 12 (Clinical) Presidential Task Force (1999). Assessment for the twenty-first century: A model curriculum. *Clinical Psychologist, 52*(4), 10–15.

Antony, M.M., & Barlow, D.H. (Eds.). (2002). *Handbook of assessment and treatment planning for psychological disorders.* New York: Guilford Press.

Barkley, R.A. (1997). Attention-deficit/hyperactivity disorder. In E.J. Mash & L.G. Terdal (Eds.), *Assessment of childhood disorders* (3rd ed., pp. 77–129). New York: Guilford Press.

Berman, W.H., Rosen, C.S., Hurt, S.W., & Kolarz, C.M. (1998). Toto, we're not in Kansas anymore: Measuring and using outcomes in behavioral health care. *Clinical Psychology: Research and Practice, 5,* 115–133.

Chambless, D.L., & Ollendick, T.H. (2001). Empirically supported psychological interventions: Controversies and evidence. *Annual Review of Psychology, 52,* 685–716.

Cone, J.D. (1988). Psychometric considerations and the multiple models of behavioral assessment. In A.S. Bellack & M. Hersen (Eds.), *Behavioral assessment: A practical handbook* (3rd ed., pp. 42–66). New York: Pergamon Press.

Cone, J.D. (1992). That was then! This is now! *Behavioral Assessment, 14,* 219–228.

Cone, J.D., & Hoier, T.S. (1986). Assessing children: The radical behavioral perspective. In R.J. Prinz (Ed.), *Advances in behavioral assessment of children and families* (Vol. 2, pp. 1–27). Greenwich, CT: JAI Press.

Dozois, D.J.A., & Dobson, K.S. (2002). Depression. In M.M. Antony & D.H. Barlow (Eds.), *Handbook of assessment and treatment planning for psychological disorders* (pp. 259–299). New York: Guilford Press.

Evans, I.M. (1985). Building systems models as a strategy for target behavior selection in clinical assessment. *Behavioral Assessment, 7,* 21–32.

Giugni, M.G. (1998). Was it worth the effort? The outcomes and consequences of social movements. *Annual Review of Sociology, 24,* 371–393.

Goldfried, M.R., & Kent, R.N. (1972). Traditional versus behavioral assessment: A comparison of methodological and theoretical assumptions. *Psychological Bulletin, 77,* 409–420.

Groth-Marnat, G. (1999). Financial efficacy of clinical assessment: Rational guidelines and issues for future research. *Journal of Clinical Psychology, 55,* 813–824.

Groth-Marnat, G. (2000). Visions of clinical assessment: Then, now, and a brief history of the future. *Journal of Clinical Psychology, 56,* 349–365.

Grove, W.M., & Meehl, P.E. (1996). Comparative efficiency of informal (subjective, impressionistic) and formal (mechanical, algorithmic) prediction procedures: The clinical-statistical controversy. *Psychology, Public Policy, and Law, 2,* 293–323.

Hayes, S.C., Barlow, D.H., & Nelson-Gray, R.O. (1999). *The scientist practitioner: Research and accountability in the age of managed care* (2nd ed.). Boston: Allyn & Bacon.

Hayes, S.C., Nelson, R.O., & Jarrett, R.B. (1987). The treatment utility of assessment: A functional approach to evaluating assessment quality. *American Psychologist, 42,* 963–974.

Haynes, S.N. (1986). The design of intervention programs. In R.O. Nelson & S.C. Hayes (Eds.), *Conceptual foundations of behavioral assessment* (pp. 386–429). New York: Guilford Press.

Haynes, S.N. (1998). The changing nature of behavioral assessment. In A.S. Bellack & M. Hersen (Eds.), *Behavioral assessment: A practical handbook* (4th ed., pp. 1–21). Needham Heights, MA: Allyn & Bacon.

Haynes, S.N., Leisen, M.B., & Blaine, D.D. (1997). Design of individualized behavioral treatment programs using functional analytic clinical case methods. *Psychological Assessment, 9,* 334–348.

Haynes, S.N., & Uchigakiuchi, P. (1993). Incorporating personality trait measures in behavioral assessment: Nuts in a fruitcake or raisins in a Mai Tai? *Behavior Modification, 17,* 72–92.

Hunsley, J. (2003). Cost-effectiveness and medical cost offset considerations in psychological service provision. *Canadian Psychology, 44,* 61–73.

Hunsley, J., & Bailey, J.M. (1999). The clinical utility of the Rorschach: Unfulfilled promises and an uncertain future. *Psychological Assessment, 11,* 266–277.

Hunsley, J., & Bailey, J.M. (2001). Whither the Rorschach? An analysis of the evidence. *Psychological Assessment, 13,* 472–485.

Hunsley, J., Lee, C.M., & Wood, J.M. (2003). Controversial and questionable assessment techniques. In S.O. Lilienfeld, S.J. Lynn, & J.M. Lohr (Eds.), *Science and pseudoscience in clinical psychology* (pp. 39–76). New York: Guilford Press.

Johnson, S.M., & Bolstad, O.D. (1973). Methodological issues in naturalistic observation: Some problems and solutions for field research. In L.A. Hamerlynck, L.C. Handy, & E.J. Mash (Eds.), *Behavior change: Methodology, concepts, and practice* (pp. 7–67). Champaign, IL: Research Press.

Kanfer, F.H. (1979). A few comments on the current status of behavioral assessment. *Behavioral Assessment, 1,* 37–39.

Kanfer, F.H. (1985). Target selection for clinical change programs. *Behavioral Assessment, 7,* 7–20.

Kanfer, F.H., & Busemeyer, J.R. (1982). The use of problem-solving and decision-making in behavior therapy. *Clinical Psychology Review, 2,* 239–266.

Kanfer, F.H., & Nay, W.R. (1982). Behavioral assessment. In G.T. Wilson & C.M. Franks (Eds.), *Contemporary behavior therapy:*

Conceptual and empirical foundations (pp. 367–402). New York: Guilford Press.

Kanfer, F.H., & Saslow, G. (1969). Behavioral diagnosis. In C.M. Franks (Ed.), *Behavior therapy: Appraisal and status* (pp. 417–444). New York: McGraw-Hill.

Kazdin, A.E. (1993). Evaluation in clinical practice: Clinically sensitive and systematic methods of treatment delivery. *Behavior Therapy, 24,* 11–45.

Kazdin, A.E. (2001). Progression of therapy research and clinical application of treatment require better understanding of the change process. *Clinical Psychology: Science and Practice, 8,* 143–151.

Kazdin, A.E., & Kendall, P.C. (1998). Current progress and future plans for developing effective treatments: Comments and perspectives. *Journal of Clinical Child Psychology, 27,* 217–226.

Mash, E.J. (1979). What is behavioral assessment? *Behavioral Assessment, 1,* 23–29.

Mash, E.J. (1985). Some comments on target selection in behavior therapy. *Behavioral Assessment, 7,* 63–78.

Mash, E.J., & Foster, S.L. (2001). Exporting analogue behavioral observation from research to clinical practice: Useful or cost-defective? *Psychological Assessment, 18,* 86–98.

Mash, E.J., & Hunsley, J. (1990). Behavioral assessment: A contemporary approach. In A.S. Bellack, M. Hersen, & A.E. Kazdin (Eds.), *International handbook of behavior modification and therapy* (2nd ed., pp. 87–106). New York: Plenum Press.

Mash, E.J., & Hunsley, J. (1993a). Assessment considerations in the assessment of failing psychotherapy: Bringing the negatives out of the darkroom. *Psychological Assessment: A Journal of Consulting and Clinical Psychology, 5,* 292–301.

Mash, E.J., & Hunsley, J. (1993b). Behavior therapy and managed mental health care: Integrating effectiveness and economics in mental health practice. *Behavior Therapy, 24,* 67–90.

Mash, E.J., Johnston, C., & Kovitz, K. (1983). A comparison of the mother-child interactions of physically abused and non-abused children during play and task situations. *Journal of Clinical Child Psychology, 12,* 337–346.

Mash, E.J., & Terdal, L.G. (Eds.) (1997a). *Assessment of childhood disorders* (3rd ed.). New York: Guilford Press.

Mash, E.J., & Terdal, L.G. (1997b). Behavioral assessment of child and family disturbance. In E.J. Mash & L.G. Terdal (Eds.), *Assessment of childhood disorders* (3rd ed., pp. 3–68). New York: Guilford Press.

McDermott, P.A. (1993). National standardization of uniform multi-situational measures of child and adolescent behavior pathology. *Psychological Assessment, 5,* 413–424.

McFall, R.M. (1986). Theory and method in behavioral assessment: The vital link. *Behavioral Assessment, 8,* 3–10.

Meyer, G.J., & Archer, R.P. (2001). The hard science of Rorschach research: What do we know and where do we go? *Psychological Assessment, 13,* 486–502.

Mischel, W. (1968). *Personality and assessment.* New York: Wiley.

Mischel, W., Shoda, Y., & Mendoz-Denton, R. (2002). Situation-behavior profiles as a locus of consistency in personality. *Current Directions in Psychological Science, 11,* 50–54.

Nelson, R.O. (1983). Behavioral assessment: Past, present, future. *Behavioral Assessment, 5,* 195–206.

Nelson, R.O., & Hayes, S.C. (1979). Some current dimensions of behavioral assessment. *Behavioral Assessment, 1,* 1–16.

Nelson-Gray, R.O., Gaynor, S.T., & Korotitsch, W.J. (1997). Behavior therapy: Distinct but acculturated. *Behavior Therapy, 28,* 563–572.

O'Donohue, W.T., & Henderson, D.A. (Eds.) (2001). *A history of the behavioral therapies: Founders' personal histories.* Reno, NV: Context Press.

Ontario Psychological Association (1998). *Ethical guidelines for psychological practice related to child custody and access.* Toronto, Ontario, Canada: Author.

Piotrowski, C. (1999). Assessment practices in the era of managed care: Current status and future directions. *Journal of Clinical Psychology, 55,* 787–796.

Polletta, F., & Jasper, J.M. (2001). Collective identity and social movements. *Annual Review of Sociology, 27,* 283–305.

Reid, J.B., Baldwin, D.V., Patterson, G.R., & Dishion, T.J. (1988). Observations in the assessment of childhood disorders. In M. Rutter, A.H. Tuma, & I.S. Lann (Eds.), *Assessment and diagnosis in child psychopathology* (pp. 156–195). New York: Guilford Press.

Strang, D., & Soule, S.A. (1998). Diffusion in organizations and social movements: From hybrid corn to poison pills. *Annual Review of Sociology, 24,* 265–290.

Taylor, S. (1999). Behavioral assessment: Review and prospect. *Behaviour Research and Therapy, 37,* 475–482.

Ullmann, L.P., & Krasner, L. (Eds.) (1965). *Case studies in behavior modification.* New York: Holt, Rinehart & Winston.

Weisz, J.R., Hawley, K.M., Pilkonis, P.A., Woody, S.R., & Follette, W.C. (2000). Stressing the (other) three Rs in the search for empirically supported treatments: Review procedures, research quality, relevance to practice and the public interest. *Clinical Psychology: Science and Practice, 7,* 243–258.

Westphal, J.D., Gulati, R., & Shortell, S.M. (1997). Customization or conformity? An institutional and network perspective on the content and consequences of TQM adoption. *Administrative Science Quarterly, 42,* 366–394.

Wittgenstein, L. (1968). *Philosophical investigations.* Oxford: Basil Blackwell.

Wilson, F.E., & Evans, I.M. (1983). The reliability of target-behavior selection in behavioral assessment. *Behavioral Assessment, 5,* 15–32.

Wolpe, J. (1986). Individualization: The categorical imperative of behavior therapy practice. *Journal of Behavior Therapy and Experimental Psychiatry, 17,* 145–153.

Wood, J.M., Garb, H.N., Lilienfeld, S.O., & Nezworski, M.T. (2002). Clinical assessment. *Annual Review of Psychology, 53,* 519–543.

Author Index

Abrams, D. B., 272, 280
Abramson, L., 13
Achenbach, T. M., 296, 297, 307, 308, 312, 367, 375, 437, 463, 476, 477
Acierno, R., 128, 133, 475
Ackerman, M. C., 454
Ackerman, M. J., 454
Ackerman, R., 129
Ackerman, S. J., 458
Acklin, M. W., 455
Adams, H. E., 111, 471, 472, 476
Adams, M., 398
Addington, D., 330
Addington, J., 330
Adrien, J-L., 395
Affleck, G., 235
Agras, S., 442
Agras, W. S., 282
Ahern, D. K., 280
Ahlburg, D. A., 350, 358
Ainsworth, M. D. S., 163, 171
Albano, A. M., 294, 295, 304, 313, 314
Albersheim, L., 171
Albert, M. L., 227
Alden, L. E., 78
Alderman, N., 331, 390
Alevizos, P., 111, 112
Alexander, J. F., 111, 155
Alford, G. S., 322, 325
Allan, E., 335
Allen, B., 392
Allen, B. A., 239
Allen, H., 393
Allen, J. B., 188
Allen, J. P., 166
Allison, D., 438
Allport, G., 201
Almquist-Parks, L., 17
Alpert, M., 335
Altmaier, E., 279
Altman, D. G., 23
Altmann, J., 113
Alveres, K. M., 359
Amador, X. F., 329, 330
Amato, P., 76
Ambrosini, P. J., 183
Ametrano, D., 247
Ametrano, I., 247
Amies, P., 282
Anbar, M., 232
Ancill, R. J., 239
Andelman, M., 390
Andersen, T. J., 458
Anderson, B., 237

Anderson, B. L., 21
Anderson, C. M., 102, 105, 395
Anderson, K. E., 165
Andreasen, N. C., 332, 475
Andrews, D. W., 146, 149, 155, 172
Andrews, L., 210
Andronis, P. T., 322
Angoff, W. H., 53
Angst, J., 474
Annatassi, A., 273
Annon, J. S., 204
Anthony, J. L., 75, 78, 80
Antony, M. M., 15, 490, 493, 497
Applebaum, M., 123
Appleby, J. D., 352
Appleby, L., 330
Archer, R. P., 458, 462, 498
Arfken, C. L., 387
Arkes, H. R., 79, 403
Arkowitz, H., 278, 280
Armendariz, G., 439
Armstrong, J. G., 458
Armstrong, J. S., 358
Aron, A., 163, 173
Aron, E., 163
Arrindell, W. A., 278
Arrington, R. E., 108, 111, 113, 117, 118, 122, 471
Arvey, R. D., 350, 358
Ary, D., 54, 108, 113, 114, 118, 119, 120
Ascione, F. R., 374
Asher, J. J., 352, 353
Asmundson, G. J. G., 95
Asmus, J. M., 390
Athayde, R., 227
Atkinson, J. W., 461, 462
Atkinson, M., 330
Auer, S. R., 39
Ault, M. H., 110
Auquier, P., 330, 331
Austin, J. T., 355
Ayllon, T., 112, 321, 325
Azrin, N. H., 116, 170
Azuma, H., 132

Baas, U., 235
Babor, T. F., 182
Bachrach, C. A., 194
Baer, D. M., 113, 118, 131
Baer, R. A., 213
Bagnato, S., 42, 46
Bagwell, C. L., 293
Baham, M., 62
Bailey, J. M., 453, 499
Bailey, J. S., 395

503

Hoffman, L. W., 146
Hofmann, S. G., 279, 281
Hofstede, G., 128
Hogansen, J., 155
Hoge, R. D., 122
Hoier, T. S., 493
Holborn, S. W., 279
Holden, B. G., 235
Holland, J. G., 60
Hollander, E., 281
Hollaway, E. L., 155
Hollenbeck, A. R., 110, 123
Hollenstein, T., 150, 151, 152
Holliday, G. A., 398
Hollon, S. D., 205, 270
Holmberg, M., 113
Holt, C. S., 277, 282
Holtzworth-Munroe, A., 11
Holz, W., 116
Holzman, P. S., 463
Honderich, T., 77
Honkoop, P. C., 235
Hope, D., 438
Hope, D. A., 163, 174, 277, 278, 281, 282, 284
Hopko, D. R., 332, 334
Hopko, S. D., 334
Hops, H., 109, 146, 148, 167
Horai, J., 477
Horn, J. L., 12
Horn, W. F., 115
Horner, M., 235
Horner, R. H., 122
Horowitz, L. M., 210
Horswill, M. S., 231
Hosokawa, M. C., 300
Hough, L., 348
Hough, L. M., 351
House, A. E., 117
Houston, T. K., 190
Houtman, I. L. D., 281
Houts, P. S., 404
Howard, R., 335
Howard, R. J., 336
Howard, W. W., 458
Howe, G. W., 168
Howell, L. A., 143
Hoyt, C. J., 44
Hoza, B., 293, 442
Hubblel, M. A., 437
Huber, M. T., 15
Hubert, L., 120
Huberty, C. J., 284
Huffcutt, A. I., 359
Hughs, T., 335
Hull, J. G., 205
Hundley, P. L., 338
Hung, C. I., 330
Hunsley, J., 167, 405, 406, 439, 440, 443, 453, 489, 491, 494, 496, 498, 499
Hunter, J., 51
Hunter, J. E., 350, 351, 354, 357, 358, 360
Hunter, R. F., 350, 357
Huntzinger, R. M., 304
Hurt, S. W., 462, 490
Huser, J., 308

Hutley, G., 393
Hutt, C., 110
Hutt, S. J., 110
Hüttner, P., 233
Hyman, R. B., 333
Hyndman, J., 393

Ialongo, N., 154
Idol-Maestas, L., 381
Ilonen, T., 458
Isaacs, M., 227
Isquith, P. K., 390
Iwamasa, G. Y., 131, 132, 133
Iwata, B. A., 65, 80, 109, 115, 122, 163, 174, 230
Izal, V., 214

Jaccard, J., 202
Jackson, D. N., 351
Jackson, H. F., 321
Jackson, W., 330
Jacob, R. G., 277, 280, 281, 282
Jacob, T., 118, 145, 173
Jacobs, R., 356
Jacobson, L., 50
Jacobson, N. S., 101, 168, 257, 272, 273, 284, 439
Jahoda, M., 441
James, L. R., 73, 75, 359
Jamison, R. N., 235
Jamner, L. D., 235
Janikowski, T. P., 228
Jansak, D. M., 458
Jansson, L., 281
Janz, T., 350
Jarrett, R., 434
Jarrett, R. B., 23, 58, 96, 103, 122, 196, 211, 237, 368, 479, 480, 492
Jasper, J. M., 497
Jeanneret, P. R., 347, 356, 358
Jefferies, S., 437
Jelicic, M., 390
Jenkins, R., 183
Jensen, A., 351
Jensen, B. J., 134
Jensen, P. S., 189
Jerremalm, A., 281
Jessel, A. S., 231
Jeste, D. V., 335
Jimerson, D. C., 281
Jobe, J. B., 194
Joffe, R. T., 281
John, R., 173
Johns, L. C., 329
Johnson, D. R., 76
Johnson, J., 205
Johnson, L., 439
Johnson, M. K., 189
Johnson, R. L., 301
Johnson, S. M., 27, 115, 116, 117, 118, 145, 153, 165, 210, 496
Johnston, C., 495
Johnston, J. M., 101, 110, 111, 119, 120
Johnston, M., 463
Joiner, T. E., 78
Joller, J. R., 398
Jolles, J., 390
Jolley, R. P., 459

Subject Index